PHILIP'S

STREET ATLAS
Lancashire

First published in 1997

George Philip Ltd, a division of
Octopus Publishing Group Ltd
2–4 Heron Quays, London E14 4JP

Second colour edition 2001
First impression 2001

ISBN 0-540-07975-8

© George Philip Ltd 2001

Ordnance Survey®

This product includes mapping data licensed
from Ordnance Survey®, with the permission of
the Controller of Her Majesty's Stationery Office.
© Crown copyright 2001. All rights reserved.
Licence number 100011710

Printed and bound in Spain
by Cayfosa-Quebecor

Contents

III **Key to map symbols**

IV **Key to map pages**

VI **Route planning**

VIII **Administrative and Postcode boundaries**

1 **Street maps** at 3½ inches to 1 mile

220 **Street maps** at 1¾ inches to 1 mile

237 **Street maps** at 3½ inches to 1 mile

239 **Index** of towns and villages

240 **Index** of streets, hospitals, industrial estates, railway stations, schools, shopping centres and universities

Digital Data

The exceptionally high-quality mapping found in this atlas is available as digital data in TIFF format, which is easily convertible to other bit mapped (raster) image formats.

The index is also available in digital form as a standard database table. It contains all the details found in the printed index together with the National Grid reference for the map square in which each entry is named and feature codes for places of interest in eight categories such as education and health.

For further information and to discuss your requirements, please contact Philip's on 020 7531 8440 or george.philip@philips-maps.co.uk

Motorway with junction number			**Railway station**
Primary route – dual/single carriageway			**Private railway station**
A road – dual/single carriageway			**Bus, coach station**
B road – dual/single carriageway			**Ambulance station**
Minor road – dual/single carriageway			**Coastguard station**
Other minor road – dual/single carriageway			**Fire station**
Road under construction			**Police station**
Pedestrianised area			**Accident and Emergency entrance to hospital**
Postcode boundaries			**Hospital**
County and unitary authority boundaries			**Place of worship**
Railway			**Information Centre** (open all year)
Tramway with tramway stop			**Parking**
Miniature railway			**Park and Ride**
Rural track, private road or narrow road in urban area			**Post Office**
Gate or obstruction to traffic (restrictions may not apply at all times or to all vehicles)			**Camping site**
Path, bridleway, byway open to all traffic, road used as a public path			**Caravan site**
The representation in this atlas of a road, track or is no evidence of the existence of a of a right of way			**Golf course**
			Picnic site
Adjoining page indicators (The colour of the arrow indicates the scale of the adjoining page - see scales below)			**Important buildings, schools, colleges, universities and hospitals**
Adjoining page indicator showing the pages adjoining the top and bottom halves of the current page			**Water name**
			Stream
			River or canal – minor and major
			Water
			Tidal water
			Woods
			Houses
			Non-Roman antiquity
			Roman antiquity

DY7

North Pier

220 84

211 207

Walsall

Prim Sch

River Medway

House

VILLA

Allot Gdns	**Allotments**	Meml	**Memorial**
Acad	**Academy**	Mon	**Monument**
Cemy	**Cemetery**	Mus	**Museum**
C Ctr	**Civic Centre**	Obsy	**Observatory**
CH	**Club House**	Pal	**Royal Palace**
Coll	**College**	PH	**Public House**
Crem	**Crematorium**	Recn Gd	**Recreation Ground**
Ent	**Enterprise**	Resr	**Reservoir**
Ex H	**Exhibition Hall**	Ret Pk	**Retail Park**
Ind Est	**Industrial Estate**	Sch	**School**
Inst	**Institute**	Sh Ctr	**Shopping Centre**
Ct	**Law Court**	TH	**Town Hall/House**
L Ctr	**Leisure Centre**	Trad Est	**Trading Estate**
LC	**Level Crossing**	Univ	**University**
Liby	**Library**	Wks	**Works**
Mkt	**Market**	YH	**Youth Hostel**

■ The dark grey border on the inside edge of some pages indicates that the mapping does not continue onto the adjacent page

■ The small numbers around the edges of the maps identify the 1 kilometre National Grid lines

The scale of the maps is 5.52 cm to 1 km
3½ inches to 1 mile 1: 18103

0   ¼   ½   ¾   1 mile

0   250m   500m   750m   1 kilometre

The scale of the maps on pages numbered in green is 2.76 cm to 1 km (1¾ inches to 1 mile) 1: 36206

0   ¼   ½   ¾   1 mile

0   250m 500m 750m 1 kilometre

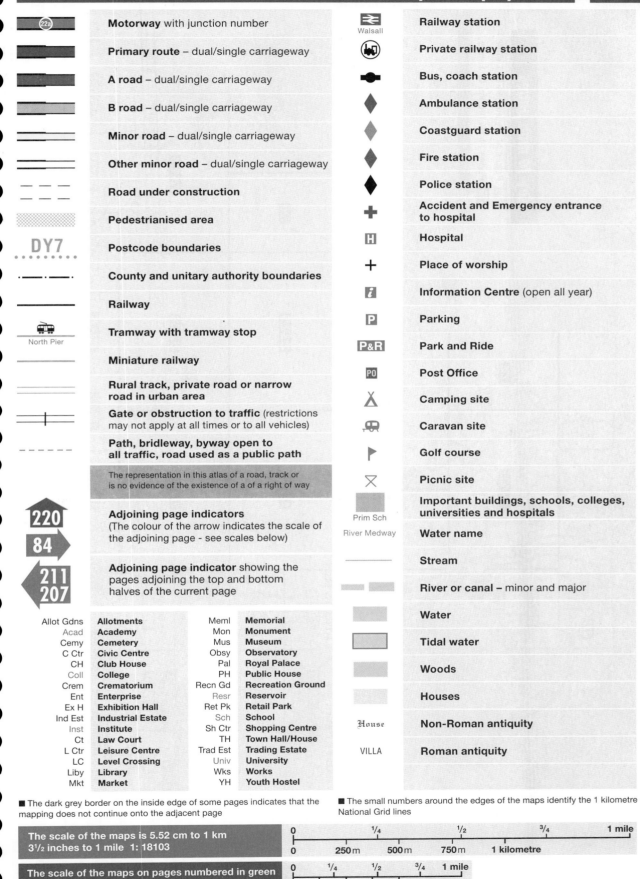

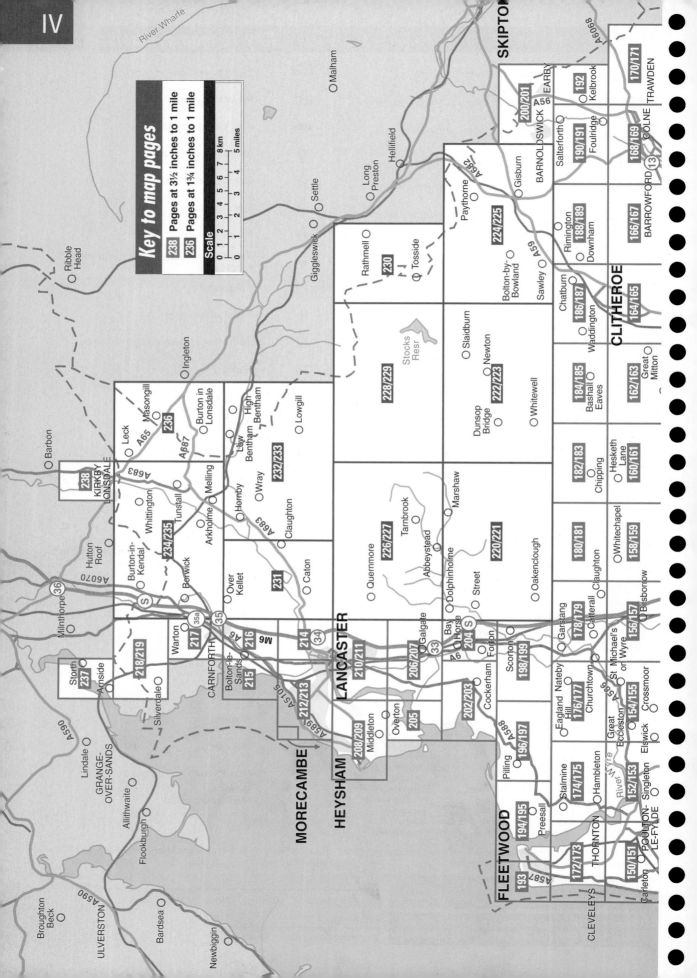

IV

Key to map pages

| 238 | Pages at 3½ inches to 1 mile |
| 236 | Pages at 1¾ inches to 1 mile |

Scale

0 1 2 3 4 5 6 7 8km
0 1 2 3 4 5 miles

River Wharfe

SKIPTON

Malham

Settle

Giggleswick

Hellifield

Long Preston

Ribble Head

Ingleton

Barbon

Masongill

Leck A65 236

Burton in Lonsdale

High Bentham

Low Bentham 232/233

Wray

Lowgill

Rathmell 230

Tosside 224/225

Paythorne

Gisburn

BARNOLDSWICK

EARBY

200/201 A56

192 Kelbrook

Salterforth 190/191 Foulridge

170/171 TRAWDEN COLNE

168/169

BARROWFORD (13)

166/167

Bolton-by-Bowland

Sawley A59

Chatburn

Rimington 188/189 Downham

186/187 Waddington

CLITHEROE

164/165

Great Mitton 162/163

228/229

Stocks Resr

Slaidburn

Newton 222/223

Whitewell

Dunsop Bridge

Bashall Eaves 184/185

Hesketh Lane 160/161

182/183 Chipping

Whitechapel 158/159

KIRKBY LONSDALE

238

A683

Hutton Roof

Whittington

Tunstall

Melling

Hornby

Claughton A683

Arkholme

234/235 Burton-in-Kendal

Borwick

Milnthorpe 36

A6070

Burton-in-Kendal (S)

35a

CARNFORTH 35

Warton 217

Bolton-le-Sands 215

216 M6

214 (34)

LANCASTER

210/211

Over Kellet 231

Caton

Quernmore

226/227 Tarnbrook

Abbeystead

Marshaw

Dolphinholme

Street

220/221

Oakenclough

180/181

Claughton

Bilsborrow 156/157

A6

St Michael's on Wyre

Catterall 178/179

Garstang

198/199 Scorton

204 (S) Forton

Bay Horse 33

Galgate

206/207

202/203

Cockerham

MORECAMBE

HEYSHAM

208/209 Middleton

Overton

205

212/213 A5105 A589

Storth 237

218/219

Silverdale

Arnside

Lindale

GRANGE-OVER-SANDS

Allithwaite

Flookburgh

Broughton Beck

ULVERSTON A590

Bardsea

Newbiggin

A590

Pilling 196/197

Preesall 194/195

FLEETWOOD 193

172/173

CLEVELEYS A587

THORNTON

Stalmine 174/175

Hambleton

River Wyre

Eagland Hill Nateby 176/177

Churchtown

Great Eccleston

Elswick 154/155 Crossmoor

Singleton 152/153

POULTON-LE-FYLDE

Carleton 150/151

A586

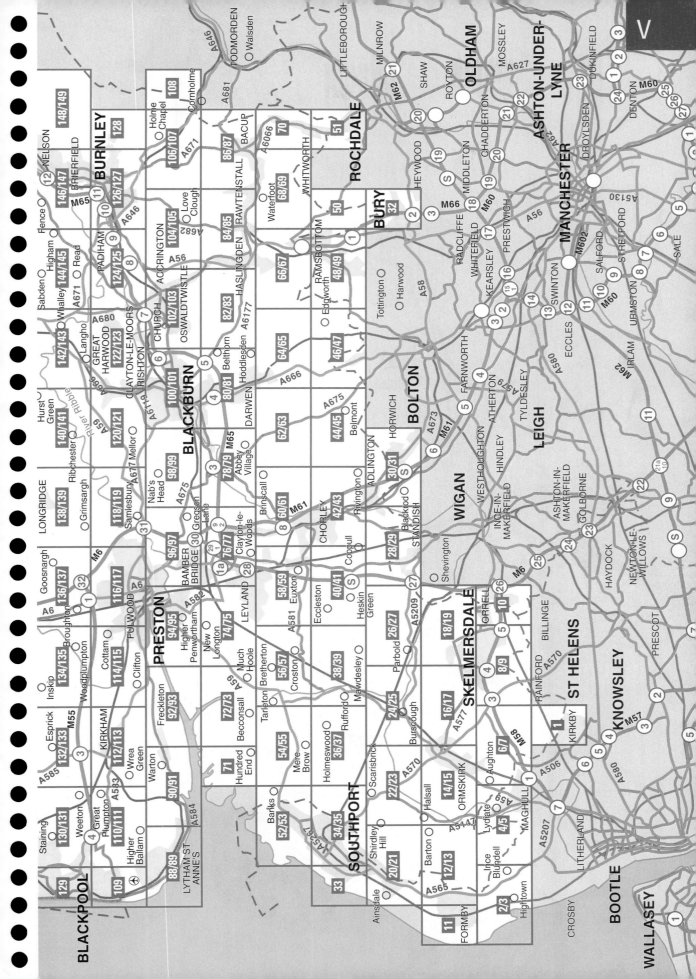

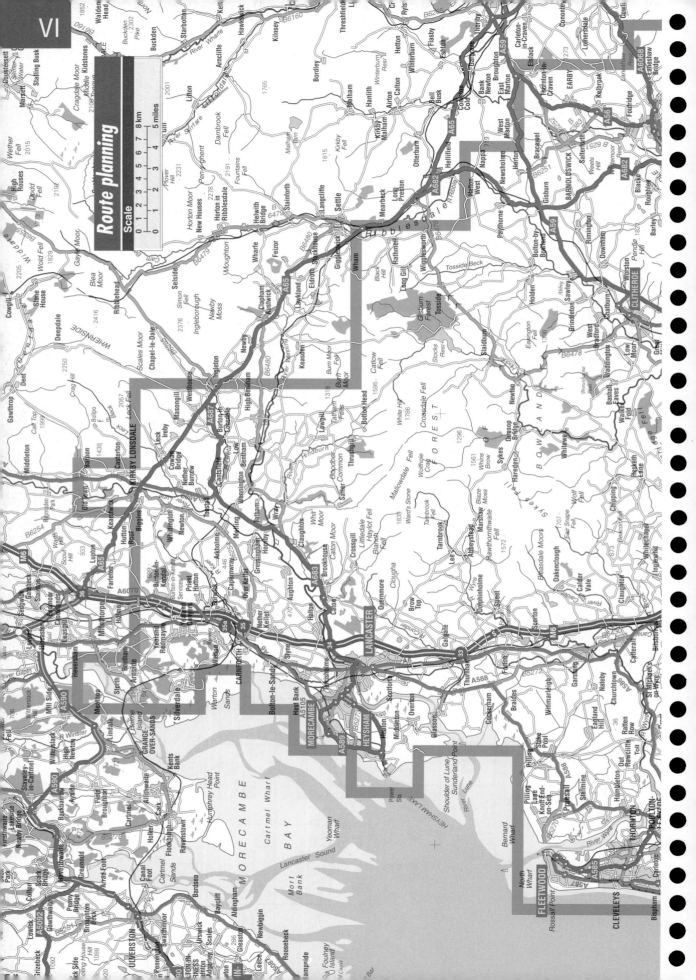

Route planning

Scale

0 1 2 3 4 5 6 7 8 km

0 1 2 3 4 5 miles

Major administrative and Postcode boundaries

County and unitary authority boundaries
District boundaries
Postcode boundaries
Area covered by this atlas

Scale

| 0 | 5 | 10 | 15 km |
| 0 | | 5 | 10 miles |

Cumbria

LA11
LA7
Arnside
Kirkby Lonsdale
Silverdale
Burton-in-Kendal
LA5
LA6
Burton in Lonsdale
Carnforth
North Yorkshire
Wray
High Bentham
LA4
Morecambe
Halton
Lancaster
Caton
Heysham
LA1
LA3
Lancaster
LA2
Overton
BD24
Galgate
Rathmell
Glasson
Dolphinholme
BD23
Forton
Dunsop Bridge
Slaidburn
Fleetwood
Pilling
Gisburn
BD23
FY7
BB7
Ribble Valley
Barnoldswick
BB18
Garstang
Bleasdale
West Bradford
Salterforth
FY6
Wyre
PR3
Downham
Cleveleys
FY5
Hambleton
Chipping
Clitheroe
Pendle
BD22
Great Eccleston
Lancashire
BB9
Colne
BB8
FY2
Carleton
Barley
Trawden
Blackpool
Goosnargh
Longridge
Whalley
Nelson
FY1
FY3
Blackpool
BB12
Weeton
Catforth
Preston
BB6
Burnley
FY4
Fylde
Kirkham
PR2
Great Harwood
BB10
Fulwood
Mellor
BB1
Hyndburn
BB11
Holme Chapel
HX7
FY8
Warton
Preston
BB2
BB5
OL14
Lytham St Anne's
PR1
Blackburn
Oswaldtwistle
Calderdale
PR4
Hoghton
South Ribble
Belthorn
OL13
Walmer Bridge
PR5
Darwen
BB3
Haslingden
BB4
Bacup
Leyland
Brinscall
Blackburn with Darwen
Rossendale
Shawforth
Banks
Tarleton
PR6
Irwell Vale
BL0
OL12
PR9
Chorley
Belmont
Ramsbottom
Tonacliffe
Southport
Holmeswood
Eccleston
PR7
Chorley
BL7
BL8
Rochdale
PR8
Chorley
BL6
BL9
Ainsdale
Burscough
L40
Parbold
Horwich
Bury
West Lancashire
WN6
Standish
Bury
Haskayne
Ormskirk
Skelmersdale
WN1
Bolton
L37
L39
Aughton
WN8
Orrell
Wigan
Formby
Skelmersdale
WN5
L38
L31
Maghull
WN11
SD
Hightown
L29
St Helens
SJ
L33
Sefton

Lancaster
Lancashire
Blackpool

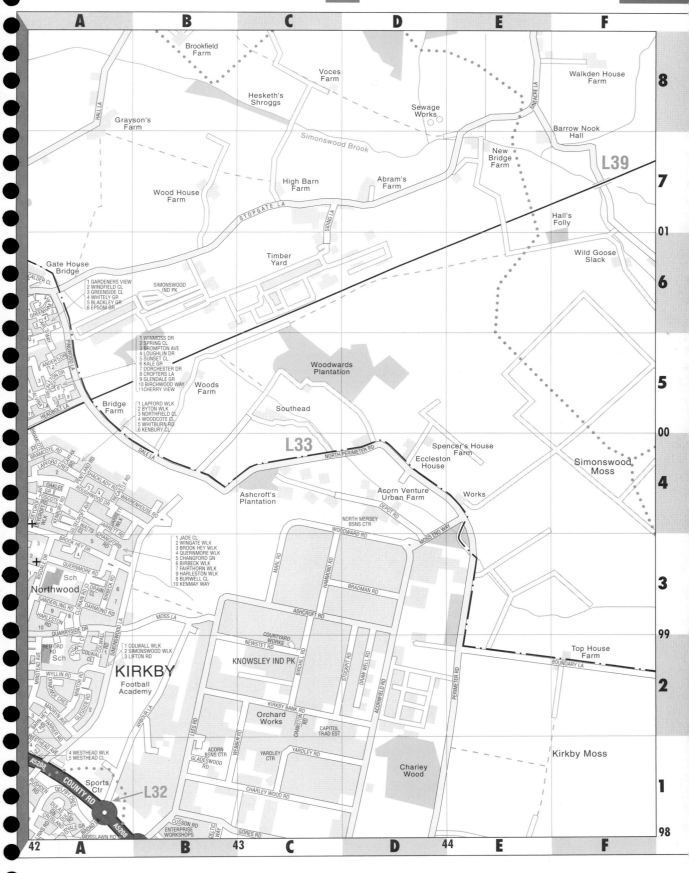

A B C D E F

8
7
01
6
5
00
4
3
99
2
1
98

Brookfield Farm

Voces Farm

Walkden House Farm

Hesketh's Shroggs

Sewage Works

Barrow Nook Hall

Grayson's Farm

Simonswood Brook

New Bridge Farm

L39

High Barn Farm

Abram's Farm

Hall's Folly

Wood House Farm

STOPGATE LA

SIDING LA

SWEACRE LA

Wild Goose Slack

Gate House Bridge

Timber Yard

1 GARDENERS VIEW
2 WINDFIELD CL
3 GREENSIDE CL
4 WHITELY GR
5 BLACKLEY GR
6 EPSOM GR

SIMONSWOOD IND PK

CALDER CL
GREENHEY
KERR SWAY

1 WINMOSS DR
2 SPRING CL
3 BROMPTON AVE
4 LOUGHLIN DR
5 SUNSET CL
6 KALE GR
7 DORCHESTER DR
8 CROFTERS LA
9 GLENDALE GR
10 BIRCHWOOD WAY
11 CHERRY VIEW

Woodwards Plantation

Woods Farm

HALL LA

PINGWOOD LA
ANDERSON CL
RECKLATON DR
ALVINA LA
HEADBOLT LA

Bridge Farm

1 LAPFORD WLK
2 BYTON WLK
3 NORTHFIELD CL
4 WOODCOTE CL
5 WHITBURN RD
6 KENBURY CL

Southead

L33

Spencer's House Farm

DALE LA

NORTH PERIMETER RD

Eccleston House

Simonswood Moss

BRAMCOTE CL
LAPFORD CRES
CARPFAX
PENTLAND AVE
SHACKLADY RD
TRECASTLE GR
WARRENHOUSE RD

Ashcroft's Plantation

Acorn Venture Urban Farm

Works

OAKLEE GR
FOSCOTE GR
DEVONPORT WAY
KENBURY WLK
GILSCROFT AVE
WATTS CL
JARRETT WLK
JARRETT RD
CHANGFORD GR
ROUGHWOOD DR

DEPOT RD

MOSS END WAY

NORTH MERSEY BSNS CTR

1 JADE CL
2 WINGATE WLK
3 BROOK HEY WLK
4 QUERNMORE WLK
5 CHANGFORD GN
6 BIRBECK WLK
7 FAIRTHORN WLK
8 HARLESTON WLK
9 BURWELL CL
10 KENMAY WAY

BROOK HEY DR

WOODWARD RD

MARL RD

HAMMOND RD

BRADMAN RD

Sch

Northwood

QUERNMORE RD
CLORAIN CL
BIRBECK CL
DARMOND RD

MOSS LA

ASHCROFT RD

SANDERLING RD
HARLESTON RD
QUARRYSIDE DR
RETFORD RD
COLWALL CT
COLWALL RD
COLWALL CL
SIMONSWOOD LA

1 COLWALL WLK
2 SIMONSWOOD WLK
3 LIFTON RD

COURTYARD WORKS
NEWSTET RD

BIRCHILL RD

STOCKPIT RD

DRAW WELL RD

ACORNFIELD RD

PERIMETER RD

Top House Farm

BOUNDARY LA

Sch

KIRKBY
Football Academy

KNOWSLEY IND PK

MINSTEAD AVE
WYLLIN RD
MADRYN AVE
ORMANDE CRES
GLESSIDE RD
MINTOR RD

ARROWE LA

LEES RD

WEBBER RD

KIRKBY BANK RD

Orchard Works

CRANSTON RD

CAPITOL TRAD EST

Kirkby Moss

BARN HEY
FARRIER RD
WESTHEAD AVE

4 WESTHEAD WLK
5 WESTHEAD CL

GLADESWOOD RD

ACORN BSNS CTR

YARDLEY CTR

YARDLEY RD

Charley Wood

A520B

COUNTY RD

Sports Ctr

L32

CHARLEY WOOD RD

RUSHDEN RD
DELBY CRES
DULAS GN
DOUGLAS DALE GR
CROSLAND RD
MOSSLAWN RD

A520B

CUSSON RD
CELTIC WAY

GORES RD

ENTERPRISE WORKSHOPS

11

A   B   C   D   E   F

8

05

7

6

05

04

5

4

03

3

02

2

03

1

02

27   A   B   28   C   D   29   E   F

Mount Pleasant

ALEXANDRA RD

ALBERT RD

ELSWORTH CL

STAPLETON RD

Marsh Farm

Range High Sch

ST LUKE'S CHURCH RD

L37

Raven Meols Hills

Raven Moels Hills Nature Reserve

Sefton Coastal Path

Cambrai Cottage

DANGER AREA

Grange Farm

Altcar Training Camp

GRANGE RD

River Alt

LC

Sefton Coastal Path

Battery Cottage

DANGER AREA

L38

Altcar Rifle Range

DANGER AREA

PARK CL

HORSE HILL LA

Sewage Works

Works

ST GEORGE'S RD

MARK RD

ST STEPHEN'S RD

CHESTER CL

KERSLAKE WAY

LOWER ALT RD

ALT RD

SCHOOL RD

NORTHDUNES

RATHBONE RD

VILLAGE WAY

RIVERSIDE

WESTWAY

BARKSIDE

THE ROAD

SANDILANDS

SANDILANDS DR

BLUNDELL AVE

WIGNALLS MEADOW

SANDHILLS

MOORHOUSES

OLD ACRE

LARKHILL

BLUNDELL GR

BRIARY CROFT

THIMBLE CK AVE

WITHINS FIELD

DANGER AREA

Formby Bank

Liverpool Bay

Hightown

ALTON CL

WHITEFI

BLUNDELL RD

BRENTWOOD CL

OAKFIELD

LANGLEY CL

RICHMOND CL

MAYFAIR CL

Sefton Coastal Path

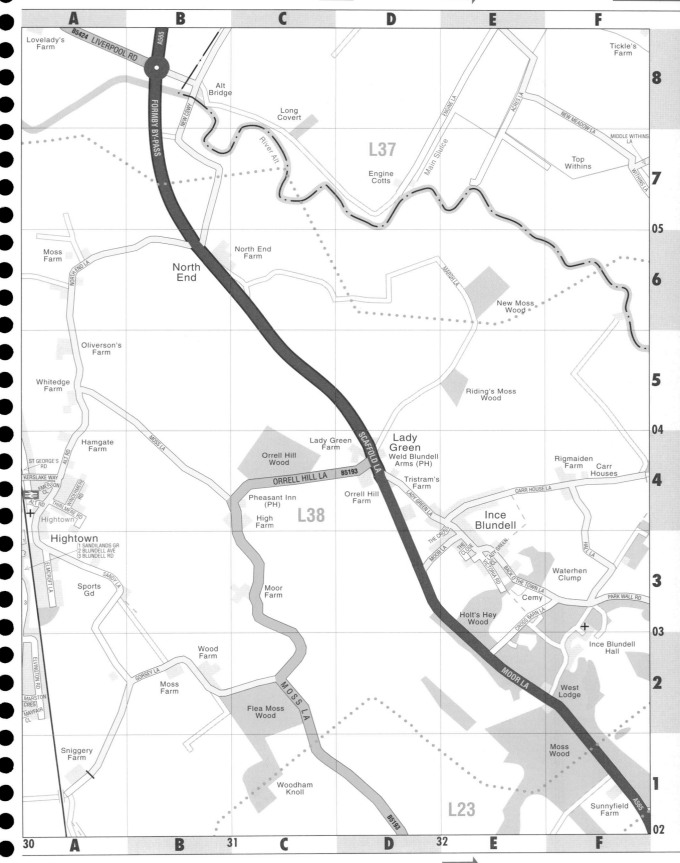

A B C D E F

Oliver's Farm

BROAD LA

RYE MOSS LA

Sewage Works

Holland's Farm

CHURCH LA

INTAKE LA

8

Lydiate Brook

MIDDLE WITHINS LA

LINACRE LA

Lydiate Wood

ACRES LA

The Withins

L37

L39

7

WITHINS LA

LOWER CARR LA

05

Cheshire Lines Path

Trans Pennine Trail

6

Altcar Meadows

Carr Wood

MONKS CARR LA

Carr Sluice

Maghull Hey Cop

Gore House Farm

PUNNELL'S LA

P CARR LA

L38

LYDIATE STATION RD

5

Searchlight Plantation

04

ALTCAR LA

L31

4

CABIN LA

Carr Side Farm

BLACKCAR LA

River Alt

L29

CARRSIDE LA

3

03

East Lodge Farm

Hunt's Brook Farm

Tower Wood

EAST LA

Broad Farm

2

PARK WALL RD

BROAD LA

Ince Blundell Park

Homer Green

L23

MOOR LA

1

LONG LA

LUNT RD

GATES LA

L23

02

A565

33 A B 34 C D 35 E F

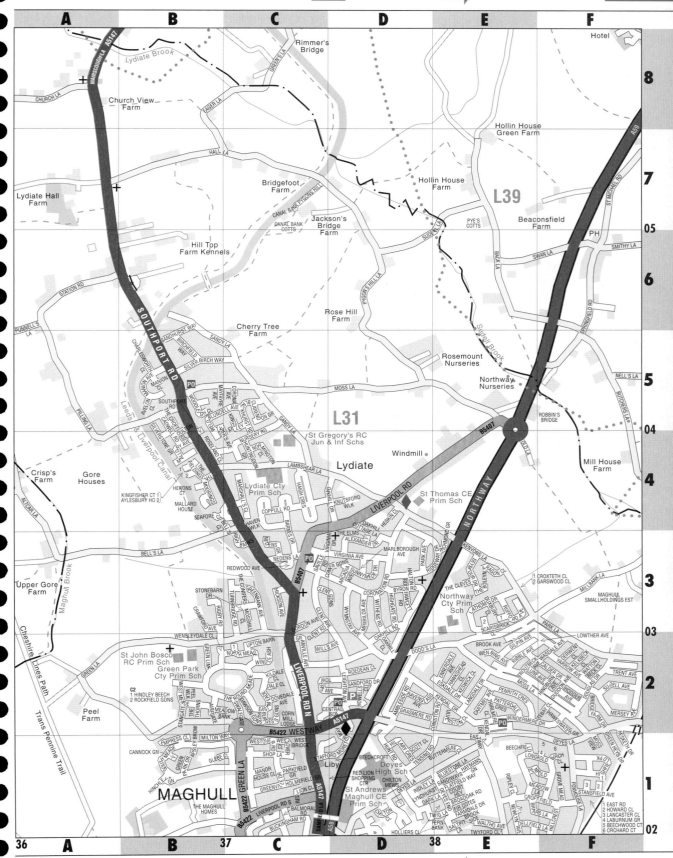

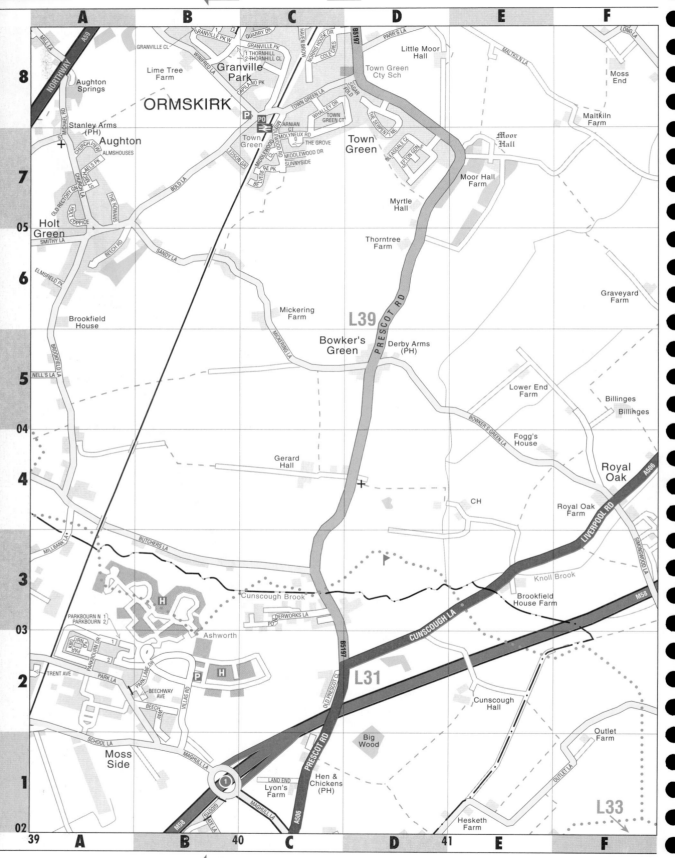

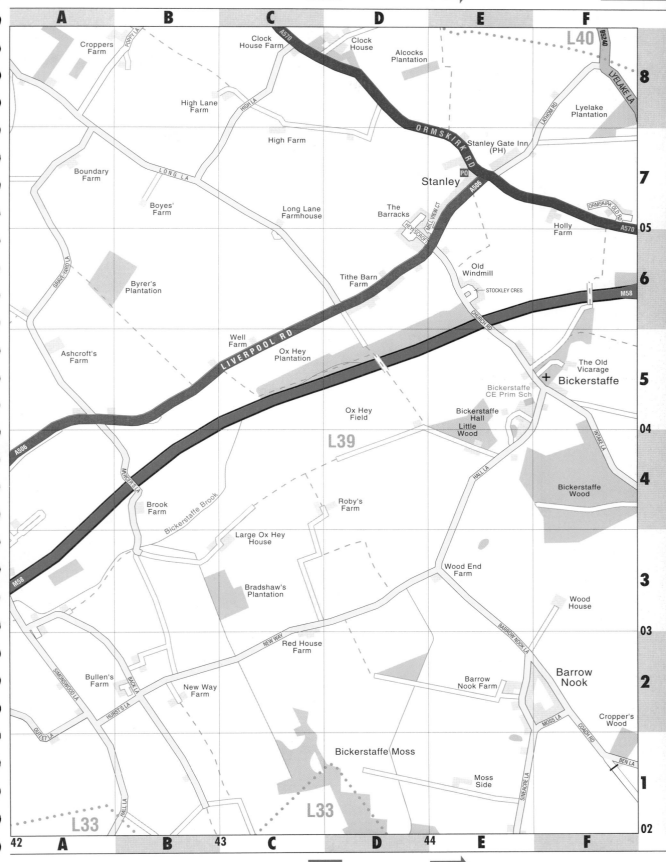

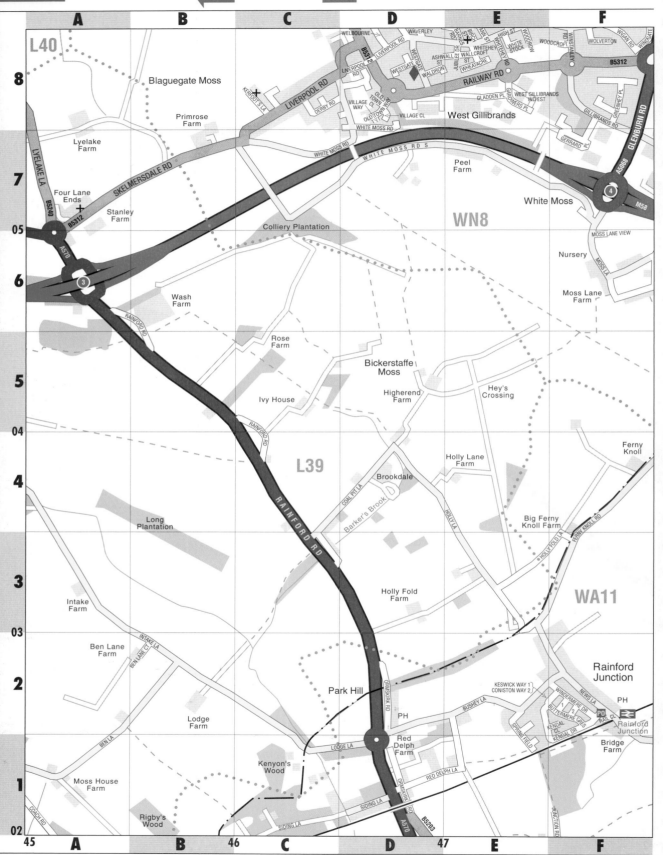

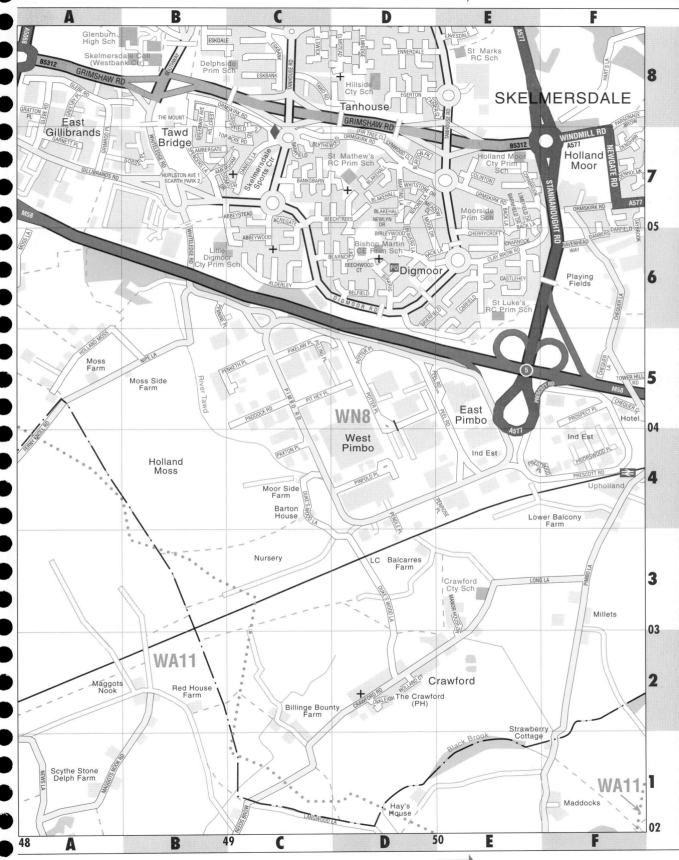

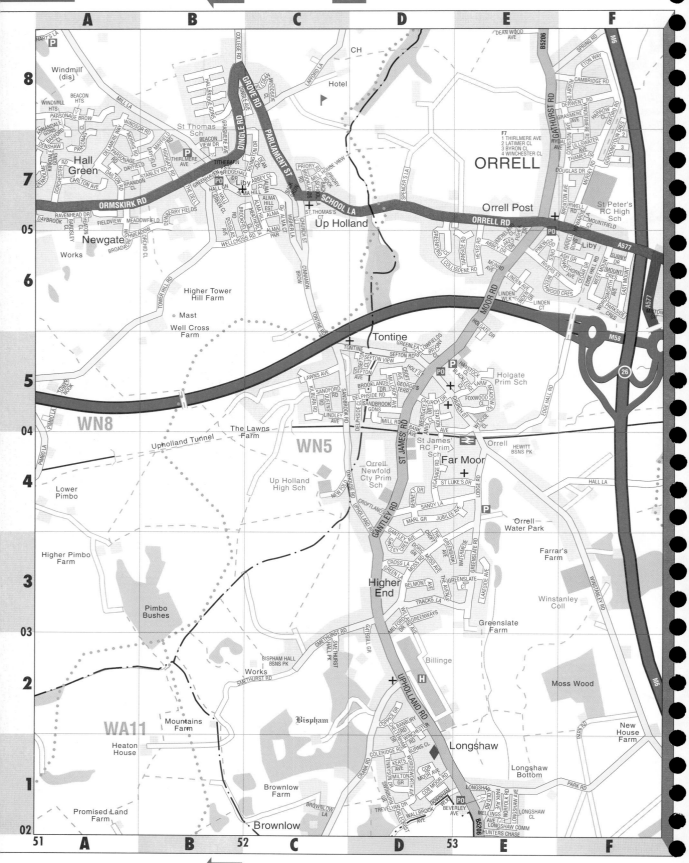

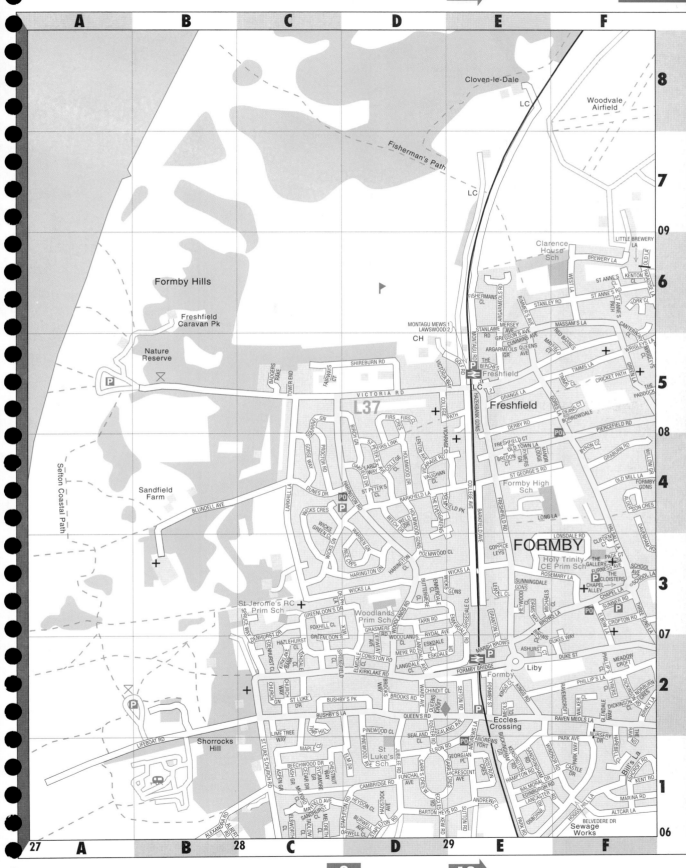

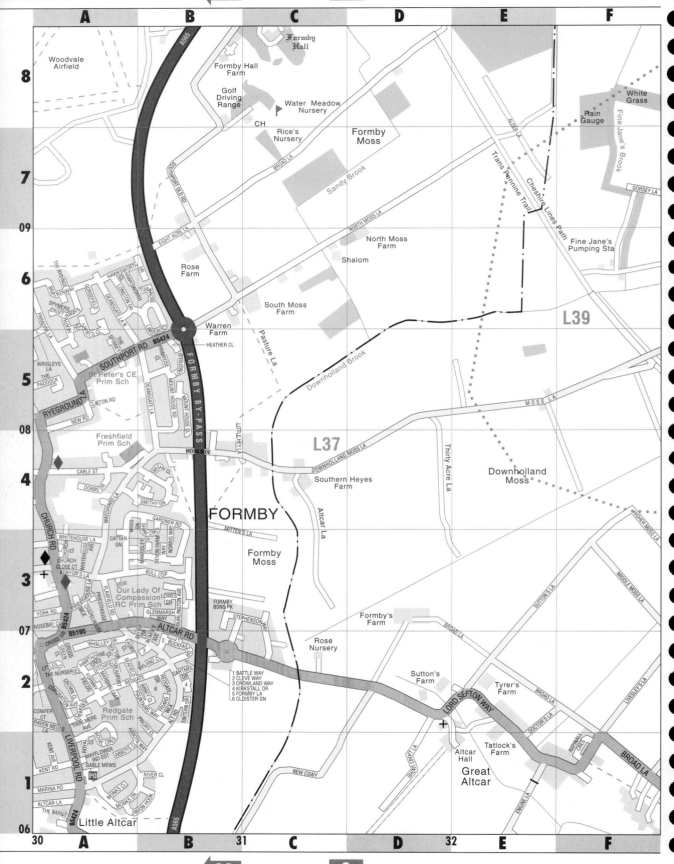

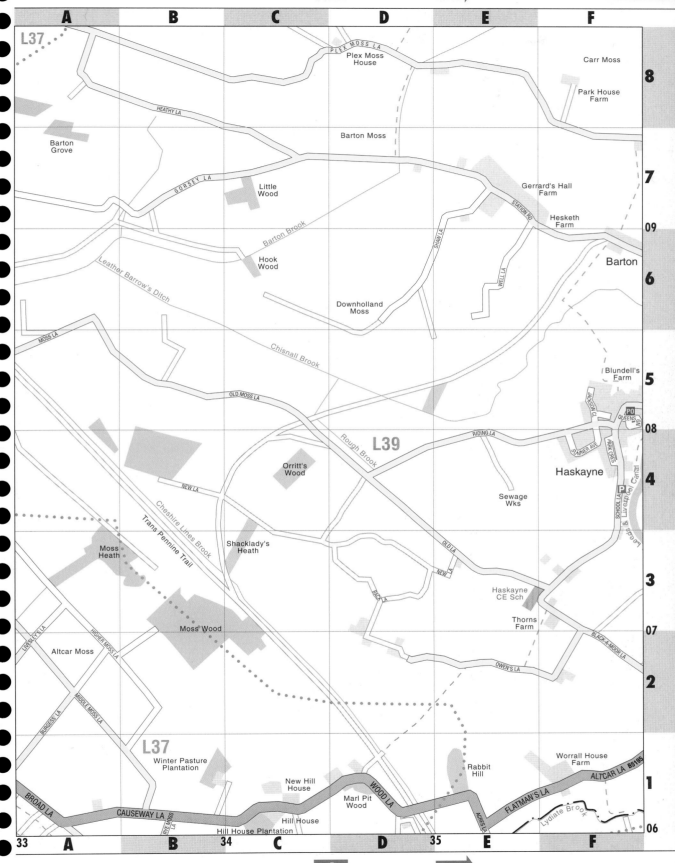

L37

A B C D E F

8

Carr Moss

Park House
Farm

Barton
Grove

HEATHY LA

Plex Moss
House

PLEX MOSS LA

Barton Moss

7

GORSEY LA

Little
Wood

Gerrard's Hall
Farm

Hesketh
Farm

STATION RD

09

Barton

Barton Brook

Hook
Wood

SHAW LA

6

WELL LA

Leather Barrow's Ditch

Downholland
Moss

MOSS LA

Chisnall Brook

Blundell's
Farm

5

JACKSON CL

PO
QUEENS GR

08

OLD MOSS LA

RIDING LA

PARK CRES

SUMNER AVE

Haskayne

L39

Rough Brook

4

Orritt's
Wood

Sewage
Wks

SCHOOL LA

P

NEW LA

Leeds & Liverpool Canal

Cheshire Lines Brook

Shacklady's
Heath

OLD LA

Haskayne
CE Sch

3

Moss
Heath

Trans Pennine Trail

NEW LA

BACK LA

Thorns
Farm

07

BLACK-A-MOOR LA

HIGHER MOSS LA

Moss Wood

OWEN'S LA

Altcar Moss

2

LIVESLEY'S LA

BURGESS LA

MIDDLE MOSS LA

L37

Winter Pasture
Plantation

Rabbit
Hill

Worrall House
Farm

ALTCAR LA B5195

1

BROAD LA

New Hill
House

WOOD LA

FLATMAN'S LA

Marl Pit
Wood

ACRES LA

Lydiate Brook

CAUSEWAY LA

RYE MOSS LA

Hill House

06

Hill House Plantation

33 A B 34 C D 35 E F

A   B   C   D   E   F

8

Halsall

CARR MOSS LA
LINAKER DR
A5147

NORTH MOOR LA
HARINGE LA

Watson House
Clock House
Primrose Hill Farm

NEW ST
Mill House Farm
Big Brick Farm
SUMMERWOOD LA
Lancashire Cycle Way
ASMALL LA
Primrose Hill
L40

Mere Lane Farm

7

Mere La
Malt House Farm
Bangor's Green
Wharton's Farm

PLEX MOSS LA
Trundle Pie La
Bangor's Green Farm
Aughton Cliffs Farm
GELL LA

09

SOUTHPORT RD
MILL BROW
Blue Bell Inn (PH)
Holly Farm
Model Farm
Trundle Pie House
NARROW LANE (CLIEVES HILLS)

6

STATION RD
SMITHY LA
HALSALL LA
Narrow Lane Farm

Wanishar Brook
Plex Lane Farm
Harker's Farm
PLEX LA
SMALL LA S
Goores Farm

WANISHAR LA
Leeds & Liverpool Canal
Shepherd's Farm
Clieves Hills Farm
BOOTH'S LA

5

Ship Inn (PH)
Gibbon's Farm
Dicconson's Farm
SHEPHERD'S LA
Lancashire Cycle Way

Moor Farm
Lowland Farm

SCHOOL LA
DELF CL
WOODS CL
ROSEMARY LA
L39
Firs La

08

DELF LA
Rosemary Farm
DICCONSON'S LA
Blundell House Farm

4

Clieves Hills
FIR TREE LA
SMALL LA

3

Downholland Hall
BYE LA
Firs Farm
FIRS LA
CLIEVES HILLS LA

Bank Farmhouse
Poplar Farm
Double Bank Farm
Clieves Hill Nursery

07

BROAD LA
FORMBY LA

2

Scarisbrick Arms (PH)
BLACK-A-MOOR LA
Works

ALTCAR LA
MAIRSCOUGH LA
Tanpit Farm
Leeds & Liverpool Canal

Downholland Cross

B5195
GREEN'S LA
Walsh Hall
B5195

Altcar Lane Farm
L31
Green's Lane Farm
Birches Brow Farm

1

Lydiate Brook
L31
A5147
MILL LA

06

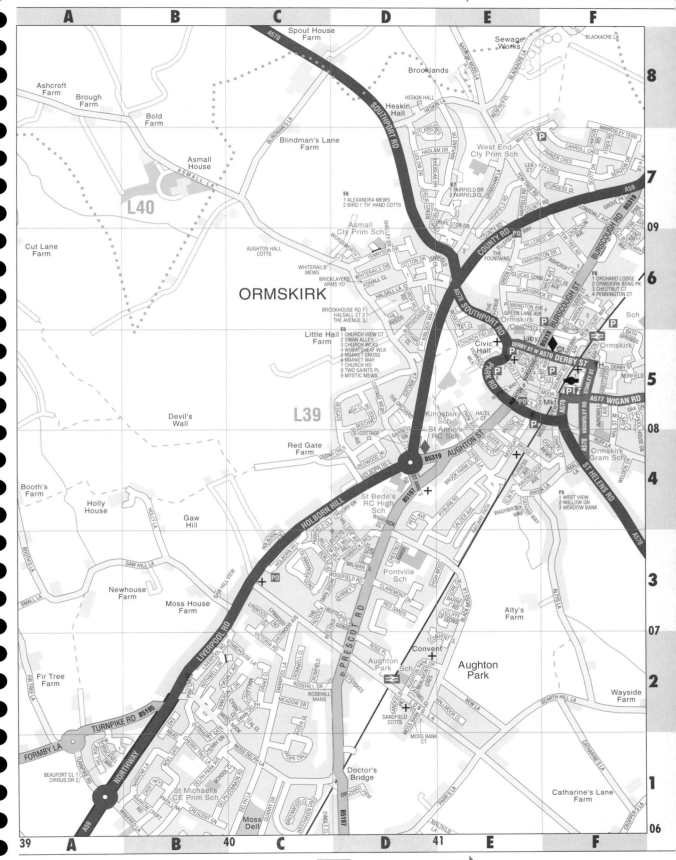

ORMSKIRK

L40

L39

Spout House Farm

Ashcroft Farm

Brough Farm

Bold Farm

Asmall House

Cut Lane Farm

Blindman's Lane Farm

Brooklands

Sewage Works

Blackacre La

Heskin Hall

West End Cty Prim Sch

Asmall Cty Prim Sch

E6
1 ALEXANDRA MEWS
2 BIRD I' TH' HAND COTTS

E7
1 FAIRFIELD DR
2 FAIRFIELD CL

Aughton Hall Cotts

Whiterails Mews

Bricklayers Arms Yd

Little Hall Farm

F6
1 ORCHARD LODGE
2 ORMSKIRK BSNS PK
3 CHESTNUT CT
4 PENNINGTON CT

BROOKHOUSE RD 1
HALSALL CT 2
THE AVENUE 3

E5
1 CHURCH VIEW CT
2 SWAN ALLEY
3 CHURCH WLKS
4 WHEATSHEAF WLK
5 MARKET CROSS
6 MARKET WAY
7 CHURCH HO
8 TWO SAINTS PL
9 MYSTIC MEWS

Civic Hall

Liby

Ormskirk

Devil's Wall

Kingsbury Sch

St Anne's RC Sch

Ormskirk Gram Sch

Red Gate Farm

Booth's Farm

Holly House

Gaw Hill

St Bede's RC High Sch

F5
1 WEST VIEW
2 WILLOW GN
3 MEADOW BANK

Newhouse Farm

Moss House Farm

Pontville Sch

Alty's Farm

Aughton Park

Wayside Farm

Fir Tree Farm

Convent

Aughton Park Sch

Doctor's Bridge

St Michael's CE Prim Sch

Moss Delf

Catharine's Lane Farm

BEAUFORT CL 1
CIRRUS DR 2

FORMBY LA

TURNPIKE RD B5195

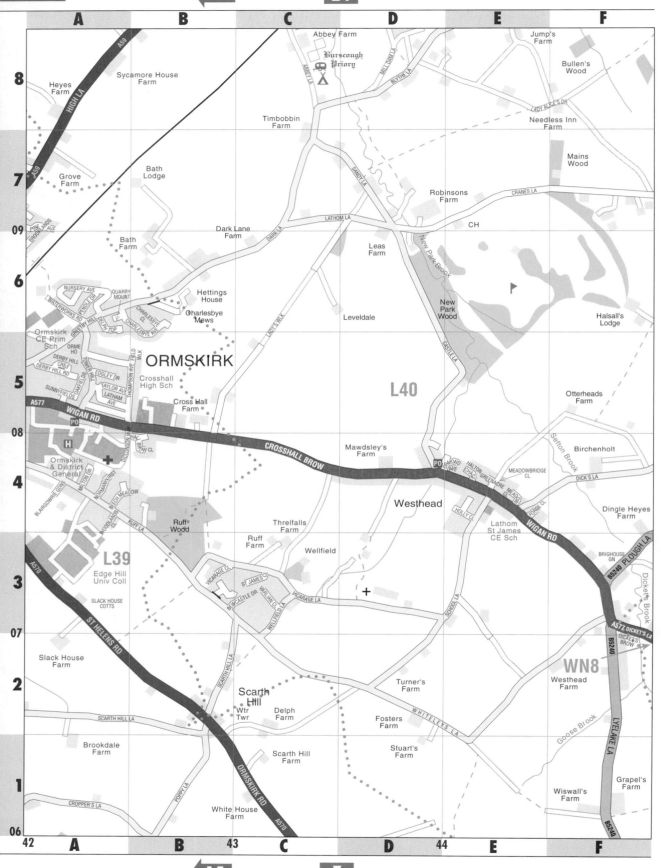

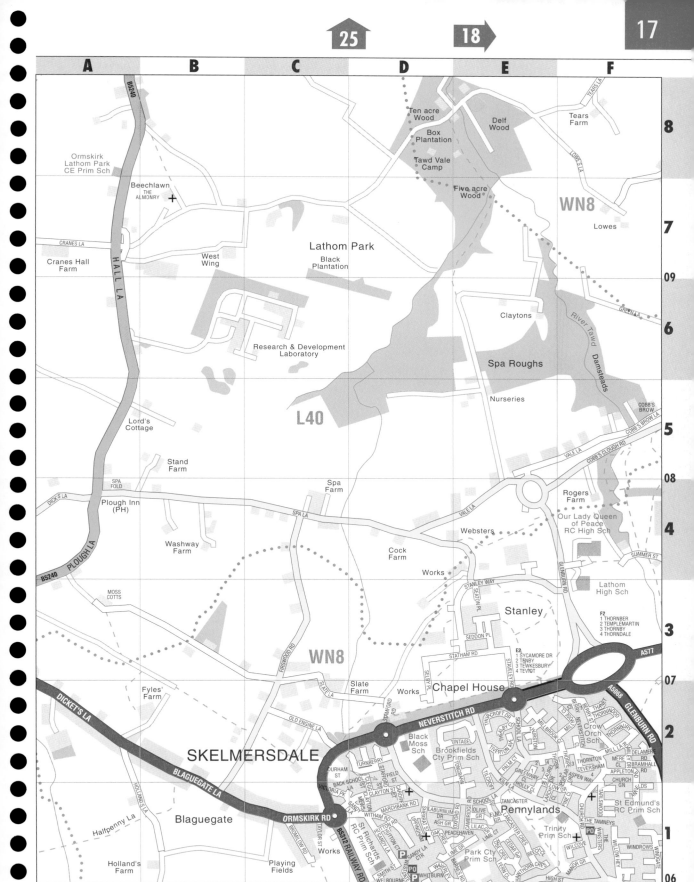

A **B** **C** **D** **E** **F**

B5240

Ten acre Wood

Delf Wood

Box Plantation

Tawd Vale Camp

Tears Farm

8

Ormskirk Lathom Park CE Prim Sch

Beechlawn THE ALMONRY

Five acre Wood

WN8

Lowes

7

HALL LA

CRANES LA

West Wing

Lathom Park

Black Plantation

09

GREEN LA

Cranes Hall Farm

River Tawd

Claytons

6

Research & Development Laboratory

L40

Spa Roughs

Damsteads

COBB'S BROW

Lord's Cottage

Nurseries

5

SPA FOLD

Stand Farm

VALE LA

COBB'S BROW LA

COBB'S CLOUGH RD

08

DICK'S LA

Plough Inn (PH)

Spa Farm

Rogers Farm

B5240

PLOUGH LA

SPA LA

VALE LA

WebSters

Our Lady Queen of Peace RC High Sch

SUMMER ST

4

Washway Farm

Cock Farm

GLENBURN RD

Lathom High Sch

MOSS COTTS

Works

Stanley Way

F2
1 THORNBER
2 TEMPLEMARTIN
3 THORNBY
4 THORNDALE

Stanley

3

FIRSWOOD RD

WN8

SEDDON PL

STATHAM RD

STANLEY RD

SEATON PL

E2
1 SYCAMORE DR
2 TENBY
3 TEWKESBURY
4 TEVIOT

A577

A5068

GLENBURN RD

07

Fyles' Farm

SLATE LA

Slate Farm

Works

Chapel House

SELBY PL

2

DICKET'S LA

OLD ENGINE LA

NEVERSTITCH RD

Black Moss Sch

Brookfields Cty Prim Sch

Crow Orch Sch

SKELMERSDALE

Durham St

TURNBERRY

STAFFORD ST

SCHOOL LA

TINTAGEL

TIVERTON

Pennylands

St Edmund's RC Prim Sch

BLAGUEGATE LA

Blaguegate

ORMSKIRK RD

BS312 RAILWAY RD

St Richards RC Prim Sch

MARCHBANK RD

Trinity Prim Sch

THE WINSTERS

WINDROWS

1

Halfpenny La

BROMILOW RD

Works

Playing Fields

P

St Richards RC Prim Sch

Park Cty Prim Sch

Holland's Farm

06

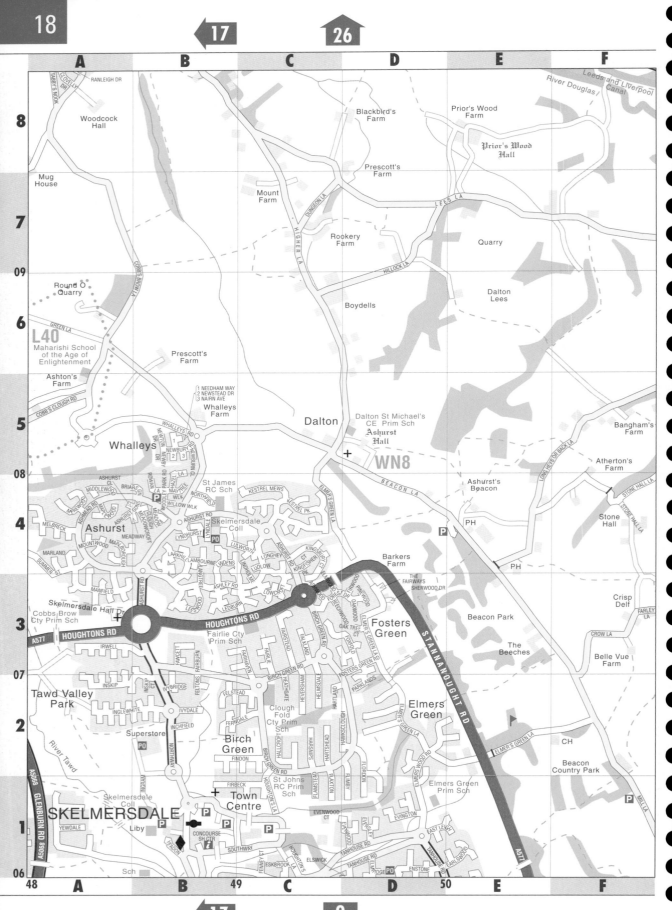

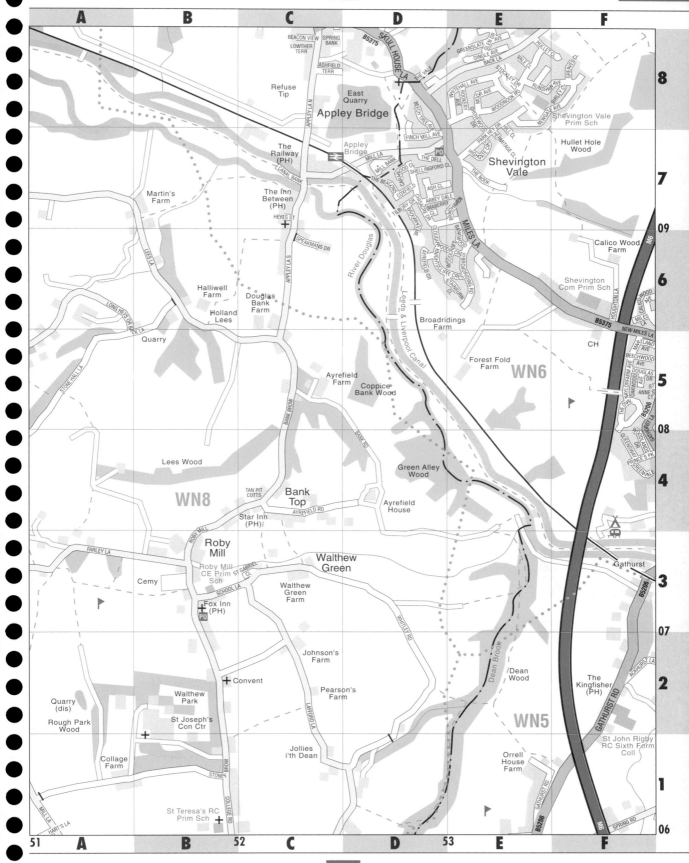

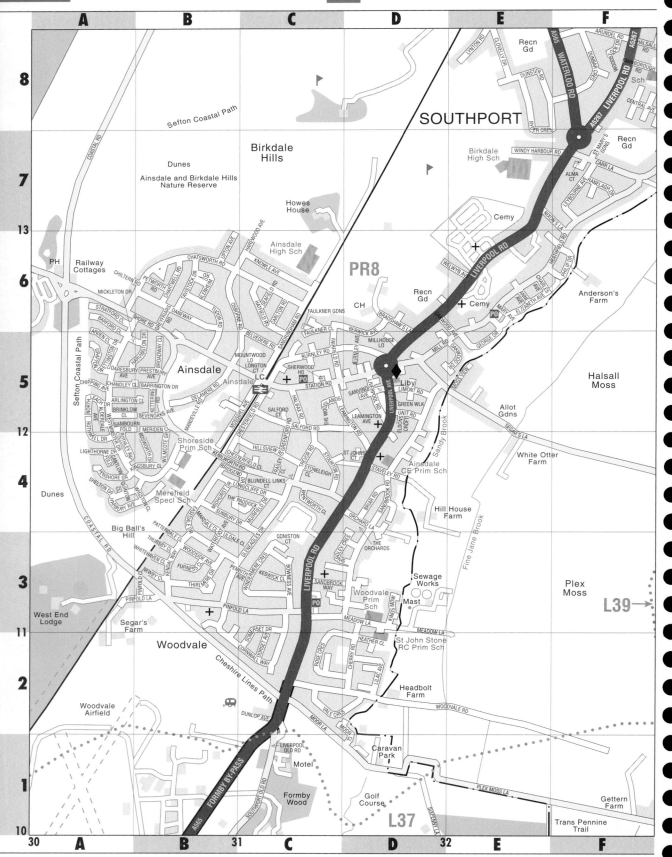

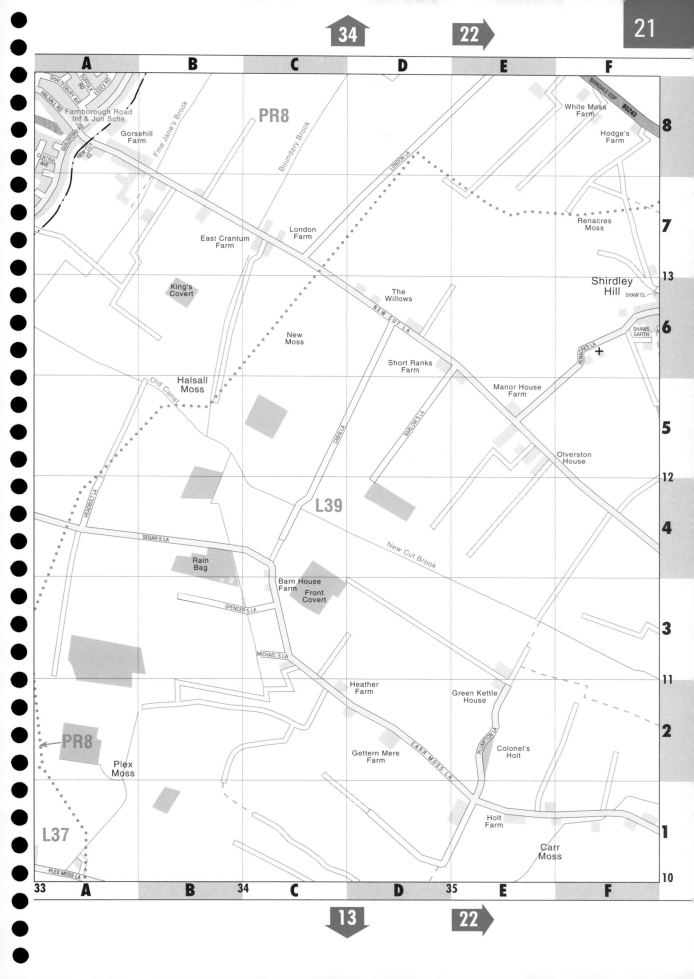

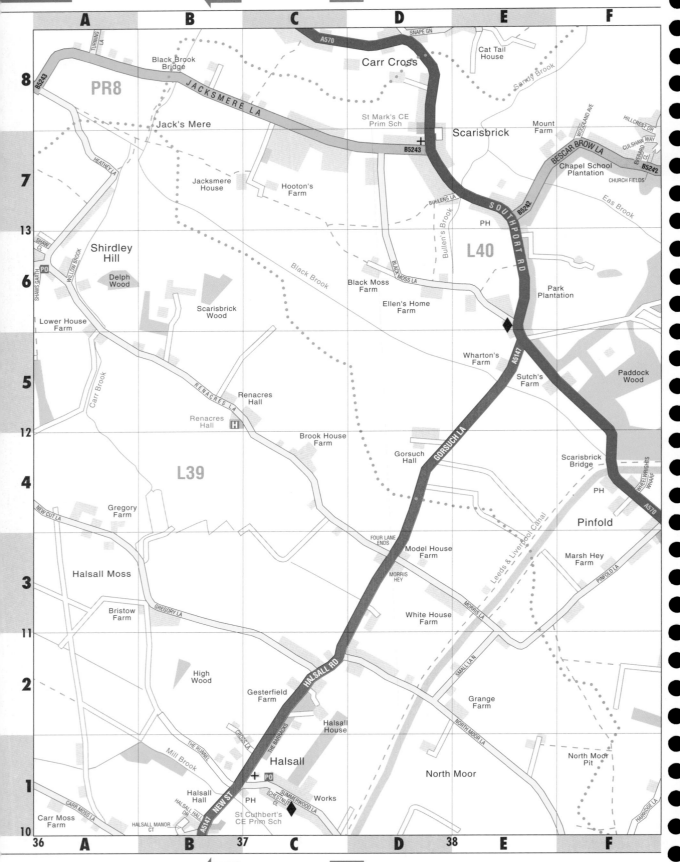

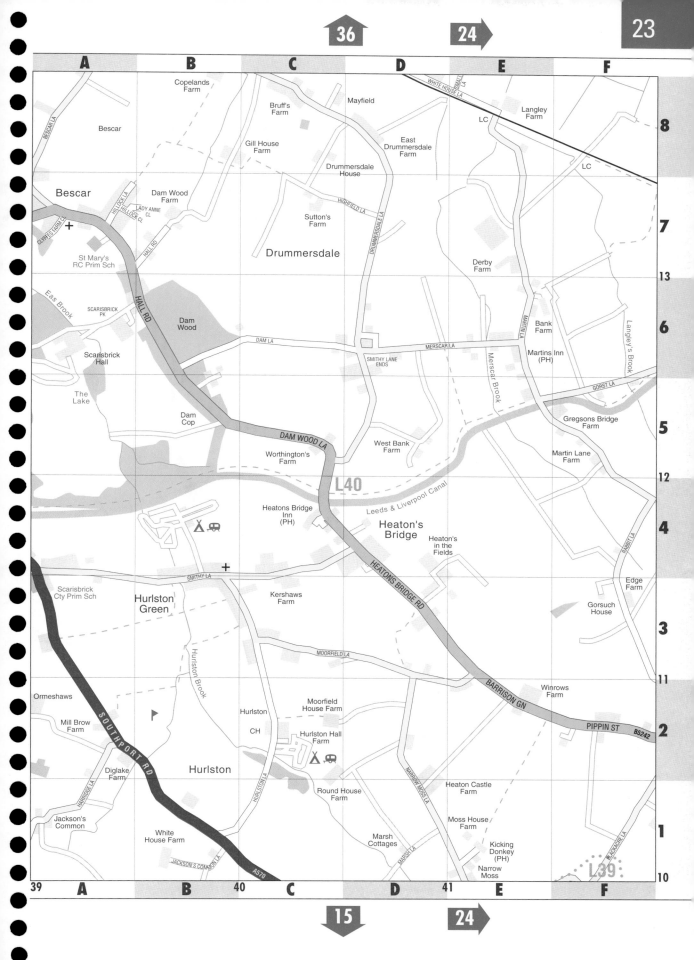

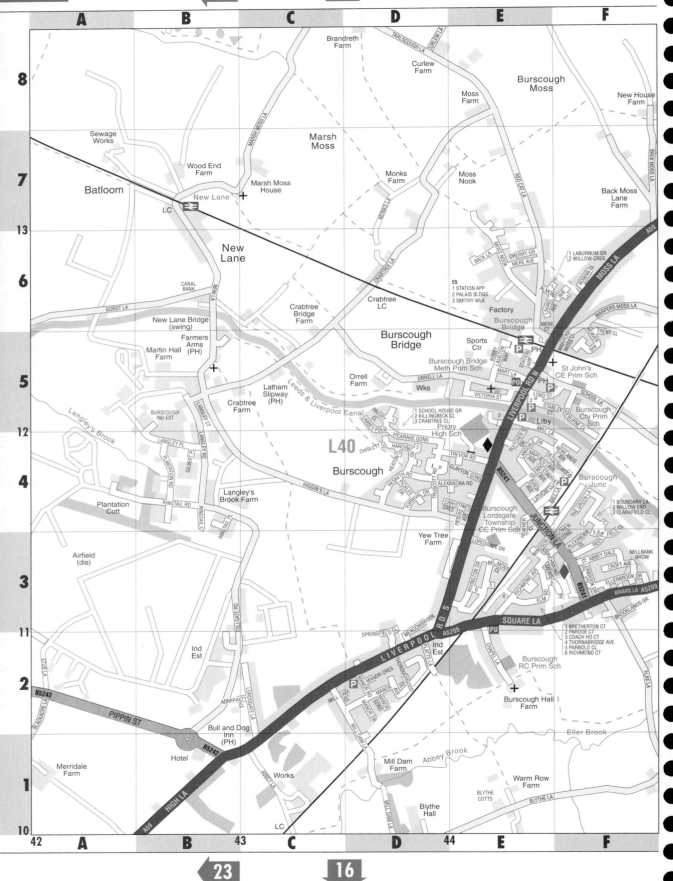

A   B   C   D   E   F

8

7

13

6

5

12

4

11

3

2

1

10

42   A   B   43   C   D   44   E   F

Brandreth Farm

Curlew Farm

Moss Farm

Burscough Moss

New House Farm

Marsh Moss

Monks Farm

Moss Nook

Sewage Works

Wood End Farm

Marsh Moss House

Batloom

New Lane

LC

New Lane

Red Cat La

Back Moss Lane Farm

Cherry Gr

Mere Ave

1 Laburnum Gr
2 Willow Cres

Moss La

Warpers Moss La

Canal Bank

Gorst La

New Lane Bridge (swing)

Crabtree Bridge Farm

Crabtree LC

Back La

E5
1 Station App
2 Palais Bldgs
3 Smithy Wlk

Factory

Burscough Bridge

Almond Ave

Rowan Ct

Trent Cl

Weaver Ct

Farmers Arms (PH)

Martin Hall Farm

Burscough Bridge

Sports Ctr

PH

Burscough Bridge Meth Prim Sch

Bobby Langton Way

P

PO

P

PH

St John's CE Prim Sch

Lord St

School La

Burscough Cty Prim Sch

Burscough Ind Est

Crabtree Farm

Latham Slipway (PH)

Orrell Farm

Orrell La

Wks

Leeds & Liverpool Canal

Victoria St

Stanley St

Liby

P

Mill La

Curbine Ct

Langley's Brook

Langley Ct

Langley Rd

Langley Pl

Gilbert Pl

Plantation Rd

Plantation Cott

Ringtail Rd

Ringtail Ct

Ringtail Pl

Langley's Brook Farm

Higgin's La

Priory Cl
Abbey Fold

1 School House Gr
2 Killingbeck Cl
3 Crabtree Cl

Vicarage Gdns

Chislett Cl

Harding Cl

Heaton Cl

L40

Burscough

Priory High Sch

Trevor Rd

Fletcher's Ct

Lancaster Dr

Map St

Hazelwood Ave

Newlands Ave

Rees Rd

The Green La

Burscough Junc

1 Boundary La
2 Willow End
3 Clarkfield Cl

Hesketh Rd

Pickles Dr

Furnival Dr

Truscott Rd

Christines Cres

Clayton Gdns

Alexandora Rd

Peters Ave

Glenroyd Ave

Glenstry Ave

Lathom Ave

Burscough Lordsgate Township CE Prim Sch

Junction La

Gover Rd

Alexander

Dover Gdns

Field Cl

Airfield (dis)

Yew Tree Farm

Lordsgate Dr

Windsor Dr

Richard

Millbank Brow

Abbey Dale

Croft Ave

Ellerbrook Dr

Briars La   A5209

Bel Mont Cl

Rivington Dr

Richmond Ave

Elm Dr

B5241

Brooklands Gr

Ind Est

Springfield Cl

Meadowbrook

Thornbrook

Platts La

A5209

Chapel La

PO

Square La

1 Bretherton Ct
2 Pardoe Ct
3 Coach Ho Ct
4 Thornabridge Ave
5 Parbold Cl
6 Richmond Ct

Burscough RC Prim Sch

Flax La

B5242

Stubi La

Blackacre La

Pippin St

Admiralty Cl

Lordsgate La

Manor Cres

Mill Dam Cl

Manor Rd

Manor Gdns

Manor Dr

Liverpool Rd S

Ind Est

Mill Dam La

Burscough Hall Farm

Eller Brook

Merridale Farm

Bull and Dog Inn (PH)

Hotel

B5242

Works

Abbey La

Mill Dam Farm

Abbey Brook

Blythe Hall

Blythe Cotts

Warm Row Farm

Blythe La

A59

High La

LC

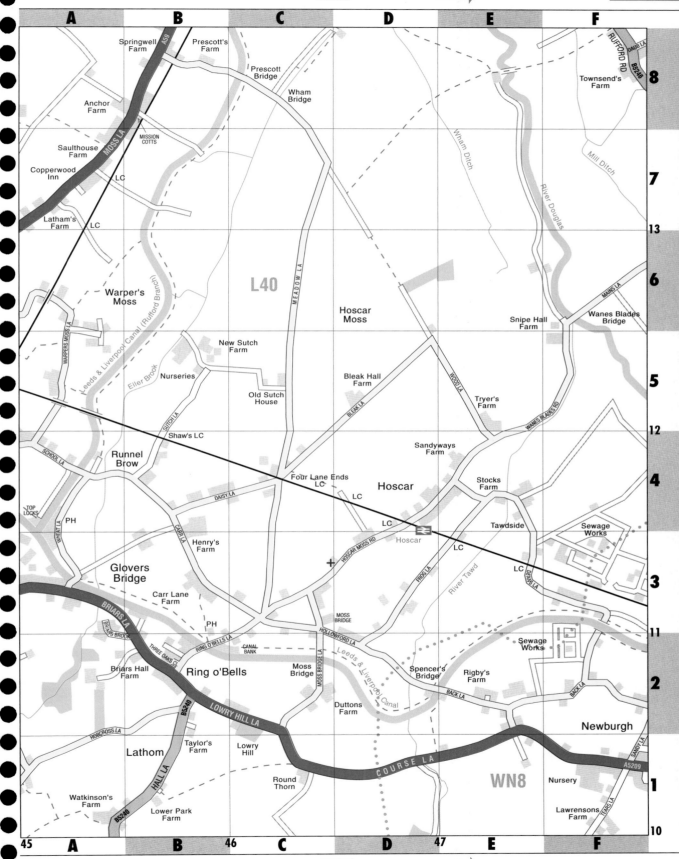

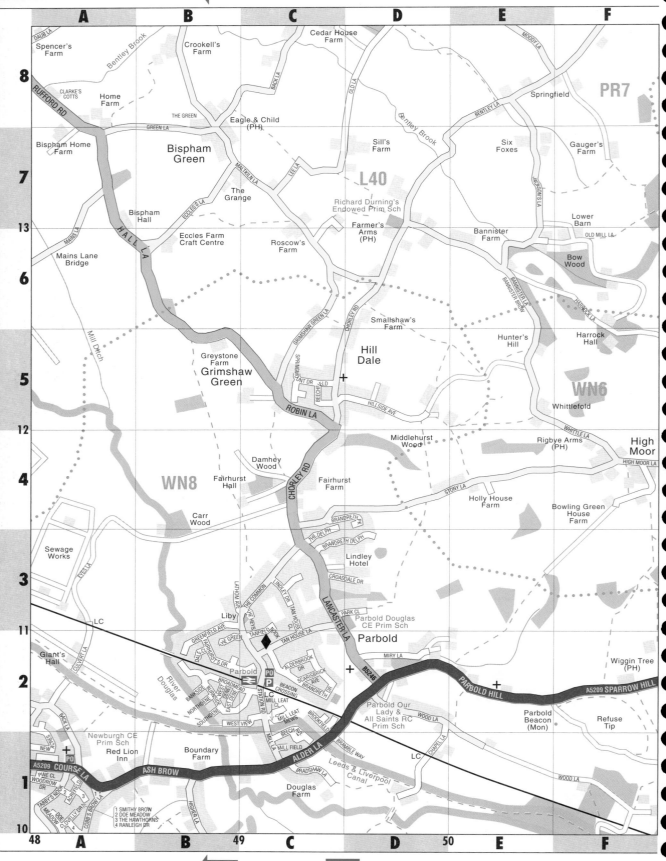

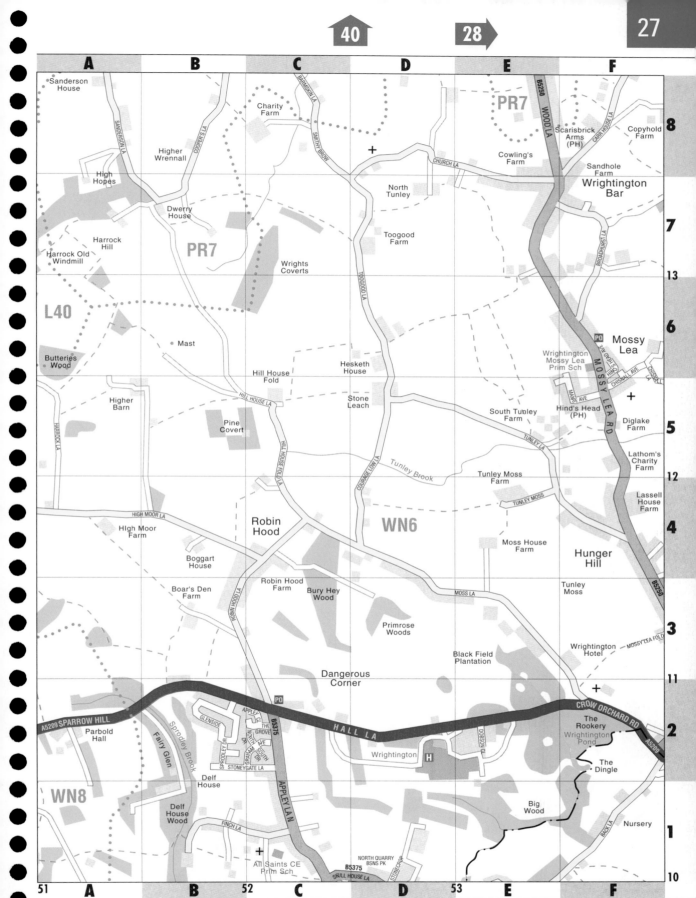

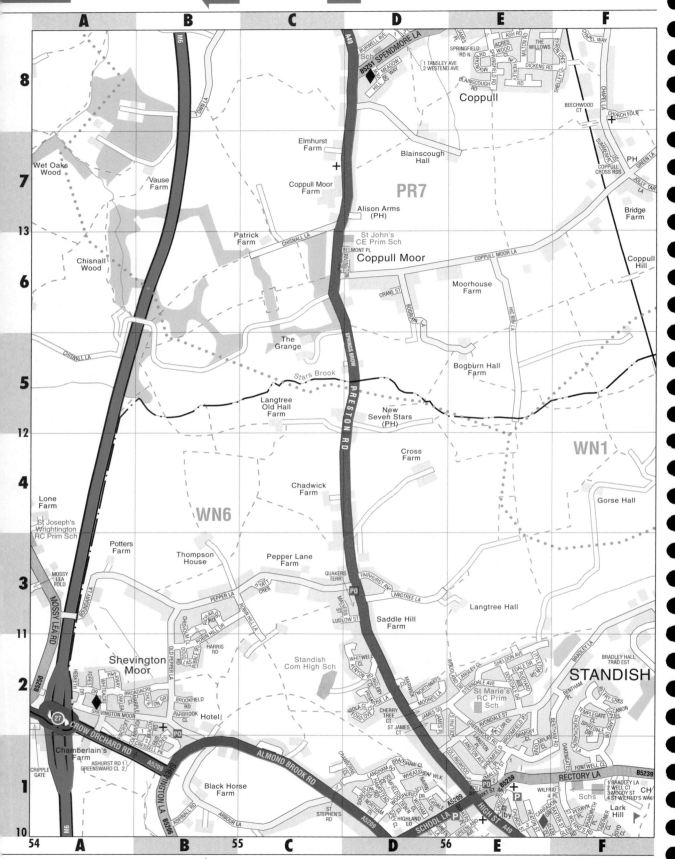

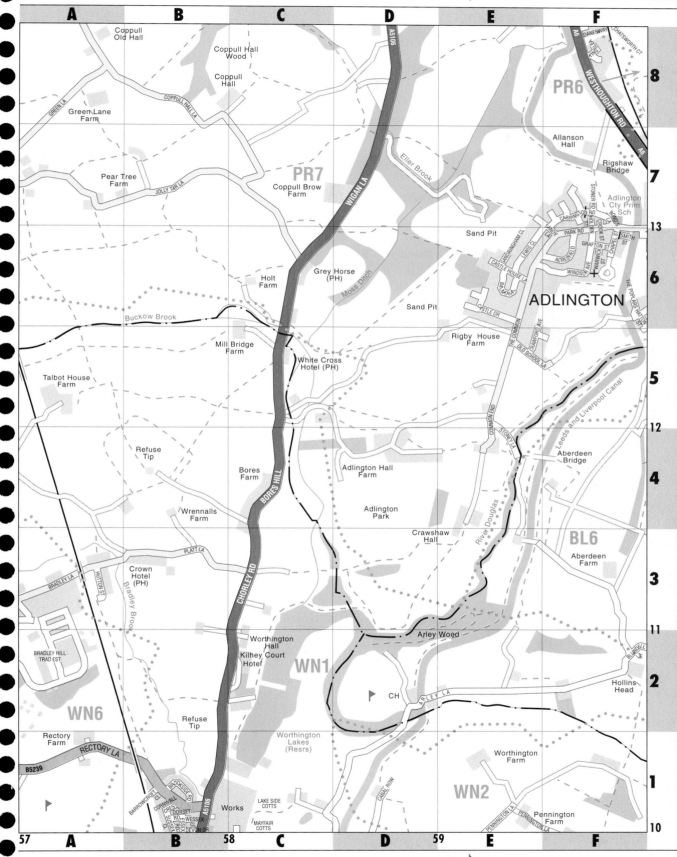

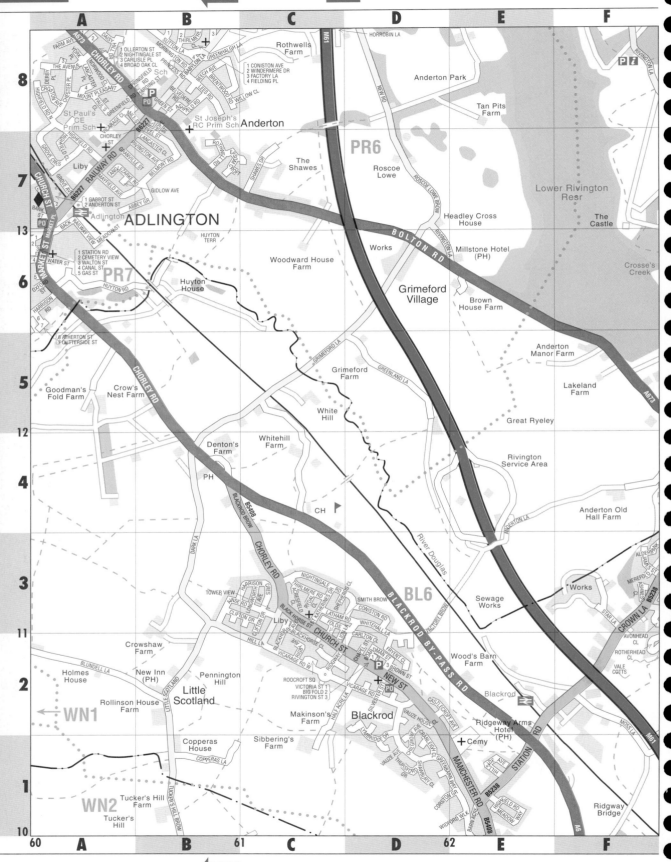

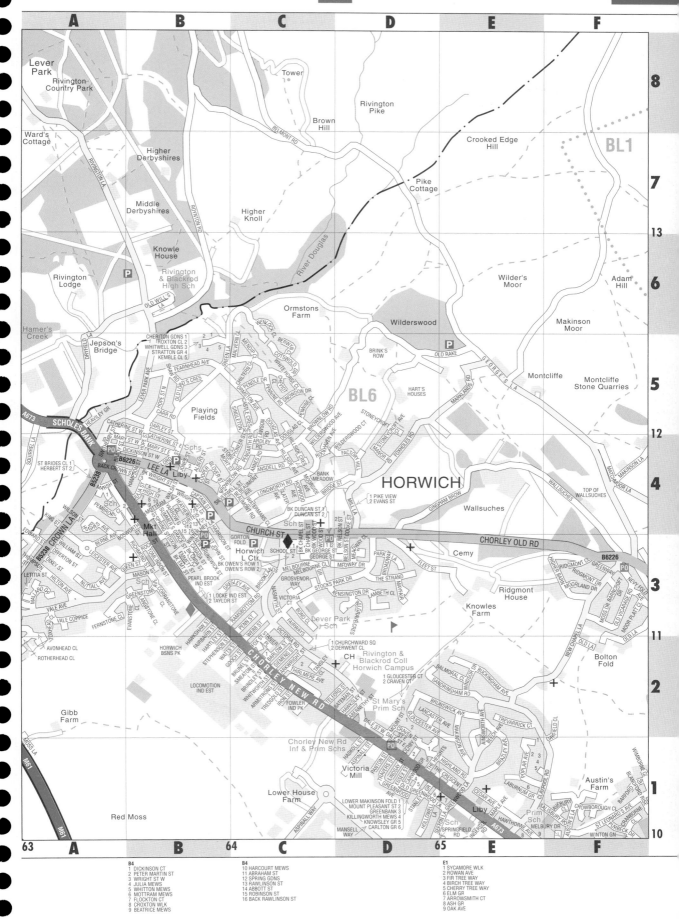

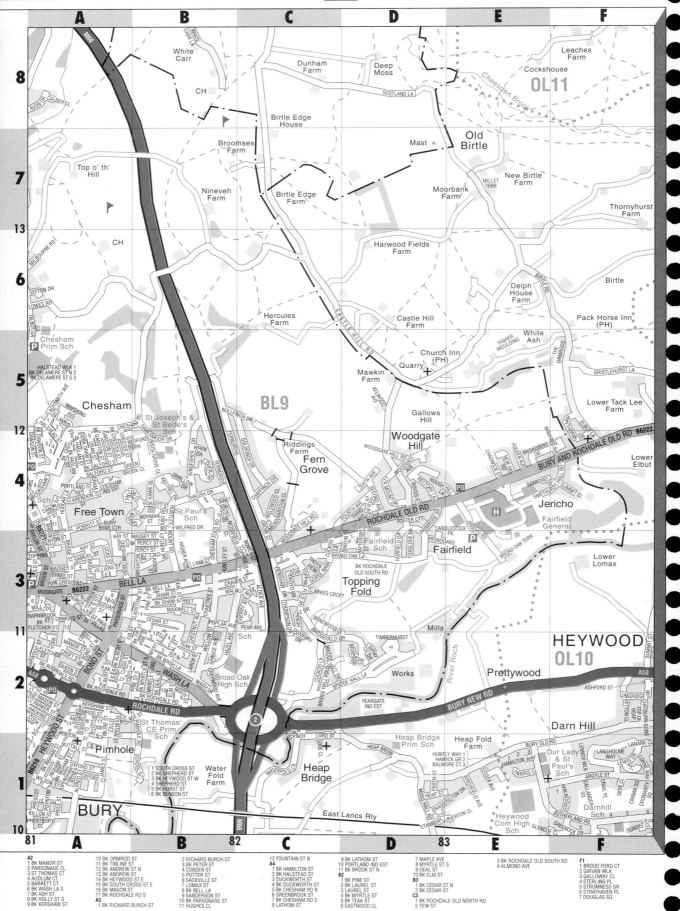

A2
1 BK MANOR ST
2 PARSONAGE CL
3 ST THOMAS CT
4 AUDLUM CT
5 BARRETT CT
6 BK WASH LA S
7 BK ASH ST
8 BK HOLLY ST S
9 BK KERSHAW ST

10 BK ORMROD ST
11 BK TINLINE ST
12 BK ANDREW ST N
13 BK ANDREW ST
14 BK HEYWOOD ST E
15 BK SOUTH CROSS ST E
16 BK MASON ST
17 BK ROCHDALE RD S
A3
1 BK RICHARD BURCH ST

2 RICHARD BURCH ST
3 BK PETER ST
4 COBDEN ST
5 POTTER ST
6 SACKVILLE ST
7 LOMAX ST
8 BK BELL LA
9 SANDERSON ST
10 BK PARSONAGE ST
11 HUGHES CL

12 FOUNTAIN ST N
A4
1 BK HAMILTON ST
2 BK HALSTEAD ST
3 DUCKWORTH ST
4 BK DUCKWORTH ST N
5 GREENBROOK ST
6 BK CHESHAM RD S
7 LATHOM ST

9 BK LATHOM ST
10 PORTLAND IND EST
11 BK BROOK ST N
B2
1 BK PINE ST
2 BK LAUREL ST
3 LAUREL ST
4 BK MYRTLE ST
5 BK TEAK ST
6 EASTWOOD CL

7 MAPLE AVE
8 MYRTLE ST S
9 DEAL ST
10 BK ELM ST
B3
1 BK CEDAR ST N
2 BK CEDAR ST
C3
1 BK ROCHDALE OLD NORTH RD
2 YEW ST

3 BK ROCHDALE OLD SOUTH RD
4 ALMOND AVE

F1
1 BROOD FORD CT
2 GIRVAN WLK
3 GALLOWAY CL
4 STERLING PL
5 STROMNESS GR
6 STRATHAVEN PL
7 DOUGLAS SQ

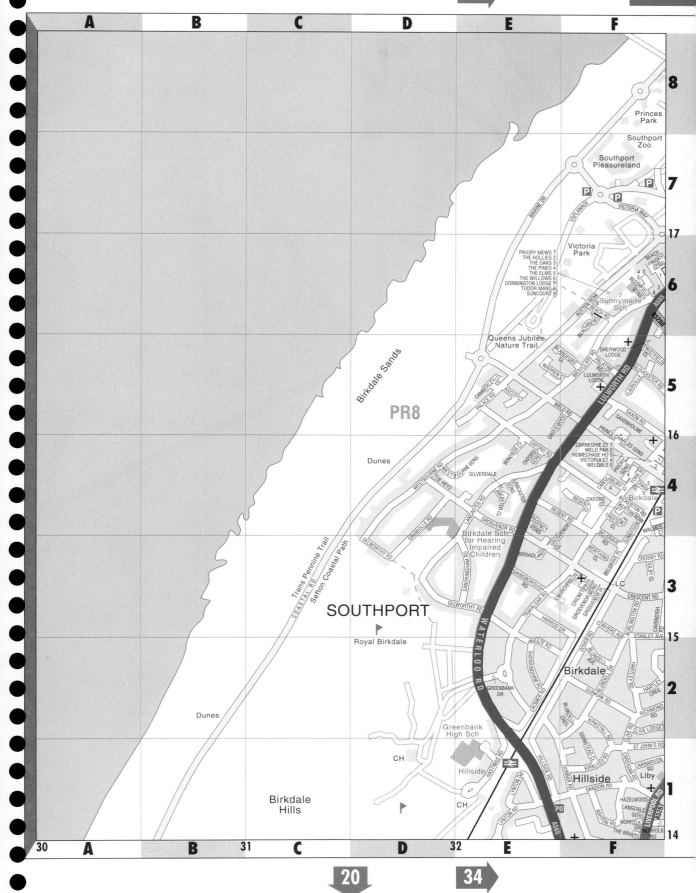

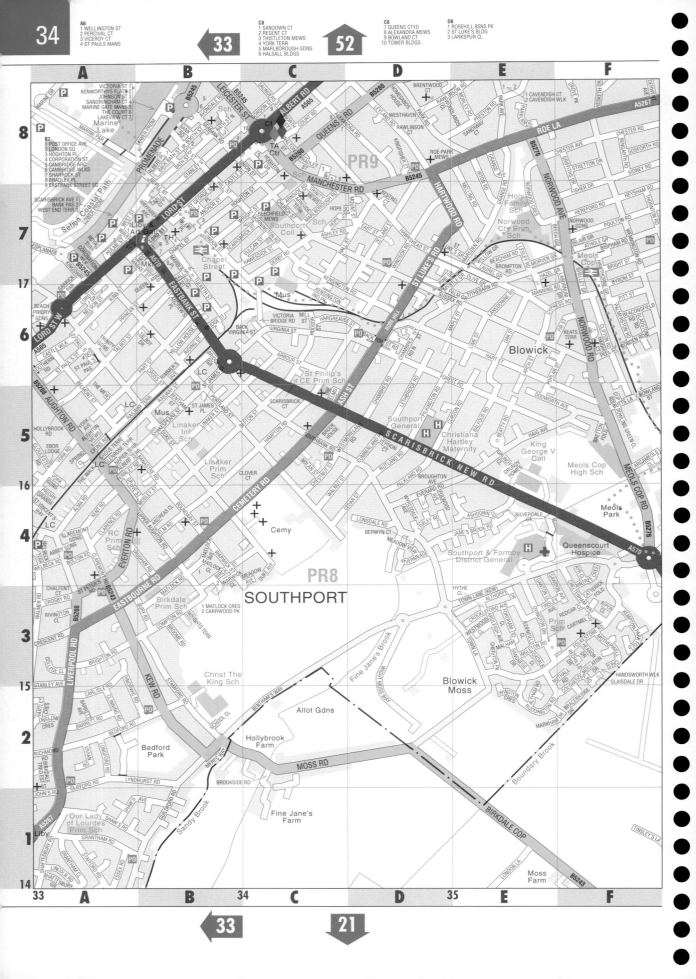

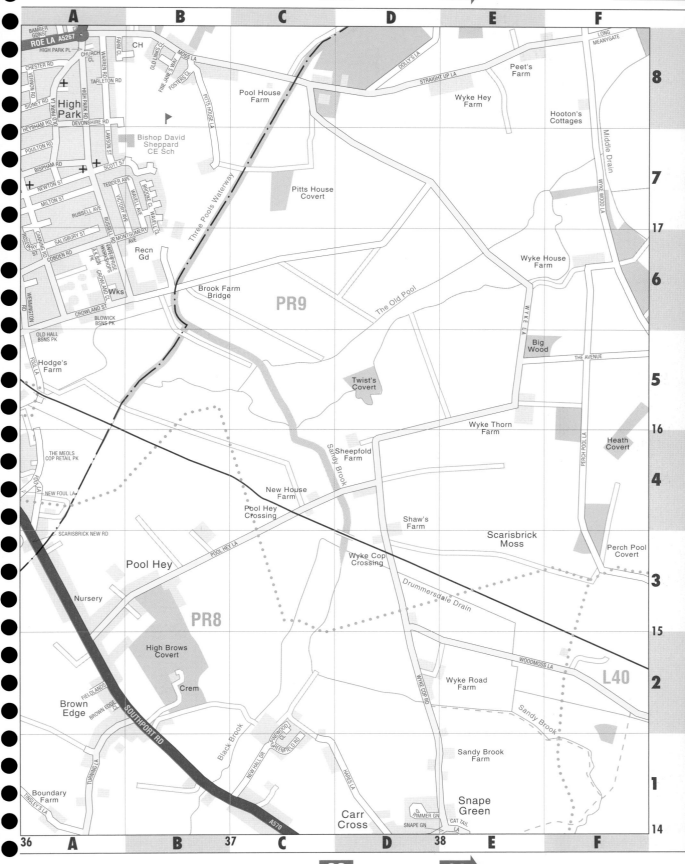

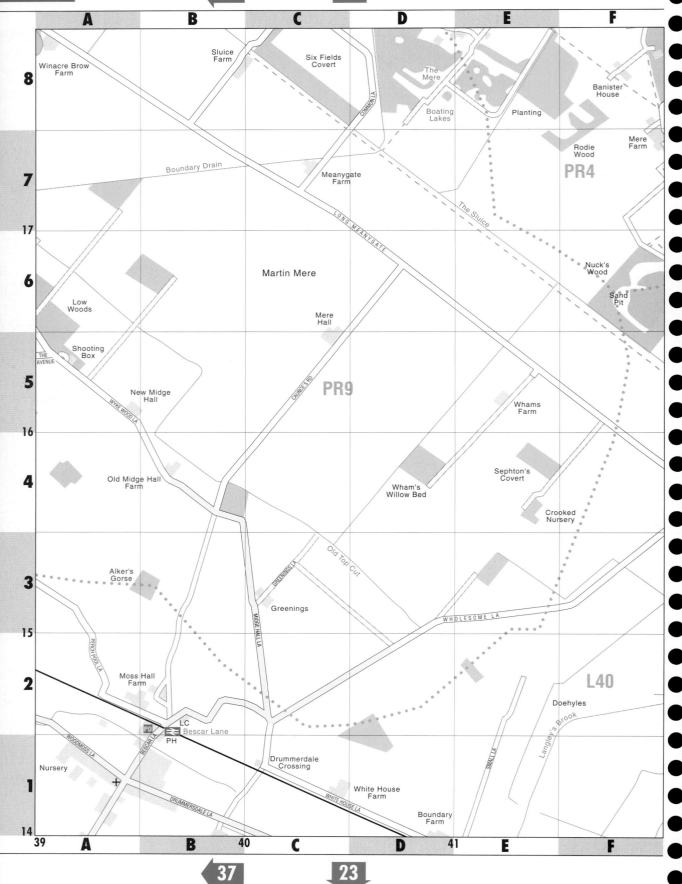

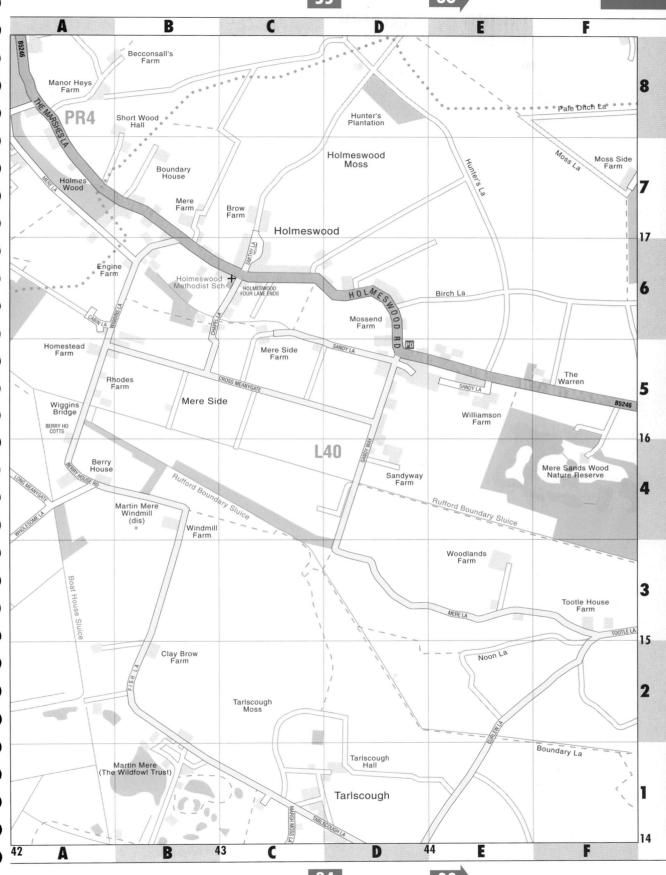

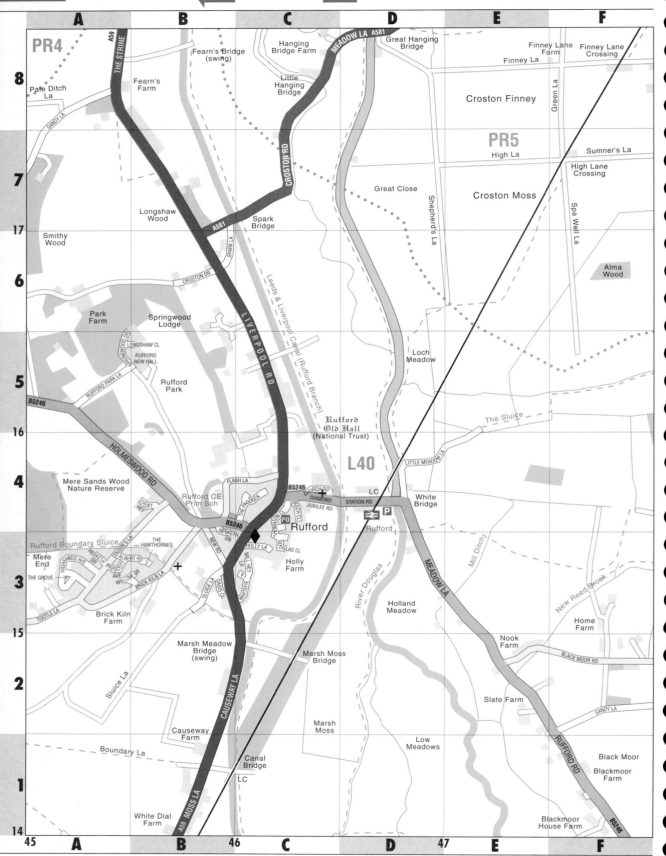

37
56

PR4

A59

THE STRINE

Pale Ditch La

SANDY LA

Fearn's Bridge (swing)

Fearn's Farm

Hanging Bridge Farm

MEADOW LA   A581

Great Hanging Bridge

Finney Lane Farm

Finney Lane Crossing

Finney La

Little Hanging Bridge

Croston Finney

PR5

Green La

High La

Sumner's La

CROSTON RD

High Lane Crossing

Smithy Wood

Longshaw Wood

A581

Spark Bridge

SPARK LA

Great Close

Shepherd's La

Croston Moss

Spa Well La

Alma Wood

CROSTON DR

Park Farm

Springwood Lodge

LONGSHAW UP

LONGSHAW CL

RUFFORD NEW HALL

LIVERPOOL RD

Leeds & Liverpool Canal (Rufford Branch)

Loch Meadow

RUFFORD PARK LA

Rufford Park

Rufford Old Hall (National Trust)

The Sluice

LITTLE MEADOW LA

L40

HOLMESWOOD RD

Mere Sands Wood Nature Reserve

Rufford CE Prim Sch

FLASH LA

THE PADDOCK

B5246

ORCH RD

DIAMOND

LC

STATION RD

White Bridge

B5246

CROFT HEY

JUBILEE RD

PO

Rufford

Rufford

Mill Ditch

New Reed Brook

Rufford Boundary Sluice

THE HAWTHORNES

COUSIN'S LA

ALBERT RD

PRESCOTT

HESKETH GN

NEW RD

SLUICE LA

OASIS CL

WHATEHE LA

WILL HEY

HOLLY LA

Holly Farm

DOUGLAS CL

River Douglas

Holland Meadow

Home Farm

Mere End

HIGH SANDS AVE

WILLOW GR

BRICK KILN LA

THE GROVE

TOOTLE LA

Brick Kiln Farm

Nook Farm

BLACK MOOR RD

Marsh Meadow Bridge (swing)

Marsh Moss Bridge

Slate Farm

SANDY LA

Sluice La

CAUSEWAY LA

Marsh Moss

Low Meadows

RUFFORD RD

Black Moor

Blackmoor Farm

Boundary La

Causeway Farm

Canal Bridge

LC

Blackmoor House Farm

B5246

A59

MOSS LA

White Dial Farm

37
25

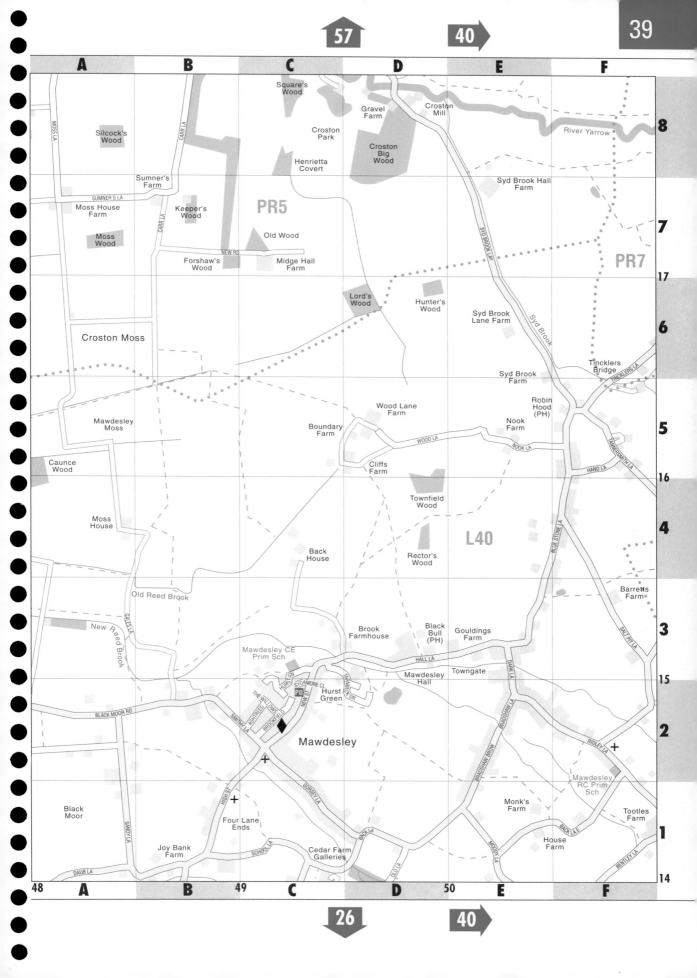

A B C D E F

8

River Yarrow

River Yarrow

River Yarrow

Eccleston Bridge

Hilton Hall Farm

Hodge Brook

7

BS250

NEW LA

WESTMINSTER PL

TOWNGATE

THE CEDARS

Blue Anchor (PH)

PO

VIEW ST

THE CROFT

LAWRENCE LA

WARWICK RD

WINDSOR RD

SANDRINGHAM RD

CONWAY RD

RICHMOND RD

WOODCOCK FOLD

PARR COTTAGE CL

Eccleston

Dig Leach Farm

Bradley Hall

PARR LA

Wood End Farm

17

THE FIELDS

GREENWAY

THE HAWTHORNS

BANNER CL

CRICKET LEA

BOUNDARY CL

G L CRES

THE CLOSE

MARSDEN CL

DOCTOR'S LA

DRAPERS AVE

Liby

Bradley Hall Wood

Bates Farm

Little Wood End Farm

BACK LA

Sibbering's Farm

RED LA

TINCKLERS

Rayner House

Eccleston Cty Prim Sch

BEECH FLDS

BEECHCROFT

REEVESWOOD

6

THE GREEN

NEW MILL ST

PO

MIDDLEWOOD CL

SAGAR ST

St Mary's CE Prim Sch

COTSWOLD CL

BRADLEY LA

New Bradley Hall Farm

Alder Hall Farm

RED HOUSE LA

HAWKSWOOD

ROCKWOOD

LARKFIELD

THE BRIARS

SNIPEWOOD

NEW ST

PARK ST

PIKE LA

WOODART LA

BELSTRING LA

CAVER'D CL

LORD ST

Sagar House

Big Wood

PR7

Woodart Bridge

Preston Nook

GROVE MILL DEVELOPMENT CTR

LANGTON BROW

SHELLY DR

VICAR'S CL

High Heys Farm

Woodcock La

5

Sherbourn House

MILL LA

LANGTON LA

Syd Brook

Heskin Bridge

16

Lang's Farm

WRENNALLS LA

Spring Wood

WHALLEY RD

Little Wood

Camelot Theme Pk

Thomson's Farm

4

Knowles' Wood

Heskin Hall

HIGHGROVE AVE

YEWLANDS AVE

PARK HALL RD

TANNERSMITH LA

Howe Brook

BANNISTER GR

Heskin Hall Farm

Pye Brook

Heskin Green

PH

Green Farm

Bimson's Farm

3

HALL GREEN LA

Heskin Old Hall Farm

HALFPENNY LA

Howe Brook House

WOOD LA

STOCKS LA

CHISNALL LA

15

PO

THE MEADOWS

WITHINGTON LA

2

Salt Pit House

L40

TOWN LA

Pyebrook Hall

Pemberton's CE Sch

School Farm

BARMSKIN LA

1

Andertons Mill

RIDLEY LA

BENTLEY LA

SANDERSON LA

COOPER'S LA

Barmskin Hall Farm

BARMSKIN LA

Kingsley House

BS250

WN6

CARR HOUSE LA

14

Brook House (PH)

51 A B 52 C D 53 E F

E1
1 GERMAN LA
2 CLEVELAND ST
3 SPRINGFIELD RD N
4 MILL ST

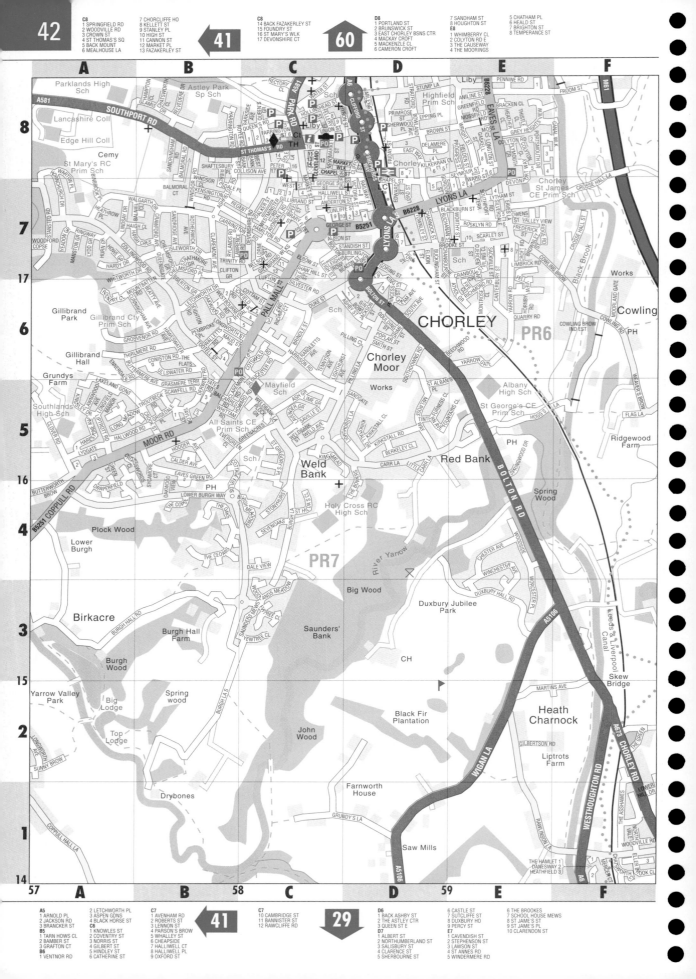

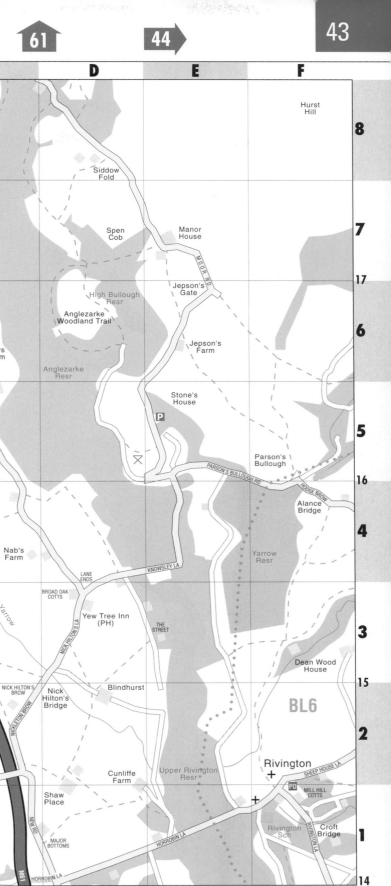

A   B   C   D   E   F

Grey
Heights

Hurst
Hill

8

Grey Heights Wood

Siddow
Fold

White
House

Works

Spen
Cob

Manor
House

7

CROSSE HALL LA

Johnson's
Farm

High Bullough
Resr

Jepson's
Gate

17

Bibbys
Farm

Anglezarke
Woodland Trail

Jepson's
Farm

6

Fish Barn
Farm

Kays
Farm

M61

Limbrick

Ainsworths
Farm

Anglezarke
Resr

Stone's
House

PH

HEAPEY FOLD LA

BACK LA

Brindles
Farm

Waring's
Farm

P

Parson's
Bullough

5

PR6

PARSON'S BULLOUGH RD

HODGE BROW

16

Holland
Fold

Hallsworth
Fold Farm

Alance
Bridge

4

LONG LA

HUT LA

OLDE STONEHEATH CT

Nab's
Farm

Yarrow
Resr

River Yarrow

Knowsley LA

LANE
ENDS

BROAD OAK
COTTS

Yew Tree Inn
(PH)

THE
STREET

3

15

CH

Nick Hilton's
Bridge

NICK HILTON'S LA

NICK HILTON'S
BROW

Nick
Hilton's
Bridge

Blindhurst

Dean Wood
House

PR7

Hall o' th' Hill
Farm

Broad Oak
Farm

BL6

2

SLACK'S LA

NICKLETON BROW

Cunliffe
Farm

Rivington

Slack's
Farm

NICKLETON

Upper Rivington
Resr

PO

SHEEP HOUSE LA

MILL HILL
COTTS

Lonsdale
Farm

Bay Horse
Hotel
(PH)

Shaw
Place

Rivington
Sch

RIVINGTON LA

Croft
Bridge

1

LOWER HILL DR

WATERFORD ST

Fairview

New
House

Springfield
Cottages

MAJOR
BOTTOMS

HORROBIN LA

A673 CHORLEY RD

BROOK ST

OLLERTON ST

DAISY HILL DR

SUTTON LA

WINDERMERE DR

THIRLMERE CL

STONEGATE FOLD

MILLBROOK
ROW

BARNLOW LA

NEW RD

HORROBIN LA

M61

14

60   A   B   61   C   D   E   62   F

43
62

A   B   C   D   E   F

8

Rushy Brow

Devil's Ditch

Anglezarke Moor

Black Lower Hill

Counting Hill

Redmond's Edge

High Shores

Limestone Clough

Standing Stones Hill

PR6

7

White Ledge Hill

BL7

Spitlers Edge

Limestone Brook

Lead Mines Clough

17

Holts Flat

6

Higher Anshaw

Sam Pasture

Will Narr

Hordern Pasture

5

River Yorrow

16

BL6

RIVINGTON RD

Hordern Stoops

4

DEAN HEAD LA

Wilcock's Farm

Moor Bottom

Sparks Bridge

Moses Cocker's

Shore

3

Bradleys

SHEEP HOUSE LA

BELMONT RD

Noon Hill Slack

15

Winter Hill Masts

HALL LA

2

Noon Hill

Rivington Hall Barn

Catter Nab

Rivington Moor

1

Brere's Meadow Pit

14

63   A   B   64   C   D   65   E   F

43
31

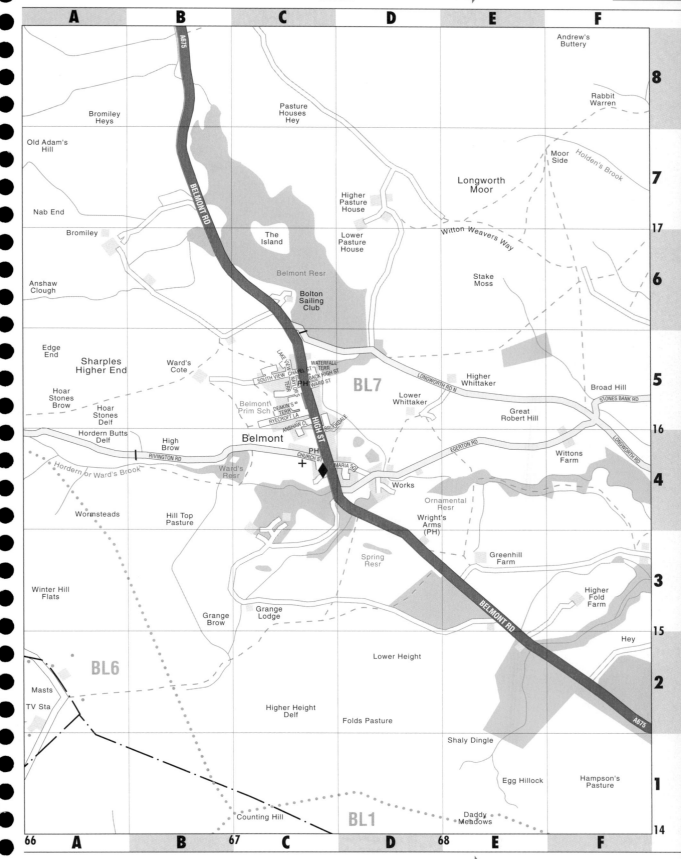

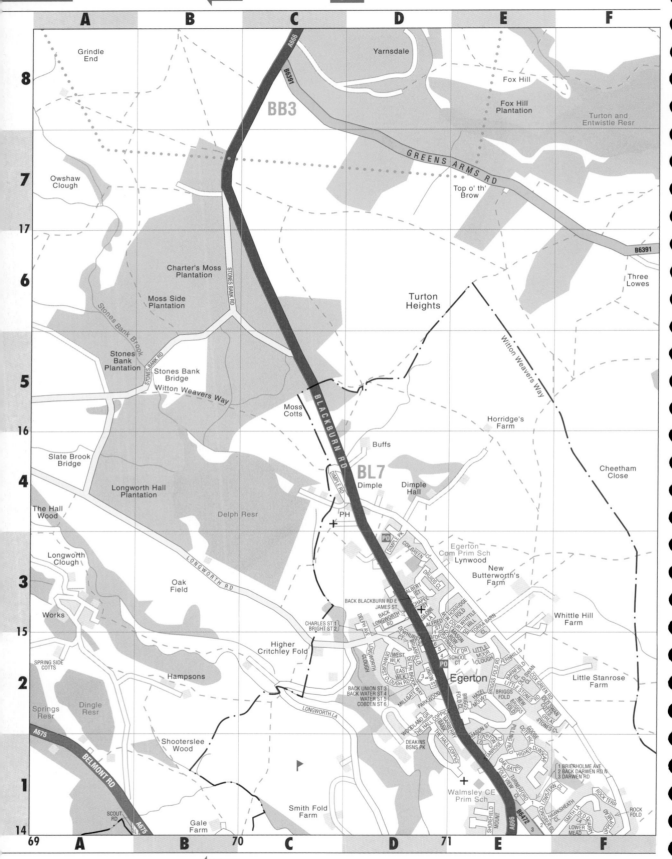

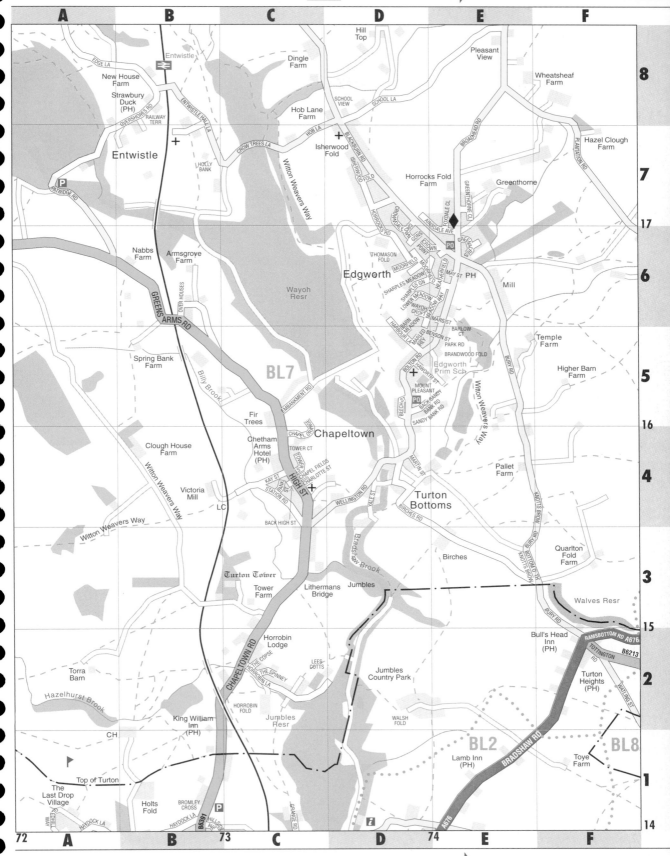

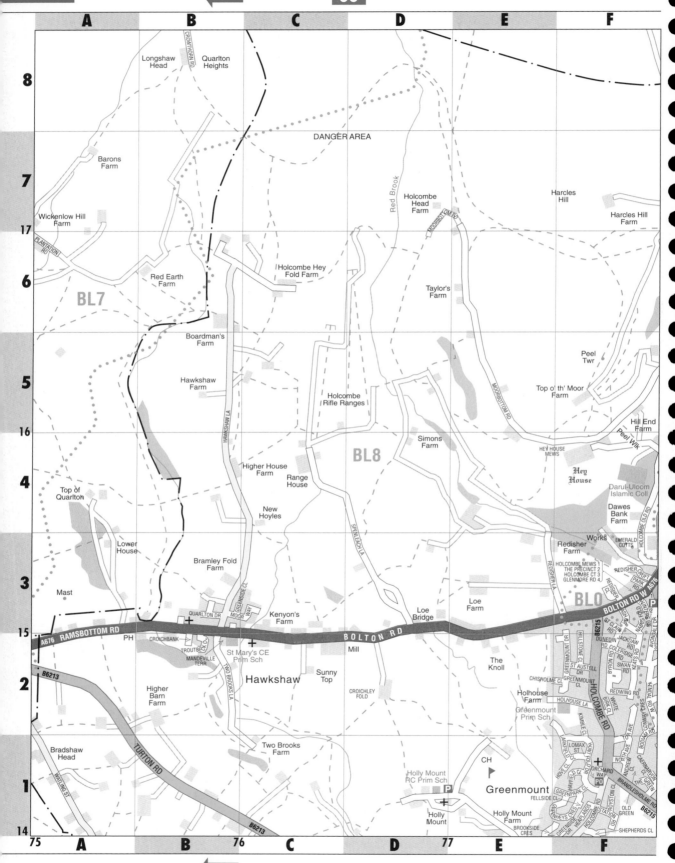

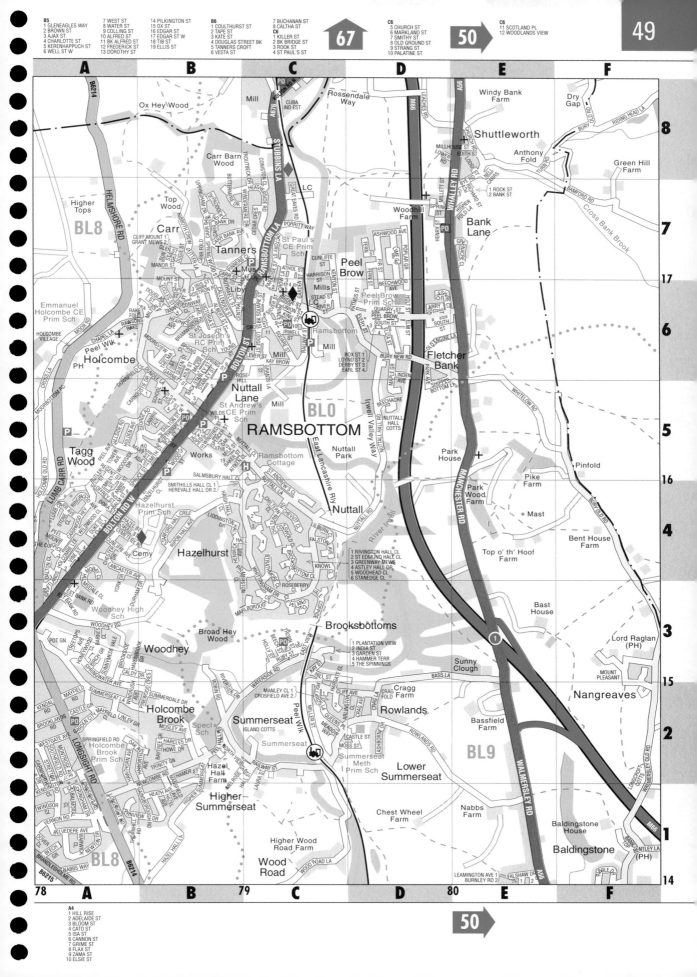

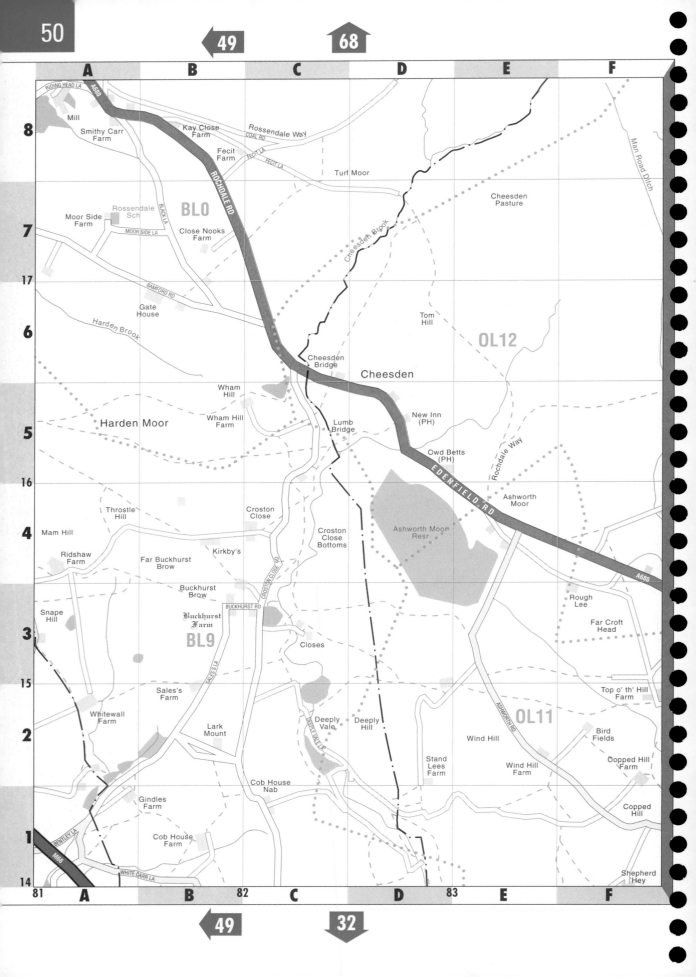

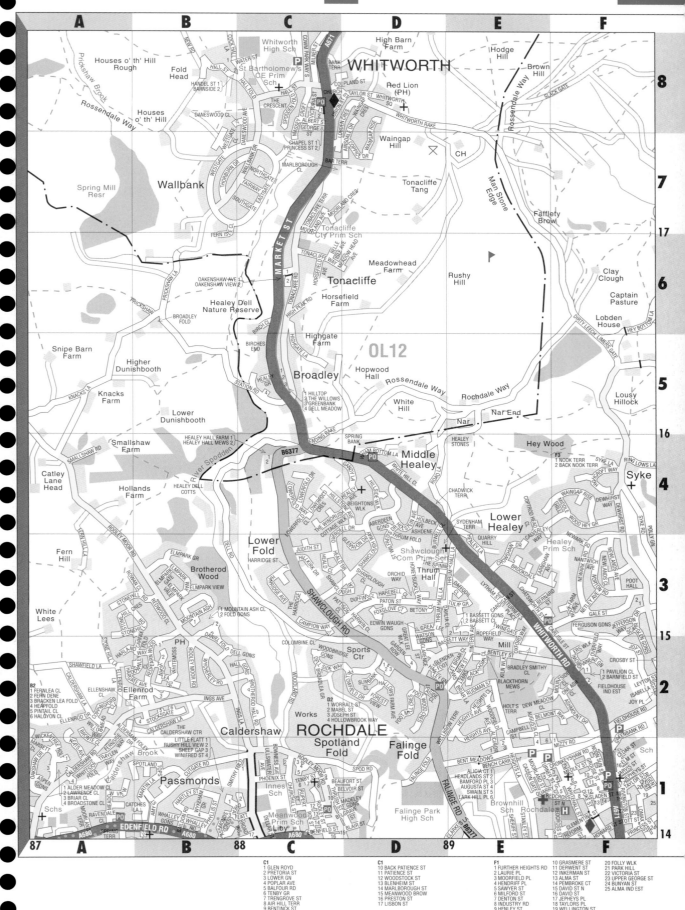

WHITWORTH

OL12

Broadley

Tonacliffe

Wallbank

Middle Healey

Lower Healey

Lower Fold

ROCHDALE

Caldershaw

Passmonds

C1
1 GLEN ROYD
2 PRETORIA ST
3 LOWER GN
4 POPLAR AVE
5 BALFOUR RD
6 TENBY GR
7 TRENGROVE ST
8 AIR HILL TERR
9 BENTINCK ST

C1
10 BACK PATIENCE ST
11 PATIENCE ST
12 WOODSTOCK ST
13 BLENHEIM ST
14 MARLBOROUGH ST
15 MEANWOOD BROW
16 PRESTON ST
17 LISBON ST

F1
1 FURTHER HEIGHTS RD
2 LAURIE PL
3 MOORFIELD PL
4 HENDRIFF PL
5 SAWYER ST
6 MILFORD ST
7 DENTON ST
8 INDUSTRY RD
9 HENLEY ST

10 GRASMERE ST
11 DERWENT ST
12 INKERMAN ST
13 ALMA ST
14 PEMBROKE CT
15 DAVID ST N
16 DAVID ST
17 JEPHEYS PL
18 TAYLORS PL
19 WELLINGTON ST

20 FOLLY WLK
21 PARK HILL
22 VICTORIA ST
23 UPPER GEORGE ST
24 BUNYAN ST
25 ALMA IND EST

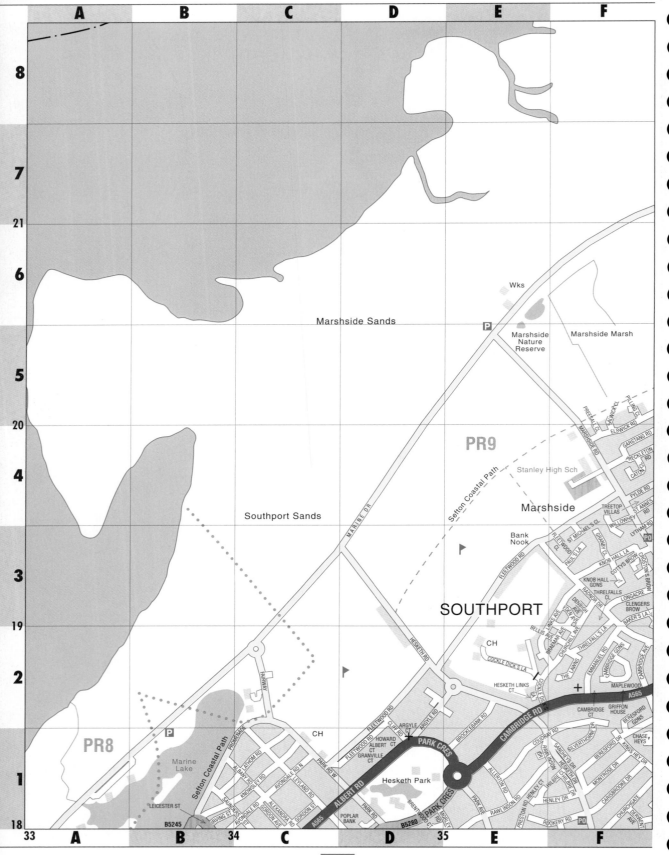

Marshside Sands

Wks

P

Marshside Nature Reserve

Marshside Marsh

PR9

Stanley High Sch

Marshside

Southport Sands

Sefton Coastal Path

Bank Nook

TREETOP VILLAS

WILLOWHEY

PO

MARINE DR

FLEETWOOD RD

SOUTHPORT

KNOB HALL LA

KNOB HALL GDNS

THRELFALLS CL

RADNOR CT

DIESBURY AVE

CLENGERS BROW

LONGACRE

BAKER'S LA

THRELFALL'S LA

CH

BELLIS AVE

HESKETH RD

COCKLE DICK'S LA

BRABHAM AVE

CHURCHILL AVE

THE LAWNS

EMMANUEL RD

CAMBRIDGE GDNS

CAMBRIDGE AVE

HESKETH LINKS CT

COCKLE DICK'S LA

MAPLEWOOD

+

A565

PR8

P

FAIRWAY

CAMBRIDGE RD

CAMBRIDGE CT

GRIFFON HOUSE

BERESFORD GDNS

CHASE HEYS

Marine Lake

Sefton Coastal Path

PROMENADE

CH

FLEETWOOD RD

ARGYLE RD

HOWARD ALBERT CT

GRANVILLE CT

BROCKLEBANK RD

PARK CRES

COUDRAY RD

RAWLINSON RD

SANDYS DR

HESKETH DR

SILVERTHORNE DR

BERESFORD DR

KINGS REY DR

MONTROSE DR

LATHOM RD

DAINTRY CL

KNOWSLEY RD

ALEXANDRA RD

ALBANY RD

AVONDALE RD N

EYLAND RD

PARK RD W

CLIFF RD

PARK RD

PARK RD

ALBERT RD

Hesketh Park

PARK AVE

ALLERTON RD

HENLEY CT

HILBRE CT

CARISBROOKE DR

CHURCHGATE

DERWENT AVE

Leicester St

SAUNDERS ST

IRVING ST

AVONDALE RD

GORDON AVE

GORDON ST

A565

POPLAR BANK

PARK RD

B5280

BRENTWOOD RD

MORLEY RD

PARK CRES

BRADMAN RD

RAWLINSON RD

PRESTON RD

HENLEY DR

HENLEY DR

ROOKERY RD

PO

B5245

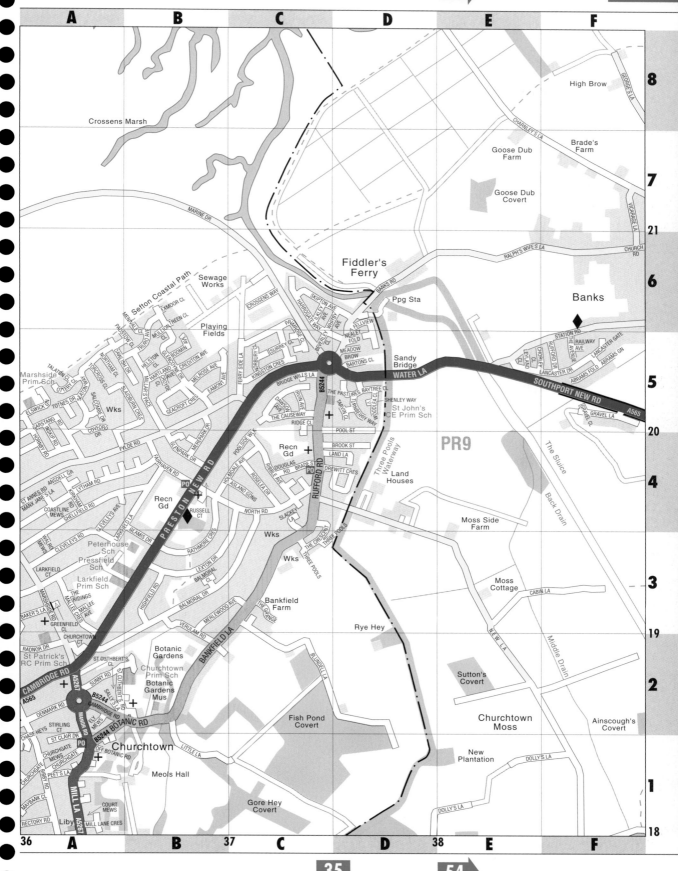

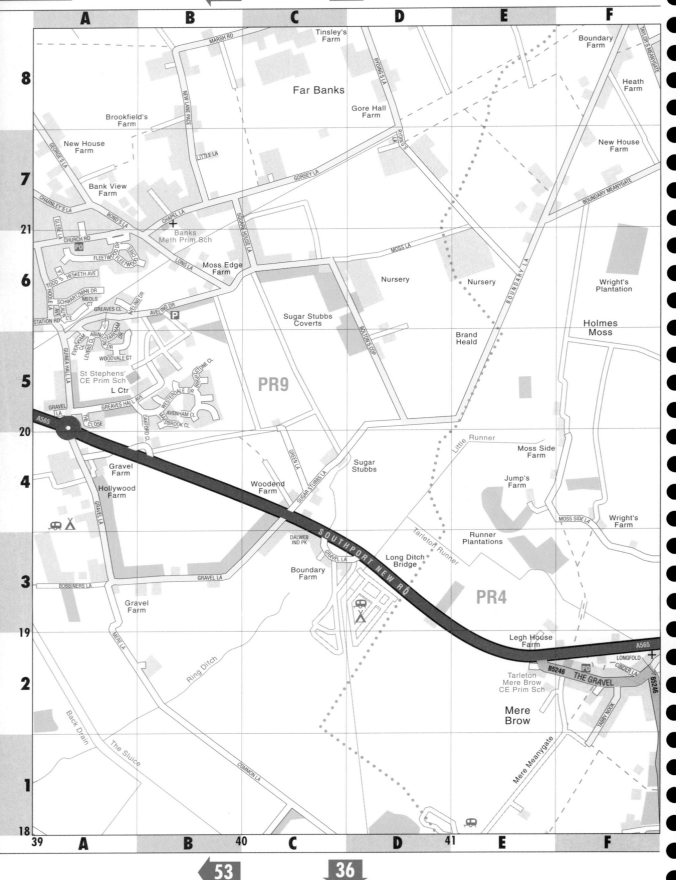

53
71

A   B   C   D   E   F

8

Tinsley's Farm

Far Banks

Boundary Farm

Heath Farm

Brookfield's Farm

Gore Hall Farm

New House Farm

New House Farm

GEORGE'S LA

7

MARSH RD

NEW LANE PACE

LITTLE LA

Bank View Farm

GORSEY LA

RYDING'S LA

CHARNLEY'S LA

BOND'S LA

CHAPEL LA

21

Banks Meth Prim Sch

MOSS LA

BOUNDARY MEANYGATE

CHURCH RD

GLEBE LA

PO

LONG LA

SOUND HOUSE LA

Moss Edge Farm

Nursery

Nursery

BOUNDARY LA

Wright's Plantation

6

FLEETWOOD DR

HESKETH AVE

FLEETWOOD

Y'S

TODD'S

SCHWARTZMAN DR

MEOLS CT

HOOLE LA

AVELING DR

GREAVES CL

P

Sugar Stubbs Coverts

Brand Heald

Holmes Moss

STATION RD

EVERSHAM

LEVENS CL

SCAUR LA

ABINGDON

CARR LANE DR

P

St Stephens' CE Prim Sch

PR9

GUINEA HALL LA

WOODVALE CT

STONE CL

5

L Ctr

WESTERDALE DR

THORN'

Little Runner

Moss Side Farm

GREAVES HALL AVE

AVENHAM CL

BROOK CL

Sugar Stubbs

Jump's Farm

Wright's Farm

GRAVEL LA

OAKFORD CL

THE CLOSE

MOSS SIDE LA

20

A565

Gravel Farm

GREEN LA

Woodend Farm

SUGAR STUBBS LA

4

Hollywood Farm

GRAVEL LA

SOUTHPORT NEW RD

Runner Plantations

Tarleton Runner

DALWEB IND PK

GRAVEL LA

Long Ditch Bridge

PR4

3

BOBBINERS LA

GRAVEL LA

Boundary Farm

Gravel Farm

MERE LA

Legh House Farm

A565

19

Ring Ditch

LONGFOLD

CINDER LA

B5246

Tarleton Mere Brow CE Prim Sch

PO

THE GRAVEL

B5246

TIBBY NOOK

2

Back Drain

Mere Brow

The Sluice

COMMON LA

Mere Meanygate

1

18

39   A   B   40   C   D   41   E   F

53
36

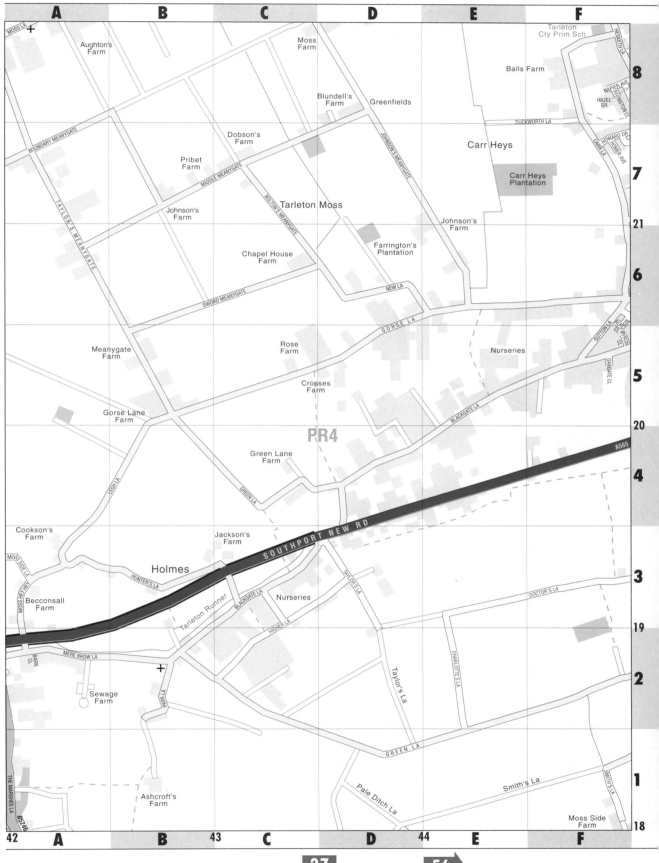

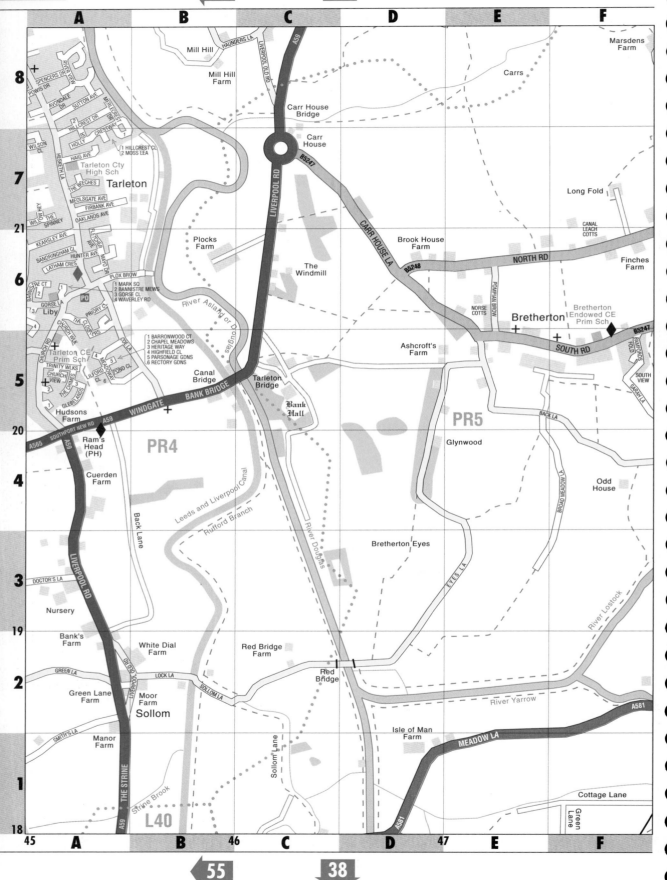

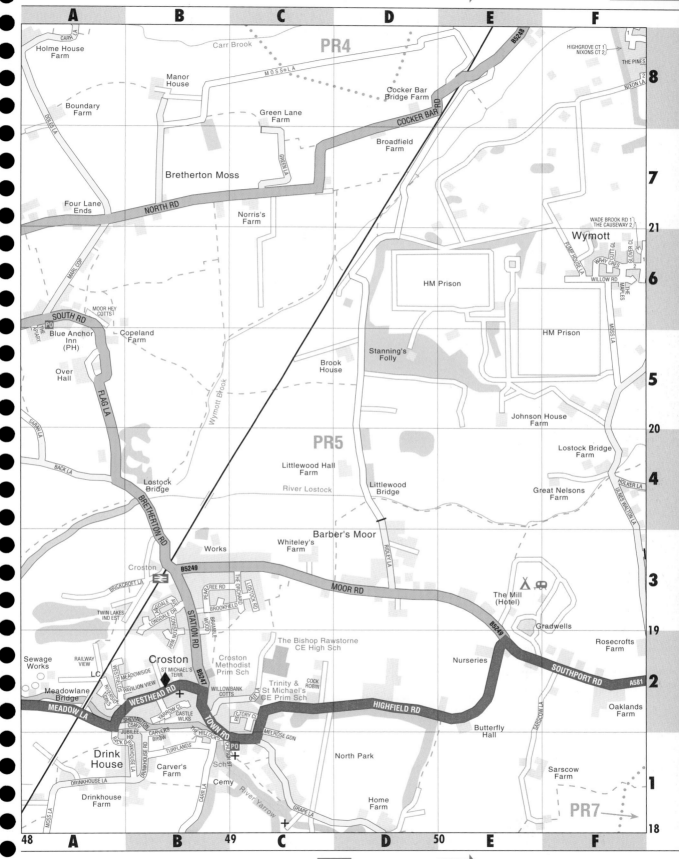

LEYLAND

Moss Side

Seven Stars

Wade Hall

Lower House

Worden Park

Worden Hall

Runshaw Moor

Newtown

Shaw Green

PR5

PR7

Wymott

Croston Farm

Miller's Farm

Calvert's Farm

Malt Kiln Farm

The Oaks

Sewage Works

Little Firs Farm

Lancester Ct

Brookfold Farm

Snubsnape Farm

Altcar Farm

Nook Farm

Culshaw's Farm

Porter's Farm

Lowe Farm

Flag Lane End Farm

Runshaw Moor Farm

Bournes Farm

Guest Farm

Blue Slates Farm

Marsh House

Nursery

Culbeck House

Folly Wood

Lydiate Farm

Nurseries

New Lane Head

Roemoor Farm

Billinge Hall Farm

Spring Lea Farm

Eccleston Hall

Ingrave Farm

Old Shaw Green

Primrose Row

Billinge Wood

St Mary's RC Sch

St Andrews CE Inf Sch

Woodlea Jun Sch

C Ctr

L Ctr

Liby

PH

Roads
DUNKIRK LA
SCHLESWIG WAY
LEYLAND LA
SOUTHPORT RD
DAWBER'S LA
LYDIATE LA
HOLKER LA
HOLLINS LA
FLAG LA
RUNSHAW LA
ALTCAR LA
CULBECK LA
FOX LA
PARKGATE DR
THE AVENUE
SHAW BROOK RD
VICTORIA PARK AVE
EMNIE LA
B5248
B5253
B5250
A581

Rivers/Brooks
River Lostock
Hollins Brook
Holker Brook
Culbeck Brook
River Yarrow

1 WESTMORLAND CL
2 DURHAM CL
3 SUFFOLK CL

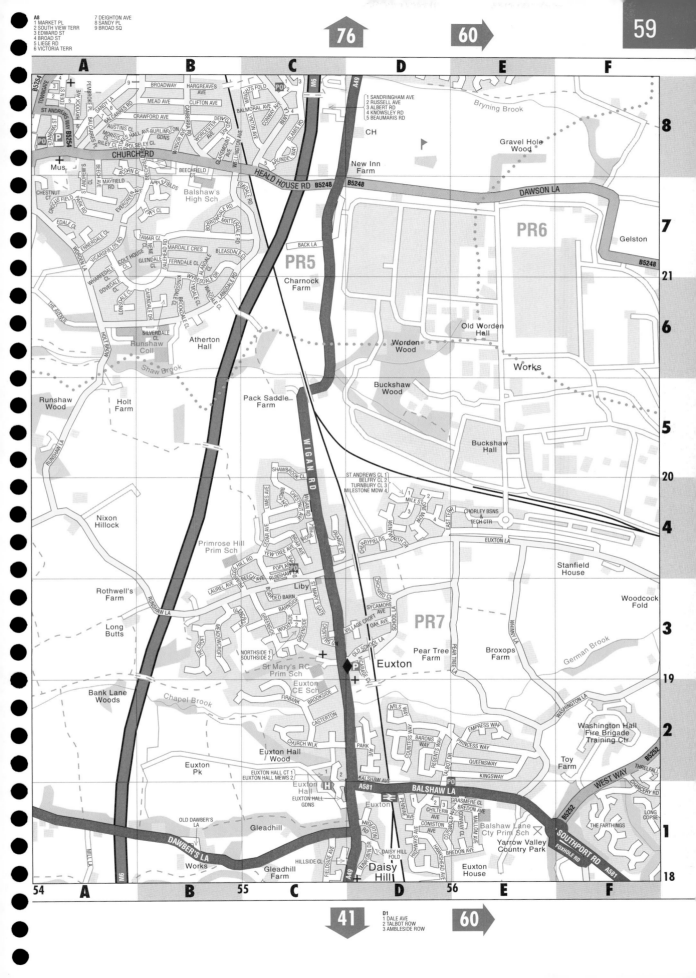

A B C D E F

8

7

21

6

5

20

4

3

19

2

1

18

57 A B 58 C D 59 E F

Whittle Hills

SMITH ST
HILLSIDE CRES
MILL LA
COW WELL LA
MOUNT PLEASANT
CARR BROOK CL
CARWOOD LA
Sch
Works
KEM MILL LA
WATKIN RD
CLIFE RD
ROCK VILLA RD
PARADISE ST
UNION
CHURCH HILL
CROSS KEY DR
CARWOOD LA
CROSS KEYS DR
BIRCHIN LA

Denham Wood

+ A6

Lisieux Hall
H
The Paddock

DAWSON LA
B5248
B5248

Lower Copthurst
LOWER COPTHURST LA
Top Lock Bridge
Top Lock (PH)
KENYON LA

P
P
Sch

Dolphin Farm
LANE
DALE ST
GRASMERE GR
SCHOOL BROW
Mill
SHAW BROW

Whittle-le-Woods

Lowe Barn

TOWN LA
TOWN LA

Higher Copthurst

COPTHURST LA
South Hill
St Chad's RC Prim Sch
A674

Shaw Hill CH
SPINNEY CL
SHAW HILL DR
SHAW HILL
THE WALLED GARDEN
PARKSIDE DR
PARKSIDE DR S
HARDACRE
PRESTON RD

Lucas Green
FARM HOUSE CL
LUCAS LA E
WARDLE CT
LUCAS LA W
Croston's Farm
LUCAS LA
DURHAM DR
MOTTRAM
STANFORD CL
ORCHARD
OLIVE CL
NEW MOSS LA
HONEYSUCKLE CL
LUPIN CL
BLUEBELL CL
FOXGLOVE
LEA RD
B6229
MOSS LA

PR6

HALLS SQ
Johnson's Hillock
RING MEWS
RING CRES
PARK LA
TANHOUSE LA
Red Cat Inn (PH)

Critchley's Farm

Moss Lane Farm

MOSS LA
B6229
PH
Hotel
MOSS TERR
GORSE CL
Leeds & Liverpool Canal
B6228
BLACKBURN RD

1 LINGWELL CL
2 CHASDEN CL
3 CATLEY CL
4 BUCKTON CL

The Sea View (PH)

HALLIWELL LA

+

Works

Hartwood Hill Farm

ALKER LA
EUXTON LA
PRESTON RD
TEMPLE WAY

+

A674
8
Knowley Bridge
Great Knowley
GUILDFORD AVE
EPSOM CL
EWELL CL
DORKING RD
BROMLEY GR
CARLETON GR
FORDHILL GN
REDGATE
MERTON GR
SUTTON GR
EALING GR

Little Knowley
PARADISE LA
HEMPET RD

CHORLEY
Hartwood
EUXTON LA
Euxton Brook
B5252
PETERSAN CT

A6
OAK DR
MAPLE
LINDEN GR
HAZEL GR
PINE GR
LABURNUM
FERN BANK
DRUMHEAD RD

MELFORD CL 1
ALPINE RD 2

Knowle Farm

KNOWLEY BROW
Knowley

PR7
WASHINGTON LA
WEST WAY
B5252
CAMOMINE CL 1
COLUMBINE CL 2
BADGERS WLK 3
CLEMATIS CL 4
MIDOS CL
GRETNA
BANASTRE
Astley Village
MILLCROFT 1
BROWNS HEY 2
TIMBER BROOK
COLIGNWOOD
LONG CROFT
MEADOW
BUCKSHAW HALL
CHANCERY RD
STUDFOLD
EDGEFOLD
FOXCOTE
FAIRWAY
HIGHFIELD RD N 1
TRIGGE HOUSE 2
LANCASTER CT 3
CHARNOCK CT 4
GILLIBRAND HOUSE 5
TALBOT HOUSE 6

Chorley and District
H
DUTCH BARN CL
CHORLEY HALL LA
HIGHFIELD RD N
HIGHFIELD RD S
THE SPINNEY
THE GROVE
THE CRESCENT
SPRINGS RD
COWSLIP WAY 1
CORNFLOWER CL 2
MILTON TERR 3
BANNERMAN TERR 4
GARFIELD TERR 5
MORRISON ST 6
SHAKESPEARE ST
POPPY AVE
COLERIDGE RD
CLAYBURN ST
NORTHGATE DR
SYCAMORE TERR

Chorley North Ind Est

BOTANY BROW
BLACKBURN BROW
BAGGANLEY LA
Baggonley Lane Farm

Buckshaw Cty Prim Sch
P
HAREWOOD
DEERFOLD
WOODMANCOTE
WOODFALL
ELMWOOD
St Michael's CE High Sch
MILLWOOD GLADE
ASTLEY RD
RAVENHILL DW
MILLFIELD RD
PARK RD
SOMERSET AVE
WATER ST
PRESTON RD
CHERRY TREE
Highfield Ind Est
No 2
Highfield
SPRINGS RD
B6229
HARPER'S LA
+
St Joseph's RC Prim Sch
CEDAR RD
THORNHILL RD
LARCH
DAISY RD
CHESTNUT AVE
St Peter's CE Prim Sch
MASON ST
St Joseph's Inf Sch
St Peter's ST
DORIS ST
CORPORATION ST
GEOFFREY ST
CARR ST
BELMONT ST
BAGGANLEY LA
P
COPPICE LA
TURTON DR
EAVES LA
B6228
RIVINGTON RD
MONTCLIFFE RD
Mills

Astley Hall
P
MEREFOLD
RAVENSTHORPE
Great Wood
River Chor
Astley Park
WOODFIELD RD 1
PARK ST 2
GARDEN TERR 3
NICHOL ST 4
CROSS ST 5
CONGRESS ST 6
WELLINGTON ST 7
WATERLOO ST 8
TRAFALGAR ST 9
St Laurence's CE Prim Sch

COMMERCIAL RD
BENGAL ST
ABBEY PARK RD
PARKER ST
BARKER ST
WATER ST
HOPE ST
SHOPE ST
A6
PO
Sports Ctr

BLACKSTONE RD
GRANVILLE ST
NAB RD
MARLBOROUGH RD
SMITHILLS CROFT
WITHNELL RD
HOLCOMBE GR
BROOK RD
FOSTER ST
Liby

1 MORRIS RD
2 GRANVILLE CT
3 FOSTERFIELD PL
4 OLD MILL TERR
5 FOSTER CT
6 COBDEN ST
7 KERSHAW ST
8 ROSSALL RD
9 TALBOT ST

M61

Works

← 59

↓ 42

D1
1 VICTORIA TERR
2 VICARAGE ST
3 WESTWELL RD
4 INGLE CL
5 RUSSELL SQ W
6 WHINFIELD AVE
7 MAYFIELD RD
8 BRIERCLIFFE RD
9 PRESTON ST

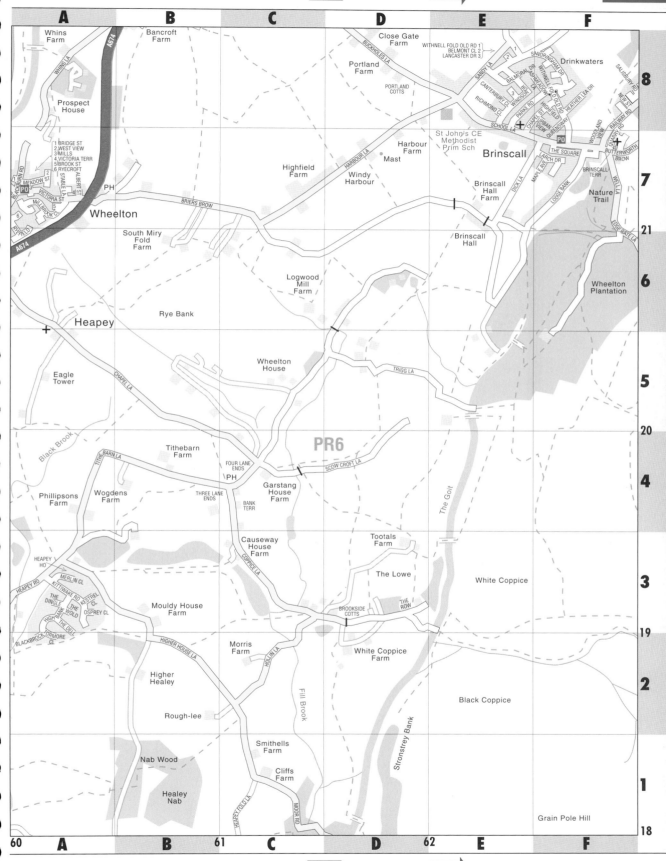

61
79

A B C D E F

8

Mount Pleasant
North East Ave
Derby St
Railway Rd
Churchill Rd
Hartington Rd
Butterworth Brow
Prospect Terr
Norcross Brow
Twist Moor La
Norcross Farm
Dole La
A675
Roddlesworth La
Roddlesworth
Wilton Weavers Way
Bolton Rd

7

21

6

Edge Gate La
Solomon's Temple
Hatch Brook
Roddlesworth Moor
Watsons
Mill La
BB3
River Roddlesworth

Withnell Moor

PR6

5

Green Hill
Cold Within Hill
Calf Hey Bridge

20

Wet Meadows
Ferney Slacks
Brown Hill
Belmont Rd A675

4

Heapey Moor
Brown Hill
Wheelton Moor

3

Drinkwaters
Great Hill

19

Black Brook

2

BL7
Adam's Delf

1

Black Hill Upper
Bromiley Pastures

18

63 A B 64 C D 65 E F

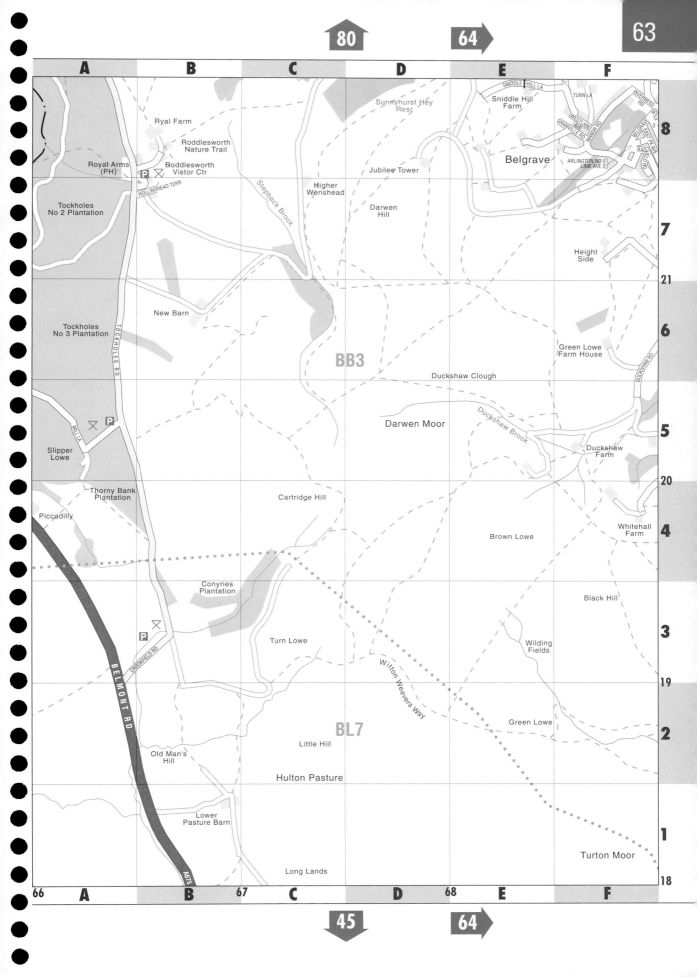

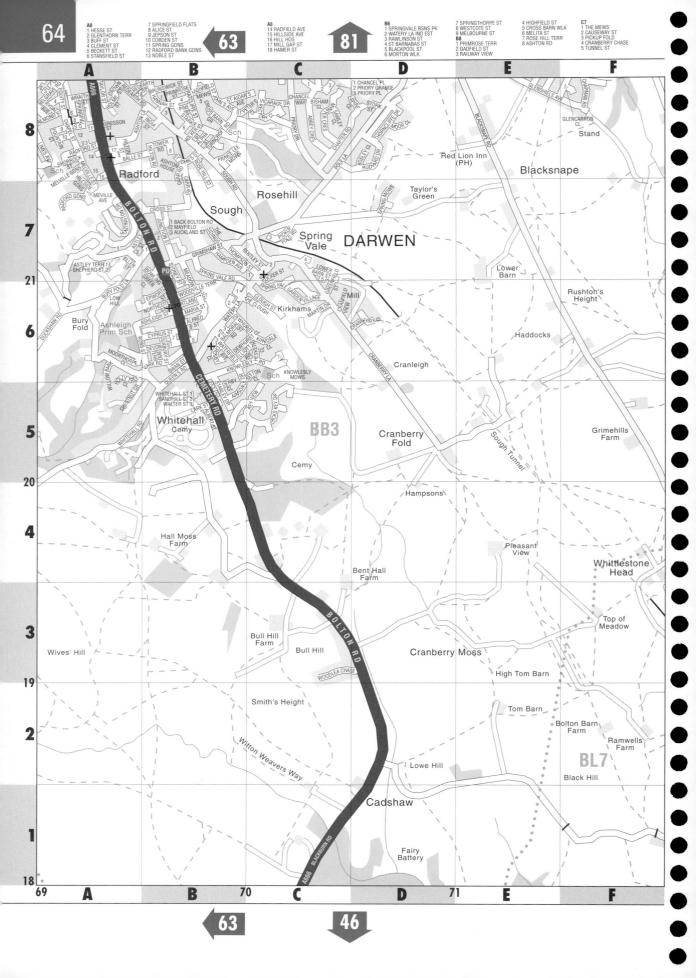

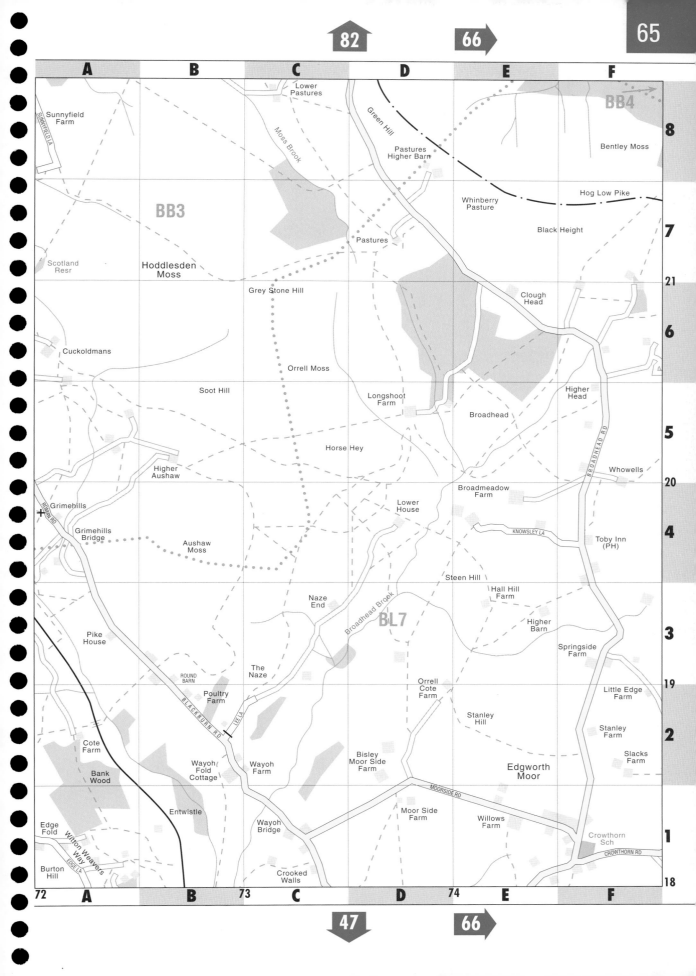

A B C D E F

8

BB4

Sunnyfield Farm

Lower Pastures

Moss Brook

Green Hill

Bentley Moss

Pastures Higher Barn

BB3

Whinberry Pasture

Hog Low Pike

Black Height

Pastures

21

Scotland Resr

Hoddlesden Moss

Grey Stone Hill

Clough Head

7

6

Cuckoldmans

Orrell Moss

Higher Head

Soot Hill

Longshoot Farm

Broadhead

5

Horse Hey

Higher Aushaw

Whowells

20

Grimehills

Broadmeadow Farm

KNOWSLEY LA

Grimehills Bridge

Aushaw Moss

Lower House

Toby Inn (PH)

4

Steen Hill

Hall Hill Farm

Naze End

Higher Barn

Pike House

BROADHEAD RD

BL7

Broadhead Brook

3

Springside Farm

ROUND BARN

The Naze

Orrell Cote Farm

Little Edge Farm

19

Poultry Farm

Stanley Hill

Stanley Farm

2

BLACKBURN RD

LEE LA

Cote Farm

Wayoh Farm

Bisley Moor Side Farm

Slacks Farm

Bank Wood

Wayoh Fold Cottage

Edgworth Moor

Entwistle

MOORSIDE RD

Edge Fold

Wayoh Bridge

Moor Side Farm

Willows Farm

Burton Hill

WITTON WEAVERS WAY

EDGE LA

Crowthorn Sch

Crooked Walls

CROWTHORN RD

1

18

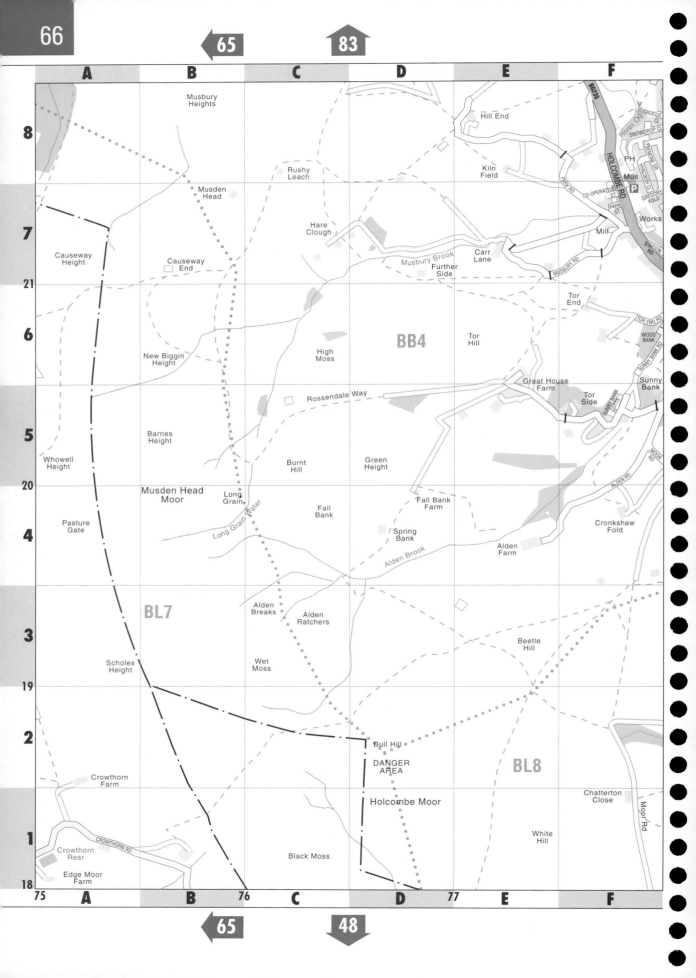

65
83

A   B   C   D   E   F

8

Musbury
Heights

Rushy
Leach

Hill End

B6235

CROCUS
CL

SNOWDROP CL

MEMORIE DR

Holcombe Rd

PH

Mus

P

Musden
Head

Kiln
Field

PARK RD

CO-OPERATIVE ST

GREGORY
FOLD

PARK
ST

Works

7

Causeway
Height

Hare
Clough

Carr
Lane

Mill

STATION RD

Causeway
End

Musbury Brook

Further
Side

MUSBURY RD

21

Tor
End

6

New Biggin
Height

High
Moss

BB4

Tor
Hill

TOR END RD

WOOD
BANK

SUNNY BANK RD

Rossendale Way

Great House
Farm

Tor
Side

Sunny
Bank

Barnes
Height

SUNNY BANK COTTAGES

5

Whowell
Height

Burnt
Hill

Green
Height

MOOR RD

20

Musden Head
Moor

Long
Grain

Fall
Bank

Fall Bank
Farm

ALDEN RD

Cronkshaw
Fold

4

Pasture
Gate

Long Grain Water

Spring
Bank

Alden Brook

Alden
Farm

BL7

Alden
Breaks

Alden
Ratchers

Beetle
Hill

3

Scholes
Height

Wet
Moss

19

2

Bull Hill

BL8

DANGER
AREA

Chatterton
Close

Moor Rd

Crowthorn
Farm

Holcombe Moor

1

CROWTHORN RD

Crowthorn
Resr

White
Hill

18

Edge Moor
Farm

Black Moss

75   A   B   76   C   D   77   E   F

65
48

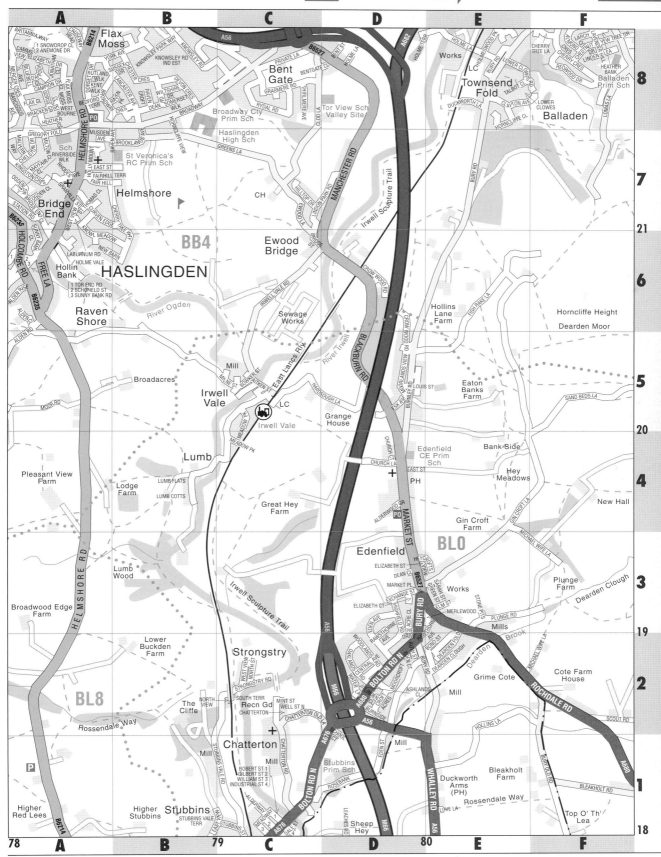

Flax Moss

Bent Gate

Townsend Fold

Balladen

Helmshore

Bridge End

BB4

Ewood Bridge

HASLINGDEN

Raven Shore

Hollin Bank

1 TOR END RD
2 SCHOFIELD ST
3 SUNNY BANK RD

River Ogden

Hollins Lane Farm

Horncliffe Height

Dearden Moor

Broadacres

Irwell Vale

Mill

LC

Grange House

Eaton Banks Farm

Sewage Works

Lumb

Pleasant View Farm

Lodge Farm

LUMB FLATS
LUMB COTTS

Great Hey Farm

Edenfield CE Prim Sch

PH

Bank Side

Hey Meadows

New Hall

Gin Croft Farm

BLO

Lumb Wood

Edenfield

Plunge Farm

Dearden Clough

Broadwood Edge Farm

Lower Buckden Farm

Strongstry

Works

Mills

Cote Farm House

BL8

Grime Cote

Mill

ROCHDALE RD

Rossendale Way

The Cliffe

Recn Gd

Chatterton

Mill

Mill

Chatterton

ROBERT ST 1
GILBERT ST 2
WILLIAM ST 3
INDUSTRIAL ST 4

Stubbins Prim Sch

Mill

Bleakholt Farm

Higher Red Lees

Higher Stubbins

Stubbins

STUBBINS VALE TERR

Duckworth Arms (PH)

Rossendale Way

Top O' Th' Lea

Sheep Hey

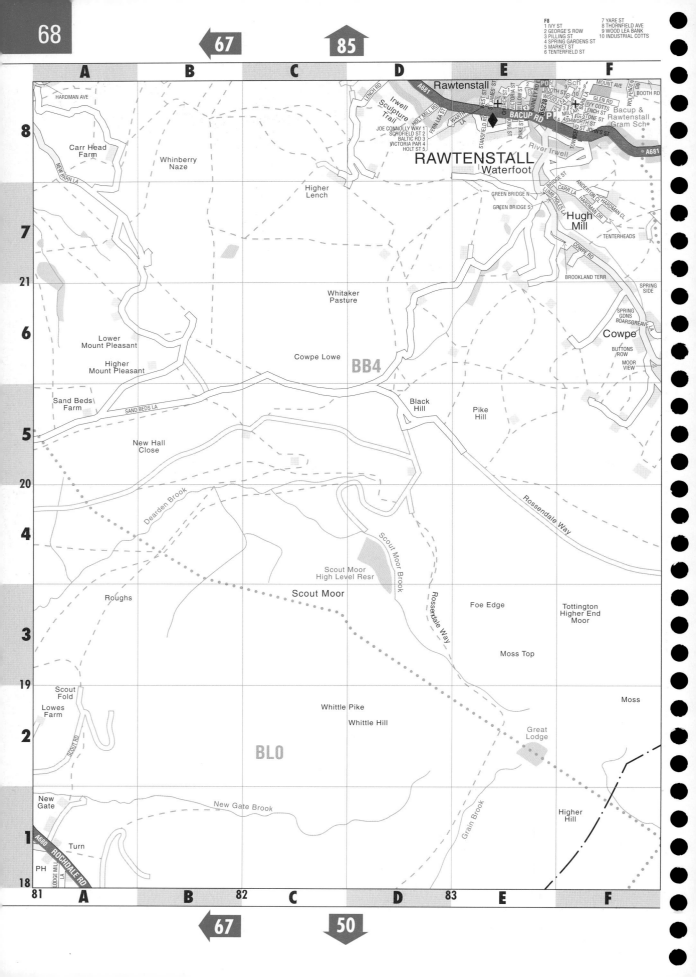

67
85

F8
1 IVY ST
2 GEORGE'S ROW
3 PILLING ST
4 SPRING GARDENS ST
5 MARKET ST
6 TENTERFIELD ST
7 YARE ST
8 THORNFIELD AVE
9 WOOD LEA BANK
10 INDUSTRIAL COTTS

HARDMAN AVE

Carr Head Farm

NEW BARN LA

Whinberry Naze

Higher Lench

Irwell Sculpture Trail

JOE CONNOLLY WAY 1
SCHOFIELD ST 2
BALTIC RD 3
VICTORIA PAR 4
HOLT ST 5

LENCH RD

HOLT MILL RD

FERN LEA RD

WHARTON LA

A681

WEST ST

ST JAMES ST

CHURCH ST

STANSFIELD RD

VICTORIA ST

WILLOW ST

PIKE ST

MILL ST

PINE ST

STONE ST

BACUP RD

B6238

P

WOOD ST

BOOTH ST

GLEN RD

IVY COTTS

LENCH ST

ASHWORTH ST

ST JOHN'S ST

MOUNT AVE

WOLFENDEN GN

BOOTH RD

Sch

Bacup & Rawtenstall Gram Sch

Rawtenstall

RAWTENSTALL
Waterfoot

River Irwell

A681

GREEN BRIDGE N
GREEN BRIDGE S

BRIDGE ST

ANDERTON CL

CARR LA

HARDMAN ST

HARDMAN DR

LIMB NOLES LA

Hugh Mill

TENTERHEADS

COWPE RD

BROOKLAND TERR

SPRING SIDE

SPRING GDNS BOARSGREAVE

Cowpe

BUTTONS ROW

MOOR VIEW

Whitaker Pasture

21

6

Lower Mount Pleasant

Higher Mount Pleasant

Cowpe Lowe

BB4

Sand Beds Farm

SAND BEDS LA

Black Hill

Pike Hill

5

New Hall Close

20

Dearden Brook

Rossendale Way

4

Scout Moor Brook

Scout Moor High Level Resr

Scout Moor

Rossendale Way

Foe Edge

Tottington Higher End Moor

Roughs

3

Moss Top

19

Scout Fold

Lowes Farm

Whittle Pike

Whittle Hill

Moss

SCOUT RD

BLO

Great Lodge

2

New Gate

New Gate Brook

Grain Brook

Higher Hill

1

A680

ROCHDALE RD

Turn

PH

LODGE MILL LA

18

67
50

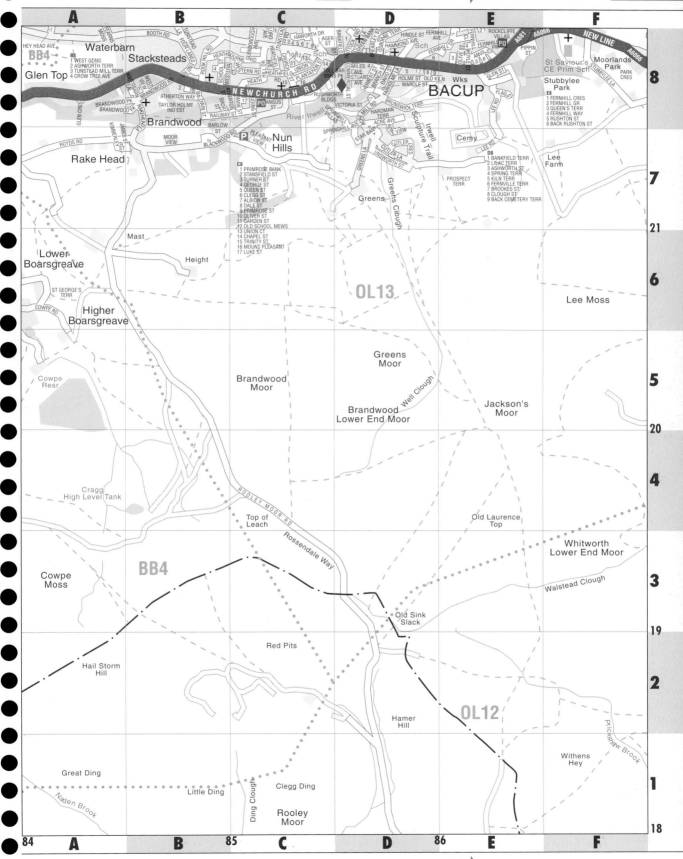

69 87

A B C D E F

8
7
21
6
5
20
4
3
19
2
18

RIBBLE ST
LAKE END RD
HOGHTON AVE
THE SIDINGS
Sch
Height Barn La
A6066
STACK LA
ROCHDALE RD
A671
Lower Stack
Higher Stack
KENYON ST 1
WHITTLES ST 2
HARRISON ST 3
NELSON ST 4
SUTCLIFFE ST 5
RAILGATE
LEE ST
WILLIAM ST
ERNEST ST
WARREN ST
Britannia Cty Prim Sch
Britannia
FAIR VIEW
P NEW LINE
A6066
DEANSGREAVE RD
Mill
PH
PRINCE ST
P
Reddish Hill
Trough Gate
Shackleton
Shackleton Holmes
OL13
Stubbylee Moss Farm
Higher Barn Moss
Brandwood Higher End Moor
Stubbylee Moss
Holden Moor
Jam Hill
Whitworth Higher End Moor
River Spodden
Freeholds
OLD LA
FREEHOLDS RD
FREEHOLDS TERR
GERTRUDE ST
PERCY ST
KNOWSLEY CRE
JANE ST
KNOTT HILL ST
EAGLEY BANK
St John with St Michael CE Prim Sch
QUARRY ST
Shawforth
MOSS SIDE ST
EDGEMOOR CL
LAND GATE
Britannia Quarries
Mast
COWM ST
Millgate Terr
PO
Shawforth Moor
Brown Hill
Ab Top
Cowm Top Farm
OAK VIEW
HEATHERLANDS
LEAVENGREAVE CT
VALLEY VIEW
SPRING SIDE
OAK ST
2K CL
OAK ST
JOHN HENRY ST
MARKET ST
Millgate
OL12
Pisgah Farm
Whitworth Lower End Moor
Little Middle Hill
Ragstone Brow
RIVERSIDE CT
BUXTON ST
Hud Clough
Cemy
BACK COWM LA
BACK LA
HIGH BARN LA
KING ST
HOYLE ST
STATION RD
MEADOW COTTS
Mill
SPODDEN COTTS
MILLFOLD
SPRING PL
CHEETHAM HILL
GRANGE
Mill
EDWARD ST
LONG ACRES LA
Brown Wardle Hill
Cowm Resr
St Anselm's RC Prim Sch
INDUSTRY ST
Tong End
THOMAS ST
JAMES ST
IND EST
ETHEL ST
ALFRED ST
MINNIE ST
Facit
Long Acres Farm
Water Ski Ctr
P
SANDBANK GARD
COWM PARK WAY N
HEDGE ROWS
KILN BANK
BURNEDGE CL
CLEGG'S CT
HILLSIDE
STONEYROYD
LONG ACRES RD
Mid Long Acres Farm
Pot Oven Farm
Rossendale Way
Limed
Cock Hall
NEW RD
BEECH CL
COCKHALL LA
TONG END
NEW WAY
COWM PARK WAY S
BANKSTOWN CL
WILLIAM ST
BARN FIELD
PRIMA CRES
CESCA ST
Mills
THORNEYLEA
ACRE ST
SHED ST
SIZE ST
CLARA ST
Slacks Farm
Rickshaw Brook
Jennie Rough
COCK HILL LA
THE GREENS
NORTH ST
MIDDLE ST
MILNER ST
JAMES ST
WHITWORTH
THE MEADOWS 1
BRIDGE ST 2
BROOKVILLE 3
BAYTREE WLK 4
HOLT ST
LLOYD ST
Liby
SCHOOL TERR
A671

69 51

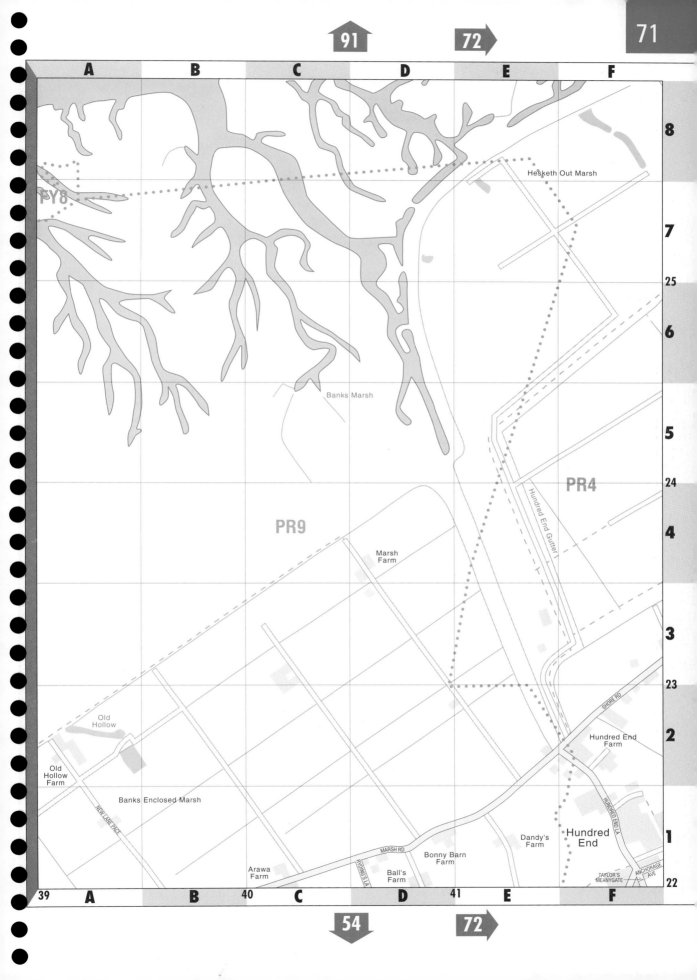

A   B   C   D   E   F

8

7

25

6

5

24

4

3

23

2

1

22

FY8

Hesketh Out Marsh

Banks Marsh

PR4

Hundred End Gutter

PR9

Marsh Farm

Old Hollow

Old Hollow Farm

Banks Enclosed Marsh

NEW LANE PACE

Arawa Farm

RYDING'S LA

MARSH RD

Ball's Farm

Bonny Barn Farm

Dandy's Farm

Hundred End Farm

SHORE RD

Hundred End

HUNDRED END LA

TAYLOR'S MEANYGATE

ANCHORAGE AVE

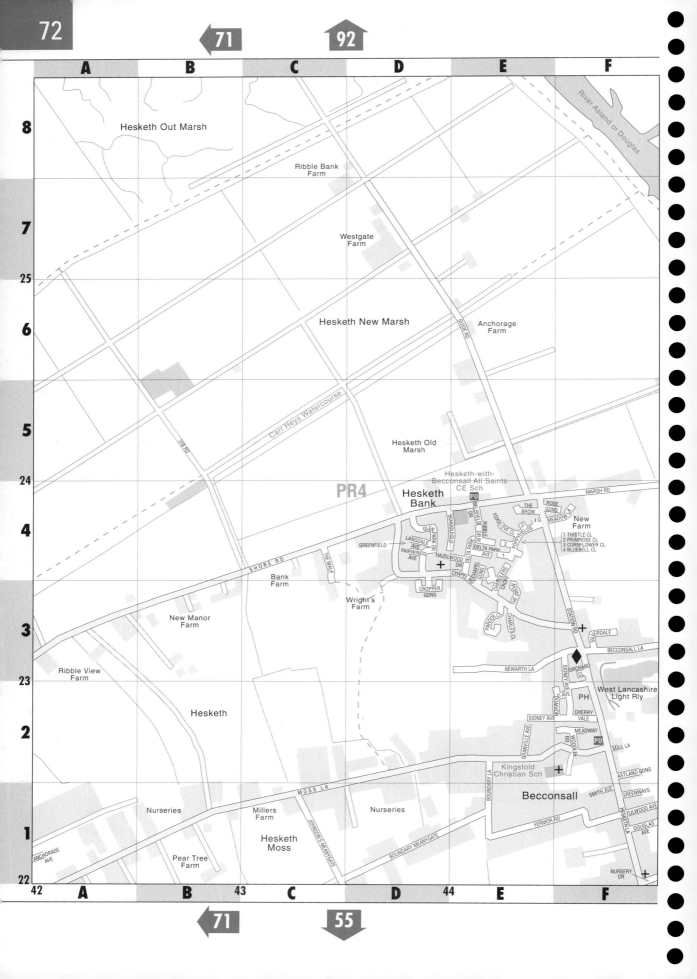

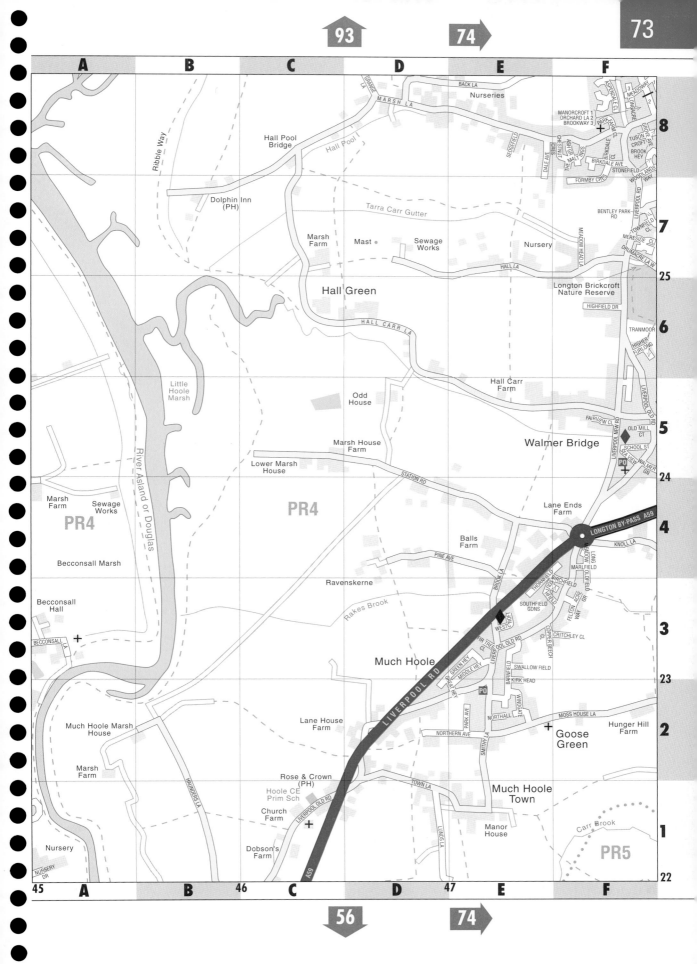

A B C D E F

8

Longton

7

25

6

5

24

4

3

23

2

1

22

48 A B 49 C 50 D E F

Longton Hall
Longton Cty Prim Sch
St Oswald's IRC Prim Sch
Cemy
Hall Pool
Church Row Chambers
Liby PO
Blackhurst Ct
Brookfield Farm
Chapel La
Chapel Wlk
Chapel Meadow
Chapel Park Rd
Brownhill La
A59
Nursery La
Moss La
Saunders La
Chapel La
Park Ave
New Longton
PO
Briarfield
The Cedars
Royalty La
Shaftesbury Av
Dickson Hey
Spinney Cl
Station Cl
Churchside
Waverley Dr
New Longton CE Prim Sch
Southfield Dr
Hugh Barn La
Hugh Barn
Hollings
Mosswah
Willow Ave
Ash Gr
Willow Farm
Thropps La
Balshaw Farm
Drumacre La W
Harrison's Farm
Drumacre La E
Thornton Barn
Long Moss La
Tarra Carr Gutter
Wholesome La
Diamond Hall Farm
Longton By-Pass
Cottam La
Six Acre La
Land La
PR4
Gill La
Wholesome Farm
Little Hoole Cty Prim Sch
Walmer Gn
June's Wlk
Gower Gr
Tristan Ave
Singleton's Farm
Midge Hall La
Dob La
Little Hoole Moss Houses
Long Fold Farm
Moss La
Wham House Farm
Wham La
Moss Farm
Moss Priory
Little Hoole Moss
Moss Farm
Station Farm
Knoll La
Moor Hey Farm
LC
Pleasant View
Midge Hall
Mill
Rakes Brook
PR5
Gabbots Farm
Moss House La
Moorhey Farm
Moss Farm
Much Hoole Moss
LC
Narrow La
Much Hoole Moss Houses
Carr La
Twenty Acre La
Moss House
Long Wham La
Moss Farm
LC
Dunkirk La
Oxen House Farm
B5248
Cocker Bar Farm
Cocker Bar
Highgrove Ct
Pintail Cl

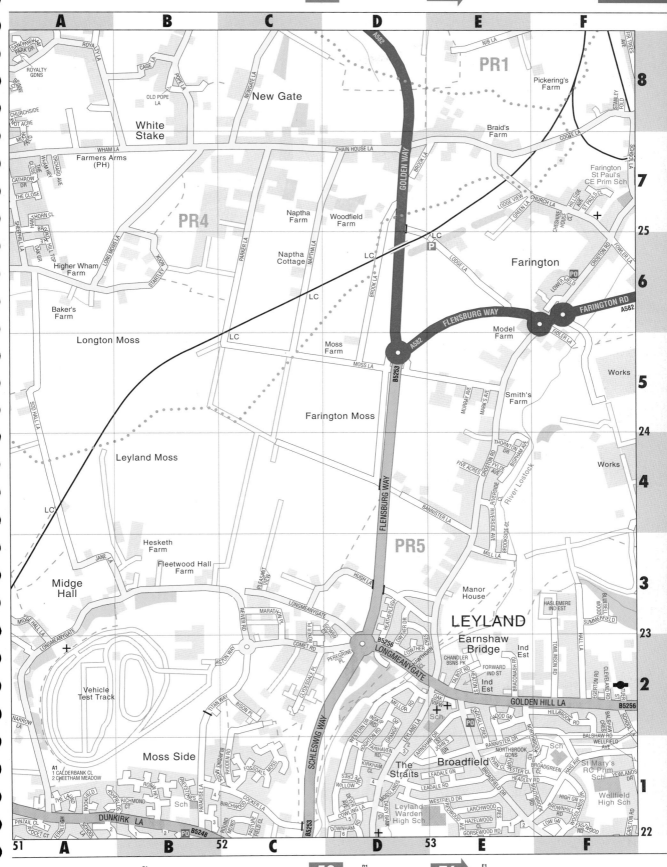

A1
1 CALDERBANK CL
2 CHEETHAM MEADOW

B1
1 BARN CROFT
2 THE MEADOWS
3 HOLMES MEADOW
4 ROSTREVOR CL

D1
1 JACKSON RD
2 MICKLEFIELD CT
3 ORRELL CL
4 HOMESTEAD CL
5 FIELDEN ST
6 LANGHOLM CL

E1
1 ELMWOOD AVE
2 BLEACHERS DR

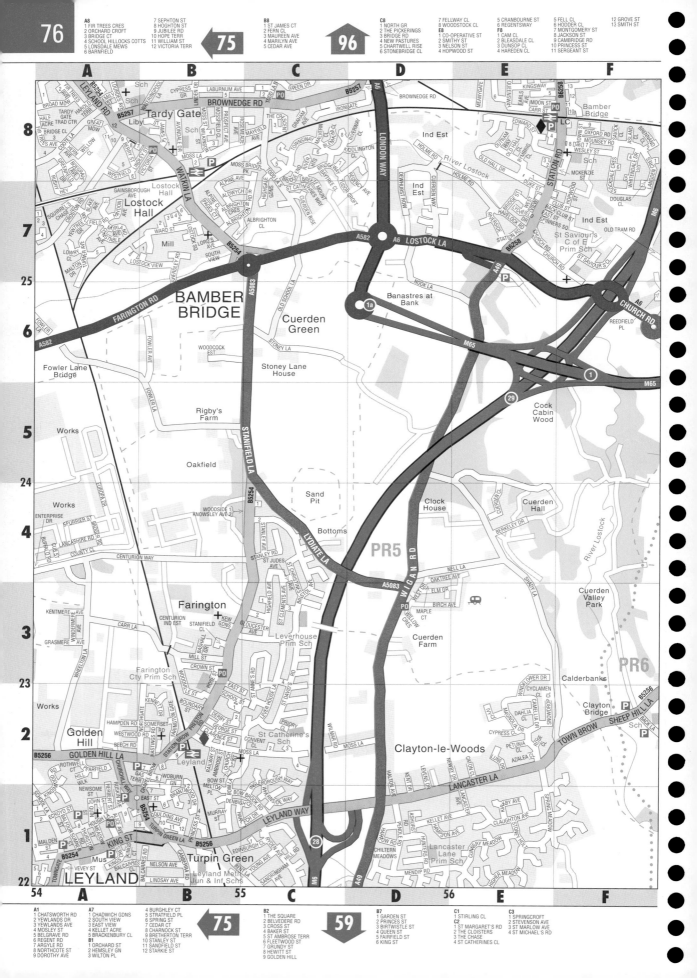

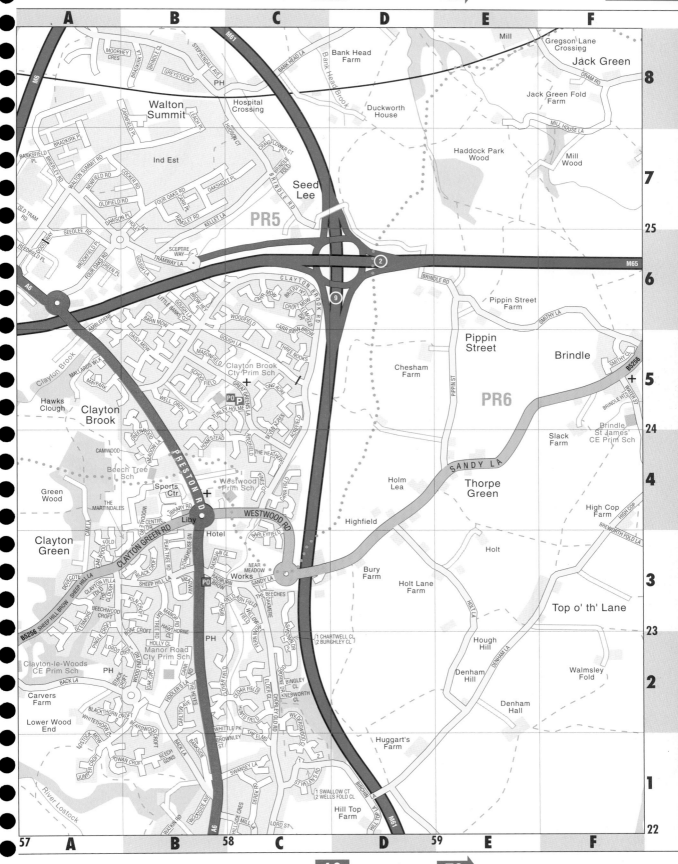

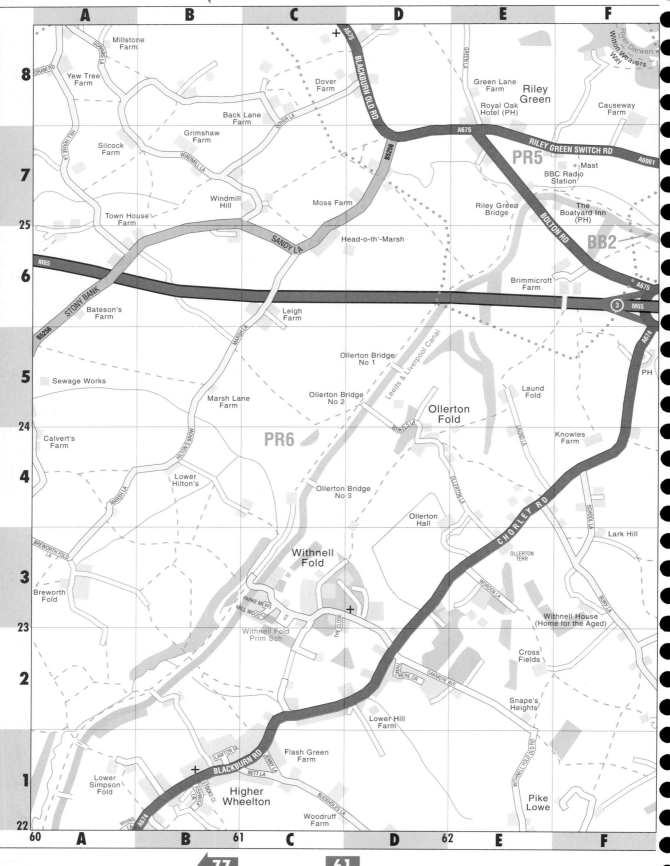

A B C D E F

8

Millstone
Farm

Yew Tree
Farm

GOWANS LA

ORAM RD

Silcock
Farm

HILL HOUSE LA

Back Lane
Farm

Grimshaw
Farm

WINDMILL LA

DOVER LA

Dover
Farm

BLACKBURN OLD RD

A675

Green Lane
Farm

GREEN LA

Riley
Green

Royal Oak
Hotel (PH)

A675

Causeway
Farm

River Darwen

Witton Weavers Way

7

Town House
Farm

Windmill
Hill

B5256

Moss Farm

RILEY GREEN SWITCH RD

A6061

PR5

Mast

BBC Radio
Station

25

SANDY LA

Head-o-th'-Marsh

Riley Green
Bridge

BOLTON RD

The
Boatyard Inn
(PH)

BB2

6

M65

STONY BANK

Bateson's
Farm

Leigh
Farm

MARSH LA

Brimmicroft
Farm

A675

3

M65

B5256

Leeds & Liverpool Canal

A674

Ollerton Bridge
No 1

PH

5

Sewage Works

Marsh Lane
Farm

Ollerton Bridge
No 2

WHIRLS LA

Ollerton
Fold

Laund
Fold

LAUND LA

24

Calvert's
Farm

MARSH LA

HILTON'S BROW

PR6

Knowles
Farm

4

Lower
Hilton's

Ollerton Bridge
No 3

OLLERTON LA

Ollerton
Hall

CHORLEY RD

SCHOOL LA

Lark Hill

3

Breworth
Fold

BREWORTH FOLD LA

Withnell
Fold

PARKE MEWS

MILL WOOD

THE CLOSE

WORDEN LA

OLLERTON
TERR

Withnell House
(Home for the Aged)

BURY LA

23

Withnell Fold
Prim Sch

Cross
Fields

2

HILL MERE DR

OAKMERE AVE

Lower Hill
Farm

Snape's
Heights

WITHNELL FOLD OLD RD

1

LAWTON CL

BLACKBURN RD

JENNY LA

BETT LA

Flash Green
Farm

A674

Lower
Simpson
Fold

ST OAKS CL

TISWICK LA

Higher
Wheelton

BUCKHOLES LA

Pike
Lowe

WHINS LA

Woodruff
Farm

22

60 A B 61 C D 62 E F

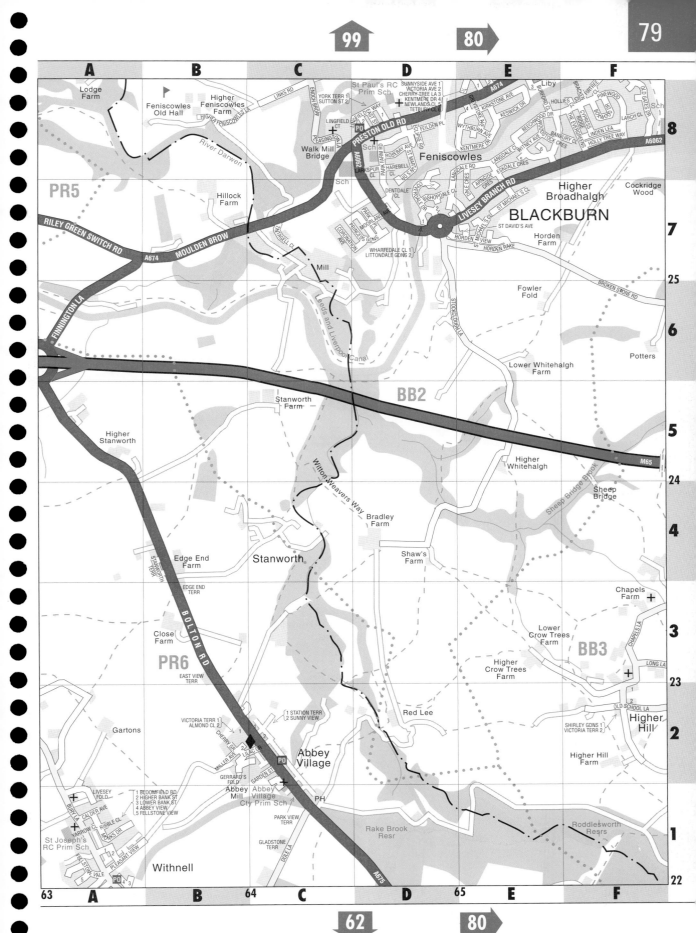

A B C D E F

Lodge
Farm
Feniscowles
Old Hall
Higher
Feniscowles
Farm
Higher Feniscowles La
LINKS RD
ENOCH BROW
York Terr 1
Sutton St 2
St Paul's RC
Prim Sch
Sunnyside Ave 1
Victoria Ave 2
Cherry Tree La 3
Kentmere Dr 4
Newlands Cl 5
Tetbury Cl 6
A674
Liby

River Darwen
PLEASINGTON LA
LINGFIELD CT
PO
FGFIELD WAY
EAST ST 1
WEST ST 2
PRESTON OLD RD
FEILDEN PL
FEILDEN ST
Sch
Kirkstone La
Keswick Dr
Kentmere Dr
Beechwood Dr
Witney Ave
Stock Cres
Holly Tree Way
Larch Cl
Sch

Hillock
Farm
Walk Mill
Bridge
A6062
Sch
LARKSPUR CL
PARK FARM RD
HAREBELL CL
HOLLY'S WD
Rosebay Ave
St Mary's
Wythburn Ave
Kentmere
Langdale Cres
Eskdale Cres
Holly Tree Way

PR5
MOORLAND RD
PRINCE'S GDNS
CORONATION AVE
Feniscowles
Higher
Broadhalgh
Cockridge
Wood

RILEY GREEN SWITCH RD
A674 MOULDEN BROW
TINTAGELL CL
Mill
DENTDALE CL
BISHOPDALE CL
LIVESEY BRANCH RD
St David's Ave
BLACKBURN
Horden
Farm
Horden
ST MICHAEL'S CH
Horden View
Horden Rake

FINNINGTON LA
WHARFEDALE CL 1
LITTONDALE GDNS 2
Fowler
Fold
BROKEN STONE RD

Leeds and Liverpool Canal
Lower Whitehalgh
Farm
Potters

BB2
Stanworth
Farm
Higher
Whitehalgh
Sheep Bridge Brook
Sheep
Bridge
M65

Higher
Stanworth
Witton Weavers Way
Higher
Whitehalgh

Edge End
Farm
STANWORTH TERR
EDGE END
TERR
Stanworth
Bradley
Farm
Shaw's
Farm
Lower
Crow Trees
Farm
Chapels
Farm
CHAPELS LA

Close
Farm
BOLTON RD
PR6
EAST VIEW
TERR
Red Lee
Higher
Crow Trees
Farm
BB3
LONG LA
OLD SCHOOL LA

Gartons
VICTORIA TERR 1
ALMOND CL 2
CHERRY GRO
MILLER AVE
LILAC CR
1 STATION TERR
2 SUNNY VIEW
SHIRLEY GDNS 1
VICTORIA TERR 2
Higher
Hill

Livesey
Fold
BURYL CL
CALDER AVE
RIBBLE CL
OAKS DR
1 BLOOMFIELD RD
2 HIGHER BANK ST
3 LOWER BANK ST
4 ABBEY VIEW
5 FELLSTONE VIEW
GERRARD'S
FOLD
GARDEN ST
PO
Abbey
Village
Abbey
Mill
Abbey
Village
Cty Prim Sch
PH
Higher Hill
Farm

St Joseph's
RC Prim Sch
YARROW CL
PLEASANT VIEW
FELLSTONE VALE
PO
PARK VIEW
TERR
Rake Brook
Resr
Roddlesworth
Resrs

Withnell
GLADSTONE
TERR
DOLE LA
A675

63   A   B   64   C   D   65   E   F

8 7 25 6 5 24 4 3 23 2 1 22

79 100

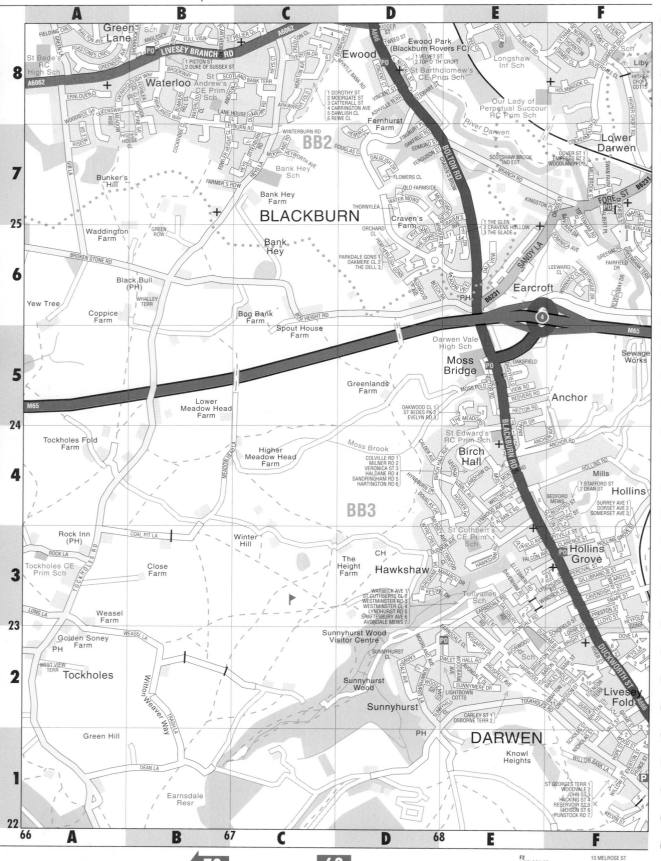

79 63

F2
1 NELSON ST
2 DOBSON ST
3 FRANCES ST
4 BROUGHTON ST
5 FINCH ST
6 DERWENT ST
7 ALEXANDRA VIEW
8 ALEXANDRA RD
9 WOOD STREET LIVESEY FOLD
10 MELROSE ST
11 MATLOCK ST
12 HIGHER LAWRENCE ST
13 ROBERT ST

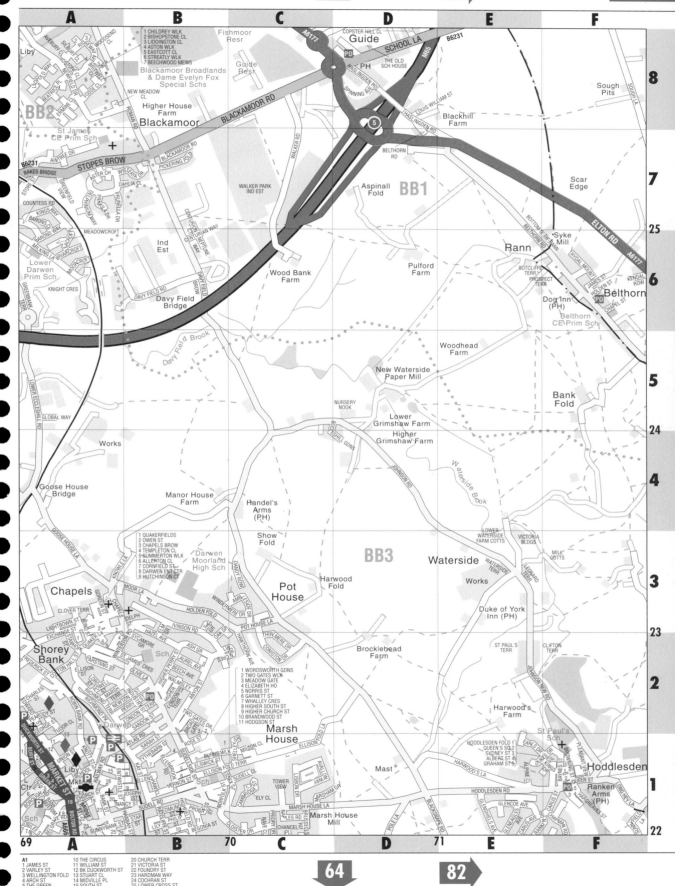

Map Labels

A | B | C | D | E | F

8 | 7 | 25 | 6 | 5 | 24 | 4 | 3 | 23 | 2 | 1 | 22

69 | 70 | 71

Liby
BB2
St James CE Prim Sch
Blackamoor Broadlands & Dame Evelyn Fox Special Schs
Higher House Farm
Blackamoor
STOPES BROW
RAKES BRIDGE
B6231
Lower Darwen Prim Sch
KNIGHT CRES
MEADOWCROFT
Ind Est
CENTURION WAY
Davy Field Bridge
Wood Bank Farm
Davy Field Brook
Goose House Bridge
GLOBAL WAY
Works
LOWER ECCLESHILL RD
Chapels
Shorey Bank
Darwen
Liby
Mkt
Sch
A666
BURY FOLD LA
MARKET ST
Marsh House
Marsh House Mill

1 CHILDREY WLK
2 BISHOPSTONE CL
3 LIDDINGTON CL
4 ASTON WLK
5 EASTCOTT CL
6 STREATLY WLK
7 BEECHWOOD MEWS

Fishmoor Resr
Guide Resr
Guide
SCHOOL LA
THE OLD SCH HOUSE
PH
BLACKAMOOR RD
WALKER RD
Walker Park Ind Est
M65
B6231
COPSTER HILL CL
HASLINGDEN RD
SPINNING JENNY
LOUIS WILLIAM ST
Blackhill Farm
BELTHORN RD
BB1
Aspinall Fold
Pulford Farm
Woodhead Farm
New Waterside Paper Mill
NURSERY NOOK
Lower Grimshaw Farm
Higher Grimshaw Farm
JOHNSON RD
ECCLESHILL GDNS
Sough Pits
SOUGH LA
Scar Edge
ELTON RD
A6177
BOTTOM O' TH' MAIN
BELTHORN RD
Rann
Syke Mill
SUTCLIFFE TERR
PROSPECT TERR
RYDAL MOUNT
JAMES ST
KENDAL ROW
Belthorn
Dog Inn (PH)
Belthorn CE Prim Sch
CHAPEL ST
Bank Fold
Waterside Brook

1 QUAKERFIELDS
2 OWEN ST
3 CHAPELS BROW
4 TEMPLETON CL
5 SUMMERTON WLK
6 ALLERTON CL
7 CORNFIELD ST
8 DARWEN ENT CTR
9 HUTCHINSON CT

Manor House Farm
Handel's Arms (PH)
Show Fold
Darwen Moorland High Sch
Pot House
Harwood Fold
BB3
Waterside
LOWER WATERSIDE FARM COTTS
VICTORIA BLDGS
MILL COTTS
Works
WATERSIDE TERR
LEONARD ST
Duke of York Inn (PH)
ST PAUL'S TERR
CLIFTON TERR
JOHNSON NEW RD

1 WORDSWORTH GDNS
2 TWO GATES WLK
3 MEADOW GATE
4 ELIZABETH HO
5 NORRIS ST
6 GARNETT ST
7 HIGHER SOUTH ST
8 HIGHER CHURCH ST
9 BRANDWOOD ST
10 HODGSON ST

Brocklehead Farm
Harwood's Farm
Mast
St Paul's Sch
HODDLESDEN FOLD
1 QUEEN'S SQ
2 SYDNEY ST
3 ALBERT ST
4 GRAHAM ST
HARWOOD'S LA
Hoddlesden
Ranken Arms (PH)
HODDLESDEN RD
GLENCOE AVE
BLACKSNAPE RD

A1
1 JAMES ST
2 VARLEY ST
3 WELLINGTON FOLD
4 ARCH ST
5 THE GREEN
6 JAMES ST W
7 ASHWORTH TERR
8 HESSE ST
9 BELGRAVE SQ
10 THE CIRCUS
11 WILLIAM ST
12 BK DUCKWORTH ST
13 STUART CL
14 MIDVILLE PL
15 SOUTH ST
16 GREEN ST E
17 CROFT ST
18 PARLIAMENT ST
19 CHURCH BANK ST
20 CHURCH TERR
21 VICTORIA ST
22 FOUNDRY ST
23 HARDMAN WAY
24 COCHRAN ST
25 LOWER CROSS ST
26 FRANKLIN ST

A B C D E F

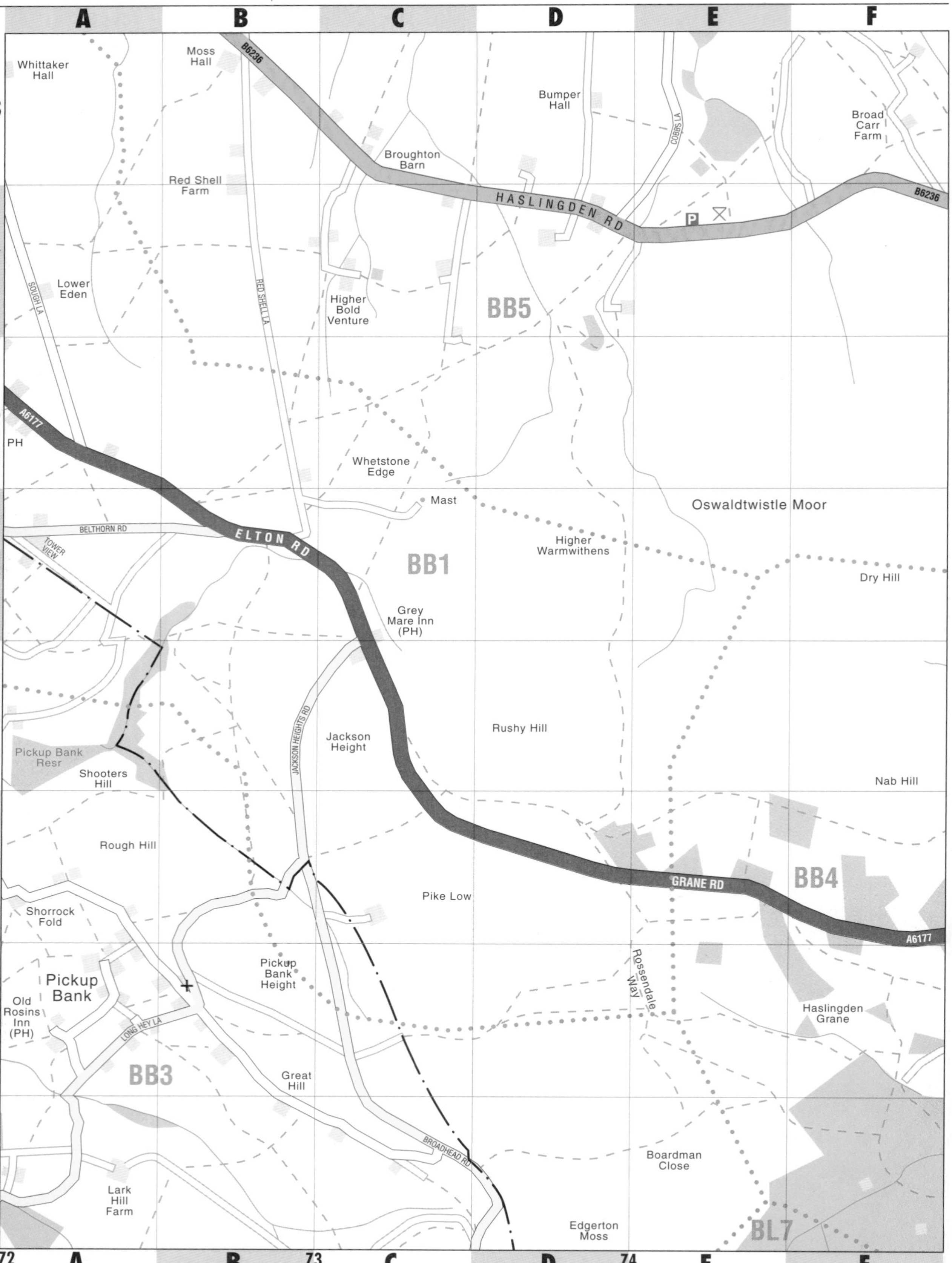

8

Whittaker Hall

Moss Hall

B6236

Bumper Hall

Broad Carr Farm

B6236

Broughton Barn

Red Shell Farm

HASLINGDEN RD

7

25

Lower Eden

SOUGH LA

RED SHELL LA

Higher Bold Venture

BB5

P

6

A6177

Whetstone Edge

Mast

Oswaldtwistle Moor

PH

BELTHORN RD

ELTON RD

Higher Warmwithens

Dry Hill

TOWER VIEW

BB1

5

24

Grey Mare Inn (PH)

Pickup Bank Resr

Shooters Hill

JACKSON HEIGHTS RD

Jackson Height

Rushy Hill

Nab Hill

4

Rough Hill

3

23

Shorrock Fold

Pike Low

GRANE RD

BB4

Pickup Bank Height

Rossendale Way

A6177

Pickup Bank

LONG HEY LA

Old Rosins Inn (PH)

Haslingden Grane

2

BB3

Great Hill

BROADHEAD RD

Boardman Close

1

Lark Hill Farm

Edgerton Moss

BL7

22

72 A B 73 C D 74 E F

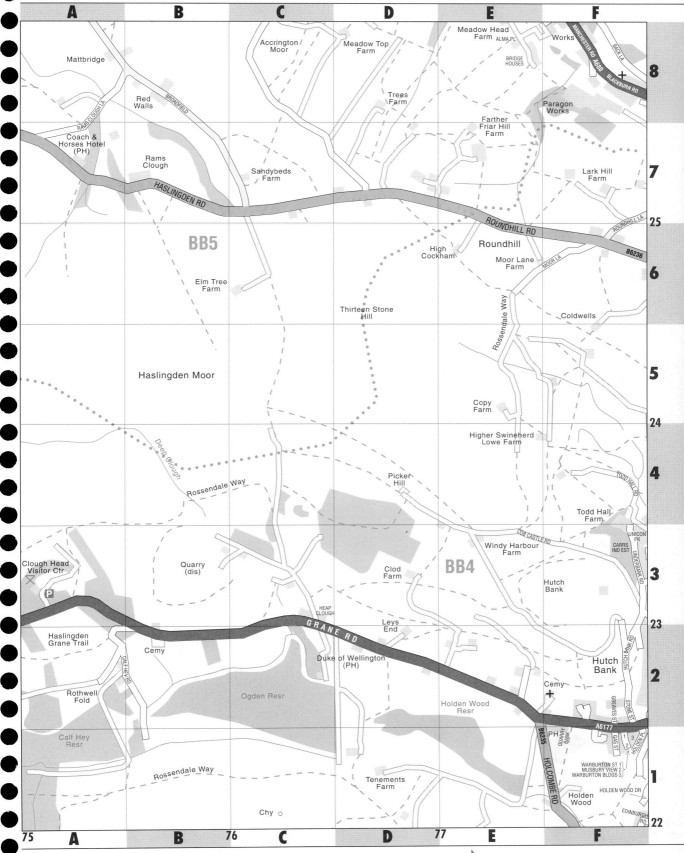

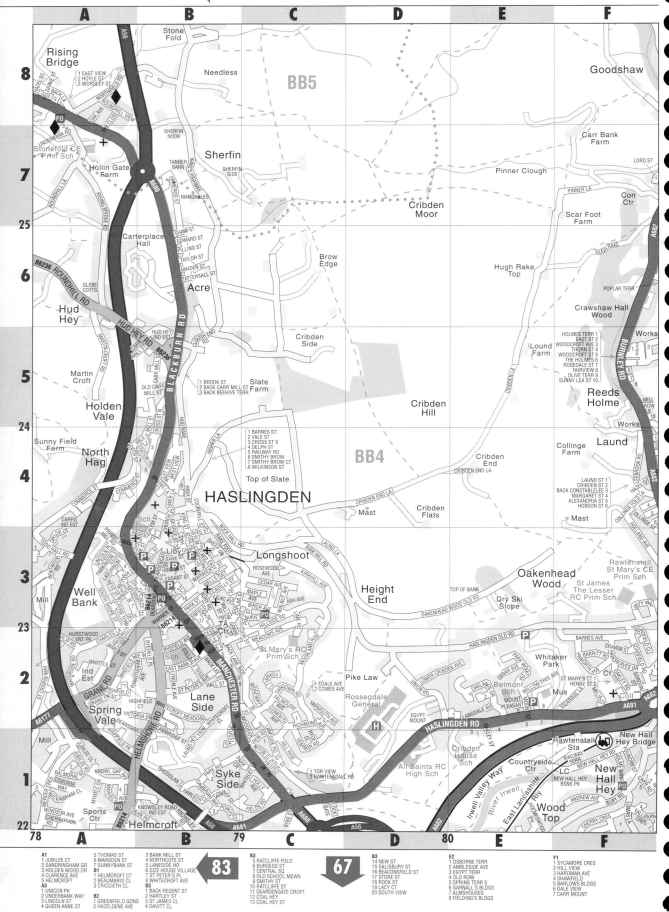

83 104

BB5

Rising Bridge

Stone Fold

Needless

1 EAST VIEW
2 HOYLE ST
3 WORSLEY ST

Goodshaw

SHERFIN NOOK

Sherfin

Carr Bank Farm

LORD ST

Stonefold CE Prim Sch

Hollin Gate Farm

TANNER BARN

SHERFIN SIDE

Pinner Clough

Carterplace Hall

SHAW ST
EDWARD ST
PILLING ST
TAYLOR ST
MAIDEN ST
TATTERSALL ST

Cribden Moor

Scar Foot Farm

Con Ctr

PINNER LA

HUGH RAKE

Acre

Brow Edge

Hugh Rake Top

POPLAR TERR

Hud Hey

GLEBE COTTS

Crawshaw Hall Wood

Cribden Side

HOLMES TERR 1
EAST ST 2
WOODCROFT AVE 3
THORN ST 4
WOODCROFT ST 5
THE HOLMES 6
ROSEDALE ST 7
FAIRVIEW 8
OLIVE TERR 9
SUNNY LEA ST 10

Works

Martin Croft

1 BROOK ST
2 BACK CARR MILL ST
3 BACK BEEHIVE TERR

Slate Farm

Lound Farm

Reeds Holme

Holden Vale

Cribden Hill

Works

Sunny Field Farm

North Hag

1 BARNES ST
2 VALE ST
3 CROSS ST S
4 DELPH ST
5 RAILWAY RD
6 SMITHY BROW
7 SMITHY BROW CT
8 WILKINSON ST

BB4

Cribden End

CRIBDEN END LA

Collinge Farm

Laund

LAUND ST 1
CRIBDEN ST 2
BACK CONSTABLELEE 3
MARGARET ST 4
ALEXANDRIA ST 5
HOBSON ST 6

Top of Slate

HASLINGDEN

Mast

Cribden Flats

Mast

Longshoot

Rosewood Ave

Oakenhead Wood

Rawtenstall St Mary's CE Prim Sch

Cedar Ave

Height End

TOP OF BANK

Dry Ski Slope

St James The Lesser RC Prim Sch

Well Bank

OAKENHEAD WOOD OLD RD

Mill

Ind Est

St Mary's RC Prim Sch

HASLINGDEN OLD RD

Barnes Ave

Whitaker Park

Spring Vale

Lane Side

1 EDALE AVE
2 COWES AVE

Pike Law

Rossendale General

Belmont Sch

ST MARY'S CT 1
HENRY ST 2

Mus

Coll

Syke Side

1 TOR VIEW
2 RAWTENSTALL RD

All Saints RC High Sch

EGYPT MOUNT

HASLINGDEN RD

Cribden House Sch

Rawtenstall Sta

New Hall Hey Bridge

Sports Ctr

Irwell Valley Way

River Irwell

East Lancashire Rly

Countryside Ctr

New Hall Hey

Wood Top

Helmcroft

83 67

A1
1 JUBILEE CT
2 SANDRINGHAM GR
3 HOLDEN WOOD DR
4 CLARENCE AVE
5 HELMCROFT
A3
1 UNICON PK
2 UNDERBANK WAY
3 LINCOLN ST
4 QUEEN ANNE CL

5 THOMAS ST
6 MARSDEN ST
7 SUNNYBANK ST
B1
1 HELMCROFT CT
2 BEAUMARIS CL
3 CRICCIETH CL
B2
1 GREENFIELD GDNS
2 HAZELDENE AVE

3 BANK MILL ST
4 NORTHCOTE ST
5 LANESIDE HO
6 SIZE HOUSE VILLAGE
7 ST PETER'S PL
8 WHITECROFT AVE
B3
1 BACK REGENT ST
2 HARTLEY ST
3 ST JAMES CL
4 DAVITT CL

B3
5 RATCLIFFE FOLD
6 BURGESS ST
7 CENTRAL SQ
8 OLD SCHOOL MEWS
9 SMITHY
10 RATCLIFFE ST
11 DEARDENGATE CROFT
12 COAL HEY
13 COAL HEY ST

B3
14 NEW ST
15 SALISBURY ST
16 BEACONSFIELD ST
17 STORE ST
18 ROCK ST
19 LACY CT
20 SOUTH VIEW

E2
1 OSBORNE TERR
2 AMBLESIDE AVE
3 EGYPT TERR
4 OLD ROW
5 SPRING TERR S
6 GARNALL'S BLDGS
7 ALMSHOUSES
8 FIELDING'S BLDGS

F1
1 SYCAMORE CRES
2 HILL VIEW
3 HARDMAN AVE
4 SHAWFIELD
5 BARLOWS BLDGS
6 DALE VIEW
7 CARR MOUNT

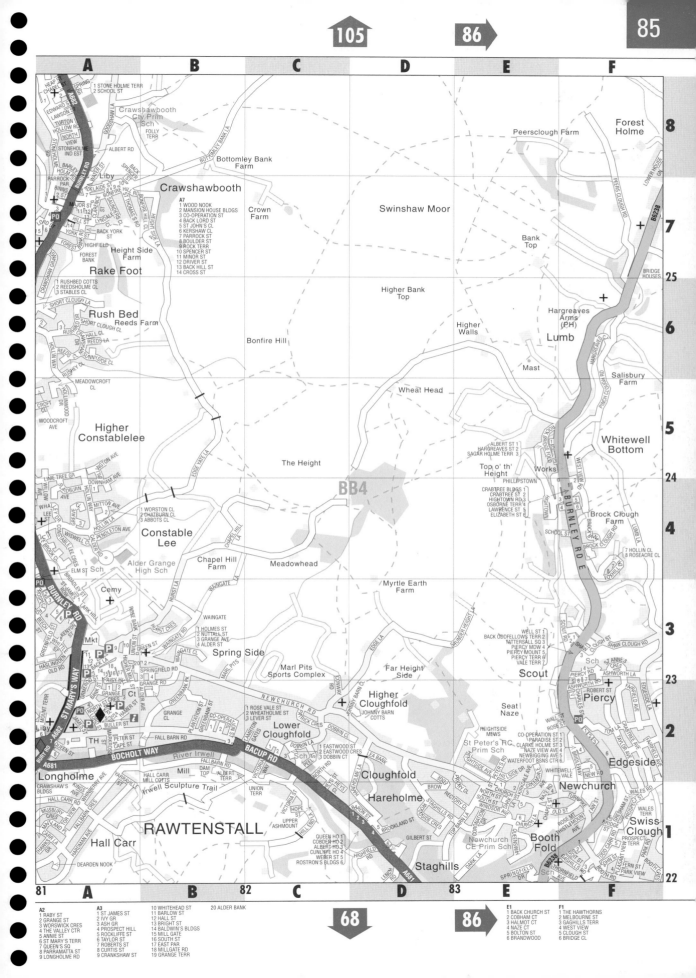

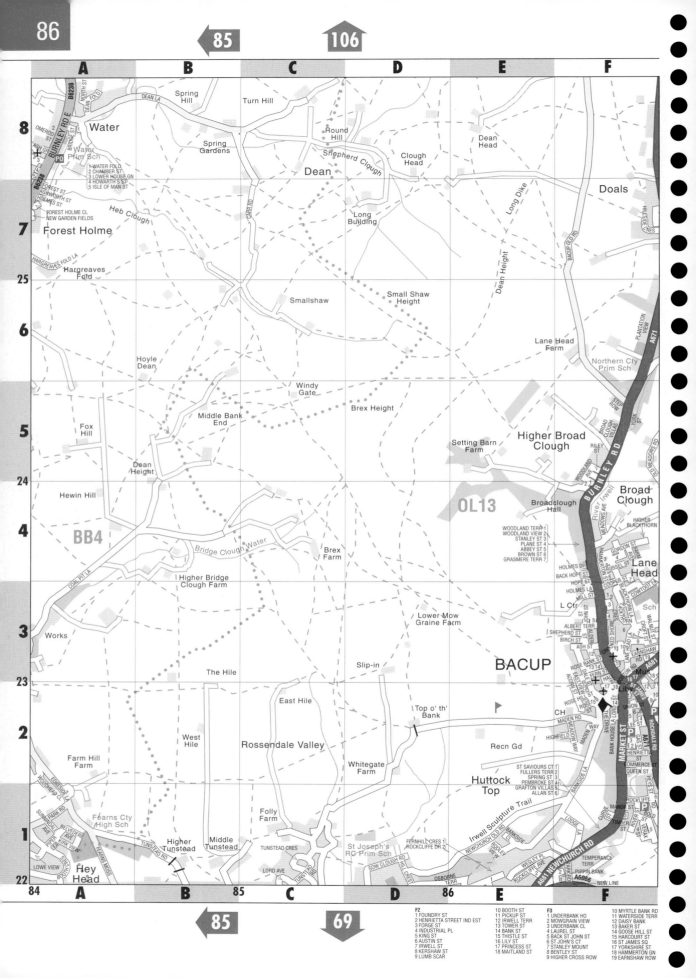

A B C D E F

8
7
25
6
5
24
4
3
23
2
1
22

Water

DEAN LA
Spring Hill
Turn Hill
Round Hill
Dean Head
Doals
Spring Gardens
Shepherd Clough
Clough Head
Dean

1 WATER FOLD
2 CHAMBER ST
3 LOWER HOUSE GN
4 HOWARTH S ST
5 ISLE OF MAN ST

FOREST ST
ASHWORTH ST
HOLMES ST
FOREST HOLME CL
NEW GARDEN FIELDS

Forest Holme
Heb Clough
Long Building
Long Dike
Dean Height

Hargreaves Fold
HARGREAVES FOLD LA
Smallshaw
Small Shaw Height
Lane Head Farm
Northern City Prim Sch

Hoyle Dean
Windy Gate
Brex Height
Setting Barn Farm
Higher Broad Clough
BROAD CLOUGH VILLAS
RILEY ST

Fox Hill
Middle Bank End
Hewin Hill
Dean Height
OL13
Broadclough Hall
Broad Clough
HIGHER BLACKTHORN

BB4
Bridge Clough Water
Brex Farm
WOODLAND TERR 1
WOODLAND VIEW 2
STANLEY ST 3
PLANE ST 4
ABBEY ST 5
BROWN ST 6
GRASMERE TERR 7
Lane Head
GORDON ST

COAL PIT LA
Higher Bridge Clough Farm
HOLMES DR
BACK HOPE ST
HOPE ST
HOLMES LA
MILL ST
L Ctr

Works
Lower Mow Graine Farm
ALBERT TERR
SHEPHERD ST
BIRCH ST
ASH ST

The Hile
Slip-in
BACUP
ROSE BANK
DALE ST
ROSE HILL ST

East Hile
Top o' th' Bank
CH
UNION ST

West Hile
Rossendale Valley
MADEN RD
THE DRIVE
Recn Gd
HIGHFIELD
MADEN WAY

Farm Hill Farm
Whitegate Farm
ST SAVIOURS CT 1
FULLERS TERR 2
SPRING ST 3
PEMBROKE ST 4
GRAFTON VILLAS 5
ALLAN ST 6
Huttock Top
HENRIETTA ST
COMMERCE ST
QUEEN ST

Fearns Cty High Sch
Folly Farm
Irwell Sculpture Trail
BANKSIDE LA

Hey Head
Higher Tunstead
Middle Tunstead
TUNSTEAD CRES
St Joseph's RC Prim Sch
FERNHILL CRES 1
ROCKCLIFFE DR 2
A681 NEWCHURCH RD
A6066
NEW LINE

LORD AVE
SOW CLOUGH RD
OSBORNE TERR
TEMPERANCE TERR
PIPPIN BANK

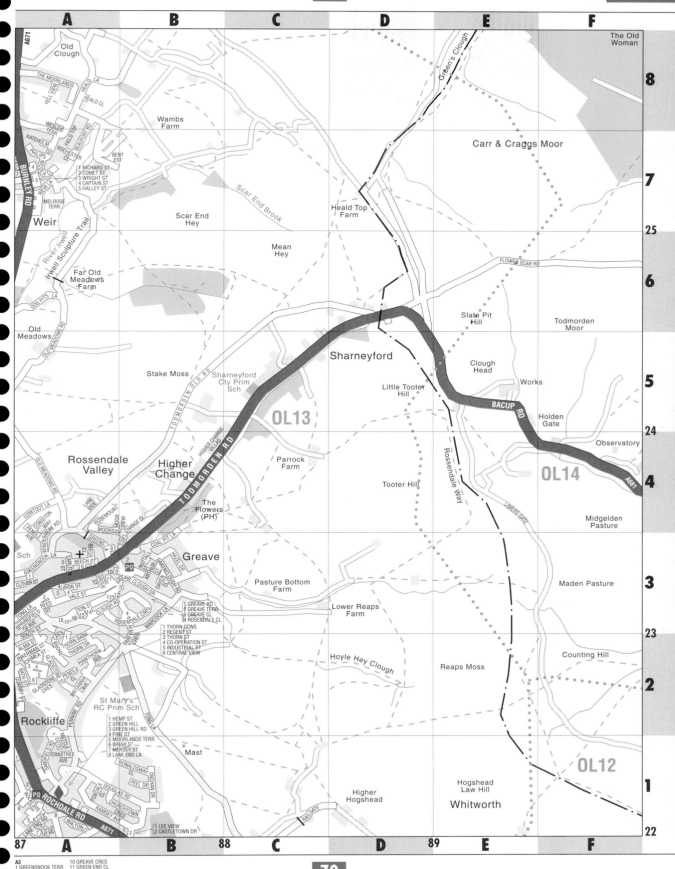

109

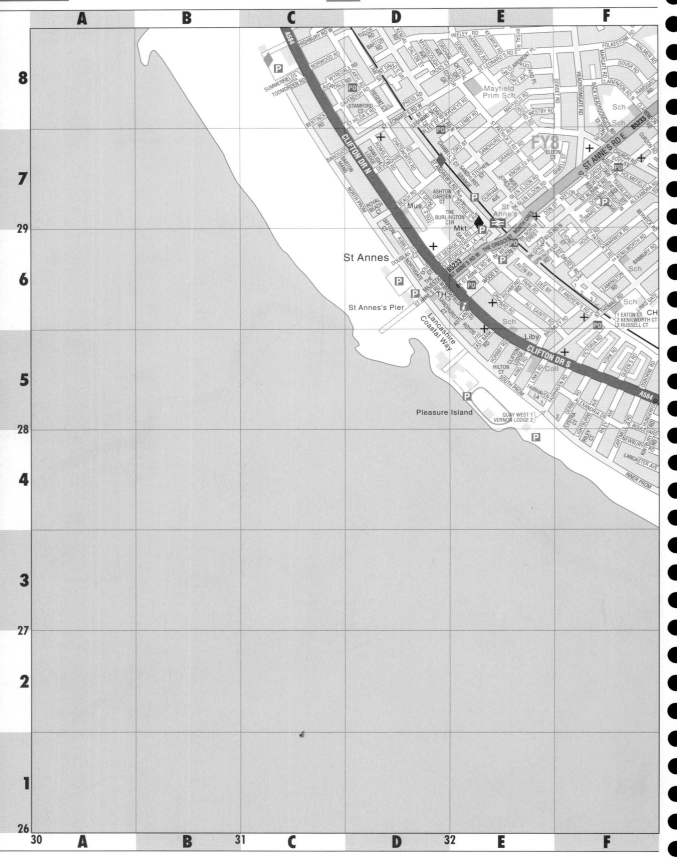

110
90

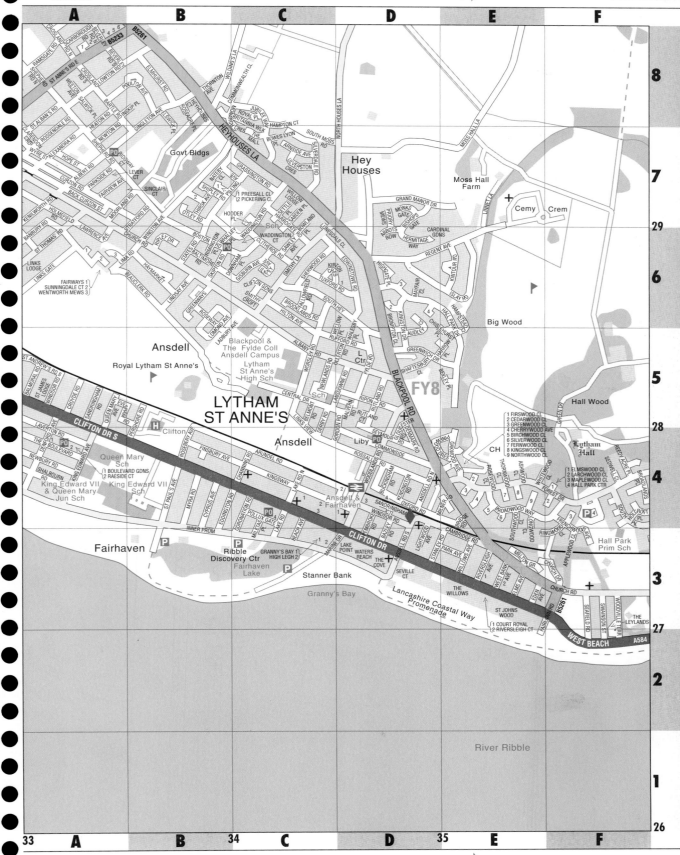

90

A8
1 BANNISTRE CL
2 BEVERLEY CT
3 TALBOT CT
4 SILVERBURN
5 FELLBOROUGH LODGE
6 GROSVENOR CT

D6
1 TUXFORD CT
2 KNIGHTSBRIDGE CL
3 BELGRAVE CL
4 TWICKENHAM PL

C4
1 WORDSWORTH CT
2 KINGSWAY CT
3 CRYSTAL LODGE
4 ST PAUL'S WLK

D4
1 BELVEDERE CT
2 PRINCES RD
3 WINDSOR LODGE
4 OXFORD CT
5 WOODLANDS CT

PR4

Smeath Hill Farm

Moss Side Villa

Brick Hill Farm

Bulwer's Wood

Wrea Brook

CARTMELL LA

Manor House Farm

PEG'S LA

Little Birks Farm

Bridge Hall Farm

Eastham Hall Farm

HUCK LA

SALTCOTES RD

B5259

BALLAM RD

Birks Farm

Eastham Hall

EASTHAM COTTS

Carr Farm

Long Wood

Liggard Brook

Birks Wood

Eastham Bridge

LODGE LA

Warton Hall Farm

Lytham Hall Park

LABURNUM AVE

LAUREL AVE

LILAC AVE

CH

GREEN DR

Cemy

Saltcotes

FY8

THE BURY

HOWGILL

COTSWOLD

WINCKLOW

GRAHAM WAY

CHEVIOT AVE

LIDUM PARK IND EST

Warton Lodge Farm

BOUNDARY RD

1 MENDIP CL
2 CHILTERN CL

Watch Wood

NORFOLK RD

Lytham CE Prim Sch

PARK VIEW RD

BELLINGHAM RD

WYKEHAM RD

OLD LYTHAM

St Peter's RC Prim Sch

St Bede's RC High Sch

EAST HOLME

GREEN HEY

TEWKESBURY DR

CHELTENHAM CRES

BREDON

MORNINGTON RD

PRESTON RD

MEADOW LA

LYTHAM RD

A584

PARK VIEW CT 1
BROOKFIELD TERR 2

MYTHOP RD

WHITECOTES

SALTCOTES RD

LYTHAM

FAIRHAVEN AVE

RIBCHESTER AVE

Lytham Dock

28

RING DYKE WAY

FOREST DR

CALF

CROFT PL

MOLYNEUX PL

SOUTH

ROOKFIELD

PAINLEY

MOORFIELD

STARFIELD

SANDACRE

ROGERLEY

ALDER

PL

CL

CL

MYTHOP AVE

BLEASDALE RD

COPELAND PL

ROTHBURY PL

PL

PENDLE

THE GLADE

ALBERT

TENNYSON AVE

BYRON

WELLINGTON

GRAVING DOCK RD

DOCK RD

MARINE IND CTR

4

SOUTH PK

GREGORY PL

Lytham

BROOK RD

BADGERS WLK E

EAST CLIFF

FRECKLETON ST

LORNE ST

NELSON

SOUTH ST

CHANDLERS REST

WATERFRONT MARINE & IND EST

Lytham

CLEVELAND RD

HAVEN RD

STATION RD

WHARF ST

WARTON ST

NORTH WARTON ST

VICTORIA ST

GROSVENOR

KENT ST

H P

3

1 2 3 4

5 6

WOOD MEWS

ASHTON ST

CECIL ST

AGNEW ST

HASTINGS PL

CLIFTON ST

HENRY ST

BANNISTER ST

ST

SOUTH WESTBY ST

UPPER WESTBY ST

Ct

WESTBY ST

SOUTH

NORTH CLIFTON ST

MARKET SQ

Liby

BATH ST

WEST ST

ST JOHN'S

SOUTH WARTON ST

EAST BEACH

Lancashire Coastal Way

SCHOOL LA

CHURCH RD

GREGSON

DUKE ST

CLIFTON

WESTWOOD

LOWTHER CRES

QUEEN ST

CENTRAL BEACH

B5259

27

A584

WEST BEACH

P

P

Lytham Lifeboat Museum

Lytham Windmill (Mus)

LB Sta

2

Jetty

River Ribble

1

26

36

37

38

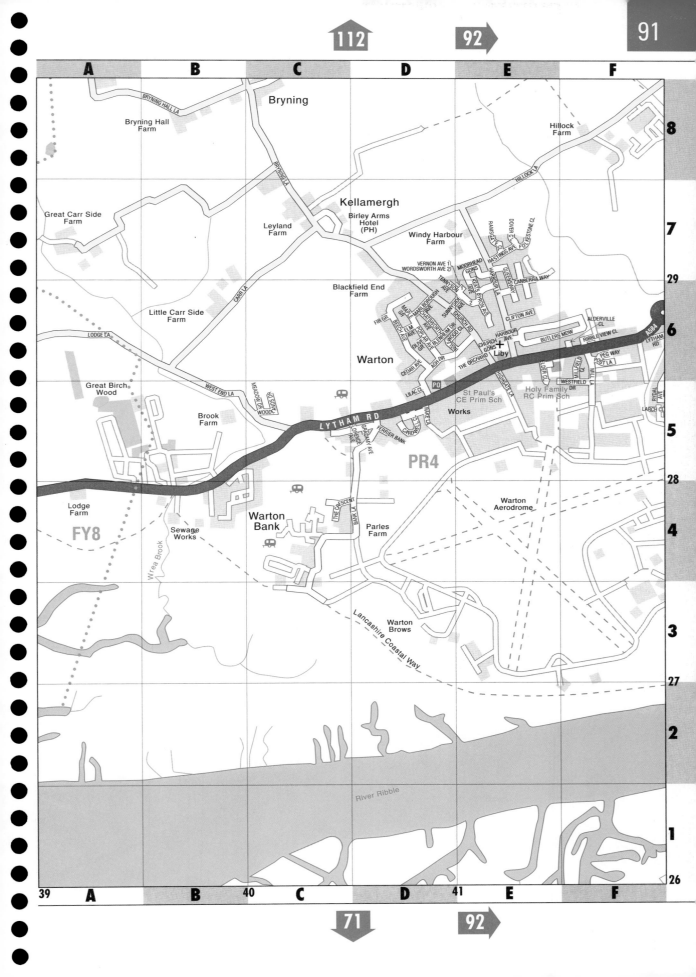

A B C D E F

BRYNING HALL LA

Bryning

Bryning Hall Farm

Great Carr Side Farm

BRYNING LA

Kellamergh

Birley Arms Hotel (PH)

Leyland Farm

Windy Harbour Farm

Blackfield End Farm

Little Carr Side Farm

CARR LA

RAMSGATE CL
DOVER CL
KESTONE CL
MOORHEAD GDNS
HASTINGS AVE
FOX
VERNON AVE 1
WORDSWORTH AVE 2
QUEENSWAY
CANBERRA WAY
HARBUR LA
BYROD AVE
KEATS
TENNYSON
MARLBOROUGH
FIR GR
ELM
BEECH AVE
CHATSWORTH
SUNNYSIDE AVE
CHURCH RD
CLIFTON AVE
ALDERVILLE CL
RIBBLE VIEW CL
BUTLERS MDW
A584
LODGE LA

LYTHAM RD

Great Birch Wood

WEST END LA

MEADOW DR
SIGNAL WOODS DR

Brook Farm

Warton

BLENHEIM DR
POPLAR AVE
OLIVERS LA
ASH GR
BIRCH AVE
WOOD CL
THE ORCHARD
HARBOUR AVE
CHURCH GDNS
Liby
CEDAR AVE
LILAC CL
PO
RAKE LA
St Paul's CE Prim Sch
Works
ELDER CL
MILLFIELD
WESTFIELD
MILL
PEG WAY
POST LA
DR
Holy Family RC Prim Sch
RYDAL AVE
LARCH CL
LYTHAM RD

FY8

Lodge Farm

Sewage Works

Wrea Brook

Warton Bank

THE CRESCENT
BANK LA
FLORENCE AVE
FERRIER BANK
NORMANDY AVE
GDNS

Parles Farm

PR4

Warton Aerodrome

Warton Brows

Lancashire Coastal Way

River Ribble

8
7
29
6
5
28
4
3
27
2
1
26

Freckleton

PR4

Nurseries

Strike Farm
Strike Lane Cty Prim Sch
Marbank Farm
Lower House Farm
Nursery

Raker House Farm

A584
Toll House Bridge
Halfpenny Hall Bridge

PRESTON NEW RD

Freckleton CE Prim Sch
Freckleton

St IVES AVE

Newton Marsh

Middle Pool

1 CLOVER DR
2 SPRING HILL
3 FOXGLOVE WAY
4 FERNDALE CL

Freckleton Marsh

Rowstorne Sports Ctr

1 QUERNMORE IND EST
2 MASON CL
3 CROFT MANOR
4 ANSBRO AVE

Grange Farm

GRANGE FARM COTTS

Caravan Pk

1 POPLAR DR
2 LARCH CL
3 BEECH DR

STONEY LA

THE CRESCENT

CHERRY LA

NAZE LANE IND EST

Pool Stream

POOL LA

Bottoms Farm

Naze Mount

Freckleton Pool

Lancashire Coastal Way

River Ribble

River Asland or Douglas

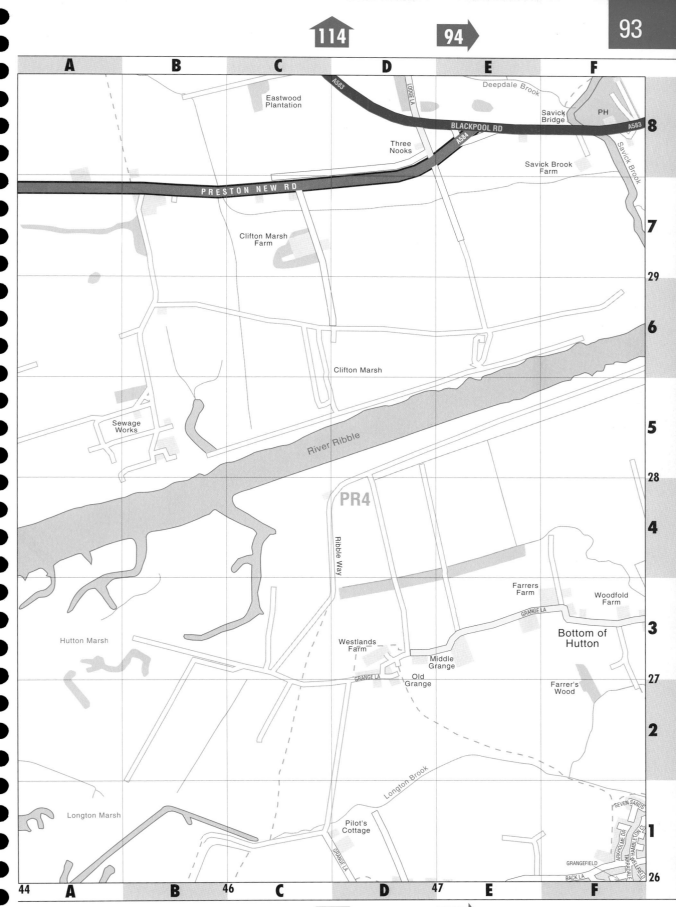

114
94

A   B   C   D   E   F

Eastwood
Plantation

A583

LODGE LA

Deepdale Brook

BLACKPOOL RD

Savick
Bridge

PH

A583   8

Three
Nooks

A584

Savick Brook
Farm

Savick Brook

PRESTON NEW RD

7

Clifton Marsh
Farm

29

6

Clifton Marsh

River Ribble

5

28

Sewage
Works

PR4

4

Ribble Way

Farrers
Farm

Woodfold
Farm

Hutton Marsh

GRANGE LA

Bottom of
Hutton

3

Westlands
Farm

Middle
Grange

Old
Grange

Farrer's
Wood

27

GRANGE LA

2

Longton Brook

Longton Marsh

Pilot's
Cottage

SEVEN SANDS

1

GRANGE LA

ARKHOLME DR

HAMBLETON CL

NEVILLE LA FLD

GRANGEFIELD

BACK LA

26

44   A   B   46   C   D   47   E   F

73
94

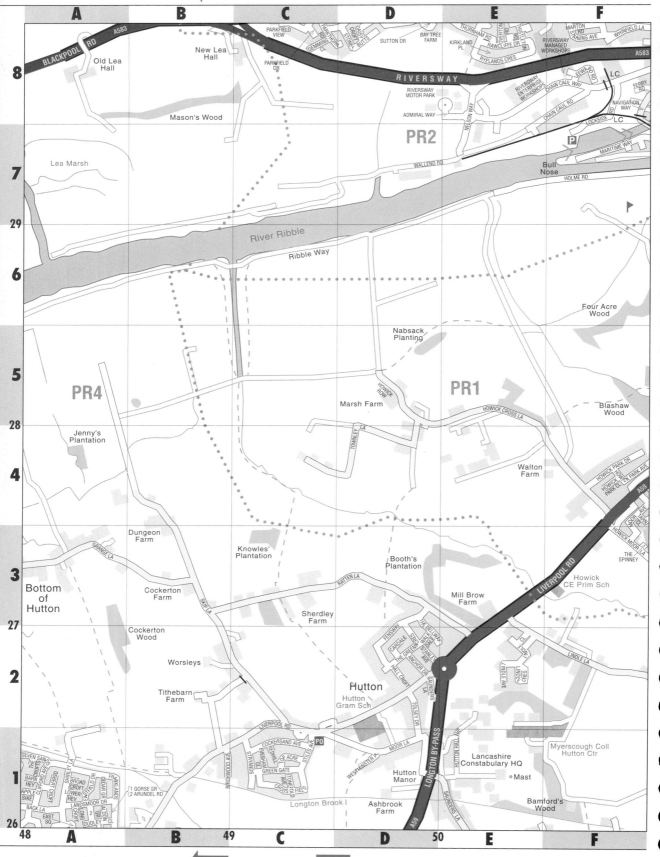

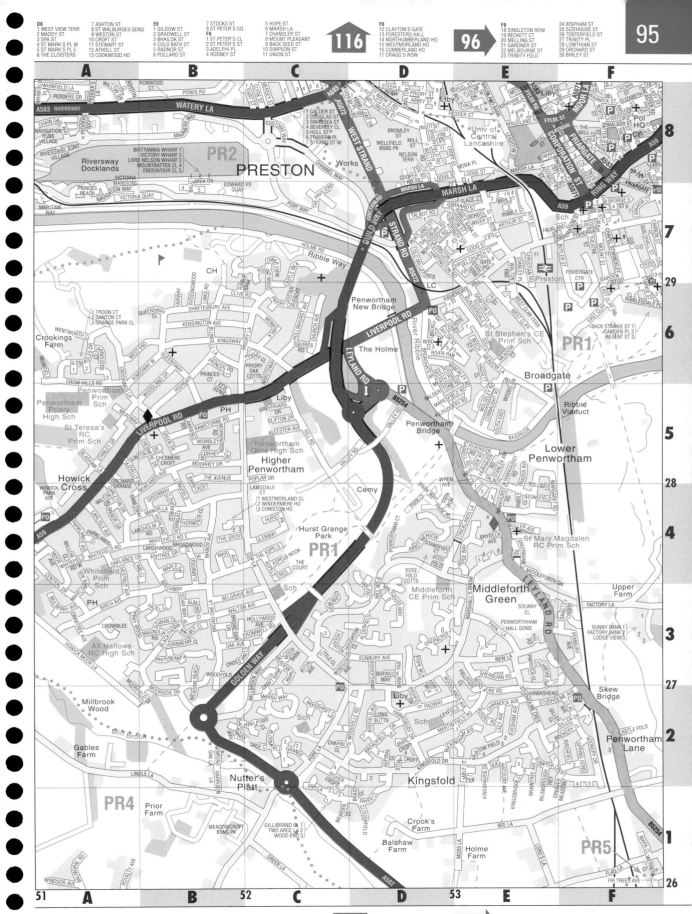

D8
1 WEST VIEW TERR
2 MADDY ST
3 SPA ST
4 ST MARK'S PL W
5 ST MARK'S PL E
6 THE CLOISTERS

7 ASHTON ST
8 ST WALBURGES GDNS
9 WESTON ST
10 CROFT ST
11 STEWART ST
12 ATHOLL ST
13 COOKWOOD HO

E8
1 GILDOW ST
2 GRADWELL ST
3 BHAILOK ST
4 COLD BATH ST
5 RADNOR ST
6 POLLARD ST

7 STOCKS ST
8 ST PETER'S SQ
F8
1 ST PETER'S CL
2 ST PETER'S SQ
3 ADELPHI PL
4 RODNEY ST

5 HOPE ST
6 MARSH LA
7 CHANDLER ST
8 MOUNT PLEASANT
9 BACK SEED ST
10 SIMPSON ST
11 UNION ST

F8
12 CLAYTON'S GATE
13 FORESTERS HALL
14 NORTHUMBERLAND HO
15 WESTMORLAND HO
16 CUMBERLAND HO
17 CRAGG'S ROW

F8
18 SINGLETON ROW
19 BECKETT CT
20 MELLING ST
21 GARDNER ST
22 MELBOURNE ST
23 TRINITY FOLD

24 BISPHAM ST
25 SIZEHOUSE ST
26 TENTERFIELD ST
27 TRINITY PL
28 LOWTHIAN ST
29 ORCHARD ST
30 BIRLEY ST

C3
1 CROMWELL AVE
2 WINGATES
3 BERRY FIELD
C2
1 ROSEMARY CT
2 SORREL CT
3 CINNAMON CT
4 BANNISTER'S BIT
5 WOODVILLE RD W

D2
1 LOWER CROFT
2 HIGHER CROFT
3 FORSHAW RD
4 CROFTERS WLK
5 OLD HEY CROFT
6 FAIRHAM AVE
7 OLDFIELD

D6
1 BEECH ST
2 RIBBLE CT
3 TAY ST
4 TYNE ST
5 CLIFTON ST
D7
1 PALEY RD
2 HUNT ST
3 CARNARVON RD

E2
1 PETERFIELD RD
2 TUSON HOUSE
3 DICKENSONS FIELD
4 THE PADDOCK
5 STURMINSTER CL
6 HAMBLEDON DR
7 WINSLOW CL
8 STUDHOLME CL

E4
1 SWALLOW AVE
2 DOVE AVE
3 LARK AVE
4 MIDDLEFORTH IND EST
5 MARSHALL'S CL
6 FINCH'S COTTS
7 PROSPECT PL
8 CHURCH BROOK HO

E6
1 BEECH TERR
2 WARTON ST
3 RIBBLE CL
4 HIND ST
5 SOUTH CLIFF ST
6 NORTH CLIFF ST
E7
1 KAY ST
2 NUTTER RD

E7
3 MARKLAND ST
4 SAVOY ST
5 RED CROSS ST
6 KINGSWOOD ST
7 BURLEIGH RD
8 LADYMAN ST
9 SPRING BANK
10 OSBOURNE ST
11 FISHERGATE CT

F2
1 GILLER FOLD
2 NORTHLEACH AVE
3 SUMPTER CT
4 CHELFORD CL
5 BURWOOD CL
F7
1 CHARNLEY ST
2 ST WILFRED ST
3 FLEET ST

4 CHAPEL WLKS
5 ST GEORGE'S SH CTR
6 FRIARGATE WLK
7 FISHERGATE WLK
8 CHEAPSIDE
9 WINCKLEY ST
10 TEMPLE CT
11 WINCKLEY CT
12 CHADDOCK ST
13 BAIRSTOW ST

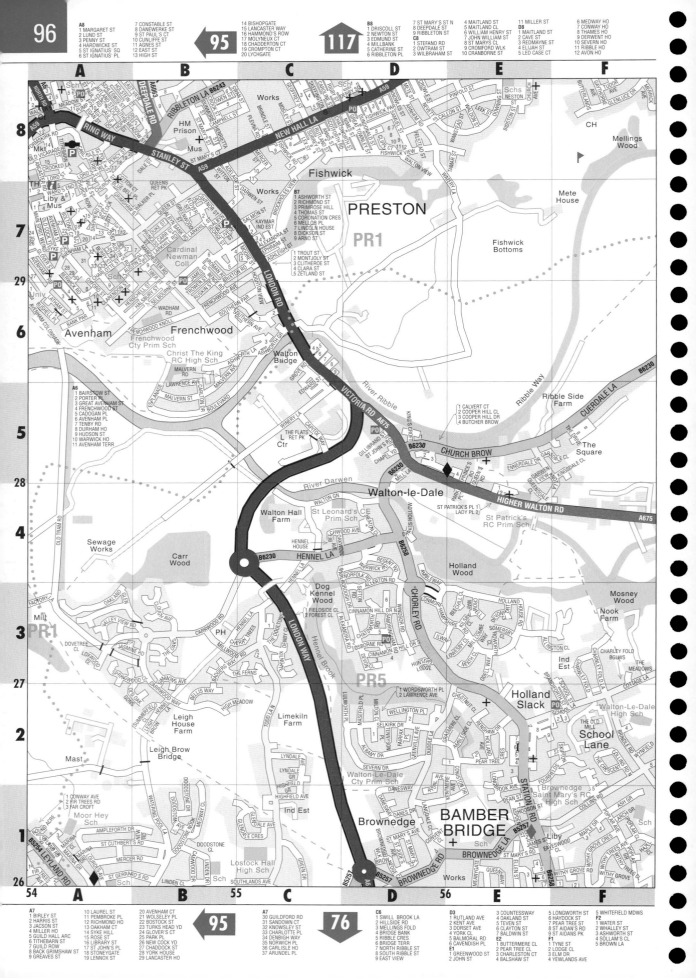

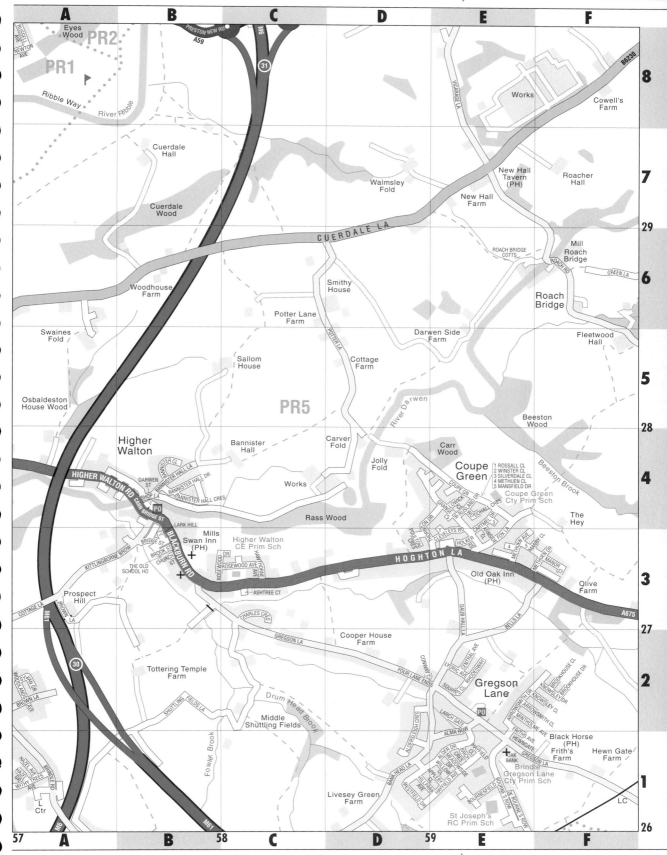

97
119

A B C D E F

8

CUERDALE LA
BB230

Sorbrose
House

Hoolster
Farm

Blue Slate
Farm

Sowerbutt's
Green

SPRING LA

Sewage
Works

Hoolster
Hill

NAB'S HEAD LA

Sewage
Works

ROUND ACRE

GREEN END

Copster
Farm

Darwen Side
Farm

Nab's Head Inn
(PH)

Nab's
Head

7

Green Lane
Farm

PO
ST JAME'S
TERR

FURTHER LA

Knight
Bottoms

GREEN LA

GOOSE FOOT CL

ALUM SCAR LA

29

Mill

BB2

Cardwell's
Farm

Knight's
Farm

Samlesbury
Bottoms

Samlesbury
Bridge

6

DARK WOOD LA

GOOSE FOOT LA

River Darwen

Simpson's
Farm

Blakey
Hey

FIRWOOD LA

Firwood
Farm

Stainton's
Farm

PR5

Wild Bottom's
Wood

5

Coppice
Farm

28

STANLEY
VILLAS

Higher
Barn

ROACH RD

Stanley
Grange

Stanley Coppice
Farm

Bolton
Hall

4

GRANGE CL

Highfields
Farm

CRIPPLE GATE LA

Tallentine
Farm

Ford

3

QUAKER BROOK LA

Quaker Brook

HOLLINS CL

GIB LA

Arthur's Wife's
Brow

WITTON WEAVERS WAY

Witton Weavers Way

Houghton
Bottoms

Rock
Gardens

LONG BARN BROW

A675 HOGHTON LA

PO

27

THE STRAITS

LITTLE DR

VIADUCT RD

Hoghton

WILLOW FIELD
THE CROFT

CHASE

LC

Hoghton
Bridge

+

LONG BARN ROW

2

Brindle
Lodge

STATION RD

FOWLER
CL

FOWLER CL

BLACKBURN OLD RD

CHAPEL LA

Boar's Head
(PH)

Barracks
Farm

+

Hoghton
Tower

Recn
Gd

Lane Side
Farm

Chapel
Bridge

1

King's
Hill

PR6

Hatchwood
Farm

A675

26

60 A B 61 C D 62 E F

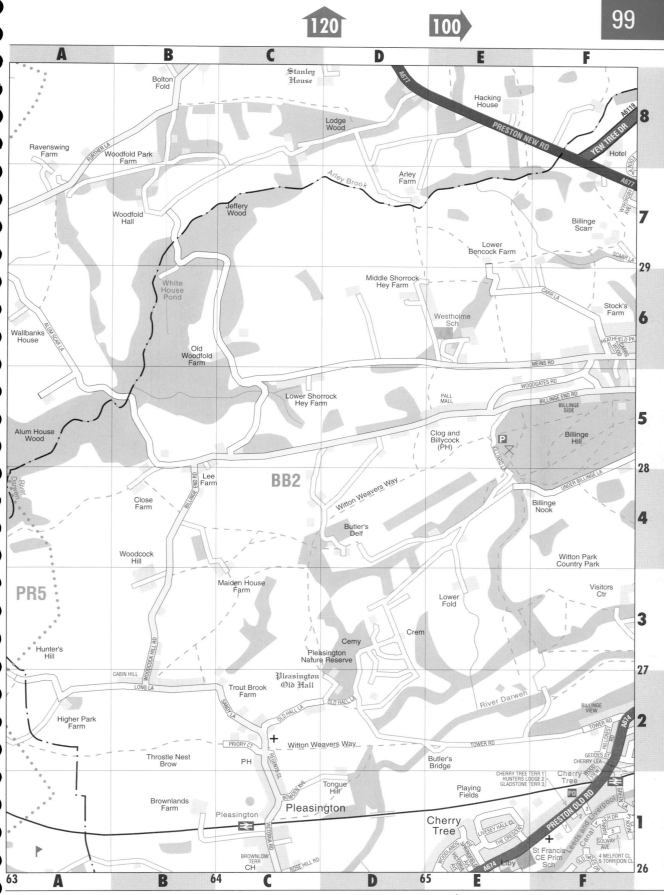

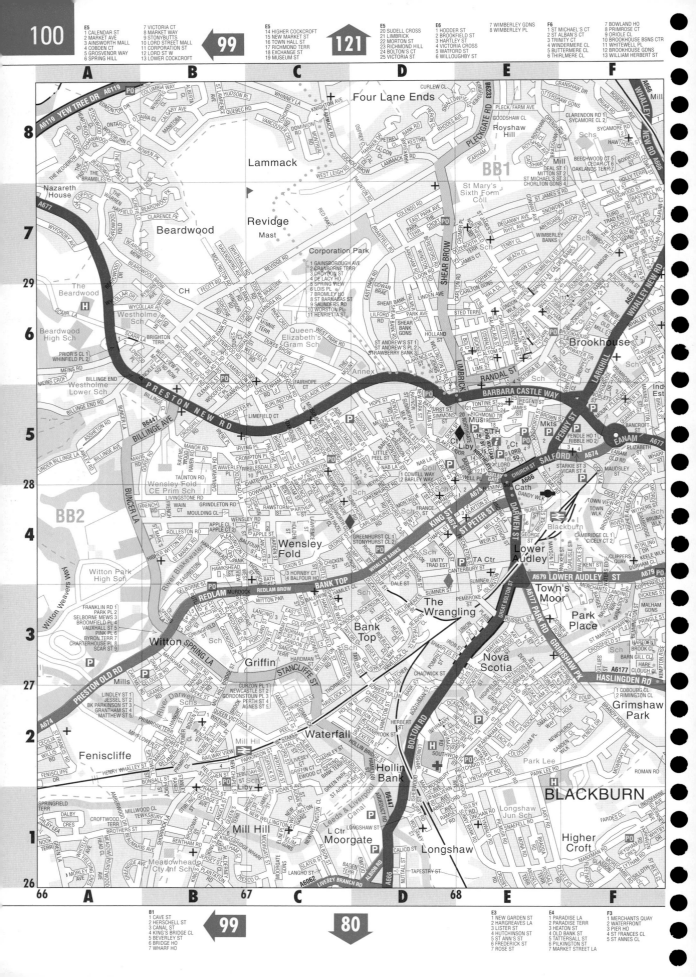

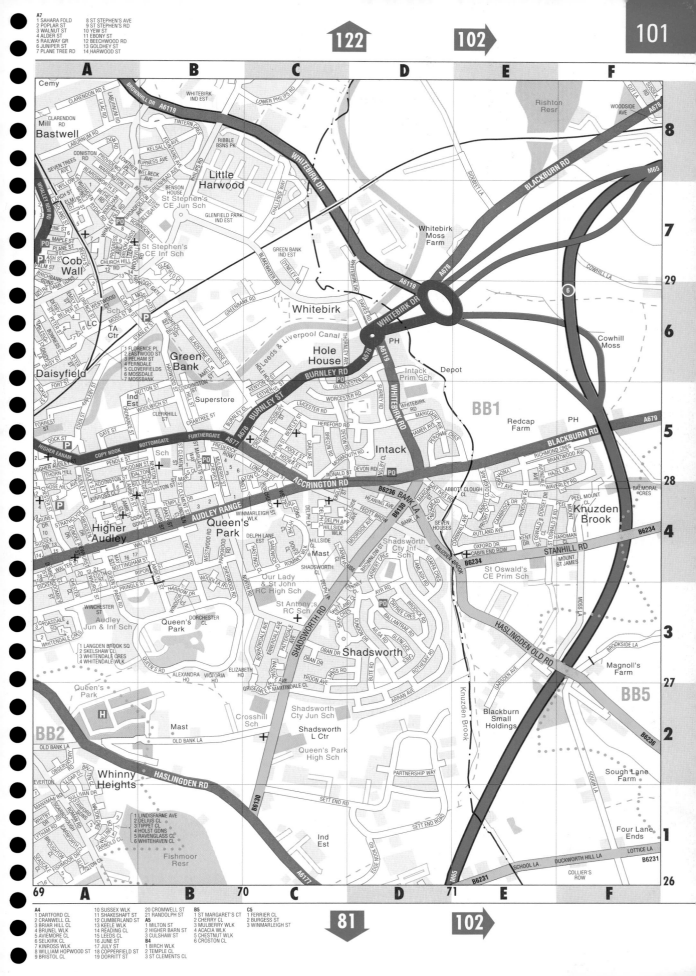

A7
1 SAHARA FOLD
2 POPLAR ST
3 WALNUT ST
4 ALDER ST
5 RAILWAY GR
6 JUNIPER ST
7 PLANE TREE RD
8 ST STEPHEN'S AVE
9 ST STEPHEN'S RD
10 YEW ST
11 EBONY ST
12 BEECHWOOD RD
13 GOLDHEY ST
14 HARWOOD ST

A4
1 DARTFORD CL
2 CRANWELL CL
3 BRIAR HILL CL
4 BRUNEL WLK
5 AVIEMORE CL
6 SELKIRK CL
7 KINROSS WLK
8 WILLIAM HOPWOOD ST
9 BRISTOL CL
10 SUSSEX WLK
11 SHAKESHAFT ST
12 CUMBERLAND ST
13 KEELE WLK
14 READING WLK
15 LEEDS CL
16 JUNE ST
17 JULY ST
18 COPPERFIELD ST
19 DORRITT ST
20 CROMWELL ST
21 RANDOLPH ST

A5
1 MILTON ST
2 HIGHER BARN ST
3 CULSHAW ST

B4
1 BIRCH WLK
2 TEMPLE ST
3 ST CLEMENTS CL

B5
1 ST MARGARET'S CT
2 CHERRY CL
3 MULBERRY WLK
4 ACACIA WLK
5 CHESTNUT WLK
6 CROSTON CL

C5
1 FERRIER CL
2 BURGESS ST
3 WINMARLEIGH ST

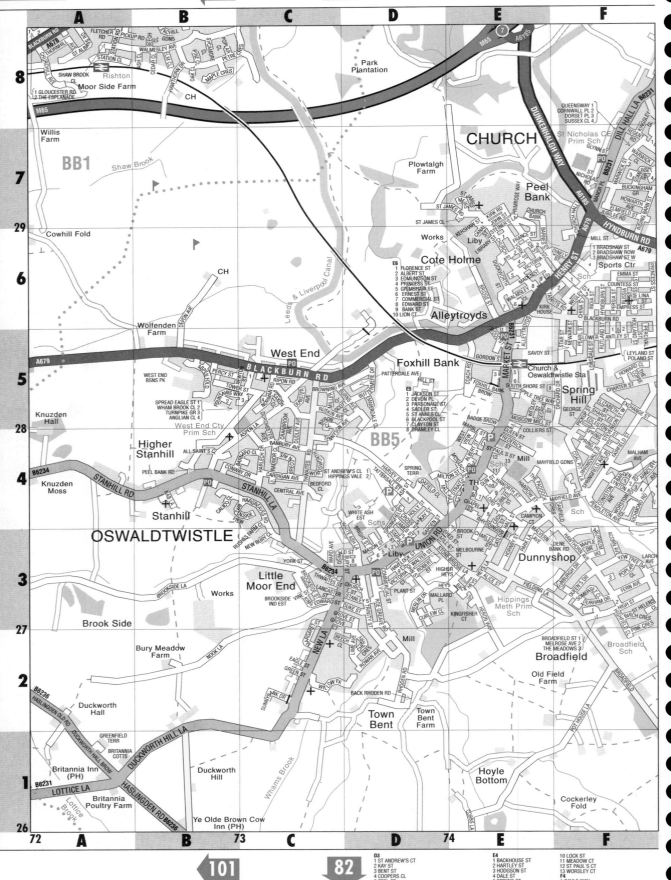

D3
1 ST ANDREW'S CT
2 KAY ST
3 BENT ST
4 COOPERS CL
5 PEEL ST
6 THOMAS ST
7 HIGHER PEEL ST
8 SMITHY BRIDGE ST
9 OAK ST

E4
1 BACKHOUSE ST
2 HARTLEY ST
3 HODGSON ST
4 DALE ST
5 SPRING ST
6 MOUNT PLEASANT ST
7 OFF MOUNT PLEASANT ST
8 WATSON ST
9 PADDOCK ST

10 LOCK ST
11 MEADOW CT
12 ST PAUL'S CT
13 WORSLEY CT
F4
1 GAYLE WAY
2 BURNSALL RD
3 REETH WAY
4 BUCKDEN RD

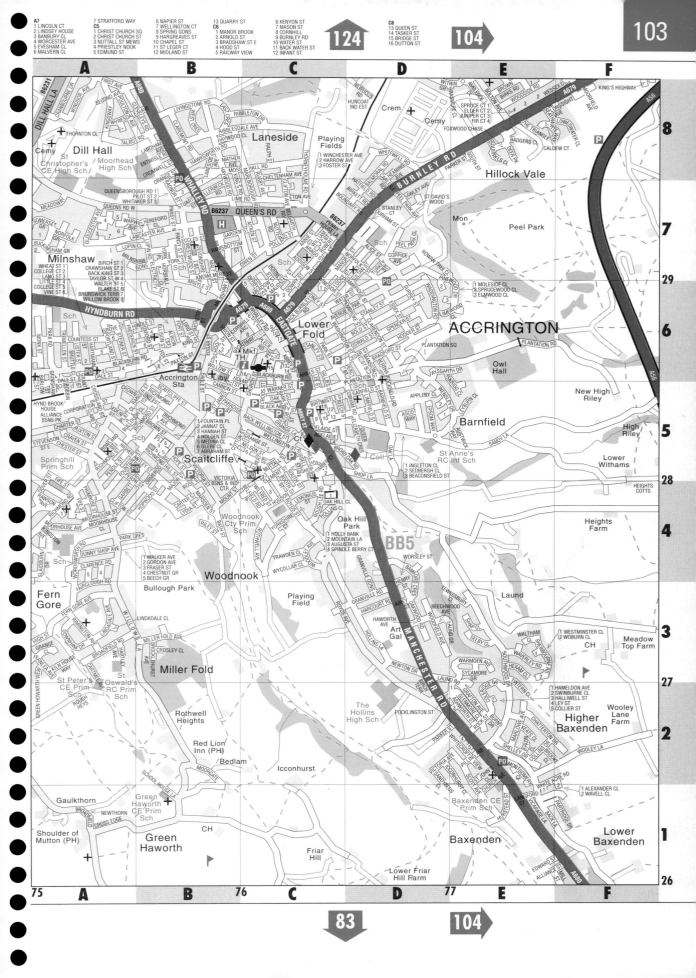

103
125

A B C D E F

8

Cronker
Plantation

Thorny
Bank

Thorny Bank
Wood

Hameldon
Scouts

BB11

7

Snipe Rake

Hameldon Common

Hapton Park

Windy
Harbour

Great Slack

29

Moleside Moor

Great Hameldon

Park Scout

Burnley Way

Great Hill

6

Moleside End
Farm

King's Highway

Masts

SANDY LA

A56

West
Farm

New Laithe
Height

5

Heights
Farm

Great
Clough

28

Higher
Hey

BB5

Higher Moor

Snipe Hole

Great Clough

4

Mitchell's House
Resrs

BB4

3

Black
Moss

KING'S HIGHWAY

Rossendale Way

Higher
Withens

Rough Hill
Farm

Works

Goodshaw
Fold

27

LOVE CLOUGH RD

SEVEN CLOG RD

Hen Heads
Farm

2

Goodshaw Hill

SPRINGBANK
GDNS

SPRING
TERR

GOODSHAW FOLD RD

New Barn

Lane Top
Farm

Limy Water

1

GOODSHAW LA

Fair Banks

Cross Edge
Farm

Gin Clough

Pewit
Hall

A56

26

78 A B 79 C D 80 E F

103
84

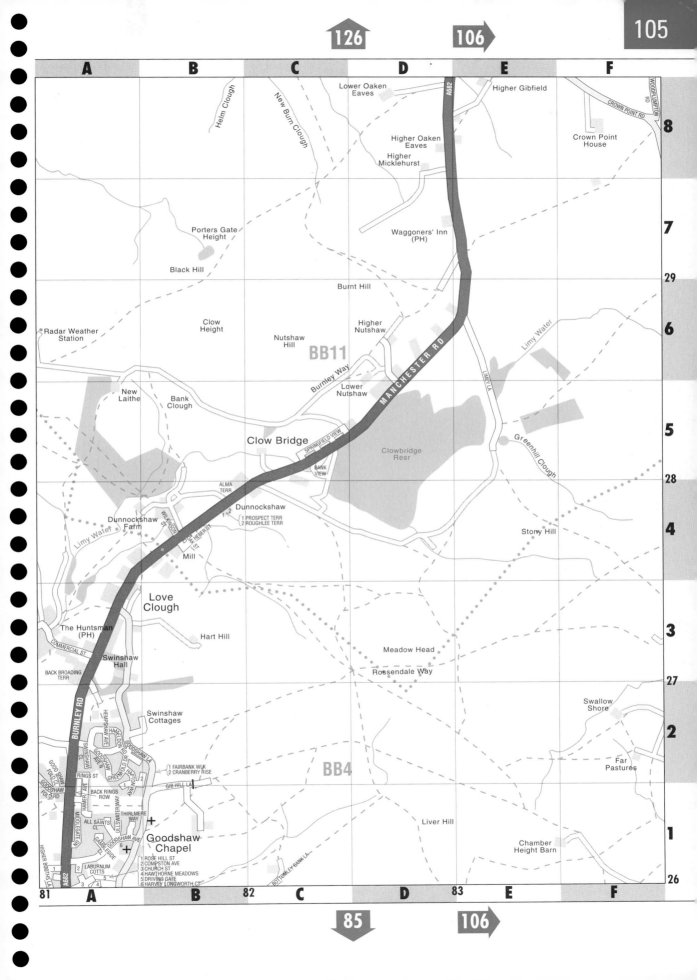

126
106
85
106

A   B   C   D   E   F

Helm Clough

New Burn Clough

Lower Oaken Eaves

Higher Gibfield

WOODPLUMPTON RD

CROWN POINT RD

8

A682

Higher Oaken Eaves

Crown Point House

Porters Gate Height

Higher Micklehurst

7

Waggoners' Inn (PH)

Black Hill

29

Burnt Hill

Clow Height

6

Radar Weather Station

Nutshaw Hill

BB11

Higher Nutshaw

Limy Water

MANCHESTER RD

Burnley Way

Lower Nutshaw

New Laithe

Bank Clough

LIMEY LA

5

Clow Bridge

SPRINGFIELD VIEW

Clowbridge Resr

Greenhill Clough

28

BANK VIEW

ALMA TERR

Dunnockshaw

Stony Hill

4

WINKINSON ST

DISH HEBER ST

Dunnockshaw Farm

1 PROSPECT TERR
2 ROUGHLEE TERR

Limy Water

Mill

Love Clough

Hart Hill

3

The Huntsman (PH)

Meadow Head

COMMERCIAL ST

Swinshaw Hall

Rossendale Way

BACK BROADING TERR

27

Swinshaw Cottages

Swallow Shore

2

BURNLEY RD

HEMPSHAW AVE

HALTON VW

GOODSHAW LA

HAMELDON RD

1 FAIRBANK WLK
2 CRANBERRY RISE

BB4

Far Pastures

GREENFOLD CT DR

GOODSHAW AVE N

GIB HILL LA

GOOD SHAW FOLD CT

RINGS ST

BACK RINGS ROW

HAMER AVE

ILLSWATER WAY

THIRLMERE WAY

Liver Hill

1

GOODSHAW AVE

ALL SAINTS CL

Goodshaw Chapel

Chamber Height Barn

HIGHER BOOTHS RD

GAMBLESIDE

MIDDLEGATE GN

LABURNUM COTTS

1 ROSE HILL ST
2 COMPSTON AVE
3 CHURCH ST
4 HAWTHORNE MEADOWS
5 DRIVING GATE
6 HARVEY LONGWORTH CT

BOTTOMLEY BANK LA

26

A682

81   A   B   82   C   D   83   E   F

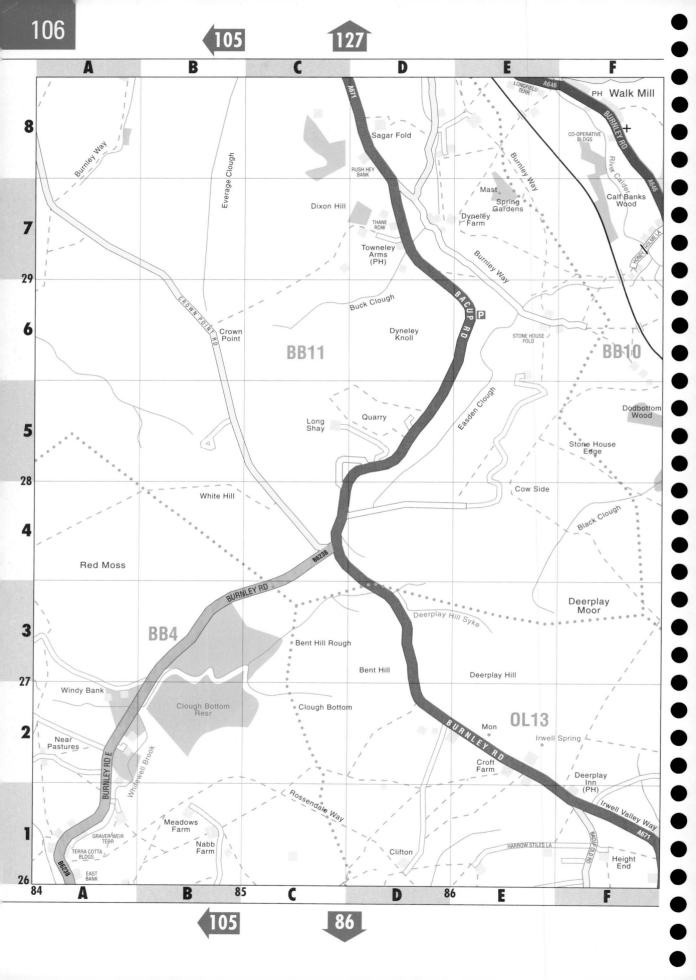

105
127

A B C D E F

8

Burnley Way

Everage Clough

A671

LONGFIELD TERR

A646

PH Walk Mill

BURNLEY RD

CO-OPERATIVE BLDGS

River Calder

Calf Banks Wood

A646

Sagar Fold

RUSH HEY BANK

Dixon Hill

THANE ROW

Burnley Way

Mast

Spring Gardens

Dyneley Farm

7

Towneley Arms (PH)

Burnley Way

HONEY HOLME LA

29

CROWN POINT RD

Buck Clough

BACUP RD

STONE HOUSE FOLD

BB10

6

Crown Point

Dyneley Knoll

P

BB11

Easden Clough

Dodbottom Wood

5

Long Shay

Quarry

Stone House Edge

28

White Hill

Cow Side

Black Clough

4

Red Moss

BB238

Deerplay Moor

Deerplay Hill Syke

BURNLEY RD

3

BB4

Bent Hill Rough

27

Bent Hill

Deerplay Hill

Windy Bank

Clough Bottom Resr

Clough Bottom

BURNLEY RD

Mon

OL13

2

Near Pastures

BURNLEY RD E

Whitewell Brook

Rossendale Way

Irwell Spring

Croft Farm

Deerplay Inn (PH)

Meadows Farm

Irwell Valley Way

1

GRAVER WEIR TERR

Nabb Farm

Clifton

HARROW STILES LA

BACUP OLD RD

Height End

A671

TERRA COTTA BLDGS

EAST BANK

B6238

26

84 A B 85 C D 86 E F

105
86

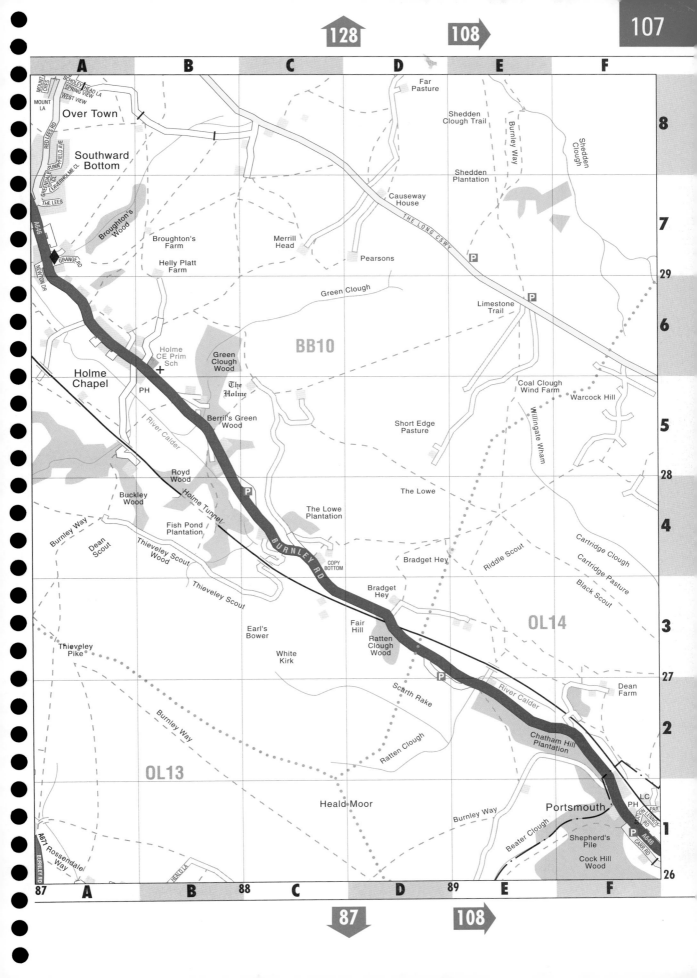

107

	A	B	C	D	E	F

BB10

Sheddon Edge

Sheddon Top

Black Hambledon

White Hill

North Grain

Hoar Side Moor

Hoar Side Top

HX7

Crooker Hill

Rush Candle Clough

Hoof Stones Height

The Lead Mine

Stiperden Moor

Lead Mine Clough

Stiperden Slack

Moss Crop

Stiperden Bar House

Moss Crop Hill

Coal Clough Wind Farm

Cold Soil

Stansfield Moor

Bent's Pasture

Coal Clough

Stiperden House Farm

Stiperden Bank

Hoppet

OL14

Burnley Way

Bank Top Farm

Paul Clough

Burnt Edge Pasture

Lower Mount Farm

Upper Mount

Mount La

Cross Hill

Higher Intake

Kebs Rd

Sportman's Arms (PH)

Coal Clough Farm

Pudsey Clough

Delf La

Hawks Stones

Keb Bridge

Sugar La

Shaw La

Gall La

Nant Wood

Coal Clough Rd

Higher Green End

Dyke Farm

Shore Law

Orchan House Farm

Brown Birks

Pudding La

Shore Gn

Blue Bell La

Shore

Blue Bell Farm

Redmires Water

Hudson Bridge

Bride Stones

Whitaker Naze

Woodbine Terr

Mount Pleasant Farm

Hartley Royd Farm

Stony La

Pudsey

Dawk Hole Wood

Pudsey Rd

Shore New Rd

Liby

Mast

Higher Hartley

Mount Zion Ct

Parkside Rd

Burnley Rd

Sch

Holme House Rd

Brighton St

Vale

Back Wood

Clunters

Lower Hartley

Joines La

Calderdale Way

Kit Hill

Lennox Rd

Tower Rd

Mount Pleasant

Stubley La

A646

Cornholme

Law St

Bridge End St

Lincoln St

Cleveland St

Rosebery St

Shackleton St

Ernest St

Fielden Rd

Ingfield Terr

A46

Cat Hole

How Gate

| 90 | A | | B | 91 | C | | D | 92 | E | | F |

107

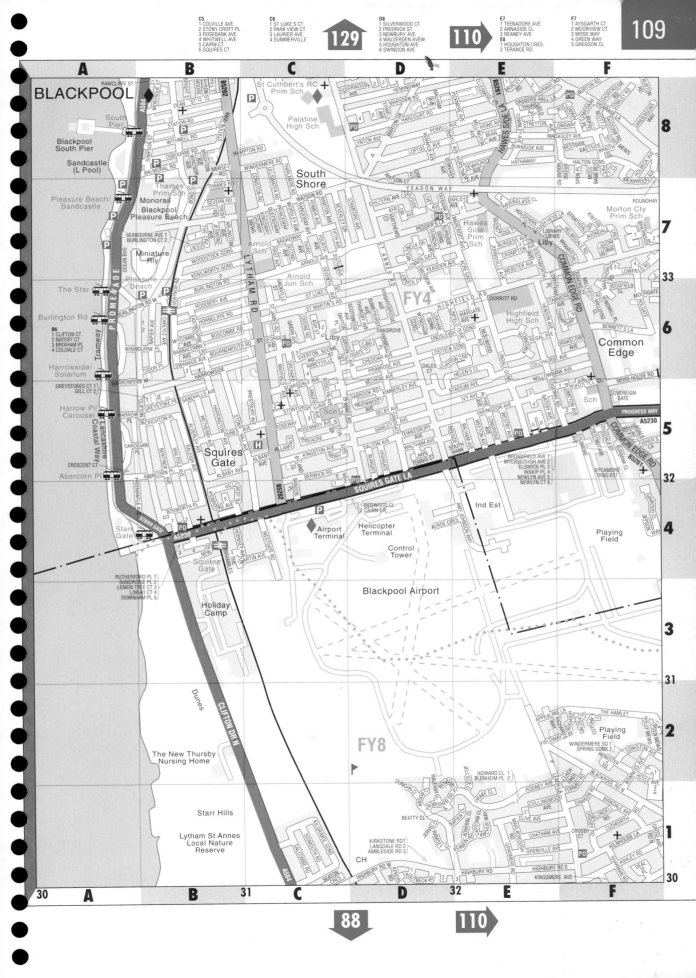

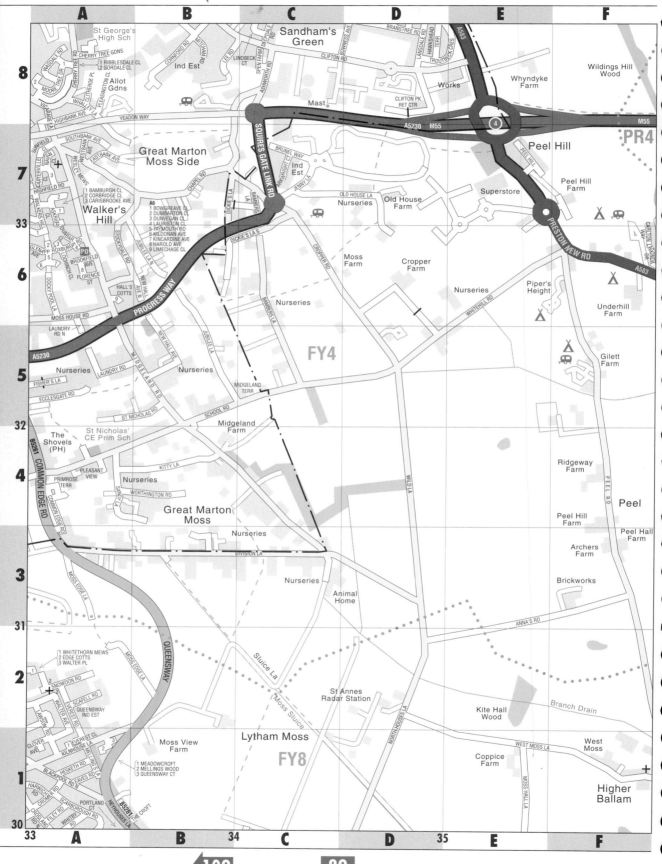

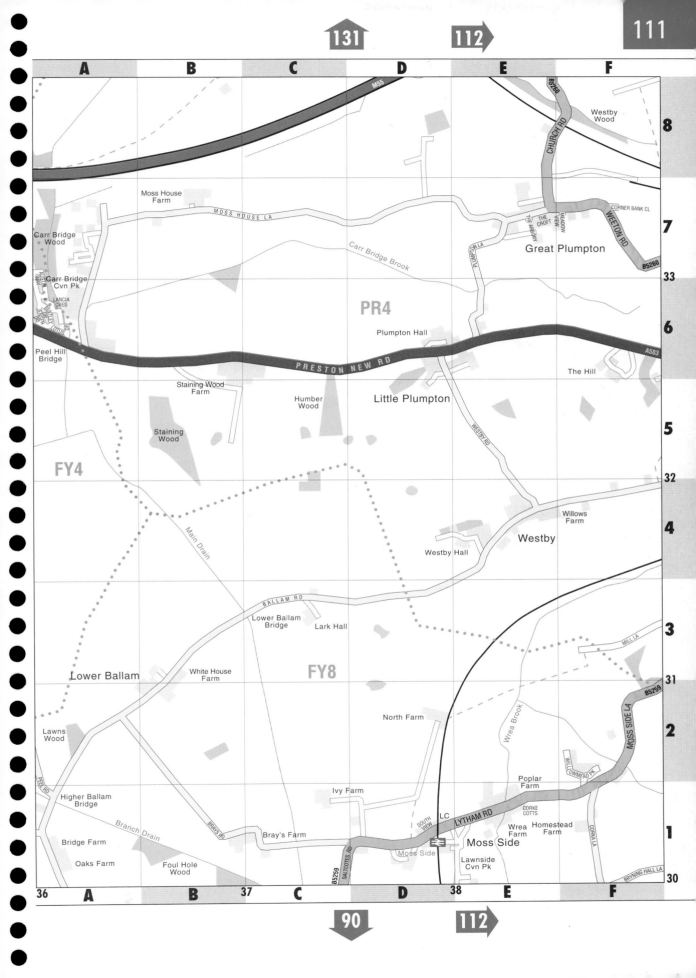

A   B   C   D   E   F

M55

B5260

CHURCH RD

Westby
Wood

8

Moss House
Farm

MOSS HOUSE LA

Carr Bridge Brook

THE ARBURY

THE CROFT

MEADOW VIEW

PLUMPTON LA

CORNER BANK CL

WEETON RD

B5260

Great Plumpton

7

Carr Bridge
Wood

33

Carr Bridge
Cvn Pk

LANCIA CRES

BENTLEY RD

LOTUS

AUSTIN

PR4

Plumpton Hall

6

A583

Peel Hill
Bridge

PRESTON NEW RD

The Hill

Staining Wood
Farm

Humber
Wood

Little Plumpton

WESTBY RD

FY4

Staining
Wood

5

32

Willows
Farm

Main Drain

Westby

4

Westby Hall

BALLAM RD

Lower Ballam
Bridge

Lark Hall

MILL LA

3

Lower Ballam

White House
Farm

FY8

31

B5259

North Farm

Wrea Brook

MOSS SIDE LA

Lawns
Wood

2

WILLOWMEAD PK

Poplar
Farm

PEEL RD

Higher Ballam
Bridge

Ivy Farm

Branch Drain

BRAYS RD

Bray's Farm

SOUTH VIEW

LC

LYTHAM RD

CORKE COTTS

Wrea
Farm

Homestead
Farm

CORKA LA

1

Bridge Farm

SALTCOTES RD

Moss Side

Moss Side

Oaks Farm

Foul Hole
Wood

Lawnside
Cvn Pk

BRYNING HALL LA

30

36   A   B   37   C   D   38   E   F

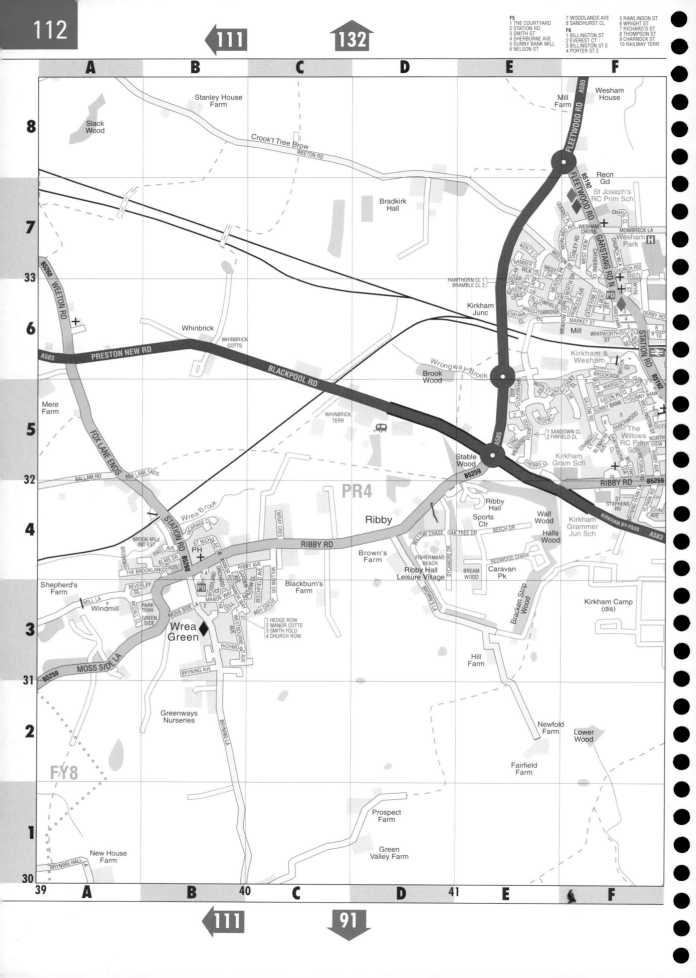

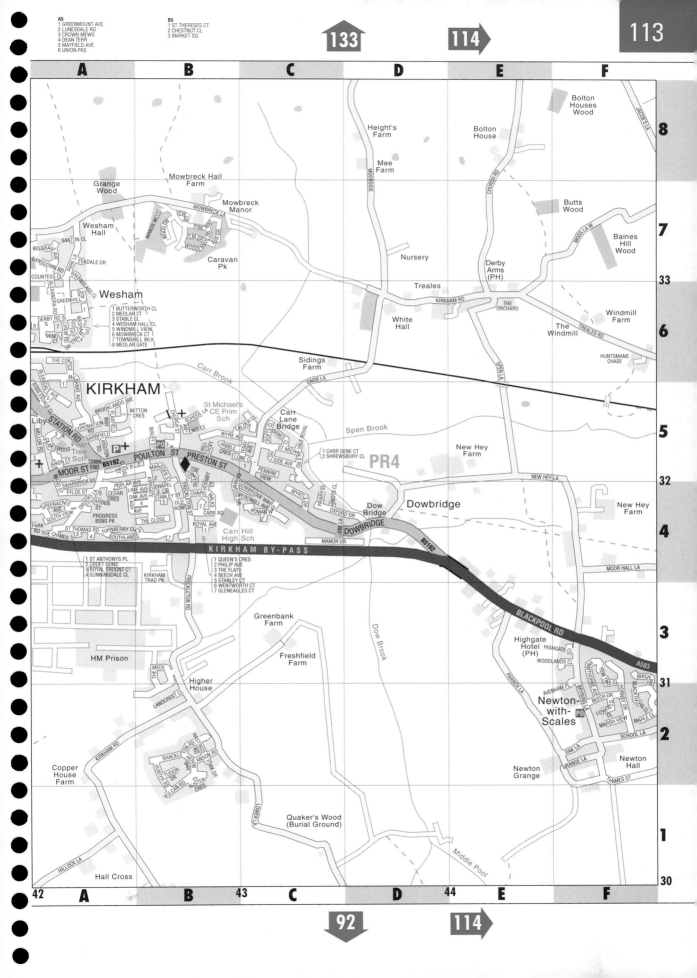

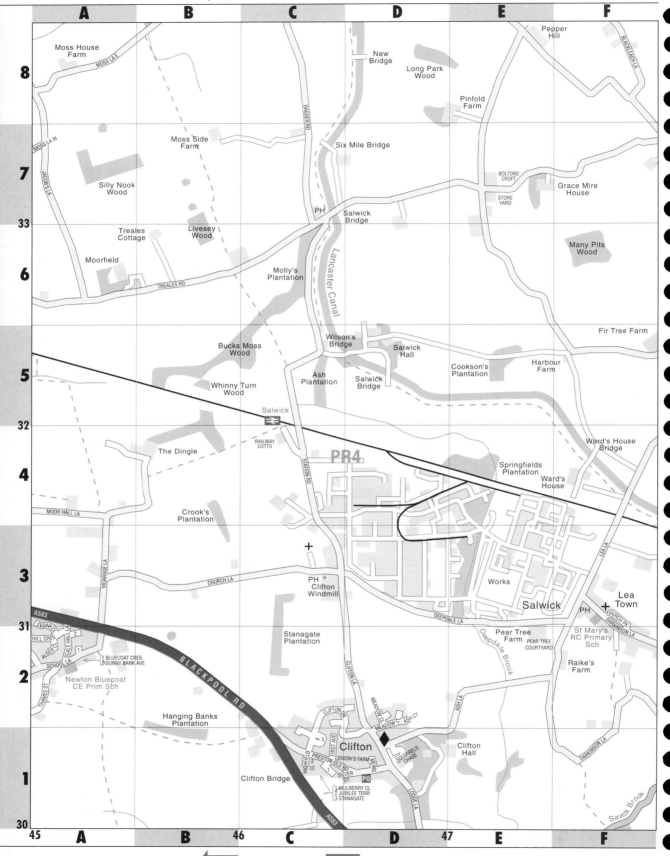

113
134

A B C D E F

8

7

33

6

5

32

4

3

31

2

1

30

45 A B 46 C D 47 E F

Moss House Farm
MOSS LA E
MOSS LA W
MOSS LA W
New Bridge
Long Park Wood
Pepper Hill
BLACKLEACH LA
DAGGER RD
Moss Side Farm
Six Mile Bridge
Pinfold Farm
BOLTONS CROFT
STORE YARD
Grace Mire House
Silly Nook Wood
PH
Salwick Bridge
Treales Cottage
Livesey Wood
Many Pits Wood
Moorfield
TREALES RD
Molly's Plantation
Lancaster Canal
Fir Tree Farm
Bucks Moss Wood
Wilson's Bridge
Salwick Hall
Cookson's Plantation
Harbour Farm
Whinny Turn Wood
Ash Plantation
Salwick Bridge
Salwick
Ward's House Bridge
The Dingle
RAILWAY COTTS
PR4
Springfields Plantation
Ward's House
STATION RD
MOOR HALL LA
Crook's Plantation
Works
LEA LA
Salwick
Lea Town
VICARAGE LA
CHURCH LA
PH
Clifton Windmill
DEEPDALE LA
PH
St Mary's RC Primary Sch
CHURCH PK
DARKINSON LA
A583
CEDAR CT
HILL CRES
ALDER CT
SCALE HALL LA
SCHOOL LA
1 BLUECOAT CRES
2 SUNNY BANK AVE
Stanagate Plantation
Pear Tree Farm
PEAR TREE COURTYARD
Raike's Farm
THAMES ST
Newton Bluecoat CE Prim Sch
BLACKPOOL RD
Deepdale Brook
CLIFTON LA
Hanging Banks Plantation
CLIFTON DR
MEADOW PL
MEADOW C
ASH CT
ASH LA
Clifton Hall
DARKINSON LA
Clifton Bridge
HIGHFIELD CL
PRESTON OLD RD
FISH LA
MEWS
SILVER ST
Clifton
Dixon's Farm
PO
SQUIRRELS CHASE
LODGE LA
1 MULBERRY CL
2 JUBILEE TERR
3 STANAGATE
A583
Swick Brook

113
93

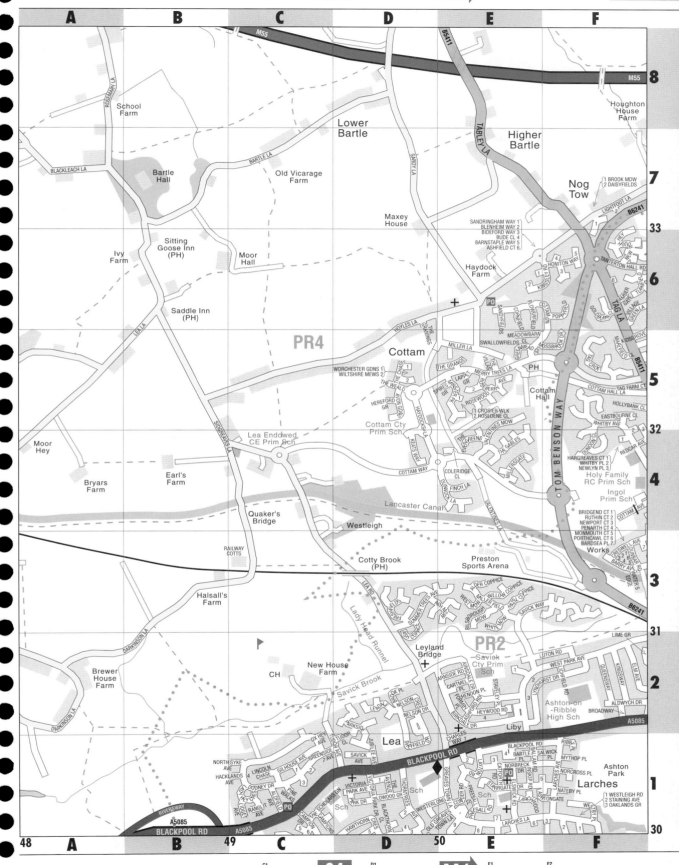

C1
1 FULFORD AVE
2 ROSE BANK
3 MAPLEBANK
4 WHITELENS AVE
5 PARKFIELD CL
6 PARKFIELD CRES
7 HARDWEN AVE

D1
1 THE CRESCENT
2 HOLMFIELD CRES
3 THORNPARK DR
4 WHITETHORN SQ
5 DAISY CROFT

E1
1 CHARLESWAY CT
2 THE PLOUGHLANDS
3 WHITEHOLME PL
4 WEETON PL
5 ROSEACRE PL
6 THE WOODLANDS
7 ALDCLIFFE RD
8 FORTON RD
9 THURNHAM RD

E2
1 GREENDALE MEWS
2 EXETER PL
3 DOWNHAM PL
4 NEWARK PL

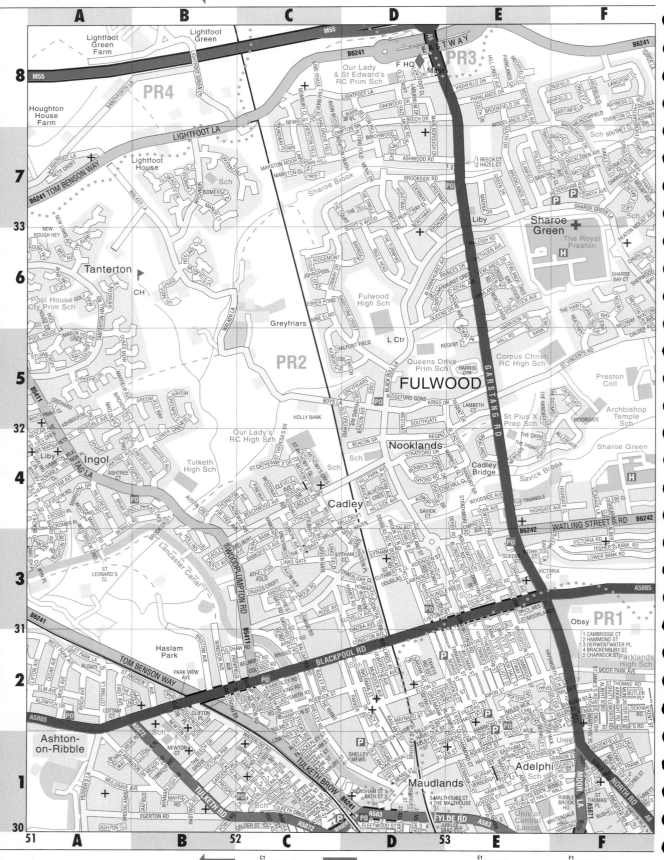

C1
1 THRELFALL ST
2 BRAMPTON ST
3 ELTON ST
4 BRUNSWICK PL
5 PECHELL ST
6 BLANCHE ST

E1
1 ADELPHI HO
2 HEYSHAM ST
3 DERWENT HALL
4 DOUGLAS HALL
5 TOWN BROOK HO

F1
1 SHELDON CT
2 PRESTON ENT CTR
3 AUGHTON WLK
4 BECKETT CT
5 HANOVER ST

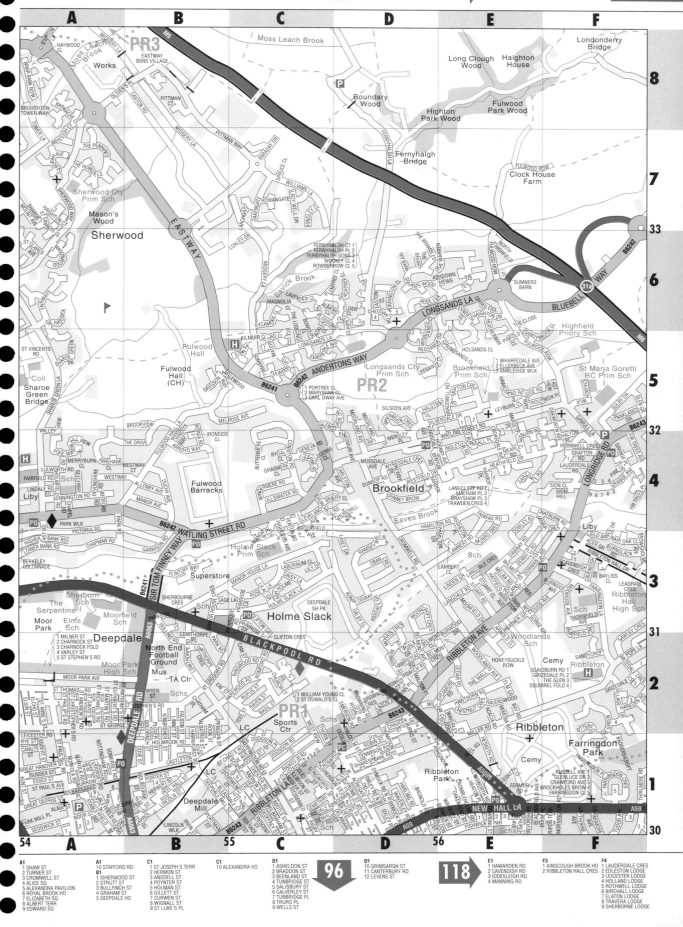

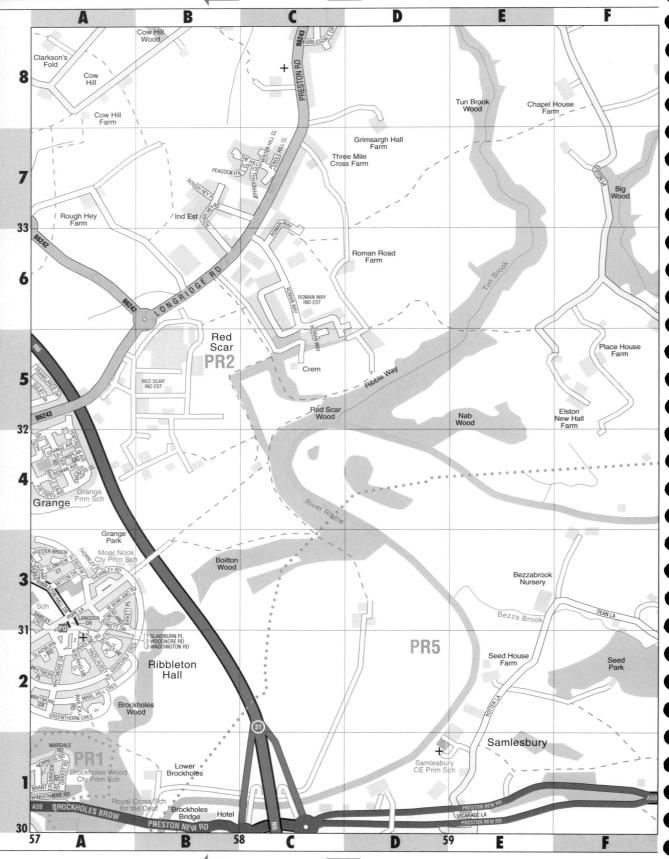

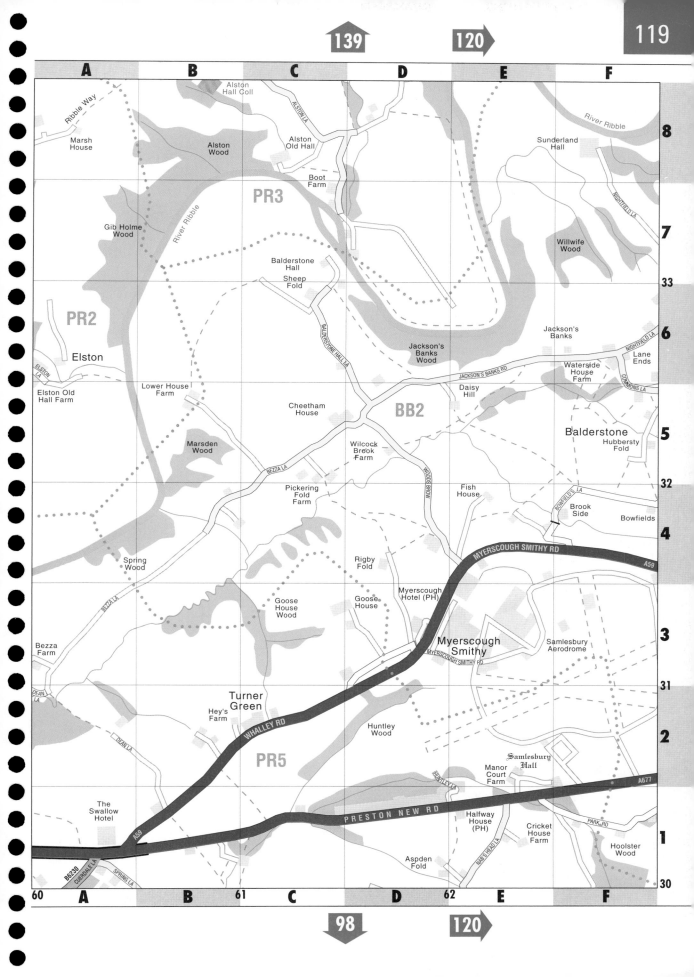

A | **B** | **C** | **D** | **E** | **F**

River Ribble

Dobridding Wood

Flashers Wood

Burr Green

New House

Showley Hall

BB1

8

Mercyfield Wood

Lower Studlehurst

Sandiford Wood

Higher Studlehurst

Park Gate

Oxendale Hall

Old Park Wood

Mire Wood

7

33

Nightfield Gate

NIGHTFIELD LA

Fletcher Fold Farm

Robert's House Farm

Carr House Farm

A59

6

Pewter House Fold

Osbaldeston Green

Balderstone

Balderstone CE Prim Sch

Smalley Fold

BB2

Rush Paddock

OSBALDESTON LA

Hawkshaw Fold

Tottering Brook

Birley Fold

5

Balderstone Grange

COMMONS LA

Sharples Farm

St Mary's RC Prim Sch

LONGSIGHT RD

Cockerham Hall

32

BOWFIELD'S LA

Holmes Farm

HIGHER COMMONS LA

Bay Horse Hotel (PH)

Osbaldeston

Abbott House Farm

ABBOTT BROW

Moor Edge

Mellor Moor

4

A59

MYERSCOUGH SMITHY RD

Mammon Wood

Mellor Brook

Sykes Holt

Calf House

Ward's Farm

Old Dad's House

Thurstons

MYERSCOUGH SMITHY RD

PH

WHALLEY RD

Mellor Brook

THE WILLOWS

Millstone Inn (Hotel)

MELLOR LA

3

FEILDENS FARM LA

PO

WOODF CL

BROADTREE CL

MELLOR BROW

ELSWICK GDNS

STOOPS FOLD

ELSWICK CLOSE

BRUNDHURST FOLD

ARLEY RISE

P

STANLEY GATE

FOURACRE

HOB GN

NICKEY LA

Mellor

31

BRANDWOOD RD

BOSBURN DR

VICTORIA TERR

Brundhurst Farm

St Mary's CE Prim Sch

Liby

ST MARY'S GDNS

PO

BROOKFIELD

CARTER FOLD

GLENDALE DR

Ottie Green Farm

2

INTACK LA

LONG MEADOW

Windmill Hotel (PH)

YERBURGH RD THWAITES AVE

CHURCH CL

CHURCH LA

GLENDALE GR

WHITECROFT LA

1

A677

PARK RD

PRESTON NEW RD

Balshaw Fold Farm

MIRE ASH BROW

Dick Dadds

Park Farm

Higher Park Farm

Moss Hall Farm

Old Doozes

FURTHER LA

A677

30

A | **B** | **C** | **D** | **E** | **F**

63 | 64 | 65

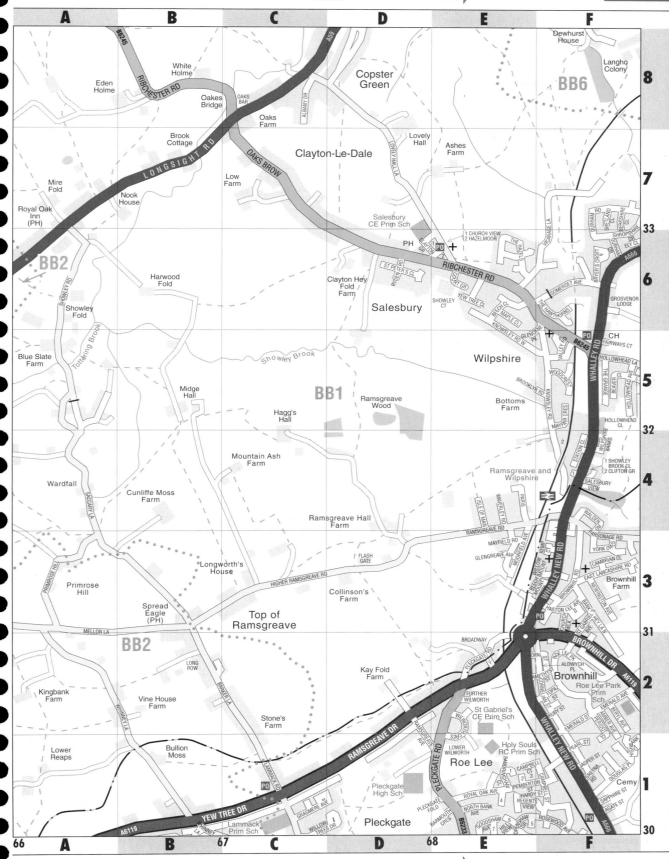

141 122

| | A | B | C | D | E | F | |

8

Dewhurst House

Langho Colony

BB6

Copster Green

B6245

RIBCHESTER RD

White Holme

Eden Holme

Oakes Bridge

OAKS BAR

Oaks Farm

Clayton-Le-Dale

ALBANY DR

A59

LOVELY HALL LA

Lovely Hall

Ashes Farm

7

Brook Cottage

LONGSIGHT RD

OAKS BROW

Low Farm

Mire Fold

Nook House

Salesbury CE Prim Sch

33

Royal Oak Inn (PH)

PH

1 CHURCH VIEW
2 HAZELMOOR

THE HAZELS

VICARAGE LA

DURHAM RD

SHETLAND

SHROPSHIRE

BERKSHIRE DR

ELY CL

A666

BB2

SHOWLEY RD

Harwood Fold

ST PETER'S CL

RYDEN AVE

PO

RIBCHESTER RD

CART GR

SOMERSET AVE

BRYER'S CROFT

GROSVENOR LODGE

6

Showley Fold

Clayton Hey Fold Farm

Salesbury

SHOWLEY CT

YEW TREE CL

BEECH CL

MAPLE CL

THE HAWTHORNS

B6245

WHALLEY RD

CH FAIRWAYS CT

Blue Slate Farm

Totiding Brook

KNOWSLEY RD W

GLENDENE PK

VALLEY RD

WOODCREST

HOLLOWHEAD LA

THE GRANGE

BEAVER

HOLLOWHEAD CL

5

Showley Brook

Midge Hall

BB1

Ramsgreave Wood

Wilpshire

Bottoms Farm

BROOKLYN RD

KNOWSLEY RD

MAYFAIR CRES

HOLLOWHEAD BANKS

WILPSHIRE RD

32

Hagg's Hall

STATION CL

1 SHOWLEY BROOK CL
2 CLIFTON GR

Wardfall

SACCARY LA

Cunliffe Moss Farm

Mountain Ash Farm

Ramsgreave and Wilpshire

SALESBURY VIEW

2

4

ISLE OF MAN

WAVERLEY RD

PARIS

WALDEN

PARSONAGE RD

Ramsgreave Hall Farm

RAMSGREAVE RD

MAYFIELD RD

GLENGREAVE AVE

MORFIELD AVE

YORK CRES

CAMBRIAN CL

EAST LANCASHIRE RD

Brownhill Farm

3

Primrose Hill

PRIMROSE HILL

Longworth's House

HIGHER RAMSGREAVE RD

Collinson's Farm

FLASH GATE

BEECH MOUNT CT

WILLOW MOUNT

WHALLEY NEW RD

PO

HASTON LEE AVE

CHURCH LA

ST GABRIEL'S LA

NEWINGTON AVE

31

MELLOR LA

Spread Eagle (PH)

BARKER LA

BB2

LONG ROW

Kay Fold Farm

BROADWAY

PLECKGATE RD

BROWNHILL DR

OPAL ST

CORNELIAN ST

AMETHYST ST

ALDWYCH PL

Brownhill

Roe Lee Park Prim Sch

A6119

2

Kingbank Farm

WHINNEY LA

Vine House Farm

Stone's Farm

RAMSGREAVE AVE

RAMSGREAVE DR

FURTHER WILWORTH

St Gabriel's CE Prim Sch

LOWER WILWORTH

Holy Souls RC Prim Sch

SANDRINGHAM RD

Roe Lee

CAMPBELL CT

PEMBERTON

OPAL ST

RUBY ST

EMERALD ST

PEARL ST

JASPER ST

AMBER AVE

BERYL AVE

PERIDOT

GRETNA RD

DOUGLAS RD

SAPPHIRE ST

HIGH BANK

Cemy

1

Lower Reaps

LAMMACK RD

Bullion Moss

PO

YEW TREE DR

A6119

WHINNEY LA

Lammack Prim Sch

GRASMERE AVE

WILLOW TREES DR

Pleckgate High Sch

Pleckgate Fold

BARMOUTH CRES

NORTH BANK AVE

Royal Oak Ave

B6233

GOODSHAW AVE

HILL ST

OPENSHAW

HARDY ST

REGENT'S VIEW

ROSEWOOD AVE

AGATE ST

A666

PO

Pleckgate

30

66 A B 67 C D 68 E F

100 122

E1
1 BLENHEIM CL
2 OUTRAM LA
3 HAYDOCK ST
4 CHATSWORTH CL
5 THORNWOOD CL
6 PENSHAW CL
7 GOODSHAW CL

121 142

A B C D E F

8

THE DALES
THE RYDINGS
LOWERFIELD
HIGHER FIELDS
FIELDS END
ROGERSFIELD
MIDFIELD
PORTLAND RD
KIRKDALE
HILLCREST RD
SPRINGDALE
WHALLEY RD
A666
ST MARY'S DR
WHINNEY LA
Higher Woodcocks
York
YORK LA
WHALLEY OLD RD
Whins Lodge
MOOR LA
Billington Moor
Whittle Hall House
BB7

7

1 LYNDALE CL
2 ANDERSON RD
3 SUTHERLAND CL
Anderton House
WHALLEY RD
Carr Hall
Snodworth
Snodworth Hall
SNODWORTH RD
Fish Moor
HAWTHORN CL
PH
OLD NAB RD
BB6

LYNDALE AVE
HAMPSHIRE CL
SUNNYSIDE AVE
RIBBLESDALE AVE
HOLLIES RD
DURHAM RD
A666

33

Snodworth Cross
Dean Clough Resr

6

Resrs
Wilpshire Moor
Little Snodworth
YORK RD
Boston Plantation
SMALLEY THORN BROW
GLINKHAM RD

5

HOLLOWHEAD LA
Parsonage Farm
RISHTON RD
YORK RD
BLACKBURN OLD RD
Dewhurst Farm

32

Parsonage Resr
PARSONAGE RD
Lower Hen Moss
HARWOOD RD
Black Law Farm

4

WARRENSIDE CL
BALMORAL AVE
BELVEDERE RD
BB1
New Inn
Bay Horse (PH)
WILPSHIRE RD
Top o' th' Heights

3

Upper Mickle Hey
Middle Mickle Hey
Height House
BLACKBURN OLD RD
Mast
Tan House
Dunscar

31

Eddy Holes

2

A6119
BROWNHILL DR
Bank Hey
RAVENSCROFT
OAKWOOD AVE
CUNLIFFE CL
SUNNY BOWER RD
WHALLEY OLD RD
Higher Cunliffe
Lower Cunliffe

1

HIGHBANK
BANK HEY
STONE HILL DR
ROWAN CL
HAZELWOOD CL
A6119
Sunny Bower
CUNLIFFE RD
CROFT HEAD RD
Whitebirk Ind Est
PHILIPS RD
LOWER PHILIPS RD
Lower Side Beet
Leeds and Liverpool Canal
Reservoir Plantation
CUT LA
Cut Farm
CONISTON WAY
DERWENT CL
SOMERSET RD

30

Cemy
Side Beet Bridge

69 A B 70 C D 71 E F

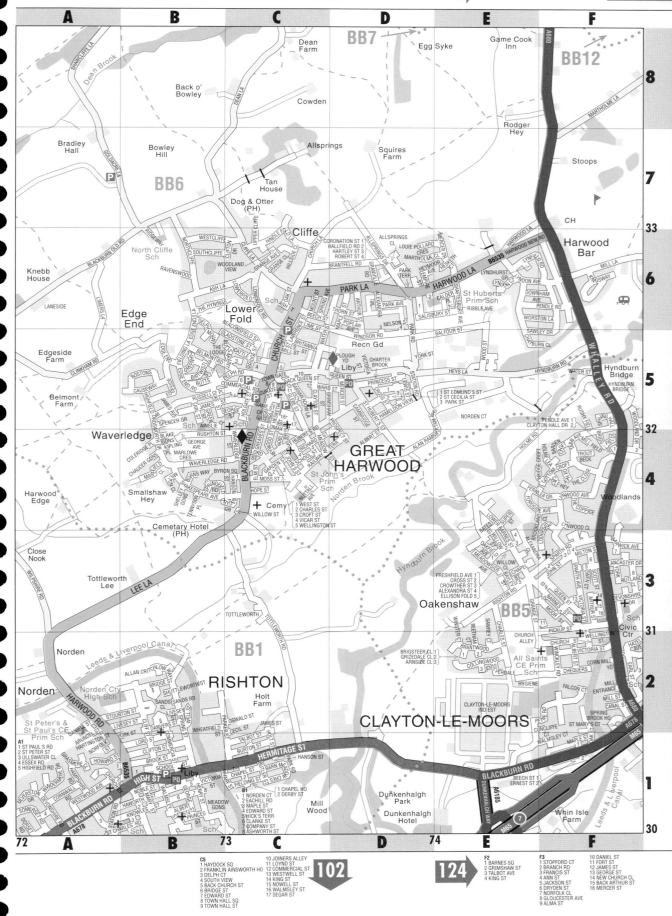

C5
1 HAYDOCK SQ
2 FRANKLIN AINSWORTH HO
3 DELPH CT
4 SOUTH VIEW
5 BACK CHURCH ST
6 BRIDGE ST
7 EDWARD ST
8 TOWN HALL SQ
9 TOWN HALL ST

10 JOINERS ALLEY
11 LOYND ST
12 COMMERCIAL ST
13 WESTWELL ST
14 KING ST
15 NOWELL ST
16 WALMSLEY ST
17 SEGAR ST

F2
1 BARNES SQ
2 GRIMSHAW ST
3 TALBOT AVE
4 KING ST

F3
1 STOPFORD CT
2 BRANCH RD
3 FRANCIS ST
4 ANN ST
5 JACKSON ST
6 DRYDEN ST
7 NORFOLK CL
8 GLOUCESTER AVE
9 ALMA ST

10 DANIEL ST
11 FORT ST
12 JAMES ST
13 GEORGE ST
14 NEW CHURCH CL
15 BACK ARTHUR ST
16 MERCER ST

8 Martholme Viaduct
Martholme
New Plantation
BB12
Dunkirk
Gooseleach Wood
The Simonstone (PH)
TUNSTEAD AVE

7 BB6
Sewage Works
River Calder
BANK TERR
SIMONSTONE LA
RAILWAY TERR
Works
BLACKBURN RD A678
SIMONSTONE BSNS PK

33 Hyndburn Brook
MILL LA
Brownsills
Syke Side Brook
Altham Bridge
NEW ROW   PH
RIVER BANK TERR
Altham St James CE Prim Sch
Altham
LANE SIDE TERR
CALDER
SYKE SIDE DR
ALTHAM BSNS PK
SHORTEN BROOK DR

6 Wind Engine Clough
Syke Side
LANESIDE
METCALF RD
Altham IND EST
VENTURE CT
SHORTEN BROOK WAY

5 Lower Moor Side
Red House Farm
The Old Engine
BURNLEY RD
BARNFIELD WAY
Houghton Barn Farm
Clayton Hall Farm
SYCAMORE CRES

32 CHESTNUT GR
Altham Bridge
ALTHAM LA

4 BB5
Altham Clough Wood
Clough Brook
M65

3 Pilkington Canal Bridge
BELL LA
Leeds and Liverpool Canal
CUMBERLAND AVE
OXFORD AVE
LANCASTER DR
DEVONSHIRE DR
PILKINGTON DR
ROSEBANK
HIGHER FIRS PL
MOORFIELD DR
MOORFIELD WAY
MOORFIELD IND EST
MOORFIELD DR
CLAYTON WAY
SEFTON CL
1 HAWTHORN BANK
2 PENDLE VIEW
3 MARTHOLME AVE
4 HENFIELD CL
5 HAWTHORN GDNS
LIVESLEY ST
ELGAR ST
WALTER ST
Huncoat
STATION RD
GRIME ROW

31 BOLD VENTURE WAY
MOORSIDE DR
PANTER CL
HAZEL DR
ENFIELD CL
CALDER
YORKSHIRE ST
LYNWOOD RD
LOWER GATE RD
TOWNELEY AVE
PENDLE VIEW
Lower Gate PH
HIGHER GATE

2 Bold Venture Farm
DUKE ST
A678
M65
WELL LA
Enfield
1 GORDON ST
2 MOUNT ST
Huncoat
PO
LC
ENFIELD RD
PROSPECT TERR
Huncoat Cty Prim Sch
Further Holker House
OAK BANK
NEWHOUSE RD
BURNLEY LA
HIGHERGATE

1 WHALLEY RD
A680
HENRY ST
WILLIAM ST
WATERLOO ST
Whinney Hill
SHERWOOD
TUNSTALL DR
GLENWOOD DR
WALTON
WHINNEY HILL RD
Works
WILLOW ST
Within Grove
1 HIGHER GATE
EAVES CL 2
HAWKSTONE CL 3
HEADINGLEY CL 4
WOODSIDE CL 5
WEDGEWOOD RD 6
KINGSWAY 7
KING'S HIGHWAY 8
TARN BROOK CL
OLD TYM
WOODSIDE RD
SPOTHOUSE LA
Griffin

30 BB231
DILL HALL LA
CHURCH LA
FIRST AVE
HARRINGTON ST
ATLAS ST
JUBILEE
A680
BEECH CRES
HAWORTH ST
1 WAREHAM CL
2 RINGWOOD CL
Huncoat IND EST
ENTERPRISE CT
OAKFIELD AVE
O AKHURST AVE
WINDERMERE AVE
OAKDENE AVE
WINTERLEY DR
BURNLEY RD A679

75   A   76   B   C   77   D   E   F

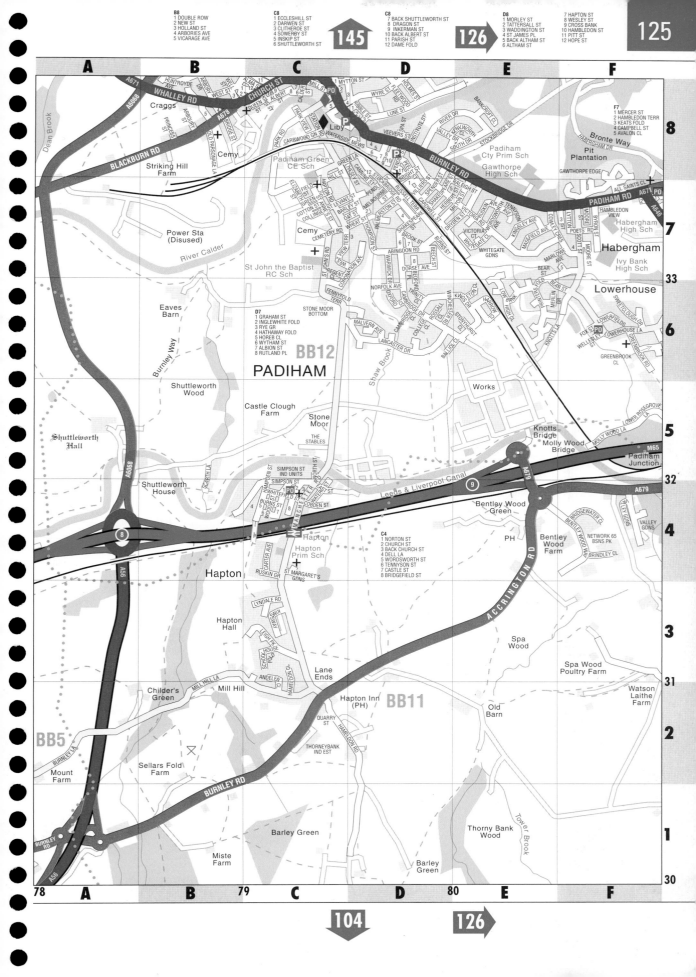

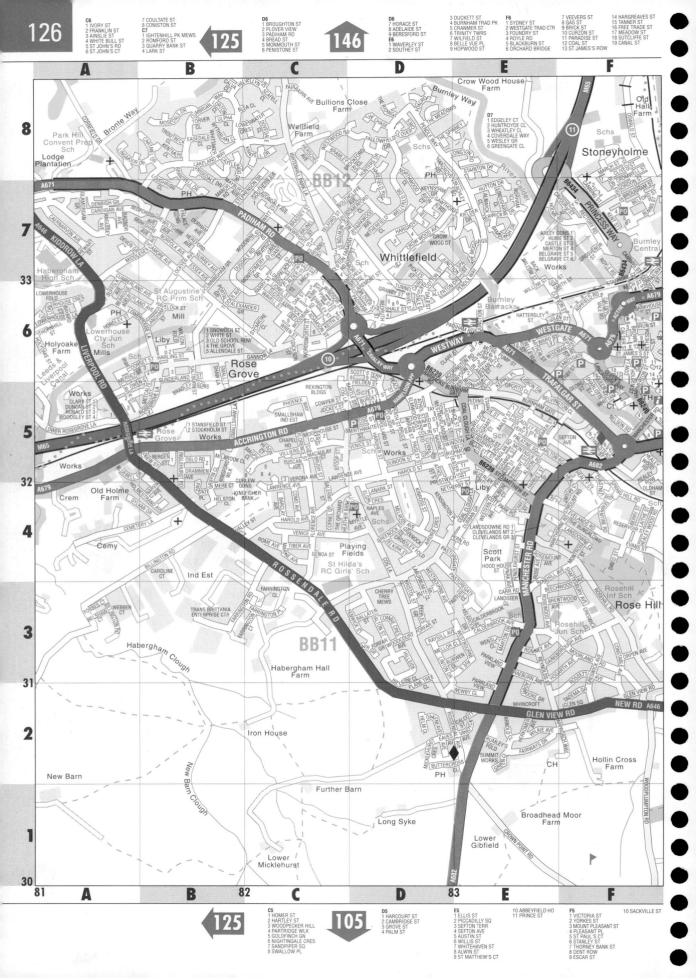

C6
1 IVORY ST
2 FRANKLIN ST
3 AINSLIE ST
4 WHITE BULL ST
5 ST JOHN'S RD
6 ST JOHN'S CT

7 COULTATE ST
8 CONISTON ST
C7
1 IGHTENHILL PK MEWS
2 ROMFORD ST
3 QUARRY BANK ST
4 LARK ST

125

D6
1 BROUGHTON ST
2 PLOVER VIEW
3 PADIHAM RD
4 BREAD ST
5 MONMOUTH ST
6 PENISTONE ST

146

D6
7 HORACE ST
8 ADELAIDE ST
9 BERESFORD ST
E6
1 WAVERLEY ST
2 SOUTHEY ST

3 DUCKETT ST
4 WHITHAM TRAD PK
5 CRANMER ST
6 TRINITY TWRS
7 WILFIELD ST
8 BELLE VUE PL
9 HOPWOOD ST

F6
1 SYDNEY ST
2 WESTGATE TRAD CTR
3 FOUNDRY ST
4 ROYLE RD
5 BLACKBURN ST
6 ORCHARD BRIDGE

7 VEEVERS ST
8 GAS ST
9 BRICK ST
10 CURZON ST
11 PARADISE ST
12 COAL ST
13 ST JAMES'S ROW

14 HARGREAVES ST
15 TANNER ST
16 FREE TRADE ST
17 MEADOW ST
18 SUTCLIFFE ST
19 CANAL ST

8
33
7
6
5
32
4
3
31
2
1
30

A 81 B 82 C D 83 E F

125

C5
1 HOMER ST
2 HARTLEY ST
3 WOODPECKER HILL
4 PARTRIDGE WLK
5 GOLDFINCH GN
6 NIGHTINGALE CRES
7 SANDPIPER SQ
8 SWALLOW PL

105

D5
1 HARCOURT ST
2 CAMBRIDGE ST
3 GROVE ST
4 PALM ST

E5
1 ELLIS ST
2 PICCADILLY SQ
3 SEFTON TERR
4 SEFTON AVE
5 AUSTIN ST
6 WILLIS ST
7 WHITEHAVEN ST
8 ALWIN ST
9 ST MATTHEW'S CT

10 ABBEYFIELD HO
11 PRINCE ST

F5
1 VICTORIA ST
2 YORKES ST
3 MOUNT PLEASANT ST
4 PLEASANT PL
5 ST PAUL'S CT
6 STANLEY ST
7 THORNEY BANK ST
8 DENT ROW
9 ESCAR ST

10 SACKVILLE ST

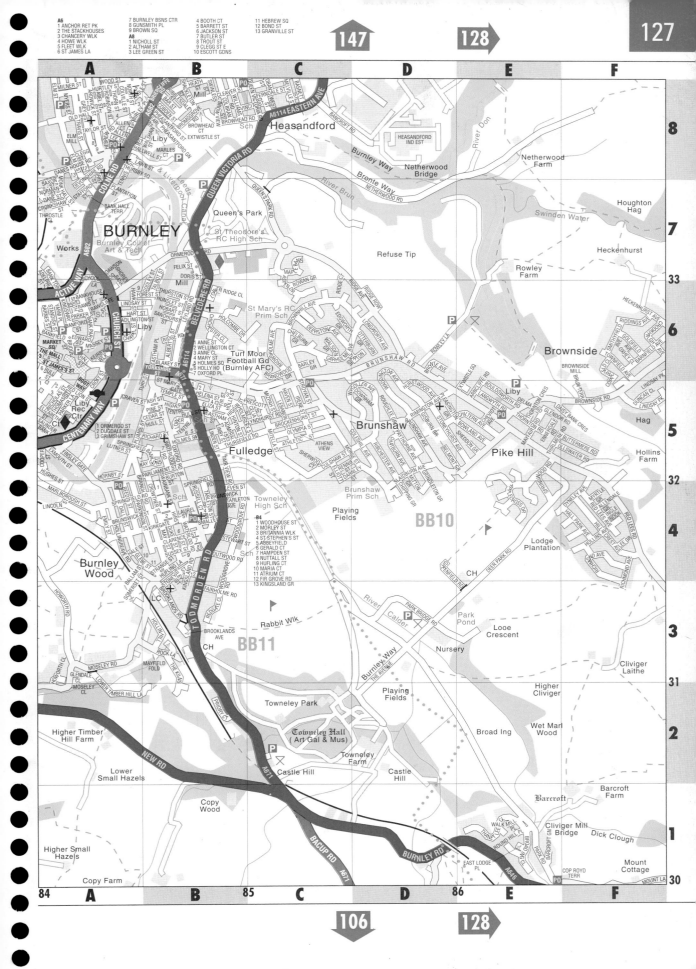

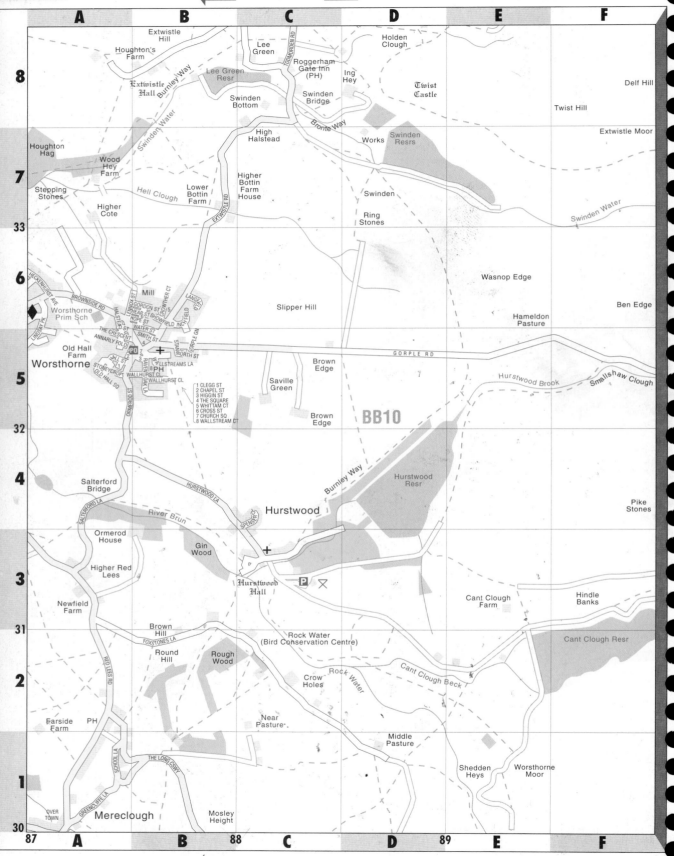

C6
1 HENTHORNE ST
2 GREENHILL PL
3 HARDMAN ST
4 HANDLEY RD
5 EDELSTON RD
6 IDDON CT
7 WHITESIDE ST
8 BEAUMOUNT CT
9 EDEN ST
10 AINLEY CT
11 SWANSON ST
12 BK COOKSON ST

C7
1 STANHOPE RD
2 SUTHERLAND VIEW
3 HAMPSTEAD MEWS
4 HANDSWORTH CT
5 GRANTHAM CT
6 ALTHORP CL
7 ST ANTHONY'S PL
8 BERESFORD ST
9 SMITHY MEWS
10 GARDENERS MEWS
11 MANOR CT
12 CROFTERS MEWS
13 GRANGE CT

14 BACK ASHBURTON RD
D7
1 KYSTON CL
2 EMPIRE GR
3 WILDMAN ST
4 CHARLES CT
5 ASHWORTH CT

D7
6 LABURNUM ST
7 CYPRESS GR
8 STIRLING CT
D8
1 WYNNWOOD AVE
2 NEWMAN RD

D8
3 DANSON GDNS
4 PENHILL CL
E7
1 CALEDONIAN CT
2 CAMPBELL AVE
3 WILLIAM ST

4 HUNTLEY AVE
5 CROYDON CT
E8
1 ST MARK'S PL
2 HUMBER AVE
3 PELHAM AVE
4 FORREST ST

150 130

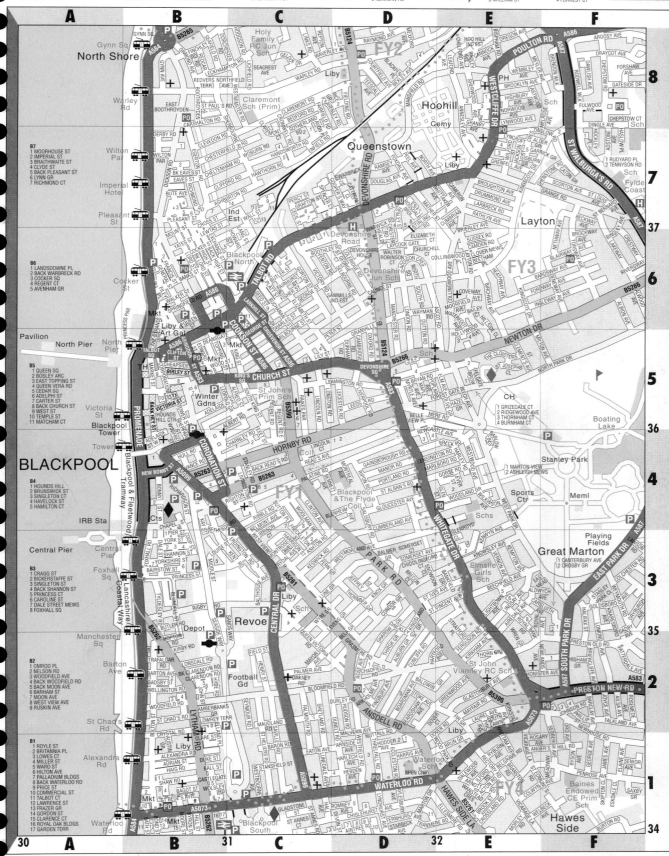

109 130

C1
1 PARKINSON WAY
2 LIGHTWOOD AVE
3 EXETER ST
C2
1 ORKNEY RD
2 DUNELT CT
C3
1 ORME ST
2 JAMESON ST

3 CHADWICK ST
C4
1 CONCORDE HO
2 WESTWELL GR
3 COURTFIELDS
4 COLLEGE CT
5 NEW CHURCH HO
6 READS CT
7 PENNINE CL
8 ANDERSON ST

C5
1 WINSTANLEY GR
2 RAIKES HILL
3 PARKER ST
4 ADELAIDE CT
5 RAIKES MEWS
6 PRIORY CT
7 ST JOHN'S CT

C6
1 HENTHORNE ST
2 GREENHILL PL
3 HARDMAN ST
4 HANDLEY RD
5 EDELSTON RD
6 IDDON CT
7 WHITESIDE ST
8 BEAUMONT CT
9 EDEN ST

10 AINLEY CT
11 SWANSON ST
12 BK COOKSON ST
D1
1 DUNSOP CL
2 BISHOP CT
3 DOUGLAS LEATHAM HOUSE
4 WESTON CL
5 WINCHESTER AVE
6 SCUDAMORE CRES

D1
1 TRURO ST
2 TAUNTON ST
3 RUGBY ST
4 DORSET ST
5 MIRFIELD GR

D4
1 HORNBY PARK CT
2 LAWN CT
3 LYCEUM AVE
4 TYNE AVE
5 GLOUCESTER CT
D5
1 DUTTON CT
2 RIDLEY ST
3 GLENWOOD ST

D2
1 LILAC AVE
2 MARINA AVE
3 DARAM HO
E1
1 BROOK ST CT
2 MANOR CT
E3
1 SPRINGFIELD CT
2 OLD MEADOW LA
3 OLD MEADOW CT

4 WHITLEY AVE
5 DEVONSHIRE SQ MEWS
F1
1 DUNMAIL AVE
2 MALTBY PL
3 JOHN HILL ST
4 BK MEADOW CT

4 WHITEGATE LODGE
5 HASLEMERE AVE
6 GODWIN AVE
7 HEREFORD AVE
8 LATHAM AVE
F2

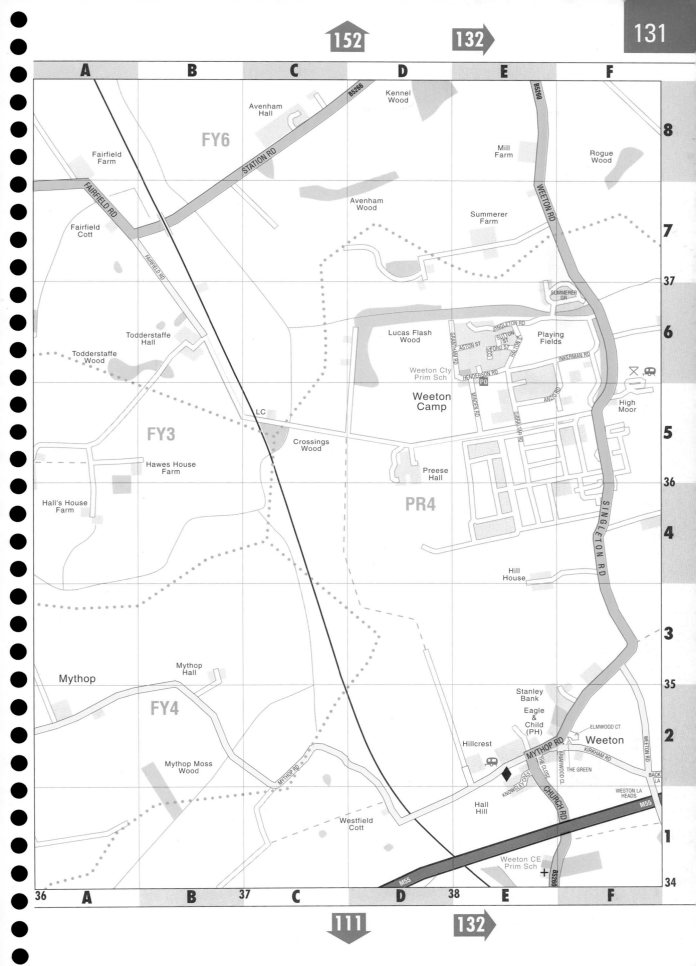

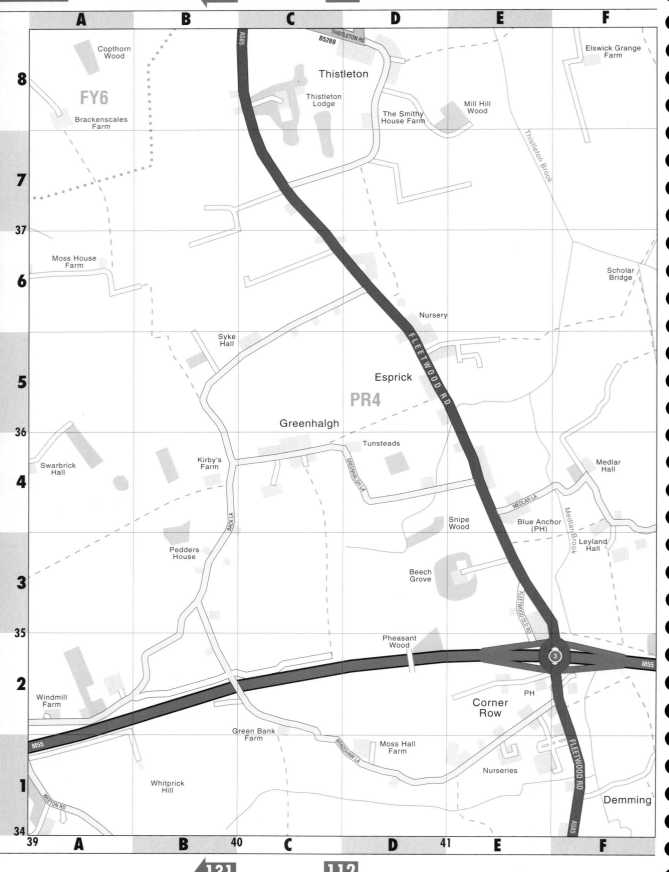

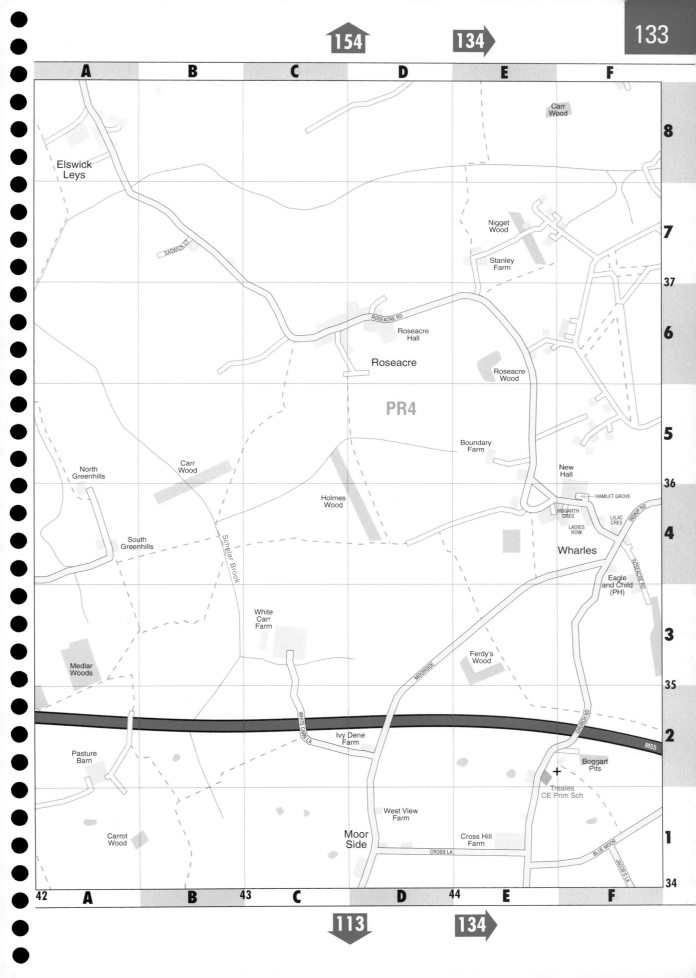

A   B   C   D   E   F

8
7
37
6
5
36
4
3
35
2
1
34

Carr Wood

Elswick Leys

SASWICK CL

Nigget Wood

Stanley Farm

ROSEACRE RD

Roseacre Hall

Roseacre

PR4

Roseacre Wood

Boundary Farm

New Hall

HAMLET GROVE

HOGARTH CRES

LILAC CRES

INSKIP RD

LADIES ROW

ROSEACRE RD

Wharles

Eagle and Child (PH)

North Greenhills

Carr Wood

Holmes Wood

South Greenhills

Scholar Brook

White Carr Farm

Medlar Woods

MOORSIDE

Ferdy's Wood

Pasture Barn

WHITE CARR LA

Ivy Dene Farm

CHURCH RD

M55

Boggart Pits

Treales CE Prim Sch

Carrot Wood

West View Farm

Moor Side

Cross Hill Farm

CROSS LA

BLUE MOOR

JACOB'S LA

42   A   B   43   C   D   44   E   F

133
155

A B C D E F

Inskip

PR3

Stavens Pool Bridge

Lower Slip Inn Farm

PO

Inskip CE Sch

B5269

WEST DR MANOR RD

SOUTH GDNS

NELSON

SCHOOL LA

HIGHFIELD AVE

WENTWORTH AVE

MILL CL

DERBY CRES

Woodplumpton Brook

8

Dead Dam Bridge

SUNNINGDALE PL

Laytus Farm

The Derby Arms (PH)

Carr House Green Common

WOODS LA

Lower House

7

PRESTON RD

Walker House Farm

Higham Side

37

Higham Side Rd

Woodsfold Bridge

Higham Nook

Old Woodsfold Farm

LEWTH LA

6

Airfield (disused)

Woodsfold

New Woodsfold Farm

B5269

GREEN LA

Raikes Farm

Inskip Wood

PR4

Moss Farm

JANE LA

5

Wolf's Farm

Brades Farm

Running Pump (PH)

CATFORTH RD

Wks

MOSS LA

INSKIP RD

36

Pointer Wood

Pop Hall Farm

CHAPEL LA

SQUARE LA

Catforth

4

Sanderson's Wood

Moss House

MILLER LA

Poultry Farm

PO

SQUARE LA

Bay Horse (PH)

Hale Hall

BAY HORSE LA

Red Lion Farm

Melling's Farm

WILLACY LA

BENSON LA

3

SALWICK RD

BENSON LA

Willacy Lane End

35

Stanley Lodge

Locking Stoops

Lancaster Canal

Roots Bridge

ROOTS LA

2

Blundell's Wood

M55

BLUE MOOR

Kellet's Bridge

Blackleach

Moss Farm

BLACKLEACH LA

M55

1

Stud Farm

Brook Wood

Stanley Grange

DAGGER RD

MOSS LA E

34

45 A B 46 C D 47 E F

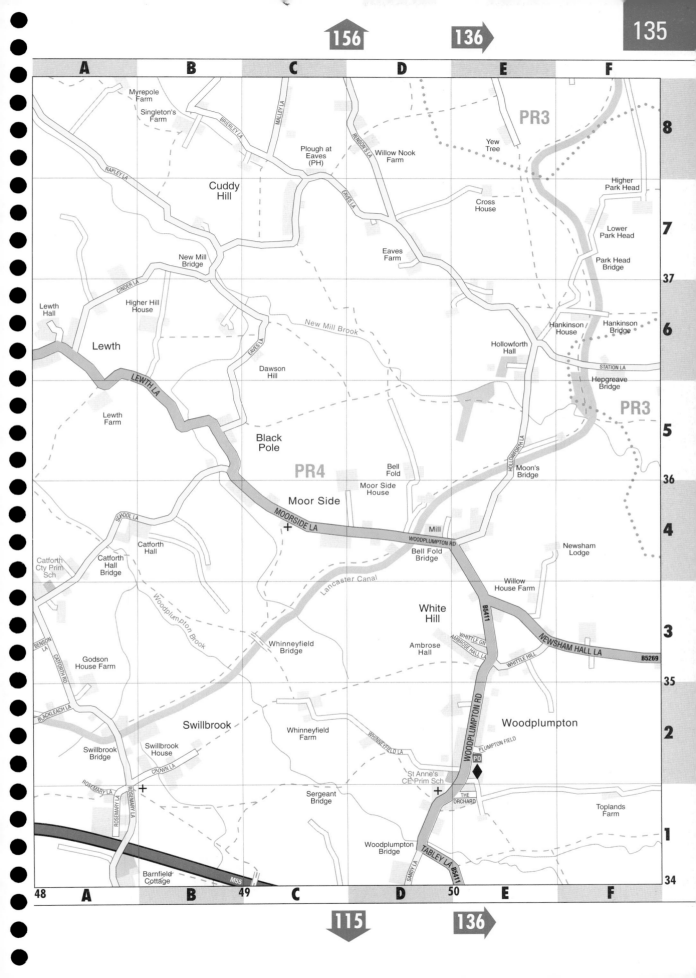

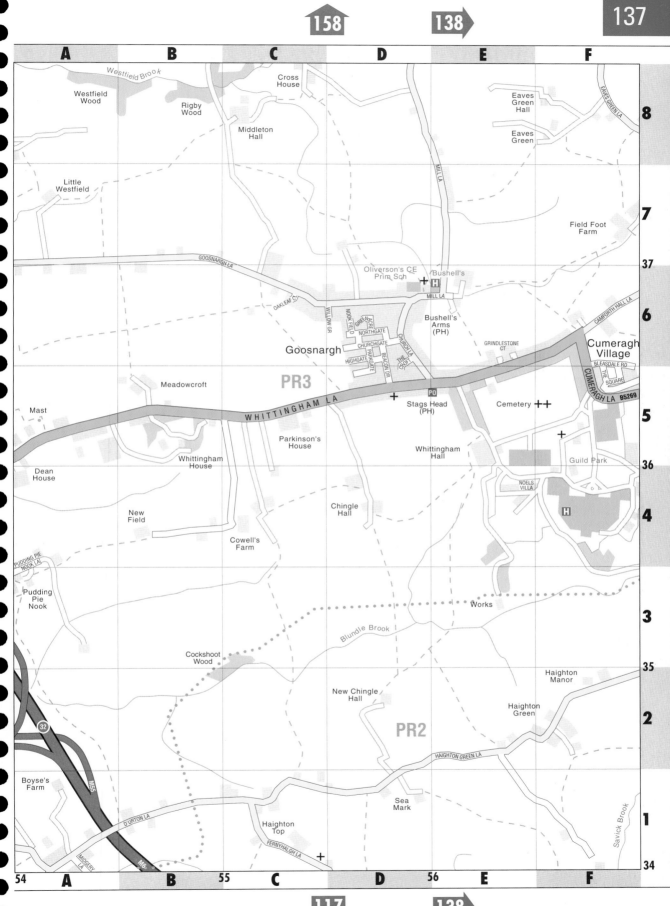

158
138

A B C D E F

8
7
37
6

5
36
4

3
35
2

1
34

Westfield Brook
Westfield Wood
Rigby Wood
Cross House
Middleton Hall
Eaves Green Hall
Eaves Green
Little Westfield
Field Foot Farm
GOOSNARGH LA
Oliverson's CE Prim Sch
Bushell's
OAKLEAF C
MILL LA
CAMFORTH HALL LA
WILLOW GR
NOOK FIELD
GREEN ACRE
NORTHGATE
CHURCHGATE
HIGHGATE
PARKGATE
BEACON DR
CHURCH LA
THE CROFT
Bushell's Arms (PH)
GRINDLESTONE CT
Cumeragh Village
Goosnargh
PR3
Meadowcroft
WHITTINGHAM LA
CUMERAGH LA
BLEASDALE RD
THE SQUARE
B5269
Mast
Stags Head (PH)
PO
Cemetery
Parkinson's House
Whittingham Hall
Dean House
Whittingham House
Guild Park
NOELS VILLA
H
New Field
Chingle Hall
Cowell's Farm
PUDDING PIE NOOK LA
Pudding Pie Nook
Works
Cockshoot Wood
Blundle Brook
Haighton Manor
New Chingle Hall
PR2
Haighton Green
32
M55
Boyse's Farm
D'URTON LA
MIDGERY LA
M6
HAIGHTON GREEN LA
Sea Mark
Savick Brook
Haighton Top
FERNYHALGH LA

54 55 56

117
138

137
159

A B C D E F

8

Cringlebrooks Farm

Tenter Hill

Sand Bank

INGLEWHITE RD
(PH)

Longridge Cty Prim Sch

BARNACRE RD

Stump Cross

Ashley La

Ashley House

Ashes Farm

EAVES GREEN LA

HALFPENNY LA

WINDSOR AVE

7

Camforth Hall Farm

CAMFORTH HALL LA

WHITTINGHAM RD

B5269

Gleadale House

TRENT ST

37

New Ashley

Higher Green Nook

BACK LA

PR3

GREEN NOOK LA

Mill

6

Back Lane Farm

CUMERAGH LA

Bottom's Farm

SHAW LA

LANGDALE RD

ESKDALE

5

B5269

Withy Trees

Blundel Brook

Pigot House

Lower Green Nook

Ind Est

HACKING DR
HEPWORTH DR

GRASMERE GR
MARDALE RD

WASDALE RD
LINDALE

BUTTERMERE DR
THIRLMERE DR
MILBECK CL

Shawe Farm

ENNERDALE RD

36

BRABINER LA

Harrison's Farm

4

Savick Brook

Daniel's Farm

3

Haighton Hall

Brabiner House Farm

Sudell's Farm

B6243

35

HAIGHTON GREEN LA

Dixons

+

Alston Lane RC Prim Sch

2

WHITTINGHAM LA

Beacon View

PR2

DIXONS LA

FELL VIEW

YEW TREE AVE

LANGDEN FOLD

Grimsargh Resrs

Woodfold Farm

ORCHARD WLK

PRESTON RD

Tun Brook

LYNWOOD AVE

PH

ELSTON LA

1

EAST VIEW

Grimsargh House

SMITH CL
NOOK

WAINGATE AVE

PO
OLD STATION CL

THE PASTURES

P ALEXANDER CT

SWALLOWFOLD

CEDAR CL
LINDALE GR

WOODLANDS GR

ELSTON GN

MAPLE GR

Salisbury Farm

34

Cow Hill

Goose Hall

Grimsargh St Michaels CE Sch

B6243

WAINGATE

TIMBER SPACE CT
BLACKLEACH AVE
ROSHAW

Grimsargh

57 A 58 B C 59 D E F

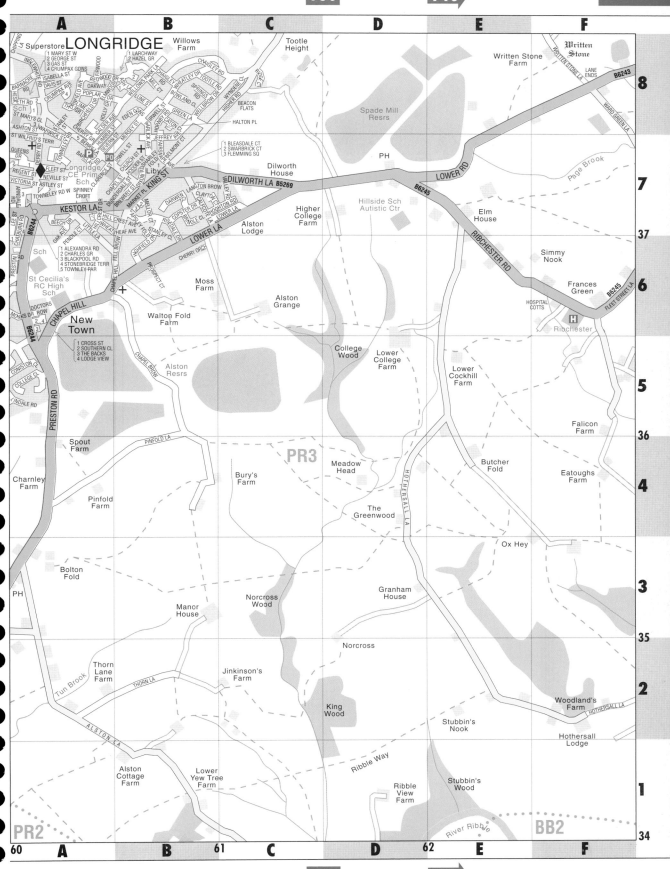

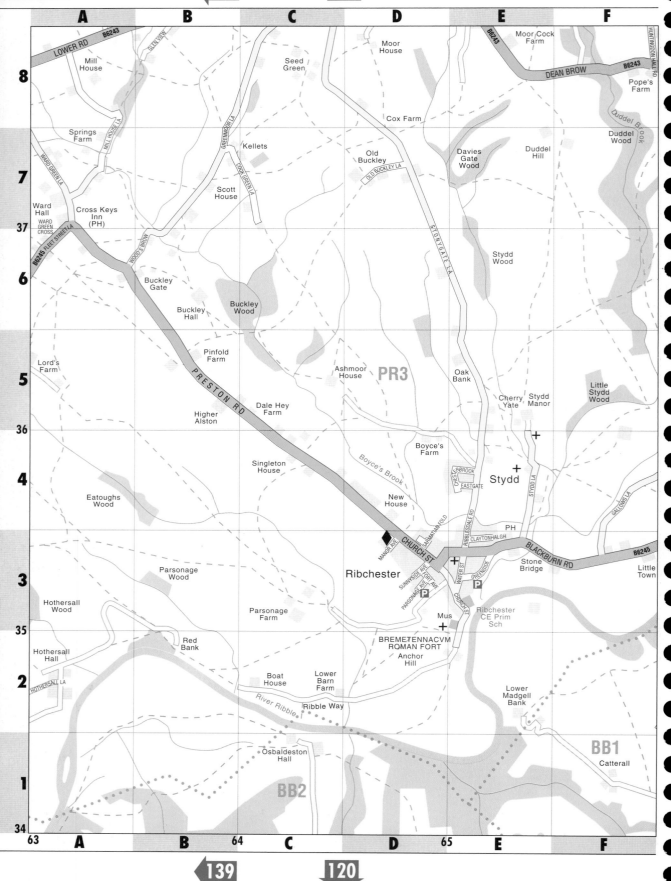

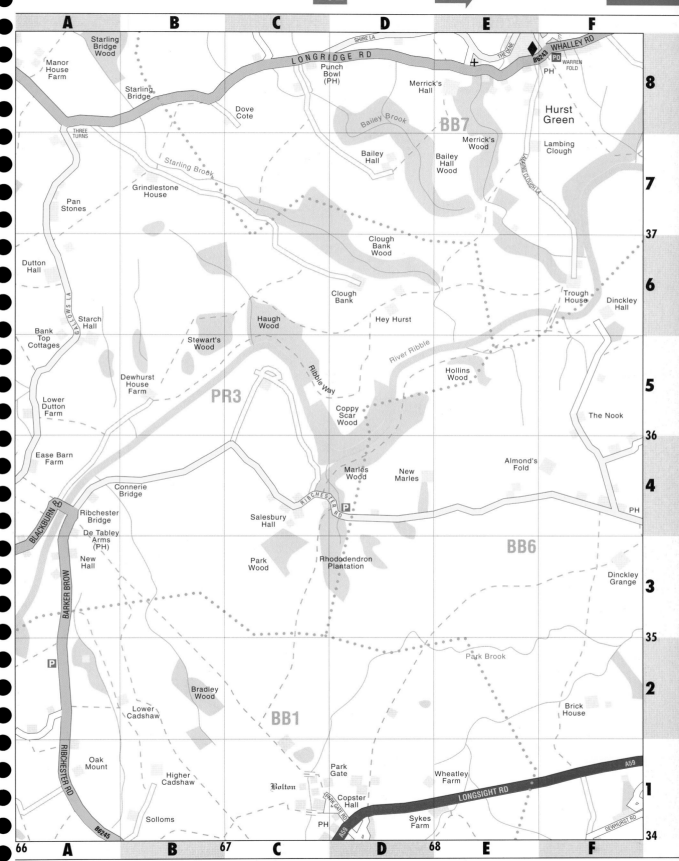

141
163

A **B** **C** **D** **E** **F**

8

Ribble Way
Jumbles

Jumbles
Rocks

Mitton
Wood

Brockhall
Wood

River Ribble

7

Hacking
Barn

Calderstones

Brockhall
Farm

37

Hacking
Wood

Hacking
Hall

BB7

Sewage
Works

PROVENCE AVE
LANCHESTER
GDNS
ST ANDREWS
RD
BELFRY
MANS

Mill
Wood

THE WOODLANDS
GLENEAGLES DR

Potter Ford
House

Bank End
Barn

6

BRADYLL CT

Bushburn
Bridge

WATLING
GATE

PRYDLE VIEW

BOWLING
GREEN
COTTS

LARKHILL

Chew
Mill

ELKER LA

Brockhall
Village

Bushburn Brook

Sewage
Works

5

Cravens

Langho
Wood

Blackburn
Rovers
Football
Academy

Aspinalls

LANG
WOODS

OLD LANGHO RD

BROOKSIDE

Sudell's
Farm

Lower
Elker

36

Dinckley Brook

Black Bull Hotel
(PH)

Old
Langho

A59

4

Gabbott's
Farm

Wardfall

Hillock
Farm

Skenning
Bridge

St Augustine's
RC High Sch

ELKER
COTTS

RIBCHESTER RD

BB6

Higher
Elker

ELKER
MEWS

NORTHCOTE RD

3

Lower
Fold

Foxfields
Hotel

35

Rileys

CHAPEL LA

Lower Fold
Wood

Petre Arms
(PH)

WHALLEY RD

St Leonard's
CE Sch

Hollin Hall
Farm

2

Monks
Barton

Laycock's
Farm

LONGSIGHT
RD

Smalley's
Farm

Langholme

WHALLEY RD

A666

Cunliffe
House Wood

LONGSIGHT RD

Doctor's Rake

Woodside

A59

Wade
Plat

Langho

1 STATION VIEW
2 TAYLOR'S BLDGS
3 OLIVE BANK
4 JUBILEE TERR
5 SPRING TERR
6 PRIMROSE TERR
7 BIRTWISTLE TERR
8 CORONATION TERR

WHALLEY OLD RD

Cronshaw

1

THE RYDINGS

Home
Farm

WHITEHALL LA

WHINNEY LA

MOOR RD

CLAYTON
ROW

ST MARY'S DR

WHALLEY RD

MOOR LA

BUSHBURN DR
CRONSHAW DR
HACKING CL
ROGERSFIELD
MIDFELD
MOOR AND RD

TUDOR
CL

A666
PO

St Mary's
RC Sch

Langho

34

69 **A** **B** 70 **C** **D** 71 **E** **F**

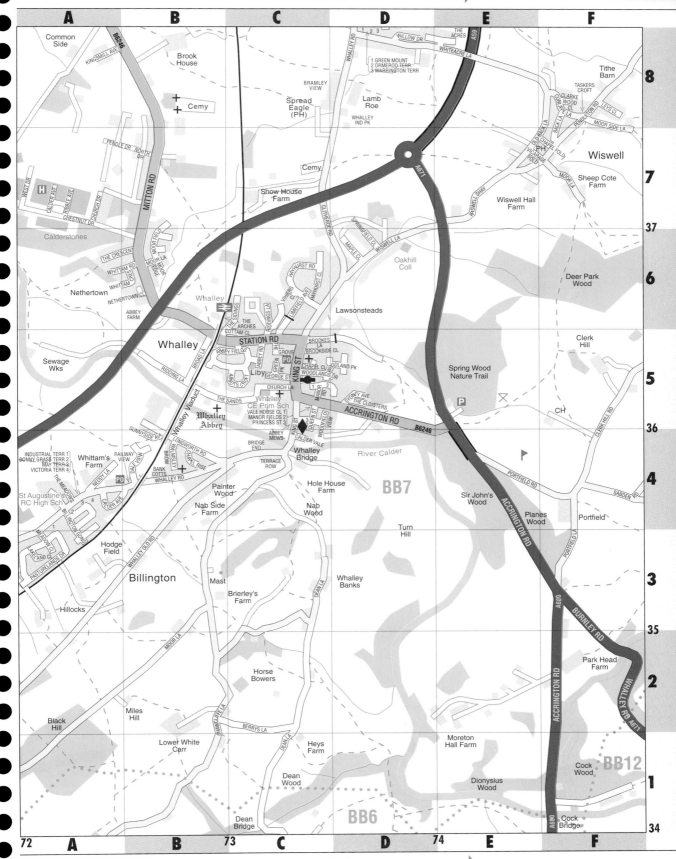

143
165

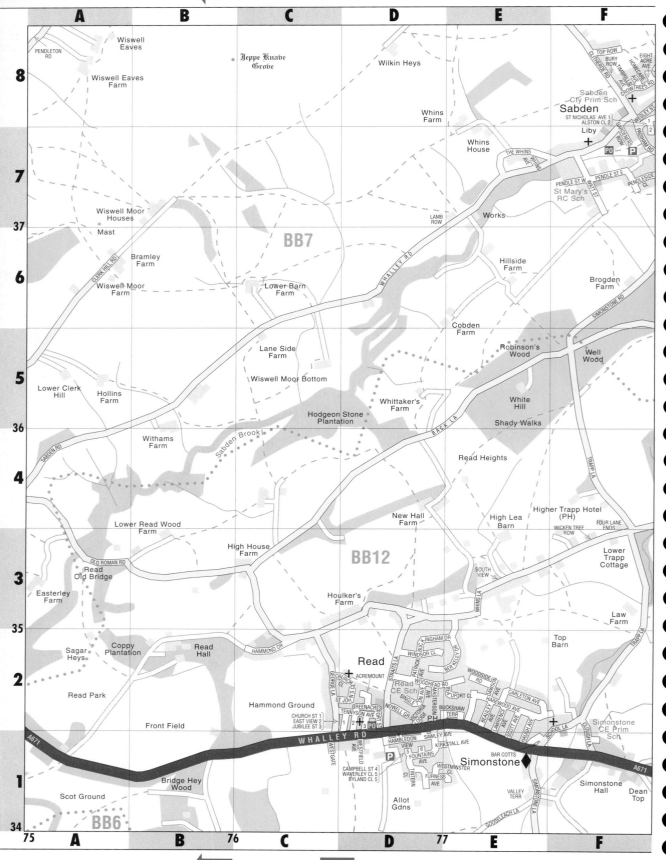

143
124

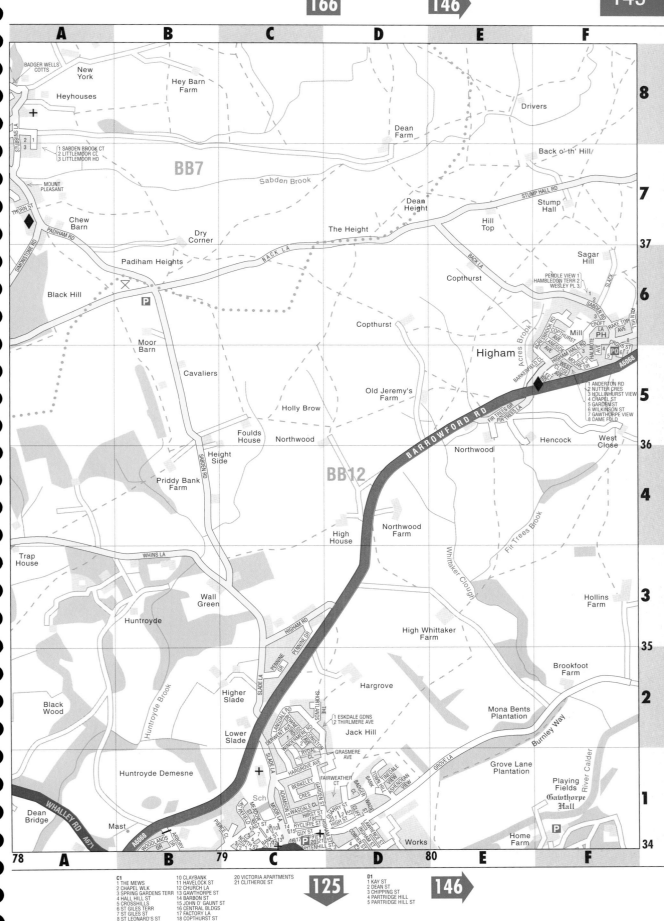

8

Badger Wells Cotts
New York
Heyhouses
Hey Barn Farm
Drivers
Dean Farm
Back o' th' Hill
BB7
Sabden Brook
1 SABDEN BROOK CT
2 LITTLEMDOR CL
3 LITTLEMDOR HO
MOUNT PLEASANT
STUBBINS LA

7
Stump Hall Rd
Dean Height
Stump Hall
Hill Top
37
Chew Barn
Dry Corner
The Height
BACK LA
Copthurst
Sagar Hill
THORN ST
PADIHAM RD
Padiham Heights

6
Black Hill
Copthurst
Copthurst
BACK LA
PENDLE VIEW 1
HAMBLEDON TERR 2
WESLEY PL 3
SIMONSTONE RD
Moor Barn
Higham
Mill
PH

5
Cavaliers
Old Jeremy's Farm
Acres Brook
1 ANDERTON RD
2 NUTTER CRES
3 HOLLINHURST VIEW
4 CRAPEL ST
5 GARDEN ST
6 WILKINSON ST
7 GAWTHORPE VIEW
8 DAME FOLD
Holly Brow
SABDEN RD
Foulds House
Northwood
BARROWFORD RD
A6068

36
Height Side
Northwood
Hencock
West Close
Priddy Bank Farm
BB12
Northwood

4
Trap House
WHINS LA
High House
Northwood Farm
Whittaker Clough
Fir Trees Brook
FIR TREES GR
FIR TREES LA

3
Wall Green
Hollins Farm
Huntroyde
HIGHAM RD
PENNINE GR
High Whittaker Farm

35
Black Wood
Higher Slade
Hargrove
Brookfoot Farm

2
Huntroyde Brook
SLADE LA
1 ESKDALE GDNS
2 THIRLMERE AVE
Jack Hill
Mona Bents Plantation
Lower Slade
Burnley Way
LANSDALE RD
DERWENT AVE
WINDERMERE AVE
RYDAL CL
GRASMERE AVE
BUTTERMERE DR
THE SHORTLANDS

1
Huntroyde Demesne
HARGROVE AVE
BERKELEY CRES
FAIRWEATHER CT
GROVE LA
Grove Lane Plantation
Playing Fields
Gawthorpe Hall
River Calder
Dean Bridge
WHALLEY RD
A671
Mast
A6068
WOODLANDS GR
ARBRY GR
Sch
Works
Home Farm

34

C1
1 THE MEWS
2 CHAPEL WLK
3 SPRING GARDENS TERR
4 HALL HILL ST
5 CROSSHILLS
6 ST GILES TERR
7 ST GILES ST
8 ST LEONARD'S ST
9 CLAYBANK FOLD
10 CLAYBANK
11 HAVELOCK ST
12 CHURCH LA
13 GAWTHORPE ST
14 BARBON ST
15 JOHN O' GAUNT ST
16 CENTRAL BLDGS
17 FACTORY LA
18 COPTHURST ST
19 HAMBERGHAM ST
20 VICTORIA APARTMENTS
21 CLITHEROE ST

D1
1 KAY ST
2 DEAN ST
3 CHIPPING ST
4 PARTRIDGE HILL
5 PARTRIDGE HILL ST

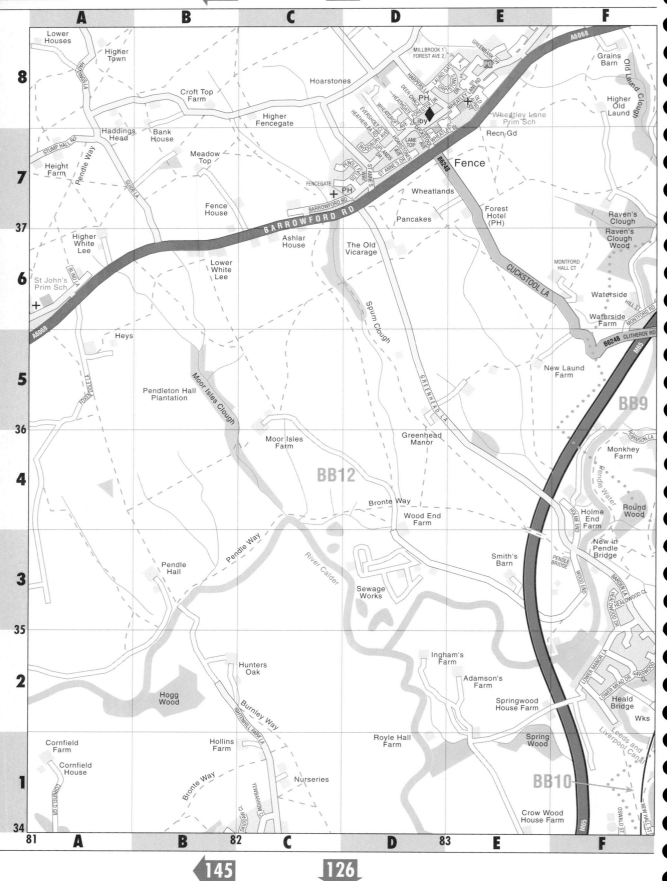

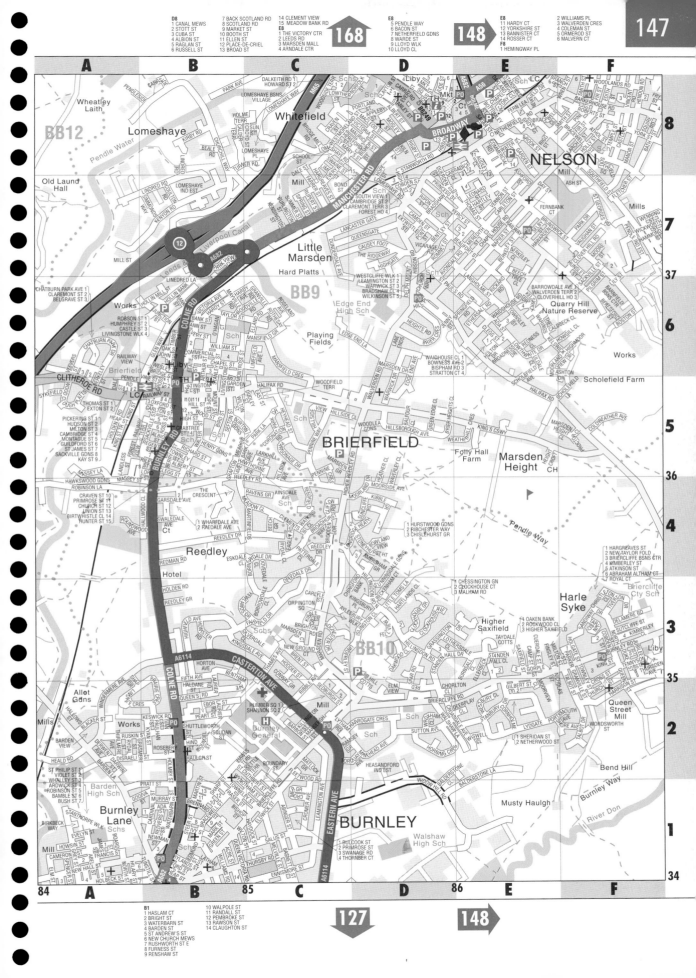

D8
1 CANAL MEWS
2 STOTT ST
3 CUBA ST
4 ALBION ST
5 RAGLAN ST
6 RUSSELL ST

7 BACK SCOTLAND RD
8 SCOTLAND RD
9 MARKET ST
10 BOOTH ST
11 ELLEN ST
12 PLACE-DE-CRIEL
13 BROAD ST

14 CLEMENT VIEW
15 MEADOW BANK RD
E8
1 THE VICTORY CTR
2 LEEDS RD
3 MARSDEN MALL
4 ARNDALE CTR

168

E8
5 PENDLE WAY
6 BACON ST
7 NETHERFIELD GDNS
8 WARDE ST
9 LLOYD WLK
10 LLOYD CL

148

E8
11 HARDY CT
12 YORKSHIRE ST
13 BANNISTER CT
14 ROSSER ST
F8
1 HEMINGWAY PL

2 WILLIAMS PL
3 WALVERDEN CRES
4 COLEMAN ST
5 ORMEROD ST
6 MALVERN CT

B1
1 HASLAM CT
2 BRIGHT ST
3 WATERBARN ST
4 BARDEN ST
5 ST ANDREW'S ST
6 NEW CHURCH MEWS
7 RUSHWORTH ST E
8 FURNESS ST
9 RENSHAW ST
10 WALPOLE ST
11 RANDALL ST
12 PEMBROKE ST
13 RAWSON ST
14 CLAUGHTON ST

127 148

8
7
37
6
5
36
4
3
35
2
1
34

A B C D E F

87 A B 88 C D 89 E F

Dry Clough

CH
MANCKNOLS WALTON
COTTAGE HOMES

Shelfield
Farm

Pinfold

Walton's
Mon

Clarion
House

Knavehill

BB9

Lower
Townhouse
Farm

Higher
Townhouse
Farm

Crawshaw
Hill
Shooters' Arms
(PH)

Southfield
Fold

Southfield

Float
Bridge

Allot
Gdns

Thaw
House

Southfield
Farm

Walverden
Reservoir

Catlow Farm

Gyll Farm

Catlow

Pothole Brook

Crawshaw La

Catlow Brook

Ford

Pendle Way

Ford

Scars
House

Pighole
Farm

Stony
Rakes

Foulds House
Farm

New
Laithe

Lane House
Farm

Hollin
Grove

Burwains
Farm

BB10

Sewage
Works

High Sym

Haggate

Lane
Bottom

Hill
Farm

Slack

Halifax Rd

Yeoman's
Farm

Long Hay
Farm

Higher
Cockden
Farm

Hanson's
Tenement

High
Ridehalgh

Banks

Rose
Cottages

Cockden

Cockden
Farm

Ingham's
Farm

Shore's
Hey

Burnley Way

Stephen
Hay

Recn
Gd

Cockden
House
Farm

Thursden Brook

Ell
Scar

River Don

Thursden

Park Wood

Cockden
Bridge

Monk Hall

Bronte Way

Shay Lane
Farm

Northbank
Farm

Elders
i' th' Row

Beadle
Hill

Bonfire
Hill

Pike
Lowe

Sweet Well
House

St John's
CE Prim
Sch

Recn
Gd

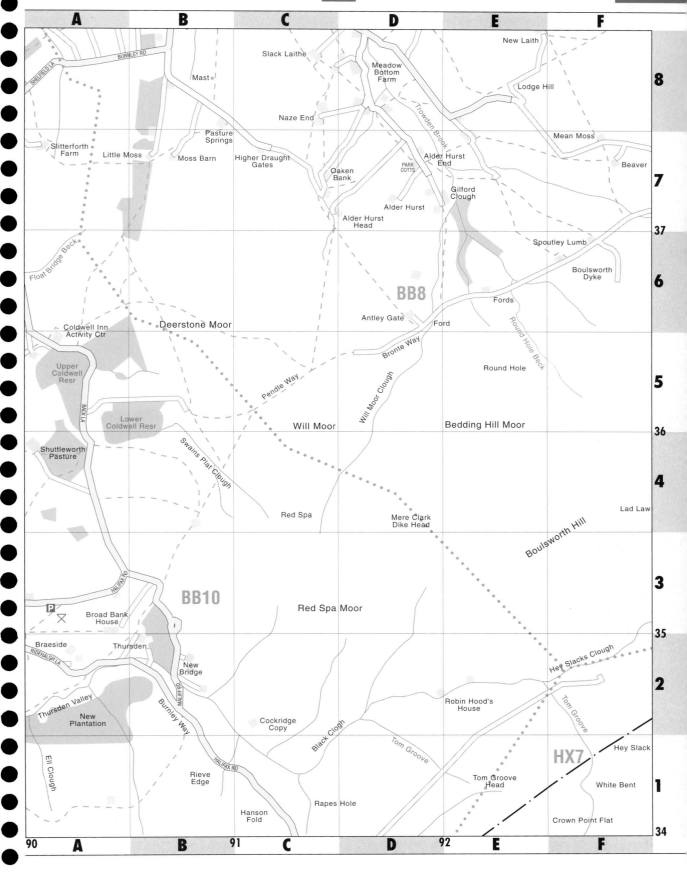

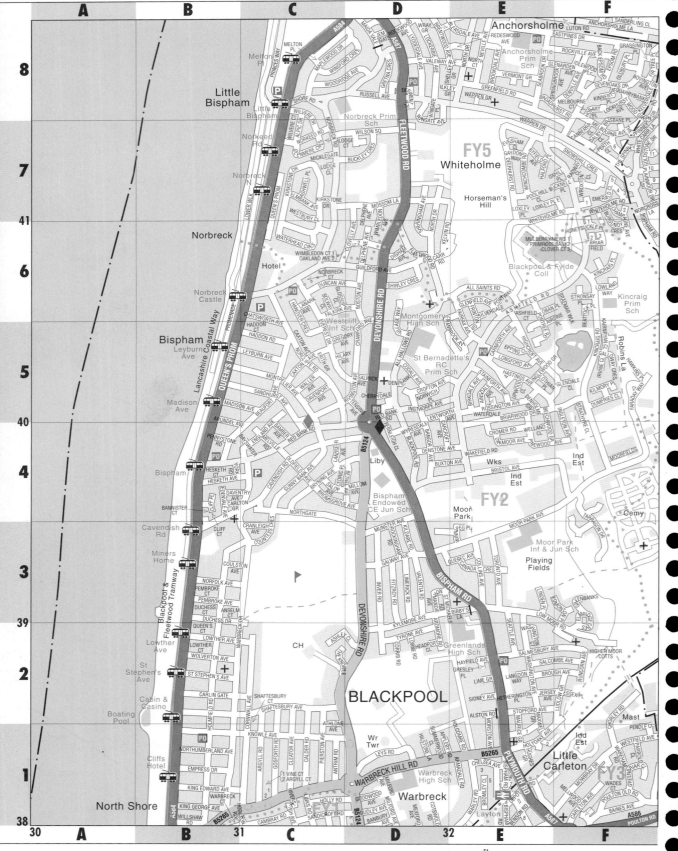

F7
1 WHEATFIELD CL
2 CHARDONNAY CRES
3 GARNET CL
4 MARBLE AVE
5 OPAL CL
6 BRIDGEWATER AVE
7 PRENTON GDNS
8 THE SHAY
9 PRIESTIELD
10 BESCOT WAY
11 SIXFIELDS

E1
1 BRODERICK AVE
2 FOX IND EST
3 CHELSEA CT
4 CHELSEA MEWS
5 BROMLEY CT
6 PEARL AVE
7 HENLEY CT
8 DELAWARE RD

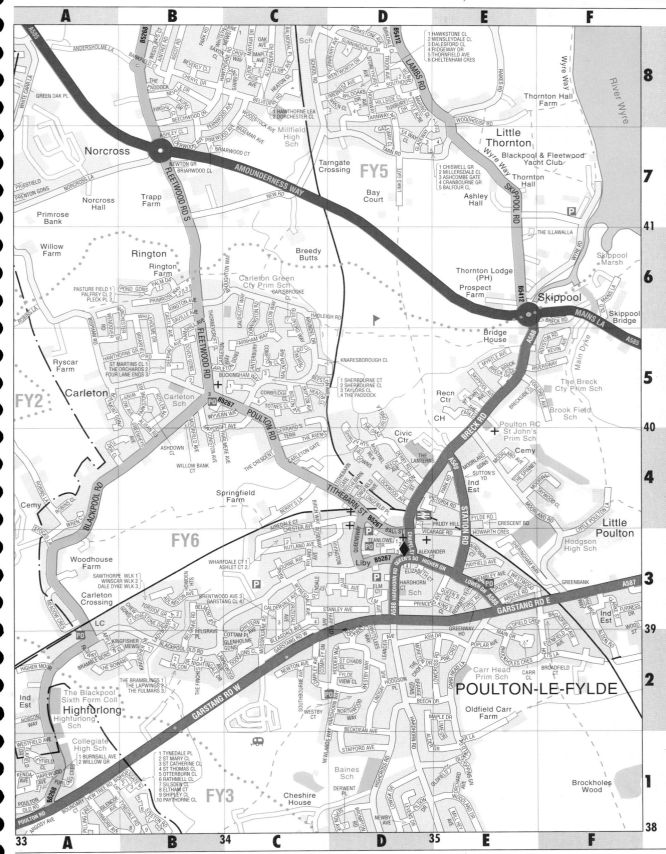

173
152
130
152

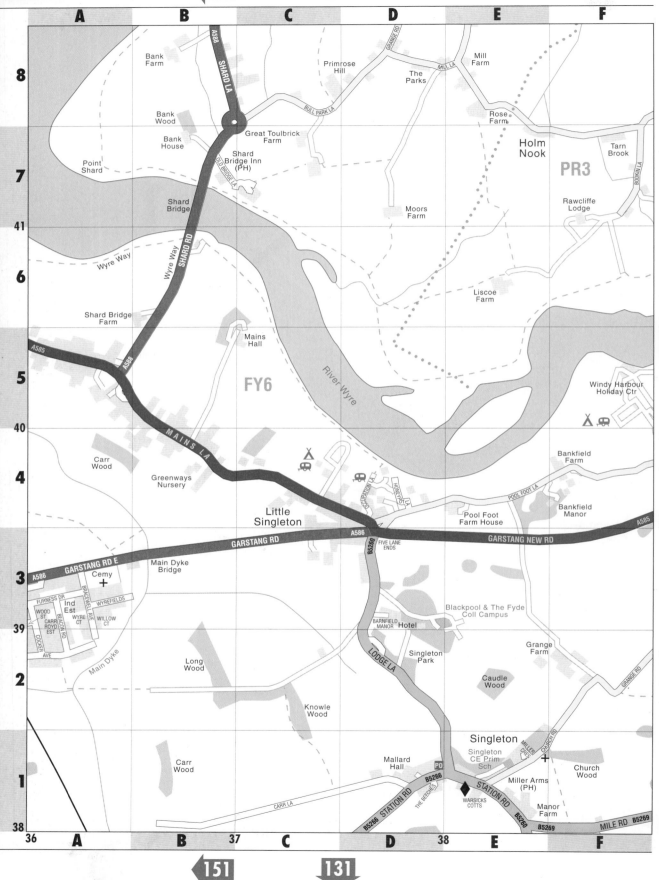

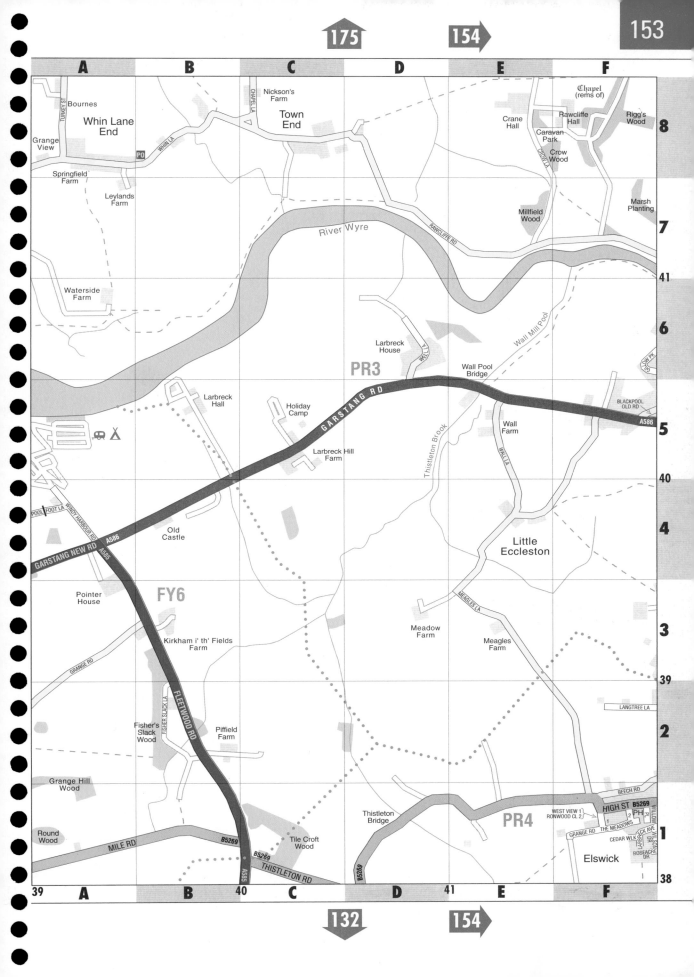

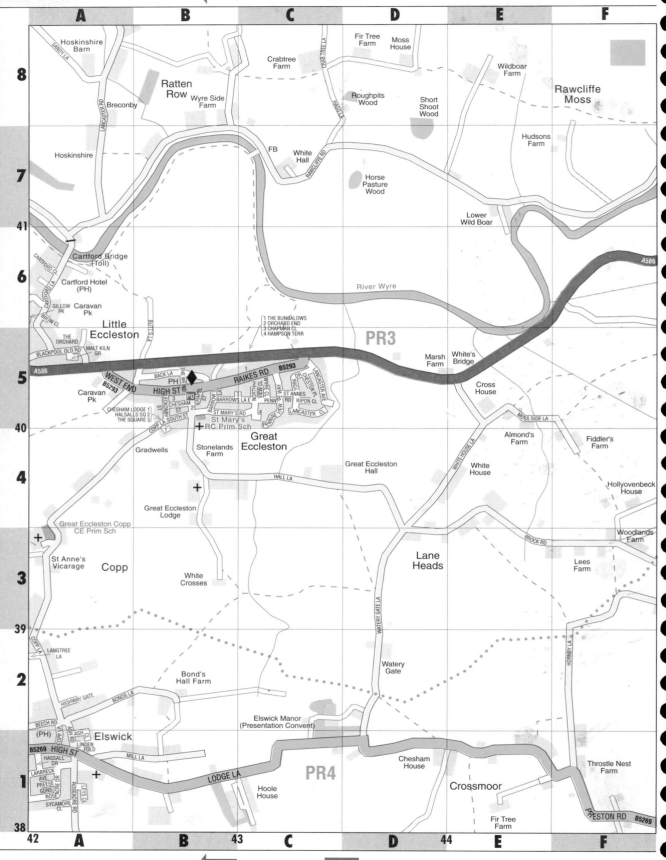

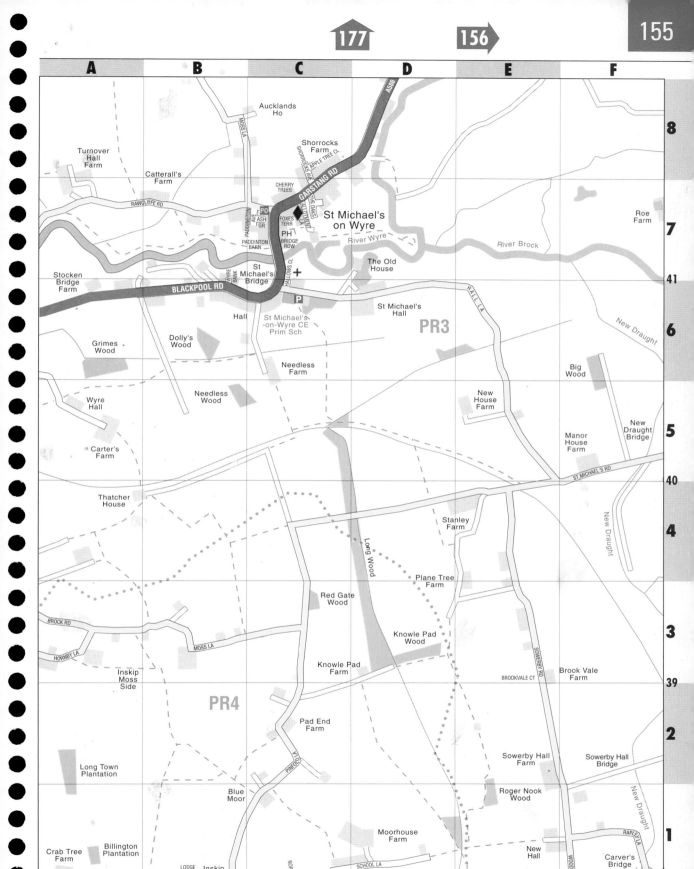

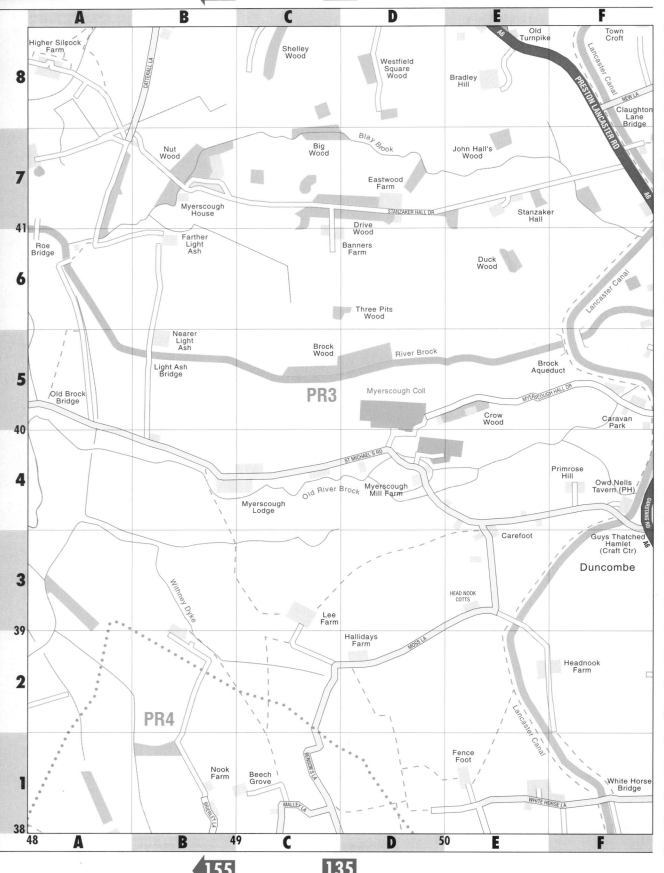

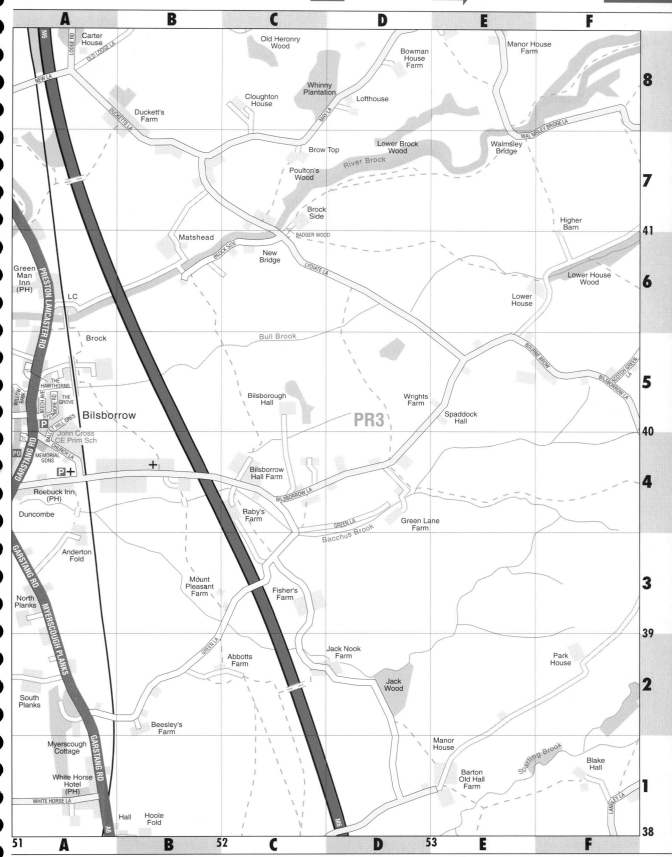

157
180

A **B** **C** **D** **E** **F**

Throstles Nest

Cloggers Farm

STANALEE LA

Lower Stanalee

BLEASDALE RD

CRUMBLEHOLM RD

Higher Oaken Head

8

WALMSLEY BRIDGE LA

Old Samuels

OAKENHEAD CL

Whitechapel

Lower Trotter Hill

Fell Side

7

Winn House

Whitechapel Cty Prim Sch

CHURCH LA

41

Higher Fairhurst

BUTTON ST

Great Plane Tree

Cross Keys Inn (PH)

Patrick House

Lower Barker

Ryeheads

Ashes Farmhouse

6

Scotch Green

SCOTCH GREEN LA

Lower Fairhurst

Factory Brook

Higher Barker

GREENFIELD LA

Syke House

5

Little Brooks House

Plane Tree

Whitechapel Brook

40

CARRON LA

Factory Bridge

SYKE HOUSE LA

Isles Field Farm

Fir Trees

BILSBORROW LA

Green Man Hotel

Inglewhite

PR3

4

Cliftons Farm

Palegate Farm

Sparling Brook

INGLEWHITE RD

Park Head

SILK MILL LA

Turner House

Higher Beesley

Lotus Hall Farm

Inglewhite Lodge

Lower Beesleys

Whinnyclough

3

Well Wood Stream

Silk Mill Bridge

Longley House Barn

39

Pointer House

LANGLEY LA

CURWEN LA

MILL LA

New House

Whinnyclough Brook

2

Goosnargh Lodge

BROADITH LA

FORD LA

Ford

Gardner's Farm

Golden Cliff

Brook Farm

Brook Bridge

HORNS LA

1

Lodge Wood

Townley Wood

Goosnargh Mill

Mill Brook

EAVES GREEN LA

Brook Cottage

38

54 **A** **B** 55 **C** **D** 56 **E** **F**

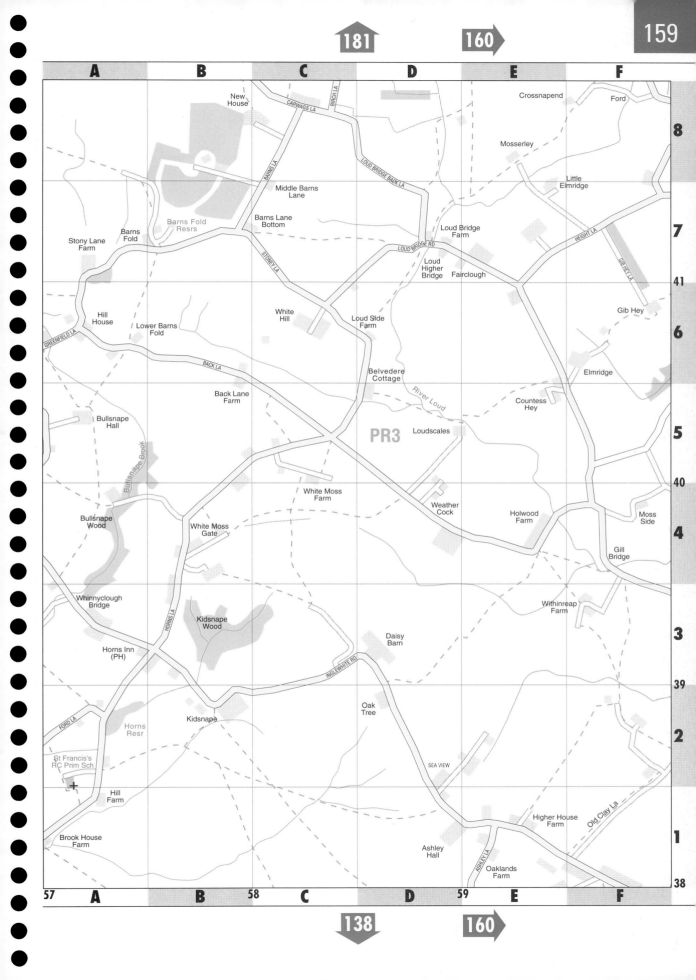

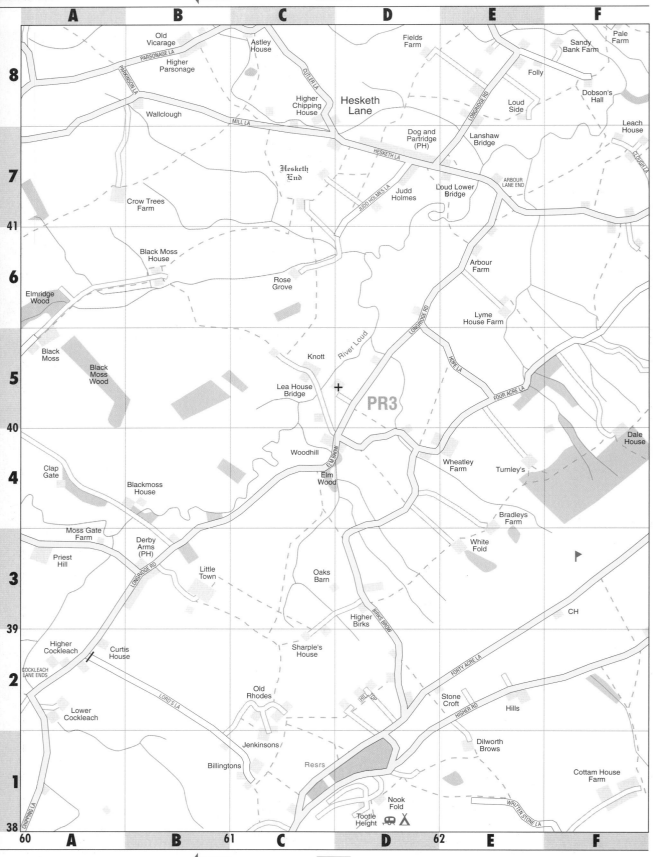

159
182

Old Vicarage

PARSONAGE LA

Astley House

CUTLER LA

Fields Farm

Sandy Bank Farm

Pale Farm

Higher Parsonage

PARKINSON LA

Higher Chipping House

Hesketh Lane

LONGRIDGE RD

Folly

Loud Side

Dobson's Hall

Wallclough

MILL LA

Dog and Partridge (PH)

Lanshaw Bridge

Leach House

CLOUGH LA

HESKETH LA

Hesketh End

JUDD HOLMES LA

Loud Lower Bridge

ARBOUR LANE END

Crow Trees Farm

Judd Holmes

Black Moss House

Rose Grove

Arbour Farm

Elmridge Wood

Knott

River Loud

LONGRIDGE RD

Lyme House Farm

Black Moss

Black Moss Wood

Lea House Bridge

HOPE LA

PR3

FOUR ACRE LA

Dale House

Woodhill

ELM BROW

Wheatley Farm

Turnley's

Clap Gate

Blackmoss House

Elm Wood

Bradleys Farm

Moss Gate Farm

Derby Arms (PH)

White Fold

Priest Hill

LONGRIDGE RD

Little Town

Oaks Barn

CH

Higher Birks

BIRKS BROW

Higher Cockleach

Curtis House

Sharple's House

FORTY ACRE LA

COCKLEACH LANE ENDS

Old Rhodes

HILL TOP

Stone Croft

HIGHER RD

Hills

Lower Cockleach

LORD'S LA

Jenkinsons

Dilworth Brows

Billingtons

Resrs

Cottam House Farm

CHIPPING LA

Nook Fold

Tootle Height

WRITTEN STONE LA

159
139

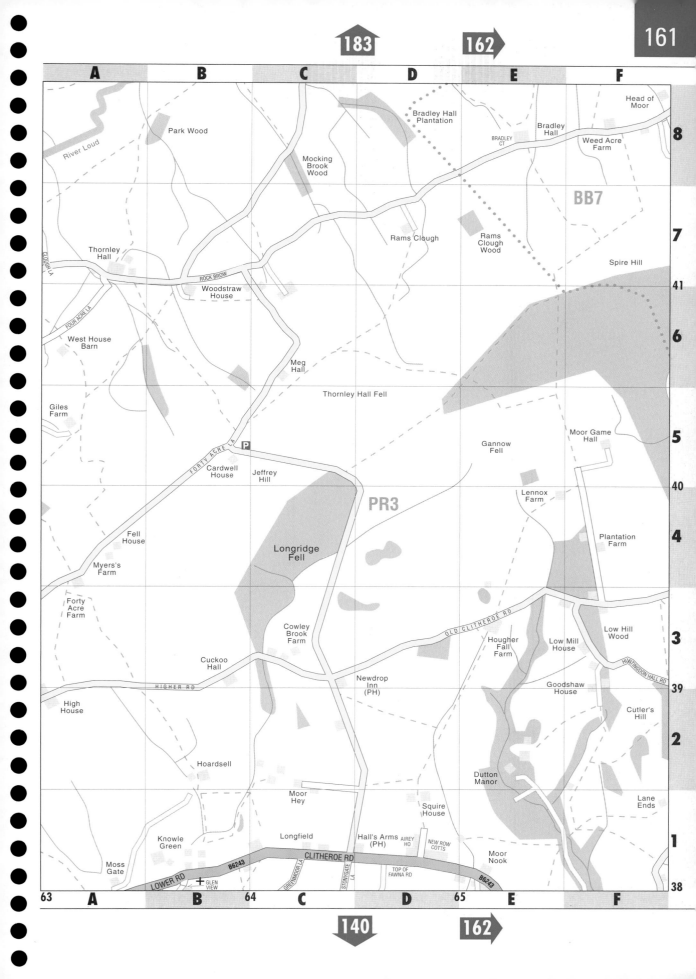

183
162

A B C D E F

Head of Moor

Bradley Hall Plantation

8

Park Wood

BRADLEY CT

Bradley Hall

Weed Acre Farm

River Loud

Mocking Brook Wood

BB7

7

Rams Clough

Rams Clough Wood

Thornley Hall

Spire Hill

CLOUGH LA

ROCK BROW

41

Woodstraw House

6

FOUR ACRE LA

West House Barn

Meg Hall

Thornley Hall Fell

Giles Farm

Moor Game Hall

5

FORTY ACRE LA

P

Gannow Fell

40

Cardwell House

Jeffrey Hill

Lennox Farm

PR3

Plantation Farm

4

Fell House

Longridge Fell

Myers's Farm

Forty Acre Farm

OLD CLITHEROE RD

Low Hill Wood

3

Cowley Brook Farm

Hougher Fall Farm

Low Mill House

Cuckoo Hall

HIGHER RD

Newdrop Inn (PH)

Goodshaw House

HUNTINGDON HALL RD

39

High House

Cutler's Hill

2

Hoardsell

Dutton Manor

Lane Ends

Moor Hey

Squire House

Knowle Green

Longfield

Hall's Arms (PH)

AIREY HO

NEW ROW COTTS

Moor Nook

1

Moss Gate

B6243

LOWER RD

GLEN VIEW

CLITHEROE RD

GREENMOOR LA

STONYGATE LA

TOP OF FAWNA RD

B6243

38

A B C D E F

63   64   65

140
162

161
184

A B C D E F

8

Bull Hill
Planetree Hall
Chapel House
Craven Heifer (PH)
Walker Fold
Rakefoot

Moss Plantation

Chaigley Hall Wood

7

Hare Hill
Longridge Fell Forest Wlk
High Beacon

41

Green Thorn Fell

6

Longridge Fell
Turner Fold

BIRDY BROW

Green Thorn
Brownslow
Nooks
Chilsey Green
Fell Side Farm House
Morton House

5

Brownslow Brook
Brook Bottom
BB7

40

Stock Bridge

4

Holly Hall
Higher Stonyhurst Park
Throstle Nest

OLD CLITHEROE RD
Intack
PR3
Crowshaw House
Higher Deer House
STOCKBRIDGE COTTS
Lower Deer House

3

Crowshaw Lodge (Resr)
Deer House Wood
Stonyhurst Park
Dashwood
Coll

39

Huntingdon Hall
Greengore
Dean Brook

2

HUNTINGDON HALL RD
Hudd Lee Wood
Hill Farm
Fox Fall Wood

Higher Hudd Lee
Mill Wood

1

Lower Hudd Lee Farm
SMITHY ROW
St Josephs RC Prim Sch
Carlinghurst
Shireburn House
Doe Hill
New House
SHIREBURN COTTS
THE AVENUE
BILSBERRY COTTS
B6243
WHALLEY RD

38

Bailey House

66 A B 67 C D 68 E F

161
141

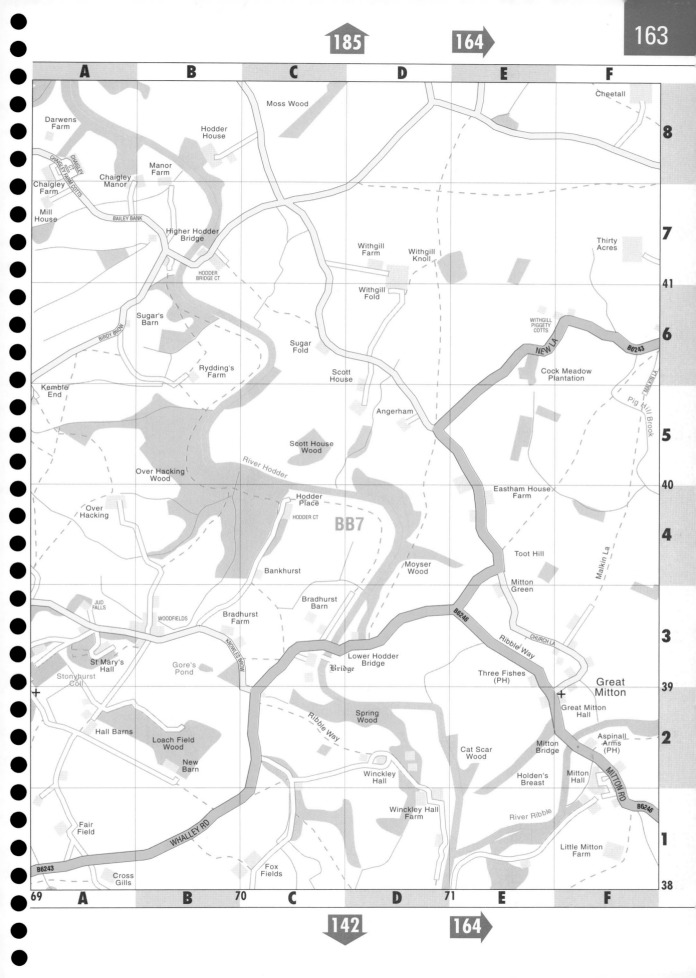

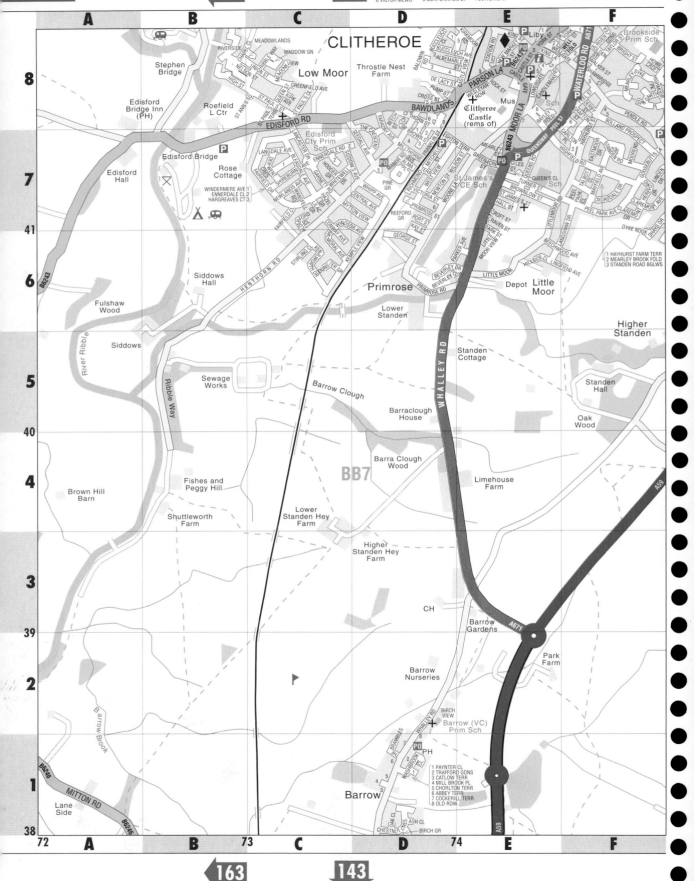

163

186

D7
1 CURZON ST
2 MONK ST
3 BARN CROFT
4 HENTHORN CL
5 DEAN MEADOW
6 VICTOR MEWS

D8
1 CARDIGAN CL
2 ALBERMARLE CT
3 BALDWIN HILL
4 MONTAGUE ST
5 WHALLEY ST
6 CORPORATION ST

7 MOSS ST
8 JOHN WALL CT
E8
1 CHURCH ST
2 HARRIS CT
3 MARKET PL
4 BOWLAND CT

5 SADDLERS MEWS
6 WILKIN SQ
7 THE EMPORIUM
8 OLD STATION CT
9 PARSONAGE COTTS
10 CARDIGAN AVE

F8
1 ALBION ST
2 DUCK ST
3 SHAW BRIDGE ST
4 PENDLE CT
5 BOLLAND CT
6 BROTHERTON MDWS

CLITHEROE

Low Moor

1 HAYHURST FARM TERR
2 MEARLEY BROOK FOLD
3 STANDEN ROAD BGLWS

1 PAYNTER CL
2 TRAFFORD GDNS
3 CATLOW TERR
4 MILL BROOK PL
5 CHORLTON TERR
6 ABBEY TERR
7 COCKERILL TERR
8 OLD ROW

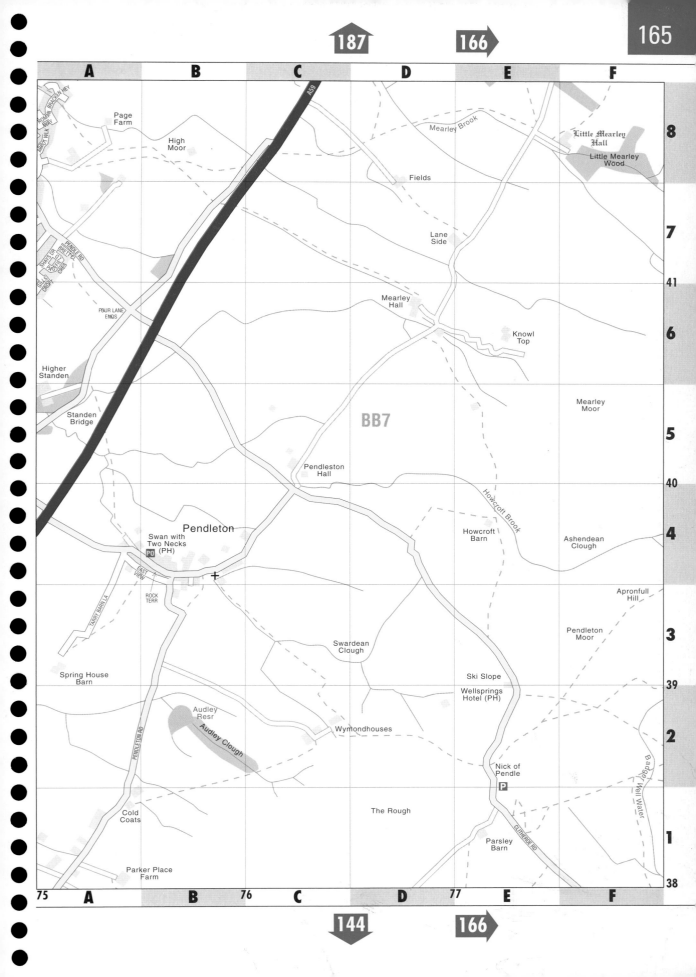

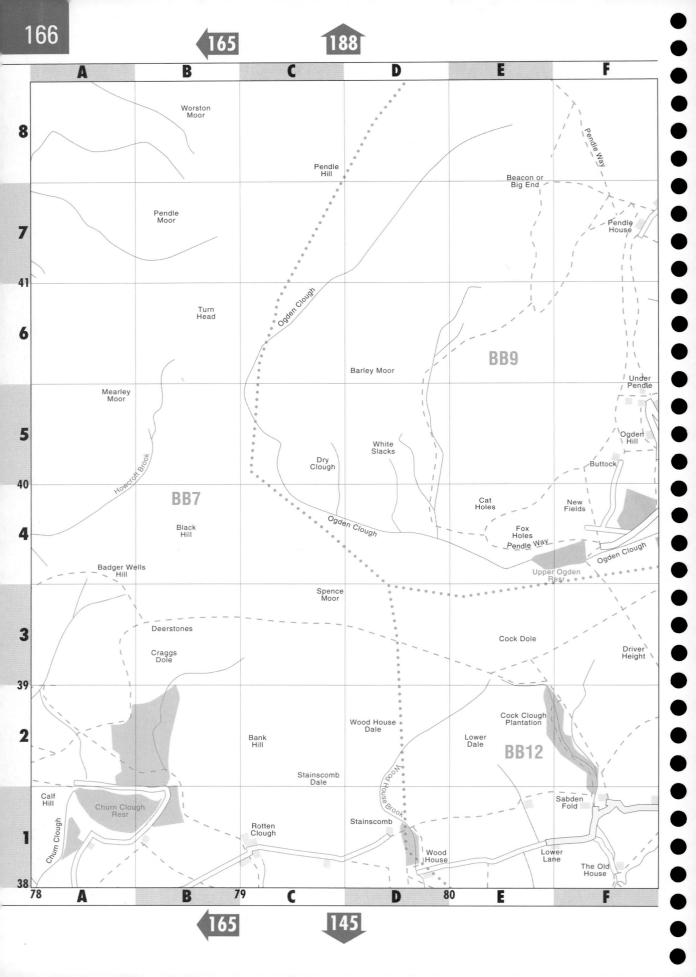

A B C D E F

8 Worston Moor

Pendle Hill

Beacon or Big End

Pendle Way

Pendle House

7 Pendle Moor

41

6 Turn Head

Ogden Clough

BB9

Under Pendle

Mearley Moor

Barley Moor

5 Howcroft Brook

White Slacks

Ogden Hill

Buttock

40

BB7

Dry Clough

Ogden Clough

Cat Holes

New Fields

4 Black Hill

Fox Holes

Pendle Way

Ogden Clough

Badger Wells Hill

Spence Moor

Upper Ogden Resr

3 Deerstones

Cock Dole

Driver Height

Craggs Dole

39

2 Bank Hill

Wood House Dale

Cock Clough Plantation

Lower Dale

BB12

Stainscomb Dale

Calf Hill

Sabden Fold

Churn Clough Resr

Rotten Clough

Stainscomb

1 Churn Clough

Wood House

Lower Lane

The Old House

38

78 A B 79 C D 80 E F

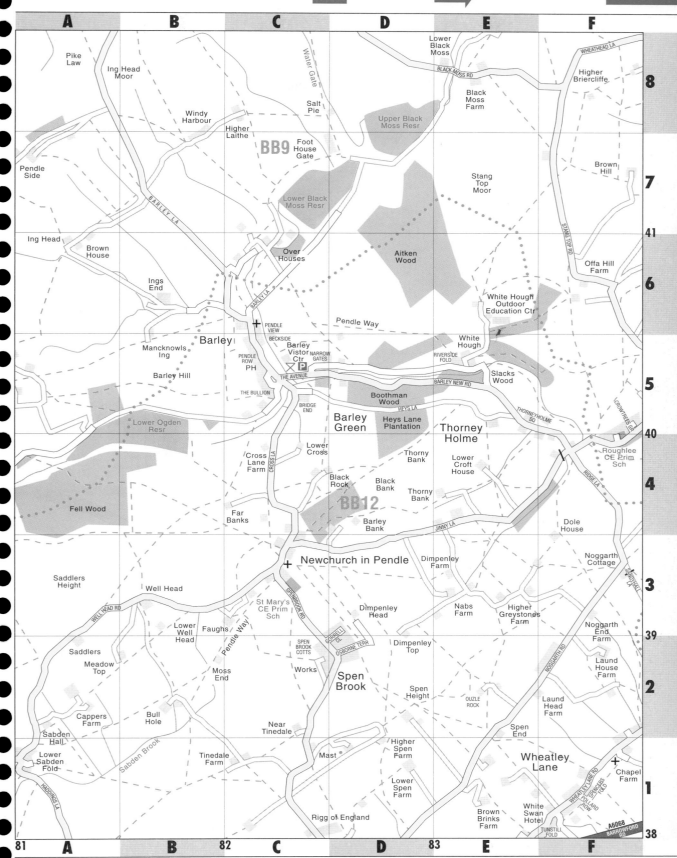

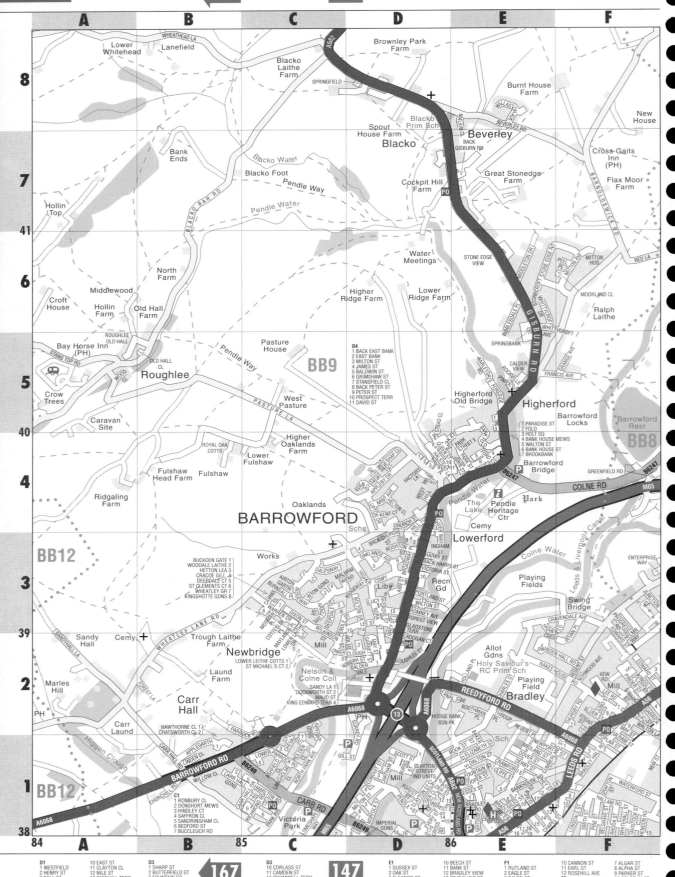

A   B   C   D   E   F

Lower
Whitehead
Lanefield
Wheathead La
Blacko
Laithe
Farm
Brownley Park
Farm
Springfield
A682
Burnt House
Farm
New
House
Blacko
Prim Sch
Spout
House Farm
Beverley
Back
Gisburn Rd
Cross Gaits
Inn
(PH)
Bank
Ends
Blacko Water
Blacko
Great Stonedge
Farm
Flax Moor
Farm
Blacko Foot
Pendle Way
Cockpit Hill
Farm
Hollin
Top
Pendle Water
Water
Meetings
Stone Edge
View
Moorland Cl
North
Farm
Middlewood
Higher
Ridge Farm
Lower
Ridge Farm
Ralph
Laithe
Croft
House
Hollin
Farm
Old Hall
Farm
Springbank
Bay Horse Inn
(PH)
Old Hall
Cl
Pasture
House
Pendle Way
BB9
Higherford
Old Bridge
Higherford
Barrowford
Locks
Barrowford
Resr
BB8
Roughlee
West
Pasture
Pasture La
Crow
Trees
Caravan
Site
Royal Oak
Cotts
Higher
Oaklands
Farm
Barrowford
Bridge
Barrowford
Water
Colne Rd
M65
Ridgaling
Farm
Fulshaw
Head Farm
Fulshaw
Lower
Fulshaw
Oaklands
Pendle
Heritage
Ctr
Park
B6247
Greenfield Rd
BB12
BARROWFORD
Schs
The
Lake
Cemy
Works
Lowerford
Colne Water
Playing
Fields
Enterprise
Way
Liby
Recn
Gd
Swing
Bridge
Sandy
Hall
Cemy
Trough Laithe
Farm
Wheatley Lane Rd
Newbridge
Mill
Allot
Gdns
Holy Saviour's
RC Prim Sch
Playing
Field
Marles
Hill
PH
Laund
Farm
Nelson &
Colne Coll
Bradley
Mill
Carr
Hall
Carr
Laund
Higgen Clough
Carr Hall Rd
Churchill Way
Reedyford Rd
A6068
BARROWFORD RD
B6249
Carr Rd
A6068
Leeds Rd
A56
BB12
A6068
Victoria
Park
Mill
Imperial
Gdns
B6249

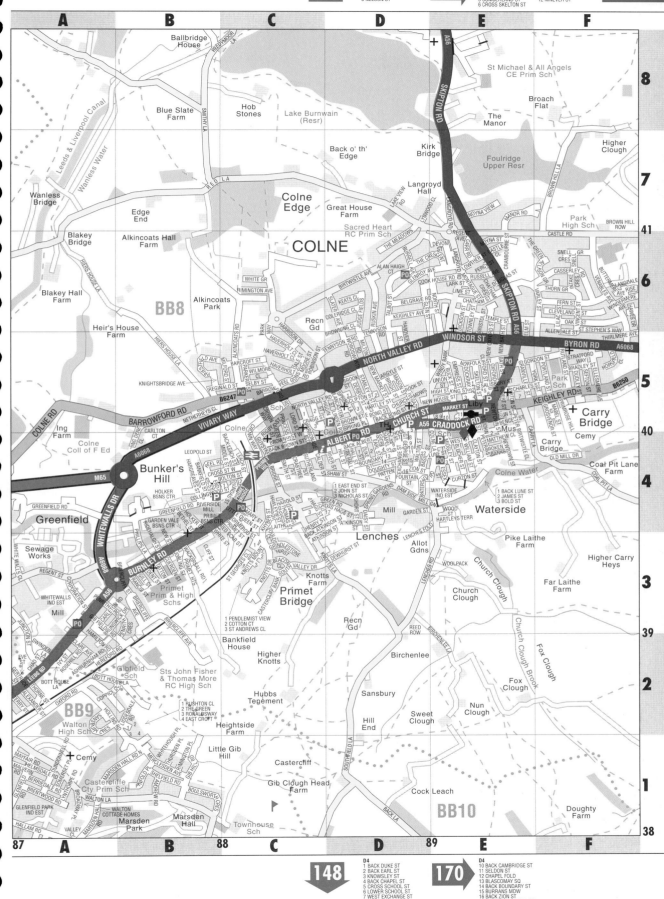

C5
1 FOTHERGILL ST
2 MOORHEAD ST
3 MELLING CT

191

D5
1 BIRTWISTLE HYDE PK
2 MITCHELL ST
3 SPRING YD
4 BACK DERBY ST
5 NELSON ST

170

E5
1 WATER ST
2 DOCKRAY CT
3 ANGEL WAY
4 DOCKRAY YD
5 CUMBERLAND ST
6 CROSS SKELTON ST

7 BIRTWISTLE FOLD
8 POST OFFICE YD
9 ARCADIA
10 MARKET PL
11 PARLIAMENT ST
12 NINEVEH ST

148

D4
1 BACK DUKE ST
2 BACK EARL ST
3 KNOWSLEY ST
4 BACK CHAPEL ST
5 CROSS SCHOOL ST
6 LOWER SCHOOL ST
7 WEST EXCHANGE ST
8 RAGLAN ST
9 CAMBRIDGE ST

170

D4
10 BACK CAMBRIDGE ST
11 SELDON ST
12 CHAPEL FOLD
13 BLASCOMAY SQ
14 BACK BOUNDARY ST
15 BURRANS MOW
16 BACK ZION ST
17 CROSS HELLIWELL ST

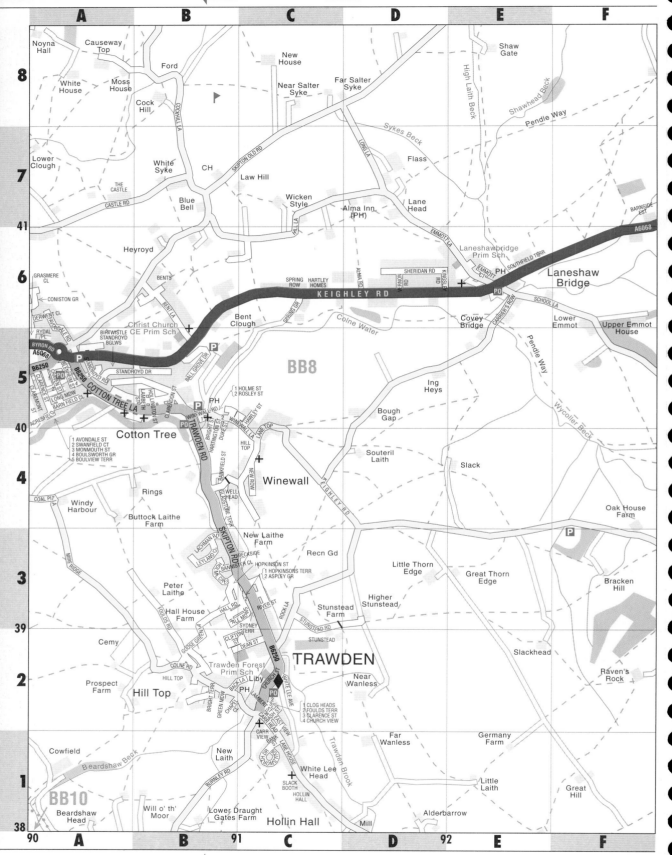

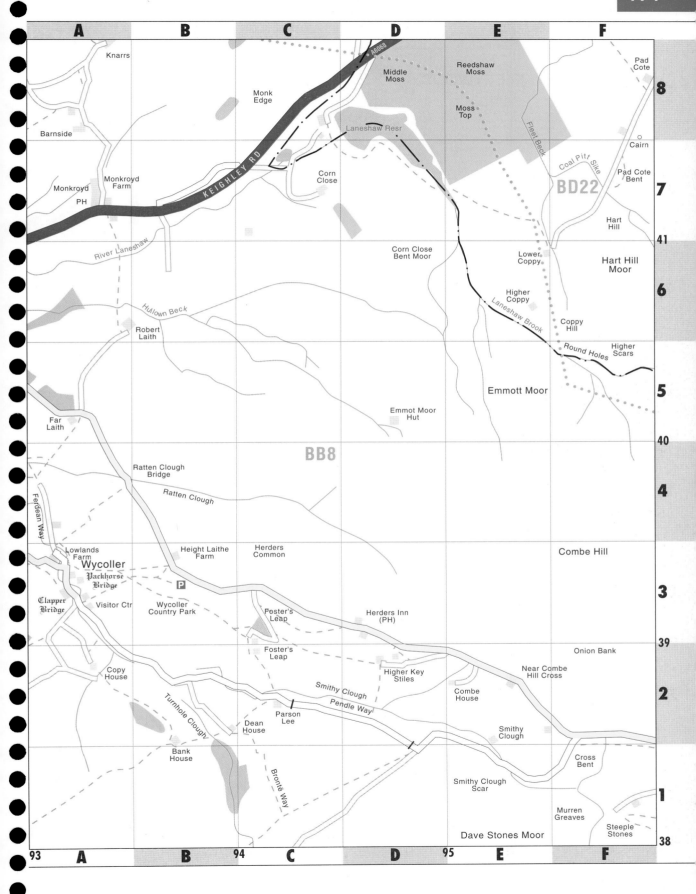

Knarrs

Barnside

Monk Edge

Monkroyd PH

Monkroyd Farm

KEIGHLEY RD

River Laneshaw

A6068

Middle Moss

Reedshaw Moss

Moss Top

Laneshaw Resr

Corn Close

Corn Close Bent Moor

Hullown Beck

Robert Laith

Far Laith

Fleet Beck

Coal Pitt Sike

BD22

Pad Cote

Cairn

Pad Cote Bent

Hart Hill

Hart Hill Moor

Lower Coppy

Higher Coppy

Coppy Hill

Laneshaw Brook

Round Holes

Higher Scars

Emmot Moor Hut

Emmott Moor

BB8

Ratten Clough Bridge

Ratten Clough

Ferndean Way

Lowlands Farm

Wycoller

Packhorse Bridge

Clapper Bridge

Visitor Ctr

P

Wycoller Country Park

Height Laithe Farm

Herders Common

Foster's Leap

Foster's Leap

Herders Inn (PH)

Combe Hill

Onion Bank

Near Combe Hill Cross

Higher Key Stiles

Combe House

Smithy Clough

Copy House

Turnhole Clough

Dean House

Parson Lee

Bank House

Brontë Way

Smithy Clough

Pendle Way

Smithy Clough Scar

Cross Bent

Murren Greaves

Steeple Stones

Dave Stones Moor

A   B   C   D   E   F

8

7

41

6

40

5

4

39

3

2

1

38

93   A   B   94   C   D   95   E   F

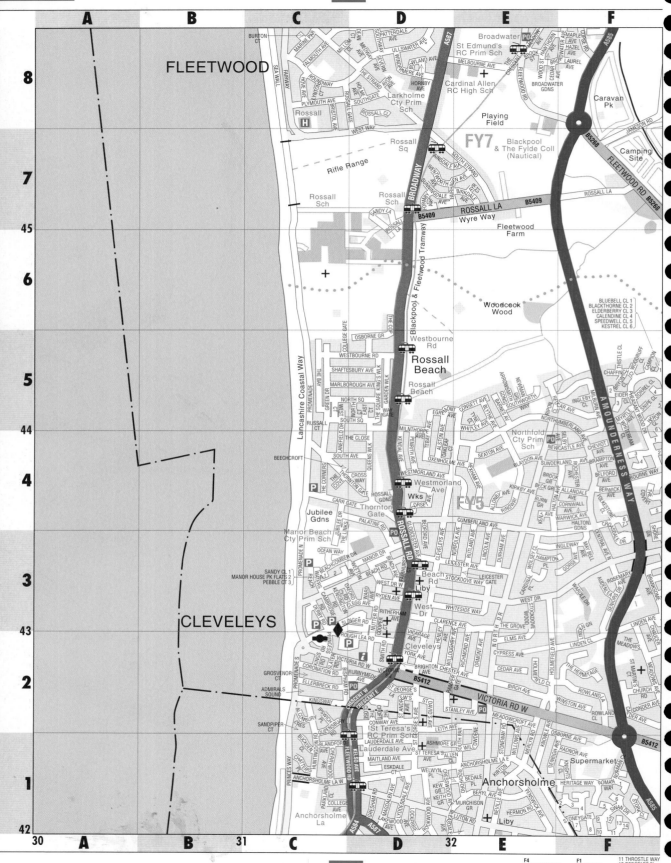

FLEETWOOD

FY7

CLEVELEYS

Rossall Beach

Anchorsholme

F4	F1	
1 REDWING AVE	1 TUDOR CL	11 THROSTLE WAY
2 CURLEW CL	2 SHERWOOD PL	12 REDSTART PL
3 WHITECREST AVE	3 RICHARDS WAY	13 KITTIWAKE CL
4 BARNFIELD CL	4 GLADSTONE WAY	14 MOORHEN PL
5 WIDGEON CL	5 POCHARD PL	
6 COLCHESTER DR	6 DOVE CL	
7 PORTSMOUTH CL	7 INGLENOOK CL	
	8 HERIOT CL	
	9 BUNTING PL	
	10 SANDPIPER PL	

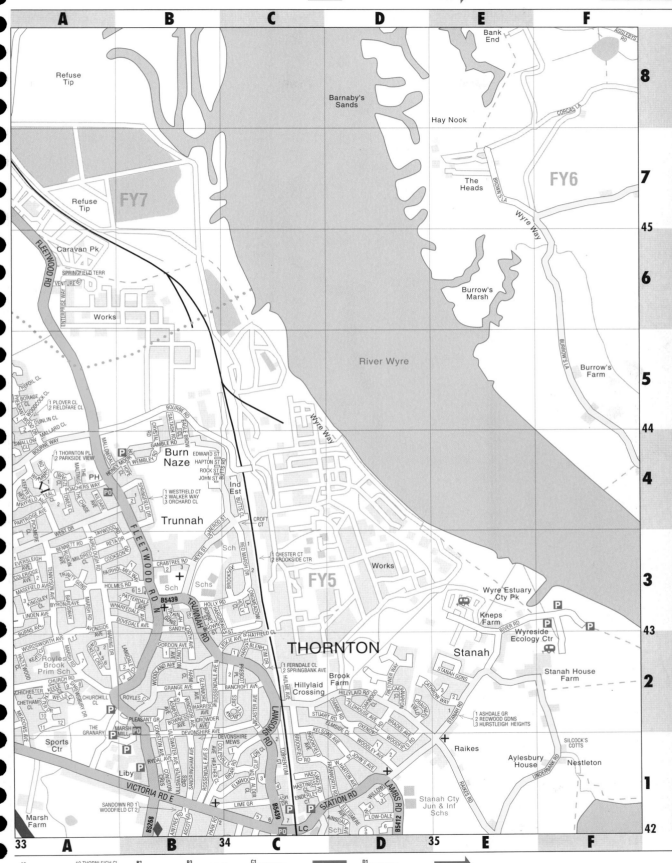

A2
1 BRAMBLE CT
2 MARSH CT
3 TOWN END
4 SANDFIELD
5 CARR HEY
6 VERONA CT
7 PENNYFARTHING LA
8 GORDONSTOUN PL
9 BENENDEN PL
10 THORNLEIGH CL
11 ROEHAMPTON CL
12 ROEDEAN CL

B2
1 CARLISLE GR
2 CHURCHILL CL
3 COUNSELL CT
4 LINADALE AVE

B3
1 FAIRHOLMES CL
2 CRABTREE ORCH
3 KINGSTON MEWS
4 LOWES CT
5 LOWESWAY
6 HOUGHTON CL
7 GRIZEDALE CT
8 ROYLES BROOK CL

C1
1 BRIAR MEWS
2 BRAY HEYS
3 EDGEWAY PL
4 LAWSONS CT
5 MAYFAIR GDNS
6 LAWSWOOD
7 THORNTON CTR

D1
1 ROSEWOOD CL
2 CHATSWORTH CL
3 WILLOW TREE GDNS
4 ACACIA CL
5 FAIRHAVEN CL
6 LAMBS HILL CL

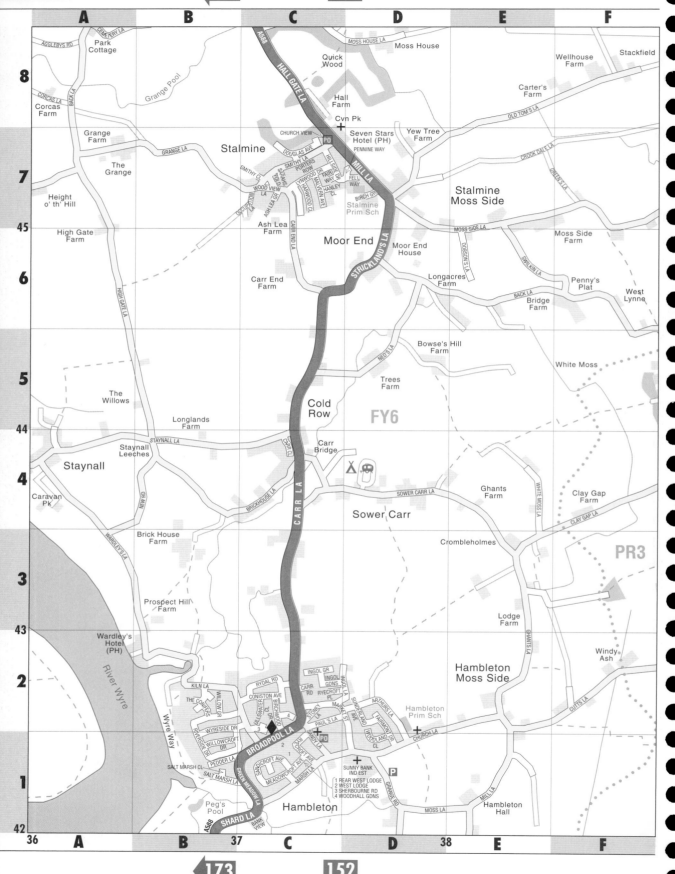

173 195

173 152

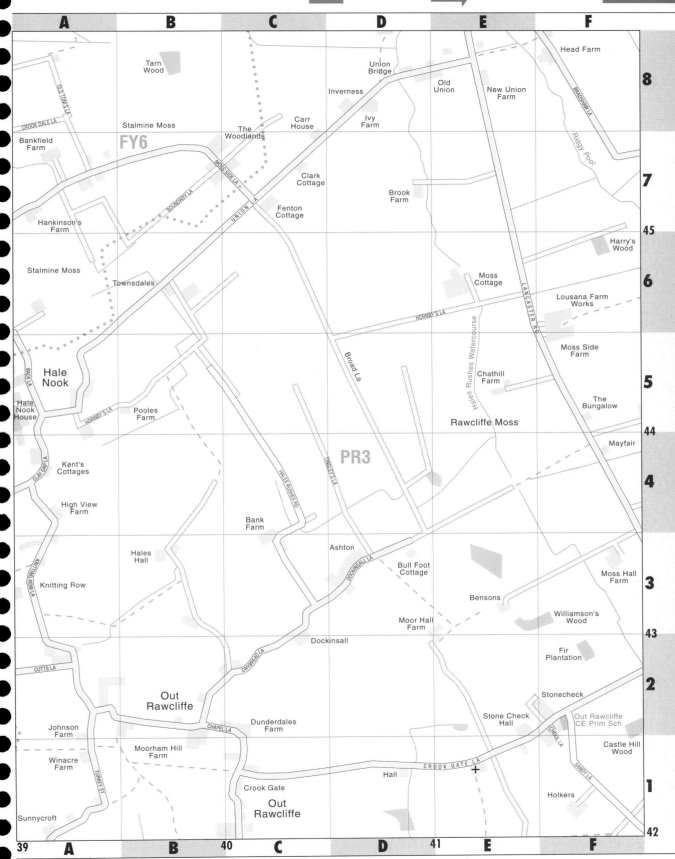

175
197

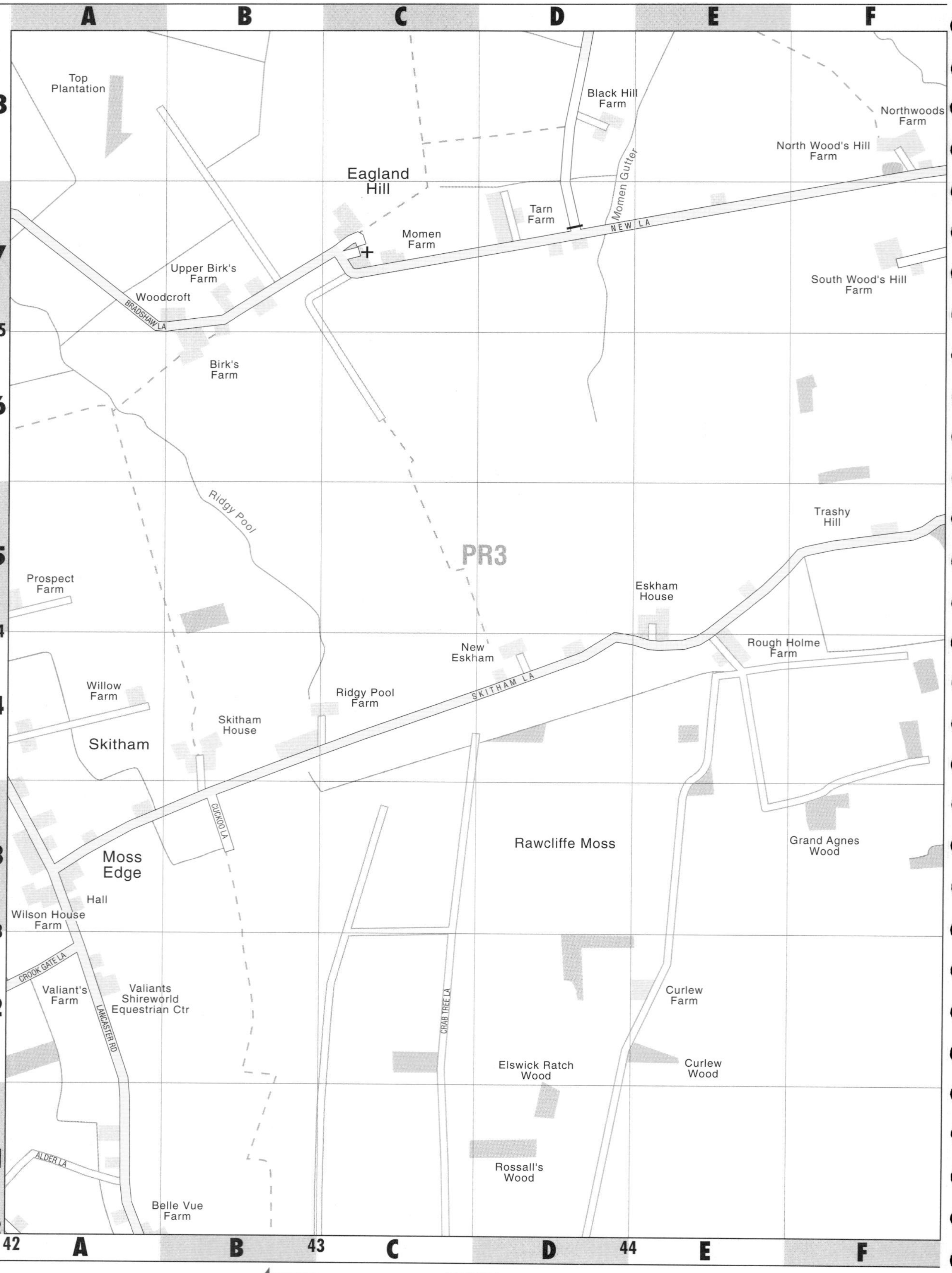

A B C D E F

8
Top Plantation
Black Hill Farm
Northwoods Farm
North Wood's Hill Farm

Eagland Hill

7
Momen Farm
Tarn Farm
Momen Gutter
NEW LA
South Wood's Hill Farm

Upper Birk's Farm
Woodcroft
BRADSHAW LA

45

Birk's Farm

6

Ridgy Pool

5
Trashy Hill

PR3

Prospect Farm
Eskham House

44
New Eskham
Rough Holme Farm

Willow Farm
Ridgy Pool Farm
SKITHAM LA

4
Skitham House

Skitham

CUCKOO LA

3
Moss Edge
Rawcliffe Moss
Grand Agnes Wood

Hall
Wilson House Farm

43
CROOK GATE LA
Valiant's Farm
Valiants Shireworld Equestrian Ctr
LANCASTER RD
CRAB TREE LA
Curlew Farm

2
Elswick Ratch Wood
Curlew Wood

1
ALDER LA
Rossall's Wood

42
Belle Vue Farm

42 A B 43 C D 44 E F

175
154

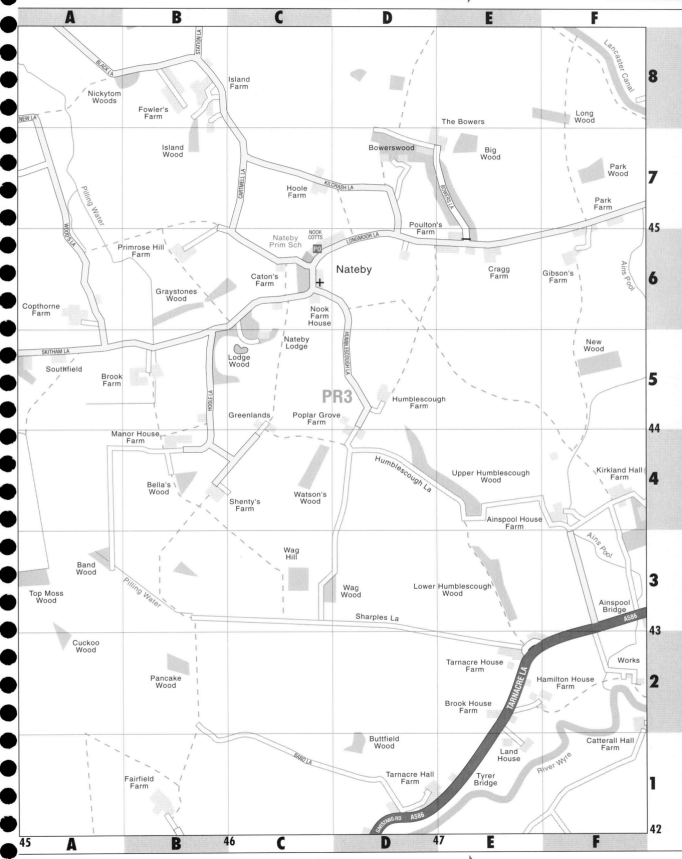

A B C D E F

8
7
45
6
5
44
4
3
43
2
1
42

Lancaster Canal

Nickytom Woods
Fowler's Farm
Island Farm
Island Wood
Hoole Farm
KILCRASH LA
STATION LA
BLACK LA
NEW LA
WOOD'S LA
CARTMELL LA
Pilling Water
Primrose Hill Farm
Nateby Prim Sch
NOOK COTTS
PO
Nateby
Caton's Farm
Graystones Wood
Copthorne Farm
Nook Farm House
Nateby Lodge
Lodge Wood
SKITHAM LA
Southfield
Brook Farm
HOOLE LA
Greenlands
Manor House Farm
PR3
Poplar Grove Farm
HUMBLESCOUGH LA
Humblescough Farm
Bella's Wood
Shenty's Farm
Watson's Wood
Humblescough La
Upper Humblescough Wood
Kirkland Hall Farm
Ainspool House Farm
Ains Pool
Band Wood
Top Moss Wood
Pilling Water
Wag Hill
Wag Wood
Lower Humblescough Wood
Ainspool Bridge
A586
Sharples La
Works
Cuckoo Wood
Pancake Wood
Tarnacre House Farm
TARNACRE LA
Hamilton House Farm
BAND LA
Buttfield Wood
Brook House Farm
Land House
Catterall Hall Farm
Fairfield Farm
Tarnacre Hall Farm
Tyrer Bridge
River Wyre
GARSTANG RD A586

The Bowers
Bowerswood
Big Wood
Long Wood
Park Wood
Park Farm
BOWERS LA
Poulton's Farm
LONGMOOR LA
Cragg Farm
Gibson's Farm
Ains Pool
New Wood

45 A B 46 C D 47 E F

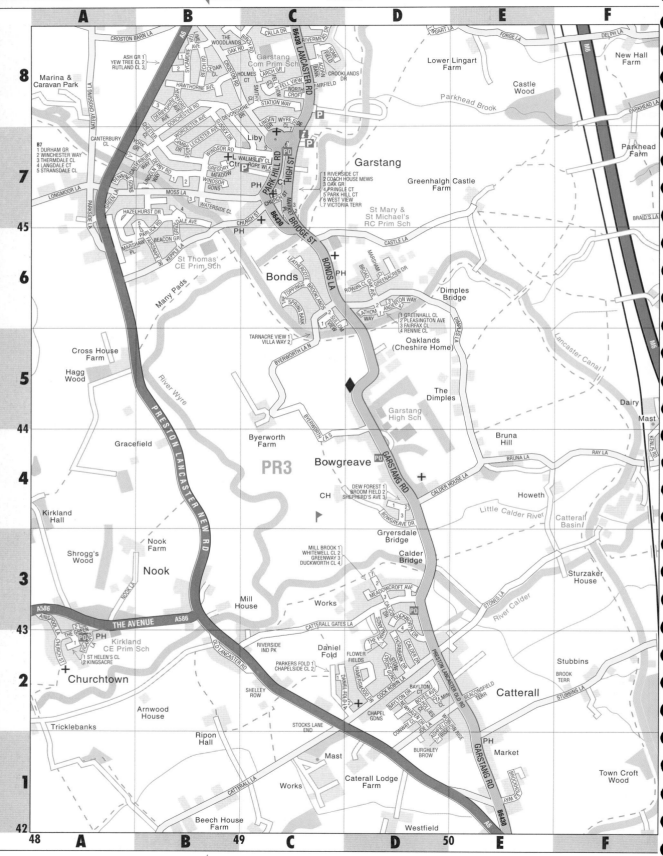

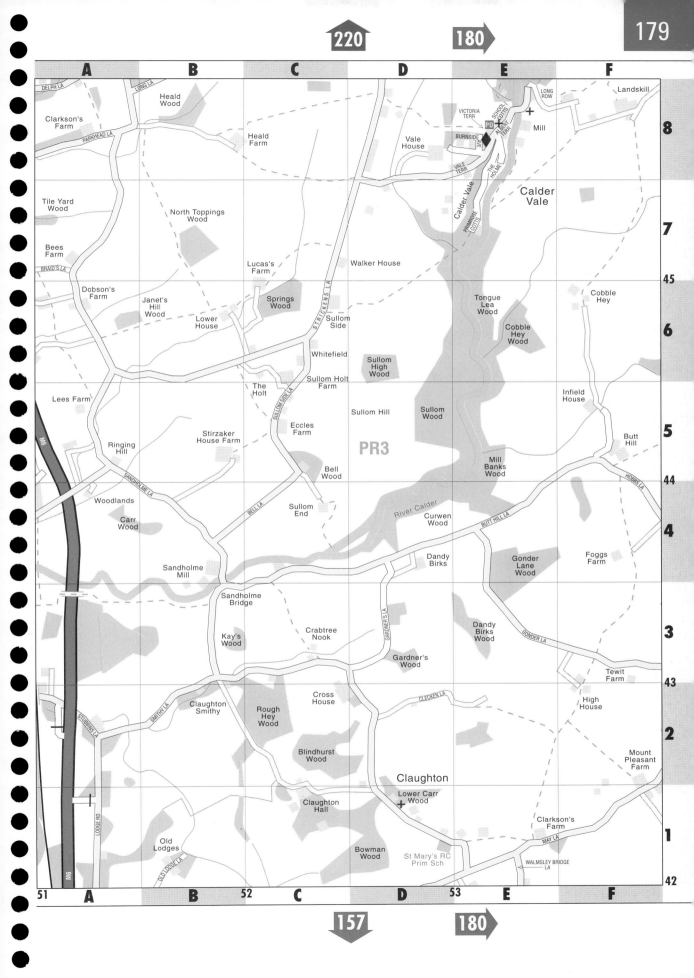

179
220

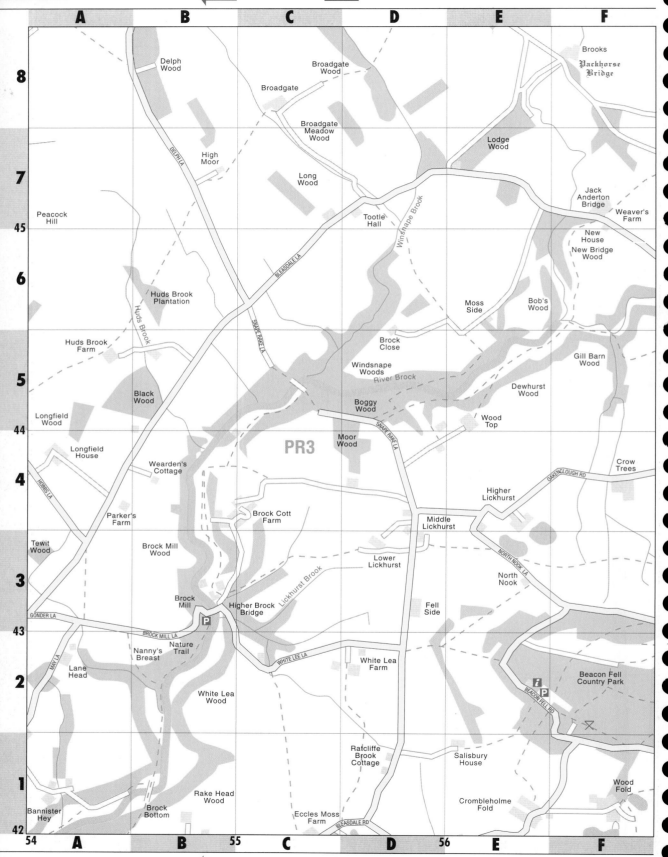

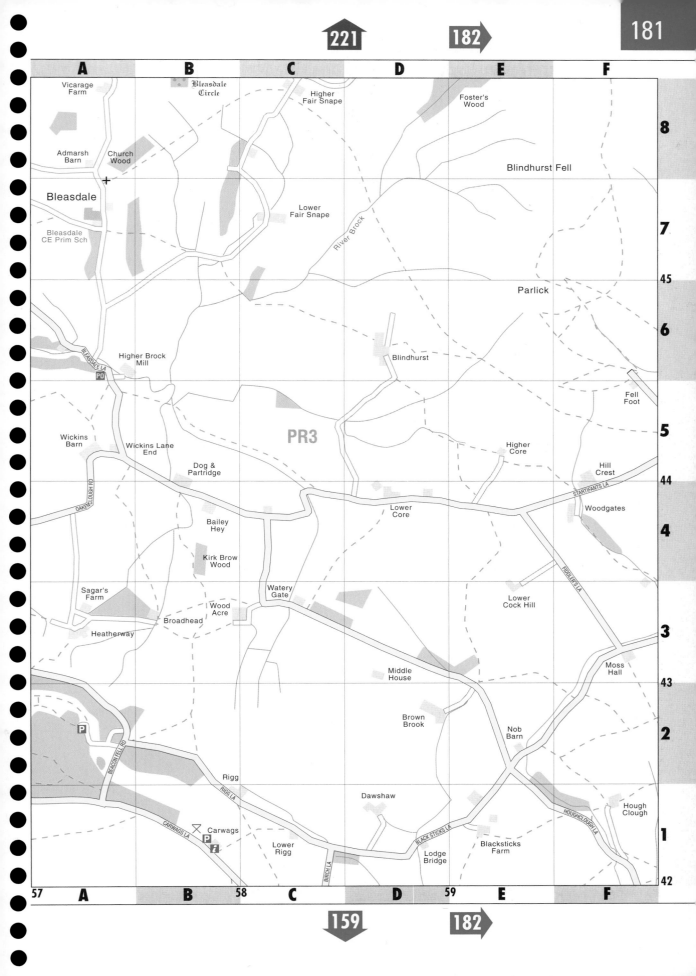

181
221

A B C D E F

8

Ward's End

Stanley

Greenough Clough

Ginney Hey

Park Gate

7

High Barn

45

Chipping Brook

Saddle End Farm

Dobson's Brook

6

Wolfen Hall

Bradley

Windy Hill Farm

Birchen Lee

Wolfen Hall Plantation

Laund Farm

Peacock Hey Farm

PR3

5

Startifants Lane End

Windy Harbour

Nan King's Farm

Leagram Hall

Startifants La

44

Fish House La

Fish House

After Lee

Works

4

Crag House

Out Lane Head

Lingey Hill

Springs House

Works

Clark House

Old Hive

The Grove

Malt Kiln Brow

Church Rake

Tweedy's Ct

3

Chipping

Kirkfield

Nirlands

Talbot St

Club La

Windy St

PH

Stanley Ct

P

PO

Green La

Green Slack

Broad Meadow

P

St Mary's RC Prim Sch

Brabins Endowed Sch

Brookfield Ct

Brooklands

Handlesteads Farm

Ferry Butts

Blackhall

43

Cold Coates

Garstang Rd

Collin's Hill La

Brickhouse Gdns

2

Cuthbert Hill

Isaac's Farm

Holton Hill

Longridge Rd

Startifants

Richmond Houses

Daub Hall

Abbot Barn

Radcliffe Hall

New House

Chipping Brook

Black House La

Parsonage La

Goose La

Sewage Works

1

Goose La Cotts

Dairy Farm

Moss La

Hall Trees Farm

42

60 A 61 B C 62 D E F

181
160

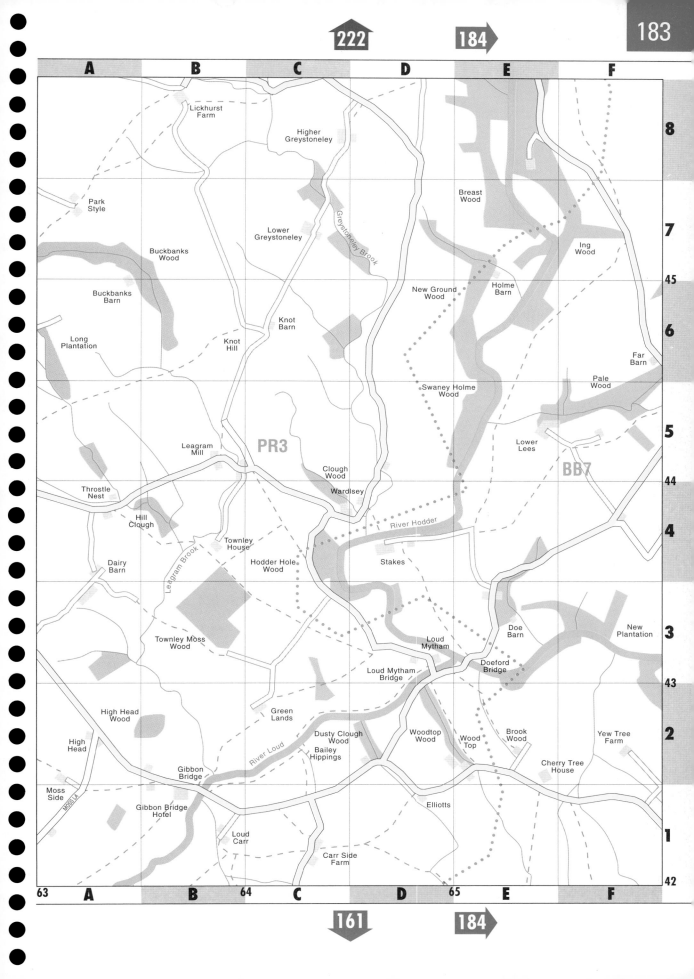

A   B   C   D   E   F

8
7
45
6
5
44
4
3
43
2
1
42

Lickhurst Farm

Higher Greystoneley

Park Style

Breast Wood

Ing Wood

Lower Greystoneley

Buckbanks Wood

Greystoneley Brook

Buckbanks Barn

New Ground Wood

Holme Barn

Far Barn

Long Plantation

Knot Barn

Knot Hill

Pale Wood

Swaney Holme Wood

Leagram Mill

PR3

Clough Wood

Wardlsey

Lower Lees

BB7

Throstle Nest

Hill Clough

River Hodder

Dairy Barn

Townley House

Hodder Hole Wood

Stakes

Leagram Brook

Doe Barn

New Plantation

Townley Moss Wood

Loud Mytham

Doeford Bridge

Loud Mytham Bridge

High Head Wood

Green Lands

Dusty Clough Wood

Woodtop Wood

Wood Top

Brook Wood

Yew Tree Farm

High Head

River Loud

Bailey Hippings

Gibbon Bridge

Cherry Tree House

Moss Side

MOSS LA

Gibbon Bridge Hotel

Loud Carr

Elliotts

Carr Side Farm

63   A   B   64   C   D   65   E   F

42

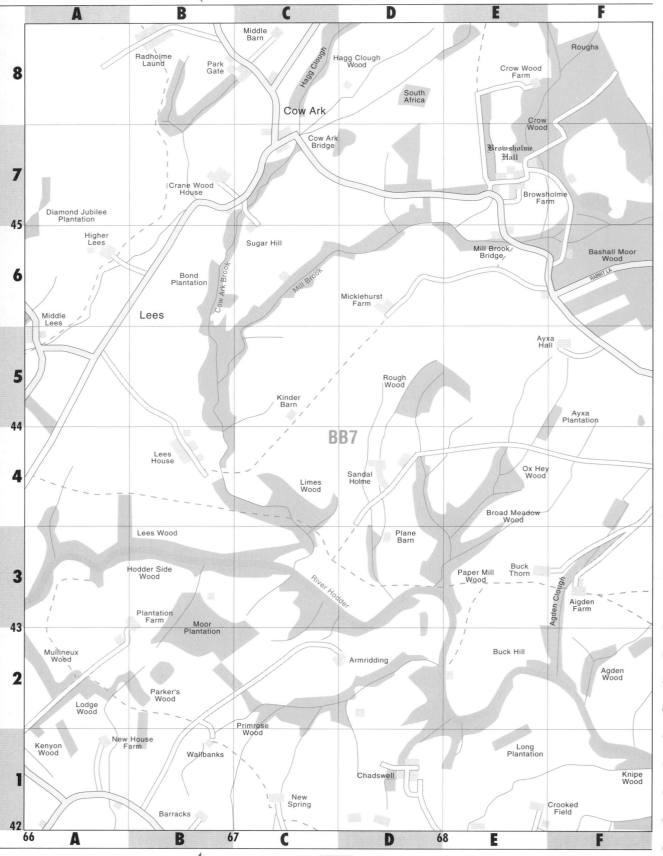

183
222
183
162

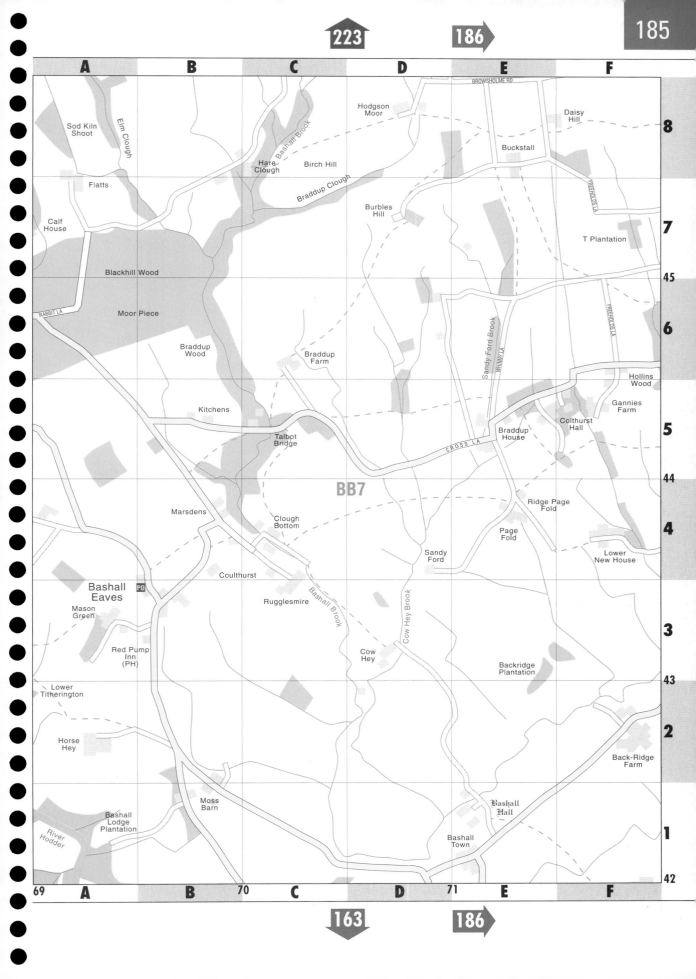

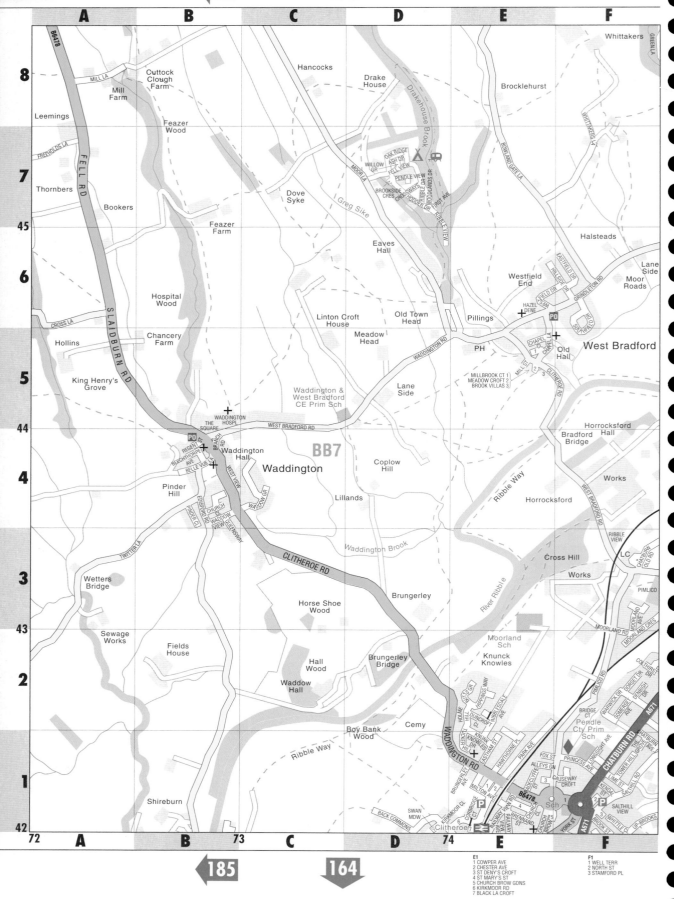

185
223

A B C D E F

8
7
45
6
5
44
4
3
43
2
1
42

72 A B 73 C D 74 E F

185
164

Whittakers
GREENLA
Brocklehurst
Drakehouse Brook
WHITTAKERS LA
BOWLAND GATE LA
Halsteads
Lane Side
Moor Roads
EASTFIELD DR
HILLSIDE DR
GRINDLETON RD
Westfield End
HAZEL DENE
PO
West Bradford
Pillings
PH
CHAPEL CL
Old Hall
MILL ST
CLITHEROE RD
MILLBROOK CT 1
MEADOW CROFT 2
BROOK VILLAS 3
Horrocksford Hall
Bradford Bridge
Works
RIBBLE VIEW
LC
WEST BRADFORD RD
Ribble Way
Horrocksford
Cross Hill
Works
PIMLICO
DARKBURN OLD RD
COLTHURST DR

Leemings
B6478
MILL LA
Cuttock Clough Farm
Mill Farm
Hancocks
Drake House
Oak Ridge
ASH DR
WILLOW GR
FELL VIEW
PENDLE VIEW
BROOKSIDE CRES
MOOR LA
Greg Sike
Feazer Wood
Dove Syke
Eaves Hall
Westfield End
Thornbers
FREEHOLDS LA
FELL RD
Bookers
Feazer Farm
Hospital Wood
CROSS LA
SLAIDBURN RD
Hollins
Chancery Farm
King Henry's Grove
Linton Croft House
Old Town Head
Meadow Head
WADDINGTON RD
Lane Side
Waddington & West Bradford CE Prim Sch
BB7
Coplow Hill
THE SQUARE
WADDINGTON HOSPL
BRANCH RD
PO
REGENT ST
BEECHTHORPE AVE
BELLE VUE
Waddington Hall
WEST VIEW
MEADOW GR
Waddington
Lillands
EDISFORD RD
PINDER CL
Pinder Hill
CHURCH OF WADDINGTON VIEW
QUEENSWAY
TWITTER LA
Wetters Bridge
Horse Shoe Wood
CLITHEROE RD
Brungerley
Waddington Brook
River Ribble
Ribble Way
Cross Hill
Works
Sewage Works
Fields House
Hall Wood
Brungerley Bridge
Moorland Sch
Knunck Knowles
MOORLAND RD
MOORLAND AVE
MOORLAND CRES
Waddow Hall
Cemy
Boy Bank Wood
WADDINGTON RD
TIPPINGS WAY
RIBBLESDALE AVE
Pendle Cty Prim Sch
BRIDGE CT
WARWICK DR
DORSET DR
SOMERSET AVE
A671
CHATBURN RD
Shireburn
SWAN MDW
BACK COMMONS
Clitheroe
KIRKMOOR RD
CARBRIDGE CT
Sch
RAILWAY VIEW
MILTON AVE
B6478
FOX ST
ALLEYS GN
CAUSEWAY CROFT
PRINCESS AVE
LIME ST
TOWER HILL
SALTHILL RD
KENDAL ST
SALTHILL VIEW
YORK ST
A671
UP-BROOKS

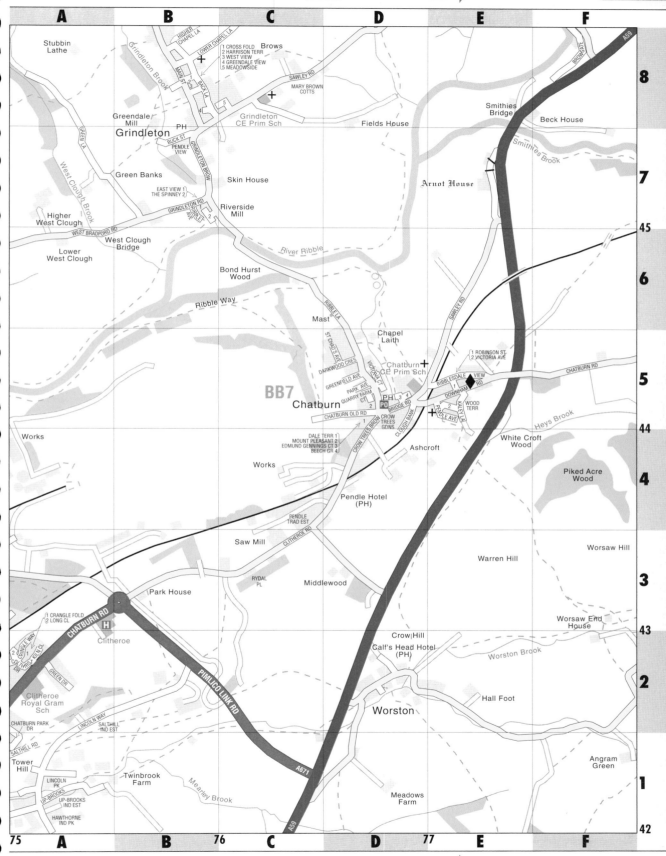

A B C D E F

8
7
45
6
5
44
4
3
43
2
1
42

Stubbin Lathe

Grindleton Brook

HIGHER CHAPEL LA
LOWER CHAPEL LA

1 CROSS FOLD
2 HARRISON TERR
3 WEST VIEW
4 GREENDALE VIEW
5 MEADOWSIDE

Brows

SAWLEY RD

MARY BROWN COTTS

Fields House

Smithies Bridge

A59
BROWGATE

Beck House

Greendale Mill

Grindleton CE Prim Sch

Smithies Brook

PH
Grindleton

MAIN ST
BACK LA
BUCK ST
PENDLE VIEW

Green Banks

GRINDLETON BROW

EAST VIEW 1
THE SPINNEY 2

Skin House

Arnot House

GREEN LA
WEST CLOUGH BROOK

Higher West Clough

GRINDLETON RD
RIBBLE A VIEW

Riverside Mill

SAWLEY RD

WEST BRADFORD RD

West Clough Bridge

Lower West Clough

River Ribble

45

Bond Hurst Wood

Ribble Way

Mast

RIBBLE LA

Chapel Laith

1 ROBINSON ST
2 VICTORIA AVE

CHATBURN RD

ST CHAD SAVE

DARKWOOD CRES

Chatburn CE Prim Sch

RIBBLESDALE VIEW

Works

GREENFIELD AVE

PARK AVE

QUARRY FARM CT

VICTORIA CT

PH
PO
BRIDGE RD

DOWNHAM RD

KALEY LA

PENDLE AVE

WOOD TERR

BB7

Chatburn

CHATBURN OLD RD

CROW TREES GDNS

White Croft Wood

44

Works

DALE TERR 1
MOUNT PLEASANT 2
EDMUND GENNINGS CT 3
BEECH GR 4

CROW TREES BROW

Ashcroft

CLOUGH BANK

Piked Acre Wood

Works

Pendle Hotel (PH)

4

PENDLE TRAD EST

Saw Mill

CLITHEROE RD

Worsaw Hill

Warren Hill

Middlewood

RYDAL PL

3

Park House

1 CRANGLE FOLD
2 LONG CL

Worsaw End House

43

CHATBURN RD

H
Clitheroe

Crow Hill

Calf's Head Hotel (PH)

Worston Brook

GRINGE WAY
GREEN DR
MRS KILN CL

PIMLICO LINK RD

2

Clitheroe Royal Gram Sch

Hall Foot

Chatburn Park Dr

LINCOLN WAY

SALTHILL IND EST

Worston

SALTHILL RD

Tower Hill

LINCOLN PK

UP-BROOKS
UP-BROOKS IND EST

Twinbrook Farm

Mearley Brook

A671

A59

Meadows Farm

Angram Green

1

HAWTHORNE IND PK

42

75 A B 76 C D 77 E F

187
224

A B C D E F

8

Swanside Beck

Kelriddin

CARRS CROFT 1
PENDLE TERR 2
STATION RD
BACK LA
PH
STOOPS LA

West Croft

Rimington

Denis Field

Low Laithe

Downham Bridge

RIMINGTON LA

Bustards Farm

7

Falshaw Wood

The Wood

Stubs Wood

New Field Wood

Mill

45

Ings Beck

Newfield Barn

GREEN LA

Hey House Wood

Torrid Bank Wood

6

Downham Green

Hey House Farm

Twiston Beck

Hall Royds Wood

Springs

Woolly Hill

Twiston Mill

CHATBURN RD

PH
PO

Smithfield Farm

TWISTON LA

5

Downham Hall

Downham

New Close

Downham Beck

P

44

BB7

Cat Gallows Wood

Lane Side

Clay House

Score Clough Beck

4

WEST LA

Hollin's Farm

Hecklin Farm

Longlands Wood

Gerna Hill

Gerna

Lane Head

PENDLE RD

Ravens Holme

3

Worsaw End

Ridding Wood

Hookcliffe Plantation

43

Radbrook

Rad Brook

Hook Cliffe

Hook Cliffe

2

Barkerfield

Moorside

1

Downham Moor

BB9

Burst Clough

42

78 A B 79 C D 80 E F

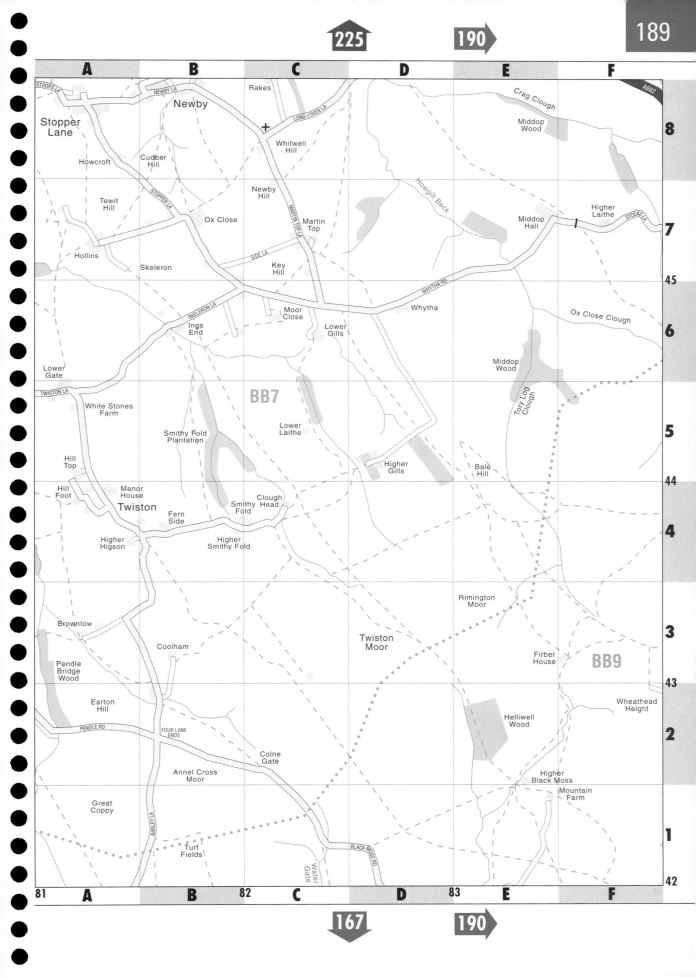

189
225

A B C D E F

8

Little Middop

Lane Side

COAL PIT LA

BROGDEN LA

Higher Clough

Brown Hill

Far New Field Edge

Hill Cloughs

ESP LA

7

Stocks House

STOCKS LA

New Field Edge Hall Farm

BB7

COAL PIT LA

Weets

FOLLY LA

Higher View Farm

New House

45

GISBURN OLD RD

Level of Weets

BB18

Ridge of Weets

Weets Hill

Prospect House

6

Crag

Duck Pond

FOLLY LA

Crag Clough

Sunny Bank

Cold Weather House

Mast

Weets House Farm

5

Sandyford

44

Craven Laithe

Greystone Moor

Star Hall

LISTER WELL RD

4

BB9

Greystone

Pendle Way

GISBURN OLD RD

3

Jackson Slack Hill

Burn Moor

Moorcock Inn (PH)

Admergill Pasture

Peel's House

Wham Clough

43

Jackson's House

Wicken Clough

Greenbank Farm

Brown House

2

Burn Moor End

Admergill Water

Higher Admergill

Higher Wheathead

Lower Admergill Farm

Tower Farm

Pasture Head Farm

Claude's Clough

Stansfield Tower

Malkin Tower

1

Height House

Blacko Hill

Blacko Hill Side

Hollin Hall

A682

42

84 A 85 B C 85 D 86 E F

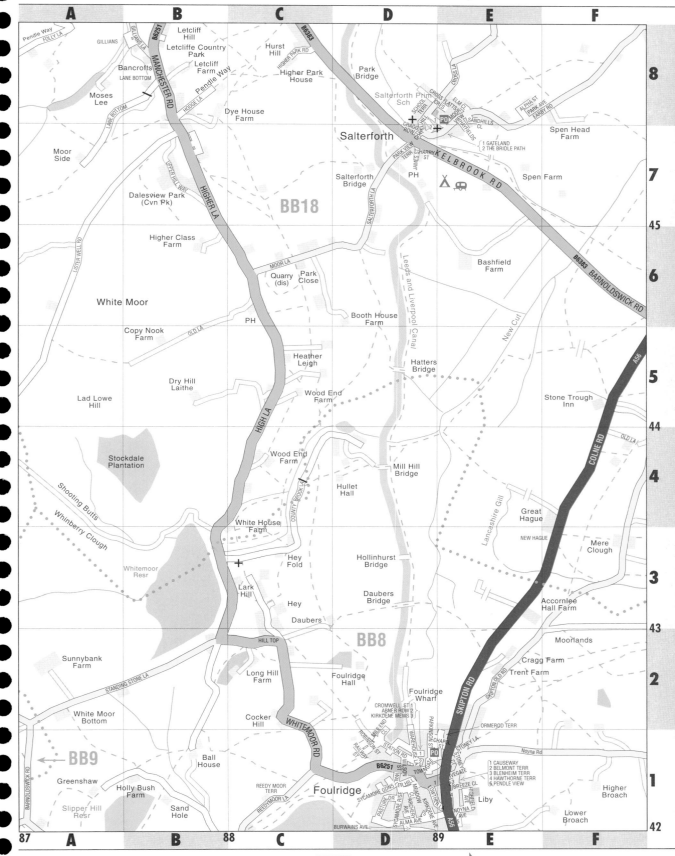

A   B   C   D   E   F

8
7
45
6
5
44
4
3
43
2
1
42

Pendle Way
FOLLY LA
GILLIANS
GILLIANS LA
B6251
Letcliff Hill
Letcliffe Country Park
Letcliff Farm
Bancrofts
LANE BOTTOM
Hurst Hill
B6383
Higher Park House
HIGHER PARK RD
Park Bridge
Moses Lee
LANE BOTTOM
MANCHESTER RD
HODGE LA
Pendle Way
Dye House Farm
Salterforth Prim Sch
CROSS FLATTS CL
ELM CL
CRESS LA
ALPHA ST
PARK AVE
EARBY RD
SANDHILLS CL
Spen Head Farm
Moor Side
UPPER HILL WAY
HIGHER LA
Salterforth
SCHOOL TERR
CRAGGS ROW
PO
1 GATELAND
2 THE BRIDLE PATH
Dalesview Park (Cvn Pk)
Salterforth Bridge
PARK TERR
PARK VIEW TERR
ST JAMES'S ST
HARRY ST
PH
KELBROOK RD
Spen Farm
Higher Class Farm
SALTERFORTH LA
B6383 BARNOLDSWICK RD
LISTER WELL RD
MOOR LA
Quarry (dis)
Park Close
Bashfield Farm
BB18
White Moor
PH
Booth House Farm
Leeds and Liverpool Canal
New Cut
A56
OLD LA
Copy Nook Farm
OLD LA
HIGH LA
Heather Leigh
Hatters Bridge
Stone Trough Inn
Dry Hill Laithe
Wood End Farm
COLNE RD
Lad Lowe Hill
Mill Hill Bridge
Lancashire Gill
Great Hague
NEW HAGUE
Mere Clough
Stockdale Plantation
Wood End Farm
COUNTY BROOK LA
Hullet Hall
Shooting Butts
White House Farm
Hollinhurst Bridge
Whinberry Clough
Accornlee Hall Farm
Whitemoor Resr
Hey Fold
Daubers Bridge
Moorlands
Lark Hill
Hey
BB8
Cragg Farm
Trent Farm
Sunnybank Farm
Daubers
SKIPTON OLD RD
SKIPTON RD
STANDING STONE LA
HILL TOP
Long Hill Farm
Foulridge Hall
Foulridge Wharf
ORMEROD TERR
White Moor Bottom
Cocker Hill
WHITEMOOR RD
CROMWELL ST 1
ABNER ROW 2
KIRKDENE MEWS 3
WAREHOUSE LA
PARRINSON ST
CHAPEL ST
STONEY LA
Noyna Rd
BB9
BARNOLDSWICK RD
Ball House
REEDY MOOR TERR
REEDYMOOR LA
RAILWAY ST
ROBINSON ST
STATION RD
WILSON ST
MILL EN
TOWNGATE
WALTERS CL
PO
LOVEGATE
B6251
SKIPTON RD
1 CAUSEWAY
2 BELMONT TERR
3 BLENHEIM TERR
4 HAWTHORNE TERR
5 PENDLE VIEW
Greenshaw
Holly Bush Farm
Sand Hole
Slipper Hill Resr
Foulridge
PASTURE RISE
SYCAMORE GDNS
SYCAMORE DR
FIR HILL
MEADOW CROFT
KIRKSTONE AVE
LOWTHER AVE
CHESTERFIELD AVE
NOYNA AVE
A56
BREEZE CL
Liby
Higher Broach
BURWAINS AVE
ALMA AVE
Lower Broach

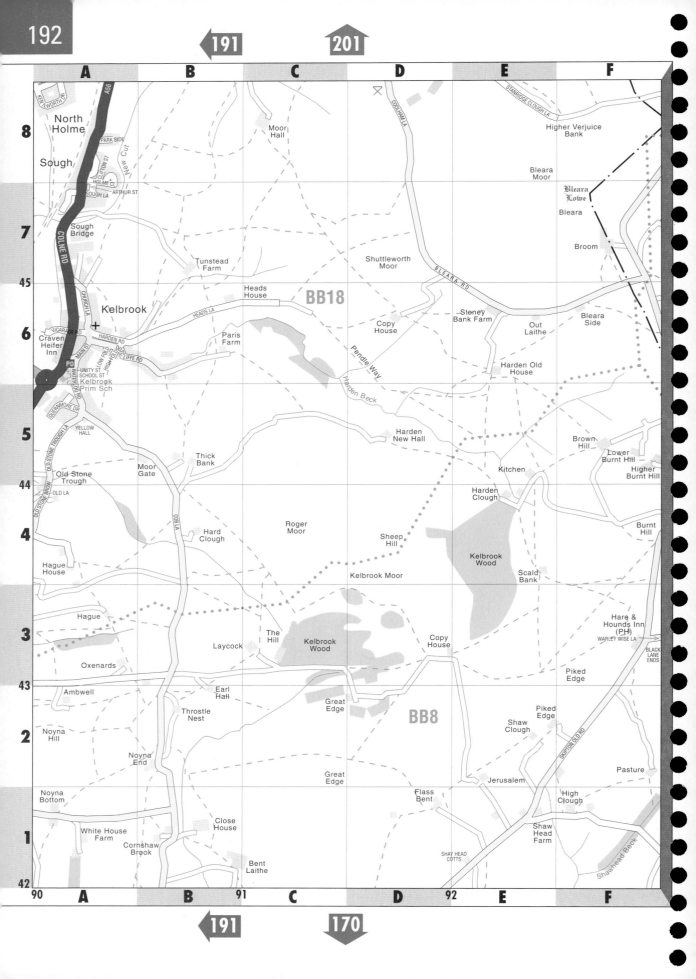

191
201

A B C D E F

8
North Holme
Sough
Moor Hall
Higher Verjuice Bank
Bleara Moor
Bleara Lowe
Bleara

PARK SIDE
KENWORTH PL
CLIFTON ST
HOLME CL
ARTHUR ST
SOUGH LA
NEW CUT

7
Sough Bridge
Tunstead Farm
Shuttleworth Moor
Broom

COLNE RD

45
Heads House
BB18
BLEARA RD

6
Kelbrook
Craven Heifer Inn
PO
Paris Farm
Copy House
Stoney Bank Farm
Out Laithe
Bleara Side

VICARAGE RD
CHURCH LA
HARDEN RD
MAIN ST
LOW FOLD
HIGH FOLD
DOTCLIFFE RD
HEADS LA

Harden Old House
Bleara Lowe

UNITY ST
SCHOOL ST
Kelbrook Prim Sch
WATERLOO RD

Pendle Way
Harden Beck

5
OVERMOOR DR
YELLOW HALL
Thick Bank
Harden New Hall
Kitchen
Brown Hill
Lower Burnt Hill
Higher Burnt Hill

44
Old Stone Trough
Moor Gate
Harden Clough

OLD STONE BROW
OLD STONE TROUGH LA
OLD LA

4
Hague House
COB LA
Hard Clough
Roger Moor
Sheep Hill
Kelbrook Wood
Scald Bank
Burnt Hill

Kelbrook Moor

3
Hague
Oxenards
The Hill
Laycock
Kelbrook Wood
Copy House
Hare & Hounds Inn (PH)
Piked Edge

WARLEY WISE LA
BLACK LANE ENDS

43
Ambwell
Earl Hall
Great Edge
BB8
Piked Edge
Shaw Clough

2
Noyna Hill
Throstle Nest
Noyna End
Great Edge
Jerusalem
Pasture
High Clough

SKIPTON OLD RD

1
Noyna Bottom
White House Farm
Cornshaw Brook
Close House
Flass Bent
Shaw Head Farm

Bent Laithe
SHAY HEAD COTTS
Shawhead Beck

42

90 A 91 B C 91 D 92 E F

191
170

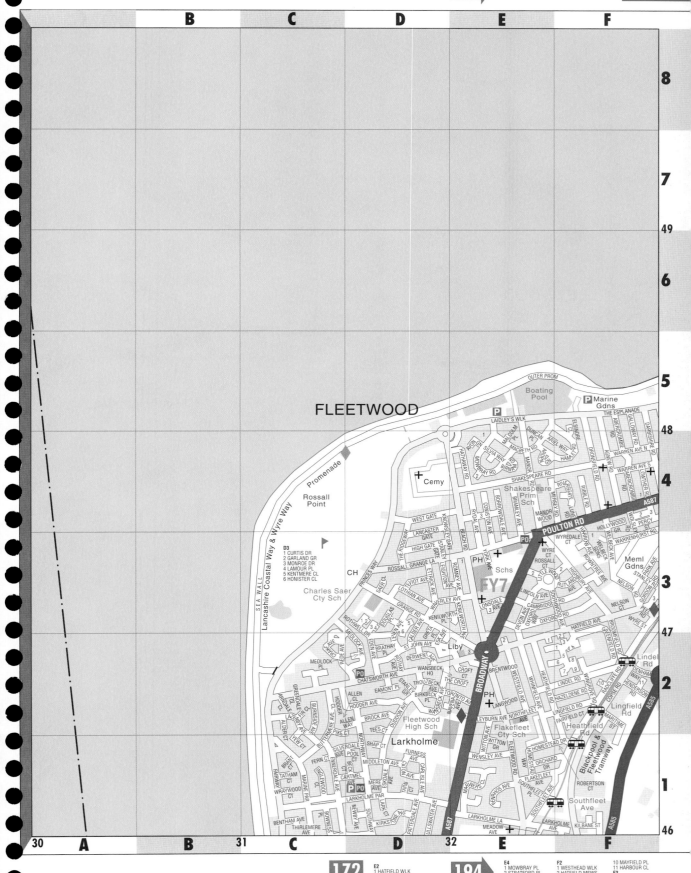

FLEETWOOD

Boating Pool

Marine Gdns

The Esplanade

Outer Prom

Promenade

Rossall Point

Cemy

Shakespeare Prim Sch

POULTON RD

A587

Meml Gdns

FY7

West Gate

Lancaster Gate

High Gate

D3
1 CURTIS DR
2 GARLAND GR
3 MONROE DR
4 LAMOUR PL
5 KENTMERE CL
6 HONISTER CL

CH

Charles Saer Cty Sch

SEA WALL

Lancashire Coastal Way & Wyre Way

Liby

BROADWAY

Lindel Rd

Lingfield Rd

Heathfield Rd

Fleetwood High Sch

Flakefleet Cty Sch

Larkholme

Blackpool & Fleetwood Tramway

Robertson Ct

Southfleet Ave

A585

A587

Bentham Ave

Thirlemere Ave

Larkholme La

Meadow Ave

Kilbane St

Larkholme Ave

A B C D E F

8

7

49

6

FLEETWOOD

Pier

5

48

4

3

47

2

1

46

33 A B 34 C D 35 E F

LB Sta
Ct
Lyndale Ct

Ferry P
Fleetwood Ferry

B5
1 WINDSOR PL
2 PHAROS GR
3 WESLEY CT
4 LIGHTHOUSE CL
5 ARTHUR ST N
6 ARTHUR ST
7 LOWER LUNE ST
8 PHAROS CT
9 ELIZABETH ST
10 CHERRY TREE CT
11 ALBERT SQ
12 NORTH ALBERT ST
13 LIFEBOAT PL

Outer Prom
The Esplanade
Pharos St
THE MOUNT
ABBOTTS WLK
BURNS RD
DRYDEN RD
CARR RD
TENNYSON RD
CHAUCER RD
PH
POULTON RD
A587
WARRENHURST RD
BELMONT RD
DEEPDALE RD
PARK VIEW
KEATING CT
Stanley Rd
BROWN ST
HERRING ARM RD

Liby
Preston St
Church St
1 MILL LA
2 CHAPMAN CT
3 CORN MILL LA
4 BRIDGE RD
5 BAY SIDE

Mus
Victoria St/Mkt
Mkt
Ferry Terminal

Blackpool & Fleetwood Tramway
AMOUNDERNESS WAY
A585
DOCK ST
Fisherman's Wlk (Arm St)
ANCHORAGE RD

1 SEAVIEW WAY
2 QUAYSIDE
3 ANCHORAGE MEWS
4 HARBOUR WAY
5 MARINA MEWS

FY7
Freeport Village

Docks

Works

Bird Sanctuary

Waste Water Treatment Works

Refuse Tip

River Wyre

Ferry P

RAMSAY CT 1
FYLDE CT 2
ASHTON CT 3
WESTBOURNE CT 4
ADDISON CT 5
OCEAN CT 6

Lancashire Coastal Way
B5270
BOURNE MAY RD
PH
ESPLANADE
WAYSIDE
ASHTON AVE
WESTBOURNE RD
WORSLEY CL
Quail Holme Rd
PARKSWAY
WYRESDALE RD
BLEASDALE RD
LINKS RD
THE GLEN
HACKENSALL RD
FAIRWAY
GH

LUNE VIEW AVE
CLARENCE AVE
WYRE
BEECH GR
ST BRADOC'S
YMEGR
PO
L Ctr Liby
SALISBURY AVE
BARTON AVE
HOLMEFIELD RD

LANCASTER RD
B5270
CONISTON AVE
GRANGE
RYDAL
KINGSTON CL
ESDALE GR
KESAD RD
DERWENT
GRASMERE RD
THIRLMERE CL
LANCASTER DR
ESDE GR
KESWICK CL
WILKINSON WAY
BUTTERMERE DR

1 PLANTATION AVE
2 ELTERWATER
3 BARTON SQ
4 SALISBURY CT

Knott End-on-Sea

FY6

MEADOW LA

Hackensall Hall

Hackensall Brows

WHINNY LA
WHINNY LA

Wyre Way

Heys Farm

Curwens Hill

Cote Walls Farm

Arm Hill

MONK'S LA

CONSCARFE CL

AGGLEBYS RD

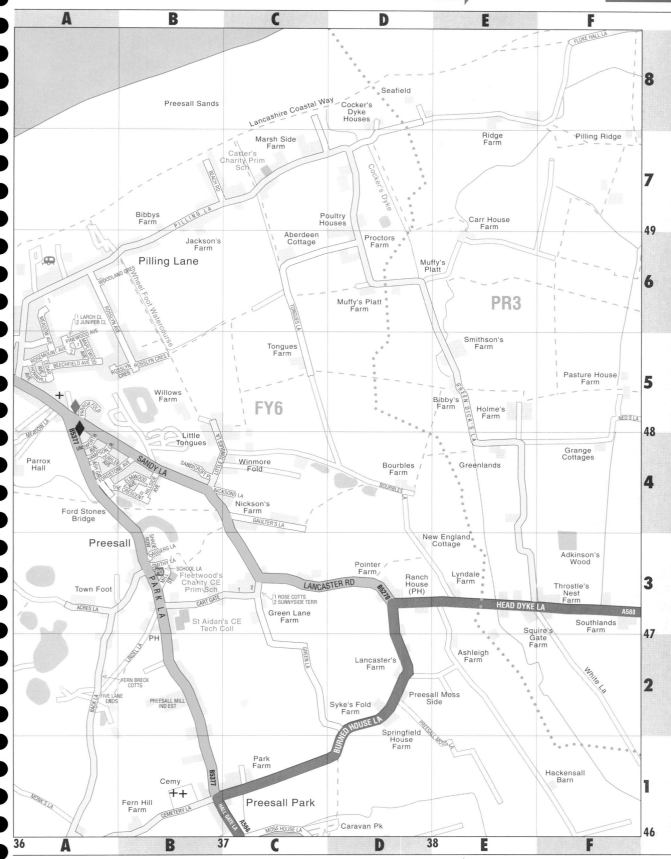

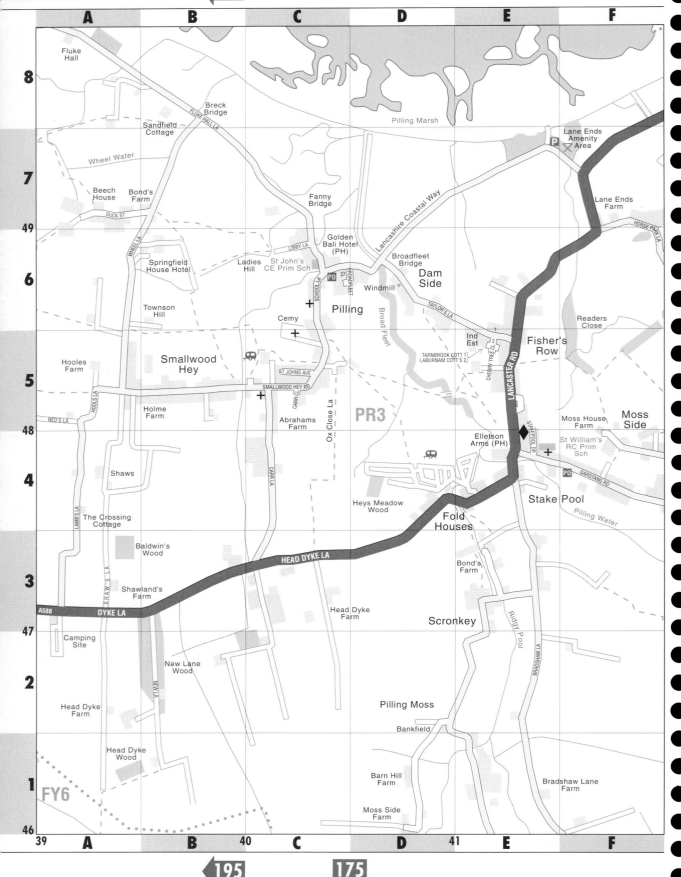

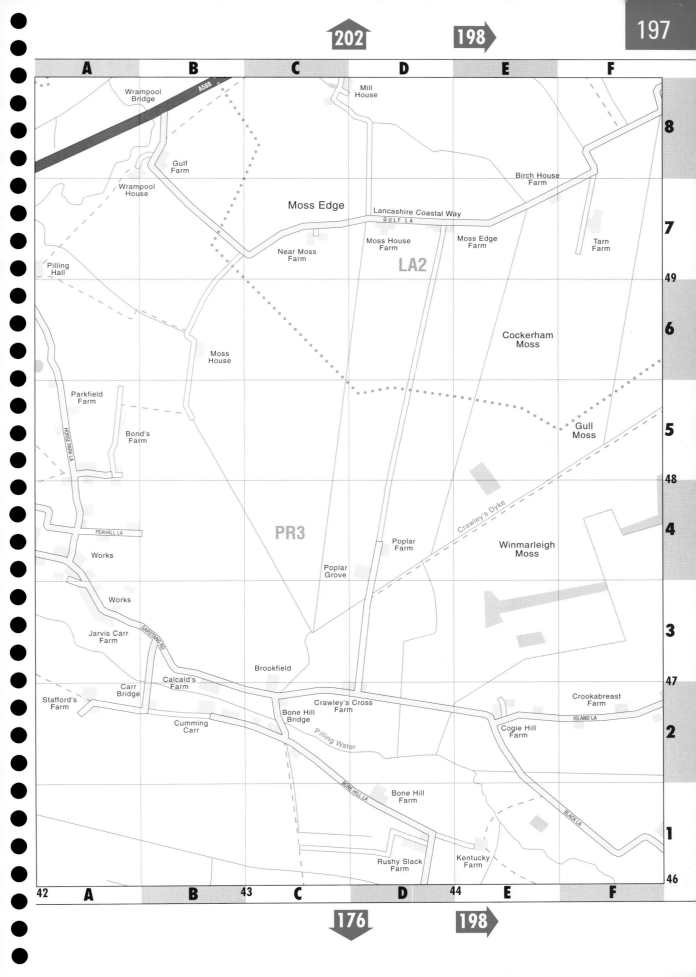

202
198

A   B   C   D   E   F

Wrampool Bridge

A588

8

Gulf Farm

Wrampool House

Mill House

Birch House Farm

Moss Edge

Lancashire Coastal Way

7

GULF LA

Moss House Farm

Moss Edge Farm

Tarn Farm

Near Moss Farm

Pilling Hall

LA2

49

Cockerham Moss

6

Moss House

Parkfield Farm

HORSE PARK LA

Bond's Farm

Gull Moss

5

48

PR3

PEAHALL LA

Crawley's Dyke

Winmarleigh Moss

Poplar Farm

4

Works

GARSTANG RD

Works

Poplar Grove

Jarvis Carr Farm

3

Brookfield

Calcald's Farm

Crawley's Cross Farm

47

Carr Bridge

Crookabreast Farm

Stafford's Farm

Bone Hill Bridge

ISLAND LA

Cumming Carr

Pilling Water

Cogie Hill Farm

2

BONE HILL LA

Bone Hill Farm

BLACK LA

1

Rushy Slack Farm

Kentucky Farm

46

176
198

197
203

A B C D E F

8

Harestones Wood

Moss Wood

Lathwaite

LA2

Lower House

Park Lane Brook

B5272

Park Lane Bridge

Park Lane Farm

7

Moss Side Stables

Hardhead

THOROUGH WAY

Patten Arms (PH)

PARK LA

49

Lee Brook

6

New Hall Farm

Hornby Wood

Morris Hill

EAST VIEW

Threlfalls Farm

SCHOOL LA

Black Pool

B5272

Depot

5

Caunce Grange

Throstle Nest

Cow Hey Wood

Winmarleigh CE Prim Sch

Hall

BROAD LA

Bent Meadow Wood

Vicarage

48

Old Hall Wood

THROSTLE NEST LA

PR3

+ Winmarleigh

CHURCH LA

4

Winmarleigh Moss

Gift Hall

Round Wood

Winmarleigh Hall

New House Farm

NEW HOUSE LA

Tyrer Farm

Sharples Hall

Wray Wood

Long Wood

Lee Brook

3

Gravel Hill Wood

ISLAND LA

Whitters Hill

Gibstick Hall

47

Island Wood

New Plantation

BROAD LA

Bell's Bridge

2

Island Farm

WHITTERS LA

Coventry

Ford Green

Lancaster Canal

Ford Green Bridge

NATEBY HALL LA

Nateby Bungalows

1

Black Lane Head

Black Wood

STATION LA

Elm Farm

Nateby Hall

Nateby Hall Bridge

BLACK LA

46

45 A B 46 C D 47 E F

197
177

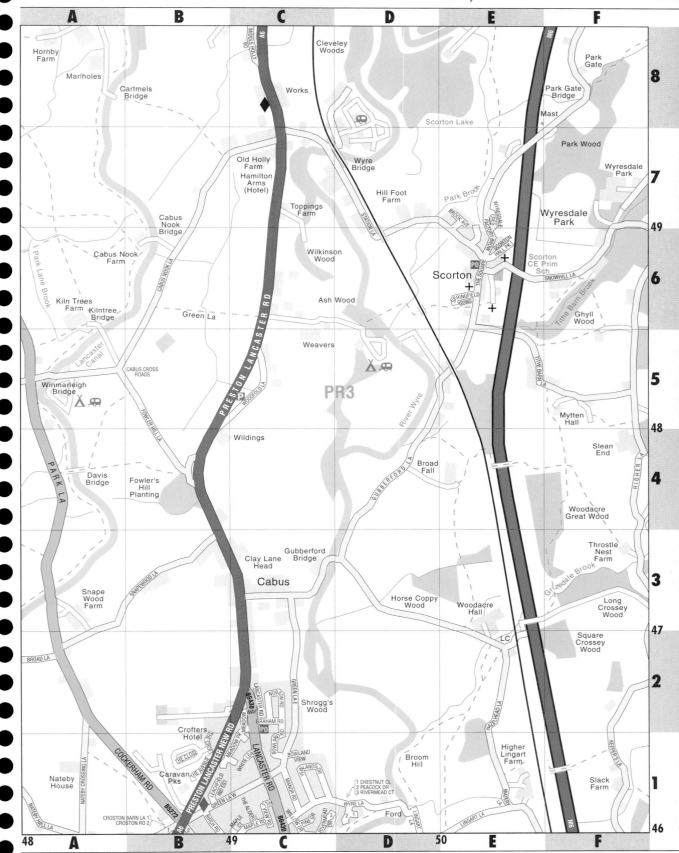

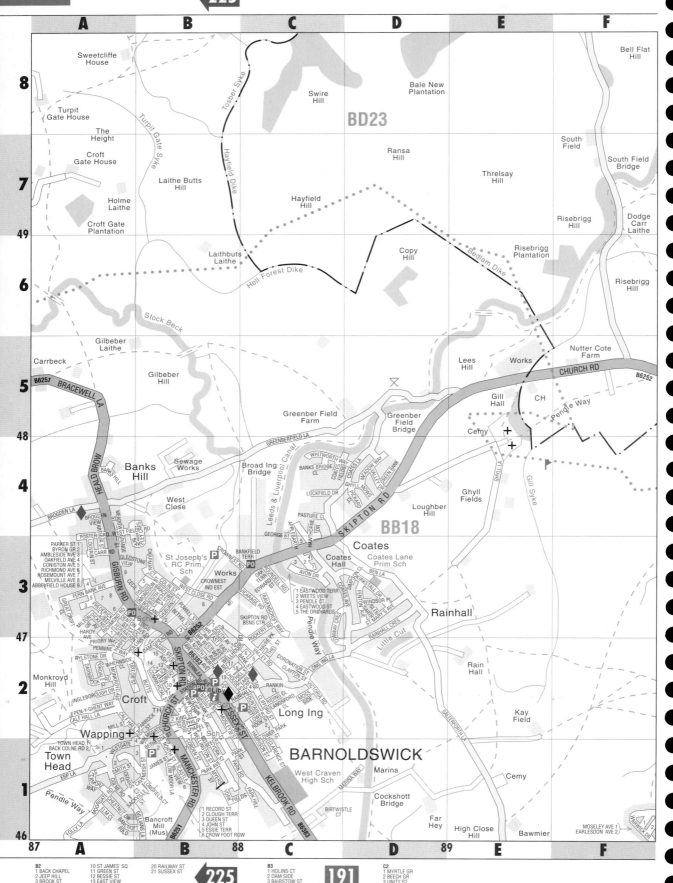

A B C D E F

8 7 49 6 5 48 4 3 47 2 1 46

87   88   89

BD23

BB18

BARNOLDSWICK

Bell Flat Hill
Sweetcliffe House
Turpit Gate House
The Height
Croft Gate House
Holme Laithe
Croft Gate Plantation
Laithe Butts Hill
Laithbuts Laithe
Swire Hill
Bale New Plantation
Ransa Hill
Threlsay Hill
South Field
South Field Bridge
Hayfield Hill
Copy Hill
Risebrigg Hill
Risebrigg Plantation
Dodge Carr Laithe
Risebrigg Hill
Hell Forest Dike
Bedlam Dike
Stock Beck
Gilbeber Laithe
Carrbeck
Gilbeber Hill
Lees Hill
Works
Nutter Cote Farm
CHURCH RD
B6252
B6257
BRACEWELL LA
Greenber Field Farm
Greenber Field Bridge
Gill Hall
CH
Pendle Way
HEALD BROW
Banks Hill
Sewage Works
Broad Ing Bridge
GREENBERFIELD LA
Cemy
Gill Syke
West Close
Loughber Hill
Ghyll Fields
Coates
Rainhall
St Joseph's RC Prim Sch
Works
CROWNEST IND EST
SKIPTON RD BSNS CTR
Coates Hall
Coates Lane Prim Sch
Monkroyd Hill
Croft
Rainhall
Rain Hall
Kay Field
Long Ing
Wapping
Town Head
Bancroft Mill (Mus)
West Craven High Sch
Marina
Cemy
Pendle Way
Cockshott Bridge
Far Hey
High Close Hill
Bawmier
MANCHESTER RD
KELBROOK RD
B6251
B6383
MOSELEY AVE 1
EARLESDON AVE 2
WARWICK DR

B2
1 BACK CHAPEL
2 JEEP HILL
3 BROOK ST
4 ORCHARD ST
5 GARDEN ST
6 MARKET ST
7 BACK SKIPTON RD
8 FORESTER'S BLDGS
9 ST JAMES' RD
10 ST JAMES' SQ
11 GREEN ST
12 BESSIE ST
13 EAST VIEW
14 PLEASANT VIEW
15 FAR EAST VIEW
16 EAST PAR
17 WELL HOUSE SQ
18 EAST HILLS ST
19 CO-OPERATIVE ST
20 RAILWAY ST
21 SUSSEX ST

B3
1 HOLINS CT
2 DAM SIDE
3 BAIRSTOW ST
4 BROGDEN ST
5 BRUCE ST
6 CORNMILL TERR
7 NORTH PAR
8 SOUTH PAR
9 MASONS WAY

C2
1 MYRTLE GR
2 BEECH GR
3 UNITY ST
4 TURNER ST
5 STUART ST
6 CRAVEN ST

1 EASTWOOD TERR
2 WEETS VIEW
3 PENDLE CT
4 EASTWOOD ST
5 THE ORCHARDS

1 RECORD ST
2 CLOUGH TERR
3 QUEEN ST
4 JOHN ST
5 ESSIE TERR
6 CROW FOOT ROW

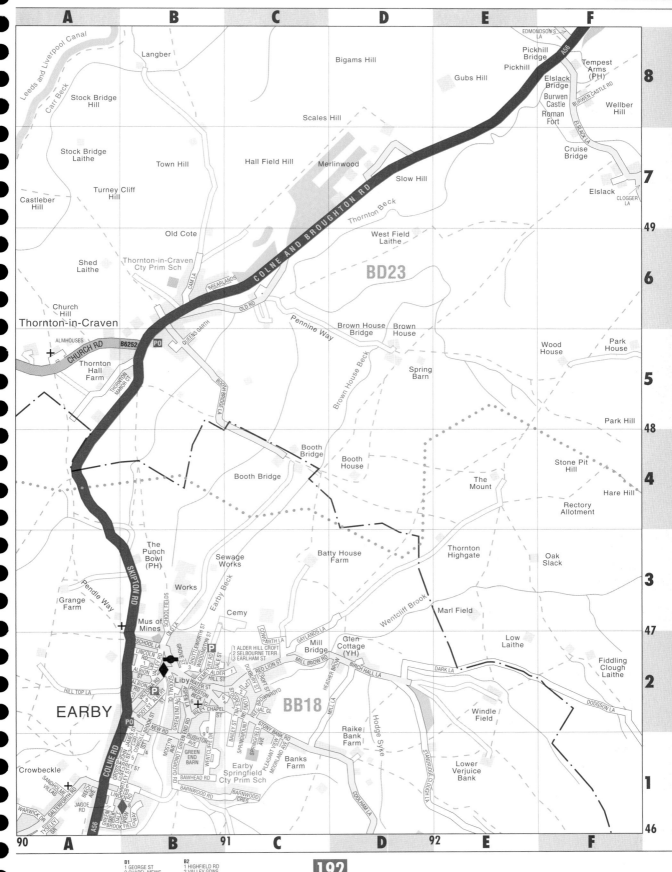

B1
1 GEORGE ST
2 CHAPEL MEWS
3 APPLEGARTH ST
4 RIVERSIDE TERR
5 WILLIAM ST
6 ROSTLE TOP RD
7 LINDEN CT
8 JAGOE MEWS
9 THE BUNGALOWS

B2
1 HIGHFIELD RD
2 VALLEY GDNS
3 LOWER CROFT ST
4 SHAW SQ
5 WELBURY CL
6 WILKINSON MOUNT
7 VICTORIA ST
8 EDWARD ST

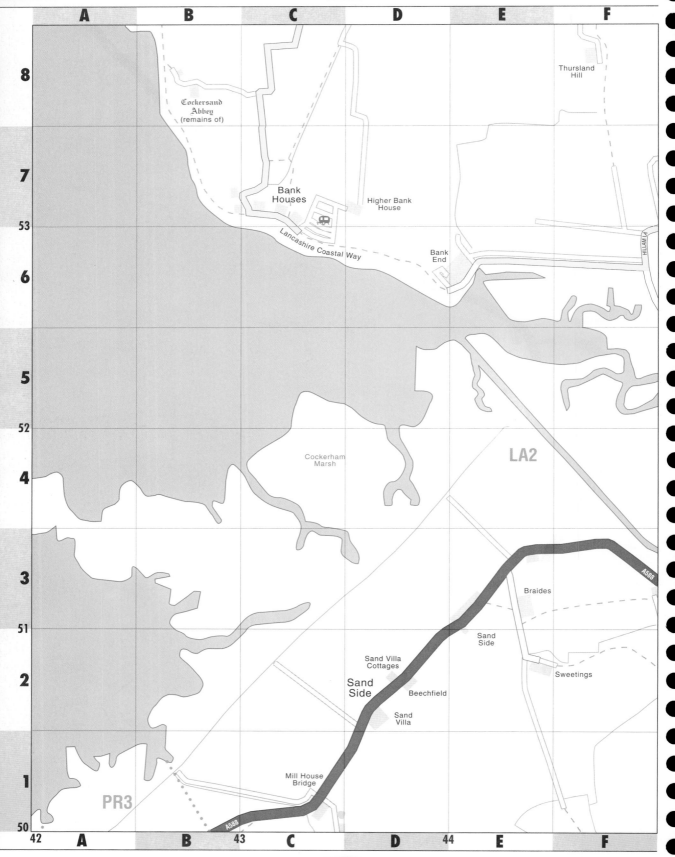

Cockersand
Abbey
(remains of)

Bank
Houses

Higher Bank
House

Thursland
Hill

Bank
End

Lancashire Coastal Way

HILLAM LA

Cockerham
Marsh

LA2

Braides

Sand
Side

Sand Villa
Cottages

Sweetings

Sand
Side

Beechfield

Sand
Villa

Mill House
Bridge

A588

PR3

A588

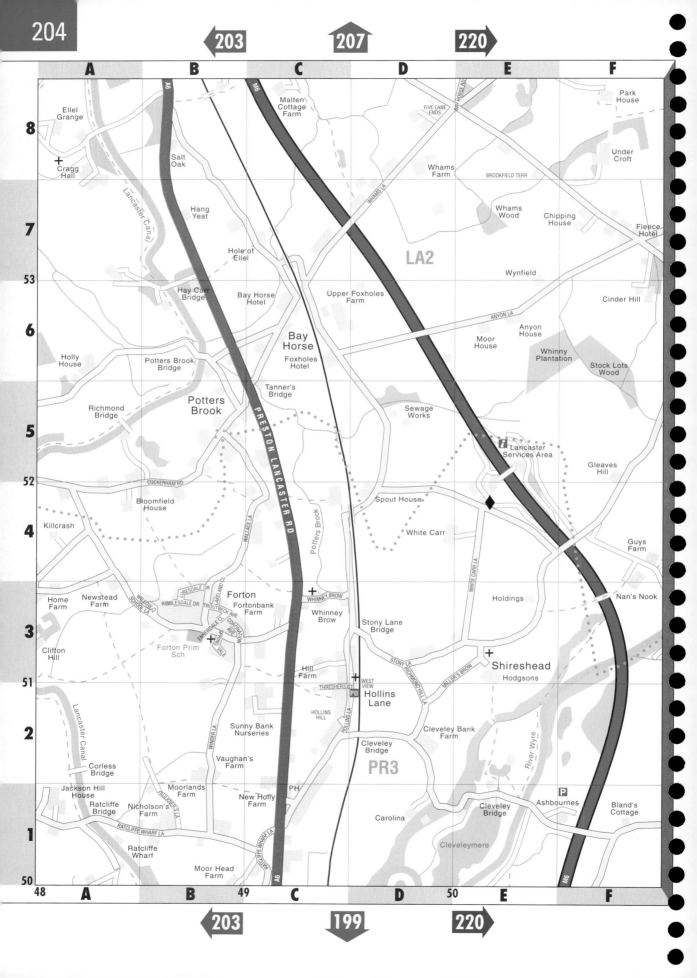

203
207
220

A B C D E F

8

Ellel
Grange

Cragg
Hall

Salt
Oak

Malten
Cottage
Farm

FIVE LANE
ENDS

BAY HORSE RD

Park
House

Whams
Farm

BROOKFIELD TERR

Under
Croft

7

Hang
Yeat

Whams
Wood

Chipping
House

Fleece
Hotel

Hole of
Ellel

LA2

53

Lancaster Canal

Hay Carr
Bridge

Bay Horse
Hotel

Upper Foxholes
Farm

ANYON LA

Cinder Hill

6

Holly
House

Potters Brook
Bridge

Bay
Horse

Foxholes
Hotel

Moor
House

Anyon
House

Whinny
Plantation

Stock Lots
Wood

Richmond
Bridge

Potters
Brook

Tanner's
Bridge

PRESTON LANCASTER RD

Sewage
Works

5

COCKERHAM RD

Lancaster
Services Area

Gleaves
Hill

52

Bloomfield
House

Potters Brook

Spout House

4

Killcrash

White Carr

Guys
Farm

WALLACE LA

WHITE CARR LA

Nan's Nook

Home
Farm

Newstead
Farm

LINESDALE DR

RIBBLESDALE DR

TROUTBECK AVE

LAKELAND CL

Forton

Fortonbank
Farm

WHINNEY BROW

Holdings

3

SCHOOL LA

WILLOW CL

BANERDALE CL

CORONATION AVE

SPRING VALE

Clifton
Hill

Forton Prim
Sch

Whinney
Brow

Stony Lane
Bridge

STONY RICHMOND HILL LA

MILLER'S BROW

Shireshead

Hodgsons

51

Hill
Farm

THRESHERS CT

PO

WEST
VIEW

Hollins
Lane

HOLLINS LA

Cleveley Bank
Farm

River Wyre

2

WINDER LA

Sunny Bank
Nurseries

HOLLINS
HILL

Cleveley
Bridge

PR3

Vaughan's
Farm

Corless
Bridge

Moorlands
Farm

PH

Carolina

Cleveley
Bridge

Ashbournes

Bland's
Cottage

Jackson Hill
House

PAULKNER'S LA

New Hoty
Farm

1

Lancaster Canal

Ratcliffe
Bridge

Nicholson's
Farm

RATCLIFFE WHARF LA

A6

Cleveleymere

Ratcliffe
Wharf

RATCLIFFE WHARF LA

Moor Head
Farm

M6

50

48 A B 49 C D 50 E F

203
199
220

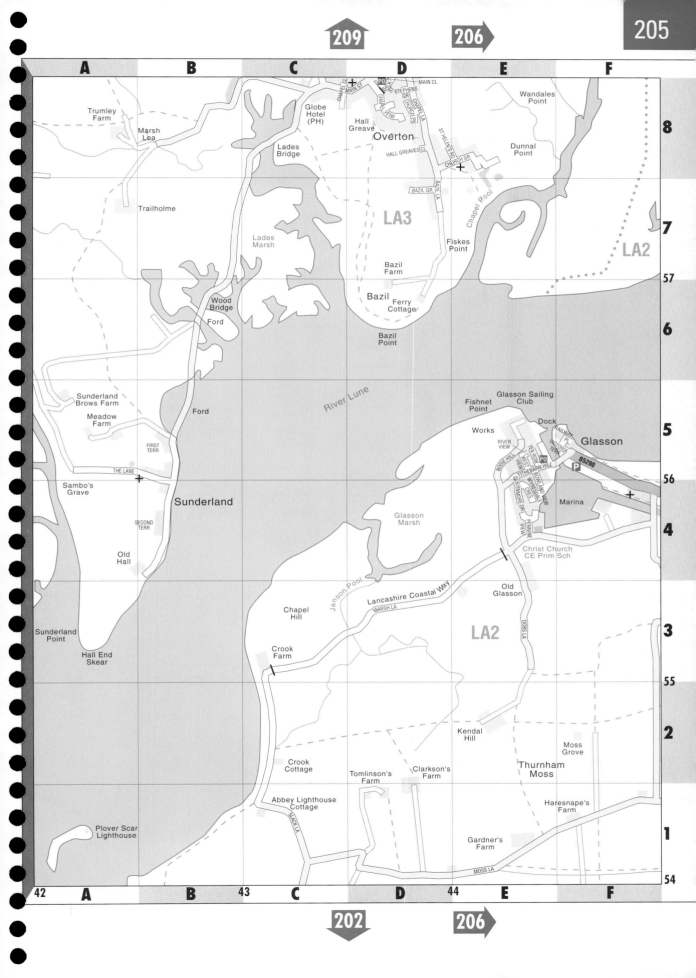

205
210

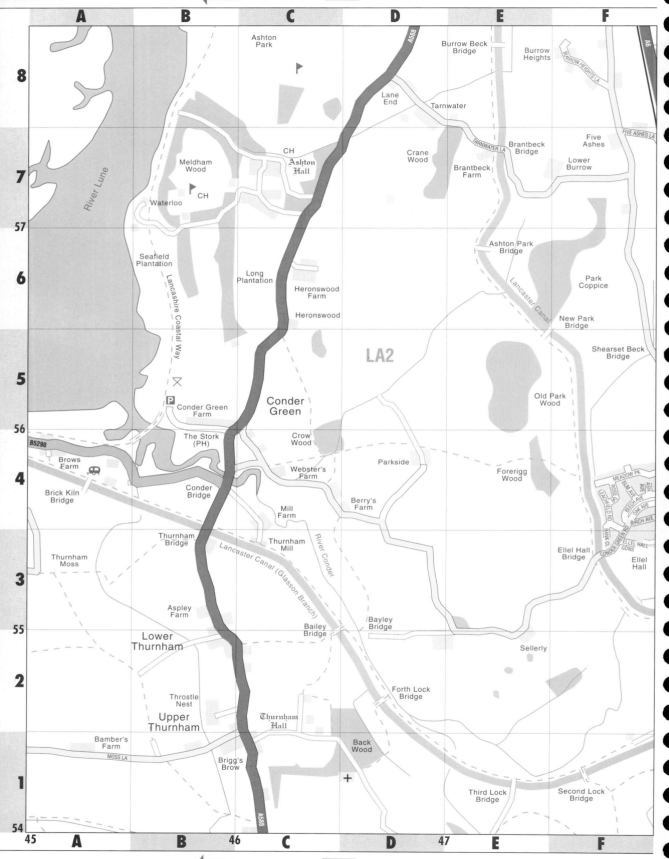

205
203

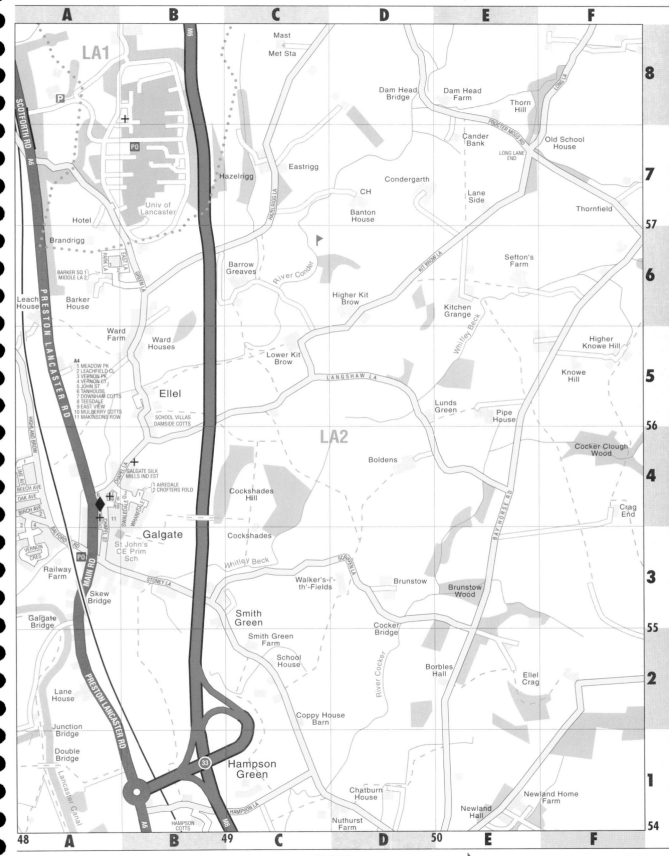

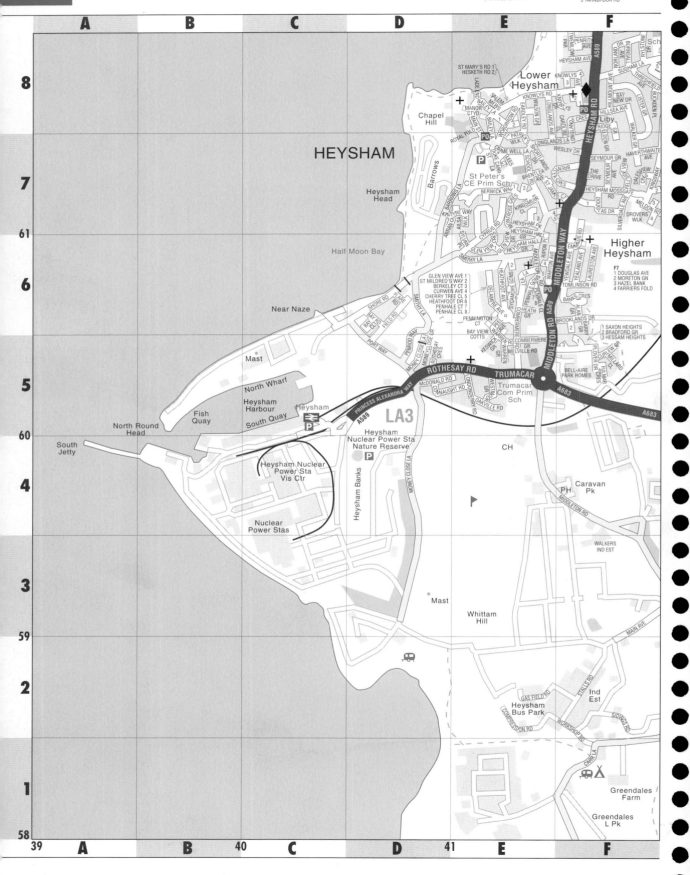

HEYSHAM

Lower Heysham

Higher Heysham

Heysham Head

Chapel Hill

Barrows

St Peter's CE Prim Sch

Half Moon Bay

Near Naze

LA3

Mast

North Wharf

Heysham Harbour

Fish Quay

South Quay

Heysham

North Round Head

South Jetty

Heysham Banks

Heysham Nuclear Power Sta Nature Reserve

Heysham Nuclear Power Sta Vis Ctr

Nuclear Power Stas

CH

Caravan Pk

PH

Whittam Hill

Mast

WALKERS IND EST

Ind Est

Heysham Bus Park

GAS FIELD RD

Greendales Farm

Greendales L Pk

ROTHESAY RD

TRUMACAR

Trumacar Com Prim Sch

PRINCESS ALEXANDRA WAY

MIDDLETON WAY

MIDDLETON RD

BELL-AIRE PARK HOMES

1 SAXON HEIGHTS
2 BRADFORD GR
3 HESSAM HEIGHTS

GLEN VIEW AVE 1
ST MILDRED'S WAY 2
BERKELEY CT 3
CURWEN AVE 4
CHERRY TREE CL 5
HEATHFOOT DR 6
PENHALE CT 7
PENHALE CL 8

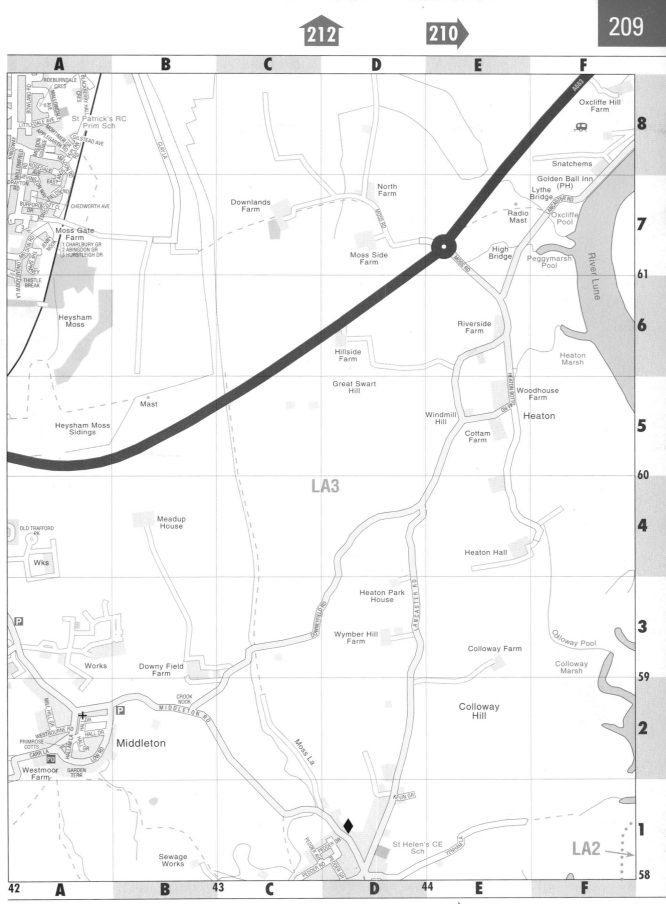

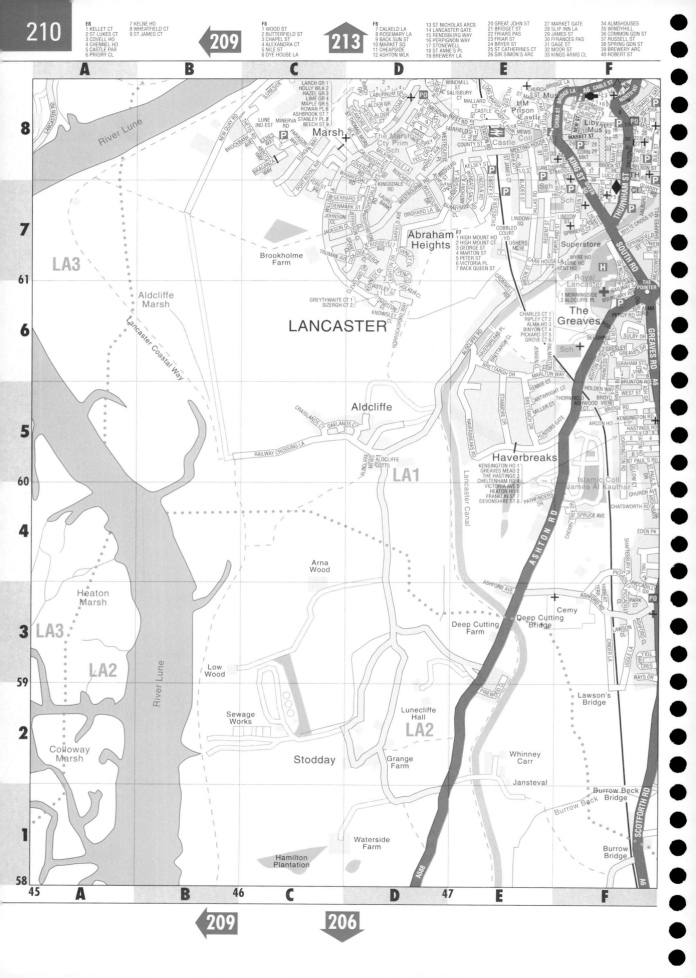

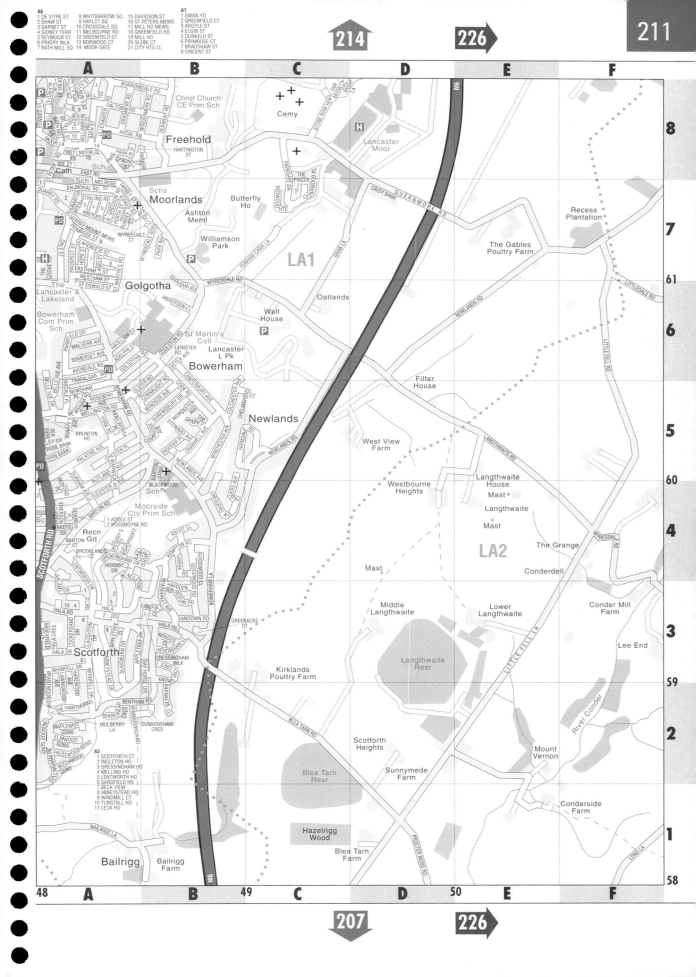

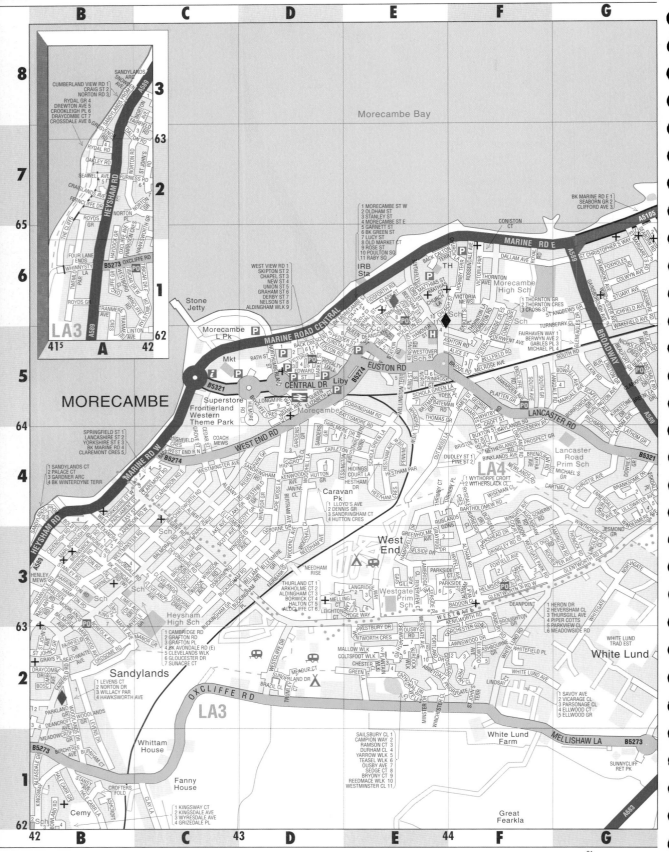

E5
1 BK QUEEN ST
2 BK LINES ST
3 WASHINGTON AVE
4 RABY ST
5 RIBBLESDALE CT
6 PRIMROSE ST
7 WHITMOOR CL

MORECAMBE

Morecambe Bay

West End

White Lund

Sandylands

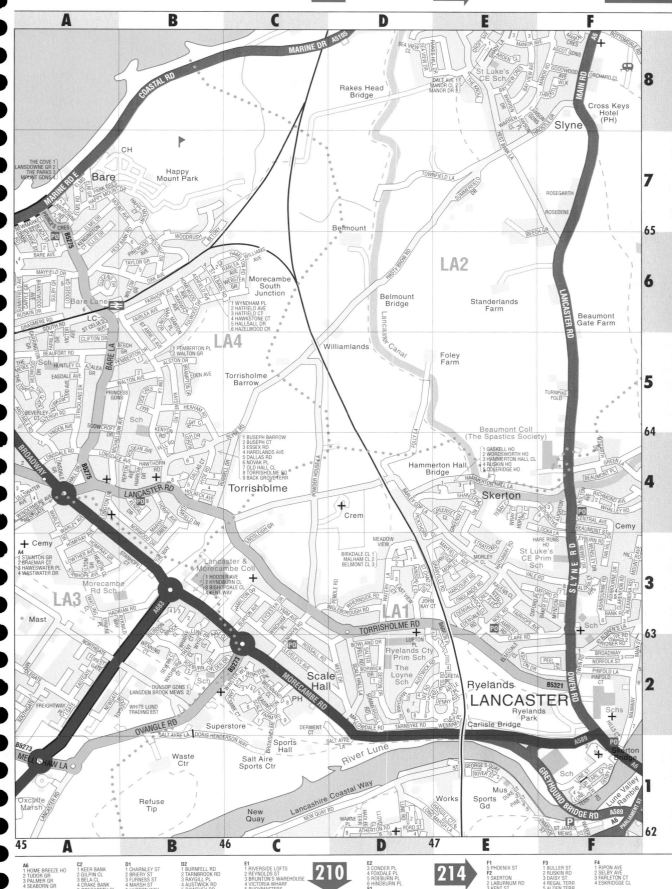

A6
1 HOME BREEZE HO
2 TUDOR GR
3 PALMER GR
4 SEABORN GR
5 LODGES CT
6 LAISTER CT

C2
1 KEER BANK
2 GILPIN CL
3 BELA CL
4 CRAKE BANK
5 GREGARETH CL
6 WINDHOLME
7 CROASDALE
8 WHITENDALE
9 BRINDLE CL

D1
1 CHARNLEY ST
2 BRIERY ST
3 FURNESS ST
4 MARSH ST
5 HUTTON WAY
6 BORDER CT
7 RICHARDS WLK
8 COWDREY MEWS

D2
1 BURNFELL RD
2 TARNBROOK RD
3 RAYGILL PL
4 AUSTWICK RD
5 RAWTHEY RD
6 MEARBECK PL
7 CROSSHILL PL
8 BROWGILL PL
9 WHITERAY RD

E1
1 RIVERSIDE LOFTS
2 REYNOLDS ST
3 BRUNTON'S WAREHOUSE
4 VICTORIA WHARF
5 BUOYMASTERS
6 THE REEDS

E2
1 UDALE PL
2 ASHDALE PL

E2
3 CONDER PL
4 FOXDALE PL
5 ROEBURN PL
6 HINDBURN PL

F1
1 CAPTAIN'S ROW
2 PARK HO
3 LORD ST
4 BACK LORD ST

F1
5 PHOENIX ST
F2
1 SKERTON
2 LABURNUM RD
3 KENT ST
4 RIVERSWAY
5 MILLRACE CT
6 SKERTON HO
7 BRIDGE HO

F3
1 BULLER ST
2 RUSKIN RD
3 DAISY ST
4 REGAL TERR
5 ALDEN TERR
6 ASHBOURNE CL
7 LINDETH GDNS
8 RICHMON HO

F4
1 RIPON AVE
2 SELBY AVE
3 FARLETON CT
4 ESKRIDDGE CL

213 216 231

A B C D E F

8

7

65

6

5

64

4

3

63

2

1

62

LA5

Ancliffe Hall

Arrow Barn

Arrow Lane Farm

Cote Beck

M6

BOTTOMDALE RD

FOUR LANE ENDS

FOUNDRY LA

ANCLIFFE LA

KELLET LA

GREEN LA

Beaumont Grange

Haverbreaks Farm

St Wilfrid's CE Prim Sch

MEADOWFIELD CL 1
HOUGHTON CT 2
WALTHAM CT 3

Meadowfield

Halton

OAK DR PINE PK
BEECH RD
PENNY STONE RD
HIGH RD
ARROW LA
POINTER GR
SYKELANDS
LIMESDALE PK
HARROWDALE
KIRKBY LONSDALE RD
SCARGILL RD
SCHOOLHOUSE LA
FELL AVE
CLOUGHA AVE
FORGEWOOD
WISP HILL GR

LA2

Dale Wood

ROWAN BANK
WILFRID'S PK
PADDOCK PINE CT
RECTORY
FACTORY ST
CHURCH ST
CHURCH BROW
NEW ST
QUARRY
RIVERSIDE CL
DENNY BANK RD

PO

1 VICTORIA PL
2 THE OLD SCHOOL

PH

LOW RD

MILL LA

Town End Mill

Halton Mills

Carus Lodge

Carus House

Halton Training Camp

River Lune

LITTLEDALE MEWS

Lune Valley Ramble

Bulk Bridge

P

Denny Beck Farm

DENNY BECK LA

A683

Denny Bank

Halton Road Bridge

Hotel

Cottam's Farm

34

Riverside Park Ind Est

Lune Aqueduct

CH

Long Bank Wood

Moss Syke Wood

Denny Beck

Old Parkside Farm

Old Parkside Fell

Works

Davies's Farm

Moor Side

ELLWOOD AVE
WHALLEY GREEN LA
HALTON RD
HILL RD
WOLSELEY ST
ANGUS RD
LANCELYN WAY
LINDON WETHERFIELD RD
CLARENDON RD
LANSIL WAY

1 HOWGILL AVE
2 MOSS PL
3 POLLARD PL

CATON RD

Lancaster Canal

LANSIL IND EST
NEWTON TERR

LA1

Ridge Wood

Ridge Farm

Ridge Lea

GRIMSHAW LA

THE RAMPARTS

Lune Riverside Park

Newton

TA Ctr

Trading Est

P

A683

Sports Ctr

KINGSWAY

A6 CATON RD

Bulk

GRIZEDALE RD

LANGDALE PL
LANGDALE RD
SCAFELL RD
CONISTON RD
AMBLESIDE RD
CARTMEL RD
SKIDDAW RD
THIRLMERE RD
LYTH RD
LOWTHER RD
HALDBECK RD
CRAG RD
DERWENT RD
LUNESDALE
LANGDALE
BOWNESS RD
FIRBANK RD
KESWICK RD
ELTERWATER PL
BUTTERMERE RD
PATTERDALE RD
PO
PO

Ridge

HONISTER RD

Newton Beck

RIDGE LA

Central Lancaster High Sch

LANCASTER

The Ridge Prim Sch

1 HERLEBECK RISE
2 LINGMOOR RD
3 MONTHALL RISE
4 RIDGE SQ
5 KESWICK CT
6 KESWICK WLK
7 THIRLEMERE CT
8 BUTTERMERE CT

HM Prison

MOOR LA

FAR MOOR LA

Stanley Farm

Stanley Farm Fell

M6

48 A B 49 C 50 D E F

213 211 231

A1
1 MARDALE RD
2 GREBE WHARF
3 GLADSTONE TERR
4 FACTORY HILL
5 ST LEONARD CT
6 DE VITRE ST
7 SWALLOW WHARF

ST LEONARD'S GATE
BULK RD
BRIDGE LA
GREEN ST
ALBION ST
KENTMERE RD
TROUTBECK RD

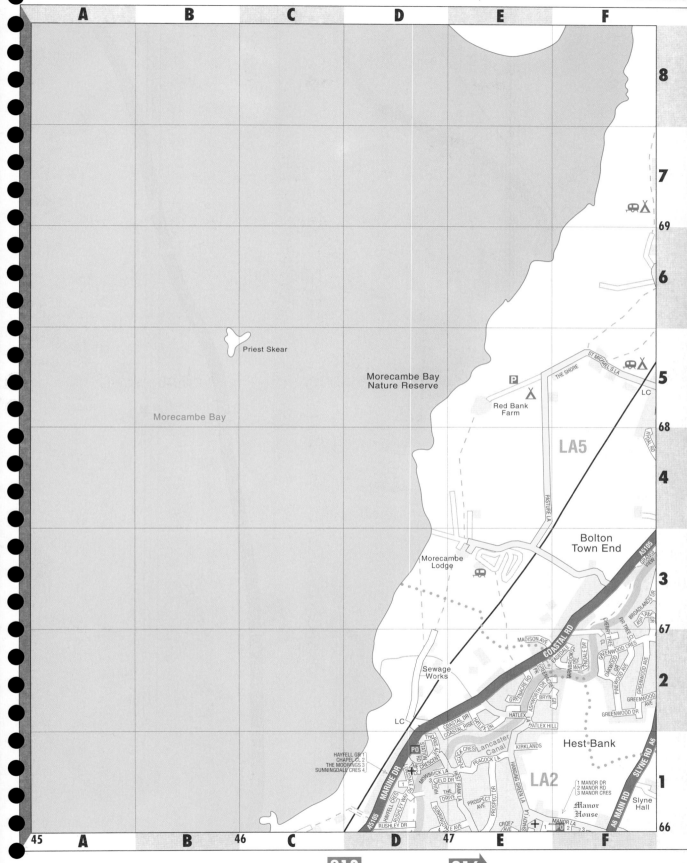

A B C D E F

8

7

69

6

Priest Skear

5

Morecambe Bay
Nature Reserve

THE SHORE

ST MICHAEL'S LA

P

Red Bank
Farm

LC

68

Morecambe Bay

PASTURE LA

LA5

RYDAL RD

4

Morecambe
Lodge

Bolton
Town End

A5105

GRANGE VIEW

3

67

Sewage
Works

MADISON AVE

COASTAL RD

BROADLANDS DR

FIR TREE CL

CHERRY TREE CL

GREENWOOD CRES

GREENWOOD AVE

EASEDALE

KENDALE DR

OAKWOOD CL

PINEWOOD AVE

GREENWOOD AVE

GREENACRE RD

KIRK

TARNBROOK CL

GREENACRE RD

BRYN

GREENWOOD DR

2

LC

COASTAL DR

COASTAL RISE

HATLEX DR

HATLEX

ASHWORTH DR

HATLEX HILL

Lancaster Canal

KIRKLANDS

Hest Bank

HAYFELL GR 1
CHAPEL CL 2
THE MOORINGS 3
SUNNINGDALE CRES 4

PO

STATION RD

THE CRESCENT

MOWBRICK LA

HEST BANK LA

PEACOCK LA

HANGING GREEN LA

LA2

1 MANOR DR
2 MANOR RD
3 MANOR CRES

SLYNE RD

A6

1

66

MARINE DR

A5105

HAYFELL WAY

RUSHLEY DR

HIGHFIELD DR

THE DRIVE

PROSPECT DR

PROSPECT AVE

SHADY LA

SUNNINGDALE AVE

CROFT AVE

MANOR LA

PO

Manor
House

Slyne
Hall

A6 MAIN RD

45 A B 46 C D 47 E F 66

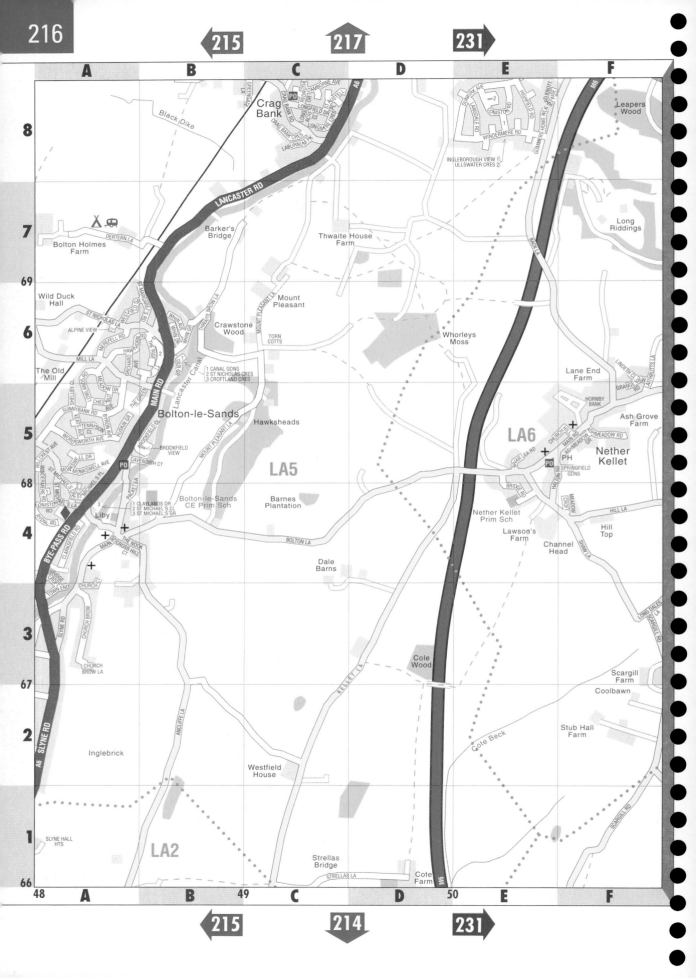

215 217 231

A B C D E F

8

7

69

6

5

68

4

3

67

2

1

66

Black Dike

GREENGATE LA

Crag Bank

PO

CAMBORNE AVE
ST AUSTELL
REDRUITH PL
LONGFIELD DR
LONGMA... CRE...
CRAG BANK CRES
LABURNUM...
CRAG BANK RD

LANCASTER RD

Barker's Bridge

DUNKIRK AVE
LANGDALE RD
CONISTON RD
= 2
HIGHFIELD RD
CONISTON RD
WIN RD KNOTT
GUMMERGS HOWE
WINDERMERE RD
INGLEBOROUGH VIEW 1
ULLSWATER CRES 2

Leapers Wood

Long Riddings

Bolton Holmes Farm

DERTERN LA

Thwaite House Farm

Wild Duck Hall

ST NICHOLAS LA
ALPINE VIEW
MEREFELL RD
ST MARGARET'S RD
WESTFIELD RD
WHIN CR
WHIN GR
WHIN LA
THWAITE BROW LA
MOUNT PLEASANT LA

Mount Pleasant

The Old Mill

MILL LA
SHELLEY CL
SUNNYBANK RD
WOODSWORTH AVE
KEATS AVE
TENNYSON CL
BYRON AVE
RUSKIN GR
CHESTNUT AVE
MEADOW DR
ORCHARD
HAWTHORN
THE GREEN
MAIN RD
HAWS HEY
THE RIDE

Crawstone Wood

TORN COTTS

1 CANAL GDNS
2 ST NICHOLAS CRES
3 CROFTLAND CRES

Lancaster Canal

Whorleys Moss

Lane End Farm

LINDETH CL
GRANGE VIEW RD
LATIBUTTS LA

Bolton-le-Sands

Hawksheads

LA5

HORNBY BANK

Ash Grove Farm

LA6

Nether Kellet

BROOKFIELD CL
BROOKFIELD VIEW
CAVENDISH CT
PO
MOUNT PLEASANT LA

CHURCH LA
MAIN RD
BRIAR LEA RD
ASHMEADOW RD
ASHMEADOW GR
PH
PO

Barnes Plantation

Bolton-le-Sands CE Prim Sch

HILLCREST AVE
WINDERMERE...
MONKSWELL PL
MON... DR
ST MICHAEL'S CRES
CONISTON RD
RYDAL RD
2
ST MICHAEL'S PL
1 CLAYLANDS DR
2 ST MICHAEL'S CL
3 ST MICHAEL'S GR

Liby

3

Nether Kellet Prim Sch

SPRINGFIELD GDNS
BRIDGE RD
WALTON CROFT
MEADOW CROFT
HILL LA

BYE-PASS RD

CLARKSFIELD RD

MAIN RD
THE NOOK
CROSS HILL
CT

BOLTON LA

Lawson's Farm

Channel Head

Hill Top

SHAW LA

Dale Barns

BRIDGE CRES
TOWN END
CHURCH RD
CHURCH BROW

Cole Wood

Scargill Farm

Coolbawn

CHURCH BROW LA

ANGLIFFE LA

KELLET LA

Gote Beck

Stub Hall Farm

LONG DALES
SCARGILL RD

SLYNE RD

Inglebrick

Westfield House

A6 SLYNE RD

SLYNE HALL HTS

LA2

Strellas Bridge

STRELLAS LA

Cote Farm

M6

SCARGILL RD

48 A B 49 C D 50 E F

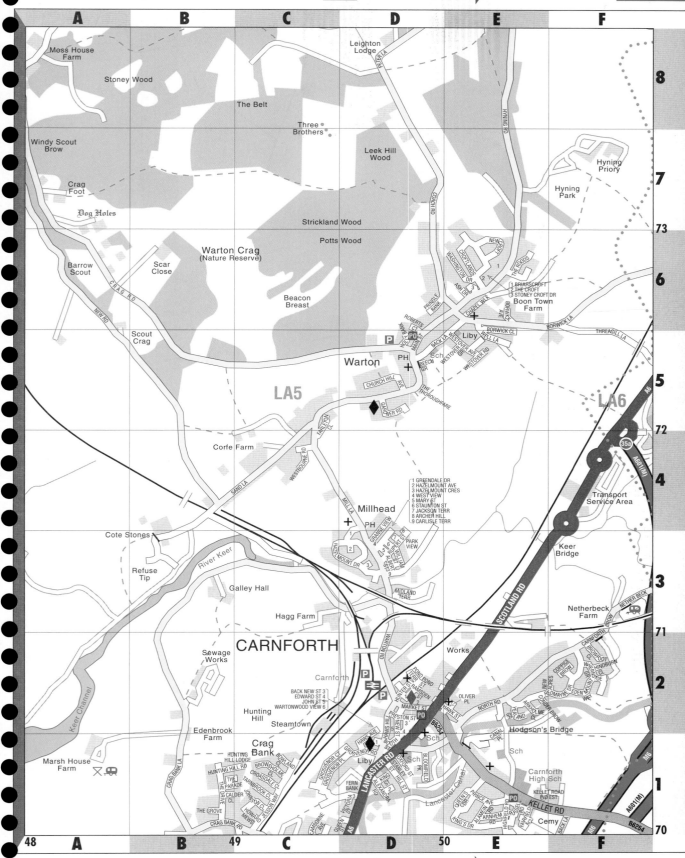

219
234
216
234

D1
1 WARTONWOOD VIEW
2 TOWPATH WLK
3 ALBERT ST
D2
1 BACK HUNTER ST
2 ASHTREES WAY
3 EDWARD ST
4 JOHN ST
5 BACK NEW ST

237

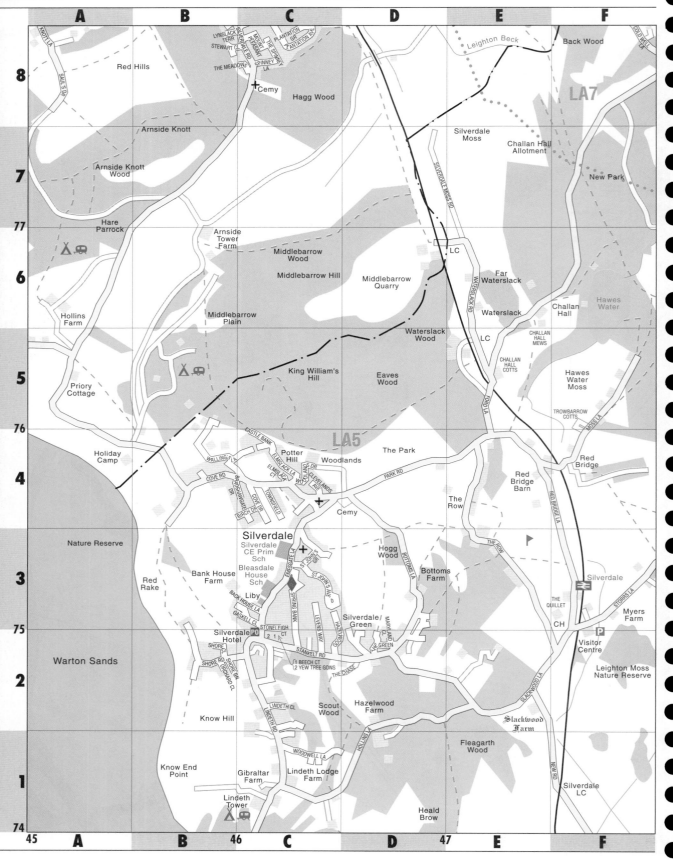

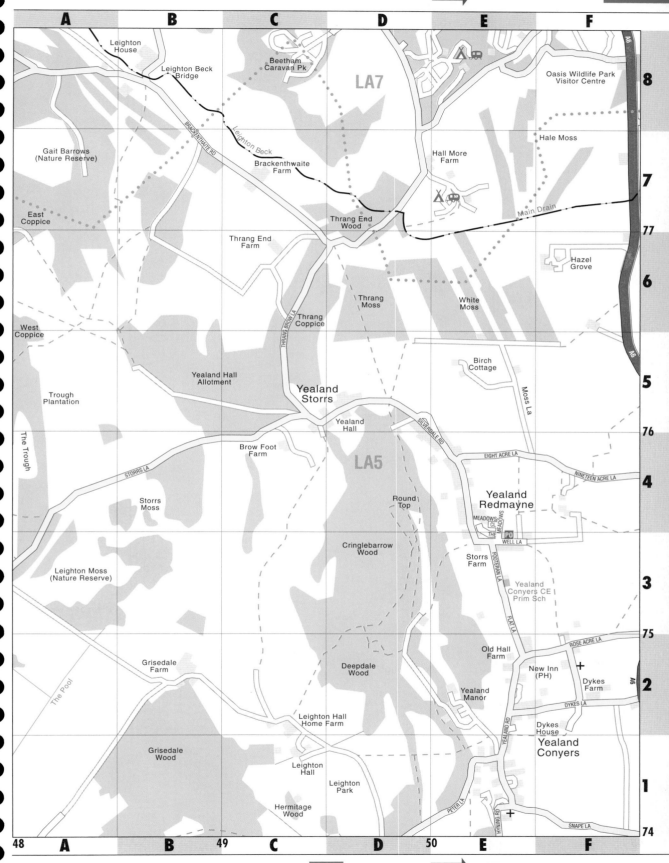

204 199
226

Scale: 1¾ inches to 1 mile
0   ¼   ½ mile
0   250m 500m 750m 1 km

Dolphinholme
PENNINE VIEW
FOUR LANE ENDS
BROOKSIDE DR
ABBEYSTEAD RD
Damas Gill
Dolphinholme CE Prim Sch
PO
CORLESS COTTS
CHURCH RD
RIVERS VIEW FOLD
WAGON RD
River Wyre
Lower Swainshead
River Wyre
Abbeystead Resr
Hawthornthwaite
Catshaw Hall
LA2
Belvidere House
Swainshead Hall
Camm House
WYRESIDE HALL
TIMBER'S LA
Bantons
Street Bridge
Street Brook
WASTE LA
Halls
Hall Gill
Fellside Farm
Street
Bracken Lea
Stonehead
Yates
Catshaw Greave
Kays Farm
Crosshill Four Lane Ends
Taylor's Farm
Isle of Skye Farm
Catshaw Fell
Foxhouses
Crosshill Farm
LONG LA
Grizedale Head
Websters
Syke's Farm
Hayshaw Fell
Lea Green
Cliftons
Ford
Harrisend Fell
Stake House Fell
Sands Bottom
Fell End
HIGHER LA
Wyresdale Park
Arbour
Stake House
Nickey Nook
The Tarn
Calder Fell
Grizedale Resr
Grizedale Lea Resr
PR3
Pedder's Wood
Grize Dale
Calder Dyke
Bleasdale Moors
Calder Side
Woodacre Pasture
Works
Hazelhurst Fell
Oakenclough
Masts
Barnacre Resrs
Oakenclough Fell
HIGHER LA
Bank Farm
OAKENCLOUGH COTTS
Moorcock Inn (PH)
Hazelhurst
Burns Farm
River Calder
Clough Heads Brook
EDISFORTH LA
Birks Farm
DELPH LA
LONG LA
Kelbrick Farm
STRICKENS LA
St John's CE Prim Sch
Rough Moor
DELPH LA
River Brock
Barnacre Lodge
Fell End
Bleasdale Tower
Clough Heads Cotts

204 199
179
180

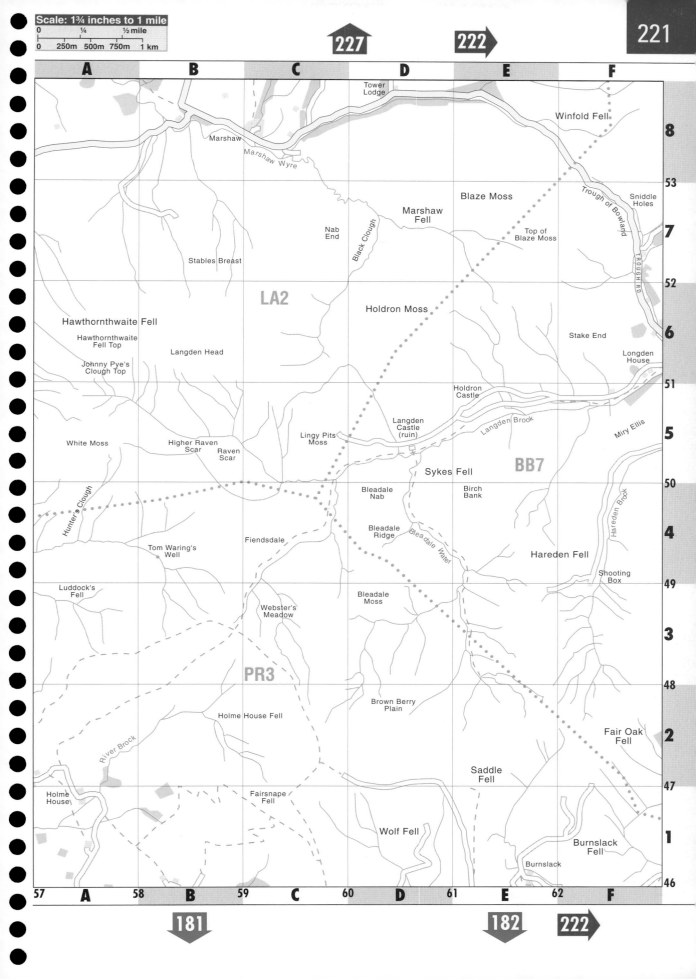

221
228

Scale: 1¾ inches to 1 mile

| 0 | ¼ | ½ mile |
| 0 | 250m 500m 750m | 1 km |

A **B** **C** **D** **E** **F**

Costy Clough

Brennand River

Burn Side

8

Whins Brow

Whin Fell

Burn Fell

53

Beatrix Fell

7

Rams Clough

Calder Moor

Burn House

The Hey

New Biggin

52

Staple Oak Fell

River Dunsop

Oxenhurst

Brunghill Moor

BACK LA

6

Sykes Farm

Sykes Nab

Bishops House

Beatrix

Back of Hill Barn

Gamble Hole Farm

51

Closes Barn

HOLME HEAD COTTS

Low Barn

Knot or Sugar Loaf

Moor End

Heaning

5

Hareden Farm

TROUGH RD

Dunsop Bridge

BB7

Boarsden

Brown Nab

Hareden Brook

Thorneyholme RC Sch

P0 P

Mossthwaite

Fober Farm

50

FORESTRY HOS 1
LANE ENDS 2
THE CRESCENT 3

Root

Thorneyholme

Knowlmere Manor

4

Mellor Knoll

River Hodder

Hodder Bank Fell

Birkett

49

Totridge

New Hay Farm

Langden Bridge

3

Birkett Fell

Ing Barn

Burholme

48

Whitmore

Hodder Bank Farm

Burholme Bridge

Crag House

2

Higher Fence Wood

Lower Fence Wood

Reed Barn Cottage

Higher Whitewell

Marl Hill

Crimpton

47

Dinkling Green Farm

New Laund

Whitewell

Marl Hill Moor

1

The Inn at Whitewell

New Laund Hill

HALL HILL

Spire Farm

PR3

Fair Oak

Wilsons

Seedalls

46

63 **A** **64** **B** **65** **C** **66** **D** **67** **E** **68** **F**

221
183
184

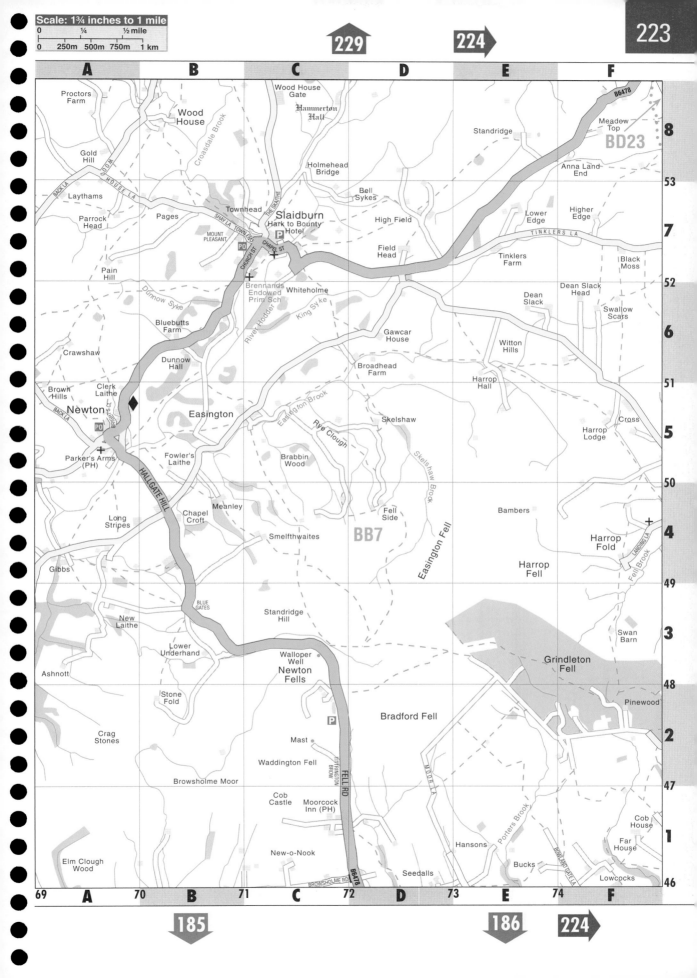

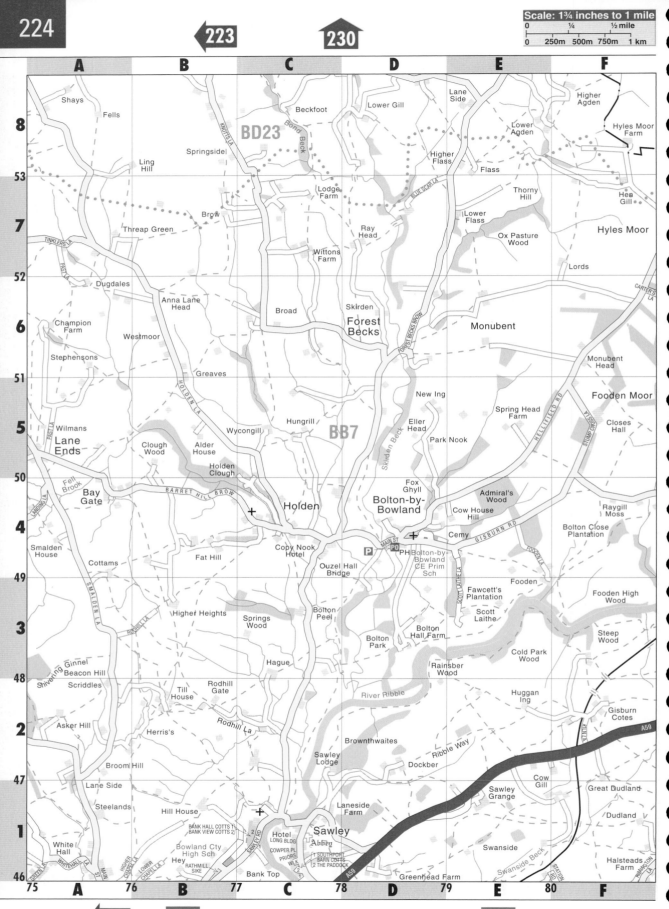

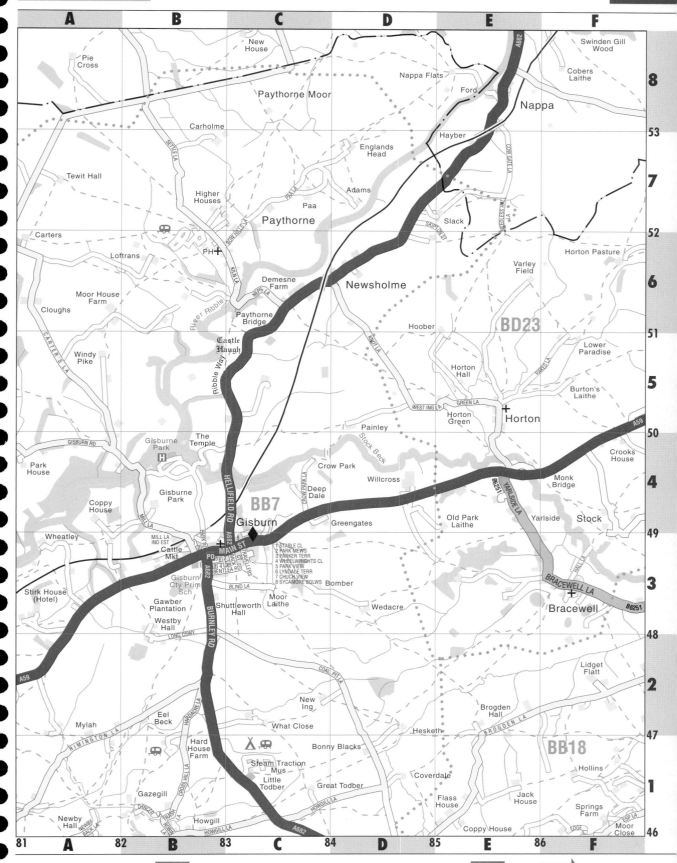

Scale: 1¾ inches to 1 mile
0   ¼   ½ mile
0   250m   500m   750m   1 km

Pie Cross
New House
Swinden Gill Wood
Nappa Flats
Cobers Laithe
Paythorne Moor
Ford
Nappa
Carholme
Hayber
Tewit Hall
Higher Houses
Englands Head
Carters
Paa
Adams
Slack
Loftrans
PH
Paythorne
Needless Hall LA
Horton Pasture
Demesne Farm
Newsholme
Varley Field
Moor House Farm
NEPS LA
Cloughs
River Ribble
Paythorne Bridge
Hoober
BD23
Windy Pike
Castle Haugh
Lower Paradise
CARTER'S LA
Ribble Way
KNOTT LA
Horton Hall
Burton's Laithe
WEST ING LA
GREEN LA
Horton Green
Horton
RAKES LA
Painley
Gisburn Rd
The Temple
Crooks House
Park House
Gisburne Park
Crow Park
Willcross
Monk Bridge
HELLIFIELD RD
Stock Beck
B6251
YARLSIDE LA
Coppy House
Gisburne Park
Deep Dale
Old Park Laithe
Yarlside
Stock
Wheatley
BB7
Gisburn
Greengates
MILL LA
MILL LA IND EST
Cattle Mkt
MAIN ST
1 STABLE CL
2 PARK MEWS
3 PARKER TERR
4 WHEELWRIGHTS CL
5 PARK VIEW
6 LYNDALE TERR
7 CHUCH VIEW
8 SYCAMORE BGLWS
Bomber
BRACEWELL LA
Bracewell
B6251
Stirk House (Hotel)
PO
BENTLEA RD
Gisburn Cty Prim Sch
BLIND LA
Moor Laithe
Wedacre
Gawber Plantation
Shuttleworth Hall
LONG CSWY
Westby Hall
BURNLEY RD
COAL PIT LA
A59
Lidget Flatt
HAGUE LA
Mylah
Eel Beck
New Ing
Brogden Hall
BROGDEN LA
RIMINGTON LA
Hard House Farm
What Close
Hesketh
BB18
Hollins
CROSS HILL LA
Steam Traction Mus
Bonny Blacks
Coverdale
Gazegill
Little Todber
Great Todber
Flass House
Jack House
Springs Farm
DANCER LA
TRASH LA
ROBIN LA
Newby Hall
NEWBY BACK LA
Howgill
HOWGILL LA
HOWGILL LA
A682
Coppy House
EDGE LA
ESP LA
Moor Close

Scale: 1¾ inches to 1 mile
0   ¼   ½ mile
0   250m   500m   750m   1 km

A   **B**   **C**   **D**   **E**   **F**

QUERNMORE RD
POSTERN GATE RD
FRIAR'S MOSS RD

Corney Hill Farm
Friar's Moss Farm
8
Knotts Farm
Askew Hill
LITTLEDALE RD
Baines Cragg
P
The Cragg
Cragg Wood
Bellhill Farm
Littledale Hall
FOXDALE BECK
Field Head

61
River Gander
Littledale
Wisp Hill
Udale Beck
Stock-a-Bank
Greenlot
Windy Clough
Conder Head

7
RIGG LA
P
Quernmore CE Prim Sch
Black Fell

60
Far Lodge
Fell End Farm
Clougha Scar
Clougha

6
Narr Lodge
Rowton Brook
Clougha Pike
Brownley Hill

WYRESDALE RD
Rowton Brook Fell

59
Quernmore
PO
QUERNMORE BROW
Brow Top Farm
Shooters Pile

LONG LA
Terrace Farm

5
Gibson's Farm
Middle Brow Top
Grit Fell

BAY HORSE RD
Hare Appletree
Lower Browtop
Hare Appletree Fell
Burrow Hill
Grizedale Head

58

4
Blackwood End
Damas Gill
LA2
Abbeystead Fell
Rotten Hill
Lee Fell

57
Longmoor
P
Twr
Westfield House

3
Yeat House Farm
PROCTER MOSS RD
Castle o' Trim
Higher Moor Head
High Moor Cross
River Grizedale
Grizedale Barn

56
Gate House Bridge
Damas Gill
Lower Moor Head

RAKEHOUSE BROW

2
Middle Crag
Lower Castle o' Trim
Borwicks
Tills Farm
Brook House
Balderstones
Grizedale Bridge
Lee

55
Hollyhead Farm
Gallows Clough
PLANTATION LA
ABBEYSTEAD LA
Summer House Head
River Wyre
Lee Bridge

LONG LA
Chapel House Farm
Abbeystead

1
Ortner
ABBEYSTEAD RD
River Wyre
Cawthorne Endowed Prim Sch
STRAIT LA
Doeholme Farm

Starbank
Lower Green Bank
Lentworth Hall
Abbeystead Resr
THE RAKE
SMITHY BROW
DOEHOLME RAKE

54
51   **A**   **52**   **B**   **53**   **C**   **54**   **D**   **55**   **E**   **56**   **F**

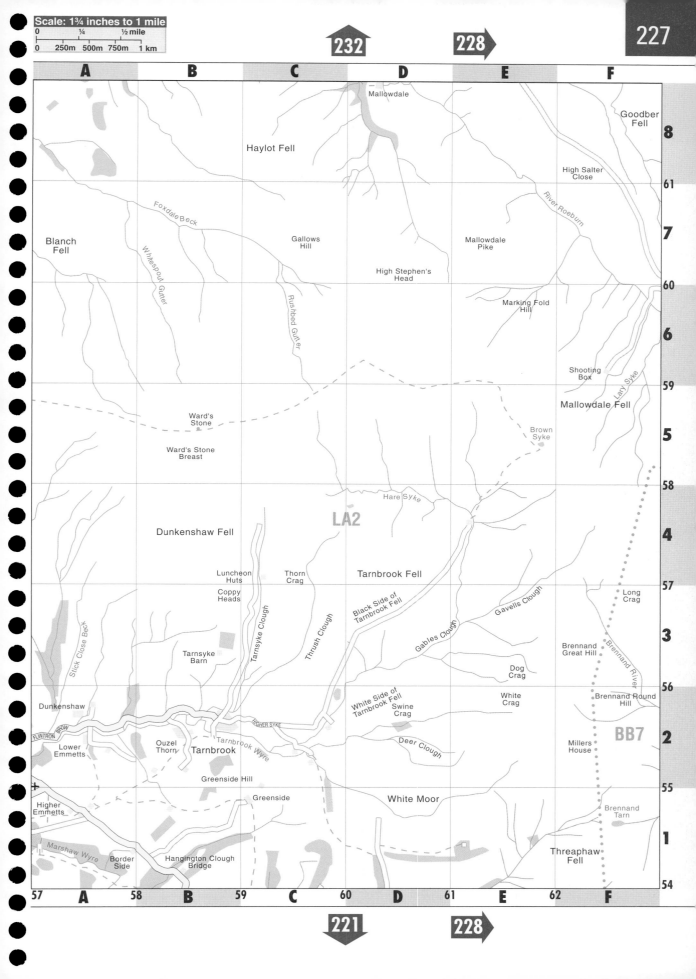

Scale: 1¾ inches to 1 mile

0   ¼   ½ mile
0   250m 500m 750m 1 km

232
228

A   B   C   D   E   F

Mallowdale

Goodber
Fell

Haylot Fell

High Salter
Close

8

61

Foxdale Beck

Gallows
Hill

Mallowdale
Pike

River Roeburn

7

Blanch
Fell

Whitespout Gutter

High Stephen's
Head

60

Rushbed Gutter

Marking Fold
Hill

6

59

Shooting
Box

Lary Syke

Ward's
Stone

Brown
Syke

Mallowdale Fell

5

Ward's Stone
Breast

58

Hare Syke

LA2

Dunkenshaw Fell

4

Luncheon
Huts

Thorn
Crag

Tarnbrook Fell

Long
Crag

57

Coppy
Heads

Black Side of
Tarnbrook Fell

Gavells Clough

Tarnsyke Clough

Gables Clough

Brennand
Great Hill

Brennand River

3

Stick Close Beck

Tarnsyke
Barn

Thrush Clough

Dog
Crag

56

White Side of
Tarnbrook Fell

Swine
Crag

White
Crag

Brennand Round
Hill

Dunkenshaw

HIGHER SYKE

BB7

2

FLINTRON BROW

Ouzel
Thorn

Tarnbrook

Tarnbrook Wyre

Deer Clough

Millers
House

Lower
Emmetts

Greenside Hill

55

Higher
Emmetts

Greenside

White Moor

Brennand
Tarn

1

Marshaw Wyre

Border
Side

Hangington Clough
Bridge

Threaphaw
Fell

54

57   A   58   B   59   C   60   D   61   E   62   F

221
228

227
233

Scale: 1¾ inches to 1 mile

0 ¼ ½ mile

0 250m 500m 750m 1 km

A **B** **C** **D** **E** **F**

Summersgill Fell

Lower Green Bank

Higher Green Bank

Botton Head

Whitray Beck

Whitray Fell

Lyne Fell Rd

8

Thrushgill Fell

New Coppy

61

Greenbank Fell

Middle Gill

River Hodder

7

Hawkshead

60

Dale Beck

LA2

Botton Head Fell

6

Salter Fell

Coumes

Far Costy Clough

59

White Hill

Lamb Hill Fell

5

Shooter's Clough

58

Esp Crag

Hard Hill Top

Little Bull Stones

Wolfhole Crag

Great Bull Stones

Reeves Edge

4

Croasdale Brook

57

Shooting Box

Brown Syke Hill

Higher Stoney Clough

Croasdale Fell

3

BB7

Brown Syke

Whitendale Hanging Stones

Whitendale Fell

Baxton Fell

Whitendale River

56

Shooting Box

Black Brook

Dane Hill Well

2

Lee End

Calf Clough

Low Fell

Brennand Fell

55

Whitendale

Brennand River

Dunsop Fell

1

Middle Knoll

54

Brennand Farm

A 63 **B** 64 **C** 65 **D** 66 **E** 67 68 **F**

227
222

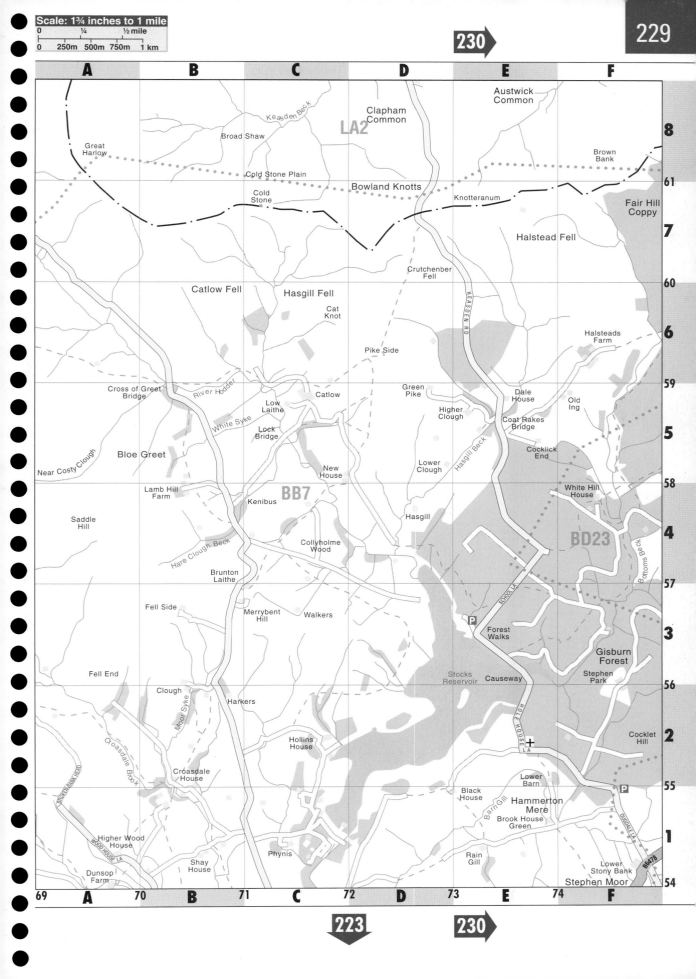

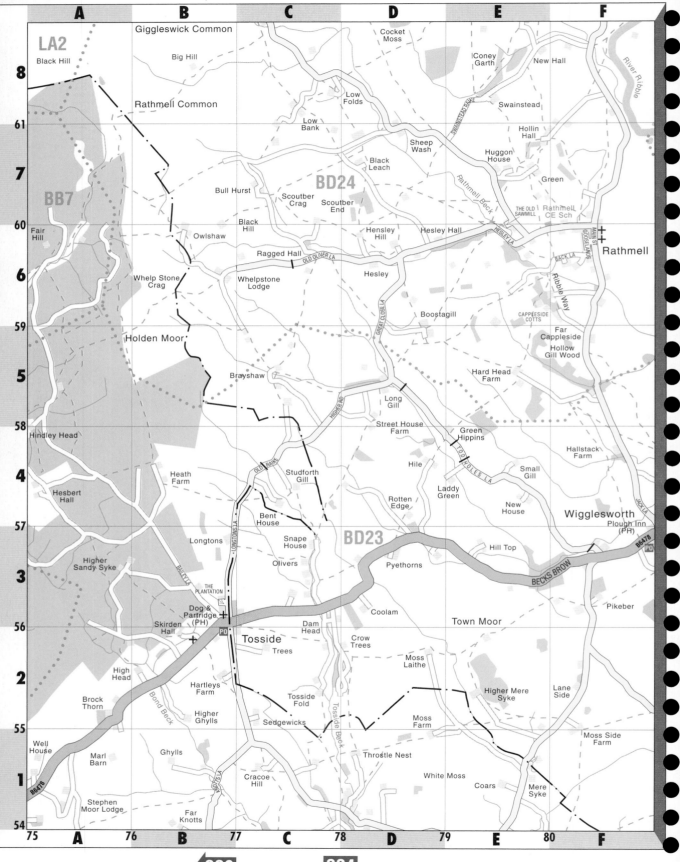

Scale: 1¾ inches to 1 mile

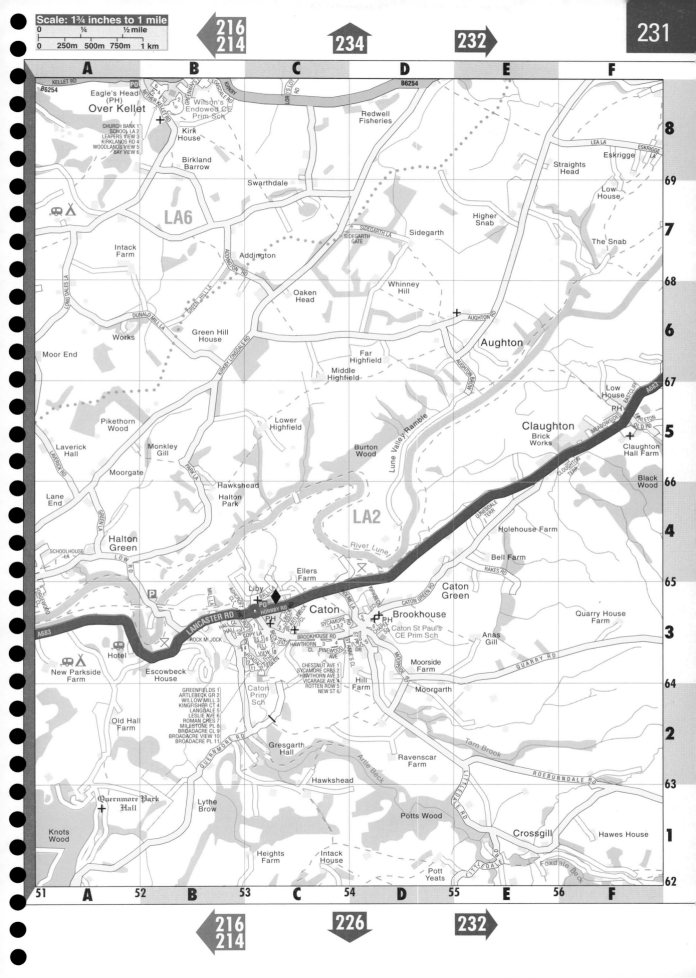

231
235

Scale: 1¾ inches to 1 mile

0 ¼ ½ mile
0 250m 500m 750m 1 km

A B C D E F

8
69
7
68
6
67
5
66
4
65
3
64
63
1
62

LA6

Clintsfield
Wennington
B6480
Tatham Bridge Inn (PH)
Raw Ridding
Castle Stede
Loyn Bridge
Park House
Tatham
Wennington Old Farm
Old Moor Rd
Hornby High Sch
Royal Oak Meadow
Kennels
Hornby Park Wood
Lune Valley Ramble
River Lune
Fleet La
Eskrigge La
Sanders La
Priory Farm
Hornby
River Wenning
Park Lane End
Park La
School Hill
Priory La
Hornby CE Prim Sch
Tatham Hall
Parkside
Russells
Sandbeds
Castle Hotel
Post Horse La
Hornby Hall
1 Stanley Dr
2 Monteagle Dr
3 Monteagle Sq
4 Castle Pk
Feathermire
Perry Moor
Melling Rd
Main St
Lancaster Rd
Station Rd
PO
Back La
Lane Head
Duck St
Gars End
Wennington Rd
River Hindburn
Agnes Ing La
Trinket La
Bottom Farm
Meal Bank
Four Score Acres
Mill Houses
Camp House
B6480
Ind Est
Butt Yeats
Lunesdale Ct
Hornby Rd
School La
George & Dragon Hotel
Wray-with-Botton Endowed Prim Sch
Wray
Main St
Roeburn Terr
Above Beck
A683
Farleton
Meadow View
Farleton Old Rd
Scale House Barn
Curwen Hall Farm
Cold Park Wood
Higher Broadwood
Cragg Hall
Claughton Hall
Hamstone Gill
Moor La
LA2
Alcocks Farm
Bellhurst
Smeer Hall
Manor House
Four Lane Ends
Leyland Farm
Claughton Moor
Outhwaite
Scale
Quarry Rd
Whit Moor
River Roeburn
Back Farm
Barkin Gate
Outhwaite Wood
Wray Wood Moor
Stauvin
Wind Farm
Thornbush
Caton Moor
Winder Wood
Harterbeck
Goodber Common
Lower Salter
Winder
Middle Salter
Roeburndale Rd
Hornby Rd
Deep Clough
Rigil Beck
Haylot Farm
High Salter

57 58 59 60 61 62

A B C D E F

231
227

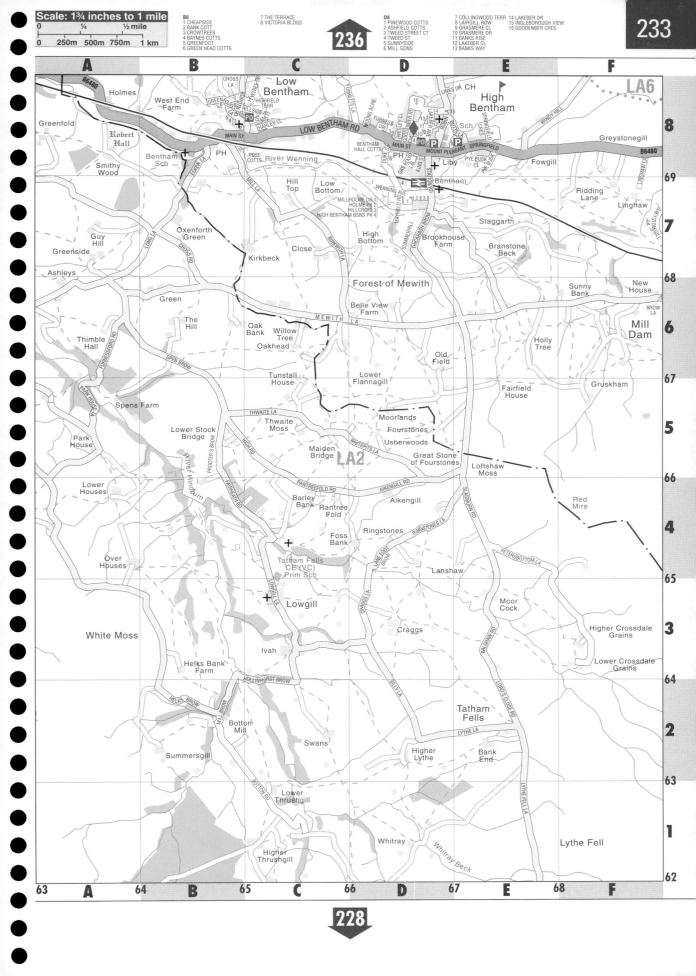

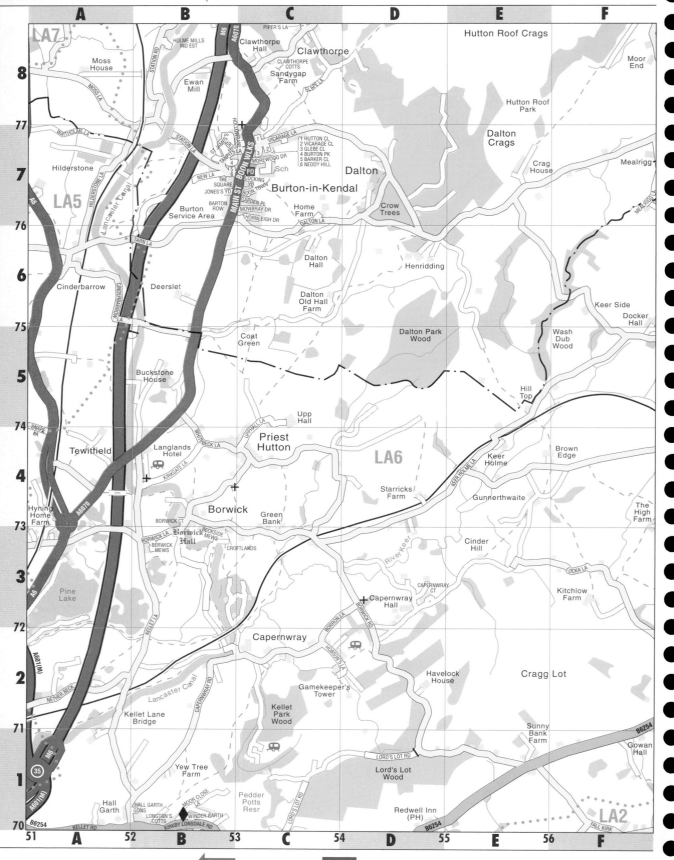

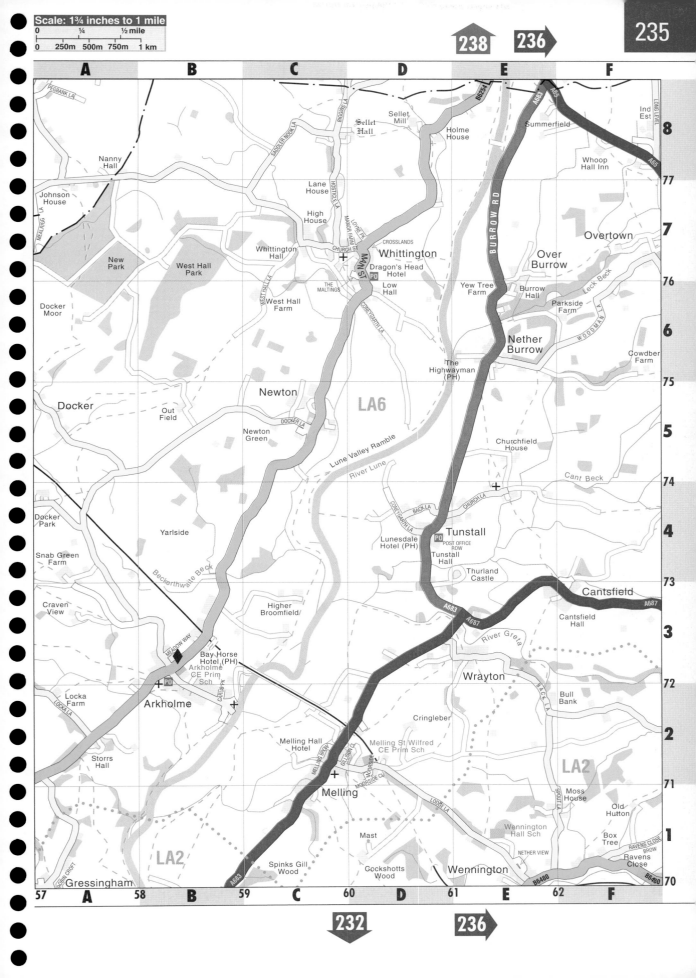

Scale: 1¾ inches to 1 mile

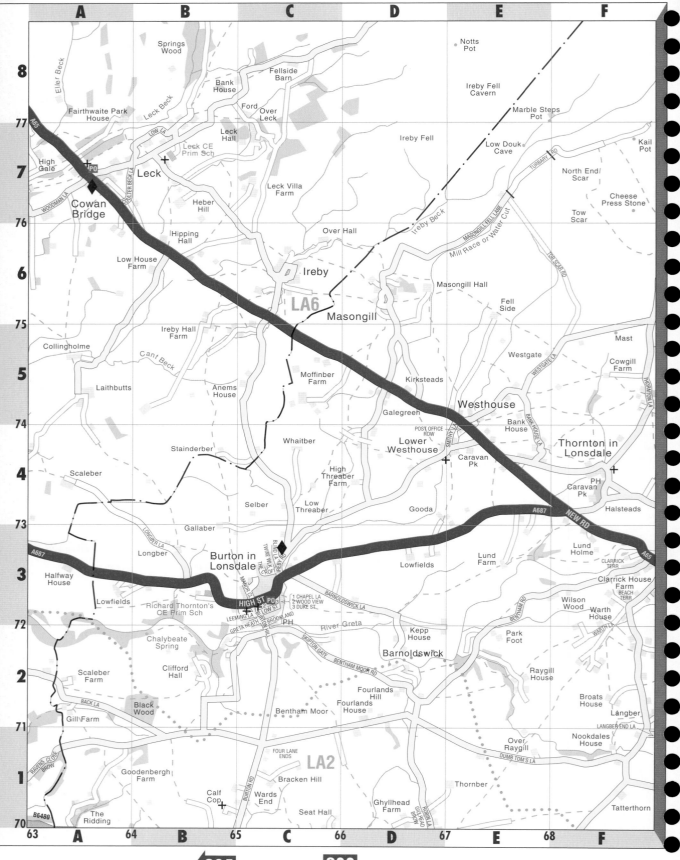

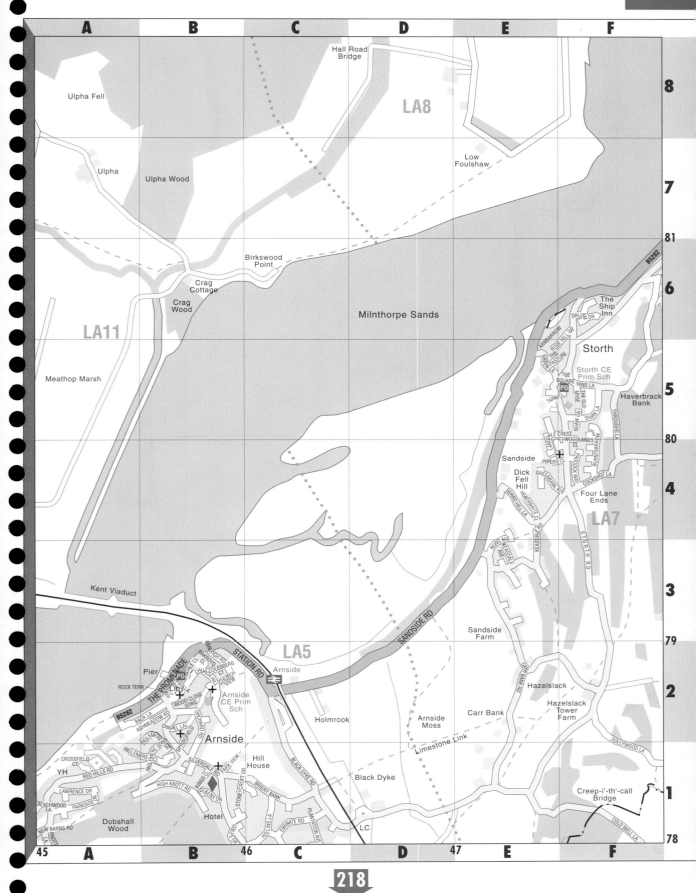

A B C D E F

8

7

81

6

LA8

Hall Road Bridge

Low Foulshaw

Ulpha Fell

Ulpha

Ulpha Wood

Birkswood Point

Crag Cottage

Crag Wood

LA11

Meathop Marsh

Milnthorpe Sands

The Ship Inn

DALT DR

ARNBARROW

ROSE HILL GR

THE GREEN LA

THE PASTURE

Storth

Storth CE Prim Sch

THE SQUARE

PO

YANS LA

TARN CL

SHAW LA

SHAW RD

SHAW RISE

THE OLD

Haverbrack Bank

5

80

LA CREST

LANT CL

WOODLANDS CL

PIPERS CL

Sandside

BURNBARROW

PADDOCK WAY

THROUGHS LA

COCKSHOT LA

Dick Fell Hill

GREENBANK AVE

HEATHWAITE RD

Four Lane Ends

LA7

GUARD HILL LA

NIVIS AVE

NEASDALE AVE

KEASDALE RD

STORTH RD

4

3

79

Kent Viaduct

SANDSIDE RD

Sandside Farm

CARR BANK RD

Hazelslack

Hazelslack Tower Farm

DOLLYWOOD LA

STATION RD

LA5

Arnside

Pier

THE PROMENADE

PO

Lib

ASHLEIGH RD

OAKROYD

CHURCH HILL CT

COLESBERG CT

CHURCH VIEW

Arnside CE Prim Sch

Holmrook

Arnside Moss

Carr Bank

2

ROCK TERR

B5282

BACK LA

ASHMEADOW RD

WOOD CLOSE GDNS

ORCHARD RD

CHAPEL LA

HIGH EAGRE GR

SPRINGFIELD

Arnside

Limestone Link

1

CROSSFIELD CT

YH

RED HILLS RD

INGLEMERE DR

INGLEMERE CL

HIGH EAGRE

SILVERDALE RD

KILLEVANS DR

PARK VIEW

STONECROFT DR

Hill House

BRIERY BANK

BLACK DYKE RD

Black Dyke

LAWRENCE DR

PARKSIDE

BEACHWOOD LA

NEW BARNS RD

KNOTT

Dobshall Wood

HIGH KNOTT RD

Hotel

KATS

HOLLINS LA

SWINATE RD

PLANTATION AVE

LC

Creep-i'-th'-call Bridge

COLD WELL LA

78

45 A B 46 C D 47 E F

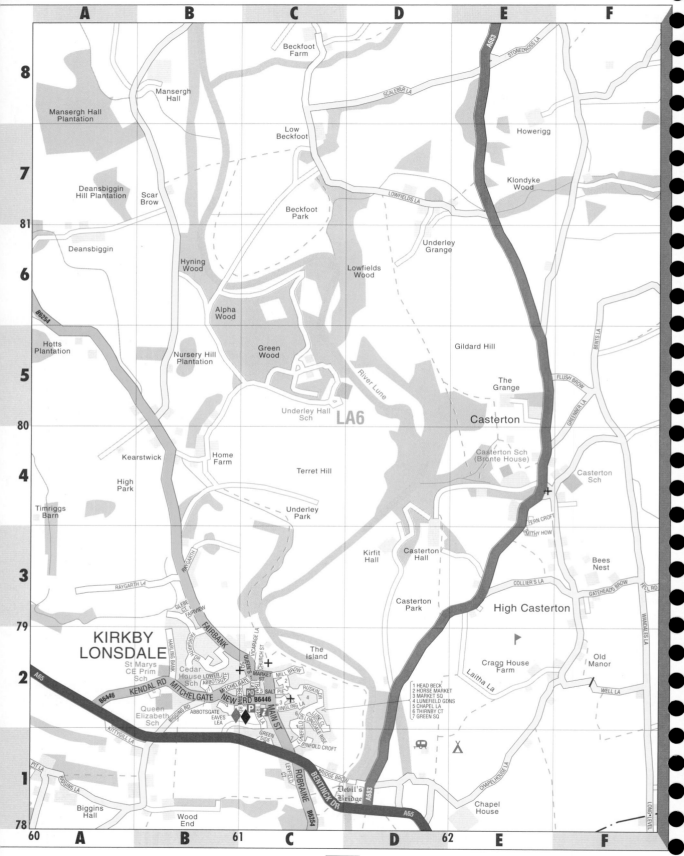

Street names are listed alphabetically and show the locality, the Postcode District, the page number and a reference to the square in which the name falls on the map page

Roberts St. 7 Rawtenstall BB4 .... 85 A3

- **Full street name** This may have been abbreviated on the map
- **Location number** If present, this indicates the street's position on a congested area of the map instead of the name
- **Town, village or locality** in which the street falls.
- **Postcode District** for the street name
- **Page number** of the map on which the street name appears
- **Grid square** in which the centre of the street falls

Schools, hospitals, sports centres, railway stations, shopping centres, industrial estates, public amenities and other places of interest are also listed. These are highlighted in magenta

Abbreviations used in the index

App	Approach	Cl	Close	Espl	Esplanade	N	North	S	South
Arc	Arcade	Comm	Common	Est	Estate	Orch	Orchard	Sq	Square
Ave	Avenue	Cnr	Corner	Gdns	Gardens	Par	Parade	Strs	Stairs
Bvd	Boulevard	Cotts	Cottages	Gn	Green	Pk	Park	Stps	Steps
Bldgs	Buildings	Ct	Court	Gr	Grove	Pas	Passage	St	Street, Saint
Bsns Pk	Business Park	Ctyd	Courtyard	Hts	Heights	Pl	Place	Terr	Terrace
Bsns Ctr	Business Centre	Cres	Crescent	Ind Est	Industrial	Prec	Precinct	Trad	Trading Est
Bglws	Bungalows	Dr	Drive		Estate	Prom	Promenade	Wlk	Walk
Cswy	Causeway	Dro	Drove	Intc	Interchange	Ret Pk	Retail Park	W	West
Ctr	Centre	E	East	Junc	Junction	Rd	Road	Yd	Yard
Cir	Circus	Emb	Embankment	La	Lane	Rdbt	Roundabout		

Town and village index

Abbey Village 79 C2	Cleveleys. 172 C3	Heysham 208 D7	Much Hoole 73 D3	Shirdley Hill 22 A6
Abbeystead 226 F1	Clifton. 114 D1	Heywood. 32 F2	Nab's Head 98 E7	Shuttleworth 49 E8
Accrington 103 E6	Clitheroe. 164 D8	High Bentham 233 E8	Nangreaves. 49 F2	Silverdale 218 C3
Adlington 30 B7	Clow Bridge 105 C5	High Casterton 238 E3	Nappa 225 E8	Simonstone. 144 E1
Altham 124 E6	Cockden 148 B2	High Cross 130 C8	Nateby 177 D6	Singleton 152 E1
Andertons Mill 40 A1	Cockerham 203 C6	Higham. 145 E5	Nelson. 147 B8	Skelmersdale 18 A1
Appley Bridge 19 C8	Cold Row 174 C5	Higher Walton 97 B4	Nether Kellet 216 F5	Slaidburn 223 C7
Arkholme 235 B2	Colne 169 C6	Higher Wheelton. 78 B1	New Lane 24 B6	Smallwood Hey 196 B5
Arnside 237 B2	Coppull 41 E2	Higherford 168 E5	New Longton 74 E8	Sollom 56 B2
Aughton 231 E6	Copster Green 121 D8	Highfurlong 151 A2	Newburgh 25 F2	Sough 192 A8
Bacup 69 E8	Corner Row. 132 E2	Hightown 2 F3	Newchurch 85 F1	Southport 34 C3
Balderstone 120 A5	Cornholme 108 B1	Hill Dale 26 D5	Newsham 136 A5	Spen Brook. 167 D2
Baldingstone. 49 F1	Cottam 115 D5	Hoddlesden. 81 F1	Newsholme 225 D6	Spring Vale. 64 C7
Bamber Bridge 96 E1	Coupe Green 97 E4	Hoghton 98 B2	Newton 223 A5	St Michael's on W. 155 C7
Bank Lane 49 E7	Cow Ark 184 C8	Hollins Lane 204 D2	Newton-with-S. 113 F2	Staining 130 E5
Banks 53 F6	Crossgill 231 E1	Holme Chapel 107 A6	Newtown. 58 A2	Stake Pool 196 E4
Barber's Moor. 57 D3	Croston. 57 B2	Holmes 55 B3	Norcross 151 A7	Stalmine 174 C7
Barley 167 B5	Cuddy Hill 135 B7	Holmeswood. 37 C7	Normoss 130 B7	Standish 28 F2
Barley Green. 167 D5	Cumeragh Village 137 F6	Hornby 232 B7	Oakenclough. 220 C2	Staynall 174 A4
Barnoldswick 200 C1	Darwen. 80 E1	Horton 225 E5	Ollerton Fold. 78 D5	Storth 237 F5
Barrow 164 D1	Dolphinholme 220 A8	Horwich 31 D4	Ormskirk. 15 C6	Street 220 A6
Barrowford 168 C4	Downham 188 B5	Hoscar 25 D4	Orrell 10 E7	Sunny Bower. 122 B1
Barton. 136 B7	Drummersdale 23 C7	Huncoat 124 E2	Osbaldeston 120 D4	Swillbrook. 135 B2
Becconsall 72 E1	Duncombe 156 F3	Hurlston 23 B2	Oswaldtwistle 102 B3	Tardy Gate 76 B8
Belmont 45 C4	Dunsop Bridge 222 C5	Hurlston Green 23 B3	Out Rawcliffe 175 C1	Tarleton 56 A7
Belthorn 81 F6	Eagland Hill 176 C8	Hurst Green 141 F8	Over Burrow 235 E7	Thistleton 132 C8
Bescar. 23 A7	Earby. 201 A2	Hutton. 94 D2	Over Kellet 231 A8	Thornton 173 D1
Beverley 168 E7	Earnshaw Bridge. 75 E2	Ince Blundell. 3 E4	Over Town 107 A8	Thornton in L 236 F4
Bickerstaffe 7 F5	Eccleston 40 D7	Inglewhite. 158 B3	Overton 205 D8	Thornton-in-C 201 A6
Billington 143 B3	Edenfield 67 D3	Inskip 134 D8	Padiham 125 C6	Thorpe Green 77 E4
Bilsborrow 157 A5	Edgworth 47 D6	Jack Green 77 F8	Parbold 26 D2	Tockholes 80 A2
Bispham Green 26 B7	Egerton 46 E2	Johnson's Hillock 60 E6	Paythorne 225 C7	Tosside 230 C2
Blackburn 100 F1	Ellel. 207 B5	Kelbrook. 192 A6	Peel 110 F4	Town End 153 C8
Blacko. 168 D7	Elswick 154 A1	Kingsfold 95 D2	Peel Hill 110 E7	Trawden. 170 C2
Blackpool 129 A4	Enfield 124 A2	Kirkby 1 A2	Pendleton 165 B4	Tunstall. 235 E4
Blackrod 30 D2	Esprick 132 D5	Kirkby Lonsdale 238 E3	Penwortham 95 C5	Turner Green 119 C2
Bolton Green. 41 C8	Euxton. 59 D3	Kirkham 113 A5	Pilling 196 C6	Waddington 186 C4
Bolton-by-B 224 D4	Fairview 43 A1	Knott End-on-S 194 E5	Pilling Lane 195 B6	Walk Mill. 106 F8
Bolton-le-S. 216 B5	Farington 75 F6	Knowle Green 161 B1	Pinfold 22 F4	Walmer Bridge 73 F5
Bonds 178 C6	Farleton 232 A6	Knowley 60 F2	Pleasington. 99 C1	Walton Summit. 77 B8
Borwick. 234 B4	Fence 146 E7	Lancaster 210 C6	Potters Brook 204 B5	Walton-le-D 96 D4
Bowgreave 178 D4	Fisher's Row 196 E5	Lane Bottom 148 B3	Poulton-le-F. 151 E2	Warton 91 D6
Bracewell 225 F3	Fleetwood 194 A6	Lane Ends 224 A5	Preesall. 195 A3	Warton, Carnforth. 217 D5
Bretherton 56 E6	Ford Green 198 F2	Lane Heads 154 D3	Preesall Park 195 C1	Water 86 A8
Brierfield 147 D5	Forest Holme 86 A7	Laneshaw Bridge 170 F6	Preston 95 C8	Waterside 81 E3
Brindle 77 F5	Formby 11 E3	Langho 142 D1	Quernmore 226 A6	Weeton 131 F2
Brinscall 61 E7	Forton 204 B3	Lea Town 114 F3	Radford 64 A8	Weeton Camp 131 D5
Broadfield 75 E1	Foulridge 191 D1	Leck 236 B7	Rainford Junction. 8 F2	Weir 87 A7
Brockhall Village 142 C5	Freckleton 92 C7	Lewth 135 A6	Rake Foot 85 A7	Wennington 235 E1
Brookbottoms 49 C3	Fulwood 116 D5	Leyland 76 A1	Ramsbottom 49 C5	West Bradford. 186 F5
Broughton. 136 D3	Galgate 207 B3	Limbrick 43 A6	Rathmell 230 F6	Westby 111 E4
Brownside 127 F6	Garstang 178 D7	Little Eccleston 154 A5	Ratten Row 154 B8	Westhead 16 D4
Burnley 127 A7	Gisburn 225 C4	Little Knowley 60 F3	Rawtenstall 85 B1	Westhouse 236 E5
Burscough 24 D4	Glasson 205 F5	Little Plumpton 111 D5	Read 144 D2	Whalley 143 B5
Burscough Bridge 24 D5	Goodshaw Chapel. 105 B1	Littledale. 226 B8	Red Scar 118 B5	Wharles. 133 F4
Burton in L 236 C3	Goosnargh 137 C6	Longridge 139 A8	Ribchester 140 D3	Wheatley Lane 167 E1
Burton-in-K 234 C7	Great Altcar 12 E1	Longshaw 10 E1	Riley Green 78 E8	Wheelton 61 A7
Bury 32 A1	Great Eccleston 154 C4	Longton 74 A8	Rimington 188 F8	White Stake 75 B7
Butt Yeats 232 B6	Great Harwood 123 D4	Lostock Hall 76 A7	Ring o'Bells. 25 B2	Whitechapel 158 D7
Cadshaw 64 D1	Great Knowley 60 E3	Low Bentham 233 C4	Rishton 123 C2	Whitehall 64 B5
Calder Vale 179 E7	Great Mitton 163 F3	Lower Ballam 111 A3	Rising Bridge 84 A8	Whitewell Bottom 85 F5
Carleton 151 A5	Great Plumpton 111 E7	Lower Bartle 115 D8	Rivington 43 F2	Whittington 235 D7
Carnforth 217 C2	Greenhalgh 132 C5	Lower Green Bank 226 B1	Rochdale. 51 C2	Whittle-le-W 60 C7
Casterton 238 E5	Gregson Lane 97 E2	Lowgill 233 C3	Royal Oak 6 F4	Whittlestone Head 64 F4
Catforth 134 F4	Grimsargh 138 D1	Lucas Green 60 C4	Rufford 38 C4	Whitworth 70 D1
Caton 231 C3	Grindleton 187 B7	Lumb 90 B3	Runshaw Moor 58 E4	Wilpshire 121 E5
Catterall 178 E2	Hale Nook 175 A5	Lytham 88 F3	Sabden 144 F8	Winewall 170 C4
Chapeltown. 47 C4	Halsall. 22 C1	Lytham St Anne's 89 E5	Salesbury 121 D6	Winmarleigh 198 E4
Charnock Green 41 C6	Halton 214 F7	Maghull 5 B1	Saltcotes 90 D5	Within Grove 124 E1
Charnock Richard. 41 D4	Halton Green 231 A4	Mawdesley 39 C2	Salterforth 191 D7	Withnell 79 B1
Chatburn. 187 D5	Hambleton 174 C1	Melling 235 C1	Salwick 114 E3	Withnell Fold 78 C3
Chipping 182 D3	Hammerton Mere 229 E1	Mellor 120 F2	Samlesbury 118 E1	Woodplumpton 135 E2
Chorley 42 D6	Hampson Green 207 C1	Mellor Brook. 120 C3	Samlesbury Bottoms 98 D6	Woodsfold 134 E6
Church 102 E7	Hapton 125 B4	Mere Brow 54 E2	Sawley 224 C1	Worsthorne. 128 A5
Churchtown 178 A2	Haskayne 13 F4	Mereclough 128 A1	Scarisbrick 22 E7	Wray 232 D6
Claughton 179 D2	Haslingden 84 B4	Mereside 130 B1	Scorton 199 E6	Wrayton 235 E3
Claughton, Lancaster . . . 231 E5	Hawkshaw. 49 C8	Middleton 209 A2	Scronkey. 196 E3	Wrea Green 112 B3
Clayton Brook 77 A5	Hesketh Bank 72 D4	Moor End 174 C6	Sharneyford 87 D5	Wrightington Bar 27 F2
Clayton Green 77 A3	Hesketh Lane 160 D3	Moor Side 133 D1	Sherwood 117 A6	Wymott 57 F6
Clayton-le-M 123 D2	Heskin Green 40 D3	Morecambe. 212 B5	Shevington 19 F5	Yealand Redmayne 219 E4
Clayton-le-W 76 D2	Hest Bank 215 F1	Moss Edge 176 A3	Shevington Moor 28 A2	
		Moss Side 75 B1		

A

A K Bsns Pk PR9 . . . . .35 A6
Aalborg Pl LA1 . . . . .210 F7
Abbey Cl Formby L37 . . . .12 B2
Orrell WN8 . . . . .10 C7
Abbey Cres BB3 . . . . .64 C8
Abbey Dale
Appley Bridge WN6 . . . . . .19 D7
Burscough L40 . . . . .24 F3
Abbey Dr WN5 . . . . .10 E6
Abbey Farm BB7 . . . . . . .143 B6
Abbey Fields BB7 . . . . . . .143 C5
Abbey Fold L40 . . . . .24 D5
Abbey Gdns PR8 . . . . .34 A4
Abbey Gr PR6 . . . . .30 B7
Abbey La L40 . . . . .24 C1
Abbey Mews BB7 . . . . . . .143 C5
Abbey Rd Blackpool FY4 . .109 D5
Whalley BB7 . . . . .143 C5
Abbey St Accrington BB5 .103 C6
Accrington, Scaitcliffe BB5 .103 C5
Bacup OL13 . . . . .86 F4
Preston PR2 . . . . .95 D8
Abbey Terr BB7 . . . . .164 D1
Abbey View PR6 . . . . .79 A1
Abbey Village
Cty Prim Sch PR6 . . . . . .79 C1
Abbey Wlk PR1 . . . . .95 D3
Abbeydale LA3 . . . . .212 E2
Abbeyfield 5 BB11 . . . . .127 B4
Abbeyfield Cl LA1 . . . . . .211 A3
Abbeyfield Ho
Barnoldswick BB18 . . . . .200 A3
10 Burnley BB11 . . . . . .126 E5
Abbeystead WN8 . . . . .9 C7
Abbeystead Dr LA1 . . . . .211 A3
Abbeystead Ho 8 LA1 . . .211 A3
Abbeystead La LA2 . . . . .226 E2
Abbeystead Rd LA2 . . . . .226 C1
Abbeyville FY4 . . . . .109 C6
Abbeyway WN8 . . . . .9 C6
Abbot Meadow PR1 . . . . . .95 D4
Abbot Wlk BB7 . . . . .165 A8
Abbots Cl Formby L37 . . . .12 A1
Kirkham PR4 . . . . .113 C4
Rawtenstall BB4 . . . . .85 A4
Abbots Croft BB7 . . . . . . .143 C5
Abbots Row FY8 . . . . .89 D6
Abbots Way Formby L37 . . .12 B1
Lancaster LA1 . . . . .210 C8
Abbotsford L39 . . . . .15 F5
Abbotsford Ave BB2 . . . . .100 D1
Abbotsford Rd FY3 . . . . . .130 A3
Abbotsgate LA6 . . . . .238 B2
Abbotsway PR1 . . . . .95 C6
Abbott Brow BB2 . . . . . . .120 E3
Abbott Clough Ave BB1 . .101 E4
Abbott Clough Cl BB1 . . .101 E4
Abbott Croft PR2 . . . . . . .116 A7
Abbott St BL6 . . . . .31 B4
Abbotts Wlk FY7 . . . . .194 A5
Abel St BB10 . . . . .127 A8
Abercorn Pl FY4 . . . . .109 A5
Abercrombie Rd FY3 . . . . .193 F4
Aberdare Cl BB1 . . . . . . .100 E7
Aberdeen Dr BB1 . . . . . . .101 A4
Aberdeen Gdns OL12 . . . . .51 D4
Aberdeen Rd LA1 . . . . . . .211 A7
Abernethy St BL6 . . . . .31 D2
Abingdon Dr PR2 . . . . . . .116 B1
Abingdon Gr LA3 . . . . . . .209 A4
Abingdon Rd BB12 . . . . . .125 D7
Abingdon St FY1 . . . . . . .129 B5
Abinger St BB10 . . . . .147 C1
Abington Dr PR9 . . . . .54 A5
Abner Row BB8 . . . . .191 D1
Abraham Altham Ct BB10 147 F3
Abraham St
Accrington BB5 . . . . .103 B5
Blackburn BB2 . . . . .100 E2
11 Horwich BL6 . . . . .31 B4
Abrams Fold PR9 . . . . .53 F5
Abrams Gn PR9 . . . . .53 F5
Acacia Cl 4 FY5 . . . . . . .173 D1
Acacia Rd PR2 . . . . .117 E2
Acacia Wlk 4 BB1 . . . . . .101 B5
Accrington & District
Golf Course BB5 . . . . . .102 B6
Accrington
& Rossendale Coll BB5 .103 D5
Accrington & Rossendale
Coll Rawtenstall Ctr BB4 .84 F2
Accrington Rd
Blackburn BB1 . . . . .101 C4
Burnley BB11 . . . . .126 C5
Hapton BB11 . . . . .125 E3
Whalley BB6,BB7 . . . . . .143 E4
Accrington Sta BB5 . . . . .103 B6
Accrington
Victoria Hospl BB5 . . . . .103 B7
Acer Gr PR2 . . . . .117 F3
Ackhurst La WN5 . . . . .19 F2
Ackhurst Rd PR7 . . . . .41 F8
Ackroyd St 10 OL14 . . . . .108 B1
Acorn Ave BB5 . . . . .102 F3
Acorn Bank PR3 . . . . .178 C8
Acorn Bsns Ctr L33 . . . . . . .1 B1
Acorn Cl PR5 . . . . .59 A8
Acorn Mews FY4 . . . . .130 D1
Acorn St Bacup OL13 . . . . .86 F2
Blackburn BB1 . . . . .101 B4
Acornfield Rd L33 . . . . .1 D2
Acre Ave OL13 . . . . .69 D8

Acre Cl BL0 . . . . .67 D3
Acre Gate FY4 . . . . .109 E7
Acre Gr PR4 . . . . .73 F3
Acre Mill Rd OL13 . . . . . . .69 D8
Acre Moss La LA4 . . . . . . .212 D4
Acre St Brierfield BB10 . . .148 A3
Burnley BB10 . . . . .147 B1
Whitworth OL12 . . . . .70 D1
Acre View OL13 . . . . .69 D7
Acrefield Blackburn BB2 . .100 A7
Clayton Brook PR5 . . . . . .77 C5
Newburgh WN8 . . . . .26 A1
Padiham BB12 . . . . .145 C1
Acregate WN8 . . . . .9 C7
Acregate La PR1 . . . . .117 C5
Acremount BB12 . . . . .144 D2
Acres La Great Altcar L37 . . .3 E8
Maghull L31,L39 . . . . .4 E7
Preesall FY6 . . . . .195 A3
Acres The BB8 . . . . .143 E8
Acresbrook Rd BB12 . . . . .145 F6
Acresfield Adlington PR7 . . .29 F6
Colne BB8 . . . . .170 A5
Acresfield Cl BL6 . . . . .30 C3
Acreswood Cl PR7 . . . . . . .28 E8
Active Way BB11 . . . . .127 A6
Acton Rd FY4 . . . . .129 E1
Ada St Blackburn BB2 . . . .100 A5
Burnley BB10 . . . . .147 B1
Nelson BB9 . . . . .147 E6
Ramsbottom BL0 . . . . .49 B5
Adamson St Burnley BB12 126 C6
Padiham BB12 . . . . .145 C1
Addington Rd LA2,LA6 . . .231 B7
Addington St BB1 . . . . . . .101 A4
Addison Cl BB2 . . . . .100 C5
Addison Cres FY3 . . . . . . .129 D6
Addison Ct FY6 . . . . .194 D5
Addison Rd FY7 . . . . .194 A3
Addison St BB5 . . . . .103 C7
Addle St LA1 . . . . .211 A4
Adelaide Ave FY5 . . . . . . .151 C8
Adelaide Cl 5 FY1 . . . . . .129 C5
Adelaide La BB5 . . . . .103 C5
Adelaide St
Accrington BB5 . . . . .103 C5
Blackpool FY1 . . . . .129 B5
8 Burnley BB11 . . . . . . .126 D6
6 Enfield BB5 . . . . .124 A1
Fleetwood FY7 . . . . .194 B5
Preston PR1 . . . . .96 B8
2 Ramsbottom BL0 . . . . . .49 A4
Rawtenstall BB4 . . . . .85 A7
Adelaide St W FY1 . . . . . .129 B4
Adelaide Terr 100 C5
Adelphi Ho 1 PR1 . . . . . .116 E1
Adelphi Pl 3 PR1 . . . . .95 F8
Adelphi St
6 Blackpool FY1 . . . . . . .129 B5
Burnley BB11 . . . . .127 A4
Lancaster LA1 . . . . .211 A6
Preston PR1 . . . . .116 E1
Standish WN6 . . . . .28 E2
Adlington Ave FY6 . . . . . .151 B3
Adlington Cty Prim Sch
PR7 . . . . .29 F7
Adlington St BB11 . . . . . .127 A6
Adlington Sta PR6 . . . . . . .30 A6
Admiral Cl FY8 . . . . .109 E1
Admiral St BB10 . . . . .127 B5
Admiral Way PR2 . . . . .94 D7
Admirals Sound FY5 . . . . .172 C2
Admiralty Cl L40 . . . . .24 C2
Adrian St FY1 . . . . .129 B1
Adstone Ave FY3 . . . . .129 F1
Agate St BB1 . . . . .121 F1
Ager St OL13 . . . . .69 C8
Agglebys Rd FY6 . . . . . . .173 F8
Agnes Ing La LA2 . . . . . . .232 D7
Agnes St Blackburn BB2 . .100 C3
11 Preston PR1 . . . . .96 A8
Agnew Rd FY7 . . . . .193 F4
Agnew St FY8 . . . . .90 A3
Aiken Ct PR4 . . . . .113 A5
Aikengill Rd LA2 . . . . .233 D4
Ailsa Ave FY4 . . . . .129 F2
Ailsa Cl PR3 . . . . .136 B8
Ailsa Rd BB1 . . . . .101 D3
Ailsa Wlk LA3 . . . . .208 E7
Ainley Ct 10 FY1 . . . . . . .129 C6
Ainscough Brook Ho 1
PR2 . . . . .117 E3
Ainsdale & Birkdale Hills
Nature Reserve PR8 . . . .20 B7
Ainsdale Ave
Blackpool FY4 . . . . .150 E5
Brierfield BB10 . . . . .147 C5
Edgworth BL7 . . . . .47 E6
Fleetwood FY7 . . . . .172 C5
Thornton FY5 . . . . .173 D1
Ainsdale CE Prim Sch
PR8 . . . . .20 D4
Ainsdale Cl LA1 . . . . .213 D3
Ainsdale Dr Darwen BB3 . . .64 B5
Preston PR2 . . . . .115 E2
Whitworth OL12 . . . . .51 D7
Ainsdale High Sch PR8 . . .20 C6
Ainsdale Sta PR8 . . . . .20 C5
Ainse Rd BL6 . . . . .30 B3
Ainslie Cl BB6 . . . . .123 B5
Ainslie Rd PR2 . . . . .116 E3
Ainslie St 8 BB12 . . . . . . .126 C6
Ainsworth Ave BL6 . . . . . .31 E2
Ainsworth Mall BB1 . . . . .100 E5
Ainsworth St BB1 . . . . . . .100 E5
Aintree Cres PR8 . . . . .34 F4
Aintree Dr BB3 . . . . .81 A7
Aintree Rd Blackpool FY4 .129 D1

Aintree Rd continued
Thornton FY5 . . . . .151 B8
Air Hill Terr 8 OL12 . . . . .51 C1
Airdrie Cres BB11 . . . . . .126 D4
Airdrie Pl FY2 . . . . .150 E6
Aire Cl LA3 . . . . .213 B3
Airedale LA2 . . . . .207 B4
Airedale Ave FY3 . . . . . . .129 E3
Airedale Ct FY6 . . . . .151 C4
Airegate L31 . . . . .5 B2
Airey Ho PR3 . . . . .161 D1
Airey St BB5 . . . . .103 D3
Airton Garth BB9 . . . . . . .168 C3
Aitken Cl BL0 . . . . .49 B5
Aitken St Accrington BB5 .103 C7
Haslingden BL0 . . . . .67 C5
Ajax St 3 BL0 . . . . .49 B5
Alamein Rd LA5 . . . . .217 E1
Alan Gr LA3 . . . . .208 F6
Alan Haigh Ct BB8 . . . . . .169 D6
Alan Ramsbottom Way
BB6 . . . . .123 E4
Alandale Cl PR5 . . . . .59 B7
Alaska St BB2 . . . . .100 E7
Albany Ave FY4 . . . . .109 B5
Albany Cl FY6 . . . . .130 E8
Albany Dr
Bamber Bridge PR5 . . . . . .96 D2
Copster Green BB1 . . . . .121 C8
Albany High Sch PR7 . . . . .42 E5
Albany Rd Blackburn BB2 .100 B6
3 Fleetwood FY7 . . . . . .193 F4
Lytham St Anne's FY8 . . . .89 C5
Morecambe LA4 . . . . . . .212 C4
Southport PR9 . . . . .52 C1
Albatros St PR1 . . . . .117 B1
Albemarle St BB7 . . . . . . .164 D8
Albemarle Ct 2 BB7 . . . . .164 D8
Albert Ho BB4 . . . . .85 D1
Albert Pl Blackburn BB3 . .80 F7
Southport PR8 . . . . .34 B8
Albert Rd
Barnoldswick BB18 . . . . .200 B2
Blackpool FY1 . . . . .129 C5
Colne BB8 . . . . .169 D4
Formby L37 . . . . .2 B8
Fulwood PR2 . . . . .116 F3
Lancaster LA1 . . . . .213 F1
Leyland PR5 . . . . .59 C8
Lytham St Anne's FY8 . . . .89 A7
Morecambe LA4 . . . . . . .212 C4
Preston PR1 . . . . .116 F2
Rawtenstall BB4 . . . . .85 A8
Rufford L40 . . . . .38 A3
Southport PR9 . . . . .52 D1
Albert Sq 11 FY7 . . . . . . .194 B5
Albert St Accrington BB5 .103 C5
Blackburn BB2 . . . . .100 C2
Brierfield BB9 . . . . .147 B5
Burnley BB11 . . . . .127 B6
Bury BL9 . . . . .32 A2
3 Carnforth LA5 . . . . . . .217 D1
Carnforth,Millhead LA5 . .217 D3
1 Chorley PR7 . . . . .42 D7
2 Church BB5 . . . . .102 E6
Clayton-le-M BB5 . . . . . .123 F2
Darwen BB3 . . . . .64 B5
Earby BB18 . . . . .201 B2
Egerton BL7 . . . . .46 D3
Fleetwood FY7 . . . . .194 B4
Great Harwood BB6 . . . . .123 D4
Hoddlesden BB3 . . . . .81 F1
Horwich BL6 . . . . .31 B4
Kirkham PR4 . . . . .112 F6
Lytham St Anne's FY8 . . . .90 C3
Nelson BB9 . . . . .147 D8
Oswaldtwistle BB5 . . . . . .102 E4
Padiham BB12 . . . . .125 C8
Ramsbottom BL0 . . . . . . .49 B6
Rishton BB1 . . . . .123 B1
Wheelton PR6 . . . . .61 A7
Whitewell Bottom BB4 . . . .85 E5
Whitworth OL12 . . . . .51 C8
Albert Terr Bacup OL13 . . .86 F3
9 Barrowford BB9 . . . . . .168 D3
Calder Vale PR3 . . . . . . .179 E8
8 Preston PR1 . . . . .117 A1
Rawtenstall BB4 . . . . .85 B2
Southport PR8 . . . . .34 A5
Alberta Cl BB2 . . . . .100 B8
Albion Ave FY3 . . . . .129 F6
Albion Ct BB1 . . . . .126 E4
Albion Mews LA1 . . . . . . .214 A1
Albion Rd Blackburn BB2 .100 D1
Earby BB18 . . . . .201 B2
Albion St Accrington BB5 .103 B6
Bacup OL13 . . . . .87 A3
7 Bacup,Stacksteads OL13 .69 C8
Blackburn BB2 . . . . .100 C1
Brierfield BB9 . . . . .147 B5
Burnley BB11 . . . . .126 E5
Chorley PR7 . . . . .42 C7
1 Clitheroe BB7 . . . . . . .164 F8
Earby BB18 . . . . .201 B2
Lancaster LA1 . . . . .214 A1
4 Nelson BB9 . . . . .147 D8
7 Padiham BB12 . . . . . . .125 D7
Albrighton Cl PR5 . . . . . . .76 B7
Albrighton Cres PR5 . . . . .76 B7
Albrighton Rd PR5 . . . . . . .76 C7
Albyn Bank Rd PR1 . . . . . .96 B7
Albyn St E PR1 . . . . .96 B7
Alcester Ave PR1 . . . . . . .95 C5
Alconbury Cres FY5 . . . . .172 C2
Aldate Gr PR2 . . . . .116 A2
Aldcliffe Cotts LA1 . . . . . .210 D5
Aldcliffe Ct LA4 . . . . .212 E3

Aldcliffe Mews LA1 . . . . .210 D5
Aldcliffe Pl LA1 . . . . .210 E7
Aldcliffe Rd Lancaster LA1 210 E6
7 Preston PR2 . . . . .115 E1
Alden Cl BB4 . . . . .67 A6
Alden Rd BB4,BL8 . . . . . . .66 F5
Alden Rise BB4 . . . . .67 A6
Alden Terr 5 LA1 . . . . . . .213 F3
Alder Bank Blackburn BB2 .100 B4
20 Rawtenstall BB4 . . . . .85 A4
Alder Cl Leyland PR5 . . . . .58 B8
Newton-with-S PR4 . . . . .114 A2
Thornton FY5 . . . . .173 C1
Alder Coppice PR2 . . . . . .115 E3
Lancaster LA1 . . . . .210 D8
Alder Dr
Charnock Richard PR7 . . . .41 D3
Gregson Lane PR5 . . . . . . .97 C3
Alder Gr Blackpool FY3 . . .129 E7
Coppull PR7 . . . . .41 F1
Huncoat BB5 . . . . .124 C2
Lancaster LA1 . . . . .210 D8
Lytham St Anne's FY8 . . . .90 A4
Poulton-le-F FY6 . . . . . . .151 D1
Alder Grange High Sch
BB4 . . . . .85 A4
Alder Hill Croft BB18 . . . .201 C4
Alder Hill St BB18 . . . . . .201 B2
Alder La Formby L37,L39 . . .12 E7
Moss Edge PR3 . . . . .176 A1
Parbold WN8 . . . . .26 C1
Alder Meadow Cl OL12 . . .51 A1
Alder Rd PR2 . . . . .118 A4
Alder St Bacup OL13 . . . . .86 F3
4 Blackburn BB1 . . . . . .101 A7
Burnley BB12 . . . . .126 C7
Rawtenstall BB4 . . . . .85 B3
Alderbank BL6 . . . . .30 F3
Alderdale Ave PR8 . . . . . .20 A5
Alderfield PR1 . . . . .95 D3
Alderford Cl BB7 . . . . . . .164 C7
Alderley WN8 . . . . .9 C6
Alderley Ave FY4 . . . . . . .109 B5
Alderley Hts LA1 . . . . . . .213 F3
Alderman Foley Dr OL12 . .51 A2
Alderney Cl BB2 . . . . .100 B1
Alders The PR3 . . . . .199 C1
Aldersleigh Cres PR5 . . . .97 C1
Alderson Cres L37 . . . . . . .11 F4
Alderville Cl PR4 . . . . .91 F6
Alderway BL0 . . . . .67 C5
Alderwood Gr BL0 . . . . . . .67 D4
Aldfield Ave PR2 . . . . . . .115 C4
Aldingham Ct LA4 . . . . . .212 E3
Aldingham Wlk LA4 . . . . .212 D5
Aldon Gr PR4 . . . . .94 A1
Aldon Rd FY6 . . . . .151 F2
Aldren's La LA1 . . . . .213 F3
Aldwych Ave FY3 . . . . . . .129 E3
Aldwych Dr
Bamber Bridge PR5 . . . . . .76 B7
Preston PR2 . . . . .116 A2
Aldwych Pl BB1 . . . . .121 F2
Alert St PR2 . . . . .116 C1
Alexander Cl
Accrington BB5 . . . . .103 E1
Burscough L40 . . . . .24 F3
Alexander Ct FY6 . . . . . . .151 D3
Alexander Dr L31 . . . . . . .5 D3
Alexander Gr BB12 . . . . . .126 B6
Alexander Pl PR2 . . . . . . .138 C1
Alexander St BB9 . . . . . . .169 A2
Alexandra Cl BB5 . . . . . . .123 E3
Alexandra Ct 4 LA1 . . . . .210 F8
Alexandra Ho
Blackburn BB1 . . . . .101 B3
10 Preston PR1 . . . . . . .117 C1
Alexandra Mews
1 Ormskirk L39 . . . . .15 E6
8 Southport PR9 . . . . . . .34 C8
Alexandra Pavilion 5
PR1 . . . . .117 A1
Alexandra Pl BB6 . . . . . . .123 D6
Alexandra Rd
Bamber Bridge PR5 . . . . . .96 D3
Blackburn BB2 . . . . .100 C6
Blackpool FY1 . . . . .129 B1
Burscough L40 . . . . .24 D4
Carnforth LA5 . . . . .217 D1
8 Darwen BB3 . . . . .80 F2
Formby L37 . . . . .11 B1
Kirkham PR4 . . . . .113 A6
Lancaster LA1 . . . . .213 F1
Longridge PR3 . . . . .139 A7
Lytham St Anne's FY8 . . . .89 A7
Morecambe LA3 . . . . . . .212 B3
Southport PR9 . . . . .34 D8
Thornton FY5 . . . . .151 C8
Alexandra St
Clayton-le-M BB5 . . . . . .123 E3
Preston PR1 . . . . .96 C7
Alexandra View 7 BB3 . . .80 F7
Alexandria Dr FY8 . . . . . . .88 F4
Alexandria St BB4 . . . . . . .84 F4
Alford Fold PR2 . . . . .116 D7
Alfred St Blackpool FY1 . .129 C5
Bury BL9 . . . . .32 A1
Darwen BB3 . . . . .64 B6
Egerton BL7 . . . . .46 D3
Lancaster LA1 . . . . .211 A8
10 Ramsbottom BL0 . . . . .49 B5
Whitworth OL12 . . . . .70 D2
Algar St BB9 . . . . .168 F2
Alice Ave PR5 . . . . .76 A1

Alice Sq 4 PR1 . . . . .117 A1
Alice St Accrington BB5 . . .103 D7
Barnoldswick BB18 . . . . .200 B2
8 Darwen BB3 . . . . .64 A8
Morecambe LA4 . . . . . . .212 F5
Oswaldtwistle BB5 . . . . . .102 E3
Alicia Cl OL12 . . . . .51 E1
Alicia Dr OL12 . . . . .51 E1
Alisan Rd FY6 . . . . .151 B5
Alker La PR7 . . . . .60 B3
Alker St PR7 . . . . .42 C7
Alkincoats Rd BB8 . . . . . .169 C5
All Hallows RC High Sch
PR1 . . . . .95 A3
All Hallows Rd FY2 . . . . . .150 D5
All Saint's Cl BB5 . . . . . . .102 B4
All Saints CE Prim Sch
Appley Bridge WN6 . . . . . .27 C1
Chorley PR7 . . . . .42 B5
Clayton-le-M BB5 . . . . . .123 F2
All Saints Cl
Padiham BB12 . . . . .125 F7
Rawtenstall BB4 . . . . .105 A1
All Saints RC High Sch
BB4 . . . . .84 D1
All Saints Rd FY2 . . . . . . .150 E6
All Saints' Rd FY4 . . . . . . .88 E6
Allan Critchlow Way BB1 123 B2
Allan St OL13 . . . . .86 F1
Allandale FY4 . . . . .109 C5
Allandale Ave FY5 . . . . . . .172 F4
Allen Cl Cleveleys FY5 . . .172 C1
Fleetwood FY7 . . . . .193 D2
Allen Ct BB10 . . . . .127 A8
Allen St BB10 . . . . .127 A8
Allen Way FY7 . . . . .193 D2
Allenbury Pl FY3 . . . . . . .130 A2
Allenby Ave PR2 . . . . .117 B4
Allenby Rd FY8 . . . . .88 E8
Allendale Gr BB10 . . . . . .127 F4
Allendale St Burnley BB12 126 B6
Colne BB8 . . . . .169 F5
Allengate PR2 . . . . .116 F4
Allerton Cl BB3 . . . . .81 A2
Allerton Dr BB12 . . . . . . .126 D6
Allerton Rd
Bamber Bridge PR5 . . . . . .96 C4
Southport PR9 . . . . .52 E1
Alleys Gn BB7 . . . . .186 E1
Alleytroyds BB5 . . . . .102 E5
Alliance Bsns Pk BB5 . . .103 A5
Alliance St BB5 . . . . .103 F1
Allington Cl PR5 . . . . .96 E3
Allison Gr BB8 . . . . .169 F6
Allonby Ave FY5 . . . . .172 E4
Allotment La PR3 . . . . . . .155 C7
Allsprings Cl BB6 . . . . . . .123 D6
Allsprings Dr BB6 . . . . . . .123 D6
Alma Ave BB8 . . . . .191 D1
Alma Cl WN8 . . . . .10 C7
Alma Ct Orrell WN8 . . . . . .10 C7
Southport PR8 . . . . .20 F7
Alma Dr PR7 . . . . .41 E4
Alma Hill WN8 . . . . .10 C7
Alma Hill Est WN8 . . . . . .10 C7
Alma Ho LA1 . . . . .210 F6
Alma Ind Est 28 OL12 . . .51 E1
Alma Par WN8 . . . . .10 C7
Alma Pl Accrington BB5 . . .83 E8
Clitheroe BB7 . . . . .164 D7
Alma Rd Lancaster LA1 . .210 F6
Laneshaw Bridge BB8 . . .170 D6
Orrell WN8 . . . . .10 C7
Southport PR8 . . . . .34 A4
Alma Row PR5 . . . . .97 E1
Alma St Bacup OL13 . . . . .87 A2
Blackburn BB2 . . . . .100 D5
9 Clayton-le-M BB5 . . . . .123 F3
Padiham BB12 . . . . .125 C8
Preston PR1 . . . . .117 A1
1 Rochdale OL12 . . . . . . .51 F1
Alma Terr BB11 . . . . .105 B4
Almhouses BD23 . . . . . . .201 A5
Almond Ave
Burscough Bridge L40 . . . .24 E6
4 Bury BL9 . . . . .32 C3
Almond Brook Rd WN6 . . .28 C1
Almond Cl
Abbey Village PR6 . . . . . . .79 B2
Fulwood PR2 . . . . .117 D6
Penwortham PR1 . . . . .95 B3
Almond Cres BB4 . . . . .67 F8
Almond St BB3 . . . . .64 A8
Almonry The L40 . . . . .17 B7
Almshouses
34 Lancaster LA1 . . . . . .210 F8
Ormskirk L39 . . . . .6 A7
7 Rawtenstall BB4 . . . . . .84 E2
Alnwick Cl BB12 . . . . .126 E7
Alpha St Darwen BB3 . . . . .64 B8
8 Nelson BB9 . . . . .168 F2
Salterforth BB18 . . . . . . .191 E8
Alpic Dr FY5 . . . . .150 C7
Alpine Ave
Bamber Bridge PR5 . . . . . .76 B7
Blackpool FY4 . . . . .109 E5
Alpine Cl
Bamber Bridge PR5 . . . . . .76 B7
Hoddlesden BB3 . . . . .81 E1
Alpine Gr PR2 . . . . .80 B8
Alpine Rd PR6 . . . . .60 E3
Alpine View LA5 . . . . .216 A6
Alsop St PR1 . . . . .116 F2
Alston Ave FY5 . . . . .172 C4
Alston Cl BB7 . . . . .144 F8
Alston Dr LA4 . . . . .213 B5
Alston Hall Coll PR3 . . . . .119 B8
Alston La PR2,PR3 . . . . . .139 A2

Alston Lane RC Prim Sch
PR3 . . . . .138 F2
Alston Rd FY2 . . . . .150 E2
Alston St PR1 . . . . .117 D1
Alt Rd Formby L37 . . . . . . .12 B2
Hightown L38 . . . . .3 A4
Altcar La Formby L37 . . . . .11 F1
Haskayne L39 . . . . .14 A2
Maghull L31 . . . . .4 F5
Runshaw Moor PR5 . . . . . .58 E5
Altcar Rd L37 . . . . .12 B2
Altham Bsns Pk BB5 . . . . .124 E6
Altham Ind Est BB5 . . . . .124 D6
Altham La BB5 . . . . .124 F4
Altham Rd Morecambe LA4 212 E3
Southport PR8 . . . . .34 E2
Altham St 2 Burnley BB10 127 A8
6 Padiham BB12 . . . . . . .125 D8
Altham St James
CE Prim Sch BB5 . . . . .124 D6
Altham Wlk LA4 . . . . .212 F3
Althorp Cl 6 FY1 . . . . . . .129 C7
Althorpe Dr PR8 . . . . .34 E3
Altom St BB1 . . . . .100 E8
Alton Cl L38 . . . . .2 F2
Altys L39 . . . . .15 F3
Alum Scar La BB2 . . . . . . .99 A6
Alvern Ave PR2 . . . . .116 D4
Alvern Cres PR2 . . . . .116 D4
Alvina La L33 . . . . .1 A5
Alwin St 8 BB11 . . . . . . .126 E6
Alwood Ave FY3 . . . . .129 F6
Amber Ave BB1 . . . . .121 F2
Amber Gate PR2 . . . . .115 F6
Amberbanks Gr FY1 . . . . .129 B2
Amberley St BB2 . . . . . . .100 C3
Amberwood PR4 . . . . . . .112 F5
Amberwood Dr BB2 . . . . .100 A1
Ambledene PR5 . . . . .77 A5
Ambleside Ave
Barnoldswick BB18 . . . . . .200 A3
Euxton PR7 . . . . .59 D1
Knott End-on-S FY6 . . . . . .194 F6
2 Rawtenstall BB4 . . . . . .84 C2
Ambleside Cl
Bamber Bridge PR5 . . . . . . .96 E2
Blackburn BB1 . . . . .101 A6
Huncoat BB5 . . . . .103 E8
Ambleside Dr BB3 . . . . . . .81 C3
Ambleside Rd
Blackpool FY4 . . . . .130 D1
Fulwood PR2 . . . . .117 C6
Lancaster LA1 . . . . .214 B2
Lytham St Anne's FY8 . . . . .109 E1
Maghull L31 . . . . .5 D2
Ambleside Wlk PR2 . . . . .117 C6
Ambrose PR5 . . . . .76 B2
Ambrose Hall La PR4 . . . .135 E3
Amelia St BB1 . . . . .101 B6
Amersham WN8 . . . . .9 C7
Amersham Cl PR4 . . . . . . .74 F8
Amersham Gr BB10 . . . . .147 D4
Amethyst St BB1 . . . . . . .121 F2
Amounderness Way
Cleveleys FY5 . . . . .172 F4
Fleetwood FY7 . . . . .194 A3
Thornton FY5 . . . . .151 C7
Ampleforth Dr PR5 . . . . . .96 A1
Amy Johnson Way FY4 . . .109 E4
Amy St OL12 . . . . .51 B1
Ancenis Ct PR4 . . . . .113 B5
Anchor Ave BB3 . . . . .80 F4
Anchor Ct PR1 . . . . .95 F7
Anchor Dr PR4 . . . . .94 D2
Anchor Gr BB3 . . . . .80 E5
Anchor Rd BB3 . . . . .80 F4
Anchor Ret Pk 1 BB11 . .127 A6
Anchor St PR9 . . . . .34 B7
Anchor Way FY8 . . . . .109 E1
Anchorage Ave PR4 . . . . . .71 F1
Anchorage Mews FY7 . . . .194 B3
Anchorage Rd FY7 . . . . . .194 B3
Anchorsholme La FY5 . . . .150 F8
Anchorsholme La E FY5 . . .172 E1
Anchorsholme La W FY5 172 C1
Anchorsholme Prim Sch
FY5 . . . . .150 E2
Anclife La LA2,LA5 . . . . . .216 B2
Andelen Cl BB11 . . . . .125 C3
Anders Dr L33 . . . . .1 A5
Andersholme La FY5 . . . . .151 A8
Anderson Cl LA1 . . . . .211 B6
Anderson Rd BB1 . . . . . . .122 A7
Anderson St 8 FY1 . . . . . .129 C4
Anderton Cl BB4 . . . . .68 F7
Anderton La BL6 . . . . .30 E4
Anderton Prim Sch PR6 . . .30 B8
Anderton Rd Euxton PR7 . . .59 D1
Higham BB12 . . . . .145 F5
Anderton St Adlington PR7 .30 A7
Chorley PR7 . . . . .42 C7
Anderton Way PR3 . . . . . .178 D6
Andertons Way PR2 . . . . .117 D5
Andreas Cl PR8 . . . . .34 B4
Andrew Ave BB4 . . . . .84 F1
Andrew Cl Blackburn BB2 . .80 B8
Ramsbottom BL8 . . . . .48 F1
Andrew Rd BB3 . . . . .169 B1
Andrew St Bury BL9 . . . . . .32 A2
Preston PR1 . . . . .117 C1
Andrews Cl L37 . . . . .11 E1
Andrews La L37 . . . . .11 E1
Andrews Yort L37 . . . . . . .11 E1
Anemone Dr BB4 . . . . .66 F8
Angel Way 3 BB8 . . . . . .169 E5
Angela St BB2 . . . . .100 B1

Anger's Hill Rd FY4 . . . . .129 F1
Angle St BB10 . . . . .127 A8
Anglesey Ave BB12 . . . . .126 A7
Anglesey St BB2 . . . . .80 B8
Anglezarke Rd PR6 . . . . . . .30 A7
Anglezarke
Woodland Trail PR6 . . . . . . .43 D6
Anglian Cl BB5 . . . . .102 C5
Angus St OL13 . . . . .69 C8
Aniline St PR6 . . . . .42 E8
Ann St Barrowford BB9 . . . .168 D3
Brierfield BB9 . . . . .147 B6
4 Clayton-le-M BB5 . . . .123 F3
Skelmersdale WN8 . . . . .8 E8
Anna's Rd FY4 . . . . .110 E3
Annan Cres FY4 . . . . .130 C1
Annandale Gdns WN8 . . . .10 A7
Annarly Fold BB11 . . . . . .128 A5
Annaside Cl 2 FY4 . . . . . .109 E7
Anne Ave PR8 . . . . .20 E6
Anne Cl BB10 . . . . .127 B5
Anne St BB11 . . . . .127 B5
Annesley Ave FY3 . . . . . . .129 E8
Annie St Accrington BB5 . . .103 C3
Ramsbottom BL0 . . . . .49 A4
5 Rawtenstall BB4 . . . . . .85 A4
Annis St PR1 . . . . .96 C8
Ansbro Ave PR4 . . . . .92 C6
Ansdell & Fairhaven Sta
FY8 . . . . .89 D4
Ansdell Cty Prim Sch FY8 .89 C5
Ansdell Gr Fulwood PR2 . . .116 C3
Southport PR9 . . . . .53 E4
Ansdell Rd Blackpool FY1 .129 D2
Horwich BL6 . . . . .31 C4
Ansdell Rd N FY8 . . . . . . .89 D4
Ansdell Rd S FY8 . . . . . . .89 D3
Ansdell St 3 PR1 . . . . . . .117 C1
Ansdell Terr BB2 . . . . . . .100 E1
Anselm Ct FY2 . . . . .150 B3
Anshaw Cl BL7 . . . . .45 C5
Anson Cl FY8 . . . . .109 D1
Anson Rd PR4 . . . . .113 B2
Anstable Rd LA4 . . . . .213 A6
Anthony Rd LA1 . . . . .210 E7
Antrim Rd FY2 . . . . .150 C1
Anvil Cl WN5 . . . . .10 D5
Anvil St OL13 . . . . .69 C8
Anzio Rd PR4 . . . . .131 C5
Apiary The PR5 . . . . .57 A6
Appealing La FY8 . . . . . . .109 E2
Apple Cl BB2 . . . . .100 C4
Apple St BB2 . . . . .100 C4
Apple St BB2 . . . . .100 C4
Apple Tree Cl PR3 . . . . . .155 D4
Apple Tree Way BB5 . . . .102 E5
Appleby Cl Accrington BB5 103 D5
Gregson Lane PR5 . . . . . . .97 C3
Appleby Dr BB9 . . . . .168 D4
Appleby Rd FY2 . . . . .150 B3
Appleby St Blackburn BB1 .101 A5
Nelson BB9 . . . . .147 B8
Preston PR1 . . . . .116 F1
Applecross Dr BB10 . . . . .127 A6
Applefields PR5 . . . . .59 B7
Applegarth
Barnoldswick BB18 . . . . . .200 C3
Barrowford BB9 . . . . .168 B1
Applegarth Rd LA3 . . . . . .209 A8
Applegarth St 3 BB18 . . .201 B1
Applesike PR4 . . . . .94 A1
Appleton Cl FY6 . . . . .151 A2
Appleton Rd WN8 . . . . . . .17 C1
Appletree Cl
Lancaster LA1 . . . . .211 A3
Penwortham PR1 . . . . .95 C2
Appletree Dr LA1 . . . . . . .211 A3
Applewood Cl FY8 . . . . . . .89 E3
Appley Bridge Sta WN6 . . .19 C7
Appley Cl WN6 . . . . .27 C2
Appley La N WN6 . . . . . . .27 C1
Appley La S WN6,WN8 . . . .19 C6
Approach Way BB11 . . . . .126 F2
Apsley Brow L31 . . . . .5 B1
Apsley Fold PR3 . . . . .139 B6
Aqueduct Rd BB2 . . . . . . .100 D1
Aqueduct St PR1 . . . . . . .116 E1
Arago St BB5 . . . . .103 C7
Aragon Cl L31 . . . . .5 E3
Arbories Ave 4 BB12 . . . .125 B8
Arbory Dr BB12 . . . . .125 B8
Arbory The PR4 . . . . .111 E7
Arbour Dr BB2 . . . . .80 D6
Arbour La Kirkby L33 . . . . . .1 B2
Shevington Moor WN6 . . . . .28 B1
Arbour Lane End PR3 . . . .160 E2
Arbour St PR8 . . . . .34 C6
Arboury St BB12 . . . . . . .125 B8
Arcadia BB8 . . . . .169 E5
Arcadia Ave L31 . . . . .5 D3
Arch St Burnley BB11 . . . .126 F6
4 Darwen BB3 . . . . .81 A1
Archbishop Hutton's
Prim Sch LA5 . . . . .217 D5
Archbishop Temple Sch
PR2 . . . . .116 F5
Archer Hill LA5 . . . . .217 D3
Archery Ave BB8 . . . . . . .191 D1
Arches The BB7 . . . . .143 B6
Arcon Ho LA1 . . . . .210 F5
Arcon Rd PR4 . . . . .41 E1
Ardee Rd PR1 . . . . .95 D6
Arden Cl Hest Bank LA2 . . .213 E8
Southport PR8 . . . . .20 A5
Arden Gn FY7 . . . . .193 E4
Ardengate LA1 . . . . .210 F4

Ardleigh Ave PR8 . . . . . . .34 E3
Ardley Rd BL6 . . . . .31 C4
Ardmore Rd FY2 . . . . .150 D2
Ardwick St BB10 . . . . . . .127 A8
Argameols Cl PR8 . . . . . . .34 F5
Argameols Rd L37 . . . . . . .11 E6
Argosy Ave FY3 . . . . .129 F8
Argosy Ct 1 FY3 . . . . . . .130 A8
Argyle Ct PR9 . . . . .52 D1
Argyle Rd 7 Leyland PR5 . .76 A1
Poulton-le-F FY6 . . . . .151 E3
Southport PR9 . . . . .52 D1
Argyle St Accrington BB5 . .103 B6
Colne BB8 . . . . .169 D5
Darwen BB3 . . . . .80 F3
Heywood OL10 . . . . .32 F1
3 Lancaster LA1 . . . . . . .211 A7
Argyll Ct FY2 . . . . .150 C1
Argyll Rd Blackpool FY2 . .150 C1
Preston PR1 . . . . .117 A1
Ariel Way FY7 . . . . .193 E4
Arkholme Ave FY1 . . . . . .129 D2
Arkholme CE Prim Sch
LA6 . . . . .235 B3
Arkholme Cl LA5 . . . . .217 E2
Arkholme Dr PR4 . . . . . . .93 F1
Arkwright Ct FY4 . . . . . . .110 C7
Arkwright Fold BB2 . . . . . .80 C8
Arkwright Rd PR1 . . . . . . .116 F2
Arkwright St
Burnley BB12 . . . . .126 C7
Horwich BL6 . . . . .31 C2
Arley Gdns BB12 . . . . . . .126 F7
Arley La WN1,WN2 . . . . . . .29 D2
Arley Rise BB2 . . . . .120 E2
Arley St PR6 . . . . .42 D8
Arlington Ave FY4 . . . . . . .109 B7
Arlington Cl
Ramsbottom BL9 . . . . .49 C2
Southport PR8 . . . . .20 A5
Arlington Rd BB3 . . . . .63 F8
Armadale Rd FY2 . . . . . . .150 E1
Armitstead Ct 3 FY8 . . . .193 F2
Armitstead Way 5 FY7 . . .193 F2
Armstrong St Horwich BL6 .31 C2
Preston PR2 . . . . .116 B2
Arnbarrow LA7 . . . . .237 E6
Arncliffe Ave BB5 . . . . . . .102 F4
Arncliffe Gr BB9 . . . . .168 C3
Arncliffe Rd Burnley BB10 .127 E5
Morecambe LA3 . . . . .212 A1
Arndale Cl FY7 . . . . .193 C2
Arndale Ctr 4 BB9 . . . . . .147 B8
Arndale Rd BB3 . . . . .139 A7
Arnhem Rd Carnforth LA5 .217 E1
Preston PR1 . . . . .96 D8
Arnian Ct L39 . . . . .6 C7
Arno St 9 PR1 . . . . .96 B7
Arnold Ave FY4 . . . . .109 C7
Arnold Cl Blackburn BB2 . .101 A1
Burnley BB11 . . . . .126 E2
Fulwood PR2 . . . . .117 E2
Arnold Jun Sch FY4 . . . . .109 C6
Arnold Pl 1 PR7 . . . . .42 A5
Arnold Rd FY8 . . . . .90 D4
Arnold Sch FY4 . . . . .109 C7
Arnold St 2 BB5 . . . . . . .103 C6
Arnott Rd Blackpool FY4 . .129 E1
Fulwood PR2 . . . . .116 C2
Arnside Ave Blackpool FY1 129 D1
Lytham St Anne's FY8 . . . . .89 C7
Arnside CE Prim Sch
LA5 . . . . .237 B2
Arnside Cl
Clayton-le-M BB5 . . . . . . .123 E2
Coupe Green PR5 . . . . .97 E4
Lancaster LA1 . . . . .211 B3
Arnside Cres Blackburn BB2 79 E8
Morecambe LA4 . . . . .212 F6
Arnside Rd Broughton PR3 136 D2
Preston PR2 . . . . .115 E2
Southport PR9 . . . . .34 C7
Arnside Sta LA5 . . . . .237 C2
Arnside Terr PR9 . . . . .34 C7
Arran Ave BB1 . . . . .101 D2
Arran Cl LA3 . . . . .208 E7
Arran St BB11 . . . . .126 E5
Arrow La LA2 . . . . .214 F7
Arrowsmith Cl PR5 . . . . . .97 C2
Arrowsmith St 7 BL6 . . . .31 C1
Arrowsmith Dr PR5 . . . . . .97 C2
Arrowsmith Gdns FY5 . . . .172 E5
Arroyo Way PR2 . . . . .117 B4
Arthur St Bacup OL13 . . . . .87 B3
Barnoldswick BB18 . . . . . .200 A3
Blackburn BB2 . . . . .100 C4
Brierfield BB9 . . . . .147 B6
Burnley BB11 . . . . .126 E6
Clayton-le-M BB5 . . . . . . .123 F3
6 Fleetwood FY7 . . . . . . .194 B5
Great Harwood BB6 . . . . . .123 D6
18 Nelson BB9 . . . . .168 C1
Preston PR1 . . . . .95 E7
Sough BB18 . . . . .192 A4
Arthur St N 5 FY7 . . . . . .194 B5
Arthur Way BB2 . . . . .100 C4
Arthurs La FY6 . . . . .174 D2
Artle Pl LA1 . . . . .213 E2
Artlebeck Cl LA2 . . . . . . .231 C3
Artlebeck Gr LA2 . . . . . . .231 C3
Artlebeck Rd LA2 . . . . . . .231 C3
Arundel Ave FY2 . . . . .150 B5
Arundel Cl FY7 . . . . .151 C5
Arundel Pl 37 PR1 . . . . . .96 A7
Arundel Rd Longton PR4 . . .94 A1
Lytham St Anne's FY8 . . . . .89 C4

Arundel Rd continued
Southport PR8 . . . . .20 F8
Arundel St BB1 . . . . .123 A6
Arundel Way PR5 . . . . .59 C8
Ascot Cl Lancaster LA1 . . .211 B4
Southport PR8 . . . . .33 E5
Ascot Gdns LA2 . . . . .213 F8
Ascot Rd Blackpool FY3 . . .129 E6
Thornton FY5 . . . . .151 B8
Ascot Way BB5 . . . . .103 D5
Ash Ave Galgate LA2 . . . . .206 F4
Haslingden BB4 . . . . .84 C3
Kirkham PR4 . . . . .113 A4
Ash Bank Cl PR3 . . . . . . .136 B8
Ash Brow WN8 . . . . .26 B1
Ash Cl Appley Bridge WN6 . .19 D7
Barrow BB7 . . . . .164 D1
Elswick PR4 . . . . .154 A1
Ormskirk L39 . . . . .15 D5
Rishton BB1 . . . . .102 B8
Ash Coppice PR2 . . . . . . .115 D2
Ash Ct PR4 . . . . .114 D2
Ash Dr
Carnforth,Warton LA5 . . . . .217 E6
Freckleton PR4 . . . . .92 A5
Freckleton,Warton PR4 . . . .91 C5
Poulton-le-F FY6 . . . . .151 E2
Thornton FY5 . . . . .173 C5
West Bradford BB7 . . . . . .186 D7
Ash Field PR2 . . . . .77 C3
Ash Gr Bamber Bridge PR5 .96 F1
Barnoldswick BB18 . . . . . .200 B2
Chorley PR7 . . . . .42 C5
Darwen BB3 . . . . .81 B2
Formby L37 . . . . .11 C1
Garstang PR3 . . . . .178 B8
8 Horwich BL6 . . . . .31 B5
Kirkham PR4 . . . . .113 B7
Lancaster LA1 . . . . .210 F5
Longton PR4 . . . . .73 F8
New Longton PR4 . . . . . . .74 F6
Orrell WN5 . . . . .10 C6
Preesall FY6 . . . . .195 A4
Ramsbottom BL0 . . . . .48 F3
3 Rawtenstall BB4 . . . . . .85 A3
Skelmersdale WN8 . . . . . . .17 D1
St Michael's on W PR3 . . . .155 C7
Water BB4 . . . . .86 A8
Wrea Green PR4 . . . . .112 C3
Ash Holme PR1 . . . . .117 C3
Ash La Clifton PR4 . . . . . .114 E2
Great Harwood BB6 . . . . . .123 B6
Longridge PR3 . . . . .139 B8
Ash Lea Gr FY6 . . . . .174 C7
Ash Mdw PR2 . . . . .115 C3
Ash Rd Coppull PR7 . . . . . .28 E8
Elswick PR4 . . . . .154 A1
Ash St Bacup OL13 . . . . . .86 F3
Blackburn BB1 . . . . .101 A7
Blackpool FY4 . . . . .109 A7
Burnley BB11 . . . . .127 B5
Bury BL9 . . . . .32 A2
Fleetwood FY7 . . . . .194 A4
Great Harwood BB6 . . . . . .123 C6
Nelson BB9 . . . . .147 B8
Oswaldtwistle BB5 . . . . . .102 A4
Southport PR8 . . . . .34 C5
Trawden BB8 . . . . .170 A4
Ash Tree Gr LA5 . . . . .215 F3
Ash Tree Wlk 18 BB9 . . . .168 D3
Ashborne Dr BL9 . . . . .49 D2
Ashbourne Cl 6 LA1 . . . . .213 F3
Ashbourne Cres PR2 . . . . .116 A5
Ashbourne Dr LA1 . . . . . .213 F3
Ashbourne Gr LA3 . . . . . .212 F2
Ashbourne Rd LA1 . . . . . .213 F3
Ashbrook St LA1 . . . . . . .210 D4
Ashburnham Rd BB8 . . . . .169 A2
Ashburton Rd FY1 . . . . . .129 B7
Ashby St PR7 . . . . .42 D6
Ashcombe Gate FY5 . . . . .151 D7
Ashcroft LA1 . . . . .212 B1
Ashcroft Ave L39 . . . . .15 F6
Ashcroft La LA2 . . . . .231 B3
Ashcroft Rd Formby L37 . . .11 F1
Kirkby L33 . . . . .1 C3
Ashdale Cl L37 . . . . .11 C2
Ashdale Gr FY5 . . . . .173 E2
Ashdale Pl 2 LA1 . . . . . . .213 E2
Ashdene OL12 . . . . .51 D4
Ashdown Cl Carleton FY6 .151 B5
Southport PR8 . . . . .34 E4
Ashdown Dr PR6 . . . . .77 C2
Ashdown Mews PR2 . . . . .117 E6
Asheldon St 1 PR1 . . . . . .117 C1
Ashendean View BB12 . . .145 D1
Ashfield PR2 . . . . .116 F8
Ashfield Ave
Lancaster LA1 . . . . .210 D7
Morecambe LA4 . . . . .213 D6
Ashfield Cl BB5 . . . . .168 C1
Ashfield Cotts 2 LA2 . . . .233 D8
Ashfield Ct Blackpool FY2 .150 E6
Fulwood PR2 . . . . .115 E4
Ashfield Rd Adlington PR6 . .30 B8
Blackpool FY2,FY5 . . . . . .150 E6
Burnley BB11 . . . . .126 F6
Chorley PR7 . . . . .42 B7
Ashfield Rise PR3 . . . . . . .178 D2
Ashfield Terr WN6 . . . . . . .19 C8
Ashfields PR5 . . . . .75 B1
Ashford Ave LA1 . . . . .210 E3
Ashford Cl LA1 . . . . .210 F3
Ashford Cres PR3 . . . . . . .136 C3
Ashford Rd Lancaster LA1 210 F3
Preston PR2 . . . . .115 E2
Ashford St Heywood OL10 . .32 F1
Nelson BB9 . . . . .147 E7

Ashgrove PR1 . . . . .117 E1
Ashlands Cl BL0 . . . . .67 D2
Ashleigh Ct PR2 . . . . .117 A7
Ashleigh Mews FY3 . . . . .129 E4
Ashleigh Prim Sch BB3 . . .64 A6
Ashleigh Rd LA5 . . . . .237 B2
Ashlet Cl 5 Darwen BB3 . . .64 B6
Preston PR1 . . . . .96 C6
Ashley Cl Blackpool FY2 . . .150 D2
Thornton FY5 . . . . .151 B7
Ashley La PR3 . . . . .138 C8
Ashley Rd
Lytham St Anne's FY8 . . . . .109 F1
Skelmersdale WN8 . . . . . . .18 B3
Southport PR9 . . . . .34 C7
Ashley St BB12 . . . . .126 F7
Ashmead Rd BB3 . . . . .18 A4
Ashmeadow Gr LA6 . . . . .216 F5
Ashmeadow La PR6 . . . . . .61 F8
Ashmeadow Rd
Arnside LA5 . . . . .237 B2
Nether Kellet LA6 . . . . . . .216 C5
Ashmoor St PR1 . . . . .116 E1
Ashmore Gr FY5 . . . . .172 C3
Ashmount Dr OL12 . . . . . .51 F2
Ashness Cl Fulwood PR2 . .116 F8
Horwich BL6 . . . . .30 F3
Ashton Ave FY6 . . . . .194 D5
Ashton Cl PR2 . . . . .95 A4
Ashton Ct Fleetwood FY6 .194 D5
Lancaster LA1 . . . . .210 F7
Ashton Dr Lancaster LA1 . .213 E2
Nelson BB9 . . . . .147 E6
Ashton Garden Ct FY8 . . . .88 E7
Ashton House BB3 . . . . . . .64 B8
Ashton La BB3 . . . . .64 A8
Ashton Meml LA1 . . . . . . .211 B7
Ashton Rd Blackpool FY1 . .129 C3
8 Darwen BB3 . . . . .64 B8
Lancaster LA1,LA2 . . . . . .210 A4
Morecambe LA4 . . . . .212 F5
Southport PR8 . . . . .33 F1
Ashton St Longridge PR3 . .139 A8
8 Lytham St Anne's FY8 . . .90 A3
7 Preston PR2 . . . . .95 D8
Ashton Wlk 12 LA1 . . . . . .210 F8
Ashton-on-Ribble
High Sch PR2 . . . . .115 F2
Ashtongate PR2 . . . . .115 F1
Ashtree Ct Fulwood PR2 . .116 A4
Higher Walton PR5 . . . . . . .97 C3
Ashtree Gr PR1 . . . . .95 B4
Ashtrees L40 . . . . .39 C2
Ashtrees Way 2 LA5 . . . . .217 D3
Ashurst Cl WN8 . . . . .18 A4
Ashurst Ct L37 . . . . .11 C4
Ashurst Gdns WN8 . . . . . . .18 B4
Ashurst Rd
Clayton-le-W PR5 . . . . . . .76 C3
Shevington Moor WN6 . . . . .28 B2
Skelmersdale WN8 . . . . . . .18 A4
Ashville Terr BB2 . . . . .80 C4
Ashwall St WN8 . . . . .8 E8
Ashwell Pl FY5 . . . . .150 C3
Ashwood WN8 . . . . .18 C3
Ashwood Ave Darwen BB3 .80 D6
Ramsbottom BL0 . . . . .49 D2
Ashwood Cl FY8 . . . . .89 E4
Ashwood Ct LA1 . . . . .210 F5
Ashwood Rd PR4 . . . . . . .116 D7
Ashworth Cl BB2 . . . . . . .100 C5
Ashworth Ct 6 FY3 . . . . .129 D7
Ashworth Dr LA2 . . . . . . .215 E2
Ashworth Gr PR1 . . . . .96 C6
Ashworth Hospl L31 . . . . . .6 B2
Ashworth La
Newchurch BB4 . . . . .85 F3
Preston PR1 . . . . .96 C6
Ashworth Rd
Blackpool FY4 . . . . .110 C8
Newchurch BB4 . . . . .85 F2
Rochdale OL11 . . . . .50 C1
Ashworth St
Accrington BB5 . . . . .103 E2
15 Bacup OL13 . . . . .87 A3
3 Bacup, Stackstead OL13 .69 D8
3 Bamber Bridge PR5 . . . .96 F2
Forest Holme BB4 . . . . . . .86 A7
1 Preston PR1 . . . . .96 B7
Rawtenstall BB4 . . . . .68 F8
8 Rishton BB1 . . . . .123 B7
Ashworth Terr
2 Bacup OL13 . . . . .69 B8
7 Darwen BB3 . . . . .81 A1
Askrigg Cl Accrington BB5 .103 C5
Blackpool FY4 . . . . .110 A7
Asland Cl PR5 . . . . .76 F8
Asland Gdns PR9 . . . . .53 C4
Asmall Cl L39 . . . . .15 C6
Asmall Cty Prim Sch L39 .15 C6
Asmall La Haskayne L39,L40 14 E8
Ormskirk L39,L40 . . . . . . .15 B1
Aspden St PR5 . . . . .96 E1
Aspels Cres PR1 . . . . .95 C4
Aspels Nook PR1 . . . . .95 C4
Aspels The PR1 . . . . .95 C4
Aspen Dr BB10 . . . . .127 C7
Aspen Fold BB5 . . . . .102 B5
Aspen Gdns 3 Chorley PR7 42 B4
Rochdale OL12 . . . . .51 A1
Aspen Gr LA1 . . . . .11 C1
Aspen La Earby BB18 . . . .201 B2
Oswaldtwistle BB5 . . . . . .102 C4
Aspendale Cl PR4 . . . . .73 F8

Aspinal Cl PR1 . . . . . . .95 D2
Aspinall Cres L37 . . . . . .12 F1
Aspinall Rd WN6 . . . . . .28 B1
Aspinall St BL6 . . . . . . .31 D1
Aspinall Way BL6 . . . . . .31 D1
Aspley Gr BB8 . . . . . . .170 C3
Asshawes The PR6 . . . . . .42 F1
Assheton Pl PR2 . . . . . .117 E4
Assheton Rd BB2 . . . . . .100 A5
Aster Ch BB3 . . . . .81 A7
Astland Gdns PR4 . . . . . .72 F2
Astland St FY8 . . . . .88 E6
Astley Cres PR4 . . . . . . .92 C6
Astley Ct LA1 . . . . .210 D6
Astley Ctr The 2 PR7 . . . .42 D6
Astley Gate BB2 . . . . . .100 E5
Astley Hall Dr BL0 . . . . . .49 C4
Astley Park Sp Sch PR7 . . .42 B8
Astley Rd PR7 . . . . .60 C1
Astley St Chorley PR6,PR7 . .60 C1
  Darwen BB3 . . . . .64 A7
  Longridge PR3 . . . . . . .139 A7
Astley Terr BB3 . . . . . . .64 A7
Aston Ave FY5 . . . . . . .173 A2
Aston St PR4 . . . . .131 E6
Aston Way PR5 . . . . .75 C2
Aston Wlk BB2 . . . . .81 A8
Athelstan Fold PR2 . . . . .116 C3
Athens View BB10 . . . . . .127 C5
Atherton Rd PR5 . . . . . . .58 D8
Atherton St Adlington PR7 . .30 A6
  Bacup OL13 . . . . .69 C8
Atherton Way OL13 . . . . . .69 B8
Athletic St BB10 . . . . . .127 C5
Athlone Ave FY2 . . . . . .150 C2
Athol Gr PR6 . . . . .42 E6
Athol St Nelson BB9 . . . .147 F8
  Ramsbottom BL0 . . . . . . .49 C7
Athol St N BB11 . . . . . .126 D5
Athol St S BB11 . . . . . .126 D5
Athole Gr PR9 . . . . .34 F7
Atholl St 3 PR1 . . . . . . .95 D8
Atkinson Art Gal PR8 . . . . .34 B7
Atkinson Liby PR8 . . . . . .34 B7
Atkinson St
  Brierfield BB10 . . . . . .147 F3
  Colne BB8 . . . . .169 C3
  Colne BB8 . . . . .169 D4
Atlas Rd BB3 . . . . .81 B1
Atlas St BB5 . . . . .124 A1
Atrium Ct 11 BB11 . . . . .127 B4
Aubigny Dr PR2 . . . . . . .116 D4
Auburn Gr FY1 . . . . . . .129 D2
Auckland St BB3 . . . . . . .64 B7
Audenlea FY5 . . . . .172 F3
Audenshaw Rd LA4 . . . . .212 F4
Audley Cl
  Lytham St Anne's FY8 . . . .89 D5
  Nelson BB9 . . . . .147 E8
Audley Jun & Inf Sch
  BB1 . . . . .101 A3
Audley La BB1 . . . . . . .101 A4
Audley Range BB1 . . . . .101 B4
Audley St BB1 . . . . . . .101 A5
Audlum Ct 4 BL9 . . . . . .32 C2
Aughton Brow LA2 . . . . .231 E6
Aughton Ct LA1 . . . . . . .213 F4
Aughton Hall Cotts L39 . . .15 C6
Aughton Mews PR8 . . . . . .34 A5
Aughton Park Dr L39 . . . . .15 D2
Aughton Park Sta L39 . . . .15 D2
Aughton Rd Aughton LA2 . .231 E6
  Southport PR8 . . . . . . .34 A5
Aughton St Fleetwood FY7 .194 B5
  Ormskirk L39 . . . . .15 E4
Aughton St Michael's
  CE Prim Sch L39 . . . . . .15 B1
Aughton Wlk 3 PR1 . . . . .116 F1
Augusta Cl OL12 . . . . . . .51 E2
Augusta St Accrington BB5 .103 C4
  Rochdale OL12 . . . . . . .51 E2
Auster Cres PR4 . . . . . . .113 B2
Austin Cres PR2 . . . . . . .116 B4
Austin Gr FY1 . . . . .129 B1
Austin St 6 Bacup OL13 . . .86 F2
  5 Burnley BB11 . . . . . .126 E5
Austin Way FY4 . . . . . . .111 A2
Austin's La PR5 . . . . .31 F1
Austins Ct PR5 . . . . .59 A8
Austwick Rd 4 LA1 . . . . .213 D2
Austwick Way BB5 . . . . . .103 E5
Avallon Way BB3 . . . . . . .81 C1
Avalon Cl BB12 . . . . . . .125 F7
Avalon Dr PR4 . . . . .92 C7
Avalwood Ave PR4 . . . . . .74 B8
Avebury Cl Blackburn BB2 . .81 A8
  Horwich BL6 . . . . .31 F1
Aveling Dr PR9 . . . . .54 A6
Avelon Cl L31 . . . . .5 B5
Avenham Ct PR9 . . . . . . .54 E5
Avenham Colonnade PR1 . .96 A6
Avenham Ct 20 PR1 . . . . .96 A7
Avenham Gr 5 FY1 . . . . .129 B6
Avenham La PR1 . . . . . . .96 A7
Avenham Pl
  Newton-with-S PR4 . . . .113 F2
  6 Preston PR1 . . . . . . .96 A6
Avenham Rd
  1 Chorley PR7 . . . . . . .42 C7
  Preston PR1 . . . . .96 A7
Avenham St 11 PR1 . . . . .96 A6
Avenue Par BB5 . . . . . . .103 D6
Avenue Rd
  Hurst Green BB7 . . . . . .162 E1
  Normoss FY3 . . . . .130 B7

Avenue The Adlington PR6 . .30 A8
  Banks PR9 . . . . .53 F5
  Barley BB12 . . . . .167 C5
  Burnley BB10,BB11 . . . . .127 D3
  Carleton FY6 . . . . .151 C4
  Churchtown PR3 . . . . . .178 A3
  Fulwood PR2 . . . . .116 A6
  Garstang PR3 . . . . .199 B1
  Leyland PR5 . . . . .59 A6
  Ormskirk L39 . . . . .15 D6
  Ormskirk L39 . . . . .15 E6
  Orrell WN5 . . . . .10 D3
  Penwortham PR1 . . . . . .95 B5
  Preston PR1 . . . . .115 D1
  Southport PR8 . . . . . . .35 F5
Aviemore Cl 5 BB1 . . . . .101 A4
Avocet Ct PR5 . . . . .75 A1
Avon Ave FY7 . . . . .172 D8
Avon Bridge PR2 . . . . . .116 C8
Avon Cl BB2 . . . . .100 D3
Avon Ct BB2 . . . . .126 D7
Avon Dr
  Barnoldswick BB18 . . . . .200 C3
  Bury BL9 . . . . .32 A8
Avon Gdns PR4 . . . . . . .115 D5
Avon Gn FY7 . . . . .193 E4
Avon Ho FY2 . . . . .96 D8
Avon Pl FY1 . . . . .129 C8
Avon St FY8 . . . . .88 E6
Avondale Ave
  Blackburn BB1 . . . . . . .101 E5
  Burnley BB12 . . . . .126 C7
Avondale Cl BB3 . . . . . . .80 C2
Avondale Cres FY4 . . . . .109 F7
Avondale Dr
  Bamber Bridge PR5 . . . . .76 B8
  Ramsbottom BL0 . . . . . . .48 F3
  Tarleton PR4 . . . . .56 A8
Avondale Mews BB3 . . . . .80 E3
Avondale Prim Sch BB3 . . .80 E2
Avondale Rd Chorley PR7 . .42 C7
  Darwen BB3 . . . . .80 E3
  Lancaster LA1 . . . . . . .211 A6
  Lytham St Anne's FY8 . . . .88 C8
  Morecambe LA3 . . . . . . .212 B3
  Nelson BB9 . . . . .147 D7
  Southport PR9 . . . . .34 B8
Avondale Rd N PR9 . . . . . .52 C1
Avondale St Colne BB8 . . .170 A5
  Standish WN6 . . . . .28 E2
Avonhead Cl BL6 . . . . . . .30 F3
Avonside Ave FY5 . . . . . .173 A3
Avonwood Cl BB3 . . . . . . .80 E2
Avroe Cres FY4 . . . . . . .109 D4
Aylesbury Ave FY4 . . . . .129 D1
Aylesbury Ho LA1 . . . . . . .5 B4
Aylesbury Wlk BB10 . . . . .147 B8
Ayr Ct PR8 . . . . .34 F4
Ayr Ct FY7 . . . . .172 E7
Ayr Gr BB11 . . . . .126 D3
Ayr Rd BB1 . . . . .101 D3
Ayr St LA1 . . . . .211 B7
Ayrefield Gr WN6 . . . . . . .19 D6
Ayrefield Rd WN8 . . . . . .19 C4
Ayrton Ave FY4 . . . . . . .109 D7
Ayrton St BB8 . . . . .169 E5
Ays-Garth Rd LA1 . . . . . .210 D8
Aysgarth Ave PR2 . . . . . .116 F7
Aysgarth Ct 1 FY4 . . . . .109 F7
Aysgarth Dr
  Accrington BB5 . . . . . . .103 D6
  Darwen BB3 . . . . .80 E2
  Lancaster LA1 . . . . . . .213 F4
Azalea Cl Clayton-le-W PR5 .76 E2
  Preston PR2 . . . . .117 C6
Azalea Gr LA4 . . . . .213 A5
Azalea Rd BB2 . . . . .100 B6

B

Babbacombe Ave FY4 . . . .109 B6
Babylon La PR6 . . . . .30 B8
Back Albert Rd BB8 . . . . .169 D4
Back Albert St Bury BL9 . . .32 A2
  10 Padiham BB12 . . . . . .125 C8
Back Alfred St 11 BL0 . . . .49 B5
Back Altham St 5 BB12 . . .125 D8
Back Andrew St 13 BL9 . . .32 A2
Back Andrew St N 12 BL9 . .32 A2
Back Arthur St 15 BB5 . . . .123 F3
Back Ash St 7 BL9 . . . . . .32 A2
Back Ashburton Rd 14
  FY1 . . . . .129 C7
Back Ashby St 1 PR7 . . . . .42 D6
Back Atkinson St BB8 . . . .169 C4
Back Avondale Rd (E)
  LA3 . . . . .212 B3
Back Avondale Rd (W)
  LA3 . . . . .212 B3
Back Bath St PR8 . . . . . . .34 B8
Back Beehive Terr BB4 . . . .84 B3
Back Bell La 8 Bury BL9 . . .32 A3
  Bury BL9 . . . . .32 B3
Back Benson St BB9 . . . . .147 D8
Back Blackburn Rd E BL7 . .46 D3
Back Bolton Rd BB3 . . . . . .64 B7
Back Bond St BB8 . . . . . .169 D5
Back Bond St W BL9 . . . . .32 A2
Back Boundary St 14
  BB8 . . . . .169 D4
Back Bourne's Row PR5 . . .97 E1
Back Bridge St 2 BL0 . . . . .49 C6
Back Broading Terr BB4 . . .105 A3
Back Brook St N 11 BL9 . . .32 A4
Back Brow WN8 . . . . .10 C7
Back Brown St 8 BB8 . . . .169 C4
Back Burnley Rd BB5 . . . .103 C6

Back Calton Terr LA4 . . . .212 E6
Back Cambridge St 10
  BB8 . . . . .169 D4
Back Canada St BL6 . . . . . .31 B3
Back Carr Mill St BB4 . . . . .84 B5
Back Cedar St 2 BL9 . . . . .32 B3
Back Cedar St 3 BL9 . . . . .32 B3
Back Cemetery Terr 9
  OL13 . . . . .69 D8
Back Chapel St
  1 Barnoldswick BB18 . . . .200 B2
  4 Colne BB8 . . . . .169 D4
  Horwich BL6 . . . . .31 C3
Back Chesham Rd N 5
  BL9 . . . . .32 A4
Back Chesham Rd S 7
  BL9 . . . . .32 A4
Back Chester St BL9 . . . . . .32 A4
Back Church St
  Barrowford BB9 . . . . . . .168 D3
  8 Blackpool FY1 . . . . . .129 B5
  5 Great Harwood BB6 . . .123 C5
  3 Hapton BB12 . . . . . . .125 C4
  1 Newchurch BB4 . . . . . .85 E1
Back Clarendon Rd FY1 . . .129 B5
Back Clayton St 9 BB9 . . .168 D1
Back Club St PR5 . . . . . . .76 E7
Back Colne Rd BB18 . . . . .200 A1
Back Commons BB7 . . . . .186 D1
Back Constablelee 84 F4
Back Cookson St 12 FY1 . .129 C6
Back Cop La FY1 . . . . . . .194 B4
Back Cowm La OL12 . . . . . .70 C3
Back Crescent St LA4 . . . .212 D5
Back Crown St BL6 . . . . . . .31 B3
Back Curzon St FY8 . . . . . .89 A7
Back Darwen Rd N BL7 . . . .46 E1
Back Deal St BL9 . . . . .32 B2
Back Delamere St N BL9 . . .32 A5
Back Delamere St S BL9 . . .32 A5
Back Derby St 4 BB8 . . . .169 D4
Back Drinkhouse La PR5 . . .57 B1
Back Duckworth St
  4 Bury BL9 . . . . .32 A4
  12 Darwen BB3 . . . . .81 A1
Back Duke St 1 BB8 . . . . .169 D4
Back Duncan St BL9 . . . . . .31 C3
Back Earl St 2 BB8 . . . . . .169 D4
Back East Bank 1 BB9 . . . .168 E7
Back Eaves St FY1 . . . . . .129 B7
Back Elm St 10 BL9 . . . . . .32 B2
Back Emmett St BL9 . . . . . .31 B3
Back Epsom Rd FY5 . . . . .150 F8
Back Fazakerley St 14 PR7 .42 C8
Back Fir St BL9 . . . . .32 B2
Back Fletcher St 3 BL9 . . . .32 A2
Back Forest Rd PR8 . . . . . .34 D6
Back Garston St BL9 . . . . . .32 A4
Back George St BL6 . . . . . .31 C3
Back Gisburn Rd BB9 . . . .168 E7
Back Glen Eldon Rd FY8 . . .88 E7
Back Green St LA4 . . . . . .212 E6
Back Grimshaw St 8 PR1 . .96 A7
Back Grove Terr LA4 . . . . .213 B4
Back Hall St BB8 . . . . . . .169 D4
Back Halstead St 2 BL9 . . .32 A4
Back Hamilton St 1 BL9 . . .32 A4
Back Harry St BB9 . . . . . .168 D3
Back Haslam St BB9 . . . . . .32 A4
Back Headroomgate Rd
  FY8 . . . . .88 F8
Back Heys BB5 . . . . .102 E3
Back Heywood St E 14
  BL9 . . . . .32 A4
Back Heywood St W BL9 . . .32 A1
Back High St Belmont BL7 . .45 C5
  Blackpool FY1 . . . . . . .129 B6
  Edgworth BL7 . . . . .47 C4
Back Hill 13 BB4 . . . . .85 A7
Back Holly St BL9 . . . . . . .32 B2
Back Holly St 3 BL9 . . . . . .32 B2
Back Hope St OL13 . . . . . .86 F4
Back House La L35 . . . . . .218 C3
Back Hunter St 1 LA5 . . . .217 D2
Back Huntley Mount Rd
  BL9 . . . . .32 B3
Back Hurst St BL9 . . . . . . .32 A1
Back Ingham St BL9 . . . . . .32 A1
Back Ingham St E BL9 . . . .32 A1
Back Kershaw St 3 BL9 . . . .32 A2
Back King St BB5 . . . . . . .103 B6
Back Knowlys Rd 2 LA3 . . .208 F8
Back La Accrington BB5 . . .103 E1
  Appley Bridge WN6 . . . . . .19 E8
  Arnside LA5 . . . . .237 B3
  Bolton Green PR7 . . . . . .41 B7
  Bretherton PR5 . . . . .56 E5
  Burscough Bridge L40 . . . .24 E6
  Carnforth LA5,LA6 . . . . . .216 E7
  Chorley PR6 . . . . .43 C6
  Clayton Green PR6 . . . . . .77 A2
  Clayton Green PR6 . . . . . .77 B1
  Cumeragh Village PR3 . . .138 B6
  Gisburn BB7 . . . . .225 C3
  Great Eccleston PR3 . . . .154 B5
  Greenhalgh PR4 . . . . . .132 B4
  Grindleton BB7 . . . . . . .187 B8
  Hale Nook FY6 . . . . . . .174 E6
  Haskayne L39 . . . . .13 D3
  Higham BB12 . . . . .145 E6
  Leyland PR5 . . . . .59 C7
  Longridge PR3 . . . . . . .159 B6
  Longton PR4 . . . . .73 E8
  Maghull L31 . . . . .5 E6
  Mawdesley L40 . . . . .39 D1
  Nelson BB10 . . . . .148 F7
  Newburgh L40,WN8 . . . . . .25 E2
  Newton PR4 . . . . .222 F6

Back La continued
  Preesall FY6 . . . . .195 A2
  Rathmell BD24 . . . . . . .230 F6
  Rawtenstall BB4 . . . . . . .85 A3
  Rimington BB7 . . . . . . .188 E8
  Royal Oak L39 . . . . .7 A2
  Sabden BB12,BB7 . . . . . .145 C6
  Skelmersdale, Digmoor WN8 . .9 D6
  Skelmersdale, Holland Moor
    WN8 . . . . .9 E7
  Trawden BB8 . . . . .170 B2
  Tunstall LA6 . . . . .235 D4
  Warton, Carnforth LA5 . . .217 D5
  Whitworth OL12 . . . . . . .70 C3
  Wiswell BB7 . . . . .143 F8
  Wray LA6 . . . . .232 C6
  Wrayton LA6 . . . . .235 D2
Back La E L40 . . . . .39 F1
Back Lane Side BB4 . . . . . .84 B2
Back Lathom St 3 BL9 . . . .32 A4
Back Laurel St 2 BL9 . . . . .32 B2
Back Leach St BB8 . . . . . .169 C4
Back Lee St BB4 . . . . .84 B2
Back Lines St 2 LA4 . . . . .212 E5
Back Longworth Rd BL7 . . .46 D3
Back Lord St
  Blackpool FY1 . . . . .129 B6
  4 Lancaster LA1 . . . . . .213 F1
  4 Rawtenstall BB4 . . . . . .85 A7
Back Lune St BB8 . . . . . .169 E4
Back Manor St 1 BL9 . . . . .32 A2
Back Marine Rd LA4 . . . . .212 C4
Back Marine Rd E LA4 . . . .212 G6
Back Mason St 16 BL9 . . . .32 A4
Back Moon Ave 5 FY1 . . .129 B2
Back Morecambe St LA4 . .212 E6
Back Moss La L40 . . . . . . .24 C7
Back Mount 5 PR7 . . . . . .42 C8
Back Myrtle St 4 BL9 . . . . .32 B2
Back Myrtle St S BL9 . . . . .32 B2
Back Nelson St BL6 . . . . . .31 D3
Back New St 5 LA5 . . . . .217 D2
Back Nook Terr 2 OL12 . . .51 F3
Back North Cres FY8 . . . . .88 E6
Back O The Town La L38 . . .3 E3
Back Oddfellows Terr BB4 . .85 F1
Back Oram St BL9 . . . . . . .32 A4
Back Ormrod St 10 BL9 . . .32 A4
Back Owen's Row BL6 . . . .31 C3
Back Oxford St BL9 . . . . . .32 A1
Back Parkinson St BB2 . . .100 B2
Back Parsonage St BL9 . . .32 A4
Back Patience St 10 OL12 . .51 C1
Back Percy St BL9 . . . . . . .32 B3
Back Peter St
  8 Barrowford BB9 . . . . . .168 C4
  3 Bury BL9 . . . . .32 A4
Back Pine St 1 BL9 . . . . . .32 B2
Back Pleasant St 6 FY1 . . .129 B7
Back Queen St
  Great Harwood BB6 . . . . .123 C5
  7 Lancaster LA1 . . . . . .210 F4
  1 Morecambe LA4 . . . . .212 E5
Back Railway View PR7 . . . .30 A7
Back Rawlinson St 16 BL6 . .31 B4
Back Read's Rd FY1 . . . . .129 C4
Back Regent St 1 BB4 . . . .84 B3
Back Rhoden Rd BB5 . . . .102 D2
Back Richard Burch St
  BL9 . . . . .32 A3
Back Rings Row BB4 . . . .105 A1
Back Rochdale
  Old North Rd 1 BL9 . . . . .32 C3
Back Rochdale Old Rd S
  BL9 . . . . .32 A3
Back Rochdale
  Old South Rd 3 Bury BL9 .32 C3
  Bury, Fairfield BL9 . . . . . .32 D3
Back Rochdale Rd BL9 . . . .32 B2
Back Rochdale Rd S 17
  BL9 . . . . .32 A2
Back Rushton St 6 OL13 . . .69 E8
Back Salford St BL9 . . . . . .32 B3
Back Sandy Bank Rd BL7 . .47 D5
Back School La Orrell WN8 .10 C7
  Skelmersdale,
    Pennylands WN8 . . . . . .17 D2
Back Scotland Rd 7
  BB9 . . . . .147 D8
Back Seed St 9 PR1 . . . . . .95 F8
Back Shannon St 4 FY1 . .129 B3
Back Shaw-Street BL9 . . . .32 B3
Back Shepherd St BL9 . . . .32 A1
Back Shuttleworth St
  BB12 . . . . .125 C8
Back Skipton St 8 BB18 200 B2
Back South Cross St E 15
  BL9 . . . . .32 A2
Back Spencer St BB4 . . . . .85 A7
Back Springfield Rd N
  FY8 . . . . .88 G6
Back Square St BL0 . . . . . .49 C6
Back St LA3 . . . . .205 D8
Back St Anne's Rd W FY8 . .88 E6
Back St John St 5 OL13 . . .86 F7
Back Stanley St BL0 . . . . . .49 B5
Back Starkie St PR1 . . . . . .95 F6
Back Sun St 9 LA1 . . . . . .210 F8
Back Teak St 5 BL9 . . . . . .32 B2
Back Tinline St 11 BL9 . . . .32 A2
Back Union St BL7 . . . . . . .46 D2
Back Virginia St 1 BB4 . . . .84 B6
Back Warbreck Rd 2
  FY1 . . . . .129 B6
Back Wash La BL9 . . . . . . .32 B2
Back Wash La S 6 BL9 . . . .32 A2
Back Water St
  11 Accrington BB5 . . . . .103 C6

Back Water St continued
  Egerton BL7 . . . . .46 D2
Back Waterloo Rd 8 FY1 129 B1
Back Wellington St BB5 . . .103 C5
Back West Cres FY8 . . . . . .88 E6
Back West End Rd N LA4 212 C4
Back Willow St BB12 . . . . .126 E6
Back Winterdyne Terr
  LA3 . . . . .212 B4
Back Wood St BL6 . . . . . . .31 C3
Back Woodfield Rd 4
  FY1 . . . . .129 B2
Back Wright St BL6 . . . . . .31 B4
Back York St
  Clitheroe BB7 . . . . .164 F8
  Rawtenstall BB4 . . . . . . .85 A7
Back Zion St 16 BB8 . . . . .169 D4
Backhouse St 1 BB5 . . . . .102 E4
Backs The PR3 . . . . .139 A6
Bacon St 6 BB9 . . . . . . .147 E6
Bacup & Rawtenstall
  Gram Sch BB4 . . . . .68 F8
Bacup Golf Course OL13 . .86 E2
Bacup Old Rd OL13 . . . . . .86 F7
Bacup Rd
  Rawtenstall BB4,OL13 . . . .68 E8
  Rawtenstall, Lower
    Cloughfold BB4 . . . . . . .85 C2
  Sharneyford OL14 . . . . . .87 E5
  Walk Mill BB11 . . . . . . .106 E6
Baddon Cl LA4 . . . . .212 F3
Baden Terr BB2 . . . . .100 D1
Badge Brow BB5 . . . . . . .102 C5
Badger Cl BB12 . . . . .145 D1
Badger Rd PR5 . . . . .76 A4
Badger St 3 BL9 . . . . .32 B3
Badger Wells Cotts BB7 . .145 A8
Badger Wood PR3 . . . . . .157 C2
Badgers Cl BB5 . . . . .103 E8
Badgers Croft PR2 . . . . . .117 F1
Badgers Rake L37 . . . . . . .11 C5
Badgers Way PR5 . . . . . . .96 B3
Badgers Wlk PR7 . . . . . . .60 A3
Badgers Wlk E PR5 . . . . . .90 C3
Badgers Wlk W 10 FY8 . . .90 B3
Bagganley La PR6 . . . . . . .60 F2
Bagnold Rd PR1 . . . . . . .117 D1
Bagot St FY1 . . . . .129 B1
Baildon Rd OL12 . . . . . . .51 B1
Bailey Bank BB7 . . . . . . .163 A7
Bailey Ct FY3 . . . . .129 E6
Bailey La Heysham LA3 . . .208 E8
  Tosside BD23 . . . . .230 B3
Bailey St Burnley BB11 . . .126 E5
  Earby BB18 . . . . .201 C2
Bailrigg La LA1 . . . . .211 A1
Baines Ave FY3 . . . . .150 F1
Baines Endowed
  CE Prim Sch FY4 . . . . . .129 F1
Baines Sch FY6 . . . . .151 D1
Baines' Endowed
  Cty Prim Sch FY5 . . . . . .173 C1
Bairstow St
  3 Barnoldswick BB18 . . .200 B3
  Blackpool FY1 . . . . .129 B3
  13 Preston PR1 . . . . . . .95 F7
Baker St 13 Bacup OL13 . . .86 F3
  Blackburn BB1 . . . . . . .101 B4
  Burnley BB11 . . . . .126 E5
  Lancaster LA1 . . . . .213 F3
  4 Leyland PR5 . . . . .76 B2
  Nelson BB9 . . . . .168 E1
  Ramsbottom BL0 . . . . . . .49 B5
Baker's La PR9 . . . . .52 F3
Bakers Ct FY4 . . . . .109 F7
Bala Cl BB1 . . . . .100 E6
Balaclava St BB1 . . . . . . .100 E6
Balcarres Cl PR5 . . . . . . .76 A1
Balcarres Pl PR5 . . . . . . .59 A8
Balcarres Rd Chorley PR7 . .42 B5
  Leyland PR5 . . . . .59 A8
  Preston PR2 . . . . .116 C2
Balderstone
  CE Prim Sch BB2 . . . . . .120 A5
Balderstone Cl BB10 . . . .147 D2
Balderstone Hall La BB2 . .119 C6
Balderstone La BB10 . . . .147 D8
Balderstone Rd
  Freckleton PR4 . . . . . . .92 B7
  Preston PR1 . . . . .95 D5
Baldwin Gr FY1 . . . . .129 D2
Baldwin Hill 3 BB7 . . . . .164 D8
Baldwin Rd BB7 . . . . . . .164 D8
Baldwin St Bacup OL13 . . .69 B8
  7 Bamber Bridge PR5 . . . .96 E1
  5 Barrowford BB9 . . . . .168 D4
  Blackburn BB2 . . . . . . .100 C3
Baldwin's Bldgs 14 BB4 . . .85 A3
Balfour Cl Brierfield BB9 . .147 D5
  Thornton FY5 . . . . .151 D7
Balfour Ho BB2 . . . . . . .100 C4
Balfour Rd Fulwood PR2 . .116 E3
  6 Rochdale OL12 . . . . . .51 C1
  Southport PR8 . . . . . . .34 E5
Balfour St Blackburn BB2 .100 C4
  Great Harwood BB6 . . . . .123 C5
  Leyland PR5 . . . . .76 A1
Balham Ave FY4 . . . . . . .109 C5
Ball La BB4 . . . . .231 C3
Ball St Blackpool FY1 . . . .129 B1
  3 Nelson BB9 . . . . .168 D1
  Poulton-le-F FY6 . . . . . .151 D3
Ball's Pl PR8 . . . . .34 B7
Balladen Prim Sch BB4 . . .67 C2
Ballam Rd
  Lower Ballam FY8 . . . . . .111 C3
  Lytham St Anne's FY8 . . . .90 B4

Ballam Rd *continued*
Preston PR2 115 E1
Ballam St BB11 127 A4
Ballantrae Rd BB1 101 D3
Ballater St BB11 126 D3
Balle St BB3 64 A8
Ballet Hill Cres PR3 157 A5
Balliol Cl BB12 125 D6
Balm St BL0 49 A4
Balmer Gr FY1 129 D3
Balmoral PR7 29 E6
Balmoral Ave
Blackburn BB1 122 A4
Clitheroe BB7 164 C6
Leyland PR5 59 C8
Morecambe LA3 212 B3
Balmoral Cl Horwich BL6 31 E2
Ramsbottom BL8 49 A1
Southport PR9 53 B3
Balmoral Cres BB1 101 F4
Balmoral Ct PR7 42 B8
Balmoral Dr Brinscall PR6 61 E8
Formby L37 11 E1
Southport PR9 53 B3
Balmoral Pl FY5 151 C8
Balmoral Rd
Accrington BB5 103 D7
5 Bamber Bridge PR5 96 D3
Blackpool FY4 109 B8
Chorley PR7 42 B8
Darwen BB3 64 B6
Eccleston PR7 40 C7
Haslingden BB4 84 A1
Lancaster LA1 211 A7
Lytham St Anne's FY8 89 A5
Maghull L31 5 C1
Morecambe LA3,LA4 212 C3
New Longton PR4 95 A1
Balmoral Terr FY7 194 B5
Balmore Ct OL10 32 E1
Balniel Cl PR7 42 A7
Balshaw Ave PR7 59 D2
Balshaw Cres PR5 75 F2
Balshaw La PR7 59 D1
Balshaw Lane Cty Prim Sch PR7 59 E1
Balshaw Rd Leyland PR5 75 F1
Lowgill LA2 233 E3
Balshaw St 4 PR5 96 E2
Balshaw's High Sch PR5 59 B7
Baltic Rd BB4 68 E8
Baltimore Rd FY8 89 B6
Bamber Ave FY2 150 C4
Bamber Bridge Meth Prim Sch PR5 76 F8
Bamber Bridge Sta PR5 76 E8
Bamber Gdns PR9 35 A8
Bamber St 2 PR7 42 B5
Bamber's Wlk PR4 112 E7
Bambers La Blackpool FY4 110 C6
Blackpool FY4 110 C7
Bamburgh Cl FY4 110 A7
Bamburgh Dr BB12 126 E7
Bamford Cl BL9 32 E4
Bamford Cres BB5 103 D4
Bamford Pl OL12 51 E1
Bamford Rd BL0 50 B6
Bamford St Burnley BB11 127 A6
Nelson BB9 148 A8
Bamfords Fold PR5 56 F5
Bamton Ave FY4 109 C7
Banastre PR7 60 A2
Banastre Rd PR8 34 B5
Banastre St 9 BB5 124 A1
Banbury Ave
Blackpool FY2 150 D1
Oswaldtwistle BB5 102 C4
Banbury Cl
3 Accrington BB5 103 A7
Blackburn BB2 79 F8
Banbury Dr PR2 116 E4
Banbury Rd Longshaw WN5 10 D2
Lytham St Anne's FY8 89 A6
Morecambe LA3 212 F3
Bancroft Ave FY5 173 C2
Bancroft Fold BB18 200 A1
Bancroft Mill (Mus) BB18 200 B1
Bancroft Rd BB10 127 C8
Bancroft St BB1 100 F5
Band La PR3 177 D1
Bangor Ave FY2 150 D4
Bangor St BB1 100 F7
Bank Ave WN5 10 D5
Bank Bottom BB3 81 A1
Bank Bridge PR4 56 B5
Bank Brow WN8 19 C5
Bank Cl Galgate LA2 206 F3
Longton PR4 74 A8
Bank Cott 2 LA2 233 B8
Bank Cotts BB7 143 B4
Bank Croft PR4 74 A8
Bank Fold BB9 168 E4
Bank Hall Cotts BB7 224 C1
Bank Hall Terr BB10 127 A7
Bank Head La PR5 97 D1
Bank Hey Cl BB1 122 A1
Bank Hey La N BB1 121 F3
Bank Hey La S BB1 122 A1
Bank Hey Sch BB2 80 C7
Bank Hey St FY1 129 B5
Bank House La Bacup OL13 86 F2
Westhouse LA6 236 E4
Bank House St BB9 168 E4
Bank La Blackburn BB1 101 D4
Warton PR4 91 D4
Bank Mdw BL6 31 C4
Bank Mill St 3 BB4 84 B2
Bank Par Burnley BB11 127 A6
Penwortham PR1 95 D3
Preston PR1 96 A6
Bank Pas PR8 34 A7
Bank Pl PR2 116 C1
Bank Rd Appley Bridge WN8 19 D4
Lancaster LA1 213 F3
Bank Sq PR8 34 B8
Bank St Accrington BB5 103 C5
Adlington PR7 30 A7
14 Bacup OL13 86 F2
Bank Lane BL0 49 E7
Barnoldswick BB18 200 C2
Brierfield BB9 147 B6
Chorley PR7 42 C8
9 Church BB5 102 E6
Darwen BB3 81 A1
Edgworth BL7 47 C4
Haslingden BB4 84 B3
11 Nelson BB9 168 E1
Padiham BB12 145 C1
Rawtenstall BB4 85 A2
Trawden BB8 170 C1
Bank Terr Knowley PR6 61 C4
Simonstone BB12 124 E8
Whitworth OL12 51 C8
Bank Top Baldingstone BL9 49 F1
Blackburn BB2 100 C4
Burnley BB11 127 A6
Bank View Hambleton FY6 174 C1
Rawtenstall BB11 105 C5
Bank View Cotts BB7 224 C1
Bankcroft Cl BB12 125 E8
Bankfield Burnley BB11 127 A6
Skelmersdale WN8 9 C7
Bankfield Ct FY5 151 B8
Bankfield Gr FY1 129 E3
Bankfield La PR9 53 B2
Bankfield St Bacup OL13 69 D8
Colne, Bunker's Hill BB8 169 B4
Colne, Winewall BB8 170 B4
Bankfield Terr
1 Bacup OL13 69 D8
Barnoldswick BB18 200 C3
Bankhouse Rd BB9 168 E1
Bankhouse St
Burnley BB11 126 F6
Burnley BB11 127 A6
Banks Bridge Cl BB18 200 C4
Banks Cres LA3 208 F6
Banks Hill BB18 200 A4
Banks Meth Prim Sch PR9 54 B7
Banks Rd Fulwood PR2 116 C3
Southport PR9 53 D6
Banks Rise 11 LA2 233 D8
Banks St Blackpool FY1 129 B6
Lane Bottom BB10 148 B3
Banks Way 13 LA2 233 D8
Banksbarn WN8 9 C7
Banksfield Ave PR2 116 C3
Banksfield Pl PR5 77 A7
Bankside Blackburn BB2 100 E2
Clayton Green PR6 77 B1
Hightown L38 2 F3
Parbold WN8 26 B2
Bankside Cl OL13 86 E1
Bankside La OL13 86 F2
Bankwood WN6 19 E6
Banner Cl PR7 40 B6
Bannerman Terr PR6 60 D2
Bannister Brow L40,WN6 26 E6
Bannister Cl
Higher Walton PR5 97 B4
Trawden BB8 170 B3
Bannister Ct
Blackpool FY2 150 B4
13 Nelson BB9 147 E8
Bannister Dr PR5 75 E1
Bannister Gn PR7 40 C3
Bannister Hall Cres PR5 97 B4
Bannister Hall Dr PR5 97 B4
Bannister Hall La PR5 97 B4
Bannister La Eccleston PR7 40 C5
Hill Dale L40,WN6 26 E6
Leyland PR5 75 E4
Bannister St
11 Chorley PR7 42 C7
Lytham St Anne's FY8 90 B3
Bannister's Bit 4 PR1 95 C2
Bannistre Cl 1 FY8 89 A8
Bannistre Ct PR4 56 A6
Bannistre Mews PR4 56 A6
Bar Cotts BB12 144 E1
Bar St BB10 127 B8
Bar Terr OL12 51 C7
Barbara Castle Way BB1 100 E5
Barberry Bank BL7 46 E2
Barbon Pl LA1 213 E2
Barbon St Burnley BB10 147 C2
14 Padiham BB12 145 C1
Barbrook Cl WN6 28 B2
Barclay Ave Blackpool FY4 129 F2
Burnley BB11 126 C4
Barclay Rd PR3 139 A7
Barcroft Gn BB10 127 E1
Barcroft St BB8 169 C5
Barden Croft BB5 123 F4
Barden Cty Inf Sch BB10 147 A1
Barden High Sch BB10 147 A2
Barden Jun Sch BB10 147 A1
Barden La BB10,BB12 147 A2
Barden Pl PR2 117 D4
Barden Rd BB5 102 F4
Barden St 4 BB10 147 B1
Barden View BB10 147 A2
Bardsea Pl PR2 115 F3
Bardsley Cl WN8 10 A7
Bardsway FY5 173 A3
Bardsway Ave FY3 129 F6
Bare Ave LA4 213 A6
Bare La LA4 213 A5
Bare Lane Sta LA4 213 A6
Barford Cl Orrell WN8 10 A7
Southport PR8 20 A6
Barford Gr BL6 31 F1
Bargee Cl BB1 100 F3
Barham St 6 FY1 129 B2
Barker Brow BB1,PR3 141 A3
Barker Cl LA6 234 B7
Barker La BB2 121 C2
Barker Sq LA2 207 A6
Barkerfield Cl BB12 145 F5
Barkerhouse Rd
Nelson BB10,BB9 148 B8
16 Nelson BB9 168 E1
Barkfield Ave L37 11 E4
Barkfield La L37 11 D4
Barley Bank St BB3 80 F2
Barley Cl BB2 100 D5
Barley Cop La LA1 213 D4
Barley Gr BB10 127 C6
Barley Holme Rd BB4 85 A8
Barley La Barley BB9 167 B7
Blackburn BB2 100 D5
Barley New Rd BB12 167 E5
Barley St BB12 125 C7
Barley Vistors Ctr BB12 167 C5
Barley Way BB2 100 D5
Barleydale Rd BB9 168 E5
Barleyfield PR5 77 C3
Barlow Cres FY3 129 E4
Barlow Ct BL7 47 E5
Barlow St Accrington BB5 103 A6
Bacup OL13 69 B7
Horwich BL6 31 C2
Preston PR1 116 E1
Preston PR1 116 F2
11 Rawtenstall BB4 85 A3
Barlow's La L39 21 D5
Barlows Bldgs 5 BB4 84 F1
Barmouth Ave FY3 130 A3
Barmouth Cres BB1 121 E1
Barmskin La PR7 40 B2
Barn Acre BL6 30 E1
Barn Cl PR4 55 A2
Barn Croft
3 Clitheroe BB7 164 D7
1 Leyland PR5 75 B1
Penwortham PR1 95 B4
Barn Field Cl BB8 170 A5
Barn Gill Cl BB1 100 F3
Barn Hey PR4 94 A1
Barn Hey Rd L33 1 A2
Barn Mdw
Clayton Brook PR5 77 B6
Edgworth BL7 47 D5
Barn Meadow Cres BB1 123 C1
Barnacre Cl Fulwood PR2 117 A8
Lancaster LA1 211 B2
Barnacre Rd PR3 139 A8
Barnard Cl BB5 102 C4
Barnbrook St BL9 32 A3
Barncroft Dr BL6 31 F3
Barnes Ave Cleveleys FY5 172 E5
Rawtenstall BB4 84 F2
Barnes Cl BL0 49 A3
Barnes Dr L31 5 C3
Barnes Rd Morecambe LA3 212 B3
Ormskirk L39 15 E3
Skelmersdale WN8 17 E1
Barnes Sq 1 BB5 123 F2
Barnes St Accrington BB5 103 C6
Burnley BB11 127 A6
Church BB5 102 E6
Clayton-le-M BB5 123 F3
Haslingden BB4 84 B4
Barnfield
6 Bamber Bridge PR5 76 A8
Kirkham PR4 113 A5
Much Hoole PR4 73 E3
Barnfield Ave BB10 127 F6
Barnfield Bsns Ctr BB9 147 F6
Barnfield Cl
4 Cleveleys FY5 172 F4
Egerton BL7 46 E2
Barnfield Dr WN8 9 E7
Barnfield Manor FY6 152 D3
Barnfield St
Accrington BB5 103 D5
Rochdale OL12 51 F2
Barnfield Way BB5 124 E5
Barnmeadow La BB6 123 C5
Barnoldswick CE Prim Sch BB18 200 B2
Barnoldswick La LA6 236 D3
Barnoldswick Rd
Beverley BB8,BB9 168 F7
Kelbrook BB18 191 F6
Barns La PR3 159 C8
Barns The L37 12 A1
Barnsfold PR2 116 D6
Barnside Euxton PR7 59 C3
Whitworth OL12 51 B8
Barnside Est BB8 170 F7
Barnstaple Way PR4 115 F6
Barnwood Cres BB18 201 C1
Barnwood Rd BB18 201 B1
Baron Rd FY1 129 C1
Baron St Darwen BB3 80 F2
Rawtenstall BB4 85 D1
Barons Cl BB3 81 A7
Barons Way Blackburn BB3 81 A6
Euxton PR7 59 D2
Barracks Rd BB11 126 D6
Barracks The L39 22 C2
Barret Hill Brow BB7 224 B4
Barret St BB18 201 A1
Barrett Ave PR8 34 A2
Barrett Ct 5 BL9 32 A2
Barrett Rd PR8 34 A2
Barrett St 5 BB10 127 A8
Barrington Dr PR8 20 B5
Barrison Gn L40 23 E2
Barritt Rd BB4 84 F2
Barronwood Ct PR4 56 A5
Barrow (VC) Prim Sch BB7 164 D2
Barrow Nook La L39 7 E2
Barrow's La PR3 154 B5
Barrowcroft Cl WN1 29 B1
Barrowdale Ave BB9 147 F7
Barrowford Rd
Barrowford BB9 168 B1
Colne BB8 169 B5
Fence BB12 146 C7
Barrowford Sch BB9 168 D3
Barrows La LA3 208 E7
Barrows La E PR3 154 B5
Barry Ave PR2 116 A3
Barry Gr LA3 208 F6
Barry St BB12 126 C7
Bartholomew Rd LA4 212 F4
Bartle La PR4 115 C7
Bartle Pl PR2 115 E1
Bartle Rd FY8 89 A8
Bartle St BB11 126 D5
Barton Ave Blackpool FY1 129 B2
Knott End-on-S FY6 194 E5
Barton Ct LA1 211 A4
Barton Gdns LA1 211 B5
Barton Heys Rd L37 11 D1
Barton La PR3 136 E7
Barton Mans FY8 88 C7
Barton Rd Lancaster LA1 211 A4
Lytham St Anne's FY8 88 D8
Barton Row LA6 234 B7
Barton Sq FY6 194 E5
Barton St BB2 100 E5
Barton Streety BB2 100 E5
Bartons Cl PR9 53 D5
Bashall Gr PR5 76 B3
Basil St Colne BB8 169 D4
Preston PR1 117 C2
Basnett St BB10 147 C1
Bass La BL9 49 D3
Bassenthwaite Rd FY3 130 C2
Bassett Way OL12 51 E2
Bastwell Rd BB1 100 F7
Bateman Gr LA4 212 E5
Bateman Rd LA4 212 E5
Bateman St BL6 31 D2
Bates St BB5 123 E3
Bath Mill La LA1 211 A8
Bath Mill Sq 7 LA1 211 A8
Bath Rd FY8 90 B3
Bath Springs L39 15 F5
Bath St Accrington BB5 103 B4
Blackburn BB2 100 C4
Blackpool FY4 129 B1
Colne BB8 169 E5
Lancaster LA1 211 A8
Lytham St Anne's FY8 90 B3
Morecambe LA4 212 D5
Nelson BB9 147 F8
Preston PR2 116 D1
Southport PR8 34 B8
Bath St N PR9 34 B8
Bathurst Ave FY3 130 A7
Bathurst St BB2 100 D5
Batridge Rd BL7 47 A7
Battersby St BL9 32 D3
Battismore Rd LA4 212 E5
Battle Way L37 12 B2
Bawdlands BB7 164 D8
Bawhead Rd BB18 201 B1
Baxenden CE Prim Sch BB5 103 E1
Baxter St WN6 28 F1
Baxtergate LA4 212 E6
Bay Cl LA3 208 D6
Bay Horse Dr LA1 211 B3
Bay Horse La PR4 134 D4
Bay Horse Rd LA2 207 E4
Bay New Dr LA3 208 F8
Bay Rd Fulwood PR2 117 E2
Heysham LA3 208 D6
Bay St BB1 101 A7
Bay The FY5 172 C5
Bay Tree Farm PR2 94 D8
Bay Tree Rd PR6 77 B3
Bay View LA6 231 B8
Bay View Ave LA2 213 E8
Bay View Cres LA2 213 E8
Bayard St BB12 126 A6
Baycliffe Cres LA4 212 D5
Bayley Fold BB7 164 E8
Bayley St BB5 123 E3
Bayliss Cl PR2 117 F3
Baylton Ct PR3 178 D2
Baylton Dr PR3 178 D2
Baynes Cotts 4 LA2 233 B8
Baynes St BB3 81 F1
Bayside FY7 194 B4
Bayswater FY2 150 C4
Baytree Cl
Bamber Bridge PR5 76 C8
Southport PR9 53 D5
Baytree Gr BL0 49 B2
Baytree Wlk OL12 70 C1
Bayview Cotts LA3 208 E6
Baywood St BB1 100 F7
Bazil Gr LA3 205 D7
Bazil La LA3 205 D7
Bazley Rd FY8 89 D3
Beach Ave Cleveleys FY5 172 D3
Lytham St Anne's FY8 89 C3
Beach Priory Gdns PR8 34 A6
Beach Rd Cleveleys FY5 172 D3
Fleetwood FY7 193 E3
Lytham St Anne's FY8 88 D7
Pilling Lane FY6 195 B7
Southport PR8 33 F6
Beach St
Lytham St Anne's FY8 90 A3
Morecambe LA4 213 A7
Beach Terr LA6 236 F3
Beacham Rd PR8 34 E7
Beachcomber Dr FY5 172 C3
Beachley Rd PR2 116 A4
Beachley Sq BB12 126 D7
Beachmews PR8 33 F6
Beachwood La LA5 237 A1
Beacon Ave PR2 116 D5
Beacon Cl BB8 169 C3
Beacon Crossing WN8 26 C2
Beacon Ctry Pk WN8 18 F2
Beacon Dr PR3 137 D6
Beacon Fell Ctry Pk PR3 180 F2
Beacon Fell Rd PR3 180 E2
Beacon Flats PR3 139 C8
Beacon Gr Fulwood PR2 116 D4
Garstang PR3 178 B6
Beacon Hts WN8 10 A8
Beacon La L40, WN8 18 D4
Beacon Rd
Poulton-le-F FY6 152 A3
Shevington Moor WN6 28 B2
Beacon St PR7 42 D7
Beacon View WN6 19 C8
Beacon View Dr WN8 10 B7
Beacons The WN6 19 D7
Beaconsfield Ave PR1 117 E1
Beaconsfield Rd PR9 34 F6
Beaconsfield St
Accrington BB5 103 D5
Great Harwood BB6 123 C5
16 Haslingden BB4 84 B3
Beaconsfield Terr
Catterall PR3 178 E2
Chorley PR6 60 D2
Beale Rd BB9 147 B8
Beamont Dr PR1 95 D8
Bean Ave FY4 109 E8
Bear St BB12 125 F6
Beardshaw Ave FY1 129 D2
Beardsworth St BB1 101 A7
Beardwood BB2 100 A8
Beardwood Brow BB2 100 B7
Beardwood Dr BB2 100 A7
Beardwood Fold BB2 100 A7
Beardwood High Sch BB2 100 A6
Beardwood Hospital The BB2 100 A6
Beardwood Mdw BB2 100 A7
Beardwood Pk BB2 100 B7
Bearncroft WN8 9 D6
Bearswood Croft PR6 77 B2
Beatie St BB9 147 B6
Beatrice Ave BB12 126 C7
Beatrice Mews 9 BL6 31 B4
Beatrice Pl BB2 81 A8
Beattock Pl FY2 150 F6
Beatty Ave PR7 42 B6
Beatty Cl FY8 109 D1
Beatty Rd PR8 34 E5
Beauclerk Rd FY8 89 B6
Beaufort L37 12 A2
Beaufort Ave FY2 150 C5
Beaufort Cl Ormskirk L39 15 A1
Simonstone BB12 144 E2
Beaufort Gr LA4 212 G5
Beaufort Rd
Morecambe LA4 213 A5
Weir OL13 87 A7
Beaufort St Nelson BB9 147 E7
Rochdale OL12 51 C1
Beauley Ave BB12 144 E2
Beauly Cl BL0 49 A2
Beaumaris Ave BB2 100 A1
Beaumaris Cl 2 BB4 84 B1
Beaumaris Rd PR5 59 C8
Beaumont Ave BL6 31 C4
Beaumont Coll (The Spastics Society) LA1 213 F4
Beaumont Cres L39 15 D2
Beaumont Ct 8 FY1 129 C6
Beaumont Gdns FY6 151 A5
Beaumont Pl LA1 213 F4
Beaumont Rd BL6 31 C4
Beaumont St LA1 213 F4
Beaver Cl BB1 121 F5
Beaver Terr 13 OL13 87 A3
Beavers La WN8 9 D6
Bebles Rd L39 15 C3
Becconsall La PR4 72 F3
Beck Ct FY7 193 D1
Beck Gr FY5 172 E4
Beck Side LA2 231 C3
Beck View 7 LA1 211 A3
Beckdean Ave FY6 151 D2
Beckenham Ct BB10 147 D3
Beckett Ct 19 PR1 95 F8
Beckett St 5 BB3 64 A8
Becks Brow BD23 230 F3
Beckside Barley BB12 167 C5
Trawden BB8 170 C3
Beckside Mews LA6 234 B3
Beckway Ave FY3 129 F7

Bective Rd LA6 . . . . .238 C2
Bedale Pl FY5 . . . . .172 E1
Beddington St **6** BB9 . . . .168 D1
Bedford Ave FY5 . . . . .172 D3
Bedford Cl BB5 . . . . .102 C4
Bedford Mews BB3 . . . . . . .80 F4
Bedford Pl Lancaster LA1 . .211 A4
 Padiham BB12 . . . . .125 D7
Bedford Rd Blackpool FY1 .129 C8
 Fulwood PR2 . . . . .117 A4
 6 Lytham St Anne's FY8 . .90 D4
 Southport PR8 . . . . .34 A2
Bedford St
 6 Barrowford BB9 . . . . . .168 C1
 Blackburn BB2 . . . . .100 C2
 Darwen BB3 . . . . .80 F4
 Egerton BL7 . . . . .46 C2
Bedford Terr Bury BL9 . . . . .32 A4
 Haslingden BB4 . . . . .67 A8
Bedfordshire Ave BB12 . . .126 B7
Bee La PR1 . . . . .95 E1
Beech Ave Adlington PR6 . . .30 B8
 Bilsborrow PR3 . . . . .157 A5
 Blackpool FY3 . . . . .129 E5
 Darwen BB3 . . . . .81 D3
 Earby BB18 . . . . .201 A1
 Euxton PR7 . . . . .59 C4
 Galgate LA2 . . . . .206 F4
 Horwich BL6 . . . . .31 E1
 Kirkham PR4 . . . . .113 B4
 Leyland PR5 . . . . .59 A7
 Parbold WN8 . . . . .26 C2
 Poulton-le-F FY6 . . . . . . .151 D4
 Warton PR4 . . . . .91 D6
Beech Cl Bacup OL13 . . . . . .87 A3
 Clitheroe BB7 . . . . .164 D8
 Oswaldtwistle BB5 . . . . . .102 C2
 Rishton BB1 . . . . .102 B8
 Rufford L40 . . . . .38 C4
 Skelmersdale WN8 . . . . . . .17 E1
 Whitworth OL12 . . . . .70 C1
 Wilpshire BB1 . . . . .121 E6
Beech Cres BB5 . . . . .124 A1
Beech Ct PR2 . . . . .116 E7
Beech Dr Freckleton L37 . . . .11 D4
 Freckleton PR4 . . . . .92 A5
 Fulwood PR2 . . . . .116 D8
 Haslingden BB4 . . . . .84 C2
 Kirkham PR4 . . . . .112 E4
 Longridge PR3 . . . . .139 A7
 Newton-with-S PR4 . . . . . .113 F2
 Poulton-le-F FY6 . . . . . . .151 D2
Beech Gdns PR6 . . . . .77 B1
Beech Gr Accrington BB5 . . .103 A4
 2 Barnoldswick BB18 . . .200 C2
 Brierfield BB10 . . . . .147 C4
 Chatburn BB7 . . . . .187 D5
 Darwen BB3 . . . . .80 D6
 Knott End-on-S FY6 . . . . .194 E6
 Lancaster LA2 . . . . .213 E6
 Morecambe LA4 . . . . .213 A5
 Preston PR2 . . . . .116 B1
 Ramsbottom BL8 . . . . .49 A1
 Southport PR9 . . . . .34 F7
 Warton, Carnforth LA5 . . .217 D5
Beech Grove Cl FY3 . . . . . .32 B4
Beech Hill Cl PR5 . . . . .96 E3
Beech Ind Est **3** OL13 . . . .87 A3
Beech Mdw L39 . . . . .16 A4
Beech Mount BB1 . . . . . . .121 F3
Beech Rd Elswick PR4 . . . . .153 F1
 Garstang PR3 . . . . .178 B8
 Halton LA2 . . . . .214 E7
 Leyland PR5 . . . . .76 A2
 Ormskirk L39 . . . . .6 A6
Beech St Accrington BB5 . . .103 C5
 Bacup OL13 . . . . .87 A3
 Barnoldswick BB18 . . . . . .200 B1
 Blackburn BB1 . . . . .101 A7
 Bury BL9 . . . . .32 B2
 Clayton-le-M BB5 . . . . . . .123 F1
 Clitheroe BB7 . . . . .164 D8
 Edgworth BL7 . . . . .47 D5
 Great Harwood BB6 . . . . . .123 C6
 Lancaster LA1 . . . . .210 D8
 10 Nelson BB9 . . . . .168 E1
 Padiham BB12 . . . . .125 D7
 1 Preston PR1 . . . . .95 D6
 Ramsbottom BL0 . . . . .49 C3
 Rawtenstall BB4 . . . . .85 A3
Beech St S PR1 . . . . .95 E6
Beech Terr **1** PR1 . . . . .95 E6
Beech Tree Ave WN6 . . . . . .19 D8
Beech Tree Cl BB9 . . . . . . .147 E7
Beech Tree Sch PR5 . . . . . .77 B4
Beechacre BL0 . . . . .49 D5
Beecham St LA4 . . . . .212 E6
Beechcroft Cleveleys FY5 .172 C4
 Maghull L31 . . . . .5 D1
Beeches The
 Clayton Green PR6 . . . . . . .77 C3
 Singleton FY6 . . . . .152 D1
 Tarleton PR4 . . . . .56 A7
Beechfield Hill Dale WN8 . . .26 C5
 Lancaster LA1 . . . . .210 D7
 Maghull L31 . . . . .5 E1
Beechfield Ave
 Blackpool FY3 . . . . .129 E3
 Knott End-on-S FY6 . . . . .195 A5
 Wrea Green PR4 . . . . .112 C4
Beechfield Cl PR5 . . . . .59 B8
Beechfield Gdns PR8 . . . . .33 F6
Beechfield Mews PR9 . . . . .34 F7
Beechfield Rd PR5 . . . . .59 C8
Beechfields PR7 . . . . .40 B6

Beeching Cl LA1 . . . . .210 F6
Beechthorpe Ave BB7 . . . .186 B4
Beechtrees WN8 . . . . .9 D7
Beechway Fulwood PR2 . . . .117 A4
 Maghull L31 . . . . .6 B2
 Penwortham PR1 . . . . .95 B3
Beechway Ave L31 . . . . .6 B2
Beechwood WN8 . . . . .18 C3
Beechwood Ave
 Accrington BB5 . . . . .103 D3
 Bamber Bridge PR5 . . . . . .96 D4
 Burnley BB10 . . . . .126 F3
 Clitheroe BB7 . . . . .164 E6
 Fulwood PR2 . . . . .116 C4
 Ramsbottom BL0 . . . . .49 D6
 Shevington WN6 . . . . .19 F5
Beechwood Cres WN6 . . . .10 E6
Beechwood Croft PR6 . . . . .77 A3
Beechwood Ct
 Blackburn BB1 . . . . .100 F1
 Coppull PR7 . . . . .28 F8
 Maghull L31 . . . . .5 F1
 Skelmersdale WN8 . . . . . . .9 D6
Beechwood Dr
 Blackburn BB2 . . . . .79 E8
 Formby L37 . . . . .11 C1
 Ormskirk L39 . . . . .15 D5
 Thornton FY5 . . . . .151 B8
Beechwood Gdns LA1 . . . .211 A2
Beechwood Gr FY2 . . . . . . .150 E4
Beechwood Mews BB1 . . . .81 A8
Beechwood Rd
 12 Blackburn BB1 . . . . . .101 A7
 Chorley PR7 . . . . .42 D6
Beenland St **3** PR1 . . . . . .117 D1
Beeston Ave FY6 . . . . .151 C5
Beetham Ct BB5 . . . . .123 E2
Beetham Pl FY3 . . . . .129 E6
Begonia St BB3 . . . . .81 B1
Beightons Wlk OL12 . . . . . .51 D4
Bela Cl **3** LA1 . . . . .213 C2
Bela Gr FY1 . . . . .129 D2
Belfield WN8 . . . . .9 D6
Belfield Rd BB5 . . . . .103 C4
Belford Ave FY5 . . . . .172 F4
Belford St BB12 . . . . .126 F7
Belfry Cl PR7 . . . . .59 D4
Belfry Cres WN6 . . . . .28 F2
Belfry Mans BB6 . . . . .142 C6
Belfry The FY8 . . . . .90 D5
Belgarth Rd BB5 . . . . .103 C7
Belgrave Ave Kirkham PR4 113 C4
 Penwortham PR1 . . . . .95 B3
Belgrave Cl Blackburn BB2 100 E1
 3 Lytham St Anne's FY8 . .89 D6
Belgrave Cres BL6 . . . . .31 D3
Belgrave Ct BB12 . . . . .126 F7
Belgrave Pl
 Poulton-le-F FY6 . . . . . . .151 B2
 Southport PR8 . . . . .33 F3
Belgrave Rd Blackpool FY4 129 C4
 Colne BB8 . . . . .169 D6
 Darwen BB3 . . . . .64 A8
 5 Leyland PR5 . . . . .76 A1
 Poulton-le-F FY6 . . . . . . .151 B3
 Southport PR8 . . . . .33 F3
Belgrave Sq **3** BB3 . . . . . . .81 A1
Belgrave St Brierfield BB9 147 A6
 Burnley BB12 . . . . .126 F7
 Haslingden BB5 . . . . .84 A8
 Nelson BB9 . . . . .168 F1
 Rochdale OL12 . . . . .51 D1
Bell La Bury BL9 . . . . .32 A3
 Claughton BB9 . . . . .179 C4
 Clayton-le-M BB5 . . . . . . .124 B4
Bell St BB4 . . . . .84 B3
Bell's Cl L31 . . . . .5 C4
Bell's La L31 . . . . .5 B3
Bell-Aire Park Homes
 LA3 . . . . .208 F5
Bellamy Ave LA4 . . . . .212 D3
Belle Isle Ave OL12 . . . . . . .51 C6
Belle View Pl FY3 . . . . .129 D5
Belle Vue Ave LA1 . . . . . . .211 A5
Belle Vue Dr LA1 . . . . .211 A5
Belle Vue La BB7 . . . . .186 B4
Belle Vue Pl **8** BB11 . . . . .126 A5
Belle Vue St
 Blackburn BB2 . . . . .100 C5
 Burnley BB11 . . . . .126 A6
Bellfield Rd LA4 . . . . .212 F5
Bellingham Rd FY8 . . . . . . .90 B4
Bellis Ave PR9 . . . . .52 F2
Bellis Way PR5 . . . . .96 B2
Bells La PR5 . . . . .97 E3
Belmont Ave
 Blackpool FY1 . . . . .129 C4
 Fulwood PR2 . . . . .117 D2
 Orrell WN5 . . . . .10 D3
 Poulton-le-F FY6 . . . . . . .151 B3
Belmont Cl Brinscall PR6 . . .61 E8
 Burscough L40 . . . . .24 E3
 Fulwood PR2 . . . . .117 D2
 Lancaster LA1 . . . . .213 D3
Belmont Cres PR2 . . . . . . .117 D2
Belmont Ct PR3 . . . . .139 B7
Belmont Dr PR6 . . . . .60 E1
Belmont Gr BB10 . . . . .127 D5
Belmont Pl PR7 . . . . .28 C6
Belmont Rd Adlington PR6 . .30 B7
 Belmont BB3,BL7 . . . . .63 A2
 Fleetwood FY7 . . . . .194 A3
 Fulwood PR2 . . . . .116 C2
 Great Harwood BB6 . . . . . .123 B5
 Horwich BL6 . . . . .31 C7
 Leyland PR5 . . . . .58 D8
 Lytham St Anne's FY8 . . . . .89 C5
 Rivington BL6 . . . . .44 C1

Belmont Sch BB4 . . . . .84 E2
Belmont St PR8 . . . . .34 A5
Belmont Terr
 7 Barrowford BB9 . . . . .168 D3
 Foulridge BB8 . . . . .191 E1
Belmont Way OL12 . . . . . . .51 E2
Belper St **1** BB1 . . . . .101 A6
Belshaw Ct **2** FY4 . . . . . .109 A6
Belthorn CE Prim Sch BB1 81 F6
Belthorn Rd BB1 . . . . .81 E6
Belton Hill PR2 . . . . .116 D8
Belvedere Ave
 Ramsbottom BL8 . . . . .49 A1
 Rawtenstall BB4 . . . . .86 A1
Belvedere Ct **1** FY8 . . . . . .89 D4
Belvedere Dr Chorley PR7 . .42 B8
 Formby L37 . . . . .11 F1
Belvedere Pk L39 . . . . .6 C7
Belvedere Rd Adlington PR6 30 B8
 Blackburn BB1 . . . . .122 A3
 Burnley BB10 . . . . .127 B6
 2 Leyland PR5 . . . . .76 B2
 Southport PR8 . . . . .20 C5
 Thornton FY5 . . . . .151 C8
Belverdale Gdns FY4 . . . . .109 F5
Belvere Ave FY3 . . . . .109 D6
Belvington Cl BB11 . . . . . .126 E5
Belvoir St OL12 . . . . .51 C1
Ben La Barnoldswick BB18 .200 D3
 Rainford Junction L39 . . . . .8 A1
Ben Lane Ct L39 . . . . .8 B2
Benbow Cl FY8 . . . . .109 C2
Bence Rd PR1 . . . . .96 B6
Bence St BB8 . . . . .169 E5
Bench Carr OL12 . . . . .51 C1
Benenden Pl **9** FY5 . . . . .173 A2
Bengal St FY7 . . . . .60 D1
Bengarth Rd PR9 . . . . .34 F8
Benjamin Hargreaves
 CE Prim Sch BB5 . . . . . .103 D5
Bennett Ave FY1 . . . . .129 C4
Bennett Dr WN5 . . . . .10 D4
Bennett Rd FY5 . . . . .173 A3
Bennett St **2** BB9 . . . . . .168 F2
Bennett's La FY4 . . . . .109 F6
Bennington St BB1,BB2 . . .100 F3
Benson Ave LA4 . . . . .212 G4
Benson House BB1 . . . . . . .101 C8
Benson La PR4 . . . . .134 F3
Benson Rd FY3 . . . . .150 E1
Benson St Blackburn BB1 . .101 B7
 Bury BL9 . . . . .32 A1
 Edgworth BL7 . . . . .47 E5
Benson's La PR4 . . . . .156 C1
Bent Est OL13 . . . . .87 A7
Bent Gap La BB2 . . . . .100 C4
Bent La Colne BB8 . . . . . . .170 B6
 Gisburn BB7 . . . . .225 C3
 Leyland PR5 . . . . .59 C8
Bent St Blackburn BB2 . . . .100 D4
 Haslingden BB4 . . . . .67 A4
 3 Oswaldtwistle BB5 . . . .102 D3
Bentgate Cl BB4 . . . . .67 D8
Bentham Ave
 Burnley BB10 . . . . .147 B3
 Fleetwood FY7 . . . . .193 C1
Bentham Cl BB2 . . . . .100 B1
Bentham Hall Cotts LA2 . .233 D8
Bentham Moor Rd LA6 . . .236 D2
Bentham Pl WN6 . . . . .28 F2
Bentham Rd
 Barnoldswick LA6 . . . . . . .236 E3
 Blackburn BB2 . . . . .100 B1
 Lancaster LA1 . . . . .211 A2
 Standish WN6 . . . . .28 F2
Bentham Sch LA2 . . . . . . .233 B8
 Southport PR8 . . . . .34 B5
Bentham Sta LA2 . . . . . . .233 D7
Bentham's Way PR8 . . . . . .34 C2
Bentinck Ave FY4 . . . . .109 B5
Bentinck Rd FY8 . . . . .88 C8
Bentinck St **9** OL12 . . . . . .51 C1
Bentlea Rd BB7 . . . . .225 C3
Bentley Dr Kirkham PR4 . . .112 C5
 Peel Hill FY4 . . . . .111 A6
Bentley La
 Andertons Mill L40,PR7 . . . .40 A1
 Bispham Green L40 . . . . . .26 E8
 Bury BL9 . . . . .50 A1
Bentley Park Rd PR4 . . . . . .73 F7
Bentley St **8** Bacup OL13 . . .86 F3
 Blackburn BB1 . . . . .101 C5
 Darwen BB3 . . . . .64 C7
 Nelson BB9 . . . . .147 D7
 Rochdale OL12 . . . . .51 C2
Bentley Wood Way BB11 . .125 F4
Bentmeadows OL12 . . . . . .51 E1
Benton Rd PR2 . . . . .117 D4
Bents BB8 . . . . .170 B6
Bents La LA6 . . . . .238 F5
Bentwood Rd BB4 . . . . .84 A3
Beresford Dr PR9 . . . . .52 F1
Beresford Gdns PR9 . . . . . .52 F2
Beresford Rd BB1 . . . . . . .100 D7
Beresford St
 8 Blackpool FY1 . . . . . .129 C7
 9 Burnley BB11 . . . . . . .126 D6
 Nelson BB9 . . . . .147 F6
Bergen St BB11 . . . . .126 B5
Berkeley Cl Chorley PR7 . . .42 D5
 Nelson BB9 . . . . .147 E7
Berkeley Colonnade PR2 117 A4
Berkeley Cres LA2 . . . . . . .145 C1
Berkeley Ct LA3 . . . . .208 E6
Berkeley Dr
 Clayton-le-W PR5 . . . . . . .76 E4

Berkeley Dr continued
 Simonstone BB12 . . . . . . .144 E2
Berkeley St Brierfield BB9 147 A5
 Nelson BB9 . . . . .147 E7
 Preston PR1 . . . . .116 E1
Berkley Cl PR4 . . . . .112 E5
Berkshire Ave BB12 . . . . . .126 B7
Berkshire Cl BB1 . . . . .121 F7
Bernard St OL12 . . . . .51 E3
Berne Ave BL6 . . . . .31 A3
Berridge Ave BB12 . . . . . . .126 A6
Berriedale Rd BB9 . . . . . . .169 A1
Berry Cl WN8 . . . . .17 E2
Berry Field **3** PR1 . . . . .95 C3
Berry Ho Cotts L40 . . . . .37 A5
Berry House Rd L40 . . . . . . .37 A4
Berry La PR3 . . . . .139 A7
Berry St Bamber Bridge PR5 76 A8
 Brierfield BB9 . . . . .147 B5
 Burnley BB11 . . . . .126 F4
 Preston PR1 . . . . .96 A7
 Skelmersdale WN8 . . . . . . .17 F2
Berry's La **6** FY6 . . . . .151 C4
Berrys La BB7 . . . . .143 C2
Bertha St BB5 . . . . .103 D6
Bertram Ave LA4 . . . . .212 D4
Bertrand Ave FY3 . . . . .130 A7
Berwick Ave Cleveleys FY5 172 F4
 Southport PR8 . . . . .20 D5
Berwick Dr Burnley BB12 . .126 E7
 Fulwood PR2 . . . . .116 D4
Berwick Rd Blackpool FY3 .109 C5
 Lytham St Anne's FY8 . . . . .88 F7
 Preston PR1 . . . . .96 A6
Berwick St PR1 . . . . .117 E1
Berwick Way LA3 . . . . .208 E7
Berwyn Ave LA4 . . . . .212 G6
Berwyn Cl BL6 . . . . .31 C5
Berwyn Ct PR8 . . . . .34 C4
Beryl Ave Blackburn BB1 . .121 F2
 Cleveleys FY5 . . . . .172 E1
Bescar Brow La L40 . . . . . .22 F7
Bescar La L40 . . . . .36 B1
Bescar La Sta L40 . . . . .36 B2
Bescot Way **10** FY5 . . . . . .150 F7
Bessie St **12** BB18 . . . . . .200 B3
Best St PR4 . . . . .112 F5
Bethel Ave FY2 . . . . .150 D4
Bethel Rd BB1 . . . . .101 A7
Bethel St
 Barnoldswick BB18 . . . . . .200 B2
 Colne BB8 . . . . .169 B4
Bethesda Cl BB2 . . . . .100 D3
Bethesda Rd FY1 . . . . .129 B3
Bethesda St
 Barnoldswick BB18 . . . . . .200 B2
 Burnley BB11 . . . . .126 F6
Betony LA4 . . . . .213 B6
Betony Cl OL12 . . . . .51 D3
Bett La PR6 . . . . .78 C1
Beulah Ave LA4 . . . . .212 G5
Bevan Pl BB9 . . . . .168 F2
Beverley Ave
 Longshaw WN5 . . . . .10 E1
 Poulton-le-F FY6 . . . . . . .130 D8
Beverley Cl Clitheroe BB7 .164 E6
 Preston PR2 . . . . .95 C8
 Southport PR9 . . . . .53 C5
 Wrea Green PR4 . . . . .112 A3
Beverley Ct
 2 Lytham St Anne's FY8 . .89 A8
 Morecambe LA4 . . . . .213 A5
Beverley Dr BB7 . . . . .164 D6
Beverley Gr FY4 . . . . .109 C7
Beverley Rd BB9 . . . . .168 E8
Beverley Rd N FY8 . . . . .89 A8
Beverley Rd S FY8 . . . . .89 A8
Beverley St Blackburn BB2 100 B1
 Burnley BB11 . . . . .126 E5
Beverly Cl FY5 . . . . .151 B8
Bewcastle Dr L40 . . . . .16 C3
Bexhill Rd PR2 . . . . .116 A4
Bexley Ave FY3 . . . . .129 D8
Bexley Pl FY8 . . . . .89 E5
Bezza St BB2,PR5 . . . . .119 C5
Bhailok St **3** PR1 . . . . .95 B8
Bibby Dr FY3 . . . . .130 E5
Bibby Rd PR9 . . . . .53 A1
Bibby's La FY2 . . . . .150 E3
Bickerstaffe
 CE Prim Sch L39 . . . . .7 E5
Bickerstaffe St **2** FY1 . . . .129 B3
Bickerton Rd PR4 . . . . .33 F4
Bicknell St LA1 . . . . .100 E6
Bideford Ave FY3 . . . . .130 A6
Bideford Way PR4 . . . . . . .115 F6
Bidston St PR1 . . . . .96 E8
Big Fold BL6 . . . . .30 D2
Bigdale Dr L33 . . . . .1 A3
Biggins La LA6 . . . . .238 A1
Biggins Rd LA6 . . . . .238 B2
Billinge Ave BB2 . . . . .100 B5
Billinge Cl BB2 . . . . .100 B5
Billinge End BB2 . . . . .100 A6
Billinge End Rd
 Blackburn BB2 . . . . .99 F5
 Pleasington BB2 . . . . .99 B4
Billinge Hospl WN5 . . . . . .10 D2
Billinge Side BB2 . . . . .99 F5
Billinge St BB1 . . . . .101 B4
Billinge View BB2 . . . . .99 F2
Billington Ave BB5 . . . . . . .85 A5
Billington Gdns BB7 . . . . .143 A4
Billington Rd BB11 . . . . . .126 B4
Billington St **1** PR4 . . . . . .112 F6
Billington St E **3** PR4 . . . .112 F6
Bilsberry Cotts BB7 . . . . . .162 F1
Bilsborough Hey PR1 . . . . . .95 C3

Bilsborough Mdw PR2 . . .115 E3
Bilsborrow La
 Bilsborrow PR3 . . . . .157 C4
 Inglewhite PR3 . . . . .157 F5
Binbrook Pl PR7 . . . . .42 A7
Binfold Croft LA6 . . . . .238 C1
Bingley Ave FY3 . . . . .129 F6
Bingley Cl PR6 . . . . .77 C2
Binns St 85 A7
Binyon Ct LA1 . . . . .210 F6
Binyon Rd LA1 . . . . .210 F5
Birbeck Rd L33 . . . . .1 A3
Birbeck Wlk L33 . . . . .1 A3
Birch Ave Blackpool L40 . . .24 E4
 Clayton-le-W PR5 . . . . . . .76 D3
 Cleveleys FY5 . . . . .172 E2
 Euxton PR7 . . . . .59 C4
 Galgate LA2 . . . . .207 A4
 Haslingden BB4 . . . . .84 C3
 Newton-with-S PR4 . . . . . .113 F3
 Penwortham PR1 . . . . .95 A3
 Preston PR2 . . . . .116 A2
Birch Cl Huncoat BB5 . . . . .124 E2
 Maghull L31 . . . . .5 F1
 Whitworth OL12 . . . . .51 C6
Birch Cres
 Gregson Lane PR5 . . . . . . .97 E3
 Oswaldtwistle BB5 . . . . . .102 F3
Birch Dr LA5 . . . . .218 C4
Birch Field PR6 . . . . .77 B3
Birch Gn L37 . . . . .11 D4
Birch Gr Barrow BB7 . . . . .164 D1
 Lancaster LA1 . . . . .210 D8
 Ramsbottom BL0 . . . . .49 A3
 Stalmine FY6 . . . . .174 D7
Birch Green Rd WN8 . . . . .18 C3
Birch Hall Ave BB3 . . . . . . .80 D4
Birch Hall La BB18 . . . . . . .201 D2
Birch La PR3 . . . . .181 C1
Birch Rd Chorley PR6 . . . . .60 E2
 Coppull PR7 . . . . .41 E1
 Garstang PR3 . . . . .178 C8
Birch St Accrington BB5 . . .103 B6
 Bacup OL13 . . . . .86 F3
 Fleetwood FY7 . . . . .194 A4
 5 Lytham St Anne's FY8 . .90 C3
 Skelmersdale WN8 . . . . . . .8 E8
 Southport PR8 . . . . .34 B4
Birch Terr BB5 . . . . .103 D2
Birch Tree Gdns FY3 . . . . .130 B2
Birch Tree Way **4** BL6 . . . . .31 E1
Birch View BB7 . . . . .164 D1
Birch Way FY6 . . . . .151 C4
Birch Wlk **1** BB1 . . . . .101 B4
Birchall Lodge **6** PR2 . . . .117 F4
Birchbank Gdns BB1 . . . . .101 A7
Birchenlee La BB8 . . . . . . .169 C2
Birches End OL12 . . . . .51 C5
Birches Rd BL7 . . . . .47 D4
Birches The L37 . . . . .11 E5
Birchfield PR4 . . . . .73 F4
Birchfield Ave OL10 . . . . . .32 E1
Birchfield Dr PR3 . . . . .139 A8
Birchfield Way L31 . . . . .5 B5
Birchill Rd L33 . . . . .1 C2
Birchin La PR6 . . . . .77 D1
Birchover Ct PR2 . . . . .116 A5
Birchtree Ave LA3 . . . . . . .212 B1
Birchway Ave FY3 . . . . . . .129 E6
Birchwood PR5 . . . . .75 C1
Birchwood Ave PR4 . . . . . . .94 B1
Birchwood Cl FY8 . . . . .89 E6
Birchwood Dr Coppull PR7 . .41 E2
 Fulwood PR2 . . . . .116 D7
 Hambleton FY6 . . . . .174 C2
Birchwood Way L33 . . . . . . .1 A1
Bird i' th' Hand Cotts **2**
 L39 . . . . .15 E6
Bird St Brierfield BB9 . . . . .147 B5
 Preston PR1 . . . . .95 D6
Birdy Brow BB7 . . . . .163 A6
Birk St PR1 . . . . .95 E5
Birkacre Brow PR7 . . . . . . .41 F2
Birkacre Rd PR7 . . . . .41 F4
Birkbeck Pl FY7 . . . . .193 D2
Birkbeck Way BB10 . . . . . .147 A1
Birkdale Ave
 Blackpool FY2 . . . . .150 E5
 Fleetwood FY7 . . . . .172 E7
 Longton PR4 . . . . .73 F8
 Lytham St Anne's FY8 . . . .109 F1
Birkdale Cl Lancaster LA1 .213 D3
 Longton PR4 . . . . .73 F8
 Thornton FY5 . . . . .151 D8
Birkdale Cop PR8 . . . . .34 E1
Birkdale Dr PR2 . . . . .115 E2
Birkdale High Sch PR8 . . .20 E7
Birkdale Prim Sch PR8 . . .34 B3
Birkdale Sch for Hearing
 Impaired Children PR8 . .33 E4
Birkdale Sta PR8 . . . . .34 F4
Birkdale Trad Est PR8 . . . .34 A2
Birkett Dr PR2 . . . . .118 A3
Birkett Pl PR2 . . . . .118 A3
Birkett Rd BB5 . . . . .103 D4
Birkett's Pl LA4 . . . . .212 F5
Birkey La L37 . . . . .11 F2
Birklands Ave LA4 . . . . . . .212 F4
Birkrig WN8 . . . . .9 D6
Birks Brow PR3 . . . . .160 D3
Birkside Way FY4 . . . . .130 C1
Birkwith La LA2 . . . . .233 C2
Birley Cl WN6 . . . . .19 F8
Birley Pl BB10 . . . . .127 A8
Birley St Blackburn BB1 . . .100 F5
 Blackpool FY1 . . . . .129 B5
 Kirkham PR4 . . . . .113 B5

Birley St *continued*
🕮 Preston PR1 . . . . .95 F8
🔳 Preston PR1 . . . . .96 A7
Birleywood WN8 . . . . .9 D6
Birnam Gn FY7 . . . . .193 E4
Birtle Rd BL9 . . . . .32 C6
Birtwhistle Cl BB9 . . . . . . .147 B5
Birtwhistle Fold 🔳 BB8 . . .169 E5
Birtwhistle Ave BB8 . . . . . .169 D6
Birtwhistle Ct BB18 . . . . . .200 C1
Birtwhistle Hyde Pk 🔳
   BB8 . . . . .169 D5
Birtwhistle St
   Accrington BB5 . . . . .103 C5
   🔳 Bamber Bridge PR5 . . . .76 B7
   Great Harwood BB6 . . . . . .123 B5
Birtwistle Standroyd
   Bglws BB8 . . . . .170 A5
Birtwhistle Terr BB6 . . . . . .142 C1
Bisham Cl BB3 . . . . .64 C8
Bishop David Sheppard
   CE Sch PR9 . . . . .35 B7
Bishop Martin
   CE Prim Sch WN8 . . . . .9 D6
Bishop Rawstorne
   CE High Sch The PR5 . . . .57 C2
Bishop St Accrington BB5 . .103 C5
   Burnley BB10 . . . . .147 B1
   Nelson BB9 . . . . .147 D8
Bishopdale Cl
   Blackburn BB2 . . . . .79 D7
   Morecambe LA3 . . . . .213 B3
Bishopdale Rd LA1 . . . . . . .210 D7
Bishopgate 🔳 PR1 . . . . .96 A8
Bishops Gate FY8 . . . . .89 D7
Bishopsgate
   Highfurlong FY3 . . . . .151 B1
   Lancaster LA1 . . . . .211 A4
Bishopstone Cl BB2 . . . . . . .81 A8
Bishopsway PR1 . . . . .95 D3
Bison Pl PR5 . . . . .75 C2
Bispham Ave PR5 . . . . .75 E4
Bispham Endowed
   CE Jun Sch FY2 . . . . .150 D4
Bispham Hall Bsns Pk
   WN5 . . . . .10 C2
Bispham Rd Blackpool FY2 .150 D3
   Blackpool, Carleton FY2 . . .150 E4
   Blackpool, Warbreck FY3 . . .129 E8
   Carleton FY5,FY6 . . . . .151 A6
   Cleveleys FY5 . . . . .172 C6
   Nelson BB9 . . . . .147 E6
   Southport PR9 . . . . .34 F7
Bispham St 🔳 PR1 . . . . .95 F8
Bittern Cl FY3 . . . . .130 B6
Bivel St BB12 . . . . .126 D6
Bk Alfred St BL0 . . . . .49 B5
Black Abbey St BB5 . . . . . .103 C5
Black Bull La PR2 . . . . .116 D5
Black Croft PR6 . . . . .77 B3
Black Dyke Rd LA5 . . . . . . .237 C1
Black Horse St
   Blackrod BL6 . . . . .30 C3
   🔳 Chorley PR7 . . . . .42 B6
Black House La
   Chipping PR3 . . . . .182 B1
   Lane Bottom BB10 . . . . . . .148 D3
Black La Nateby PR3 . . . . . .177 A8
   Ramsbottom BL0 . . . . .50 B7
Black Lane Croft BB7 . . . . .186 E1
Black Lane Ends BB8 . . . . .192 F3
Black Moor Rd L40 . . . . .39 C4
Black Moss La
   Ormskirk L39 . . . . .15 E3
   Scarisbrick L40 . . . . .22 C6
Black Moss Sch WN8 . . . . . .17 D2
Black Sticks La PR3 . . . . . .181 D1
Black-a-Moor La L39 . . . . . .14 A2
Blackacre La L39, L40 . . . . .15 E8
Blackamoor Broadlands
   & Dame Evelyn Fox
   Special Schs BB1 . . . . .81 B8
Blackamoor Rd BB1 . . . . . . .81 C8
Blackberry Hall Cres LA3 209 A8
Blackberry Way PR1 . . . . . . .95 B2
Blackbrook PR6 . . . . .61 A2
Blackburn Brow PR6 . . . . . . .60 E3
Blackburn Cath
   BB1 . . . . .100 E4
Blackburn Coll BB2 . . . . . .100 D5
Blackburn Old Rd
   Blackburn BB1 . . . . .122 D3
   Great Harwood BB1,BB6 . . .122 F5
   Hoghton PR5 . . . . .98 C2
Blackburn Rd
   Accrington BB5 . . . . .103 A6
   Accrington BB5 . . . . .103 C6
   Blackburn BB1 . . . . .101 E8
   Clayton-le-M BB5 . . . . . . .123 E1
   Darwen BB3 . . . . .80 E4
   Edenfield BL0,BB4 . . . . . . .67 D5
   Egerton BL7 . . . . .46 C4
   Great Harwood BB6 . . . . . .123 C4
   Great Knowley PR6 . . . . . . .60 E4
   Haslingden BB4,BB5 . . . . . .84 B5
   Higher Walton PR5 . . . . . . .97 B3
   Higher Wheelton PR6 . . . . .78 C1
   Oswaldtwistle BB5,BB1 . . . .102 C5
   Padiham BB12 . . . . .125 A8
   Ribchester PR3 . . . . .140 E3
   Rishton BB1 . . . . .123 A1
   Wheelton PR6 . . . . .60 F6
   Whittlestone Head BB3,BL7 . .65 B2
Blackburn Royal Infmy
   BB2 . . . . .100 D2
Blackburn St
   Blackburn BB1 . . . . .100 E6

Blackburn St *continued*
🔳 Burnley BB11 . . . . .126 F6
Chorley PR6 . . . . .42 E7
Blackburn Sta BB1 . . . . . . .100 F4
Blackcar La L29 . . . . .4 B3
Blacker St BB10 . . . . .147 A2
Blackfen Pl FY2 . . . . .129 D8
Blackfield Rd PR4 . . . . .92 B6
Blackgate La Holmes PR4 . . .55 C3
   Tarleton PR4 . . . . .55 E5
Blackhorse Ave BL6 . . . . . . .30 C2
Blackhorse Cl BL6 . . . . .30 C3
Blackhurst Ct PR4 . . . . .74 B8
Blackhurst La PR4 . . . . .134 F1
Blackledge Cl WN5 . . . . .10 E5
Blackley St L33 . . . . .1 A6
Blacko Bar Rd BB9 . . . . . . .168 B3
Blacko Prim Sch BB9 . . . . .168 D8
Blackpool & Fleetwood
   Tramway FY2 . . . . .150 B2
Blackpool & Fleetwood
   Yacht Club FY5 . . . . .151 F7
Blackpool & Fylde Coll
   Blackpool FY2 . . . . .150 E6
   Fleetwood FY7 . . . . .194 A4
Blackpool & Fylde Coll
   of F Ed FY8 . . . . .88 E5
Blackpool & The Fyde
   Coll Campus FY6 . . . . . . .152 D3
Blackpool & The Fylde
   Coll Blackpool FY1 . . . . . .129 C4
   Blackpool FY1 . . . . .129 D4
Blackpool & The Fylde
   Coll (Nautical) FY7 . . . . .172 E7
Blackpool & The Fylde
   Coll Ansdell Campus
   FY8 . . . . .89 C5
Blackpool Airport FY4 . . . .109 D3
Blackpool Central Pier
   FY1 . . . . .129 A3
Blackpool North Pier
   FY1 . . . . .129 A5
Blackpool North Sta FY1 129 C6
Blackpool Old Rd
   Little Eccleston PR3 . . . . . .154 A5
   Poulton-le-F FY6 . . . . .151 B2
Blackpool
   Pleasure Beach FY4 . . . .109 B7
Blackpool Rd
   Blackpool FY2 . . . . .150 D4
   Blackpool, Carleton FY6 . . .151 A4
   Clifton PR4 . . . . .93 E8
   Longridge PR3 . . . . .139 A7
   Lytham St Anne's FY8 . . . . .89 D5
   Newton-with-S PR4 . . . . . .114 B2
   Preston PR1,PR2 . . . . .116 C2
   Preston, Larches PR2 . . . . .115 E1
   St Michael's on W PR3 . . . .155 B6
   Wrea Green PR4 . . . . .112 C6
Blackpool Rd N FY8 . . . . . .109 F2
Blackpool Sixth Form
   Coll The FY3 . . . . .151 A2
Blackpool South Pier
   FY4 . . . . .109 A8
Blackpool South Sta FY4 129 B1
Blackpool St
   🔳 Church BB5 . . . . .102 E5
   🔳 Darwen BB3 . . . . .64 B6
Blackpool Tower FY1 . . . . .129 B5
Blackpool Tramway FY1 . . .129 A4
Blackpool Zoo FY3 . . . . . . .130 A4
Blackrod Brow BL6 . . . . .30 B4
Blackrod By-Pass Rd BL6 . . .30 D2
   Blackrod BL6 . . . . .30 E2
Blacksnape Rd BB3 . . . . .81 D2
Blackstone Rd PR6 . . . . .60 E1
Blackthorn Cl
   Cleveleys FY5 . . . . .172 F5
   Newton-with-S PR4 . . . . . .113 F2
   Preston PR2 . . . . .115 D1
   Rochdale OL12 . . . . .51 E2
Blackthorn Cres OL13 . . . . . .86 F3
Blackthorn Croft PR6 . . . . . .77 A2
Blackthorn Dr PR1 . . . . .95 B3
Blackthorn La OL13 . . . . . . .86 F3
Blackthorn Mews OL12 . . . . .51 E2
Blackwood Pl LA1 . . . . .211 B5
Blackwood Rd OL13 . . . . . . .69 B7
Blades St LA1 . . . . .210 F4
Blaguegate La WN8 . . . . .17 B2
Blainscough Rd PR7 . . . . . . .28 E8
Blair Gr PR9 . . . . .34 F7
Blair St OL12 . . . . .51 D1
Blairgowrie Gdns L39 . . . . .16 A4
Blairway Ave FY3 . . . . .129 F6
Blake Ave PR5 . . . . .76 A7
Blake Gdns BB6 . . . . .123 B4
Blake St BB5 . . . . .103 B6
Blakehall WN8 . . . . .9 D7
Blakeley Cres BB18 . . . . . .200 B3
Blakewater Rd BB1 . . . . . . .101 C7
Blakey Moor BB2 . . . . .100 D5
Blakey St BB11 . . . . .127 B6
Blakiston St FY7 . . . . .194 A4
Blanche St 🔳 PR2 . . . . .116 C1
Blandford Ave FY5 . . . . . . .172 C1
Blandford Cl PR8 . . . . .33 F5
Blandford Rise BL6 . . . . .30 C2
Blannell St BB11 . . . . .126 F1
Blascomay Sq 🔳 BB8 . . . . .169 D4
Blashaw La PR1 . . . . .95 A5
Blaydike Moss FY5 . . . . .75 B1
Blaydon Ave FY5 . . . . .172 E4
Blaydon Pk WN8 . . . . .9 D7
Blea Cl BB12 . . . . .126 B8
Blea Tarn Pl 🔳 LA4 . . . . . .212 G4

Blea Tarn Rd LA1,LA2 . . . .211 C2
Bleachers Dr 🔳 PR5 . . . . . .75 E1
Bleak La L40 . . . . .25 D5
Bleakholt Rd BL0 . . . . .67 F1
Bleara Rd BB18 . . . . .192 D7
Bleasdale Ave
   Cleveleys FY5 . . . . .150 E8
   Clitheroe BB7 . . . . .164 C7
   Kirkham PR4 . . . . .113 A5
   Poulton-le-F FY6 . . . . .151 C2
   Staining FY3 . . . . .130 E5
Bleasdale CE Prim Sch
   PR3 . . . . .181 A7
Bleasdale Cl
   🔳 Bamber Bridge PR5 . . . .76 F8
   Leyland PR25 . . . . .59 B7
   Ormskirk L39 . . . . .6 D7
Bleasdale Ct PR3 . . . . .139 B7
Bleasdale Gr LA3 . . . . .212 B1
Bleasdale House Sch
   LA5 . . . . .218 C3
Bleasdale La PR3 . . . . .180 C6
Bleasdale Rd
   Cumeragh Village PR3 . . . .137 F6
   Knott End-on-S FY6 . . . . . .194 D5
   Lytham St Anne's FY8 . . . . .90 C4
   Whitechapel PR3 . . . . .158 C8
Bleasdale St E PR1 . . . . . . .117 C1
Blelock St PR1 . . . . .96 A7
Blenheim Ave
   Blackpool FY1 . . . . .129 D4
   Kirkham PR4 . . . . .112 F5
Blenheim Cl
   Bamber Bridge PR5 . . . . . . .76 C8
   Blackburn BB1 . . . . .121 E1
Blenheim Dr Thornton FY5 173 C2
   Warton PR4 . . . . .91 D6
Blenheim Pl FY8 . . . . .109 E1
Blenheim Rd PR8 . . . . .20 B6
Blenheim St Colne BB8 . . . .170 A5
   🔳 Rochdale OL12 . . . . .51 C1
Blenheim Terr BB8 . . . . . . .191 E1
Blenheim Way PR4 . . . . . . .115 E6
Blessed Sacrament
   RC Prim Sch PR2 . . . . . . .117 F3
Blind La Burton in L LA6 . . .236 C3
   Gisburn BB7 . . . . .225 C3
   Higham BB12 . . . . .146 A6
Blindman's La L39 . . . . .15 C7
Bloom St 🔳 BL0 . . . . .49 A4
Bloomfield Ct PR1 . . . . .116 E2
Bloomfield Grange PR1 . . . .95 C2
Bloomfield Pk LA5 . . . . .217 D1
Bloomfield Rd
   Blackpool FY1 . . . . .129 C2
   Withnell BB6 . . . . .79 A1
Bloomfield Road
   Football Gd
   (Blackpool FC) FY1 . . . .129 C2
Blossom Ave FY4 . . . . .109 F7
Blossoms The PR7 . . . . . . .117 C6
Blowick Bsns Pk PR9 . . . . .35 A6
Blucher St BB5 . . . . .169 E4
Blue Bell La OL14 . . . . .108 D2
Blue Bell Pl PR1 . . . . .96 A7
Blue Gates BB7 . . . . .223 B3
Blue Moor PR4 . . . . .134 A2
Blue Scar La BB7 . . . . .224 D7
Blue Stone La L40 . . . . .39 F4
Bluebell Ave BB4 . . . . .67 A8
Bluebell Cl Cleveleys FY5 . .172 F5
   Hesketh Bank PR4 . . . . .72 E4
   Lucas Green PR6 . . . . .60 C5
Bluebell Gr BB11 . . . . .126 A5
Bluebell Way PR2 . . . . .117 F6
Bluebell Wood PR5 . . . . .75 F3
Bluecoat Cres PR4 . . . . . . .114 A2
Bluestone La L31 . . . . .5 E1
Blundell Ave Formby L37 . . .11 B4
   Hightown L38 . . . . .2 F3
   Southport PR8 . . . . .33 F2
Blundell Cres PR8 . . . . .33 F2
Blundell Dr PR8 . . . . .33 F2
Blundell Gr L38 . . . . .2 F3
Blundell La Blackrod BL6 . . .30 A2
   Penwortham PR1 . . . . .95 B6
   Southport PR9 . . . . .53 C2
Blundell Links Ct PR8 . . . . .20 C4
Blundell Rd Fulwood PR2 . .116 E3
   Hightown L38 . . . . .2 F3
   Lytham St Anne's FY8 . . . . .109 F1
Blundell St FY1 . . . . .129 B3
Blythe Ave FY5 . . . . .172 E5
Blythe Cotts L40 . . . . .24 E1
Blythe La L40 . . . . .24 E1
Blythewood WN8 . . . . .9 D7
Board St BB10 . . . . .147 A1
Boarded Barn PR7 . . . . .59 C3
Boardman Av FY2 . . . . .129 D2
Boardman St BL6 . . . . .30 D2
Boarsgreave La BB4 . . . . . . .68 F6
Bobbin Cl BB5 . . . . .103 A5
Bobbin Mill Cl 🔳 OL14 . . .108 D1
Bobbin St OL14 . . . . .108 C1
Bobbiners La PR9 . . . . .54 A3
Bobby Langton Way L40 . . .24 C5
Bocholt Way BB4 . . . . .85 A2
Bodiam Rd BL8 . . . . .48 F2
Bodie Hill LA2 . . . . .205 E5
Bodkin La PR3 . . . . .152 F7
Bodmin Ave PR9 . . . . .53 B5
Bodmin St PR1 . . . . .117 D1
Boegrave Ave PR5 . . . . .76 A8
Bog Height Rd BB3 . . . . . . .80 C6
Bogburn La PR7 . . . . .28 D6
Boland St BB1 . . . . .101 A7
Bold La L39 . . . . .6 B7
Bold St Accrington BB5 . . . .103 D6

Bold St *continued*
   Bacup OL13 . . . . .86 F1
   Blackburn BB1 . . . . .100 E6
   Bury BL9 . . . . .32 A3
   Colne BB8 . . . . .169 E4
   Fleetwood FY7 . . . . .194 B5
   Morecambe LA3 . . . . .212 B4
   Preston PR1 . . . . .116 D1
   Southport PR9 . . . . .34 E4
Bold Venture Way BB5 . . . .124 A3
Boleyn Ct FY3 . . . . .130 A2
Boleyn The L31 . . . . .5 E3
Bolland Cl 🔳 BB7 . . . . .164 F8
Bolland Prospect BB7 . . . . .164 F7
Bolland St BB18 . . . . .200 B3
Bolton Ave Accrington BB5 124 D1
   Carleton FY6 . . . . .151 C5
   Lancaster LA1 . . . . .213 F4
Bolton Cl PR3 . . . . .139 B7
Bolton Croft PR5 . . . . .58 B8
Bolton Gr BB9 . . . . .168 D3
Bolton La LA5 . . . . .216 C4
Bolton Rd Abbey Village PR6 79 B3
   Adlington BL60,PR6 . . . . . . .30 D6
   Blackburn BB2 . . . . .100 D8
   Blackburn, Ewood BB2,BB3 . .80 E7
   Cadshaw BB3 . . . . .64 C3
   Chorley PR6 . . . . .42 E4
   Darwen BB3 . . . . .64 B7
   Edgworth BL7 . . . . .47 D5
   Ramsbottom BL8 . . . . .48 D2
   Riley Green PR5,PR6 . . . . . .78 E6
   Southport PR8 . . . . .34 A4
Bolton Rd N BL0 . . . . .49 B6
Bolton Rd W BL0,BL8 . . . . . .49 A4
Bolton St Blackpool FY1 . . .129 B2
   Chorley PR7 . . . . .42 C7
   Colne BB8 . . . . .169 C4
   🔳 Newchurch BB4 . . . . .85 E1
   Ramsbottom BL0 . . . . .49 B6
Bolton's Cop PR9 . . . . .54 D5
Bolton's Ct 🔳 BB1 . . . . . . .100 E5
Bolton's Meanygate PR4 . . .55 C7
Bolton-by-Bowland
   CE Prim Sch BB7 . . . . . . .224 D4
Bolton-le-Sands
   CE Prim Sch LA5 . . . . . . .216 B4
Boltons Croft PR4 . . . . .114 E7
Boltons Ct PR1 . . . . .96 A7
Bombay St BB2 . . . . .100 C3
Bonchurch St BB1 . . . . .101 C4
Bond Cl BL6 . . . . .31 C3
Bond St Blackpool FY4 . . . .109 B7
   🔳 Blackpool BB10 . . . . . . .127 A8
   Bury BL9 . . . . .32 A2
   Colne BB8 . . . . .169 D5
   Darwen BB3 . . . . .81 A2
   Edenfield BL0 . . . . .67 E2
   Lancaster LA1 . . . . .211 A8
   Nelson BB9 . . . . .147 D7
Bond's La Adlington PR7 . . . .29 F7
   Banks PR9 . . . . .54 C4
Bonds St PR9 . . . . .54 C5
Bonds The PR3 . . . . .178 C6
Bone Croft PR8 . . . . .77 B3
Bone Hill La PR3 . . . . .197 D1
Bonfire Hill Cl BB4 . . . . .85 B7
Bonfire Hill Rd BB4 . . . . . . .85 B7
Bonney St FY1 . . . . .173 B3
Bonny Grass Terr BB7 . . . .143 A4
Bonny St FY1 . . . . .129 B4
Bonsall St BB2 . . . . .100 B2
Boome St FY4 . . . . .109 C6
Boon Town L40 . . . . .234 C7
Boon Wlks LA6 . . . . .234 C7
Boot St BB18 . . . . .201 B2
Boot Way BB11 . . . . .127 A5
Booth Bridge La BD23 . . . .201 B5
Booth Cres BB4 . . . . .86 A1
Booth Ct 🔳 BB10 . . . . .127 A8
Booth Rd OL13 . . . . .86 F2
Booth St Accrington BB5 . . .103 C4
   🔳 Bacup OL13 . . . . .86 F2
   Carnforth LA5 . . . . .217 D1
   Haslingden BB4 . . . . .84 A4
   🔳 Nelson BB9 . . . . .147 D8
   Rawtenstall BB4 . . . . .68 E8
   Southport PR8 . . . . .34 B8
Booth's La L39 . . . . .14 F4
Boothley Rd FY1 . . . . .129 D6
Boothman Pl BB9 . . . . .168 E2
Boothman St BB2 . . . . .100 D2
Boothroyden FY1 . . . . .129 B8
Bootle St PR1 . . . . .117 C1
Borage Cl FY5 . . . . .173 A5
Border Ct 🔳 LA1 . . . . .213 D1
Bores Hill WN1 . . . . .29 C4
Borough Rd BB3 . . . . .81 A1
Borron La LA2 . . . . .234 C3
Borrowdale Ave
   Blackburn BB1 . . . . .101 C3
   Fleetwood FY7 . . . . .193 D6
Borrowdale Cl
   🔳 Accrington BB5 . . . . . . .124 D1
   Brierfield BB10 . . . . .147 C3
Borrowdale Dr BB10 . . . . . .147 C4
Borrowdale Gr LA4 . . . . . . .212 G5
Borrowdale Rd
   Blackpool FY4 . . . . .130 B1
   Lancaster LA1 . . . . .211 A8
   Leyland PR25 . . . . .59 B7
Borwick Ave LA5 . . . . .217 E6
Borwick Cl LA5 . . . . .217 E6
Borwick Ct Borwick LA6 . . .234 B4
   Morecambe LA4 . . . . .212 E3
Borwick Dr LA6 . . . . .234 B3

Borwick Mews LA6 . . . . . . .234 B3
Borwick Rd LA6 . . . . .234 D3
Bosburn Dr BB2 . . . . .120 C2
Boscombe Ave LA3 . . . . . . .212 B2
Boscombe Rd FY4 . . . . .109 B6
Bosley Arc 🔳 FY1 . . . . .129 B5
Bosley Cl BB3 . . . . .64 D8
Bostock St 🔳 PR1 . . . . .96 A7
Boston Ave FY2 . . . . .150 D6
Boston Rd Bacup OL13 . . . . .86 F3
   Lytham St Anne's FY8 . . . . .89 B6
Boston St BB9 . . . . .147 F6
Bostons BB6 . . . . .123 B5
Bostonway FY4 . . . . .109 F8
Bosworth Dr PR8 . . . . .20 B4
Bosworth Pl FY4 . . . . .109 B4
Bosworth St BL6 . . . . .31 B4
Botanic Gardens Mus PR9 53 B2
Botanic Rd PR9 . . . . .53 B2
Botany Brow PR6 . . . . .60 D2
Bott House La BB8,BB9 . . . .169 A2
Bottom o' th' Knotts
   Brow BL7 . . . . .47 E3
Bottom o' th' Rann BB1 . . .81 F6
Bottomdale Rd LA2 . . . . . . .214 A8
Bottomgate BB1 . . . . .101 B5
Bottomley Bank La BB4 . . . .85 B8
Bottomley St BB9 . . . . .147 E8
Bottoms La LA5 . . . . .218 D3
Botton Rd LA2 . . . . .233 C1
Boulder St BB4 . . . . .85 A7
Bouldsworth Rd BB10 . . . . .127 E5
Boulevard PR1 . . . . .96 B5
Boulevard Gdns FY8 . . . . . . .89 A4
Boulevard The FY8 . . . . .89 A4
Boulsworth Cres BB9 . . . . .169 B1
Boulsworth Dr BB8 . . . . . . .170 C1
Boulsworth Gr BB8 . . . . . . .170 A5
Boulview Terr BB8 . . . . .170 A5
Boundary Cl Eccleston PR7 . .40 B6
   New Longton PR4 . . . . .74 F4
Boundary Ct FY3 . . . . .151 A1
Boundary La
   Becconsall PR4 . . . . .72 C1
   Burscough L40 . . . . .24 F4
   Hale Nook FR6,PR3 . . . . . .175 B7
   Holmes PR4,PR9 . . . . .54 E6
   Kirkby L33 . . . . .1 F2
   Shevington Moor WN6 . . . . .28 A3
Boundary Meanygate
   Becconsall PR4 . . . . .72 C1
   Holmes PR4 . . . . .54 F7
Boundary Rd
   Accrington BB5 . . . . .103 D7
   Fulwood PR2 . . . . .116 D3
   Lancaster LA1 . . . . .210 F6
   Lytham St Anne's FY8 . . . . .90 E5
Boundary St Burnley BB10 147 C2
   Colne BB8 . . . . .169 D4
   Leyland PR25 . . . . .76 B2
   Southport PR8 . . . . .34 B4
Bourbles La FY6 . . . . .195 D4
Bourne Brow PR3 . . . . .157 E5
Bourne May Rd FY6 . . . . . . .194 D5
Bourne Rd FY5 . . . . .173 B5
Bourne Way FY5 . . . . .173 A4
Bourne's Row PR5 . . . . .97 E1
Bournemouth Rd FY4 . . . . .109 B6
Bournesfield PR5 . . . . .97 E1
Bovington Ave FY5 . . . . . . .150 F8
Bow Brook Rd PR5 . . . . .76 C1
Bow Hills La BB7 . . . . .225 C6
Bow La Leyland PR5 . . . . . . .76 B1
   Preston PR1 . . . . .95 E7
Bow St PR5 . . . . .76 B2
Bowden Ave BB2 . . . . .99 C1
Bowen St BB2 . . . . .100 B2
Bower Cl BB2 . . . . .100 B2
Bower St Blackburn BB2 . . .100 B2
   Bury BL9 . . . . .32 C3
Bowerham
   Com Prim Sch LA1 . . . . . .211 A6
Bowerham La LA1,LA2 . . . .211 B3
Bowerham Rd LA1 . . . . .211 A5
Bowers La PR3 . . . . .177 E7
Bowers The PR7 . . . . .42 D4
Bowes Lyon Pl FY8 . . . . .89 C7
Bowfell Ave LA4 . . . . .212 G5
Bowfell Cl FY4 . . . . .130 D1
Bowfield's La BB2 . . . . .119 F4
Bowgreave Cl 🔳 FY4 . . . . .110 A6
Bowgreave Dr PR3 . . . . . . .178 D4
Bowker St BL0 . . . . .67 C5
Bowker's Green La L39 . . . .6 E4
Bowland Ave
   Burnley BB10 . . . . .127 E5
   Chorley PR6 . . . . .42 D8
   Fleetwood FY7 . . . . .172 D8
Bowland Cl
   Carnforth LA5 . . . . .217 C1
   Longridge PR3 . . . . .139 B8
Bowland Cres FY3 . . . . .130 A8
Bowland Ct
   🔳 Clitheroe BB7 . . . . .164 E8
   🔳 Southport PR8 . . . . .34 C8
Bowland Cty High
   Sch BB7 . . . . .224 B1
Bowland Dr LA1 . . . . .213 D2
Bowland Gate La LA6 . . . . .186 C2
Bowland Ho 🔳 BB1 . . . . . .100 F6
Bowland Pl Fulwood PR2 . . .118 A4
   Lytham St Anne's FY8 . . . . .89 C6
Bowland Rd Fulwood PR2 . .118 A3
   Garstang PR3 . . . . .199 C1
   Heysham LA3 . . . . .209 A8

Bowland View
Brierfield BB9 . . . .**147** D4
Garstang PR3 . . . .**199** C1
Glasson LA2 . . . .**205** E4
Bowlers Cl PR2 . . . .**117** C5
Bowlers Wlk OL12 . . . . . .**51** F2
Bowling Green Cl
Darwen BB3 . . . .**64** B7
Southport PR8 . . . .**34** F5
Bowling Green Cotts
BB6 . . . .**142** C6
Bowlingfield PR2 . . . . . .**116** A6
Bowness Ave
Blackpool FY4 . . . .**130** D1
Lytham St Anne's FY8 . . . .**109** F2
Nelson BB9 . . . .**147** E6
Rochdale OL12 . . . .**51** C1
Southport PR8 . . . .**20** C3
Thornton FY5 . . . .**173** B2
Bowness Cl BB1 . . . .**101** A6
Bowness Pl FY7 . . . .**193** C1
Bowness Rd Fulwood PR1 .**116** A6
Lancaster LA1 . . . .**214** A1
Padiham BB12 . . . .**145** C2
Bowood Ct FY3 . . . .**130** B7
Bowran St PR1 . . . .**95** F8
Box St BL0 . . . .**49** D6
Boxer Pl PR5 . . . .**75** C2
Boxwood Dr BB2 . . . .**79** F8
Boxwood St BB1 . . . .**100** F8
Boyd Cl WN6 . . . .**28** F1
Boyes Ave PR3 . . . .**178** D2
Boyle St BB1 . . . .**100** F6
Boys La PR2 . . . .**116** C5
Brabiner La PR2,PR3 . . . .**138** B4
Brabins Endowed Sch
PR3 . . . .**182** E3
Bracebridge PR8 . . . .**34** F2
Bracewell Ave FY6 . . . . .**152** A3
Bracewell Cl BB9 . . . . . .**147** E8
Bracewell La BB23 . . . . .**225** F3
Bracewell Rd PR2 . . . . . .**117** E5
Bracewell St
Barnoldswick BB18 . . . . . .**200** B3
Burnley BB10 . . . .**147** B6
Nelson BB9 . . . .**147** F8
Bracken Cl Blackburn BB2 . .**79** E8
Chorley PR6 . . . .**42** E8
Bracken Dr PR4 . . . .**92** D7
Bracken Gr BB4 . . . .**67** A8
Bracken Hey BB7 . . . .**165** A8
Bracken Lea Fold 🖪 OL12 .**51** B2
Brackenbury Cl 🖪 PR5 . . . .**76** A7
Brackenbury Rd PR1,PR2 .**116** E3
Brackenbury St PR1 . . . .**116** F2
Brackenthaite Rd
LA5,LA7 . . . .**219** B7
Brackenway L37 . . . .**12** A6
Bracknel Way L39 . . . .**15** A1
Braconash Rd PR5 . . . . . .**75** C2
Bradda Rd BB2 . . . .**100** E1
Braddon St 🖪 PR1 . . . . .**117** D1
Brade St PR9 . . . .**53** C4
Brades Ave FY5 . . . .**173** D2
Brades La PR4 . . . .**92** D7
Bradford Gr LA3 . . . .**208** F6
Bradford St BB5 . . . .**103** D6
Bradkirk La PR5 . . . .**77** B8
Bradkirk Pl PR5 . . . .**77** A7
Bradley Cty Prim Sch
BB9 . . . .**168** E1
Bradley Fold 🖪 BB9 . . . . .**168** E1
Bradley Gdns BB12 . . . . .**126** B5
Bradley Hall Rd BB9 . . . .**168** F1
Bradley Hall Trad Est
WN6 . . . .**28** F2
Bradley Hill Trad Est WN6 .**29** A4
Bradley La Eccleston PR7 . .**40** D6
Standish WN6 . . . .**28** F2
Bradley Pl 🖪 PR8 . . . .**34** B7
Bradley Rd BB9 . . . .**168** E1
Bradley Rd E BB9 . . . .**168** E1
Bradley Smithy Cl OL12 . . .**51** E2
Bradley St Colne BB8 . . . .**169** F5
Southport PR9 . . . .**34** C8
Bradley View 🖪 BB9 . . . .**168** E1
Bradman Rd L33 . . . .**1** D3
Bradshaw Brow L40 . . . . .**39** E2
Bradshaw Cl
Blackburn BB1 . . . .**100** E4
Nelson BB9 . . . .**147** E7
Standish WN6 . . . .**28** D1
Bradshaw La
Corner Row PR4 . . . .**132** D1
Eagland Hill PR3 . . . .**176** A7
Mawdesley L40 . . . .**39** E2
Parbold WN8 . . . .**26** C1
Scronkey PR3 . . . .**196** A2
Bradshaw Rd BL7 . . . .**47** E1
Thornton FY5 . . . .**173** A4
Bradshaw Row BB5 . . . . .**102** F6
Bradshaw St Church BB5 . .**102** F6
🖪 Lancaster LA1 . . . .**211** A7
Nelson BB9 . . . .**147** D7
Bradshaw St E 🖪 BB5 . . .**103** C6
Bradshaw St W BB5 . . . . .**102** F6
Bradshaw's La PR8 . . . . . .**20** D6
Bradshawgate Dr LA5 . . .**218** C4
Brady St BL6 . . . .**31** A4
Bradyll Ct BB6 . . . .**142** C6
Braefield Cres PR4 . . . . .**112** E6
Braemar Ave Southport PR9 .**52** E2
Thornton FY5 . . . .**151** C2
Braemar Ct 🖪 LA4 . . . . . .**213** A4
Braemar Wlk FY2 . . . .**150** F2

Braemore Dr BL9 . . . .**32** D2
Braeside BB2 . . . .**100** C6
Braewood Cl BL9 . . . .**32** D2
Braganza Way LA1 . . . . . .**210** C8
Braid Cl PR1 . . . .**95** D1
Braid's La PR3 . . . .**179** A7
Braidhaven WN6 . . . .**19** E7
Braintree Ave PR1 . . . .**95** E2
Braith Cl FY4 . . . .**109** F8
Braithwaite St 🖪 FY1 . . .**129** B7
Bramble Cl PR4 . . . .**112** E6
Bramble Ct
Penwortham PR1 . . . .**95** E2
🖪 Thornton FY5 . . . .**173** A2
Bramble Gdns FY6 . . . . . .**151** A2
Bramble St BB10 . . . .**147** A1
Bramble Way WN8 . . . .**26** C1
Brambles The
Barrow BB7 . . . .**164** D1
Blackburn BB2 . . . .**100** A8
Blackpool FY8 . . . .**109** B4
Coppull PR7 . . . .**41** F2
Preston PR2 . . . .**117** D6
Bramblewood PR5 . . . .**57** B2
Bramblings The FY6 . . . . .**151** B2
Bramcote Cl L33 . . . .**1** A4
Bramcote Rd L33 . . . .**1** A4
Bramhall Rd WN8 . . . .**17** C1
Bramley Ave Burnley BB12 .**126** C8
Fleetwood FY7 . . . .**193** A4
Bramley Cl 🖪 BB5 . . . . . .**102** E5
Bramley View BB7 . . . . . .**143** C8
Brampton Ave FY5 . . . . . .**172** F4
Brampton Dr LA4 . . . .**213** B5
Brampton St 🖪 PR2 . . . . .**116** C1
Bramwell Rd PR4 . . . .**92** B6
Bramworth Ave BL0 . . . . . .**49** B6
Branch Rd
Blackburn BB2,BB3 . . . .**80** E7
Burnley BB7 . . . .**127** B4
🖪 Clayton-le-M BB2 . . . . .**123** F3
Mellor Brook BB2 . . . .**120** C2
Waddington BB7 . . . .**186** B4
Branch St Bacup OL13 . . . .**69** D8
Nelson BB9 . . . .**147** F8
Brancker St 🖪 PR7 . . . . . .**42** A5
Brandiforth St PR5 . . . . . .**96** F2
Brandlesholme Rd BL8 . . .**49** A1
Brandon Cl WN8 . . . .**10** A7
Brandreth Delph WN8 . . . .**26** C3
Brandreth Dr WN8 . . . .**26** C2
Brandreth Pk WN8 . . . .**26** D4
Brandreth Pl WN6 . . . .**28** F1
Brandwood 🖪 BB4 . . . .**85** E1
Brandwood Fold BL7 . . . . .**47** E5
Brandwood Gr BB10 . . . . .**127** C6
Brandwood Pk OL13 . . . . . .**69** B8
Brandwood Rd OL13 . . . . . .**69** B8
Brandwood St BB3 . . . .**81** B1
Brandy House Brow BB2 .**100** F2
Branksome Ave FY5 . . . . .**172** F3
Branksome Dr LA4 . . . . . .**212** G4
Branston Rd FY4 . . . .**129** E1
Branstree Rd FY4 . . . .**130** C1
Brant Cl FY7 . . . .**193** C1
Brant Rd PR1 . . . .**118** A1
Brantfell Dr BB12 . . . .**126** B8
Brantfell Rd
Blackburn BB1 . . . .**100** D7
Great Harwood BB6 . . . . . .**123** B4
Brantwood BB5 . . . .**123** E2
Brantwood Ave
Blackburn BB1 . . . .**101** F5
Morecambe LA4 . . . .**213** A6
Brantwood Dr
Lancaster LA1 . . . .**211** A2
Leyland PR5 . . . .**76** B1
Brassey St BB12 . . . .**126** C7
Brathay Pl FY7 . . . .**193** D2
Bray St PR2 . . . .**116** C1
Brays Heys 🖪 FY5 . . . . . .**173** C1
Brays Rd FY8 . . . .**111** B1
Brayshaw Pl PR2 . . . .**117** E4
Brazil Cl LA3 . . . .**212** D2
Brazley Ave BL6 . . . .**31** E1
Bread St 🖪 BB12 . . . .**126** D6
Bream Wood PR4 . . . .**112** A4
Brearlands BD23 . . . .**201** B6
Brearley St OL13 . . . .**69** D8
Breck Cl FY6 . . . .**151** F5
Breck Cty Prim Sch The
FY6 . . . .**151** F5
Breck Dr FY6 . . . .**151** E5
Breck Rd Blackpool FY3 . . .**129** B7
Poulton-le-F FY6 . . . .**151** F6
Breckside Cl FY5 . . . .**151** E5
Brecon Ave BB5 . . . .**102** C4
Brecon Cl FY1 . . . .**129** D3
Brecon Rd BB1 . . . .**101** C5
Bredon Ave PR7 . . . .**59** E1
Bredon Cl FY8 . . . .**90** D5
Bredon Ct L37 . . . .**11** D4
Breeze Cl Foulridge BB8 . .**171** A1
Thornton FY5 . . . .**173** A4
Breeze Mount PR5 . . . .**76** C8
Breeze Rd PR8 . . . .**33** E2
Brenbar Cres OL12 . . . .**70** D1
Brendjean Rd LA4 . . . . . .**212** F4
Brendon Wlk FY3 . . . .**129** F8
Brennand Cl
Bamber Bridge PR5 . . . .**76** F8
Lancaster LA1 . . . .**213** C2
Brennand St Burnley BB10 .**147** B1
Clitheroe BB7 . . . .**186** E1
Brennands Endowed
Prim Sch BB7 . . . .**223** C7
Brent St BB10 . . . .**147** C6
Brentlea Ave LA3 . . . .**208** E7

Brentlea Cres LA3 . . . . . .**208** E7
Brentwood FY7 . . . .**193** E2
Brentwood Ave
Burnley BB11 . . . .**126** E3
Cleveleys FY5 . . . .**150** D8
Poulton-le-F FY6 . . . .**151** C3
Brentwood Cl L38 . . . .**2** F2
Brentwood Ct PR9 . . . .**52** D1
Brentwood Rd
Adlington PR6 . . . .**30** B8
Nelson BB9 . . . .**169** A1
Bretherton Cl PR5 . . . .**58** C8
Bretherton Ct L40 . . . .**24** F3
Bretherton Endowed
CE Prim Sch PR5 . . . .**56** F6
Bretherton Rd PR5 . . . .**57** B4
Bretherton Terr 🖪 PR5 . . .**76** B1
Brett Cl BB7 . . . .**165** A7
Brettarch Dr LA1 . . . .**210** E5
Brettargh Cl LA1 . . . .**210** E6
Brettargh Dr LA1 . . . .**210** E6
Bretton Fold PR8 . . . .**34** F5
Brewery Arc 🖪 LA1 . . . . .**210** F8
Brewery La Formby L37 . . . .**11** F6
🖪 Lancaster LA1 . . . .**210** F8
Brewery St Blackburn BB2 .**100** D5
Longridge PR3 . . . .**139** B7
Breworth Fold La PR6 . . . .**78** A3
Briar Ave PR7 . . . .**59** C4
Briar Bank Row PR2 . . . .**117** A8
Briar Cl OL12 . . . .**51** A1
Briar Croft PR4 . . . .**74** A7
Briar Field FY2 . . . .**150** F6
Briar Gr PR2 . . . .**116** A4
Briar Hill Cl 🖪 BB1 . . . . .**101** A4
Briar Lea Rd LA6 . . . .**216** E5
Briar Mews 🖪 FY5 . . . . . .**173** C1
Briar Rd Blackburn BB1 . . .**100** F8
Southport PR8 . . . .**20** D4
Thornton FY5 . . . .**173** C1
Briar St OL13 . . . .**87** A1
Briarcroft BB3 . . . .**81** A6
Briarfield BB4 . . . .**46** D2
Briarfield Rd FY6 . . . .**151** B5
Briars Brook L40 . . . .**25** A2
Briars Gn WN8 . . . .**18** B4
Briars La Maghull L31 . . . . . .**5** E1
Ring o'Bells L40 . . . .**25** A3
Briars The Eccleston PR7 . . .**40** C6
Fulwood PR2 . . . .**117** D6
Southport PR8 . . . .**33** F1
Briarscroft LA5 . . . .**217** E6
Briarwood PR4 . . . .**92** A6
Briarwood Cl Leyland PR5 . .**58** E8
Weeton PR4 . . . .**131** F2
Briarwood Ct FY5 . . . .**151** B7
Briarwood Dr FY2 . . . .**150** E5
Briary Croft L38 . . . .**2** F3
Brick Kiln La L40 . . . .**38** B3
Brick St 🖪 Burnley BB11 . .**126** F6
Bury BL9 . . . .**32** A3
Brickcroft La PR5 . . . .**57** B3
Brickhouse Gdns PR3 . . .**182** E3
Brickhouse La FY6 . . . . . .**174** C4
Bricklayers Arms Yd L39 . .**15** D6
Bridge Ave L39 . . . .**15** E5
Bridge Bank 🖪 PR1 . . . . . .**96** C6
Bridge Brow LA6 . . . .**238** C1
Bridge Cl
Bamber Bridge PR5 . . . .**76** A8
🖪 Rawtenstall BB4 . . . .**85** F1
Bridge Croft
Bolton-le-S LA5 . . . .**216** A4
Clayton-le-M BB5 . . . .**123** E4
Bridge Ct
🖪 Bamber Bridge PR5 . . . .**76** A8
Clitheroe BB7 . . . .**186** F2
🖪 Lytham St Anne's FY8 . . . .**90** A4
Bridge End
Bamber Bridge PR5 . . . .**76** C8
Barley BB12 . . . .**167** C5
Whalley BB7 . . . .**143** C4
Bridge End Rd BB4 . . . .**67** A7
Bridge End St OL14 . . . . .**108** C1
Bridge Farm Dr L31 . . . .**5** F2
Bridge Gr PR8 . . . .**34** B6
Bridge Hall Dr BL9 . . . .**32** C2
Bridge Hall Fold BL9 . . . . .**32** C2
Bridge Hall La BL9 . . . .**32** D2
Bridge Ho Blackburn BB2 .**100** B1
🖪 Lancaster LA1 . . . .**213** F2
🖪 Saltcotes BB5 . . . .**90** D4
Bridge House Rd FY4 . . . .**109** F8
Bridge Houses
Accrington BB5 . . . .**83** E8
Whitewell Bottom BB4 . . . . .**85** F7
Bridge La LA1 . . . .**210** E4
Bridge Mill Rd BB9 . . . . . .**147** C6
Bridge Rd
🖪 Bamber Bridge PR5 . . . .**76** C8
Chatburn BB7 . . . .**187** D5
Fleetwood FY7 . . . .**194** B4
Lancaster LA1 . . . .**210** F5
Lytham St Anne's FY8 . . . . .**89** E4
Morecambe LA4 . . . .**212** F5
Nether Kellet LA6 . . . .**216** E4
Preston PR2 . . . .**116** C2
Bridge Row PR3 . . . .**155** C7
Bridge St
🖪 Accrington BB5 . . . .**103** C6
Bamber Bridge PR5 . . . .**76** E7
Blackburn BB1 . . . .**100** E4
Brierfield BB9 . . . .**147** B5
Burnley BB11 . . . .**127** A6
Bury BL9 . . . .**32** A3
Church BB5 . . . .**102** E6
Colne BB8 . . . .**169** C4
Darwen BB3 . . . .**81** A1

Bridge St continued
Garstang PR3 . . . .**178** C6
🖪 Great Harwood BB6 . . . .**123** C5
Haslingden BB4 . . . .**67** C6
Higher Walton PR5 . . . .**97** B3
Horwich BL6 . . . .**31** C4
Newchurch BB4 . . . .**85** F1
Ormskirk L39 . . . .**15** E4
Padiham BB12 . . . .**125** B8
Ramsbottom BL0 . . . .**49** C6
Rawtenstall BB4 . . . .**68** E7
Rishton BB1 . . . .**123** B2
Southport PR8 . . . .**34** B6
Water BB4 . . . .**86** A8
Wheelton PR6 . . . .**61** A7
Whitworth OL12 . . . .**70** C1
Bridge Terr 🖪 PR1 . . . . . .**96** C6
Bridge Wills La PR9 . . . . . .**53** C5
Bridgefield Dr BL9 . . . .**32** D2
Bridgefield St 🖪 BB6 . . .**125** C4
Bridgehall Dr WN8 . . . .**10** B7
Bridgemill Rd BB1 . . . . . .**100** F4
Bridgend Ct PR2 . . . .**115** F3
Bridgend Dr PR8 . . . .**20** B4
Bridget St 🖪 LA1 . . . .**210** F8
Bridgewater Ave 🖪 FY5 . .**150** F7
Bridgewater BB11 . . . .**125** F4
Bridgeway PR5 . . . .**76** C8
Bridle Path The BB18 . . . .**191** D7
Bridleway BB5 . . . .**85** F2
Brief St BB10 . . . .**127** A8
Brier Cres BB9 . . . .**147** D6
Brier Dr LA3 . . . .**208** E7
Brier Field FY2 . . . .**150** F6
Brier Hill Cl 🖪 BB1 . . . . .**101** A4
Brier Heights Cl BB9 . . . .**147** D5
Briercliffe Ave
Blackpool FY3 . . . .**129** E7
Nelson BB8 . . . .**169** B3
Briercliffe Bsns Ctr BB10 .**147** C4
Briercliffe Cty Sch BB10 .**147** F3
Briercliffe Rd
Brierfield BB10 . . . .**147** D2
Burnley BB10 . . . .**147** C1
🖪 Chorley PR6 . . . .**60** D1
Briercliffe St BB8 . . . .**169** B3
Brierfield New Longton PR4 .**74** F8
Skelmersdale WN8 . . . .**9** D6
Brierfield Mansfield
High Sch BB9 . . . .**147** B6
Brierfield Reedley
Cty Sch BB10 . . . .**147** C4
Brierfield Sta BB9 . . . . . .**147** B5
Brierholme Ave BL7 . . . . . .**46** E1
Brierley Ave FY3 . . . .**129** E7
Brierley La PR4 . . . .**135** B8
Brierley Rd PR5 . . . .**77** A7
Brierley St PR2 . . . .**116** D1
Briers Brow PR6 . . . .**61** B7
Briery Bank LA5 . . . .**237** C1
Briery Cl PR2 . . . .**117** C4
Briery Hey PR5 . . . .**77** C6
Briery St 🖪 LA1 . . . .**213** D1
Brieryfield Rd PR1 . . . .**95** D8
Brigg Field BB5 . . . .**123** F4
Briggs Fold BL7 . . . .**46** E2
Briggs Fold Cl BL7 . . . .**46** E2
Briggs Fold Rd BL7 . . . .**46** E2
Briggs Rd PR2 . . . .**116** C2
Brighouse Cl L39 . . . .**15** D6
Brighouse Gn L39 . . . .**16** F3
Bright St Blackburn BB1 . . .**101** B6
Blackpool FY4 . . . .**109** B8
🖪 Burnley BB10 . . . .**147** B1
Bury BL9 . . . .**32** A3
Clitheroe BB7 . . . .**164** F8
Colne BB8 . . . .**169** D5
Colne, Cotton Tree BB8 . . . .**170** B5
Darwen BB3 . . . .**80** F2
Egerton BL7 . . . .**46** D2
Oswaldtwistle BB5 . . . .**102** D3
Padiham BB12 . . . .**125** D4
🖪 Rawtenstall BB4 . . . .**85** A3
Southport PR9 . . . .**34** F7
Bright Terr BB8 . . . .**170** B2
Bright's Cl BB7 . . . .**223** A5
Brighton Ave
Blackpool FY4 . . . .**109** B8
Cleveleys FY5 . . . .**172** D2
Lytham St Anne's FY8 . . . . .**88** F7
Brighton Cres PR2 . . . . . .**116** A3
Brighton Rd
Brierfield BB10 . . . .**147** C3
Southport PR8 . . . .**34** A3
Brighton St Bury BL9 . . . . .**32** B3
🖪 Chorley PR6 . . . .**42** E8
Cornholme OL14 . . . .**108** C1
Brighton Terr
Blackburn BB2 . . . .**100** B6
Darwen BB3 . . . .**80** E2
Brightstone Cl PR9 . . . . . .**54** B5
Brigsteer Cl BB5 . . . .**123** E2
Brindle Cl
🖪 Lancaster LA1 . . . .**213** C2
Longridge PR3 . . . .**139** B7
Walton Summit PR5 . . . .**77** B8
Brindle Fold PR5 . . . .**77** C7
Brindle Gregson Lane
Cty Prim Sch PR5 . . . .**97** E1
Brindle Hts PR6 . . . .**77** F5
Brindle Rd
Bamber Bridge PR5 . . . .**96** F2
Walton Summit PR5,PR6 . . . .**77** C7
Brindle St Blackburn BB2 .**100** C1
Chorley PR7 . . . .**42** C6
Preston PR1 . . . .**96** C2
Brindle St James'
CE Prim Sch PR6 . . . .**77** F5
Brindley Cl BB11 . . . .**125** F4
Brindley St BL6 . . . .**31** C5

Brink's Row BL6 . . . .**31** D5
Brinklow Cl PR8 . . . .**20** A5
Brinscall Terr PR6 . . . .**61** F7
Brinwell Rd FY4 . . . .**130** B1
Brisbane Pl FY5 . . . .**150** F7
Brisbane St 🖪 BB5 . . . . .**124** A1
Bristol Ave Blackpool FY2 .**150** E4
Fleetwood FY7 . . . .**172** C8
Leyland PR5 . . . .**76** C3
Bristol Cl 🖪 BB1 . . . .**101** A4
Bristol St Burnley BB11 . . .**126** D3
Colne BB8 . . . .**169** E5
Morecambe LA4 . . . .**212** F4
Bristow Ave PR2 . . . .**116** B2
Britannia Ave OL13 . . . .**87** A2
Britannia Cotts BB5 . . . . .**102** A1
Britannia Cty Prim Sch
OL13 . . . .**70** C8
Britannia Pl 🖪 FY1 . . . . .**129** B1
Britannia St BB6 . . . .**123** C5
Britannia Way BB4 . . . .**67** A8
Britannia Wlk
🖪 Burnley BB11 . . . .**127** B4
Lytham St Anne's FY8 . . . . .**89** C8
British in India Mus BB8 .**169** E5
British Lawnmower Mus
PR8 . . . .**34** B4
Brittannia Dr PR2 . . . .**95** B7
Brittannia Wharf PR2 . . . . .**95** B8
Britten Cl BB2 . . . .**101** A2
Britten St BB3 . . . .**80** F2
Britwell Cl BB2 . . . .**81** A8
Brixey St PR1 . . . .**95** D6
Brixham Pl 🖪 FY4 . . . . . .**109** B6
Brixton Rd PR1 . . . .**96** B7
Broad Clough Villas OL13 . .**86** F5
Broad Croft PR4 . . . .**94** A1
Broad Gate BB3 . . . .**81** B2
Broad Ing OL12 . . . .**51** C1
Broad Ing Cl BB10 . . . . . .**127** E1
Broad La Ford Green BB3 . .**198** F2
Formby L37 . . . .**12** E2
Formby L37,L38 . . . .**4** A8
Haskayne L39 . . . .**14** B7
Kirkby L32 . . . .**1** A1
Maghull L29 . . . .**4** C2
Whalley BB7 . . . .**143** B5
Winmarleigh PR3 . . . .**198** F5
Broad Mdw
Bamber Bridge PR5 . . . .**76** A8
Chipping PR3 . . . .**182** D3
Broad Meadow La PR5 . . . .**56** F4
Broad Oak Ave PR3 . . . . .**178** D6
Broad Oak Cl PR8 . . . .**30** A8
Broad Oak Cotts PR6 . . . . .**43** D3
Broad Oak Gn PR1 . . . .**95** B3
Broad Oak High Sch BL9 . .**32** B2
Broad Oak La Bury BL9 . . . .**32** D3
Penwortham PR1 . . . .**95** B3
Penwortham, Nutter's
Platt PR4 . . . .**95** B2
Staining FY3 . . . .**130** D5
Broad Oak Rd BB5 . . . . . .**103** D5
Broad Oak Terr BL9 . . . . . .**32** E3
Broad Sq 🖪 PR5 . . . .**59** A8
Broad St 🖪 Leyland PR5 . . .**59** A8
🖪 Nelson BB9 . . . .**147** D8
Broadacre Caton LA2 . . . . .**231** C3
Orrell WN8 . . . .**10** A6
Shevington Moor WN6 . . . . .**28** B2
Broadacre Cl LA2 . . . .**231** C3
Broadacre Pl LA2 . . . .**231** C3
Broadacre View LA2 . . . . .**231** C3
Broadbent Dr BL9 . . . .**32** E4
Broadfield Accrington BB5 . .**83** B8
Broughton PR3 . . . .**136** B2
Oswaldtwistle BB5 . . . .**102** F2
Broadfield Ave
Blackpool FY4 . . . .**109** F5
Poulton-le-F FY6 . . . .**151** F3
Broadfield Ct FY6 . . . .**151** F3
Broadfield Dr Leyland PR5 . .**75** E1
Penwortham PR1 . . . .**95** D2
Broadfield Jun Sch PR5 . . .**75** F1
Broadfield Rd BB5 . . . . . .**103** A3
Broadfield Sch BB5 . . . . .**102** F2
Broadfield St BB5 . . . .**102** F3
Broadfleet Ct PR3 . . . .**196** C6
Broadfold Ave BB1 . . . . . .**101** B7
Broadgate PR1 . . . .**95** D6
Broadgreen Cl PR5 . . . .**59** A8
Broadhead Rd BB3,BL7 . . . .**65** F5
Broadhurst La WN6 . . . . . .**27** F7
Broadhurst Rd FY5 . . . . . .**150** E8
Broadhurst Way
BB10,BB9 . . . .**147** C4
Broadith La PR3 . . . .**158** E1
Broadlands PR8 . . . .**33** E3
Broadlands Dr LA5 . . . . . .**215** F3
Broadlands Pl PR4 . . . .**89** F4
Broadlea Gr OL12 . . . .**51** C2
Broadley Fold OL12 . . . .**51** B6
Broadley St BB4 . . . .**85** A3
Broadmead WN8 . . . .**26** B2
Broadness Dr BB9 . . . . . .**147** E6
Broadoak Rd L31 . . . .**5** D1
Broadoaks BL9 . . . .**32** D3
Broadpool La FY6 . . . .**174** C1
Broadriding Rd WN6 . . . . . .**19** E6
Broadstone Cl OL12 . . . . . .**51** A1
Broadstone Cl BB2 . . . . . .**120** C3
Broadtree Cl BB8 . . . .**170** B2
Broadwater Ave FY7 . . . . .**172** F8
Broadwater Gdns FY7 . . . .**172** E8
Broadway Accrington BB5 . .**103** B6
Blackburn BB1 . . . .**121** C4
Blackpool FY4 . . . .**109** C2
Fleetwood FY7 . . . .**193** E2

Broadway *continued*
Fulwood PR2 116 D7
Haslingden BB4 67 B8
Horwich BL6 31 D3
Lancaster LA1 213 F2
Leyland PR5 59 B8
Morecambe LA4 212 G5
Nelson BB9 147 D8
Preston PR2 115 F2
Broadway Cl PR8 20 B5
Broadway Cres BB4 67 A8
Broadway Cty Prim Sch BB4 67 C8
Broadway Pl
Barrowford BB9 168 D3
Nelson BB9 169 A1
Broadway St BB2 100 B1
Broadwood Cl PR1 95 B4
Broadwood Dr PR2 116 F7
Broadwood Way FY8 89 E4
Brock Ave FY7 193 D2
Brock Bank BB4 85 F4
Brock Cl LA1 213 E3
Brock Clough Rd BB4 85 F4
Brock Mill La PR3 180 B2
Brock Rd Chorley PR6 60 D1
Lane Heads PR3,PR4 154 E3
Brock Side PR3 157 C6
Brock St LA1 210 F8
Brockbank Ave LA1 210 C8
Brockenhurst St BB10 127 C5
Brockholes Brow
PR1,PR2 118 A1
Brockholes Cres FY6 151 E2
Brockholes View PR1 96 C7
Brockholes Way PR3 178 E1
Brockholes Wood Cty Prim Sch PR1 118 A1
Brocklebank Rd PR9 52 E2
Brocklehurst Ave BB5 103 B3
Brocklewood Ave FY6 130 D8
Brockway FY6 151 D2
Brockway Ave FY3 129 F6
Broderick Ave 1 FY2 150 E1
Brodick Rd BB1 101 D3
Brogden La BB18 225 E2
Brogden St 4 BB18 200 B3
Brogden View BB18 200 A4
Broken Bank Head BB7 229 A2
Broken Banks BB8 169 E4
Broken Stone Rd BB2,BB3 80 A6
Bromilow Rd WN8 17 C1
Bromley Cl FY2 150 E1
Bromley Cross BL7 47 B1
Bromley Ct 5 FY2 150 E1
Bromley Gn PR6 60 F4
Bromley Ho BB2 100 C5
Bromley Rd FY8 88 F6
Bromley St Blackburn BB2 100 C5
Preston PR1 95 D8
Brompton Ave L33 1 A5
Brompton Cl FY8 89 D5
Brompton Rd
Poulton-le-F FY6 130 D8
Southport PR8 34 E7
Bromsgrove Ave FY2 150 C4
Bromsgrove Rd BB10 127 B8
Bronte Ave BB10 127 D6
Bronte Cl OL12 51 A1
Brood Ford Ct 1 OL10 32 F1
Brooden Dr BB10 147 C4
Brook Ave Maghull L31 5 E2
Morecambe LA3 212 C3
Scorton PR3 199 E7
Brook Croft PR2 116 B4
Brook Farm Cl L39 15 E4
Brook Field Sch FY6 151 F5
Brook Field Way BB18 201 B1
Brook Gr Cleveleys FY5 172 E4
Morecambe LA3 212 C3
Brook Hey PR4 73 F8
Brook Hey Dr L33 1 A3
Brook Hey Wlk L33 1 A3
Brook Ho PR8 34 C5
Brook La
Charnock Richard PR7 41 C4
Farington PR4,PR5 75 D6
Farington PR4,PR5 75 D7
Much Hoole PR4 73 E3
Ormskirk L39 15 E4
Brook Mdw PR4 115 F7
Brook Mill Ind Est PR4 112 B4
Brook Pl PR2 115 D2
Brook Rd
Lytham St Anne's FY8 90 C3
Morecambe LA3 212 C3
Brook Side L31 5 E1
Brook St Adlington PR6 43 A1
3 Barnoldswick BB18 200 B2
Blackburn BB2 100 B2
Blackpool FY4 129 E1
Bury BL9 32 A3
Clitheroe BB7 186 F1
Colne BB8 169 D5
Earby BB18 201 B2
Fleetwood FY7 172 E8
Haslingden BB4 84 B5
Higher Walton PR5 97 B3
Kirkham PR4 112 F6
Lancaster LA1 210 E7
Nelson BB9 147 E8
Oswaldtwistle BB5 102 E3
Padiham BB12 125 D7
Preston PR1 116 E2
Rishton BB1 123 B1
Southport PR9 53 D4
Wheelton PR6 61 A7
Brook St Ct 1 FY4 129 E1
Brook St N PR2 116 D3
Brook Terr PR3 178 F2
Brook Villas BB7 186 E5
Brookbank BB9 168 E4
Brookdale Adlington PR6 43 A1
Belmont BL7 45 C5
New Longton PR4 75 A6
Rochdale OL12 51 E3
Brookdale Ave FY5 150 E8
Brookdale Cl PR5 59 B6
Brooke Cl Accrington BB5 103 E2
Southport PR9 35 B7
Brooke St PR6 42 E7
Brookes La BB7 143 C5
Brookes St 7 OL13 69 D8
Brookes The 6 PR6 42 E7
Brookfield Croston PR5 57 B3
Mawdesley L40 39 C2
Mellor BB2 120 E2
Parbold WN8 26 C2
Brookfield Ave
Blackpool FY4 110 A6
Fulwood PR2 117 C4
Thornton FY5 173 C1
Brookfield Cl LA5 216 B5
Brookfield Ct PR3 182 E3
Brookfield Dr PR2 116 E8
Brookfield La L39 6 A5
Brookfield Pl PR5 77 A6
Brookfield Prim Sch PR2 117 E5
Brookfield Rd Orrell WN8 10 B7
Shevington Moor WN6 28 B2
Thornton FY5 173 C1
Brookfield St
2 Blackburn BB1 100 E6
4 Cornholme OL14 108 C1
Preston PR1 116 F1
Brookfield Terr
Hampson Green LA2 204 E8
Lytham St Anne's FY8 90 B4
Brookfield View LA5 216 B5
Brookfields Cty Prim Sch WN8 17 D2
Brookford Cl BB12 126 D8
Brookhouse Bsns Ctr 10 BB1 100 F6
Brookhouse Cl
Blackburn BB1 100 F6
Gregson Lane PR5 97 F2
Brookhouse Dr PR5 97 F2
Brookhouse Gdns 12 BB1 100 F6
Brookhouse La BB1 100 F6
Brookhouse Prim Sch BB1 100 F7
Brookhouse Rd Caton LA2 231 C3
Ormskirk L39 15 D6
Brookhouse St PR2 116 D1
Brookland LA6 236 C3
Brookland Cl BB5 123 F4
Brookland St BB4 85 D1
Brookland Terr BB4 68 F7
Brooklands Chipping PR3 182 F3
Horwich BL6 31 C3
Ormskirk L39 16 A6
Preston PR2 116 A1
Brooklands Ave
Burnley BB11 127 B3
Fulwood PR2 116 F7
Haslingden BB4 67 B7
Kirkham PR4 113 A5
Brooklands Ct LA1 211 A4
Brooklands Dr Bonds PR3 178 C6
Heysham LA3 208 F6
Orrell WN5 10 D5
Brooklands Gr L40 24 F3
Brooklands Rd
Burnley BB11 127 B3
Lytham St Anne's FY8 89 C6
Orrell WN8 10 C7
Ramsbottom BL0 49 A2
Brooklands Terr BB1 101 A7
Brooklands The PR4 112 B4
Brooklyn Ave FY3 129 E8
Brooklyn Rd BB1 121 F5
Brooks Rd L37 11 D2
Brooks Way L37 11 D2
Brooksbottom Cl BL0 49 C4
Brookshaw St BL9 32 A4
Brookside
Brockhall Village BB6 142 C5
Coppull PR7 41 F1
Euxton PR7 59 C2
Kirkham PR4 112 F6
Thornton FY5 173 C3
Brookside Cl Leyland PR5 75 E3
Ramsbottom BL0 49 A3
Whalley BB7 143 C5
Brookside Cotts PR7 61 D3
Brookside Cres
Ramsbottom BL8 48 E1
West Bradford BB7 186 D7
Brookside Ctr FY5 173 C3
Brookside Dr LA2 220 A8
Brookside Ind Est BB5 102 C3
Brookside La BB5 102 B3
Brookside Prim Sch BB7 164 F8
Brookside Rd
Fulwood PR2 116 D7
Southport PR8 34 C2
Standish WN1 29 B1
Brookside St BB5 102 C3
Brookside View BB5 102 B4
Brookvale Ct PR3 155 E3
Brookview PR2 117 B5
Brookville OL12 70 C1
Brookway Blackburn BB2 80 B8
Longton PR4 73 F8
Wrea Green PR4 112 A4
Broom Field PR3 178 D4
Broome Rd PR8 34 B3
Broomfield Mill St PR1 116 F1
Broomfield Pl
Blackburn BB2 100 B3
Standish WN6 28 E1
Broomfield Rd
Fleetwood FY7 193 F2
Standish WN6 28 E2
Broomflat Cl WN6 28 E1
Broomholme WN6 19 D7
Brotherod Hall Rd OL12 51 C2
Brothers St BB2 100 A1
Brotherton Mdws 6 BB7 164 F8
Brough Ave FY2 150 F2
Brougham St BB12 126 F7
Broughton Ave
Blackpool FY3 129 E7
Southport PR8 34 D4
Broughton Cl BB2 101 A1
Broughton Gr LA3 212 F3
Broughton High Sch PR3 136 C2
Broughton in Amounderness CE Prim Sch PR3 136 D1
Broughton St
1 Burnley BB12 126 D6
4 Darwen BB3 80 F2
Preston PR1 116 E2
Broughton Tower Way
PR2 117 A8
Broughton Way FY6 151 C6
Brow Cl PR3 154 A6
Brow Edge BB4 85 D1
Brow Hey PR5 77 B6
Brow La LA2 233 F6
Brow The PR4 72 E4
Brow View BB10 127 B8
Browfoot Cl LA5 217 F2
Browgate BB7 187 F8
Browgill Pl 8 LA1 213 D2
Browhead Ct BB10 127 B8
Browhead Rd BB10 127 B8
Brown Birks Rd BB5 103 E8
Brown Birks St 15 OL14 108 B1
Brown Edge Cl PR8 35 A2
Brown Hill La BB8 169 F7
Brown Hill Row BB8 169 F7
Brown La
Bamber Bridge PR5 97 A2
Higher Walton PR5 97 A3
Brown Sq 9 BB11 127 A6
Brown St Accrington BB5 103 B5
Bacup OL13 86 F4
Bamber Bridge PR5 76 F8
Blackburn BB1 100 E5
Blackrod BL6 30 D2
Burnley BB11 126 F6
Chorley PR6 42 D8
Clitheroe BB7 164 D7
Fleetwood FY7 194 A3
2 Ramsbottom BL0 49 B5
Thornton FY5 173 B3
Brown St E BB8 169 D5
Brown St W BB8 169 C4
Brown's La Kirkham PR4 112 D3
Thornton FY6 173 E7
Brownedge Cl PR5 96 D1
Brownedge La PR5 96 E1
Brownedge Rd PR5 76 B8
Brownedge Saint Mary's RC High Sch PR5 96 E1
Brownedge Wlk PR5 96 D1
Brownhill Ave BB10 127 C6
Brownhill Dr BB1 122 A1
Brownhill La PR4 74 D7
Brownhill Rd
Blackburn BB1 121 F3
Leyland PR5 75 F1
Brownhill Sch OL12 51 E1
Browning Ave
4 Lytham St Anne's FY8 90 D4
Oswaldtwistle BB5 102 C5
3 Thornton FY5 173 A3
Browning Cl BB8 169 D6
Browning Cres PR1 117 D2
Browning Rd PR1 117 D2
Browning St BB3 81 F1
Brownley St Chorley PR6 42 E7
Clayton Green PR6 77 B1
Brownlow La WN5 10 C1
Brownlow Rd BL6 31 C5
Brownlow St
Blackburn BB1 101 D4
Clitheroe BB7 164 E7
Brownlow Terr BB2 99 C1
Brownroyd BB18 201 C2
Browns Hey PR7 60 A2
Brownside Mill BB10 127 F6
Brownside Rd BB10 127 F5
Brows Cl L37 11 E3
Brows La L37 11 E3
Browsholme LA1 213 C2
Browsholme Ave
Burnley BB10 127 C6
Fulwood PR2 117 F3
Browsholme Cl
Carnforth LA5 217 C1
Normoss FY3 130 B8
Browsholme Hall BB7 184 E7
Browsholme Rd BB7 223 C1
Broxfield Ct FY8 88 D6
Broxton Ave WN5 10 F7
Broyd View LA1 210 F5
Bruce St
5 Barnoldswick BB18 200 B3
Blackburn BB1 101 B6
Burnley BB11 126 D5
Brun Gr FY1 129 E1
Brun St BB11 126 F6
Brun Terr BB10 127 F5
Bruna La PR3 178 E4
Brundhurst Fold BB2 120 E2
Brunel Dr BB1 101 A4
Brunel St Burnley BB12 126 C7
Horwich BL6 31 C2
Brunel Way FY4 110 C7
Brunel Wlk BB1 100 F4
Brungerley Ave BB7 186 E1
Brunshaw Ave BB10 127 D5
Brunshaw Prim Sch BB10 127 D4
Brunshaw Rd BB10 127 D6
Brunswick Ave BL6 31 E2
Brunswick Dr BB8 169 A3
Brunswick Pl 4 PR2 116 C1
Brunswick Rd LA3 212 B3
Brunswick St
Blackburn BB2 100 D4
2 Blackpool FY1 129 B4
Burnley BB11 127 A4
2 Chorley PR6 42 D8
Darwen BB3 64 B8
Nelson BB9 147 E7
Brunswick Terr
Accrington BB5 103 B6
Bacup OL13 69 D8
Brunton Ho LA1 211 A5
Brunton Rd LA1 210 F6
Brunton's Warehouse LA1 213 E1
Brush St BB11 126 C5
Brussels Rd BB3 81 C1
Bryan Rd FY3 129 D5
Bryan St BB2 100 E2
Brydeck Ave PR1 95 E4
Bryer St 24 LA1 210 F8
Bryer's Croft BB1 121 F6
Bryn Gr LA2 215 E2
Bryning & Warton St Paul's CE Prim Sch PR4 91 D6
Bryning Ave
Blackpool FY2 150 C4
Wrea Green PR4 112 B3
Bryning Fern La PR4 112 F4
Bryning Hall La
Saltcotes, Moss Side FY8 111 F1
Warton PR4 91 B8
Wrea Green FY8,PR4 112 A1
Bryning La
Newton-with-S PR4 113 F2
Wrea Green PR4 112 B2
Bryony Cl Cleveleys FY5 172 F5
Orrell WN5 10 D5
Bryony Ct LA3 212 E2
Buccleuch Ave BB7 164 D8
Buccleuch Cl BB7 164 D8
Buccleuch Rd 7 BB9 168 C1
Buccleuch St BB11 126 E5
Buchanan St
Blackpool FY1 129 C6
Chorley PR6 42 D7
7 Ramsbottom BL0 49 B6
Buck St Burnley BB11 126 E5
Colne BB8 169 E5
Grindleton BB7 187 B7
Buckden Cl FY5 172 C1
Buckden Gate BB9 168 C3
Buckden Pl LA3 208 F8
Buckden Rd 4 BB5 102 F4
Buckfast Dr L37 12 B2
Buckholes La PR6 78 C1
Buckhurst Rd BL9 50 C3
Buckingham Ave
Horwich BL6 31 E2
Penwortham PR1 95 E2
Buckingham Cl BB4 84 A1
Buckingham Dr BB12 144 D2
Buckingham Gr
Church BB5 102 F7
Formby L37 11 E1
Morecambe LA3 212 C3
Buckingham Pl LA3 212 C3
Buckingham Rd
Lytham St Anne's FY8 89 D4
Maghull L31 5 C1
Morecambe LA3,LA4 212 C3
Buckingham St PR6 42 D7
Buckingham Way FY6 151 C5
Bucklands Ave PR2 116 D2
Buckley Cres FY5 150 D7
Bucknell Pl FY5 150 F7
Buckshaw Cty Prim Sch PR7 60 A2
Buckshaw Hall Cl PR7 60 B2
Buckshaw Terr BB12 144 E2
Buckton Cl PR6 60 C6
Bude Cl PR4 115 F6
Buff St 3 BB3 64 A8
Buffalo Rd PR5 76 A4
Bulcock St BB10 147 C1
Bulk Rd LA1 214 A1
Bulk St LA1 210 F8
Bull Cop L37 12 B3
Bull Park La FY6 152 C8
Bull St BB11 127 A6
Bullens La L40 22 E7
Buller Ave PR1 95 E4
Buller St 1 Lancaster LA1 213 F3
Rawtenstall BB4 85 A2
Bullfinch Dr BL9 32 B5
Bullfinch St 3 PR1 117 B1
Bullion The BB12 167 C5
Bullough Cl BB5 103 A5
Bulmer St PR2 116 C2
Buncer La BB2 100 A4
Bungalows The
Burnley BB11 126 F4
9 Earby BB18 201 B1
Great Eccleston PR3 154 C5
Bunker St PR4 92 C6
Bunkers Hill Cl BB2 80 B8
Bunting Pl 9 FY5 172 F1
Bunyan St 24 OL12 51 F1
Buoymaster 5 LA1 213 E1
Burbank Cl FY4 109 F5
Burdett St BB11 126 D5
Burdock Wlk LA3 212 E2
Burford Cl Blackburn BB2 79 E8
Blackpool FY3 130 A7
Burford Dr LA3 209 A7
Burgate FY4 109 D5
Burgess Ave FY4 109 E7
Burgess Gdns L31 5 C2
Burgess St
2 Blackburn BB1 101 C5
6 Haslingden BB4 84 B3
Burgess' La L37 13 A2
Burgh Hall Rd PR7 42 A3
Burgh La PR7 42 C4
Burgh La S PR7 42 B2
Burgh Meadows PR7 42 C4
Burghley Brow PR3 178 D1
Burghley Cl PR6 77 C2
Burghley Ct 4 PR5 76 B1
Burgundy Cres FY5 150 F7
Burholme Cl PR2 118 A2
Burholme Pl PR2 118 A2
Burholme Rd PR2 118 A2
Burleigh PR1 95 E7
Burleigh Rd 4 PR1 95 E7
Burleigh St BB12 126 F7
Burlington Ave Formby L37 12 B3
Morecambe LA4 212 G5
Burlington Ct FY4 109 B7
Burlington Ctr The FY8 88 E6
Burlington Gdns PR5 59 B8
Burlington Gr LA4 212 G5
Burlington Rd
Blackpool FY4 109 B6
Southport PR8 33 F3
Burlington Rd W FY4 109 A6
Burlington St
Blackburn BB2 100 C5
Chorley PR7 42 D7
Nelson BB9 147 C7
Burn Gr FY5 172 E4
Burn Naze Cty Prim Sch FY5 173 B3
Burnage Gdns FY4 109 D7
Burned House La FY6 195 D2
Burnedge Cl OL12 70 D2
Burneside Cl LA4 212 F4
Burnfell Rd 1 LA1 213 D2
Burnham Cl BB11 126 E5
Burnham Ct Blackpool FY3 129 E5
Morecambe LA3 212 B1
Burnham Gate BB11 126 D5
Burnham Trad Pk 4 BB11 126 E6
Burnley Ave PR8 20 D5
Burnley Barracks Sta BB12 126 E6
Burnley Bsns Ctr 7 BB11 127 A6
Burnley Central Sta BB12 126 F7
Burnley Cl BB1 101 B5
Burnley Coll of Art & Tech BB11 127 A7
Burnley General Hospl BB10 147 C2
Burnley La BB11,BB5 125 A2
Burnley Rd Accrington, Hillock Vale BB5 103 D8
9 Accrington, Lower Fold BB5 103 C6
Baldingstone BL9 49 E1
Blackburn BB1 101 C6
Brierfield BB10,BB9 147 B5
Brierfield, Harle Syke BB10 147 F3
Burnley BB10,BB11 127 D1
Clayton-le-M BB5 124 C5
Colne BB8,BB9 169 B3
Edenfield BL0 67 D5
Gisburn BB7 225 B3
Hapton BB11 125 B1
Holme Chapel BB10,OL14,BB11,OL13 107 C4
Padiham BB12 125 D8
Rawtenstall, Goodshaw Fold BB4 105 A2
Rawtenstall, Reeds Holme BB4 84 F5
Southport PR8 20 C5
Trawden BB8 170 B1
Weir BB11,BB4 106 C3
Whalley BB6 143 F3
Burnley Rd E
Rawtenstall BB4 68 E8
Water BB4 106 A2
Whitewell Bottom BB4 85 F4
Burnley St BB1 101 C5
Burnley Wood Prim Sch BB11 127 B4
Burns Ave
Lytham St Anne's FY8 90 D4
Oswaldtwistle BB5 102 D5
Thornton FY5 173 A3
Burns Cl WN5 10 D1
Burns Dr BB5 103 E2
Burns Pl FY4 109 F8

Burns Rd FY7 ....194 A5
Burns St Burnley BB12 ...126 F7
  Hapton BB12 ....125 C4
  Nelson BB9 ....168 D1
  Padiham BB12 ....125 D7
  Preston PR1 ....117 D2
Burns Way BB6 ....123 B4
Burns Wlk BB3 ....81 B1
Burnsall Ave
  Blackpool FY3 ....151 A1
  Heysham LA3 ....208 F8
Burnsall Cl BB10 ......147 E3
Burnsall Pl
  Barrowford BB9 ......168 C3
  Fulwood PR2 ....117 E4
Burnsall Rd 2 BB5 ....102 F4
Burnside Edenfield BL0 ...67 D2
  Parbold WN8 ....26 B2
Burnside Ave
  Blackpool FY4 ....109 E4
  Calder Vale PR3 .....179 E8
  Fleetwood FY7 ....193 C2
  Fulwood PR2 ....117 F3
Burnside Way PR1 ......95 D3
Burnslack Rd PR2 ......117 F3
Burntbarrow LA7 ....237 E6
Burrans Mdw 15 BB8 ...169 D4
Burrell Ave BB8 ....169 D6
Burrington Cl PR2 ....117 D6
Burrow Rd
  Over Burrow LA6 .....235 E7
  Preston PR1 ....117 A1
Burrow's La FY6 ......173 F5
Burscough Bridge
  Meth Prim Sch L40 ...24 E5
Burscough Bridge Sta L40 24 E5
Burscough Cty Prim Sch
  L40 ....24 F5
Burscough Ind Est L40 ...24 B5
Burscough Junc Sta L40 24 E5
Burscough Lordsgate
  Township CE Prim Sch
  L40 ....24 E3
Burscough RC Prim Sch
  L40 ....24 E2
Burscough Rd L39 .....15 F7
Burscough St L39 .....15 F6
Burton Ave LA1 ....213 C3
Burton Ct FY7 ....172 C8
Burton Gdns BB9 ......147 B5
Burton Hill LA6 ......236 C3
Burton Morewood
  Prim Sch LA6 ....234 C7
Burton Pk LA6 ....234 B7
Burton Rd Blackpool FY4 ...129 F1
  Burton in L LA2 .....236 C1
  Low Bentham LA2 ....233 B8
Burton St Burnley BB11 ...127 B5
  Rishton BB1 ....123 C1
Burwains Ave BB8 .....191 D1
Burwell Ave Coppull PR7 ...28 D8
  Formby L37 ....11 D1
Burwell Cl Kirkby L33 ...1 A3
  Rochdale OL12 ......51 D4
Burwen Castle Rd BD23 ...201 E8
Burwen Cl BB11 ....126 D3
Burwood Cl 5 PR1 ....95 F2
Burwood Dr Blackpool FY3 130 A6
  Fulwood PR2 ....117 E3
Bury Bsns Ctr BL9 ....32 A4
Bury Fold La BB3 .....64 A6
Bury La PR6 ....78 F3
Bury New Rd
  Heywood BL9,OL10 ...32 E2
  Ramsbottom BL0 .....49 D6
Bury Old Rd Edenfield BL0 ...67 F1
  Heywood BL9,OL10 ...32 E1
  Nangreaves BL0,BL9 ...49 F4
Bury Rd Edenfield BL0 ...67 D3
  Edgworth BL7 ....47 C3
  Haslingden BB4 .....84 B3
  Rawtenstall BB4 ....67 E7
  Southport PR8 ....34 B3
Bury Row BB7 ....144 F8
Bury St Darwen BB3 ...81 A1
  Oswaldtwistle BB5 ...102 D3
Buseph Barrow LA4 ...213 B4
Buseph Ct LA4 ....213 B4
Buseph Dr LA4 ....213 B4
Bush La Freckleton PR4 ...92 B5
  Freckleton PR4 .....92 B6
Bush St BB10 ....147 B1
Bushburn Dr BB6 .....142 C1
Bushby's La L37 .....11 C2
Bushby's Pk L37 .....11 D2
Bushell Pl PR1 ......96 A6
Bushell St PR1 ......116 F1
Bushell's Hosp PR3 ...137 E6
Bushey La WA11 ......8 E2
Bussel Rd PR1 ....95 E2
Butcher Brow PR5 ....96 E5
Butchers La L39 .....6 B3
Bute Ave FY1 ....129 B7
Bute Rd BB1 ....101 D3
Bute St BB11 ....126 D3
Butler Pl PR1 ....116 F2
Butler Rd FY1 ....129 B3
Butler St Blackpool FY1 ...129 C6
  7 Burnley BB10 .....127 A8
  Preston PR1 ....95 F7
  Ramsbottom BL0 .....49 A5
  Rishton BB1 ....123 C1
Butlers Mdw PR4 .....91 E6
Butt Hill La PR3 ....179 E4

Butt's La PR3 ....154 B5
Buttercross Cl BB11 ...126 D2
Butterfield Gdns L39 ...15 D3
Butterfield St
  2 Barrowford BB9 ...168 D3
  2 Lancaster LA1 ....210 F8
Butterfly Ho LA1 ....211 B7
Butterlands PR1 .....96 F8
Buttermere Ave
  Chorley PR7 ....42 B6
  Colne BB8 ....169 F6
  Fleetwood FY7 ......193 C2
  2 Morecambe LA4 ...212 G4
Buttermere Cl
  1 Bamber Bridge PR5 ...96 E2
  5 Blackburn BB1 ....100 F6
  Formby L37 ....11 D3
  Fulwood PR2 ....117 C4
  Maghull L31 ....5 E1
Buttermere Cres WA11 ...8 F2
Buttermere Ct LA1 ...214 B1
Buttermere Dr
  Knott End-on-S FY6 ...194 F5
  Oswaldtwistle BB5 ...102 D5
  Ramsbottom BL0 .....49 B7
Buttermere Rd
  Burnley BB10 ....127 F5
  Lancaster LA1 ......214 B1
  Longridge PR3 ......138 F5
Butterworth Brow
  Brinscall PR6 ......62 A7
  Chorley PR7 ....42 A4
Butterworth Cl PR4 ...113 A6
Buttons Row BB4 .....68 F6
Butts Barnoldswick BB18 ...200 B2
  Great Harwood BB6 ...123 B5
Butts Cl FY5 ....173 C4
Butts Gr BB7 ....186 E2
Butts La High Bentham LA2 233 E8
  Southport PR8 ......34 F5
Butts Mount BB6 .....123 C5
Butts Rd FY5 ....173 C4
Buxton Ave FY2 ......150 D4
  Morecambe LA4 .....212 F4
  Whitworth OL12 .....70 D3
Bye La L39 ....14 C3
Bye Rd BL0 ....49 E8
Bye-Pass Rd LA5 .....216 A4
Byerworth La BB5 ....178 C5
Byerworth La S PR3 ...178 C4
Byfield Ave FY5 .....150 E7
Byland Cl Blackpool FY4 ...109 C5
  Formby L37 ....12 B2
  Read BB12 ....144 D1
Bymbrig Cl PR5 .....76 E8
Byrom St Blackburn BB2 ...100 D4
  Southport PR9 .....53 F3
Byron Ave Bolton-le-S LA5 ...216 A5
  Lytham St Anne's FY8 ...90 D4
  Thornton FY5 ......173 A3
  Warton PR4 ....91 E6
Byron Cl Accrington BB5 ...103 E2
  Formby L37 ....11 F4
  3 Orrell WN5 ......10 F7
  Oswaldtwistle BB5 ...102 C5
  Tarleton PR4 ......55 F5
Byron Cres PR7 .....28 F8
Byron Gr BB18 ......200 A3
Byron Rd Colne BB8 ...169 F5
  Maghull L31 ....5 D3
  Morecambe LA3 ....212 B3
  Ramsbottom BL8 ....48 F2
Byron Sq BB6 ....123 B4
Byron St Blackpool FY4 ...129 B1
  Chorley PR6 ....42 D8
  Fleetwood FY7 .....194 A5
  Padiham BB12 ......125 F7
Byron Terr BB2 .....100 B3
Byton Wlk L33 ......1 A4

C

Cabin End Row BB1 ...101 E4
Cabin Hill BB2 .....99 B2
Cabin La Holmeswood L40 ...37 A6
  Maghull L31 ....4 F4
  Southport, Churchtown Moss
  PR9 ....53 F3
  Southport, Halsall Moss L39 ...21 C5
Cable St Formby L37 ...12 A4
  Lancaster LA1 .....210 F8
  Southport PR8 .....33 F3
Cabus Cross Roads PR3 ...199 A5
Cabus Nook La PR3 ...199 B6
Cadby Ave FY3 .....129 F2
Cadley Ave PR2 ....116 B3
Cadley Cswy PR2 ...116 C4
Cadley Dr PR2 .....116 B3
Cadogan Pl 5 PR1 ...96 A6
Cadogan St BB9 .....168 D2
Cadshaw Cl BB1 ....100 E8
Cadwell Rd L31 ....5 B5
Caernarfon Cl FY5 ...173 D2
Caernarvon Ave BB12 ...126 A7
Caernarvon Cl BL8 ...48 F1
Caernarvon Rd BB4 ...84 A1
Cage La PR4 ....75 B8
Cairn Ct 5 FY4 ....109 C5
Cairn Gr FY4 ......109 C4
Cairndale Dr PR5 ...59 B6
Cairns Cl BB9 .....168 C3
Cairnsmore Ave PR1 ...117 F1
Cairo St BB12 .....126 D6
Caister Cl WN8 ....9 E8
Calcott St BB11 ...126 E6
Caldbeck Cl BB9 ...147 E6

Caldbeck Rd LA1 ...214 B1
Calder Ave Billington BB7 ...143 A4
  Chorley PR7 ....42 B5
  Cleveleys FY5 .....172 F2
  Darwen BB3 ....80 D4
  Fleetwood FY7 ....193 D3
  Freckleton PR4 ...92 A5
  Fulwood PR2 ......116 F6
  Longridge PR3 ....139 A8
  Ormskirk L39 .....15 E4
  Whalley BB7 ......143 A7
  Withnell PR6 .....79 A1
Calder Banks BB1 ...100 F7
Calder Cl Bury BL9 ...32 A8
  Carnforth LA5 ....217 B1
  Kirkby L33 ....1 A6
  Kirkham PR4 ......113 C5
  Lytham St Anne's FY8 ...109 F2
  Nelson BB9 ....168 D1
Calder Ct BB5 .....124 E6
Calder Dr Catterall PR3 ...178 D2
  Lancaster LA3 ....213 B2
  Maghull L31 ......5 F2
Calder House La PR3 ...178 D4
Calder Pl BB6 .....123 C6
Calder Rd Blackpool FY2 ...150 C4
  Rawtenstall BB4 ...85 A4
Calder St Blackburn BB1 ...100 F7
  Burnley BB11 .....126 F6
  Colne BB8 ....169 C4
  Nelson BB9 ....168 D1
  Padiham BB12 .....125 C8
  Preston PR2 ......116 C1
Calder Terr BB9 ...147 B8
Calder Vale
  Barrowford BB9 ...168 D2
  Whalley BB7 ......143 A7
Calder Vale Rd BB12 ...126 F6
Calder View BB9 ...168 E5
Calderbank Cl 1 PR5 ...75 A1
Calderbrook Ave BB11 ...126 E3
Calderbrook Pl BB11 ...126 E3
Calderdale Way OL14 ...108 F1
Caldershaw Ctr The OL12 ...51 B2
Caldershaw La OL12 ...51 A2
Caldershaw Prim Sch
  OL12 ....51 A1
Caldershaw Rd OL11,OL12 ...51 A1
Calderstones Hospl BB7 ...143 A7
Calderview Ave FY5 ...151 C3
Calderview Sch BB12 ...126 F8
Caldew Cl BB5 .....103 E8
Caldicott Way FY6 ...151 C6
Caldy Dr BL8 ......49 A3
Caleb St 6 BB9 ....168 E1
Caledonian Ave 1 PR1 ...129 E7
Calendar St 1 BB1 ...100 E5
Calendine Cl FY5 ...172 F5
Calf Croft Pl FY8 ...90 A4
Calf Hall La BB18 ...200 A2
Calf Hall Rd BB18 ...200 A2
Calf Hey BB5 ......123 F4
Calf Hey Rd BB4 ...83 B2
Calfcote La PR3 ...139 B7
Calgary Ave BB2 ...100 B8
Calico Cl BB5 .....102 B4
Calico Dr PR3 .....178 D3
Calico St BB2 .....100 C4
Calico Wood Ave WN6 ...19 F6
Calkeld La 7 LA1 ...210 F8
Calla Dr PR3 ......178 C8
Callander Sq OL10 ...32 F1
Callender St BL0 ...49 B6
Callon St PR1 .....96 E8
Caltha St 8 BL0 ...49 B6
Calva St BB12 .....126 B8
Calverley St 6 PR1 ...117 D1
Calverley Way OL12 ...51 E4
Calvert Ct PR5 ....96 D5
Calvert Pl FY3 ....130 A7
Cam Cl 1 PR5 .....76 F8
Cam La Clayton Green PR6 ...77 A4
  Thornton-in-C BD23 ...201 B6
Cam St PR1 ....117 C2
Cam Wood Fold PR6 ...77 A3
Cambell's Ct FY8 ...88 E7
Camberley Cl PR8 ...33 E5
Camborne Ave LA5 ...216 C8
Camborne Ct FY3 ...130 B2
Camborne Pl PR4 ...92 B6
Cambray Rd FY1 ...150 C1
Cambrian Cl BB1 ...121 F3
Cambrian Way BB4 ...84 B1
Cambridge Arc 5 PR8 ...34 B7
Cambridge Ave
  Lancaster LA1 .....211 B5
  Southport PR9 ....52 F2
Cambridge Cl
  Blackburn BB1 ....100 F4
  Padiham BB12 .....125 D6
  Preston PR1 ......116 F2
Cambridge Ct
  Preston PR1 ......116 F2
  Southport PR9 ....52 F2
Cambridge Dr
  Blackburn BB1 ....101 E4
  Garstang PR3 .....178 B7
  Padiham BB12 .....125 D6
Cambridge Gdns PR9 ...52 F2
Cambridge Rd
  9 Bamber Bridge PR5 ...76 F8
  Blackpool FY1 ....129 D5
  Cleveleys FY5 ....172 F2
  Fleetwood FY7 ....193 B3
  Formby L37 ......11 D1
  Lytham St Anne's FY8 ...89 E3
  Morecambe LA3 ...212 B3
  Orrell WN5 ....10 F8

Cambridge Rd continued
  Skelmersdale WN8 ...17 E1
  Southport PR8 ....52 E2
Cambridge St
  Accrington BB5 ...103 D6
  Blackburn BB1 ....100 F4
  Brierfield BB9 ....147 B5
  2 Burnley BB11 ...126 D5
  10 Chorley PR7 ...42 C7
  9 Colne BB8 .....169 D4
  Darwen BB3 ......81 C1
  Great Harwood BB6 ...123 D5
  Haslingden BB4 ...84 B1
  Nelson BB9 ......147 D7
  Preston PR1 .....116 E2
Cambridge Wlk PR1 ...116 E2
Cambridge Wlks 6 PR8 ...34 B7
Camden Pl PR1 ....95 F6
Camden Rd FY3 ...129 E6
Camden St
  11 Barrowford BB9 ...168 D3
  Nelson BB9 ......147 D7
Camellia Dr PR5 ...76 E2
Cameron Ave FY3 ...129 E7
Cameron Croft 6 PR6 ...42 D8
Cameron St BB10 ...147 A1
Camforth Hall La PR3 ...138 A7
Camms View BB4 ...67 A8
Camomine Cl PR7 ...60 A3
Camp St BB10 ....147 B8
Campbell Ave 2 FY3 ...129 E7
Campbell St
  Blackburn BB1 ....121 F1
  4 Padiham BB12 ...125 F7
  Preston PR1 .....96 B8
  Read BB12 ....144 D1
  Rochdale OL12 ...51 C2
Campion Cl FY5 ...172 F5
Campion Ct BB5 ...102 E4
Campion Dr Haslingden BB4 67 A8
  Preston PR2 .....115 C1
Campion Way
  Morecambe LA3 ...212 C1
  Rochdale OL12 ...51 C3
Campions The PR2 ...115 C1
Camwood PR5 .....77 B4
Camwood Dr PR5 ...96 B1
Canada Cres FY2 ...150 E3
Canada St BL6 ....31 A1
Canal Bank
  Appley Bridge WN6 ...19 C7
  New Lane L40 ....24 B6
  Ring o'Bells L40 ...25 C2
Canal Bank Cotts L31 ...5 C7
Canal Gdns LA5 ...216 B6
Canal Leach Cotts PR5 ...56 F6
Canal Mews 1 BB9 ...147 D8
Canal Pl LA5 .....217 C1
Canal Row WN2 ...29 D1
Canal Side BB3 ...168 D2
Canal St Adlington PR7 ...30 A6
  Blackburn BB2 ...100 B1
  19 Burnley BB11 ...126 F6
  Church BB5 ......102 E6
  Clayton-le-M BB5 ...123 F2
  Canal Wlk PR6 ...42 F8
Canalside BB1 ....100 F3
Canberra Cl FY5 ...150 F7
Canberra Rd PR5 ...59 B8
Canberraway PR4 ...91 E7
Candlemakers Ct BB7 ...164 E8
Candlestick Pk BL9 ...32 D4
Cann Bridge St PR5 ...97 B4
Canning Rd PR9 ...35 A4
Canning St Burnley BB12 ...126 F7
  Padiham BB12 ...125 D7
Cannock Ave FY3 ...129 E8
Cannock Gn L31 ...5 B1
Cannon Hill PR2 ...116 C1
Cannon St Accrington BB5 ...103 B5
  11 Chorley PR7 ...42 C8
  10 Nelson BB9 ...168 F1
  Preston PR1 .....95 F7
  6 Ramsbottom BL0 ...49 A4
Canon Cl WN6 ....28 C2
Canon St BL9 .....32 A4
Canterbury Ave
  Blackpool FY3 ...129 F3
  Lancaster LA1 ...211 B5
Canterbury Cl Brinscall PR6 61 E8
  Carleton FY6 ....151 C5
  Formby L37 .....11 F5
  Garstang PR3 ...178 A7
  Southport PR8 ...33 F4
Canterbury Rd 11 PR1 ...117 D1
Canterbury St
  Blackburn BB2 ...100 E4
  Chorley PR6 .....42 D4
Canterbury Way PR3 ...178 B7
Cantlow Fold PR8 ...20 A4
Cantsfield Ave PR2 ...116 B4
Canute St PR1 ...117 A1
Cape St BB4 .....85 A2
Capernwray Ct LA6 ...234 D3
Capernwray Rd LA6 ...234 B2
Capilano Pk L39 ...6 C8
Capitol Trad Est L31 ...1 C2
Capitol Way PR1,PR5 ...96 C5
Appleside Cotts BD24 ...230 E6
Capstan Cl FY8 ...109 E1
Captain St Horwich BL6 ...31 B4
  Weir OL13 ....87 A7
Captain's Row 1 LA1 ...213 F1
Carawood Cl WN6 ...19 C7
Carcroft Ave FY2 ...150 D4
Cardale Ave PR4 ...94 D2
Cardiff St WN8 ...17 D1

Cardigan Ave
  Burnley BB12 ....126 A7
  10 Clitheroe BB7 ...164 E8
  Oswaldtwistle BB5 ...102 C4
Cardigan Cl 1 BB7 ...164 D8
Cardigan Pl FY4 ...109 A5
Cardigan Rd PR8 ...33 F1
Cardigan St Preston PR2 ...116 D1
  Rochdale OL12 ...51 E3
Cardinal Allen
  RC High Sch FY7 ...172 E8
Cardinal Gdns FY8 ...89 D6
Cardinal Newman Coll
  PR1 ....96 B7
Cardinal Pl FY5 ...172 E3
Cardinal St BB10 ...147 B1
Cardwell Cl PR4 ...91 D5
Cardwell Pl BB2 ...100 E5
Cardwell St BB12 ...125 D7
Carfax Fold OL12 ...51 B2
Carfax Rd L33 ....1 A4
Carfield WN8 .....9 E6
Carham Rd BB1 ...100 E8
Carholme Ave BB10 ...127 C6
Carisbrooke Ave FY4 ...110 A7
Carisbrooke Cl FY6 ...151 C6
Carisbrooke Dr PR9 ...52 F1
Carl Oway Ave PR2 ...117 C5
Carl's Way L33 ...1 A4
Carleton Ave
  Blackpool FY3 ...150 F1
  Fulwood PR2 ....117 C4
  Simonstone BB12 ...144 E2
Carleton Dr PR1 ...95 A4
Carleton Gate FY6 ...151 C4
Carleton Gdns FY6 ...151 B5
Carleton Green
  Cty Prim Sch FY6 ...151 C6
Carleton Rd
  Great Knowley PR6 ...60 F3
  Nelson BB8 ......169 A3
Carleton Sch FY6 ...151 B5
Carleton St
  Morecambe LA4 ...212 D4
  Nelson BB9 ......147 E7
Carleton Way FY6 ...151 B5
Carley St BB3 ....80 E2
Carlin Gate FY2 ...150 B2
Carlinghurst Rd BB2 ...100 C4
Carlisle Ave
  Fleetwood FY7 ...193 D1
  Penwortham PR1 ...95 A4
Carlisle Gr 1 FY5 ...173 B2
Carlisle Ho 38 PR1 ...96 A7
Carlisle Pl PR6 ...30 A8
Carlisle Rd Accrington BB5 103 D7
  Southport PR8 ...34 A4
Carlisle St Blackburn BB1 ...100 F4
  Preston PR1 .....96 A8
  Rochdale OL12 ...51 E3
Carlisle Terr LA5 ...217 D2
Carlton Ave
  Clayton Green PR6 ...77 B2
  Orrell WN8 ......10 A7
Carlton Cl BL6 ...30 D2
Carlton Ct BB8 ...169 B5
Carlton Dr PR1 ...96 B5
Carlton Gdns BB1 ...100 E6
Carlton Gr Blackpool FY2 ...150 B4
  Horwich BL6 .....31 D1
Carlton Pl BB7 ...164 F7
Carlton Rd Blackburn BB1 ...100 E6
  Leyland PR5 .....58 F8
  Lytham St Anne's FY8 ...88 F7
  Southport PR8 ...20 C6
Carlton St Bacup OL13 ...87 A3
  Brierfield BB9 ...147 B5
  Preston PR2 .....95 D8
Carluke St BB1 ...101 C5
Carlyle Ave FY4 ...109 B6
Carlyle St BB10 ...147 C3
Carmel Cl L39 ...15 D2
Carnarvon Rd
  Blackburn BB2 ...100 B5
  3 Preston PR1 ...95 D7
  Southport PR8 ...33 F1
Carneghie Ct PR8 ...33 F4
Carnfield Pl PR5 ...77 B8
Carnforth Ave FY2 ...150 E5
Carnforth Brow LA5 ...217 F2
Carnforth Cl BB2 ...101 A1
Carnforth Dr BL8 ...49 A2
Carnforth High Sch LA5 ...217 E1
Carnforth Sta LA5 ...217 D2
Carnoustie Cl PR2 ...116 B7
Carnoustie Ct PR1 ...95 A6
Carnoustie Dr BL0 ...49 B5
Caroline Cl LA3 ...208 F8
Caroline Ct BB11 ...126 B4
Caroline St
  6 Blackpool FY1 ...129 B3
  Preston PR1 .....96 C8
Carr Bank Ave BL0 ...49 B7
Carr Bank Dr BL0 ...49 B7
Carr Bank Rd
  Ramsbottom BL0 ...49 B7
  Storth LA7 ......237 E2
Carr Barn Brow PR5 ...77 C6
Carr Brook Ct PR6 ...60 B8
Carr Cl Cold Row FY6 ...174 C4
  Poulton-le-F FY6 ...151 E2
  Smallwood Hey PR3 ...196 C5
Carr Dr PR4 .....112 E7
Carr End La FY6 ...174 C6
Carr Field PR5 ...77 C6
Carr Fold BL0 ...49 B7
Carr Gate FY5 ...172 C4

Carr Hall Dr BB9 . . . . .168 C1
Carr Hall Gdns BB9 . . . . . .168 B1
Carr Hall Rd BB9 . . . . .168 B1
Carr Hall St BB4 . . . . .84 A5
Carr Head BB8 . . . . .170 C2
Carr Head La FY6 . . . . .151 E2
Carr Hey 5 FY5 . . . . .173 A2
Carr Hill High Sch PR4 . .113 B4
Carr House La
 Bretherton PR5 . . . . .56 D6
 Heskin Green WN6 . . . . . .40 E4
 Ince Blundell L38 . . . . .3 E4
 Lancaster LA1 . . . . .210 A2
Carr La Blackburn BB2 . . . .99 F6
 Chorley PR7 . . . . .42 D5
 Cold Row PR6 . . . . .174 C4
 Croston PR5 . . . . .39 B8
 Heysham LA3 . . . . .208 E7
 Kirkham PR4 . . . . .113 C6
 Leyland PR5 . . . . .76 A3
 Maghull L31 . . . . .4 F5
 Middleton LA3 . . . . .208 A4
 Much Hoole PR4 . . . . .74 A1
 Rawtenstall, Hall Carr BB4 .85 A1
 Rawtenstall, Hugh Mill BB4 .68 F7
 Ring o'Bells L40 . . . . .25 B3
 Singleton FY6 . . . . .152 C1
 Smallwood Hey LA3 . . . .196 C4
 Southport PR8 . . . . .20 F7
 Tarleton PR4 . . . . .55 F7
 Warton PR4 . . . . .91 B6
Carr Mdw PR5 . . . . .77 C6
Carr Mill St BB4 . . . . .84 B5
Carr Moss La Haskayne L39 14 B8
 Southport L39 . . . . .21 D2
Carr Mount 7 BB4 . . . . . . .84 F1
Carr Pl 77 B7
Carr Rd Barnoldswick BB18 200 A3
 Blackpool FY5 . . . . .150 D6
 Burnley BB11 . . . . .126 E3
 Clayton Green PR6 . . . . . .77 B2
 Colne BB8 . . . . .169 E6
 Cornholme OL14 . . . . . . .107 F1
 Darwen BB3 . . . . .64 B8
 Fleetwood FY7 . . . . .194 A4
 Hambleton FY6 . . . . .174 C2
 Horwich BL6 . . . . .31 B5
 Kirkham PR4 . . . . .113 B4
 Nelson BB9 . . . . .168 C1
 Rawtenstall BB4 . . . . .84 F1
 Water BB4 . . . . .86 C7
Carr Royd Est FY6 . . . . . .152 A3
Carr Side La L29 . . . . .4 A3
Carr St Bamber Bridge PR5 .76 E8
 Blackburn BB1 . . . . .100 E6
 Chorley PR6 . . . . .60 E1
 Preston PR1 . . . . .96 B7
 Ramsbottom BL0 . . . . . . .49 B7
Carr View BB8 . . . . .170 C1
Carr's Cres L37 . . . . .11 B1
Carr's Cres W L37 . . . . . . .11 D1
Carradice CI BB9 . . . . .147 E8
Carradon Dr WN6 . . . . .28 E1
Carrfield Villas 4 OL14 . .108 A1
Carrick Mews FY3 . . . . . . .130 B2
Carrier's Row BB8 . . . . . . .170 E6
Carrington Ave BB2 . . . . . .80 C8
Carrington Gr LA4 . . . . . .213 A6
Carrington Rd
 Adlington PR7 . . . . .29 F7
 Chorley PR7 . . . . .42 C7
Carrol St PR1 . . . . .117 B1
Carroll Cres L39 . . . . .15 F7
Carron La PR3 . . . . .158 A4
Carrs Croft BB7 . . . . .188 E8
Carrs Ind Est BB4 . . . . . . .84 A4
Carrs Wood BB2 . . . . .99 F6
Carrside BB9 . . . . .147 E8
Carrwood Dr PR4 . . . . . . .113 B4
Carrwood Gn BB12 . . . . . .125 C8
Carrwood Hey BL0 . . . . . . .49 A4
Carrwood Pk PR8 . . . . .34 B4
Carrwood Rd PR1,PR5 . . . .96 B3
Carrwood Way PR5 . . . . . .96 B2
Carry La BB8 . . . . .169 E4
Carshalton Rd FY1 . . . . . .129 B8
Carson Rd FY4 . . . . .130 A1
Cart Gate FY6 . . . . .195 B3
Carter Ave BB11 . . . . .125 C4
Carter Fold BB2 . . . . .120 E2
Carter St Accrington BB5 . .103 B4
 7 Blackpool FY3 . . . . . . .129 B5
 Burnley BB12 . . . . .126 C7
Carter's
 Charity Prim Sch FY6 . .195 C7
Carter's La BB7 . . . . .225 A5
Carterville CI FY4 . . . . . . .110 A7
Cartford Ct PR3 . . . . .154 A6
Cartford La PR3 . . . . .154 A6
Cartmel Ave
 Accrington BB5 . . . . .103 A3
 Fleetwood FY7 . . . . .193 D1
 Maghull L31 . . . . .5 E2
Cartmel CI PR8 . . . . .34 F3
Cartmel Dr Burnley BB12 . .126 B8
 Coupe Green PR5 . . . . . . .97 E4
 Formby L37 . . . . .12 B2
Cartmel Pl
 Morecambe LA4 . . . . . . .212 G4
 Preston PR2 . . . . .115 E1
Cartmel Rd Blackburn BB2 100 A3
 Lancaster LA1 . . . . .214 B2
 Leyland PR5 . . . . .58 D8
Cartmell La Nateby PR3 . . .177 C7
 Saltcotes, Moss Side FY8 . .90 E8
 Lytham St Anne's FY8 . . . .88 F5

Cartwright Ct LA1 . . . . . .210 E5
Carus Ave BB3 . . . . .81 E1
Carus Pk LA6 . . . . .235 B2
Carus St BB3 . . . . .81 E1
Carvers Brow PR5 . . . . . . .57 B1
Carwags La PR3 . . . . .159 C8
Carwood Gr BL6 . . . . .31 D1
Carwood La PR6 . . . . .60 C8
Caryl Rd FY8 . . . . .88 D8
Caryle Gr LA4 . . . . .213 A6
Casserley Rd BB8 . . . . . . .169 F6
Casson Gate OL12 . . . . . . .51 E1
Casterclliffe
 Cty Prim Sch BB9 . . . . .169 B1
Castercliffe Rd BB9 . . . . . .148 B8
Casterton PR7 . . . . .59 C2
Casterton Ave BB10 . . . . . .147 C3
Casterton Prim Sch
 BB10 . . . . .147 C3
Casterton Sch LA6 . . . . . .238 F4
Castle Ave FY6 . . . . .151 E4
Castle Bank LA5 . . . . .218 C4
Castle CI BB8 . . . . .169 E6
Castle Cres BL6 . . . . .31 C5
Castle Ct LA1 . . . . .210 E8
Castle Dr Adlington PR7 . . .29 E6
Castle Fold PR1 . . . . .95 F2
Castle Gate BB7 . . . . .164 E8
Castle Gr LA4 . . . . .213 A6
Castle Hill LA1 . . . . .210 E8
Castle Hill Rd BL9 . . . . . . .32 C5
Castle House La PR7 . . . . . .29 E6
Castle La Bonds PR3 . . . . .178 C6
 Staining FY3 . . . . .130 D5
 Westhead L40 . . . . .16 E5
Castle Mount PR2 . . . . . . .116 F7
Castle Par 5 LA1 . . . . . . .210 E8
Castle Park Mews LA1 . . .210 E8
Castle Pk Hornby LA2 . . . .232 B7
 Lancaster LA1 . . . . .210 E8
Castle Rd BB8 . . . . .170 A7
Castle St Brierfield BB9 . . .147 B6
 Burnley BB12 . . . . .126 F7
 6 Chorley PR7 . . . . .42 C8
 Clitheroe BB7 . . . . .164 E8
 7 Hapton BB12 . . . . .125 C4
 Nelson BB9 . . . . .147 F8
 Preston PR1 . . . . .116 F1
 Ramsbottom BL9 . . . . . . .49 D2
 Southport PR9 . . . . .34 B8
Castle View
 Barnoldswick BB18 . . . . .200 B1
 Clitheroe BB7 . . . . .164 E8
Castle Wlk Penwortham PR1 95 C7
 Southport PR8 . . . . .34 A6
Castle Wlks PR5 . . . . .57 B2
Castlecroft Ave BL6 . . . . . .30 D2
Castlegate FY1 . . . . .129 B1
Castlehey WN8 . . . . .9 E6
Castlerigg Dr BB12 . . . . . .126 B8
Castlerigg Pl FY4 . . . . . . .130 C1
Castleton Rd PR1 . . . . . . .117 C1
Castletown Dr OL13 . . . . . .87 B1
Cat Tail La PR8 . . . . .35 E1
Catches La OL11 . . . . .51 B1
Catforth Ave FY4 . . . . . . .130 B1
Catforth Cty Prim Sch
 PR4 . . . . .135 A4
Catforth Rd Catforth PR4 . .134 F5
 Preston PR2 . . . . .115 C1
Catharine's La L39 . . . . . . .15 F1
Cathedral Dr LA3 . . . . . . .212 E2
Cathedral PC Prim Sch
 LA1 . . . . .211 A7
Catherine CI PR4 . . . . . . .112 F7
Catherine St
 6 Chorley PR7 . . . . .42 C6
 Kirkham PR4 . . . . .112 F6
 5 Preston PR1 . . . . .96 B8
Catherine St E BL6 . . . . . .31 B4
Catherine St W BL6 . . . . . .31 B5
Cathrow Dr PR4 . . . . .75 A7
Catley CI PR6 . . . . .60 C5
Catlow Hall St BB5 . . . . . .102 E4
Catlow Terr BB7 . . . . .164 D1
Cato St 4 BL0 . . . . .49 A4
Caton Ave FY7 . . . . .193 D6
Caton CI Clayton-le-W PR5 . .76 E2
 Longridge PR3 . . . . .139 B8
 Southport PR9 . . . . .52 F4
Caton Gr FY3 . . . . .129 F7
Caton Green Rd LA2 . . . . .231 D3
Caton Prim Sch LA2 . . . . .231 C3
Caton Rd
 Lancaster, Bulk LA1 . . . . .214 A1
 Lancaster, Newton LA1 . . .214 B4
Caton St Paul's
 CE Prim Sch LA2 . . . . . .231 D3
Cattan Gn L37 . . . . .12 B3
Catterall CI FY1 . . . . .129 D7
Catterall Gates La PR3 . . .178 C3
Catterall La PR3 . . . . .178 C1
Catterall St BB2 . . . . .80 C8
Catterick Fold PR8 . . . . . . .34 F3
Cattle St BB6 . . . . .123 C5
Caunce Ave PR9 . . . . .54 A6
Caunce St FY1,FY3 . . . . . .129 D6
Caunce's Rd PR9 . . . . .36 C5
Causeway Foulridge BB8 . .191 D1
 Great Harwood BB6 . . . . .123 B5
Causeway Ave PR2 . . . . . .116 C4
Causeway Croft BB7 . . . . .186 F1
Causeway Head BB4 . . . . . .67 A8
Causeway La Haskayne L37 13 B1

Causeway La continued
 Rufford L40 . . . . .38 B2
Causeway St 2 BB3 . . . . . .64 C7
Causeway The
 3 Chorley PR6 . . . . .42 E8
 Southport PR9 . . . . .53 C5
 Wymott PR5 . . . . .57 F6
Causey Foot BB9 . . . . . . .147 D7
Cavalry Way BB11 . . . . . .126 C6
Cave St Blackburn BB2 . . .100 B1
 2 Preston PR1 . . . . .96 B8
Cavendish Cres PR2 . . . . .117 F3
Cavendish Ct
 Bolton-le-S LA5 . . . . .216 A5
 Southport PR9 . . . . .34 E8
Cavendish Dr PR2 . . . . . . .117 F3
Cavendish Pl
 6 Bamber Bridge PR5 . . . .96 D3
 Blackburn BB2 . . . . .100 B3
Cavendish Rd
 Blackpool FY2 . . . . .150 C4
 Lytham St Anne's FY8 . . . .88 D8
 Morecambe LA3 . . . . . . .212 B3
 2 Preston PR1 . . . . .117 E1
 Southport PR8 . . . . .33 F3
Cavendish St
 Barnoldswick BB18 . . . . .200 B1
 1 Chorley PR6 . . . . .42 E7
 Darwen BB3 . . . . .80 F3
 Lancaster LA1 . . . . .210 D8
Cavendish Wlk PR9 . . . . . .34 E8
Cavour St BB2 . . . . .126 F7
Cawthorne Endowed
 Prim Sch LA2 . . . . .226 F1
Cawthorne St LA1 . . . . . . .210 E8
Caxton Ave FY2 . . . . .150 C5
Caxton Rd PR2 . . . . .117 B8
Cecil Ct FY8 . . . . .90 A3
Cecil St Barnoldswick BB18 200 B3
 Blackpool FY1 . . . . .129 C7
 4 Lytham St Anne's FY8 . .90 A3
 Oswaldtwistle BB5 . . . . . .102 E4
 Rishton BB1 . . . . .123 C2
Cecilia Rd BB2 . . . . .100 A2
Cecilia St PR1 . . . . .117 D1
Cedar Ave
 5 Bamber Bridge PR5 . . . .76 B8
 Cleveleys FY5 . . . . .172 E2
 Euxton PR7 . . . . .59 C4
 Fleetwood FY7 . . . . .172 E8
 Haslingden BB4 . . . . .84 C3
 Horwich BL6 . . . . .31 E1
 Knott End-on-S FY6 . . . .195 A5
 Poulton-le-F FY6 . . . . . . .130 D8
 Preston PR2 . . . . .116 A2
 Rawtenstall BB4 . . . . .84 E2
 Warton PR4 . . . . .91 D6
Cedar CI Garstang PR3 . . .178 B8
 Grimsargh PR2 . . . . .138 D1
 Newton-with-S PR4 . . . . .114 A3
 Rishton BB1 . . . . .102 B8
Cedar Cres Kirkham PR4 . .113 A4
 Ormskirk L39 . . . . .15 D4
 Ramsbottom BL0 . . . . . . .49 C7
Cedar Ct Blackburn BB1 . . .100 F7
 7 Farington PR5 . . . . .76 B1
Cedar Dr L37 . . . . .11 C1
Cedar Farm Galleries L40 .39 C1
Cedar Field PR6 . . . . .77 C2
Cedar Gr Longton PR4 . . . .94 A1
 Orrell WN5 . . . . .10 F6
 Skelmersdale WN8 . . . . . . .9 C8
Cedar House Sch LA6 . . . .238 B2
Cedar Rd Chorley PR6 . . . .60 D2
 Fulwood PR2 . . . . .117 C2
 Lancaster LA1 . . . . .210 D8
Cedar Sq 5 FY1 . . . . .129 B1
Cedar St Accrington BB5 . .103 D6
 Blackburn BB1 . . . . .100 F8
 Burnley BB11 . . . . .127 B5
 Bury BL9 . . . . .32 A3
 Bury BL9 . . . . .32 B3
 Morecambe LA4 . . . . . . .212 C4
 Rochdale OL12 . . . . .51 F1
 Southport PR8 . . . . .34 D4
Cedar Way PR1 . . . . .95 B3
Cedar Wlk PR4 . . . . .153 F1
Cedars CI BB8 . . . . .200 A1
Cedars Cty Inf Sch The
 BB1 . . . . .201 B2
Cedars The Chorley PR7 . . .42 B4
 Eccleston PR7 . . . . .40 B7
 New Longton PR4 . . . . . . .74 F8
Cedarwood CI FY8 . . . . . . .89 E4
Cedarwood Dr PR5 . . . . . . .58 E8
Cedarwood Pl LA1 . . . . . .211 C7
Cedric PI FY2 . . . . .150 C4
Celia St BB10 . . . . .127 C5
Cemetery La Burnley BB11 126 A4
 Preesall Park FY6 . . . . . .195 B1
Cemetery Rd Earby BB18 . .201 B2
 Padiham BB12 . . . . .125 C7
 Preston PR1 . . . . .117 C1
 Ramsbottom BL0 . . . . . . .49 A4
 Southport PR8 . . . . .34 C4
 Whitehall BB3 . . . . .64 B5
Cemetery View PR7 . . . . . .30 A6
Centenary Way PR7 . . . . . .30 A6
Central Ave Clitheroe BB7 . .164 D7
 Edenfield BL0 . . . . .67 D2
 Gregson Lane PR5 . . . . . .97 E2
 Kirkham PR4 . . . . .112 F6
 Lancaster LA1 . . . . .213 F4
 Oswaldtwistle BB5 . . . . . .102 C4
 Southport PR8 . . . . .20 F8
Central Ave N FY5 . . . . . .172 C4
Central Beach FY8 . . . . . . .90 B3
Central Bldgs 16 BB12 . . .145 C1

Central Dr Blackpool FY1 . .129 C3
 Lytham St Anne's FY8 . . . .89 C5
 Morecambe LA4 . . . . . . .212 C5
 Penwortham PR1 . . . . . . .95 A4
Central Lancaster
 High Sch 214 B1
Central Sq
 7 Haslingden BB4 . . . . . .84 B3
 Maghull L31 . . . . .5 D2
Central St BL0 . . . . .49 C6
Central View OL13 . . . . . . .87 B4
Centre Dr PR6 . . . . .77 B4
Centurian Way BB1 . . . . . .81 B6
Centurion Ct BB1 . . . . .81 B7
Centurion Ind Est PR5 . . . .76 B3
Centurion Way PR5 . . . . . .76 A4
Ceres Way LA1 . . . . .210 C8
Chad St BB8 . . . . .169 A2
Chadderton Ct 18 PR1 . . . .96 A8
Chaddock St 27 PR1 . . . . . .96 A7
Chadfield Rd FY1 . . . . . . .129 D2
Chadwich Gdns 1 PR5 . . .76 A7
Chadwick St
 Blackburn BB2 . . . . .100 D3
 3 Blackpool FY1 . . . . . . .129 C5
 Bury BL9 . . . . .32 E4
Chadwick Terr OL12 . . . . . .51 D4
Chaffinch CI FY5 . . . . .172 F5
Chaffinch Ct FY3 . . . . . . .130 B6
Chaffinch Dr BL9 . . . . .32 C4
Chaigley Ct BB7 . . . . .163 A8
Chaigley Farm Cotts BB7 163 A8
Chaigley Rd PR3 . . . . .139 B8
Chain Caul Rd PR2 . . . . . . .94 F8
Chain Caul Way PR2 . . . . .94 F8
Chain House La PR4 . . . . . .75 D7
Chain La PR3 . . . . .130 E4
Chalfont Ct PR8 . . . . .34 A3
Chalfont Fold PR8 . . . . . . .34 A3
Challan Hall Cotts LA5 . . .218 E5
Challan Hall Mews LA5 . .218 E5
Challenge Way BB1 . . . . . .101 C7
Chamber St BB8 . . . . .86 A8
Chambres Rd PR8 . . . . . . .34 D5
Chambres Rd N PR8 . . . . .34 D6
Champagne Ave FY5 . . . . .150 F7
Chancel Pl BB3 . . . . .64 C8
Chancel Way BB3 . . . . .64 C8
Chancery Rd PR7 . . . . .60 B2
Chancery Wlk 3 BB1 . . . . .127 A6
Chandler Bsns Pk PR5 . . . .75 E2
Chandler St 7 PR1 . . . . . . .95 F8
Chandlers Croft PR4 . . . . .72 E4
Chandlers Rest FY8 . . . . . .90 D3
Chandley CI PR8 . . . . .20 A5
Change CI OL13 . . . . .87 B4
Changford Gn L33 . . . . .1 A3
Changford Rd L33 . . . . .1 A3
Channel Way PR2 . . . . .95 C8
Channing Rd FY8 . . . . .89 C4
Chapel Alley L37 . . . . .11 F1
Chapel Brow Leyland PR5 . .76 B2
 Longridge PR3 . . . . .139 A7
Chapel CI Clitheroe BB7 . . .164 B8
 Hest Bank LA2 . . . . .215 D1
 Kirkham PR4 . . . . .112 F7
 Overton LA3 . . . . .205 C8
 Trawden BB8 . . . . .170 B2
 West Bradford BB7 . . . . .186 E5
 Whalley BB7 . . . . .143 C5
Chapel Ct BB10 . . . . .148 A3
Chapel Fields BL7 . . . . . . .47 C4
Chapel Fold 12 Colne BB8 .169 D4
 Wiswell BB7 . . . . .143 F7
Chapel Gdns Catterall PR3 178 D2
 Hesketh Bank PR4 . . . . . .72 E4
Chapel Grange BL7 . . . . . .47 C4
Chapel Hill Longridge PR3 .139 A6
 Salterforth BB18 . . . . . . .191 D7
Chapel Hill La BB4 . . . . . . .85 B4
Chapel Ho BB11 . . . . .126 C5
Chapel House BB1 . . . . . . .123 C1
Chapel House Rd BB9 . . . .147 E7
Chapel La Arnside LA5 . . . .237 B2
 Banks PR9 . . . . .54 B7
 Burscough PR9 . . . . .24 E2
 Burton in L LA6 . . . . .236 C3
 Catforth PR4 . . . . .134 D4
 Coppull PR7 . . . . .41 F1
 Formby L37 . . . . .11 F3
 Galgate LA2 . . . . .207 B4
 Grindleton BB7 . . . . .187 B8
 Hoghton PR5 . . . . .98 D2
 Holmeswood L40 . . . . . . .37 B6
 Kirkby Lonsdale LA6 . . . .238 C2
 Kirkham PR4 . . . . .113 B4
 Langho BB6 . . . . .142 B2
 Longton PR4 . . . . .74 C8
 New Longton PR4 . . . . . . .74 E8
 Out Rawcliffe PR3 . . . . . .175 B3
 Overton LA3 . . . . .205 D8
 Parbold WN8 . . . . .26 D1
 Ramsbottom BL8 . . . . . . .49 A6
 West Bradford BB7 . . . . .186 E5
 Wheelton PR6 . . . . .61 B5
Chapel Meadow PR4 . . . . .74 C8
Chapel Meadows PR4 . . . .56 A5
Chapel Mews
 2 Earby BB18 . . . . .201 B1
 Ormskirk L39 . . . . .15 F4
Chapel Park Rd PR4 . . . . . .74 D8
Chapel Rd Blackpool FY4 . .110 B7
 Fulwood PR2 . . . . .117 A4
 Hesketh Bank PR4 . . . . . .72 E4
Chapel Rise BB7 . . . . .143 B4
Chapel Sq LA2 . . . . .231 D3
Chapel St
 10 Accrington BB5 . . . . .103 C5

Chapel St continued
 Adlington PR7 . . . . .29 F6
 14 Bacup OL13 . . . . .69 C8
 Barnoldswick BB18 . . . . .200 B2
 Belmont BL7 . . . . .45 C5
 Belthorn BB1 . . . . .81 F6
 Blackburn BB2 . . . . .100 D4
 Blackpool FY1 . . . . .129 D4
 Blackrod BL6 . . . . .30 D2
 Brierfield BB9 . . . . .147 B6
 Brinscall PR6 . . . . .61 F8
 Burnley BB11 . . . . .127 A6
 Chorley PR7 . . . . .42 C8
 Clayton-le-M BB5 . . . . . .123 E3
 Colne BB8 . . . . .169 D4
 Coppull PR7 . . . . .41 E1
 Darwen BB3 . . . . .64 A8
 Earby BB18 . . . . .201 B2
 Egerton BL7 . . . . .46 D3
 Foulridge BB8 . . . . .191 E1
 Galgate LA2 . . . . .207 A3
 Great Eccleston PR3 . . . .154 B5
 Haslingden BB4 . . . . .84 B3
 Higham BB12 . . . . .145 F5
 Horwich BL6 . . . . .31 C3
 3 Lancaster LA1 . . . . . . .210 F8
 Longridge PR3 . . . . .139 B7
 Lytham St Anne's FY8 . . . .90 A3
 Morecambe LA4 . . . . . . .212 C5
 Nelson BB9 . . . . .147 E8
 Newchurch BB4 . . . . .85 E1
 Ormskirk L39 . . . . .15 F4
 Oswaldtwistle BB5 . . . . . .102 E4
 Poulton-le-F FY6 . . . . . . .151 D3
 Preston PR1 . . . . .95 F7
 Rawtenstall BB4 . . . . .85 A8
 Rishton BB1 . . . . .123 C1
 Slaidburn BB7 . . . . .223 C7
 Southport PR8 . . . . .34 B7
 Whitworth OL12 . . . . .51 C8
 Worsthorne BB10 . . . . . .128 A5
Chapel Street Ct 2 FY6 . .151 D3
Chapel Street Ave PR8 . . . .34 B7
Chapel View LA3 . . . . .205 D8
Chapel Way PR7 . . . . .28 F8
Chapel Wlk Coppull PR7 . . .41 D8
 Longton PR4 . . . . .74 D8
 2 Padiham BB12 . . . . . . .145 C1
 Warton, Carnforth LA5 . . .217 E6
Chapel Wlks Kirkham PR4 .113 B4
 4 Preston PR1 . . . . .95 F7
Chapel Yd PR5 . . . . .96 D5
Chapelhouse La LA6 . . . . .238 E1
Chapelhouse Wlk L37 . . . .12 A3
Chapels BB3 . . . . .81 A3
Chapels Brow BB3 . . . . . . .81 A3
Chapels La BB3 . . . . .79 F3
Chapelside CI PR3 . . . . . . .178 C2
Chapeltown Rd BL7 . . . . . .47 C2
Chapman CI PR3 . . . . .154 C5
Chapman Ct
 Barnoldswick BB18 . . . . .200 B3
 Fleetwood FY7 . . . . .194 B4
Chapman Rd Fulwood PR2 117 A3
 Hoddlesden BB3 . . . . .81 F1
Chapter Rd BB3 . . . . .64 C8
Chardonnay Cres 2 FY5 . .150 F7
Charlbury Gr LA3 . . . . . . .209 A7
Charles Ave PR8 . . . . .20 C6
Charles CI PR4 . . . . .72 E3
Charles Cres PR5 . . . . .97 C3
Charles Ct
 4 Blackpool FY3 . . . . . . .129 D7
 Lancaster LA1 . . . . .210 F6
Charles Gr PR3 . . . . .139 A7
Charles La BB4 . . . . .84 A2
Charles Saer
 Com PrimSch FY7 . . . . .193 D3
Charles St Blackburn BB2 . .100 C2
 Blackpool FY1 . . . . .129 C6
 Clayton-le-M BB5 . . . . . .123 E2
 Colne BB8 . . . . .169 E5
 Darwen BB3 . . . . .81 A2
 Egerton BL7 . . . . .46 D2
 Great Harwood BB6 . . . . .123 C4
 Lancaster LA1 . . . . .210 F6
 Morecambe LA4 . . . . . . .212 F5
 Nelson BB9 . . . . .168 E2
 Newchurch BB4 . . . . .85 F2
 Oswaldtwistle BB5 . . . . . .102 E3
Charles Way PR2 . . . . .115 E1
Charlesbye Ave L39 . . . . . .16 B6
Charlesbye CI L39 . . . . . . .16 B6
Charleston Ct 3 PR5 . . . . .96 E2
Charlesway Ct 1 PR2 . . . .115 E1
Charlesworth CI L31 . . . . . .5 B5
Charley Fold Bglws PR5 . . .96 F3
Charley Wood Rd L33 . . . . .1 C1
Charlotte Pl 38 PR1 . . . . . .96 A7
Charlotte St
 Blackburn BB1 . . . . .100 E6
 Burnley BB11 . . . . .126 F5
 Edgworth BL7 . . . . .47 C4
 Preston PR1 . . . . .96 A7
 4 Ramsbottom BL0 . . . . .49 B5
Charlotte's La PR4 . . . . . . .55 E2
Charnley CI PR1 . . . . .95 C2
Charnley Fold PR5 . . . . . . .96 F3
Charnley Fold La PR5 . . . . .96 F3
Charnley Rd FY1 . . . . .129 C4
Charnley St Blackburn BB2 100 C2
 1 Lancaster LA1 . . . . . . .213 D1
 1 Preston PR1 . . . . .95 F7
Charnley's La PR9 . . . . . . .53 E2
Charnock Ave PR1 . . . . . . .95 E2

Charnock Brow PR7 41 C7
Charnock Fold PR1 117 A2
Charnock House PR7 60 C2
Charnock Richard CE Prim Sch PR7 41 D4
Charnock St Chorley PR6 42 D7
9 Kirkham PR4 112 F6
8 Leyland PR5 76 B1
Preston PR1 116 F2
Charnwood Ave FY3 130 A7
Charnwood Cl BB2 100 A8
Charter Brook BB6 123 D5
Charter La PR7 41 D3
Charter St BB5 103 A5
Charterhouse Pl BB2 100 B3
Chartwell Cl PR6 77 C2
Chartwell Rd PR8 20 B6
Chartwell Rise 5 PR5 76 C8
Chasden Cl PR6 60 C5
Chase Cl PR8 33 F4
Chase Heys PR9 53 A1
Chase The Burnley BB12 126 D8
Cottam PR4 115 D5
3 Leyland PR5 76 C2
Normoss FY3 130 C7
Silverdale LA5 218 D2
Thornton FY5 173 A4
Chatburn Ave
Burnley BB10 127 D5
Clitheroe BB7 186 F1
Chatburn CE Prim Sch BB7 187 D5
Chatburn Cl
Great Harwood BB6 123 E5
Normoss FY3 130 B8
Rawtenstall BB4 85 A4
Chatburn Gdns OL10 32 F2
Chatburn Old Rd BB7 187 D5
Chatburn Park Ave BB9 147 A6
Chatburn Park Dr
Brierfield BB9 147 A6
Clitheroe BB7 187 A2
Chatburn Rd
Chatburn BB7 187 F5
Clitheroe BB7 187 A3
Fulwood PR2 117 F4
Longridge PR3 139 A7
Chatburn St BB2 100 C5
Chatham Ave FY8 109 E1
Chatham Cres BB8 169 E6
Chatham Pl 5 Chorley PR6 42 E8
Preston PR1 117 B2
Chatham St Colne BB8 169 E6
Nelson BB9 168 D1
Chatsworth Ave
Blackpool FY2 150 C6
Fleetwood FY7 193 D2
Warton PR4 91 D6
Chatsworth Cl
Barrowford BB9 168 B1
Blackburn BB1 121 E1
Chorley PR7 42 B8
2 Thornton FY5 173 D1
Chatsworth Ct PR6 42 F1
Chatsworth Rd
Bamber Bridge PR5 96 D3
Lancaster LA1 210 F4
1 Leyland PR5 76 A1
Lytham St Anne's FY8 88 D7
Morecambe LA4 212 C4
Southport PR8 20 B6
Chatsworth St Preston PR1 96 D8
Rochdale OL12 51 E3
Chatteris Pl FY5 172 C1
Chatterton BL0 67 C2
Chatterton Dr BB5 103 E2
Chatterton Old La BL0 67 C2
Chatterton Rd BL0 67 C1
Chaucer Ave FY5 172 F2
Chaucer Cl PR7 40 B6
Chaucer Gdns BB6 123 B4
Chaucer Prim Sch FY7 194 A4
Chaucer Rd FY7 194 A4
Chaucer St PR1 117 D2
Cheam Ave PR7 42 D6
Cheapside Blackpool FY1 129 B5
6 Chorley PR7 42 C7
Formby L37 12 A2
11 Lancaster LA1 210 F8
1 Low Bentham LA2 233 B8
8 Preston PR1 95 F7
Cheddar Ave FY4 109 D6
Cheddar Dr PR2 117 D6
Chedworth Ave LA3 209 A7
Cheetham Hill OL12 70 D3
Cheetham Meadow PR5 58 B8
Cheetham St BB2 100 C5
Chelburn Gr BB10 127 C6
Chelford Ave FY3 129 E8
Chelford Cl 4 PR1 95 F2
Chelmsford Cl LA1 211 B5
Chelmsford Gr PR7 42 B7
Chelmsford Pl PR7 42 B7
Chelmsford Wlk PR5 58 A8
Chelsea Ave FY2 150 E1
Chelsea Ct 3 FY2 150 E1
Chelsea Mews 4 FY2 150 E1
Chelston Dr BB4 67 A7
Cheltenham Ave BB5 103 C8
Cheltenham Cres
Lytham St Anne's FY8 90 D5
Thornton FY5 151 D8
Cheltenham Dr WN5 10 D2
Cheltenham Rd
Blackburn BB2 100 C5
Cheltenham Rd *continued*
Blackpool FY1 129 B7
Lancaster LA1 210 F5
Cheltenham Way PR8 34 F3
Chennel Ho 4 LA1 210 E8
Chepstow Ct FY3 129 F8
Chepstow Rd FY3 129 F8
Chequer Cl WN8 9 F5
Chequer La WN8 9 F6
Chequers BB5 123 F2
Chequers Ave LA1 211 B4
Cheriton Field PR2 116 C7
Cheriton Gdns BL6 31 B5
Cheriton Pk PR8 34 E3
Cherry Ave BL9 32 C3
Cherry Cl
2 Blackburn BB1 101 B5
Fulwood PR2 117 D6
Kirkham PR4 112 E5
Cherry Cres
Oswaldtwistle BB5 102 D2
Rawtenstall BB4 67 F8
Cherry Gn L39 15 B1
Cherry Gr Abbey Village PR6 79 B2
Burscough Bridge L40 24 E6
Longridge PR3 139 A7
Cherry La PR4 92 B4
Cherry Lea BB2 99 F2
Cherry Orch PR3 139 B6
Cherry Rd PR8 20 D2
Cherry St BB1 101 B5
Cherry Tree Cl
Fisher's Row PR3 196 E5
Hest Bank LA5 215 F2
Heysham LA3 208 E6
Cherry Tree Ct
Blackpool FY4 130 B1
10 Fleetwood FY7 194 B5
Standish WN6 28 D2
Cherry Tree Dr LA1 210 F4
Cherry Tree Gdns FY4 110 A8
Cherry Tree Gr PR6 60 C3
Cherry Tree La
Blackburn BB2 79 E8
Ormskirk L39 15 B1
Rawtenstall BB4 67 F8
Cherry Tree Mews BB11 126 D3
Cherry Tree Rd FY4 130 A1
Cherry Tree Rd N FY4 130 A1
Cherry Tree Sta BB2 99 F1
Cherry Tree Terr BB2 99 F1
Cherry Tree Way
Haslingden BB4 67 B7
5 Horwich BL6 31 E1
Cherry Trees
Bamber Bridge PR5 96 C3
St Michael's on W PR3 155 C7
Cherry Vale PR4 72 F2
Cherry View L33 1 A5
Cherry Wood PR1 95 A3
Cherryclough Way BB2 80 B8
Cherrycroft WN8 9 E6
Cherrydale FY2 150 D5
Cherryfields PR7 59 D4
Cherrywood Ave
Cleveleys FY5 172 C1
Lytham St Anne's FY8 89 E4
Cherrywood Cl PR5 58 E8
Cheryl Dr FY5 151 B8
Chesham Cres BL9 32 A3
Chesham Dr PR4 74 F8
Chesham Fold Rd BL9 32 B4
Chesham Ind Est BL9 32 A4
Chesham Prim Sch BL9 32 A5
Chesham Rd BL9 32 A5
Chesham St PR3 154 B5
Cheshire Ct BL0 49 D6
Cheshire House Cl PR5 75 F7
Chesmere Croft PR1 95 B5
Chesmere Dr PR1 95 B5
Chessington Gn BB10 147 D3
Chester Ave Chorley PR7 42 E4
Cleveleys FY5 172 E2
Clitheroe BB7 186 E1
Poulton-le-F FY6 151 C4
Southport PR9 34 F8
Chester Cl Blackburn BB1 101 A3
Garstang PR3 178 B7
Morecambe LA3 212 E2
Chester Cres BB4 67 B8
Chester Ct FY5 173 C3
Chester Dr BL0 49 A4
Chester Pl Adlington PR6 30 A8
Great Eccleston PR3 154 C5
Lancaster LA1 211 A5
Chester Rd Blackpool FY3 129 D6
Preston PR1 117 C1
Southport PR9 34 F8
Chester St Accrington BB5 103 A5
Blackburn BB1 101 A4
Bury BL9 32 A4
Chesterbrook PR3 140 E4
Chesterfield Cl PR8 20 C4
Chesterfield Rd
Blackpool FY1 129 C7
Southport PR8 20 C5
Chestnut Ave
Blackpool FY4 109 F5
Bolton-le-S LA5 216 A5
Bury BL9 32 B2
Caton LA2 231 C3
Chorley PR6 60 E2
Euxton PR7 59 C4
Penwortham PR1 95 A4
Chestnut Cl
Bamber Bridge PR5 96 E2
Garstang PR3 199 D1
Halsall L39 22 C1
Chestnut Cl *continued*
2 Kirkham PR4 113 B5
Chestnut Cres
Barrow BB7 164 D1
Fulwood PR2 117 E2
Longton PR4 73 F8
Chestnut Ct Leyland PR5 59 A7
3 Ormskirk L39 15 F6
Chestnut Dr
Barnoldswick BB18 200 A1
Fulwood PR2 116 D7
Morecambe LA4 213 B6
Rawtenstall BB4 67 F8
Whalley BB7 143 A7
Chestnut Gdns BB1 100 F7
Chestnut Gr
Accrington BB5 103 A4
Clayton-le-M BB5 124 A4
Darwen BB3 64 A5
Lancaster LA1 210 D8
Chestnut Grange L39 15 D3
Chestnut Rise BB11 126 F4
Chestnut St PR8 34 C5
Chestnut Way L37 11 C1
Chestnut Wlk 5 BB1 101 B5
Chestnuts The PR7 41 F2
Chethams Cl FY5 173 A2
Chevassut Cl BB9 168 C1
Cheviot Ave Burnley BB10 127 E5
Cleveleys FY5 172 F4
Saltcotes FY8 90 E5
Cheviot Cl Horwich BL6 31 C5
Ramsbottom BL0 49 C4
Cheviot St PR1 95 C8
Chew Gdns FY6 151 B3
Chichester Cl
Burnley BB10 127 B6
Thornton FY5 173 A2
Chicken St BB2 100 C4
Chiddlingford Ct FY1 129 D3
Childrey Wlk BB2 81 A8
Chilgrove Ave BL6 30 D1
Chiltern Ave
Blackpool FY4 109 D7
Burnley BB10 127 E5
Euxton PR7 59 D1
Poulton-le-F FY6 151 C3
Chiltern Cl Horwich BL6 31 C5
Lytham St Anne's FY8 90 D5
Ramsbottom BL0 49 C4
Chiltern Meadow PR5 76 D1
Chiltern Rd
Ramsbottom BL0 49 C4
Southport PR8 20 B6
Chilton Cl L31 5 D1
Chilton Mews L31 5 D1
Chimes The Kirkham PR4 113 A4
Tarleton PR4 56 A5
China St Accrington BB5 102 F6
Lancaster LA1 210 F8
Chindit Cl L37 11 D2
Chindits Way PR2 117 B4
Chines The PR2 116 E4
Chingford Bank BB10 147 D3
Chingle Cl PR2 117 E6
Chipping Ave PR8 20 A5
Chipping Ct 4 FY3 130 A8
Chipping Gr Burnley BB10 127 D4
Normoss FY3 130 A8
Chipping La PR3 139 A8
Chipping St 3 BB12 145 D1
Chisacre Dr WN6 19 D7
Chisholm Cl WN6 28 B2
Chisholme Cl BL8 48 F2
Chislehurst Ave FY4 129 D1
Chislehurst Gr BB10 147 D4
Chislehurst Pl FY8 89 E5
Chislett Cl L40 24 D4
Chisnall Ave WN6 27 F6
Chisnall La Coppull PR7 28 C6
Heskin Green PR7 40 F2
Wrightington Bar WN6 28 A5
Chiswell Gr FY5 151 D8
Chiswick Gr FY3 130 B2
Chitheroe Rd PR3 161 C1
Chorcliffe Ho 7 PR7 42 C8
Chorley & District Hospl PR7 60 C2
Chorley Bsns & Tech Ctr PR7 59 E4
Chorley Cl PR9 53 F5
Chorley Golf Course PR6 43 A3
Chorley Hall Rd PR7 60 C2
Chorley Info Ctr PR7 42 C8
Chorley La PR7 41 D3
Chorley New Rd BL6 31 C2
Chorley New Rd Inf Sch BL6 31 D2
Chorley New Rd Prim Sch BL6 31 D2
Chorley North Ind Est PR6 60 D3
Chorley Old Rd
Clayton Green PR6 77 C2
Horwich BL6 31 E3
Chorley Rd Adlington PR6 30 A8
Adlington, Blackrod BL6,PR7 30 B5
Bamber Bridge PR5 96 D3
Blackpool FY3 150 F2
Hill Dale L40,WN8 26 D6
Ollerton Fold BB2,PR6 78 E4
Parbold WN8 26 C4
Standish WN1 29 C3
Chorley St PR6 30 B8
Chorley St James CE Prim Sch PR6 42 E7
Chorley Sta PR6 42 D8
Chorley West Bsns Pk PR7 41 F8
Chorlton Cl BB10 147 D2
Chorlton Gdns BB1 100 F7
Chorlton St BB1 100 F7
Chorlton Terr BB7 164 D1
Christ Church CE Prim Sch Carnforth LA5 217 D1
Glasson LA2 205 E4
Lancaster LA1 211 B8
Christ Church CE Sch LA1 211 A8
Christ Church Prim Sch BB8 170 B5
Christ Church Sq 1 BB5 103 C5
Christ Church St
2 Accrington BB5 103 C5
6 Bacup OL13 87 A3
Preston PR1 95 E7
Christ The King RC High Sch PR1 96 B6
Christ The King RC Prim Sch Blackpool FY3 130 A7
Burnley BB11 126 E3
Christ The King Sch PR8 34 B2
Christian Rd PR1 95 E7
Christiana Hartley Maternity Hospl PR8 34 D5
Christie Ave LA4 212 G4
Christines Cres L40 24 E4
Christleton Cl BB10 147 F3
Church & Oswaldtwistle Sta BB5 102 E5
Church Alley BB5 123 F2
Church Ave
Accrington BB5 103 E2
Lancaster LA1 210 F4
Penwortham PR1 95 C6
Preston PR1 96 E8
Church Bank LA6 231 B8
Church Bank St 19 BB3 81 A1
Church Brook House 8 PR1 95 E4
Church Brow
Bolton-le-S LA5 216 A3
Clitheroe BB7 186 E1
Halton LA2 214 E6
Walton-le-D PR5 96 E5
Church Brow Cl LA5 216 A3
Church Brow Gdns BB7 186 E1
Church Cl Clitheroe BB7 186 E1
Dolphinholme LA2 220 A8
Formby L37 12 A3
Freckleton PR4 92 A6
Mellor BB2 120 E2
Ramsbottom BL0 49 B5
Read BB12 144 D2
Southport PR9 35 A8
Waddington BB7 186 B4
Church Close Ct L37 12 A3
Church Ct Bolton-le-S LA5 216 A3
Edenfield BL0 67 D4
Preston PR1 117 C2
Church Dr
Lytham St Anne's FY8 89 F3
Orrell WN5 10 D5
Whalley BB7 143 A7
Church Fields Bescar L40 22 F7
Ormskirk L39 15 E5
Church Fold
Charnock Richard PR7 41 E4
Coppull PR7 28 F8
Church Gdns PR4 91 E6
Church Gn Formby L37 11 C2
Skelmersdale WN8 17 F1
Church Gr LA3 205 E8
Church Hall BB5 102 F7
Church Hill Arnside LA5 237 B2
Nether Kellet LA6 216 F5
Whittle-le-W PR6 60 C7
Church Hill Ave LA5 217 D5
Church Hill Rd
Blackburn BB1 101 A7
Ormskirk L39 15 D6
Church Ho 7 L39 15 E5
Church House Mus PR3 136 D1
Church La Accrington BB5 124 A1
Bilsborrow PR3 157 A4
Broughton PR3 136 D1
Charnock Richard PR7 41 D4
Edenfield BL0 67 D4
Farington PR5 75 F7
Goosnargh PR3 137 D6
Great Harwood BB6 123 C6
Great Mitton BB7 163 E3
Hambleton FY6 174 D1
Kelbrook BB18 192 A6
Maghull L31 5 A8
Mellor BB2 120 E2
Morecambe LA4 212 E6
Newchurch BB4 85 E1
Newton-with-S PR4 114 B3
Ormskirk L39 6 A7
12 Padiham BB12 145 C1
Tunstall LA6 235 E4
Whalley BB7 143 C5
Whitechapel PR3 158 E7
Winmarleigh PR3 198 E4
Wrightington Bar WN6 27 D8
Church Mdws BB8 169 D5
Church Pk Lea Town PR4 114 F3
Overton LA3 205 D8
Church Raike PR3 182 E3
Church Rd
Bamber Bridge PR5 76 E7
Bamber Bridge PR5 76 F6
Banks PR9 54 A6
Bickerstaffe L39 7 E6
Formby L37 12 A5
Kirkham PR4 112 F7
Leyland PR5 59 A8
Church Rd *continued*
Lytham FY8 89 F3
Lytham St Anne's FY8 89 B6
Rufford L40 38 C4
Shuttleworth BL0 49 E8
Singleton FY6 152 F1
Skelmersdale WN8 17 F1
Tarleton PR4 56 A5
Thornton FY5 173 A2
Thornton-in-C BD23 201 A5
Warton PR4 91 D6
Weeton PR4 131 F1
Wharles PR4 133 F2
Church Row Preston PR1 96 A7
Wrea Green PR4 112 B4
Church Row Chambers PR4 74 A8
Church Sq BB10 128 B5
Church St Accrington BB5 103 C5
Adlington PR7 30 A7
Bacup OL13 69 C8
Barnoldswick BB18 200 B2
Barrowford BB9 168 D4
Belmont BL7 45 C4
Blackburn BB1 100 E5
Blackpool FY1 129 C5
Blackrod BL6 30 C2
Brierfield BB9 147 B5
Brierfield, Harle Syke BB10 147 F2
Burnley BB11 127 A6
Bury BL9 32 A3
Chorley PR7 42 C7
Church BB5 102 E6
Churchtown PR3 178 A2
Clayton-le-M BB5 123 F2
1 Clitheroe BB7 164 E8
Colne BB8 169 D5
Croston PR5 57 B1
Darwen BB3 81 A1
Fleetwood FY7 194 B4
Garstang PR3 178 C7
Goodshaw Chapel BB4 105 A1
Great Harwood BB6 123 C5
Halton LA2 214 D6
2 Hapton BB12 125 C4
Haslingden BB4 84 B4
Higher Walton PR5 97 B3
Horwich BL6 31 C3
Kirkby Lonsdale LA6 238 C2
Kirkham PR4 113 B5
Lancaster LA1 210 F8
Leyland PR5 76 B2
Longridge PR3 139 B7
Morecambe LA4 212 E6
Newchurch BB4 85 E1
Ormskirk L39 15 E5
Orrell, Far Moor WN5 10 E5
Orrell, Up Holland WN8 10 C7
Oswaldtwistle BB5 102 D3
Padiham BB12 125 C8
1 Poulton-le-F FY6 151 D3
Preston PR1 96 A7
5 Ramsbottom BL0 49 C6
Rawtenstall BB4 68 E8
Read BB12 144 D2
Rishton BB1 123 A1
Slaidburn BB7 223 C7
Southport PR9 34 C7
Standish WN6 28 E1
Trawden BB8 170 C2
Whittington LA6 235 C7
Whitworth OL12 51 C8
Church Terr 20 BB3 81 A1
Church View Arnside LA5 237 B2
Gisburn BB7 225 B3
Ormskirk L39 6 A7
Salesbury BB1 121 E6
Stalmine FY6 174 C7
Tarleton PR4 56 A5
Trawden BB8 170 C2
Church View Ct 1 L39 15 E5
Church Way Formby L37 11 C2
Nelson BB9 147 D6
Church Wlk Blackburn BB1 121 F3
Euxton PR7 59 C2
Kirkham PR4 112 F7
Preston PR2 117 F5
Tarleton PR4 56 A6
Church Wlks 3 L39 15 E5
Churchfield PR2 116 F6
Churchfields PR8 33 F3
Churchgate
Goosnargh PR3 137 D6
Southport PR9 52 F1
Churchgate Mews PR9 53 A1
Churchill Ave Rishton BB1 102 A8
Southport PR9 52 F2
Churchill Cl 2 FY5 173 B2
Churchill Ct FY3 129 D6
Churchill Dr PR2 117 D4
Churchill Rd
Barrowford BB9 168 B1
Brinscall PR6 62 A8
Fulwood PR2 117 C4
Churchill St OL11,OL12 51 C1
Churchill Way Leyland PR5 76 A2
Nelson BB9 147 B8
Churchlands La WN6 28 F1
Churchside PR4 74 F8
Churchtown Cres OL13 87 B1
Churchtown Ct PR9 53 A2
Churchtown Prim Sch PR9 53 B2
Churchward Sq BL6 31 C2
Churton Gr WN6 28 B2
Cicely Ct BB1 100 F4
Cicely La BB1 100 F5
Cicely St BB1 100 F4

Cinder La Lancaster LA1 . .210 F3
Lewth PR4 . . . . .135 A6
Mere Brow PR4 . . . . .54 F2
Cinderbarrow La LA5,LA6 234 A6
Cinnamon Brow WN8 . . . . .10 C6
Cinnamon Ct **3** PR1 . . . . .95 C2
Cinnamon Hill Dr N PR5 . .96 D3
Cinnamon Hill Dr S PR5 . .96 D3
Cintra Ave PR2 . . . . .116 D3
Cintra Terr PR2 . . . . .116 D3
Circus The **10** BB3 . . . . . . .81 A1
Cirrus Dr L39 . . . . .15 A1
City Hts Cl **21** LA1 . . . . . .211 A8
Clairane Ave PR2 . . . . . .116 E6
Clairville PR8 . . . . .33 F5
Clancut La PR7 . . . . .41 F2
Clanfield PR2 . . . . .116 E7
Clara St Preston PR1 . . . . .96 C7
Whitworth OL12 . . . . .70 D1
Clare Ave BB8 . . . . .169 A2
Clare Rd LA1 . . . . .213 E2
Clare St Blackpool FY1 . . .129 B1
Burnley BB11 . . . . .126 D6
Claremont Ave Chorley PR7 42 B7
Clitheroe BB7 . . . . .164 F7
Claremont Cres LA4 . . . . .212 C4
Claremont Ct FY1 . . . . . .129 C7
Claremont Dr
Clitheroe BB7 . . . . .164 F7
Ormskirk L39 . . . . .15 D3
Claremont Gdns PR8 . . . . .34 A4
Claremont Pl FY8 . . . . . . .88 E8
Claremont Rd
Accrington BB5 . . . . .103 B8
Blackpool FY1 . . . . .129 C8
Chorley PR7 . . . . .42 B5
Morecambe LA4 . . . . . . .212 C4
Southport PR8 . . . . .34 A4
Claremont Sch (Prim)
FY1 . . . . .129 C8
Claremont St
Brierfield BB9 . . . . .147 A6
Burnley BB12 . . . . .126 D6
Colne BB8 . . . . .170 A5
Claremont Terr BB9 . . . . .147 D7
Claremount Ave PR5 . . . . .59 B8
Clarence Ave
Cleveleys FY5 . . . . .172 D3
4 Haslingden BB4 . . . . . .84 A1
Knott End-on-S FY6 . . . . .194 E5
Clarence Ct **15** FY4 . . . . .129 B1
Clarence House Sch L37 . .11 F6
Clarence Pk BB2 . . . . . . .100 B7
Clarence Rd
Accrington BB5 . . . . .103 A4
Southport PR8 . . . . .34 A4
Clarence St
Barnoldswick BB18 . . . . .200 C1
Blackburn BB1 . . . . .100 D6
Burnley BB11 . . . . .127 B4
4 Chorley PR7 . . . . .42 D7
Colne BB8 . . . . .170 A5
Darwen BB3 . . . . .80 F3
Lancaster LA1 . . . . .211 A7
Leyland PR5 . . . . .76 B2
Morecambe LA4 . . . . . . .212 E5
Rawtenstall BB4 . . . . .85 A2
Rochdale OL12 . . . . .51 D2
Trawden BB8 . . . . .170 C2
Clarendon Gr L31 . . . . .5 C5
Clarendon Rd
Blackburn BB1 . . . . .100 F8
Blackpool FY1 . . . . .129 B3
Lancaster LA1 . . . . .213 F3
Lytham St Anne's FY8 . . . .89 A8
Clarendon Rd E
Blackburn BB1 . . . . .101 A8
Morecambe LA4 . . . . . . .212 C4
Clarendon Rd W LA3 . . . .212 B4
Clarendon St
Accrington BB5 . . . . .103 D6
Bury BL9 . . . . .32 A4
10 Chorley PR6 . . . . . . .42 E7
Colne BB8 . . . . .170 B5
Preston PR1 . . . . .96 A6
Claret St BB5 . . . . .103 A5
Clark St LA4 . . . . .212 E6
Clarke Holme St BB4 . . . . .85 F2
Clarke St Poulton-le-F FY6 .192 F1
6 Rishton BB1 . . . . .123 B1
Clarke Wood Cl BB7 . . . .143 F8
Clarke's Cotts L40 . . . . . . .26 A8
Clarke's La OL12 . . . . .51 E1
Clarkes Croft BL9 . . . . . . .32 C3
Clarkfield Cl L40 . . . . .24 F3
Clarkfield Dr LA4 . . . . . . .212 G5
Clarksfield Rd LA5 . . . . . .216 A4
Clarrick Terr LA6 . . . . . . .236 F3
Clary St BB12 . . . . .126 A5
Claughton Ave PR5 . . . . . .76 E1
Claughton Dr LA1 . . . . . .211 A3
Claughton St **14** BB10 . . .147 B1
Clawthorpe Cotts LA6 . . .234 C8
Clay Brow Rd WN8 . . . . . . .9 E6
Clay Gap La FY6,PR3 . . . .174 F4
Clay La LA3 . . . . .209 B8
Clay St BB11 . . . . .126 C5
Claybank **10** BB12 . . . . . .145 C1
Claybank Fold **9** BB12 . . .145 C1
Clayburn Cl PR6 . . . . .60 E2
Claylands Dr LA5 . . . . . . .216 A4
Claypool Prim Sch BL6 . . . .31 F1
Claypool Rd BL6 . . . . .31 E1
Clayton Ave Leyland PR5 . .58 D7
Rawtenstall BB4 . . . . .67 C4
Clayton Brook
Cty Prim Sch PR5 . . . . . .77 B5

Clayton Brook Rd PR5 . . . .77 C6
Clayton Cl **11** BB9 . . . . . .168 D1
Clayton Cres FY4 . . . . . . .109 E6
Clayton Ct PR3 . . . . .139 B7
Clayton Gdns L40 . . . . . . .24 E4
Clayton Green Rd PR6 . . . .77 B3
Clayton Hall Dr BB5 . . . . .123 F4
Clayton Mews WN8 . . . . . .17 D1
Clayton Row BB6 . . . . . . .142 D1
Clayton St
6 Bamber Bridge PR5 . . . .96 E1
Barnoldswick BB18 . . . . .200 C2
Blackburn BB2 . . . . .100 E4
Colne BB8 . . . . .169 E4
1 Enfield BB5 . . . . .124 A1
Great Harwood BB6 . . . . .123 C5
18 Nelson BB9 . . . . . . .168 D1
7 Oswaldtwistle BB5 . . . .102 E5
Skelmersdale WN8 . . . . . .17 D1
Clayton Street Ind Units
BB9 . . . . .168 D1
Clayton Villa Fold PR6 . . . .77 A3
Clayton Way BB5 . . . . . . .124 A3
Clayton's Gate **12** PR1 . . . .95 F8
Clayton-le-Moors
Ind Est BB5 . . . . .123 E2
Clayton-le-Woods
CE Prim Sch PR6 . . . . . . .77 A2
Clayton-le-Woods
Westwood Prim Sch
PR5 . . . . .77 C4
Claytongate PR7 . . . . .41 F2
Claytonhalgh PR3 . . . . . .140 E3
Cleator Ave FY2 . . . . .150 C1
Cleaver St Blackburn BB1 . .100 F5
Burnley BB10 . . . . .127 B8
Clegg Ave FY5 . . . . .172 D3
Clegg St **6** Bacup OL13 . . .69 C8
Brierfield BB9 . . . . .147 B5
Burnley BB10 . . . . .127 A8
Haslingden BB4 . . . . .84 B3
Kirkham PR4 . . . . .113 A5
Nelson BB9 . . . . .147 E6
Skelmersdale WN8 . . . . . .17 D1
Whitworth OL12 . . . . .70 C2
Worsthorne BB10 . . . . . . .128 A5
Clegg St E **9** BB10 . . . . .127 A8
Clegg's Ct OL12 . . . . .70 C2
Clematis Cl PR7 . . . . .60 A3
Clematis St BB8 . . . . .170 C2
Clement St Accrington BB5 103 C5
4 Darwen BB3 . . . . .64 A8
Clement View **14** BB9 . . . .147 D8
Clementina St OL12 . . . . . .51 F1
Clements Dr BB10 . . . . . .147 C4
Clengers Brow PR9 . . . . . .53 A3
Clent Ave L31 . . . . .5 C3
Clent Gdns L31 . . . . .5 C3
Clent Rd L31 . . . . .5 C3
Clerk Hill Rd BB7 . . . . . . .143 F5
Clerkhill St BB1 . . . . .101 B5
Cleve Way L37 . . . . .12 B2
Clevedon Rd
Blackpool FY1 . . . . .129 B7
Fulwood PR2 . . . . .116 A4
Cleveland Ave PR2 . . . . .117 C4
Cleveland Cl BL0 . . . . .49 C3
Cleveland Dr LA1 . . . . . . .210 D7
Cleveland Rd Leyland PR5 . .75 C2
Lytham St Anne's FY8 . . . .90 B3
Cleveland St Chorley PR7 . .42 C8
Colne BB8 . . . . .169 F6
2 Coppull PR7 . . . . .41 E1
Cornholme OL14 . . . . . . .108 B1
Clevelands Ave
Morecambe LA3 . . . . . . .212 C3
Silverdale LA5 . . . . .218 C4
Clevelands Gr
Burnley BB11 . . . . .126 E4
Morecambe LA3 . . . . . . .212 C3
Clevelands Mt BB11 . . . . .126 E4
Clevelands Rd BB11 . . . . .126 F4
Clevelands Wlk LA3 . . . . .212 C3
Cleveleys Ave
Cleveleys FY5 . . . . .172 D3
Fulwood PR2 . . . . .116 C4
Lancaster LA1 . . . . .213 C4
Southport PR9 . . . . .53 A4
Cleveleys Rd
Accrington BB5 . . . . .103 B8
Blackburn BB2 . . . . .100 F1
Coupe Green PR5 . . . . . . .97 E3
Southport PR9 . . . . .53 A3
Cleves Ct FY3 . . . . .130 A2
Cleves The L31 . . . . .5 C3
Clieves Hills La L39 . . . . . .14 E3
Clifden Ct L37 . . . . .11 F3
Cliff Ave BL9 . . . . .49 C2
Cliff Ct FY2 . . . . .150 B4
Cliff Mount BL0 . . . . .49 B7
Cliff Pl FY2 . . . . .150 B4
Cliff Rd PR9 . . . . .52 D1
Cliff St Colne BB8 . . . . . .169 B3
Padiham BB12 . . . . .145 D1
Preston PR1 . . . . .95 D6
Rishton BB1 . . . . .123 B2
Cliffe Ct PR1 . . . . .96 D8
Cliffe Dr PR6 . . . . .60 B8
Cliffe La BB6 . . . . .123 C6
Cliffe St BB9 . . . . .168 E1
Clifford Ave Longton PR4 . .94 A1
Morecambe LA4 . . . . . . .212 G6
Clifford Rd Blackpool FY1 . .129 C7
Southport PR8 . . . . .34 A2
Clifford St
Barnoldswick BB18 . . . . .200 C2

Clifford St continued
Chorley PR7 . . . . .42 D8
Colne BB8 . . . . .169 E5
Cliffs The LA3 . . . . .212 A2
Clifton Ave Accrington BB5 130 C7
Blackpool FY4 . . . . .130 C1
Leyland PR5 . . . . .59 B8
Preston PR2 . . . . .116 A2
Warton PR4 . . . . .91 E6
Clifton Cl FY5 . . . . .173 C1
Fulwood PR1 . . . . .117 C2
Clifton Cres Blackpool FY3 130 A2
1 Blackpool FY4 . . . . . .109 B6
3 Lytham St Anne's FY8 . .90 D3
Clifton Cty Prim Sch FY8 .89 C6
Clifton Dr Blackpool FY4 . .109 B5
Great Harwood BB6 . . . . .123 C6
Lytham St Anne's FY8 . . . .89 D3
Morecambe LA4 . . . . . . .213 A5
Penwortham PR1 . . . . .95 C5
Clifton Dr N FY8 . . . . . . .109 B2
Clifton Dr S FY8 . . . . .88 E5
Clifton Gdns FY8 . . . . . . .89 C6
Clifton Gn PR4 . . . . .114 C2
Clifton Gr Chorley PR7 . . . .42 B7
Fulwood PR1 . . . . .117 C3
Clifton Hospl FY8 . . . . . . .89 B5
Clifton La FY8 . . . . .114 D2
Clifton Lodge FY8 . . . . . . .88 E5
Clifton Par FY8 . . . . .90 B3
Clifton Pk Ret Ctr FY4 . . .110 D8
Clifton Pl Freckleton PR4 . .92 B6
Fulwood PR2 . . . . .116 B2
Clifton Rd Blackpool FY4 . .110 C8
Brierfield BB9 . . . . .147 C4
Burnley BB12 . . . . .126 C4
Fleetwood FY7 . . . . .194 A3
Formby L37 . . . . .12 A5
Southport PR8 . . . . .34 F6
Clifton Sq **4** FY8 . . . . . . .90 B3
Blackpool FY1 . . . . .129 B5
Burnley BB12 . . . . .126 F6
Colne BB8 . . . . .169 D5
Darwen BB3 . . . . .80 D4
Lytham St Anne's FY8 . . . .90 B3
5 Preston PR1 . . . . .95 D6
Rishton BB1 . . . . .123 B1
Sough BB18 . . . . .192 A8
Trawden BB8 . . . . .170 C2
Clifton Terr BB3 . . . . .81 E2
Clifton Wlk **6** FY8 . . . . . . .90 B3
Clinkham Rd BB6 . . . . . . .123 A5
Clinning Rd PR8 . . . . .34 A2
Clinton Ave FY1 . . . . .129 C4
Clinton St BB1 . . . . .101 A6
Clippers Quay BB1 . . . . . .100 F4
Clitheroe Castle BB7 . . . .164 E8
Clitheroe Castle Mus
BB7 . . . . .164 E8
Clitheroe Hospl BB7 . . . . .187 A3
Clitheroe Pl FY4 . . . . .110 A8
Clitheroe Rd
Brierfield BB9 . . . . .147 A5
Chatburn BB7 . . . . .187 C3
Lytham St Anne's FY8 . . . .89 C6
Sabden BB7 . . . . .165 E1
Waddington BB7 . . . . . . .186 C3
West Bradford BB7 . . . . . .186 F5
Whalley BB7 . . . . .143 C7
Clitheroe Royal Gram Sch
Clitheroe BB7 . . . . .186 F1
Clitheroe BB7 . . . . .187 A3
Clitheroe St
3 Padiham BB12 . . . . . .125 C8
Preston PR1 . . . . .96 C7
Clitheroe Sta BB7 . . . . . .186 E1
Clitheroes La PR4 . . . . . . .92 B6
Clive Ave FY8 . . . . .109 E1
Clive Lo PR8 . . . . .33 F2
Clive Rd Penwortham PR1 . .95 B6
Southport PR8 . . . . .33 F2
Clive St BB12 . . . . .126 F8
Clockhouse Ave BB10 . . .147 D3
Clockhouse Ct BB10 . . . .147 D3
Clockhouse Gr BB10 . . . .147 D3
Clod La BB4 . . . . .67 C8
Clods Carr La FY6 . . . . . .194 F3
Clog Heads BB8 . . . . .170 C2
Clogger La BD23 . . . . . . .201 F7
Cloister Dr BB3 . . . . .81 C1
Cloister Gn L37 . . . . .12 B2
Cloisters LA3 . . . . .212 F2
Cloisters The
Blackpool FY3 . . . . .129 E5
Formby L37 . . . . .11 F3
2 Leyland PR5 . . . . .76 C2
3 Preston PR2 . . . . .95 D8
Tarleton PR4 . . . . .56 A6
Whalley BB7 . . . . .143 D5
Clorain Cl L33 . . . . .1 A3
Clorain Rd L33 . . . . .1 A3
Close The Banks PR9 . . . . .54 A5
Clayton-le-M BB5 . . . . . . .123 F4
Cleveleys FY5 . . . . .172 D2
Cleveleys, Rossall
Beach FY5 . . . . .172 D4
Fulwood PR2 . . . . .117 E6
Garstang PR3 . . . . .199 B1
Haslingden BB5 . . . . .84 A8
Ince Blundell L38 . . . . .3 E3
Kirkham PR4 . . . . .113 B4
New Longton PR4 . . . . . . .75 A7
Weeton PR4 . . . . .131 C2
Withnell Fold PR6 . . . . . . .78 C3
Clough Acre PR7 . . . . .60 A2

Clough Ave PR1 . . . . .96 B3
Clough Bank BB7 . . . . . . .187 D5
Clough End Rd BB4 . . . . . .84 B5
Clough Fold Cty Prim Sch
WN8 . . . . .18 C2
Clough Head Visitor Ctr
BB4 . . . . .83 A3
Clough La
Hesketh Lane PR3 . . . . . .161 A7
Simonstone BB7 . . . . . . .144 F1
Clough Rd Bacup OL13 . . . .87 A3
Nelson BB9 . . . . .148 A8
Clough St **8** Bacup OL13 . . .69 D8
Burnley BB11 . . . . .126 D5
Darwen BB3 . . . . .64 C6
6 Newchurch BB4 . . . . . .85 F1
Clough Terr BB18 . . . . . . .200 B1
Clough The
Clayton Green PR6 . . . . . .77 A3
Darwen BB3 . . . . .64 C6
Clougha Ave Halton LA2 . .214 F7
Lancaster LA1 . . . . .211 B6
Cloughfield PR1 . . . . .95 D1
Cloughfold Cty Prim Sch
BB4 . . . . .85 C2
Cloughton Terr **31** FY1 . . .129 F6
Cloughwood Cres WN6 . . . .19 D6
Clovelly Ave
Blackpool FY5 . . . . .150 D6
Fulwood PR2 . . . . .116 D2
Clovelly Dr Newburgh WN8 .26 A1
Penwortham PR1 . . . . .95 A5
Skelmersdale WN8 . . . . . .18 A8
Southport PR8 . . . . .20 E8
Clover Ave FY8 . . . . .110 A1
Clover Crescent BB12 . . .126 D8
Clover Ct Blackpool FY2 . .150 F6
Southport PR8 . . . . .34 E5
Clover Dr PR4 . . . . .92 D7
Clover Field PR6 . . . . .77 B2
Clover Hill Rd BB9 . . . . . .147 F2
Clover Mews FY3 . . . . . . .129 E6
Clover Rd PR7 . . . . .42 A5
Clover St OL13 . . . . .87 A3
Clover Terr BB3 . . . . .81 A3
Cloverfield PR1 . . . . .95 B4
Cloverfields BB1 . . . . .101 A6
Cloverhill Ho BB9 . . . . . . .147 F7
Club La PR3 . . . . .182 E3
Club St Bamber Bridge PR5 .76 F7
Cornholme OL14 . . . . . . .108 B1
Clucas Gdns L39 . . . . .15 E6
Clyde St Blackburn BB2 . . .100 B3
4 Blackpool FY1 . . . . . .129 B7
Preston PR2 . . . . .95 C8
Clydesdale Pl PR5 . . . . . .75 C2
Clyffes Farm Cl L40 . . . . . .23 A7
Co-operation St
Bacup OL13 . . . . .87 A2
Newchurch BB4 . . . . .85 E7
3 Rake Foot BB4 . . . . . .85 A7
Rawtenstall BB4 . . . . .85 B5
Co-operative Bldgs BB10 106 F8
Co-operative St
1 Bamber Bridge PR5 . . . .76 E8
10 Barnoldswick BB18 . . .200 B2
Haslingden BB4 . . . . .66 F7
Coach Ho Ct L40 . . . . .24 E3
Coach Mews LA4 . . . . . . .212 C4
Coach Rd Bickerstaffe L39 . . .7 F1
Church BB5 . . . . .102 E5
Warton, Carnforth LA5 . . .217 D7
Coal Clough Jun
& Inf Sch BB11 . . . . .126 D5
Coal Clough La BB11 . . . .126 E4
Coal Clough Rd OL14 . . . .108 B2
Coal Hey BB4 . . . . .84 B3
Coal Hey St **18** BB4 . . . . . .84 B3
Coal Pit La Accrington BB5 102 F4
Bacup OL13 . . . . .87 B2
Barnoldswick BB7 . . . . . .190 B7
Colne BB8 . . . . .169 F4
Darwen BB3 . . . . .80 B3
Gisburn BB7 . . . . .225 D2
Rawtenstall BB4 . . . . .86 A4
Skelmersdale L39 . . . . . . .148 A8
Coal Rd BL0 . . . . .50 C8
Coal St **12** BB11 . . . . . . .126 F6
Coastal Dr LA2 . . . . .215 E2
Coastal Rd
Hest Bank LA2,LA5 . . . . .215 F2
Morecambe LA4 . . . . . . .213 B8
Southport, Birkdale PR8 . . .33 C3
Southport, Woodvale PR8 . .20 A4
Coastal Rise LA2 . . . . . . .215 E2
Coastline Mews PR9 . . . . .53 A4
Coates Ave BB18 . . . . . . .200 C3
Coates Fields BB18 . . . . .200 C4
Coates La BB18 . . . . .200 C4
Coates Lane Prim Sch
BB18 . . . . .200 D3
Cob Castle Rd BB4 . . . . . .83 E3
Cob La BB8,BB18 . . . . . . .192 B4
Cob Moor Ave WN5 . . . . . .10 D1
Cob Moor Rd WN5 . . . . . . .10 D1
Cobb's Brow L40 . . . . .17 F5
Cobb's Brow La WN8 . . . . .18 B6
Cobb's Clough Rd L40 . . . .17 F7
Cobbled Court Yd LA1 . . .210 E7
Cobbs Brow
Cty Prim Sch WN8 . . . . . .18 A3
Cobbs La BB5 . . . . .82 E8
Cobden Ct **3** BB1 . . . . . .100 E5
Cobden Ho BB4 . . . . .85 D1
Cobden Rd PR9 . . . . .35 A6
Cobden St Bacup OL13 . . . .70 D8
Barnoldswick BB18 . . . . .200 B1
Brierfield BB10 . . . . .147 F3

Cin-Col 251

Cobden St continued
Burnley BB10 . . . . .127 B8
4 Bury BL9 . . . . .32 A3
Chorley PR6 . . . . .60 E1
10 Darwen BB3 . . . . . . .64 A8
Egerton BL7 . . . . .46 D2
Hapton BB12 . . . . .125 C4
Nelson BB9 . . . . .147 D7
Padiham BB12 . . . . .145 D1
Cobham Ct **2** BB4 . . . . . .85 E1
Cobham Rd BB5 . . . . .103 D5
Cobourg Cl BB2 . . . . .100 F2
Cochran St **24** BB3 . . . . . .81 A1
Cock Hall La OL12 . . . . . . .51 C8
Cock Robin PR5 . . . . .57 C2
Cock Robin La PR3 . . . . . .178 D2
Cocker Ave FY6 . . . . .152 A2
Cocker Bar Rd PR5 . . . . . .57 C8
Cocker Rd PR5 . . . . .75 C1
Cocker Rd PR5 . . . . .77 B7
Cocker Sq **3** FY1 . . . . . . .129 B6
Darwen BB3 . . . . .64 C7
Cockerham Parochial
CE Prim Sch LA2 . . . . . .203 D4
Cockerham Rd
Garstang PR3 . . . . .199 B1
Potters Brook LA2,PR3 . . .204 B4
Cockerham Wlk FY3 . . . . .130 A8
Cockerill St BB4 . . . . .84 B4
Cockermouth Cl BB7 . . . . .80 F7
Cockersand Ave PR4 . . . . .94 C1
Cockersand Dr LA1 . . . . .211 A3
Cockhall La OL12 . . . . .70 C1
Cockhill La BB8 . . . . .170 B8
Cocking Yd LA6 . . . . .234 C7
Cockle Dick's La PR4 . . . .52 E2
Cockleach Lane Ends
PR3 . . . . .160 A2
Cockridge Cl BB2 . . . . . . .80 B7
Cockshot La LA7 . . . . . . .237 F4
Codale Ave FY2 . . . . .150 D5
Coddington St BB1 . . . . . .101 B5
Coe La PR4 . . . . .56 A5
Cog La BB11 . . . . .126 D4
Cog St BB11 . . . . .126 D5
Colbran St Burnley BB10 . .127 B8
10 Nelson BB9 . . . . .168 F2
Colburne Cl L40 . . . . .24 F5
Colchester Ave LA1 . . . . .211 B5
Colchester Dr **6** FY5 . . . .172 F4
Colchester Rd
Blackpool FY3 . . . . .129 F3
Southport PR8 . . . . .34 F3
Cold Bath St **4** PR1 . . . . .95 E8
Cold Well La LA7 . . . . . . .237 F1
Coldale Ct **4** FY4 . . . . . .109 B6
Coldstream Pl BB2 . . . . . .100 D7
Coldweather Ave BB9 . . . .147 F5
Coldwell Inn Activity Ctr
BB10 . . . . .149 A5
Cole Cres L39 . . . . .6 C3
Colebatch PR2 . . . . .116 D5
Coleman St **4** BB9 . . . . . .147 F8
Colenso Rd Blackburn BB1 100 D7
Fulwood PR2 . . . . .116 C2
Coleridge Ave FY5 . . . . . .173 A3
Coleridge Cl Colne BB8 . . .169 D6
Cottam PR4 . . . . .115 E4
Coleridge Dr BB5 . . . . . . .103 E8
Coleridge Pl BB6 . . . . . . .123 E4
Coleridge Rd
Blackpool FY1 . . . . .129 D6
Longshaw WN5 . . . . .10 D1
Ramsbottom BL8 . . . . .48 F2
Coleridge St BB2 . . . . . . .100 C3
Coles Dr LA5 . . . . .237 B1
Colesberg Ct LA5 . . . . . . .237 B2
Coleshill Ave BB10 . . . . . .127 D5
Colesville Ave FY5 . . . . . .173 B1
Colin St Barnoldswick BB18 200 B3
Burnley BB11 . . . . .126 D5
Colinmander Gdns L39 . . . .15 C3
Colinton WN8 . . . . .9 E7
Colldale Terr BB4 . . . . .84 B2
College Ave Cleveleys FY5 172 C1
Formby L37 . . . . .11 E4
College Cl Formby L37 . . . .11 D4
Longridge PR3 . . . . .139 A3
Padiham BB12 . . . . .125 D6
Southport PR8 . . . . .34 A3
College Ct Accrington BB5 103 A6
4 Blackpool FY1 . . . . . .129 C4
Fulwood PR1 . . . . .116 F2
College Gate FY5 . . . . . . .172 C5
College Path L37 . . . . .11 D5
College Rd WN8 . . . . .19 B1
College St Accrington BB5 .103 A6
7 Cornholme OL14 . . . .108 C1
Collegiate High Sch FY3 .151 A1
Collier St BB5 . . . . .103 A6
Collier's La L39 . . . . .238 E3
Collier's Row BB1 . . . . . . .101 F1
Colliers St BB5 . . . . .102 E5
Collin's Hill La PR3 . . . . . .182 A3
Colling St **9** BL0 . . . . .49 B5
Collinge Fold La BB4 . . . . .84 F4
Collinge St Padiham BB12 .125 C7
Rawtenstall BB4 . . . . .84 F4
Collingham Pk LA1 . . . . . .211 A2
Collingwood BB5 . . . . . . .123 E2
Collingwood Ave
Blackpool FY3 . . . . .129 E6
Lytham St Anne's FY8 . . . .109 E1

Collingwood Pl FY3 .... 129 E6
Collingwood Rd PR7 .... 42 B7
Collingwood St
Colne BB8 .... 169 C4
Standish WN6 .... 28 E1
Collingwood Terr 7 LA2 .... 233 D8
Collins Ave FY2 .... 150 E3
Collins Dr BB5 .... 103 E2
Collins Rd PR5 .... 96 F1
Collins Rd N PR5 .... 96 F2
Collinson St PR1 .... 117 C1
Collisdene Rd WN5 .... 10 E6
Collison Ave PR7 .... 42 C8
Collyhurst Ave FY4 .... 109 E6
Colman Ct PR1 .... 95 D6
Colnbrook WN6 .... 28 B1
Colne & Broughton Rd
BD23 .... 201 C6
Colne Coll of F Ed BB8 .... 169 A5
Colne Golf Course BB8 .... 170 B8
Colne La BB8 .... 169 E4
Colne Rd
Barnoldswick BB18 .... 200 A1
Barrowford BB8,BB9 .... 168 F4
Brierfield BB9 .... 147 B6
Burnley BB10,BB11 .... 127 A8
Burnley, Burnley Lane BB10 .... 147 B3
Sough BB18 .... 192 A7
Trawden BB8 .... 170 B2
Colne Sta BB8 .... 169 C4
Colt House Cl PR5 .... 59 A7
Colthirst Dr BB7 .... 187 A2
Coltsfoot Dr PR6 .... 60 D2
Coltsfoot Wlk LA3 .... 212 E2
Columbia Way BB2 .... 100 B8
Columbine Cl Chorley PR7 .... 60 A3
Rochdale OL12 .... 51 C3
Colville Ave 1 FY4 .... 109 C5
Colville Rd BB3 .... 80 E4
Colville St BB10 .... 127 A8
Colwall Cl L33 .... 1 A2
Colwall Rd L33 .... 1 A2
Colwall Wlk L33 .... 1 A2
Colwyn Ave Blackpool FY4 .... 129 E1
Morecambe LA4 .... 212 G6
Colwyn Pl PR2 .... 116 A3
Colyton Cl PR6 .... 42 E8
Colyton Rd PR6 .... 42 E8
Colyton Rd E 2 PR6 .... 42 E8
Combermere Gr LA3 .... 208 E5
Combermere Rd LA3 .... 208 E6
Comer Gdns L31 .... 5 C3
Comet Rd PR5 .... 75 C2
Comet St OL13 .... 87 A7
Commerce St Bacup OL13 .... 86 F2
Haslingden BB4 .... 84 A4
Commercial Rd
Chorley PR7 .... 60 C1
Great Harwood BB6 .... 123 C5
Nelson BB9 .... 147 E8
Commercial St Bacup OL13 .... 69 D8
Barnoldswick BB18 .... 200 B2
10 Blackpool FY1 .... 129 B1
Brierfield BB9 .... 147 B6
7 Church BB5 .... 102 E6
12 Great Harwood BB6 .... 123 C5
Oswaldtwistle BB5 .... 102 D3
Rawtenstall BB4 .... 105 A3
Rishton BB1 .... 123 B1
Common Bank
Employment Area PR7 .... 41 F8
Common Bank La PR7 .... 41 F8
Common Edge Rd FY4 .... 109 F6
Common End PR7 .... 29 E5
Common Gdn St 36 LA1 .... 210 F8
Common La PR9 .... 54 C1
Common The Adlington PR7 .... 29 E5
Parbold WN8 .... 26 C3
Commons La BB2 .... 120 B5
Commonside FY8 .... 89 D4
Commonwealth Cl FY8 .... 89 C8
Como Ave BB11 .... 126 C4
Company St 7 BB1 .... 123 B1
Compley Ave FY6 .... 151 C2
Compley Gn FY6 .... 151 C2
Compression Rd LA3 .... 208 E2
Compston Ave BB4 .... 105 A1
Compton Cl FY6 .... 151 C5
Compton Gn PR2 .... 116 D7
Compton Rd PR8 .... 34 B3
Comrie Cres BB11 .... 126 D3
Concorde Ho 1 FY1 .... 129 C4
Concourse Sh Ctr WN8 .... 18 B1
Conder Ave FY5 .... 172 F2
Conder Brow LA5 .... 217 E2
Conder Green Rd LA2 .... 206 F3
Conder Pl 3 LA1 .... 213 E2
Conder Rd PR2 .... 115 E1
Condor Gr Blackpool FY1 .... 129 D3
Lytham St Anne's FY8 .... 88 E8
Conduit St BB9 .... 168 D1
Coneygarth La
Tunstall LA6 .... 235 D4
Whittington LA6 .... 235 D6
Congleton Cl FY4 .... 130 B1
Congress St PR7 .... 60 C1
Conifer Ct L37 .... 12 A2
Conifers The Barton PR3 .... 136 B8
Hambleton FY6 .... 174 B2
Kirkham PR4 .... 113 B5
Maghull L31 .... 5 C3
Conisber Cl BL7 .... 46 E1
Coniston Ave
Accrington BB5 .... 102 F4
Adlington PR6 .... 30 B8

Coniston Ave *continued*
Barnoldswick BB18 .... 200 A3
Carleton FY6 .... 151 B4
Euxton PR7 .... 59 D1
Fleetwood FY7 .... 193 E4
Fulwood PR2 .... 116 D2
Hambleton FY6 .... 174 C2
Knott End-on-S FY6 .... 194 E6
Lytham St Anne's FY8 .... 109 F2
Orrell WN5 .... 10 F7
Padiham BB12 .... 145 C2
Thornton FY5 .... 173 B1
Coniston Cl Longridge PR3 .... 139 A5
Ramsbottom BL0 .... 49 C7
Coniston Cres FY5 .... 173 B1
Coniston Ct
Morecambe LA4 .... 212 F6
Southport PR8 .... 20 C3
Coniston Dr
Bamber Bridge PR5 .... 96 E2
Darwen BB3 .... 81 C2
Coniston Gr BB8 .... 170 A6
Coniston Ho PR1 .... 95 B4
Coniston Rd
Blackburn BB1 .... 101 A8
Blackpool FY4 .... 109 C7
Blackrod BL6 .... 30 D3
Bolton-le-S LA5 .... 216 A4
Carnforth LA5 .... 216 E8
Chorley PR7 .... 42 B6
Formby L37 .... 11 D2
Fulwood PR2 .... 117 C4
Lancaster LA1 .... 214 A2
Maghull L31 .... 5 E2
Morecambe LA4 .... 212 F6
Coniston St 8 BB12 .... 126 C6
Coniston Way Bacup OL13 .... 87 A4
Croston PR5 .... 57 B3
Rainford Junction WA11 .... 8 F2
Rishton BB1 .... 122 F1
Connaught Rd
Heysham LA3 .... 208 D5
Lancaster LA1 .... 211 B5
Preston PR1 .... 95 E5
Consett Ave FY5 .... 172 E5
Constable Ave
Bamber Bridge PR5 .... 76 A7
Burnley BB11 .... 126 F3
Constable Lee Cres BB4 .... 85 A4
Constable Lee St Paul's
CE Sch BB4 .... 85 A4
Constable St 7 PR1 .... 96 A8
Convent Cl
Bamber Bridge PR5 .... 96 D1
Leyland PR5 .... 76 C2
Ormskirk L39 .... 15 E2
Convent Cres FY3 .... 130 A8
Conway Ave
Bamber Bridge PR5 .... 96 A1
Blackburn BB1 .... 100 E7
Cleveleys FY5 .... 172 D2
Clitheroe BB7 .... 164 C6
Leyland PR5 .... 59 C8
Normoss FY3 .... 130 B7
Conway Cl Catterall PR3 .... 178 D2
Euxton PR7 .... 59 E1
Haslingden BB4 .... 84 B1
Ramsbottom BL0 .... 49 B6
Conway Cres
Barnoldswick BB18 .... 200 C3
Ramsbottom BL8 .... 48 F2
Conway Ct PR5 .... 97 D2
Conway Dr Bury BL9 .... 32 D2
Fulwood PR2 .... 116 C6
Oswaldtwistle BB5 .... 102 B4
Conway Gr BB10 .... 147 C3
Conway Ho 7 PR1 .... 96 D8
Conway Rd Eccleston PR7 .... 40 C7
Rawtenstall BB4 .... 85 C2
Conyers Ave PR8 .... 33 F3
Cook Gdns BB1 .... 101 B4
Cook Green La PR3 .... 140 C7
Cook House Rd BB8 .... 169 E6
Cook St BL9 .... 32 A2
Cooke St BL6 .... 31 D4
Cookson Cl PR4 .... 92 B6
Cookson Rd FY5 .... 173 B3
Cookson St FY1 .... 129 C5
Cookwood Ho 13 PR1 .... 95 D8
Coolham La BB18 .... 201 D1
Coolidge Ave LA1 .... 210 D7
Coombes The PR2 .... 116 F5
Coop St FY1 .... 129 B3
Cooper Ct FY5 .... 172 D3
Cooper Hill Cl PR5 .... 96 D5
Cooper Hill Dr PR5 .... 96 D5
Cooper Rd PR1 .... 95 D8
Cooper St Bacup OL13 .... 86 F4
Burnley BB11 .... 127 A5
Horwich BL6 .... 31 B4
Nelson BB9 .... 168 E1
Cooper's La PR7 .... 27 B8
Cooper's Way FY1 .... 129 D7
Coopers Cl 4 BB5 .... 102 D3
Coote La PR5 .... 75 F7
Cop La Fleetwood FY7 .... 194 A4
Penwortham PR1 .... 95 C4
Cop Lane CE Prim Sch
PR1 .... 95 C3
Cop Rd PR8 .... 34 F5
Cop Royd Terr BB10 .... 127 F1
Cop The FY5 .... 172 D6
Copeland Dr WN6 .... 28 F1
Copeland Pl FY8 .... 90 C4
Copp La PR3,PR4 .... 154 A2
Copper Beech Cl PR4 .... 73 E3
Copperas La BL6 .... 30 B1
Copperfield Cl BB10 .... 127 F6

Copperfield St BB1 .... 100 F3
Copperwood Way PR7 .... 41 F7
Coppice Ave BB5 .... 103 D7
Coppice Brow LA5 .... 217 F2
Coppice Cl Chorley PR6 .... 60 E1
Nelson BB9 .... 169 A2
Coppice Dr Longshaw WN5 .... 10 D2
Whitworth OL12 .... 51 D7
Coppice La PR6,PR7 .... 61 C3
Coppice Leys L37 .... 11 E3
Coppice St BL9 .... 32 C3
Coppice The
Blackburn BB2 .... 100 A7
Clayton-le-M BB5 .... 123 F4
Fulwood PR2 .... 116 B4
Kirkham PR4 .... 113 A6
Longton PR4 .... 74 A7
Morecambe LA4 .... 213 A5
Ramsbottom BL0 .... 49 A4
Coppingford Cl OL12 .... 51 A2
Coppins Gn FY6 .... 151 E1
Coppull & District
Cty Prim Sch PR7 .... 41 E1
Coppull Cross Rds PR7 .... 28 F7
Coppull Hall La PR7 .... 42 A1
Coppull Moor La PR7 .... 28 E6
Coppull Parish Church
Prim Sch PR7 .... 41 F1
Coppull Rd Chorley PR7 .... 42 A4
Maghull L31 .... 5 C4
Copse Rd FY7 .... 193 F2
Copse The Accrington BB5 .... 102 F5
Chorley PR7 .... 42 B4
Edgworth BL7 .... 47 C2
Copster Dr PR3 .... 139 B7
Copster Hill Cl BB1 .... 81 D8
Copthurst Ave BB12 .... 145 F6
Copthurst La PR6 .... 60 F7
Copthurst St 18 BB12 .... 145 C1
Coptrod Head Cl OL12 .... 51 E4
Copy Bottom BB10 .... 107 C4
Copy La LA2 .... 231 C3
Copy Nook BB1 .... 101 A5
Coral Cl FY4 .... 130 A1
Corbridge Cl
Blackpool FY4 .... 110 A7
Carleton FY6 .... 151 C5
Corbridge Ct BB7 .... 186 E1
Corcas La FY6 .... 173 F8
Cork Rd LA1 .... 211 B5
Cork St BL9 .... 32 A2
Corka La FY8 .... 111 F1
Corke Cotts FY8 .... 111 E1
Corlass St 10 BB9 .... 168 D3
Corless Cotts LA2 .... 220 A8
Corn Mill La FY7 .... 194 B4
Corn Mill Lo L31 .... 5 C2
Corn Mill Yd BB5 .... 123 F2
Cornbrook WN8 .... 9 E7
Corncroft PR1 .... 95 C3
Cornel Gr BB11 .... 126 C4
Cornelian St BB1 .... 121 F2
Corner Bank Cl PR4 .... 111 F7
Corners The FY5 .... 172 C4
Cornfield PR4 .... 115 E6
Cornfield Cl PR4 .... 72 E4
Cornfield Gr BB12 .... 126 A8
Cornfield St BB3 .... 81 B2
Cornflower Cl PR6 .... 60 D2
Cornford Rd FY4 .... 110 B8
Cornhill 8 BB5 .... 103 C6
Cornhill Arc BB5 .... 103 B6
Cornholme BB10 .... 147 E2
Cornholme Jun
& Infs Sch OL14 .... 108 A1
Cornholme Terr 9 OL14 .... 108 B1
Cornmill Terr 6 BB18 .... 200 B3
Cornthwaite Rd PR2 .... 116 E3
Cornwall Ave
Blackburn BB1 .... 101 E4
Blackpool FY2 .... 150 C2
Cleveleys FY5 .... 172 F4
Cornwall Cres WN1 .... 29 B1
Cornwall Pl Blackpool FY3 .... 130 B2
Church BB5 .... 102 F7
Cornwall Rd BB1 .... 123 A1
Cornwall Way PR8 .... 20 C2
Corona Ave L31 .... 5 C5
Coronation Ave
Blackburn BB2 .... 79 C7
Formby L37 .... 12 A2
Forton PR3 .... 204 B3
Padiham BB12 .... 125 C7
Coronation Cres 5 PR1 .... 96 B7
Coronation Gr BB4 .... 85 E1
Coronation Pl 6 BB9 .... 168 D3
Coronation Rd
Brierfield BB9 .... 147 C5
Cleveleys FY5 .... 172 C2
Kirkham PR4 .... 113 A5
Lytham St Anne's FY8 .... 89 C4
Maghull L31 .... 5 D3
Coronation St
Barnoldswick BB18 .... 200 C2
Blackpool FY1 .... 129 B4
Great Harwood BB6 .... 123 D6
Coronation Terr BB6 .... 142 C1
Coronation Way LA1 .... 214 A4
Coronation Wlk PR8 .... 34 A7
Corporation St
Accrington BB5 .... 103 A5
10 Blackburn BB2 .... 100 E5
Blackpool FY1 .... 129 B5
Chorley PR6 .... 60 D1
6 Clitheroe BB7 .... 164 D8
Nelson BB8 .... 169 A3
Preston PR1 .... 95 F8
4 Southport PR8 .... 34 B7

Corpus Christi
RC High Sch PR2 .... 116 E5
Corranstone Cl BL6 .... 31 B3
Corrib Rd FY2 .... 150 D2
Corringham Rd LA4 .... 212 E5
Corston Gr BL6 .... 30 D1
Corwen Cl BB1 .... 100 E7
Cosford St PR4 .... 131 E6
Cotswold Ave PR7 .... 59 D1
Cotswold Cl Eccleston PR7 .... 40 D6
Ramsbottom BL0 .... 49 C4
Cotswold Dr BL6 .... 31 C5
Cotswold Rd
Blackpool FY2 .... 150 D1
Chorley PR7 .... 42 C6
Lytham St Anne's FY8 .... 90 D5
Cottage Cl L39 .... 15 D4
Cottage Fields PR7 .... 42 B5
Cottage La
Bamber Bridge PR5 .... 96 F3
Ormskirk L39 .... 15 D5
Cottage Mews L39 .... 15 D5
Cottage Wlk OL12 .... 51 C4
Cottam Ave PR2 .... 116 A4
Cottam Cl
Lytham St Anne's FY8 .... 109 F2
Whalley BB7 .... 143 C5
Cottam Ct PR2 .... 116 A2
Cottam Cty Prim
Sch PR4 .... 115 D5
Cottam Gn PR4 .... 115 F6
Cottam Hall La PR2 .... 115 F5
Cottam La PR2 .... 116 A2
Cottam Pl FY6 .... 151 C2
Cottam St PR7 .... 42 C6
Cottam Way PR4 .... 115 D4
Cottesloe Pl BB9 .... 168 C3
Cottesmore Pl FY3 .... 130 A6
Cottom Croft BB5 .... 123 F4
Cotton Ct Colne BB8 .... 169 C3
Preston PR1 .... 96 A8
Cotton Dr L39 .... 15 D6
Cotton Hall St BB3 .... 81 A2
Cotton St Accrington BB5 .... 103 B5
Burnley BB12 .... 126 D7
Padiham BB12 .... 125 C7
Cotton Tree La BB8 .... 170 A5
Cottys Brow PR9 .... 52 F3
Coudray Rd PR9 .... 52 E1
Coulston Ave FY2 .... 150 B3
Coulston Rd LA1 .... 211 B6
Coultate St 7 BB12 .... 126 C6
Coulter Beck La LA6 .... 236 A7
Coulthurst St 1 BL0 .... 49 B6
Coulton Rd BB9 .... 147 B7
Counsell Ct 3 FY5 .... 173 B2
Countess Cl PR4 .... 113 A7
Countess Cres FY2 .... 150 C3
Countess Rd BB3 .... 81 A7
Countess St BB5 .... 103 A6
Countess Way PR7 .... 59 D2
Countessway 3 PR5 .... 96 E1
Country Side Ctr BB4 .... 84 E1
County Brook La
BB8,BB18 .... 191 C4
County Cl PR5 .... 76 A4
County Rd Kirkby L32 .... 1 A1
Ormskirk L39 .... 15 E6
County St LA1 .... 210 E8
Coupe Gn PR5 .... 97 E4
Coupe Green
Cty Prim Sch PR5 .... 97 E4
Coupland St OL12 .... 51 C8
Courage Low La WN6 .... 27 D5
Course La L40,WN8 .... 25 D1
Court Gr BB1 .... 121 E6
Court Hey L31 .... 5 E1
Court Mews PR9 .... 53 A1
Court Rd PR9 .... 34 C8
Court Royal FY8 .... 89 E3
Court The Fulwood PR2 .... 116 C7
Penwortham PR1 .... 95 C4
Southport PR9 .... 34 B8
Courtfield L39 .... 15 D7
Courtfield Ave FY2 .... 129 D8
Courtfields 3 FY1 .... 129 C4
Courtgreen L39 .... 15 D7
Courtyard The
8 Bacup OL13 .... 87 A3
1 Kirkham PR4 .... 112 F5
Courtyard Wks L33 .... 1 C2
Cousin's La L40 .... 38 A3
Cove Dr LA5 .... 218 C4
Cove Rd LA5 .... 218 B4
Cove The Cleveleys FY5 .... 172 C4
Lytham St Anne's FY8 .... 89 D3
Morecambe LA4 .... 213 A7
Covell Ho 3 LA1 .... 210 E8
Coventry St 2 PR7 .... 42 C6
Coverdale Dr BB2 .... 79 D7
Coverdale Rd LA1 .... 210 D8
Coverdale Way BB12 .... 126 D7
Covert The FY5 .... 172 F4
Coveway Ave FY3 .... 129 E6
Cow Gate La BD23 .... 225 E7
Cow Well La PR6 .... 60 B8
Cowan Brae BB1 .... 100 D6
Cowdrey Mews 8 LA1 .... 213 D1
Cowell Way BB2 .... 100 D5
Cowes Ave BB4 .... 84 C2
Cowgarth La BB18 .... 201 C2
Cowgill St 16 Bacup OL13 .... 87 A3
Earby BB18 .... 201 B1
Cowhill La BB1 .... 101 F7
Cowley Cres BB12 .... 125 E7
Cowley Rd Blackpool FY4 .... 109 F8
Fulwood PR2 .... 117 E4
Cowling Brow PR6 .... 42 E7

Cowling Brow Ind Est PR6 .... 42 F6
Cowling La PR5 .... 75 D1
Cowling Rd PR6 .... 42 F6
Cowm Park Way N OL12 .... 70 D2
Cowm Park Way S OL12 .... 70 C1
Cowm St OL12 .... 70 E5
Cowpe Rd BB4 .... 68 F7
Cowper Ave BB7 .... 186 E1
Cowper Pl BB7 .... 224 C1
Cowper St Blackburn BB1 .... 100 F7
Burnley BB11 .... 126 C5
Cowslip Way PR6 .... 60 D2
Cowtoot La OL13 .... 87 A4
Cox Green Cl BL7 .... 46 D3
Cox Green Rd BL7 .... 46 E2
Coxfield WN6 .... 19 D7
Coyford Dr PR9 .... 53 A4
Crab Tree La PR3 .... 176 C2
Crabtree Ave Bacup OL13 .... 87 A1
Newchurch BB4 .... 85 F2
Penwortham PR1 .... 95 A3
Crabtree Bldgs BB4 .... 85 F4
Crabtree Cl L40 .... 24 D4
Crabtree La L40 .... 24 D6
Crabtree Orch 2 FY5 .... 173 B3
Crabtree Rd FY5 .... 173 B3
Crabtree St Blackburn BB1 .... 101 B5
Brierfield BB9 .... 147 B5
Bury BL9 .... 32 B3
Colne BB8 .... 169 C4
Whitewell Bottom BB4 .... 85 F4
Cracoe Gill BB9 .... 168 C3
Craddock Rd BB8 .... 169 E5
Crag Ave BL9 .... 49 D2
Crag Bank Cres LA5 .... 216 C8
Crag Bank La LA5 .... 217 B1
Crag Fold BL9 .... 49 D2
Crag La BL9 .... 49 D2
Crag Rd Lancaster LA1 .... 214 B1
Warton, Carnforth LA5 .... 217 A6
Cragg Row BB18 .... 191 D7
Cragg St 1 Blackpool FY1 .... 129 B3
Colne BB8 .... 169 C5
Cragg's Row 17 PR1 .... 95 F8
Craggs La LA2 .... 233 D3
Craig St LA3 .... 212 A3
Craigflower Ct PR5 .... 77 C7
Craiglands Ave LA3 .... 212 A2
Craiglands Ct LA1 .... 210 C5
Crail Pl OL10 .... 32 F1
Crake Ave FY7 .... 193 C2
Crake Bank 4 LA1 .... 213 C2
Cranberry Chase 4 BB3 .... 64 C7
Cranberry Cl BB3 .... 64 D6
Cranberry La BB3 .... 64 D6
Cranberry Rise BB4 .... 105 A2
Cranborne Cl Horwich BL6 .... 31 F1
Standish WN6 .... 28 D1
Cranborne St
5 Bamber Bridge PR5 .... 76 E8
10 Preston PR1 .... 96 C8
Cranborne Terr BB2 .... 100 C6
Cranbourne Dr
Chorley PR6 .... 42 E7
Church BB5 .... 103 A8
Cranbourne Gr FY5 .... 151 E7
Cranbourne St Chorley PR6 .... 42 D7
Colne BB8 .... 169 E6
Cranbrook Ave
Blackpool FY2 .... 150 E5
Oswaldtwistle BB5 .... 102 C4
Cranbrook St BB2 .... 100 D2
Crane St PR7 .... 28 D6
Cranes La L40 .... 16 E7
Cranfield View BB3 .... 64 C6
Crangle Fold BB7 .... 187 A2
Crank Rd WN5 .... 10 D1
Crankshaw St 9 BB4 .... 85 A3
Cranleigh Ave FY2 .... 150 C3
Cranleigh Cl BL6 .... 30 D1
Cranmer St 5 BB11 .... 126 E6
Cranshaw Dr BB1 .... 100 F8
Cranston Rd L33 .... 1 C2
Cranwell Ave LA1 .... 211 B5
Cranwell Cl 2 BB1 .... 101 A4
Cranwell Ct PR4 .... 112 F5
Craven Cl PR2 .... 116 F7
Craven Ct BL6 .... 31 D2
Craven St Accrington BB5 .... 103 A5
6 Barnoldswick BB18 .... 200 C2
Brierfield BB9 .... 147 B5
Burnley BB11 .... 127 A5
Bury BL9 .... 32 C3
Clitheroe BB7 .... 164 E7
Colne BB8 .... 170 A5
Nelson BB9 .... 147 C8
Rawtenstall BB4 .... 84 F2
Craven St E BL6 .... 31 D2
Craven's Ave BB2 .... 80 D6
Craven's Brow BB2 .... 80 E7
Cravendale Ave BB9 .... 168 F3
Cravens Hollow BB2 .... 80 D6
Cravens Hollows BB2 .... 80 E6
Crawford Ave
Adlington PR7 .... 29 E5
Blackpool FY2 .... 150 D5
Chorley PR7 .... 42 B7
Leyland PR5 .... 59 B8
Maghull L31 .... 5 B3
Preston PR1 .... 117 F1
Crawford Cty Sch WN8 .... 9 E3
Crawford Rd WN8 .... 9 D2
Crawford St BB9 .... 168 E1
Crawshaw Dr BB4 .... 85 A6
Crawshaw Grange BB4 .... 85 A7
Crawshaw La BB10 .... 148 D6
Crawshaw St BB5 .... 103 B6
Crawshaw's Bldgs BB4 .... 85 A1

Crawshawbooth
Cty Prim Sch BB4 . . . . . .85 A8
Crediton Ave PR9 . . . . . . .53 B5
Crediton Cl BB2 . . . . .80 C8
Crescent Ave L37 . . . . . . .11 E1
Crescent Ct FY4 . . . . . . .109 A5
Crescent E FY5 . . . . .172 C2
Crescent Gn L39 . . . . .15 B1
Crescent The
  Bamber Bridge PR5 . . . . .96 C2
  Blackburn BB2 . . . . .99 E1
  Blackpool FY4 . . . . .109 B7
  Brierfield BB10 . . . . . . .147 B4
  Carleton FY6 . . . . .151 C4
  Chorley PR7 . . . . .60 C2
  Clitheroe BB7 . . . . .164 D7
  Colne BB8 . . . . .169 E6
  Dunsop Bridge BB7 . . . . .222 C5
  Fleetwood FY7 . . . . . . .172 E8
  Freckleton PR4 . . . . .92 C5
  Hest Bank LA2 . . . . . . .215 D1
  Horwich BL6 . . . . .31 E1
  Lostock Hall PR5 . . . . . . .76 C8
  Lytham St Anne's FY8 . . . .88 E6
  Preesall FY6 . . . . .195 B4
  Preston, A-on-Ribble PR2 .116 B2
  1 Preston, Lea PR2 . . . .115 D1
  Southport PR9 . . . . .53 C3
  Warton PR4 . . . . .91 C4
  Whalley BB7 . . . . .143 A6
  Whitworth OL12 . . . . .51 C8
  Worsthorne BB10 . . . . . .128 A5
Crescent W FY5 . . . . . . .172 D2
Cressell Pk WN6 . . . . .28 B1
Cressingham Wlk LA1 . . . .211 B3
Cresswood Ave FY5 . . . . .172 D1
Crestway Blackpool FY3 . . .129 F6
  Tarleton PR4 . . . . .56 C4
Creswell Ave PR2 . . . . . .115 F3
Creswick Ave BB11 . . . . . .126 F3
Creswick Cl BB11 . . . . . .126 F3
Crewdson St BB3 . . . . . . .80 F2
Crewgarth Rd LA3 . . . . . .212 E2
Cribben End La BB4 . . . . . .84 D4
Cribden House Sch BB4 . . .84 E1
Cribden La BB4 . . . . .84 E5
Cribden St BB4 . . . . .84 B1
Criccieth Cl **3** BB4 . . . . . .84 B1
Crichton Pl FY4 . . . . . . .109 B5
Cricket Path Formby L37 . .11 F5
  Southport PR8 . . . . .33 F3
Cricketers Gn PR7 . . . . . . .40 B6
Crimbles La LA2 . . . . . . .203 B3
Crime Well La LA3 . . . . . .208 F2
Crimea St OL13 . . . . .87 A2
Cringle Way FY7 . . . . . . .187 A2
Cripple Gate WN6 . . . . . . .28 A2
Cripple Gate La PR5 . . . . . .98 C4
Critchley Cl PR4 . . . . .73 F1
Croasdale **1** LA1 . . . . . .213 C2
Croasdale Ave
  Brierfield BB10 . . . . . . .147 C2
  Fulwood PR2 . . . . .117 E4
Croasdale Cl LA5 . . . . . .217 C1
Croasdale Dr
  Cleveleys FY5 . . . . .172 F4
  Clitheroe BB7 . . . . .164 F7
  Parbold WN8 . . . . .26 C3
Croasdale Sq BB1 . . . . . .101 A3
Croasdale Wlk FY3 . . . . . .130 B8
Crockleford Ave PR8 . . . . .34 E3
Crocus Cl BB4 . . . . .66 F8
Crocus Field PR5 . . . . .59 A7
Croft Acres BL0 . . . . .67 D2
Croft Ave Burscough L40 . .24 C4
  Hest Bank LA2 . . . . . . .213 E8
  Orrell WN5 . . . . .10 D5
Croft Bank PR1 . . . . .95 C3
Croft Butts La PR4 . . . . . . .92 C6
Croft Cl BB4 . . . . .85 A5
Croft Ct Fleetwood FY7 . . .193 E2
  Thornton FY5 . . . . .173 C3
Croft Field L31 . . . . .5 E1
Croft Gdns PR4 . . . . .113 A4
Croft Head Rd BB1 . . . . . .122 B1
Croft Hey L40 . . . . .38 B4
Croft Heys L39 . . . . .15 B1
Croft La BB12 . . . . .145 F6
Croft Manor PR4 . . . . .92 C6
Croft Mdw PR5 . . . . .77 C6
Croft Rd PR6 . . . . .42 E7
Croft St Bacup OL13 . . . . . .86 F3
  Burnley BB11 . . . . .127 A5
  Bury BL9 . . . . .32 A2
  Clitheroe BB7 . . . . .164 E7
  17 Darwen BB3 . . . . . . .81 A1
  Earby BB18 . . . . .201 C2
  Great Harwood BB6 . . . . .123 C4
  Morecambe LA4 . . . . . . .212 F5
  10 Preston PR1 . . . . . . .95 D8
  Preston PR1 . . . . .95 E8
Croft The Blackburn BB1 . .100 D7
  Burton in L LA6 . . . . . . .236 C3
  Carnforth LA5 . . . . .217 E6
  Caton LA2 . . . . .231 C3
  Cleveleys FY5 . . . . .172 D2
  Eccleston PR7 . . . . .40 C7
  Euxton PR7 . . . . .59 B3
  Fleetwood FY7 . . . . . . .193 E2
  Garstang PR3 . . . . .199 B1
  Goosnargh PR3 . . . . . . .137 D6
  Great Plumpton PR4 . . . .111 E2
  Hoghton PR5 . . . . .98 B2

Croft The continued
  Lytham St Anne's FY8 . . . .110 B1
  Maghull L31 . . . . .5 B5
  Orrell WN5 . . . . .10 D3
  Poulton-le-F FY6 . . . . . .151 D2
Croft Way FY5 . . . . .151 C8
Crofters Fold Galgate LA2 .207 B4
  Morecambe LA3 . . . . . . .212 B1
  Preston PR1 . . . . .116 C2
Crofters Gn Euxton PR7 . . .59 C3
  Preston PR1 . . . . .116 C2
Crofters La L33 . . . . .1 C7
Crofters Mews **12** FY1 . . .129 C7
Crofters Wlk **4** PR1 . . . . .95 D2
Croftgate PR2 . . . . .116 F5
Croftland Gdns LA5 . . . . .216 B6
Croftlands Borwick LA6 . . .234 B3
  Orrell WN5 . . . . .10 D4
  Ramsbottom BL0 . . . . . . .49 A3
  Warton, Carnforth LA5 . . .217 E6
Crofton Ave L39 . . . . .15 F7
Crofts Cl PR4 . . . . .113 C5
Crofts The PR4 . . . . .94 A1
Croftson Ave L39 . . . . . . .15 F7
Croftwood Terr BB2 . . . . .100 A1
Croichbank BB1 . . . . .48 B2
Croichley Fold BL8 . . . . . . .48 C5
Cromarty Sq OL10 . . . . . . .32 F1
Crombleholme Rd PR1 . . .117 E1
Cromer Ave BB10 . . . . . .147 C1
Cromer Gr BB10 . . . . . . .147 C1
Cromer Pl Blackburn BB1 . .100 E7
  Fulwood PR2 . . . . .117 D2
Cromer Rd Blackpool FY2 . .150 A4
  Lytham St Anne's FY8 . . . .110 A1
  Southport PR8 . . . . .33 E2
Cromfield L39 . . . . .15 C2
Cromford Wlk **9** PR1 . . . .96 C8
Crompton Ave FY4 . . . . . .109 E7
Crompton Ct **10** PR1 . . . . .96 A8
Crompton Pl BB2 . . . . . . .100 C5
Crompton St PR1 . . . . . .117 C1
Cromwell Ave **1** PR1 . . . . .95 C3
Cromwell Cl L39 . . . . .15 C2
Cromwell Rd
  Blackpool FY1 . . . . .129 C7
  Fulwood PR2 . . . . .117 D3
  Lancaster LA1 . . . . .210 E6
  Penwortham PR1 . . . . . . .95 C3
Cromwell St
  Accrington BB5 . . . . . . .103 B8
  20 Blackburn BB1 . . . . .101 A4
  Burnley BB12 . . . . .126 F8
  Foulridge BB8 . . . . .191 D1
  3 Preston PR1 . . . . . . .117 A1
Cromwell Terr **12** BB9 . . .168 D3
Cronkeyshaw Rd OL12 . . . .51 F1
Cronkshaw St BB10 . . . . .127 A7
Cronshaw Dr BB6 . . . . . . .142 C1
Crook Dale La FY6 . . . . . .174 F2
Crook Gate La PR3 . . . . . .175 C1
Crook Nook La L33 . . . . . .209 B2
Crook St Adlington PR7 . . . .29 F7
  Chorley PR7 . . . . .42 B5
  Preston PR1 . . . . .96 B8
Crookall Cl **7** FY7 . . . . . .193 F2
Crooked La PR1 . . . . .96 A8
Crooked Shore OL13 . . . . .86 F3
Crookfield Rd BL7 . . . . . . .63 B3
Crookhalgh Ave BB10 . . . .127 F6
Crookhey Gdns LA2 . . . . .203 E3
Crookhey Hall Sch LA2 . . .203 E3
Crookings La PR1 . . . . . . .95 A6
Crooklands Dr PR3 . . . . . .178 C8
Crookleigh Pl LA3 . . . . . .212 A2
Croos St BB5 . . . . .103 C5
Cropper Gdns PR4 . . . . . . .72 D3
Cropper Rd FY4 . . . . .110 C6
Cropper's La L39 . . . . .16 A1
Cropton Rd L37 . . . . .11 F3
Crosby Cl BB3 . . . . .64 B6
Crosby Cl FY8 . . . . .109 F1
Crosby Gr FY3 . . . . .129 F3
Crosby Pl PR2 . . . . .116 A4
Crosby Rd Blackburn BB2 . .100 C1
  Lytham St Anne's FY8 . . . .109 F1
  Southport PR8 . . . . .34 A4
Crosby St OL12 . . . . .51 F2
Crosfield Ave BL9 . . . . . . .49 C2
Crosier Wlk PR4 . . . . . . .115 E5
Crosland Rd L32 . . . . .1 A1
Crosland Rd N FY8 . . . . . .89 A8
Crosland Rd S FY8 . . . . . .89 A8
Crosley Cl BB5 . . . . .103 B3
Cross Bank 3 BB12 . . . .125 D8
Cross Barn Gr BB3 . . . . . . .64 B8
Cross Barn La L38 . . . . .3 E3
Cross Barn Wlk **5** BB3 . . . .64 B8
Cross Brow PR7 . . . . .41 C8
Cross Edge BB5 . . . . .103 A1
Cross Field PR4 . . . . .94 C1
Cross Flatts Cres BB18 . . .191 E8
Cross Fold BB7 . . . . .187 B8
Cross Gates BB6 . . . . . . .123 C5
Cross Gn L37 . . . . .12 A2
Cross Green Cl L37 . . . . . .12 A2
Cross Green Rd PR2 . . . . .116 E6
Cross Hagg St BB8 . . . . . .169 C4
Cross Halls PR1 . . . . .95 C3
Cross Helliwell St **17**
  BB8 . . . . .169 D4
Cross Hill Ct LA5 . . . . . . .216 A4
Cross Hill
  Four Lane Ends PR3 . . . .220 B6
Cross Hill La BB7 . . . . . . .225 B1
Cross Hos PR7 . . . . .41 C8
Cross Keys Dr PR6 . . . . . .60 C2
Cross La
  Barley Green BB12 . . . . .167 C4

Cross La continued
  Halsall L39 . . . . .22 C1
  Low Bentham LA2 . . . . . .233 B8
  Moor Side PR4 . . . . .133 D1
  Orrell WN5 . . . . .10 D3
  Ramsbottom BL8 . . . . . . .49 A6
  Salterforth BB18 . . . . . .191 E8
  Waddington BB7 . . . . . . .185 E5
Cross Meanygate L40 . . . . .37 C5
Cross Rd LA2 . . . . .233 B7
Cross School St **5** BB8 . .169 D4
Cross Skelton St **6** BB8 . .169 E5
Cross St **4** Bacup OL13 . . .87 A3
  Blackburn BB3 . . . . .80 F7
  Blackpool FY1 . . . . .129 B7
  Brierfield BB7 . . . . .147 B5
  Brierfield, Harle Syke BB10 .147 F3
  Chorley PR7 . . . . .60 C1
  Clayton-le-M BB5 . . . . . .123 E3
  Clitheroe BB7 . . . . .164 D8
  Darwen BB3 . . . . .64 B7
  Earby BB18 . . . . .201 A1
  Fleetwood FY7 . . . . . . .194 B5
  Great Harwood BB6 . . . . .123 D5
  Higham BB12 . . . . .145 F6
  8 Leyland PR5 . . . . . . .76 B2
  Longridge PR3 . . . . .139 A6
  Lytham St Anne's FY8 . . . .88 D8
  Morecambe LA4 . . . . . . .212 F5
  Nelson BB9 . . . . .147 D8
  Oswaldtwistle BB5 . . . . .102 D4
  Preston PR1 . . . . .95 F7
  Ramsbottom BL0 . . . . . . .49 C6
  14 Rawtenstall BB4 . . . . .85 A7
  Southport PR8 . . . . .34 B6
  Standish WN6 . . . . .28 E1
  Worsthorne BB10 . . . . . .128 B6
Cross St N BB4 . . . . .84 B5
Cross St S BB4 . . . . .84 B4
Cross St W BB8 . . . . .169 B4
Cross Swords Cl PR7 . . . . .42 A5
Cross The L38 . . . . .3 E4
Cross Way FY5 . . . . .172 D4
Crossdale Ave LA3 . . . . . .212 A2
Crossdale Sq **10** LA1 . . . .211 A8
Crosse Hall La PR6 . . . . . .42 F7
Crosse Hall St PR6 . . . . . .42 F7
Crossens Way PR9 . . . . . .53 C6
Crossfield Ct LA5 . . . . . . .237 A1
Crossfield Rd WN8 . . . . . . .9 C8
Crossfield St BB2 . . . . . .100 F3
Crosshall Brow L40 . . . . . .16 C4
Crosshall High Sch L39 . . . .16 B5
Crosshill Pl **7** LA1 . . . . .213 D2
Crosshill Rd BB2 . . . . . . .100 B5
Crosshill Sch BB1 . . . . . . .101 C2
Crosshills **5** BB12 . . . . .145 C1
Crossing The PR5 . . . . . . .98 B2
Crossland Rd FY4 . . . . . .129 E1
Crossland St BB5 . . . . . . .103 A5
Crosslands L46 . . . . .235 D7
Crossley Fold BB11 . . . . . .126 D4
Crossways BB7 . . . . .186 D7
Croston Ave PR6 . . . . .30 A8
Croston Barn La PR3 . . . . .178 A8
Croston Cl **6** BB1 . . . . . .101 B5
Croston Close Rd
  BL9,OL12 . . . . .50 C4
Croston Dr L40 . . . . .38 B6
Croston La PR7 . . . . .41 B2
Croston Meth Prim Sch
  PR5 . . . . .57 B2
Croston Rd Croston L40,PR5 38 C7
  Farington PR5 . . . . .75 F6
  Garstang PR3 . . . . .178 B8
  Leyland PR5 . . . . .75 E4
Croston St BB1 . . . . .101 C5
Croston Sta PR5 . . . . .57 B3
Croston's Brow PR9 . . . . . .52 F3
Crow Foot Row BB18 . . . .200 B1
Crow Hills Rd PR1 . . . . . . .95 A6
Crow La Ramsbottom BL0 . . .49 C6
  Skelmersdale WN8 . . . . . .18 F3
  Town End PR3 . . . . .153 E8
Crow Orch Cty Prim Sch
  WN8 . . . . .17 F2
Crow Orchard Rd WN6 . . . .28 A1
Crow Park La BB7 . . . . . .225 C4
Crow Tree Ave **4** OL13 . . .69 B8
Crow Trees Brow BB7 . . . .187 D4
Crow Trees Gdns BB7 . . . .187 D5
Crow Trees La BL7 . . . . . . .47 C7
Crow Wood Ave BB12 . . . .126 D7
Crow Wood Cl BB12 . . . . .126 E7
Crow Wood Rd BB4 . . . . . .67 D6
Crowborough Pl BL6 . . . . . .31 F1
Crowder Ave FY5 . . . . . . .173 B2
Crowell Way PR5 . . . . . . .96 E3
Crowland Cl PR9 . . . . . . .35 A6
Crowland St PR9 . . . . . . .35 A6
Crowland Way L37 . . . . . . .12 B2
Crowle St PR1 . . . . .96 D8
Crown Cl L37 . . . . .12 A2
Crown Gdns BL7 . . . . .47 D6
Crown La Fleetwood FY7 . . .194 B4
  Horwich BL6 . . . . .31 A4
  Swillbrook PR4 . . . . .135 B2
Crown Mews **3** PR4 . . . . .113 A5
Crown Point BL7 . . . . .47 D6
Crown Point Rd BB11 . . . .126 E1
Crown St Accrington BB5 . .103 B5
  3 Chorley PR7 . . . . . . .42 C8
  Darwen BB3 . . . . .64 B4
  Leyland PR5 . . . . .76 B3
  Preston PR1 . . . . .95 F8
Crown Way BB8 . . . . .169 C6
Crowndale BL7 . . . . .47 D7
Crownest Ind Est BB18 . . .200 B3

Crownest Rd BB18 . . . . . .200 C3
Crownlee PR1 . . . . .95 A3
Crowshaw Dr BB5 . . . . . . .103 B7
Crowther St Burnley BB11 . .127 B4
  Clayton-le-M BB5 . . . . . .123 E3
Crowthorn Rd BL7 . . . . . . .66 A1
Crowthorn Sch BL7 . . . . . .65 F1
Crowtrees **3** LA2 . . . . . .233 B8
Crowtrees Gr BB9 . . . . . . .167 F5
Crowtrees Rd BB7 . . . . . .144 F8
Croxteth Cl L31 . . . . .5 E3
Croxton Wlk BL6 . . . . .31 B4
Croyde Cl PR9 . . . . .53 B5
Croyde Rd FY8 . . . . .89 A5
Croydon Rd **6** FY3 . . . . .129 E7
Croydon St BB2 . . . . .100 C5
Crumbleholme Rd PR3 . . .180 E1
Crummock Pl **2** FY4 . . . . .130 C1
Crummock Rd PR2 . . . . . .118 A1
Crumpax Ave PR3 . . . . . .139 A8
Crumpax Gdns PR3 . . . . . .139 A8
Crystal Gr FY8 . . . . .88 C4
Crystal Lodge **3** FY8 . . . . .89 C4
Crystal Rd Blackpool FY1 . .129 C8
  Thornton FY5 . . . . .173 B5
Cub St PR5 . . . . .76 A4
Cuba Ind Est BL0 . . . . . . .49 C8
Cuba St **3** BB9 . . . . .147 D8
Cuckoo Brow BB1 . . . . . . .100 D8
Cuckoo La Bury BL9 . . . . . .32 C2
  Moss Edge PR3 . . . . . . .176 B3
Cuckstool La BB12 . . . . . .146 B3
Cudworth Rd FY8 . . . . . . .109 F1
Cuerdale La PR1,PR5 . . . . .97 D6
Cuerdale St BB10 . . . . . . .147 E3
Cuerden Ave PR5 . . . . . . .58 D7
Cuerden Cl PR5 . . . . .76 E4
Cuerden Rise PR5 . . . . . . .76 C7
Cuerden St Chorley PR6 . . .42 E7
  Colne BB8 . . . . .169 B3
Cuerden Valley Pk PR5 . . . .76 F3
Cuerden Way PR5 . . . . . . .76 D7
Culbeck La PR7 . . . . .58 F2
Culshaw St
  3 Blackburn BB1 . . . . .101 A5
  Burnley BB10 . . . . .127 C5
Culshaw Way L40 . . . . . . .22 F7
Culvert La WN8 . . . . .26 A2
Cumberland Ave
  Blackpool FY1 . . . . .129 D4
  Burnley BB12 . . . . .126 A6
  Clayton-le-M BB5 . . . . . .124 A3
  Cleveleys FY5 . . . . .172 E4
  Leyland PR5 . . . . .58 E7
Cumberland Ho **16** PR1 . . .95 F8
Cumberland Rd PR8 . . . . . .34 E5
Cumberland St
  12 Blackburn BB1 . . . .101 A4
  5 Colne BB8 . . . . .169 E5
  Nelson BB9 . . . . .168 E1
Cumberland View Rd
  LA3 . . . . .212 A3
Cumbrian Ave FY3 . . . . . .129 D4
Cumbrian Way BB12 . . . . .126 B8
Cumeragh La PR3 . . . . . .138 C6
Cummins Ave L37 . . . . . . .11 C5
Cumpstey St BB2 . . . . . . .100 E3
Cuncliffe Ct BB5 . . . . . . .123 F2
Cunliffe Ave BL0 . . . . . . .49 A4
Cunliffe Cl BB1 . . . . .122 B1
Cunliffe Ho BB4 . . . . .85 D1
Cunliffe La BB7 . . . . .143 F8
Cunliffe Rd Blackburn BB1 .122 C1
  Blackpool FY1 . . . . .129 D2
Cunliffe St Chorley PR7 . . .42 D7
  Preston PR1 . . . . .96 A8
  Ramsbottom BL0 . . . . . . .49 C7
Cunnery Meadow PR5 . . . .76 E1
Cunningham Ave PR7 . . . . .42 A6
Cunningham Gr BB12 . . . .126 B6
Cunscough La L31, L39 . . . . .6 C3
Curate St Chorley PR6 . . . .60 E1
  Great Harwood BB6 . . . . .123 C5
Curlew Cl Blackburn BB1 . .100 E8
  2 Cleveleys FY5 . . . . . .172 F4
  Leyland PR5 . . . . .58 C7
  Oswaldtwistle BB5 . . . . .102 D3
Curlew Gdns BB11 . . . . . .126 C5
Curlew Gr LA3 . . . . .208 F5
Curlew La L40 . . . . .37 E2
Curteis St BL6 . . . . .31 B4
Curtis Dr FY7 . . . . .193 D3
Curtis St **8** BB4 . . . . . . .85 A3
Curve St OL13 . . . . .86 F1
Curven Edge BB4 . . . . . . .67 A7
Curwen Ave LA3 . . . . .208 E6
Curwen La PR3 . . . . .158 C2
Curwen St PR1 . . . . .117 C1
Curzon Rd
  Lytham St Anne's FY8 . . . .89 A7
  Poulton-le-F FY6 . . . . . .151 E3
  Southport PR8 . . . . .34 E5
Curzon St **10** Burnley BB11 126 F6
  1 Clitheroe BB7 . . . . . .164 D7
  Colne BB8 . . . . .169 E4
Cusson Rd L33 . . . . .1 B1
Custom House La FY7 . . . .194 C5
Customs Way PR7 . . . . . . .95 C8
Cut La Haskayne L39, L40 . .14 C5
  Rishton BB1 . . . . .122 F1
Cutgate Rd OL12 . . . . . . .51 D1
Cutler Cl BB2 . . . . .100 C5
Cutler Cres OL13 . . . . . . .69 D7
Cutler La Bacup OL13 . . . . .69 D7
  Hesketh Lane PR3 . . . . . .160 C8
Cutt Cl PR5 . . . . .57 F6

Cutts La FY6 . . . . .174 F2
Cyclamen Cl PR5 . . . . .76 E2
Cygnet Cl L39 . . . . .15 C2
Cygnet Ct L33 . . . . .1 A2
Cypress Ave FY5 . . . . . . .172 E2
Cypress Cl
  Clayton-le-W PR5 . . . . . .76 E2
  Fulwood PR2 . . . . .118 A4
Cypress Gr
  Bamber Bridge PR5 . . . . .76 B8
  7 Blackpool FY3 . . . . .129 D2
Cypress Rd PR8 . . . . .34 F6
Cypress Ridge BB2 . . . . . .79 F8
Cyprus Ave FY5 . . . . .89 B4
Cyprus Rd LA3 . . . . .208 D2
Cyprus St BB3 . . . . .64 B6

D

D'urton La PR2,PR3 . . . . .136 F1
Daffodil Cl Haslingden BB4 .67 A8
  Rochdale OL12 . . . . .51 E3
Dagger Rd PR4 . . . . .114 C8
Daggers Hall La FY4 . . . . .109 E8
Daggers La FY6 . . . . .195 B3
Dahlia Cl Blackburn BB3 . . .81 B7
  Clayton-le-W PR5 . . . . . .76 E2
  Rochdale OL12 . . . . .51 D3
Dailton Rd WN8 . . . . .10 A7
Daisy Bank **12** Bacup OL13 .86 F3
  Lancaster LA1 . . . . .211 D7
Daisy Bank Cl PR5 . . . . . . .75 D1
Daisy Bank Cres BB10 . . . .127 E5
Daisy Bank St **18** OL14 . . .108 B1
Daisy Croft PR2 . . . . .94 D8
Daisy Fold PR6 . . . . .60 E2
Daisy Hill BB4 . . . . .85 A3
Daisy Hill Dr PR6 . . . . . . .30 A8
Daisy Hill Fold PR7 . . . . . .59 D1
Daisy La Blackburn BB1 . . .100 F6
  Preston PR1 . . . . .117 C3
  Ring o'Bells L40 . . . . . . .25 B4
Daisy Mdw PR5 . . . . .77 B5
Daisy St Blackburn BB1 . . .101 A6
  Colne BB8 . . . . .169 D4
  3 Lancaster LA1 . . . . . .213 F3
Daisyfield Prim Sch BB1 . .101 A6
Daisyfield St BB3 . . . . . . .80 E5
Daisyfields PR4 . . . . .115 F7
Dalby Cl Cleveleys FY5 . . . .150 F7
  Fulwood PR2 . . . . .117 D3
Dalby Cres BB2 . . . . .100 A1
Dalby Lea BB2 . . . . .100 A1
Dale Ave Euxton PR7 . . . . .59 D1
  Hest Bank LA2 . . . . . . .213 E8
  Longton PR4 . . . . .73 D6
Dale Cl Burnley BB12 . . . .126 D6
  Maghull L31 . . . . .5 C2
  Parbold WN8 . . . . .26 B2
Dale Cres BB2 . . . . .79 E7
Dale Dyke Wlk FY6 . . . . . .151 B3
Dale La 1 B4
Dale St Accrington BB5 . . .103 A6
  Bacup OL13 . . . . .86 F3
  8 Bacup, Stacksteads OL13 .69 C8
  Blackburn BB2 . . . . .100 D4
  Blackpool FY1 . . . . .129 B3
  Brierfield BB9 . . . . .147 A5
  Burnley BB12 . . . . .126 D6
  Colne BB8 . . . . .169 C5
  Earby BB18 . . . . .201 B2
  Haslingden BB4 . . . . .84 B3
  Lancaster LA1 . . . . .211 A7
  Nelson BB9 . . . . .147 C8
  4 Oswaldtwistle BB5 . . .102 E4
  Preston PR1 . . . . .96 B8
  Ramsbottom BL0 . . . . . . .67 C1
Dale St E BL6 . . . . .31 D2
Dale St W BL6 . . . . .31 D2
Dale Street Mews **7** FY1 129 B3
Dale Terr BB7 . . . . .187 D5
Dale View Billington BB7 . .143 B4
  Chorley PR7 . . . . .42 C4
  Darwen BB2,BB3 . . . . . . .80 E6
  Earby BB18 . . . . .201 A1
  6 Rawtenstall BB4 . . . . .84 F1
Dalecrest WN5 . . . . .10 D1
Dalegarth Cl FY4 . . . . . . .130 C1
Dalehead Rd PR5 . . . . . . .59 B7
Dales Ct FY4 . . . . .109 D6
Dales The BB6 . . . . .122 A8
Dalesford BB4 . . . . .84 B1
Dalesford Cl FY5 . . . . . . .151 C8
Dalesview Cres LA3 . . . . .208 F7
Dalesview Park (Cvn Pk)
  BB18 . . . . .191 B7
Dalesway BB9 . . . . .168 C3
Dalewood Ave FY4 . . . . . .129 D5
Dalglish Dr BB2 . . . . .80 D7
Dalkeith Ave FY3 . . . . . . .130 A2
Dalkeith Rd BB9 . . . . . . .147 C8
Dall St BB11 . . . . .127 A4
Dallam Ave LA4 . . . . .212 F6
Dallam Dr LA7 . . . . .237 F6
Dallas Ct LA4 . . . . .213 C4
Dallas Rd Lancaster LA1 . .210 E7
  Morecambe LA4 . . . . . . .213 B4
Dallas Road Sch LA1 . . . . .210 E7
Dallas St PR1 . . . . .116 A3
Dalmore Rd PR2 . . . . . . .116 A3
Dalton Ave FY4 . . . . .109 D5
Dalton Cl Blackburn BB1 . .101 B5
  Ramsbottom BL0 . . . . . . .49 A4
Dalton La LA6 . . . . .234 C7

Dalton Rd Lancaster LA1 211 A8
Morecambe LA3 212 A3
Dalton Sq LA1 210 F8
Dalton St Burnley BB11 126 D3
Lytham St Anne's FY8 88 D8
Nelson BB9 168 E1
Dalton St Michael's CE Prim Sch WN8 18 D5
Dalweb Ind Pk PR9 54 C3
Dam Head Rd BB18 200 B2
Dam La L40 23 C6
Dam Side
2 Barnoldswick BB18 200 B3
Colne BB8 169 D4
Dam Top BB4 85 B2
Dam Wood La L40 23 C5
Dame Fold Higham BB12 145 F6
12 Padiham BB12 125 C8
Damfield La L31 5 C1
Damside Cotts LA2 207 B5
Damside St LA1 210 F8
Danbers WN8 9 F6
Dancer La BB7 225 B1
Dandy Row BB3 81 C3
Dandy Wlk BB1 100 E4
Dane Hall La PR7 58 D2
Dane St BB10 127 A7
Danes Cl PR4 113 C5
Danes Dr PR5 96 D1
Danes House Rd BB10 127 A8
Danesbury Pl 4 FY1 129 C5
Danesmoor Dr BL9 32 B4
Danesway
Bamber Bridge PR5 96 D1
Chorley PR7 42 F1
Penwortham PR1 95 A4
Daneswood Ave OL12 51 C8
Daneswood Cl OL12 51 C8
Daneway PR8 20 B6
Danewerke St 8 PR1 96 A8
Daniel Fold OL12 51 B2
Daniel Fold La PR3 178 D2
Daniel St
10 Clayton-le-M BB5 123 F3
Whitworth OL12 70 D2
Daniell St BB1 123 A2
Daniels La WN8 9 C7
Danson Gdns 3 FY2 129 D8
Danvers St BB1 123 B2
Daram Ho 3 FY1 129 D2
Darbishire Rd FY7 193 F4
Daresbury Ave PR8 20 A5
Darfield WN8 9 F7
Dark La Blackrod BL6 30 B3
Earby BB18 201 E2
Johnson's Hillock PR6 60 E6
Maghull L31 5 E1
Mawdesley L40 39 E3
Newchurch BB4 85 E1
Ormskirk L40 16 C6
Dark Wood La PR5 98 B6
Darkinson La
Lea Town PR4 114 F1
Preston PR4 115 B2
Darkwood Cres BB7 187 D5
Darley Ave FY4 109 E7
Darley St BL6 31 B5
Darlington St PR7 41 E1
Darmond Rd L33 1 A3
Darnbrook Rd BB18 200 A2
Darnhill Cty Prim Sch OL10 32 F1
Darnley St BB10 127 C5
Dart St PR2 95 C8
Dartford Cl 1 BB1 101 A4
Dartmouth Cl PR4 112 F5
Darul-Uloom Islamic Coll BL8 48 F4
Darwen Cl PR3 139 B7
Darwen Ent Ctr BB3 81 A2
Darwen Golf Course BB3 80 C3
Darwen L Ctr BB3 81 A1
Darwen Moorland High Sch BB3 81 B3
Darwen Rd BL7 46 E1
Darwen St Blackburn BB2 100 E4
Higher Walton PR5 97 B4
2 Padiham BB12 125 C8
Preston PR1 96 C7
Darwen Sta BB3 81 A1
Darwen Vale High Sch BB3 80 E5
Darwen View PR5 96 E5
Darwin St BB10 147 A2
Daub Hall La PR5 97 E3
Daub La L40 39 A1
Dauntesey Ave FY3 130 A6
Davenham Rd Darwen BB3 80 E8
Formby L37 11 F3
Davenport Ave FY2 150 C5
Daventry Ave FY2 150 B4
David St Bacup OL13 69 D8
11 Barrowford BB9 168 D4
Burnley BB11 126 F4
16 Rochdale OL12 51 F1
David St N 15 OL12 51 F1
Davidson St 15 LA1 211 A8
Davies Rd BB1 101 D6
Davis St PR3 139 A8
Davitt Cl 4 BB4 84 B3
Davy Field Brow BB1 81 B6
Davy Field Rd BB1 81 B6
Dawber's La PR7 58 E2
Dawlish Ave FY3 129 F8
Dawlish Cl BB2 80 C8
Dawlish Dr PR9 53 A5
Dawlish Lodge FY8 88 D7
Dawlish Pl PR2 116 A3
Dawnay Rd PR2 117 E3
Dawson Ave
Simonstone BB12 144 E2
Southport PR9 53 C5
Dawson Gdns L31 5 C2
Dawson La PR6,PR7 59 E7
Dawson Pl PR5 77 A7
Dawson Rd
Lytham St Anne's FY8 109 F1
Ormskirk L39 15 F7
Dawson Sq BB11 127 A7
Dawson St BL9 32 A4
Dawson Wlk PR1 116 F1
Day St BB9 147 E7
Daybrook WN8 9 F7
Dayfield WN8 10 B7
Dayton Pl FY4 109 C6
De Lacy Ho BB2 100 C5
De Lacy St Clitheroe BB7 164 D8
Preston PR2 116 D2
De Vitre St 6 LA1 214 A1
Deakin's Terr BL7 45 C5
Deakins Bsns Pk BL7 46 D1
Deal Pl FY8 109 F1
Deal St Blackburn BB1 100 F7
9 Bury BL9 32 B2
Dean Brow PR3 140 F8
Dean Cl Edenfield BL0 67 D3
Orrell WN8 10 C7
Dean Ct FY7 172 D8
Dean Fold BB4 86 A8
Dean Head La BL6 44 A4
Dean La Billington BB6,BB7 143 C1
Darwen BB3 80 B1
Samlesbury PR5 118 F3
Water BB4 86 B8
Dean Mdw 5 BB7 164 D7
Dean Rd BB4 84 B1
Dean St Bamber Bridge PR5 96 E1
Blackpool FY4 109 B8
Burnley BB11 126 E6
Darwen BB3 80 F4
2 Padiham BB12 145 D1
Trawden BB8 170 C2
Dean Terr 4 PR4 113 A5
Dean Wood Ave WN5 10 E8
Deancroft Ave LA3 212 B2
Deanpoint LA3 212 F3
Deans Ct L37 11 F5
Deans La L40,WN8 25 E3
Deansgate Blackpool FY1 129 B5
Morecambe LA4 212 E5
Deansgate La L37 12 B5
Deansgate La N L37 12 A6
Deansgrave BB4 84 B1
Deansgreave Rd OL13 70 B7
Dearden Clough BL0 67 E2
Dearden Fold BL0 67 E2
Dearden Nook BB4 85 A1
Deardengate BB4 84 B3
Deardengate Croft 11 BB4 84 B3
Deben Cl WN6 28 D1
Deborah Ave PR2 117 A7
Dee Rd LA1 213 D2
Dee St FY8 88 E6
Deepdale Ave FY6 151 B5
Deepdale Ct BB9 168 C3
Deepdale Cty Inf Sch PR1 117 B2
Deepdale Cty Jun Sch PR1 117 B2
Deepdale Dr BB10 147 C4
Deepdale Gn BB9 168 C3
Deepdale Ho 5 PR1 117 B1
Deepdale La PR4 114 E3
Deepdale Mill PR1 117 B1
Deepdale Mill St PR1 117 B1
Deepdale Rd
Blackpool FY4 130 C1
Fleetwood FY7 194 A3
Preston PR1 117 B2
Deepdale Sh Pk PR1 117 C3
Deepdale St 8 PR1 96 B8
Deeply Vale La BL9 50 C2
Deer Chace BB12 146 D8
Deer Park La LA2 232 B7
Deer Park Rd BB10 127 E4
Deer Pk BB5 103 E8
Deerfold PR7 60 B2
Deerhurst Rd FY5 150 E7
Deerplay Cl BB10 147 E2
Deerstone Ave BB10 127 C6
Deerstone Rd BB9 148 B8
Deeside FY4 109 E5
Deganwy Ave BB1 100 E7
Deighton Ave 7 PR5 59 A8
Deighton Rd PR7 42 B6
Delamere Ave LA3 208 E6
Delamere Cl BB2 100 B2
Delamere Pl PR6 42 D8
Delamere Rd
Brierfield BB10 147 F3
Skelmersdale WN8 17 F2
Southport PR8 20 B5
Delamere St BL9 32 A5
Delamere Way WN8 10 A7
Delany Dr PR4 92 A6
Delaware Rd 8 FY3 150 E1
Delaware St PR1 117 D1
Delf La Cornholme OL14 108 D3
Haskayne L39 14 A4
Delfby Cres L32 1 A1
Delius Cl BB2 101 A1
Dell Gdns OL12 51 B2
Dell La 4 BB12 125 C4
Dell Mdw OL12 51 C5
Dell Rd OL12 51 B3
Dell Side Way OL12 51 C2
Dell The Appley Bridge WN6 19 D7
Blackburn BB2 80 D6
Fulwood PR2 116 D7
Knowley PR6 61 A3
Orrell WN8 10 B7
Wrea Green PR4 112 B3
Dellar St OL12 51 C1
Dellfield La L31 5 E1
Dellway The PR4 94 D2
Delma Rd BB10 127 E5
Delph App BB1 101 C4
Delph Ave BL7 46 D3
Delph Brook Way BL7 46 D2
Delph Cl BB1 101 C4
Delph Common Rd L39 15 C1
Delph Ct 3 BB6 123 C5
Delph La Blackburn BB1 101 C3
Blackburn BB1 101 C4
Charnock Green PR7 41 D6
Coppull PR7 41 E5
Formby L37 11 C3
Garstang PR3 178 F8
Oakenclough PR3 180 B7
Ormskirk L39 15 C1
Delph Lane Est BB1 101 C4
Delph Mount
Great Harwood BB6 123 B6
Nelson BB9 147 D6
Delph Park Ave L39 15 B1
Delph Rd BB6 123 C5
Delph St Darwen BB3 81 B3
Haslingden BB4 84 B4
Delph The WN8 26 C3
Delph Top L39 16 A6
Delph Way PR6 60 C7
Delphene Ave FY5 150 D6
Delphinium Way BB3 81 A7
Delphside Cl WN5 10 D5
Delphside Prim Sch WN8 9 C8
Delphside Rd WN5 10 D5
Delta La FY7 194 A4
Delta Park Ave PR4 72 E4
Delta Park Dr PR4 72 E4
Deltic Way L33 1 B1
Delves La BB10 148 E7
Demming Cl PR2 94 C8
Denbigh Ave
Cleveleys FY5 172 E1
Southport PR9 52 F3
Denbigh Cl PR5 76 B1
Denbigh Dr BB7 186 F2
Denbigh Gr BB12 126 A7
Denbigh Way 34 PR1 96 A7
Denby Cl PR5 96 C3
Dene Bank Rd BB5 102 E3
Dene The Blackburn BB2 100 B7
Hurst Green BB7 141 E8
Denebank FY2 150 D5
Deneway Ave FY3 129 F6
Denford Ave Leyland PR5 59 B8
Lytham St Anne's FY8 89 A4
Denham La PR6 77 E2
Denham Way FY7 193 F2
Denholme Orrell WN8 10 A7
Skelmersdale WN8 9 F7
Denholme Gr FY2 150 E5
Denis St LA1 211 A8
Denmark Rd
Lytham St Anne's FY8 89 D4
Southport PR9 53 A2
Denmark St LA1 210 D7
Dennis Gr LA4 212 D4
Denny Ave LA1 213 E2
Denny Bank LA2 214 E5
Denny Beck La LA2 214 E5
Denshaw WN8 9 F7
Denstone Ave FY2 150 D4
Dent Row 8 BB11 126 F5
Dent St BB8 169 B3
Denton St
Barnoldswick BB18 200 A3
7 Rochdale OL12 51 F1
Denville Ave FY5 150 F8
Denville Rd Blackburn BB2 100 D5
Preston PR1 117 C1
Denville St BB2 100 D5
Depot Rd Blackpool FY3 150 E1
Kirkby L33 1 D4
Derbe Rd FY8 88 F5
Derby Cl BB3 64 B5
Derby Cres PR4 134 C8
Derby Hill Cres L39 16 A5
Derby Hill Rd L39 16 A5
Derby Pl PR6 30 A8
Derby Rd Blackpool FY1 129 B7
Cleveleys FY5 172 C3
Formby L37 11 E5
Fulwood PR2 116 E3
Garstang PR3 178 B7
Kirkham PR4 113 A6
Lancaster LA1 213 F1
Longridge PR3 139 A7
Lytham St Anne's FY8 89 C5
Poulton-le-F FY6 151 D4
Skelmersdale WN8 8 C8
Southport PR9 34 C7
Derby Sq PR1 96 D8
Derby St Accrington BB5 103 C6
Blackburn BB1 101 A6
Brinscall PR6 62 A8
Burnley BB11 126 E5
Clitheroe BB7 164 F8
Colne BB8 169 D5
Horwich BL6 31 D1
Leyland PR5 76 B2
Derby St *continued*
Morecambe LA4 212 D5
Nelson BB9 168 E1
Ormskirk L39 15 F5
Preston PR1 96 A8
Ramsbottom BL0 49 D6
Rishton BB1 123 C1
Derby St W L39 15 E5
Derbyshire Ave PR3 178 B8
Derek Rd PR6 77 C1
Derham St BB2 100 E3
Derry Rd PR2 117 E3
Dertern La LA5 216 A7
Derwent Ave
Burnley BB10 147 A2
Fleetwood FY7 193 D2
Formby L37 11 D2
Morecambe LA4 212 F5
Padiham BB12 145 C2
Southport PR9 52 F1
Derwent Cl Colne BB8 170 A6
Freckleton PR4 92 A6
Horwich BL6 31 C2
Knott End-on-S FY6 194 F6
Maghull L31 5 F2
Rishton BB1 122 F1
Derwent Cres BB7 164 C7
Derwent Ct LA1 213 C2
Derwent Dr Freckleton PR4 92 A6
Longridge PR3 138 F5
Derwent Hall 3 PR1 116 E1
Derwent Ho 9 PR1 96 D8
Derwent Pl Cleveleys FY5 150 D8
Poulton-le-F FY6 151 D1
Derwent Rd Chorley PR7 42 B5
Lancaster LA1 211 B8
Lytham St Anne's FY8 110 A1
Orrell WN5 10 F8
Derwent St 6 Darwen BB3 80 F2
11 Rochdale OL12 51 F1
Derwentwater Pl PR1 116 F2
Dever Ave PR5 75 D1
Devereux Prep Sch BB9 147 D8
Devon Ave Fleetwood FY7 193 E3
Oswaldtwistle BB5 102 B6
Devon Cl PR5 96 D3
Devon Cres BB4 67 B8
Devon Dr WN1 29 B1
Devon Farm Way L37 12 B3
Devon Gr BB12 126 A7
Devon Pl 2 Church BB5 102 E5
Lancaster LA1 211 A4
Devon Rd BB1 101 C5
Devon St Blackpool FY4 129 D1
Colne BB8 169 E6
Darwen BB3 64 B6
Devona Ave FY4 130 B1
Devonport Cl PR5 96 E3
Devonport Rd BB2 100 C5
Devonport Way PR6 42 E8
Devonshire Ave FY5 173 B2
Devonshire Ct 17 PR7 42 C8
Devonshire Dr
Clayton-le-M BB5 124 A3
Garstang PR3 178 B8
Devonshire Ho FY3 129 D6
Devonshire Jun Sch FY3 129 D6
Devonshire Mews FY5 173 B1
Devonshire Pl PR1 117 E1
Devonshire Rd
Blackpool FY2 150 D2
Burnley BB10 127 A8
Chorley PR7 42 C7
Fulwood PR2 117 A4
Lytham St Anne's FY8 88 D7
Morecambe LA3 212 C3
Rishton BB1 123 A1
Southport PR9 35 A8
Devonshire Road Hospl FY1 129 D7
Devonshire Sq FY3 129 D5
Devonshire Square Mews 5 FY3 129 D5
Devonshire St
Accrington BB5 103 B7
Lancaster LA1 210 F5
Dew Forest PR3 178 D4
Dew Meadow Cl OL12 51 E2
Dewberry Fields WN8 10 B7
Dewhirst Rd OL12 51 F4
Dewhirst Way OL12 51 F4
Dewhurst Ave FY4 109 E8
Dewhurst Cl BB3 64 C6
Dewhurst Clough Rd BL7 46 D2
Dewhurst Ct BL7 46 D3
Dewhurst Rd BB6 141 F1
Dewhurst Row PR5 76 D7
Dewhurst St
Blackburn BB1 101 A4
Colne BB8 169 D3
Darwen BB3 64 B6
Preston PR2 116 D1
Deycroft Ave L33 1 A4
Deycroft Wlk L33 1 A4
Deyes End L31 5 E1
Deyes High Sch L31 5 D1
Deyes La Maghull L31 5 D1
Maghull, Moss Side L31 5 F1
Diamond Jubilee Rd L40 38 C4
Dianne Rd FY5 173 D2
Dib Rd PR4 72 B5
Dibbs Pocket PR4 92 D7
Dicconson Terr 5 FY8 90 B3
Dicconson Way L39 16 A5
Dicconson's La L39 14 D4
Dick La PR6 61 E7
Dick's La L40 16 F4
Dickens Ave BB18 200 A3
Dickens Rd PR7 28 E8
Dickens St BB1 101 A3
Dickensons Field 3 PR1 95 E2
Dicket's Brow L40 16 F3
Dicket's La WN8, L40 17 A2
Dickie's La FY4 110 B7
Dickie's La S FY4 110 C6
Dickinson Cl
Blackburn BB2 100 C3
Formby L37 11 F2
Dickinson Ct 1 BL6 31 B4
Dickinson Rd L37 11 F2
Dickinson St BB2 100 D3
Dickinson St W BL6 31 B4
Dickson Ave PR1 117 D2
Dickson Hey PR4 74 F8
Dickson Rd FY1 129 B7
Dickson St Burnley BB12 126 C6
Colne BB8 169 E6
8 Preston PR1 96 B7
Dickson St W BL6 31 A4
Didsbury St BB1 101 C5
Digham Ave FY5 150 D6
Digmoor Dr WN8 9 C7
Digmoor Rd WN8 9 D6
Dill Hall La BB5 102 F7
Dilworth La PR3 139 C7
Dimmock St BB2 100 C2
Dimple Pk BL7 46 D3
Dimple Rd BL7 46 C4
Dimples La PR3 178 E5
Dinckley Gr FY1 129 D3
Dinckley Sq BB2 100 B6
Dinely St BB5 102 F6
Dingle Ave
Appley Bridge WN6 19 E8
Blackpool FY3 129 F8
Orrell WN8 10 C8
Dingle Cl L39 15 C1
Dingle Rd WN8 10 B7
Dingle The Fulwood PR2 116 D7
Knowley PR6 61 A3
Dinmore Ave FY3 130 A8
Dinmore Pl FY3 130 A7
Dinorwic Rd PR8 34 A2
Dirty Leech OL12 51 F6
Disraeli St BB10 147 A2
Ditchfield L37 12 A2
Division La FY4 110 C3
Dixey St BL6 31 A3
Dixon Rd PR3 139 B7
Dixon St Barrowford BB9 168 C3
Blackburn BB2 100 C4
Horwich BL6 31 B3
Dixon's Farm Mews PR4 114 D1
Dixons La PR2 138 C2
Dob Brow PR7 41 F4
Dob La PR4 74 A4
Dobbin Cl BB4 85 C2
Dobbin La BB4 85 C2
Dobbs Dr L37 12 A4
Dobs La LA2 205 E3
Dobson Ave FY8 88 E8
Dobson Cl WN6 27 E2
Dobson St 2 BB3 80 F2
Dobson's La FY6 174 E6
Dock Ave FY7 194 A2
Dock Rd FY8 90 D4
Dock St Blackburn BB1 101 A5
Fleetwood FY7 194 B4
Docker La LA6 235 C5
Dockinsall La PR3 175 D3
Dockray Ct 2 BB8 169 E5
Dockray St BB8 169 E5
Dockray Yd 4 BB8 169 E5
Docky Pool La FY4 110 A6
Doctor's La Eccleston PR7 40 B6
Great Altcar L37 12 E2
Sollom PR4 55 F3
Doctors Row PR3 139 A6
Dodd Way PR5 77 A6
Dodd's La L31 5 D2
Dodgeons Cl FY6 151 C2
Dodgson La BB18 201 F2
Dodgson Pl PR1 117 C1
Dodgson Rd PR1 117 C1
Dodney Dr PR2 115 C1
Dodson Rd FY3 130 B7
Dodworth Ave PR8 34 E5
Doe Meadow WN8 26 A1
Doeholme Rake LA2 226 F1
Dog Pits La OL13 87 A6
Dole La Abbey Village PR6 79 C1
Chorley PR7 42 C8
Doles La PR3 57 A7
Dolls House & Fleetwood Mus FY7 194 C5
Dolly's La PR9 35 D8
Dollywood La LA7 237 F1
Dolphinholme CE Prim Sch LA2 220 A8
Dombey St Blackburn BB1 101 A3
Blackburn BB1 101 A4
Dominica Ave BB3 80 F6
Dominion Rd BB2 100 C8
Don St FY8 88 E7
Doncaster Rd FY3 130 A3
Donnington Lo PR8 33 F6
Donnington Rd
Carleton FY6 151 C6
Lytham St Anne's FY8 88 F7
Donshort Mews 2 BB9 168 C1
Doodstone Ave PR5 96 B1
Doodstone Cl PR5 96 B1
Doodstone Dr PR5 96 B1
Doodstone Nook PR5 96 B1
Dora St BL0 49 A4
Dorchester Ave BB5 102 C4

Dorchester Cl
Blackburn BB1 . . . . 101 B3
Thornton FY5 . . . . 151 C8
Dorchester Dr L33 . . . . 1 A5
Dorchester Gdns LA3 . . . . 212 F2
Dorchester Rd
Blackpool FY1 . . . . 129 B8
Garstang PR3 . . . . 178 B8
Orrell WN8 . . . . 10 A7
Doric Gn WN5 . . . . 10 D3
Doris Henderson Way
LA3 . . . . 213 B2
Doris St Burnley BB11 . . . . 127 B7
Chorley PR6 . . . . 60 D1
Dorking Rd PR6 . . . . 60 F4
Dorman Rd PR2 . . . . 117 E3
Dorothy Ave 9 PR5 . . . . 76 A1
Dorothy St Blackburn BB2 . . 80 C8
13 Ramsbottom BL0 . . . . 49 B5
Dorrington Rd LA1 . . . . 210 F5
Dorritt Rd FY4 . . . . 109 E6
Dorritt St 19 BB1 . . . . 101 A4
Dorset Ave
3 Bamber Bridge PR5 . . . . 96 D3
Cleveleys FY5 . . . . 172 D4
Darwen BB3 . . . . 80 F3
Padiham BB12 . . . . 125 D7
Southport PR8 . . . . 20 C2
Dorset Dr Blackburn BB1 . . 101 E4
Clitheroe BB7 . . . . 186 F2
Haslingden BB4 . . . . 67 A8
Dorset Pl BB5 . . . . 102 F7
Dorset Rd
Lytham St Anne's FY8 . . . . 88 F8
Preston PR1 . . . . 117 A1
Rishton BB1 . . . . 123 A1
Standish WN1 . . . . 29 B1
Dorset St 10 Blackpool FY4 129 D1
Burnley BB12 . . . . 126 A6
Dotcliffe Rd BB18 . . . . 192 A6
Double Row 1 BB12 . . . . 125 B8
Doughty St BB8 . . . . 169 D4
Douglas Ave Becconsall PR4 72 F1
Blackpool FY3 . . . . 129 D7
1 Heysham LA3 . . . . 208 F7
Horwich BL6 . . . . 31 C5
Orrell WN8 . . . . 10 B7
Stalmine FY6 . . . . 174 C7
Douglas Cl
Bamber Bridge PR5 . . . . 76 F7
Blackburn BB2 . . . . 80 D7
Horwich BL6 . . . . 31 C5
Rufford L40 . . . . 38 C3
Douglas Ct PR2 . . . . 116 D3
Douglas Dr Freckleton PR4 . 92 B6
Heysham LA3 . . . . 208 F7
Maghull L31 . . . . 5 F2
Ormskirk L39 . . . . 15 D7
Orrell WN5 . . . . 10 F7
Shevington WN6 . . . . 19 F5
Douglas Gr BB3 . . . . 80 D4
Douglas Hall 4 PR1 . . . . 116 E1
Douglas Leatham Ho 3
FY1 . . . . 129 D1
Douglas Pl Blackburn BB1 . 121 F1
Fleetwood FY7 . . . . 193 D3
Douglas Rd Bacup OL13 . . . . 87 A1
Brierfield BB10 . . . . 148 A3
Fulwood PR2 . . . . 116 D3
Shevington Moor WN6 . . . . 28 B2
Southport PR9 . . . . 53 C4
Douglas Rd N PR2 . . . . 116 D3
Douglas Sq 7 OL10 . . . . 32 F1
Douglas St Colne BB8 . . . . 169 E6
Lytham St Anne's FY8 . . . . 88 D6
Preston PR2 . . . . 95 C8
Ramsbottom BL0 . . . . 49 B6
Douglas St Back 4 BL0 . . . . 49 B6
Douglas Way BB10 . . . . 148 A3
Doultons The PR5 . . . . 96 C3
Dove Ave 2 PR1 . . . . 95 E4
Dove Cl 6 FY5 . . . . 172 F1
Dove Dr BL9 . . . . 32 B4
Dove La BB3 . . . . 80 F2
Dove St
Lytham St Anne's FY8 . . . . 88 D6
Preston PR1 . . . . 117 B1
Dove Tree Ct FY4 . . . . 130 B1
Dovecote PR6 . . . . 77 A3
Dovedale Ave
Blackpool FY3 . . . . 130 C2
Fulwood PR2 . . . . 116 A5
Maghull L31 . . . . 5 C2
Thornton FY5 . . . . 173 B3
Dovedale Cl
Brierfield BB10 . . . . 147 C4
Burnley BB12 . . . . 126 C8
Fulwood PR2 . . . . 116 A4
Leyland PR5 . . . . 59 A6
Dovedale Dr WN6 . . . . 28 E2
Dover Cl Blackburn BB1 . . 101 C4
Ramsbottom BL8 . . . . 49 A1
Warton PR4 . . . . 91 E7
Dover Ct FY1 . . . . 129 D2
Dover Gdns FY6 . . . . 151 B5
Dover La PR5,PR6 . . . . 78 C8
Dover Rd Blackpool FY1 . . 129 E2
Lytham St Anne's FY8 . . . . 88 F8
Southport PR8 . . . . 33 F2
Dover St Accrington BB5 . . 103 A4
Blackburn BB3 . . . . 80 F7
Nelson BB9 . . . . 168 E1
Dovestone Dr FY6 . . . . 151 B3
Dovetree Cl PR1 . . . . 96 A3
Dowbridge PR4 . . . . 113 C4
Dowbridge Way PR4 . . . . 113 C5
Downes Gr LA4 . . . . 212 G4
Downeyfield Rd LA3 . . . . 209 C3
Downfield Cl BL0 . . . . 49 B6
Downham Ave
Great Harwood BB6 . . . . 123 F6
Rawtenstall BB4 . . . . 85 A4
Downham Cotts 7 LA2 . . 207 A4
Downham Dr BB5 . . . . 103 A3
Downham Gr BB10 . . . . 127 D5
Downham Pl
Lytham St Anne's FY8 . . . . 89 C6
3 Preston PR2 . . . . 115 E2
Downham Rd
Chatburn BB7 . . . . 187 E5
Leyland PR5 . . . . 75 D1
Downham St BB2 . . . . 100 C4
Downham Wlk WN5 . . . . 10 D1
Downholland Moss La
L37 . . . . 12 C4
Downing Ct PR3 . . . . 136 C3
Downing St PR1 . . . . 96 E8
Downley Cl OL12 . . . . 51 B2
Downs The FY6 . . . . 151 D4
Dowry St BB5 . . . . 103 C6
Dragon St 8 BB12 . . . . 125 C8
Drake Cl
Lytham St Anne's FY8 . . . . 109 E1
Ormskirk L39 . . . . 15 C2
Drakelowe Ave FY4 . . . . 109 F6
Drakes Croft PR2 . . . . 116 C3
Drakes Hollow PR5 . . . . 96 D4
Drammen Ave BB11 . . . . 126 B5
Draperfield PR7 . . . . 42 A4
Drapers Ave PR7 . . . . 40 C6
Draw Well Rd L33 . . . . 1 D2
Draycombe Ct LA3 . . . . 212 A2
Draycombe Dr LA3 . . . . 212 B2
Draycot Ave FY3 . . . . 129 F8
Drayton Rd LA3 . . . . 209 A7
Drew St BB11 . . . . 126 B5
Drewitt Cres PR9 . . . . 53 D4
Drewton Ave LA3 . . . . 212 A2
Drinkhouse La PR5 . . . . 57 A1
Drinkhouse Rd PR5 . . . . 57 B1
Driscoll St 1 PR1 . . . . 96 B8
Drive The Bacup OL13 . . . . 86 F2
Carnforth LA5 . . . . 217 B1
Edenfield BL0 . . . . 67 D3
Fulwood PR2 . . . . 117 B4
Hest Bank LA2 . . . . 215 E1
Heysham LA3 . . . . 208 F7
Longton PR4 . . . . 74 A8
Walton-le-D PR5 . . . . 96 F5
Driver St 12 BB4 . . . . 85 A7
Driving Gate BB4 . . . . 105 A1
Dronsfield Rd FY7 . . . . 193 F4
Drovers Wlk LA3 . . . . 208 F7
Druids Cl BL7 . . . . 46 D3
Drumacre La E PR4 . . . . 74 D6
Drumacre La W PR4 . . . . 74 A6
Drumhead Rd PR6 . . . . 60 D2
Drummersdale La L40 . . . . 23 D7
Drummond Ave FY3 . . . . 129 E7
Drybread La PR3 . . . . 175 C2
Dryburgh Ave FY3 . . . . 129 F3
Dryden Gr BB6 . . . . 123 C4
Dryden Rd FY7 . . . . 194 A4
Dryden St
6 Clayton-le-M BB5 . . . . 123 F3
Padiham BB12 . . . . 125 E7
Dryfield La BL6 . . . . 31 A5
Dubdon Cl LA3 . . . . 213 B3
Duchess Ct FY2 . . . . 150 B3
Duchess Dr FY2 . . . . 150 B3
Duchess St BB3 . . . . 80 F7
Duchy Ave PR2 . . . . 117 B4
Ducie Pl PR1 . . . . 117 F1
Duck St 2 Clitheroe BB7 . . 164 F8
Smallwood Hey PR3 . . . . 196 A7
Wray LA2 . . . . 232 D6
Duckett St 3 BB11 . . . . 126 E6
Ducketts La PR3 . . . . 157 B8
Duckshaw Rd BB3 . . . . 63 F6
Duckworth Cl PR3 . . . . 178 D3
Duckworth Dr PR3 . . . . 178 D3
Duckworth Hall
Brow BB5 . . . . 102 A1
Duckworth Hill La BB5 . . 102 B1
Duckworth La
Rawtenstall BB4 . . . . 67 E8
Tarleton PR4 . . . . 55 F8
Duckworth St
Barrowford BB9 . . . . 168 D2
Blackburn BB2 . . . . 100 D3
3 Bury BL9 . . . . 32 A4
Church BB5 . . . . 102 E6
Darwen BB3 . . . . 80 F2
Duddle La PR5 . . . . 96 D2
Duddon Ave Darwen BB3 . . 80 E3
Fleetwood FY7 . . . . 193 D2
Maghull L31 . . . . 5 F2
Dudley Ave Blackpool FY2 . 150 D1
Oswaldtwistle BB5 . . . . 102 C4
Dudley Cl PR4 . . . . 94 A1
Dudley St Brierfield BB9 . . 147 C5
Colne BB8 . . . . 169 F5
Morecambe LA4 . . . . 212 F4
Duerden St BB9 . . . . 147 D7
Duffins Cl OL12 . . . . 51 D3
Dugdale Ct FY4 . . . . 109 F5
Dugdale La BB7 . . . . 229 F1
Dugdale Rd BB12 . . . . 126 C7
Dugdale St BB11 . . . . 127 A5
Dugie St BL0 . . . . 49 B7
Duke Ave PR8 . . . . 34 C4
Duke of Sussex St BB2 . . 80 B8
Duke St Bamber Bridge PR5 . 76 E7
Blackburn BB2 . . . . 100 D5
Blackpool FY1 . . . . 129 B1
Brierfield BB10 . . . . 147 F3
Duke St *continued*
Burnley BB11 . . . . 127 B4
Burton in L LA6 . . . . 236 C3
Chorley PR7 . . . . 42 C6
Clayton-le-M BB5 . . . . 124 A2
Colne BB8 . . . . 169 D4
Formby L37 . . . . 11 F2
Great Harwood BB6 . . . . 123 B5
Heysham LA3 . . . . 208 E7
High Bentham LA2 . . . . 233 D8
Lancaster LA1 . . . . 213 E1
Oswaldtwistle BB5 . . . . 102 D3
Preston PR1 . . . . 96 B7
Ramsbottom BL0 . . . . 49 A4
Rawtenstall BB4 . . . . 68 E8
Rochdale OL12 . . . . 51 F1
Southport PR8 . . . . 34 B5
Trawden BB8 . . . . 170 B5
Duke St Cty Prim Sch PR7 42 C6
Duke's Wood La WN8 . . . . 9 D3
Dukes Brow BB2 . . . . 100 C6
Dukes Ct BB2 . . . . 100 B6
Dukes Dr BB3 . . . . 81 F1
Dukes Mdw PR2 . . . . 116 A5
Dukes Way L37 . . . . 11 F2
Dulas Gn L32 . . . . 1 A1
Dulas Rd L32 . . . . 1 A1
Dumb Tom's La LA6 . . . . 236 E1
Dumbarton Cl 2 FY4 . . . . 110 A6
Dumbarton Rd LA1 . . . . 211 A7
Dumfries Cl FY2 . . . . 150 F5
Dunald Mill La LA2,LA6 . . 231 B6
Dunbar Cl FY4 . . . . 110 A6
Dunbar Cres PR8 . . . . 20 F8
Dunbar Dr Fulwood PR2 . . 116 D4
2 Heysham LA3 . . . . 208 E7
Dunbar Rd Fulwood PR2 . . 115 F3
Southport PR8 . . . . 33 F1
Duncan Ave FY2 . . . . 150 C6
Duncan Cl Brownside BB10 127 F5
Lytham St Anne's FY8 . . . . 109 D1
Duncan Pl FY7 . . . . 193 E4
Duncan St Burnley BB12 . . 126 A5
Horwich BL6 . . . . 31 C3
Duncroft Cl BB7 . . . . 186 E2
Dundas St BB8 . . . . 169 C4
Dundee Cl OL10 . . . . 32 F1
Dundee Dr BB1 . . . . 101 A4
Dundee La BL0 . . . . 49 B6
Dundee St LA1 . . . . 211 A7
Dunderdale Ave BB9 . . . . 147 C7
Dunderdale St PR3 . . . . 139 B7
Dundonald St PR1 . . . . 96 D8
Dundonnell Rd BB9 . . . . 169 A1
Dunedin Rd BL8 . . . . 48 F2
Dunelt Ct 2 FY1 . . . . 129 C2
Dunelt Rd FY1 . . . . 129 D2
Dunes Ave FY4 . . . . 109 B5
Dunes Dr L37 . . . . 11 C4
Dungeon La WN8 . . . . 18 C7
Dunham Dr PR6 . . . . 60 C6
Dunkeld St 5 LA1 . . . . 211 A7
Dunkenhalgh Way
Church BB5 . . . . 102 E7
Clayton-le-M BB5 . . . . 123 E1
Dunkenshaw Cres LA1 . . . . 211 B2
Dunkirk Ave Carnforth LA5 216 E8
Fulwood PR2 . . . . 116 C3
Dunkirk La PR5 . . . . 75 A1
Dunkirk Rd PR8 . . . . 33 F2
Dunlin Cl FY5 . . . . 173 A5
Dunlop Ave PR8 . . . . 20 C2
Dunmail Ave 1 FY3 . . . . 129 F2
Dunmore St PR1 . . . . 96 B8
Dunnock La PR4 . . . . 115 E4
Dunny Shop Ave BB5 . . . . 103 A4
Dunoon Cl PR2 . . . . 115 F4
Dunoon Dr BB1 . . . . 101 D3
Dunoon St BB11 . . . . 126 D5
Dunrobin Dr PR7 . . . . 59 D1
Dunscar Dr PR6 . . . . 60 E1
Dunsop Cl
3 Bamber Bridge PR5 . . . . 76 F8
1 Blackpool FY1 . . . . 129 D1
Dunsop Ct 2 FY1 . . . . 129 D1
Dunsop Rd PR2 . . . . 117 D4
Dunsop St BB1 . . . . 100 F7
Dunster Ave BB5 . . . . 102 C5
Dunster Gr BB7 . . . . 164 C6
Dunster Rd PR8 . . . . 20 E8
Dunvegan Cl 3 FY4 . . . . 110 A6
Durban Gr BB11 . . . . 126 E4
Durham Ave Burnley BB12 126 B7
Cleveleys FY5 . . . . 172 E3
Lancaster LA1 . . . . 211 A4
Lytham St Anne's FY8 . . . . 88 E7
Durham Cl Blackburn BB1 . 100 F4
Leyland PR5 . . . . 58 E6
Morecambe LA3 . . . . 212 E2
Durham Dr
Oswaldtwistle BB5 . . . . 102 F3
Ramsbottom BL0 . . . . 49 B3
Wilpshire BB1 . . . . 121 F6
Durham Gr PR3 . . . . 178 B7
Durham Ho 8 PR1 . . . . 96 A6
Durham Rd Blackpool FY1 . 129 D5
Darwen BB3 . . . . 80 F2
Wilpshire BB1 . . . . 121 F7
Durham St
Accrington BB5 . . . . 103 D7
Skelmersdale WN8 . . . . 17 D2
Durley Rd FY1 . . . . 129 D2
Durn St 1 OL14 . . . . 108 A1
Dutch Barn Cl PR7 . . . . 60 B2
Dutton Ct 1 FY3 . . . . 129 D5
Dutton Rd FY3 . . . . 129 D5
Dutton St 16 BB5 . . . . 103 C6
Duxbury Cl L31 . . . . 5 E3
Duxbury Dr BL9 . . . . 32 C2
Duxbury Hall Rd PR7 . . . . 42 E3
Duxbury Ho 8 PR6 . . . . 42 D7
Duxbury Jubilee Pk PR7 . . 42 D3
Duxbury St Darwen BB3 . . 64 B6
Earby BB18 . . . . 201 C2
Dye House La 6 LA1 . . . . 210 F8
Dyer St PR4 . . . . 112 F5
Dyers La L39 . . . . 15 E4
Dyke La PR3 . . . . 196 A3
Dyke Nook BB7 . . . . 164 F6
Dykes La LA5 . . . . 219 F2
Dymock Rd PR1 . . . . 117 D1
Dymock Rd N PR1 . . . . 117 D1
Dyneley Ave BB10 . . . . 127 F4
Dyneley Rd BB1 . . . . 101 C7
Dyson St BB2 . . . . 100 E2

E

Eachill Gdns BB1 . . . . 102 B8
Eachill Rd 2 BB1 . . . . 123 B1
Eager La L31 . . . . 5 B8
Eagle Brow Cl FY5 . . . . 173 B4
Eagle St Accrington BB5 . . 103 B5
Blackburn BB1 . . . . 101 C4
2 Nelson BB9 . . . . 168 F1
Oswaldtwistle BB5 . . . . 102 C2
Eagles The FY6 . . . . 151 E5
Eagley Bank OL12 . . . . 70 E6
Eagley Rd BB10 . . . . 147 C4
Ealing Gr PR6 . . . . 60 F3
Eamont Ave PR9 . . . . 53 B5
Eamont Pl FY7 . . . . 193 D2
Eanam BB1 . . . . 100 F5
Eanam Old Rd BB1 . . . . 100 F5
Earby Rd BB18 . . . . 191 F8
Earby Springfield
Cty Prim Sch BB18 . . . . 201 C1
Eardley Rd LA3 . . . . 208 E8
Earl Rd BL0 . . . . 49 B6
Earl St Barnoldswick BB18 . 200 C2
Blackburn BB1 . . . . 100 E6
Burnley BB10 . . . . 127 B8
Clayton-le-M BB5 . . . . 123 F2
Colne BB8 . . . . 169 D4
Great Harwood BB6 . . . . 123 B5
Lancaster LA1 . . . . 213 F1
11 Nelson BB9 . . . . 168 F1
Preston PR1 . . . . 95 F8
Ramsbottom BL0 . . . . 49 D6
Earlesdon Ave BB18 . . . . 200 F1
Earlham St BB18 . . . . 201 C2
Earls Ave PR5 . . . . 76 E8
Earls Dr BB3 . . . . 81 E1
Earls Way PR7 . . . . 59 D2
Earlsway FY3 . . . . 130 D5
Earlswood WN8 . . . . 18 E1
Earnsdale Ave BB3 . . . . 80 D2
Earnsdale Cl BB3 . . . . 80 E2
Earnsdale Rd BB3 . . . . 80 E3
Earnshaw Ave OL12 . . . . 51 E3
Earnshaw Bridge
Cty Infs Sch PR5 . . . . 75 E2
Earnshaw Dr PR5 . . . . 75 D1
Earnshaw Rd OL13 . . . . 86 F3
Earnshaw Row 19 OL13 . . . . 86 F3
Easby Cl L37 . . . . 12 A2
Easdale Ave LA4 . . . . 213 A5
Easedale Cl Burnley BB12 . 126 B8
Hest Bank LA5 . . . . 215 F2
Easedale Dr PR8 . . . . 20 B4
Easington LA1 . . . . 213 C2
Easington Cres FY3 . . . . 130 B8
East Ave BB18 . . . . 200 B2
East Bank
2 Barrowford BB9 . . . . 168 D4
Water BB4 . . . . 106 A1
East Bank Ave BB4 . . . . 84 B2
East Bank Rd FY8 . . . . 88 E5
East Beach FY8 . . . . 90 C3
East Boothroyden Rd FY1 . . 129 B8
East Cecil St FY8 . . . . 90 A3
East Chorley Bsns Ctr 3
PR6 . . . . 42 D8
East Cliff PR1 . . . . 95 F6
East Cliff Rd PR1 . . . . 95 F6
East Cliffe FY8 . . . . 90 C3
East Cres BB5 . . . . 103 B8
East Croft BB9 . . . . 169 B2
East Ct FY5 . . . . 172 D5
East Dene WN8 . . . . 26 B2
East End St BB8 . . . . 169 C4
East Gate BB4 . . . . 84 B3
East Hills St 18 BB18 . . . . 200 B2
East Holme FY8 . . . . 90 C4
East La Ellel LA2 . . . . 207 B6
Maghull L29 . . . . 4 B2
East Lancashire Rd BB1 . 121 F3
East Lancashire Rly
BL0 . . . . 49 C5
East Leigh WN8 . . . . 18 D1
East Lodge Pl BB10 . . . . 127 E1
East Mead Blackpool FY3 . . 129 F3
Ormskirk L39 . . . . 15 B2
East Meade L31 . . . . 5 C2
East Mount WN5 . . . . 10 F6
East Par
16 Barnoldswick BB18 . . . . 200 B2
17 Rawtenstall BB4 . . . . 85 A3
East Park Ave
Blackburn BB1 . . . . 100 D7
Darwen BB3 . . . . 63 F8
East Park Dr FY3 . . . . 130 A5
East Park Rd BB1 . . . . 100 D6
East Rd Fulwood PR2 . . . . 117 A3
Lancaster LA1 . . . . 211 A8
East Rd *continued*
Maghull L31 . . . . 5 F1
East Sq PR4 . . . . 94 A1
East St Bamber Bridge PR5 . 76 E7
Blackburn BB2 . . . . 100 C3
Blackburn, Feniscowles BB2 . 79 D8
Brierfield BB9 . . . . 147 C5
Edenfield BL0 . . . . 67 D4
Hapton BB12 . . . . 125 C4
Haslingden BB4 . . . . 67 A7
Leyland PR5 . . . . 76 B1
Leyland, Farington PR5 . . . . 76 B2
Morecambe LA3 . . . . 212 B4
10 Nelson BB9 . . . . 168 D1
Padiham BB12 . . . . 145 C1
12 Preston PR1 . . . . 96 A8
Rawtenstall BB4 . . . . 84 F5
Southport PR9 . . . . 34 D7
East Terr PR7 . . . . 59 D4
East Topping St 3 FY1 . . . 129 B5
East View Bacup OL13 . . . . 86 F2
13 Barnoldswick BB18 . . . . 200 B2
9 Galgate LA2 . . . . 207 A4
Grimsargh PR2 . . . . 138 B1
Grindleton BB7 . . . . 187 B7
Haslingden BB4 . . . . 84 A8
3 Lostock Hall PR5 . . . . 76 A7
Pendleton BB7 . . . . 165 B4
Preston PR1 . . . . 96 A8
Preston, Brookfield PR2 . . 117 F5
9 Preston, Frenchwood PR1 . 96 C6
Ramsbottom, Brooksbottoms
BL0 . . . . 49 C3
Ramsbottom, Stubbins BL0 . . 67 C1
Read BB12 . . . . 144 D2
Trawden BB8 . . . . 170 C2
Winmarleigh PR3 . . . . 198 F6
East View Ct LA1 . . . . 213 D3
East View Terr PR6 . . . . 79 B3
East Ward Com Prim Sch
BL9 . . . . 32 B2
East Way PR6 . . . . 42 D8
East Wlk BL7 . . . . 46 D2
Eastbank Ave FY4 . . . . 110 A7
Eastbank St PR8 . . . . 34 B6
Eastbank Street Sq 9
PR8, PR9 . . . . 34 B7
Eastbourne Cl PR2 . . . . 115 F5
Eastbourne Rd
Blackpool FY4 . . . . 109 B6
Southport PR8 . . . . 34 A3
Eastcliff LA2 . . . . 231 F5
Eastcott Cl BB2 . . . . 81 A8
Eastern Ave BB10 . . . . 147 C1
Eastfield Dr Longton PR4 . . 94 A1
West Bradford BB7 . . . . 186 F6
Eastgate Accrington BB5 . . 103 C6
Fulwood PR2 . . . . 116 E4
Morecambe LA3 . . . . 213 A2
Ribchester PR3 . . . . 140 E4
Whitworth OL12 . . . . 51 C7
Eastham Cotts FY8 . . . . 90 D6
Eastham Pl BB11 . . . . 127 B6
Eastham St Burnley BB10 . 127 B5
Clitheroe BB7 . . . . 186 E1
Lancaster LA1 . . . . 211 A7
Preston PR1 . . . . 116 E1
Eastlands Heysham LA3 . . 209 A7
Leyland PR5 . . . . 58 C7
Eastmoor Dr BB7 . . . . 164 F7
Easton Cl PR2 . . . . 117 D6
Eastpines Dr FY5 . . . . 150 F8
Eastside FY4 . . . . 109 F8
Eastway Freckleton PR4 . . . . 92 A6
Fulwood PR2,PR3 . . . . 117 B6
Maghull L31 . . . . 5 E1
Eastway Bsns Village
PR2 . . . . 117 B8
Eastwood Ave
Blackpool FY3 . . . . 129 E8
2 Fleetwood FY7 . . . . 193 F3
Eastwood Cl 6 BL9 . . . . 32 B2
Eastwood Cres BB4 . . . . 85 C2
Eastwood Rd PR5 . . . . 75 F1
Eastwood St
Barnoldswick BB18 . . . . 200 C3
Blackburn BB1 . . . . 101 A6
Rawtenstall BB4 . . . . 85 C2
Eastwood Terr BB18 . . . . 200 C3
Eaton Ave FY1 . . . . 129 C1
Eaton Ct FY8 . . . . 88 F6
Eaton Pl PR4 . . . . 112 F5
Eaton Way FY6 . . . . 130 E8
Eaves Ave BB11 . . . . 126 D2
Eaves Cl BB5 . . . . 124 F1
Eaves Green La PR3 . . . . 137 F8
Eaves Green Rd PR7 . . . . 42 B5
Eaves La Chorley PR6 . . . . 42 E8
Cuddy Hill PR4 . . . . 135 D7
Fulwood PR2 . . . . 116 E3
Eaves Lane Hospl PR6 . . . . 42 E8
Eaves Lea LA6 . . . . 238 B2
Eaves Rd FY8 . . . . 110 A1
Eaves St FY1 . . . . 129 B7
Eavesdale WN8 . . . . 9 E8
Eaveswood Cl PR5 . . . . 96 E1
Ebony St 11 BB1 . . . . 101 A7
Ebor Lo PR8 . . . . 34 A5
Ebor St BB10 . . . . 147 B2
Eccles Rd L37 . . . . 11 D1
Eccles St Accrington BB5 . . 103 B7
Blackburn BB2 . . . . 100 E3
Preston PR1 . . . . 117 C1
Ramsbottom BL0 . . . . 49 B6
Eccles's La L40 . . . . 26 B7

Ecclesgate Rd FY4 . . . . .110 A5
Ecclshill Gdns BB3 . . . . . .81 C4
Eccleshill St 1 BB12 . . . .125 C8
Eccleston Cty Prim Sch
PR7 . . . . .40 B6
Eccleston Rd FY1 . . . . . .129 D1
Eclipse Rd BB2 . . . . .79 D8
Ecroyd Rd PR2 . . . . .116 C2
Ecroyd St Leyland PR5 . . . .76 A1
Nelson BB9 . . . . .147 C8
Edale Ave BB4 . . . . .84 C2
Edale Cl PR5 . . . . .59 A7
Edale Ct PR1 . . . . .116 F1
Edale Dr WN6 . . . . .28 E2
Eddington Rd FY8 . . . . . . .89 B4
Eddleston Cl FY3 . . . . . .130 D5
Edelston Rd 5 FY1 . . . . .129 C6
Eden Ave Edenfield BL0 . . . .67 D3
Fleetwood FY7 . . . . .193 D2
Lytham St Anne's FY8 . . . .89 E3
Morecambe LA4 . . . . .213 B5
Southport PR9 . . . . .52 F2
Eden Cl BB9 . . . . .168 D4
Eden Ct BL0 . . . . .67 D2
Eden Gdns PR3 . . . . .139 B8
Eden Gr LA5 . . . . .216 B6
Eden Hall PR1 . . . . .116 E1
Eden Mount Way LA5 . . .217 F2
Eden Pk Blackburn BB2 . . . .99 F8
Lancaster LA1 . . . . .210 F4
Eden St Accrington BB5 . . .103 A5
Blackburn BB1 . . . . .101 A5
9 Blackpool FY1 . . . . . . .129 C6
Edenfield BL0 . . . . .67 D1
Leyland PR5 . . . . .59 A8
Edenfield Ave FY6 . . . . . .151 C7
Edenfield CE Prim Sch
BL0 . . . . .67 D4
Edenfield Cl PR8 . . . . . . .34 E3
Edenfield Rd
Ramsbottom OL11, OL12 . . . .50 E4
Rochdale OL11, OL12 . . . . .51 B1
Edenfield Rd OL11, OL12 . . .51 C1
Edenhurst Cl L37 . . . . . . .11 C2
Edenhurst Dr L37 . . . . . . .11 C2
Edensor Terr BB3 . . . . . . .80 F2
Edenvale Ave FY2 . . . . . .150 B4
Edenvale Cres LA1 . . . . .213 E3
Edenvale Rd LA1 . . . . . . .213 E3
Edenway PR2 . . . . .116 D7
Edgar St Accrington BB5 . . .103 B6
Huncoat BB5 . . . . .124 C4
Nelson BB9 . . . . .168 F2
16 Ramsbottom BL0 . . . . .49 B5
Edgar St W 17 BL0 . . . . .49 B5
Edge Cotts FY8 . . . . .110 A2
Edge End BB6 . . . . .123 B5
Edge End Ave BB9 . . . . . .147 D6
Edge End High Sch BB9 .147 D6
Edge End La
Brierfield BB9 . . . . .147 D6
Great Harwood BB6 . . . . .123 B6
Edge End Rd BB6 . . . . . .123 B5
Edge End Terr BB2 . . . . . .79 B3
Edge Gate La PR6 . . . . . . .62 A6
Edge Hall Rd WN5 . . . . . . .10 E5
Edge Hill Coll PR7 . . . . . . .42 A8
Edge Hill Univ Coll L39 . .16 A3
Edge La Bacup OL13 . . . . .70 C8
Barnoldswick BB8 . . . . . .225 F1
Edgworth BL7 . . . . .47 A8
Rawtenstall BB4 . . . . .85 D3
Edge Nook Rd BB1 . . . . .101 D1
Edge Yate La BB4 . . . . . . .85 B5
Edgecott Cl LA3 . . . . .209 A4
Edgefield PR7 . . . . .60 B2
Edgefield Ct FY3 . . . . . . .130 B8
Edgehill Cl PR2 . . . . .116 D4
Edgehill Cres PR5 . . . . . . .75 E2
Edgehill Dr PR2 . . . . .116 D4
Edgeley Dr BB12 . . . . . . .126 D7
Edgemoor Cl OL12 . . . . . .70 E5
Edgeside BB6 . . . . .123 B5
Edgeside La BB4 . . . . .85 F2
Edgeware Rd BB2 . . . . . .100 C6
Edgeway Pl 3 FY5 . . . . .173 C1
Edgeway Rd FY4 . . . . . . .109 C5
Edgley Dr L39 . . . . .16 A5
Edgworth Gr BB10 . . . . .127 C6
Edgworth Prim Sch BL7 . .47 D5
Edinburgh Cl PR5 . . . . . . .76 C1
Edinburgh Dr BB5 . . . . . .102 F3
Edinburgh Rd Formby L37 . .11 E1
Haslingden BB4 . . . . .83 F1
Edisford Cty Prim Sch
BB7 . . . . .164 C7
Edisford Rd Clitheroe BB7 .164 C8
Waddington BB7 . . . . . . .186 B4
Edison St BB3 . . . . .80 F1
Edith St Barnoldswick BB18 .200 B3
Blackburn BB1 . . . . .101 A4
Nelson BB9 . . . . .147 F8
Shuttleworth BL0 . . . . . . .49 E8
Edleston Lodge 2 PR2 . .117 F4
Edleston St BB5 . . . . .102 F4
Edmondsen Pl 4 FY7 . . .193 F2
Edmondson St BB3 . . . . .200 B3
Edmondson's La BD23 . . .201 F8
Edmonton Dr BB2 . . . . . .100 A8
Edmonton Pl FY2 . . . . . .150 F3
Edmund Gennings Ct
BB7 . . . . .187 D5
Edmund St
5 Accrington BB5 . . . . . .103 C5
Blackburn BB2 . . . . .80 D7

Edmund St continued
Burnley BB10 . . . . .147 B1
Darwen BB3 . . . . .81 B1
3 Preston PR1 . . . . .96 B8
Edmundson St
Blackburn BB2 . . . . .100 C5
3 Church BB5 . . . . .102 E6
Edward Ct BB5 . . . . .102 E6
Edward Sq 9 PR1 . . . . . .117 A1
Edward St Accrington BB5 .103 E1
12 Bacup OL13 . . . . .87 A3
Bamber Bridge PR5 . . . . . .76 E8
Barnoldswick BB18 . . . . .200 C3
Blackpool FY1 . . . . .129 B5
Burnley BB11 . . . . .127 A6
4 Carnforth LA5 . . . . . . .217 D2
Chorley PR6 . . . . .42 D7
Darwen BB3 . . . . .81 A2
8 Earby BB18 . . . . .201 B2
7 Great Harwood BB6 . . .123 C5
Haslingden BB4 . . . . .84 B6
Horwich BL6 . . . . .31 A3
Lancaster LA1 . . . . .211 A8
1 Leyland PR5 . . . . .59 A8
Lytham St Anne's FY8 . . . .88 F7
Morecambe LA4 . . . . .212 D5
Nelson BB9 . . . . .168 F2
Preston PR1 . . . . .95 F8
Rawtenstall BB4 . . . . .85 A8
Thornton FY5 . . . . .173 B4
Walton-le-D PR1 . . . . .96 C5
Whitworth OL12 . . . . .70 D2
Edward VII Quay PR2 . . . .95 B7
Edwell Ave FY4 . . . . .109 B8
Edwin Waugh Gdns OL12 .51 D3
Edwinstowe Rd FY8 . . . . .89 D6
Egan St PR1 . . . . .96 A8
Egbert St PR1 . . . . .117 A1
Egerton St WN8 . . . . .9 D8
Egerton Com Prim Sch
BL7 . . . . .46 D3
Egerton Gr PR7 . . . . .42 B6
Egerton Lo BL7 . . . . .46 E1
Egerton Rd Belmont BL7 . . .45 E4
Blackpool FY1 . . . . .129 B7
Leyland PR5 . . . . .75 F2
Preston PR2 . . . . .116 B1
Egremont Ave FY5 . . . . . .172 D5
Egypt Mount BB4 . . . . . . .84 D2
Egypt Terr 3 BB4 . . . . . . .84 E2
Eider Cl FY5 . . . . .172 F5
Eidsforth La PR3 . . . . . . .220 A1
Eidsforth Rd LA4 . . . . . . .212 E6
Eight Acre Ave BB7 . . . . .144 B8
Eight Acre La Formby L37 . .12 B6
Yealand Redmayne LA5 . . .219 E4
Eildon Dr FY6 . . . . .151 D1
Elaine Ave FY4 . . . . .129 F1
Elaton Lodge 7 PR2 . . . .117 F4
Elbow La L37 . . . . .11 F3
Elbow St PR7 . . . . .42 C7
Elbut La BL9 . . . . .32 F5
Elcho St PR1 . . . . .117 A1
Elder Cl Clayton Green PR6 . .77 C2
Fulwood PR2 . . . . .117 D6
Warton PR4 . . . . .91 E6
Elder Ct BB5 . . . . .103 E8
Elder St BB9 . . . . .168 F2
Elderberry Cl FY5 . . . . . .172 F5
Elderwood Ave FY5 . . . . .151 B7
Eldon Ct FY8 . . . . .88 F7
Eldon Cty Prim Sch PR1 .116 E2
Eldon Gr LA3 . . . . .208 D3
Eldon Rd BB1 . . . . .100 D7
Eldon St Chorley PR6 . . . . .42 D7
Preston PR1, PR2 . . . . . . .116 D2
Eldons Croft PR8 . . . . . . .20 D5
Eldwick St BB10 . . . . .147 C1
Eleanor St Blackburn BB1 .100 F5
3 Nelson BB9 . . . . .168 E1
Electricity St BB5 . . . . . .103 B6
Elgar Cl BB2 . . . . .101 A2
Elgin Cres BB11 . . . . .126 D4
Elgin Pl FY3 . . . . .130 C4
Elgin St 4 Lancaster LA1 . .211 A7
Preston PR1 . . . . .117 A2
Elijah St 4 PR1 . . . . .96 D8
Elim Ct 4 FY8 . . . . .90 C3
Elim Gdns BB2 . . . . .100 C1
Elim Pl BB2 . . . . .100 C1
Eliza St Burnley BB10 . . . .127 B5
Ramsbottom BL0 . . . . .49 D6
Elizabeth Ave PR8 . . . . . .20 E6
Elizabeth Cl FY3 . . . . . . .130 D6
Elizabeth Ct Blackpool FY3 .129 D6
Edenfield BL0 . . . . .67 D3
Poulton-le-F FY6 . . . . . . .151 D3
Elizabeth Dr BB4 . . . . . . .67 A8
Elizabeth Ho
Blackburn BB1 . . . . .101 B3
Darwen BB3 . . . . .81 B1
Elizabeth Sq 7 PR1 . . . . .117 A1
Elizabeth St
Accrington BB5 . . . . .102 F5
Blackburn BB1 . . . . .100 F5
Blackpool FY1 . . . . .129 C6
Burnley BB11 . . . . .127 A5
Edenfield BL0 . . . . .67 D3
9 Fleetwood FY7 . . . . . . .194 B5
Nelson BB9 . . . . .168 E1
Padiham BB12 . . . . .125 C7
Preston PR1 . . . . .95 F8
Whitewell Bottom BB4 . . . .85 F4
Elker Cotts BB7 . . . . .142 F4
Elker La BB7 . . . . .142 F5
Elker Mews BB7 . . . . .142 F3

Elkfield Dr FY3 . . . . .151 A1
Elkin Rd LA4 . . . . .212 G5
Elland Pl FY1 . . . . .129 B1
Elland Rd BB9 . . . . .147 C6
Ellel Hall Gdns LA2 . . . .206 F3
Ellen Ct PR1 . . . . .116 F2
Ellen St Bamber Bridge PR5 .96 E1
Darwen BB3 . . . . .64 A7
11 Nelson BB9 . . . . .147 D8
Preston PR1 . . . . .116 E1
Preston PR1 . . . . .116 F2
Ellenbrook Cl PR6 . . . . . . .42 F1
Ellenrod Dr OL12 . . . . . . .51 A2
Ellenrod La OL12 . . . . . . .51 A2
Ellenshaw Cl Darwen BB3 . .81 B1
Rochdale OL12 . . . . .51 A2
Eller Brook Cl PR6 . . . . . .42 F1
Ellerbeck Ave PR7 . . . . . .117 E5
Ellerbeck Cl BB10 . . . . . .147 C1
Ellerbeck Rd BB5 . . . . . .103 B7
Ellerbreck Rd FY5 . . . . . .172 C2
Ellerbrook Dr L40 . . . . . . .24 F3
Ellerbrook Rd BB3 . . . . . . .81 B1
Ellerbrook Way L39 . . . . . .15 E6
Ellerslie Rd PR2 . . . . .116 B1
Ellesmere Ave Colne BB8 .169 F5
Thornton FY5 . . . . .173 D1
Ellesmere Gr LA4 . . . . . .212 D3
Ellesmere Rd
Blackpool FY4 . . . . .129 E1
Darwen BB3 . . . . .80 E3
Morecambe LA4 . . . . .212 C4
Elletson St FY5 . . . . .151 D4
Elliott Ave BB3 . . . . .64 B6
Elliott Cl PR1 . . . . .116 E2
Elliott St Burnley BB10 . . .127 C5
Preston PR1 . . . . .116 E1
Preston PR1 . . . . .116 E2
Elliott Wlk PR1 . . . . .116 E2
Ellis Dr LA4 . . . . .213 A6
Ellis St Barnoldswick BB18 .200 D1
1 Burnley BB11 . . . . .126 E5
19 Ramsbottom BL0 . . . . .49 B5
Ellisland FY4 . . . . .130 C1
Ellison Fold BB5 . . . . . . .123 A3
Ellison Fold La BB3 . . . . . .81 C1
Ellison Fold Terr BB3 . . . . .81 B1
Ellison St Accrington BB5 .103 B6
Darwen BB3 . . . . .81 A2
Ellwood Ave
Lancaster LA1 . . . . .214 A4
Morecambe LA3 . . . . .212 F2
Ellwood Ct LA3 . . . . .212 G2
Ellwood Gr LA3 . . . . .212 F2
Elm Ave Blackpool FY3 . . .129 E5
Galgate LA2 . . . . .206 F4
Poulton-le-F FY6 . . . . . . .151 D3
Preston PR1 . . . . .116 A2
Warton PR4 . . . . .91 D6
Elm Brow PR3 . . . . .160 C4
Elm Cl Barnoldswick BB18 .200 A1
Haslingden BB4 . . . . .84 B3
Rishton BB1 . . . . .102 B8
Salterforth BB18 . . . . . . .191 E8
Elm Ct FY6 . . . . .151 D3
Elm Dr
3 Bamber Bridge PR5 . . . .96 F1
Formby L37 . . . . .11 D1
Elm Gr Chorley PR6 . . . . . .60 E2
Clayton-le-W PR5 . . . . .76 D3
Darwen BB3 . . . . .81 B3
Fulwood PR2 . . . . .117 E2
6 Horwich BL6 . . . . .31 E1
Kirkham PR4 . . . . .113 B7
Morecambe LA4 . . . . .213 A7
Skelmersdale WN8 . . . . . .17 E1
Elm Pl L39 . . . . .15 E4
Elm Rd Burscough L40 . . . .24 E3
Southport PR8 . . . . .34 B4
Elm St 7 Bacup OL13 . . . . .87 A3
Blackburn BB1 . . . . .101 A4
Burnley BB10 . . . . .127 A8
Bury BL9 . . . . .32 B2
Colne BB8 . . . . .169 E6
Edenfield BL0 . . . . .67 E3
Fleetwood FY7 . . . . .194 A4
Great Harwood BB6 . . . . .123 C4
Haslingden BB4 . . . . .84 B3
9 Nelson BB9 . . . . .168 E1
Ramsbottom BL0 . . . . .49 D6
Rawtenstall BB4 . . . . .85 A4
Rochdale OL12 . . . . .51 F1
Whitworth OL12 . . . . .70 D2
Elm View BB10 . . . . .147 D2
Elmbank Ave FY5 . . . . . .150 C7
Elmcroft La L38 . . . . .3 A3
Elmdale Cl L37 . . . . .11 D2
Elmer's Green La
Skelmersdale, Dalton WN8 . .18 C4
Skelmersdale, Elmers
Green WN8 . . . . .18 D2
Elmers Green Prim Sch
WN8 . . . . .18 D1
Elmers Wood Rd WN8 . . . .18 D2
Elmfield Dr PR5 . . . . .77 C6
Elmfield St BB5 . . . . .102 F7
Elmhurst Rd FY8 . . . . .89 B8
Empark Gate OL12 . . . . . .51 B3
Empark Gr OL12 . . . . .51 B3
Empark Vale OL12 . . . . . . .51 B3
Empark View OL12 . . . . . .51 B3
Empark Way OL12 . . . . . . .51 B3
Elmridge WN8 . . . . .9 D8
Elmridge Cres FY2 . . . . .150 F3
Elms Ave Cleveleys FY5 . . .172 E2
Lytham St Anne's FY8 . . . .89 E3
Elms Ct LA4 . . . . .213 A7
Elms Dr Morecambe LA4 . .213 A7

Elms Dr continued
Wrea Green PR4 . . . . .112 B4
Elms Sch LA4 . . . . .213 A7
Elms Sch PR1 . . . . .117 A3
Elms The Clayton Green PR6 .77 C1
Maghull L31 . . . . .5 D3
Southport PR8 . . . . .34 C5
Southport, Birkdale PR8 . . . .33 F6
Elmsdale Cl LA1 . . . . .213 E2
Elmsfield Pk L39 . . . . .6 A6
Elmside Cl FY5 . . . . .173 C1
Elmslack Cl LA5 . . . . .218 C4
Elmslack La LA5 . . . . .218 C4
Elmsley St PR1 . . . . .116 E2
Elmslie Girls Sch FY3 . . .129 E3
Elmstead WN8 . . . . .9 D8
Elmswood Cl FY8 . . . . . . .89 F4
Elmwood Chorley PR7 . . . . .60 B1
Longridge PR3 . . . . .139 A8
Skelmersdale WN8 . . . . . .18 C3
Elmwood Ave
1 Leyland PR5 . . . . .75 E1
Preesall FY6 . . . . .195 B4
Elmwood Cl BB5 . . . . .103 D6
Elmwood Ct PR4 . . . . .131 C6
Elmwood Dr
Penwortham PR1 . . . . .95 B4
Thornton FY5 . . . . .173 C1
Elmwood Gdns LA1 . . . . .211 A2
Elmwood St BB11 . . . . . .126 D5
Elsby Ave FY5 . . . . .151 C8
Elsie St 10 BL0 . . . . .49 A4
Elsinore Cl FY7 . . . . .193 C6
Elslack La BD23 . . . . .201 F7
Elson Rd L37 . . . . .11 D1
Elston Ave FY3 . . . . .130 A8
Elston Gn PR2 . . . . .138 E1
Elston La PR2 . . . . .118 F7
Elswick WN8 . . . . .9 C8
Elswick Gdns BB2 . . . . . .120 D3
Elswick Gn PR9 . . . . .53 A5
Elswick Lodge BB2 . . . . .120 E3
Elswick Pl Blackpool FY4 . .109 B8
Lytham St Anne's FY8 . . . .89 B8
Elswick Rd Leyland PR5 . . .58 D8
Preston PR2 . . . . .115 C1
Southport PR9 . . . . .52 F4
Elswick St BB3 . . . . .81 B1
Elsworth Cl L37 . . . . .2 C8
Elterwater Pl
Blackpool FY3 . . . . .130 C2
Lancaster LA1 . . . . .214 A1
Eltham St FY3 . . . . .151 B1
Elton Rd BB1, BB4 . . . . . . .82 B5
Elton St 3 PR2 . . . . .116 C1
Elvaston Way FY6 . . . . . .151 C6
Elvington Rd L38 . . . . .3 A2
Ely Cl Darwen BB3 . . . . . . .81 C1
Wilpshire BB1 . . . . .121 F6
Ely Mews PR9 . . . . .53 A2
Embankment Rd BL7 . . . . .47 C5
Emerald Ave BB1 . . . . . . .121 F2
Emerald Cl FY5 . . . . .150 F7
Emerald Cotts BL8 . . . . . .48 F3
Emerald St BB1 . . . . .121 F2
Emerson Ave FY4 . . . . . .109 D7
Emerson Cl L38 . . . . .3 A4
Emerson Rd PR1 . . . . . . .117 C2
Emerson St LA1 . . . . .211 A4
Emesgate La LA5 . . . . . . .218 C3
Emily St Bamber Bridge PR5 .76 A8
Blackburn BB1 . . . . .101 A6
Burnley BB1 . . . . .127 A4
Emma St BB5 . . . . .102 F6
Emmanuel Holcombe
CE Prim Sch BL8 . . . . . .49 A6
Emmanuel Rd PR9 . . . . . . .52 F2
Emmanuel St PR1, PR2 . . .116 E2
Emmaus Rd LA3 . . . . .208 F6
Emmerdale Cl BB5 . . . . . .102 D5
Emmett St Horwich BL6 . . . .31 A3
Preston PR1 . . . . .116 F1
Emmott Cl BB8 . . . . .170 E6
Emmott La BB8 . . . . .170 D6
Emnie La PR5 . . . . .58 C7
Empire Gr 2 FY3 . . . . . . .129 D7
Empire St BB6 . . . . .123 D6
Emporium The 7 BB7 . . . .164 E8
Empress Ave PR2 . . . . . . .116 E4
Empress Cl L31 . . . . .5 B1
Empress Dr FY2 . . . . .150 B3
Empress St Accrington BB5 .102 F6
Blackburn BB3 . . . . .80 F7
Colne BB8 . . . . .169 E5
Empress Way PR7 . . . . . . .59 E2
End St BB8 . . . . .169 B4
Endcliffe Rd LA4 . . . . . . .212 F5
Endeavour Ct PR2 . . . . . . .95 B7
Enderley Ct FY5 . . . . .173 C1
Ending Rake OL12 . . . . . . .51 C4
Endsleigh Gdns FY4 . . . .109 E6
Endsleigh Gr LA1 . . . . . . .213 C3
Enfield Cl Eccleston PR7 . . .40 C5
Huncoat BB5 . . . . .124 C4
Enfield Rd Accrington BB5 .124 D2
Blackpool FY1 . . . . .129 C7
Engine La L37 . . . . .3 E8
England Ave FY2 . . . . . . .150 C4
English Martyrs' Pl PR1 .116 F2
English Martyrs'
RC Prim Sch PR1 . . . . . .116 E1
Ennerdale WN8 . . . . .9 D8
Ennerdale Ave
Blackburn BB1 . . . . .101 C3
Fleetwood FY7 . . . . .193 C1
Maghull L31 . . . . .5 E2
Morecambe LA4 . . . . .212 G4

Ennerdale Cl
Clitheroe BB7 . . . . .164 C7
Formby L37 . . . . .11 D3
Forton PR3 . . . . .204 B3
Knott End-on-S FY6 . . . . .194 F6
Lancaster LA1 . . . . .214 B2
Leyland PR5 . . . . .59 A7
Ennerdale Dr Ormskirk L39 .15 B2
Walton-le-D PR5 . . . . .96 E5
Ennerdale Rd
Blackpool FY4 . . . . .130 C1
Burnley BB10 . . . . .127 E5
Chorley PR7 . . . . .42 A6
Clitheroe BB7 . . . . .164 C7
Formby L37 . . . . .11 E3
Longridge PR3 . . . . .138 F5
Ennismore St BB10 . . . . .147 C1
Enoch Brow BB2 . . . . .79 C8
Enstone WN8 . . . . .18 C1
Enterprise Ct BB5 . . . . . .124 D1
Enterprise Dr PR5 . . . . . . .76 A4
Enterprise Way
Nelson BB8 . . . . .168 F3
Thornton FY7 . . . . .173 A6
Enterprise Workshops
Kirkby L33 . . . . .1 B1
Southport PR9 . . . . .35 A6
Entwisle Rd BB5 . . . . .103 B8
Entwistle Hall La BL7 . . . .47 B8
Entwistle St BB3 . . . . .81 A1
Entwistle Sta BL7 . . . . . . .47 B8
Ephraim St PR1 . . . . .96 C7
Epping Cl FY2 . . . . .150 E5
Epping Pl PR6 . . . . .42 D8
Epsom Croft PR6 . . . . .60 F4
Epsom Ct PR6 . . . . .30 B7
Epsom Gr L33 . . . . .1 A6
Epsom Rd FY5 . . . . .150 F8
Epsom Way BB5 . . . . .103 C5
Epworth St BB3 . . . . .64 B6
Equity St BB3 . . . . .64 A8
Erdington Rd FY1 . . . . . . .129 C3
Erith Gr FY2 . . . . .150 C5
Ermine Cl BB2 . . . . .81 A8
Ermine Pl LA3 . . . . .213 A3
Ernest St Bacup OL13 . . . . .70 C8
6 Church BB5 . . . . .102 E6
Clayton-le-M BB5 . . . . . . .123 F1
Cornholme OL14 . . . . . . .108 C1
Ernlouen Cl BB2 . . . . .80 A8
Erskine Rd PR6 . . . . .60 E1
Escar St 9 BB11 . . . . .126 F5
Escott Gdns 10 BB10 . . . .127 A8
Esher Pond PR2 . . . . .116 C6
Eshton Terr BB7 . . . . .164 E7
Esk Ave Edenfield BL0 . . . . .67 D5
Fleetwood FY7 . . . . .193 D2
Eskbank WN8 . . . . .9 C8
Eskbrook WN8 . . . . .18 C1
Eskdale WN8 . . . . .9 B8
Eskdale Ave
Fleetwood FY7 . . . . .193 D1
Ormskirk L39 . . . . .15 C2
Eskdale Cl Blackpool FY4 . .129 F1
Brierfield BB10 . . . . .147 C4
Formby L37 . . . . .11 D2
Fulwood PR2 . . . . .116 F8
Eskdale Cres BB2 . . . . . . .79 E8
Eskdale Ct FY5 . . . . .172 D1
Eskdale Dr Formby L37 . . . .11 D2
Kirkham PR4 . . . . .113 A7
Maghull L31 . . . . .5 E2
Eskdale Gdns BB12 . . . . .145 C2
Eskdale Gr FY6 . . . . .194 F6
Eskdale Pl LA4 . . . . .212 G4
Eskdale Rd Leyland PR5 . . .59 C2
Longridge PR3 . . . . .138 F6
Eskew La LA2 . . . . .233 B8
Eskham Cl PR4 . . . . .112 C6
Eskrigge Cl 4 LA1 . . . . . .213 F4
Eskrigge La LA2 . . . . .232 A8
Esp La BB8 . . . . .225 F1
Esplanade
Knott End-on-S FY6 . . . . .194 D6
Preston PR1 . . . . .96 B5
Southport PR8 . . . . .33 F7
Esplanade The
Fleetwood FY7 . . . . .194 A5
Rishton BB1 . . . . .102 A8
Essex Ave Burnley BB12 . .126 B7
Heywood OL10 . . . . .32 E1
Essex Cl BB8 . . . . .200 D3
Essex Pl FY2 . . . . .150 E5
Essex Rd Morecambe LA4 .213 B4
4 Rishton BB1 . . . . .123 A1
Southport PR8 . . . . .21 A8
Standish WN1 . . . . .29 B1
Essex St Accrington BB5 . .103 D6
Barnoldswick BB18 . . . . .200 B2
Colne BB8 . . . . .169 E4
Darwen BB3 . . . . .81 C1
Horwich BL6 . . . . .31 D1
Nelson BB9 . . . . .168 E1
Preston PR1 . . . . .117 A1
Essie Terr BB18 . . . . .200 B1
Essington Ave LA4 . . . . . .212 D4
Est Bank Rd BL0 . . . . .49 A3
Esther St BB1 . . . . .101 C5
Ethel St Barnoldswick BB18 .200 C2
Whitworth OL12 . . . . .70 D2
Ethersall Rd BB9 . . . . . . .147 E6
Eton Ave BB5 . . . . .103 C7
Eton Cl BB12 . . . . .125 C6
Eton Pk PR2 . . . . .117 C5
Eton Way WN5 . . . . .10 F8
Ettington Dr PR8 . . . . .20 A5
Ettrick Ave FY7 . . . . .193 D3
Euro Trad Est BB1 . . . . . .100 F7

Europa Dr PR5 76 A4
Europa Way LA1 210 C8
Euston Rd LA4 212 E5
Euston St PR1 95 E7
Euxton CE Sch PR7 59 C2
Euxton Hall Ct PR7 59 C2
Euxton Hall Gdns PR7 59 C1
Euxton Hall Hospl PR7 59 C1
Euxton Hall Mews PR7 59 C2
Euxton La Chorley PR7 60 B3
Euxton PR7 59 E4
Euxton Sta PR7 59 D1
Evans St Burnley BB11 126 F4
Horwich BL6 31 D4
Preston PR2 116 D1
Evanstone Cl BL6 31 B3
Eve St BB9 169 A2
Evelyn Rd BB3 80 E5
Evelyn St BB10 147 A1
Evenwood WN8 18 D1
Evenwood Ct WN8 18 C1
Everard Cl L40 22 F7
Everard Rd PR8 34 D4
Everest Cl FY8 110 A1
Everest Ct 2 PR4 112 F6
Everest Dr FY2 150 C5
Everest Rd FY8 110 A2
Evergreen Ave PR5 59 A7
Evergreen Cl PR7 42 B5
Evergreens The
Blackburn BB2 79 F8
Formby L37 11 D4
Fulwood PR4 115 E4
Eversham Cl PR9 54 A5
Eversholt Cl BB12 146 D7
Eversleigh Ave FY5 173 A3
Eversleigh St PR1 116 E1
Eversley WN8 18 D1
Everton BB2 101 A1
Everton Rd Blackpool FY4 109 C6
Southport PR8 34 A4
Everton St BB3 80 F1
Every St Brierfield BB9 147 B6
Burnley BB11 126 E5
Nelson BB9 147 C8
Nelson BB9 147 D8
Ramsbottom BL0 49 D6
Evesham Ave PR1 95 E2
Evesham Cl
5 Accrington BB5 103 A7
Blackpool FY5 150 E7
Hutton PR4 94 C1
Evesham Rd
Lytham St Anne's FY8 89 A5
Normoss FY3 130 B7
Evington WN8 18 D1
Ewell Cl PR6 60 F4
Ewood BB2 100 D1
Ewood Ct BB2 100 C2
Ewood La BB4 67 C7
Ewood Park (Blackburn Rovers FC) BB2 80 D8
Exchange St
Accrington BB5 102 F5
18 Blackburn BB1 100 E5
Blackpool FY1 129 B6
Colne BB8 169 D4
Darwen BB3 81 A2
Edenfield BL0 67 D3
Exe St PR1 117 B2
Exeter Ave LA1 211 B6
Exeter Dr FY5 173 A2
Exeter Pl 2 PR2 115 E2
Exeter St Blackburn BB2 100 D2
3 Blackpool FY4 129 C1
Exmoor Cl PR9 53 B6
Exmouth St BB11 127 A5
Exton St BB9 147 A5
Extwistle Rd BB10 128 B7
Extwistle Sq BB10 127 E5
Extwistle St Burnley BB10 127 B8
Nelson BB9 147 D7
Eyes La Bretherton PR5 56 E3
Newburgh WN8 26 A3

F

Factory Bank PR1 95 F3
Factory Brow Blackrod BL6 30 D3
Scorton PR3 199 E6
Factory Hill Horwich BL6 31 D4
4 Lancaster LA1 214 A1
Factory La Adlington PR6 30 B8
Barrowford BB9 168 D4
17 Padiham BB12 145 C1
Penwortham PR1 95 F3
Factory St BL0 49 C7
Fair Hill BB4 67 A7
Fair Oak Cl PR2 117 F3
Fair View OL13 70 C8
Fair View Cres OL13 87 B3
Fair View Rd BB11 127 B5
Fair Way FY6 174 C7
Fairacres WN6 28 B1
Fairbairn Ave BB12 126 C8
Fairbairn St BL6 31 B3
Fairbank LA6 238 B2
Fairbank Gr LA4 212 D3
Fairbank Wlk BB4 105 A2
Fairburn WN8 18 B3
Fairclough Rd
Accrington BB5 103 A3
Thornton FY5 173 A3
Fairfax Ave FY2 150 E5
Fairfax Cl PR3 178 D6
Fairfax Pl PR5 96 D2
Fairfax Rd PR2 117 E4
Fairfield PR3 178 C8
Fairfield Ave
Newchurch BB4 85 F2
Normoss FY3 130 B7
Poulton-le-F FY6 151 D3
Fairfield Cl Carnforth LA5 217 E1
Clitheroe BB7 164 C7
Lancaster LA1 210 E8
2 Ormskirk L39 15 E7
Fairfield Ct FY7 193 F2
Fairfield Dr
Brierfield BB10 147 C3
Bury BL9 32 D3
Clitheroe BB7 164 C7
1 Ormskirk L39 15 E7
Preston PR2 116 B2
Fairfield General Hospl BL9 32 E4
Fairfield Gr LA3 212 B2
Fairfield Prim Sch BL9 32 D3
Fairfield Rd Blackpool FY1 129 C8
Fulwood PR2 117 A4
Lancaster LA1 210 E8
Leyland PR5 58 F8
Morecambe LA3 212 B2
Nelson BB9 148 B8
Poulton-le-F FY6 130 F7
Southport PR8 20 C5
Fairfield St Accrington BB5 102 F4
5 Bamber Bridge PR5 76 B7
Fairfields Dr BB3 80 F6
Fairgarth Dr LA6 238 B2
Fairham Ave 6 PR1 95 D2
Fairhaven WN8 18 C3
Fairhaven Ave FY7 172 D7
Fairhaven Cl 5 FY5 173 D1
Fairhaven La FY8 88 E5
Fairhaven Lake FY8 89 C3
Fairhaven Rd
Blackburn BB2 100 F1
Leyland PR5 75 D1
Lytham St Anne's FY8 88 F5
Penwortham PR1 95 E5
Southport PR9 53 B4
Fairhaven Way LA4 212 G5
Fairheath Rd LA2 233 B4
Fairhill Terr BB4 67 A7
Fairholme Rd BB11 127 B3
Fairholmes Cl FY5 173 B3
Fairholmes Way 1 FY5 173 B3
Fairhope Ave
Lancaster LA1 213 E3
Morecambe LA4 213 B6
Fairhope Ct BB2 100 C6
Fairhurst Ave WN6 28 D3
Fairhurst Ct FY5 172 D3
Fairhurst St FY1 129 C6
Fairhurst's Dr WN8 26 B2
Fairlawn Rd FY8 89 F3
Fairlea Ave LA4 213 B6
Fairlie WN8 18 C3
Fairlie Cty Prim Sch WN8 18 C3
Fairmont Dr FY6 174 D2
Fairsnape Ave PR3 139 B7
Fairsnape Dr PR3 178 B6
Fairsnape Rd FY8 90 D4
Fairstead WN8 18 C3
Fairthorn Wlk L33 1 A3
Fairview
Kirkby Lonsdale LA6 238 B3
Rawtenstall BB4 84 F5
Fairview Ave FY8 89 A7
Fairview Cl PR4 73 F5
Fairway Chorley PR7 60 C2
Fleetwood FY7 193 C1
Penwortham PR1 95 B6
Poulton-le-F FY6 151 A2
Southport PR8 52 C2
Whitworth OL12 51 C7
Fairway Gdns FY6 194 D5
Fairway Rd FY4 109 E8
Fairways Fulwood PR2 117 A6
Horwich BL6 31 C3
Lytham St Anne's FY8 89 A6
Fairways Ave PR3 136 C3
Fairways Ct Formby L37 11 C5
Wilpshire BB1 121 F5
Fairways Dr BB11 126 E2
Fairways The WN8 18 D3
Fairweather Ct BB12 145 D1
Fairwinds Ave PR4 72 D4
Falcon Ave BB3 80 E3
Falcon Cl Blackburn BB1 100 D8
Bury BL9 32 B4
Falcon Ct BB5 123 F2
Falcon Dr FY6 151 B2
Falcon St PR1 117 B2
Falinge Fold OL12 51 D1
Falinge Park High Sch OL12 51 D1
Falinge Rd OL12 51 E1
Falkirk Ave FY2 150 C6
Falkland WN8 18 C3
Falkland Ave FY4 129 F2
Falkland Rd PR8 34 D5
Falkland St PR1 95 F7
Fall Barn Rd BB4 85 B2
Fall Kirk LA2 234 F1
Fallbarn Cres BB4 85 A1
Fallbarn Rd BB4 85 B2
Fallowfield Cl PR4 112 E6
Fallowfield Dr
Burnley BB12 126 D8
Rochdale OL12 51 D2
Fallowfield Rd FY8 89 C6
Falmouth Ave
Fleetwood FY7 172 C8
Haslingden BB4 84 C2
Falmouth Rd FY1 129 C2
Falshaw Dr BL9 49 E1
Falstone Ave BL0 49 C4
Far Croft PR5 96 A1
Far East View 15 BB18 200 B2
Far Field PR1 95 D3
Far La PR1 95 C2
Far Moor La LA1 211 C8
Far Nook PR6 60 B7
Faraday Ave BB7 164 D8
Faraday Dr PR2 117 C7
Faraday St BB12 126 D7
Faraday Way FY2 150 F5
Fardes Cl BB2 100 F1
Fareham Cl PR2 117 A4
Fareham Dr PR9 54 A5
Farholme La OL13 69 D8
Faringdon Ave FY4 109 E5
Farington Ave PR5 58 D7
Farington Cty Prim Sch PR5 76 B3
Farington Gate PR5 76 B2
Farington Rd PR5 76 A6
Farington St Paul's CE Prim Sch PR5 75 F7
Farleton Cl LA5 217 C5
Farleton Ct 3 LA1 213 F4
Farleton Old Rd LA2 232 A5
Farley La Orrell WN8 19 A3
Skelmersdale WN8 18 F3
Farm Ave Adlington PR6 30 A8
Bacup OL13 86 F4
Farm Cl Southport PR9 35 A8
Thornton FY5 173 B2
Farm House Cl
Blackburn BB1 101 C4
Lucas Green PR6 60 C6
Farm Meadow Rd WN5 10 E5
Farmdale Dr L31 5 E1
Farmdale Rd LA1 211 B5
Farmend Cl PR4 74 B8
Farmer's Row BB2 80 B7
Farnborough Rd PR8 20 F8
Farnborough Road Inf & Jun Schs PR8 21 A8
Farnell Pl FY4 109 D6
Farnham Way FY6 151 C5
Farnlea Dr LA4 213 A5
Farnworth Rd FY5 173 D1
Farrer St BB9 147 C7
Farrier Rd L33 1 A2
Farriers Fold 4 LA3 208 F7
Farringdon Cl PR1 117 F1
Farringdon Cres PR1 117 F1
Farringdon La PR2 117 F3
Farringdon Pl PR1 117 F1
Farrington Cl BB11 126 C3
Farrington Ct BB11 126 C3
Farrington Dr L39 15 E6
Farrington Pl BB11 126 C3
Farrington Rd BB11 126 B3
Farrington St PR7 42 C8
Farthings The PR7 59 F1
Faulkner Cl PR8 20 C6
Faulkner Gdns PR8 20 C6
Faulkner's La PR3 204 B1
Favordale Rd BB8 170 A5
Fawcett WN8 18 B3
Fawcett Cl BB2 100 D3
Fawcett Rd L31 5 D3
Fayles Gr FY4 130 A1
Fazackerley St PR2 116 C1
Fazakerley St 18 PR7 42 C8
Fearnhead Ave BL6 31 A3
Fearns Cty High Sch OL13 86 A1
Fearns Moss BB4,OL13 86 A1
Fecit La BL0 50 C8
Fecitt Brow BB1 101 D4
Fecitt Rd BB2 100 B6
Federation St BB18 200 A3
Feilden Pl BB2 79 D8
Feilden St BB2 100 D5
Feildens Farm La BB2 120 B3
Felgate Brow FY3 129 E5
Felix St BB11 127 B7
Fell Brow PR3 139 B7
Fell Cl 5 PR5 76 F8
Fell Rd High Casterton LA6 238 F3
Morecambe LA4 213 B4
Waddington BB7 186 A6
Fell View Brierfield BB10 147 D3
Caton LA2 231 C3
Chorley PR6 42 E6
Garstang PR3 178 C8
Grimsargh PR2 138 C2
Weir OL13 87 A7
West Bradford BB7 186 D7
Fell View Cl PR3 178 C8
Fell Way FY6 174 D7
Fellborough Lodge 5 FY8 89 A8
Fellery St PR7 42 C8
Fellgate LA3 213 A2
Fellside Cl BL8 48 F1
Fellside View LA3 208 F7
Fellstone Vale PR6 79 A1
Fellstone View PR6 79 A1
Fellview PR9 53 D6
Fellway Cl 7 PR5 76 C8
Felstead WN8 18 B2
Felstead St PR1 96 D8
Felton Way PR4 73 F3
Feltons WN8 18 B2
Fenber Ave FY4 109 C7
Fencegate BB12 146 C7
Fengrove PR4 74 A8
Fenham Carr La LA1 211 C7
Feniscliffe Dr BB2 100 A2
Feniscowles Cty Jun Sch BB2 79 C7
Feniscowles Prim Sch BB2 79 D8
Fenney Ct WN8 18 C1
Fennyfold Terr BB12 125 C6
Fensway PR4 94 D2
Fenton Ave BB18 200 D3
Fenton Rd Blackpool FY1 129 C6
Fulwood PR2 117 C4
Fenton St LA1 210 E8
Fenwick St BB11 126 D3
Ferguson Gdns OL12 51 F3
Ferguson Rd FY1 129 E2
Ferguson St BB2 80 D7
Fermor Rd Becconsall PR4 72 E1
Preston PR1 117 E1
Fern Ave BB5 102 F3
Fern Bank Carnforth LA5 217 D1
Chorley PR6 60 D3
Lancaster LA1 211 A5
Maghull L31 5 E1
Fern Bank Ave BB18 200 A3
Fern Breck Cotts FY6 195 A2
Fern Cl
2 Bamber Bridge PR5 76 B8
Skelmersdale WN8 17 E1
Fern Croft LA6 238 E4
Fern Ct FY7 193 C1
Fern Dene 2 OL12 51 B2
Fern Gore Ave BB5 103 A3
Fern Gr FY1 129 C3
Fern Hill La OL12 51 A3
Fern Isle Cl OL12 51 B6
Fern Lea BB9 147 E8
Fern Lea St BB4 68 D8
Fern Mdw PR6 77 C2
Fern Rd BB11 126 E4
Fern St Bacup OL13 86 F3
Colne BB8 169 F6
Newchurch BB4 85 F1
Ramsbottom BL0 49 D7
Fern Terr BB4 84 A3
Fernbank Ct BB9 147 E7
Ferncliffe Dr LA3 212 A2
Ferndale Blackburn BB1 101 A6
Skelmersdale WN8 18 C2
Ferndale Ave FY4 109 D7
Ferndale Cl Freckleton PR4 92 D7
Leyland PR5 59 B7
Thornton FY5 173 C2
Ferndale St BB10 127 C8
Ferngrove BL9 32 B5
Fernhill Ave OL13 69 E8
Fernhill Cl OL13 69 E8
Fernhill Cres 1 OL13 69 E8
Fernhill Dr OL13 69 E8
Fernhill Gr 2 OL13 69 E8
Fernhill Pk OL13 69 E8
Fernhill Way 4 OL13 69 E8
Fernhills BL7 46 E2
Fernhurst Ave FY4 129 D1
Fernhurst Gate L39 15 B1
Fernhurst St BB2 80 D8
Fernlea Ave
Barnoldswick BB18 200 B2
Oswaldtwistle BB5 103 A3
Fernlea Cl Blackburn BB2 80 B8
1 Rochdale OL12 51 B2
Fernlea Dr BB5 123 F4
Fernleigh PR5 58 A8
Fernleigh Cl FY2 150 D4
Fernley Rd PR8 34 A5
Ferns The Bacup OL13 87 A1
Bamber Bridge PR5 96 C3
Preston PR2 116 C2
Fernside Way OL12 51 A1
Fernstone Cl BL6 31 A3
Fernview Dr BL0 49 A1
Fernville Terr 6 OL13 69 D8
Fernwood Ave FY5 151 B8
Fernwood Cl FY8 89 E4
Ferny Knoll Rd WA11 8 F4
Fernyhalgh Ct PR2 117 D6
Fernyhalgh Gdns PR2 117 D6
Fernyhalgh La PR2 117 D7
Fernyhalgh Pl PR2 117 D6
Ferrier Bank PR4 91 D5
Ferrier Cl 1 BB1 101 C5
Ferry Rd PR2 94 F8
Ferry Side La PR9 53 C5
Ffrances Pas 30 LA1 210 F8
Fiddler's La Chipping PR3 181 F4
Clayton Green PR6 77 B2
Fidler La PR5 75 F5
Field Cl L40 24 F3
Field Maple Dr PR2 117 F3
Field Rd LA3 208 D6
Field St Blackburn BB2 100 B2
Blackpool FY1 129 C2
Padiham BB12 125 C7
Skelmersdale WN8 17 D2
Field Top OL13 87 A7
Field Wlk L39 16 B5
Fielden St Burnley BB11 126 D5
Chorley PR6 42 E8
5 Leyland PR5 75 D1
Fieldfare Cl
Penwortham PR1 95 E3
Thornton FY5 173 A5
Fieldhouse Ave FY5 173 D2
Fieldhouse Ind Est OL12 51 F2
Fieldhouse Rd OL12 51 F2
Fielding Cres BB2 100 A1
Fielding La
Great Harwood BB6 123 B5
Oswaldtwistle BB5 102 E3
Fielding Pl PR6 30 B8
Fielding Rd FY1 129 D8
Fielding St BB1 123 C1
Fieldings Bldgs 8 BB4 84 E2
Fieldings The L31 5 B4
Fieldlands PR8 35 A2
Fields End BB6 122 C8
Fields Rd BB4 84 C1
Fields The PR7 40 B7
Fieldsend LA3 209 A7
Fieldside Ave PR7 59 C1
Fieldside Cl PR5 96 C3
Fieldview WN8 10 A7
Fieldway FY8 109 E2
Fife Cl PR6 42 E6
Fife St Accrington BB5 103 A4
Barrowford BB9 168 C1
Fifth Ave Blackpool FY4 109 C7
Burnley BB10 147 B3
Bury BL9 32 D4
Filberts Cl PR2 116 C3
Filberts The PR2 116 C3
File St PR7 42 C7
Filey Pl Blackpool FY1 129 B6
Fulwood PR2 116 A4
Filey Rd FY8 110 A1
Filton Gr LA3 213 A3
Finch Cl BB1 100 E6
Finch La Appley Bridge WN6 27 B1
Cottam PR4 115 E4
Finch Mill Ave WN6 19 D7
Finch St 5 BB3 80 F2
Finch's Cotts 6 PR1 95 E4
Finches The FY6 151 B2
Finchley Rd FY1 129 B8
Findon WN8 18 C2
Fine Jane's Way PR9 35 B8
Finnington La BB2 79 A6
Finsbury Ave
Blackpool FY1 129 D2
Lytham St Anne's FY8 89 B4
Finsbury Pl BB2 80 D8
Finsley Gate BB11 127 A5
Finsley St BB10 147 E3
Fir Cl FY7 193 C2
Fir Cotes L31 5 E1
Fir Ct BB5 103 E8
Fir Gr Blackpool FY1 129 E2
Warton PR4 91 D6
Fir Grove Rd 12 BB11 127 B4
Fir St Burnley BB10 127 B5
Bury BL9 32 A2
Haslingden BB4 84 B3
Nelson BB9 147 F8
Ramsbottom BL0 49 D7
Southport PR8 34 F6
Fir Tree Ave PR2 116 B4
Fir Tree Cl Hest Bank LA5 215 F2
Much Hoole PR4 73 E3
Skelmersdale WN8 9 D7
Fir Tree La Haskayne L39 14 F3
Ormskirk L39 15 A2
Fir Tree Pl FY5 150 F8
Fir Tree Way 3 BL6 31 E1
Fir Trees Ave
Bamber Bridge PR5 76 A8
Fulwood PR2 118 A4
Fir Trees Cres 1 PR5 76 A8
Fir Trees Gr BB12 145 E5
Fir Trees La BB12 145 E5
Fir Trees Pl PR2 117 F4
Fir Trees Rd PR5 96 A1
Firbank PR7 59 C2
Firbank Ave PR4 56 A7
Firbank Rd LA1 214 A1
Firbeck WN8 18 C1
Fircroft WN6 28 A2
Firfield Cl PR4 112 E5
Firs Cl L37 11 D5
Firs Cres L37 11 D5
Firs La L39 14 E3
Firs Link L37 11 D4
Firshill Cl FY5 151 B8
First Ave Blackpool FY4 109 C7
Church BB5 103 A8
Clifton PR4 114 C1
Poulton-le-F FY6 151 E3
Preston PR2 116 A2
West Bradford BB7 186 D7
Wrea Green PR4 112 B4
First Terr LA3 205 B5
Firswood Cl FY8 89 E4
Firswood Rd L40, WN8 17 C3
Firtree Cl Blackburn BB2 79 F8
Chorley PR7 42 C3
Firwood Longridge PR3 139 A8
Skelmersdale WN8 18 D3
Firwood La PR5 98 B5
Fish House La PR3 182 B5
Fish La L40 37 B2
Fish Rake La BL0,BB4 67 E6
Fisher Dr Orrell WN5 10 E7
Southport PR9 34 F7
Fisher Slack La FY6 153 B2
Fisher St FY1 129 C6
Fisher's La FY4 110 A5
Fishergate PR1 95 F7
Fishergate Ct 11 PR1 95 E7
Fishergate Ctr PR1 95 F7
Fishergate Hill PR1 95 E6
Fishergate Wlk 7 PR1 95 F7
Fishermans Cl L37 11 E6
Fishermans Reach PR4 112 D4
Fishmoor Dr BB2,BB3 80 F8
Fishwick Cty Prim Sch PR1 117 E1

Fishwick La PR6 ....78 B1
Fishwick Par PR1 ....96 D8
Fishwick Rd PR1 ....96 C8
Fishwick View PR1 ....96 D8
Fitchfield PR1 ....95 F2
Fitzgerald St PR1 ....117 C1
Fitzroy Rd FY2 ....150 D3
Fitzroy St PR1 ....95 E7
Five Acres PR5 ....75 E4
Five Lane Ends
  Hampson Green LA2 ....204 D8
  Preesall FY6 ....195 A2
  Singleton FY6 ....152 D4
Flag La Bamber Bridge PR1 .95 F1
  Bretherton PR5 ....57 A5
  Limbrick PR6 ....42 F5
  Runshaw Moor PR5,PR7 ...58 D4
Flag St OL13 ....69 E8
Flakefleet Ave FY7 .....193 E1
Flakefleet Prim Sch FY7 .193 E2
Flamstead WN8 ....18 C1
Flare Rd LA3 ....208 D6
Flash Gate BB1 ....121 D3
Flash La L40 ....38 B4
Flat La LA5 ....219 E4
Flatfield Way L31 ....5 E1
Flatman's La L39 ....17 E5
Flats Ret Pk The PR1,PR5 .96 C5
Flats The Chorley PR7 ...42 B6
  Kirkham PR4 ....113 B4
Flax Cl BB4 ....67 A8
Flax La L40 ....24 F2
Flax Moss Cl BB4 ....67 A8
Flax St BL0 ....49 A4
Flaxfield Rd L37 ....12 A3
Flaxfield Way PR4 .....113 A5
Flaxton WN8 ....18 C1
Fleet La LA2 ....204 A4
Fleet St Blackpool FY1 .129 C4
  Chorley PR7 ....42 C7
  Horwich BL6 ....31 D3
  Longridge PR3 ....139 A7
  Lytham St Anne's FY8 ..88 D4
  Nelson BB9 ....168 E1
  Preston PR1 ....95 F7
Fleet Street La PR3 ....140 A6
Fleet Wlk BB11 ....127 A6
Fleetgreen LA1 ....213 E3
Fleetwood Cl
  Blackburn BB2 ....100 F1
  Southport PR9 ....52 F3
Fleetwood Cres PR9 .....54 A4
Fleetwood Dr PR9 ......54 A6
Fleetwood High Sch FY7 193 D2
Fleetwood High Sch
  Beach Rd Site FY7 ....193 E3
Fleetwood Hospl 194 B5
Fleetwood Old Rd PR4 ..132 E3
Fleetwood Rd
  Blackpool FY5 ....150 D7
  Burnley BB10 ....147 C6
  Carleton FY6 ....151 B5
  Esprick PR4 ....132 C6
  Fleetwood FY7 ....193 E1
  Kirkham PR4 ....112 F7
  Padiham BB12 ....125 D8
  Southport PR9 ....52 E3
  Thornton FY7 ....173 A6
Fleetwood Rd N FY5 ....173 B3
Fleetwood Rd S FY5 ....151 B7
Fleetwood St
  Leyland PR5 ....76 B2
  Preston PR2 ....116 D1
Fleetwood's Charity
  Prim CE Sch FY6 .....195 B3
Fleming Sq BB2 ....100 E4
Flemming Sq PR3 ......139 B7
Flensburg Way
  Farington PR5 ....75 E6
  Leyland PR5 ....75 D4
Fletcher Ave PR4 ......56 A6
Fletcher Rd Preston PR1 .117 C1
  Rishton BB1 ....102 A4
Fletcher St Blackburn BB2 100 D3
  Bury BL9 ....32 A2
  Nelson BB9 ....147 F7
Fletcher's Dr L40 ......24 E4
Flett St PR2 ....116 C1
Flimby WN8 ....18 D1
Flimby Cl BB2 ....80 F8
Flintoff Way PR1 ......117 B3
Flintron Brow LA2 .....227 D4
Flip Rd BB4 ....84 A2
Flockton Ct BL6 ....31 B4
Flordon WN8 ....18 D1
Florence Ave
  Burnley BB11 ....126 C4
  Warton PR4 ....91 D5
Florence Pl BB1 ....101 A6
Florence St Blackburn BB1 101 A6
  Blackpool FY4 ....110 A6
  Burnley BB11 ....126 C5
  Church BB5 ....102 E6
Flower Fields PR3 .....178 C2
Flower Scar Rd OL14 ...87 E6
Flowerfield PR4 ....115 E6
Flowers Cl BB2 ....80 D7
Floyd Rd PR2 ....117 E3
Floyer St PR1 ....95 F7
Fluke Hall La PR3 .....196 B8
Flush Brow LA6 ....238 F5
Fold BB9 ....168 E5
Fold Gdns OL12 ....51 B4
Fold House Caravan Pk
  PR3 ....196 D4

Fold View BL7 ....46 E1
Folds BL6 ....30 C3
Folds St BB12 ....126 F8
Foldside PR4 ....92 C7
Folkestone Cl
  Cleveleys FY5 ....172 F4
  Warton PR4 ....91 D1
Folkestone Rd
  Lytham St Anne's FY8 ..88 F8
  Southport PR8 ....34 F3
Folly La Barnoldswick BB8 .190 F7
  Lancaster LA1,LA2 ....213 D4
Folly Terr BB4 ....85 B8
Folly Wlk PR4 ....51 F1
Fontwell Cl WN6 ....28 F1
Fooden La BB7 ....224 E4
Foot Mill Cres OL12 ...51 D2
Foot Wood Cres OL12 ...51 D2
Football Mus Deepdale
  Preston The PR1 .....117 B2
Footeran La LA5 ......219 E3
Forbes Ct BB11 ....126 A3
Ford La Goosnargh PR3 .158 F2
  Silverdale LA5 ....218 E5
Ford St Barrowford BB9 .168 A5
  Burnley BB10 ....147 B1
  Lancaster LA1 ....213 D1
Fordham Cl PR8 ....34 E3
Fordside Ave BB5 .....123 E4
Fordstone Ave FY5 ....195 A4
Fordway Ave FY3 .....129 F6
Fore St BB3 ....80 F7
Foregate PR2 ....116 E4
Foreside BB9 ....168 E5
Forest Ave BB12 ......146 E8
Forest Bank BB4 ....85 A7
Forest Bank Rd BB4 ....85 A7
Forest Becks Brow BB7 .224 D6
Forest Cl PR5 ....96 C3
Forest Dr
  Lytham St Anne's FY8 ..89 F4
  Shevington Moor WN6 ...28 A2
  Skelmersdale WN8 .....18 C3
Forest Gate Blackpool FY3 .129 E5
  Morecambe LA3 ....213 A2
Forest Gr PR3 ....136 B8
Forest Ho BB9 ....147 D7
Forest Holme Cl BB4 ...86 A7
Forest La BB9 ....168 B2
Forest Pk LA1 ....210 C2
Forest Rd PR8 ....34 D6
Forest St Burnley BB11 .127 B6
  Forest Holme BB4 .....86 A7
  Nelson BB9 ....168 D1
Forest View
  Barrowford BB9 ......168 D3
  Brierfield BB9 ....147 A5
  Rochdale OL12 ....51 D2
Forest Way PR2 ....116 F6
Forester Dr BB12 .....146 D8
Forester's Bldgs BB18 .200 B2
Foresters Hall PR1 ....95 F8
Forestry Houses BB7 ..222 C5
Forestway PR5 ....58 F8
Forfar Gr BB11 ....126 D3
Forfar St BB11 ....126 D3
Forge Cl L40 ....16 E4
Forge La PR3 ....178 E8
Forge St OL13 ....86 F2
Forgewood Cl LA2 ....231 A3
Forgewood Dr LA2 ....214 F6
Formby Ave FY7 ......172 D7
Formby Bridge L37 ....11 E2
Formby Bsns Pk L37 ...12 B3
Formby By-Pass
  Formby L37 ....12 B5
  Hightown L37, L38 .....3 B8
Formby Cl BB2 ....80 F8
Formby Cres PR4 ......73 F8
Formby Fields L37 .....12 A2
Formby Gdns L37 ......11 F4
Formby La Formby L37 ..12 B2
  Haskayne L39 ....14 E2
Formby Pl PR2 ....115 E2
Formby Rd FY8 ....109 F1
Formby St L37 ....11 E2
Formby High Sch L37 ..11 E4
Formby Sta L37 ....11 E2
Forrest Ct FY3 ....129 E8
Forrest St BB1 ....101 A5
Forrester Cl PR5 ......75 E1
Forshaw Ave
  Blackpool FY3 ....129 F8
  Lytham St Anne's FY8 ..88 D8
Forshaw Cl FY7 ......193 F2
Forshaw Rd PR1 ....95 D2
Fort Ave PR3 ....140 D3
Fort St Accrington BB5 .103 B6
  Blackburn BB1 ....101 A6
  Clayton-le-M BB5 ....123 F3
  Clitheroe BB7 ....164 D7
  Read BB12 ....144 D7
Forton Primary Sch PR3 .204 B3
Forton Rd PR2 ....115 E1
Forty Acre La PR3 ....161 B5
Forward Ind Est PR5 ...75 E2
Foscote Rd L33 ....1 A4
Fossdale Moss PR5 .....75 C1
Fosse Cl BB1,BB2 ....81 A8
Foster Croft PR5 ....95 C6
Foster Ct Bury BL9 .....32 C4
  Chorley PR7 ....60 E1
Foster Rd
  Barnoldswick BB18 ...200 A3
  Formby L37 ....11 D2
Foster St Accrington BB5 .103 C7
  Chorley PR7 ....60 E1
Fosterfield Pl PR6 .....60 E1

Fosters Cl PR9 ....35 B8
Fosters Green Rd WN8 ..18 D3
Fothergill St BB8 .....169 C5
Foul La PR8,PR9 ....35 A5
Fouldrey Ave FY6 .....151 F5
Foulds Cl BB8 ....169 C3
Foulds Rd BB8 ....170 B3
Foulds Terr BB8 ......170 C2
Foulridge Wharf BB8 ..191 D2
Foundry La Halton LA2 .214 C4
  Halton LA2 ....214 D6
Foundry St Bacup OL13 .86 F2
  Blackburn BB2 ....100 D4
  Blackburn BB11 .....126 F6
  Chorley PR7 ....42 C8
  Darwen BB3 ....81 A1
  Rawtenstall BB4 ......84 F1
Fountain Pl BB5 ......103 B5
Fountain Sq BB9 ......168 D3
Fountain St
  Accrington BB5 ......103 A5
  Barnoldswick BB18 ...200 C2
  Bury BL9 ....32 A2
  Colne BB8 ....169 D4
  Darwen BB3 ....64 A8
  Nelson BB9 ....168 E1
  Fountain St N BL9 .....32 A3
Fountains Ave
  Blackburn BB1 ....101 B8
  Read BB12 ....144 D1
Fountains Cl PR7 ....42 D5
Fountains The L39 .....15 E6
Fountains Way Formby L37 .12 B2
  Oswaldtwistle BB5 ...102 B5
Four Acre La PR3 .....160 E5
Four Lane Ends
  Barley BB7 ....189 B2
  Burton in L LA2 .....236 C1
  Carleton FY6 ....151 B5
  Charnock Richard PR7 ..41 C4
  Clitheroe BB7 ....165 A6
  Dolphinholme LA2 ....220 A8
  Gregson Lane PR5 ....97 D2
  Halsall L39 ....22 D3
  Halton LA2 ....214 B7
  Knowley PR6 ....61 C4
  Morecambe LA3 ......212 A1
  Sabden BB12 ....144 F4
  Wray LA2 ....232 E4
Four Lanes End Rd OL13 .86 F7
Four Oaks Rd PR5 ......77 B7
Fouracre BB2 ....120 E2
Fourfields PR5 ....96 E2
Fourth Ave Blackpool FY4 .109 C7
  Bury BL9 ....32 D4
Fowler Ave PR5 ....76 B6
Fowler Cl PR5 ....98 C2
Fowler Height Cl BB2 ..80 B7
Fowler Hill La PR3 ....199 B5
Fowler Ind Pk BL6 .....31 C2
Fowler La Farington PR5 ..75 F6
  Leyland PR5 ....76 B5
Fowler St PR2 ....116 D3
Fox Gr LA3 ....212 B3
Fox Ind Est FY2 ......129 C8
Fox La Coupe Green PR5 ..97 E3
  Leyland PR5 ....58 E7
Fox Lane Ends PR4 ....112 A5
Fox St Accrington BB5 .103 B6
  Burnley BB12 ....125 F6
  Clitheroe BB7 ....186 E1
  Horwich BL6 ....31 C2
  Preston PR1 ....95 F7
Foxcote PR7 ....60 C2
Foxcroft BB12 ....126 D8
Foxdale Ave FY3 .....129 D7
Foxdale Cl Bacup OL13 ..87 A1
  Edgworth BL7 ....47 E7
  Southport PR8 ....34 E3
Foxdale Gr PR1 ....117 D3
Foxdale Pl LA1 ....213 E2
Foxen Dole La BB12 ...146 A5
Foxes Terr PR3 ....155 C7
Foxfield Ave LA4 .....212 F3
Foxfield Cl BB5 ......102 D4
Foxfold WN8 ....18 D3
Foxglove Cl
  Hesketh Bank PR4 .....72 E4
  Standish WN6 ....28 D2
Foxglove Ct OL12 ......51 D3
Foxglove Dr Bury BL9 ..32 D3
  Lucas Green PR6 ......60 C5
Foxglove Way PR4 ......92 D7
Foxhall Rd FY1 ....129 B3
Foxhall Sq FY1 ....129 B3
Foxhill Bank Brow BB5 .102 E5
Foxhill Cl L37 ....11 C3
Foxhill Dr BB4 ....85 F4
Foxhole Rd PR7 ....41 F8
Foxholes Rd Horwich BL6 .31 C4
  Morecambe LA4 ......212 G6
Foxhouse La L31 ....5 F1
Foxhouse St BB2 ......100 C5
Foxleigh PR5 ....58 D7
Foxstones Cres BB2 ....80 A8
Foxstones La BB10 ...128 B2
Foxwell Cl BB4 ....84 C2
Foxwood Chase BB5 ...103 E8
Foxwood Cl WN5 ....10 E5
Foxwood Dr PR4 ......112 E5
Foxwood The PR7 ......41 C1
Frailey Cl PR8 ....34 D4
France St Blackburn BB2 .100 D4
  Church BB5 ....102 E6
Frances St BB3 ....80 F2
Francis Ave BB9 ......168 E5
Francis St Blackburn BB2 .100 B1
  Blackpool FY4 ....129 B6

Francis St continued
  Burnley BB10 ....147 A1
  Clayton-le-M BB5 ....123 F3
  Colne BB8 ....169 B3
  Preston PR1 ....116 C1
Frank St
  Barnoldswick BB18 ...200 B2
  Enfield BB5 ....124 A1
  Preston PR1 ....116 F1
Franklands PR4 ....94 A1
Franklands Dr PR2 ....118 A5
Franklands Fold PR4 ...74 A8
Franklin Ainsworth
  Ho BB6 ....123 C5
Franklin Rd BB2 ....100 B3
Franklin St
  Burnley BB12 ....126 C6
  Clitheroe BB7 ....164 D7
  Darwen BB3 ....81 A1
  Lancaster LA1 ....210 F5
Fraser Ave PR1 ....95 E5
Fraser St Accrington BB5 .103 A4
  Burnley BB10 ....147 B1
Frazer Gr FY4 ....129 B1
Freckleton CE Prim Sch
  PR4 ....92 C7
Freckleton Ct FY8 .....90 C3
Freckleton Dr L33 ......1 A5
Freckleton Rd
  Kirkham PR4 ....113 B3
  Southport PR9 ....52 F4
Freckleton St
  Blackburn BB2 ....100 E4
  Blackpool FY1 ....129 C3
  Kirkham PR4 ....113 B4
  Lytham St Anne's FY8 ..90 C3
Frederick Row BB1 ....101 B5
Frederick St
  Accrington BB5 ......103 A6
  Barnoldswick BB18 ...200 A3
  Blackburn BB2 ....100 E3
  Blackpool FY4 ....109 D8
  Chorley PR7 ....42 E7
  Darwen BB3 ....81 A7
  Oswaldtwistle BB5 ...102 E4
  Ramsbottom BL0 ....49 B5
Fredora Ave FY3 .....130 A2
Free La BB4 ....67 A6
Free Trade St BB11 ...126 F6
Freeholds La
  Waddington BB7 .....185 F6
  Waddington BB7 .....185 F7
Freeholds Rd OL12 .....70 E6
Freeholds Terr OL12 ...70 E6
Freeman's La PR7 ......41 E3
Freemantle Ave FY4 ..109 B4
Freightway LA3 ....213 A2
French Cl BB2 ....100 B4
French Rd BB2 ....100 B4
Frenchwood Ave
  Lytham St Anne's FY8 ..89 F3
  Preston PR1 ....96 B6
Frenchwood Cty Prim Sch
  PR1 ....96 B6
Frenchwood Knoll PR1 ..96 B6
Frenchwood St PR1 .....96 B6
Freshfield Ave BB5 ...123 C3
Freshfield Ct L37 .....11 E4
Freshfield Prim Sch L37 .12 A4
Freshfield Rd L37 .....11 E4
Freshfield Sta L37 ....11 E5
Freshfields PR2 ......115 D3
Friar St PR4 ....210 F8
Friar's Moss Rd LA2 ..226 A8
Friar's Pas LA1 ......210 F8
Friargate Preston PR1 ..95 F7
  Preston PR1 ....95 F8
Friargate Wlk PR1 .....95 F7
Friars The PR2 ....116 E4
Friars Wlk L37 ....12 B2
Friary Cl PR4 ....113 C4
Friday St PR6 ....42 D8
Fieldhurst Rd OL14 ...108 C1
Frinton Gr FY2 ....150 E6
Friths Ave PR5 ....97 E1
Frobisher Dr FY8 .....109 D1
Frog La L40 ....25 D3
Frome St PR1 ....117 D1
Frontierland
  Western Theme Pk LA4 .212 C5
Froom St PR6 ....42 F8
Fry St BB9 ....147 F8
Fryent Cl BL6 ....30 D2
Fryer Cl PR1 ....95 D1
Fulford Ave FY4 .....109 B4
Fulham St BB9 ....168 F2
Full View BB2 ....80 B8
Fullers Terr OL13 .....86 F1
Fulmar Cres LA3 .....208 F5
Fulmars The FY6 .....151 B2
Fulshaw Rd PR2 ......116 B2
Fulwood & Cadley
  Prim Sch PR2 ....116 D4
Fulwood Ave
  Becconsall PR4 ....72 F1
  Blackpool FY3 ....129 F8
  Southport PR8 ....34 D4
Fulwood Dr LA4 ......212 F3
Fulwood Hall Hospl PR2 .117 C5
Fulwood Hall La PR2 ..117 B4
Fulwood High Sch PR2 .116 D6
Fulwood Hts PR2 .....117 C5
Fulwood Row PR2 ....117 E6
Funchal Ave L37 ......11 D1
Furlong Cres FY3 .....151 A1
Furlong La FY6 ......151 D5
Furness Ave
  Blackburn BB1 ....101 B8

Furness Ave continued
  Fleetwood FY7 ....193 D1
  Formby L37 ....11 F3
  Normoss FY3 ....130 A8
  Ormskirk L39 ....15 E4
  Read BB12 ....144 D1
Furness Cl Chorley PR7 ..42 D5
  Southport PR8 ....20 B3
Furness Ct FY3 ....130 A8
Furness Dr
  High Bentham LA2 ....233 D8
  Poulton-le-F FY6 ....152 A3
Furness Rd LA3 ......212 A2
Furness St
  Burnley BB10 ....147 B1
  Lancaster LA1 ....213 D1
Furnessford Rd LA2 ..233 A6
Furnival Dr L40 ....24 D4
Further Ends Rd PR4 ...92 B6
Further Heights Rd
  OL12 ....51 F1
Further La BB2,PR5 ....99 A8
Further Wilworth BB1 .121 E2
Furthergate BB1 ......101 B5
Fushetts La LA2 ......233 D8
Fylde Ave PR5 ....75 E4
Fylde Coast Hospl FY3 .129 F7
Fylde Ct PR4 ....194 D5
Fylde Rd
  Lytham St Anne's FY8 ..89 D5
  Poulton-le-F FY6 ....151 E4
  Preston PR1,PR2 .....116 D1
  Southport PR9 ....53 B4
Fylde School Cotts FY3 .130 C8
Fylde St Kirkham PR4 ..113 A4
  Preston PR1 ....95 E8
Fylde View Cl FY6 ....151 D2

G

Gabbot St PR7 ....30 A7
Gable Mews L37 ....12 A1
Gables Pl LA4 ....212 G5
Gables The PR4 ....115 E4
Gadfield St BB3 ....64 B8
Gadsby St FY1 ....129 B2
Gage St LA1 ....210 F8
Gaghills Rd BB4 ....85 F1
Gaghills Terr BB4 ....85 F1
Gainsborough Ave
  Bamber Bridge PR5 ....76 A7
  Blackburn BB2 ....100 C6
  Burnley BB11 ....126 F3
  Morecambe LA4 ......212 G6
Gainsborough Rd
  Blackpool FY1 ....129 D4
  Ramsbottom BL0 ....49 B1
  Southport PR8 ....33 E3
Gaisgill Ave LA4 .....212 E3
Gait Barrows
  (Nature Reserve) LA7 .219 A7
Gale St OL12 ....51 F3
Gales La L40 ....39 A3
Galgate Silk Mills
  Ind Est LA2 ....207 B4
Gall La OL14 ....108 C3
Gallery The L37 ....11 F3
Galligreaves St BB2 ..100 D3
Galligreaves Way BB2 .100 D3
Galloway Cl OL10 ......32 F1
Galloway Cres FY5 ...150 F5
Galloway Rd FY7 .....193 F5
Gallows La PR3 ......141 A6
Galway Ave FY2 ......150 D3
Gamble Rd FY5 ......173 B4
Gambleside Cl BB4 ...105 A1
Game St BB6 ....123 C5
Gamull La PR2 ....117 F5
Gandy La OL12 ....51 D4
Gannow La BB12 .....126 C6
Gantley Ave WN5 ......10 D3
Gantley Cres WN5 .....10 D3
Gantley Rd WN5 ......10 D4
Ganton Cl PR8 ....34 E3
Ganton Ct PR1 ....95 A6
Garbett St BB5 ....103 A4
Garden Ave PR4 ......112 B4
Garden City BL0 ....49 A2
Garden Pl LA6 ....234 C2
Garden Row OL12 ......51 D2
Garden St Abbey Village PR6 79 C2
  Accrington BB5 ......103 B5
  Bacup OL13 ....69 C8
  Bamber Bridge PR5 ....76 B7
  Barnoldswick BB18 ...200 B2
  Blackburn BB2 ....100 C4
  Brierfield BB9 ......147 B5
  Brookbottoms BL0 .....49 C3
  Colne BB8 ....169 D4
  Great Harwood BB6 ...123 C4
  Higham BB12 ....145 F5
  Kirkham PR4 ....113 A4
  Lytham St Anne's FY8 ..88 E6
  Nelson BB9 ....147 E8
  Oswaldtwistle BB5 ...102 D4
  Padiham BB12 ....145 C1
  Preston PR1 ....95 F7
  Ramsbottom BL0 ....49 C6
Garden Terr
  Blackpool FY4 ....129 B1
  Chorley PR7 ....60 C1
  Heysham LA3 ....209 A2
Garden Vale Bsns Ctr
  BB8 ....169 B4
Garden Wlk Cleveleys FY5 172 D5
  Preston PR2 ....116 B2
Gardeners Mews FY1 .129 C7

Gardeners Row BB7 . . . . . .144 F7
Gardeners View L33 . . . . .1 A6
Gardens Gr LA4 . . . . .212 D4
Gardiners Pl WN8 . . . . .8 E8
Gardner Arc LA3 . . . . .212 B4
Gardner Rd Formby L37 . . . .12 B4
　Lancaster LA1 . . . . .213 F2
　Morecambe LA3 . . . . .212 B3
　Warton, Carnforth LA5 . . .217 D5
Gardner St 21 PR1 . . . . .95 F8
Gardner's La PR3 . . . . .179 D3
Garfield Ave LA1 . . . . .210 D7
Garfield Ct FY3 . . . . .130 C2
Garfield Dr LA4 . . . . .213 B4
Garfield St Accrington BB5 103 C3
　8 Cornholme OL14 . . . . . .108 C1
　Fleetwood FY7 . . . . .194 B5
Garfield Terr PR6 . . . . .60 D2
Garland Gr FY7 . . . . .193 D3
Garnall's Bldgs 6 BB4 . . . .84 E2
Garnet Cl FY5 . . . . .150 F7
Garnet St 8 LA1 . . . . .211 A8
Garnett Gn L39 . . . . .15 D4
Garnett Pl WN8 . . . . .9 A7
Garnett Rd BB7 . . . . .164 C7
Garnett St Barrowford BB9 168 D2
　Darwen BB3 . . . . .81 B1
　Morecambe LA4 . . . . .212 E6
　Ramsbottom BL0 . . . . .49 B5
Garrick Dr FY3 . . . . .129 E7
Garrick Par PR8 . . . . .34 A6
Garrick St BB9 . . . . .168 F2
Garrison Rd PR2 . . . . .117 B3
Gars End LA2 . . . . .232 D6
Gars The LA2 . . . . .232 B6
Garsdale Ave BB10 . . . . . . .147 B4
Garsdale Cl PR5 . . . . .96 E5
Garsdale Rd PR2 . . . . .117 E4
Garsden Ave BB1 . . . . .101 E3
Garstang Cl FY6 . . . . .151 D4
Garstang Com Prim Sch
　PR3 . . . . .178 C8
Garstang High Sch PR3 . . .178 D4
Garstang New Rd FY6 . . . .152 E3
Garstang Rd
　Bilsborrow PR3 . . . . .157 A4
　Bowgreave PR3 . . . . .178 D4
　Catterall PR3 . . . . .178 E1
　Chipping PR3 . . . . .182 C2
　Cockerham LA2,PR3 . . . . .203 E2
　Fulwood PR1,PR2,PR3 . . .116 C5
　Kirkham PR4 . . . . .112 F6
　Little Eccleston PR3,FY6 . .153 C5
　Newsham PR3 . . . . .136 B4
　Singleton FY6 . . . . .152 C3
　Southport PR9 . . . . .53 A5
　St Michael's on W PR3 . . .155 C7
　Stake Pool PR3 . . . . .197 B3
Garstang Rd E FY6 . . . . . . .151 E3
Garstang Rd N PR4 . . . . . . .112 F7
Garstang Rd S PR4 . . . . . . .112 F6
Garstang Rd W FY3,FY6 . . .151 B2
Garstang St BB3 . . . . .81 A2
Garston St BL9 . . . . .32 A4
Garstone Croft PR2 . . . . . . .116 D6
Garswood Cl
　Brierfield BB12 . . . . .146 F2
　Maghull L31 . . . . .5 E3
Garton Ave FY4 . . . . .109 D6
Gas Field Rd LA3 . . . . .208 E2
Gas House La LA2 . . . . .233 D8
Gas St Adlington PR7 . . . . . .30 A6
　Bacup OL13 . . . . .86 F2
　8 Burnley BB11 . . . . .126 F6
　Haslingden BB4 . . . . .83 F1
　Longridge PR3 . . . . .139 A8
Gas Terr PR5 . . . . .76 B2
Gaskell Cl LA5 . . . . .218 C3
Gaskell Cres PR5 . . . . .173 A2
Gaskell Ho LA1 . . . . .213 A8
Gaskell Rd PR1 . . . . .95 E5
Gaskell St PR6 . . . . .42 E5
Gate Ho PR1 . . . . .95 E7
Gate St BB1 . . . . .101 A4
Gategill Gr WN5 . . . . .10 D3
Gateheads Brow LA6 . . . . . .238 F3
Gateland BB18 . . . . .191 D8
Gates La L29 . . . . .4 C1
Gateside Ct 2 FY3 . . . . . . .130 A8
Gateside Dr FY3 . . . . .129 F8
Gateway Cl FY5 . . . . .151 D7
Gathurst La WN6 . . . . .19 F5
Gathurst Rd Fulwood PR2 116 C2
　Gathurst WN5 . . . . .19 F2
　Orrell WN5 . . . . .10 E8
Gaulter's La FY6 . . . . .195 C4
Gaw Hill La L39 . . . . .15 B3
Gaw Hill View L39 . . . . . . .15 B3
Gawthorpe Edge BB12 . . . .125 E8
Gawthorpe Hall BB12 . . . .145 F1
Gawthorpe High Sch
　BB12 . . . . .125 E8
Gawthorpe Rd BB12 . . . . . .126 D7
Gawthorpe St 18 BB12 . . . .145 F1
Gawthorpe View BB12 . . . .145 F5
Gaydon Way FY5 . . . . .150 E7
Gaylands La BB18 . . . . . . .201 C2
Gayle Way 1 BB5 . . . . . . .102 F4
Gaythorne Ave PR1 . . . . . . .96 F8
Geddes St BB2 . . . . .99 F2
Geldof Dr FY1 . . . . .129 C8
General St FY1 . . . . .129 B6
Geneva Rd PR2 . . . . .117 C4
Genoa St BB11 . . . . .126 C4
Geoffrey St Bury BL9 . . . . . .32 A4
　Chorley PR6 . . . . .60 E1
　Preston PR1 . . . . .96 C8

Geoffrey St continued
　Ramsbottom BL0 . . . . . . .49 A4
George Ave Blackpool FY4 .129 F1
　Great Harwood BB6 . . . . .123 B4
George Dr PR8 . . . . .20 E5
George La BB12 . . . . .144 C8
George Rd BL0 . . . . .49 B5
George St Accrington BB5 .102 F4
　4 Bacup OL13 . . . . .69 C8
　Barnoldswick BB18 . . . . .200 C4
　Blackburn BB2 . . . . .100 E4
　Blackpool FY1 . . . . .129 C5
　Blackpool FY1 . . . . .129 C5
　Burnley BB11 . . . . .126 F5
　Chorley PR7 . . . . .42 C7
　13 Clayton-le-M BB5 . . . .123 F3
　Clitheroe BB7 . . . . .164 D6
　Darwen BB3 . . . . .81 A2
　1 Earby BB18 . . . . .201 B1
　Great Harwood BB6 . . . . .123 C5
　Haslingden BB4 . . . . .84 B3
　Horwich BL6 . . . . .31 C3
　4 Lancaster LA1 . . . . . . .210 F7
　Leyland PR5 . . . . .76 B2
　Longridge PR3 . . . . .139 A8
　9 Lytham St Anne's FY8 . . .90 B3
　Morecambe LA4 . . . . .212 F5
　Oswaldtwistle BB5 . . . . . .102 E5
　Preston PR1 . . . . .96 B7
　Rishton BB1 . . . . .123 B1
　Whalley BB7 . . . . .143 C5
　Whitworth OL12 . . . . .51 C8
George St W BB2 . . . . .100 D4
George's La Banks PR9 . . . .54 A7
　Horwich BL6 . . . . .31 E5
George's Rd PR1 . . . . .95 F7
George's Row 2 BB4 . . . . . .68 F8
George's Terr WN5 . . . . . . .10 D5
Georgian Pl L37 . . . . .11 E1
Gerald Ct 6 BB11 . . . . . . .127 B4
German La
　Bolton Green PR7 . . . . . . .41 D7
　1 Coppull PR7 . . . . .41 E1
Gerrard Pl WN8 . . . . .8 F7
Gerrard St Lancaster LA1 .210 D7
　Preston PR1 . . . . .95 E7
Gerrard's Fold PR6 . . . . . . .79 B2
Gerrard's Terr PR5 . . . . . . .151 C4
　Whitworth OL12 . . . . .70 E6
Ghants La FY6 . . . . .174 E2
Ghyll La BB18 . . . . .200 E4
Ghyll Mdws BB18 . . . . . . .200 A3
Gib Field Rd BB8 . . . . .169 A3
Gib Hey La PR3 . . . . .159 F7
Gib Hill La BB4 . . . . .105 B2
Gib Hill Rd BB9 . . . . .169 B1
Gib La Blackburn BB2 . . . . .80 A7
　Hoghton PR5 . . . . .98 C3
Gibfield Sch BB8 . . . . .169 E1
Gibraltar Rd PR4 . . . . .131 E5
Gibraltar St BB2 . . . . .100 B6
Gibson St BB9 . . . . .168 F2
Giddygate La L31 . . . . .6 B1
Gidlow Ave PR6 . . . . .30 A7
Gilbert Pl L40 . . . . .24 B4
Gilbert St 4 Brierfield BB10 .147 E2
　4 Chorley PR7 . . . . .42 C6
　Ramsbottom BL0 . . . . . . .67 C4
　Rawtenstall BB4 . . . . .85 D1
Gilbertson Rd PR7 . . . . . . .42 E2
Gildabrook Rd 1 FY8 . . . . .109 D5
Gilderdale Ct 2 FY8 . . . . . .90 C4
Gildow St 1 PR1 . . . . .95 E8
Giles St Clitheroe BB7 . . . .164 E1
　Nelson BB9 . . . . .168 E1
Gilhouse Ave PR2 . . . . .115 C1
Gill Ct FY4 . . . . .109 B5
Gill La PR4 . . . . .74 C5
Gill Nook PR4 . . . . .74 A5
Gill St Burnley BB12 . . . . . .126 E6
　Colne BB8 . . . . .169 B3
　Nelson BB9 . . . . .168 D1
Gillcroft PR7 . . . . .40 B7
Giller Cl PR1 . . . . .95 F2
Giller Dr PR1 . . . . .95 F2
Giller Fold 1 PR1 . . . . .95 F2
Gillett St 6 PR1 . . . . .117 C1
Gillhead Brow LA2 . . . . . . .236 D1
Gillians BB18 . . . . .191 B8
Gillians La BB18 . . . . .191 B8
Gillibrand Cl PR1 . . . . .95 C1
Gillibrand Cty Prim Sch
　PR7 . . . . .42 B6
Gillibrand Ho PR7 . . . . .60 C2
Gillibrand St Chorley PR7 . .42 C7
　Darwen BB3 . . . . .80 F3
　Walton-le-D PR1,PR5 . . . .96 D5
Gillibrand Wlks PR7 . . . . . .42 C7
Gillibrands Rd WN8 . . . . . . .9 A7
Gillies St
　Accrington BB5 . . . . .103 C6
　Blackburn BB2 . . . . .100 F3
Gillison Cl LA6 . . . . .235 C2
Gillow Ct LA1 . . . . .210 F5
Gillow Pk PR3 . . . . .153 F6
Gillow Rd PR4 . . . . .112 F5
Gills Croft BB7 . . . . .165 A4
Gilpin Ave L31 . . . . .5 C4
Gilpin Cl 1 LA4 . . . . .213 C2
Gilsecroft Ave L33 . . . . .1 A4
Gilstead Ave LA3 . . . . .209 A8
Gin Bow PR7 . . . . .42 D6
Gin Croft La BL0 . . . . .67 E4
Gingham Brow BL6 . . . . . . .31 E4
Girvan Gr BB11 . . . . .126 D5
Girvan Wlk 2 OL10 . . . . . . .32 F1
Gisburn Ave FY8 . . . . .89 C6

Gisburn Cty Prim Sch
　BB7 . . . . .225 C3
Gisburn Gr Blackpool FY3 .129 E7
　Burnley BB10 . . . . .127 D5
Gisburn Old Rd
　Barnoldswick BB7,BB9 . . .190 C5
　Foulridge BB9 . . . . .190 E4
Gisburn Rd
　Barnoldswick BB18 . . . . .200 A3
　Barrowford BB9 . . . . .168 E5
　Bolton-by-B BB7 . . . . . . .224 E4
　Fulwood PR2 . . . . .117 E4
Gisburn Road
　Com Prim Sch BB18 . . . .200 B3
Gisburn St
　Barnoldswick BB18 . . . . .200 B3
　Blackburn BB2 . . . . .100 C4
Gisburne Park Hospl
　. . . . . .225 B4
Gladden Pl WN8 . . . . .8 E6
Glade The Blackburn BB2 . .80 D6
　Morecambe LA4 . . . . .213 A5
Glades The FY8 . . . . .90 C4
Gladeswood Rd L33 . . . . . . .1 B1
Gladeway FY5 . . . . .151 D7
Gladstone Cres OL13 . . . . .87 A2
Gladstone Rd PR9 . . . . .34 F6
Gladstone St Bacup OL13 . .87 A2
　Blackburn BB1 . . . . .101 B6
　Blackpool FY4 . . . . .129 C1
　Bury BL9 . . . . .32 B3
　2 Cornholme OL14 . . . . . .108 B1
　Great Harwood BB6 . . . . .123 C5
Gladstone Terr
　Abbey Village PR6 . . . . . . .79 C1
　Barrowford BB9 . . . . .168 D3
　Blackburn BB1 . . . . .99 F1
　Colne BB8 . . . . .170 B4
　3 Lancaster LA1 . . . . . . .214 A1
Gladstone Way 4 FY5 . . . .172 F1
Glaisdale Dr PR8 . . . . .34 F3
Glamis Dr Chorley PR7 . . . .42 B8
　Southport PR9 . . . . .53 B3
Glamis Rd PR5 . . . . .59 C8
Glamorgan Gr BB12 . . . . . .126 A7
Glasson Cl BB2 . . . . .100 F1
Glastonbury Ave FY1 . . . . .129 C3
Glebe Cl Accrington BB5 . .103 B5
　Burton-in-K LA6 . . . . .234 C7
　Fulwood PR2 . . . . .116 F4
　Maghull L31 . . . . .5 B1
　Standish WN6 . . . . .28 C1
Glebe Cotts BB4 . . . . .84 A6
Glebe Ct
　Kirkby Lonsdale LA6 . . . .238 B3
　20 Lancaster LA1 . . . . . .211 A8
Glebe La Banks PR9 . . . . . .54 A7
　Kirkham PR4 . . . . .113 C4
Glebe Pl PR8 . . . . .34 B7
Glebe Rd Skelmersdale WN8 .9 A8
　Standish WN6 . . . . .28 C1
Glebe St Burnley BB11 . . . .127 B4
　Great Harwood BB6 . . . . .123 C5
Glebe The PR5 . . . . .58 B8
Glebelands PR4 . . . . .56 A5
Gledhill Way BL7 . . . . .47 A1
Glendale View BB18 . . . . . .200 A3
Glegside Rd L33 . . . . .1 A2
Glen Cottage
　(Youth Hostel) BB18 . . .201 D2
Glen Cres OL13 . . . . .69 A8
Glen Dr WN6 . . . . .19 E8
Glen Eldon Rd FY8 . . . . . . .88 E7
Glen Garth BB18 . . . . .200 D3
Glen Gdns OL12 . . . . .51 F2
Glen Gr PR2 . . . . .117 F5
Glen Park Dr PR4 . . . . .72 D4
Glen Rd BB4 . . . . .68 F8
Glen Royd Cl OL12 . . . . . . .51 C1
Glen Sq BB11 . . . . .126 F2
Glen St Bacup OL13 . . . . . . .69 E8
　Blackpool FY3 . . . . .129 E4
　Burnley BB11 . . . . .126 E6
　Colne BB8 . . . . .169 D6
　Ramsbottom BL0 . . . . . . .49 B7
Glen The Blackburn BB2 . . .80 D6
　Caton LA2 . . . . .231 D1
　Fulwood PR2 . . . . .117 F2
　Knott End-on-S FY6 . . . . .194 E4
Glen View PR3 . . . . .140 B8
Glen View Ave LA3 . . . . . . .208 E6
Glen View Cres LA3 . . . . . .208 E6
Glen View Dr LA3 . . . . .208 E6
Glen View Rd BB11 . . . . . .126 E2
Glen View St 1 OL14 . . . . .108 B1
Glen Way BB9 . . . . .147 B6
Glenapp Ave FY4 . . . . .110 A6
Glenarden Ave FY5 . . . . . . .150 F8
Glenavon Dr OL12 . . . . .51 D3
Glenborough Ave OL13 . . . .69 C8
Glenbrook St BB2 . . . . .80 B8
Glenburn High Sch WN8 . . .9 B8
Glenburn Rd WN8 . . . . .18 A1
Glencarron St BB3 . . . . . . .64 F8
Glencoe Ave
　Blackpool FY3 . . . . .151 A1
　Hoddlesden BB3 . . . . .81 C1
Glencoe Cl OL13 . . . . .32 F1
Glencourse Dr PR2 . . . . . . .117 C5
Glencoyne Dr PR9 . . . . .53 B5
Glencroft PR7 . . . . .59 C3
Glencross Pl FY4 . . . . .109 E7
Glendale Ave PR5 . . . . .96 C1
Glendale Cl Blackpool FY2 .150 F5
Glendale Cres PR5 . . . . .96 C1

Glendale Dr BB2 . . . . .120 E2
Glendale Gr Fulwood PR2 .117 D2
　Kirkby L33 . . . . .1 A5
Glendale Way L37 . . . . .11 F2
Glenden Foot OL12 . . . . . . .51 D2
Glendene Pk BB1 . . . . .121 E5
Glendor Rd BB10 . . . . .127 E5
Gleneagles Ave BB3 . . . . . . .81 E1
Gleneagles Ct PR4 . . . . . . .113 E4
Gleneagles Dr
　Fulwood PR2 . . . . .116 B7
　Morecambe LA4 . . . . .212 G6
　Penwortham PR1 . . . . .95 A6
　Southport PR8 . . . . .20 C3
Gleneagles Way 1 BL0 . . . .49 B5
Glenfield Ave FY2 . . . . .150 E6
Glenfield Cl BB1 . . . . .101 B7
Glenfield Park Ind Est
　Blackburn BB1 . . . . .101 B7
　Nelson BB9 . . . . .169 A1
Glenfield Rd BB9 . . . . .169 A1
Glengarry 7 FY8 . . . . .90 C3
Glengreave Ave BB1 . . . . . .121 E5
Glenholme Gdns FY6 . . . . .151 C2
Glenluce Cres BB1 . . . . . . .101 D3
Glenluce Dr PR1 . . . . .96 F8
Glenmarsh Way L37 . . . . . .12 B3
Glenmere Cres FY5 . . . . . .150 C7
Glenmore PR6 . . . . .77 A3
Glenmore Ave FY5 . . . . . . .173 B2
Glenmore Cl BB5 . . . . .103 E2
Glenmore Rd BL0 . . . . .48 F2
Glenpark Dr PR9 . . . . .53 B4
Glenrose Terr PR8 . . . . .34 A5
Glenroyd Ave BB8 . . . . . . .169 D6
Glenroyd Cl FY3 . . . . .129 E3
Glenroyd Dr L40 . . . . .24 C4
Glenshiels Ave BB3 . . . . . . .64 E8
Glenside BB9 . . . . .27 B2
Glenthorn Terr 2 BB3 . . . . .64 A8
Glentworth Rd E LA4 . . . . .212 G3
Glentworth Rd W LA4 . . . . .212 F3
Glenview Cl PR2 . . . . .118 A3
Glenview Ct PR2 . . . . .118 A3
Glenway PR1 . . . . .95 C4
Glenwood St 3 FY3 . . . . . .129 D5
Global Way BB3 . . . . .81 A5
Globe La BL7 . . . . .46 D3
Glossop Cl FY2 . . . . .150 C6
Gloucester Ave
　Accrington BB5 . . . . .103 A7
　Blackpool FY1 . . . . .129 D4
　8 Clayton-le-M BB5 . . . .123 F3
　Cleveleys FY5 . . . . .172 D3
　Horwich BL6 . . . . .31 D2
　Lancaster LA1 . . . . .211 A4
　Leyland PR5 . . . . .76 C3
Gloucester Ct
　5 Blackpool FY1 . . . . . . .129 D4
　Horwich BL6 . . . . .31 D2
Gloucester Dr LA3 . . . . . . .212 B3
Gloucester Rd
　Blackburn BB1 . . . . .101 C5
　Chorley PR7 . . . . .42 C6
　Lytham St Anne's FY8 . . . .89 D4
　Rishton BB1 . . . . .102 A8
　Southport PR8 . . . . .33 F5
Glover Cl PR5 . . . . .57 F6
Glover St Horwich BL6 . . . . .31 B4
　Preston PR1 . . . . .96 A7
Glover's Ct 24 PR1 . . . . . . .96 A7
Glynn St BB5 . . . . .102 F7
Godiva St BB10 . . . . .147 A1
Godley St BB11 . . . . .127 B6
Godwin Ave 6 FY3 . . . . . . .129 E3
Goe La PR4 . . . . .92 B6
Goit St Blackburn BB2 . . . .100 C3
　Newchurch BB4 . . . . .85 F1
Goitside BB9 . . . . .168 E1
Golbourne St PR1 . . . . .117 B1
Goldacre La BB6 . . . . .123 A4
Goldcrest Cl PR2 . . . . .115 C4
Golden Hill 9 PR5 . . . . .76 B2
Golden Hill La PR5 . . . . . . .75 F2
Golden Way
　Farington PR1,PR4 . . . . . .75 D7
　Penwortham PR1 . . . . .95 C3
Goldfield Ave BB10 . . . . . . .127 F6
Goldfinch Dr BL9 . . . . .32 C4
Goldfinch Gn 5 BB11 . . . . .126 C5
Goldfinch St PR1 . . . . .117 B1
Goldhey St BB1 . . . . .101 A7
Goldsboro Ave FY3 . . . . . . .129 C5
Goldstone Dr FY5 . . . . .150 F7
Golf Rd L37 . . . . .11 C5
Golf View PR2 . . . . .116 A6
Golgotha Rd LA1 . . . . .211 A6
Gonder La PR3 . . . . .179 E3
Gooch St BL6 . . . . .31 C3
Good Shaw Fold Cl BB4 . .105 A2
Goodall Cl BB18 . . . . .201 B4
Goodenber Cres 18 LA2 . .233 D8
Goodenber Rd LA2 . . . . . . .233 D8
Goodshaw Ave
　Blackburn BB1 . . . . .121 E5
　Rawtenstall BB4 . . . . .105 A1
Goodshaw Ave N BB4 . . . .105 A2
Goodshaw Chapel BB4 . . .105 B1
Goodshaw Cl BB1 . . . . . . .100 E8
Goodshaw Fold Rd BB4 . .104 F2
Goodshaw La
　Accrington BB5 . . . . .104 C1
　Rawtenstall BB4 . . . . .105 B2
Goodwood Ave
　Blackpool FY3 . . . . .150 D1
　Fulwood PR2 . . . . .116 F7
　Hest Bank LA2 . . . . .213 F8

Goodwood Cl LA1 . . . . .211 B4
Goodwood Rd LA1 . . . . . . .211 B4
Goose Cote Hill BL7 . . . . . .46 E1
Goose Foot Cl PR5 . . . . .98 D7
Goose Foot La PR5 . . . . .98 C6
Goose Green Ave PR7 . . . . .41 F1
Goose Green La BB8 . . . . . .170 B2
Goose Hill St 14 OL13 . . . . .86 F3
Goose House La BB3 . . . . . .81 A3
Goose La PR3 . . . . .182 E1
Goose La Cotts PR3 . . . . . .182 E1
Goosebutts La BB7 . . . . . . .164 C7
Gooselands BD24 . . . . .230 F6
Gooseleach La BB12 . . . . . .144 C2
Goosnargh La PR3 . . . . . . .137 B7
Gordale Cl
　Barnoldswick BB18 . . . . .200 A2
　Blackpool FY4 . . . . .110 A8
Gorden St 11 OL13 . . . . . . .69 C8
Gordon Ave
　Accrington BB5 . . . . .103 A4
　Maghull L31 . . . . .5 C3
　Southport PR9 . . . . .52 C1
　Thornton FY5 . . . . .173 B2
Gordon Rd Fleetwood FY7 .193 F3
　Lytham St Anne's FY8 . . . .89 D4
　8 Nelson BB9 . . . . .168 C1
Gordon St Bacup OL13 . . . .86 F4
　14 Blackpool FY4 . . . . . . .129 B1
　Burnley BB12 . . . . .126 F7
　Chorley PR6 . . . . .42 D7
　Church BB5 . . . . .102 E5
　Clayton-le-M BB5 . . . . . .124 A2
　Colne BB8 . . . . .169 F5
　Darwen BB3 . . . . .81 A3
　Preston PR1 . . . . .116 E1
　Rawtenstall BB4 . . . . .84 F2
　Southport PR9 . . . . .34 C8
　Worsthorne BB10 . . . . . . .128 B6
Gordon Way OL10 . . . . .32 F1
Gordonstoun Cres WN5 . . .10 F7
Gordonstoun Pl
　Blackburn BB1 . . . . .100 C3
　8 Thornton FY5 . . . . .173 A2
Gore Cl BL9 . . . . .32 C1
Gore Dr L39 . . . . .15 E3
Gores La L37 . . . . .11 F5
Gores Rd L33 . . . . .1 C1
Goring St PR7 . . . . .42 D7
Gorple Gn BB10 . . . . .128 B5
Gorple Rd BB10 . . . . .128 D5
Gorple St BB10 . . . . .147 E5
Gorrell Cl BB12 . . . . .167 D2
Gorse Ave FY5 . . . . .172 F3
Gorse Bank BL9 . . . . .32 C3
Gorse Cl Great Knowley PR6 60 E5
　Tarleton PR4 . . . . .56 A6
Gorse Gr Fulwood PR2 . . . .117 E3
　Haslingden BB4 . . . . .67 A8
　Longton PR4 . . . . .94 A1
Gorse La PR4 . . . . .55 D5
Gorse Rd Blackburn BB2 . .100 B3
　Blackpool FY3 . . . . .129 E4
Gorse St BB1 . . . . .101 B6
Gorse Way L37 . . . . .11 A2
Gorsefield L37 . . . . .12 A6
Gorsewood PR5 . . . . .75 E1
Gorsey La Banks PR9 . . . . .54 C7
　Haskayne L39 . . . . .13 B7
　Hightown L38 . . . . .3 B2
　Mawdesley L40 . . . . .39 C1
Gorsey Pl WN8 . . . . .9 B7
Gorst La L40,PR9 . . . . .24 A6
Gorsuch La L39,L40 . . . . . .22 C5
Gorton Fold BL6 . . . . .31 C3
Gorton St FY1 . . . . .129 C6
Gosforth Rd Blackpool FY2 150 C1
　Southport PR9 . . . . .34 F8
Gough La Clayton Brook PR5 77 C5
　Walton Summit PR5 . . . . . .77 B6
Goulding Ave PR5 . . . . .76 B1
Goulding St PR7 . . . . .42 D6
Gowans La PR6 . . . . .78 A8
Gower Ct PR5 . . . . .75 D3
Gower Gdns L40 . . . . .24 F3
Gower Gr PR4 . . . . .74 A5
Goyt St FY8 . . . . .88 F7
Grab La LA1 . . . . .211 C7
Graburn Rd L37 . . . . .11 F4
Gracamy Ave PR4 . . . . .91 D5
Grace St BL6 . . . . .31 B3
Gradwell St 2 PR1 . . . . . . .95 E8
Grafton Ave
　Accrington BB5 . . . . .103 E2
　Brierfield BB10 . . . . .147 B5
Grafton Ct 3 Chorley PR7 . .42 B5
　Darwen BB3 . . . . .80 F2
Grafton Dr PR8 . . . . .20 A5
Grafton Pl LA3 . . . . .212 B3
Grafton Rd Fulwood PR2 . .117 F4
　Morecambe LA4 . . . . .212 B3
Grafton St Adlington PR7 . . .29 F6
　Blackburn BB2 . . . . .100 D2
　Blackpool FY1 . . . . .129 C7
　Clitheroe BB7 . . . . .164 F8
　Nelson BB9 . . . . .168 F1
　Preston PR1 . . . . .95 E6
Grafton Villas OL13 . . . . . . .86 F3
Graham Ave
　Appley Bridge WN6 . . . . . .27 C2
　Bamber Bridge PR5 . . . . . .76 C8
Graham Rd PR8 . . . . .199 C2
Graham St Hoddlesden BB3 .81 F1
　Lancaster LA1 . . . . .210 F6
　Morecambe LA4 . . . . .212 D5

Graham St *continued*
1 Padiham BB12 .125 D7
4 Preston PR1 .117 B1
Grampian Way FY8 .90 D5
Granary The FY5 .173 A2
Granby Ave FY3 .129 E8
Granby Cl PR9 .52 F3
Granby St BB12 .126 D6
Grand Manor Dr FY8 .89 D7
Grane Pk BB4 .84 A2
Grane Rd BB4 .83 C2
Grane St BB4 .84 B2
Grange Ave
Barrowford BB9 .168 F5
Fulwood PR2 .117 F4
Fulwood PR2 .118 A4
Great Harwood BB6 .123 C6
Rawtenstall BB4 .85 B3
Southport PR9 .34 E8
Thornton FY5 .173 B2
Grange Cl
Great Harwood BB6 .123 C6
Hoghton PR5 .98 B4
Knott End-on-S FY6 .194 F6
Oswaldtwistle BB5 .103 A3
Rawtenstall BB4 .85 B2
Grange Cres BB4 .85 A2
Grange Ct 13 FY1 .129 C7
Grange Dr Coupe Green PR5 97 E4
Euxton PR7 .59 C4
Grange Farm Cotts PR4 .92 E5
Grange Gdns FY6 .151 D2
Grange La Accrington BB5 .103 C5
Formby L37 .11 E5
Longton PR4 .93 D3
Newton-with-S PR4 .113 F2
Stalmine FY6 .174 B7
Grange Park Cl PR1 .95 A6
Grange Park
Cty Prim Sch FY3 .130 A7
Grange Pl PR2 .117 F4
Grange Prim Sch PR2 .118 A4
Grange Rd Blackburn BB2 .100 B2
Blackpool FY3 .129 F7
Edgworth BL7 .47 C1
Elswick PR4 .153 F1
Fleetwood FY7 .193 D3
Fulwood PR2 .116 C3
Hambleton FY6 .174 D1
Hightown L38 .2 E6
Leyland PR5 .75 D2
Lytham St Anne's FY8 .88 E7
Over Town BB10 .107 A7
Rawtenstall BB4 .85 B2
Singleton FY6 .153 A3
Southport PR9 .34 E7
Whitworth OL12 .70 D3
Grange St
Accrington BB5 .103 C5
Barnoldswick BB18 .200 A3
Burnley BB11 .126 E5
Clayton-le-M BB5 .123 E3
Morecambe LA4 .213 A6
2 Rawtenstall BB4 .85 A2
Grange Terr 19 BB4 .85 A3
Grange The Cottam PR4 .115 E5
Southport PR9 .53 C3
Wilpshire BB1 .121 F5
Grange View
Carnforth LA5 .217 D3
Hest Bank LA5 .215 F3
Grange View Rd LA6 .216 F6
Grangefield PR4 .93 F1
Granings The PR4 .115 D6
Granny's Bay FY8 .89 C3
Grant Cl LA1 .210 D7
Grant Dr PR4 .74 A5
Grant Mews BL0 .49 B7
Grant Rd BB2 .100 B3
Grant St Accrington BB5 .103 A6
Burnley BB11 .126 E5
Grantham Cl PR8 .34 A1
Grantham Rd
5 Blackpool FY1 .129 C7
Southport PR8 .34 A1
Grantham St BB2 .100 B2
Granton Cl L37 .11 E3
Granton Wlk PR2 .116 A4
Grants La BL0 .49 C6
Granville Ave
Becconsall PR4 .72 E2
Maghull L31 .5 C2
Granville Cl L39 .6 B8
Granville Ct Chorley PR6 .60 E1
Southport PR9 .52 D1
Granville Gdns BB5 .103 D3
Granville Pk L39 .6 C8
Granville Pk W L39 .6 B8
Granville Rd
Accrington BB5 .103 D3
Blackburn BB2 .100 B5
Blackpool FY1 .129 D5
Brierfield BB9 .147 C6
Chorley PR6 .60 E1
Darwen BB3 .63 F8
Great Harwood BB6 .123 D6
Lancaster LA1 .213 E3
Morecambe LA3 .212 B3
Southport PR8 .33 D4
Granville St Adlington PR6 .30 A7
Brierfield BB10 .147 F2
13 Burnley BB10 .127 A8
Colne BB8 .169 E5
Haslingden BB4 .67 A7
Grape La PR5 .57 C1
Grasmere Ave
Blackburn BB1 .121 C1
3 Fleetwood FY7 .193 E4
Leyland PR5 .76 A3
Orrell WN5 .10 F8
Orrell, Hall Green WN8 .10 B7
Padiham BB12 .145 C1
Thornton FY5 .173 B2
Grasmere Cl
Accrington BB5 .103 D8
Bamber Bridge PR5 .96 D2
Colne BB8 .170 A5
Euxton PR7 .59 E1
Fulwood PR2 .117 C4
9 High Bentham LA2 .233 D8
Rishton BB1 .123 A1
Grasmere Dr 10 LA2 .233 D8
Grasmere Gr
Longridge PR3 .138 F5
Whittle-le-W PR6 .60 B7
Grasmere Rd
Blackpool FY1 .129 D2
Formby L37 .11 D3
Haslingden BB4 .67 C8
Knott End-on-S FY6 .194 F6
Lancaster LA1 .211 A8
Lytham St Anne's FY8 .109 E1
Maghull L31 .5 D2
Morecambe LA4 .213 A6
Grasmere St Burnley BB10 147 A2
10 Rochdale OL12 .51 F1
Grasmere Terr Bacup OL13 .86 F4
Chorley PR7 .42 B5
Grassington Dr
Brierfield BB10 .147 D3
Bury OL10 .32 D1
Grassington Pl FY5 .150 F8
Grassington Rd FY8 .89 C7
Gratton Pl WN8 .9 A8
Grave-Yard La L39 .7 A6
Gravel Cl PR9 .53 F5
Gravel La Banks PR9 .53 F5
Banks PR9 .54 B3
Gravel The PR4 .54 F2
Graver Weir Terr BB4 .106 A1
Graving Dock Rd FY8 .90 D4
Gravners Field FY5 .173 D2
Grayrigg Dr LA4 .212 E3
Grays Pl LA3 .212 B2
Great Arley Sp Sch FY5 .173 B3
Great Avenham St 3 PR1 .96 A6
Great Bolton St BB2 .100 E3
Great Close
La BD23,BD24 .230 D6
Great Croft Cl BB18 .200 A3
Great Eaves Rd BL0 .49 C7
Great Eccleston Copp
CE Prim Sch PR3 .154 A3
Great Flatt OL12 .51 B1
Great George St
Colne BB8 .169 D5
Preston PR1 .117 A1
Great Gill PR4 .74 A5
Great Greens La PR5 .77 C5
Great Hanover St PR1 .117 A1
Great Harwood
Golf Course BB6 .123 F7
Great Harwood Prim Sch
BB6 .123 B5
Great Hey PR4 .73 D3
Great John St 20 LA1 .210 F8
Great Lee OL12 .51 D3
Great Lee Wlk OL12 .51 D2
Great Mdw
Bamber Bridge PR5 .76 A8
Chorley PR7 .60 A2
Great Shaw St PR1 .95 F8
Great Stone of Fourstones
LA2 .233 D5
Great Stones Cl BL7 .46 E2
Great Townley St PR1 .96 D8
Great Tunstead PR4 .74 A7
Great Wood
Cty Prim Sch LA4 .213 A5
Greave Cl Bacup OL13 .87 B3
Rawtenstall BB4 .85 A4
Greave Clough Cl 9
OL13 .87 A3
Greave Clough Dr OL13 .87 B3
Greave Cres 10 OL13 .87 A3
Greave Rd OL13 .87 B3
Greave Terr OL13 .87 B3
Greaves Cl Banks PR9 .54 A6
Shevington Vale WN6 .19 F8
Greaves Dr LA1 .210 F6
Greaves Hall Ave PR9 .54 A5
Greaves Mead LA1 .210 F5
Greaves Mdw PR1 .95 E2
Greaves Rd LA1 .210 F6
Greaves St
Great Harwood BB6 .123 C4
Haslingden BB4 .83 F2
9 Preston PR1 .96 A7
Greaves-Town La PR2 .115 E1
Grebe Cl FY3 .130 B7
Grebe Wharf 2 LA1 .214 A1
Green Acre PR3 .137 D6
Green Acres PR4 .92 C7
Green Ave FY4 .109 C6
Green Bank Bacup OL13 .69 D8
Barnoldswick BB18 .200 D4
Green Bank Ind Est BB1 .101 C7
Green Bridge N BB4 .68 E7
Green Bridge S BB4 .68 E7
Green Brook Cl BL9 .32 A4
Green Cl BB11 .126 E2
Green Close Pk BB2 .100 C2
Green Dick's La PR3 .195 E5
Green Dr
Bamber Bridge PR5 .96 C1
Barton PR3 .136 B8
Cleveleys FY5 .172 C5
Clitheroe BB7 .187 A2
Fulwood PR2 .116 E7
Lytham St Anne's FY8 .89 F5
Penwortham PR1 .95 B5
Poulton-le-F FY6 .130 E8
Saltcotes FY8 .90 C5
Green Edge Cl BB9 .147 D5
Green End PR5 .98 E7
Green End Ave BB18 .201 B2
Green End Barn BB18 .201 B1
Green End Cl 11 OL13 .87 A3
Green End Rd BB18 .201 B1
Green Gate Fulwood PR2 .116 C3
Hutton PR4 .94 C1
Green Haworth
CE Prim Sch BB5 .103 B1
Green Haworth
Golf Course BB5 .103 B1
Green Head Cotts 6 LA2 233 B8
Green Hey
Lytham St Anne's FY8 .90 D4
Much Hoole PR4 .73 E3
Green Heys Dr L31 .5 F1
Green Hill OL13 .87 A1
Green Hill La LA2,LA6 .231 B6
Green Hill Rd OL13 .87 A1
Green Howarth
View BB5 .103 A3
Green La Banks PR9 .54 C4
Bilsborrow PR3 .157 B2
Bispham Green L40 .26 B7
Blackburn BB2 .100 A1
Bretherton PR5 .57 C7
Chipping PR3 .182 F3
Coppull PR7 .29 A8
Downham BB7 .188 B6
Ellel LA1,LA2 .207 B6
Farington PR5 .75 E7
Formby L37 .11 F5
Freckleton PR4 .92 C6
Garstang PR3 .178 A7
Grindleton BB7 .187 A7
Halton Green LA2 .231 A4
Holmes PR4 .55 C4
Horton BD23 .225 E5
Horwich BL6 .31 B5
Lancaster LA1,LA2 .214 A6
Longridge PR3 .139 B8
Maghull L31 .5 A2
Maghull L31 .5 C1
Morecambe LA3 .212 E2
Ormskirk L39 .15 E6
Orrell WN5 .10 D3
Padiham BB12 .125 C8
Penwortham PR4 .95 C1
Preesall FY6 .195 C2
Riley Green PR5 .78 E8
Samlesbury Bottoms PR5 .98 B7
Skelmersdale L40 .18 A6
Sollom PR4 .55 D1
Standish WN6 .28 D1
Storth LA7 .237 E5
Woodsfold PR4 .134 E6
Green La E PR3 .199 C2
Green La The L40 .24 F4
Green La W Freckleton PR4 .92 B5
Garstang PR3 .199 B1
Green Lane Ave L39 .15 E6
Green Link L31 .5 B2
Green Mdw BB8 .170 B2
Green Meadow La FY6 .174 C1
Green Mount BB6 .143 D8
Green Nook La PR3 .138 F6
Green Oak Pl FY5 .151 A8
Green Park Cty Prim Sch
L31 .5 B2
Green Park Dr L31 .5 B1
Green Pk BB7 .143 C5
Green Pl PR5 .77 A6
Green Rd BB8 .169 D4
Green Row BB3 .80 B6
Green Side
Kirkby Lonsdale LA6 .238 C1
Wrea Green PR4 .112 B3
Green Sq LA6 .238 C1
Green St Adlington PR6 .30 B8
11 Barnoldswick BB18 .200 B2
Burnley BB10 .147 B1
Chorley PR7 .42 A5
Darwen BB3 .81 A1
Edenfield BL0 .67 E3
Great Harwood BB6 .123 B5
Lancaster LA1 .214 A1
Lytham St Anne's FY8 .90 A3
Morecambe LA4 .212 E6
Oswaldtwistle BB5 .102 C2
Padiham BB12 .125 C7
Rawtenstall BB4 .85 A3
Green St E 16 BB3 .81 A1
Green The Adlington PR6 .42 F2
Bispham Green L40 .26 B8
Bolton-le-S LA5 .216 B5
Churchtown PR3 .178 A2
Colne BB8 .169 F6
5 Darwen BB3 .81 A1
Eccleston PR7 .40 C6
Fulwood PR2 .117 F2
Hesketh Bank PR4 .72 E3
Nelson BB9 .169 B2
Parbold WN8 .26 B2
Ramsbottom BL8 .48 F1
Silverdale LA5 .218 D2
Weeton PR4 .131 F2
Green Way 4 FY4 .109 F7
Green Wlk Earby BB18 .201 A1
Southport PR8 .20 D5
Green's La Haskayne L31 .14 C1
Stalmine FY6 .174 F7
Greenacre Blackburn BB3 .80 F6
Westhead L40 .16 E4
Greenacre Cl BL0 .49 E7
Greenacre Ct LA1 .211 B3
Greenacre Pk LA2 .215 E2
Greenacre Rd LA2 .215 E2
Greenacre St BB7 .164 E7
Greenacres Chorley PR7 .42 C5
Edgworth BL7 .47 E6
Fulwood PR2 .116 B7
Read BB12 .144 D2
Greenacres Ave PR4 .113 A4
Greenacres Dr PR3 .178 D6
Greenacres The PR4 .94 D2
Greenbank Horwich BL6 .31 D1
Poulton-le-F FY6 .151 E3
Whitworth OL12 .51 C5
Greenbank Ave Maghull L31 .5 C3
Orrell WN5 .10 D3
Preston PR1 .116 D2
Storth LA7 .237 E4
Greenbank Dr Fence BB12 146 E8
Southport PR8 .33 E2
Greenbank High Sch PR8 .33 E1
Greenbank Pk BB4 .85 B2
Greenbank Pl PR1 .116 E1
Greenbank Rd
Blackburn BB1 .101 B6
Penwortham PR1 .95 E4
Rochdale OL12 .51 F2
Greenbank Sch OL12 .51 F1
Greenbank St
Preston PR1 .116 D2
Preston PR1 .116 E1
Rawtenstall BB4 .85 B2
Greenbank Terr BB3 .80 F6
Greenbanks FY2 .150 F3
Greenbarn Way BL6 .30 D1
Greenber La LA6 .238 F5
Greenberfield La BB18 .200 C4
Greenbriar Cl FY3 .150 F1
Greenbrook Cl BB12 .125 F6
Greenbrook Rd BB12 .125 F6
Greenbrook St 6 BL9 .32 A4
Greencliffe La BB10 .128 A1
Greencroft PR1 .95 D3
Greendale Ave BB4 .85 E2
Greendale Cl
Fleetwood FY7 .193 C2
Over Town BB10 .107 A7
Greendale Dr LA5 .217 D3
Greendale Mews 1 PR2 .115 E2
Greendale View BB7 .187 B8
Greenfield PR4 .72 D4
Greenfield Ave
Chatburn BB7 .187 D5
Clitheroe BB7 .164 C8
Parbold WN8 .26 B2
Greenfield Cl PR9 .53 A3
Greenfield Ct 2 LA1 .211 A7
Greenfield Dr PR5 .76 A8
Greenfield Gdns 1 BB4 .84 B2
Greenfield Ho 18 LA1 .211 A8
Greenfield La PR3 .159 A6
Greenfield Rd
Adlington PR6 .30 A8
Burnley BB10 .127 D4
Chorley PR6 .42 E8
Cleveleys FY5 .150 E8
Colne BB8 .169 B4
Fleetwood FY7 .193 F2
Nelson BB8 .169 A4
Southport PR8 .35 C1
Greenfield St Darwen BB3 .64 C6
Haslingden BB4 .84 B3
12 Lancaster LA1 .211 A8
Rawtenstall BB4 .85 A3
Greenfield Terr
3 Cornholme OL14 .108 A1
Oswaldtwistle BB5 .102 A1
Greenfield View BB3 .81 A7
Greenfield Way PR2 .116 B5
Greenfields LA2 .231 C3
Greenfields Cres PR4 .112 E6
Greenfinch Ct FY3 .130 B6
Greenfold Dr BB4 .105 A2
Greenfoot 5 LA2 .233 B8
Greenfoot La LA2 .233 B8
Greenford Cl WN5 .10 D6
Greenford Rd PR8 .20 C4
Greengate Cl BB12 .126 D7
Greengate La LA5 .216 C8
Greenhalgh La
Adlington PR6 .30 B8
Greenhalgh PR4 .132 D4
Greenhall Cl PR3 .178 D6
Greenham Ave L33 .1 A6
Greenhaven WN8 .10 B7
Greenhead Ave BB1 .101 B7
Greenhead La BB12 .146 D5
Greenhey Pl WN8 .8 F8
Greenheys Ave FY6 .151 B4
Greenheys Cres BL8 .48 F1
Greenhill BB6 .123 B5
Greenhill Ave PR4 .113 A6
Greenhill Pl 2 FY1 .129 C6
Greenholme Ave LA4 .212 E3
Greenhurst Cl BB2 .100 D4
Greenings La PR9 .36 C3
Greenland Ave WN6 .28 E1
Greenland La PR6 .30 D5
Greenlands Cres PR2 .117 E3
Greenlands
Cty Prim Sch PR2 .117 E3
Greenlands High Sch
FY2 .150 E2
Greenlea Cl WN5 .10 D5
Greenlea Dr LA4 .212 G5
Greenloon's Dr L37 .11 C3
Greenloon's Wlk L37 .11 C2
Greenmead Cl PR4 .115 E5
Greenmoor La PR3 .140 B7
Greenmount Ave
1 Kirkham PR4 .113 A5
1 Thornton FY5 .173 A3
Greenmount Cl BL8 .48 F2
Greenmount Dr BL8 .48 F2
Greenmount Prim Sch
BL8 .48 F2
Greenock Cl BB11 .126 D4
Greenock Dr OL10 .32 F1
Greenock St BB11 .126 D4
Greenpark Cl BL8 .48 F1
Greens Arms Rd BB3,BL7 .46 E7
Greens La
Bacup, Lane Head OL13 .87 A3
Bacup, Nun Hills OL13 .69 D7
Haslingden BB4 .67 C7
Greens The OL12 .70 C1
Greenset Cl LA1 .213 E4
Greenside Euxton PR7 .59 C3
Fulwood PR4 .115 D4
Ribchester PR3 .140 E3
Greenside Ave
Blackburn BB2 .80 A8
Preston PR2 .115 C1
Greenside Cl Kirkby L33 .1 A6
Ramsbottom BL8 .48 B3
Greenside Dr BL8 .48 F1
Greenside Gdns PR5 .58 B7
Greenslate Ave WN6 .19 E8
Greenslate Ct WN5 .10 E3
Greenslate Rd WN5 .10 E3
Greensnook La OL13 .87 A3
Greensnook Mews 5
OL13 .87 A3
Greensnook Terr 1 OL13 .87 A3
Greenstone Ave BL6 .31 B3
Greensward Cl WN6 .28 B1
Greensway PR3 .136 C3
Greenthorn Cres PR2 .118 A2
Greenthorne Cl BL7 .47 E7
Greenvale WN6 .19 F4
Greenville Dr L31 .5 C1
Greenway Catterall PR3 .178 D3
Eccleston PR7 .40 B7
Fulwood PR2 .116 D7
Horwich BL6 .31 F3
Penwortham PR1 .95 B4
Greenway Ave WN8 .9 B8
Greenway Cl WN8 .17 E2
Greenway Ho FY6 .151 E3
Greenway Mews BL0 .49 C4
Greenway St BB3 .80 F3
Greenways Becconsall PR4 .72 F1
Lytham St Anne's FY8 .89 B6
Orrell WN5 .10 D3
Over Kellet LA6 .231 B8
Greenwich Dr FY8 .89 D5
Greenwood PR5 .77 B4
Greenwood Ave
Blackpool FY1 .129 E2
Hest Bank LA5 .215 F2
Horwich BL6 .31 D1
Greenwood Cl
Lytham St Anne's FY8 .89 E4
Ormskirk L39 .15 C1
Greenwood Cres LA5 .215 F2
Greenwood Dr LA5 .215 F2
Greenwood La BL6 .31 E1
Greenwood Rd WN6 .28 E2
Greenwood St
1 Bamber Bridge PR5 .96 E1
Preston PR1 .96 B7
Greetby Hill L39, L40 .16 A6
Greetby Pl WN8 .9 A8
Gregareth Cl 5 LA1 .213 C2
Gregory Ave FY2 .150 C5
Gregory Fold BB4 .67 A7
Gregory La L39 .22 B3
Gregory Meadow PR3 .178 B7
Gregory Pl FY8 .90 A3
Gregory's Ct LA1 .211 A4
Gregson Cl 5 FY4 .109 F7
Gregson Dr 3 FY7 .193 F2
Gregson La Blackburn BB2 100 D5
Gregson Lane PR5 .97 E1
Higher Walton PR5 .97 C2
Gregson Rd LA1 .211 A7
Gregson St Darwen BB3 .64 A8
Lytham St Anne's FY8 .90 A3
Gregson Way PR2 .117 B5
Gregson's Ave L37 .11 E5
Grenfell Ave FY3 .129 E7
Grenville Ave
Bamber Bridge PR5 .96 D2
Lytham St Anne's FY8 .109 E1
Gresham Rd FY5 .172 D1
Gresham St BB4 .85 F1
Gresley Ave BL6 .31 B3
Gresley Ct LA1 .210 F6
Gresley Pl FY2 .150 E2
Gressingham Dr LA1 .211 A4
Gressingham Ho 3 LA1 .211 A3
Greta Heath LA6 .236 C3
Greta Pl Fleetwood FY7 .193 D3
Lancaster LA1 .213 E2
Gretdale Ave FY8 .88 E8
Gretna Cres FY5 .150 D8
Gretna Rd BB1 .121 F1
Grey Heights View PR6 .42 E8
Grey St Barrowford BB9 .168 D3

Grey St continued
Burnley BB10 . . . .**127** A8
Greyfriars Ave PR2 . . . . . .**116** D5
Greyfriars Cres PR2 . . . . .**116** D5
Greyfriars Dr PR1 . . . . . .**95** C5
Greyfriars Rd PR8 . . . .**20** B6
Greyhound Bridge Rd
LA1 . . . .**213** F1
Greystock Ave PR2 . . . . . .**116** E6
Greystock Cl PR5 . . . .**77** B8
Greystoke Ave BB5 . . . . . .**79** E8
Greystoke Pl FY4 . . . .**109** B5
Greystokes L39 . . . .**15** D2
Greystokes Ct FY4 . . . . . .**109** B5
Greystonegill La LA2 . . . .**233** F7
Greystones PR5 . . . .**75** B1
Greystones Dr BB12 . . . . .**146** E8
Greythwaite Ct LA1 . . . . .**210** D6
Greywood Ave BL9 . . . .**32** B2
Griffin Cl Accrington BB5 .**124** F1
Burnley BB11 . . . .**126** B5
Bury BL9 . . . .**32** B4
Griffin Ct BB2 . . . .**100** C2
Griffin Park Prim Sch
BB2 . . . .**100** B3
Griffin St BB2 . . . .**100** B3
Griffiths Dr PR9 . . . .**34** F8
Griffon Ho PR9 . . . .**52** F2
Grime Row BB5 . . . .**124** F2
Grime St Chorley PR7 . . . . .**42** D6
Darwen BB3 . . . .**80** F2
7 Ramsbottom BL0 . . . . . .**49** A4
Grimeford La BL6,PR6 . . . .**30** C5
Grimrod Pl WN8 . . . .**9** A7
Grimsargh St **10** PR1 . . . .**117** D1
Grimsargh St Michaels
CE Sch PR2 . . . .**138** C1
Grimshaw Green La
L40,WN8 . . . .**26** C6
Grimshaw La L39 . . . .**15** E7
Grimshaw Pk BB2 . . . .**100** F3
Grimshaw Rd WN8 . . . .**9** D8
Grimshaw St
Accrington BB5 . . . .**103** A5
6 Barrowford BB9 . . . . . .**168** D4
Burnley BB11 . . . .**127** A5
5 Church BB5 . . . .**102** E6
2 Clayton-le-M BB5 . . . . .**123** F2
Darwen BB3 . . . .**64** B7
Great Harwood BB6 . . . . .**123** C5
Preston PR1 . . . .**96** A7
Grindleton Ct PR3 . . . . . .**137** E6
Grindlestone Hirst BB8 . .**169** C3
Grindleton Brow BB7 . . . .**187** B7
Grindleton CE Prim Sch
BB7 . . . .**187** C8
Grindleton Cl FY3 . . . . . .**130** B8
Grindleton Gr BB10 . . . . .**127** D5
Grindleton Rd
Blackburn BB2 . . . .**100** C4
Grindleton BB7 . . . .**187** B7
West Bradford BB7 . . . . . .**186** F6
Gringley Rd LA4 . . . .**212** F3
Grinstead Cl PR8 . . . .**33** F1
Grisedale Ave BB1 . . . . . .**101** C2
Grisedale Cl L37 . . . .**11** E3
Grisedale Dr BB12 . . . . . .**126** B8
Grisedale Pl PR7 . . . .**42** B5
Grizedale Ave
Garstang PR3 . . . .**178** B7
Poulton-le-F FY6 . . . .**151** C3
Grizedale Cl
Clayton-le-M BB5 . . . .**123** E2
Fulwood PR2 . . . .**117** F2
Grizedale Cres PR2 . . . . . .**118** A2
Grizedale Ct Blackpool FY3 **129** E5
7 Thornton FY5 . . . .**173** B3
Grizedale Pl Fulwood PR2 .**117** F2
Morecambe LA3 . . . .**212** B4
Grizedale Rd
Blackpool FY4 . . . .**130** C1
Lancaster LA1 . . . .**214** B2
Grosvenor Cl PR8 . . . .**33** E3
Grosvenor Ct
Carnforth LA5 . . . .**217** C1
Cleveleys FY5 . . . .**172** C2
6 Lytham St Anne's FY8 . .**89** A8
Grosvenor Gdns PR8 . . . . .**33** F3
Grosvenor Lodge BB1 . . . .**121** F6
Grosvenor Park
Cty Prim Sch LA3 . . . . . .**213** B2
Grosvenor Pl
Carnforth LA5 . . . .**217** C1
Preston PR2 . . . .**116** B2
Southport PR8 . . . .**33** F3
Grosvenor Rd
Carnforth LA5 . . . .**217** D1
Chorley PR7 . . . .**42** B6
Morecambe LA3 . . . .**212** A3
Southport PR8 . . . .**33** E4
Grosvenor St
Blackpool FY1 . . . .**129** C5
Burnley BB12 . . . .**126** F7
Colne BB8 . . . .**169** F5
Lytham St Anne's FY8 . . . . .**90** C3
Preston PR1 . . . .**96** B7
Grosvenor Way
4 Blackburn BB1 . . . . . .**100** E5
Horwich BL6 . . . .**31** F4
Grouse St OL12 . . . .**51** F1
Grove Ave Adlington PR6 . .**30** A7
Longton PR4 . . . .**73** F8
Grove Cres PR6 . . . .**30** A7
Grove Ct Lancaster LA1 . . .**210** F6
Oswaldtwistle BB5 . . . .**102** C3
Grove La BB12 . . . .**145** E1

Grove Mead L31 . . . .**5** F1
Grove Mill
Development Ctr PR7 . . . . .**40** C5
Grove Pk Ormskirk L39 . . . .**15** F7
Southport PR9 . . . .**34** F8
Grove Rd Orrell WN8 . . . . .**10** C8
Preston PR1 . . . .**96** C6
Grove St Accrington BB5 . .**103** A6
Bacup OL13 . . . .**87** A3
12 Bamber Bridge PR5 . . .**76** F8
Barrowford BB9 . . . .**168** D3
Blackburn BB2 . . . .**100** C2
3 Burnley BB11 . . . .**126** D5
Bury BL9 . . . .**32** C3
Earby BB18 . . . .**201** B3
Leyland PR5 . . . .**58** D8
Lytham St Anne's FY8 . . . . .**88** F7
Morecambe LA4 . . . .**212** C4
Nelson BB9 . . . .**147** E8
Oswaldtwistle BB5 . . . .**102** D3
Southport PR8 . . . .**34** A4
Grove Terr PR8 . . . .**34** A5
Grove The
Appley Bridge WN6 . . . . . .**27** C2
Bilsborrow PR3 . . . .**157** A5
Burnley BB12 . . . .**126** B6
Carnforth LA5 . . . .**217** B1
Chipping PR3 . . . .**182** D4
Chorley PR7 . . . .**60** C2
Cleveleys FY5 . . . .**172** E3
Clitheroe BB7 . . . .**186** F1
Lancaster LA1 . . . .**211** A7
Ormskirk L39 . . . .**6** C7
Penwortham PR1 . . . .**95** B4
Preston PR2 . . . .**116** B1
Rufford L40 . . . .**38** A3
Whalley BB7 . . . .**143** C5
Grovewood PR8 . . . .**33** E5
Grovewood Dr WN6 . . . . . .**19** E8
Grundy Cl PR8 . . . .**34** E5
Grundy Homes PR8 . . . . . .**34** E5
Grundy Mews FY4 . . . .**109** C7
Grundy St 7 PR5 . . . .**76** B2
Grundy's La PR7 . . . .**42** D1
Guard Hill La LA7 . . . .**237** E4
Gubberford La PR3 . . . . . .**199** D4
Guernsey Ave BB2 . . . . . .**100** F1
Guide La BB12 . . . .**146** A7
Guide Rd PR4 . . . .**72** C5
Guide Sq BB1 . . . .**81** B8
Guild Hall Arc 5 PR1 . . . .**96** A7
Guild Park Hosp PR3 . . . .**137** F5
Guild Row 7 PR1 . . . .**96** A7
Guild Way PR1 . . . .**95** D7
Guildford Ave
Blackpool FY2 . . . .**150** D6
Great Knowley PR6 . . . .**60** E4
Guildford Rd
30 Preston PR1 . . . .**96** A7
Southport PR8 . . . .**34** B2
Guildford Way FY6 . . . . . .**151** C6
Guildhall St PR1 . . . .**95** F7
Guilford St BB9 . . . .**147** B5
Guinea Hall La PR9 . . . . . .**54** A5
Gulf La LA2,PR3 . . . .**197** D7
Gummers Howe Wlk LA5 **216** E8
Gunsmith Pl 8 BB11 . . . . .**127** A6
Gurney St BB2 . . . .**100** B3
Guy St BB12 . . . .**145** C1
Guys Thatched Hamlet
(Craft Ctr) PR3 . . . .**156** F3
Guysyke BB8 . . . .**169** C4
Gynn Ave FY1 . . . .**129** B8
Gynn Sq FY1 . . . .**129** B8

H

Habergham Dr BB12 . . . . .**125** F8
Habergham High Sch
BB12 . . . .**126** A7
Habergham High Sch
& Sixth Form Ctr BB12 .**125** F7
Habergham St 10 BB12 . . .**145** C1
Hackensall Rd FY6 . . . . . .**194** E5
Hacking Cl BB6 . . . .**142** C1
Hacking Dr PR3 . . . .**138** F5
Hacking St Bury BL9 . . . . . .**32** A2
Darwen BB3 . . . .**80** F1
3 Nelson BB9 . . . .**168** F1
Hacklands Ave PR2 . . . . . .**115** C1
Haddings La BB12 . . . .**146** A8
Haddon Ct FY2 . . . .**150** C5
Haddon Pl PR2 . . . .**116** D3
Haddon Rd FY2 . . . .**150** C5
Hadlee Terr LA1 . . . .**213** D1
Hadleigh Rd FY6 . . . .**151** C6
Hadrian Rd LA3 . . . .**213** B3
Hadstock Ave L37 . . . .**11** D1
Hagg La PR3 . . . .**154** C8
Hagg St BB8 . . . .**169** C4
Haig Ave Lancaster LA1 . . .**210** D8
Leyland PR5 . . . .**75** F1
Preston PR2 . . . .**116** D2
Southport PR8 . . . .**34** E5
Tarleton PR4 . . . .**56** A7
Haig Rd FY1 . . . .**129** B1
Haig St BB1 . . . .**75** F1
Haigh Cl PR7 . . . .**42** A1
Haigh Cres Chorley PR7 . . .**42** B7
Maghull L31 . . . .**5** C4
Haigh Ct PR8 . . . .**34** F6
Haigh Hall Cl BL0 . . . .**49** B4
Haighton Ct PR2 . . . .**117** A7
Haighton Dr PR2 . . . .**117** A7
Haighton Green La PR2 . .**137** E2
Hail St BL0 . . . .**49** A4
Hala Cres LA1 . . . .**211** A3

Hala Gr LA1 . . . .**211** A3
Hala Hill LA1,LA2 . . . .**211** B3
Hala Rd LA1 . . . .**211** A3
Hala Sq LA1 . . . .**211** A3
Halcyon Cl 6 OL12 . . . .**51** B2
Haldane Rd BB3 . . . .**80** E4
Haldane St BB10 . . . .**147** B2
Halden Rd LA3 . . . .**212** B3
Hale Carr Gr LA4 . . . .**212** B1
Hale Carr La LA4 . . . .**212** B1
Hale St BB11 . . . .**127** A4
Hales Rushes Rd PR3 . . . .**175** C4
Half Acre PR5 . . . .**76** A8
Half Acre La BL6 . . . .**30** C2
Halford Pl FY5 . . . .**150** E7
Halfpenny La
Andertons Mill PR7 . . . .**40** B3
Longridge PR3 . . . .**138** F8
Halifax Rd Brierfield BB9 . .**147** C5
Lane Bottom BB10 . . . . . .**148** D3
Lane Bottom BB10 . . . . . .**149** B1
Nelson BB10,BB9 . . . .**147** E5
Southport PR8 . . . .**20** C5
Halifax St FY3 . . . .**129** F3
Hall Ave FY4 . . . .**129** C1
Hall Brow Cl L39 . . . .**16** B4
Hall Carr La PR4 . . . .**73** D6
Hall Carr Mill Cotts BB4 . .**85** B2
Hall Carr Rd BB4 . . . .**85** A1
Hall Cl Caton LA2 . . . .**231** B3
Rawtenstall BB4 . . . .**85** A6
Hall Coppice The BL7 . . . .**46** E1
Hall Croft PR4 . . . .**94** D2
Hall Dr Caton LA2 . . . .**231** B3
Heysham LA3 . . . .**209** A2
Morecambe LA4 . . . .**213** A4
Hall Fold OL10 . . . .**51** C8
Hall Garth Cl LA6 . . . .**234** A1
Hall Garth Gdns LA6 . . . .**234** B1
Hall Gate PR7 . . . .**60** A2
Hall Gate La FY6 . . . .**174** C8
Hall Gdns OL12 . . . .**51** C2
Hall Gn WN8 . . . .**10** B7
Hall Gr LA3 . . . .**209** A2
Hall Greaves Cl LA3 . . . . .**205** D8
Hall Green Cl WN8 . . . .**10** B7
Hall Green La L40,PR7 . . . .**40** A3
Hall Hill BB7 . . . .**222** D1
Hall Hill St 4 BB12 . . . . . .**145** C1
Hall La Appley Bridge WN6 .**27** D2
Bickerstaffe L39 . . . .**7** E4
Bispham Green L40,WN8 . . .**26** A6
Bracewell BD23 . . . .**225** F3
Great Eccleston PR3 . . . . .**154** C4
Ince Blundell L38 . . . .**3** F3
Kirkby L33 . . . .**1** A8
Leyland PR5 . . . .**75** F2
Longton PR4 . . . .**73** E7
Maghull L31 . . . .**5** B7
Mawdesley L40 . . . .**39** D3
Orrell WN5 . . . .**10** F4
Rivington BL6 . . . .**44** A2
Royal Oak L39 . . . .**7** B1
Skelmersdale L40 . . . .**17** A4
St Michaels on W PR3 . . . .**155** E6
Hall Mdws BB8 . . . .**170** C3
Hall Park Ave BB10 . . . . . .**127** F4
Hall Park Ctr FY8 . . . .**89** F4
Hall Park Dr FY8 . . . .**89** E6
Hall Park Prim Sch FY8 . . .**89** F3
Hall Pk LA1 . . . .**210** F4
Hall Rd Bescar L40 . . . .**23** B6
Fulwood PR2 . . . .**116** E5
Penwortham PR1 . . . .**95** E3
Trawden BB8 . . . .**170** B3
Hall St Bacup OL13 . . . .**86** F3
Blackburn BB2 . . . .**100** E2
Burnley BB11 . . . .**127** A6
Clitheroe BB7 . . . .**164** E7
Colne BB8 . . . .**169** D4
Haslingden BB4 . . . .**84** B2
Morecambe LA4 . . . .**212** E6
Preston PR1 . . . .**116** C1
Ramsbottom BL0 . . . .**49** C2
12 Rawtenstall BB4 . . . . . .**85** A3
Southport PR9 . . . .**34** C7
Whitworth OL12 . . . .**51** B8
Whitworth OL12 . . . .**51** C8
Worsthorne BB10 . . . .**128** C5
Hall's Cotts FY4 . . . .**110** A6
Hallam Cres BB9 . . . .**148** A8
Hallam La LA2 . . . .**209** A2
Hallam Rd BB9 . . . .**148** A8
Hallam St BB5 . . . .**124** A1
Hallbridge Gdns WN8 . . . .**10** B8
Hallcroft WN8 . . . .**18** C2
Halley Rd BB3 . . . .**80** E3
Halley St OL13 . . . .**87** A7
Hallfield Rd BB6 . . . .**123** D6
Hallgate Hill BB7 . . . .**223** B4
Halliwell Ct 7 PR7 . . . .**42** C7
Halliwell La PR6 . . . .**60** C4
Halliwell Pl 8 PR7 . . . .**42** C7
Halliwell St
Accrington BB5 . . . .**103** E2
Chorley PR7 . . . .**42** C7
Hallmoor Cl L39 . . . .**15** C4
Hallows Cl PR3 . . . .**155** C6
Hallows Farm Ave OL12 . .**51** D2
Hallows St BB10 . . . .**147** A2
Halls Sq PR6 . . . .**60** E3
Hallsall Dr LA4 . . . .**213** B6
Hallsalls Sq PR3 . . . .**154** B5
Hallwell St BB10 . . . .**127** A8
Hallwood Cl BB10 . . . .**147** B4
Hallwood Rd PR7 . . . .**42** A5
Halmot Ct 3 BB4 . . . .**85** E1
Halmote Ave BB12 . . . . . .**145** F5

Halsall Bldgs 6 PR9 . . . . . .**34** C8
Halsall Ct L39 . . . .**15** D6
Halsall Hall Dr L39 . . . .**22** B1
Halsall La Formby L37 . . . . .**11** C1
Haskayne L39 . . . .**14** D6
Ormskirk L39 . . . .**15** D6
Halsbury St PR1 . . . .**96** B6
Halstead Cl BB9 . . . .**168** D4
Halstead La BB9 . . . .**168** D4
Halstead Rd PR2 . . . .**117** E5
Halstead St Burnley BB11 .**126** F5
Bury BL9 . . . .**32** A4
Worsthorne BB10 . . . .**128** A6
Halstead Wlk BL9 . . . .**32** A5
Halton Ave
Clayton-le-W PR5 . . . .**76** D1
Cleveleys FY5 . . . .**172** E4
Halton Chase L40 . . . .**16** E4
Halton Ct LA4 . . . .**212** E3
Halton Gdns Blackpool FY4 **109** F8
Cleveleys FY5 . . . .**172** F4
Halton Pl Fulwood PR2 . . .**117** F4
Longridge PR3 . . . .**139** B8
Halton Rd Lancaster LA1 . .**214** A4
Maghull L31 . . . .**5** D3
Nether Kellet LA6 . . . .**216** E5
Halton St PR4 . . . .**131** E6
Hambledon Dr 6 PR1 . . . . .**95** E2
Hambledon St 10 BB12 . . .**125** D8
Hambledon Terr
Higham BB12 . . . .**145** F6
2 Padiham BB12 . . . .**125** F7
Hambledon View
Padiham BB12 . . . .**125** F7
Read BB12 . . . .**144** D1
Hambleton Prim Sch
FY6 . . . .**174** D2
Hameldon App BB11 . . . . .**126** D5
Hameldon Ave BB5 . . . . . .**103** E2
Hameldon Cl BB11 . . . . . .**125** D5
Hameldon Rd
Hapton BB11 . . . .**125** D8
Rawtenstall BB4 . . . .**105** A2
Hameldon View BB6 . . . .**123** D5
Rawtenstall BB4 . . . .**105** A1
Hamer Ave Blackburn BB1 .**101** D5
Hamer Rd PR2 . . . .**116** D3
Hamer St 18 Darwen BB3 . . .**64** A8
Ramsbottom BL0 . . . .**49** B2
Rawtenstall BB4 . . . .**85** A2
Hamerswood Dr PR3 . . . .**178** C2
Hamilton Ct
5 Blackpool FY1 . . . .**129** B4
8 Saltcotes FY8 . . . .**90** D4
Hamilton Dr LA1 . . . .**213** C3
Hamilton Gr PR2 . . . .**117** C3
Hamilton Rd
Barrowford BB9 . . . .**168** C1
Chorley PR7 . . . .**42** C7
Fulwood PR2 . . . .**117** C3
Morecambe LA4 . . . .**213** C6
Nelson BB8 . . . .**169** A2
Hamilton St BB2 . . . .**100** D2
Hamilton Way OL10 . . . . . .**32** E1
Hamlet Cl BB2 . . . .**100** C3
Hamlet Gr PR4 . . . .**133** F4
Hamlet Rd FY7 . . . .**193** F4
Hamlet The Chorley PR7 . . .**42** F1
Lytham St Anne's FY8 . . . .**109** F2
Hammer Terr BL0 . . . .**49** C3
Hammerton Gn 18 OL13 . . .**86** F3
Hammerton Hall Cl LA1 . .**213** E4
Hammerton Hall La LA1 . .**213** E4
Hammerton Pl FY3 . . . . . .**130** A8
Hammerton St Bacup OL13 .**86** F4
Burnley BB11 . . . .**126** F5
Hammond Cl OL13 . . . .**69** D8
Hammond Ct PR1 . . . .**116** E1
Hammond Dr BB12 . . . . . .**144** C2
Hammond Rd L33 . . . .**1** C3
Hammond St Nelson BB9 . .**147** F7
Preston PR1 . . . .**116** E1
Preston PR1 . . . .**116** E1
Preston PR1 . . . .**116** F2
Hammond's Row 16 PR1 . . .**96** A8
Hampden Ave BB3 . . . .**64** B7
Hampden Rd PR5 . . . .**76** A2
Hampden St
7 Burnley BB11 . . . .**127** B4
Hapton BB12 . . . .**125** C4
Hampsfell Dr LA4 . . . .**212** E3
Hampshire Cl BB1 . . . .**122** A7
Hampshire Pl FY4 . . . .**109** F6
Hampshire Rd
Bamber Bridge PR5 . . . . . .**96** D3
Rishton BB1 . . . .**123** A1
Hampson Ave PR5 . . . .**76** D1
Hampson Cotts LA2 . . . . .**207** B1
Hampson Gr FY6 . . . .**195** A4
Hampson La LA2 . . . .**207** C1
Hampson St BL6 . . . .**31** B4
Hampson Terr PR2 . . . . . .**154** C5
Hampstead Cl FY8 . . . .**89** E6
Hampstead Mews 3 FY1 **129** C7
Hampstead Rd
Fulwood PR2 . . . .**117** D2
Standish WN6 . . . .**28** D1
Hampton Cl PR7 . . . .**42** B8
Hampton Ct FY8 . . . .**89** C8
Hampton Pl FY5 . . . .**172** C4
Hampton Rd
Blackpool FY4 . . . .**109** C8
Formby L37 . . . .**11** C1
Morecambe LA3 . . . .**212** B3

Hampton Rd continued
Southport PR8 . . . .**34** C5
Hampton St PR2 . . . .**116** C2
Hanbury St PR2 . . . .**116** C1
Hancock St BB2 . . . .**100** C3
Hand La L40 . . . .**39** F5
Handbridge The PR2 . . . . .**116** C5
Handel St OL12 . . . .**51** B8
Handley Rd 4 FY1 . . . .**129** C6
Handsworth Ct 4 FY1 . . . .**129** C7
Handsworth Rd FY1 . . . . . .**129** C7
Handsworth Wlk PR8 . . . . .**34** F3
Hanging Green La LA2 . . .**215** E1
Hanley Cl FY6 . . . .**174** C7
Hannah St Accrington BB5 .**103** B5
14 Bacup OL13 . . . .**87** A3
Darwen BB3 . . . .**64** B8
Hanover Cres FY2 . . . .**150** C5
Hanover St Colne BB8 . . . .**169** D5
Morecambe LA4 . . . .**212** E5
5 Preston PR1 . . . .**116** F1
Hanson St
Great Harwood BB6 . . . . .**123** C4
Rishton BB1 . . . .**123** C1
Hanstock Cl WN5 . . . .**10** E5
Hants La L39 . . . .**15** E6
Happy Mount Ct LA4 . . . . .**213** B7
Happy Mount Dr LA4 . . . . .**213** A7
Hapton
CE Meth Prim Sch BB11 **125** C4
Hapton Rd BB12 . . . .**125** C7
Hapton St
7 Padiham BB12 . . . .**125** D8
Thornton FY5 . . . .**173** B4
Hapton Sta BB11 . . . .**125** C4
Hapton Way BB4 . . . .**105** A2
Harbour Ave PR4 . . . .**91** E6
Harbour Cl 11 FY7 . . . .**193** F2
Harbour Ho 4 FY8 . . . .**90** F4
Harbour La Brinscall PR6 . .**61** D7
Edgworth BL7 . . . .**47** D5
Warton PR4 . . . .**91** E6
Harbour Way FY7 . . . .**194** B3
Harbury Ave PR8 . . . .**20** A4
Harcles Dr BL0 . . . .**49** B2
Harcourt Mews 10 BL6 . . . .**31** B4
Harcourt Rd
Accrington BB5 . . . .**103** D3
Blackburn BB2 . . . .**100** C6
Blackpool FY4 . . . .**109** D8
Lancaster LA1 . . . .**213** E3
Harcourt St 15 Bacup OL13 .**86** F3
1 Burnley BB11 . . . .**126** D5
Preston PR1 . . . .**116** E1
Hard Knott Rise LA5 . . . . .**216** E8
Hardacre La
Lucas Green PR6 . . . .**60** C5
Rimington BB7 . . . .**225** B2
Hardacre St L39 . . . .**15** F6
Hardcastle Rd PR2 . . . . . .**116** E3
Harden Rd BB18 . . . .**192** A6
Hardhorn Ct FY6 . . . .**151** D3
Hardhorn Rd FY6 . . . .**151** D2
Hardhorn Way FY6 . . . . . .**151** D2
Harding Rd L40 . . . .**24** D4
Harding St PR6 . . . .**30** B8
Hardlands Ave LA4 . . . . . .**213** B4
Hardman Ave
Rawtenstall BB4 . . . .**85** A1
Hardman Cl Blackburn BB1 **101** F4
Rawtenstall,Hugh Mill BB4 . .**68** A8
Hardman Dr BB4 . . . .**68** F7
Hardman St
Blackburn BB2 . . . .**100** C3
3 Blackpool FY1 . . . .**129** C6
Hardman Terr OL13 . . . . . .**69** D8
Hardman Way 22 BB3 . . . . .**81** A1
Hardsough La BL0 . . . .**67** D5
Hardwen Ave 7 PR2 . . . . .**115** C1
Hardwicke St 4 PR1 . . . . . .**96** A8
Hardy Ave
Barnoldswick BB18 . . . . . .**200** A3
Brierfield BB9 . . . .**147** B6
Hardy Ct 11 BB9 . . . .**147** E8
Hardy Dr PR7 . . . .**42** A7
Hardy St Blackburn BB1 . . .**121** F1
Brierfield BB9 . . . .**147** B6
Hare Clough Cl BB2 . . . . .**100** F3
Hare Runs Ho LA1 . . . . . .**213** F3
Harebell Cl Blackburn BB2 . .**79** D8
Formby L37 . . . .**11** F1
Rochdale OL12 . . . .**51** D3
Hareden Brook Cl BB1 . . .**100** F3
Hareden Cl 4 PR5 . . . .**76** F8
Hareden Rd PR2 . . . .**117** F2
Hareholme La BB4 . . . .**85** D2
Hares La PR8 . . . .**35** D1
Harestone Ave PR7 . . . . . .**42** A5
Harewood PR7 . . . .**60** B2
Harewood Ave
Blackpool FY3 . . . .**151** A1
Lancaster LA1 . . . .**211** A3
Morecambe LA3 . . . .**212** B2
Simonstone BB12 . . . .**144** E2
Southport PR8 . . . .**20** C6
Harewood Cl FY6 . . . .**151** C5
Harewood Rd PR1 . . . .**117** C2
Hargate Ave OL12 . . . .**51** A2
Hargate Cl BB4 . . . .**49** C2
Hargate Rd FY5 . . . .**173** C2
Hargher Clough Jun Sch
BB11 . . . .**126** D5
Hargher St BB11 . . . .**126** D5

Hargreaves Ave PR5 . . . . . .59 B8
Hargreaves Ct
Clitheroe BB7 . . . . .164 C7
Fulwood PR2 . . . . .115 F4
Whitewell Bottom BB4 . . . .85 F6
Hargreaves Dr BB4 . . . . . .84 F2
Hargreaves Fold La BB4 . .86 A7
Hargreaves La ☑ BB2 . . .100 E3
Hargreaves Rd BB5 . . . . .102 C4
Hargreaves St
☑ Accrington BB5 . . . . . . .103 C5
Brierfield BB10 . . . . .147 F3
☑ Burnley BB11 . . . . .126 F6
Colne BB8 . . . . .169 B4
Haslingden BB4 . . . . .84 B3
Hoddlesden BB3 . . . . .81 F1
Nelson BB9 . . . . .147 C7
Southport PR8 . . . . .34 C6
Thornton FY5 . . . . .173 B3
Whitewell Bottom BB4 . . . .85 E5
Hargrove Ave
Burnley BB12 . . . . .126 D7
Padiham BB12 . . . . .145 C1
Hargrove Rd BB12 . . . . . .126 D8
Harington Cl L37 . . . . .11 D3
Harington Gn L37 . . . . .11 D3
Harington Rd L37 . . . . .11 D4
Harland St PR2 . . . . .116 D3
Harland Way OL12 . . . . . . .51 B2
Harlech Ave FY1 . . . . . . .129 D1
Harlech Cl BB4 . . . . .84 B1
Harlech Dr Leyland PR5 . . .76 C1
Oswaldtwistle BB5 . . . . . .102 C4
Harleston Rd L33 . . . . .1 A3
Harleston Wlk L33 . . . . .1 A3
Harley Cl LA2 . . . . .233 C8
Harley Rd FY3 . . . . .129 E4
Harley St BB12 . . . . .126 C6
Harling Bank LA6 . . . . . . .238 B2
Harling Rd PR1 . . . . .117 D1
Harling St BB12 . . . . .126 B6
Harold Ave
☑ Blackpool FY4 . . . . . . .110 A6
Burnley BB11 . . . . .126 C4
Harold Dr Burnley BB11 . .126 D5
Colne BB8 . . . . .169 C4
Harold Terr PR5 . . . . .76 A8
Harper St BB18 . . . . .200 A3
Harper's La PR6 . . . . .60 D1
Harperley PR7 . . . . .60 B2
Harpers La BB12 . . . . . . .146 D8
Harridge Ave OL12 . . . . . .51 C3
Harridge La L39,L40 . . . . .23 A1
Harridge St OL12 . . . . .51 C3
Harridge The OL12 . . . . . .51 C3
Harrier Dr BB1 . . . . .100 D8
Harriet St BB11 . . . . .126 E5
Harrington Ave FY4 . . . . .109 E5
Harrington Rd Chorley PR7 .42 B8
Morecambe LA3 . . . . .212 B3
Harrington St
Accrington BB5 . . . . .124 A1
Preston PR1 . . . . .116 F1
Harris Ave FY1 . . . . .129 D1
Harris Cl OL10 . . . . .32 E1
Harris Ct ☑ BB7 . . . . . . .164 E8
Harris Ctr PR2 . . . . .116 B7
Harris Cty Prim Sch PR2 .116 B7
Harris Mus PR5 . . . . .96 A7
Harris Rd Fleetwood FY7 . .194 A4
☑ Preston PR1 . . . . .96 A7
Harrison Ave FY5 . . . . . .173 B2
Harrison Cres Blackrod BL6 30 C3
Morecambe LA3 . . . . .212 A1
Harrison Dr BB8 . . . . . . .169 C6
Harrison La PR4 . . . . .95 B2
Harrison Rd Adlington PR7 .30 A6
Chorley PR7 . . . . .42 C6
Fulwood PR2 . . . . .117 B1
Harrison St Bacup OL13 . .70 B8
Barnoldswick BB18 . . . . . .200 C1
Blackburn BB2 . . . . .100 D4
Blackpool FY1 . . . . .129 C3
Brierfield BB10 . . . . .147 F2
☑ Cornholme OL14 . . . . .108 B1
Horwich BL6 . . . . .31 B4
Ramsbottom BL0 . . . . . . .49 C7
Harrison Terr BB7 . . . . . .187 B8
Harrock La L40,WN6 . . . . .26 F6
Harrock Rd PR5 . . . . .76 D1
Harrod Dr PR8 . . . . .33 E3
Harrogate Cres BB10 . . . .147 D2
Harrogate Rd FY8 . . . . . . .89 C7
Harrogate Way PR9 . . . . .53 C6
Harrop Pl PR2 . . . . .117 E4
Harrow Ave
Accrington BB5 . . . . .103 C4
Fleetwood FY7 . . . . .193 F3
Padiham BB12 . . . . .125 E6
Harrow Cl Orrell WN5 . . . .10 F8
Harrow Gr LA4 . . . . .213 B4
Harrow Pl Blackpool FY4 . .109 A5
Lytham St Anne's FY8 . . . .89 E5
Harrow St BB5 . . . . .102 E4
Harrow Stiles La OL13 . . .106 E1
Harrowside Pk LA2 . . . . . .214 F7
Harrowside FY4 . . . . .109 B6
Harrowside W FY4 . . . . . .109 A5
Harry St Barrowford BB9 . .168 D3
Salterforth BB18 . . . . .191 D7
Harsnips WN8 . . . . .18 C2
Hart St Blackburn BB1 . . . .100 F4
Burnley BB11 . . . . .127 A6

Hart St continued
Southport PR8 . . . . .34 E6
Hart's Hos BL6 . . . . .31 D5
Hart's La WN8 . . . . .9 F8
Hartford Ave FY1 . . . . . . .129 D2
Hartington Rd
Brinscall PR6 . . . . .62 A8
Darwen BB3 . . . . .80 E4
Preston PR1 . . . . .95 D7
Hartington St
Brierfield BB9 . . . . .147 B5
Colne BB8 . . . . .170 B5
Lancaster LA1 . . . . .211 B8
Rishton BB1 . . . . .123 A1
Hartland WN8 . . . . .18 C2
Hartland Ave PR9 . . . . . . .53 B5
Hartlands Cl BB10 . . . . . .147 D3
Hartley Ave BB5 . . . . .103 A3
Hartley Cres PR8 . . . . . . .33 F2
Hartley Homes BB8 . . . . .170 C6
Hartley Rd PR8 . . . . .33 F2
Hartley St
☑ Blackburn BB1 . . . . . . .100 E6
☑ Burnley BB11 . . . . .126 C5
Colne BB8 . . . . .169 D5
Earby BB18 . . . . .201 B3
Great Harwood BB6 . . . . .123 D5
☑ Haslingden BB4 . . . . . . .84 B3
Horwich BL6 . . . . .31 B3
Nelson BB9 . . . . .147 E7
☑ Oswaldtwistle BB5 . . . .102 E4
Rochdale OL12 . . . . .51 B1
Hartleys Terr BB8 . . . . . .169 E4
Hartmann St BB5 . . . . . .103 A6
Hartshead WN8 . . . . .18 C2
Hartwood Gn PR6 . . . . . . .60 C3
Hartwood Rd PR6 . . . . . . .34 D7
Harvest Dr PR6 . . . . .60 C6
Harvey Longworth Ct
BB4 . . . . .105 A1
Harvey St ☑ Nelson BB9 . .168 C1
Oswaldtwistle BB5 . . . . . .102 D4
Harvington Dr PR8 . . . . . .20 B5
Harwich Rd FY8 . . . . .110 A1
Harwin Cl OL12 . . . . .51 D3
Harwood Ave FY8 . . . . . . .88 E8
Harwood Cl FY6 . . . . .174 C7
Harwood Gate BB5 . . . . . .101 B6
Harwood La BB6 . . . . .123 E6
Harwood New Rd BB1 . . .123 C6
Harwood St Rishton BB1 . .123 A2
Wilpshire BB1 . . . . .122 D4
Harwood St
☑ Blackburn, Cob Wall BB1 101 A7
Blackburn, Green Bank BB1 .101 B6
Darwen BB3 . . . . .80 E2
Harwood's La BB3 . . . . . . .81 E1
Hasgill Ct LA1 . . . . .213 E1
Haskayne CE Sch L39 . . . .13 E3
Haskoll St BL6 . . . . .31 D1
Haslam Ct ☑ BB10 . . . . . .147 B1
Haslam Dr L39 . . . . .15 D7
Haslam St BL9 . . . . .32 A4
Haslemere Ave ☑ FY3 . . .129 E3
Haslemere Ind Est PR5 . . .75 F3
Haslingden Grane Trail
BB4 . . . . .83 A2
Haslingden High Sch BB4 .67 B8
Haslingden Old Rd
Blackburn BB1,BB5 . . . . . .101 E3
Haslingden BB4 . . . . .84 E2
Haslingden Prim Sch BB4 .84 B2
Haslingden Rd
Blackburn BB1,BB2 . . . . . .101 B2
Oswaldtwistle BB5 . . . . . .82 D7
Rawtenstall BB4 . . . . .84 E2
Haslingden St James
CE Prim Sch BB4 . . . . . . .84 B3
Haslow Pl FY3 . . . . .129 F7
Hassall Dr PR4 . . . . .154 A1
Hassett Cl PR1 . . . . .95 E6
Hastings Ave
Blackpool FY2 . . . . .150 E5
Warton PR4 . . . . .91 E7
Hastings Cl Blackburn BB1 101 C4
Thornton FY5 . . . . .173 C1
Hastings Pl FY8 . . . . .90 A3
Hastings Rd Kirkham PR4 .113 B2
Lancaster LA1 . . . . .210 F5
Leyland PR5 . . . . .76 B2
Preston PR2 . . . . .116 B1
Southport PR8 . . . . .33 E1
Thornton FY5 . . . . .173 C1
Hastings The LA1 . . . . . . .210 F5
Haston Lee Ave BB1 . . . .121 F3
Hasty Brow Rd LA2 . . . . .213 D6
Hatfield Ave
Fleetwood FY7 . . . . .193 F3
Morecambe LA4 . . . . .213 B6
Hatfield Cl FY5 . . . . .173 C2
Hatfield Ct LA4 . . . . .213 B6
Hatfield Gdns ☑ FY7 . . . .193 E2
Hatfield Mews ☑ FY7 . . .193 E2
Hatfield Rd
Accrington BB5 . . . . .103 D7
Fulwood PR2 . . . . .117 D3
Southport PR8 . . . . .20 C6
Hatfield Wlk ☑ FY7 . . . . .193 E2
Hathaway
Fleetwood FY7 . . . . .193 E4
Lancaster LA1 . . . . .213 E3
Hathaway FY4 . . . . .109 E8
Hathaway Fold ☑ BB12 . .125 D7
Hathaway Rd
Fleetwood FY7 . . . . .193 E4
Lancaster LA1 . . . . .213 E3
Hatlex Dr LA2 . . . . .215 E2
Hatlex Hill LA2 . . . . .215 E2
Hatlex La LA2 . . . . .215 E2
Hattersley St BB11 . . . . . .126 E6
Hatton St PR7 . . . . .29 F6

Haugh Ave BB12 . . . . . . .144 E2
Haulgh St BB10 . . . . .147 B2
Haunders La PR4 . . . . . . .73 B1
Havelock Cl BB2 . . . . . .100 D3
Havelock Rd
Bamber Bridge PR5 . . . . . .76 E7
Penwortham PR1 . . . . . . .95 E5
Havelock St
Blackburn BB2 . . . . .100 C2
☑ Blackpool FY1 . . . . . . .129 B4
Burnley BB12 . . . . .126 B6
Lancaster LA1 . . . . .211 A6
Oswaldtwistle BB5 . . . . . .102 D3
☑ Padiham BB12 . . . . . . .145 C1
Preston PR1 . . . . .116 D2
Preston PR1 . . . . .116 E2
Preston PR1 . . . . .116 F2
Haven Brow L39 . . . . .6 C8
Haven Rd FY8 . . . . .90 C3
Haven St BB10 . . . . .127 C5
Haven Wlk L31 . . . . .5 C4
Havenbrook Gr BL0 . . . . .49 A3
Haverbreaks Pl LA1 . . . . .210 E6
Haverbreaks Rd LA1 . . . .210 E6
Haverholt Cl BB8 . . . . . . .169 C5
Haverholt Rd BB8 . . . . . .169 C5
Haverthwaite Ave LA3 . . .208 F7
Havre Pk BB18 . . . . .200 C2
Hawarden Ave LA4 . . . . .212 F5
Hawarden Rd ☑ PR1 . . . .117 C1
Hawarden St BB9 . . . . . .147 E7
Hawes Dr BB8 . . . . .169 F6
Hawes Side La FY4 . . . . .109 E8
Hawes Side Prim Sch
FY4 . . . . .109 E7
Hawes Terr BB10 . . . . . . .147 B2
Hawesside St PR9 . . . . . . .34 C7
Haweswater Ave PR7 . . . .42 B6
Haweswater Gr L31 . . . . . .5 E7
Haweswater Pl ☑ LA4 . . .213 A4
Haweswater Rd ☑ BB5 . .124 F1
Hawick Gr OL10 . . . . .32 E1
Hawk Cl BL9 . . . . .32 B4
Hawk St Burnley BB11 . . .127 A6
Carnforth LA5 . . . . .217 E2
Hawkeshead Cl BB2 . . . .100 B4
Hawkhurst Ave PR2 . . . . .116 D6
Hawkhurst Cres PR2 . . . .116 D6
Hawkhurst Rd
Penwortham PR1 . . . . . . .95 E5
Preston PR1 . . . . .117 B1
Hawkins Cl PR1 . . . . .116 E1
Hawkins Pl FY2 . . . . .150 F5
Hawkins St Blackburn BB2 100 B2
Preston PR1 . . . . .116 E1
Hawks Dr BB4 . . . . .85 A1
Hawksbury Dr PR1 . . . . . .95 D2
Hawksclough WN8 . . . . . .18 D2
Hawkshaw Ave BB3 . . . . .80 E3
Hawkshaw Bank Rd BB1 100 D8
Hawkshaw La BL8 . . . . . .48 B5
Hawkshaw St BL6 . . . . . .31 B3
Hawkshead PR1 . . . . .95 E3
Hawkshead Ave PR7 . . . . .59 D1
Hawkshead Cl L37 . . . . . . .5 C2
Hawkshead Dr LA4 . . . . .212 F3
Hawkshead Rd
Fulwood PR2 . . . . .117 E5
Knott End-on-S FY6 . . . . .194 F6
Hawkshead St
Blackburn BB2 . . . . .100 B4
Southport PR8, PR9 . . . . . .34 D7
Hawkshead Terr FY4 . . . .110 D8
Hawksheath Cl BL7 . . . . .46 E1
Hawksley St BL6 . . . . . . .31 D2
Hawkstone Cl
Accrington BB5 . . . . .124 F1
Thornton FY5 . . . . .151 D8
Hawkstone Ct LA4 . . . . . .213 B6
Hawkswood PR7 . . . . .40 B6
Hawksworth Gdns BB9 . .147 A4
Hawksworth Ave LA3 . . . .212 A4
Hawksworth Cl L37 . . . . . .12 A6
Hawksworth Dr L37 . . . . . .12 A6
Hawksworth Gr LA3 . . . .212 A2
Hawksworth Rd BB5 . . . .103 B8
Hawley Gn OL12 . . . . .51 D2
Hawley St Colne BB8 . . . .169 C4
Winewall BB8 . . . . .170 C5
Haworth Ave
Accrington BB5 . . . . .103 D3
Ramsbottom BL0 . . . . . . .49 A2
Rawtenstall BB4 . . . . .84 F2
Haworth Dr OL13 . . . . . . .69 C8
Haworth St
Accrington BB5 . . . . .124 A1
Edgworth BL7 . . . . .47 D5
Oswaldtwistle BB5 . . . . . .102 E4
Rishton BB1 . . . . .123 B1
Haws Ave LA5 . . . . .217 D1
Haws Hill LA5 . . . . .217 D1
Hawthorn Ave Caton LA2 .231 C3
Darwen BB3 . . . . .81 C2
Edenfield BL0 . . . . .67 D2
Fleetwood FY7 . . . . .172 E8
Orrell WN5 . . . . .10 F6
Oswaldtwistle BB5 . . . . . .102 F3
Ramsbottom BL0 . . . . . . .49 A2
Hawthorn Bank BB5 . . . .124 A3
Hawthorn Cl Caton LA2 . .231 C3
Kirkham PR4 . . . . .112 E6
Langho BB6 . . . . .122 D8
Leyland PR5 . . . . .75 D2
New Longton PR4 . . . . . . .75 A7
Hawthorn Cres
Preston PR2 . . . . .115 D1
Skelmersdale WN8 . . . . . .17 E1
Hawthorn Dr BB1 . . . . . .102 B8

Hawthorn Gdns BB5 . . . .124 A3
Hawthorn Rd Bacup OL13 .87 A2
Blackpool FY1 . . . . .129 C2
Bolton-le-S LA5 . . . . .216 A6
Fulwood PR2 . . . . .117 E2
Morecambe LA4 . . . . .213 B4
Hawthorn St BB1 . . . . . . .100 F8
Hawthorne Ave
Brierfield BB10 . . . . .147 C5
Garstang PR3 . . . . .178 B8
Higher Walton PR5 . . . . . .97 C3
Horwich BL6 . . . . .31 E1
Newton-with-S PR4 . . . . .113 F3
Hawthorne Cl
Barrowford BB9 . . . . .168 B1
Clayton Green PR6 . . . . . .77 B3
Nelson BB9 . . . . .148 B8
Hawthorne Cres L37 . . . . .12 A2
Hawthorne Dr BB18 . . . . .200 C4
Hawthorne Gr
☑ Barrowford BB9 . . . . . .168 D3
Carleton FY6 . . . . .151 B5
Southport PR9 . . . . .34 E7
Hawthorne Ind Pk BB7 . .187 A1
Hawthorne Lea FY5 . . . . .151 C8
Hawthorne Mdws
BB4 . . . . .105 A1
Hawthorne Pl BB7 . . . . . .186 E1
Hawthorne Rd
Burnley BB11 . . . . .126 F4
Thornton FY5 . . . . .151 C8
Hawthorne Terr BB8 . . . .191 E4
Hawthornes Cty Jun Sch
BB1 . . . . .100 F8
Hawthornes The L40 . . . . .38 B3
Hawthorns The
Bilsborrow PR3 . . . . .157 A5
Eccleston PR7 . . . . .40 B7
Fulwood PR2 . . . . .116 F6
Lancaster LA1 . . . . .211 A2
Newburgh WN8 . . . . .26 A1
☑ Newchurch BB4 . . . . . .85 F1
Wilpshire BB1 . . . . .121 F6
Haworth Art Gall
BB5 . . . . .103 D3
Haydock Ave PR5 . . . . . . .59 C4
Haydock Gr LA3 . . . . .212 A1
Haydock La BL7 . . . . .47 B1
Haydock Rd LA1 . . . . . . .211 B3
Haydock Sq ☑ BB6 . . . . .123 C5
Haydock St
☑ Bamber Bridge PR5 . . . .96 E2
Blackburn BB1 . . . . .121 E1
Burnley BB10 . . . . .147 C1
Haydocks La PR4 . . . . . . .115 D5
Haydon Ave PR5 . . . . .76 A7
Hayfell Ave LA4 . . . . .212 F3
Hayfell Cres LA2 . . . . . . .215 D1
Hayfell Gr LA2 . . . . .215 D1
Hayfield BB2 . . . . .100 A7
Hayfield Ave
Blackpool FY2 . . . . .150 E2
Gregson Lane PR5 . . . . . .97 E1
Poulton-le-F FY6 . . . . . . .151 E3
Hayfield Cl
Gregson Lane PR5 . . . . . .97 E1
Ramsbottom BL0 . . . . . . .48 E1
Hayfield Rd L39 . . . . .15 E7
Hayfields BB18 . . . . .191 E8
Hayhurst Cl BB7 . . . . . . .143 C6
Hayhurst Farm Terr BB7 .164 F3
Hayhurst Rd BB7 . . . . . . .143 C6
Hayhurst St BB7 . . . . . . .164 F3
Hayling Pl PR2 . . . . .116 A4
Haylot Dr LA2 . . . . .214 F7
Haylot Sq ☑ LA1 . . . . . . .211 A8
Haymans Gn L31 . . . . .5 E1
Haymarket FY8 . . . . .89 B6
Haysworth St PR1 . . . . . .116 F2
Haywood Cl
Accrington BB5 . . . . .103 D8
Sherwood PR2 . . . . .117 A8
Haywood Rd BB5 . . . . . . .103 B8
Hazekbank Gdns L37 . . . .11 E5
Hazel Ave
Bamber Bridge PR5 . . . . . .97 A1
Bury BL9 . . . . .32 B3
Clayton-le-M BB5 . . . . . .123 F2
Darwen BB3 . . . . .81 B2
Fleetwood FY7 . . . . .172 F8
Ramsbottom BL0 . . . . . . .49 B1
Hazel Bank ☑ BB3 . . . . .208 F7
Hazel Cl Bamber Bridge PR5 .96 F1
Blackburn BB2 . . . . .100 C4
Penwortham PR1 . . . . . . .95 B3
Hazel Coppice PR2 . . . . .115 E3
Hazel Ct Fulwood PR2 . . .116 E7
Ormskirk L39 . . . . .15 E5
Hazel Dene BB6 . . . . .186 E6
Hazel Gr Bacup OL13 . . . .87 B3
Bamber Bridge PR5 . . . . . .97 A1
Blackburn BB1 . . . . .101 F5
Blackpool FY3 . . . . .129 E5
Chorley PR6 . . . . .60 C3
Clayton-le-M BB5 . . . . . .124 A2
Clitheroe BB7 . . . . .164 C7
Fulwood PR2 . . . . .118 A4
Lancaster LA1 . . . . .210 D8
Longridge PR3 . . . . .139 B8
Rawtenstall BB4 . . . . .84 F4
Southport PR8 . . . . .34 E7
Tarleton PR4 . . . . .55 F8
Hazel Hall La BL0 . . . . . . .49 E1
Hazel La WN8 . . . . .18 A4
Hazel Mount LA2 . . . . . . .46 E2
Hazel St Haslingden BB5 . .84 A8
Ramsbottom BL0 . . . . . . .49 A4
Hazeldene Ave ☑ BB4 . . .84 B2

Hazeldene Rd FY7 . . . . . .193 F2
Hazelhead La PR3 . . . . . .199 E2
Hazelhurst Dr PR3 . . . . . .178 A7
Hazelhurst Prim Sch BL0 .49 A4
Hazelhurst Rd PR2 . . . . . .118 A2
Hazelmere Cty F HQ PR2 116 D8
Hazelmere Rd
Fulwood PR2 . . . . .116 D8
Preston PR1 . . . . .116 A1
Hazelmoor BB1 . . . . .121 E6
Hazelmount Ave LA5 . . . .217 D3
Hazelmount Cres LA5 . . .217 D3
Hazelmount Dr LA5 . . . . .217 C3
Hazelrigg La LA2 . . . . . . .207 C7
Hazels The Coppull PR7 . .41 E1
Wilpshire BB1 . . . . .121 E6
Hazelwood Silverdale LA5 .218 C2
Southport PR8 . . . . .33 F1
Hazelwood Ave L40 . . . . .24 E4
Hazelwood Cl
Blackburn BB1 . . . . .122 A1
Leyland PR5 . . . . .75 E1
Hazelwood Dr
Hesketh Bank PR4 . . . . . .72 E4
Morecambe LA4 . . . . .213 B6
Hazelwood Gdns LA1 . . . .211 A2
Hazelwood Rd BB9 . . . . .148 A8
Hazlehurst Cl L37 . . . . . . .11 C2
Hazlewood Cl FY5 . . . . . .173 A2
Head Beck LA6 . . . . .238 C2
Head Dyke La PR3 . . . . . .196 C3
Head Nook Cotts PR3 . . .156 E3
Headbolt La Kirkby L33 . . . .1 A5
Southport PR8 . . . . .21 A4
Headfort Cl FY2 . . . . .150 D2
Headingley Cl BB5 . . . . . .124 F1
Headlands St OL12 . . . . . .51 E1
Headley Rd PR5 . . . . .75 E1
Headroomgate Rd FY8 . . .88 F8
Heads La BB18 . . . . .192 B6
Heald Brow BB18 . . . . . .200 A4
Heald Cl Rochdale OL12 . .51 C3
Weir OL13 . . . . .87 A8
Heald Dr OL12 . . . . .51 C3
Heald House Rd PR5 . . . . .59 C7
Heald La OL13 . . . . .87 A8
Heald Rd BB10,BB12 . . . .147 A2
Heald St Blackpool FY3 . .129 D6
☑ Chorley PR6 . . . . .42 E8
Healdwood Cl BB12 . . . . .146 F3
Healdwood Dr BB12 . . . . .146 F3
Healey Ave OL12 . . . . .51 D4
Healey Ct BB11 . . . . .126 F5
Healey Dell Cotts OL12 . . .51 B4
Healey Dell
Nature Reserve OL12 . . . .51 B6
Healey Gr OL12 . . . . .51 C5
Healey Hall Farm OL12 . . .51 C4
Healey Hall Mews OL12 . . .51 C4
Healey La OL12 . . . . .51 E3
Healey Mount BB11 . . . . .126 F4
Healey Row OL12 . . . . . . .51 B3
Healey Row BB11 . . . . . .126 F5
Healey St FY3 . . . . .129 D7
Healey Stones OL12 . . . . .51 B4
Healey Wood Cty Inf Sch
BB11 . . . . .126 F4
Healey Wood Rd BB11 . . .126 F4
Heaning Ave
Accrington BB5 . . . . .103 D8
Blackburn BB1 . . . . .101 D4
Heanor Dr PR8 . . . . .34 F3
Heap Bridge
Cty Prim Sch BL9 . . . . . .32 D1
Heap Brow BL9 . . . . .32 D1
Heap Clough BB4 . . . . . . .83 C3
Heap St Brierfield BB9 . . .147 A5
Burnley BB10 . . . . .147 B1
Bury BL9,OL10 . . . . .32 D1
Rawtenstall BB4 . . . . .85 A8
Worsthorne BB10 . . . . . . .128 B6
Heapey Fold La PR6 . . . . .43 C7
Heapey Ho PR6 . . . . .61 A3
Heapey Rd PR6 . . . . .60 F2
Heapfold ☑ OL12 . . . . . . .51 B2
Heaplands BL8 . . . . .48 F1
Heapworth Ave BL0 . . . . .49 B6
Heartwood Cl BB2 . . . . . .100 A8
Heasandford
Cty Prim Sch BB10 . . . . .127 B8
Heasandford Ind Est
Burnley BB10 . . . . .127 C8
Burnley BB10 . . . . .147 D2
Heath Ave BL0 . . . . .49 B6
Heath Gr LA3 . . . . .208 E6
Heath Hill Dr OL13 . . . . . .69 C8
Heath St BB10 . . . . .127 B8
Heathbourne Rd OL13 . . .69 C8
Heather Bank
Burnley BB11 . . . . .126 C4
Rawtenstall BB4 . . . . .67 A4
Heather Brow BB18 . . . . .201 D2
Heather Cl Brierfield BB9 .147 D4
Burscough L40 . . . . .24 E4
Chorley PR6 . . . . .42 E8
Formby L37 . . . . .12 B5
Haslingden BB4 . . . . .67 A8
Horwich BL6 . . . . .31 B4
Southport PR8 . . . . .20 D2
Thornton FY5 . . . . .173 B1
Heather Gr PR2 . . . . .117 E3
Heather Lea Dr PR6 . . . . .61 F8
Heatherfield BL7 . . . . .47 E6
Heatherlands OL12 . . . . . .70 D4
Heatherlea Cl WN8 . . . . . .10 C7
Heatherlea Rd BB12 . . . .146 D2
Heatherleigh Gdns BB2 . . .80 D6

Heathers The PR5 ....77 C4
Heatherside Rd BL0 .....49 C7
Heatherway PR2 ....117 E6
Heatherways L37 ....12 A6
Heathey La L39,PR8 .....22 A7
Heathfield PR6 ....42 F1
Heathfield Ave OL13 ....69 C8
Heathfield Cl L37 ....12 A6
Heathfield Dr PR2 ......117 E4
Heathfield Pk BB2 ....99 F6
Heathfield Rd Bacup OL13 .69 C8
Fleetwood FY7 ....193 E2
Southport PR8 ....20 F6
Heathfoot Ave LA3 .....208 E6
Heathfoot Dr LA3 ......208 E6
Heathgate Fence BB2 ...146 D8
Skelmersdale WN8 .....18 C2
Heathrow PI PR7 ....42 A7
Heathway Ave FY3 .....129 E6
Heathy La L39 ....13 B8
Heatley Cl BB2 ....100 D3
Heatley St PR1 ....95 F8
Heaton Bottom Rd LA3 .209 E5
Heaton Cl
Bamber Bridge PR5 .....96 D4
Burscough L40 ....24 D4
Carleton FY6 ....151 C5
Morecambe LA3 ....213 A3
Orrell WN8 ....10 A7
Thornton FY5 ....151 C8
Heaton Ho LA1 ....210 F5
Heaton Mount Ave PR2 .116 F7
Heaton Pl 117 E1
Heaton Rd Lancaster LA1 .210 F5
Lytham St Anne's FY8 ..89 A8
Heaton St
3 Blackburn BB2 ......100 E4
Leyland PR5 ....75 E2
Standish WN6 ....28 E1
Heatons Bridge Rd L40 .23 D3
Heaviley Gr BL6 ....31 A5
Hebden Ave FY1 ....129 D1
Heber St BB11 ....105 B4
Hebrew Rd BB10 ....127 A8
Hebrew Sq 11 BB10 ....127 A8
Heckenhurst Ave BB10 .128 A6
Hector Rd BB3 ....80 E5
Hedge Row PR4 ....112 B3
Hedgerow The BB2 .....100 A8
Hedgerows PR5 ....58 A8
Heeley Rd FY8 ....88 E8
Height Barn La OL13 ...70 A4
Height Croft BB7 ......147 E5
Height La PR3 ....159 F7
Height Side La BB4 .....85 B7
Heights Ave OL12 ......51 E2
Heights Cl OL12 ....51 E2
Heights Cotts BB5 .....103 F4
Heights La OL12 ....51 E1
Heights Rd BB9 ....147 D6
Heights The BL6 ....31 D1
Heightside Ave BB4 .....85 E2
Heightside Mews BB4 ...85 E2
Helen's Cl FY4 ....109 E6
Helena St BB10 ....127 E4
Helks Brow LA2 ....233 B2
Hellifield PR2 ....116 F7
Hellifield Rd
Bolton-by-B BB7 ....224 F4
Gisburn BB7 ....225 C4
Helm Cl BB11 ....126 D2
Helmcroft 5 BB4 ....84 A1
Helmcroft Ct 1 BB4 ....84 B1
Helmn Way BB9 ....168 F2
Helmsdale WN8 ....18 C2
Helmsdale Cl BL0 ....49 A4
Helmsdale Rd
Blackpool FY4 ....109 F2
Nelson BB9 ....169 A1
Helmshore Prim Sch BB4 .67 A7
Helmshore Rd
Haslingden BB4 ....67 A1
Ramsbottom BL0,BL8,BB4 .67 A3
Helmshore Textile Mus
BB4 ....66 F8
Helmside Ave LA4 .....212 F3
Helmsley Gn 2 PR5 .....76 B1
Helston Cl Burnley BB11 .126 B4
Southport PR9 ....53 B5
Helton Cl BB9 ....168 D4
Helvellyn Dr BB12 .....126 C8
Hemingway FY4 ....109 D8
Hemingway PI 1 BB9 ...147 F8
Hemp St OL13 ....87 A1
Hempshaw Ave BB4 ....105 A2
Henderson Rd
Fleetwood FY7 ....193 F2
Weeton Camp PR4 .....131 E6
Henderson St PR1 .....116 E2
Hendon PI PR2 ....115 E2
Hendon Rd BB9 ....147 F8
Hendriff PI 4 OL12 .....51 F1
Hendry La 2 BB2 ....80 D7
Henfield Cl BB5 ....124 A1
Henley Ave FY5 ....172 D2
Henley Ct
7 Blackpool FY2 ......150 E1
Southport PR9 ....52 E1
Henley Dr PR9 ....52 F1
Henley Mews LA3 .....212 B3
Henley St 9 OL12 ....51 F1
Henley House PR5 ......96 C4
Hennel La
Bamber Bridge PR5 .....96 B2
Bamber Bridge PR5 .....96 C3

Hennel La continued
Bamber Bridge PR5 .....96 C4
Henrietta St Bacup OL13 .86 F2
Blackburn BB2 ....100 C5
Preston PR1 ....96 B8
Henrietta Street Ind Est
OL13 ....86 F2
Henry Gdns BB9 ....147 B5
Henry St Accrington BB5 .103 D3
Bank Lane BL0 ....49 D7
Blackpool FY1 ....129 C2
Church BB5 ....102 F6
Colne BB8 ....169 C4
Enfield BB5 ....124 A2
Lancaster LA1 ....210 F7
Lytham St Anne's FY8 ..90 A3
2 Nelson BB9 ....168 D1
Rawtenstall BB4 ....84 F2
Rishton BB1 ....123 B1
Henry Whalley St BB2 .100 A2
Henson Ave FY5 ....109 E6
Henthorn Cl 4 BB7 ....164 D7
Henthorn Rd BB7 ......164 C6
Henthorne St 1 FY1 ...129 C6
Henwick Hall Ave BL0 ..49 B4
Herbert St Bacup OL13 ..69 D8
Blackburn BB2 ....100 D2
Burnley BB11 ....126 E5
Horwich BL6 ....31 B4
Leyland PR5 ....76 A1
Padiham BB12 ....125 D7
Preston PR1 ....117 B1
Hereford Ave
7 Blackpool FY3 ......129 C3
Burnley BB12 ....126 B7
Garstang PR3 ....178 B8
Hereford Cl BB5 ....103 B7
Hereford Dr BB7 ......164 F7
Hereford Gr PR4 ......115 C5
Hereford Rd
Blackburn BB1 ....101 C5
Nelson BB8,BB9 ....169 A2
Southport PR9 ....34 F7
Hereford St BB9 ....147 C8
Herevale Hall Dr BL0 ...49 B4
Heriot Cl 8 FY5 ....172 F1
Heritage Way
Cleveleys FY5 ....172 F1
Tarleton PR4 ....56 A5
Herkomer Ave BB11 ...126 E2
Herlbeck Rise LA1 .....214 B2
Hermitage Cl WN6 .....19 E7
Hermitage St BB1,BB5 .123 C1
Hermitage The FY5 ....172 F2
Hermitage Way FY8 ....89 D6
Hermon Rd FY5 ....172 E1
Hermon St
2 Preston PR1 ....117 C1
Preston PR1 ....117 D1
Hern Ave PR5 ....76 A8
Heron Cl Blackburn BB1 .100 D8
Cleveleys FY5 ....172 F1
Heron Ct BB11 ....126 C5
Heron Dr LA4 ....212 F3
Heron Way Blackpool FY3 .130 B6
Kirkham PR4 ....113 C3
Oswaldtwistle BB5 ....102 E3
Herons Ct L31 ....5 B4
Heronsyke LA1 ....213 F4
Herring Arm Rd FY7 ..194 A2
Herschel Ave BB12 ....126 C8
Herschell St
Blackburn BB2 ....100 B1
Preston PR1 ....96 B6
Hertford St BB2 ....100 C1
Hesketh Ave Banks PR9 .54 A6
Blackpool FY2 ....150 B4
Hesketh Cl Darwen BB3 .64 C6
Preston PR2 ....117 E1
Hesketh Ct Blackpool FY2 .150 B4
Great Harwood BB6 ...123 E6
Hesketh Dr Maghull L31 ..5 F1
Rufford L40 ....38 A3
Shevington Moor WN6 .28 A2
Southport PR9 ....52 F1
Hesketh Gn L40 ....38 B4
Hesketh La Becconsall PR4 .72 F1
Hesketh Lane PR3 ....160 D7
Tarleton PR4 ....56 A7
Hesketh Links Ct PR9 ..52 E2
Hesketh PI FY7 ....194 B5
Hesketh Rd
Burscough L40 ....24 D4
Fulwood PR2 ....117 E1
Heysham LA3 ....208 E8
Longridge PR3 ....139 A8
Lytham St Anne's FY8 .110 A1
Southport PR9 ....52 D2
Hesketh St
Great Harwood BB6 ...123 C5
Preston PR1 ....116 C1
Hesketh-with-Becconsall
All Saints CE Sch PR4 .72 E4
Heskin Cl L31 ....5 D4
Heskin Hall Ct L39 .....15 D8
Heskin La L39 ....15 D8
Hesley La BD24 ....230 E6
Hessam Hts LA3 ....208 F5
Hesse St 1 BB3 ....64 A8
Hest Bank La LA2 .....213 E7
Hest Bank Rd LA4 ....213 A6
Hester Cl L38 ....2 F4
Hestham Ave LA4 .....212 E4
Hestham Cres LA4 ....212 E4
Hestham Dr LA4 ......212 E4
Hestham Par LA4 .....212 E4
Hetherington PI FY2 ..150 E2
Hetton Lea BB9 ....168 C3

Heversham WN8 ....18 C2
Heversham Ave PR2 ...116 F7
Heversham Cl
Lancaster LA1 ....211 B3
Morecambe LA4 ......212 F3
Hewart Dr BL9 ....32 C3
Hewart St BB11 ....126 A7
Hewitt Bsns Pk WN5 ...10 E4
Hewitt St BB5 ....76 B2
Hewlett Ave FY5 ....41 D1
Hewlett St PR7 ....41 D1
Hewngate PR5 ....97 E1
Hexam Ave BB5 ....103 E3
Hexham Ave FY5 .....172 E4
Hexham Rd LA4 ....213 B5
Hey Bottom La OL12 ...51 F6
Hey End PR4 ....74 F8
Hey Head Ave BB4 .....69 A8
Hey House Mews BL8 ..48 F4
Hey St BB9 ....168 E1
Heycrofts View BL0 ....67 E3
Heydon Cl L37 ....11 D1
Heyes Rd WN5 ....10 E6
Heyes WN6 ....19 C7
Heyes The PR7 ....77 B2
Heyescroft L39 ....7 D6
Heyfold Gdns BB3 .....80 F3
Heyhead St BB9 ....147 C5
Heyhouses Ct FY8 .....89 B8
Heyhouses Endowed
CE Inf Sch FY8 ....88 F7
Heyhouses Endowed
CE Jun Sch FY8 ....88 F8
Heyhouses La FY8 ......89 C7
Heyhurst Rd BB2 ......100 D5
Heymoor Ave BB6 .....123 D6
Heys BB5 ....102 D3
Heys Cl Blackburn BB2 ..80 C7
Rawtenstall BB4 ....85 C1
Heys Ct BB2 ....80 C8
Heys La Barley Green BB12 167 D5
Blackburn BB2,BB3 ....80 C7
Darwen BB3 ....80 F2
Great Harwood BB6 ...123 E5
Heys St Bacup OL13 ....86 F1
Haslingden BB4 ....84 A3
Rawtenstall BB4 ....85 C1
Thornton FY5 ....173 B3
Heys The Coppull PR7 ..41 F2
Parbold WN8 ....26 C3
Southport PR9 ....33 C4
Heysham Ave 208 F8
Heysham Cres BB2 ....100 F1
Heysham Cty High Sch
LA3 ....212 C3
Heysham Hall Dr LA3 .208 E6
Heysham Hall Gr LA3 .208 E7
Heysham Mossgate Rd
LA3 ....208 F7
Heysham Nuclear
Power Sta
Nature Reserve LA3 ..208 D4
Heysham Nuclear
Power Sta Vis Ctr LA3 .208 C4
Heysham Pk LA3 ......208 E7
Heysham Rd
4 Heysham LA3 ....208 E7
Morecambe LA3 ......212 A2
Southport PR9 ....34 F7
Heysham St 2 PR1 ....116 E1
Heysham Sta LA3 .....208 C5
Heywood Cl L37 ....11 E3
Heywood Com High Sch
OL10 ....32 E1
Heywood Rd PR2 .....115 E2
Heywood St Bury BL9 ..32 A1
Great Harwood BB6 ...123 C4
Heyworth Ave BB2 .....80 C7
Hibbert Terr LA1 ......210 F3
Hibson Rd Nelson BB9 .147 D8
Nelson, Little Marsden BB9 .147 D7
Hic Bibi La PR7 ....28 E6
Hick's Terr 5 BB1 ....123 B1
Hickory St BB1 ....100 F7
Hickson Ave L31 ....5 C3
Hidings Court La LA4 ..212 E4
Hiers House La BB8 ...169 B5
Higgin St Burnley BB10 .127 B5
Colne BB8 ....169 D5
Worsthorne BB10 .....128 B5
Higgin's La L40 ....24 C4
High Bank PR6 ....61 A3
High Banks L31 ....5 C3
High Barn La L40 ....70 C3
High Bentham Bsns Pk
LA2 ....233 D7
High Bentham Prim Sch
LA2 ....233 D8
High Cl PR3 ....125 E6
High Cop PR6 ....77 F4
High Ct LA4 ....213 B5
High Fold BB18 ....192 A6
High Gate La FY6 .....174 A6
High Gn PR5 ....75 F1
High Knott Rd LA5 ....237 B1
High La Bickerstaffe L39 ..7 C8
Ormskirk L39, L40 ......16 A8
Salterforth BB18 ......191 C5
High Legh FY8 ....89 C3
High Mdw PR5 ....96 B2
High Moor La WN6 .....27 B4
High Moss L39 ....15 E3
High Mount 2 LA1 ....210 F7
High Mount Ho 1 LA1 .210 F7
High Park PI PR9 ......35 A8
High Park Rd PR9 .....35 A8
High Peak Rd OL12 ....51 C6

High Rd Halton LA2 ...214 E7
Knowle Green PR3 ....161 E2
Lowgill LA2 ....233 C5
High St Belmont BL7 ...45 C4
Blackburn BB1 ....100 E5
Blackpool FY1 ....129 B6
Brierfield BB9 ....147 B5
Clitheroe BB7 ....164 B8
Colne BB8 ....169 C5
Darwen BB3 ....81 A1
Edgworth BL7 ....47 C4
Elswick PR4 ....153 F1
Fleetwood FY7 ....194 B4
Garstang PR3 ....178 C2
Great Eccleston PR3 ..154 B5
Haslingden BB4 ....84 B4
Horwich BL6 ....31 B4
Lancaster LA1 ....210 F7
Mawdesley L40 ....39 B1
Nelson BB9 ....147 D2
Oswaldtwistle BB5 ....102 F3
Padiham BB12 ....145 D1
13 Preston PR1 ....96 A8
Rishton BB1 ....123 B1
Skelmersdale WN8 .....17 C1
Standish WN6 ....28 E1
High Warren LA2 ......210 F7
Highbank Ave FY4 .....110 A8
Highbank BB1 ....121 F1
Highbury Ave
Blackpool FY3 ....129 E8
Fleetwood FY7 ....193 F2
Highbury Rd BB5 ......109 E1
Highbury Rd E FY8 ...109 E1
Highbury Rd W FY8 ..109 E1
Highcroft Ave FY2 ....150 E5
Highcross Ave FY6 ....130 D8
Highcross Hill FY6 ....130 D8
Highcross Rd FY6 ....151 D1
Higher Antley St BB5 ..103 B5
Higher Audley St BB1 .100 F4
Higher Bank Rd PR2 ..116 F3
Higher Bank St
Blackburn BB2 ....100 B6
Withnell PR6 ....79 A1
Higher Barn BL6 ....31 F3
Higher Barn St 2 BB1 .101 A5
Higher Blackthorn OL13 .86 F7
Higher Booths La BB4 .105 A4
Higher Change Villas
OL13 ....87 B4
Higher Chapel St 2 BB4 .224 A1
Higher Church St BB3 ..81 B1
Higher Cockcroft 13 BB1 .100 E5
Higher Commons La
BB2 ....120 C4
Higher Croft Kingsfold PR1 .95 C2
2 Kingsfold PR1 ....95 D2
Higher Croft Cotts BB3 .80 F8
Higher Croft Rd BB2,BB3 .80 F8
Higher Cross Row 9 OL13 86 F1
Higher Cswy BB9 .....168 D3
Higher Dunscar BL7 ...46 E1
Higher Eanam BB1 ....101 A5
Higher Feniscowles La
BB2 ....79 B8
Higher Field BB6 .....122 C8
Higher Firs BB5 ....124 A3
Higher Fold La BL0 ....49 E7
Higher Furlong PR4 ...73 F6
Higher Gate BB5 .....124 F1
Higher Gate Rd BB5 ..124 F1
Higher Gn FY6 ....151 E3
Higher Greenfield PR2 .116 B5
Higher Heys BB5 .....102 E3
Higher House Cl BB2 ..80 A7
Higher House La PR6,PR7 .61 B2
Higher La
Barnoldswick BB18 ...191 B7
Haslingden BB4 ....84 B4
Holmes PR4 ....55 C3
Orrell WN8 ....10 C7
Scorton PR3 ....199 F4
Skelmersdale WN8 .....17 D2
Higher Lawrence St 12
BB3 ....80 F2
Higher London Terr BB3 .81 B2
Higher Mdw PR5 ....76 E1
Higher Mill St BB4 .....85 A4
Higher Moor Cotts FY2 .150 F2
Higher Moor Rd FY3 ..151 A2
Higher Moss La L37 ....13 A4
Higher Moulding BL9 ..32 E5
Higher Park Rd BB18 .191 C6
Higher Peel St 7 BB5 .102 D3
Higher Perry St BB3 ...81 B2
Higher Ramsgreave Rd
BB1 ....121 C2
Higher Rd Longridge PR3 .160 E2
Tosside BB4 ....230 C5
Higher Reedley Rd
BB10,BB9 ....147 D5
Higher Row BL9 ....32 B3
Higher Saxifield BB10 .147 E3
Higher South St BB3 ...81 A1
Higher Summerseat BL0 .49 B2
Higher Syke LA2 .....227 C2
Higher Tentre BB11 ..127 B5
Higher Walton
CE Prim Sch PR5 ......97 C3
Higher Walton Rd PR5 .96 A4
Higher Witton Rd BB2 .100 B4

Highergate Cl BB5 ....124 F2
Highfield Bacup OL13 ..86 F2
Brinscall PR6 ....61 F8
Great Harwood BB6 ..123 B5
Rawtenstall BB4 ....85 A7
Highfield Ave
Bamber Bridge PR5 ....96 C1
Brierfield BB10 ....147 B3
Foulridge BB8 ....191 E1
Fulwood PR2 ....117 C4
Inskip PR4 ....134 C8
Leyland PR5 ....76 C3
Highfield Cl Adlington PR6 .30 A7
Clifton PR4 ....114 C1
Oswaldtwistle BB5 ....102 F3
Tarleton PR4 ....56 A5
Highfield Cres
5 Barrowford BB9 ....168 D3
Morecambe LA4 ......212 C4
Nelson BB9 ....168 E3
Highfield Ct BB4 ....84 A2
Highfield Dr Fulwood PR2 .116 E8
Hest Bank LA2 ....215 D1
Longridge PR3 ....139 B6
Longton PR4 ....73 F6
Penwortham PR1 ....95 D2
Highfield Gdns BB2 ...100 E2
Highfield Gr PR5 ....96 C2
Highfield High Sch FY3 .109 E6
Highfield Ind Est PR7 ..60 D2
Highfield La L40 ....23 D7
Highfield Mews BB3 ....64 B8
Highfield Pk
Haslingden BB4 ....84 A1
Maghull L31 ....5 F1
Highfield Prim Sch PR2 .42 E8
Highfield Priory Sch PR2 117 F5
Highfield Rd Adlington PR6 .30 A7
Blackburn BB2 ....100 D3
Blackpool FY4 ....109 E6
Blackrod BL6 ....30 E1
Carnforth LA5 ....216 E8
Clitheroe BB7 ....164 F7
Croston PR5 ....57 D2
Darwen BB3 ....81 B3
1 Earby BB18 ....201 B2
Edenfield BL0 ....67 D3
Ormskirk L39 ....15 E7
Rawtenstall BB4 ....85 D1
5 Rishton BB1 ....123 A1
Southport PR9 ....53 B3
Highfield Rd N
Adlington PR6 ....30 A8
Chorley PR7 ....60 C2
Highfield Rd S PR7 ....60 C1
Highfield St 4 Darwen BB3 64 B8
Haslingden BB4 ....84 A2
Highfield Terr LA2 ....233 C8
Highfurlong Sch FY3 ..151 A2
Highgale Gdns PR5 ....76 C2
Highgate Blackpool FY4 .109 D5
Goosnargh PR3 ....137 D6
Nelson BB9 ....147 D7
Penwortham PR1 ....95 B5
Highgate Ave PR2 ....116 E4
Highgate Cl Fulwood PR2 .116 F4
Newton-with-S PR4 ...113 F3
Highgate Cres WN6 ....19 E7
Highgate PI 1 FY8 .....89 D6
Highgate Rd Maghull L31 ..5 D3
Orrell WN8 ....10 B7
Highgrove Ave PR7 ....40 F4
Highgrove Cl LA4 ....212 D4
Highgrove Ct PR5 .....57 F4
Highland Ave PR1 ......95 B4
Highland Brow LA2 ...207 A4
Highland Lo WN6 ......28 C1
Highland Rd BL6 ....31 E1
Highmeadow WN8 .....10 A6
Highmoor BB9 ....147 F6
Highmoor Pk BB7 ....164 F6
Highrigg Dr PR3 ......136 F1
Highsands Ave L40 .....38 A3
Hightown BB4 ....85 E4
Hightown Rd BB4 .....85 F4
Hightown Sta L38 ....3 A4
Highway Gate PR4 ....154 A2
Highways Ave PR7 .....59 D1
Higson St BB2 ....100 D5
Hilary Ave FY2 ....150 C5
Hilary St BB10 ....147 A1
Hilbre Cl PR9 ....52 F1
Hilbre Dr PR9 ....52 F1
Hilderstone La LA5 ...234 A7
Hildrop Rd 7 BB9 ....168 F1
Hill Cl WN6 ....19 E8
Hill Cres PR4 ....114 A2
Hill Crest OL13 ....86 D1
Hill Crest Ave
Burnley BB10 ....127 F4
Fulwood PR2 ....116 E8
Longridge PR3 ....139 A7
Hill Croft PR4 ....113 B5
Hill End La BB4 ....85 C1
Hill Hos 16 BB3 ....64 A8
Hill House Fold La WN6 .27 C5
Hill House La
Appley Bridge WN6 ....27 A7
Jack Green PR6 ....78 A7
Hill La Blackrod BL6 ...30 C4
Colne BB8 ....170 C7
Nether Kellet LA6 ....216 F4
Hill PI BB9 ....147 D6

Hill Rd Lancaster LA1 213 F3
Leyland PR5 76 C1
Penwortham PR1 95 D4
Hill Rd S PR1 95 D3
Hill Rise Haslingden BB4 84 C1
1 Ramsbottom BL0 49 A4
Hill Rise View L39 15 A1
Hill Side LA1 210 E8
Hill St Accrington BB5 103 C5
Barnoldswick BB18 200 C2
Blackburn BB1 101 B5
Blackpool FY4 129 B1
Brierfield BB9 147 B5
Brierfield, Fence BB9 146 F6
Carnforth LA5 217 D1
Colne BB8 169 D4
3 Enfield BB5 124 A1
Oswaldtwistle BB5 102 D5
Padiham BB12 125 C8
Preston PR1 95 F8
Ramsbottom BL9 49 C3
Rawtenstall BB4 85 A7
Southport PR9 34 B7
Hill Top Barrowford BB9 168 D4
Colne BB8 170 C4
Foulridge BB8 191 C2
Longridge PR3 160 D2
New Longton PR4 75 A6
Trawden BB8 170 B2
Hill Top Cl PR4 92 D7
Hill Top La Earby BB18 201 A2
Whittle-le-W PR6 60 D8
Hill View Blackburn BB1 121 E1
2 Rawtenstall BB4 84 F1
Hill View Dr PR7 28 D8
Hill View Rd PR3 199 C1
Hill Wlk PR5 76 A2
Hillam La LA2 203 B7
Hillary Cres L31 5 D1
Hillbrook Rd PR5 75 F2
Hillcrest Maghull L31 5 F4
Skelmersdale WN8 9 B8
Hillcrest Ave
Bolton-le-S LA5 216 A5
Fulwood PR2 116 A4
Hillcrest Cl PR4 56 A8
Hillcrest Dr Bescar L40 22 F7
Longridge PR3 139 A7
Tarleton PR4 56 A8
Hillcrest Rd Blackburn BB2 99 F2
Blackpool FY4 109 B4
Langho BB6 122 C8
Ormskirk L39 15 E6
Hillcroft Fulwood PR2 116 C7
High Bentham LA2 233 D7
Hilldean WN8 10 C8
Hillingdon Rd BB10 147 D3
Hillingdon Rd N BB10 147 D3
Hillkirk Dr OL12 51 C3
Hillmount Ave LA3 208 F8
Hillock Cl L40 23 A7
Hillock La Bescar L40 23 A7
Skelmersdale WN8 18 D7
Warton PR4 91 E7
Hillocks The PR5 57 B1
Hillpark Ave Fulwood PR2 116 D4
Gregson Lane PR5 97 D1
Hills Ct LA1 213 F1
Hills The PR2 118 C7
Hillsborough Ave BB9 147 D5
Hillsea Ave LA3 208 F8
Hillside BB11 126 D3
Hillside Ave
Blackburn BB1 101 C4
Blackrod BL6 30 E1
Brierfield BB10 147 C5
15 Darwen BB3 64 A8
Edgworth BL7 47 B1
Farington PR5 75 F7
Fulwood PR2 116 D4
Hill Dale WN8 26 D5
Horwich BL6 31 C4
Kirkham PR4 113 C5
Ormskirk L39 15 D3
Preesall FY6 195 B4
Hillside Cl Blackburn BB1 101 C4
Blackpool FY3 129 E6
Brierfield BB9 147 C5
Burnley BB11 126 D2
Clitheroe BB7 164 E6
Euxton PR7 59 C1
Great Harwood BB6 123 C6
Thornton FY5 151 D8
Hillside Cres Horwich BL6 31 C4
Weir OL13 86 F7
Whittle-le-W PR6 60 C8
Hillside Cty Sch WN8 9 D8
Hillside Dr Newchurch BB4 85 E2
Stalmine FY6 174 C7
West Bradford BB7 186 F6
Hillside Gdns BB3 64 A7
Hillside Rd Haslingden BB4 84 C3
Low Bentham LA2 233 C8
2 Preston PR1 96 C6
Ramsbottom BL0 49 A5
Southport PR8 33 E1
Hillside Sch Autistic Ctr
PR3 139 D7
Hillside Sta PR8 33 E1
Hillside View BB9 147 C5
Hillside Way OL12 70 C1
Hillside Wlk
Blackburn BB1 101 C4
Rochdale OL12 51 D4
Hillstone Ave OL12 51 D4
Hillstone Cl BL8 48 F2
Hillsview Rd PR8 20 C4
Hilltop OL12 51 C5
Hilltop Dr BB4 67 C7
Hilltop Wlk L39 15 C3
Hillview Rd PR4 113 A6
Hillylaid Rd FY5 173 D2
Hilmont Terr BB1 100 F7
Hilmore Rd LA4 212 D5
Hilstone La FY2 150 D1
Hilton Ave
6 Blackpool FY1 129 B1
Horwich BL6 31 A3
Lytham St Anne's FY8 89 C6
Hilton Ct FY8 88 E5
Hilton Rd BB3 64 B8
Hilton St BB3 64 A8
Hilton's Brow PR6 78 B4
Hinchley Gn L31 5 B1
Hind St Burnley BB10 147 B2
4 Preston PR1 95 E6
Hind's Head Ave WN6 27 F6
Hindburn Ave L31 5 F2
Hindburn Cl LA5 217 F2
Hindburn Pl 6 LA1 213 E2
Hinde St LA1 214 A1
Hindle Fold La BB6 123 C6
Hindle St Accrington BB5 103 B6
Bacup OL13 69 D8
Darwen BB3 80 F2
Haslingden BB4 84 B3
Hindley Beech 1 L31 5 C2
Hindley Cl PR2 117 C7
Hindley Ct 3 BB9 168 C1
Hindley St 5 PR7 42 C6
Hinton St BB10 127 B5
Hippings Meth Prim Sch
BB5 102 E3
Hippings Vale BB5 102 D4
Hippings Way BB7 186 E2
Hirst St Burnley BB11 127 B4
6 Cornholme OL14 108 B1
Padiham BB12 145 C1
Hoarstones Ave BB12 146 D7
Hob Gn BB2 120 F2
Hob La BL7 47 C7
Hobart Pl FY5 150 F8
Hobart St BB11 127 B6
Hobbs La PR3 180 A4
Hobcross La L40 25 A2
Hobson St BB4 84 F4
Hobson's La LA6 234 C2
Hockley Pl FY3 129 F7
Hodder Ave Blackpool FY1 129 D1
Chorley PR7 42 B5
Fleetwood FY7 193 D2
Maghull L31 5 F2
Morecambe LA3 213 B3
Hodder Bridge Ct BB7 163 B7
Hodder Brook PR2 118 A3
Hodder Cl
6 Bamber Bridge PR5 76 F8
Fleetwood FY7 193 C2
Hodder Ct BB7 163 C4
Hodder Dr BB7 186 D7
Hodder Gr Clitheroe BB7 164 C7
Darwen BB3 80 E4
Hodder Pl Blackburn BB1 100 F6
Lancaster LA1 211 B5
Lytham St Anne's FY8 89 C7
Hodder St Accrington BB5 103 D6
1 Blackburn BB1 100 E6
Brierfield BB10 147 C3
Longridge PR3 139 B7
Hodder Way FY6 151 D2
Hoddlesden Fold BB3 81 F1
Hoddlesden Rd BB3 81 E1
Hodge Bank Bsn Pk BB9 168 D2
Hodge Brow BL6 43 F4
Hodge La BB18 191 B8
Hodge St PR8 34 B7
Hodgson Ave PR4 92 A5
Hodgson High Sch FY6 151 F3
Hodgson Pl FY6 151 D2
Hodgson Rd FY1 129 C8
Hodgson St Darwen BB3 81 B1
3 Oswaldtwistle BB5 102 E4
Hodson St
Bamber Bridge PR5 96 E1
Southport PR8 34 C6
Hogarth Ave BB11 126 F3
Hogarth Cres PR4 133 F4
Hogg's La PR7 42 E5
Hoggs Hill La L37 11 F1
Hoghton Ave OL13 70 A8
Hoghton Cl Lancaster LA1 210 D6
Lytham St Anne's FY8 109 F2
Hoghton Gr PR9 34 C8
Hoghton La PR5 97 D3
Hoghton Pl 3 PR9 34 B7
Hoghton Rd Leyland PR5 75 D1
Longridge PR3 139 C7
Hoghton St
8 Bamber Bridge PR5 76 A8
Southport PR9 34 C7
Hoghton Twr PR5 98 E1
Hoghton View PR1 96 C6
Holbeck Ave
Blackpool FY4 109 F8
Morecambe LA4 213 B4
Rochdale OL12 51 D4
Holbeck St BB10 147 A1
Holborn Dr L39 15 C3
Holborn Hill L39 15 C4
Holcombe Brook
Prim Sch BL0 49 A2
Holcombe Ct BL0 48 F2
Holcombe Dr BB10 127 B6
Holcombe Gr PR6 60 E1
Holcombe Lee BL0 49 A4
Holcombe Mews BL0 48 F3
Holcombe Old Rd BL8,BL0 49 A5
Holcombe Rd
Blackpool FY2 150 E1
Haslingden BB4 66 F8
Ramsbottom BL8 48 F2
Holcombe Village BL8 49 A6
Holcroft Pl FY8 89 F4
Holden Ave Bury BL9 32 E4
Ramsbottom BL0 49 A5
Holden Cl BB9 168 C1
Holden Fold BB3 81 B3
Holden La BB7 224 B5
Holden Pl BB4 83 F1
Holden Rd Brierfield BB9 147 A5
Brierfield, Reedley BB10 147 B3
Holden St Accrington BB5 103 B5
Adlington PR7 29 F7
Belthorn BB1 81 F6
Blackburn BB2 100 C4
Burnley BB11 126 F5
Clitheroe BB7 164 F8
Holden Way LA1 210 F5
Holden Wood Dr BB4 83 F1
Hole House La BB7 229 E2
Hole House St BB1 101 C5
Holgate FY4 109 F6
Holgate Dr WN5 10 E6
Holgate Prim Sch WN5 10 E5
Holgate St Brierfield BB10 147 F3
Great Harwood BB6 123 C5
Holhouse La BL8 48 F2
Holker Bsns Ctr BB8 169 B4
Holker Cl Coupe Green PR5 97 E3
Lancaster LA1 210 D6
Holker La PR5 58 B4
Holker St Colne BB8 169 B4
Darwen BB3 64 B8
Holland Ave
Bamber Bridge PR5 96 E2
Rawtenstall BB4 84 F3
Holland Ct WN8 9 D2
Holland House Rd PR5 96 E3
Holland Lodge 4 PR2 117 F4
Holland Moor
Cty Prim Sch WN8 9 E7
Holland Moss WN8 9 A5
Holland Pl BB9 168 E2
Holland Rd PR2 116 C1
Holland St Accrington BB5 102 F6
Blackburn BB1 100 D6
3 Padiham BB12 125 B8
Holland's La WN8 17 A1
Holliers Cl L31 5 E1
Hollies Cl Blackburn BB2 79 F8
Catterall PR3 178 D2
Hollies Rd BB1 122 A7
Hollies The PR8 33 F6
Hollin Bank BB9 147 B6
Hollin Bridge St BB2 100 D2
Hollin Hall BB8 170 C1
Hollin Hill BB11 127 B3
Hollin La Knowley PR7 61 C2
Rawtenstall BB4 85 A4
Hollin Mill St BB9 147 B6
Hollin St BB2 100 C2
Hollin Way Rawtenstall,
Constable Lee BB4 85 A4
Rawtenstall, Rush Bed BB4 85 A6
Hollingreave Rd BB11 127 A4
Hollings PR4 74 F7
Hollington St BB8 170 B5
Hollinhead Cres PR2 116 B4
Hollinhurst Ave PR1 95 C6
Hollinhurst Brow LA2 233 C2
Hollinhurst View BB12 145 F5
Hollins Ave BB10 127 F4
Hollins Cl Accrington BB5 103 C4
Hoghton PR5 98 C3
Hollins Ct 1 BB18 200 B3
Hollins Gr PR2 116 B3
Hollins Grove St BB3 80 F3
Hollins High Sch The
BB5 103 D2
Hollins Hill PR3 204 C2
Hollins La Accrington BB5 103 D3
Arnside LA5 237 C1
Edenfield BL0 67 E2
Hollins Lane PR3 204 C2
Runshaw Moor PR5 58 C4
Hollins Rd
Barnoldswick BB18 200 A2
Darwen BB3 80 F4
Nelson BB9 169 A2
Preston PR1 117 B2
Hollinshead St PR7 42 C8
Hollinshead St Sch PR7 42 C8
Hollinshead Terr BB3 63 B7
Hollinwood Dr BB4 85 A5
Hollowbrook Way 4 OL12 51 D2
Hollowell La BL6 31 D1
Hollowford La L40 25 D2
Hollowforth La PR4 135 E5
Hollowhead Ave BB1 121 F5
Hollowhead Cl BB1 121 F5
Hollowhead La BB1 122 A5
Hollowrane LA6 234 C7
Holly Ave BB4 84 C1
Holly Bank Accrington BB5 103 C4
Edgworth BL7 47 B7
Fulwood PR2 116 C5
Warton, Carnforth LA5 217 D5
Holly Cl Clayton Green PR6 77 B2
Skelmersdale WN8 17 E1
Thornton FY5 173 C3
Westhead L40 16 E4
Holly Cres PR7 41 E2
Holly Fold La L39, WA11 8 E3
Holly Gr Longridge PR3 139 A8
Tarleton PR4 56 A7
Holly Ho BB11 127 B5
Holly La Ormskirk L39 15 B4
Rufford L40 38 C3
Skelmersdale L39, WA11 8 E4
Holly Mews FY8 109 F2
Holly Mount BB4 67 A7
Holly Mount RC Prim Sch
BL8 48 D1
Holly Pl PR5 77 B6
Holly Rd Blackpool FY1 150 C1
Thornton FY5 173 B3
Holly St Blackburn BB1 100 F7
Burnley BB10 127 B5
Bury BL9 32 A2
Nelson BB9 147 F8
Oswaldtwistle BB5 102 D4
Ramsbottom BL0 49 C3
Holly Terr BB1 100 F8
Holly Tree Cl BB3 64 A6
Holly Tree Way BB2 79 F8
Holly Wlk LA1 210 D8
Hollybank Cl PR2 115 F5
Hollybrook Rd PR8 34 A5
Hollywood Ave
Blackpool FY3 129 E5
Penwortham PR1 95 C3
Hollywood Gr FY7 193 F4
Holman St 5 PR1 117 C1
Holmbrook Cl BB2 80 F8
Holmby St BB10 147 B2
Holmdale Ave PR9 53 C4
Holme Ave FY7 172 D8
Holme Bank BB4 84 F1
Holme CE Prim Sch
BB10 107 B6
Holme Cl BB18 192 A7
Holme Cres BB8 170 B3
Holme End BB12 146 F4
Holme Head Cotts BB7 222 C5
Holme Hill BB7 186 E2
Holme House Rd OL14 108 C1
Holme La Caton LA2 231 C3
Haslingden BB4 67 D8
Rawtenstall BB4 67 E8
Holme Lea BB5 123 F4
Holme Mills Ind Est LA6 234 B8
Holme Pk LA2 233 D7
Holme Rd
Bamber Bridge PR5 76 E8
Burnley BB12 126 E7
Clayton-le-M BB5 123 E4
Penwortham PR1,PR2 95 C7
Holme Slack La PR1 117 C3
Holme Slack Prim Sch
PR1 117 C3
Holme St Accrington BB5 103 C6
Bacup OL13 69 D8
Barrowford BB9 168 D2
Colne BB8 170 B5
Darwen BB3 64 A8
Nelson BB9 147 E8
Holme Terr Nelson BB9 147 C8
Rawtenstall BB4 67 D8
Holme The PR3 179 E7
Holme Vale BB4 67 A6
Holmefield Ave FY5 172 E2
Holmefield Cl FY5 172 E2
Holmefield Ct 8 BB9 168 D3
Holmefield Gr L31 5 C1
Holmefield Rd
Knott End-on-S FY6 194 E5
Lytham St Anne's FY8 89 A7
Holmes Ct Fulwood PR1 116 E3
Garstang PR3 178 C8
Holmes Dr OL13 86 F4
Holmes La OL13 86 F3
Holmes Mdws 3 PR5 75 B1
Holmes Rd FY5 173 B3
Holmes Sq BB10 127 B5
Holmes St Burnley BB11 127 B5
Forest Holme BB4 86 A7
Padiham BB12 125 D8
Rawtenstall BB4 85 B3
Holmes Terr BB4 84 F5
Holmes The BB4 84 F5
Holmestrand Ave BB11 126 B4
Holmeswood PR4 113 A5
Holmeswood Cres PR3 136 B8
Holmeswood
Four Lane Ends L40 37 C6
Holmeswood
Meth Sch L40 37 C6
Holmeswood Pk BB4 67 E8
Holmeswood Rd L40 37 D6
Holmfield Cres 2 PR2 115 D1
Holmfield Pk L37 11 D4
Holmfield Rd
Blackpool FY2 150 B2
Fulwood PR2 117 A4
Holmrook Rd PR1 117 B1
Holmsley St BB10 127 B5
Holmwood Cl L37 11 D3
Holmwood Gdns L37 11 D4
Holsands Cl PR2 117 E6
Holst Gdns BB2 101 A1
Holstein Ave OL12 51 D4
Holstein St PR1 96 A8
Holt Ave PR7 41 F2
Holt Brow PR5 59 A6
Holt Coppice L39 6 A7
Holt La PR6 77 E3
Holt Mill Rd BB4 68 D8
Holt Sq BB9 168 E5
Holt St Orrell WN5 10 D5
Holt St *continued*
Ramsbottom BL0 49 D6
Rawtenstall BB4 68 E8
Rishton BB1 123 C1
Whitworth OL12 70 C1
Holt St W BL0 49 B5
Holt's Terr OL12 51 E2
Holts La FY6 151 F2
Holy Cross RC High Sch
PR7 42 C4
Holy Family RC Jun Sch
FY1 129 C8
Holy Family RC Prim Sch
Fulwood PR2 115 F4
Southport PR9 34 E7
Warton PR4 91 E6
Holy Saviour's
RC Prim Sch BB9 168 E2
Holy Souls RC Prim Sch
BB1 121 E1
Holy Trinity CE Prim Sch
Burnley BB11 126 E5
Darwen BB3 81 A1
Formby L37 11 F3
Southport PR9 34 C8
Holy Trinity RC Prim Sch
BB9 147 C5
Holy Trinity RC Sch BB9 147 B5
Holy Trinity Stacksteads
CE Prim Sch OL13 69 C8
Holyoake Ave FY2 150 E1
Holyoake St Burnley BB12 126 A6
2 Cornholme OL14 108 A1
Home Breeze Ho 1
LA4 213 A6
Home Farm Cl LA2 232 D6
Home Field PR3 178 C8
Homecare Ave BB7 144 F8
Homechase Ho PR8 33 F4
Homer Ave PR4 55 F7
Homer St 1 BB11 126 C5
Homesands Ho PR9 34 D8
Homestead PR5 77 B4
Homestead Cl 4 PR5 75 D1
Homestead Dr FY7 193 E1
Homestead The 9 FY8 90 A3
Homestead Way FY7 193 E1
Homewood Ave LA4 213 B6
Homfray Ave LA3 213 A3
Homfray Gr LA3 213 A3
Honey Hole BB2 100 E2
Honey Holme La BB10 106 F7
Honey Moor Dr FY5 173 B4
Honeypot La FY6 152 D4
Honeysuckle Cl PR6 60 B5
Honeysuckle Pl FY2 150 F6
Honeysuckle Row PR2 117 E2
Honeysuckle Way OL12 51 D3
Honeywood Cl BL0 49 A3
Honister Ave FY3 129 F2
Honister Cl FY7 193 D3
Honister Rd
Brierfield BB10 147 B3
Lancaster LA1 214 B2
Honister Sq FY8 109 F2
Honiton Ave BB2 80 C8
Honiton Way PR4 115 F6
Hoo Hill Ind Est FY3 129 E8
Hood House St BB11 126 E4
Hood St 4 BB5 103 C6
Hoole CE Prim Sch PR4 73 C1
Hoole La Banks PR9 54 A6
Nateby PR3 177 B5
Hools La PR3 196 A5
Hope Cl FY5 173 B4
Hope La PR3 160 E5
Hope Sq PR9 34 D7
Hope St Accrington BB5 103 B5
Adlington PR6 30 B8
Bacup OL13 86 F4
Blackburn BB2 100 D5
Brierfield BB9 147 B5
Chorley PR7 60 C1
Darwen BB3 80 F1
Great Harwood BB6 123 C4
Haslingden BB4 84 B2
Horwich BL6 31 B4
Lancaster LA1 211 A7
Lytham St Anne's FY8 89 A7
Morecambe LA4 212 F4
Nelson BB9 147 D8
12 Padiham BB12 125 D8
5 Preston PR1 95 F8
Ramsbottom BL0 49 B5
Rawtenstall BB4 85 C1
Southport PR9 34 C7
Worsthorne BB10 128 B6
Hope St N BL6 31 B5
Hope Terr
10 Bamber Bridge PR5 76 A8
Blackburn BB2 100 C6
Hopkinson St BB8 170 B3
Hopkinsons Terr BB8 170 C3
Hopton Rd FY1 129 B2
Hopwood Ave BL6 31 C4
Hopwood St
Accrington BB5 103 B4
4 Bamber Bridge PR5 76 E8
Bamber Bridge PR5 76 F7
Blackburn BB2 100 E3
9 Burnley BB11 126 E6
Preston PR1 96 A8
Horace St 7 BB12 126 D6
Horden Rake BB2 79 E7
Horden View BB2 79 E7
Hordley St BB12 126 A6
Horeb Cl 5 BB12 125 D7
Hornbeam Cl PR1 95 B3

Hornby Ave
　Fleetwood FY7 . . . . .172 D8
　Fulwood PR2 . . . . .117 E4
Hornby Bank Hornby LA2 .232 B8
　Nether Kellet LA6 . . . . . . .216 F5
Hornby CE Prim Sch LA2 232 B7
Hornby Croft PR5 . . . . .58 B8
Hornby Ct Blackburn BB2 . .100 C4
　Kirkham PR4 . . . . .113 A4
　Lancaster LA1 . . . . .213 E4
Hornby Dr Lancaster LA1 .211 A4
　Newton-with-S PR4 . . . . . .113 F2
Hornby Hall Ct LA2 . . . . . .232 B7
Hornby High Sch LA2 . . . .232 B7
Hornby La PR4 . . . . .154 F2
Hornby Park Ct ■ FY3 . . .129 C4
Hornby Rd Blackburn FY1 .129 C4
　Caton LA2 . . . . .231 C3
　Chorley PR6 . . . . .42 E6
　Longridge PR3 . . . . .139 B8
　Lytham St Annes FY8 . . . . .88 E5
　Southport PR9 . . . . .53 A4
　Wray LA2 . . . . .232 D1
　Wray LA2 . . . . .232 D6
Hornby St Burnley BB11 . .127 A5
　Oswaldtwistle BB5 . . . . . .102 E3
Hornby Terr LA4 . . . . .212 F6
Hornby's La
　Hale Nook PR3 . . . . .175 A5
　Moss Edge PR3 . . . . .175 D6
Hornchurch Dr PR7 . . . . . .42 A7
Horncliffe Cl BB4 . . . . .67 E8
Horncliffe Rd FY4 . . . . . . .109 B6
Horncliffe View BB4 . . . . . .67 B8
Horne St BB5 . . . . .103 C7
Horning Cres BB10 . . . . . .147 D2
Horns La PR3 . . . . .159 B3
Hornsea Cl PR2 . . . . .116 A4
Hornsey Ave FY8 . . . . . . .109 B4
Horridge Fold BL7 . . . . . . .46 E3
Horrobin Fold BL7 . . . . . . .47 C2
Horrobin La Adlington PR6 .30 C8
　Edgworth BL7 . . . . .47 C2
　Rivington PR6,BL6 . . . . . . .43 E1
Horrocks Rd BL7 . . . . .47 D6
Horrocksford Way LA1 . . .210 D6
Horse Mkt LA6 . . . . .238 C2
Horse Park La PR3 . . . . . .197 A5
Horsebridge Rd PR7 . . . . .130 B8
Horsefield Ave OL12 . . . . . .51 C6
Horsfall Ave ■ FY8 . . . . . .90 A3
Horsfall Cl BB5 . . . . .103 B7
Horsfield Cl BB8 . . . . .169 F5
Horton Ave BB10 . . . . .147 B3
Horwich Bsns Pk BL6 . . . . .31 B2
Horwich L Ctr BL6 . . . . . . .31 C3
Horwich Parish
　CE Prim Sch BL6 . . . . .31 C4
Hoscar Moss Rd L40 . . . . . .25 D3
Hoscar Sta L40 . . . . .25 D4
Hospital Cotts PR3 . . . . . .139 F6
Hosticle La LA6 . . . . .235 C7
Hothersall La PR3 . . . . . . .139 D4
Hough La PR5 . . . . .76 A1
Houghclough La PR3 . . . . .181 F1
Houghton Ave ■ FY4 . . . .109 D8
Houghton Cl PR1 . . . . .95 C3
Houghton Cres ■ FY4 . . . .109 D8
Houghton Ct Halton LA2 . .214 E7
　■ Thornton FY5 . . . . .173 B3
Houghton La WN6 . . . . . . .19 F6
Houghton Rd PR1 . . . . .95 C3
Houghton St ■ PR6 . . . . . .42 D8
Houghton's La WN8 . . . . . .18 C1
Houghtons Rd WN8 . . . . . .18 B3
Houldsworth Rd PR2 . . . . .116 E3
Hounds Hill ■ FY1 . . . . . .129 B4
Hounds Hill Ctr FY1 . . . . .129 B5
Houseman Pl FY4 . . . . . . .109 E7
Hove Ave FY7 . . . . .172 C4
Hove Cl BL8 . . . . .48 F1
Hove Rd FY8 . . . . .88 F6
Howard Cl Accrington BB5 .102 F5
　Lytham St Annes FY8 . . . .109 E1
　Maghull L31 . . . . .5 F1
Howard Ct PR9 . . . . .52 D1
Howard Dr PR4 . . . . .55 F7
Howard Mews LA5 . . . . . .217 C1
Howard St Blackpool FY1 .129 C6
　Burnley BB11 . . . . .126 D5
　Nelson BB9 . . . . .147 C6
　Rishton BB1 . . . . .123 A1
　Rochdale OL12 . . . . .51 F1
Howards La WN5 . . . . .10 F7
Howarth Ave BB5 . . . . . . .102 F7
Howarth Cres FY6 . . . . . . .151 E3
Howarth Rd PR2 . . . . .116 D3
Howarth's St BB4 . . . . .86 A8
Howden Hts FY6 . . . . .151 B3
Howe Ave FY4 . . . . .109 E8
Howe Croft BB7 . . . . .164 F8
Howe Dr BL0 . . . . .49 B2
Howe Gr PR7 . . . . .42 A7
Howe Wlk ■ BB11 . . . . . .127 A6
Howells Cl L31 . . . . .5 D2
Howgill Ave LA1 . . . . .214 A4
Howgill Cl BB9 . . . . .147 F6
Howgill La BB7 . . . . .225 C1
Howgill Way PR7 . . . . .90 D5
Howgills The PR2 . . . . . . .117 A7
Howick CE Prim Sch PR1 .94 F3
Howick Cross La PR1 . . . . .94 E5
Howick Moor La PR1 . . . . .95 A3
Howick Park Ave PR1 . . . . .94 F4
Howick Park Cl PR1 . . . . . .94 F4
Howick Park Dr PR1 . . . . . .94 F4
Howick Row PR2 . . . . .94 D5

Howorth Cl BB11 . . . . .127 A3
Howorth Rd BB11 . . . . . . .127 A3
Howsin Rd BB10 . . . . .147 A1
Hoylake Cl PR2 . . . . .116 B6
Hoyle Ave FY8 . . . . .109 F2
Hoyle St Bacup OL13 . . . . .69 E8
　Haslingden BB5 . . . . .84 A8
　Whitworth OL12 . . . . .70 D3
Hoyles La PR4 . . . . .115 D6
Hozier St BB1 . . . . .101 C5
Hubert Pl LA1 . . . . .210 D8
Hubie St BB12 . . . . .126 F7
Huck La FY8 . . . . .90 E7
Hud Hey Ind Est BB4 . . . . .84 B5
Hud Hey Rd BB4 . . . . .84 B5
Hudcar La BL9 . . . . .32 A4
Hudson Ct PR5 . . . . .77 C8
Hudson Pl BB2 . . . . .100 B8
Hudson Rd FY1 . . . . .129 D2
Hudson St Accrington BB5 .103 C4
　Brierfield BB9 . . . . .147 B5
　Burnley BB11 . . . . .126 D5
　■ Cornholme OL14 . . . . .108 C1
　■ Preston PR1 . . . . .96 A6
Hufling Ct ■ BB11 . . . . . .127 B4
Hufling La BB11 . . . . .127 B4
Hugh Barn La PR4 . . . . . . .74 F7
Hugh La PR5 . . . . .75 D3
Hugh Rake BB4 . . . . .84 F6
Hughes Ave BL6 . . . . .31 A4
Hughes Cl ■ BL9 . . . . .32 A3
Hughes Gr FY2 . . . . .150 E1
Hughes St BB11 . . . . .127 A5
Hull Rd FY1 . . . . .129 B4
Hull St Burnley BB11 . . . . .127 B5
　Preston PR2 . . . . .95 C8
Hullet St WN6 . . . . .19 E8
Hulme Ave FY5 . . . . .173 C2
Hulme St PR8 . . . . .34 A7
Hulton Dr BB9 . . . . .147 E6
Humber Ave ■ FY3 . . . . . .129 E8
Humber Sq BB10 . . . . .147 C2
Humber St PR3 . . . . .139 A2
Humblescough La PR3 . . . .177 D5
Humphrey St BB9 . . . . . . .147 B6
Huncoat Bsns Pk BB5 . . . .124 D1
Huncoat Cty Prim Sch
　BB5 . . . . .124 F2
Huncoat Ind Est BB5 . . . . .103 D8
Huncoat Sta BB5 . . . . .124 E2
Hundred End La PR4,PR9 . .71 F1
Hungerford Rd FY8 . . . . . . .88 F5
Hunslet St Burnley BB11 . .127 B6
　Nelson BB9 . . . . .147 F7
Hunt Fold Dr BL8 . . . . .48 F1
Hunt Rd L31 . . . . .5 D1
Hunt St ■ PR1 . . . . .95 D7
Hunter Ave PR4 . . . . .56 A6
Hunter Rd PR4 . . . . .113 B2
Hunter St
　Brierfield BB10,BB9 . . . . . .147 B5
　Carnforth LA5 . . . . .217 D2
Hunter's La PR4 . . . . .55 B3
Hunters Chase WN5 . . . . . .10 E1
Hunters Dr BB12 . . . . .126 D8
Hunters Fold PR4 . . . . .74 A5
Hunters Gn BL0 . . . . .48 F3
Hunters Lodge BB2 . . . . . . .99 F1
Hunters Rd PR5 . . . . .76 B1
Hunting Hill Lodge LA5 . . .217 C1
Hunting Hill Rd LA5 . . . . .217 B1
Huntingdon Gr L31 . . . . . . .5 C4
Huntingdon Hall Rd PR3 . .162 A2
Huntingdon Rd FY5 . . . . . .172 C1
Huntingdon Dr BB3 . . . . . .64 A7
Huntingdon Terr OL14 . . . .108 C1
Huntley Ave ■ FY3 . . . . . .129 E7
Huntley Cl LA4 . . . . .213 A5
Huntley La PR5 . . . . .119 E1
Huntley Mount Rd BL9 . . . .32 B3
Huntley St BL9 . . . . .32 B3
Huntly Way OL10 . . . . .32 E1
Huntroyde Ave BB12 . . . . .125 B8
Huntroyde Cl BB12 . . . . . .126 D7
Hunts Field PR6 . . . . .77 C2
Huntsmans Chase PR4 . . .113 F4
Hurlston Ave WN8 . . . . .9 C4
Hurlston Dr L39 . . . . .15 E7
Hurlston La L40 . . . . .23 C1
Hurn Gr PR7 . . . . .42 A7
Hurst Brook PR7 . . . . .41 F1
Hurst Cres BB4 . . . . .85 B3
Hurst Gn L40 . . . . .39 C2
Hurst La BB4 . . . . .85 B3
Hurst Pk PR1 . . . . .95 C4
Hurst's La L39 . . . . .7 B2
Hurstead St BB5 . . . . .103 E1
Hurstleigh Dr LA3 . . . . . . .209 A4
Hurstleigh Hts FY5 . . . . . .173 E2
Hurstmere Ave FY4 . . . . . .109 D7
Hurstway PR2 . . . . .116 D7
Hurstway Cl PR2 . . . . .116 D7
Hurstwood Ave
　Blackburn BB2 . . . . .100 A1
　Burnley BB10 . . . . .127 D5
Hurstwood Ent Pk BB4 . . . .84 A2
Hurstwood Gdns BB9 . . . .147 D4
Hurstwood La BB10 . . . . . .128 B4
Hurtley St BB10 . . . . .127 A8
Hut La PR6 . . . . .43 B3
Hutch Bank Rd BB4 . . . . . .83 F2
Hutchinson Ct BB3 . . . . . . .81 A3
Hutchinson St ■ BB2 . . . .100 E3
Hutton Cl LA6 . . . . .234 C7
Hutton Cres LA4 . . . . .212 D4
Hutton Ct WN8 . . . . .17 D1

Hutton Dr BB12 . . . . .126 E7
Hutton Gr LA4 . . . . .212 D4
Hutton Gram Sch PR4 . . . . .94 D2
Hutton Hall Ave PR4 . . . . . .94 E1
Hutton Rd WN8 . . . . .17 D1
Hutton St Blackburn BB1 . .101 B5
　Standish WN1 . . . . .29 A3
Hutton Way
　■ Lancaster LA1 . . . . .213 D1
　Ormskirk L39 . . . . .15 C5
Huyton Rd PR6,PR7 . . . . . .30 A6
Huyton Terr PR6 . . . . .30 B6
Hyacinth Cl BB4 . . . . .66 F8
Hyatt Cres WN8 . . . . .28 C3
Hyde Rd Blackpool FY1 . . .129 B2
　Morecambe LA4 . . . . .213 B4
Hygiene BB5 . . . . .123 C2
Hynd Brook Ho BB5 . . . . .103 A5
Hyndburn Bridge BB5 . . . .123 F5
Hyndburn Cl LA3 . . . . .213 B3
Hyndburn Dr BB3 . . . . .80 D4
Hyndburn Park
　Cty Prim Sch BB5 . . . . . . .103 A6
Hyndburn Rd
　Accrington BB5 . . . . .103 A6
　Church BB5 . . . . .102 F6
　Great Harwood BB6 . . . . .123 F5
Hyndburn St BB5 . . . . . . .102 F6
Hyning Rd LA5 . . . . .217 E8
Hynings The BB6 . . . . .123 B6
Hythe Cl Blackburn BB1 . .101 C4
　Southport PR8 . . . . .34 E3

I

Ibbison Ct FY1 . . . . .129 C3
Icconhurst Cl BB5 . . . . . . .103 E2
Ice St BB1 . . . . .100 E7
Iddesleigh Rd ■ PR1 . . . . .117 E1
Iddon Ct ■ FY1 . . . . .117 E1
Idlewood Pl FY5 . . . . .150 F8
Idstone Cl BB2 . . . . .81 A8
Ightenhill Jun Sch BB12 .126 C6
Ightenhill Park La
　Burnley BB11 . . . . .126 C8
　Padiham BB12 . . . . .146 C2
Ightenhill Pk Mews ■
　. . . . . .126 C7
Ightenhill Prim Inf Sch
　BB12 . . . . .126 C6
Ightenhill St BB12 . . . . . . .145 C1
Ilford Rd FY4 . . . . .129 E1
Ilkley Ave
　Lytham St Annes FY8 . . . . .89 C6
　Southport PR9 . . . . .53 C6
Ilkley Gr FY5 . . . . .150 E8
Illawalla The FY5 . . . . .151 E6
Illingworth Rd PR1 . . . . . .117 E1
Ilway PR5 . . . . .96 E3
Imperial Gdns BB9 . . . . . .168 D1
Imperial St ■ FY1 . . . . . . .129 B7
Ince Cres L37 . . . . .11 D3
Ince La PR7 . . . . .40 C6
Inch Field BB10 . . . . .128 B6
Inchfield WN8 . . . . .18 B2
India St Accrington BB5 . . .102 F6
　Darwen BB3 . . . . .64 B8
　Ramsbottom BL0 . . . . .49 C3
Industrial Cotts ■ BB4 . . . .68 F8
Industrial Pl ■ OL13 . . . . . .86 F2
Industrial St Bacup OL13 . . .87 A2
　Ramsbottom BL0 . . . . .67 C1
Industrial Terr BB7 . . . . . .143 A4
Industry Rd ■ OL12 . . . . . .51 F1
Industry St Darwen BB3 . . .81 B2
　Whitworth OL12 . . . . .70 D2
Infant St ■ BB5 . . . . .103 C6
Infimary Rd BB2 . . . . .100 D3
Infirmary Cl BB2 . . . . .100 D2
Infirmary St BB2 . . . . .100 E4
Ing Dene Cl BB8 . . . . .169 B4
Ingersol Rd BL6 . . . . .31 E1
Ingfield Terr OL14 . . . . . . .108 C1
Ingham Brow BL6 . . . . .31 F4
Ingham St ■ Barrowford BB9 168 D1
　Bury BL9 . . . . .32 A1
　Padiham BB12 . . . . .145 D1
Ingleby Cl Cleveleys FY5 . .172 F5
　Standish WN6 . . . . .28 D2
Inglehurst Rd BB11 . . . . . .126 B5
Inglemere Cl LA5 . . . . .237 B1
Inglemere Dr LA5 . . . . .237 B2
Inglemere Gdns LA5 . . . . .237 B1
Inglenook Cl ■ FY5 . . . . . .172 F1
Ingleton Ave FY5 . . . . .150 F4
Ingleton Cl BB5 . . . . .103 D5
Ingleton Dr LA1 . . . . .211 A4
Ingleton Ho ■ LA1 . . . . . . .211 A3
Ingleton Rd Fulwood PR2 .117 E4
　Southport PR8 . . . . .34 E3
Ingleway FY5 . . . . .172 F3
Ingleway Ave FY3 . . . . . . .129 F6
Inglewhite WN8 . . . . .18 A2
Inglewhite Fold ■ BB12 . . .125 D7
Inglewhite Rd PR3 . . . . . . .159 C3
Inglewood Cl Bury BL0 . . . .32 C4
　Fleetwood FY7 . . . . .193 C1

Inglewood Cl continued
　Warton PR4 . . . . .91 D6
Inglewood Gr FY2 . . . . . . .150 E2
Ingol Gdns FY6 . . . . .174 C2
Ingol Gr FY6 . . . . .174 C2
Ingol La FY6 . . . . .174 D2
Ingol Prim Sch PR2 . . . . . .115 F4
Ingot St PR1 . . . . .95 D8
Ingram WN8 . . . . .18 B1
Ings Ave
　Barnoldswick BB18 . . . . . .200 B3
　Rochdale OL12 . . . . .51 B2
Ings La OL12 . . . . .51 C2
Ingthorpe Ave FY2 . . . . . .150 D5
Inkerman Rd PR4 . . . . .131 F6
Inkerman St Bacup OL13 . . .87 A2
　Blackburn BB1 . . . . .100 C6
　■ Padiham BB12 . . . . .125 C8
　Preston PR2 . . . . .116 D2
　■ Rochdale OL12 . . . . .51 F1
Inner Prom FY8 . . . . .89 B3
Innes Sch OL12 . . . . .51 C1
Inskip Cl WN8 . . . . .18 A2
Inskip Ct BB4 . . . . .18 B2
Inskip Pl Blackpool FY4 . . .109 E5
　Lytham St Annes FY8 . . . . .89 A8
　Preston PR2 . . . . .115 E1
　Southport PR9 . . . . .53 A4
　Wharles PR4 . . . . .134 A5
Inskip St ■ BB12 . . . . .125 C8
Institute St BB12 . . . . .125 D8
Intack La BB2 . . . . .120 B2
Intack Prim Sch BB1 . . . . .101 D5
Intack Rd PR4 . . . . .74 B8
Intake Cres BB8 . . . . .169 F6
Intake La Maghull L39 . . . . .4 E8
　Skelmersdale L39 . . . . .8 B2
Inver Rd FY2 . . . . .150 D3
Inverness Rd BB3 . . . . .63 F8
Ipswich Pl FY5 . . . . .172 C2
Ipswich Rd PR2 . . . . .117 D2
Ireby Rd LA6 . . . . .236 C3
Irene Pl BB2 . . . . .100 B5
Irene St BB10 . . . . .127 C5
Iris St BL0 . . . . .49 B6
Iron St Blackburn BB2 . . . .100 E3
　Horwich BL6 . . . . .31 C5
Irongate PR5 . . . . .76 C8
Ironside Cl PR2 . . . . .117 B4
Irton Rd PR9 . . . . .34 E8
Irvin Ave PR9 . . . . .53 C5
Irvin St PR1 . . . . .117 B1
Irvine Cl FY2 . . . . .150 F5
Irvine Ct ■ BB9 . . . . .168 F2
Irving Pl BB2 . . . . .100 B5
Irving St PR9 . . . . .52 B1
Irwell WN8 . . . . .18 A3
Irwell Rd WN5 . . . . .10 F7
Irwell St ■ Bacup OL13 . . . .86 F2
　Burnley BB10 . . . . .147 A6
　Longridge PR3 . . . . .139 B7
　Longridge PR3 . . . . .139 B8
　Lytham St Annes FY8 . . . . .88 F7
　Ramsbottom BL0 . . . . .49 C6
Irwell Terr ■ OL13 . . . . . . .86 F2
Irwell Vale Rd BL0 . . . . . . .67 C6
Irwell Vale Sta BL0 . . . . . .67 C5
Isa St ■ BL0 . . . . .49 B4
Isabella St Longridge PR3 .139 A8
　Rochdale OL12 . . . . .51 F2
Isherwood Fold BL7 . . . . . .47 D7
Isherwood St
　Blackburn BB2 . . . . .100 D1
　■ Preston PR1 . . . . .117 B1
　Preston PR1 . . . . .117 C1
Islamic Coll Jamea Al
　Kauthar ■ 210 F5
Island Cotts BL9 . . . . .49 C6
Island La PR3 . . . . .198 B3
Islay Rd FY8 . . . . .89 E6
Isle of Man BB1 . . . . .121 E4
Isle of Man St BB4 . . . . . . .86 A7
Isleworth Dr PR7 . . . . .42 A7
Islington Dr BB2 . . . . .100 E3
Islington Cl BB10 . . . . .147 D3
Ivan St BB10 . . . . .147 B2
Ivegate Colne BB8 . . . . . . .169 D5
　Foulridge BB8 . . . . .191 E1
Ivinson Rd BB3 . . . . .81 B3
Ivory St ■ BB12 . . . . .126 C6
Ivy Ave Blackpool FY4 . . . .109 E5
　Haslingden BB4 . . . . .84 C3
Ivy Bank PR2 . . . . .96 B7
Ivy Bank High Sch BB12 .125 F7
Ivy Cl PR5 . . . . .76 E2
Ivy Cotts BB4 . . . . .68 F8
Ivy Gr ■ BB4 . . . . .85 A3
Ivy St Blackburn BB2 . . . .100 E3
　Burnley BB10 . . . . .147 B1
　Nelson BB9 . . . . .169 A2
　■ Rawtenstall BB4 . . . . . . .68 F8
　Southport PR8 . . . . .34 D6
Ivy Terr BB3 . . . . .64 B6
Ivybridge WN8 . . . . .18 B2
Ivydale WN8 . . . . .18 B2

J

Jack La BD23 . . . . .230 F4
Jackdaw Rd BL8 . . . . .48 F2
Jacks Key Dr BB3 . . . . .64 C5
Jacksmere La L40,PR8 . . . .22 B8
Jackson Cl Haskayne L39 . .13 F5
　Lancaster LA1 . . . . .210 C7
Jackson Heights Rd BB1 . .82 B4
Jackson Rd ■ Chorley PR7 .42 A5

Hor-Joh 265

Jackson Rd continued
　■ Leyland PR5 . . . . .75 D1
Jackson St
　■ Bamber Bridge PR5 . . . .76 F8
　Blackpool FY3 . . . . .129 E7
　■ Burnley BB10 . . . . .127 A8
　Chorley PR7 . . . . .42 D6
　■ Church BB5 . . . . .102 E5
　■ Clayton-le-M BB5 . . . . .123 F3
Jackson Terr LA5 . . . . .217 D3
Jackson's Banks Rd BB2 .119 E6
Jackson's Common La
　L40 . . . . .23 B1
Jackson's La L40 . . . . .26 C1
Jacob St BB5 . . . . .103 C5
Jacob's La PR4 . . . . .114 A7
Jacson St ■ PR1 . . . . .96 A7
Jade Cl L33 . . . . .1 A3
Jagoe Mews ■ BB18 . . . . .201 B1
Jagoe Rd BB18 . . . . .201 A1
James Ave Blackpool FY4 .129 F1
　Great Harwood BB6 . . . . .123 B5
James Pl Coppull PR7 . . . . .28 E8
　Standish WN6 . . . . .28 D2
James Sq WN6 . . . . .28 D2
James St Bacup OL13 . . . . .69 B7
　Bamber Bridge PR5 . . . . . .96 E1
　Barnoldswick BB18 . . . . . .200 B1
　■ Barrowford BB9 . . . . . .168 D4
　Belthorn BB1 . . . . .81 A4
　Blackburn BB1 . . . . .100 C5
　Burnley BB10 . . . . .147 A1
　Bury BL9 . . . . .32 A1
　■ Clayton-le-M BB5 . . . . .123 F3
　Colne BB8 . . . . .169 E4
　■ Darwen BB3 . . . . .81 A1
　Earby BB18 . . . . .201 B1
　Egerton BL7 . . . . .46 D3
　Great Harwood BB6 . . . . .123 B5
　Haslingden BB4 . . . . .84 A2
　Horwich BL6 . . . . .30 F3
　Huncoat BB5 . . . . .124 E2
　■ Lancaster LA1 . . . . .210 F8
　Morecambe LA4 . . . . .212 F5
　Oswaldtwistle BB5 . . . . . .102 D3
　Preston PR1 . . . . .96 B7
　Rawtenstall BB4 . . . . .85 A2
　Rishton BB1 . . . . .123 C1
　Salterforth BB18 . . . . .191 D7
　Whitworth OL12 . . . . .70 D2
James St W ■ BB3 . . . . . . .81 A1
Jameson Rd FY7 . . . . .194 A1
Jameson St ■ FY1 . . . . . . .129 C3
Jane La Catforth PR4 . . . . .134 E5
　Leyland PR5 . . . . .75 A3
Jane St OL12 . . . . .70 E6
Jane's Brook Rd PR8 . . . . . .34 C4
Janice Dr PR2 . . . . .116 D7
Janine Cl LA4 . . . . .212 D4
Jannat Cl BB5 . . . . .103 B5
Jarrett Rd L33 . . . . .1 A4
Jarrett Wlk L33 . . . . .1 A4
Jarvis St OL12 . . . . .51 F1
Jasmine Rd PR1 . . . . .96 A3
Jasper St BB1 . . . . .121 F1
Jefferson Cl LA1 . . . . .210 D7
Jefferson Way OL12 . . . . . .51 F3
Jeffrey Ave PR3 . . . . .139 B7
Jeffrey Hill Cl PR2 . . . . . . .118 C2
Jeffrey Sq FY1 . . . . .129 D3
Jellicoe Cl FY1 . . . . .109 E1
Jem Gate FY5 . . . . .150 D8
Jemmett St PR1 . . . . .116 F2
Jenny La Blackpool FY4 . . .110 C7
　Higher Wheelton PR6 . . . . .78 C1
Jenny Nook LA3 . . . . .209 A7
Jenny St BB9 . . . . .147 D6
Jensen Cl LA1 . . . . .210 E6
Jensen Dr FY4 . . . . .111 A6
Jepheys Pl ■ OL12 . . . . . . .51 F1
Jepheys St OL12 . . . . .51 F1
Jepp Hill ■ BB18 . . . . .200 B2
Jepps Ave PR3 . . . . .136 B8
Jepps La PR3 . . . . .136 B8
Jepson St ■ BB3 . . . . .64 A8
Jepson Way FY4 . . . . .109 E4
Jericho Rd BL9 . . . . .32 E4
Jersey Ave FY2 . . . . .150 E2
Jersey St BB2 . . . . .100 B1
Jervis Cl FY8 . . . . .109 D1
Jesmond Ave FY4 . . . . . . .109 B7
Jesmond Gr LA4 . . . . .212 G3
Jessel St BB2 . . . . .100 B2
Jesson Way LA5 . . . . .217 C1
Jevington Way LA3 . . . . . .209 A4
Jib Hill Cotts BB10 . . . . . .147 D2
Jingling La LA6 . . . . .238 C2
Jinny La BB12 . . . . .167 E4
Jobling St BB8 . . . . .169 B3
Jockey St BB11 . . . . .126 E5
Joe Connolly Way BB4 . . . .68 E8
Joe La PR3 . . . . .178 D2
John Cross CE Prim Sch
　PR3 . . . . .157 A4
John Henry St OL12 . . . . . .70 D4
John Hill St ■ FY4 . . . . . . .129 F2
John Kay Ct LA1 . . . . .213 D3
John o' Gaunt
　St ■ BB12 . . . . .145 C1
John St
　■ Bamber Bridge PR5 . . . .96 E1
　Barnoldswick BB18 . . . . . .200 B1
　Barrowford BB9 . . . . .168 E4
　Blackpool FY1 . . . . .129 B2
　Brierfield BB9 . . . . .147 B6

John St continued
4 Carnforth LA5 ....217 D2
Church BB5 ....102 E7
Clayton-le-M BB5 ....123 F3
Colne BB8 ....169 C4
Coppull PR7 ....41 E1
Darwen BB3 ....80 F2
Earby BB18 ....201 B1
5 Galgate LA2 ....207 A4
Haslingden BB4 ....84 B3
Leyland PR5 ....76 A1
Newchurch BB4 ....85 F1
Oswaldtwistle BB5 ....102 D3
Thornton FY5 ....173 B4
Whitworth OL12 ....70 D2
John Wall Ct 8 BB7 ......164 D8
John William St 7 PR1 ....96 C8
Johnny Barn Cl BB4 ....85 D2
Johnny Barn Cotts BB4 ....85 D2
Johnson Cl Carnforth LA5 .217 C1
Lancaster LA1 ....210 C7
Johnson New Rd BB3 ....81 E2
Johnson Rd Blackpool FY4 .129 F2
Waterside BB3 ....81 D4
Johnson St PR9 ....34 B8
Johnson's
Meanygate PR4 ....55 D7
Johnspool PR2 ....116 C6
Johnston Cl BB2 ....100 C5
Johnston St BB2 ....100 C5
Johnsville Ave FY4 ....109 E7
Joiner's Row BB2 ....100 E3
Joiners Alley 10 BB6 .....123 C5
Jolly Tar La PR7 ....29 B7
Jonathan Cl BB4 ....67 A8
Jones St BL6 ....31 B4
Jones' Gr FY7 ....194 B5
Jones's Yd LA6 ....234 B7
Joseph St Barrowford BB9 .168 D2
Darwen BB3 ....81 B1
3 Rochdale OL12 ....51 D2
Joy Pl OL12 ....51 F2
Joy St Ramsbottom BL0 ....49 B6
Rochdale OL12 ....51 F2
Joyce Ave FY4 ....129 F2
Jubilee Ave Ormskirk L39 ..15 F6
Orrell WN5 ....10 A4
Preesall FY6 ....195 A4
Preston PR2 ....115 D1
Jubilee Cl BB4 ....84 A1
Jubilee Ct 1 BB4 ....84 A1
Jubilee Cts PR5 ....58 E8
Jubilee Dr Cleveleys FY5 .172 C4
Skelmersdale WN8 ....8 E8
Jubilee Ho PR5 ....57 B1
Jubilee La FY4 ....110 B5
Jubilee La N FY4 ....110 B6
Jubilee Rd
9 Bamber Bridge PR5 ....76 A8
Church BB5 ....102 F7
Formby L37 ....11 D1
Haslingden BB4 ....84 A1
Jubilee St Blackburn BB1 .100 E4
Brierfield BB10 ....147 F3
Darwen BB3 ....81 A1
Enfield BB5 ....124 A1
Oswaldtwistle BB5 ....102 E4
Read BB12 ....144 D2
Jubilee Terr Clifton PR4 .114 C1
Freckleton PR4 ....92 C7
Langho BB6 ....142 D1
Jubilee Trad Est PR1 .....116 E1
Jubilee Way FY8 ....89 C8
Jud Falls BB7 ....163 A3
Judd Holmes La PR3 ....160 D7
Jude St BB9 ....147 D8
Judeland PR7 ....60 A2
Judge Fields BB8 ....169 D6
Judith St OL12 ....51 C3
Julia Mews 4 BL6 ....31 B4
Julia St BL6 ....31 B4
July St 17 BB1 ....101 A4
Jumbles Ctry Pk BL7 ......47 D2
Jumps La OL14 ....108 E1
Junction La L40 ....24 E3
Junction Rd Preston PR2 ...95 D7
Rainford Junction WA11 .....8 F1
Junction St Brierfield BB9 .147 B6
Burnley BB12 ....126 E6
Burnley, Whittlefield BB12 .126 E7
Darwen BB3 ....64 B7
Nelson BB8 ....169 A3
June Ave FY4 ....130 A1
June St 16 BB1 ....101 A4
June's Wlk PR4 ....74 A5
Juniper Cl FY6 ....195 A5
Juniper Croft PR6 ....77 A1
Juniper Ct BB5 ....103 E8
Juniper St 6 BB1 ....101 A7
Juno St BB9 ....168 F2
Jutland St PR1 ....96 A8

K

Kairnryan Cl FY2 ....150 F5
Kale Gr L33 ....1 A5
Kaley La BB7 ....187 E5
Kane St PR2 ....116 C1
Kate St 3 BL0 ....49 B6
Kateholm OL13 ....87 A7
Kay Brow BL0 ....49 C6
Kay Gdns BB11 ....127 B5
Kay St Blackburn BB2 ....100 E3
Blackpool FY1 ....129 B4

Kay St continued
Brierfield BB9 ....147 B5
Bury BL9 ....32 A3
Clitheroe BB7 ....164 D6
Darwen BB3 ....81 B1
Edgworth BL7 ....47 C4
2 Oswaldtwistle BB5 ......102 D4
1 Padiham BB12 ....145 D1
1 Preston PR1 ....95 E7
Ramsbottom BL0,BL9 ....49 C5
Rawtenstall BB4 ....85 A2
Kaymar Ind Est PR1 ....96 C7
Kayswell Rd LA4 ....213 B5
Kearsley Ave PR4 ....56 A6
Keasdale Ave LA7 ....237 E3
Keasdale Rd LA7 ....237 E3
Keasden Ave FY4 ....109 D7
Keasden Rd BB7 ....229 E6
Keating Ct FY7 ....194 A3
Keats Ave Bolton-le-S LA5 .216 A5
Longshaw WN5 ....10 D1
Rochdale OL12 ....51 A1
Warton PR4 ....91 E6
Keats Cl Accrington BB5 ..103 E2
Colne BB8 ....169 D6
Eccleston PR7 ....40 D5
Thornton FY5 ....173 A2
Keats Fold 3 BB12 ....125 F7
Keats Rd BL8 ....48 F2
Keats Terr PR8 ....34 F6
Keats Way PR4 ....115 D4
Kebs Rd OL14 ....108 E3
Keele Cl FY5 ....173 A2
Keele Wlk BB1 ....100 F4
Keeper's Hey FY5 ....173 A4
Keeper's La PR3 ....199 F1
Keer Bank 1 LA1 ....213 C2
Keer Holme La LA6 ....234 E4
Keighley Ave BB8 ....169 D6
Keighley Rd Colne BB8 ...169 F5
Laneshaw Bridge BB8 .....170 D6
Trawden BB8 ....170 C4
Keirby Wlk BB11 ....127 A6
Keith Gr FY5 ....172 D1
Keith St BB2 ....126 C6
Kelbrook Dr BB11 ....126 E3
Kelbrook Prim Sch BB18 ..192 A6
Kelbrook Rd BB18 ....191 E4
Kelkbeck Cl L31 ....5 F2
Kellaway Pl BB11 ....126 E6
Kellet Acre 4 PR5 ....76 A7
Kellet Ave PR5 ....76 D1
Kellet Ct 1 LA1 ....210 E8
Kellet La
Bolton-le-S LA5,LA2 .....216 C3
Borwick LA6 ....234 B3
Walton Summit PR5 ....77 B7
Over Kellet LA6 ....234 A8
Kellet Rd Carnforth LA5 ..217 C1
Over Kellet Ind Est LA5 ..217 F1
Kellett St 8 PR7 ....42 C8
Kelmarsh Cl FY3 ....130 B2
Kelne Ho 7 LA1 ....210 E8
Kelsall Ave BB1 ....101 B8
Kelsey St LA1 ....210 E8
Kelso Ave FY5 ....172 D1
Kelsons Ave FY5 ....173 C2
Kelswick Dr BB9 ....147 E6
Kelverdale Rd FY5 ....150 D6
Kelvin Rd FY5 ....150 D6
Kelvin St BB3 ....80 F1
Kelwood Ave BL9 ....32 D5
Kem Mill La PR6 ....60 B8
Kemble Cl BL6 ....31 B5
Kemp Ct BB1 ....121 F3
Kemp St FY7 ....194 B4
Kemple View BB7 ....164 D6
Kempton Ave FY3 ....129 E3
Kempton Park Fold PR8 ...34 F3
Kempton Rd LA1 ....211 B4
Kempton Rise BB1 ....100 F3
Kenbury Cl L33 ....1 A4
Kenbury Rd L33 ....1 A4
Kendal Ave
Barrowford BB9 ....168 D4
Blackpool FY3 ....151 A1
Cleveleys FY5 ....172 C4
Kendal Cl WA11 ....8 F2
Kendal Dr Maghull L31 .....5 E2
Morecambe LA4 ....213 B4
Rainford Junction WA11 ....8 F2
Kendal Rd
Kirkby Lonsdale LA6 .....238 B2
Lytham St Anne's FY8 ....109 D1
Ramsbottom BL0 ....49 A2
Kendal Rd W BL0 ....48 F2
Kendal Row BB1 ....81 F6
Kendal St Blackburn BB1 .100 E6
Clitheroe BB7 ....186 F1
5 Nelson BB9 ....168 D1
Preston PR1 ....95 E8
Kendal Way PR4 ....20 B3
Kenilworth Ave FY7 ......193 E3
Kenilworth Cl BB12 ......125 E8
Kenilworth Ct FY8 ....88 F6
Kenilworth Dr
Clitheroe BB7 ....164 C6
Earby BB18 ....192 A8
Kenilworth Gdns FY4 .....109 B7
Kenilworth Pl
Fleetwood FY7 ....193 E3
Lancaster LA1 ....211 A5
Kenilworth Rd
Lytham St Anne's FY8 .....88 F6
Morecambe LA3 ....212 F3
Southport PR8 ....20 B4
Kenlis Rd PR3 ....178 F4
Kenmay Way L33 ....1 A3
Kenmure Pl PR1 ....116 F2

Kennedy Cl LA1 ....210 D6
Kennet Dr PR2 ....116 F8
Kennett Dr PR5 ....76 B2
Kennington Cty Prim Sch
PR2 ....117 A4
Kennington Rd PR2 ....117 A4
Kensington Ave PR1 ....95 B6
Kensington Cl BL8 ....49 A1
Kensington Ct LA4 ....213 A6
Kensington Dr BL6 ....31 D3
Kensington Ho LA1 ....210 F5
Kensington Ind Pk PR9 ....34 C6
Kensington Rd
Blackpool FY1 ....129 E4
Chorley PR7 ....42 B7
Cleveleys FY5 ....172 C3
Formby L37 ....11 E1
Lancaster LA1 ....210 F5
Lytham St Anne's FY8 .....89 D4
Morecambe LA4 ....212 E5
Southport PR9 ....34 C6
Kensington St BB1 ....147 C7
Kent Ave
2 Bamber Bridge PR5 ......96 D3
Cleveleys FY5 ....172 E4
Formby L37 ....12 A1
Kent Ct BB9 ....168 D4
Kent Dr Blackburn BB1 ...101 E4
Clayton-le-W PR5 ....76 D1
Kent Ho LA1 ....210 F7
Kent Rd Blackpool FY1 ...129 C3
Formby L37 ....12 A1
Southport PR8 ....34 A4
Kent St Blackburn BB1 ...100 F4
Burnley BB12 ....126 F7
Fleetwood FY7 ....194 B5
3 Lancaster LA1 ....213 F2
Preston PR1 ....116 F2
Kent Way LA3 ....213 B3
Kent Wlk BB4 ....67 A8
Kent's Cl PR4 ....112 E7
Kentmere Ave
Bamber Bridge PR5 ....96 E1
Leyland PR5 ....76 A4
Kentmere Cl Burnley BB12 .126 B8
Fleetwood FY7 ....193 D3
Kentmere Dr Blackburn BB2 .79 E8
Blackpool FY4 ....130 C1
Longton PR4 ....74 B8
Kentmere Gr 1 LA4 ....212 G4
Kentmere Rd LA1 ....214 A1
Kenton Cl L37 ....11 F6
Kenwood Ave LA4 ....212 D4
Kenworthys Flats PR8 .....34 B8
Kenwyn Ave FY3 ....129 E3
Kenyon La PR6 ....60 F7
Kenyon Rd
Morecambe LA4 ....213 B5
Nelson BB9 ....147 B7
Standish WN6 ....28 D2
Kenyon St
6 Accrington BB5 ....103 C6
Bacup OL13 ....70 B8
Blackburn BB1 ....101 C6
Bury BL9 ....32 A3
Ramsbottom BL0 ....49 C6
Rawtenstall BB4 ....85 A3
Kenyon's La L37 ....12 A3
Kenyons La L31 ....5 E3
Keppel Pl BB11 ....126 E6
Kepple La PR3 ....178 B6
Kerenhappuch St 5 BL0 ...49 B5
Kerfoot's La WN8 ....8 C8
Kerr Pl PR1 ....95 D8
Kershaw Cl BB3 ....80 D8
Kershaw St 6 Bacup OL13 ..86 F2
6 Bamber Bridge PR5 ......76 B7
Bury BL9 ....32 A2
Chorley PR6 ....60 E1
Church BB5 ....102 E7
Kerslake Way L38 ....3 A4
Kerslea Ave FY3 ....130 D8
Kerton Row PR8 ....33 F4
Keston Gr FY4 ....109 C5
Kestor La PR3 ....139 A7
Kestrel Cl
Blackburn BB1 ....100 D8
Cleveleys FY5 ....172 F5
Knowley PR6 ....61 A3
Kestrel Ct BB9 ....168 C5
Kestrel Dr Bury BL9 ......32 B4
Darwen BB3 ....80 D3
Kestrel Mews WN8 ....18 C4
Kestrel Pk WN8 ....18 C4
Keswick Cl Accrington BB5 .124 D1
Maghull L31 ....5 E2
Southport PR8 ....20 C3
Keswick Ct LA1 ....214 B1
Keswick Dr BB2 ....79 E8
Keswick Gr Heysham LA3 ..208 E5
Knott End-on-S FY6 ......194 F5
Keswick Rd Blackpool FY1 .129 B2
Burnley BB10 ....147 B2
Lancaster LA1 ....214 B1
Lytham St Anne's FY8 .....88 E8
Keswick Way WA11 ....8 F2
Keswick Wlk LA1 ....214 B1
Kettering Rd PR8 ....20 B5
Kevin Ave FY6 ....151 F5
Kevin Gr LA3 ....209 D1
Kew Ct PR5 ....96 D5
Kew Gr FY5 ....172 D1
Kew Rd Formby L37 ....11 D1
Nelson BB9 ....168 F2
Southport PR8 ....34 B3
Kew Woods Prim Sch PR8 ..34 F3
Key View BB8 ....64 C5
Keynsham Gr BB12 ....126 D7

Khyber St BB8 ....169 C4
Kibble Cres BB10 ....147 C3
Kibble Gr BB9 ....147 D4
Kibboth Crew BL0 ....49 B7
Kidbrooke Ave FY4 ....109 B4
Kiddington Cl PR5 ....76 D8
Kiddrow La BB12 ....126 A7
Kidsgrove PR2 ....115 F5
Kielder Ct 3 FY8 ....90 C4
Kielder Dr BB12 ....126 E7
Kilbane St FY7 ....193 F1
Kilburn Rd WN5 ....10 C5
Kilcrash La PR3 ....177 D7
Kildale Cl L31 ....5 C2
Kildare Ave FY5 ....173 A4
Kildare Rd FY2 ....150 D3
Kilgrimol Gdns FY8 ......109 C1
Kilkerran Cl PR6 ....42 D5
Killer St 1 BL0 ....49 C6
Killiard La BB2 ....99 E5
Killingbeck Cl L40 ....24 D4
Killington St BB5 ....147 C2
Killingworth Mews BL6 ....31 D1
Killon St FY3 ....32 A1
Kilmory Pl FY2 ....150 F5
Kilmuir Cl PR2 ....117 C5
Kiln Bank OL12 ....70 C2
Kiln Bank La OL12 ....70 C2
Kiln Cl BB7 ....187 A2
Kiln Croft PR6 ....77 B3
Kiln Hill BB12 ....145 F6
Kiln House Way BB5 ......103 A3
Kiln La Hambleton FY6 ...174 B2
Paythorne BB7 ....225 C6
Rimington BB7 ....224 F2
Skelmersdale WN8 ....17 E1
Wray LA2 ....232 D6
Kiln St Nelson BB9 ......147 D8
Ramsbottom BL0 ....49 B5
Kiln Terr 5 OL13 ....69 D8
Kiln Wlk OL12 ....51 E2
Kilnbank Ave LA4 ....212 D5
Kilngate PR5 ....96 C3
Kilnhouse La FY8 ....110 A1
Kilns The BB11 ....127 B3
Kilruddery Rd PR1 ....95 E5
Kilsby Cl PR5 ....96 E3
Kilworth Ht FY7 ....116 C5
Kimberley Ave FY4 ....109 D5
Kimberley Cl BB10 ....147 F3
Kimberley Rd PR2 ....116 C8
Kimberley St Bacup OL13 ..69 A7
Brierfield BB10 ....147 F3
Kimberly Cl PR4 ....92 B6
Kimble Cl BL8 ....48 F2
Kime St BB12 ....126 C6
Kincardine Ave 7 FY4 ...110 A6
Kincraig Pl FY2 ....150 F6
Kincraig Prim Sch FY2 ...150 F6
Kincraig Rd FY2 ....150 F5
Kindonan Ave LA4 ....110 A6
King Edward Ave
Blackpool FY2 ....150 B1
Lytham St Anne's FY8 .....89 A4
King Edward St BB5 .....102 C3
King Edward Terr BB9 ....168 D2
King Edward VII & Queen
Mary Jun Sch FY8 ......89 A4
King Edward VII Sch FY8 ..89 B4
King George Ave FY2 .....150 B1
King George V Coll PR8 ...34 E5
King La BB7 ....164 E8
King St Accrington BB5 ..103 B6
5 Bacup OL13 ....86 F2
6 Bamber Bridge PR5 ......76 B7
Barnoldswick BB18 ....200 B2
Blackburn BB2 ....100 D4
Blackpool FY1 ....129 C5
Brierfield BB9 ....147 A5
Brierfield, Harle Syke BB10 .147 F3
Carnforth LA5 ....217 D1
Chorley PR7 ....42 D6
Clitheroe BB7 ....164 E8
Colne BB8 ....169 E5
Fleetwood FY7 ....194 A4
14 Great Harwood BB6 ....123 C5
Haslingden BB4 ....84 B4
High Bentham LA2 ....233 D8
Horwich BL6 ....31 A4
Lancaster LA1 ....210 F8
Leyland PR5 ....76 A1
Longridge PR3 ....139 B7
Morecambe LA4 ....212 E5
Padiham BB12 ....125 C8
Ramsbottom BL0 ....49 C6
Rawtenstall BB8 ....68 E8
Southport PR8 ....34 A6
Whalley BB7 ....143 C5
Whitworth OL12 ....70 D3
King Street Terr BB9 ....147 A5
King William St BB1 .....100 E5
King's Bridge Cl BB2 ...100 B1
King's Bridge St BB2 ....100 B1
King's Cl FY5 ....151 E2
King's Cres LA3 ....212 B3
King's Croft PR5 ....96 D5
King's Cswy BB9 ....147 E5
King's Dr LA5 ....217 E1
King's Highway
Accrington BB5 ....104 B2
Huncoat BB5 ....104 B3
King's Rd Accrington BB5 .103 B7
Blackburn BB2 ....100 B1
Lytham St Anne's FY8 .....88 E5
King's Sq FY1 ....129 C5

King's Wlk FY5 ....172 D5
Kingfisher Bank BB11 ....126 C4
Kingfisher Cl BB1 ....100 D8
Kingfisher Ct Maghull L31 ..5 B4
Oswaldtwistle BB5 ....102 C3
Southport PR9 ....34 D8
Kingfisher Dr Bury BL9 ...32 B4
Poulton-le-F FY6 ....151 B2
Kingfisher Mews FY6 ....151 B2
Kingfisher Pk WN8 ....18 C4
Kingfisher St PR1 ....117 B1
Kings Arms Cl 33 LA1 ....210 F8
Kings Ave BB4 ....85 A1
Kings Cl Arnside LA5 ....237 B1
Formby L37 ....11 E2
Kings Cres PR5 ....76 A1
Kings Ct PR5 ....76 A1
Kings Dr Fulwood PR2 ...116 D5
Hoddlesden BB3 ....81 F1
Padiham BB12 ....125 E6
Kings Hey Dr PR9 ....52 F1
Kings Mdw PR8 ....20 D3
Kings Rd Cleveleys FY5 ..172 C2
Formby L37 ....11 E2
Kingsacre PR3 ....178 A3
Kingsbridge Cl PR1 ....95 D2
Kingsbridge Wharfe BB2 .100 B1
Kingsbury Cl PR8 ....20 B4
Kingsbury Ct WN8 ....18 C4
Kingsbury Pl BB10 ....147 D3
Kingsbury Sch L39 ....15 C5
Kingscote Dr FY3 ....129 E7
Kingsdale Ave
Brierfield BB10 ....147 C3
Fulwood PR2 ....117 D5
Morecambe LA3 ....212 B1
Kingsdale Cl Leyland PR5 .59 B6
Walton-le-D PR5 ....96 F5
Kingsdale Rd LA1 ....210 D7
Kingsfold Christian Sch
PR4 ....72 F2
Kingsfold Dr PR1 ....95 D2
Kingsfold Prim Sch PR1 ...95 D2
Kingshaven Dr PR1 ....95 E2
Kingshotte Gdns BB9 ....168 C3
Kingsland Gr
Blackpool FY1 ....129 D3
13 Burnley BB11 ....127 B4
Kingsland Rd BB11 ......127 B4
Kingslea PR7 ....29 F8
Kingsley Ave BB12 ......125 E7
Kingsley Cl Church BB5 ..102 F7
Maghull L31 ....5 C5
Thornton FY5 ....173 A3
Kingsley Dr PR7 ....42 A5
Kingsley Rd Blackpool FY3 .130 B2
Cottam PR4 ....115 F6
Kingsley St BB9 ....168 F2
Kingsmead Blackburn BB1 .101 D4
Chorley PR7 ....42 C5
Kingsmede FY4 ....109 E6
Kingsmere Ave FY8 ......109 F1
Kingsmill Ave BB7 ......143 A8
Kingsmuir Ave PR2 ......117 D4
Kingsmuir Cl LA3 ....208 E7
Kingston Ave
Accrington BB5 ....103 A4
Blackpool FY4 ....109 C5
Kingston Cl FY4 ....194 F6
Kingston Cres
Haslingden BB4 ....67 A7
Southport PR9 ....53 C5
Kingston Dr FY8 ....89 D6
Kingston Mews 3 FY5 ....173 B3
Kingston Pl BB3 ....80 F7
Kingsway Accrington BB5 .103 A8
Bamber Bridge PR5 ....76 E8
Blackburn BB3 ....81 A7
Blackpool FY4 ....109 C7
Burnley BB11 ....127 A6
Cleveleys FY5 ....172 C2
Euxton PR7 ....59 E2
Great Harwood BB6 ......123 F6
Hapton BB11 ....125 C3
Heysham LA3 ....209 A8
Huncoat BB5 ....124 F1
Lancaster LA1 ....214 A1
Leyland PR5 ....58 E7
2 Lytham St Anne's FY8 ...89 C4
Penwortham PR1 ....95 B6
Preston PR2 ....115 F2
Southport PR8 ....34 A7
Kingsway Ave PR3 ....136 C3
Kingsway Ct
Broughton PR3 ....136 C3
Lytham St Anne's FY8 .....89 C4
Morecambe LA3 ....212 B1
Kingsway Sports Ctr LA1 .214 A1
Kingsway W PR1 ....95 B6
Kingswood Cl FY8 ....89 E4
Kingswood Rd PR5 ....76 A2
Kingswood St 6 PR1 ......95 E7
Kinloch Way L39 ....15 D6
Kinnerton Pl FY5 ....150 F8
Kinross Cl BB1 ....101 A4
Kinross Cres FY4 ....130 A1
Kinross St BB11 ....126 D4
Kinross Wlk 7 BB1 ......101 A4
Kintbury Rd FY8 ....88 F4
Kintour Rd FY8 ....89 E6
Kintyre Cl FY4 ....109 F7
Kintyre Way LA3 ....208 E2
Kipling Dr FY3 ....130 B2
Kipling Pl BB6 ....123 B4
Kirby Dr PR4 ....92 B6
Kirby Rd Blackburn BB2 ..100 D1
Blackpool FY1 ....129 B2
Nelson BB9 ....147 B8

Kirk Ave BB7 . . . . .164 C8
Kirk Head PR4 . . . . .73 E2
Kirk Hill Rd PR4 . . . . .84 C3
Kirk House BB5 . . . . .102 E6
Kirk Rd BB5 . . . . .102 E1
Kirk View BB4 . . . . .86 A1
Kirkbeck Cl LA2 . . . . .231 D3
Kirkby Ave
  Clayton-le-W PR5 . . . . . . .76 E1
  Cleveleys FY5 . . . . .172 E4
Kirkby Bank Rd L33 . . . . . .1 C2
Kirkby Londsdale Rd LA2 214 F7
Kirkby Lonsdale Rd
  Caton LA2,LA6 . . . . .231 B6
  Over Kellet LA6 . . . . .234 B1
Kirkdale Ave
  Lytham St Anne's FY8 . . . .88 F7
  Newchurch BB4 . . . . .85 E1
Kirkdale Cl BB3 . . . . .64 C6
Kirkdale Gdns WN8 . . . . . .10 A7
Kirkdale Rd BB6 . . . . .122 C8
Kirkdene Ave BB8 . . . . . . .191 D1
Kirkdene Mews BB8 . . . . . .191 D1
Kirkes Rd LA1 . . . . .211 A7
Kirkfell Dr BB12 . . . . .126 C8
Kirkfield PR3 . . . . .182 D3
Kirkgate Burnley BB11 . . . .127 B4
  Kirkham PR4 . . . . .113 B4
Kirkgate La LA6 . . . . .234 B4
Kirkham & Wesham
  Cty Prim Sch PR4 . . . . . . .112 F5
Kirkham & Wesham Sta
  PR4 . . . . .112 F6
Kirkham Ave FY1 . . . . .129 E2
Kirkham By-Pass PR4 . . . . .113 B4
Kirkham Cl PR5 . . . . .75 D1
Kirkham Gram Jun Sch
  PR4 . . . . .112 F4
Kirkham Gram Sch PR4 . . .112 F5
Kirkham Rd Freckleton PR4 .92 B8
  Kirkham PR4 . . . . .113 E6
  Kirkham, Freckleton PR4 . .113 A2
  Southport PR9 . . . . .53 A4
  Weeton PR4 . . . . .131 F2
Kirkham St PR1 . . . . .95 E8
Kirkham Trad Pk PR4 . . . . .113 B4
Kirkhill Ave BB4 . . . . .84 C3
Kirklake Bank L37 . . . . . . .11 C2
Kirklake Rd L37 . . . . .11 D2
Kirkland & Catterall
  St Helen's CE Prim Sch
  PR3 . . . . .178 A2
Kirkland Pl PR2 . . . . .94 E8
Kirklands Chipping PR3 . . . .182 E3
  Hest Bank LA2 . . . . .215 F1
Kirklands Rd LA1 . . . . .231 B8
Kirklees Rd PR8 . . . . .33 F1
Kirkmoor Cl BB7 . . . . .186 D1
Kirkmoor Rd BB7 . . . . .164 E8
Kirkstall Ave
  Blackpool FY1 . . . . .129 E2
  Read BB12 . . . . .144 D1
Kirkstall Cl PR7 . . . . .42 D5
Kirkstall Dr
  Barnoldswick BB18 . . . . . .200 D3
  Chorley PR7 . . . . .42 D5
  Formby L37 . . . . .12 B2
Kirkstall Rd Chorley PR7 . . .42 D5
  Southport PR8 . . . . .33 F2
Kirkstone Ave
  Blackburn BB2 . . . . .79 E8
  Fleetwood FY7 . . . . .193 D1
Kirkstone Dr
  Blackpool FY5 . . . . .150 C7
  Morecambe LA4 . . . . .212 G5
Kirkstone Rd FY8 . . . . .109 D1
Kirton Cres FY8 . . . . .89 C6
Kirton Pl FY5 . . . . .172 E4
Kit Brow La LA2 . . . . .207 D6
Kittiwake Cl ⅓ FY5 . . . . . .172 E1
Kittiwake Rd PR6 . . . . .61 A3
Kittlingborne Brow PR5 . . .97 A3
Kitty La FY4 . . . . .110 B4
Kittygill La LA6 . . . . .238 A1
Knacks La OL12 . . . . .51 A5
Knaresboro Ave FY3 . . . . . .129 F3
Knaresborough Cl FY6 . . . .151 D5
Knebworth Cl PR6 . . . . . . .77 C2
Knight Cres BB3 . . . . .81 A6
Knighton Ave LA2 . . . . .100 C8
Knights Cl FY5 . . . . .172 E1
Knightsbrdige Ave PR4 . . .112 E6
Knightsbridge Ave
  Blackpool FY4 . . . . .109 D6
  Colne BB8 . . . . .169 B5
Knightsbridge Cl
  Kirkham PR4 . . . . .112 E6
  ⅔ Lytham St Anne's FY8 . . .89 D6
Knightscliffe Cres WN6 . . .19 D6
Knitting Row La PR3 . . . . . .175 D6
Knob Hall Gdns PR9 . . . . . .52 E3
Knob Hall La PR9 . . . . .52 E3
Knoll La PR4 . . . . .74 A4
Knoll The LA2 . . . . .213 E8
Knot Acre PR4 . . . . .75 A8
Knot La
  Newsholme BB7,BD23 . . . .225 D5
  Walton-le-D PR5 . . . . . . .96 F5
Knott Hill St OL12 . . . . . . .70 E6
Knott La LA5 . . . . .218 A8
Knott St BB3 . . . . .81 A1
Knotts Brow BL7 . . . . .47 F4
Knotts Dr BB8 . . . . .169 C3
Knotts La
  Bolton-by-B BB7,BD23 . . . .224 D8
  Colne BB8 . . . . .169 D3
  Padiham BB12 . . . . .125 E6
Knotts Mount BB8 . . . . . . .169 C3

Knowe Hill Cres LA1 . . . . .211 B3
Knowl Cl BL0 . . . . .49 C4
Knowl Gap Ave BB4 . . . . . .84 A1
Knowl Mdw BB4 . . . . .67 A6
Knowle Ave Blackpool FY2 150 C1
  Cleveleys FY5 . . . . .172 E2
  Southport PR8 . . . . .20 C6
Knowle La BB3 . . . . .81 A3
Knowle The FY2 . . . . .150 C2
Knowles Brow BB7 . . . . . . .163 B3
Knowles Rd FY8 . . . . .88 E7
Knowles St ⅟ Chorley PR7 .42 C6
  Preston PR1 . . . . .96 D8
  Rishton BB1 . . . . .123 B1
Knowlesly Mdws BB3 . . . . .64 C6
Knowlesly Rd BB3 . . . . . . .64 B6
Knowley Brow PR6 . . . . . . .60 C1
Knowlmere St BB5 . . . . . . .103 B7
Knowlys Ave LA3 . . . . .208 F8
Knowlys Cres ⅘ LA3 . . . . . .208 F8
Knowlys Dr ⅔ LA3 . . . . .208 F8
Knowlys Gr LA3 . . . . .208 F8
Knowlys Rd LA3 . . . . .208 E8
Knowsley Ave
  Blackpool FY3 . . . . .129 C3
  Leyland PR5 . . . . .76 C8
Knowsley Cl
  Gregson Lane PR5 . . . . . . .97 C2
  Lancaster LA1 . . . . .210 D6
Knowsley Cres
  Thornton FY5 . . . . .173 C2
  Weeton PR4 . . . . .131 E2
  Whitworth OL12 . . . . .70 E6
Knowsley Dr PR5 . . . . .97 C2
Knowsley Gate FY7 . . . . . .193 D4
Knowsley Gr BL6 . . . . .31 D1
Knowsley Ind Pk L33 . . . . .1 C2
Knowsley La Edgworth BL7 .65 C4
  Rivington PR6 . . . . .43 E4
Knowsley Park Way BB4 . .67 B8
Knowsley Rd
  Haslingden BB4 . . . . .67 B8
  Leyland PR5 . . . . .59 C8
  Ormskirk L39 . . . . .15 F5
  Southport PR9 . . . . .52 C1
  Wilpshire BB1 . . . . .121 C5
Knowsley Rd East BB4 . . . .67 B8
Knowsley Rd W BB1 . . . . . .121 C5
Knowsley Road Ind Est
  . . . . .84 B1
Knowsley St ⅓ Colne BB8 169 D4
  ⅔ Preston PR1 . . . . .96 A7
Knox Gr FY1 . . . . .129 D3
Knunk Knowles Dr BB7 . . .186 E1
Knutsford Rd FY3 . . . . .130 B2
Knutsford Wlk L31 . . . . . . .5 C4
Knuzden Brook BB1 . . . . . .101 D4
Korea Rd PR2 . . . . .117 B4
Kumara Cres FY4 . . . . .130 D1
Kyan St BB10 . . . . .147 B3
Kylemore Ave FY2 . . . . . . .150 D3
Kyston Cl ⅟ FY1 . . . . .129 D7

L

Laburnam Cotts PR3 . . . . .196 E5
Laburnum Ave
  Bamber Bridge PR5 . . . . . .76 B8
  Lytham St Anne's FY8 . . . .90 B5
Laburnum Cl
  Burnley BB11 . . . . .126 D3
  Fulwood PR1 . . . . .117 C3
Laburnum Dr
  Fulwood PR2 . . . . .116 D8
  Oswaldtwistle BB5 . . . . . .102 F3
  Skelmersdale WN8 . . . . . .17 D1
Laburnum Gr
  Burscough Bridge L40 . . . .24 E6
  Horwich BL6 . . . . .31 E1
  Lancaster LA1 . . . . .210 D8
  Maghull L31 . . . . .5 F1
  Southport PR8 . . . . .34 F7
Laburnum Pk LA5 . . . . . . .216 C8
Laburnum Rd
  Blackburn BB1 . . . . .101 A8
  Chorley PR6 . . . . .60 D3
  Haslingden BB4 . . . . .67 A7
  ⅔ Lancaster LA1 . . . . . . .213 F2
Laburnum St
  ⅟ Blackpool FY3 . . . . .129 D7
  Haslingden BB4 . . . . .84 A3
Lacey Ct ⅘ BB4 . . . . .84 B3
Lachman Rd BB8 . . . . .170 B3
Lacy Ave PR1 . . . . .95 C2
Ladbrooke Gr BB11 . . . . . .126 E2
Ladbury Ave FY8 . . . . .89 B5
Lade End LA3 . . . . .208 E8
Ladies Row PR4 . . . . .133 F4
Ladies Wlk LA1 . . . . .214 A2
Lady Alice's Dr L40 . . . . . .16 E8
Lady Anne Cl L40 . . . . .23 B7
Lady Crosse Dr PR6 . . . . . .60 C7
Lady Green Cl L38 . . . . . . .3 E3
Lady Green La L38 . . . . . . .3 D4
Lady Hey Cres PR2 . . . . . .115 C1
Lady Pl PR5 . . . . .96 E4
Lady St PR5 . . . . .95 F8
Lady Well Dr PR2 . . . . .117 C7
Lady's Wlk L40 . . . . .16 C6
Ladybower La FY6 . . . . . . .151 B3
Ladyman St ⅟ PR1 . . . . . . .95 E7
Ladysmith Ave BL9 . . . . . .32 A5
Ladysmith Rd PR2 . . . . . . .116 C2
Ladywell St FY1 . . . . .95 E8
Lafford La WN8 . . . . .19 C2
Lagonda Dr FY4 . . . . .110 F6
Lagonda Way FY4 . . . . . . .110 F6

Laidley's Wlk FY7 . . . . . . .193 E5
Lairgill Row ⅛ LA2 . . . . . . .233 D8
Laister Ct ⅔ LA2 . . . . .213 A6
Laithbutts La LA6 . . . . .216 F5
Laithe St Burnley BB11 . . . .126 F4
  Colne BB8 . . . . .169 C4
Lake Ave LA1 . . . . .212 C4
Lake Gr LA4 . . . . .212 C4
Lake Point FY8 . . . . .89 D3
Lake Rd
  Lytham St Anne's FY8 . . . .89 C4
  Morecambe LA3 . . . . .212 C3
Lake Rd N FY8 . . . . .89 C4
Lake Side Cotts WN1 . . . . .29 C1
Lake View BL7 . . . . .45 C5
Lake View Rd BB8 . . . . . . .169 D7
Lakeber Ave LA2 . . . . .233 D8
Lakeber Cl LA2 . . . . .233 D8
Lakeber Dr ⅟⅘ LA2 . . . . . . .233 D8
Lakeland Cl Billington BB7 143 A3
  Forton PR3 . . . . .204 B3
Lakeland Gdns PR7 . . . . . .42 A5
Lakeland Way BB12 . . . . . .126 B8
Lakes Dr WN5 . . . . .10 E6
Lakeside Ave WN5 . . . . . . .10 E3
Lakeview Ct PR9 . . . . .34 B4
Lakeway FY3 . . . . .129 F6
Lakewood Ave FY5 . . . . . . .172 D1
Lamaleach Dr PR4 . . . . . . .92 A6
Lamb Row BB7 . . . . .144 E7
Lamb's La PR3 . . . . .196 A4
Lambert Ct PR2 . . . . .117 E3
  Lancaster LA1 . . . . .213 E3
Lambert St BB8 . . . . .170 C2
Lambeth Cl Blackburn BB1 101 A4
  Horwich BL6 . . . . .31 D1
Lambeth Ct PR2 . . . . .116 E5
Lambeth St Blackburn BB1 101 A4
  Blackburn BB1 . . . . .101 B4
  Colne BB8 . . . . .170 B5
Lambing Clough La BB7 . . .141 E7
Lambourne PR4 . . . . .18 A4
Lambridge Cl LA4 . . . . .212 E3
Lambs Hill Cl ⅔ FY5 . . . . . .173 D1
Lambs Rd FY5 . . . . .151 D8
Lambshear La L31 . . . . . . .5 C4
Lambton Gates BB4 . . . . . .85 C2
Lamlash Rd BB1 . . . . .101 C4
Lammack Prim Sch BB1 . . .121 C1
Lammack Rd
  Blackburn BB1 . . . . .100 C8
  Blackburn BB1 . . . . .100 B8
Lamour FY1 . . . . .193 D3
Lanark Ave FY2 . . . . .150 C6
Lanark Cl OL10 . . . . .32 F1
Lanark St BB11 . . . . .126 D1
Lancambe Dr LA1 . . . . . . .213 C2
Lancashire Coll PR4 . . . . . .42 A8
Lancashire Constabulary
  HQ PR4 . . . . .94 C1
Lancashire Rd PR5 . . . . . . .76 A4
Lancashire St LA4 . . . . . . .212 B4
Lancaster & Lakeland
  Nuffield Hospl The LA1 . . .211 A7
Lancaster & Morecambe
  Coll LA1 . . . . .213 B3
Lancaster & Morecambe
  Coll (Annexe) LA4 . . . . . . .212 E5
Lancaster Ave
  Accrington BB5 . . . . .103 B7
  Clayton-le-W PR5 . . . . . . .76 E1
  Great Eccleston PR3 . . . . .154 C5
  Haslingden BB4 . . . . .67 B8
  Horwich BL6 . . . . .31 D1
  Lytham St Anne's FY8 . . . .88 F4
  Ramsbottom BL0 . . . . . . .49 A4
  Thornton FY5 . . . . .173 C2
Lancaster Castle LA1 . . . . .210 E8
Lancaster Cl Adlington PR6 .30 D7
  Great Eccleston PR3 . . . . .154 C5
  Knott End-on-S FY6 . . . . . .194 F5
  Maghull L31 . . . . .5 F1
  Southport PR8 . . . . .33 F4
Lancaster Cres WN8 . . . . .17 E1
Lancaster Ct PR7 . . . . .60 C2
Lancaster Dr Banks PR9 . . .53 F5
  Brinscall PR6 . . . . .61 E8
  Clayton-le-M BB5 . . . . . . .124 A3
  Clitheroe BB7 . . . . .164 C7
  Padiham BB12 . . . . .125 D6
Lancaster Gate
  Banks PR9 . . . . .53 F5
  Fleetwood FY7 . . . . .193 D4
  ⅟⅘ Lancaster LA1 . . . . . . .210 F8
  Nelson BB9 . . . . .147 D7
Lancaster Gdns PR8 . . . . . .33 E4
Lancaster
  Girls' Gram Sch LA1 . . . . .210 E7
  Lancaster Ho ⅔⅘ PR1 . . . .96 A7
Lancaster L PR1 . . . . .211 B6
Lancaster La
  Clayton-le-W PR5 . . . . . . .76 E2
  Parbold WN8 . . . . .26 C3
Lancaster Lane Prim Sch
  PR5 . . . . .76 D1
Lancaster Maritime Mus
  LA1 . . . . .213 E2
Lancaster Moor Hospl
  LA1 . . . . .211 D8
Lancaster Pl Adlington PR6 .30 D7
  Blackburn BB2 . . . . .100 B5
Lancaster Rd
  Blackpool FY3 . . . . .130 A3
  Carnforth LA5 . . . . .216 B7
  Caton LA2 . . . . .231 B3
  Cockerham LA2 . . . . .203 C6
  Fisher's Row PR3 . . . . . . .196 E5

Lancaster Rd continued
  Formby L37 . . . . .11 E1
  Garstang PR3 . . . . .199 C1
  Hornby LA2 . . . . .232 D2
  Knott End-on-S FY6 . . . . .194 F5
  Lancaster LA3 . . . . .209 D1
  Lancaster, Slyne LA2 . . . .213 F6
  Morecambe LA4 . . . . .212 F5
  Morecambe,
    Torrisholme LA4 . . . . . . .213 B4
  Moss Edge PR3 . . . . .175 E6
  Preesall PR3 . . . . .195 C3
  Preston PR1 . . . . .95 F8
  Preston PR1 . . . . .96 A8
  Ratten Row PR3 . . . . .154 A8
  Southport PR8 . . . . .33 E4
Lancaster Rd N PR1 . . . . . .116 F1
Lancaster Road
  Prim Sch LA4 . . . . .212 G4
Lancaster
  Royal Gram Sch LA1 . . . .211 A8
Lancaster
  Royal Gram Sch LA1 . . . .211 B7
Lancaster St
  Blackburn BB2 . . . . .100 C4
  Colne BB8 . . . . .169 D5
  Coppull PR7 . . . . .41 F1
  Oswaldtwistle BB5 . . . . . .102 C3
Lancaster Way ⅟⅘ PR1 . . . .96 A8
Lancastergate PR5 . . . . . . .58 F8
Lanchester Gdns BB6 . . . . .142 C6
Lancia Cres FY4 . . . . .111 A6
Lancing Pl BB2 . . . . .100 C3
Land End L31 . . . . .6 C1
Land Gate OL12 . . . . .70 F5
Land La New Longton PR4 . .74 D5
  Southport PR9 . . . . .53 D4
Landcrest Cl PR4 . . . . .113 B2
Landless St BB9 . . . . .147 A5
Landing La BB7 . . . . .223 F4
Landseer Ave FY2 . . . . . . .150 C4
Landseer Cl BB11 . . . . .126 E3
Landseer Pl PR1 . . . . .117 C1
Landsmoor Dr PR4 . . . . . . .94 A1
Lane Bottom BB18 . . . . . . .191 B8
Lane End La OL13 . . . . . . .87 A1
Lane End Rd OL13 . . . . . . .70 A8
Lane Ends Brierfield BB9 . . .147 B6
  Dunsop Bridge BB7 . . . . . .222 C5
  Longridge PR3 . . . . .139 F8
  Rivington PR6 . . . . .43 D4
Lane Ends Ct ⅔ FY4 . . . . . .129 E1
Lane Foot Brow LA2 . . . . . .233 D4
Lane Head LA2 . . . . .232 D6
Lane Head La OL13 . . . . . .86 F3
Lane House BB8 . . . . .170 C1
Lane House Cl BB2 . . . . . . .80 B8
Lane Side OL13 . . . . .87 A4
Lane The LA3 . . . . .205 A5
Lane Top Colne BB8 . . . . . .170 C5
  Fence BB12 . . . . .146 D7
Lanedale PR4 . . . . .74 A8
Lanefield Dr FY5 . . . . .172 C4
Laneshaw Cl BB3 . . . . .80 E4
Laneshawbridge
  Prim Sch LA4 . . . . .170 E6
Laneside Altham BB5 . . . . .124 D6
  Great Harwood BB6 . . . . .123 A6
Laneside Ave
  Accrington BB5 . . . . .103 B8
  Higham BB12 . . . . .145 F6
Laneside Ho ⅘ BB4 . . . . . .84 B2
Laneside Rd BB4 . . . . .84 C1
Lang St Accrington BB5 . . . .103 A6
  Blackpool FY1 . . . . .129 C6
Lang Woods BB6 . . . . .142 C5
Langber End La LA6 . . . . . .236 F1
Langcliffe Rd PR2 . . . . .117 E4
Langdale Cl
  Clitheroe BB7 . . . . .164 C7
  Croston PR5 . . . . .57 B3
  Formby L37 . . . . .11 D2
  Hesketh Bank PR4 . . . . . .72 C4
  Rawtenstall BB4 . . . . .84 C2
Langdale Cl
  ⅔ Accrington BB5 . . . . . . .124 D1
  Bamber Bridge PR5 . . . . . .96 D1
  Blackburn BB2 . . . . .79 E8
  Formby L37 . . . . .11 D2
  Freckleton PR4 . . . . .92 A6
  Thornton FY5 . . . . .173 C2
Langdale Cres PR7 . . . . . . .117 E3
Langdale Crest LA7 . . . . . .237 E5
Langdale Ct
  ⅔ Fleetwood FY7 . . . . . . .193 E2
  Garstang PR3 . . . . .178 B7
  Penwortham PR1 . . . . .95 D8
Langdale Dr Burscough L40 .24 E4
  Maghull L31 . . . . .5 E2
Langdale Gdns PR8 . . . . . .33 F1
Langdale Gr PR6 . . . . .60 B7
Langdale Pl
  ⅟ Blackpool FY4 . . . . .130 C1
  Lancaster LA1 . . . . .214 A2
Langdale Rd
  Blackburn BB2 . . . . .79 E8
  Blackpool FY3 . . . . .130 C1
  Carnforth LA5 . . . . .216 D8
  Fulwood PR2 . . . . .117 E3
  Lancaster LA1 . . . . .214 A2
  Leyland PR5 . . . . .59 B6
  Longridge PR3 . . . . .138 F5
  Lytham St Anne's FY8 . . . .109 D1
  Morecambe LA4 . . . . .212 G5
  Padiham BB12 . . . . .145 C2
Langdale Rise BB8 . . . . . . .169 F6

Langden Brook Mews
  LA3 . . . . .213 A3
Langden Brook Sq BB1 . . . .101 A3
Langden Cres PR5 . . . . .76 F8
Langden Dr PR2 . . . . .118 A3
Langden Fold PR2 . . . . . . .138 D1
Langdon Way FY2 . . . . . . .150 E2
Langfield BB10 . . . . .128 B6
Langfield Ave FY4 . . . . . . .109 C5
Langfield Cl PR2 . . . . .116 E1
Langford St BB5 . . . . .103 C1
Langham Ave BB5 . . . . . . .103 B8
Langham Rd
  Blackburn BB1 . . . . .100 D7
  Standish WN6 . . . . .28 D1
Langham St BB12 . . . . .126 B6
Langho St BB2 . . . . .100 C1
Langho Sta BB6 . . . . .142 C1
Langholm Cl ⅔ PR5 . . . . . . .75 C1
Langholme Cl BB9 . . . . . . .168 C1
Langholme Rd PR1 . . . . . . .95 B4
Langholme Way BB9 . . . . . .147 E6
Langley Cl Hightown L38 . . .2 C1
  Standish WN6 . . . . .28 E2
Langley Ct L40 . . . . .24 E4
Langley La Goosnargh PR3 136 F6
  Inglewhite PR3 . . . . .158 B2
Langley Pl L40 . . . . .24 E4
Langley Rd Burscough L40 . .24 E4
  Lancaster LA1 . . . . .211 A7
Langport Cl PR2 . . . . .116 E5
Langridge Way LA4 . . . . . .212 E3
Langroyd Rd BB8 . . . . .169 E6
Langshaw Dr BB7 . . . . . . .164 F6
Langshaw La LA2 . . . . .207 D5
Langstone Cl BL6 . . . . .31 B3
Langthwaite Rd LA1,LA2 . . .211 C5
Langton Ave WN6 . . . . .28 E1
Langton Brow
  Eccleston PR7 . . . . .40 D5
  Longridge PR3 . . . . .139 B7
Langton Cl Eccleston PR7 . .40 D5
  Lancaster LA1 . . . . .214 A4
  Leyland PR5 . . . . .58 C8
Langton Pl WN6 . . . . .28 E1
Langton Rd PR4 . . . . .113 A5
Langton St PR1 . . . . .95 D7
Langtree WN8 . . . . .18 B3
Langtree La Elswick PR4 . . .153 F2
  Standish WN6 . . . . .28 D3
Langwood FY7 . . . . .193 E2
Langwood La WA11 . . . . . .9 C1
Langworth Rd BB10 . . . . . .127 E5
Lansborough Cl PR5 . . . . . .58 B8
Lansbury Pl ⅟ BB9 . . . . . . .168 F4
Lansdown Hill PR2 . . . . . . .116 C7
Lansdown Rd PR4 . . . . . . .113 A7
Lansdown Cl BB11 . . . . . . .126 F4
Lansdowne Gr LA4 . . . . . . .213 A7
Lansdowne Pl ⅟ FY1 . . . . . .129 B6
Lansdowne Rd
  Burnley BB11 . . . . .126 E4
  Lytham St Anne's FY8 . . . .89 D5
  Morecambe LA4 . . . . .213 A7
  Southport PR8 . . . . .34 C6
Lansdowne St BB2 . . . . . . .100 B3
Lansil Ind Est LA1 . . . . . . .214 A3
Lansil Way LA1 . . . . .214 A3
Lanterns The FY4 . . . . . . .151 D4
Lapford Cres L33 . . . . .1 A4
Lapford Wlk L33 . . . . .1 A4
Lappet Gr PR4 . . . . .115 E5
Lapwings The FY6 . . . . . . .151 B2
Larbreck Ave PR4 . . . . .154 A1
Larbreck Rd FY3 . . . . .129 E7
Larch Ave Chorley PR6 . . . .60 E2
  Oswaldtwistle BB5 . . . . . .102 F3
Larch Cl Blackburn BB2 . . . .79 F8
  Freckleton PR4 . . . . .92 A5
  Knott End-on-S FY6 . . . . . .195 A5
  Rawtenstall BB4 . . . . .67 B8
  Skelmersdale WN8 . . . . . .17 E1
Larch Dr PR6 . . . . .61 F7
Larch Gate PR5 . . . . .97 E2
Larch Gr Bamber Bridge PR5 96 F1
  Garstang PR3 . . . . .178 C3
  Lancaster LA1 . . . . .210 D8
Larch St Blackburn BB1 . . . .101 A7
  Burnley BB12 . . . . .126 C7
  Bury BL9 . . . . .32 A7
  Nelson BB9 . . . . .147 F8
  Southport PR8 . . . . .34 E6
Larch Way L37 . . . . .11 D4
Larches Ave PR2 . . . . .115 F1
Larches La PR2 . . . . .115 E1
Larches The BB1 . . . . .100 F7
Larchgate PR2 . . . . .117 C7
Larchway PR3 . . . . .139 B8
Larchwood Lancaster LA1 . .211 B4
  Penwortham PR1 . . . . .95 B4
  Preston PR2 . . . . .115 E1
Larchwood Cl FY8 . . . . .89 E4
Larchwood Cres PR5 . . . . . .75 E1
Largs Rd BB1 . . . . .101 C3
Lark Ave ⅔ PR1 . . . . .95 E4
Lark Hill Blackburn BB1 . . . .100 F6
  Higher Walton PR5 . . . . . .97 B3
  Rawtenstall BB4 . . . . .85 A3
Lark Hill Pl OL12 . . . . .70 E6
Lark Hill ⅘ Burnley BB12 . . .126 C7
  Colne BB8 . . . . .169 E6
  Darwen BB3 . . . . .64 B5

Larkfield PR7 ....40 B6
Larkfield Cl BL8 ....48 F1
Larkfield Ct PR9 ......53 A3
Larkfield PR9 ....53 A3
Larkfield Prim Sch PR9 .53 A3
Larkhill
 Brockhall Village BB6 ...142 C5
 Skelmersdale WN8 .....18 B4
Larkhill Ave BB10 .....147 C5
Larkhill Gr L38 ....2 F3
Larkhill La L37 ....11 C4
Larkhill Rd PR1 ....96 B7
Larkhill St Blackpool FY1 .129 C6
 Preston PR1 ....96 B7
Larkholme Ave FY7 ....193 E1
Larkholme
 Cty Prim Sch FY7 .....172 D8
Larkholme La FY7 .....193 E1
Larkholme Par FY7 ....193 D1
Larkspur Cl
 Blackburn BB2 ....79 D8
 3 Blackpool FY3 ......34 D6
Last Drop Village The BL7 .47 A1
Latham Ave
 8 Blackpool FY3 ......129 E3
 Ormskirk L39 ....16 A5
Latham Cres PR4 ......56 A6
Latham Rd BL6 ....30 C3
Latham St Burnley BB10 .147 B1
 Preston PR1 ....96 A6
Lathom Ave
 Morecambe LA4 ....212 G4
 Parbold WN8 ....26 B3
Lathom Cl L40 ....24 E4
Lathom Dr L31 ....5 E3
Lathom Gr LA4 ....212 G4
Lathom High Sch WN8 .17 F3
Lathom La L40 ....16 C7
Lathom Rd Bickerstaffe L39 .7 F8
 Southport PR9 ....52 C1
Lathom St 8 BL9 .....32 A4
Lathom St James CE Sch
 L40 ....16 E4
Lathom Way PR3 ......178 D6
Latimer Cl 2 WN5 .....10 F7
Latimer Dr PR4 ....74 F7
Lauderdale Ave FY5 ...172 D1
Lauderdale Cres 1 PR2 .117 F4
Lauderdale Rd PR2 ....117 F4
Lauderdale St PR1 .....95 E6
Laund Gate BB12 ......146 D8
Laund Gr BB5 ....103 D3
Laund Hey View BB4 ....84 B1
Laund La Haslingden BB4 .84 C3
 Ollerton Fold PR6 ......78 E4
Laund Rd BB5 ....103 D3
Laund St BB4 ....84 F4
Laund The PR5 ....75 A1
Laundry Rd N FY4 .....110 A5
Laura St BL0 ....49 C2
Laurel Ave Blackpool FY1 .129 C6
 Burscough Bridge L40 ..24 E6
 Darwen BB3 ....81 B2
 Euxton PR7 ....59 B3
 Fleetwood FY7 ....172 F8
 Lytham St Anne's FY8 ..90 B5
Laurel Bank LA1 ......210 D7
Laurel Bank Ave PR2 ..116 C3
Laurel Dr
 Skelmersdale WN8 .....17 E2
 Thornton FY5 ....151 B8
Laurel Gr PR8 ....34 E7
Laurel St 4 Bacup OL13 .86 F3
 Burnley BB11 ....127 B4
 3 Burnley BL9 ....32 B2
 10 Preston PR1 ......96 A7
Laurels The PR7 ......41 F3
Laureston Ave LA4 ....208 F6
Laurie Pl 2 OL12 .....51 F1
Laurier Ave 3 FY4 ....109 C6
Laurier Rd BB10 ......147 B2
Lauriston Cl 4 FY4 ....110 A6
Lavender Cl PR2 ......117 C6
Lavender Gr PR7 ......42 C5
Lavender Hill BB4 .....67 F8
Laverick Rd LA2 ......231 A5
Laverton Cl OL10 .....32 E1
Laverton Rd PR4 ......89 A4
Law St Cornholme OL14 .108 B1
 Newchurch BB4 ....85 F1
Lawley Rd PR2 ....100 A5
Lawn Ct 2 FY1 ....129 D4
Lawn St BB10 ....127 A8
Lawn Tennis Ct FY4 ...109 D5
Lawns Ave WN5 ......10 C5
Lawns The PR9 ....52 F2
Lawnswood Ave
 Lancaster LA1 ....211 A3
 Poulton-le-F FY6 ......151 C2
Lawnswood Cres PR3 ..130 C2
Lawnswood Dr LA3 ....212 F2
Lawnwood Ave PR7 ....42 A5
Lawrence Ave
 Bamber Bridge PR5 ....96 D2
 Burnley BB11 ....126 C4
 Burnley BB11 ....126 C5
 Lytham St Anne's FY8 ..89 A6
 Preston PR1 ....96 B5
 Simonstone BB12 .....144 E2
Lawrence Cl OL12 .....51 A1
Lawrence Ct LA5 ......237 A1
Lawrence La PR7 ......40 C7
Lawrence Rd Chorley PR7 .42 B7
 Penwortham PR1 ......95 E1
Lawrence Row FY7 ....194 A4

Lawrence St
 Blackburn BB2 ....100 C4
 12 Blackpool FY4 .....129 B1
 Fulwood PR2 ....116 D3
 Padiham BB12 ....145 D1
 Whitewell Bottom BB4 ..85 F4
Lawrie Ave BL0 ....49 B5
Lawson Cl LA1 ....210 F3
Lawson Gdns LA2 .....213 E8
Lawson Pl LA2 ....213 E8
Lawson Rd Blackpool FY3 .130 A3
 Horwich BL6 ....31 C4
 Lytham St Anne's FY8 ..110 A3
Lawson St 3 Chorley PR6 .42 E7
 Preston PR1 ....95 F8
 Rawtenstall BB4 ......85 A8
 Southport PR9 ....35 A7
Lawsons Ct 4 FY5 ....173 C1
Lawsons Rd FY5 ......173 C2
Lawswood Formby L37 .11 E5
 6 Thornton FY5 ......173 C1
Lawton Cl PR6 ....78 B1
Laxey Gr PR1 ....117 D3
Laxey Rd BB2 ....100 E1
Laycock Gate LA2 .....129 D6
Layton Cty Prim Sch FY3 .129 E4
Layton Rd Blackpool FY3 .129 E6
 Preston PR2 ....115 E1
Layton Sta FY2 ....150 E1
Lazenby Ave FY7 .....193 C2
Lea Bank BB4 ....85 D2
Lea Cres L39 ....15 F7
Lea Ct L39 ....15 E7
Lea Cty Prim Sch PR2 ..115 D1
Lea Dr BB2 ....80 E6
Lea Endowed
 CE Prim Sch PR4 .....115 C4
Lea La
 Claughton, Lancaster LA2 .231 F8
 Heysham LA3 ....208 E6
 Lea Town PR4 ....115 B5
Lea Mount Dr BL9 ....32 D4
Lea Rd Lucas Green PR6 ..60 C5
 Preston PR2,PR4 .....115 D3
Lea Way Cl FY5 ....151 D7
Leach Cres FY8 ......109 F2
Leach La FY8 ....109 E1
Leach Pl PR5 ....77 B8
Leach St Blackburn BB2 .100 E2
 Colne BB8 ....169 C4
Leaches Rd BL0 ......49 D8
Leachfield Cl 2 LA2 ...207 A4
Leachfield Ind Est PR3 .199 B1
Leachfield Rd LA2 ....206 F4
Leacroft BB3 ....81 A6
Lead Mines Clough PR6 .44 A7
Leadale PR2 ....115 D2
Leadale Cl WN6 ......28 D1
Leadale Gn PR5 ......75 E1
Leadale Rd PR5 ......75 E1
Leaford Ave FY3 .....129 E8
Leafy Cl PR5 ....59 B7
Leagram Cres PR4 ....118 A3
Leamington Ave
 Baldingstone BL9 .....49 E1
 Burnley BB10 ....147 C1
 Southport PR8 ....20 D5
Leamington Rd
 Blackburn BB2 ....100 B6
 Blackpool FY1 ....129 C6
 Lytham St Anne's FY8 ..88 F6
 Morecambe LA4 ....212 G3
 Southport PR8 ....20 D5
Leamington St BB9 ...147 E7
Leander Ave FY6 .....151 D2
Leapers View LA6 ....231 B8
Leaside Cl OL12 ......51 D2
Leathercote PR3 ......178 C6
Leathwood L31 ....5 E1
Leavengreave Ct OL12 .70 D4
Leaver St BB12 ....126 A5
Leaverholme Cl BB10 .107 A7
Leavesley Rd FY1 ....129 D8
Lebanon St BB10 .....127 C5
Leck CE Prim Sch LA6 ..236 B7
Leck Ho 11 LA1 ......211 A3
Leckhampton Rd FY1 ..129 B8
Leckonby St PR3 .....154 B5
Ledbury Rd FY3 ......130 B7
Ledbury WN8 ....18 B3
Ledson Gr L39 ....6 B7
Lee Brook Cl BB4 .....85 A4
Lee Gr BB10 ....127 F4
Lee Green St 3 BB10 ..127 A8
Lee La Bispham Green L40 .26 C7
 Great Harwood BB1 ...123 B3
 Horwich BL6 ....31 B4
 Whittlestone Head BL7 .65 B2
Lee Rd Bacup OL13 ...69 E8
 Blackpool FY4 ....110 B8
 Nelson BB9 ....168 F2
Lee St Accrington BB5 ..103 C6
 Bacup OL13 ....86 F2
 Barrowford BB9 ......168 D3
 Longridge PR3 ....139 A7
 Rawtenstall BB4 ......85 A4
Lee View OL13 ....87 B1
Lee's St OL13 ....70 C8
Leebrook Rd BB4 .....84 F4
Leeds Cl 15 BB1 .....101 A4
Leeds Rd Blackpool FY1 .129 D5
 2 Nelson BB9 ....147 B8
 Nelson BB9 ....168 F1
Leehouse Dr FY6 .....130 D8
Leek St PR1 ....96 E8
Leeming La LA6 ......236 C3
Lees Cotts BL7 ....47 C2

Lees Ct LA3 ....208 E7
Lees La WN8 ....18 E7
Lees Rd Adlington PR6 ..30 B8
 Kirkby L33 ....1 B2
Lees The BB10 ....107 A7
Leeson Ave PR7 ......41 D4
Leeswood WN8 ......18 E3
Leet Rd BB12 ....145 F5
Leeward Cl BB3 ......80 F6
Leeward Rd PR2 .....94 B3
Legh La PR4 ....55 B4
Leicester Ave
 Cleveleys FY5 ....172 E3
 Garstang PR3 ....178 B7
 Horwich BL6 ....31 A3
Leicester Gate FY5 ...172 E3
Leicester Lodge 3
 PR2 ....117 F4
Leicester Rd
 Blackburn BB1 ....101 C5
 Blackpool FY1 ....129 D5
 Preston PR1 ....117 A1
Leicester St PR9 .....34 B8
Leigh Brow PR6 ......96 B2
Leigh Pk BB11 ....125 C3
Leigh Row PR7 ....42 C7
Leigh St PR7 ....42 C7
Leighton Ave
 Fleetwood FY7 ....193 D3
 Maghull L31 ....5 D2
Leighton Ct LA4 ......212 D3
Leighton Dr LA1 ......210 D7
Leighton Hall LA5 ....219 C1
Leighton Moss
 (Nature Reserve) LA5 .219 A3
Leighton St PR1 ......95 E8
Leinster Rd LA1 ......211 A5
Leith Ave FY5 ....172 A2
Lemon Tree Ct FY8 ...109 B4
Lemonius St BB5 .....103 C4
Lench Rd BB4 ....68 F8
Lench St BB4 ....68 F8
Lenches Fold BB8 ....169 D4
Lenches Rd BB8 .....169 D3
Lendel Cl L37 ....11 E3
Lennon St 3 PR7 .....42 C7
Lennox Ct FY4 ....109 D6
Lennox Gate FY4 .....109 D7
Lennox Rd OL14 .....108 A1
Lennox St 19 Preston PR1 .96 A7
 Worsthorne BB10 ....128 A6
Lennox Wlk OL10 ....32 F1
Lenton Ave L37 ......11 D4
Lentworth Ave FY2 ...150 D5
Lentworth Dr PR1 ....211 A4
Lentworth Ho 5 LA1 ..211 A3
Leonard St
 Barnoldswick BB18 ...200 B2
 Nelson BB9 ....147 E7
Leonard Terr BB3 .....81 E3
Leopold Gr FY1 ......129 B5
Leopold Rd BB2 ......100 B6
Leopold St BB8 ......169 B4
Leopold Way BB2 ....81 A8
Lesley Rd PR8 ....34 A7
Leslie Ave Caton LA2 ..231 C3
 Thornton FY5 ....173 C2
Letchworth Dr PR7 ...42 B6
Letchworth Pl 2 PR7 ..42 B6
Letcliffe Ctry Pk BB18 .191 B8
Lethbridge Rd PR8 ...34 D5
Letitia St BL6 ....31 A3
Levant St BB12 ......125 C7
Leven Ave FY7 ....193 D3
Leven Gr BB3 ....80 E4
Leven St BB11 ....127 B4
Levens Cl Banks PR9 ..54 A5
 Blackburn BB2 ....80 F8
 Lancaster LA1 ....210 D7
 Poulton-le-F FY6 .....130 E8
Levens Ct LA3 ....212 B2
Levens Dr
 Clayton-le-W PR5 .....76 D2
 Morecambe LA3 ......212 B2
 Poulton-le-F FY6 .....151 D1
Levens Gr FY1 ....129 D3
Levens St 12 PR1 ....117 D1
Levens Way LA5 .....218 C3
Levensgarth Ave PR2 ..116 F8
Lever House La PR5 ..76 C2
Lever Park Ave BB5 ...31 B5
Lever Park Sch BL6 ...31 C3
Lever St Blackpool FY3 .129 E4
 Ramsbottom BL0 .....49 C6
 Rawtenstall BB4 ......85 A8
Leverhouse Prim Sch PR5 .76 C3
Levine Ave FY4 ......130 A1
Lewis Cl PR7 ....29 E6
Lewis Dr OL10 ....32 F1
Lewis St BB6 ....123 D5
Lewis Textile Mus BB1 .100 E5
Lewtas St FY1 ....129 B6
Lewth La PR4 ....135 B5
Lex St PR1 ....96 C8
Lexton Dr PR9 ....53 B3
Ley Ct LA1 ....210 D8
Ley St BB5 ....103 E2
Leybourne Ave PR8 ..20 F7
Leyburn Ave
 Blackpool FY2 ....150 C5
 Fleetwood FY7 ....172 F8
 Fulwood PR2 ....116 C8
Leyburn Cl Accrington BB5 .103 E5
Leyburn Rd Blackburn BB2 .80 C7
 Lancaster LA1 ....213 F3
Leycester Dr LA1 .....213 C3
Leyfield PR1 ....95 E2

Leyfield Cl FY3 ....151 A1
Leyfield Ct LA6 ......238 C1
Leyfield Rd PR5 ......58 F8
 Trawden BB8 ....170 B3
Leyland Cl Southport PR9 .53 E5
Leyland Golf Course PR5 .59 D8
Leyland La Leyland PR5 ..58 D7
 Leyland PR5 ....75 D2
 Runshaw Moor PR5,PR7 .58 B8
Leyland Meth Inf Sch PR5 76 B1
Leyland
 Meth Jun Sch PR5 ....76 B1
Leyland Rd Burnley BB11 .127 B6
 Penwortham PR1 .....95 E3
 Southport PR9 ....52 C1
Leyland St BB5 ....102 F5
Leyland Sta PR5 .....76 B2
Leyland Warden
 High Sch PR5 ....75 E1
 Ormskirk L39 ....15 F5
Leyland Way Leyland PR5 .76 C1
Leylands The FY8 ....89 F2
Leys Cl Elswick PR4 ..154 A1
 Wiswell BB7 ....143 F8
Leys Rd FY2 ....150 D1
Leyster St LA4 ....212 F5
Leyton Ave PR5 ......58 D7
Leyton St OL12 ......51 F1
Libby La PR3 ....196 C6
Library Mews FY4 ....109 E7
Library Rd PR6 ....77 B4
Library St Chorley PR7 ..42 C7
 Church BB5 ....102 E6
 16 Preston PR1 ......96 A7
Lichen Cl PR7 ....41 D4
Lichfield Ave LA4 ....212 G6
Lichfield Rd Blackpool FY3 129 C8
 Chorley PR7 ....42 C6
 Preston PR2 ....115 C1
Liddesdale Rd BB9 ...169 B2
Liddington Cl BB2 ....81 A8
Liddington Hall Dr BL0 .49 B4
Lidget Ave PR2 ......115 C1
Lidum Park Ind Est FY8 ..90 E5
Liege Rd 5 PR5 ......59 A8
Lifeboat Pl 18 FY7 ...194 B5
Lifeboat Rd L37 ......11 B1
Lifton Rd L33 ....1 A2
Lightbown Ave FY3 ...129 E3
Lightbown Cotts BB3 ..80 E2
Lightbown St BB3 ....81 A3
Lightburne Ave FY8 ...88 F5
Lightfoot Cl PR2 .....116 D8
Lightfoot Green La PR4 .116 B8
Lightfoot La PR2,PR4 .116 B8
Lighthorne Dr PR8 ...20 A4
Lighthouse Cl 4 FY7 ..194 B5
Lighthurst Ave PR7 ...42 C6
Lighthurst La PR7 ....42 D5
Lightwood Ave
 2 Blackpool FY3 .....129 C1
 Lytham St Anne's FY8 ..89 D3
Lilac Ave 1 Blackpool FY1 .129 D2
 Haslingden BB4 ......84 B3
 Lytham St Anne's FY8 ..90 B5
 Penwortham PR1 .....95 F2
 Southport PR8 ....20 D2
Lilac Cl PR4 ....91 D5
Lilac Cres PR4 ....133 F4
Lilac Gr Abbey Village PR6 .79 C7
 Clitheroe BB7 ....164 C7
 Darwen BB3 ....81 B3
 Fulwood PR1 ....117 C3
 Skelmersdale WN8 ....17 E1
Lilac Rd BB1 ....101 A8
Lilac St BB8 ....169 F6
Lilac Terr 2 OL13 ....69 D8
Lilburn Cl BL0 ....49 C4
Lilford Cl PR4 ....56 A5
Lilford Rd BB1 ....100 D6
Lily Gr Fulwood PR1 ..117 C3
 Lancaster LA1 ....211 A3
Lily St 18 Bacup OL13 ..86 F2
 Blackpool FY1 ....129 C5
 Darwen BB3 ....81 B1
 Nelson BB9 ....147 F6
Lima Rd FY8 ....89 B6
Lima St BL9 ....32 B3
Limbrick 21 Blackburn BB1 100 E5
 Blackburn BB1 ......100 E6
Limbrick Rd PR6 .....42 E7
Lime Ave Galgate LA2 ..207 A4
 Kirkham PR4 ....113 B4
 Oswaldtwistle BB5 ....102 D2
Lime Chase PR2 .....116 C8
Lime Cl PR1 ....95 B4
Lime Ct WN8 ....17 E1
Lime Gr Blackpool FY2 ..150 E2
 Chorley PR7 ....42 C5
 Garstang PR3 ....178 C8
 Lancaster LA1 ....210 D8
 Longridge PR3 ....139 A8
 Lytham St Anne's FY8 ..88 D8
 Poulton-le-F FY6 .....151 E2
 Preston PR2 ....115 F2
 Ramsbottom BL0 .....49 D7
 Skelmersdale WN8 ....17 E1
 Thornton FY5 ....173 C1
Lime Rd Accrington BB5 .103 C7
 Haslingden BB4 ......84 C3
Lime St Blackburn BB1 ..100 E6
 Clitheroe BB7 ....186 F1
 Colne BB8 ....169 C6
 Great Harwood BB6 ...123 C6
 Nelson BB9 ....147 C8
 Southport PR8 ....34 E6
Lime Tree Gr BB4 ....85 A4
Lime Tree Way L37 ...11 C4

Limebrest Ave FY5 ...151 D8
Limechase Cl 9 FY4 ..110 A6
Limefield Ave
 Brierfield BB9 ....147 C6
 Whalley BB7 ....143 C6
Limefield Cl BB2 .....100 B5
Limefield Dr WN8 ....9 E7
Limefield St BB5 .....103 D5
Limerick Rd FY3 .....150 D3
Limers Gate Rochdale OL12 .51 F5
 Sharneyford OL14 ....87 E4
Limers La BB6 ....123 A6
Limes Ave Darwen BB3 ..64 A8
 Euxton PR7 ....59 C4
 Morecambe LA3 ......212 B3
Limestone Trail BB10 ..107 E6
Limewood Cl BB5 ....103 D6
Limey La BB11 ....105 E6
Limont Rd PR8 ......20 D5
Lina St BB5 ....102 F6
Linacre La L37 ....4 B7
Linadale Ave 4 FY5 ..173 B2
Linaker Dr L39 ......14 B8
Linaker Inf Sch PR8 ..34 B5
Linaker Prim Sch PR8 .34 B5
Linaker St PR8 ......34 B5
Linby St BB10 ....127 B5
Lincoln Ave Cleveleys FY5 .172 E3
 Fleetwood FY7 ....193 E3
Lincoln Chase PR2 ...115 C1
Lincoln Cl Blackburn BB1 .101 B4
 Morecambe LA4 .....212 G3
Lincoln Ct Blackpool FY1 .129 C4
 1 Preston PR5 ....103 A7
Lincoln Ho 7 PR1 ....96 B7
Lincoln Pk BB7 ......187 A1
Lincoln Pl BB4 ....84 A3
Lincoln Rd Blackburn BB1 .101 B4
 Blackpool FY1 ....129 C5
 Earby BB18 ....201 B2
 Lancaster LA1 ....210 E7
 Southport PR8 ....34 A1
Lincoln St Burnley BB11 .127 A4
 Cornholme OL14 .....108 B1
 3 Haslingden BB4 ....84 A3
 Preston PR1 ....117 B1
Lincoln Way Clitheroe BB7 187 A2
Lincoln Wlk PR1 .....117 B1
Lindadale Ave BB5 ...103 A4
Lindadale Cl BB5 ....103 A3
Lindale Ave PR2 .....138 E1
Lindale Cl LA5 ....237 B2
Lindale Cres BB10 ...147 A2
Lindale Gdns FY4 ....109 E6
Lindale Rd Fulwood PR2 .117 A4
 Longridge PR3 ....138 F5
Lindbeck Ct FY4 .....110 C8
Lindbeck Rd FY4 ....130 C1
Lindel La FY6 ....195 B2
Lindel Rd FY7 ....193 F2
Linden Ave Blackburn BB1 100 D6
 Cleveleys FY5 ....172 F3
 Orrell WN5 ....10 E6
 Ramsbottom BL0 .....49 D6
Linden Cl
 Bamber Bridge PR5 ...96 B1
 Barrowford BB9 ......168 B1
 Cleveleys FY5 ....172 F2
 Edenfield BL0 ....67 D2
Linden Cres BB3 .....81 C2
Linden Ct 7 Earby BB18 ..201 B1
 Orrell WN5 ....10 E6
Linden Dr
 Bamber Bridge PR5 ...96 B1
 Clitheroe BB7 ....164 F7
Linden Fold PR4 .....154 A1
Linden Gn FY5 ......172 F2
Linden Gr Chorley PR6 ..60 D3
 Fulwood PR2 ....117 E3
 Garstang PR3 ....178 C8
 Orrell WN5 ....10 E6
Linden Lea Blackburn BB2 .79 F8
 Rawtenstall BB4 ......77 F8
Linden Mews FY8 ....109 F2
Linden Pl FY2 ....150 E3
Linden Rd Colne BB8 ..169 D5
 Earby BB18 ....201 B1
Linden St BB10 ......127 B5
Linden Wlk WN5 .....10 E6
Lindens WN8 ....18 B4
Lindeth Cl
 Nether Kellet LA6 ....216 F6
 Silverdale LA5 ....218 C2
Lindeth Gdns 7 LA1 ..213 F3
Lindeth Rd LA5 ......218 C2
Lindholme WN8 ......18 C3
Lindisfarne Ave BB2 ..100 F1
Lindisfarne Cl BB12 ..126 E7
Lindle Ave PR4 ......94 E2
Lindle Cl PR4 ....94 E2
Lindle Cres PR4 .....94 E2
Lindle La PR4 ....95 A2
Lindley Ave WN5 ....10 C5
Lindley Dr WN8 .....26 D1
Lindley St
 Bamber Bridge PR5 ...76 B8
 Blackburn BB2 ....100 B2
Lindon Park Rd BB4 ..67 C7
Lindow Sq LA1 ......210 E7
Lindow St LA1 ....210 F7
Lindred Rd BB9 .....147 B2
Lindsay Ave Blackpool FY3 129 E3
 Leyland PR5 ....76 B1
 Lytham St Anne's FY8 ..89 B6
 Poulton-le-F FY6 .....151 D2
Lindsay Ct Blackpool FY8 .109 B4
 Morecambe LA3 ......212 F2

Lindsay Dr PR7 42 A7
Lindsay Pk BB10 127 F5
Lindsay St Burnley BB11 127 A6
Horwich BL6 31 D1
Lindsey Ho 2 BB5 103 A7
Linedred La BB9 147 B7
Lines St LA4 212 E5
Linfield Terr FY4 109 E6
Lingart La PR3 199 D1
Lingdales L37 12 B5
Lingfield Ave BB7 164 E6
Lingfield Cl LA1 211 B3
Lingfield Ct BB2 79 C8
Lingfield Rd FY7 193 F2
Lingfield Way BB2 79 D8
Linghaw La LA2 233 F8
Lingmoor Dr BB12 126 A8
Lingmoor Rd LA1 214 B1
Lingwell Cl PR6 60 C5
Links Ave PR9 52 F3
Links Dr LA2 233 D8
Links Field PR2 116 C3
Links Gate Fulwood PR2 116 C3
Lytham St Anne's FY8 89 A6
Thornton FY5 151 D7
Links Lodge FY8 89 A6
Links Rd Blackburn BB2 79 C8
Blackpool FY1 129 C8
Kirkby L32 1 A1
Knott End-on-S FY6 194 D5
Lytham St Anne's FY8 88 E5
Penwortham PR1 95 B6
Links The FY5 172 C4
Links View FY8 89 C5
Linkside Ave BB9 148 B8
Linley Gr BL0 49 A2
Linnet Cl FY3 130 B6
Linnet Dr BL9 32 B4
Linnet La FY8 89 E7
Linnet St PR1 117 B2
Linton Ave LA3 212 A1
Linton Dr BB11 126 D3
Linton Gdns BB9 168 C3
Linton Gr PR1 95 B5
Linton St PR2 116 D3
Lion Ct 10 BB5 102 E6
Lion La BL6 30 C2
Lion St BB5 102 E6
Lionel St BB12 126 C6
Lions Ct 1 FY8 90 D4
Liptrott Rd PR7 42 A5
Lisbon Dr Burnley BB11 126 E5
Darwen BB3 81 C1
Lisbon St 17 OL12 51 C1
Lisieux Hall Hospl PR6 60 A7
Lister Gr LA3 208 F8
Lister St Accrington BB5 103 A6
3 Blackburn BB2 100 E3
Lister Well Rd BB18 191 A6
Little Acre Longton PR4 74 A8
Thornton FY5 151 D8
Little Banks Cl PR5 77 B6
Little Brewery La L37 11 F6
Little Carr La PR7 42 D5
Little Cl PR1 95 C3
Little Digmoor Cty Prim Sch WN8 9 B6
Little Fell La LA2 211 E3
Little Fell Rd LA1,LA2 211 F6
Little Flatt OL12 51 B1
Little Hey La L37 12 B4
Little Hoole Cty Prim Sch PR4 74 A5
Little La Banks PR9 54 B7
Longridge PR3 139 A7
Southport PR9 53 B1
Little Meadow La L40 38 D4
Little Moor BB7 164 E6
Little Moor Clough BL7 46 E2
Little Moor View BB7 164 E6
Little Peel St BB2 100 D5
Little Poulton La FY6 151 F4
Little Queen St BB8 169 C4
Little Scotland BL6 30 B2
Little St BB5 103 A6
Little Stones Rd BL7 46 E2
Little Toms La BB10 147 D3
Little Tongues La FY6 195 B4
Little Twining PR4 74 A7
Little Wood FY7 193 E3
Littledale Ave LA3 209 A8
Littledale Mews LA2 214 B6
Littledale Rd Crossgill LA2 231 E1
Littledale LA2 226 C8
Littlemoor Cl BB7 145 A8
Littlemoor Ho BB7 145 A7
Littlemoor Rd BB7 164 E7
Littleton Gr WN6 28 E2
Littondale Gdns BB2 79 D7
Liverpool Ave PR8 20 D5
Liverpool New Rd PR4 73 F5
Liverpool Old Rd
Much Hoole PR4 73 C1
Much Hoole PR4 73 E3
Sollom PR4 56 B2
Southport PR8 20 C1
Walmer Bridge PR4 73 F5
Liverpool Rd Bickerstaffe L39 7 C5
Blackpool FY1 129 D5
Burnley BB12 126 A6
Formby L37 12 A1
Hightown L37 3 A8
Hutton PR1,PR4 94 F3
Longton PR4 73 F7
Maghull L31 5 D4
Much Hoole PR4 73 D2
Ormskirk L39 15 B2
Penwortham PR1 95 B5
Liverpool Rd *continued*
Preston PR1 95 D6
Royal Oak L39 6 F4
Rufford L40 38 C5
Skelmersdale WN8 8 C8
Sollom PR4 56 A3
Southport PR8 20 F8
Liverpool Rd N
Burscough Bridge L40 24 E5
Maghull L31 5 C2
Liverpool Rd S
Burscough L40 24 D2
Maghull L31 5 C1
Livesey Branch Rd BB2 80 D8
Livesey Ct BB2 100 C2
Livesey Fold PR6 79 A1
Livesey Hall Cl BB2 99 E1
Livesey St
11 Lytham St Anne's FY8 90 A3
Padiham BB12 125 C8
Preston PR1 96 B7
Rishton BB1 123 B2
Livesley's La
Great Altcar L37 12 F2
Haskayne L37 13 A2
Livet Ave FY4 109 D7
Livingstone Rd
Accrington BB5 103 B8
Blackburn BB2 100 B4
Blackpool FY1 129 C4
Livingstone St BB9 147 B5
Livingstone Wlk BB9 147 B6
Lloyd Cl Lancaster LA1 213 D1
10 Nelson BB9 147 E8
Lloyd St Darwen BB3 80 F3
Whitworth OL12 70 C1
Lloyd Wlk 9 BB9 147 E8
Lloyd's Ave LA4 212 D4
Lobden Cres OL12 51 D8
Lochinch Cl FY4 110 A6
Lock Gate BB4 84 C1
Lock La PR4 56 B2
Lock St 10 BB5 102 E4
Locka La Arkholme LA6 234 F3
Lancaster LA1 213 F4
Locke Ind Est BL6 31 B3
Lockerbie Ave FY5 150 D8
Lockfield Dr BB18 200 C4
Lockhart Rd PR1 116 F2
Lockhurst Ave FY5 150 F8
Lockside BB2 100 D2
Lockside Rd PR2 94 F8
Lockwood Ave FY6 151 D4
Lockyer Ave BB12 126 B7
Locomotion Ind Est BL6 31 B2
Lodge Bank PR6,PR7 61 F7
Lodge Cl
2 Bamber Bridge PR5 96 F1
Blackpool FY5 150 C7
Freckleton PR4 92 B7
Lodge Ct Blackpool FY5 150 C7
Inskip PR4 155 B1
Staining FY3 130 D5
Lodge La Bacup OL13 86 F1
Clifton PR4 114 D1
Elswick PR4 154 B1
Farington PR5 75 E6
Melling LA2 235 D1
Rainford Junction L39,WA11 8 D1
Singleton FY6 152 D2
Warton FY8 90 F5
Lodge Mill La BL0 68 A1
Lodge Rd Catterall PR3 179 A1
Orrell WN5 10 E4
Lodge St Accrington BB5 103 C7
Lancaster LA1 210 F8
Preston PR1 95 E8
Ramsbottom BL0 49 C6
Shuttleworth BL0 49 E8
Lodge View Farington PR5 75 E7
Longridge PR3 139 A6
Penwortham PR1 95 F3
Lodges Gr 5 LA4 213 A6
Lodgeside BB5 123 F3
Lodgings The PR2 117 C5
Lodore Rd FY4 109 C6
Lofthouse Way FY7 194 A4
Loftos Ave FY4 109 D8
Logwood St BB1 100 F7
Lois Pl BB2 100 C5
Lomas La BB4 67 F8
Lomax St 7 Bury BL9 32 A3
Great Harwood BB6 123 C5
Ramsbottom BL8 48 F1
Rochdale OL12 51 F1
Lomeshaye Bsns Village BB9 147 C8
Lomeshaye Cty Jun Sch BB9 147 C8
Lomeshaye Ind Est BB9 147 B7
Lomeshaye Pl BB9 147 C8
Lomeshaye Rd BB9 147 D7
Lomeshaye Way BB9 147 C8
Lomond Ave Blackpool FY3 129 F2
Lytham St Anne's FY8 89 B5
London La PR8 21 D8
London Rd Blackburn BB1 100 E6
Blackpool FY3 129 D6
Preston PR1 96 C6
London Sq 2 PR8 34 B7
London St Fleetwood FY7 194 B4
Southport PR8, PR9 34 B7
London Terr BB3 81 B2
London Way PR1,PR5 96 C3
London Wlk BB1 100 E6
Londonderry Rd LA3 208 E5
Long Acre PR5 77 C5
Long Acre Cl LA5 216 C8
Long Acre Pl FY8 90 A4
Long Acres Dr OL12 70 D2
Long Barn Brow PR5 98 E2
Long Barn Row PR5 98 E2
Long Bldg BB7 224 A1
Long Butts PR1 95 D2
Long Cl Clitheroe BB7 187 A2
Leyland PR5 58 A8
Long Copse PR7 59 F1
Long Croft Barton PR3 136 B8
Longton PR4 94 A1
Long Croft Mdw PR7 60 B2
Long Cswy BB7 225 B2
Long Cswy The BB10 107 D7
Long Dales La LA6 231 A6
Long Gn BB18 201 C2
Long Hey La BB1,BB3 82 A2
Long Heys or Back La WN8 18 F5
Long Ing La BB18 200 C2
Long La Abbeystead LA2 226 F1
Banks PR9 54 B6
Bickerstaffe L39 7 B7
Darwen BB3 80 A3
Formby L37 11 E4
Laneshaw Bridge BB8 170 D7
Limbrick PR6 43 B4
Low Bentham LA2 233 B7
Maghull L29 4 B1
Oakenclough PR3 220 B1
Ormskirk L39 6 F8
Pleasington BB2 99 B2
Quernmore LA2 226 A5
Skelmersdale WN8 9 E3
Street PR3 220 B5
Long Lane End LA2 207 E7
Long Level LA6 235 F8
Long Lover La BB7 189 C8
Long Marsh La LA1 213 D1
Long Mdw Chorley PR7 42 A5
Colne BB8 170 A5
Kirkham PR4 112 E5
Mellor Brook BB2 120 B2
Much Hoole PR4 73 F4
Long Meanygate PR9 36 C7
Long Moss PR5 58 A8
Long Moss La PR4 75 A6
Long Row Blackburn BB2 121 B2
Calder Vale PR3 179 E8
Long Wham La PR4 74 D1
Longacre Longton PR4 73 F8
Southport PR9 52 F3
Longacres La OL12 70 D2
Longber La LA6 236 B3
Longbrook Ave PR5 96 E1
Longcliffe Dr PR8 20 C4
Longcroft Cotts BL9 49 F1
Longfield Formby L37 12 B5
Fulwood PR2 116 F8
Penwortham PR1 95 B4
Longfield Ave Coppull PR7 41 E2
Poulton-le-F FY6 151 D4
Longfield Ct BB18 200 B1
Longfield Dr LA5 216 C8
Longfield Manor PR7 42 A5
Longfield Pl FY6 151 D4
Longfield Terr BB10 106 E8
Longfold Maghull L31 5 E1
Mere Brow PR4 54 F2
Longford Ave FY2 150 E5
Longford Rd PR8 34 A2
Longhey WN8 18 C4
Longholme Rd 9 BB4 85 A2
Longhouse La FY6 130 D8
Longlands Ave LA3 208 E8
Longlands Cres LA3 208 F8
Longlands La LA3 208 E7
Longlands Rd LA1 213 E3
Longley Cl PR2 116 F8
Longmeadow La
Heysham LA3 209 A7
Thornton FY5 173 C3
Longmeanygate Leyland,
Earnshaw Bridge PR5 75 D2
Leyland, Midge Hall PR5 75 A2
Longmere Cres LA5 216 C8
Longmire Way LA4 212 D5
Longmoor La PR3 177 E6
Longridge Ave FY4 109 E5
Longridge CE Prim Sch PR3 139 A7
Longridge Cty Prim Sch PR3 138 F8
Longridge Dr OL10 32 F2
Longridge Fell Forest Wlk PR3 162 C7
Longridge Golf Course PR3 160 F3
Longridge Heath BB10,BB9 147 D4
Longridge High Sch PR3 139 A6
Longridge Rd
Fulwood PR2 118 B6
Hurst Green BB7,PR3 141 D8
Longridge PR3 160 C4
Longroyd Rd BB18 201 B1
Longsands Cty Prim Sch PR2 117 D5
Longsands La PR2 117 E6
Longshaw Ave WN5 10 E1
Longshaw Cl
Longshaw WN5 10 E1
Rufford L40 38 A5
Longshaw Comm WN5 10 E1
Longshaw Inf Sch BB2 80 E8
Longshaw Jun Sch BB2 100 E1
Longshaw La BB2 100 D2
Longshaw Old Rd WN5 10 E1
Longshaw St BB2 100 D1
Longsight Ave
Clitheroe BB7 186 F1
Huncoat BB5 103 E8
Longsight Rd Langho BB6 142 B2
Langho BB6 142 D2
Osbaldeston BB1,BB2 120 E4
Ramsbottom BL0 49 A2
Longton Ave FY5 173 B2
Longton Brickcroft Nature Reserve PR4 73 F7
Longton By-Pass PR4 74 C6
Longton Cl BB1 101 C5
Longton Ct PR8 20 C5
Longton Cty Prim Sch PR4 74 A8
Longton Dr Formby L37 12 A6
Morecambe LA4 213 A4
Longton Rd Blackpool FY1 129 C5
Burnley BB12 126 E8
Longton St Blackburn BB1 101 C5
Chorley PR6 42 E8
Longton's Cotts LA6 234 B1
Longtons La BD23 230 B3
Longway FY4 109 F8
Longwood Cl FY8 89 E4
Longworth Ave
Blackrod BL6 30 C3
Burnley BB10 127 D6
Coppull PR7 41 F2
Longworth Clough BL7 46 D2
Longworth La BL7 46 C2
Longworth Rd
Billington BB7 143 B4
Egerton BL7 46 B3
Horwich BL6 31 C4
Longworth Rd N BL7 45 D5
Longworth St
5 Bamber Bridge PR5 96 E2
Chorley PR7 42 B6
Preston PR1 117 C1
Lonmore PR5 96 D3
Lonsdale Ave
Fleetwood FY7 193 E3
Morecambe LA4 213 A4
Ormskirk L39 15 F7
Lonsdale Cl PR5 59 A6
Lonsdale Cres 3 FY7 193 E3
Lonsdale Dr PR5 57 B3
Lonsdale Gdns 4 BB9 168 D3
Lonsdale Gr LA4 213 A4
Lonsdale Mews 5 PR5 76 A8
Lonsdale Pl LA1 211 A5
Lonsdale Rd Blackpool FY1 129 B2
Formby L37 11 F3
Hest Bank LA2 215 D1
Morecambe LA4 213 A4
Preston PR1 117 C1
Southport PR8 34 D4
Lonsdale Rise LA6 238 C2
Lonsdale St
Accrington BB5 102 F5
Burnley BB12 126 C7
Nelson BB9 168 F1
Lord Ave OL13 86 C1
Lord Nelson Wharf PR2 95 B8
Lord Sefton Way L37 12 E2
Lord Sq BB1 100 E5
Lord St Accrington BB5 103 B6
Bacup OL13 86 F2
Blackburn BB2 100 E5
Blackpool FY1 129 B6
Brierfield BB9 147 B5
Burscough Bridge L40 24 E5
Bury BL9 32 C1
Chorley PR6 42 D7
Clayton Green PR6 77 C1
Colne BB8 169 C5
Darwen BB3 81 A2
Eccleston PR7 40 C5
Fleetwood FY7 194 B4
Great Harwood BB6 123 C4
Horwich BL6 31 B4
3 Lancaster LA1 213 F1
Lytham St Anne's FY8 88 E7
Morecambe LA4 212 E6
Oswaldtwistle BB5 102 E4
Preston PR1 96 A8
Rawtenstall BB4 85 A2
Rawtenstall, Rake Foot BB4 85 A7
Rishton BB1 123 B1
Southport PR8, PR9 34 B7
Lord St W
11 Blackburn BB2 100 E5
Southport PR8 34 A6
Lord Street Cty Prim Sch BB8 169 C5
Lord Street Mall 9 BB1 100 E5
Lord Street Prim Sch BL6 31 B4
Lord's Ave PR5 76 B7
Lord's Close Rd LA2 233 E2
Lord's La
Bamber Bridge PR1 95 E1
Longridge PR3 160 B2
Lord's Lot Rd
Over Kellet LA6 234 C1
Over Kellet LA6 234 D1
Lord's Wlk PR1 96 A8
Lords Croft PR6 77 A2
Lordsgate Dr L40 24 E3
Lordsgate La L40 24 C2
Lordsome Rd LA3 212 B2
Lorne Rd FY2 150 D2
Lorne St Chorley PR7 42 C7
Darwen BB3 80 F2
Lytham St Anne's FY8 90 D4
Lorne Way OL10 32 F1
Lorraine Ave PR2 116 E3
Lorton Cl Burnley BB12 126 B8
Fulwood PR2 116 F6
Lostock Gdns FY4 109 E6
Lostock Hall Cty Prim Sch PR5 96 B1
Lostock Hall High Sch PR5 96 C1
Lostock Hall Sta PR5 76 B8
Lostock La PR5 76 D7
Lostock Mdw PR6 77 A1
Lostock Rd PR5 57 C3
Lostock Sq PR5 76 B7
Lostock View PR5 76 B7
Lothersdale Cl BB10 147 D3
Lothian Ave FY7 193 D3
Lothian Pl FY2 150 E5
Lottice La BB5,BB1 102 A1
Lotus Dr FY4 111 A6
Loud Bridge Back La PR3 159 D8
Loud Bridge Rd PR3 159 D7
Loughlin Dr L33 1 A5
Loughrigg Cl BB12 126 B7
Loughrigg Terr FY4 130 C1
Louie Pollard Cres BB6 123 D6
Louis St BL0 67 D5
Louis William St BB1 81 D8
Louise St FY1 129 B3
Loupsfell Dr LA4 212 F4
Lourdes Ave PR5 96 A1
Louvain St BB18 200 A3
Lovat Rd PR1 116 F2
Love Clough Rd BB4 104 F2
Love La BL0 67 E1
Lovely Hall La BB1 121 D7
Low Bank BB12 125 E6
Low Bentham Prim Sch LA2 233 B8
Low Bentham Rd LA2 233 C8
Low Croft PR3 136 B2
Low Fold BB18 192 A6
Low Gn PR5 75 F1
Low Hill BB3 64 A6
Low La Leck LA6 236 B7
Morecambe LA4 213 B5
Low Moor La BB18 200 B1
Low Moor Rd FY2 150 E3
Low Rd Halton Green LA2 231 A4
Heysham LA3 209 A2
Low St LA6 236 C3
Lowcroft WN8 18 C3
Lowcross Rd FY6 151 E2
Lowe View BB4 86 A1
Lowe's La WN8 17 F8
Lower Abbotsgate LA6 238 B2
Lower Alt Rd L38 2 F4
Lower Antley St BB5 102 F5
Lower Ashworth Cl BB2 100 C4
Lower Audley St BB1,BB2 100 F4
Lower Bank Rd PR2 116 F3
Lower Bank St PR6 79 A1
Lower Barn St BB3 64 C7
Lower Barnes St BB5 123 E4
Lower Burgh Way PR7 42 B4
Lower Carr La L37 4 B7
Lower Chapel La BB7 187 B8
Lower Clough St BB9 168 D2
Lower Clowes BB4 67 E8
Lower Clowes Rd BB4 67 E8
Lower Cockcroft 12 BB2 100 E5
Lower Copthurst La PR6 60 E7
Lower Cribden Ave BB4 84 D2
Lower Croft 1 PR1 95 D2
Lower Croft St 3 BB18 201 B2
Lower Cross St 25 BB3 81 A1
Lower Darwen Prim Sch BB3 81 A6
Lower East Ave BB18 200 B3
Lower Eccleshill Rd BB3 81 A5
Lower Field PR5 75 F6
Lower Gate Rd BB5 124 F2
Lower Gn Poulton-le-F FY6 151 E3
3 Rochdale OL12 51 C1
Lower Greenfield PR2 116 B5
Lower Hazel Cl BB2 100 C4
Lower Hey PR4 94 A1
Lower Hill Dr PR6 43 A1
Lower Hollin Bank St BB2 100 D2
Lower House Gn BB4 86 A8
Lower House Rd PR5 58 E8
Lower La Freckleton PR4 92 D7
Haslingden BB4 84 B4
Kirkham PR4 113 C1
Longridge PR3 139 B7
Lower Laithe Dr BB9 168 C3
Lower Leithe Cotts BB9 168 C2
Lower Lune St 7 FY7 194 B5
Lower Makinson Fold BL6 31 D1
Lower Manor La BB12 146 F2
Lower Mdw BL7 47 D6
Lower Mead BL7 46 F1
Lower Mead Dr BB12 146 F2
Lower North Ave BB18 200 B2
Lower Park St BB18 200 C2
Lower Parrock Rd BB9 168 C1
Lower Philips Rd BB1 101 C8
Lower Prom Southport PR8 34 A7
Southport PR8 34 B8
Lower Rd Longridge PR3 139 E7
Ramsbottom BL0 49 E8
Lower Ridge Cl BB10 127 B6
Lower Rook St BB18 200 C2
Lower Rosegrove La BB12 126 A5

Lower School St 6 BB8 .169 D4
Lower Tentre BB11 ... 127 B5
Lower Timber Hill La
BB11 ... 127 A2
Lower Waterside
Farm Cotts BB3 ... 81 E3
Lower West Ave BB18 ... 200 B2
Lower Wilworth BB1 ... 121 E1
Lower Wlk FY2 ... 150 C7
Lowerfield BB6 ... 122 C8
Lowerfields BB12 ... 125 F6
Lowerfold BB6 ... 123 C6
Lowerfold Cl OL12 ... 51 C4
Lowerfold Cres OL12 ... 51 C4
Lowerfold Dr OL12 ... 51 C4
Lowerfold Rd BB6 ... 123 C6
Lowerfold Way OL12 ... 51 C4
Lowergate BB7 ... 164 E8
Lowerhouse Cres BB12 ... 126 A6
Lowerhouse Cty Jun Sch
BB12 ... 126 A6
Lowerhouse Fold BB12 ... 126 A6
Lowerhouse La
Burnley, Lowerhouse BB12 .125 F6
Burnley, Rose Grove BB12 ... 126 B6
Lowes Ct 3 Blackpool FY1 .129 B1
4 Thornton FY5 ... 173 B3
Lowes Gn L37 ... 12 B3
Lowes Park Golf Course
BL9 ... 32 A7
Lowes Rd BL9 ... 32 A6
Lowesby Cl PR5 ... 96 E3
Loweswater Cl BB5 ... 103 F8
Loweswater Cres BB12 ... 126 B8
Loweswater Dr 5 LA4 ... 212 G4
Lowesway Blackpool FY4 ... 109 F8
5 Thornton FY5 ... 173 B3
Lowfield Cl PR4 ... 113 F2
Lowfield Rd FY4 ... 109 F7
Lowfields La LA6 ... 238 D7
Lowgill La LA2 ... 233 C3
Lowick Cl PR5 ... 97 E4
Lowick Dr FY6 ... 151 D1
Lowland Way FY2 ... 150 F6
Lowlands Rd
Bolton-le-S LA5 ... 216 A5
Morecambe LA4 ... 212 F4
Lowndes St PR1 ... 116 E2
Lowood Gr PR2 ... 115 D1
Lowood Lodge 7 FY8 ... 90 A3
Lowood Pl BB2 ... 100 A6
Lowrey Terr FY1 ... 129 B2
Lowry Cl PR5 ... 76 A7
Lowry Hill La L40 ... 25 B2
Lowstead Pl FY4 ... 109 E6
Lowstern Cl BL7 ... 46 E1
Lowther Ave
Blackpool FY2 ... 150 B2
Maghull L31 ... 5 F2
Morecambe LA3 ... 213 A3
Lowther Cres PR5 ... 75 D2
Lowther Ct Blackpool FY2 .150 B2
5 Lytham St Anne's FY8 ... 90 A3
Lowther Dr PR5 ... 75 D3
Lowther La BB8 ... 191 D1
Lowther Pl BB1 ... 101 A8
Lowther Rd Fleetwood FY7 193 F4
Lancaster LA1 ... 214 B1
Lowther St Colne BB8 ... 169 E6
Nelson BB9 ... 147 C8
Preston PR2 ... 116 C1
Lowther Terr
Appley Bridge WN6 ... 19 C8
Lytham St Anne's FY8 ... 90 A3
Lowthian St 28 PR1 ... 95 F8
Lowthorpe Cres PR1 ... 117 B2
Lowthorpe Pl PR1 ... 117 B2
Lowthorpe Rd PR1 ... 117 B2
Lowthwaite Dr BB9 ... 147 E6
Lowton Rd FY8 ... 89 A8
Loxham Gdns FY4 ... 109 D6
Loxley Gn PR2 ... 117 C6
Loxley Pl FY5 ... 150 E7
Loxley Pl E FY5 ... 150 F7
Loxley Rd PR8 ... 34 D4
Loxwood Cl PR5 ... 96 A3
Loynd St
11 Great Harwood BB6 ... 123 C5
Ramsbottom BL0 ... 49 D6
Loyne Pk LA6 ... 235 D7
Loyne Sch The LA1 ... 213 D2
Lubbock St BB12 ... 126 C6
Lucas Ave PR7 ... 41 D8
Lucas La E PR6 ... 60 C6
Lucas La W PR6 ... 60 C5
Lucas St BL9 ... 32 A3
Lucerne Cl PR2 ... 117 C4
Lucerne Rd PR2 ... 117 C4
Lucy St Barrowford BB9 ... 168 D3
Lancaster LA1 ... 210 F8
Morecambe LA4 ... 212 E6
Ludlow WN8 ... 18 C4
Ludlow Dr L39 ... 15 D7
Ludlow Gr FY2 ... 150 F2
Ludlow St WN6 ... 28 D3
Luke St 17 OL13 ... 69 C8
Lulworth WN8 ... 18 C4
Lulworth Ave
Blackpool FY3 ... 130 A3
Preston PR2 ... 116 D2
Lulworth Ho PR8 ... 33 F5
Lulworth Pl PR5 ... 96 D2
Lulworth Rd Fulwood PR2 .117 A4
Southport PR8 ... 33 F5
Lumb Carr Ave BL0,BL8 ... 49 A4
Lumb Carr Rd BL0,BL8 ... 49 A4
Lumb Cotts BL0 ... 67 B4
Lumb Flats BL0 ... 67 B4
Lumb Holes La BB4 ... 68 E7
Lumb La BB4 ... 85 F4
Lumb Scar 9 OL13 ... 86 F2
Lund St Blackburn BB2 ... 100 C4
2 Preston PR1 ... 96 A8
Lunds La PR4 ... 73 D1
Lune Ave L31 ... 5 E2
Lune Cl
Kirkby Lonsdale LA6 ... 238 C2
Kirkham PR4 ... 113 C5
Lune Dr Clayton-le-W PR5 ... 76 E2
Morecambe LA3 ... 213 B3
Lune Gr FY1 ... 129 C3
Lune Ho LA1 ... 210 F7
Lune Ind Est LA1 ... 210 C8
Lune Rd Fleetwood FY7 ... 193 F4
Lancaster LA1 ... 213 D1
Lune St Colne BB8 ... 169 E4
Lancaster LA1 ... 213 F1
Longridge PR3 ... 139 B8
Padiham BB12 ... 125 D8
Preston PR1 ... 95 F7
Lune Terr LA1 ... 213 F1
Lune View FY6 ... 194 E6
Lunedale Ave FY1 ... 129 C1
Lunefield Dr LA6 ... 238 C1
Lunefield Gdns LA6 ... 238 C2
Lunesdale Cl FY8 ... 89 C7
Lunesdale Ct
Butt Yeats LA2 ... 232 B6
Lancaster LA1 ... 214 B1
Lunesdale Dr PR3 ... 204 B3
Lunesdale Rd 2 PR4 ... 113 A5
Lunesdale Terr LA2 ... 231 E4
Lunesdale View LA2 ... 214 F7
Luneside LA1 ... 210 C8
Lunt Rd L29 ... 4 C1
Lupin Cl Accrington BB5 ... 103 A7
Lucas Green PR6 ... 60 B5
Lupin Rd BB5 ... 103 B7
Lupton Dr BB9 ... 168 D4
Lupton Pl LA1 ... 213 D3
Lupton St PR7 ... 42 C6
Lutner St BB11 ... 127 A5
Luton Rd Cleveleys FY5 ... 172 E1
Preston PR2 ... 115 F2
Lutwidge Ave PR1 ... 117 C1
Lyceum Ave 3 FY3 ... 129 D4
Lychfield Dr PR5 ... 76 E7
Lychgate 20 PR1 ... 96 A8
Lydd Gr PR7 ... 42 A7
Lyddesdale Ave FY5 ... 150 D8
Lydgate Brierfield BB10 ... 147 E2
Chorley PR7 ... 42 A5
Lydia St BB5 ... 103 B4
Lydiate Cty Prim Sch L31 ... 5 C4
Lydiate La Bilsborrow PR3 .157 C6
Leyland PR5 ... 76 C4
Newtown PR7 ... 58 B1
Lydiate Lane End PR7 ... 58 B2
Lydiate Station Rd L31 ... 4 E5
Lydric Ave PR5 ... 97 E2
Lyelake La L40 ... 16 F2
Lymbridge Dr BL6 ... 30 D1
Lyme Gr FY6 ... 194 E5
Lymm Ave LA1 ... 213 C3
Lyncroft Cres FY3 ... 129 E7
Lyndale WN8 ... 18 B4
Lyndale Ave
Bamber Bridge PR5 ... 96 C2
Haslingden BB4 ... 84 B2
Wilpshire BB1 ... 122 A7
Lyndale Cl Leyland PR5 ... 59 B6
Rawtenstall BB4 ... 85 A7
Wilpshire BB1 ... 122 A7
Lyndale Ct FY7 ... 194 B5
Lyndale Gr PR5 ... 96 C2
Lyndale Rd BB11 ... 125 C3
Lyndale Terr BB7 ... 225 B3
Lynden Ave LA4 ... 213 A5
Lyndeth Cl PR2 ... 117 E6
Lyndhurst Maghull L31 ... 5 D1
Skelmersdale WN8 ... 18 B4
Lyndhurst Ave
Blackburn BB1 ... 101 E5
Blackpool FY4 ... 129 D1
Lyndhurst Dr PR2 ... 115 E2
Lyndhurst Gr BB6 ... 123 E6
Lyndhurst Rd
Blackburn BB2 ... 100 E2
Burnley BB10 ... 127 C5
Darwen BB3 ... 80 E3
Darwen BB3 ... 80 F3
Southport PR8 ... 34 B2
Lyndon Ave BB6 ... 123 E6
Lyndon Ct BB6 ... 123 E6
Lynfield Rd BB6 ... 123 E6
Lynn Gr 6 FY1 ... 129 B7
Lynn Pl PR2 ... 117 D2
Lynslack Terr LA5 ... 218 B8
Lynthorpe Rd
Blackburn BB2 ... 100 E2
Nelson BB9 ... 169 A1
Lynton Ave Blackpool FY4 .109 D8
Leyland PR5 ... 59 C8
Lynton Ct FY7 ... 172 C8
Lynton Dr PR8 ... 33 E1
Lynton Rd Accrington BB5 .102 F4
Southport PR8 ... 33 E1
Lynwood Ave
Blackpool FY3 ... 129 E8
Clayton-le-M BB5 ... 123 F4
Darwen BB3 ... 80 E4
Grimsargh PR2 ... 138 C2
Ormskirk L39 ... 15 C3
Lynwood Cl
Clayton-le-M BB5 ... 123 F4
Colne BB8 ... 169 D7
Darwen BB3 ... 80 E3
Skelmersdale WN8 ... 9 D7
Lynwood Dr FY6 ... 174 C7
Lynwood End L39 ... 15 C3
Lynwood Rd
Blackburn BB2 ... 100 B6
Huncoat BB5 ... 124 E2
Lyons La S PR7 ... 42 D7
Lyons Rd PR8 ... 34 A5
Lystra Ct FY8 ... 88 F5
Lyth Rd LA1 ... 214 B2
Lythall Ave FY8 ... 90 D4
Lytham CE Prim Sch FY8 .90 B4
Lytham Cl PR2 ... 116 D3
Lytham Hall FY8 ... 89 F4
Lytham Lifeboat Mus FY8 .90 C3
Lytham Rd Blackburn BB2 .100 F1
Blackpool FY1,FY4 ... 109 C6
Brierfield BB10 ... 147 C2
Freckleton PR4 ... 92 B6
Fulwood PR2 ... 116 D3
Saltcotes, Moss Side FY8 ... 111 E1
Southport PR9 ... 53 A4
Warton FY8,PR4 ... 91 D5
Lytham St Chorley PR6 ... 42 E7
Rochdale OL12 ... 51 E3
Lytham St Anne's
High Sch FY8 ... 89 C5
Lytham St Anne's Local
Nature Reserve FY8 ... 109 B1
Lytham St Annes L Ctr
FY8 ... 89 D5
Lytham Sta FY8 ... 90 A3
Lytham Windmill (Mus)
FY8 ... 90 C3
Lythcoe Ave PR2 ... 116 C4
Lythe Fell Ave LA2 ... 214 F7
Lythe Fell Rd LA2 ... 228 F8
Lythe La LA2 ... 233 E2
Lytles Cl L37 ... 12 A2
Lytton St BB12 ... 125 F7

M

Mabel St Colne BB8 ... 169 F5
2 Rochdale OL12 ... 51 D2
Maberry Cl WN6 ... 19 D7
Macaulay St BB11 ... 126 C5
Macauley Ave FY4 ... 109 F8
Macbeth Rd FY7 ... 193 E4
Mackay Croft 4 PR6 ... 42 D8
Mackenzie Cl 5 PR6 ... 42 D8
Maclaren Cl FY3 ... 130 D5
Macleod St BB9 ... 147 D8
Maddy St 2 PR1 ... 95 D8
Madeley Gdns OL12 ... 51 C1
Maden Rd OL13 ... 86 F2
Maden St BB5 ... 102 E6
Maden Way OL13 ... 86 F2
Madison Ave
Blackpool FY2 ... 150 B5
Hest Bank LA5 ... 215 E2
Madryn Ave L33 ... 1 A2
Maesbrook Cl PR9 ... 54 B5
Mafeking Ave BL9 ... 32 A5
Mafeking Rd PR2 ... 116 C2
Magdalen Ave FY5 ... 172 D1
Maggots Nook Rd WA11 ... 9 A1
Maghull Homes The L31 ... 5 B1
Maghull La L31 ... 6 B1
Maghull Smallholdings Est
L31 ... 5 F3
Magnolia Cl PR2 ... 117 C6
Magnolia Dr PR5 ... 76 E2
Magnolia Rd PR1 ... 95 B3
Magpie Cl BB11 ... 126 C5
Maharishi School of the
Age of Enlightenment
L40 ... 18 A5
Maida Vale FY5 ... 150 D8
Maiden St BB4 ... 84 B6
Main Ave LA3 ... 208 F3
Main Cl LA3 ... 205 D8
Main Dr FY6 ... 151 E2
Main Rd Bolton-le-S LA5 ... 216 B5
Galgate LA2 ... 207 A3
Hest Bank LA2 ... 215 F1
Nether Kellet LA6 ... 216 F5
Main Sprit Weind PR1 ... 96 A7
Main St Bolton-by-B BB7 ... 224 D4
Burton-in-K LA6 ... 234 B7
Cockerham LA2 ... 203 D4
Gisburn BB7 ... 225 C3
Grindleton BB7 ... 187 B8
Heysham LA3 ... 208 E8
High Bentham LA2 ... 233 D8
Hornby LA2 ... 232 B7
Kelbrook BB18 ... 192 A6
Kirkby Lonsdale LA6 ... 238 C2
Lancaster LA1 ... 213 F2
Low Bentham LA2 ... 233 B8
Overton LA3 ... 205 D8
Rathmell BD24 ... 230 F6
Warton, Carnforth LA5 ... 217 D5
Whittington LA6 ... 235 D7
Wray LA2 ... 232 D6
Mains La Bispham Green L40 26 A6
Poulton-le-F FY6 ... 152 B4
Mainway LA1 ... 213 F2
Mairscough La L39 ... 14 B1
Maitland Ave FY5 ... 172 D1
Maitland Cl 5 PR1 ... 96 C8
Maitland Pl BB4 ... 85 A1
Maitland St 18 Bacup OL13 .86 F2
Maitland St *continued*
4 Preston PR1 ... 96 C8
1 Preston PR5 ... 96 D8
Majestic The FY8 ... 88 D6
Major St Accrington BB5 ... 103 B4
Ramsbottom BL0 ... 49 B6
Rawtenstall BB4 ... 85 A7
Makinson Ave BL6 ... 31 E1
Makinson La BL6 ... 31 F4
Makinsons Row 11 LA2 ... 207 A4
Malcolm Pl FY7 ... 193 E4
Malcolm St PR1 ... 117 D1
Malden St PR5 ... 76 A1
Maldern Ave FY6 ... 151 C5
Maldon Pl PR2 ... 117 D2
Malham Ave
Accrington BB5 ... 102 F4
Blackpool FY4 ... 109 D8
Malham Cl Lancaster LA1 .213 D3
Southport PR8 ... 34 E3
Malham Gdns BB1 ... 100 F3
Malham Pl PR2 ... 117 E4
Malham Rd BB10 ... 147 D3
Malham Wend BB9 ... 168 C3
Maliff Rd BB10 ... 149 B2
Malkin Cl BB9 ... 168 E8
Malkin La BB7 ... 163 F6
Mall The Burnley BB11 ... 127 A6
Fulwood PR2 ... 117 E2
Lytham St Anne's FY8 ... 89 C7
Mallard Cl Leyland PR5 ... 58 D8
Ormskirk L39 ... 15 C2
Thornton FY5 ... 173 A4
Mallard Ct Blackpool FY3 ... 130 B6
Lancaster LA1 ... 210 E8
Mallard Dr BL6 ... 31 A3
Mallard Ho L31 ... 5 B4
Mallard Pl BB5 ... 102 D3
Mallards Wlk PR5 ... 77 A5
Mallee Ave PR9 ... 53 A3
Mallee Cres PR9 ... 53 A3
Malley La PR4 ... 135 C8
Mallom Ave PR7 ... 59 E1
Mallory Ave L31 ... 5 B4
Mallow Wlk LA3 ... 212 E2
Mallowdale FY5 ... 173 A4
Mallowdale Ave LA3 ... 209 A8
Mallowdale Rd LA1 ... 213 D2
Malt Kiln Brow PR3 ... 182 E4
Malt Kiln Gr PR3 ... 154 A5
Malt St BB5 ... 103 B7
Maltby Pl 2 FY4 ... 129 F2
Malthouse Ct PR2 ... 116 D1
Malthouse The PR2 ... 116 D1
Malthouse Way PR1 ... 95 D3
Maltings The Longton PR4 ... 73 F8
Thornton FY5 ... 173 A4
Whittington LA6 ... 235 D7
Maltkiln La
Bispham Green L40,WN8 ... 26 C7
Ormskirk L39 ... 6 E8
Malton Dr PR5 ... 76 A7
Malvern Ave
Blackburn BB2 ... 100 D1
Blackpool FY1 ... 129 D2
Lancaster LA1 ... 211 A6
Oswaldtwistle BB5 ... 102 E3
Padiham BB12 ... 125 D6
Preston PR1 ... 96 B6
Stalmine FY6 ... 174 C7
Malvern Cl
6 Accrington BB5 ... 103 A7
Bamber Bridge PR5 ... 76 C8
Horwich BL6 ... 31 C5
Malvern Ct 6 BB9 ... 147 F8
Malvern Rd
Lytham St Anne's FY8 ... 89 D5
Nelson BB9 ... 169 A1
Preston PR1 ... 96 B6
Malvern St Preston PR1 ... 96 B5
Standish WN6 ... 28 D3
Malvern Way BB4 ... 67 A7
Manby Cl PR5 ... 97 E3
Manchester Rd
Accrington BB5 ... 103 D3
Barnoldswick BB18 ... 200 B1
Blackpool FY3 ... 129 D6
Blackrod BL6 ... 30 E1
Burnley BB11 ... 126 E4
Clow Bridge BB11 ... 105 D6
Hapton BB11,BB12 ... 125 C4
Haslingden, Ewood
Bridge BB4 ... 67 D7
Haslingden, Lane Side BB4 ... 84 B2
Nelson BB9 ... 147 D7
Preston PR1 ... 96 B7
Ramsbottom BL0,BL9 ... 49 E4
Southport PR9 ... 34 C7
Manchester Road Sta
BB11 ... 126 F5
Mancknols St BB9 ... 148 A7
Mancknols Walton
Cottage Homes BB9 ... 148 B8
Mandella Ct BB1 ... 100 E6
Mandeville Rd PR8 ... 20 B5
Mandeville Terr BL8 ... 48 B2
Manfield WN8 ... 18 A3
Manghales BB4 ... 84 B7
Manion Ave L31 ... 5 B5
Manion Cl L31 ... 5 B5
Manitoba Cl BB2 ... 100 B8
Manley Cl BL9 ... 49 C2
Manner Sutton St BB1 ... 100 F5
Manning Rd
4 Preston PR1 ... 117 E1
Southport PR8 ... 34 E6
Manor Ave Burscough L40 ... 24 D2
Fulwood PR2 ... 117 B4
Manor Ave *continued*
Hest Bank LA2 ... 213 E8
Penwortham PR1 ... 95 B4
Ribchester PR3 ... 140 D3
Manor Beach
Cty Prim Sch FY5 ... 172 D3
Manor Brook 1 BB5 ... 103 C6
Manor Cl Burton in L LA6 ... 236 C3
Coupe Green PR5 ... 97 F3
Hest Bank LA2 ... 213 E8
Manor Cotts PR4 ... 112 B3
Manor Cres Burscough L40 .24 D2
Hest Bank LA2 ... 213 F8
Manor Ct 11 Blackpool FY1 129 C7
3 Blackpool, Hawes
Side FY4 ... 129 E1
Fulwood PR2 ... 116 B7
Manor Ctyd LA3 ... 208 E8
Manor Dr Burscough L40 ... 24 D2
Cleveleys FY5 ... 172 D3
Hest Bank LA2 ... 213 E8
Kirkham PR4 ... 113 C4
Manor Farm LA6 ... 235 D7
Manor Fields BB7 ... 143 C5
Manor Gdns L40 ... 24 D2
Manor Gr Morecambe LA3 .212 C2
Penwortham PR1 ... 95 A4
Skelmersdale WN8 ... 17 F1
Manor House Cl
Leyland PR5 ... 58 B8
Maghull L31 ... 5 C1
Manor House Cres PR1 ... 117 B3
Manor House Dr WN8 ... 9 E3
Manor House La PR1 ... 117 C3
Manor House Park Flats
FY5 ... 172 C3
Manor La Hest Bank LA2 ... 215 F1
Penwortham PR1 ... 95 B4
Manor Lo L37 ... 11 E4
Manor Pk PR2 ... 117 C4
Manor Pl BB5 ... 102 F7
Manor Rd Blackburn BB2 ... 100 B5
Blackpool FY1 ... 129 D4
Burnley BB12 ... 126 B7
Burscough L40 ... 24 D2
Clayton Green PR6 ... 77 B3
Clitheroe BB7 ... 164 D7
Colne BB8 ... 169 E7
Darwen BB3 ... 63 F8
Fleetwood FY7 ... 193 E4
Garstang PR3 ... 199 C1
Hest Bank LA2 ... 213 F8
Horwich BL6 ... 31 D4
Inskip PR4 ... 134 C8
Southport PR9 ... 53 A2
Whalley BB7 ... 143 C5
Wrea Green PR4 ... 112 B4
Manor Road
Cty Prim Sch PR6 ... 77 B2
Manor St Accrington BB5 ... 103 D7
Bacup OL13 ... 86 F1
Bury BL9 ... 32 A2
Nelson BB9 ... 147 F8
Ramsbottom BL0 ... 49 B7
Manor Steet BB9 ... 147 F8
Manor Way PR4 ... 112 B3
Manor Wood
Fleetwood FY7 ... 193 E4
Kirkham PR4 ... 113 B7
Manorcroft PR4 ... 73 F8
Manse Ave WN6 ... 27 F5
Mansell Way BL6 ... 31 D1
Mansergh St BB10 ... 147 C2
Mansfield Ave BL0 ... 49 B2
Mansfield Cres BB9 ... 147 C6
Mansfield Dr PR5 ... 97 E3
Mansfield Gr BB9 ... 147 C6
Mansfield Rd FY3 ... 129 D8
Mansion House Bldgs 2
BB4 ... 85 A7
Mansion St S BB5 ... 103 D6
Manston Gr PR7 ... 42 A7
Manx Jane's La PR9 ... 53 A4
Manxman Rd BB2 ... 100 F1
Maple Ave Blackpool FY3 .129 D5
Brinscall PR6 ... 61 F7
Burscough L40 ... 24 E4
7 Bury BL9 ... 32 B2
Fleetwood FY7 ... 172 F8
Haslingden BB4 ... 84 C3
Horwich BL6 ... 31 E1
Morecambe LA3 ... 212 B2
Thornton FY5 ... 151 C8
Maple Bank BB10 ... 127 C7
Maple Cl Formby L37 ... 11 C1
Newton-with-S PR4 ... 113 F2
Whalley BB7 ... 143 D6
Wilpshire BB1 ... 121 E6
Maple Cres BB1 ... 102 B8
Maple Ct Farington PR5 ... 76 D3
Garstang PR3 ... 199 C1
Maple Dr
Bamber Bridge PR5 ... 96 F1
Oswaldtwistle BB5 ... 102 F3
Poulton-le-F FY6 ... 151 E2
Maple Gr Chorley PR6 ... 60 D3
Fulwood PR2 ... 118 A4
Grimsargh PR2 ... 138 D1
Lancaster LA1 ... 210 D8
Penwortham PR1 ... 95 B4
Ramsbottom BL0 ... 49 D6
Warton PR4 ... 91 D6
Maple Rd PR3 ... 199 C1
Maple St Blackburn BB1 ... 101 A7
Clayton-le-M BB5 ... 123 F1
Great Harwood BB6 ... 123 D6
3 Rishton BB1 ... 123 B1
Southport PR8 ... 34 E6

Maplebank 3 PR2 115 C1
Maples The PR5 57 F6
Maplewood
Skelmersdale WN8 18 A4
Southport PR9 52 F2
Maplewood Ave FY6 195 A5
Maplewood Cl Leyland PR5 58 E8
Lytham St Anne's FY8 89 F4
Maplewood Dr FY5 150 C8
Maplewood Gdns LA1 211 A2
Marabou Dr BB3 80 E3
Marathon Pl PR5 75 C3
Marble Ave 4 FY5 150 F7
Marble Pl PR8 34 B7
Marble St BB5 102 E4
March St BB12 126 F8
Marchbank Rd WN8 17 D1
Marchwood Rd FY3 130 B8
Marcroft Ave FY4 109 E7
Mardale Ave
Blackpool FY4 130 C1
Morecambe LA4 212 G5
Mardale Cl PR8 20 B4
Mardale Cres PR5 59 B7
Mardale Rd Fulwood PR1 118 A1
1 Lancaster LA1 214 A1
Longridge PR3 138 F5
Maresfield Rd PR1 95 E5
Margaret Rd PR1 95 E4
Margaret St
Blackburn BB1 101 D4
Oswaldtwistle BB5 102 C2
1 Preston PR1 96 A8
Rawtenstall BB4 84 F4
Margate Ave FY4 109 E6
Margate Rd Fulwood PR2 116 A4
Lytham St Anne's FY8 88 F8
Maria Ct 10 BB11 127 B4
Maria Sq BL7 45 D4
Maria St BB3 64 B6
Marians Dr L39 15 E7
Maricourt Ave BB1 101 D5
Marilyn Ave 4 PR5 76 B8
Marina Ave
2 Blackpool FY1 129 D2
Poulton-le-F FY3 130 D8
Marina Cl PR5 96 A1
Marina Dr
Bamber Bridge PR5 96 A1
Fulwood PR2 116 E7
Marina Gr PR5 96 A1
Marina Mews FY7 194 B3
Marina Rd L37 11 F1
Marina Way BB18 200 D1
Marine Ave BB11 126 C4
Marine Dr Hest Bank LA2 215 D1
Lytham St Anne's FY8 89 D3
Southport PR8 33 E7
Southport, Marshside
PR8, PR9 52 D4
Marine Gate Mans PR9 34 B8
Marine Ind Ctr FY8 90 D4
Marine Par Fleetwood FY7 193 C1
Southport PR8 34 A8
Marine Rd E LA4 212 F6
Marine Rd W LA3,LA4 212 C4
Marine Road Central
LA4 212 D5
Mariners Cl FY7 193 E1
Mariners Way PR2 95 B8
Marino Cl FY5 151 D8
Maritime St FY7 193 F2
Maritime Way PR2 94 F7
Mark Cl PR1 95 F1
Mark Rd L38 2 F4
Mark Sq PR4 56 A6
Mark St Bacup OL13 69 C8
Burnley BB10 147 B1
Mark's Ave PR5 75 E5
Market Ave 2 BB1 100 E5
Market Cross 5 L39 15 E5
Market Gate 27 LA1 210 F8
Market Pl Adlington PR7 30 A7
12 Chorley PR7 42 C8
3 Clitheroe BB7 164 E8
10 Colne BB8 169 E5
Edenfield BL0 67 D3
Garstang PR3 178 C7
1 Leyland PR5 59 A8
Longridge PR3 139 B7
3 Poulton-le-F FY6 151 D3
Ramsbottom BL0 49 C7
Standish WN6 28 E1
Market Sq Burnley BB11 127 A6
Kirkby Lonsdale LA6 238 C2
3 Kirkham PR4 113 B5
10 Lancaster LA1 210 F8
Lytham St Anne's FY8 90 A3
Nelson BB9 147 D8
Market St Adlington PR7 30 A6
Bacup OL13 86 F2
6 Barnoldswick BB18 200 B2
Blackpool FY1 129 B5
Carnforth LA5 217 D2
Chorley PR7 42 C7
Church BB5 102 E5
Colne BB8 169 E5
Darwen BB3 81 A1
Edenfield BL0 67 D4
Hambleton FY6 174 C2
Kirkby Lonsdale LA6 238 C2
Kirkham PR4 112 F6
Lancaster LA1 210 F8
Morecambe LA4 212 D5
9 Nelson BB9 147 D8
Preston PR1 95 F8
5 Rawtenstall BB4 68 F8
Southport PR8 34 B7
Market St *continued*
Standish WN6 28 E1
Whitworth OL12,OL13 70 D4
Market St W PR1 95 F8
Market Street La 7 BB2 100 E4
Market Way
7 Blackburn BB1 100 E5
6 Ormskirk L39 15 E5
Market Wlk PR7 42 C8
Markham Dr PR8 34 E2
Markham Rd BB2 100 B3
Markham St PR2 116 C1
Markland St
3 Preston PR1 95 E7
6 Ramsbottom BL0 49 C6
Marklands Rd BL6 31 E5
Markross St BB4 85 A2
Marl Ave PR1 95 B4
Marl Cop PR5 57 A6
Marl Croft PR1 95 D2
Marl Gr WN5 10 D4
Marl Hill Cres PR2 118 A2
Marl Pits BB4 85 B3
Marl Pits Sports Complex
BB4 85 C3
Marl Rd L33 1 C3
Marland WN8 18 A4
Marlboro Rd FY3 129 E4
Marlborough WN8 18 A4
Marlborough Ave
Cleveleys FY5 172 D5
Maghull L31 5 D3
Warton PR4 91 D6
Marlborough Cl
Ramsbottom BL0 49 C3
Whitworth OL12 51 C7
Marlborough Dr
Bamber Bridge PR5 96 D3
Fulwood PR2 116 D7
Marlborough Gdns 5 PR9 34 C8
Marlborough Rd
Accrington BB5 103 C7
Lytham St Anne's FY8 109 E1
Morecambe LA3 212 B3
Southport PR9 34 C7
Marlborough St
Burnley BB11 127 A4
Chorley PR6 60 E1
14 Rochdale OL12 51 C1
Marled Hey BL7 47 D5
Marles Ct BB10 127 B8
Marlfield PR4 73 F4
Marlfield Cl PR2 115 F5
Marlhill Rd FY3 130 B8
Marlin St 5 BB9 168 F2
Marlowe Ave
Accrington BB5 103 E2
Padiham BB12 125 F7
Marlowe Cres BB6 123 B4
Marlton Rd BB2 100 D1
Marlton Way LA1 210 E6
Marple Cl WN6 28 B2
Marquis Cl BB3 80 F7
Marquis Dr PR4 92 C7
Marquis St PR4 112 F5
Marron Cl PR5 58 E8
Mars St BL7 47 E6
Marsden Cl PR7 40 B7
Marsden Cres BB9 148 A8
Marsden Ct BB10 147 C3
Marsden Dr BB9 147 D6
Marsden Gr BB9 147 C5
Marsden Hall Rd BB9 148 A8
Marsden Hall Rd N BB9 169 B1
Marsden Hall Road S
BB9 148 A8
Marsden Height Cl BB9 147 F5
Marsden Mall 3 BB9 147 E8
Marsden Park
Golf Course BB9 148 C8
Marsden Prim Sch BB9 147 D7
Marsden Rd Blackpool FY4 109 D8
Brierfield BB10 147 C3
Southport PR9 34 E7
Marsden St
Accrington BB5 103 B4
Blackburn BB2 100 B2
6 Haslingden BB4 84 A3
Kirkham PR4 113 B5
Marsett Cl OL12 51 A1
Marsett Pl PR2 117 E5
Marsh Brows L37 11 E2
Marsh Cl LA2 203 B4
Marsh Cres LA4 213 B4
Marsh Ct 2 FY5 173 A2
Marsh Cty Prim Sch The
LA1 210 D8
Marsh Dr PR4 92 D7
Marsh Gates PR4 92 D7
Marsh Hos LA2 203 B4
Marsh House La BB3 81 C1
Marsh La Brindle PR6 78 B5
Cockerham LA2 203 B4
Glasson LA2 205 D3
Hambleton FY6 174 C1
Hightown L37, L38 3 E6
Longton PR4 73 D8
Ormskirk L40 23 D1
Preston PR1 95 E7
6 Preston PR1 95 F8
Marsh Mill FY5 173 B2
Marsh Moss La L40 24 C7
Marsh Rd Banks PR9 71 D1
Hesketh Bank PR4 72 F4
Thornton FY5 173 A2
Marsh St Blackburn BB1 100 E6
Horwich BL6 31 A4
4 Lancaster LA1 213 D1
Marsh Terr BB3 81 A2
Marsh View PR4 113 F2
Marsh Way PR1 95 C2
Marshall Ave BB5 124 F2
Marshall Gr PR2 116 A4
Marshall's Brow PR1 95 E3
Marshall's Cl Maghull L31 5 C4
5 Penwortham PR1 95 E4
Marshallsay L37 12 A2
Marsham Cl PR3 178 D6
Marsham Gr BB3 81 C1
Marshaw Pl PR3 178 A6
Marshaw Rd LA1 213 D2
Marshdale Rd FY4 109 F7
Marshes La The PR4 37 A8
Marshside
Nature Reserve PR9 52 E5
Marshside Prim Sch PR9 53 A5
Marshside Rd PR9 52 F4
Marston Cl PR2 116 C7
Marston Cres L38 3 A2
Marston Moor PR2 116 C7
Mart La L40 24 E5
Martholme Ave BB5 124 A3
Martholme Cl BB6 123 D6
Martholme La BB6 123 F8
Martin Ave FY8 109 C4
Martin Croft Rd BB4 84 A5
Martin Dr BB3 64 C6
Martin Field Rd PR1 95 E2
Martin La
Drummersdale L40 23 E6
Rochdale OL12 51 B1
Martin Mere
(The Wildfowl Trust) L40 37 B1
Martin St Burnley BB10 147 B1
Bury BL9 32 D3
Edgworth BL7 47 D4
Martin Top La BB7 189 C7
Martindale Cl BB1 101 C2
Martindales The PR6 77 B3
Martinfield PR2 116 F8
Martinfields BB10 147 C4
Martinique Dr BB3 80 F6
Martins Ave PR7 42 E2
Martins La WN8 9 D7
Martland Ave WN6 19 F5
Marton Dr Blackpool FY4 109 D8
Burnley BB11 126 E3
Morecambe LA4 213 B6
Marton Pl LA4 213 B6
Marton Rd PR2 94 F8
Marton St 4 LA1 210 F7
Marton View FY3 129 E4
Marwick Cl WN6 28 D2
Mary Ave PR8 20 E6
Mary Brown Cotts BB7 187 C8
Mary St Blackburn BB1 101 A4
Burnley BB10 127 B5
Carnforth LA5 217 D3
Colne BB8 169 C4
Lancaster LA1 210 F8
Ramsbottom BL0 49 B5
Rishton BB1 123 B1
Mary St E BL6 31 B4
Mary St W Horwich BL6 31 A4
Longridge PR3 139 A8
Marybank Cl PR2 117 C5
Maryland Cl LA5 218 D2
Masefield Ave
Padiham BB12 125 E7
Thornton FY5 173 A3
Masefield Cl BB6 123 B4
Masefield Pl PR5 96 D2
Mason Cl PR4 92 C6
Mason Hill View PR2 117 A4
Mason House Cres PR2 116 A5
Mason Row BL7 46 E2
Mason St
7 Accrington BB5 103 C6
Bury BL9 32 A2
Chorley PR6 60 E2
Colne BB8 169 D5
Egerton BL7 46 E1
Horwich BL6 31 B3
Oswaldtwistle BB5 102 D3
Masonfield PR5 77 B5
Masongill Fell Lane LA6 236 E7
Masons Ct 1 FY7 193 E3
Masons Way 9 BB18 200 B3
Masonwood PR2 117 A6
Massam's La L37 11 F6
Massey Croft OL12 51 C8
Massey La BB9 147 A5
Massey St Brierfield BB9 147 A4
Burnley BB11 127 A6
Bury BL9 32 B3
Masterson Ave BB12 144 D2
Matcham Ct 11 FY1 129 B5
Matchmoor La BL6 31 F4
Mather Ave BB5 103 B8
Mather St FY3 129 D7
Mathias Ct LA4 212 E6
Matlock Ave PR8 34 B4
Matlock Cl PR8 34 B4
Matlock Cres PR8 34 B4
Matlock Gr BB10 147 C2
Matlock Pl PR2 116 A5
Matlock Rd PR8 34 B4
Matlock St 11 BB3 80 F2
Matterdale Rd PR5 59 B7
Matthew Cl BB8 169 E4
Matthew St BB2 100 B2
Matthews Ct FY4 109 D7
Matthias St LA4 212 E6
Mattock Cres LA4 213 B5
Maud St Barrowford BB9 168 D2
Chorley PR7 42 B6
Maudland Bank PR1 95 E8
Maudland Rd
Blackpool FY1 129 C2
Preston PR1 95 E8
Maudsley St
Accrington BB5 103 C6
Blackburn BB1 100 F5
Maureen Ave 3 PR5 76 B8
Maurice Gr FY2 150 E1
Maurice St BB9 147 D8
Mavis Dr PR7 41 E2
Mavis Rd BB2 100 A5
Mawdesley CE Prim Sch
L40 39 C3
Mawdesley RC Prim Sch
L40 39 F2
Mawdsley Cl L37 12 B3
Mawdsley Terr L39 15 F7
Maxwell Gr FY2 150 E2
Maxwell St BL9 32 B3
May Bell Ave FY5 172 F3
May La Bilsborrow PR3 157 C8
Claughton PR3 179 E1
May St Barrowford BB9 168 D2
Blackburn BB1 101 A4
Burnley BB11 127 B4
Edgworth BL7 47 E6
Nelson BB9 168 F2
May Terr BB7 143 A4
Maybank Cl PR9 53 A1
Maybury Ave BB12 126 B7
Maycroft Ave FY6 151 B5
Mayfair BL6 31 D3
Mayfair Cl Haslingden BB4 67 A7
Hightown L38 2 F2
Lytham St Anne's FY8 89 D6
Mayfair Cotts WN1 29 C1
Mayfair Cres BB1 121 F5
Mayfair Dr FY5 151 C8
Mayfair Gdns 5 FY5 173 C1
Mayfair Rd Blackpool FY1 129 E2
Burnley BB10 127 E5
Nelson BB9 169 A1
Mayfayre Ave L31 5 B5
Mayfield BB3 64 B7
Mayfield Ave Adlington PR6 30 A7
Bamber Bridge PR5 76 C8
Blackpool FY4 109 C5
Clitheroe BB7 164 F7
Formby L37 11 C1
Fulwood PR2 116 A5
Fulwood PR2 116 B4
Haslingden BB4 84 A1
5 Kirkham PR4 113 A5
Lancaster LA1 213 E3
Oswaldtwistle BB5 102 F4
Thornton FY5 173 A4
Mayfield Cl BL0 49 A2
Mayfield Ct L37 11 F5
Mayfield Dr LA4 213 A6
Mayfield Fold BB11 127 B3
Mayfield Gdns BB5 102 F4
Mayfield Pl 10 FY7 193 F2
Mayfield Prim Sch FY8 88 E8
Mayfield Rd
Blackburn BB1 121 E3
7 Chorley PR6 60 D1
High Bentham LA2 233 D7
Leyland PR5 59 A7
Lytham St Anne's FY8 88 E8
Orrell WN8 10 B7
Preston PR2 116 B1
Ramsbottom BL0 49 A2
Mayfield Sch PR7 42 C6
Mayfield St BB2 100 E3
Mayflower Ave PR1 95 A3
Mayflower Ind Est L37 12 A1
Mayflower St BB2 100 B2
Maylands Pl BB9 168 C3
Maylands Sq LA4 212 F4
Maynard St PR1,PR2 116 D2
Mayo Dr PR4 56 A6
Mayor Ave FY1 129 C2
Maypark PR5 77 A5
Mayson St BB1 100 E4
Maytree Wlk WN8 18 B4
Mayville Rd BB9 147 B6
McCall Cl PR4 112 A3
McDonald Rd LA3 208 D5
McKenzie St PR5 76 F8
Mead Ave PR5 59 B8
Meadow Ave
Fleetwood FY7 193 E1
Knott End-on-S FY6 195 A6
Southport PR8 34 C4
Meadow Bank Maghull L31 5 B2
3 Ormskirk L39 15 F5
Penwortham PR1 95 C3
Meadow Bank Ave BB10 147 B5
Meadow Bank Rd 15 BB9 147 D8
Meadow Bolton PR5 58 A8
Meadow Brow PR9 53 D5
Meadow Cl Accrington BB5 124 F1
Billington BB7 143 A3
Brierfield BB10 147 C4
Clifton PR4 114 D2
Foulridge BB8 191 D1
Skelmersdale WN8 9 D7
Westhead L40 16 E4
Wrea Green PR4 112 B3
Meadow Clough WN8 18 B4
Meadow Cotts OL12 70 D3
Meadow Court Rd LA4 212 F3
Meadow Cr PR4 112 F6
Meadow Cres FY6 151 A3
Meadow Croft
Nether Kellet LA6 216 F4
West Bradford BB7 186 E5
Meadow Ct
11 Oswaldtwistle BB5 102 E4
Preston PR1 95 E6
Meadow Dr
Bolton-le-S LA5 216 A5
Ormskirk L39 15 C2
Warton PR4 91 C5
Meadow Field PR1 95 E2
Meadow Gate BB3 81 B2
Meadow Gdns BB1 123 B1
Meadow Head Ave OL12 51 D6
Meadow Head Cl BB2 100 A1
Meadow Head La
Darwen BB3 80 B4
Longton PR4 73 F7
Meadow La
Clayton Brook PR5 77 B4
Croston PR5 56 E1
Hesketh Bank PR4 72 F4
Hoscar L40 25 C6
Knott End-on-S FY6 194 F4
Lytham St Anne's FY8 90 E4
Maghull L31 5 F1
Rufford L40 38 D3
Southport PR8 20 D3
Meadow Pk Galgate LA2 206 F4
Garstang PR3 199 C1
Haslingden BL0 67 C4
Kirkham PR4 112 E6
Staining FY3 130 D5
Meadow Reach PR1 95 B2
Meadow Rise BB2 80 A8
Meadow St
Accrington BB5 103 C6
Adlington PR7 30 A6
Barnoldswick BB18 200 A4
17 Burnley BB11 126 F6
Darwen BB3 64 B6
Great Harwood BB6 123 C4
Lancaster LA1 210 D8
Leyland PR5 76 A1
Padiham BB12 145 C1
Preston PR1 96 A8
Wheelton PR6 61 A7
Meadow Vale PR5 58 A8
Meadow View
Clitheroe BB7 164 C8
Farleton LA2 232 A6
Great Plumpton PR4 111 F7
Lancaster LA1 213 D3
Rochdale OL12 51 A1
Southport PR8 34 D4
Meadow Way
Arkholme LA6 235 B3
Bacup OL13 86 F2
Barnoldswick BB18 200 D4
Blackrod BL6 30 E1
Coppull PR7 28 D8
Edgworth BL7 47 E6
Garstang PR3 199 C2
Ramsbottom BL9 49 C2
Meadoway Church BB5 103 A7
Longton PR4 73 F8
Tarleton PR4 56 A5
Meadowbarn Cl PR4 115 E5
Meadowbridge Cl L40 16 E4
Meadowbrook
Blackpool FY3 130 C2
Burscough L40 24 D2
Meadowbrook Cl BL9 32 C4
Meadowcroft
Blackburn BB3 81 A6
Euxton PR7 59 B3
Formby L37 11 F2
Lytham St Anne's FY8 110 A1
Skelmersdale WN8 18 B4
Meadowcroft Ave
Catterall PR3 178 D3
Cleveleys FY5 172 E2
Hambleton FY6 174 C1
Meadowcroft Bsns Pk
PR4 95 B1
Meadowcroft Cl BB4 85 A5
Meadowcroft Gr LA3 212 B1
Meadowcroft Rd PR5 58 D7
Meadowfield Fulwood PR2 116 F8
Halton LA2 214 E7
Orrell WN8 10 A7
Meadowfield Cl LA2 214 E7
Meadowfields BB2 80 D7
Meadowhead Cty Inf Sch
BB2 100 B1
Meadowhead Jun Sch
BB2 80 B8
Meadowlands
Charnock Richard PR7 41 D4
Clitheroe BB7 164 C8
Meadows Ave Bacup OL13 86 F4
Cleveleys FY5 172 F2
Haslingden BB4 84 C2
Meadows Cl LA5 219 E4
Meadows The
Arnside LA5 218 C8
Bamber Bridge PR5 96 F3
Billington BB7 143 A4
Burnley BB12 126 D8
Cleveleys FY5 172 F2
Colne BB8 169 D6
Darwen BB3 80 E5
Elswick PR4 153 F1
Heskin Green PR7 40 E2
2 Leyland PR5 75 B1
Oswaldtwistle BB5 102 F3
Whitworth OL12 70 C1
Yealand Redmayne LA5 219 E3

Meadowside
Claughton, Lancaster LA2 ..231 F5
Croston PR5 ....57 A2
Grindleton BB7 ....187 C8
Lancaster LA1 ....210 F7
Walmer Bridge PR4 ....74 A5
Meadowside Ave BB5 ...123 E3
Meadowside Dr PR5 .....97 E1
Meadowside Rd LA4 ....212 E3
Meads Rd PR2 ....116 B1
Meadup Ct LA3 ....212 D2
Meadway Becconsall PR4 ..72 F2
Blackpool FY4 ....129 F1
Clayton Green PR6 ....77 B3
Penwortham PR1 ....95 A5
Ramsbottom BL0 ....67 C1
Skelmersdale WN8 ....18 A4
Meadway Cl BL6 ....31 D3
Meagles La PR3,PR4 .....153 E3
Mealhouse La 6 PR7 .....42 C8
Mealrigg La LA6 ....235 A7
Meanwood Ave FY4 ....109 F7
Meanwood Brow 15 OL12 ..51 C1
Meanwood Prim Sch
OL12 ....51 C1
Meanygate PR5 ....96 E1
Mearbeck Pl 6 LA1 ......213 D2
Mearley Brook Fold BB7 .164 F7
Mearley Rd PR2 ....117 E4
Mearley St BB7 ....164 F1
Mearley Syke BB7 ....164 F8
Meath Rd PR1 ....95 D6
Mede The PR4 ....113 B3
Medina Cl BB5 ....103 B5
Medlar Cl PR4 ....112 E6
Medlar Ct PR4 ....113 A6
Medlar Gate PR4 ....113 A6
Medlar La PR4 ....132 E4
Medley St OL12 ....51 F1
Medlock Ave FY7 ....193 D2
Medlock Pl FY7 ....193 D2
Medway PR2 ....116 F6
Medway Ave FY7 ....172 D8
Medway Cl PR5 ....96 B1
Medway Dr BL6 ....31 D3
Medway Ho 6 PR1 ....96 D8
Meeting House La LA1 ...210 E8
Meins Croft BB2 ....100 A6
Meins Rd BB2 ....99 F6
Melba Rd PR2 ....117 E3
Melbert Ave PR2 ....116 C3
Melbourne Ave
Cleveleys FY5 ....150 F7
Fleetwood FY7 ....172 E8
Melbourne Cl BL6 ....31 C3
Melbourne Ct FY5 ....150 E8
Melbourne Gr BL6 ....31 C3
Melbourne Rd 11 LA1 ....211 A8
Melbourne St Darwen BB3 ..64 B6
5 Enfield BB5 ....124 A1
2 Newchurch BB4 ....85 F1
Oswaldtwistle BB5 ....102 D3
Padiham BB12 ....125 D7
22 Preston PR1 ....95 F8
9 Whitehall BB3 ....64 B6
Melbreck WN8 ....18 A4
Melbury Dr BL6 ....31 F1
Meldon Grange LA3 ......209 A8
Meldon Rd Heysham LA3 .209 A7
Heysham LA3 ....209 A8
Meldreth Cl L37 ....11 C1
Melford Cl PR6 ....60 F3
Melford Dr WN5 ....10 D3
Melfort Cl BB2 ....99 F1
Melia Cl BB4 ....84 F2
Melita St 6 BB3 ....64 B8
Melling Brow LA4 ....235 C2
Melling Ct 3 Colne BB8 .169 C5
Morecambe LA4 ....212 D3
Melling Ho 6 LA1 ....211 A3
Melling Rd Hornby LA2 ...232 B7
Southport PR9 ....34 E2
Melling St 20 PR1 ....95 F8
Melling St Wilfred
CE Prim Sch LA6 ....235 D2
Melling's La FY8 ....110 A1
Mellings PR1 ....96 C6
Mellings Ave WN5 ....10 E1
Mellings Fold 3 PR1 ......96 C6
Mellings Wood FY8 ....110 A1
Mellishaw La LA3 ....212 G1
Mellor Brow BB2 ....120 D2
Mellor Cl Burnley BB11 ..126 D3
Standish WN6 ....28 E2
Mellor Ct PR3 ....139 B7
Mellor La BB2 ....120 F3
Mellor Pl 6 PR1 ....96 B7
Mellor Rd Kirkham PR4 ...113 A5
Leyland PR5 ....75 D2
Mellowfield Sch PR9 ......34 C7
Mellwood Ave FY3 ....150 F1
Melrose Ave
Blackpool FY3 ....129 E8
Burnley BB11 ....126 D4
Fulwood PR2 ....117 C6
Morecambe LA4 ....212 F5
Oswaldtwistle BB5 ....102 F3
Southport PR9 ....53 B5
Melrose Gdn PR5 ....57 C2
Melrose St 10 Darwen BB3 ..80 F2
Lancaster LA1 ....211 A7
Ramsbottom BL0 ....49 B2
Melrose St OL13 ....87 A7
Melrose Way PR7 ....42 D5
Melton Gr FY8 ....89 E3

Melton Pl Cleveleys FY5 ..150 C8
Leyland PR5 ....76 B1
Melville Ave BB18 ....200 A3
Melville Dr BB2 ....100 D5
Melville Gdns BB3 ....64 A8
Melville Rd Blackpool FY2 .150 C4
Heysham LA3 ....208 E5
Melville St Burnley BB10 .147 C1
Darwen BB3 ....64 A8
Memorial Gdns PR3 ....157 A4
Memory Cl PR4 ....92 B7
Menai Dr PR2 ....116 D7
Mendip Cl Horwich BL6 ....31 C5
Saltcotes PR4 ....90 E5
Mendip Rd PR5 ....76 D1
Menivale Cl PR9 ....53 B5
Meols Cl L37 ....11 E2
Meols Cop High Sch PR8 ...35 A4
Meols Cop Rd PR8,PR9 ...34 F4
Meols Cop Retail Pk The
PR9 ....35 A4
Meols Cop Sta PR9 ....34 F7
Meols Ct PR9 ....54 A6
Meolsgate Ave PR4 ....56 A7
Mercer Cres BB4 ....67 A8
Mercer Ct PR7 ....42 F1
Mercer Dr BB6 ....123 E6
Mercer Pl PR5 ....96 A1
Mercer St 11 Burnley BB12 .125 F7
18 Clayton-le-M BB5 ....123 F3
Great Harwood BB6 ......123 D5
Preston PR1 ....96 C8
Mercer's La L39 ....7 B4
Merchants Landing BB1 ..100 F3
Merchants Quay 11 BB1 ..100 F3
Merclesden Ave BB9 ......169 B1
Mere Ave
Burscough Bridge L40 .....24 E6
Fleetwood FY7 ....193 D1
Mere Brook FY3 ....130 E5
Mere Brow La PR4 ....55 A2
Mere Cl Broughton PR3 ...136 C3
Skelmersdale WN8 ....17 F2
Mere Ct Burnley BB11 ....126 B4
Burscough Bridge L40 .....24 E5
Mere Fold PR7 ....41 D3
Mere La Banks PR9 ....54 A2
Holmeswood PR4 ....37 A7
Rufford L40 ....37 E3
Mere Park Ct FY3 ....130 A2
Mere Rd Blackpool FY3 ...129 D5
Formby L37 ....11 D2
Mere Sands Wood
Nature Reserve L40 ......37 F4
Meredith St BB9 ....147 E7
Merefell Rd LA5 ....216 A6
Merefield PR7 ....60 A1
Merefield Specl Sch PR8 ..20 F3
Merefold PR4 ....30 F3
Mereland Cl WN5 ....10 E6
Mereland Rd FY3 ....130 A2
Merepark Dr PR9 ....53 B4
Meres Way PR8 ....34 B2
Mereside Inf Sch FY4 ....130 B1
Mereside Rd PR4 ....73 F7
Merewood WN8 ....18 A4
Meriden Cl PR8 ....20 B5
Merlecrest Dr PR4 ....56 A8
Merlewood BL6 ....67 E3
Merlewood Ave PR9 ....53 B3
Merlin Cl PR6 ....61 A3
Merlin Dr BB5 ....102 D3
Merlin Gr Leyland PR5 .....58 C8
Padiham BB12 ....125 E6
Merlin Rd BB2 ....100 B6
Merlyn Rd FY5 ....172 E1
Merrick Ave PR1 ....96 F8
Merrilox Ave L31 ....5 D3
Merry Trees La PR2,PR4 ..115 E5
Merryburn Cl PR2 ....117 A4
Merscar La L40 ....23 D6
Mersey Ave Darwen BB3 ...80 D3
Formby L37 ....11 E6
Maghull L31 ....5 F2
Mersey Rd Blackpool FY4 .109 B8
Fleetwood FY7 ....193 H4
Orrell WN5 ....10 F7
Mersey St Bacup OL13 .....87 A1
Burnley BB12 ....126 A6
Longridge PR3 ....139 B8
Preston PR2 ....95 C8
Merton Ave PR2 ....116 F6
Merton Gr PR6 ....60 F3
Merton St Burnley BB12 ..126 F7
4 Nelson BB9 ....168 D1
Messenger St BB9 ....148 A7
Meta St BB2 ....100 E2
Metcalf Dr BB5 ....124 D6
Metcalfe St BB12 ....126 B5
Mete St PR1 ....96 D8
Methuen Ave
Coupe Green PR5 ....97 E3
Fulwood PR2 ....116 E6
Methuen Cl PR5 ....97 E3
Methuen Dr PR5 ....97 F3
Metropolitan Bsns Pk
FY3 ....130 B2
Metropolitan Dr FY3 .....130 B2
Mettle Cote OL13 ....87 A1
Meville Ave BB3 ....64 A7
Mewith La LA2 ....233 C6
Mews The Morecambe LA4 .213 A5
1 Padiham BB12 ....145 C1
1 Radford BB3 ....64 C7
Southport PR8 ....34 A5
Mexford Ave FY2 ....129 D8
Meyler Ave FY3 ....129 E8
Michael Pl LA4 ....212 G5

Michael Wife La
Edenfield BL0 ....67 F2
Edenfield BL0 ....67 F3
Michael's La L39 ....21 C3
Michaels Cl L37 ....11 E3
Michaelson Ave LA4 ......213 A4
Mickering La L39 ....6 C5
Mickleden Ave PR2 ....116 F7
Mickleden Rd FY4 ....130 C1
Micklefield Ct 2 PR5 ......75 D1
Micklegate PR5 ....75 D1
Micklehurst Cres BB11 ..126 D2
Middle Hey PR4 ....73 E3
Middle Holly Rd PR3 .....199 C8
Middle La LA2 ....207 A6
Middle Meanygate PR4 ....55 C7
Middle Moss La
Great Altcar L37 ....12 F3
Haskayne L37 ....13 A2
Middle St Blackpool FY1 ..129 B3
Colne BB8 ....169 C4
Lancaster LA1 ....210 F8
Whitworth OL12 ....70 D1
Middle Withins La L37, L38 .4 A7
Middlefield PR5 ....58 A8
Middleforth CE Prim Sch
PR1 ....95 D3
Middleforth Gn PR1 ....95 E4
Middleforth Ind Est 4
PR1 ....95 E4
Middlegate LA3 ....213 A2
Middlegate Gn BB4 ....105 A1
Middlesex Ave BB12 .....126 B7
Middleton Ave FY7 ....193 D1
Middleton Dr BB9 ....168 E6
Middleton Rd
Heysham LA3 ....208 E5
Heysham, Middleton LA3 ..209 B2
Middleton Tower
Holiday Ctr LA3 ....208 E1
Middleton Way LA3 ....208 F6
Middlewood WN8 ....18 A4
Middlewood Cl
Eccleston PR7 ....40 C6
Ormskirk L39 ....6 C7
Middlewood Dr L39 ....6 C7
Middlewood Rd L39 ....6 C7
Midfield BB6 ....122 C8
Midge Hall La
Drummersdale PR9 ....36 C3
Leyland PR4,PR5 ....74 F4
Midgeland Rd FY4 ....110 B5
Midgeland Terr FY4 ....110 B5
Midgery La Fulwood PR2 ..117 B7
Fulwood PR2,PR3 ....117 A8
Midgley St BB8 ....169 E4
Midhurst Dr PR8 ....20 B4
Midland St
12 Accrington BB5 ....103 C5
Nelson BB9 ....168 E1
Midland Terr LA5 ....217 D3
Midsummer St BB2 ....100 C5
Midville Pl 14 BB3 ....81 A1
Milbanke Ave PR4 ....113 A5
Milbourne Rd BL9 ....32 A6
Milbourne St FY1 ....129 C5
Milbrook Cl BB11 ....126 B5
Milburn Ave FY5 ....172 F5
Mildred Cl FY5 ....173 A3
Mile End Cl BB8 ....191 D1
Mile End Row BB2 ....100 B6
Mile Rd FY6 ....153 A1
Mile Stone Mdw PR7 ....59 D4
Miles Ave OL13 ....69 D8
Miles La WN6 ....19 E6
Miles St PR1 ....116 F2
Miles Wlk PR1 ....116 E2
Milestone Mdw PR7 ....59 D4
Milestone Pl LA2 ....231 C3
Miletas Pl FY8 ....89 C4
Milford Ave FY2 ....150 D1
Milford Cl L37 ....11 C1
Milford St Colne BB8 ....169 C5
6 Rochdale OL12 ....51 F1
Milk St BL0 ....49 B5
Milking La BB3 ....81 A6
Milking Stile La LA1 ....210 D8
Mill Bank WN6 ....19 D7
Mill Brook PR3 ....178 D3
Mill Brook Pl BB7 ....94 C8
Mill Brow Haskayne L39 ...14 A7
Kirkby Lonsdale LA6 .....238 C2
Lowgill LA2 ....233 B2
Mill Brow Rd BB18 ....201 C2
Mill Cl PR4 ....134 C8
Mill Ct PR3 ....139 B8
Mill Cotts BB3 ....81 F3
Mill Dam Cl L40 ....24 C2
Mill Dam La L40 ....16 D8
Mill Entrance BB5 ....123 F2
Mill Field Clayton-le-M BB5 .123 F1
Parbold WN8 ....26 C1
Mill Gap St 8 BB3 ....64 A8
Mill Gate Fulwood PR2 ...116 D3
15 Rawtenstall BB4 ....85 A3
Mill Gdns 6 LA2 ....233 D8
Mill Gn BB2 ....169 D4
Mill Haven PR2 ....116 D3
Mill Hey Ave FY6 ....151 E1
Mill Hey La LA4 ....238 D2
Mill Hill Oswaldtwistle BB5 102 E4
Preston PR1 ....95 E8
Mill Hill Bridge St BB2 ..100 B2
Mill Hill Cotts BL6 ....43 F1

Mill Hill Gr LA3 ....209 A2
Mill Hill La BB11 ....125 B3
Mill Hill St BB2 ....100 B2
Mill Hill Sta BB2 ....100 B2
Mill Ho 15 LA1 ....211 A8
Mill Ho Mews 17 LA1 .....211 A8
Mill House La
Clayton Brook PR6 ....77 F8
Longridge PR3 ....140 A8
Mill House View WN8 .....10 C7
Mill La Appley Bridge WN6 ..19 D7
Becconsall PR4 ....72 F2
Blackburn BB2 ....100 E4
Bolton Green PR7 ....41 A8
Bolton Green PR7 ....59 A1
Bolton-le-S LA5 ....216 A6
Burscough L40 ....24 E4
Carnforth LA5 ....217 D4
Caton LA2 ....231 B3
Clayton Green PR6 ....77 C1
Coppull PR7 ....41 E2
Darwen BB3 ....63 A5
Eccleston PR7 ....40 C5
Elswick PR4 ....154 B1
Fleetwood FY7 ....194 B4
Fulwood PR2 ....116 C4
Gisburn BB7 ....225 B4
Goosnargh PR3 ....137 G6
Great Harwood BB6 ......124 A6
Halton LA2 ....214 F6
Hambleton FY6 ....174 E1
Haskayne L39 ....14 F1
Hesketh Lane PR3 ....160 C8
Heskin Green PR7 ....41 A2
Horwich BL6 ....31 D4
Leyland PR5 ....58 D8
Leyland PR5 ....75 E3
Low Bentham LA2 ....233 C7
Orrell WN8 ....10 A8
Parbold WN8 ....26 C1
Skelmersdale,
Pennylands WN8 ....17 F2
Southport PR9 ....53 A1
Staining FY5 ....130 D5
Stalmine FY6 ....174 D7
Waddington BB7 ....186 A8
Walton-le-D PR5 ....96 D5
Warton PR4 ....91 F6
Wrea Green PR4 ....112 A3
Mill La Ind Est BB7 .....225 B3
Mill Lane Cres PR9 ....53 A1
Mill Leat Cl WN8 ....26 C2
Mill Leat Mews WN8 ......26 C2
Mill Rd Orrell WN5 ....10 D5
Southport PR8 ....20 D5
Mill Row BB4 ....84 F5
Mill St Accrington BB5 ...103 F1
Adlington PR6 ....30 B8
Bacup OL13 ....86 F3
Barnoldswick BB18 ......200 A2
Barrowford BB9 ....168 D4
Church BB5 ....102 F6
Clayton-le-M BB5 ....123 F2
4 Coppull PR7 ....41 E1
Great Harwood BB6 ......123 C5
Haslingden BB4 ....84 B5
Kirkham PR4 ....113 A5
Lancaster LA1 ....211 A8
Leyland, Farington PR5 ...76 B3
Leyland, Seven Stars PR5 ..58 D8
Ormskirk L39 ....15 F5
Oswaldtwistle BB5 ......102 D3
Padiham BB12 ....125 C8
Preesall FY6 ....195 B3
Preston PR1 ....95 D8
Ramsbottom BL0 ....49 A4
Southport PR8 ....34 C6
West Bradford BB7 ......186 E5
Mill The PR1 ....95 F8
Mill View PR4 ....92 B7
Mill View Ct L39 ....7 E6
Mill Wood Cl PR6 ....78 C3
Mill Yd BL9 ....32 A3
Millar Barn La BB4 ....68 F8
Millar's Pace PR9 ....53 B5
Millard Cl LA3 ....208 F5
Millbank Fulwood PR2 ....116 C3
4 Preston PR1 ....96 B8
Millbank Brow L40 ....24 F3
Millbank La L31, L39 ....5 F3
Millbrook BB12 ....146 E8
Millbrook Cl
Skelmersdale WN8 ....17 E2
Wheelton PR6 ....61 A7
Millbrook Ct BB7 ....186 E5
Millbrook Mews 11 FY8 ...90 C3
Millbrook Row PR6 ....43 B1
Millbrook St BB3 ....80 F7
Millbrook Way PR1 ....95 C3
Millcombe Way PR5 ....96 E3
Millcroft Chorley PR7 .....60 A2
Fulwood PR2 ....116 D4
Millcroft Ave WN5 ....10 D5
Milldyke Cl FY4 ....109 F6
Miller Ave PR6 ....79 B2
Miller Cl BB5 ....102 C5
Miller Cres FY5 ....152 E1
Miller Ct LA1 ....210 E5
Miller Field PR2 ....115 E3
Miller Fold Ave BB5 ......103 B3
Miller Ho 6 PR1 ....96 A7
Miller La Catforth PR4 ....134 E4
Fulwood PR2 ....115 E5
Miller Rd PR1,PR2 ....117 C3
Miller St 4 Blackpool FY1 .129 B1
11 Preston PR1 ....96 C8
Ramsbottom BL9 ....49 C2

Miller's Brow PR3 ....204 E3
Millers Ct L39 ....15 F5
Millersdale Cl FY5 ....151 E7
Millersgate PR4 ....115 C4
Millet Terr BL9 ....32 E7
Millett St BL0 ....49 D7
Millfield Cl PR4 ....91 F6
Millfield High Sch FY5 ..151 C8
Millfield Rd Blackpool FY4 .109 F6
Chorley PR7 ....60 C1
Millfold OL12 ....70 D2
Millgate BL7 ....46 D2
Millgate Rd 18 BB4 ....85 A3
Millgate Terr OL12 ....70 E5
Millham St BB1 ....100 E6
Millholme Dr LA2 ....233 D7
Millhouse Lo PR8 ....20 D5
Millhouse St BL0 ....49 E8
Millington Ave FY4 ....109 E8
Millom Ave FY2 ....150 D4
Millom Cl FY7 ....172 C8
Millrace Ct 5 LA1 ....213 F2
Millrose St WN8 ....17 F2
Mills PR6 ....61 A7
Mills St OL12 ....70 D1
Millstone Cl PR7 ....41 F1
Millthorne Ave BB7 ......164 D7
Millwood Cl BB2 ....100 A1
Millwood Glade PR7 ....60 B1
Millwood Rd PR1,PR5 .....96 B3
Milman Cl L39 ....15 D3
Milne St BL0 ....67 C5
Milner Rd Darwen BB3 .....80 E4
Lytham St Anne's FY8 .....89 E4
Milner St Burnley BB10 ..127 A8
Preston PR1 ....117 A2
Whitworth OL12 ....51 C8
Whitworth OL12 ....70 C1
Milnshaw Gdns BB5 ......103 B7
Milnshaw La BB5 ....103 B6
Milnthorpe Ave FY5 ......172 D5
Milton Ave Blackpool FY3 .129 F5
Clitheroe BB7 ....186 E1
2 Thornton FY5 ....173 A3
Milton Cl
Bamber Bridge PR5 ....96 D2
Darwen BB3 ....81 C1
Great Harwood BB6 ......123 B4
Haslingden BB4 ....67 A7
Milton Cres FY6 ....130 D8
Milton Ct PR7 ....41 E1
Milton Dr L39 ....16 A4
Milton Gr
Barnoldswick BB18 ......200 A3
Longshaw WN5 ....10 D1
Orrell WN5 ....10 F6
Milton Rd Colne BB8 .....169 D5
Coppull PR7 ....28 E8
Milton St
3 Barrowford BB9 ....168 D4
1 Blackburn BB1 ....101 A5
Brierfield BB9 ....147 B5
Brierfield, Harle Syke BB10 .147 F3
Clayton-le-M BB5 ....123 F3
Fleetwood FY7 ....194 A4
Nelson BB9 ....168 D1
Oswaldtwistle BB5 ......102 E4
Padiham BB12 ....125 E7
Ramsbottom BL0 ....49 B6
Southport PR9 ....35 A7
Milton Terr PR6 ....60 D2
Milton Way L31 ....5 B1
Mimosa Cl PR7 ....60 A3
Mimosa Rd PR2 ....117 E2
Mincing La BB2 ....100 E4
Minden Rd PR4 ....131 E5
Minehead Ave BB10 ......147 D2
Minerva Rd LA1 ....210 C8
Minnie St OL12 ....70 D2
Minnie Terr BB2 ....100 C6
Minor St 11 BB4 ....85 A7
Minstead Ave L33 ....1 A2
Minster Cres BB3 ....64 C8
Minster Dr LA3 ....212 G4
Minster Pk PR4 ....115 E5
Minstrel Wlk FY6 ....151 D4
Mint Ave BB9 ....168 D4
Mint St BL0 ....67 C2
Mintholme Ave PR5 ....97 E2
Mintor Rd L33 ....1 A2
Mire Ash Brow BB2 ......120 D1
Mire Ridge BB8 ....170 A3
Mirfield Gr 11 FY4 ....129 D1
Miry La WN8 ....26 D2
Mission Cotts L40 ....25 B8
Mitcham Rd FY4 ....110 B8
Mitchelgate LA6 ....238 B2
Mitchell St Burnley BB12 .126 C6
Clitheroe BB7 ....164 D7
2 Colne BB8 ....169 D5
Mitella St BB10 ....127 C5
Mitre St BB11 ....126 E6
Mitten's La L37 ....12 B3
Mitton Ave
Barrowford BB9 ....168 F6
Rawtenstall BB4 ....85 A4
Mitton Cl OL10 ....32 F2
Mitton Cres PR4 ....113 A5
Mitton Dr PR2 ....118 A3
Mitton Gn BB3 ....127 D5
Mitton Hos BB9 ....168 F6
Mitton Rd
Great Mitton BB7 ....163 F2
Whalley BB7 ....143 B2
Mitton St BB1 ....100 F7
Mizpah St BB10 ....127 C5
Mizzy Rd OL12 ....51 F1
Moira Cres PR2 ....117 F4

Moleside Cl BB5 103 D6
Mollington Rd BB2 100 B7
Molly Wood La BB11 125 F5
Molyneux Ct 17 PR1 96 A8
Molyneux Dr FY4 109 D7
Molyneux Pl FY8 90 A4
Molyneux Rd L39 6 C7
Mona Pl PR1 95 E8
Mona Rd BB2 100 E1
Monarch Cres FY8 89 B8
Monarch St BB5 102 E4
Money Close La LA3 208 D4
Moneyclose Gr LA3 208 D5
Monk Hall St BB10 127 A7
Monk St Accrington BB5 103 A6
2 Clitheroe BB7 164 D7
Monk's La FY6 195 A1
Monkroyd Ave BB18 200 A2
Monks Carr La L37, L38 4 A6
Monks Cl L37 12 A1
Monks Dr Formby L37 12 A1
Longridge PR3 139 A6
Withnell PR6 79 A1
Monks Gate FY8 89 D7
Monks La L40 24 D7
Monks Wlk PR1 95 C6
Monkswell Ave LA5 216 A5
Monkswell Dr LA5 216 A5
Monkswood Ave LA4 213 A5
Monmouth Ct PR2 115 F3
Monmouth Rd BB1 101 C5
Monmouth St
5 Burnley BB12 126 D6
Colne BB8 170 A5
Monroe Dr FY7 193 D3
Montagu Mews L37 11 E5
Montagu Rd L37 11 E5
Montague Cl BB2 100 D4
Montague Rd BB11 126 E5
Montague St
Blackburn BB2 100 D5
Blackpool FY4 109 B8
Brierfield BB9 147 B5
4 Clitheroe BB7 164 D8
Colne BB8 169 E6
Montcliffe Rd PR6 60 E1
Monteagle Dr LA2 232 B7
Monteagle Sq LA2 232 B7
Montford Ct BB12 146 F6
Montford Rd BB9 146 F6
Montgomery Ave PR9 35 B6
Montgomery Cl BB5 103 E2
Montgomery Gr BB12 126 C7
Montgomery High Sch FY2 150 D5
Montgomery St 7 PR5 76 F8
Monthall Rise LA1 214 B1
Montjoly St PR1 96 C7
Monton Rd BB3 80 E4
Montpelier Ave FY2 150 C5
Montreal Ave FY1 129 D4
Montreal Rd BB2 100 C8
Montrose Ave
Blackpool FY1 129 C3
Ramsbottom BL0 49 A2
Montrose Cl PR6 42 E6
Montrose Cres LA3 208 E7
Montrose Dr PR9 52 F1
Montrose St
Blackburn BB2 100 C3
Brierfield BB9 147 B6
Burnley BB11 126 F4
Moody La L40 39 E1
Moody St WN6 28 E1
Moon Ave 7 FY1 129 B2
Moon St PR5 76 E8
Moons Acre LA2 233 D8
Moor Ave
Appley Bridge WN6 19 E8
Penwortham PR1 95 A4
Moor Cl Darwen BB3 64 D8
Lancaster LA1 211 A8
Southport PR8 20 D2
Moor Close La LA6 234 B1
Moor Dr WN8 9 D7
Moor Edge BB7 143 B6
Moor End Cty Prim Sch BB5 102 D4
Moor Field
New Longton PR4 75 A7
Whalley BB7 143 B6
Moor Gate 14 LA1 211 A8
Moor Hall La PR4 113 F4
Moor Hall St PR1 116 E2
Moor Hey Cotts PR5 57 A6
Moor Hey Sch PR5 96 A1
Moor La Billington BB6,BB7 143 B2
Butt Yeats LA2 232 C5
Clitheroe BB7 164 E8
Darwen BB3 81 B3
Haslingden BB4 83 F6
Hutton PR4 94 D1
Ince Blundell L38, L23 3 E2
Lancaster LA1 211 A8
Langho BB6 122 E8
Maghull L29 4 D1
Padiham BB12 145 C1
Preston PR1 116 F1
Salterforth BB18 191 C6
Southport PR8 20 C2
Waddington BB7 223 D2
West Bradford BB7 186 D7
Whalley BB7 143 B6
Wiswell BB7 143 F7
Moor Nook Cty Prim Sch PR2 118 A3
Moor Park Ave
Blackpool FY2 150 E4
Moor Park Ave *continued*
Preston PR1 117 A2
Moor Park High Sch PR1 117 A2
Moor Park Inf & Jun Sch FY2 150 E3
Moor Platt Cl BL6 31 F3
Moor Rd Barber's Moor PR5 57 D3
Chorley PR7 42 B5
Haslingden BB4 66 F5
Orrell WN5 10 E6
Ramsbottom BL8 49 A6
Rivington PR6 43 E7
Moor Side La
Ramsbottom BL0 50 A7
Wiswell BB7 143 F7
Moor St Clayton-le-M BB5 123 F3
Kirkham PR4 113 A5
32 Lancaster LA1 210 F8
Ormskirk L39 15 F5
Moor View Bacup OL13 87 A4
Bacup, Brandwood OL13 69 B7
Rawtenstall BB4 68 F6
Salterforth BB18 191 E8
Moor Way BL8 48 C3
Moorbottom Rd BL8 48 E5
Moorbrook Sch PR2 116 E3
Moorbrook St PR1 116 E1
Moorcroft Blackburn BB3 81 A6
Broughton PR3 136 B2
Edenfield BL0 67 D2
Moorcroft Cres PR2 117 D3
Moore Dr PR8 145 F5
Moore St Blackpool FY4 129 B1
Colne BB8 169 C5
Nelson BB9 147 F7
Padiham BB12 125 F7
Preston PR1 96 C7
Moore Tree Dr FY4 110 A8
Moorend BB7 164 F7
Moores La WN6 28 D2
Moorfield BL7 47 D6
Moorfield Ave
Blackburn BB1 121 E3
Blackpool FY3 129 E6
Carleton FY6 151 B4
Huncoat BB5 103 F8
Moorfield Cl
Clayton-le-M BB5 124 B3
Fulwood PR2 116 E8
Preston PR1 95 A2
Moorfield Dr
Clayton-le-M BB5 124 B3
Fulwood PR2 117 E3
Lytham St Anne's FY8 90 A4
Moorfield Ind Est BB5 124 B3
Moorfield La L40 23 C3
Moorfield Pl 3 OL12 51 F1
Moorfield Rd
Clayton-le-M BB5 124 B3
Leyland PR5 58 C8
Moorfield Sch PR1 117 A3
Moorfield Way BB5 124 B3
Moorfields Blackpool FY2 150 F4
Chorley PR6 60 E1
Moorfields Ave PR2 116 E8
Moorgate Accrington BB5 103 B2
Blackpool FY4 109 F6
Bury BL9 32 A3
Fulwood PR2 116 F5
Ormskirk L39 15 E4
Moorgate Gdns BB2 100 C1
Moorgate Rd BB18 200 A1
Moorgate St BB2 100 C1
Moorhead Gdns PR4 91 E7
Moorhead High Sch BB5 103 A7
Moorhead St 2 BB8 169 C5
Moorhen Pl 14 FY5 172 F1
Moorhey Cres
Penwortham PR1 95 B5
Walton Summit PR5 77 A8
Moorhey Dr PR1 95 B5
Moorhouse Ave BB5 103 A4
Moorhouse Cl BB5 103 A4
Moorhouse St
Accrington BB5 103 A4
1 Blackpool FY1 129 B7
Burnley BB11 126 C5
Moorhouses L38 2 F3
Mooring The 4 PR6 42 E8
Moorings The
Burnley BB12 126 E7
Hest Bank LA2 215 D1
Maghull L31 5 B4
Moorland Ave
Blackburn BB2 79 D7
Clitheroe BB7 186 F3
Darwen BB3 80 D2
Earby BB18 201 C1
Fulwood PR2 117 D4
Poulton-le-F FY6 151 E4
Whitworth OL12 51 C7
Moorland Cl BB9 168 F6
Moorland Cres
Clitheroe BB7 186 F2
Fulwood PR2 117 D4
Whitworth OL12 51 C7
Moorland Dr
Brierfield BB9 147 D4
Horwich BL6 31 F3
Moorland Gate PR6 42 F6
Moorland Gdns FY6 151 E4
Moorland Rd
Blackburn BB2 80 C7
Burnley BB11 126 F3
Clitheroe BB7 186 F2
Langho BB6 142 C1
Lytham St Anne's FY8 89 A7
Poulton-le-F FY6 151 F4
Moorland Rise BB4 84 C2
Moorland Sch BB7 186 E2
Moorland St OL12 51 E1
Moorland Terr OL12 51 A1
Moorland View BB9 147 E6
Moorlands PR1 116 E3
Moorlands Gr LA3 212 B3
Moorlands Terr OL13 87 A1
Moorlands The OL13 87 A8
Moorlands View BL0 67 D5
Moorside Melling LA6 235 D2
Moor Side PR4 133 D3
Moorside Ave
Blackburn BB1 101 D4
Brierfield BB9 147 D4
Fulwood PR2 117 F3
Horwich BL6 31 C4
Moorside Cl LA6 235 D2
Moorside Cres OL13 87 A4
Moorside Cty Prim Sch LA1 211 B4
Moorside Dr Enfield BB5 124 A2
Preston PR1 95 B2
Moorside La PR4 135 C4
Moorside Prim Sch WN8 9 E7
Moorside Rd Caton LA2 231 D3
Edgworth BL7 65 E1
Moorsview BL0 49 B6
Moorthorpe Cl BB3 64 A6
Moorview Cl BB10 147 E2
Moorview Ct 2 FY4 109 F7
Moorway FY6 151 F4
Moray Cl BL0 49 A4
Morecambe Bay Com Prim Sch LA4 212 E5
Morecambe Bay Nature Reserve LA5 215 D5
Morecambe High Sch LA4 212 F6
Morecambe L Pk LA4 212 C5
Morecambe Rd
Blackburn BB2 100 F1
Lancaster LA3,LA1 213 C2
Morecambe Rd Sch LA3 213 B3
Morecambe St E LA4 212 E6
Morecambe St W LA4 212 E6
Morecambe Sta LA4 212 D5
Moresby Ave FY3 130 B7
Moreton Dr
Poulton-le-F FY6 151 D2
Staining FY3 130 D5
Moreton Gn 2 LA3 208 F7
Moreton St BB5 103 B6
Morewood Dr LA6 234 C7
Morland Ave
Bamber Bridge PR5 76 A7
Kirkham PR4 112 F7
Morley Ave BB2 100 A1
Morley Cl LA1 213 E3
Morley Rd Blackpool FY4 129 E1
Lancaster LA1 213 E3
Southport PR9 34 E8
Morley St 2 Burnley BB11 127 B4
1 Padiham BB12 125 D8
Morningside LA1 210 E7
Mornington Rd
Adlington PR6 30 B8
Lytham St Anne's FY8 90 E4
Penwortham PR1 95 B5
Preston PR1 117 F1
Southport PR9 34 C7
Morris Cl PR5 59 A8
Morris Cres PR2 117 D2
Morris Ct PR2 117 D2
Morris Hey L39 22 D3
Morris La L39,L40 22 E3
Morris Rd Chorley PR6 60 E1
Fulwood PR2 117 D2
Orrell WN8 10 A7
Morrison St PR6 60 D2
Morse St BB10 127 D5
Morston Ave FY2 150 E1
Mort St BL6 31 B4
Mortimer Gr LA3 209 A8
Morton Cty Prim Sch FY4 109 F7
Morton St 22 BB1 100 E5
Morton Wlk 6 BB3 64 B6
Morven Gr PR8 34 E7
Moscow Mill St BB5 102 E5
Mosedale Dr BB12 126 B8
Moseley Ave BB18 200 F1
Moseley Cl BB11 127 A2
Moseley Rd BB11 127 A3
Mosley Ave BL0 49 B2
Mosley St
Barnoldswick BB18 200 B2
Blackburn BB2 100 E2
4 Leyland PR5 76 A1
Nelson BB9 147 D8
Preston PR1 96 C8
Southport PR8 34 B4
Mosman Pl BB9 168 C3
Moss Acre Rd PR1 95 E2
Moss Ave Orrell WN5 10 D3
Preston PR2 116 A2
Moss Bank Coppull PR7 41 E1
Ormskirk L39 15 D2
Moss Bank Ct L39 15 D2
Moss Bank Pl FY4 109 F8
Moss Bridge L40 25 C3
Moss Bridge La L40 25 C2
Moss Bridge Pk PR5 76 C8
Moss Cl Chorley PR6 42 E8
Haslingden BB4 67 A8
Moss Cotts L40 17 A3
Moss Delph La L39 15 C1
Moss Dr BL6 31 F3
Moss Edge La
Blackpool FY4 110 A3
Lytham St Anne's FY8 110 B2
Moss End Way L33 1 D3
Moss Fold Rd BB3 80 E5
Moss Gate BB1 101 B6
Moss Gn L37 12 B4
Moss Hall La FY8 89 E7
Moss Hall Rd BB5 103 C8
Moss Hey Hey PR4 55 A3
Moss House La
Great Plumpton PR4 111 C7
Much Hoole PR4 74 B2
Stalmine FY6 174 D8
Moss House Rd
Blackpool FY4 110 A6
Broughton PR4 136 B2
Moss La Appley Bridge WN6 27 E3
Bamber Bridge PR5 76 B8
Banks PR9 54 D6
Becconsall PR4 72 C1
Bickerstaffe L39 7 F2
Blackburn BB1,BB5 101 F3
Blackrod BL6 30 F2
Bretherton PR5 57 C8
Burscough L40 25 A7
Burton-in-K LA5 234 A8
Catforth PR4 134 D5
Chipping PR3 183 A1
Clayton-le-W PR5 76 D2
Coppull PR7 41 E1
Croston PR5 39 A8
Duncombe PR3 156 D2
Farington PR5 75 D5
Formby L37, L39 12 E5
Garstang PR3 178 B7
Glasson LA2 205 E1
Hambleton FY6 174 D1
Hightown L38, L23 3 C2
Inskip PR4 155 B3
Kingsfold PR1 95 E1
Kirkby, Northwood L33 1 B3
Leyland PR5 76 C2
Lucas Green PR6 60 D5
Maghull L31 5 E2
Maghull, Lydiate L31 5 D5
New Longton PR4 74 E7
Silverdale LA5 218 F5
Skelmersdale WN8 8 F6
Southport PR9 35 B8
St Michael's on W PR3 155 B8
Walmer Bridge PR4 74 C4
Wymott PR5 57 F5
Moss La E PR4 114 A8
Moss La W PR4 113 F7
Moss Lane View WN8 8 F6
Moss Lea PR4 56 A7
Moss Nook
Burscough Bridge L40 24 E6
Ormskirk L39 15 C2
Moss Pl LA1 214 A4
Moss Rd Lancaster LA3 209 D7
Orrell WN5 10 D3
Southport PR8 34 C2
Moss Side
Barnoldswick BB18 200 C2
Formby L37 12 B4
Moss Side Cty Prim Sch PR5 75 B1
Moss Side La
Hale Nook FR6,PR3 175 C7
Lane Heads PR3 154 E5
Mere Brow PR4 54 F4
Stalmine FY6 174 E7
Wrea Green PR4 112 A3
Moss Side St OL12 70 E5
Moss Side Sta FY8 111 D1
Moss Side Way PR5 58 C8
Moss St Bamber Bridge PR5 76 B8
Blackburn BB1 101 A6
7 Clitheroe BB7 164 D8
Great Harwood BB6 123 C4
Preston PR1 95 E8
Ramsbottom BL9 49 D2
Moss Terr PR6 60 E5
Moss View Maghull L31 5 F1
Ormskirk L39 15 E4
Southport PR8 20 E5
Moss Way 3 FY4 109 F7
Mossbank BB1 101 A6
Mossbourne Rd FY6 151 C2
Mossbrook Dr PR4 115 F5
Mossdale BB1 101 A6
Mossdale Ave PR2 117 D4
Mossfield Cl
Bamber Bridge PR5 76 B8
Bury BL9 32 B4
Mossfield Rd PR6 42 E8
Mossgate Cty Prim Sch
Heysham LA3 208 F8
Morecambe LA3 212 B1
Mossgiel Ave PR8 20 B5
Mosshill Cl L31 5 C3
Mosslands PR5 75 D1
Mosslawn Rd L32 1 A1
Mosslea Dr PR3 136 B8
Mossom La FY5 150 D7
Mossway PR4 74 F7
Mossy Lea Fold WN6 28 A3
Mossy Lea Rd WN6 27 F5
Mostyn St BB3 80 E4
Motherwell Cres PR8 34 F3
Mottram Cl PR6 60 C5
Mottram Mews 6 BL6 31 B4
Mottram St BL6 31 B4
Moulden Brow BB2 79 B7
Moulding Cl BB2 100 B4
Mounsey Rd PR5 76 F8
Mount Ave Lancaster LA1 213 F3
Morecambe LA4 213 B7
Rawtenstall BB4 68 F8
Mount Carmel Prep Sch L39 15 D2
Mount Carmel RC High Sch BB5 103 A4
Mount Cres Orrell WN5 10 F6
Over Town BB10 107 A8
Mount Gdns LA4 213 A7
Mount House Cl L37 12 B5
Mount House Rd L37 12 B5
Mount La Burnley BB10 127 F1
Cornholme OL14 108 C3
Over Town BB10 107 A8
Mount Pleasant
Adlington PR6 30 A8
Arnside LA5 218 C8
16 Bacup OL13 69 C8
Blackburn BB1 100 F5
Brinscall PR6 62 A8
Chatburn BB7 187 D5
Edgworth BL7 47 D5
High Bentham LA2 233 D8
Nangreaves BL9 49 F3
8 Preston PR1 95 F8
Rawtenstall BB4 84 E2
Sabden BB7 145 A7
Slaidburn BB7 223 B7
Whittle-le-W PR6 60 C8
Mount Pleasant La LA5 216 B5
Mount Pleasant Prim Sch BB5 123 F2
Mount Pleasant St
3 Burnley BB11 126 F5
Cornholme OL14 108 A1
Horwich BL6 31 D1
6 Oswaldtwistle BB5 102 E4
Mount Rd Burnley BB11 126 F4
Fleetwood FY7 194 A5
Mount St Accrington BB5 103 B4
13 Barrowford BB9 168 D3
Blackpool FY1 129 B6
Brierfield BB9 147 B5
Clayton-le-M BB5 124 A2
Fleetwood FY7 194 A4
Great Harwood BB6 123 C6
Horwich BL6 31 D2
Preston PR1 95 F7
Ramsbottom BL0 49 B6
Rawtenstall BB4 84 E2
Southport PR9 34 D7
Mount St James BB1 101 F4
Mount Terr BB4 85 A2
Mount The Blackburn BB2 100 C6
Fleetwood FY7 194 A5
Skelmersdale WN8 9 B8
Mount Zion Ct OL14 108 A1
Mountain Ash OL12 51 B3
Mountain Ash Cl OL12 51 B3
Mountain La BB5 103 C4
Mountain Rd PR7 28 E8
Mountbatten Cl PR2 95 B7
Mountbatten Rd PR7 42 B6
Mountfield Ct WN5 10 F7
Mountside Cl OL12 51 F2
Mountwood WN8 18 A4
Mountwood Lo PR8 20 C5
Mowbray Ave BB2 100 F2
Mowbray Dr Blackpool FY3 150 F1
Burton-in-K LA6 234 C7
Mowbray Pl 1 FY7 193 E4
Mowbray Rd FY7 193 E4
Mowbreck Ct PR4 113 A6
Mowbreck La PR4 113 B7
Mowbrick La LA2 215 D1
Mowgrain View 2 OL13 86 F3
Muirfield PR1 95 A6
Muirfield Cl PR2 116 B6
Muirfield Dr PR8 20 C4
Mulberry Ave PR1 95 A3
Mulberry Cl PR4 114 C1
Mulberry Cotts 10 LA2 207 A4
Mulberry La LA1 211 A2
Mulberry Mews FY2 150 F6
Mulberry St BB1 101 B5
Mulberry Wlk 3 BB1 101 B5
Mulgrave Ave PR2 116 A1
Mullion Cl PR9 53 B5
Muncaster Rd PR1 116 F2
Munro Ave WN5 10 E6
Munro Cres PR2 117 E3
Munster Ave FY2 150 D3
Murchison Gr FY5 172 E1
Murdock Ave PR2 116 D2
Murdock St BB2 100 B4
Murray Ave PR5 75 E5
Murray St Burnley BB10 147 B1
Leyland PR5 76 B1
Preston PR1 116 E1
Musbury Cres BB4 85 A1
Musbury Rd BB4 66 F7
Musbury View BB4 83 F1
Musden Ave BB4 67 A7
Museum of Mines BB18 201 B2
Museum St 19 BB1 100 E5
Myers St
Barnoldswick BB18 200 B1
Burnley BB10 127 A8
Myerscough Ave
Blackpool FY4 109 F5
Lytham St Anne's FY8 88 D8
Myerscough Coll PR3 156 D5
Myerscough Coll - Hutton Ctr PR4 94 F1

Myerscough Hall Dr PR3 156 E5
Myerscough Planks PR3 .157 A2
Myerscough Smithy Rd
 BB2 . . . . .119 E4
Myndon St LA1 . . . . .213 F3
Myra Ave LA4 . . . . .212 F4
Myra Rd FY8 . . . . .89 B4
Myrtle Ave Blackpool FY3 .129 D5
 Burnley BB11 . . . . .126 D4
 Cleveleys FY5 . . . . .172 F4
 Poulton-le-F FY6 . . . . . . .151 E5
Myrtle Bank Inf Sch
 BB11 . . . . .126 D4
Myrtle Bank Rd
 🔟 Bacup OL13 . . . . .86 F3
 Blackburn BB2 . . . . .80 C8
Myrtle Dr PR4 . . . . .113 C4
Myrtle Gdns BL9 . . . . .32 B2
Myrtle Gr
 🛈 Barnoldswick BB18 . . . .200 C2
 Burnley BB10 . . . . .127 F4
 Haslingden BB4 . . . . .84 A1
 Morecambe LA3 . . . . . . .212 C3
 Southport PR9 . . . . .34 E7
Myrtle St N BL9 . . . . .32 B2
Myrtle St S 🞵 BL9 . . . . . . .32 B2
Mystic Mews 🞹 L39 . . . . . .15 C5
Mythop Ave FY8 . . . . .90 C4
Mythop Cl 🛈 FY8 . . . . .90 C4
Mythop Pl PR2 . . . . .115 F1
Mythop Rd
 Lytham St Anne's FY8 . . . . .90 C4
 Weeton FY4,PR4 . . . . . . .131 C2
Mythop Village FY4 . . . . .130 F2
Mytton St BB12 . . . . .125 D8
Mytton View BB7 . . . . . . .164 D7

N

Naarian Ct BB1 . . . . .100 F7
Nab La Blackburn BB2 . . . .100 D5
 Oswaldtwistle BB5 . . . . . .102 B4
Nab Rd PR6 . . . . .60 E1
Nab's Head La PR5 . . . . . . .98 E8
Nabbs Fold BL8 . . . . .48 F3
Nabbs Way BL8 . . . . .49 A1
Nairn Ave WN8 . . . . .18 B5
Nairn Cl Blackpool FY4 . . .110 A7
 Standish WN6 . . . . .28 D1
Nairne St BB11 . . . . .126 D5
Nancy St BB3 . . . . .81 B1
Nansen Rd Blackburn BB2 .100 B3
 Fleetwood FY7 . . . . .194 A3
Nantwich Ave OL12 . . . . . .51 F3
Napier Ave Blackpool FY4 .109 B6
 Tarleton PR4 . . . . .55 F8
Napier Cl FY8 . . . . .109 E1
Napier St
 🞺 Accrington BB5 . . . . . .103 C5
 Nelson BB9 . . . . .147 E7
Napier Terr PR8 . . . . .34 A5
Naples Ave BB11 . . . . . . .126 D4
Naples Rd BB3 . . . . .81 C1
Naptha La PR4 . . . . .75 C6
Narcissus Ave BB4 . . . . . . .67 A8
Nares Rd BB2 . . . . .100 B3
Nares St PR2 . . . . .116 C1
Narrow Croft Rd L39 . . . . .15 B1
Narrow Gates BB12 . . . . .167 C5
Narrow La Leyland PR5 . . . .74 F2
 Ormskirk L39 . . . . .15 B1
Narrow Lane
 (Clieves Hills) L39 . . . . . .14 E6
Narrow Moss La L39, L40 . .15 E8
Narvik Ave BB11 . . . . . . .126 B4
Nasmyth St BL6 . . . . .31 C3
Nateby Ave FY4 . . . . .109 C5
Nateby Cl Longridge PR3 . .138 F8
 Lytham St Anne's FY8 . . . . .89 A7
Nateby Crossing La PR3 .178 A8
Nateby Ct 🛈 FY4 . . . . . . .109 B6
Nateby Hall La PR3 . . . . .198 F1
Nateby Pl PR2 . . . . .115 F1
Nateby Prim Sch PR3 . . . .177 C6
Nature Trail PR6 . . . . .61 F7
Nave Cl BB3 . . . . .81 C1
Navena Ave FY7 . . . . .193 E2
Navigation Bsns Village
 PR2 . . . . .95 A8
Navigation Way
 Blackburn BB1 . . . . .100 F3
 Preston PR2 . . . . .95 A7
Naylor's Terr BL7 . . . . .45 C5
Naylorfarm Ave WN6 . . . . .19 F5
Naze Ct 🞵 BB4 . . . . .85 E1
Naze La E PR4 . . . . .92 B6
Naze La E PR4 . . . . .92 C5
Naze Lane Ind Est PR4 . . . .92 C4
Naze Rd BB4 . . . . .85 E1
Naze View Ave BB4 . . . . . .85 F2
Nealet Fold PR9 . . . . .53 D5
Near Mdw PR2 . . . . .77 C3
Neargates PR7 . . . . .41 D3
Neath Cl Bamber Bridge PR5 96 E3
 Blackburn BB1 . . . . .100 E7
Ned's La Cold Row FY6 . . .174 D5
 Smallwood Hey PR3 . . . .196 A5
Neddy Hill LA6 . . . . .234 B7
Neddy La BB7 . . . . .143 A4
Nedens Gr L31 . . . . .5 C3
Nedens La L31 . . . . .5 C3
Needham Ave LA4 . . . . . .212 D3
Needham Rise LA4 . . . . . .212 D3
Needham Way WN8 . . . . . .18 B5

Needless Hall La BD23 . .225 E7
Nell Carrs BL0 . . . . .49 E8
Nell La PR5 . . . . .76 E4
Nell's La L39 . . . . .5 F5
Nelson & Colne Coll BB9 168 D2
Nelson & Colne FE Coll
 BB8 . . . . .169 D5
Nelson Ave PR5 . . . . .76 B1
Nelson Cres PR2 . . . . . . .115 D2
Nelson Ct FY7 . . . . .193 F3
Nelson Dr PR2 . . . . .115 D2
Nelson Gdns PR4 . . . . . . .134 C8
Nelson Golf Course BB9 .147 E4
Nelson Rd
 🞺 Blackpool FY1 . . . . . . .129 B2
 Brierfield BB10 . . . . .148 A4
 Chorley PR7 . . . . .42 C7
 Fleetwood FY7 . . . . .193 F3
Nelson Sq BB11 . . . . .126 E4
 Bacup OL13 . . . . .70 C8
 🞺 Bamber Bridge PR5 . . .76 C8
 Clitheroe BB7 . . . . .164 B8
 🞵 Colne BB8 . . . . .169 D5
 🛈 Darwen BB3 . . . . .80 F2
 Great Harwood BB6 . . . . .123 D6
 Horwich BL6 . . . . .31 D3
 🞷 Padiham BB12 . . . . . .112 F5
 Lancaster LA1 . . . . .210 F8
 Lytham St Anne's FY8 . . . . .90 D3
 Morecambe LA4 . . . . . . .212 D5
 Southport PR8 . . . . .34 A6
Nelson Sta BB9 . . . . .147 E8
Nelson Terr PR1 . . . . .95 D8
Nelson Way PR2 . . . . .94 B8
Nene Cl PR5 . . . . .59 B7
Neps La BB7 . . . . .225 C6
Neptune St BB11 . . . . . . .126 F6
Neptune Way BB3 . . . . . . .81 B6
Nesswood Ave FY4 . . . . . .109 E6
Neston St PR1 . . . . .96 E8
Nether Beck LA6 . . . . . . .234 A2
Nether Kellet Prim Sch
 LA6 . . . . .216 E4
Nether Kellet Rd LA6 . . . .231 B8
Nether View LA2 . . . . . . .235 E1
Netherby St BB11 . . . . . . .126 E4
Netherfield Cl BB12 . . . . .126 D7
Netherfield Gdns 🞷 BB9 .147 B8
Netherfield Rd BB9 . . . . . .147 E8
Netherheys Cl BB8 . . . . . .169 B5
Netherlands Rd LA4 . . . . .212 F4
Netherley Rd PR7 . . . . . . .28 E8
Nethertown St BB7 . . . . . .126 D7
Netherwood Rd BB10 . . . .127 D7
Netherwood St BB10 . . . . .147 E2
Nethway Ave FY3 . . . . . . .129 F6
Netley Ave OL12 . . . . .51 F3
Network 65 Bsns Pk
 BB11 . . . . .125 F4
Neverstitch Cl WN8 . . . . . .17 D2
Neverstitch Rd WN8 . . . . .17 D2
Nevett St PR1 . . . . .96 D8
Neville Ave FY5 . . . . .172 E1
Neville Dr FY5 . . . . .151 B8
Neville St PR3 . . . . .139 A7
Nevy Fold Ave BL6 . . . . . . .31 F3
New Acres Carnforth LA5 .217 F2
 Newburgh WN8 . . . . .26 A1
New Bank Rd BB2 . . . . . . .100 B6
New Barn Barn 67 B6
New Barn La BB4 . . . . .68 A8
New Barns Rd LA5 . . . . . .237 A1
New Bath St BB8 . . . . . . .169 E6
New Bonny St FY1 . . . . . .129 B4
New Briggs Fold BL7 . . . . .46 E2
New Brown St 🞷 BB9 . . . .168 D1
New Brunswick St BL6 . . . .31 B3
New Bury Ct BB5 . . . . . . .102 C3
New Chapel La BL6 . . . . . . .31 F2
New Chapel St BB2 . . . . . .100 B2
New Church Ct 🞴 BB5 . . .123 F3
New Church Ho 🞷 FY1 . . .129 C4
New Church Mews 🞶
 BB10 . . . . .147 B1
New Cock Yd 🞲 PR1 . . . . .96 A7
New Court Dr BL7 . . . . . . .46 E3
New Court Way L39 . . . . . .15 F5
New Cswy L37, L38 . . . . . . .3 B8
New Cut Cl PR8 . . . . .21 A8
New Cut La L39, PR8 . . . . .21 D6
New Fold WN5 . . . . .10 C4
New Foul La PR8 . . . . .35 A4
New Garden Fields BB4 . . .86 A7
New Garden St 🛈 BB2 . . .100 E3
New Ground Ct BB10 . . . . .147 C3
New Hague BB18 . . . . . . .191 F3
New Hall Ave FY4 . . . . . . .110 B5
New Hall Ave N FY4 . . . . .110 B6
New Hall Dr PR8 . . . . .35 C1
New Hall Hey Bsns Pk
 BB4 . . . . .84 F1
New Hall Hey Rd BB4 . . . . .84 F1
New Hall La PR1 . . . . .96 C8
New Hall Rd BL9 . . . . .32 E4
New Hall St BB10,BB12 . . .147 A1
New Hey La PR4 . . . . .113 C5
New House La PR3 . . . . . .198 F4
New House St BB8 . . . . . .169 E5
New La Burton-in-K LA6 . . .234 B7
 Duncombe PR3 . . . . .156 F8
 Eagland Hill PR3 . . . . . . .176 D7
 Great Mitton BB7 . . . . . .163 E6
 Haskayne L39 . . . . .13 E3
 New Lane L40 . . . . .24 B6
 Newtown PR7 . . . . .58 A1
 Ormskirk L39 . . . . .15 E2

New La continued
 Oswaldtwistle BB5 . . . . . .102 C2
 Penwortham PR1 . . . . . . .95 E3
 Smallwood Hey PR3 . . . .196 B2
 Southport PR9 . . . . .53 E3
 Tarleton PR4 . . . . .55 D6
New Lane Head PR5 . . . . . .58 A2
New Lane Pace PR9 . . . . . .54 B8
New Lane Sta L40 . . . . . . .24 B7
New Line OL13 . . . . .70 B8
New Links Ave PR2 . . . . . .116 A6
New Longton
 CE Prim Sch PR4 . . . . . .74 F7
New Market St
 🞶 Blackburn BB1 . . . . . . .100 E5
 Chorley PR7 . . . . .42 C8
 Clitheroe BB7 . . . . .164 E8
 Colne BB8 . . . . .169 D5
New Meadow Cl BB1 . . . . .81 A8
New Meadow La L37 . . . . . .3 F8
New Miles La WN5 . . . . . . .19 F5
New Mill St Blackburn BB1 100 F6
 Eccleston PR7 . . . . .40 C6
New Moss La PR6 . . . . . . .60 C5
New Oxford St BB8 . . . . . .169 E6
New Park St BB2 . . . . .100 D5
New Pastures 🞴 PR5 . . . .76 C8
New Quay Rd LA1 . . . . . . .210 B8
New Rd Adlington PR6 . . . .30 D7
 Bamber Bridge PR5 . . . . . .96 B1
 Blackpool FY8 . . . . .109 B4
 Burnley BB11 . . . . .127 B2
 Coppull PR7 . . . . .41 F3
 Cornholme OL14 . . . . . . .108 C4
 Croston PR5 . . . . .39 B7
 Earby BB18 . . . . .201 B2
 Formby L37 . . . . .12 A5
 Kirkby Lonsdale LA6 . . . . .238 C2
 Lancaster LA1 . . . . .210 F8
 Newchurch BB4 . . . . .85 F2
 Rufford L40 . . . . .38 B3
 Silverdale LA5 . . . . .218 F1
 Staynall LA1 . . . . .174 B4
 Thornton FY5 . . . . .151 C7
 Thornton in L LA6 . . . . . .236 F4
 Warton, Carnforth LA5 . . .217 A6
 Whitworth OL12 . . . . .70 B1
New Rough Hey PR2 . . . . .115 F6
New Row Altham BB5 . . . . .124 C6
 Colne BB8 . . . . .170 C4
New Row Cotts PR3 . . . . . .161 D1
New Scotland Rd BB8 . . . .168 E1
New St Blackrod BL6 . . . . . .30 D2
 Brinscall PR6,PR7 . . . . . . .61 F8
 Carnforth LA5 . . . . .217 D2
 Caton LA2 . . . . .231 D3
 Colne BB8 . . . . .169 B3
 Eccleston PR7 . . . . .40 C6
 Halton LA2 . . . . .214 C6
 Haskayne L39 . . . . .14 B8
 🞳 Haslingden BB4 . . . . . .84 B3
 Lancaster LA1 . . . . .210 F8
 Mawdesley L40 . . . . .39 C2
 Morecambe LA4 . . . . . . .212 D5
 Nelson BB9 . . . . .168 F1
 🞳 Padiham BB12 . . . . . .125 B8
 Rochdale OL12 . . . . .51 E2
New Summerseat House
 Specl Sch BL0 . . . . .49 B2
New Taylor Fold BB5 . . . . .147 F3
New Way Royal Oak L39 . . . .7 C2
 Whitworth OL12 . . . . .70 C1
New Wellington Cl BB2 .100 C1
New Wellington Gdns
 BB2 . . . . .100 C1
New Wellington St BB2 . .100 C1
Newark Pl Fulwood PR2 . . .116 D8
 🞴 Preston PR2 . . . . .115 E2
Newark Rd OL12 . . . . .51 F3
Newark Sq OL12 . . . . .51 F3
Newark St BB5 . . . . .102 F5
Newarth La PR4 . . . . .72 E3
Newbigging Ave BB4 . . . . .85 F2
Newburgh CE Prim Sch
 WN8 . . . . .26 A1
Newburn Cl WN8 . . . . .18 B5
Newbury Ave 🞳 FY4 . . . . .109 D8
Newbury Ct PR2 . . . . .116 C8
Newbury Gn PR2 . . . . . . .116 C8
Newbury Rd
 Lytham St Anne's FY8 . . . . .89 A4
 Skelmersdale WN8 . . . . . .18 B5
Newby Ave Fleetwood FY7 193 D1
 Poulton-le-F FY6 . . . . . . .151 D1
Newby Back La BB7 . . . . .225 A1
Newby Cl Burnley BB11 . . .126 E2
 Southport PR8 . . . . .20 B3
Newby Dr Clayton-le-W PR5 .76 E2
 Lancaster LA1 . . . . .213 F3
 Skelmersdale WN8 . . . . . .18 B5
Newby La BB7 . . . . .189 B8
Newby Pl Blackpool FY4 . . .130 B1
 Fulwood PR2 . . . . .117 D4
Newcastle Ave
 Blackpool FY3 . . . . .129 D4
 Cleveleys FY5 . . . . .172 F4
Newcastle St BB2 . . . . . . .100 C3
Newchurch CE Prim Sch
 BB4 . . . . .85 E1
Newchurch Cl BB2 . . . . . .100 F2
Newchurch Old Rd OL13 . .86 C1
Newchurch Rd Bacup OL13 69 C8
 Rawtenstall BB4 . . . . .85 C2
Newcombe Rd BL0 . . . . . . .49 B2
Newcroft LA5 . . . . .217 E6
Newfield Dr
 Blackburn BB1,BB2 . . . . . .81 A8
 Nelson BB9 . . . . .147 E8

Newfield Rd PR5 . . . . .77 A7
Newgate Fulwood PR2 . . . .116 E4
 Morecambe LA3 . . . . . . .213 A2
Newgate Ave WN6 . . . . . . .19 E8
Newgate La PR4 . . . . .75 C8
Newgate Rd WN8 . . . . .9 F7
Newhaven Dr PR3 . . . . . . .178 D7
Newhouse Rd
 Accrington BB5 . . . . .124 D1
 Blackpool FY4 . . . . .129 F2
Newington Ave BB1 . . . . . .121 F3
Newlands PR7 . . . . .40 C6
Newlands Ave
 Blackpool FY3 . . . . .129 F2
 Burscough L40 . . . . .24 F4
 Clitheroe BB7 . . . . .164 C7
 Lancaster LA1 . . . . .211 B5
 Penwortham PR1 . . . . . . .95 B5
 Rochdale OL12 . . . . .51 F3
Newlands Cl Blackburn BB2 79 E8
 Rochdale OL12 . . . . .51 F3
Newlands Rd
 Lancaster LA1 . . . . .211 E6
 Lancaster, Newlands LA1 .211 C5
 Lytham St Anne's FY8 . . . . .89 C5
 Morecambe LA4 . . . . . . .212 F4
Newlands Way FY6 . . . . . .151 C1
Newlyn Ave Blackpool FY4 109 E5
 Maghull L31 . . . . .5 E1
Newlyn Cl FY4 . . . . .109 E5
Newlyn Dr WN8 . . . . .9 D7
Newlyn Pl PR2 . . . . .115 F5
Newman Gr FY5 . . . . .172 E5
Newman Rd 🞴 FY1 . . . . . .129 D8
Newman St BB10 . . . . . . .147 B1
Newmarket Ave LA1 . . . . .211 B3
Newmarket St LA4 . . . . . .213 A7
Newport Ct PR2 . . . . .115 F3
Newport St BB9 . . . . .168 E1
News La WA11 . . . . .8 F2
Newsham Hall La PR4 . . . .135 F3
Newsham Pl LA1 . . . . .211 A5
Newsham Rd LA1 . . . . . . .211 A5
Newsham St PR2 . . . . . . .116 D1
Newsome St PR5 . . . . .76 A1
Newstead Dr WN8 . . . . . . .18 B5
Newstet Rd L33 . . . . .1 C2
Newthorn BB5 . . . . .103 A1
Newton Ave
 Poulton-le-F FY6 . . . . . . .151 C2
 Preston PR1 . . . . .97 A8
Newton Bluecoat
 CE Prim Sch PR4 . . . . . .114 A2
Newton Cl Freckleton PR4 . .92 C7
 Leyland PR5 . . . . .58 B8
Newton Ct PR2 . . . . .116 C8
Newton Dr Accrington BB5 103 D3
 Blackpool FY3 . . . . .129 E5
 Over Town BB10 . . . . . . .107 A7
 Ramsbottom BL8 . . . . . . .49 A1
 Skelmersdale WN8 . . . . . .18 B5
Newton Dr E FY3 . . . . . . .130 A7
Newton Gr FY5 . . . . .151 D7
Newton Pl FY3 . . . . .130 A7
Newton Rd
 Lytham St Anne's FY8 . . . . .89 A7
 Preston PR2 . . . . .116 B2
Newton St Blackburn BB1 .101 B5
 Burnley BB12 . . . . .126 C7
 Clitheroe BB7 . . . . .164 D7
 Darwen BB3 . . . . .81 B2
 Oswaldtwistle BB5 . . . . . .102 C5
 🞴 Preston PR1 . . . . .96 B8
 Southport PR9 . . . . .35 A7
Newton Terr LA1 . . . . .214 A3
Newtown BB18 . . . . .200 B2
Newtown St BB8 . . . . .169 E5
Nib La PR1 . . . . .75 E8
Nichol St PR7 . . . . .60 C1
Nicholas St
 Brierfield BB10 . . . . .147 B3
 Burnley BB11 . . . . .127 A5
 Colne BB8 . . . . .169 C4
 Darwen BB3 . . . . .80 F1
Nicholl St 🛈 BB10 . . . . . .127 A8
Nicholson Cres LA4 . . . . .212 G5
Nick Hilton's La PR6 . . . . .43 D3
Nickey La BB2 . . . . .120 F2
Nickleton Brow PR6 . . . . .43 C2
Nicksons La FY6 . . . . .195 B4
Nicola Cl OL13 . . . . .87 C2
Nightfield La BB2 . . . . . . .119 F6
Nightingale Cres 🞶
 BB11 . . . . .126 C5
Nightingale Dr FY6 . . . . . .151 B2
Nightingale Rd BL6 . . . . . .30 C3
Nightingale St PR1 . . . . . .30 A8
Nile St 🞵 Lancaster LA1 . .210 F8
 🞷 Nelson BB9 . . . . .168 D1
 Preston PR1 . . . . .96 A7
Nimes St PR1 . . . . .96 D8
Nine Elms PR2 . . . . .116 C6
Nineteen Acre La LA5 . . . .219 F4
Nineveh St 🞷 BB8 . . . . . .169 E5
Nipe La WN8 . . . . .9 B5
Nithside FY4 . . . . .130 C1
Niton Cl BB4 . . . . .84 C1
Nixon La BB5 . . . . .58 A8
Nixon's La PR8 . . . . .20 A7
Nixons Ct PR5 . . . . .57 F8
Nixons La WN8 . . . . .9 D7
Noble St 🞳 Darwen BB3 . . .64 A8
 Great Harwood BB6 . . . . .123 C4
 Rishton BB1 . . . . .123 B1
Noblett St 🞵 FY7 . . . . . . .193 F2
Noblett St BB1 . . . . .100 F5
Noel Gate L39 . . . . .15 B1
Noel Jones Ct FY8 . . . . . . .88 C7

Noel Rd LA1 . . . . .213 E3
Noel Sq PR2 . . . . .117 E1
Noels Villa FY5 . . . . .137 E4
Noggarth Rd BB12 . . . . . .167 F2
Nolan St PR8 . . . . .34 C5
Nook Cotts PR3 . . . . .177 C6
Nook Cres PR2 . . . . .138 C1
Nook Farm Ave OL12 . . . . .51 F3
Nook Field PR3 . . . . .137 D6
Nook Glade PR2 . . . . .138 C1
Nook La Bamber Bridge PR5 76 D6
 Blackburn BB2 . . . . .99 F1
 Churchtown PR3 . . . . . . .178 A3
 Mawdesley L40 . . . . .39 E5
 Oswaldtwistle BB5 . . . . . .102 B2
Nook Terr Blackburn BB2 . .100 A1
 🛈 Rochdale OL12 . . . . . .51 F3
Nook The
 Appley Bridge WN6 . . . . . .19 E7
 Bolton-le-S LA5 . . . . .216 A4
 Staining FY3 . . . . .130 D5
Nookfield PR5 . . . . .75 A1
Nookfield Cl FY8 . . . . .90 A4
Nooklands PR2 . . . . .116 E4
Noon Sun St OL12 . . . . . . .51 F1
Noor St PR1 . . . . .117 A1
Nora St BB9 . . . . .168 D3
Norbreck Cl BB2 . . . . .80 F8
Norbreck Ct FY5 . . . . .150 C6
Norbreck Dr PR2 . . . . .115 E1
Norbreck Prim Sch FY5 . .150 D8
Norbreck Rd FY5 . . . . .150 C7
Norburn Cres L37 . . . . .11 F2
Norbury Cl PR9 . . . . .53 C5
Norcliffe Rd FY2 . . . . .150 C5
Norcross Brow PR6 . . . . . .62 B8
Norcross La FY5 . . . . .151 A7
Norcross Pl PR2 . . . . .115 F1
Norden Ct
 Great Harwood BB6 . . . . .123 E5
 🛈 Rishton BB1 . . . . .123 B1
Norden Cty High Sch
 BB1 . . . . .123 A2
Norfield L39 . . . . .15 F5
Norfolk Ave Blackpool FY2 150 B3
 Burnley BB12 . . . . .126 B7
 Cleveleys FY5 . . . . .172 E3
 Morecambe LA3 . . . . . . .212 B2
 Padiham BB12 . . . . .125 D6
Norfolk Cl
 🞷 Clayton-le-M BB5 . . . .123 F3
 Leyland PR5 . . . . .58 E7
Norfolk Gr Church BB5 . . .103 A7
 Southport PR8 . . . . .33 F1
Norfolk Rd
 Bamber Bridge PR5 . . . . . .96 D4
 Blackpool FY3 . . . . .130 A2
 Longshaw WN5 . . . . .10 E1
 Lytham St Anne's FY8 . . . . .90 C5
 Preston PR1 . . . . .117 A1
 Southport PR8 . . . . .33 F1
Norfolk St Accrington BB5 .103 D7
 Blackburn BB2 . . . . .100 C2
 Colne BB8 . . . . .169 E5
 Darwen BB3 . . . . .81 B1
 Lancaster LA1 . . . . .213 F2
 Nelson BB9 . . . . .168 D1
 Rishton BB1 . . . . .123 A1
Norham Cl BB12 . . . . .126 E7
Norkeed Rd FY5 . . . . .150 C7
Norland Dr LA3 . . . . .208 F8
Norman Cl FY5 . . . . .172 F1
Norman Rd BB5 . . . . .102 C5
Norman St Blackburn BB2 .100 C3
 Burnley BB10 . . . . .127 A7
 Bury BL9 . . . . .32 B4
Normandie Ave FY2 . . . . .150 D3
Normandy Rd PR4 . . . . . .136 B3
Normanhurst L39 . . . . . . .16 A4
Normington Cl L31 . . . . . . .5 C4
Normoss Ave FY3 . . . . . . .130 A7
Normoss Rd FY3 . . . . .130 C7
Norris House Dr L39 . . . . . .6 C8
Norris St 🛈 Chorley PR7 . . .42 C6
 Darwen BB3 . . . . .81 B1
 Fulwood PR2 . . . . .116 D3
 Preston PR1 . . . . .116 E2
Norris Way L37 . . . . .12 B3
Norse Cotts PR5 . . . . .56 E6
North Albert St 🞶 FY7 . . .194 B5
North Albion St FY7 . . . . .194 A4
North Ave
 Barnoldswick BB18 . . . . .200 B2
 Blackpool FY3 . . . . .129 D4
 Ramsbottom BL8 . . . . . . .48 F1
North Bank Ave BB1 . . . . .121 E1
North Church St 🞵 FY7 . . .194 B5
North Cliff St 🞶 PR1 . . . . .95 E6
North Cliffe Sch BB6 . . . . .123 B6
North Clifton St FY8 . . . . . .90 B3
North Cres FY8 . . . . .88 E6
North Croft PR3 . . . . .178 C8
North Ct Blackpool FY5 . . .150 E8
 Cleveleys FY5 . . . . .172 D5
North Dr Appley Bridge WN6 27 C2
 Blackpool FY5 . . . . .150 D6
 Cleveleys FY5 . . . . .172 E2
 Inskip PR4 . . . . .155 C1
 Kirkham PR4 . . . . .112 F6
 Whalley BB7 . . . . .143 B7
North East Ave PR6 . . . . . .62 A8
North End Football Gd
 (Preston North End FC)
 PR1 . . . . .117 B2
North End La L38 . . . . .3 A6
North Gr 🛈 PR5 . . . . .76 C8
North Highfield PR2 . . . . .117 E6
North Houses La FY8 . . . . .110 D1

North Leach Dr PR8 . . . .20 A5
North Meade L31 . . . . . . .5 C2
North Meadowside PR4 . .74 A6
North Mersey Bsns Ctr L33 1 D4
North Moor La L39 . . . . . .22 E2
North Moss La L37 . . . . . .12 D7
North Nook La PR3 . . . .180 E3
North Par **7** BB18 . . . . .200 B3
North Park Ave BB9 . . . .168 C1
North Park Dr FY3 . . . . .129 F5
North Perimeter Rd L33 . . .1 D4
North Prom FY7 . . . . .88 D7
North Quarry Bsns Pk
WN6 . . . . .27 D2
North Rd Blackburn BB1 . .101 C3
  Bretherton PR5 . . . . .57 B7
  Carnforth LA5 . . . . .217 E2
  Lancaster LA1 . . . . . . .210 F8
  Preston PR1 . . . . .116 F1
  Rawtenstall BB4 . . . . . . .85 C2
  Southport PR9 . . . . .53 C4
North Ribble St **7** PR1 . .96 C6
North Road Sch LA5 . . . .217 D1
North Shore Golf Course
  FY2 . . . . .150 C3
  Cleveleys FY5 . . . . .172 D5
North Sq Blackpool FY3 . .129 F5
North St
  Barnoldswick BB18 . . . .200 B1
  Brierfield BB10 . . . . . . .147 F3
  Burnley BB10 . . . . .147 A1
  Chorley PR7 . . . . .60 D2
  Clitheroe BB7 . . . . .186 F1
  Colne BB8 . . . . .169 E6
  Fleetwood FY7 . . . . . . .194 B5
  Hapton BB12 . . . . .125 C5
  Haslingden BB4 . . . . . . .84 C1
  Morecambe LA4 . . . . . .212 E5
  14 Nelson BB9 . . . . . .168 D1
  Newchurch BB4 . . . . . . .85 E1
  Padiham BB12 . . . . .145 C1
  Preston PR1 . . . . .95 F8
  Ramsbottom BL0 . . . . . .67 C2
  Rawtenstall BB4 . . . . . . .85 A2
  Southport PR9 . . . . .34 C8
  Water BB4 . . . . .86 A8
  Whitworth OL12 . . . . . . .70 C1
North Syke Ave PR2 . . . .115 C1
North Vale PR6 . . . . .42 F1
North Valley Rd BB8 . . . .169 D5
North View Kirkham PR4 . .112 F5
  Leyland PR5 . . . . .58 F8
  Ramsbottom, Higher
    Summerseat BL0 . . . . .49 B2
  Ramsbottom, Strongstry BL0 .67 C2
  Rawtenstall BB4 . . . . . . .85 A8
North View Cl PR3 . . . . .154 C5
North Warton St FY8 . . . .90 C3
Northall PR4 . . . . .73 E2
Northam Cl PR9 . . . . .53 A5
Northbrook Gdns PR5 . . . .75 E1
Northbrook Rd PR5 . . . . .75 F1
Northcliffe BB6 . . . . . . .123 B6
  Preston PR1 . . . . .95 D7
Northcote Rd Langho BB6 142 C3
Northcote St Darwen BB3 . .64 B8
  4 Haslingden BB4 . . . .84 B2
  8 Leyland PR5 . . . . . . .76 A1
Northdene WN8 . . . . .26 B2
Northdunes L38 . . . . .2 F4
Northenden Rd PR7 . . . . .41 F2
Northern Ave PR4 . . . . . .73 E2
Northern Cty Prim Sch
  OL13 . . . . .86 F6
Northfield WN8 . . . . .18 B4
Northfield Ave FY1 . . . . .129 B8
Northfield Cl L33 . . . . .1 A4
Northfield Rd
  Blackburn BB1 . . . . . . .100 E7
  Haslingden BB5 . . . . . . .84 A4
Northfleet Ave FY7 . . . . .193 E2
Northfold Cty Prim Sch
  FY5 . . . . .172 E4
Northgate
  14 Blackburn BB2 . . . .100 E5
  Blackpool FY2 . . . . .150 B4
  Goosnargh PR3 . . . . . . .137 D6
  Leyland PR5 . . . . .76 B2
  Lytham St Anne's FY8 . . .88 D4
  Morecambe LA3 . . . . . .213 A4
  Whitworth OL12 . . . . . . .51 C7
Northgate Dr PR6 . . . . . .60 E2
Northlands Fulwood PR2 . 116 E6
  Leyland PR5 . . . . .58 C7
Northleach Ave **2** PR1 . .95 F2
Northside PR7 . . . . .59 C3
Northumberland Ave
  Blackpool FY2 . . . . .150 B1
  Cleveleys FY5 . . . . .172 F5
Northumberland
  House PR1 . . . . .95 F8
Northumberland St
  2 Chorley PR7 . . . . . . .42 D7
  Morecambe LA4 . . . . . .212 D5
Northway Broughton PR3 .136 C3
  Fleetwood FY7 . . . . . . .193 D1
  Fulwood PR2 . . . . .116 D7
  Maghull L31, L39 . . . . . . .5 E4
  Ormskirk L39 . . . . .15 A1
  Skelmersdale WN8 . . . . .18 B2
Northway Cty Prim Sch L31 5 E2
Northways WN6 . . . . .28 D2
Northwood Cl
  Burnley BB12 . . . . .126 D7
  Lytham St Anne's FY8 . . .89 E4
Northwood Way FY6 . . . .151 D2
Norton Ave LA3 . . . . . . .212 A3
Norton Dr LA3 . . . . .212 B2

Norton Gr LA3 . . . . .212 A2
Norton Pl LA3 . . . . .212 A2
Norton Rd Garstang PR3 .199 C2
  Morecambe LA3 . . . . . .212 A2
  Rochdale OL12 . . . . .51 F3
Norton St **1** BB12 . . . .125 C4
Norwich Pl Blackpool FY2 .150 D5
  35 Preston PR1 . . . . . .96 A7
Norwich St BB1 . . . . . . .100 F7
Norwood Ave
  Becconsall PR4 . . . . . . .72 F2
  Blackburn BB2 . . . . . . .100 E2
  Blackpool FY3 . . . . .129 E8
  Burnley BB9 . . . . .168 F2
  Southport PR9 . . . . .34 C7
Norwood Cl PR6 . . . . . . .30 A8
Norwood Cres PR9 . . . . . .34 E7
Norwood Cty **13** LA1 . . .211 A8
Norwood Cty Prim Sch
  PR9 . . . . .34 E7
Norwood Dr LA4 . . . . . . .213 B3
Norwood Gdns PR9 . . . . .34 F7
Norwood Rd
  Lytham St Anne's FY8 . . .88 C8
  Southport PR8, PR9 . . . .34 F6
Notre Dame Gdns BB1 . . .101 A3
Nottingham Rd PR1 . . . . .117 A1
Nottingham St BB1 . . . . .101 A4
Novak Pl LA4 . . . . .213 B4
Nowell Gr BB12 . . . . . . .144 D2
Nowell St **15** BB6 . . . . .123 C5
Noyna Ave BB8 . . . . . . .191 E1
Noyna Rd BB8 . . . . .191 E1
Noyna St BB8 . . . . .169 E6
Noyna View BB8 . . . . . . .169 E6
Nun's St LA1 . . . . .211 A8
Nuns Ave LA7 . . . . .237 F5
Nurseries The L37 . . . . . .12 A2
Nursery Ave L39 . . . . . . .16 A6
Nursery Cl Coppull PR7 . .41 E4
  Leyland PR5 . . . . .58 F8
Nursery Dr Becconsall PR4 .72 F1
  Formby L37 . . . . .11 F2
Nursery La PR4 . . . . .74 E8
Nursery Nook BB3 . . . . . .81 D5
Nursery Rd L31 . . . . .5 C4
Nuthall Rd BB4 . . . . .34 F3
Nuttall Ave
  Great Harwood BB6 . . . .123 C4
  Horwich BL6 . . . . .31 A3
Nuttall Cl BL0 . . . . .49 C5
Nuttall Hall Cotts
  Ramsbottom BL0 . . . . . .49 D5
Nuttall Hall Rd BL0 . . . . .49 D5
Nuttall La BL0 . . . . .49 C4
Nuttall Rd Blackpool FY1 .129 D2
  Ramsbottom BL0 . . . . . .49 D4
Nuttall St Accrington BB5 .103 C5
  Bacup OL13 . . . . .87 B3
  Blackburn, Ewood BB2 . . .80 D8
  Blackburn, Longshaw BB2 .100 D1
  8 Burnley BB11 . . . . . .127 B4
  Bury BL9 . . . . .32 A1
  Rawtenstall BB4 . . . . . . .85 B3
Nuttall St Mews **3** BB5 .103 C5
Nutter Cres BB12 . . . . . .145 F5
Nutter Rd Accrington BB5 .103 C7
  Cleveleys FY5 . . . . .172 D5
  2 Preston PR1 . . . . . . .95 E7

O

O'Hagan Ct BB9 . . . . . . .147 B6
Oak Ave Blackpool FY4 . .109 C6
  Euxton PR7 . . . . .59 D3
  Galgate LA2 . . . . .206 F4
  Haslingden BB5 . . . . . . .84 A8
  8 Horwich BL6 . . . . . . .31 B1
  Kirkham PR4 . . . . .113 B4
  Longridge PR3 . . . . .139 A7
  Morecambe LA4 . . . . . .213 B6
  Ormskirk L39 . . . . .15 C4
  Penwortham PR1 . . . . . .95 B3
  Ramsbottom BL0 . . . . . .49 A2
  Thornton FY5 . . . . .151 C8
Oak Bank
  Accrington BB5 . . . . . . .124 D2
  Gregson Lane PR5 . . . . . .97 E1
Oak Cl Barrow BB7 . . . . .164 D1
  Rishton BB1 . . . . .102 B8
  Whitworth OL12 . . . . . . .70 D4
Oak Cres WN8 . . . . .17 D1
Oak Croft PR6 . . . . .77 B2
Oak Dr Chorley PR6 . . . . .60 C3
  Freckleton PR4 . . . . .92 A5
  Halton LA2 . . . . .214 F7
Oak Gates BL7 . . . . .46 E1
Oak Gn L39 . . . . .15 F5
Oak Gr Darwen BB3 . . . . .81 B2
  Garstang PR3 . . . . .178 C7
  New Longton PR4 . . . . . .75 A6
Oak Hill Cl BB5 . . . . . . .103 D5
Oak La Accrington BB5 . . .103 D5
  Newton-with-S PR4 . . . . .113 F2
Oak Rd PR3 . . . . .178 B8
Oak Ridge BB7 . . . . .186 D7
Oak St Accrington BB5 . . .103 C5
  Blackburn BB1 . . . . . . .100 F7
  Brierfield BB9 . . . . .147 B6
  Burnley BB12 . . . . .126 C6
  Clayton-le-M BB5 . . . . . .123 F1
  Colne BB8 . . . . .169 F6
  Fleetwood FY7 . . . . . . .194 A4
  Great Harwood BB6 . . . .123 C6
  2 Nelson BB9 . . . . . . .168 D1
  9 Oswaldtwistle BB5 . . .102 D3
  Preston PR1 . . . . .96 A7

Oak St continued
  Ramsbottom BL0 . . . . . .49 B5
  Rawtenstall BB11 . . . . .105 B4
  Southport PR8 . . . . .34 E6
  Whitworth OL12 . . . . . . .70 D5
Oak Terr BB18 . . . . .200 C3
Oak Tree Ct WN8 . . . . . . .18 D3
Oak Tree Dr BB4 . . . . . .112 E4
Oak View Leyland PR5 . . . .75 E2
  Whitworth OL12 . . . . . . .70 D4
Oakdene Ave BB5 . . . . . .124 E1
Oaken Bank BB10 . . . . . .147 E3
Oaken Cl OL13 . . . . .87 B3
Oakenclough Cotts PR3 .220 C2
Oakenclough Rd
  Bacup OL13 . . . . .87 B3
  Chipping PR3 . . . . .180 E4
Oakeneaves Ave BB11 . . .126 D2
Oakengate PR2 . . . . .117 C7
Oakengates BB4 . . . . . . .28 F1
Oakenhead Cl PR3 . . . . .158 D7
Oakenhead St PR1 . . . . .117 C5
Oakenhead Wood Old Rd
  BB4 . . . . .84 E3
Oakenhurst Rd BB2 . . . . .100 D4
Oakenshaw Ave OL12 . . . .51 C6
Oakenshaw View OL12 . . .51 C6
Oakfield Fulwood PR2 . . .116 F7
  Preston PR2 . . . . .116 B1
Oakfield Ave
  Accrington BB5 . . . . . . .124 E1
  Barnoldswick BB18 . . . .200 A3
  Clayton-le-M BB5 . . . . . .123 E3
Oakfield Cl BL6 . . . . .31 F2
Oakfield Cres BB5 . . . . . .102 F4
Oakfield Dr Formby L37 . . .11 F4
  Leyland PR5 . . . . .58 B8
Oakfield Rd Blackburn BB2 .80 D7
  Hightown L38 . . . . .2 F2
Oakfields L39 . . . . .16 A5
Oakford Cl PR9 . . . . .54 B5
Oakgate Cl PR4 . . . . .55 F5
Oakgrove FY4 . . . . .109 D6
Oakham Ct **13** PR1 . . . . .96 A7
Oakhill Cl L31 . . . . .5 D2
Oakhill Coll BB7 . . . . . . .143 D2
Oakhill Cottage La L31 . . . .5 D4
Oakhill Dr L31 . . . . .5 D4
Oakhill Rd L31 . . . . .5 D3
Oakhurst Ave BB5 . . . . . .124 E1
Oakland Ave FY5 . . . . . . .150 D6
Oakland Glen PR1 . . . . . .96 A3
Oakland St
  4 Bamber Bridge PR5 . . .96 E1
  Nelson BB9 . . . . .147 E8
Oaklands Ave
  Barrowford BB9 . . . . . . .168 D3
  Tarleton PR4 . . . . .56 A7
Oaklands Ct LA1 . . . . . . .210 C5
Oaklands Dr
  Penwortham PR1 . . . . . .95 A4
  Rawtenstall BB4 . . . . . . .84 E2
Oaklands Gr PR2 . . . . . .115 F1
Oaklands Rd BL0 . . . . . . .67 D2
Oaklands Terr BB1 . . . . .100 F7
Oaklea WN6 . . . . .28 A2
Oakleaf Cl PR3 . . . . .137 C6
Oakleaf Ct FY5 . . . . .172 D4
Oakleaf Way FY4 . . . . . .130 D1
Oaklee Gr L33 . . . . .1 A4
Oakleigh WN8 . . . . .9 D2
Oakleigh Terr **8** OL14 . .108 B1
Oakley Rd Morecambe LA3 212 A2
Oakley St BB4 . . . . .84 E2
Oakmere PR6 . . . . .77 C3
Oakmere Ave PR6 . . . . . .78 C2
Oakmere Cl BB2 . . . . . . .80 D6
Oakmoor Ave FY2 . . . . . .150 E4
Oakridge Cl PR2 . . . . . .116 F7
Oakroyd Cl LA5 . . . . .237 B2
Oaks Bar BB1 . . . . .121 C8
Oaks Brow BB1 . . . . .121 C7
Oaks The
  Bamber Bridge PR1 . . . . .96 B3
  Chorley PR7 . . . . .42 B4
  Leyland PR5 . . . . .58 A7
  Poulton-le-F FY6 . . . . . .151 D4
  Southport PR8 . . . . .33 F6
  St Michael's on W PR3 . .155 C7
Oaksfield BB3 . . . . .80 E5
Oakshaw Dr OL12 . . . . . . .51 A1
Oakshott Pl FY5 . . . . .77 B7
Oaktree Ave
  Clayton-le-W PR5 . . . . . .76 D4
  Fulwood PR2 . . . . .116 A4
Oaktree Cl PR2 . . . . . . .116 A4
Oakville Rd LA3 . . . . . . .208 E5
Oakway PR3 . . . . .139 A8
Oakwood WN8 . . . . .18 D3
Oakwood Ave
  Bamber Bridge PR5 . . . . .96 C4
  Blackburn BB1 . . . . . . .122 B1
  Lytham St Anne's FY8 . . .89 E4
  Shevington WN6 . . . . . . .19 F5
  Southport PR8 . . . . .20 D6
Oakwood Cl Blackpool FY4 109 F4
  Brierfield BB10 . . . . . . .147 D3
  Darwen BB3 . . . . .80 E5
  Thornton FY5 . . . . .173 D2
Oakwood Dr Fulwood PR2 116 D8
Oakwood Gdns LA1 . . . . .211 A2
Oakwood Gr LA5 . . . . . . .215 F2
Oakwood Rd
  Accrington BB5 . . . . . . .103 D3
  Chorley PR7 . . . . .42 B6
  Coppull PR7 . . . . .41 F2

Oakwood View PR7 . . . . .42 B4
Oakworth Ave PR2 . . . . .117 F5
Oasis Cl L40 . . . . .38 B3
Oasis Wildlife Park
  Visitor Ctr LA7 . . . . . . .219 F8
Oat St BB12 . . . . .125 D7
Oban Cres PR7 . . . . .117 D3
Oban Ct PR2 . . . . .138 D1
Oban Dr BB1 . . . . .101 C3
Oban Pl FY2 . . . . .150 E6
Oban St BB10 . . . . .127 C8
Observatory Rd BB2 . . . . .101 A2
Occupation La
  Moor End FY6 . . . . .174 C7
  Singleton FY6 . . . . .152 D4
Ocean Bvd FY4 . . . . .109 A7
Ocean Ct FY6 . . . . .194 D5
Ocean Way FY5 . . . . .172 C3
Odell Way PR5 . . . . .96 E3
Off Botanic Rd PR9 . . . . .53 A1
Off Mount Pleasant St
  BB5 . . . . .102 E4
Offerton St BL6 . . . . .31 A3
Ogden Cl BB4 . . . . .67 A7
Ogden Dr BB4 . . . . .67 A7
Old Acre L38 . . . . .2 F3
Old Back La BB7 . . . . . . .143 F7
Old Bank La
  Blackburn BB1,BB2 . . . .101 B2
  Blackburn BB2 . . . . . . .101 A2
Old Bank St **4** BB2 . . . .100 E4
Old Boundary Way L39 . . .15 F6
Old Bridge La FY6 . . . . .152 B6
Old Bridge Way PR6 . . . . .60 E1
Old Buckley La PR3 . . . .140 D7
Old Carr Mill St BB4 . . . . .84 B5
Old Clitheroe Rd PR3 . . .161 E3
Old Cock Yd PR1 . . . . . . .96 A7
Old Croft PR2 . . . . .116 D8
Old Dawber's La PR7 . . . .59 B1
Old Engine La
  Ramsbottom BL0 . . . . . .49 D6
  Skelmersdale WN8 . . . . .17 C2
Old Farmside BB2 . . . . . .80 D7
Old Gates Dr BB2 . . . . . .79 F8
Old Greaves-Town La
  PR2 . . . . .115 C1
Old Green BL8 . . . . .48 F1
Old Greenwood La BL6 . . .31 D1
Old Ground St **8** BL0 . . .49 A5
Old Hall Bsns Pk WN8 . . .35 A5
Old Hall Cl
  Bamber Bridge PR5 . . . . .76 E8
  Morecambe LA4 . . . . . .213 B4
  Roughlee BB9 . . . . .168 B5
Old Hall Dr Accrington BB5 124 F1
  Bamber Bridge PR5 . . . . .76 E8
Old Hall La
  Charnock Green PR7 . . . .41 B6
  Pleasington BB2 . . . . . . .99 C2
Old Hall Sq BB10 . . . . . .128 A5
Old Hall St BB10 . . . . . .127 A8
Old Hey Croft **5** PR1 . . .95 D2
Old Hive PR5 . . . . .182 D4
Old House La FY4 . . . . . .110 D7
Old Kiln OL13 . . . . .69 D8
Old La Bispham Green L40 .26 D7
  Earby BB18 . . . . .201 B2
  Formby L37 . . . . .11 F6
  Haskayne L39 . . . . .13 E3
  Horwich BL6 . . . . .31 F2
  Kelbrook BB18 . . . . .191 F4
  Maghull L31 . . . . .5 E4
  Salterforth BB18 . . . . . .191 B5
  Whitworth OL12,OL13 . . .70 E6
Old Lancaster La PR2 . . .116 F1
Old Lancaster Rd PR3 . . .178 D1
Old Langho Rd BB6 . . . . .142 C5
Old Laund St BB12 . . . . .146 E8
Old Links Cl PR9 . . . . . . .35 B8
Old Lodge La PR3 . . . . . .157 A8
Old Lord's Cres BL6 . . . . .31 B5
Old Lostock La PR5 . . . . .76 E7
Old Mains La FY6 . . . . . .151 F6
Old Market Ct LA4 . . . . .212 E6
Old Meadow Ct **3** FY3 . .129 E3
Old Meadow La **2** FY3 . .129 E3
Old Meadows Rd OL13 . . .87 A5
Old Mill Ct PR4 . . . . .73 F5
Old Mill Dr BB8 . . . . . . .169 F4
Old Mill Hill L39 . . . . . . .15 D3
Old Mill La Formby L37 . . .11 F4
  Hill Dale L40 . . . . .26 F6
Old Mill St BB1 . . . . . . .100 F6
Old Mill Terr PR6 . . . . . .60 E1
Old Mill The PR5 . . . . . . .96 F2
Old Millstones PR1 . . . . .95 D7
Old Moor Rd LA2 . . . . . .232 F8
Old Moss La L39 . . . . . . .13 C5
Old Myse The LA7 . . . . .237 F5
Old Nab Rd BB6 . . . . . . .122 E8
Old Oak Gdns PR1 . . . . . .96 A2
Old Oliver La BD24 . . . . .230 C6
Old Orchard PR2 . . . . . .116 D5
Old Park La PR9 . . . . . . .35 A8
Old Parsonage La BB12 .125 B8
Old Pepper La WN6 . . . . .28 B2
Old Pope La PR4 . . . . . . .75 B8
Old Prescot Cl L31 . . . . . .6 C2
Old Quarry La BL7 . . . . . .46 F1
Old Raike BD23 . . . . . . .230 C1
Old Rake BB5 . . . . .31 E5
Old Rd BD23 . . . . .201 C6
Old Rectory Gn L39 . . . . . .6 E2
Old Roman Rd BB12,BB7 .144 A3
Old Row Barrow BB7 . . . .164 D1
  Kirkham PR4 . . . . .113 B4
  4 Rawtenstall BB4 . . . .84 E2

Old Sawmill The BD24 . . .230 E7
Old Sch Mews **8** BB4 . . .84 B3
Old School Cl PR5 . . . . . .58 A8
Old School Ho The PR5 . . .97 B3
Old School La
  Adlington PR7 . . . . .29 C5
  Bamber Bridge PR5 . . . . .76 C6
  Euxton PR7 . . . . .59 D3
  Tockholes BB3 . . . . .99 F2
Old School Mews **12** OL13 .69 C8
Old School Row BB12 . . .126 B6
Old School The LA2 . . . . .214 E6
Old St BB4 . . . . .85 F1
Old Station Cl PR2 . . . . .138 D1
Old Station Ct **8** BB7 . . .164 E8
Old Stone Brow BB18 . . . .192 A4
Old Stone Trough La
  BB18 . . . . .192 A5
Old Swan Cl BL7 . . . . . . .46 E2
Old Swan Cotts BL7 . . . . .46 E2
Old Tom's La PR5 . . . . . .174 E8
Old Town Cl WN8 . . . . . . .8 D2
Old Town La L37 . . . . . . .11 E4
Old Town Way WN8 . . . . . .8 D2
Old Trafford Pk LA3 . . . .209 A4
Old Tram Rd
  Bamber Bridge PR5 . . . . .76 F7
  Preston PR1 . . . . .96 A4
Old Vicarage PR1 . . . . . . .96 A8
Old Vicarage Rd BL6 . . . .31 F3
Old Will's La BL6 . . . . . . .31 B6
Oldbury Pl FY5 . . . . .150 E6
Olde Stoneheath Ct PR6 . .43 B4
Oldfield **7** Penwortham PR1 .95 D2
Oldfield Ave
  Blackpool FY2 . . . . .150 C4
  Darwen BB3 . . . . .80 E3
Oldfield Carr La FY6 . . . .151 E1
Oldfield Cl FY6 . . . . .151 E1
Oldfield Cres FY6 . . . . . .151 E3
Oldfield Rd PR5 . . . . .77 A7
Oldham St Burnley BB11 .126 F4
  Morecambe LA4 . . . . . .212 D6
Olivant St BB12 . . . . . . .126 C7
Olive Bank BB6 . . . . .142 D1
Olive Cl PR6 . . . . .60 C5
Olive Gr Blackpool FY3 . .129 E5
  Skelmersdale WN8 . . . . .17 E1
  Southport PR8 . . . . .34 E7
  Warton PR4 . . . . .91 A6
Olive La BB3 . . . . .81 B2
Olive Rd LA1 . . . . .213 F2
Olive St OL13 . . . . .69 E8
Olive Terr BB4 . . . . .84 F5
Oliver Pl LA5 . . . . .217 E2
Oliver St **10** OL13 . . . . . .69 C8
Oliver's Pl PR2 . . . . .117 B8
Olivers Pl PR2 . . . . .117 A8
Oliverson's Ce Prim Sch
  PR3 . . . . .137 D6
Ollerton Cl PR6 . . . . .78 E4
Ollerton Rd FY8 . . . . .89 D5
Ollerton St PR6 . . . . .43 A1
Ollerton Terr PR6 . . . . . . .78 E3
Olympia St BB10 . . . . . . .127 C5
Omerod St BB4 . . . . .86 A8
Omrod Pl **1** FY1 . . . . . .129 B2
Onchan Dr OL13 . . . . . . .87 B1
Onchan Rd BB2 . . . . .100 E1
One Ash Cl OL12 . . . . . . .51 F2
Onslow Cres PR8 . . . . . . .34 A2
Onslow Rd FY3 . . . . .129 F7
Ontario Cl BB2 . . . . .100 A8
Oozebooth Terr BB1 . . . .100 E7
Oozehead La BB2 . . . . . .100 B5
Opal Cl **5** FY5 . . . . .150 F7
Opal St BB1 . . . . .121 F2
Openshaw Dr BB1 . . . . . .100 E8
Openshaw St BL9 . . . . . . .32 A1
Oporto Cl BB11 . . . . .126 E5
Oram Rd PR5 . . . . .77 F8
Oram St BL9 . . . . .32 A4
Orange St BB5 . . . . .103 B8
Orchard Ave
  Blackpool FY4 . . . . .109 C6
  Bolton-le-S LA5 . . . . . . .216 A6
  New Longton PR4 . . . . . .75 A7
  Poulton-le-F FY6 . . . . . .151 D4
Orchard Bridge **6** BB11 .126 F6
Orchard Cl Becconsall PR4 .72 F2
  Blackburn BB2 . . . . .80 D6
  Euxton PR7 . . . . .59 D3
  Freckleton PR4 . . . . .92 A6
  Fulwood PR2 . . . . .116 A5
  Hest Bank LA2 . . . . .213 F8
  Silverdale LA5 . . . . .218 C5
  Thornton FY5 . . . . .173 B4
  Wrea Green PR4 . . . . . .112 B3
Orchard Croft **2** PR5 . . .76 A8
Orchard Ct L31 . . . . .5 F1
Orchard Dr Fleetwood FY7 193 C1
  Lucas Green PR6 . . . . . .60 C5
  Oswaldtwistle BB5 . . . . .102 F5
Orchard End PR3 . . . . . .154 C5
Orchard Grange PR1 . . . .95 A5
Orchard La Lancaster LA1 .210 F8
  Longton PR4 . . . . .73 F8
  Southport PR9 . . . . .20 D4
Orchard Lo **1** L39 . . . . . .15 F6
Orchard Rd Arnside LA5 . .237 D2
  Lytham St Anne's FY8 . . .88 E6
Orchard St
  4 Barnoldswick BB18 . .200 B3
  Great Harwood BB6 . . . .123 C4

Orchard St continued
1 Leyland PR5 . . . .**76** B1
29 Preston PR1 . . . .**95** F4
Orchard The Burnley BB11 **126** C4
Croston PR5 . . . .**57** C3
Kirkham PR4 . . . .**113** E6
Little Eccleston PR3 . . . . . .**154** A5
Ormskirk L39 . . . .**15** D5
Warton PR4 . . . .**91** E6
Woodplumpton PR4 . . . . . .**135** E1
Orchard View L39 . . . .**15** D1
Orchard Way BL8 . . . .**48** F1
Orchard Wlk PR2 . . . .**138** C2
Orchards The
Barnoldswick BB18 . . . . . .**200** C3
Carleton FY6 . . . .**151** B5
Southport PR8 . . . .**20** D4
Orchid Cl WN8 . . . .**10** B6
Orchid Way OL12 . . . .**51** D3
Ord Ave FY4 . . . .**129** F1
Ord Rd PR2 . . . .**116** C2
Orders La PR4 . . . .**113** A4
Ordnance St BB1 . . . .**101** A5
Oregon Ave FY3 . . . .**129** E8
Oriole Cl 9 BB1 . . . .**100** F6
Orkney Cl BB1 . . . .**101** D3
Orkney Rd 1 FY1 . . . .**129** C2
Orme Ho L39 . . . .**16** A5
Orme St 1 FY1 . . . .**129** C3
Ormerod Rd BB10,BB11 . .**127** D3
Ormerod St
Accrington BB5 . . . .**103** B5
Burnley BB11 . . . .**127** A5
Colne BB8 . . . .**169** C4
Haslingden BB4,BB5 . . . . . .**84** B7
5 Nelson BB9 . . . .**147** F8
Rawtenstall BB4 . . . .**85** A2
Thornton FY5 . . . .**173** B4
Worsthorne BB10 . . . .**128** A5
Ormerod Terr
Barrow BB6 . . . .**143** D8
Foulridge BB8 . . . .**191** E1
Ormond Ave
Blackpool FY1 . . . .**129** B8
Westhead L40 . . . .**16** A4
Ormond St BL9 . . . .**32** A3
Ormonde Cres L33 . . . .**1** A2
Ormont Ave FY5 . . . .**172** E4
Ormrod St BL9 . . . .**32** A2
Ormrods The BL9 . . . .**32** F5
Orms Way L37 . . . .**11** E3
Ormsby Cl WN6 . . . .**28** E2
Ormskirk & District
General Hospl **16** A4
Ormskirk Bsns Pk 2 L39 . .**15** F5
Ormskirk CE Prim Sch
L39 . . . .**16** A6
Ormskirk Coll L39 . . . .**15** E5
Ormskirk Gram Sch L39 . .**15** F4
Ormskirk Lathom Park
CE Prim Sch L40 . . . .**17** A8
Ormskirk Old Rd L39 . . . . . .**7** F7
Ormskirk Rd Bickerstaffe L39 **7** E1
Orrell WN8 . . . .**10** A7
Preston PR1 . . . .**96** A8
Rainford Junction WA11 . . . .**8** D1
Skelmersdale,
Blaguegate WN8 . . . .**17** C1
Skelmersdale, Tanhouse WN8 . .**9** D7
Ormskirk Sta L39 . . . .**15** F5
Ormskirk Tourist
Information Ctr L39 . . . . . .**15** F5
Ormston Ave BL6 . . . .**31** C5
Orpen Ave BB11 . . . .**126** F3
Orpington Sq BB10 . . . . . .**147** C3
Orrell Cl 3 PR5 . . . .**75** D1
Orrell Gdns WN5 . . . .**10** F6
Orrell Hill La L38 . . . .**3** C4
Orrell La L40 . . . .**24** D5
Orrell Newfold
Cty Prim Sch WN5 . . . .**10** D4
Orrell Rd WN5 . . . .**10** E7
Orrell Sta WN5 . . . .**10** E4
Orrell Water Pk WN5 . . . . . .**10** E4
Orrest Rd PR1 . . . .**118** A1
Orton Ct BB9 . . . .**168** D4
Orwell Cl L37 . . . .**11** D1
Osbaldeston La BB2 . . . . . .**120** D5
Osbert Croft PR4 . . . .**94** A1
Osborne Cres LA3 . . . .**212** C3
Osborne Dr PR6 . . . .**77** C2
Osborne Gr Cleveleys FY5 .**172** D5
Morecambe LA4 . . . .**212** D3
Osborne Rd
Bamber Bridge PR5 . . . .**96** D3
Blackburn BB2 . . . .**100** B6
Cleveleys FY5 . . . .**172** D5
Formby L37 . . . .**11** E5
Lytham St Anne's FY8 . . . . .**88** F5
Morecambe LA3,LA4 . . . . .**212** C3
Southport PR8 . . . .**20** B6
Osborne St 10 PR1 . . . .**95** E7
Osborne Terr Bacup OL13 . .**69** D8
Darwen BB3 . . . .**80** E2
1 Rawtenstall BB4 . . . .**84** E2
Spen Brook BB12 . . . .**167** D2
Whitewell Bottom BB4 . . . . .**85** F4
Osborne Way BB4 . . . .**84** A1
Osbourne Rd FY4 . . . .**109** B8
Osbourne Way PR1 . . . . . .**117** A1
Oscar St 4 FY4 . . . .**129** F2
Oslo Rd BB11 . . . .**126** B5
Osprey Cl Blackburn BB1 . .**100** D8
Knowley PR6 . . . .**61** A3

Oswald Rd
Lytham St Anne's FY8 . . . . .**90** D4
Preston PR2 . . . .**116** C1
Oswald St Accrington BB5 .**103** D6
Blackburn BB1 . . . .**100** E6
Burnley BB12 . . . .**126** F8
Oswaldtwistle BB5 . . . .**102** D3
Rishton BB1 . . . .**123** C1
Oswaldtwistle Mill BB5 . . .**102** E4
Otley Rd FY3 . . . .**89** B7
Ottawa Cl BB2 . . . .**100** A8
Otterburn Cl FY3 . . . .**151** B1
Otterburn Gr BB10 . . . . . .**127** D6
Otterburn Rd BB2 . . . .**80** C7
Otters Cl PR2 . . . .**117** F2
Ottershaw Gdns BB1 . . . . .**100** E8
Ottery Cl PR9 . . . .**53** A5
Otway St PR1 . . . .**116** E2
Oulton Cl L31 . . . .**5** B4
Our Lady & St Edward's
RC Prim Sch PR2 . . . .**116** D8
Our Lady & St Gerard's
RC Prim Sch BB5 . . . .**76** A8
Our Lady & St John
RC High Sch BB1 . . . .**101** C3
Our Lady & St Paul's
RC Prim Sch OL10 . . . .**32** F1
Our Lady Of Compassion
RC Prim Sch L37 . . . .**12** A3
Our Lady of Lourdes RC
Prim Sch Carnforth LA5 . .**217** E1
Southport PR8 . . . .**34** A1
Our Lady of Perpetual
Succour RC Prim Sch
BB2 . . . .**80** E8
Our Lady of the
Assumption
RC Prim Sch FY4 . . . .**109** F5
Our Lady Queen of Peace
RC High Sch WN8 . . . .**17** F4
Our Lady Star of the Sea
RC Prim Sch FY8 . . . .**88** F4
Our Lady's RC High Sch
Fulwood PR2 . . . .**116** C4
Lancaster LA1 . . . .**213** F1
Ousby Ave LA3 . . . .**212** A2
Ousby Rd LA3 . . . .**212** A2
Ouseburn Rd BB2 . . . .**80** C8
Out La PR5 . . . .**57** C2
Out Moss La LA4 . . . .**212** E4
Out Rawcliffe
CE Prim Sch PR3 . . . .**175** F2
Outer Prom FY7 . . . .**193** E5
Outlet La L31, L39 . . . .**6** F1
Outram La BB1 . . . .**121** E1
Outram Way PR5 . . . .**76** E8
Outwood Rd BB11 . . . .**127** B4
Ouzle Rock BB12 . . . .**167** E2
Oval The WN6 . . . .**19** F5
Ovangle Rd LA3 . . . .**213** B2
Over Hos BL7 . . . .**47** B6
Over Town BB10 . . . .**128** A1
Overdale Gr FY3 . . . .**130** A8
Overdell Dr OL12 . . . .**51** C4
Overfield Way OL12 . . . .**51** F2
Overshores Rd BL7 . . . .**47** B8
Overton Rd PR2 . . . .**94** E8
Ovington Dr PR8 . . . .**34** E3
Owen Ave L39 . . . .**15** F6
Owen Ct BB5 . . . .**123** F3
Owen Rd LA1 . . . .**213** F2
Owen St Accrington BB5 . . .**103** C6
Burnley BB12 . . . .**126** A5
Darwen BB3 . . . .**81** A3
Preston PR1 . . . .**96** B8
Owen's La L39 . . . .**13** E2
Owen's Row BL6 . . . .**31** C3
Owens Dr PR6 . . . .**42** E7
Owlet Hall Rd BB3 . . . .**80** E2
Owtram St 2 PR1 . . . .**96** C8
Ox Hey BB5 . . . .**123** F4
Ox Hey Ave PR2 . . . .**115** C1
Ox St 16 BL0 . . . .**49** B5
Oxcliffe Ave LA3 . . . .**212** A1
Oxcliffe Gr LA3 . . . .**212** A1
Oxcliffe Rd LA3 . . . .**212** C2
Oxendale Rd FY5 . . . .**173** D2
Oxenholme Ave FY5 . . . . . .**172** D4
Oxenhurst Rd FY3 . . . .**130** A8
Oxford Ave BB5 . . . .**124** A3
Oxford Cl Blackburn BB1 . .**100** F4
Padiham BB12 . . . .**125** D6
Oxford Ct
4 Lytham St Anne's FY8 . . .**89** D4
Southport PR8 . . . .**33** F4
Oxford Dr Blackburn BB1 . .**101** E4
Kirkham PR4 . . . .**113** C4
Oxford Gdns PR8 . . . .**33** E4
Oxford Pl Burnley BB10 . . .**127** B5
Lancaster LA1 . . . .**213** E3
Oxford Rd
Bamber Bridge PR5 . . . .**76** F8
Blackpool FY1 . . . .**129** C5
Burnley BB11 . . . .**127** B5
Cleveleys FY5 . . . .**172** D3
Fleetwood FY7 . . . .**193** E3
Fulwood PR2 . . . .**116** A4
Lytham St Anne's FY8 . . . . .**88** D4
Lytham St Anne's,
Ansdell FY8 . . . .**89** D4
Nelson BB9 . . . .**169** A2
Orrell WN5 . . . .**10** F8
Skelmersdale WN8 . . . .**17** E1
Southport PR8 . . . .**33** E4
Oxford St Accrington BB5 . .**103** B6
Adlington PR7 . . . .**30** A6
Brierfield BB9 . . . .**147** B5

Oxford St continued
Bury BL9 . . . .**32** A1
Carnforth LA5 . . . .**217** D1
9 Chorley PR7 . . . .**42** C7
Colne BB8 . . . .**169** C5
Darwen BB3 . . . .**80** F4
Lancaster LA1 . . . .**213** F3
Morecambe LA4 . . . .**212** E6
Preston PR1 . . . .**96** A6
Oxford Way Fleetwood FY7 **193** E3
Rochdale OL12 . . . .**51** E2
Oxhey Cl BB10 . . . .**127** F6
Oxheys Ind Est PR1 . . . . . .**116** D2
Oxheys St PR1 . . . .**116** D2
Oxhill Pl FY5 . . . .**150** F7
Oxhouse Rd WN5 . . . .**10** D4
Oxley Cl PR4 . . . .**112** F5
Oxley Rd PR1 . . . .**117** D1
Oxley Rd N PR1 . . . .**117** D1

P

Paa La BB7 . . . .**225** C7
Packet La LA5 . . . .**216** A4
Paddington Ave PR3 . . . . . .**155** C7
Paddington Barn PR3 . . . . .**155** C7
Paddock Ave PR5 . . . .**58** A8
Paddock Dr FY3 . . . .**130** C2
Paddock Rd WN8 . . . .**9** C5
Paddock St 9 BB5 . . . .**102** E4
Paddock The
Blackburn BB2 . . . .**100** A8
Carleton FY6 . . . .**151** C5
Formby L37 . . . .**12** A5
Fulwood PR2 . . . .**117** A6
Ormskirk L39 . . . .**15** C3
Oswaldtwistle BB5 . . . .**102** E4
4 Penwortham PR1 . . . .**95** E2
Ramsbottom BL0 . . . .**49** B7
Rufford L40 . . . .**38** C4
Sawley BB7 . . . .**224** C1
Southport PR8 . . . .**20** C4
Thornton FY5 . . . .**151** B8
Paddock Way LA7 . . . .**237** F4
Padgate Pl BB11 . . . .**126** B4
Padiham Green CE Sch
BB12 . . . .**125** C8
Padiham Rd Burnley BB12 .**126** D6
Burnley, Whittlefield BB12 . .**126** C7
3 Burnley,
Whittlefield BB12 . . . .**126** D6
Padiham BB12 . . . .**125** F7
Sabden BB7 . . . .**145** A7
Padstow Cl PR9 . . . .**53** A5
Padway PR1 . . . .**95** D2
Page Ct L37 . . . .**11** F3
Pagefield Cres BB7 . . . . . .**165** A7
Pages Ct PR5 . . . .**76** B7
Paignton Rd BB1 . . . .**100** D7
Painley Cl FY8 . . . .**90** A4
Paisley St BB11 . . . .**126** D5
Palace Ct LA3 . . . .**212** B4
Palace Gdns BB12 . . . .**126** B7
Palace Rd PR8 . . . .**33** F5
Palace St Burnley BB12 . . .**126** C7
Bury BL9 . . . .**32** A2
Palais Bldgs 2 L40 . . . .**24** C5
Palatine Ave LA1 . . . .**211** A5
Palatine Cl FY3 . . . .**130** C6
Palatine High Sch FY4 . . . .**109** C8
Palatine Rd Blackburn BB2 **100** C5
Blackpool FY1 . . . .**129** C4
Cleveleys FY5 . . . .**172** D4
Southport PR8 . . . .**33** F5
Palatine Sq BB11 . . . .**126** E5
Palatine St 10 BL0 . . . .**49** C6
Paley Rd 1 PR1 . . . .**95** D7
Palfrey Cl FY6 . . . .**151** B6
Pall Mall Blackburn BB2 . . .**99** E5
Chorley PR7 . . . .**42** C6
Palladium Bldgs 7 FY1 . . .**129** B1
Palm Ct WN8 . . . .**17** E2
Palm Dr FY5 . . . .**151** B6
Palm Gr PR8 . . . .**34** E6
Palm St Blackburn BB1 . . .**101** A7
4 Burnley BB10 . . . .**127** E1
Palma St 4 OL14 . . . .**108** B1
Palmaston Cl LA1 . . . .**210** E6
Palmer Ave FY1 . . . .**129** C2
Palmer Gr 3 LA4 . . . .**213** A6
Palmer St BB1 . . . .**100** D6
Palmerston Cl BL0 . . . .**49** C4
Palmerston Rd PR9 . . . .**34** F6
Palmerston St BB12 . . . . . .**125** D7
Pansy St N BB5 . . . .**103** B7
Pansy St S BB5 . . . .**103** B7
Panton St BL6 . . . .**31** D1
Parade The LA5 . . . .**217** B1
Paradise Cl PR6 . . . .**60** C8
Paradise La
1 Blackburn BB2 . . . .**100** E4
Formby L37 . . . .**12** A6
Leyland PR5 . . . .**75** B1
Paradise St
Accrington BB5 . . . .**103** B5
Barrowford BB9 . . . .**168** E5
Blackburn BB2 . . . .**100** D4
11 Burnley BB11 . . . .**126** F6
Little Knowley PR6 . . . .**60** F3
Newchurch BB4 . . . .**85** F2
Ramsbottom BL0 . . . .**49** C7
Paradise Terr 2 BB2 . . . . .**100** E4
Paragon Way LA1 . . . .**210** C8
Parbold Cl Blackpool FY3 . .**150** F1
Burscough L40 . . . .**24** E3
Parbold Douglas
CE Prim Sch WN8 . . . .**26** D3

Parbold Hill WN8 . . . .**26** E2
Parbold Our Lady
All Saints RC Prim Sch
WN8 . . . .**26** C2
Parbold Sta WN8 . . . .**26** C2
Pardoe Cl PR4 . . . .**72** E3
Pardoe Ct L40 . . . .**24** F3
Paris BB1 . . . .**121** E4
Parish St 11 BB12 . . . .**125** C8
Park Ave
Barnoldswick BB18 . . . . . .**200** B1
Barrowford BB9 . . . .**168** C1
Blackburn BB1 . . . .**100** D6
Burnley BB11 . . . .**126** E4
Chatburn BB7 . . . .**187** D5
Clitheroe BB7 . . . .**186** E1
Euxton PR7 . . . .**59** D2
Fleetwood FY7 . . . .**193** F3
Formby L37 . . . .**11** F1
Great Harwood BB6 . . . . . .**123** D6
Haslingden BB4 . . . .**84** B1
Lancaster LA1 . . . .**211** B7
Longshaw WN5 . . . .**10** E1
Lytham St Anne's FY8 . . . . .**89** E3
Maghull L31 . . . .**5** D3
Much Hoole PR4 . . . .**73** C2
New Longton PR4 . . . .**74** F8
Ormskirk L39 . . . .**15** E5
Preston PR1 . . . .**117** B2
Ramsbottom BL0 . . . .**49** D6
Salterforth BB18 . . . .**191** E8
Southport PR9 . . . .**34** E8
Park Bridge Rd BB10 . . . . .**127** D3
Park Cl Hightown L37 . . . .**2** E8
Parbold WN8 . . . .**26** D3
Penwortham PR1 . . . .**95** D4
Park Cotts BB8 . . . .**149** D7
Park Cres Accrington BB5 . .**103** A5
Bacup OL13 . . . .**69** F8
Blackburn BB2 . . . .**100** C6
Haskayne L39 . . . .**13** F4
Haslingden BB4 . . . .**84** C1
Morecambe LA4 . . . .**213** A4
Southport PR9 . . . .**52** D3
Park Ct LA1 . . . .**210** F3
Park Cty Prim Sch
Colne BB8 . . . .**169** F5
Skelmersdale WN8 . . . .**17** E1
Park Dr Brierfield BB9 . . . . .**147** C5
Nelson BB9 . . . .**147** F7
Preston PR2 . . . .**115** D1
Park Farm Cl PR4 . . . .**73** F8
Park Farm Rd BB2 . . . .**79** D8
Park Gate Rd BB1 . . . .**141** D1
Park Hall L Ctr PR7 . . . .**41** A4
Park Hall Rd PR7 . . . .**40** F3
Park Hey Dr WN6 . . . .**19** E7
Park High Sch BB8 . . . .**169** F6
Park Hill
Barnoldswick BB18 . . . . . .**200** C1
21 Rochdale OL12 . . . .**51** F1
Park Hill
Convent Prep Sch BB12 **126** A8
Park Hill Ct PR3 . . . .**178** C7
Park Hill Rd PR3 . . . .**178** C7
Park Ho 2 LA1 . . . .**213** F1
Park House La LA2 . . . .**233** A5
Park La
Brierfield BB10,BB9 . . . . . .**147** C5
Caton LA2 . . . .**231** B5
Ellel LA2 . . . .**207** A6
Garstang PR3 . . . .**199** A4
Great Harwood BB6 . . . . . .**123** D6
Holmes BB4 . . . .**55** B2
Horwich BL6 . . . .**31** D3
Kirkham PR4 . . . .**113** A7
Maghull L31 . . . .**5** F3
Oswaldtwistle BB5 . . . .**102** E3
Penwortham PR1 . . . .**95** E3
Preesall FY6 . . . .**195** B3
Wennington LA2 . . . .**232** E8
Park Lane Dr L31 . . . .**6** B2
Park Lane End L31 . . . .**232** E8
Park Lee Hospl BB2 . . . . . .**100** E2
Park Lee Rd BB2 . . . .**100** E2
Park Link L39 . . . .**15** B1
Park Mews BB7 . . . .**225** B3
Park Mill Pl PR1 . . . .**117** A1
Park Pl
Blackburn, Feniscowles BB2 .**79** D7
Blackburn, Wilton BB2 . . . .**100** B3
25 Preston PR1 . . . .**96** A7
Walton-le-D PR5 . . . .**96** E4
Park Rd Accrington BB5 . . .**103** A6
Adlington PR7 . . . .**29** F6
Bacup OL13 . . . .**86** F1
Barnoldswick BB18 . . . . . .**200** B1
Blackburn BB2 . . . .**100** E3
Blackpool FY1 . . . .**129** D3
Burnley BB10 . . . .**127** E1
Chorley PR7 . . . .**42** C8
Coppull PR7 . . . .**41** E1
Darwen BB3 . . . .**64** B6
Edgworth BL7 . . . .**47** C5
Formby L37 . . . .**11** E1
Fulwood PR2 . . . .**117** A4
Gisburn BB7 . . . .**225** B3
Great Harwood BB6 . . . . . .**123** D5
Haslingden BB4 . . . .**66** F7
Kirkham PR4 . . . .**112** F4
Lancaster LA1 . . . .**211** A8
Leyland PR5 . . . .**59** A7
Longshaw WN5 . . . .**10** F1
Lytham St Anne's FY8 . . . . .**88** E6
Mellor Brook BB2,PR5 . . . .**120** A1
Morecambe LA4 . . . .**213** A6
Newchurch BB4 . . . .**85** F1
Ormskirk L39 . . . .**15** E5

Park Rd continued
Padiham BB12 . . . .**125** C8
Penwortham PR1 . . . .**95** D4
Poulton-le-F FY6 . . . .**151** E4
Ramsbottom BL0 . . . .**48** F3
Rishton BB1 . . . .**123** C1
Silverdale LA5 . . . .**218** D4
Southport PR9 . . . .**34** D8
Thornton FY5 . . . .**173** B1
Park Rd W PR9 . . . .**52** C1
Park Sch FY3 . . . .**129** E4
Park Side BB18 . . . .**192** A8
Park Sq LA1 . . . .**211** A8
Park Sreet E BB5 . . . .**168** E4
Park St Accrington BB5 . . .**103** C6
Barnoldswick BB18 . . . . . .**200** B1
Barrowford BB9 . . . .**168** D4
Chorley PR7 . . . .**60** C1
Clitheroe BB7 . . . .**164** E7
Eccleston PR7 . . . .**40** C6
Great Harwood BB6 . . . . . .**123** D5
Haslingden BB4 . . . .**84** B3
Haslingden, Bridge End BB4 .**66** F7
Lytham St Anne's FY8 . . . . .**90** B3
Park Stone Rd PR3 . . . .**136** C3
Park Terr Blackburn BB1 . .**100** D7
Great Harwood BB6 . . . . . .**123** D6
Wrea Green PR4 . . . .**112** B3
Park View Arnside LA5 . . . .**237** B1
Carnforth LA5 . . . .**217** D3
Gisburn BB7 . . . .**225** B3
Newchurch BB4 . . . .**85** F1
Padiham BB12 . . . .**125** C8
Penwortham PR1 . . . .**95** D4
Park View Ave PR2 . . . .**116** B2
Park View Cl BB9 . . . .**147** B7
Park View Cotts FY8 . . . . . .**90** B4
Park View Ct 2 FY4 . . . . . .**109** C6
Park View Rd FY8 . . . .**90** B4
Park View Terr
Abbey Village PR6 . . . .**79** C1
Salterforth BB18 . . . .**191** D7
Park Wall Rd L29, L38 . . . . . .**4** B2
Park Way Colne BB8 . . . . . .**169** C6
Formby L37 . . . .**11** F1
Penwortham PR1 . . . .**95** D4
Park Wlk PR7 . . . .**117** A4
Park Wood Dr BB4 . . . .**84** E2
Parkbourn L31 . . . .**6** A2
Parkbourn Dr L31 . . . .**6** A2
Parkbourn N L31 . . . .**6** A2
Parkbourn Sq L31 . . . .**6** A2
Parkdale Gdns BB2 . . . .**80** D6
Parke Mews PR6 . . . .**78** C3
Parke Rd PR6 . . . .**61** E8
Parker Ave BB7 . . . .**164** E6
Parker Cres L39 . . . .**15** F7
Parker La Burnley BB11 . . .**127** A5
New Longton PR4 . . . .**75** C6
Parker St Accrington,
Higher Baxenden BB5 . . . . .**103** E2
Accrington, Hillock Vale BB5 **103** E8
Barnoldswick BB18 . . . . . .**200** A3
3 Blackpool FY1 . . . .**129** C5
Brierfield BB10 . . . .**147** F3
Burnley BB11 . . . .**127** A6
Bury BL9 . . . .**32** A2
Chorley PR7 . . . .**60** C1
Colne BB8 . . . .**169** C5
Lancaster LA1 . . . .**211** A8
9 Nelson BB9 . . . .**168** F2
Preston PR2 . . . .**116** D2
Rishton BB1 . . . .**123** C2
Parker Terr BB7 . . . .**225** B3
Parkers Fold PR3 . . . .**178** C2
Parkfield Ave PR3 . . . .**137** D5
Parkfield Cl Leyland PR5 . . .**58** C8
Ormskirk L39 . . . .**15** C4
5 Preston PR2 . . . .**115** C1
Parkfield Cres 6 PR2 . . . . .**115** C1
Parkfield Dr
Lancaster LA1 . . . .**211** A6
Preston PR2 . . . .**94** C8
Parkfield Gr L31 . . . .**5** C1
Parkfield View PR2 . . . .**94** C8
Parkgate PR3 . . . .**137** D5
Parkgate Dr
Lancaster LA1 . . . .**211** C7
Leyland PR5 . . . .**58** F7
Parkhead La PR3 . . . .**179** A8
Parkinson La PR3 . . . .**160** B8
Parkinson St
Blackburn BB2 . . . .**100** C2
Burnley BB11 . . . .**127** A4
Foulridge BB8 . . . .**191** D1
Haslingden BB4 . . . .**84** A3
Parkinson Way 1 FY4 . . . .**129** C1
Parkland Cl FY5 . . . .**172** C1
Parkland Gr LA3 . . . .**212** B2
Parkland View BB11 . . . . . .**126** E2
Parklands
Skelmersdale WN8 . . . .**18** D2
Southport PR9 . . . .**34** E8
Parklands Ave PR1 . . . .**95** A4
Parklands Cl PR1 . . . .**95** A4
Parklands Dr PR2 . . . .**116** E8
Parklands Gr PR2 . . . .**116** E8
Parklands High Sch
Chorley PR7 . . . .**42** A8
Preston PR1 . . . .**116** F2
Parklands The PR3 . . . .**178** D3
Parklands Way BB2 . . . .**80** B8
Parks The LA4 . . . .**213** A7
Parkside Fulwood PR1 . . . .**117** B3
Morecambe LA4 . . . .**212** F3
Preston PR2 . . . .**115** D2
Parkside Ave PR7 . . . .**42** C8
Parkside Cl 12 OL14 . . . . .**108** B1

Parkside Cres WN5 ....10 F6
Parkside Ct LA4 ....212 F3
Parkside Dr Arnside LA5 .237 A1
  Lucas Green PR6 ....60 B6
Parkside Dr S PR6 ....60 B6
Parkside La PR3 ....178 A7
Parkside Rd
  Cornholme OL14 ....108 B1
  Lytham St Anne's FY8 ....89 A7
  Nelson BB9 ....148 B8
Parkside View FY5 ....173 A4
Parkstone Ave
  Carleton FY6 ....151 B5
  Thornton FY5 ....151 D8
Parksway FY6 ....194 D5
Parkthorn Rd PR2 ....94 C8
Parkview Cl LA4 ....212 E3
Parkway Blackpool FY3 ...130 A6
  Shevington Moor WN6 .....28 A2
Parkwood BL7 ....46 D2
Parkwood Ave BB12 .....126 D7
Parkwood Rd BB1 ....101 A6
Parliament St
  Burnley BB11 ....127 B5
  11 Colne BB8 ....169 E5
  18 Darwen BB3 ....81 A1
  Lancaster LA1 ....213 F1
  Morecambe LA3 ....212 B4
  Orrell WN8 ....10 C7
Parlick Ave PR3 ....139 B7
Parlick Rd Fulwood PR2 ..118 A2
  Garstang PR3 ....178 B6
Parr Cottage Cl PR7 .....40 C7
Parr La PR7 ....40 C7
Parramatta St 8 BB4 .....85 A2
Parrock Cl PR1 ....95 E3
Parrock Par 85 A7
Parrock Rd BB9 ....168 C2
Parrock St
  Barnoldswick BB18 .....200 B2
  10 Nelson BB9 ....168 E1
  7 Rawtenstall BB4 ......85 A7
Parrox Fold FY6 ....195 A5
Parrox La PR4 ....113 E2
Parson La BB7 ....164 E8
Parson's Brow 4 PR7 ....42 C7
Parson's Bullough Rd
  PR6,BL6 ....43 E5
Parsonage Ave PR3 .....140 D3
Parsonage Brow WN8 .....10 A8
Parsonage Ct 2 Bury BL9 .32 A2
  Morecambe LA3 ....212 F2
  Orrell WN8 ....10 A7
Parsonage Cotts 9 BB7 ..164 E8
Parsonage Dr BB10,BB9 ..147 C5
Parsonage Gdns PR4 .....56 A5
Parsonage La PR3 ....182 C1
Parsonage Rd BB1 ......122 A4
Parsonage St Bury BL9 ...32 A3
  3 Church BB5 ....102 E5
  Colne BB8 ....169 C4
Part St PR8 ....34 B6
Parth St OL10 ....32 D1
Partnership Way BB1 ....101 D2
Partridge Ave FY5 .....173 A4
Partridge Dr FY5 ......103 F1
Partridge Hill 4 BB12 ..145 D1
Partridge Hill St 5 BB12 145 D1
Partridge Wlk 4 BB11 ..126 C5
Passmonds Cres
  OL11,OL12 ....51 B1
Past La Lane Ends BB7 ..224 A6
  Lane Ends BB7 ....224 A7
Pasture Cl
  Barnoldswick BB18 .....200 C4
  Burnley BB11 ....126 E3
Pasture Dr BB8 ....191 D1
Pasture Field FY6 ......151 B6
Pasture Field Cl PR5 ....75 C1
Pasture La
  Barrowford BB9 ....168 C5
  Hest Bank LA5 ....215 E1
Pasture The LA7 ....237 E5
Pasturegate BB11 ......126 E3
Pasturegate Ave BB11 ...126 E4
Pasturelands Dr BB7 ....143 A3
Pastures The
  Blackburn BB2 ....100 A8
  Grimsargh PR2 ....138 D1
  Southport PR9 ....53 D5
Paterson St BB2 ....100 E1
Pathfinders Dr LA1 .....210 E4
Patience St 11 OL12 .....51 C1
Patmos St BL0 ....49 D6
Paton St OL12 ....51 D3
Patrick Ave BB12 ......144 D2
Patrick Cres BB4 ....85 C2
Patten St Blackburn BB1 .101 C5
  Colne BB8 ....169 D4
  Preston PR1 ....95 F8
Patterdale Ave
  Blackburn BB1 ....101 C3
  Blackpool FY3 ....129 F2
  Fleetwood FY7 ....193 D1
  Oswaldtwistle BB5 .....102 D5
  Thornton FY5 ....173 B3
Patterdale Cl
  Brierfield BB10 ....147 C4
  Southport PR8 ....20 B3
Patterdale Cres L31 ......5 E2
Patterdale Rd LA1 ......214 B1
Pattison Cl OL12 ....51 D3
Paul's La Hambleton FY6 .174 C2
  Southport PR9 ....52 F4
Paulhan St BB10 ....147 B2
Pavey Cl FY4 ....109 F8
Pavilion Cl OL12 ....51 F2

Pavilion View PR5 ....57 B2
Pavilions The PR2 ....95 C7
Paxton Pl WN8 ....9 C4
Paxton St BB5 ....103 B6
Paynter Cl Barrow BB7 ..164 D1
  Enfield BB5 ....124 A2
Paythorne Ave BB10 ....127 D5
Paythorne Cl FY3 ......151 B1
Peabody St BB3 ....81 A2
Peace St BB11 ....126 D5
Peacehaven WN8 ....17 E1
Peachtree Cl PR2 ......117 D6
Peacock Cres LA2 ......215 E1
Peacock Dr PR3 ....199 D1
Peacock Hall Rd PR5 ....58 D7
Peacock Hill Cl PR2 ....118 C7
Peacock La LA2 ....215 E1
Peahall La PR3 ....197 A4
Pear Ave BL9 ....32 C3
Pear 16 OL14 ....108 B1
Pear St 17 OL14 ....108 B1
Pear Tree Ave PR7 ......41 F3
Pear Tree Cl 2 PR5 .....96 E2
Pear Tree Cres PR5 .....96 E2
Pear Tree Croft PR4 .....74 A8
Pear Tree Ctyd PR4 ....114 A2
Pear Tree La PR7 ....59 E3
Pear Tree Rd PR6 ....77 B3
Pear Tree St PR4 ......113 A5
Pear Tree St 7 PR5 .....96 E2
Pearfield PR5 ....76 A2
Pearl Ave 6 FY2 ....150 E1
Pearl Brook Ind Est BL6 .31 B3
Pearl St Accrington BB5 .102 F5
  Blackburn BB1 ....121 F1
Pearson St Blackburn BB2 100 D4
  Bury BL9 ....32 B3
Peart St BB10 ....147 B2
Peartree Rd PR5 ....57 B3
Pebble Ct FY5 ....172 C3
Pechell St 5 PR2 ......116 C1
Pedder Ave LA3 ....209 C1
Pedder Dr LA3 ....209 D1
Pedder Gr LA3 ....209 D1
Pedder La FY6 ....174 B1
Pedder Rd LA3 ....209 C1
Pedder St Morecambe LA4 212 D5
  Preston PR2 ....95 E8
Pedder's La Blackpool FY4 109 D7
  Preston PR2 ....116 A1
Pedders Gr PR2 ....95 A8
Pedders La PR2 ....95 A8
Pedders Way PR2 ....95 A8
Peebles Gr BB11 ......126 D3
Peel Ave Blackpool FY3 ..129 D7
  Heysham LA3 ....208 E6
  Lancaster LA1 ....213 F2
  Ramsbottom BL0 ....49 A5
Peel Bank Rd BB5 ......102 B4
Peel Brow BL0 ....49 D6
Peel Brow Prim Sch BL0 .49 D6
Peel Cl BB2 ....80 E8
Peel Cres LA1 ....210 D4
Peel Dr OL13 ....87 B1
Peel Gdns BB8 ....169 C5
Peel Hall Rd BL0 ....49 A4
Peel Hall St PR1 ....117 B1
Peel Hill FY4 ....110 E7
Peel Mount Blackburn BB1 101 F4
  Ramsbottom BL0 ....49 A4
Peel Mount Ct BB1 .....101 F4
Peel Park Ave
  Accrington BB5 ....103 D7
  Clitheroe BB7 ....164 F7
Peel Park Cl
  Accrington BB5 ....103 D7
  Clitheroe BB7 ....164 F7
Peel Park Cty Prim Sch
  BB5 ....103 D7
Peel Pl BB9 ....168 F6
Peel Rd Colne BB8 .....169 B4
  Fleetwood FY7 ....193 F3
  Peel FY4 ....110 F4
  Skelmersdale WN8 ....9 E5
Peel St Accrington BB5 ..103 C6
  Adlington PR6 ....30 B8
  Blackburn BB2 ....100 C2
  Chorley PR7 ....42 C7
  Clitheroe BB7 ....164 E8
  Haslingden BB4 ....84 A3
  5 Oswaldtwistle BB5 ...102 D3
  Padiham BB12 ....125 D8
  Preston PR2 ....95 E8
  Rawtenstall BB4 ....85 C2
  Southport PR8 ....34 F6
Peel Twr BL8 ....48 F5
Peel Wlk L31 ....5 B2
Peers Clough Rd BB4 ....85 F7
Peet Ave L39 ....15 D4
Peet's La PR9 ....53 A1
Peg Way PR4 ....91 F6
Peg's La FY8 ....90 B8
Pegbank La LA6 ....235 A8
Pelham Ave 3 FY3 .....129 E8
Pelham St BB1 ....101 A6
Pemberton Dr LA4 .....213 B5
Pemberton Pl LA4 .....213 B5
Pemberton St BB1 .....121 E1
Pemberton's CE Sch PR7 .40 E2
Pembroke Ave
  Blackpool FY2 ....150 B3
  Morecambe LA4 ....212 G6
Pembroke Cl BL6 ....31 A4
Pembroke Ct
  Blackpool FY2 ....150 B3
  14 Rochdale OL12 ......51 F2
Pembroke Pl Chorley PR7 .42 B6
  Leyland PR5 ....59 A8

Pembroke Pl continued
  11 Preston PR1 ....96 A7
Pembroke Rd FY8 ....89 D4
Pembroke St
  Accrington BB5 ....103 D6
  Bacup OL13 ....86 F1
  Blackburn BB1 ....100 E3
  12 Burnley BB10 ......147 B1
Pembury Ave PR1 ....95 F3
Pen-y-Ghent Way BB18 .200 D4
Penarth Ct PR2 ....115 F3
Pendle Ave Bacup OL13 ..87 A3
  Chatburn BB7 ....187 E5
  Clayton-le-M BB5 .....123 F4
Pendle Bridge LA2 .....146 F3
Pendle Cl Bacup OL13 ...87 A2
  Blackpool FY3 ....150 D3
Pendle Comm Hosp BB 168 E1
Pendle Ct
  Barnoldswick BB18 .....200 C3
  4 Clitheroe BB7 ....164 F8
  Kirkham BB7 ....113 A6
  Longridge PR3 ....139 A7
Pendle Cty Prim Sch BB7 186 F1
Pendle Dr Blackburn BB2 .100 F2
  Horwich BL6 ....31 C5
  Ormskirk L39 ....16 A6
  Whalley BB7 ....143 A7
Pendle Fields BB12 .....146 D1
Pendle Hill Cl PR2 ....118 C7
Pendle House BB1 ......100 F3
Pendle Ind Est BB9 ....147 F7
Pendle Pl
  Lytham St Anne's FY8 ...90 C4
  Skelmersdale WN8 ....9 D4
Pendle Rd Brierfield BB9 .147 A5
  Clayton-le-W PR5 ......76 D1
  Clitheroe BB7 ....165 A4
  Downham BB7 ....188 D3
  Great Harwood BB6 ....123 F6
  Lancaster LA1 ....213 D3
  Nelson BB9 ....147 E7
  Oswaldtwistle BB5 .....102 B5
  Preston PR1 ....96 A3
  Ramsbottom BL0 ....49 B5
  Whitworth OL12 ....70 E6
Pendle Row BB12 ......167 C5
Pendle St Accrington BB5 .103 A5
  Barrowford BB9 ....168 C3
  Blackburn BB1 ....101 A4
  Nelson BB9 ....168 D1
  Padiham BB12 ....125 D8
Pendle St E BB7 ....144 F7
Pendle St W BB7 ......144 F7
Pendle Terr BB7 ....188 E8
Pendle Trad Est BB7 ...187 C4
Pendle View Barley BB12 .167 C6
  Brockhall Village BB6 ..142 C6
  Clayton-le-M BB5 .....124 A3
  Foulridge BB8 ....191 E1
  Grindleton BB7 ....187 B7
  Higham BB12 ....145 F6
  Huncoat BB5 ....124 F7
  West Bradford BB7 ....186 D7
Pendle Way Burnley BB12 .126 E6
  5 Nelson BB9 ....147 E8
Pendlehurst St BB11 ...126 E4
Pendlemist View BB8 ...169 C3
Pendleside BB9 ....147 B8
Pendleside Cl BB7 .....144 F7
Pendleton Ave
  Accrington BB5 ....102 F4
  Rawtenstall BB4 ....85 A4
Pendleton Rd
  Pendleton BB7 ....165 A2
  Wiswell BB7 ....143 F8
Penfold L5 ....5 E1
Pengarth Rd BL6 ....31 C4
Penguin St PR1 ....117 B2
Penhale Cl LA3 ....208 E6
Penhale Ct LA3 ....208 E6
Penhale Gdns LA3 .....208 E6
Penhill Cl 4 FY2 ......129 D8
Penistone St 6 BB12 ...126 D6
Penketh Pl WN8 ....9 C5
Penn St BB1 ....31 C3
Pennine Ave PR7 ....59 D1
Pennine Cl
  7 Blackpool FY1 ......129 C4
  Horwich BL6 ....31 C5
Pennine Cres BB5 .....147 C5
Pennine Gdns PR3 .....178 A7
Pennine Gr LA2 ....145 C2
Pennine Pl WN8 ....9 B6
Pennine Rd Bacup OL13 ..87 A2
  Chorley PR6 ....42 E8
  Horwich BL6 ....31 C5
Pennine View
  Dolphinholme LA2 .....220 A8
  Glasson LA2 ....205 E4
  Great Eccleston PR3 ...154 C5
  Kirkham PR4 ....113 C5
  Morecambe LA4 ....212 E4
Pennine Way
  Barnoldswick BB18 .....200 A2
  Brierfield BB9 ....147 C5
  Great Eccleston PR3 ...154 C5
  Stalmine FY6 ....174 D7
Pennines The PR2 .....117 A7
Pennington Ave L39 .....15 E6
Pennington Ct
  Heysham LA3 ....208 A5
  4 Ormskirk L39 ....15 F6
Pennington La WN2 .....29 E1
Penny House La BB5 ...103 C7
Penny St Blackburn BB1 .100 F5
  Lancaster LA1 ....210 F7
  3 Preston PR1 ....96 A8
Penny Stone Rd LA2 ...214 C2
Pennyfarthing 7 FY5 ..173 A2
Pennystone Rd FY2 ....150 B4
Penrhos Ave FY7 ......193 E1

Penrhyn Rd LA1 ....213 C2
Penrith Ave Cleveleys FY5 .172 C4
  Heysham LA3 ....208 F8
  Southport PR8 ....20 C3
Penrith Cres Maghull L31 ..5 E2
  Nelson BB8 ....169 B3
Penrith Rd BB8 ....169 A3
Penrod Way LA3 ....208 F8
Penrose Ave FY4 ......129 F1
Penrose Pl WN8 ....9 E4
Penshaw Cl LA1 ....121 E1
Penswick Ave FY5 .....172 E1
Pentland Rd L33 ....1 A4
Penwortham Broad Oak
  Cty Prim Sch PR1 .....95 C2
Penwortham Ct PR1 .....95 D4
Penwortham
  Girls High Sch PR1 ....95 C5
Penwortham Hall Gdns
  PR1 ....95 E3
Penwortham Prim Sch
  PR1 ....95 A5
Penwortham Priory
  High Sch PR1 ....95 A5
Penzance St BB2 ......100 B2
Peplow Rd LA3 ....209 A8
Pepper La WN6 ....28 B3
Perch Pool La PR9 ......35 F4
Percival St Accrington BB5 102 F4
  Blackburn BB2 ....100 F7
  Darwen BB3 ....80 F3
Percy Rd LA1 ....210 F6
Percy St Accrington BB5 .103 B6
  Blackburn BB2 ....100 D8
  Blackpool FY1 ....129 C2
  Bury BL9 ....32 B3
  9 Chorley PR7 ....42 D7
  Colne BB8 ....169 E6
  Fleetwood FY7 ....193 F4
  Nelson BB9 ....147 E7
  Oswaldtwistle BB5 .....102 B5
  Preston PR1 ....96 A4
  Ramsbottom BL0 ....49 B5
  Whitworth OL12 ....70 E6
Peregrine Dr BB3 ....80 D3
Peregrine Pl PR5 ....75 D2
Peridot Cl BB1 ....121 F2
Perimeter Rd L33 ....1 E2
Peronne Cres BB1 .....101 D5
Perpignon Way 10 LA1 .210 F8
Perry St BB10 ....81 B2
Perryn Pl WN6 ....28 F1
Pershore Gdns FY3 ....130 B8
Pershore Gr PR8 ....20 A4
Pershore Rd FY8 ....89 B5
Persia St BB5 ....102 F6
Perth Cl FY5 ....150 F7
Perth St Accrington BB5 .103 A5
  Blackburn BB2 ....100 C3
  Burnley BB11 ....126 D5
  Lancaster LA1 ....211 A2
  8 Nelson BB9 ....168 F1
Peter Birtwistle Cl BB8 .169 E5
Peter La LA5 ....219 E1
Peter Martin St 2 BL6 ..31 B4
Peter St
  9 Barrowford BB9 .....168 D4
  Blackburn BB1 ....101 A6
  Blackpool FY1 ....129 C4
  Colne BB8 ....169 C4
  6 Rawtenstall BB4 .....85 A2
Peterfield Rd 1 PR1 .....95 C2
Peterhouse Sch PR9 ....53 B3
Peters Ave L40 ....24 C4
Petersan Ct PR7 ....60 C3
Petersbottom La LA2 ...233 D3
Petre Cres BB1 ....102 B8
Petre Rd BB5 ....123 F2
Petrel Cl BB1 ....100 D8
Petunia Cl PR5 ....76 E2
Petworth Rd PR8 ....20 B6
Pharos Ct 8 FY7 ......194 B5
Pharos Gr 2 FY7 ......194 B5
Pharos Pl FY7 ....194 B5
Pharos St FY7 ....194 B5
Pheasant Wood Dr FY5 .172 F5
Pheasantford Gn BB10 ..127 D8
Pheasantford St BB10 ..127 B8
Philip Ave PR4 ....113 B4
Philip Dr PR8 ....20 F6
Philip St
  Barnoldswick BB18 .....200 B2
  Darwen BB3 ....81 B1
Philips Rd Blackburn BB1 .101 B8
  Weir OL13 ....87 A7
Phillip St FY4 ....129 D2
Phillip's Cl L37 ....11 F2
Phillip's La L37 ....11 F1
Phillips La BB8 ....169 B3
Phillipstown BB4 ....85 E4
Phoenix St
  5 Lancaster LA1 ....213 F1
  Rochdale OL12 ....51 C1
Phoenix Way BB11 .....126 C5
Phyllis St OL12 ....51 B1
Piazza The LA1 ....211 C2
Piccadilly LA1 ....210 F3
Piccadilly Cl LA1 .....210 F3
Piccadilly Gr LA1 .....210 F3
Piccadilly Rd BB11 ....126 C4
Piccadilly Sq 2 BB11 ..126 E5
Piccadilly St BB4 ....84 B3
Pickard Cl BB18 ......200 D4
Pickard St LA1 ....210 F5
Pickering Cl FY8 ....89 B7

Pickering Fold BB1 .....81 B7
Pickering St BB9 ......147 E5
Pickerings The 2 PR5 ..76 C8
Pickles Dr L40 ....24 C4
Pickles St BB12 ......126 D7
Pickmere Ave FY4 .....109 E8
Pickmere Cl FY5 ......173 A4
Pickthorn Cl LA1 .....213 D4
Pickup Fold 3 BB3 .....64 C7
Pickup Fold Rd BB3 ....64 C7
Pickup Rd BB1 ....102 A8
Pickup St Accrington BB5 .102 F5
  11 Bacup OL13 ....86 F2
  Blackburn BB1 ....101 A5
  Clayton-le-M BB5 .....123 F3
Picton St BB2 ....80 B8
Pier Ho 3 BB1 ....100 F3
Pier La LA5 ....237 A2
Pier St FY1 ....129 B3
Pierce Cl Lancaster LA1 .210 F7
  Padiham BB12 ....145 C1
Piercefield Rd L37 ......11 F5
Piercy Mdw BB4 ....85 F3
Piercy Mount BB4 ......85 F3
Piercy Rd BB4 ....85 F3
Piercy Terr BB4 ....85 F3
Pierston Ave FY2 .....150 C1
Pike Ct FY7 ....193 C2
Pike View BL6 ....31 C4
Pikelaw Pl WN8 ....9 C5
Pilgrim St BB9 ....147 E6
Pilkington Dr BB5 ....124 A3
Pilkington Rd PR8 ......34 C5
Pilkington St
  6 Chorley PR7 ....42 D7
  14 Ramsbottom BL0 .....49 B5
Pilling Ave Accrington BB5 103 E2
  Lytham St Anne's FY8 ...89 C7
Pilling Cl Chorley PR7 ...42 D6
  Southport PR9 ....52 F5
Pilling Cres FY3 ......130 A8
Pilling Field BL7 ....46 E1
Pilling La Chorley PR7 ...42 D6
  Maghull L31 ....5 A5
  Pilling Lane FY6 ......195 B2
Pilling Pl WN8 ....9 C5
Pilling St Haslingden BB4 ..84 B6
  3 Rawtenstall BB4 .....68 F8
Pilmuir Rd BB2 ....100 A1
Pilot St BB5 ....103 B7
Pimbo La Orrell WN8 ....10 A4
  Skelmersdale WN8 ......9 F3
Pimbo Rd WN8 ....9 C5
Pimhole Rd BL9 ....32 B2
Pimlico BB7 ....186 F3
Pimlico Link Rd BB7 ...187 C2
Pimlico Rd BB7 ....186 F2
Pinch Clough Rd BB4 ...85 F5
Pincock Brow PR7 ......41 C8
Pincock St PR7 ....41 C8
Pinder Cl BB7 ....186 B4
Pinder Cl BB9 ....168 F2
Pine Ave Blackpool FY1 .129 E2
  Much Hoole PR4 ....73 D4
  Ormskirk L39 ....15 F7
Pine Cl Fulwood PR2 ...117 F4
  Halton LA2 ....214 E6
  Newburgh WN8 ....26 A1
  Rishton BB1 ....102 B8
  Skelmersdale WN8 ......17 F1
Pine Cres
  Oswaldtwistle BB5 .....102 F3
  Poulton-le-F FY6 .....151 E3
Pine Crest L39 ....15 B2
Pine Dr L39 ....15 F6
Pine Gr Chorley PR6 ....60 D3
  Clitheroe BB7 ....164 D7
  Garstang PR3 ....199 C1
  Ormskirk L39 ....15 F7
  Southport PR9 ....34 C1
Pine Lake LA6 ....234 A3
Pine St Bacup OL13 .....87 A1
  Blackburn BB1 ....101 A7
  Burnley BB11 ....127 B5
  Bury BL9 ....32 B2
  Darwen BB3 ....64 B8
  Haslingden BB4 ....84 C3
  Lancaster LA1 ....213 E1
  Morecambe LA4 ....212 F4
  Nelson BB9 ....147 F8
Pine St S BL9 ....32 B2
Pine Way PR4 ....113 B7
Pine Wlks PR2 ....115 C1
Pines Cl PR5 ....77 C4
Pines The Leyland PR5 ..58 A8
  Southport PR8 ....33 F6
Pineway PR2 ....116 C4
Pinewood Blackburn BB2 .79 F8
  Skelmersdale WN8 ......18 D3
Pinewood Ave
  Blackpool FY2 ....150 E4
  Broughton PR3 ....136 C3
  Caton LA2 ....231 C3
  Formby L37 ....11 D1
  Hest Bank LA5 ....215 F2
  Knott End-on-S FY6 ...195 B3
  Morecambe LA4 ....213 B6
  Thornton FY5 ....151 B2
Pinewood Cl Formby L37 .11 D2
  Lancaster LA2 ....210 C2
  Southport PR8 ....35 C1
Pinewood Cotts 11 LA2 .233 D8
Pinewood Cres
  Leyland PR5 ....58 E8

Pinewood Cres *continued*
Lytham St Anne's FY8 . . . . . .**89** D4
Orrell WN5 . . . .**10** E6
Ramsbottom BL0 . . . .**49** B2
Pinewood Dr BB5 . . . .**103** E6
Pinfold Barrowford BB9 . . . .**168** E5
Longton PR4 . . . .**74** A8
Pinfold Cl Preston PR2 . . . . .**117** E5
Southport PR8 . . . .**20** B3
Pinfold Ct LA3 . . . .**213** B2
Pinfold La Inskip PR4 . . . . . .**155** C2
Lancaster LA1 . . . .**213** F2
Longridge PR3 . . . .**139** B4
Pinfold L40 . . . .**22** F3
Southport PR8 . . . .**20** B3
Pinfold Pl Nelson BB9 . . . . .**169** B1
Skelmersdale WN8 . . . .**9** D4
Pinfold St PR1 . . . .**96** E8
Pingle Croft PR6 . . . .**77** A2
Pingwood La L33 . . . .**1** A5
Pink Pl BB2 . . . .**100** B3
Pink St BB12 . . . .**126** C6
Pinnacle Dr BL7 . . . .**46** E2
Pinner La BB4 . . . .**84** F7
Pinners Cl BL0 . . . .**49** B7
Pintail Cl Moss Side PR5 . . . .**75** A1
5 Rochdale OL12 . . . .**51** B2
Pioneer St BL6 . . . .**31** C4
Piper Cotts LA4 . . . .**212** F3
Piper Lea BB4 . . . .**86** A1
Piper's La LA6 . . . .**234** C8
Pipers Cl LA7 . . . .**237** E4
Pippin Bank OL13 . . . .**86** F1
Pippin St Ormskirk L40 . . . . .**24** A2
Thorpe Green PR6 . . . .**77** E5
Pit Hey Pl WN8 . . . .**9** C5
Pitt St Lancaster LA1 . . . . .**210** F8
11 Padiham BB12 . . . .**125** D8
Preston PR1 . . . .**95** E7
Southport PR9 . . . .**34** F6
Pittman Ct PR2 . . . .**117** B8
Pittman Way PR2,PR3 . . . . .**117** C7
Pitts House La PR9 . . . .**35** B8
Pittsdale Ave FY3 . . . .**130** A2
Pitville St BB3 . . . .**80** F3
Place-de-Criel **12** BB9 . . .**147** D8
Plain Pl BB2 . . . .**100** A8
Plainmoor Dr FY5 . . . .**150** F7
Plane St Bacup OL13 . . . .**86** F4
Blackburn BB1 . . . .**101** A4
Plane Tree Cl BB11 . . . .**126** D3
Plane Tree Rd **7** BB1 . . . .**101** A4
Planet Earth OL14 . . . .**87** F4
Plant St Oswaldtwistle BB5 . .**102** D3
Preston PR2 . . . .**116** C1
Plantain Wlk LA3 . . . .**212** E2
Plantation Ave
Arnside LA5 . . . .**218** C8
Knott End-on-S FY6 . . . . . .**194** E5
Plantation Gr LA5 . . . .**218** C8
Plantation La LA2 . . . .**226** D1
Plantation Rd
Accrington BB5 . . . .**103** E6
Blackburn BB2 . . . .**100** B1
Burscough L40 . . . .**24** B4
Edgworth BL7 . . . .**47** F7
Plantation Sq BB5 . . . .**103** D6
Plantation St
Accrington BB5 . . . .**103** D6
Bacup OL13 . . . .**69** C8
Burnley BB10 . . . .**127** A7
6 Nelson BB9 . . . .**168** F1
Rawtenstall BB4 . . . .**85** B2
Plantation The BD23 . . . . .**230** B3
Plantation View
Bacup OL13 . . . .**86** F6
Ramsbottom BL0 . . . .**49** C3
Platt Cl BB5 . . . .**103** A5
Platt La WN1 . . . .**29** B3
Platt St FY1 . . . .**129** C6
Platten Gr LA4 . . . .**212** F5
Platts La L40 . . . .**24** D2
Pleasant Gr FY5 . . . .**173** B2
Pleasant Pl **4** BB11 . . . . .**126** F5
Pleasant St Blackpool FY1 .**129** B7
Haslingden BB4 . . . .**84** B3
2 Lytham St Anne's FY8 . . .**90** B3
Pleasant View Bacup OL13 .**69** C7
14 Barnoldswick BB18 . . .**200** B3
Blackpool FY4 . . . .**110** A4
Coppull PR7 . . . .**41** F2
Earby BB18 . . . .**201** C1
Hoddlesden BB3 . . . .**81** F1
Leyland PR5 . . . .**75** C3
Newchurch BB4 . . . .**85** F1
Withnell PR6 . . . .**79** A1
Pleasington Ave PR3 . . . .**178** D6
Pleasington Cl
Blackburn BB2 . . . .**100** B4
Blackpool FY4 . . . .**110** A8
Pleasington Gr BB10 . . . .**127** D5
Pleasington La BB2 . . . .**79** C8
Pleasington
Nature Reserve BB2 . . . . .**99** D3
Pleasington Rd BB2 . . . .**99** C1
Pleasington St BB2 . . . . . .**100** B4
Pleasington Sta BB2 . . . . . .**99** C1
Pleasure Beach Sta FY4 .**109** B6
Pleck Farm Ave BB1 . . . . .**100** E8
Pleck Pl FY6 . . . .**151** B6
Pleck Rd BB5 . . . .**103** C6
Pleckgate Fold BB1 . . . . . .**121** E1
Pleckgate High Sch BB1 .**121** D1
Pleckgate Rd BB1 . . . .**121** E1
Plevna Rd PR1 . . . .**96** C8

Plex La L39 . . . .**14** C5
Plex Moss La L39 . . . .**13** D8
Plock Gn PR7 . . . .**42** C5
Plough La L40, WN8 . . . .**17** A4
Plough Yd BB6 . . . .**123** D5
Plover Cl FY5 . . . .**173** A5
Heysham LA3 . . . .**208** F5
Plover Dr Bury BL9 . . . .**32** B4
Plover St Burnley BB12 . . . .**126** D6
Preston PR1 . . . .**117** B1
Plover View **2** BB12 . . . . .**126** D6
Plovers Way FY3 . . . .**130** B6
Plox Brow PR4 . . . .**56** A6
Plumbe St BB11 . . . .**127** A5
Plumpton Ave FY4 . . . .**109** F5
Plumpton Field PR4 . . . . .**135** E2
Plumpton La
Great Plumpton PR4 . . . . . .**111** E7
Shirdley Hill L39 . . . .**21** E2
Plumpton Rd PR2 . . . .**116** C2
Plumtree Cl PR2 . . . .**117** C6
Plunge Rd BL0 . . . .**67** E3
Plungington Rd PR1,PR2 .**116** E7
Plymouth Ave FY7 . . . .**172** C8
Plymouth Gr PR6 . . . .**42** E8
Plymouth Rd FY2,FY3 . . . . .**150** E1
Poachers Way FY5 . . . .**173** A4
Pochard Pl **5** FY5 . . . .**172** F1
Pocklington St BB5 . . . . . .**103** D2
Podiham Cty Prim Sch
BB12 . . . .**125** E8
Poets' Rd BB12 . . . .**125** F7
Pointer Ct LA1 . . . .**210** F6
Pointer Gr LA2 . . . .**214** F7
Pointer The LA1 . . . .**210** F6
Poland St BB5 . . . .**102** F6
Pole La BB3 . . . .**64** C8
Pole St Preston PR1 . . . .**96** A8
Standish WN6 . . . .**28** E1
Polefield PR2 . . . .**116** E7
Police St BB3 . . . .**81** A1
Pollard Pl LA1 . . . .**214** A4
Pollard Row BB12 . . . .**167** F1
Pollard St Accrington BB5 . .**103** C7
Burnley BB11 . . . .**126** D5
4 Nelson BB9 . . . .**168** E1
6 Preston PR1 . . . .**95** E8
Pollards La BL9 . . . .**49** C2
Pollux Gate FY8 . . . .**89** C4
Polly Gn OL12 . . . .**51** F3
Polperro Dr PR4 . . . .**92** A6
Pomfret St Blackburn BB2 .**100** D3
Burnley BB11 . . . .**126** E6
Pompian Brow PR5 . . . .**56** E6
Pond Cl PR4 . . . .**56** A5
Pond Gdns FY6 . . . .**151** B6
Pond St LA5 . . . .**217** D2
Pond Terr LA5 . . . .**217** D2
Pont St BB9 . . . .**147** D7
Pontville Sch L39 . . . .**15** D3
Pool Cl FY7 . . . .**193** D1
Pool Foot La FY6 . . . .**152** E4
Pool Hey La PR8, PR9 . . . . . .**35** B3
Pool House Ct PR2 . . . . . .**116** A6
Pool House
Cty Prim Sch PR2 . . . . . .**116** A6
Pool House La PR2 . . . .**116** A5
Pool La PR4 . . . .**92** A4
Pool St PR9 . . . .**53** D5
Poole Rd PR2 . . . .**117** A4
Poole St BB1 . . . .**101** C5
Poolhill Cl FY5 . . . .**150** E7
Poolside Wlk PR9 . . . .**53** C5
Pool Hall OL12 . . . .**51** F3
Pope La Fulwood PR2 . . . . . .**118** A3
Penwortham PR1 . . . .**95** C2
Pope Wlk PR1 . . . .**95** D3
Poplar Ave
Bamber Bridge PR5 . . . .**96** F1
Blackpool FY3 . . . .**129** D5
Bury BL9 . . . .**32** B3
Euxton PR7 . . . .**59** C4
Great Harwood BB6 . . . .**123** D6
Horwich BL6 . . . .**31** E1
Kirkham PR4 . . . .**113** A4
Longton PR4 . . . .**74** B8
Poulton-le-F FY6 . . . .**151** E2
4 Rochdale OL12 . . . .**51** C1
Warton PR4 . . . .**91** D6
Poplar Bank PR9 . . . .**52** D1
Poplar Cl
Bamber Bridge PR5 . . . .**96** F1
Oswaldtwistle BB5 . . . .**102** F3
Rishton BB1 . . . .**102** B8
Poplar Dr Freckleton PR4 . . .**92** A5
Longridge PR3 . . . .**139** A4
Penwortham PR1 . . . .**95** C5
Skelmersdale WN8 . . . .**17** F1
Poplar Gr
Bamber Bridge PR5 . . . .**96** F1
Fulwood PR2 . . . .**118** A4
Ramsbottom BL0 . . . .**49** D7
Poplar St Blackburn BB1 . . .**100** F7
2 Blackburn BB1 . . . .**101** A7
Chorley PR7 . . . .**42** D6
Haslingden BB4 . . . .**84** B3
Nelson BB9 . . . .**168** F1
Southport PR8 . . . .**34** E6
Poplar Terr BB4 . . . .**84** F6
Poplars The PR7 . . . .**29** F6
Poppy Ave PR6 . . . .**60** D2
Poppy La L39 . . . .**16** B1
Poppyfield PR4 . . . .**115** F6
Poppyfields PR4 . . . .**72** E4
Porritt Ave LA1 . . . .**210** D8
Porritt St Bury BL9 . . . .**32** A4

Porritt Way BL0 . . . .**49** C7
Port Royal Ave LA1 . . . . . .**210** C8
Port Way Heysham LA3 . . . .**208** D5
Preston PR2 . . . .**95** C7
Portal Gr BB12 . . . .**126** B6
Porter Pl **2** PR1 . . . .**96** A6
Porter St Accrington BB5 . . .**102** F5
Preston PR1 . . . .**117** B1
Porter St E **4** PR4 . . . .**112** F6
Porters Row FY6 . . . .**174** C7
Portfield La BB6 . . . .**143** F3
Portfield Rd BB7 . . . .**143** E4
Porthcawl Cl PR4 . . . .**115** F3
Portland Cotts PR6 . . . .**61** D8
Portland Ct FY4 . . . .**110** A1
Portland Dr LA3 . . . .**212** E2
Portland Ind Est **10** BL9 . . .**32** A4
Portland Rd Blackpool FY1 .**129** D4
Langho BB6 . . . .**122** C8
Portland St
Accrington BB5 . . . .**103** A6
Barrowford BB9 . . . .**168** D3
Blackburn BB2 . . . .**100** C3
Bury BL9 . . . .**32** A4
11 Chorley PR6 . . . .**42** D8
Colne BB8 . . . .**169** F5
Darwen BB3 . . . .**64** B6
Lancaster LA1 . . . .**210** F7
Nelson BB9 . . . .**147** D8
Preston PR1 . . . .**95** D7
Southport PR9 . . . .**34** B5
Portman St PR1 . . . .**117** B1
Portree Cl PR2 . . . .**117** C5
Portree Cres BB1 . . . .**101** D3
Portree Rd FY2 . . . .**150** E5
Portsmouth Ave BB10 . . . .**147** E2
Portsmouth Cl **7** FY5 . . . .**172** F4
Portsmouth Dr PR6 . . . .**42** E8
Portway FY2 . . . .**150** E6
Post Horse La LA2 . . . .**232** B7
Post La PR4 . . . .**91** F6
Post Office Ave **11** PR9 . . . .**34** B7
Post Office Row
Tunstall LA6 . . . .**235** D4
Westhouse LA6 . . . .**236** E4
Post Office Yd **8** BB8 . . . .**169** E5
Postern Gate Rd LA2 . . . . .**226** A8
Pot Gn BL0 . . . .**49** A3
Pot House La Darwen BB3 . . .**81** C7
Oswaldtwistle BB5 . . . .**102** F2
Potter La Coupe Green PR5 . .**97** D5
Samlesbury PR5 . . . .**118** C4
Potter Pl WN8 . . . .**9** D5
Potter St **5** BL9 . . . .**32** A3
Poulton Ave
Accrington BB5 . . . .**103** A8
Lytham St Anne's FY8 . . . . . .**89** B8
Poulton Cres PR5 . . . .**97** D3
Poulton Gr FY7 . . . .**194** A4
Poulton Old Rd FY3 . . . . . .**150** F1
Poulton RC St John's
Prim Sch FY6 . . . .**151** C5
Poulton Rd Blackpool FY3 .**129** E8
Carleton FY6 . . . .**151** C5
Fleetwood FY7 . . . .**193** F4
Morecambe LA4 . . . .**212** E5
Southport PR9 . . . .**34** F7
Poulton Sq LA4 . . . .**212** E6
Poulton St Fleetwood FY7 .**194** A4
Kirkham PR4 . . . .**113** B5
Preston PR2 . . . .**116** C1
Poulton-le-Fylde
CE Prim Sch FY6 . . . .**151** D3
Poulton-le-Fylde Sta
FY6 . . . .**151** D4
Poulton-le-Sands
CE Prim Sch LA4 . . . .**212** E6
Powder House La
LA1,LA4 . . . .**213** C4
Powderworks La L31 . . . .**6** C3
Powell Ave FY4 . . . .**109** D8
Powell St
Barnoldswick BB18 . . . . . .**200** B3
Burnley BB11 . . . .**126** E4
Darwen BB3 . . . .**81** A2
Powis Dr PR4 . . . .**56** A8
Powis Rd PR2 . . . .**95** B8
Powys Cl BB4 . . . .**84** B1
Poynter St **4** PR1 . . . .**117** C1
Poynton St BL9 . . . .**32** A1
Prairie Cres BB10 . . . .**147** B2
Pratt St BB10 . . . .**147** B1
Precinct The BL0 . . . .**48** F3
Preesall Cl
Lytham St Anne's FY8 . . . . . .**89** B7
Preston PR2 . . . .**115** C1
Southport PR9 . . . .**52** F4
Preesall Mill Ind Est FY6 .**195** D2
Preesall Moss La FY6 . . . .**195** D2
Preesall Rd PR2 . . . .**115** C1
Preese Gdns PR4 . . . .**154** A1
Premier Way FY6 . . . .**151** F3
Prenton Gdns
7 Blackpool FY5 . . . .**150** F7
Norcross FY5 . . . .**151** A7
Prescot Cl BL9 . . . .**32** A1
Prescot Gn L39 . . . .**15** D3
Prescot Pl Blackpool FY3 . .**130** A2
Thornton FY5 . . . .**173** C2
Prescot Rd L31,L39 . . . .**6** D6
Prescott Ave L40 . . . .**38** A3
Prescott Rd WN8 . . . .**9** F4
Prescott St BB10 . . . .**127** C5
Press Rd FY8 . . . .**88** D8
Pressfield Sch PR9 . . . .**53** A3
Prestbury Ave
Blackpool FY4 . . . .**109** C5
Southport PR8 . . . .**20** B5

Prestbury Cl BL9 . . . .**32** A1
Prestbury Dr LA3 . . . .**212** E2
Preston Beck BB18 . . . .**201** B2
Preston Coll PR2 . . . .**116** F5
Preston Coll
Trinity Building PR1 . . . .**95** F8
Preston Coll
Winkley Building PR1 . . . .**95** F7
Preston Ent Ctr **2** PR1 . . .**116** C1
Preston Golf Course PR2 **117** A6
Preston Lancaster
New Rd LA1 . . . .**178** B4
Preston Lancaster
Old Rd PR3 . . . .**178** D2
Preston Lancaster Rd
Bilsborrow PR3 . . . .**157** A6
Cabus PR3 . . . .**199** C5
Galgate LA2 . . . .**207** A5
Potters Brook LA2,PR3 . . . .**204** C5
Preston New Rd
Blackburn BB2 . . . .**100** B5
Blackpool FY1,FY3 . . . .**130** C2
Clifton PR4 . . . .**93** C7
Freckleton PR4 . . . .**92** D7
Little Plumpton PR4 . . . . . .**111** C6
Mellor Brook BB2, PR5 . . . .**119** D1
Peel Hall FY4 . . . .**110** E7
Samlesbury PR2,PR5 . . . . .**118** E1
Southport PR9 . . . .**53** B4
Preston Nook PR7 . . . .**40** C5
Preston Old Rd
Blackburn BB2 . . . .**79** D8
Blackpool FY3 . . . .**130** A2
Clifton PR4 . . . .**114** C1
Freckleton PR4 . . . .**92** C6
Preston Rd
Charnock Richard PR7 . . . . .**41** C4
Chorley PR6,PR7 . . . .**60** C2
Clayton Brook PR5,PR6,PR7 . .**77** B3
Grimsargh PR2,PR3 . . . . . .**138** E2
Inskip PR4 . . . .**134** D7
Leyland PR5 . . . .**76** B2
Longridge PR3 . . . .**139** A5
Lucas Green PR6 . . . .**60** C4
Lytham St Anne's FY8 . . . . . .**90** D4
Ribchester PR3 . . . .**140** B5
Southport PR9 . . . .**34** E8
Standish PR7,WN6 . . . .**28** D5
Preston St Carnforth LA5 . .**217** D2
9 Chorley PR6 . . . .**60** D1
Darwen BB3 . . . .**80** F3
Fleetwood FY7 . . . .**194** B4
Kirkham PR4 . . . .**113** B5
16 Rochdale OL12 . . . .**51** C1
Preston Sta PR1 . . . .**95** E7
Prestwich St BB5 . . . .**126** E5
Prestwood Pl WN8 . . . .**9** F4
Pretoria St **2** OL12 . . . .**51** C1
Price Cl LA1 . . . .**213** E3
Price St **9** Blackpool FY1 .**129** B1
Bury BL9 . . . .**32** A1
Prickshaw OL12 . . . .**51** B6
Prickshaw La OL12 . . . .**51** B6
Priestfield Ave BB8 . . . . . .**169** B5
Priesthouse Cl L37 . . . .**12** A3
Priesthouse La L37 . . . .**12** A3
Priestfield **8** Blackpool FY5 **150** F7
Norcross FY5 . . . .**151** A7
Priestley Nook **4** BB5 . . . .**103** C5
Primet Bridge BB8 . . . .**169** C4
Primet Bsns Ctr BB8 . . . . .**169** B4
Primet High Sch BB8 . . . . .**169** B3
Primet Hill BB8 . . . .**169** C4
Primet Hts BB9 . . . .**169** B3
Primet Prim Sch BB8 . . . . .**169** B3
Primet St BB8 . . . .**169** C4
Primrose Ave FY4 . . . .**109** D6
Primrose Bank
1 Bacup OL13 . . . .**69** C8
Blackburn BB1 . . . .**100** F6
Blackpool FY2 . . . .**150** F6
Primrose Cl
Blackburn BB2 . . . .**100** B2
Formby L37 . . . .**12** B5
Hesketh Bank PR4 . . . .**72** E4
Southport PR9 . . . .**53** C6
Primrose Cotts
Calder Vale PR3 . . . .**179** E7
Middleton LA3 . . . .**209** A2
Primrose Ct
8 Blackburn BB1 . . . .**100** F6
6 Lancaster LA1 . . . .**211** A7
Morecambe LA4 . . . .**212** E5
Primrose Dr
Blackburn BB1 . . . .**100** F5
Bury BL9 . . . .**32** D4
Primrose Gr PR1 . . . .**117** C3
Primrose Hill Colne BB8 . . .**169** F5
Mellor BB2 . . . .**121** A3
3 Preston PR1 . . . .**96** B7
Primrose Hill Prim Sch
PR7 . . . .**59** B4
Primrose Hill Rd PR7 . . . . .**59** B4
Primrose Hill Sch BB10 . .**147** D2
Primrose La Fulwood PR1 .**117** C3
Standish WN6 . . . .**28** D2
Primrose Rd
Clitheroe BB7 . . . .**164** D6
Fulwood PR1 . . . .**117** C3
Primrose Row PR7 . . . .**58** F1
Primrose St
Accrington BB5 . . . .**103** A4
9 Bacup OL13 . . . .**69** C8
Brierfield BB9 . . . .**147** B5
Burnley BB10 . . . .**147** C1
Chorley PR6 . . . .**42** D6
Clitheroe BB7 . . . .**164** D7
Darwen BB3 . . . .**64** B8

Primrose St *continued*
Lancaster LA1 . . . .**211** A7
6 Morecambe LA4 . . . . . .**212** E5
Primrose Terr
Blackburn BB2 . . . .**100** B2
Blackpool FY4 . . . .**110** A4
Langho BB6 . . . .**142** C1
1 Radford BB3 . . . .**64** B8
Primrose Way
Carleton FY6 . . . .**151** B6
Church BB5 . . . .**102** E7
Primula Dr BB3 . . . .**81** A7
Prince Ave LA5 . . . .**217** E1
Prince Charles Gdns PR8 .**33** F4
Prince Lee Mdws BB3 . . . . .**64** B8
Prince St Bacup OL13 . . . . . .**70** D7
11 Burnley BB11 . . . .**126** E5
Darwen BB3 . . . .**80** F1
Ramsbottom BL0 . . . .**49** C6
Prince's Pk WN6 . . . .**19** F4
Prince's Rd PR5 . . . .**96** E5
Prince's St BB2 . . . .**100** D4
Princes Cres LA4 . . . .**213** A7
Princes Ct PR1 . . . .**95** B6
Princes Dr PR2 . . . .**116** E6
Princes Rd
2 Lytham St Anne's FY8 . . .**89** D4
Penwortham PR1 . . . .**95** B6
Princes Reach PR2 . . . .**95** A7
Princes St Rishton BB1 . . . .**123** B1
Southport PR8 . . . .**34** A6
Princes Way
Cleveleys FY5 . . . .**172** C1
Fleetwood FY7 . . . .**193** D3
Princess Alexandra Way
LA3 . . . .**208** D5
Princess Ave
Clitheroe BB7 . . . .**186** F1
Kirkham PR4 . . . .**112** F6
Lancaster LA1 . . . .**210** F6
Poulton-le-F FY6 . . . .**151** D3
Princess Ct **5** FY1 . . . .**129** B3
Princess Gdns
Blackburn BB2 . . . .**79** C7
Morecambe LA4 . . . .**213** A5
Princess Par FY1 . . . .**129** B6
Princess Rd Adlington PR6 . .**30** B8
Cleveleys FY5 . . . .**172** C2
Princess St Accrington BB5 **102** F6
17 Bacup OL13 . . . .**86** F7
10 Bamber Bridge PR5 . . .**76** F8
2 Bamber Bridge, Lostock
Hall PR5 . . . .**76** B7
Blackburn BB2 . . . .**100** C2
Blackpool FY1 . . . .**129** B3
Chorley PR7 . . . .**42** D6
4 Church BB5 . . . .**102** E6
Colne BB8 . . . .**169** C4
Great Harwood BB6 . . . .**123** D5
Haslingden BB4 . . . .**84** B2
Leyland PR5 . . . .**76** B1
Nelson BB9 . . . .**147** D7
Padiham BB12 . . . .**125** B8
Preston PR1 . . . .**96** B7
Rochdale OL12 . . . .**51** F1
Whalley BB7 . . . .**143** C5
Whitworth OL12 . . . .**51** C8
Princess Way
Burnley BB12 . . . .**126** F7
Euxton PR7 . . . .**59** E2
Princeway FY4 . . . .**109** C7
Pringle Bank LA5 . . . .**217** D6
Pringle Ct PR3 . . . .**178** C2
Pringle St BB1 . . . .**101** A3
Pringle Wood PR3 . . . .**136** C2
Prinny Hill Rd BB4 . . . .**84** A3
Printers Fold BB12 . . . .**125** E6
Prior's Cl BB2 . . . .**100** A6
Priors Wlk BB7 . . . .**224** C1
Priorsgate LA3 . . . .**212** F2
Priorswood Pl WN8 . . . .**9** F4
Priory Cl Blackburn BB1 . . .**101** E4
Burscough L40 . . . .**24** D5
Formby L37 . . . .**12** B2
6 Lancaster LA1 . . . .**210** E8
Leyland PR5 . . . .**76** C2
Morecambe LA3 . . . .**212** F2
Newchurch BB4 . . . .**85** E2
Penwortham PR1 . . . .**95** C6
Tarleton PR4 . . . .**56** A6
Priory Cres PR1 . . . .**95** C6
Priory Ct **7** Blackpool FY1 .**129** C5
Burnley BB11 . . . .**127** B2
Pleasington BB2 . . . .**99** C2
Priory Dr BB3 . . . .**64** C8
Priory Gate FY4 . . . .**109** C6
Priory Gdns PR8 . . . .**33** F4
Priory Gr L39 . . . .**15** D4
Priory Grange Darwen BB3 .**64** C8
Southport PR8 . . . .**34** A4
Priory High Sch L40 . . . .**24** E5
Priory La Hornby LA2 . . . . .**232** B7
Penwortham PR1 . . . .**95** C6
Priory Mews
Lytham St Anne's FY8 . . . . . .**89** D7
Southport PR8 . . . .**33** F6
Priory Nook WN8 . . . .**10** C7
Priory Oak Cotts PR1 . . . . .**95** C6
Priory Pl BB3 . . . .**64** C8
Priory Rd WN8 . . . .**10** C7
Priory St **5** Nelson BB9 . . .**168** F1
Preston PR2 . . . .**95** D8
Priory Way BB18 . . . .**200** A2
Priory Wlk **6** LA1 . . . .**211** A8
Pritchard St
Blackburn BB2 . . . .**100** E2
Burnley BB11 . . . .**126** E5
Private La BB4 . . . .**67** C8

Procter Moss Rd
Lancaster LA2 . . . . .211 D1
Lower Green Bank LA2 . . .226 B3
Procter St BB2 . . . . .100 F3
Procter's Brow LA2 . . . . . .233 B5
Procter Cl BB9 . . . . .147 F5
Proctor Rd L37 . . . . .11 C4
Progress Ave BB1 . . . . . . .101 A7
Progress Bsns Pk PR4 . . . .113 A4
Progress Ct FY3 . . . . .130 B8
Progress Rd BB9 . . . . .168 F3
Progress St Chorley PR6 . . .42 B1
Darwen BB3 . . . . .81 B1
Progress Way FY4 . . . . . . .110 B6
Promenade Blackpool FY1 .129 B5
Blackpool, Bispham FY2 . . .86 F2
Blackpool, South Shore FY4 109 A6
Cleveleys FY5 . . . . .172 C5
Southport PR8,PR9 . . . . . . .34 B8
Promenade N FY5 . . . . . . .172 C3
Promenade Rd FY7 . . . . . .194 A5
Promenade S FY5 . . . . . . .172 C2
Promenade The LA5 . . . . . .237 B2
Prospect Ave
Bamber Bridge PR5 . . . . . .76 B8
Darwen BB3 . . . . .80 E2
Hest Bank LA2 . . . . .215 E1
Prospect Ct PR3 . . . . .139 B6
Prospect Dr LA2 . . . . .215 E1
Prospect Gr LA4 . . . . .212 F4
Prospect Hill
Haslingden BB4 . . . . .84 A2
4 Rawtenstall BB4 . . . . . . .85 A3
Prospect Pl
7 Penwortham PR1 . . . . . .95 E4
Preston PR2 . . . . .116 B1
Skelmersdale WN8 . . . . .9 F5
Prospect Rd BB4 . . . . .85 A3
Prospect St
Great Harwood BB6 . . . . .123 D5
Lancaster LA1 . . . . .211 A7
Newchurch BB4 . . . . .85 F1
Prospect Terr Bacup OL13 . .69 E7
10 Barrowford BB9 . . . . . .168 D4
Belthorn BB1 . . . . .81 F6
Brinscall PR6 . . . . .62 A8
Huncoat BB5 . . . . .124 E2
Newchurch BB4 . . . . .85 F1
Rawtenstall BB4 . . . . . . .105 B4
Provence Ave BB6 . . . . . . .142 C6
Providence St BB1 . . . . . . .101 A8
Prudy Hill FY6 . . . . .151 D4
Prunella Dr BB3 . . . . .81 A7
Pudding La OL14 . . . . .108 C2
Pudding Pie Nook La
PR3 . . . . .136 F4
Pudsey Rd OL14 . . . . .108 B2
Pump House La PR5 . . . . . . .57 F6
Pump St Blackburn BB2 . . .100 D4
Burnley BB10 . . . . .126 E6
Clitheroe BB7 . . . . .164 D8
Preston PR1 . . . . .96 A8
Punnell's La L31 . . . . .4 F5
Punstock Rd BB3 . . . . .80 F1
Purbeck Dr BL6 . . . . .31 F1
Pye Busk La LA2 . . . . .233 E8
Pye Busk Cl LA2 . . . . .233 E8
Pye's Cotts L39 . . . . .5 E7
Pygon's Hill La L31 . . . . .5 D6

Q

Quaile Holme Rd FY6 . . . .194 E5
Quaker Brook La PR5 . . . . .98 A3
Quaker La BB3 . . . . .81 A2
Quakerfields BB3 . . . . .81 A2
Quakers Terr WN6 . . . . .28 D3
Quakers' Pl WN6 . . . . .28 E1
Quarlton Dr BL8 . . . . .48 B3
Quarry Bank BB4 . . . . .83 F1
Quarry Bank St 8 BB12 . .126 C7
Quarry Dr L39 . . . . .15 C1
Quarry Farm Ct BB7 . . . . .187 D5
Quarry Hill OL12 . . . . .51 E3
Quarry Hill
Nature Reserve BB9 . . . .147 F6
Quarry Mount L39 . . . . .16 A4
Quarry Mount Mews LA1 211 A7
Quarry Rd Brinscall PR7 . . . .61 F7
Caton LA2 . . . . .231 E3
Chorley PR6 . . . . .42 E6
Halton LA2 . . . . .214 E6
Lancaster LA1 . . . . .211 A7
Quarry St
13 Accrington BB5 . . . . . .103 C5
Bacup OL13 . . . . .87 A2
Blackburn BB1 . . . . .100 F5
Hapton BB11 . . . . .125 C2
Padiham BB12 . . . . .145 D1
Ramsbottom BL0 . . . . .49 D6
Rochdale OL12 . . . . .51 E1
Whitworth OL12 . . . . .70 E6
Quarrybank FY5 . . . . .150 F8
Quarryside Dr L33 . . . . .1 A3
Quay West FY8 . . . . .88 E5
Quayle Ave FY4 . . . . .109 E8
Quayside FY7 . . . . .194 B3
Quebec Ave FY2 . . . . .150 E3
Quebec Rd BB2 . . . . .100 B8
Queen Anne St
4 Haslingden BB4 . . . . . . .84 A3
Southport PR8 . . . . .34 B7
Queen Elizabeth Cres
BB5 . . . .
Queen Elizabeth Ct LA4 . .212 D5
Queen Elizabeth Sch LA6 238 B2

Queen Elizabeth's
Gram Sch BB2 . . . . .100 C6
Queen Elizabeth's
Gram Sch (Annexe)** BB2 100 D6
Queen Ho BB4 . . . . .85 D1
Queen Mary Ave FY8 . . . . . .89 A5
Queen Mary Sch FY8 . . . . . .89 A4
Queen Sq
1 Blackpool FY1 . . . . . . .129 B5
Lancaster LA1 . . . . .210 F7
Queen St
18 Accrington BB5 . . . . . .103 C5
Bacup OL13 . . . . .86 F2
5 Bacup, Stacksteads OL13 .69 C8
4 Bamber Bridge PR5 . . . .76 B7
Barnoldswick BB18 . . . . . .200 B1
Barrowford BB9 . . . . .168 D4
Blackpool FY1 . . . . .129 B6
Brierfield BB10 . . . . .147 F2
Burnley BB11 . . . . .126 F5
Bury BL9 . . . . .32 A2
Carnforth LA5 . . . . .217 D1
Clayton-le-M BB5 . . . . . . .123 F3
Clitheroe BB7 . . . . .164 C8
Colne BB8 . . . . .169 C4
Darwen BB3 . . . . .80 F2
Fleetwood FY7 . . . . .194 A4
Great Harwood BB6 . . . . .123 D5
Hoddlesden BB3 . . . . .81 F1
Horwich BL6 . . . . .31 B3
Lancaster LA1 . . . . .210 F7
Lytham St Anne's FY8 . . . . .90 A3
Morecambe LA4 . . . . .212 E5
Nelson BB9 . . . . .168 E1
Ormskirk L39 . . . . .15 E4
Oswaldtwistle BB5 . . . . . .102 E4
Padiham BB12 . . . . .125 D3
Preston PR1 . . . . .96 B7
Ramsbottom BL0 . . . . .49 B6
Rawtenstall BB4 . . . . .85 A2
Whalley BB7 . . . . .143 C5
Queen St E 8 PR7 . . . . . . .42 C6
Queen Street Mill BB10 . . .147 F2
Queen Vera Rd 4 FY1 . . . .129 B5
Queen Victoria Hospl
LA4 . . . . .212 E5
Queen Victoria Rd
Blackpool FY1 . . . . .129 C2
Burnley BB10 . . . . .127 B8
Burnley BB10 . . . . .147 B1
Queen Victoria St BB2 . . . .100 B2
Queen's Cl Clitheroe BB7 . .164 E7
Poulton-le-F FY6 . . . . . . .151 E5
Queen's Cres PR4 . . . . . . .113 B4
Queen's Ct FY2 . . . . .150 B2
Queen's Dr Carnforth LA5 . .217 E1
Oswaldtwistle BB5 . . . . . .102 F3
Queen's Gr PR7 . . . . .42 C8
Queen's Lancashire Way
BB11 . . . . .126 F6
Queen's Park High Sch
BB1 . . . . .101 C2
Queen's Park Hospl BB1 . .101 A2
Queen's Park Rd
Blackburn BB1 . . . . .101 A3
Burnley BB10 . . . . .127 C7
Queen's Prom FY2 . . . . . .150 B5
Queen's Rd
Accrington BB5 . . . . .103 C7
Blackburn BB1 . . . . .101 B3
Burnley BB10 . . . . .147 B2
Chorley PR7 . . . . .42 C8
Darwen BB3 . . . . .64 B6
Formby L37 . . . . .11 D2
Fulwood PR2 . . . . .116 E3
Lytham St Anne's FY8 . . . . .88 F5
Walton-le-D PR5 . . . . .96 E4
Queen's Sq Hoddlesden BB3 81 F1
Kirkby Lonsdale LA6 . . . . .238 C2
Poulton-le-F FY6 . . . . . . .151 D3
7 Rawtenstall BB4 . . . . . .85 A2
Queen's Terr
3 Bacup OL13 . . . . .69 E8
Blackburn BB2 . . . . .100 B1
Fleetwood FY7 . . . . .194 C5
Queens Ave L37 . . . . .11 E5
Queens Croft L37 . . . . .11 D2
Queens Ct PR2 . . . . .116 E3
Queens Ctyd 7 PR9 . . . . . .34 C8
Queens Dr Arnside LA5 . . . .237 B1
Fulwood PR2 . . . . .116 D6
Longridge PR3 . . . . .139 A7
Morecambe LA4 . . . . .213 A6
Staining FY3 . . . .
Queens Drive Prim Sch
PR2 . . . . .116 D6
Queens Garth BD23 . . . . . .201 B5
Queens Gn L39 . . . . .13 F5
Queens Jubilee
Nature Trail PR8 . . . . . . .33 E5
Queens Pl Kirkham PR4 . . . .112 F7
Ramsbottom BL9 . . . . .49 C2
Queens Rd Clitheroe BB7 . .164 E7
Orrell WN5 . . . . .10 C5
Southport PR9 . . . . .34 C8
Queens Rd W BB5 . . . . . . .103 A7
Queens Ret Pk PR1 . . . . . . .96 B7
Queens Wlk FY5 . . . . .172 D4
Queensberry Rd BB11 . . . .126 E5
Queensborough Rd BB5 . . .103 B7
Queensbury Rd FY5 . . . . . .172 C2
Queenscourt Ave PR1 . . . . .95 E2
Queenscourt Hospice PR8 34 F4
Queensdale Cl PR5 . . . . . . .96 E4
Queensgate Chorley PR7 . . .42 B7
Nelson BB9 . . . . .147 D7
Queensway
Bamber Bridge PR5 . . . . . .96 E1

Queensway continued
Blackburn BB2 . . . . .80 A8
Blackpool FY4 . . . . .109 C7
Brinscall PR6 . . . . .61 F8
Church BB5 . . . . .102 F7
Clitheroe BB7 . . . . .164 E7
Euxton PR7 . . . . .59 E2
Leyland PR5 . . . . .58 E7
Lytham St Anne's FY4,FY8 . .110 B2
Newchurch BB4 . . . . .85 E1
Penwortham PR1 . . . . .95 B6
Poulton-le-F FY6 . . . . . . .151 D3
Preston PR2 . . . . .115 F2
Shevington WN6 . . . . .19 F4
Waddington BB7 . . . . .186 B4
Warton PR4 . . . . .91 E7
Queensway Cl PR1 . . . . . . .95 B6
Queensway Ct PR1 . . . . . . .95 B6
Queensway Ind Est FY8 . . .110 A2
Quernmore Ave FY3 . . . . . .130 A3
Quernmore Brow LA2 . . . .226 B5
Quernmore CE Prim Sch
LA2 . . . . .226 A3
Quernmore Dr
Glasson LA2 . . . . .205 E4
Kelbrook BB18 . . . . .192 A5
Quernmore Ind Est PR4 . . .92 C6
Quernmore Rd Caton LA2 . .231 B2
Kirkby L33 . . . . .1 A3
Lancaster LA1,LA2 . . . . . .211 D7
Quernmore Wlk L33 . . . . . . .1 A3
Quillet The LA5 . . . . .218 F3
Quin St PR5 . . . . .76 A1
Quinton Cl PR8 . . . . .20 A4

R

Rabbit La Burscough L40 . . .23 C4
Cow Ark BB7 . . . . .184 F6
Raby Sq LA4 . . . . .212 E6
Raby St 4 Morecambe LA4 212 E5
1 Rawtenstall BB4 . . . . . .85 A2
Radburn Brow PR6 . . . . . . .77 B3
Radburn Ct PR6 . . . . .77 B3
Radcliffe Rd FY7 . . . . .193 F2
Radclyffe St BB2 . . . . .186 E1
Radfield Ave 14 BB3 . . . . . .64 E1
Radfield Rd BB3 . . . . .63 F8
Radford Bank Gdns
12 BB3 . . . . .64 A8
Radford Gdns BB3 . . . . . . .64 A7
Radford St BB3 . . . . .64 A8
Radley Ave FY3 . . . . .129 E8
Radnor Ave Burnley BB12 . .126 A7
Cleveleys FY5 . . . . .172 F1
Radnor Cl BB5 . . . . .102 C4
Radnor Dr PR9 . . . . .52 F3
Radnor St Accrington BB5 . .103 B7
5 Preston PR1 . . . . .95 E8
Radway Cl FY5 . . . . .150 F7
Radworth Cres FY4 . . . . . .130 B1
Raeburn Ave BB11 . . . . . . .126 E3
Raedale Ave BB10 . . . . . . .147 B4
Raeside Ct FY8 . . . . .89 A4
Raglan Rd Burnley BB11 . . .126 E5
Morecambe LA4 . . . . .212 B3
Raglan St 8 Colne BB8 . . . .169 C4
5 Nelson BB9 . . . . .147 D8
Preston PR2 . . . . .116 D2
Raikes Hill 2 FY1 . . . . . . .129 C5
Raikes Hill Dr LA2 . . . . . . .213 E8
Raikes Mews 6 FY1 . . . . . .129 C5
Raikes Par FY1 . . . . .129 C5
Raikes Rd
Great Eccleston PR3 . . . . .154 C5
Preston PR1 . . . . .117 C1
Thornton FY5 . . . . .151 E8
Rail Cl WA11 . . . . .8 E1
Railgate OL13 . . . . .70 C8
Railton Ave BB2 . . . . .80 A8
Railway App L15 . . . . .15 F5
Railway Ave PR9 . . . . .53 F5
Railway Cotts Coppull PR7 . .41 F1
Preston PR1 . . . . .115 C3
Salwick PR4 . . . . .114 C4
Railway Crossing La LA1 210 C5
Railway Gr 5 BB1 . . . . . . .101 A7
Railway Path L39 . . . . .15 E4
Railway Pl LA2 . . . . .205 F5
Railway Rd
Adlington PR6,PR7 . . . . . .30 A7
Blackburn BB1 . . . . .100 E5
Brinscall PR6 . . . . .62 A8
Chorley PR6 . . . . .60 D1
Darwen BB3 . . . . .81 A1
Haslingden BB4 . . . . .84 B4
Ormskirk L39 . . . . .15 F5
Skelmersdale WN8 . . . . .8 E8
Railway St Bacup OL13 . . . .69 B8
20 Barnoldswick BB18 . . . .200 B2
Brierfield BB9 . . . . .147 B5
Burnley BB11 . . . . .126 F7
Chorley PR7 . . . . .42 D7
Foulridge BB8 . . . . .191 D1
Lancaster LA1 . . . . .210 F6
Leyland PR5 . . . . .76 B2
Nelson BB9 . . . . .147 E1
Ramsbottom BL0 . . . . .49 C6
Ramsbottom,
Summerseat BL0,BL9 . . . . .49 C2
Southport PR8 . . . . .34 B5
Railway Terr
Brierfield BB9 . . . . .147 B5
Edgworth BL7 . . . . .47 B8
Great Harwood BB6 . . . . .123 C4
10 Kirkham PR4 . . . . . . .112 F6
Rawtenstall BB4 . . . . .84 F1

Railway Terr continued
Simonstone BB12 . . . . . . .124 D8
Southport PR8 . . . . .34 A5
Railway View
5 Accrington BB5 . . . . . .103 C6
Billington BB7 . . . . .143 B4
Blackburn BB2 . . . . .100 B2
Brierfield BB9 . . . . .147 B6
Croston PR5 . . . . .57 A2
3 Radford BB3 . . . . .64 B8
Railway View Ave BB7 . . . .186 E1
Railway View Rd BB7 . . . . .186 E1
Rainford By-pass WA11 . . . .8 A3
Rainford Junc WA11 . . . . . . .8 F2
Rainford Rd L39, WA11 . . . . .8 C4
Rainhall Cres BB18 . . . . . .200 B3
Rainhall Rd BB18 . . . . .200 B2
Rainhall Rd
Com Prim Sch BB18 . . . .200 B2
Rake Fold BL0 . . . . .49 A6
Rake Foot BB4 . . . . .84 B3
Rake La PR4 . . . . .91 D5
Rake The LA2 . . . . .226 E1
Rake Top Ave BB12 . . . . . .145 F6
Rakehead La OL13 . . . . . . .69 B8
Rakehouse Brow LA2 . . . .226 F2
Rakes Bridge BB3 . . . . .81 A7
Rakes House Rd BB9 . . . . .168 F2
Rakes La BD23 . . . . .225 F5
Rakes Rd LA2 . . . . .231 E4
Raleigh Ave FY4 . . . . .109 B5
Raleigh Cl FY8 . . . . .109 D1
Raleigh Rd PR2 . . . . .116 E6
Raleigh St BB12 . . . . .125 E7
Ralph St BB5 . . . . .103 C8
Ralph's Wife's La PR9 . . . . .53 E6
Ramparts The LA1 . . . . . . .214 A2
Ramper Gate FY5 . . . . . . .172 C2
Rams Clough La BB5 . . . . . .83 A8
Ramsay Ct FY3 . . . . .194 D5
Ramsbottom
Cottage Hospl BL0 . . . . . .49 C5
Ramsbottom
Heritage Ctr Mus BL0 . . . .49 C7
Ramsbottom La BL0 . . . . . . .49 C7
Ramsbottom Rd
Horwich BL6 . . . . .31 C3
Ramsbottom BL8,BL7 . . . . .48 A3
Ramsbottom St BB5 . . . . . .103 B7
Ramsbottom Sta BL0 . . . . . .49 C6
Ramsden St LA2 . . . . .217 D2
Ramsey Ave Bacup OL13 . . .87 A1
Blackpool FY3 . . . . .129 D7
Fulwood PR1 . . . . .117 D3
Ramsey Cl PR2 . . . . .109 D1
Ramsey Gr BB10 . . . . .147 C2
Ramsey Rd BB2 . . . . .100 D1
Ramsgate Cl PR4 . . . . .91 E7
Ramsgate Rd FY8 . . . . .89 A8
Ramsgreave & Wilpshire
Sta BB1 . . . . .121 F4
Ramsgreave Ave BB1 . . . . .121 D2
Ramsgreave Dr BB1 . . . . . .121 D1
Ramsgreave Rd BB1 . . . . . .121 E4
Ramshill Ave FY6 . . . . . . .151 E5
Ramson Ct LA3 . . . . .212 E2
Ranaldsway PR5 . . . . .58 D8
Randal St BB1 . . . . .100 E6
Randall St 9 BB10 . . . . . . .147 B1
Randolph St 21 BB1 . . . . . .101 A4
Ranelagh Dr PR8 . . . . .20 F7
Range High Sch L37 . . . . . . .2 B7
Ranger St BB5 . . . . .103 B5
Rangeway Ave FY4 . . . . . .109 C7
Ranglet Rd PR5 . . . . .77 B7
Ranglets Ave PR7 . . . . .42 C6
Ranglit Ave PR2 . . . . .115 C1
Rankin Cl BB18 . . . . .200 C2
Rankin Dr BB3 . . . . .81 C1
Ranlea Ave LA4 . . . . .213 C6
Ranleigh Dr
Newburgh WN8 . . . . .26 A1
Skelmersdale WN8 . . . . . .18 A8
Rannoch Dr BB2 . . . . .99 F1
Rantreefold Rd LA2 . . . . . .233 C4
Rapley La PR4 . . . . .135 A8
Ratcliffe Fold 5 BB4 . . . . . .84 B3
Ratcliffe St Darwen BB3 . . . .64 B8
10 Haslingden BB4 . . . . . .84 B3
Ratcliffe Wharf La PR3 . . . .204 A1
Rathbone Rd L38 . . . . .2 F4
Rathlyn Ave FY3 . . . . .129 C8
Rathmell CE Sch BD24 . . . .230 E7
Rathmell Cl FY3 . . . . .151 B1
Rathmill Sike BB7 . . . . . . .224 B1
Rathmore Cres PR9 . . . . . . .53 B3
Ratten La PR4 . . . . .94 D3
Raven Ave BB4 . . . . .67 A7
Raven Croft BB4 . . . . .67 B8
Raven Meols La L37 . . . . . . .11 F2
Raven Oak La BB10 . . . . . .128 B5
Raven Pk BB4 . . . . .67 B8
Raven Rd BB2 . . . . .100 B5
Raven St 3 Nelson BB9 . . .168 F1
Preston PR1 . . . . .117 C2
Raven's Cl FY3 . . . . .130 B7
Ravendale Cl OL12 . . . . .51 A1
Ravenglass Ave L31 . . . . . . .5 D7
Ravenglass Cl
Blackburn BB2 . . . . .101 A1
Blackpool FY4 . . . . .109 E7
Kirkham PR4 . . . . .113 A7
Ravenhead Dr WN8 . . . . . . .10 A7
Ravenhead Way WN8 . . . . . .9 F6
Ravenhill Dr PR7 . . . . .60 C1
Ravens Cl LA1 . . . . .213 E3

Ravens Close Brow LA2 . .235 F1
Ravens Gr BB10 . . . . .147 C4
Ravens The L37 . . . . .11 F2
Ravens Wood BB2 . . . . . . .100 B5
Ravenscroft L37 . . . . .11 F2
Ravenscroft Ave L39 . . . . . .15 E4
Ravenscroft Cl BB1 . . . . . .122 A1
Ravenscroft Way BB18 . . . .200 C3
Ravensthorpe PR7 . . . . .60 A1
Ravenswing Ave BB2 . . . . .100 B7
Ravenswood Fulwood PR2 117 E2
Great Harwood BB6 . . . . .123 B6
Ravenswood Ave FY3 . . . . .130 B7
Ravenwood Ave FY4 . . . . . .109 C5
Rawcliffe Dr PR2 . . . . .94 E8
Rawcliffe Rd
12 Chorley PR7 . . . . .42 C7
Ratten Row PR3 . . . . . . .154 C7
Rawcliffe St Blackpool FY4 109 B8
Burnley BB11 . . . . .127 A6
Rawlinson Ct PR9 . . . . .34 D8
Rawlinson Gr PR9 . . . . .52 F1
Rawlinson La PR6 . . . . .42 E1
Rawlinson Rd PR9 . . . . .52 E1
Rawlinson St
3 Darwen BB3 . . . . .64 B6
13 Horwich BL6 . . . . .31 B5
5 Kirkham PR4 . . . . .112 F6
Raws St BB11 . . . . .127 A6
Rawson Ave BB5 . . . . .103 A4
Rawson St 18 BB10 . . . . . .147 B1
Rawsons Rake BL0,BL8 . . . .49 A6
Rawsthorne Ave
Edenfield BL0 . . . . .67 D2
Haslingden BB4 . . . . .84 B2
Rawstorne Cl PR4 . . . . .92 A7
Rawstorne Rd PR1 . . . . .95 B5
Rawstorne St BB2 . . . . . . .100 C4
Rawstron St OL12 . . . . .70 C1
Rawtenstall Rd BB4 . . . . . . .84 C1
Rawtenstall St Mary's
CE Prim Sch BB4 . . . . . . .84 F3
Rawtenstall Sta BB4 . . . . . .84 F1
Rawthey Rd 5 LA1 . . . . . . .213 D2
Ray La PR3 . . . . .178 F4
Raybourne Ave FY6 . . . . . .151 C3
Raygarth La LA6 . . . . .238 B2
Raygarth La LA6 . . . . .238 A3
Raygill Ave BB11 . . . . .126 C3
Raygill Pl 3 LA1 . . . . .213 D2
Raymond Ave FY2 . . . . . . .129 D8
Raynor St BB2 . . . . .100 D5
Rays Dr LA1 . . . . .210 F3
Read CE Sch BB12 . . . . . . .144 D2
Read St 2 BB5 . . . . .124 A1
Read's Ave FY1 . . . . .129 C5
Reading Cl 14 BB1 . . . . . . .101 A4
Reads Ct 6 FY1 . . . . .129 C5
Reaney Ave 3 FY4 . . . . . . .109 E7
Rear West Lodge FY6 . . . . .174 C1
Record St BB18 . . . . .200 B1
Rectory Cl Chorley PR7 . . . . .42 C8
Croston PR5 . . . . .57 C2
Darwen BB3 . . . . .64 C8
Newchurch BB4 . . . . .85 E1
Rectory Gdns
Cockerham LA2 . . . . .203 C5
Tarleton PR4 . . . . .56 A5
Rectory La Bury BL9 . . . . . .32 D4
Standish WN1,WN6 . . . . . .29 A1
Rectory Paddock LA2 . . . . .214 E6
Rectory Rd Blackpool FY4 . .129 E1
Burnley BB12 . . . . .126 F7
Southport PR9 . . . . .53 A1
Red Bank Rd FY2 . . . . .150 C4
Red Barnes L37 . . . . .11 F5
Red Bridge La LA5 . . . . . . .218 F4
Red Cat La L40 . . . . .24 E7
Red Cross St 5 PR1 . . . . . . .95 E7
Red Delph La WA11 . . . . . . .8 E1
Red Fold L39 . . . . .15 C2
Red Hills Rd LA5 . . . . .237 A1
Red House La PR7 . . . . .40 B6
Red La Colne BB8 . . . . . . .169 B7
Eccleston PR7 . . . . .40 E6
Red Lees Ave BB10 . . . . . .127 F4
Red Lees Rd BB10 . . . . . . .128 A2
Red Lion Cl L31 . . . . .5 C1
Red Lion Shopping Ctr L31 5 C1
Red Lion St Burnley BB11 . .127 A5
Earby BB18 . . . . .201 C2
Red Marsh Dr FY5 . . . . . . .173 C3
Red Marsh Sp Sch FY5 . . .173 B3
Red Rake BB1 . . . . .100 C8
Red Sands L39 . . . . .15 D3
Red Scar Ind Est PR2 . . . . .118 B5
Red Scar St BB5 . . . . .169 C4
Red Shell La BB1,BB5 . . . . .82 B7
Red Spar Rd BB10 . . . . . . .147 D3
Redcar Ave Cleveleys FY5 . .172 F5
Fulwood PR2 . . . . .116 A4
Redcar Cl PR4 . . . . .34 F3
Redcar Rd Blackpool FY1 . .129 B8
Lancaster LA1 . . . . .211 B3
Redcliffe Gdns L39 . . . . . . .15 E3
Redcross St OL12 . . . . .51 F1
Redcross St N OL12 . . . . . . .51 F1
Rede Ave FY7 . . . . .193 C2
Redearth Rd BB3 . . . . .64 A8
Redearth St BB3 . . . . .64 A8
Redeswood Ave FY5 . . . . . .150 E8
Redgate Formby L37 . . . . . . .12 A2
Ormskirk L39 . . . . .15 D5
Redgate Cl BB11 . . . . .127 B3

Redgate Dr L37 . . . . .12 B2
Redgate Prim Sch L37 . . .12 A2
Redhill PR4 . . . . .94 C1
Redhill Gn PR6 . . . . .60 E3
Redhills Dr PR8 . . . . .34 F3
Redisher Cl BL0 . . . . .48 F3
Redisher Croft BL0 . . . . . . .48 F3
Redisher La BL8 . . . . .48 E3
Redlam BB2 . . . . .100 B3
Redlam Brow BB2 . . . . . . .100 C3
Redman Rd BB10 . . . . .147 B4
Redmayne Dr LA5 . . . . .217 F2
Redmayne St 3 PR1 . . . . . .96 D8
Redness Cl BB9 . . . . .147 E6
Redruth St BB12 . . . . .126 D6
Redsands Dr PR2 . . . . .117 D5
Redstart Pl 12 FY5 . . . . . . .172 F1
Redvers Rd BB3 . . . . .80 E5
Redvers St Burnley BB10 . .147 B1
  Lancaster LA1 . . . . .210 D8
Redvers Terr FY1 . . . . .129 B8
Redwing Ave 1 FY5 . . . . . .172 F4
Redwing Rd BL8 . . . . .48 F2
Redwood Ave Leyland PR5 .58 E8
  Maghull L31 . . . . .5 C3
Redwood Chase PR4 . . . . .112 E4
Redwood Dr Blackpool FY4 109 C4
  Rochdale OL12 . . . . .51 B3
Redwood Dr
  Longridge PR3 . . . . .139 A8
  Morecambe LA4 . . . . .213 A5
  Ormskirk L39 . . . . .15 D4
  Rawtenstall BB4 . . . . .67 F8
Redwood Gdns FY5 . . . . . .173 E2
Redwood Hts LA1 . . . . . . .211 C7
Reed Row BB8 . . . . .169 D3
Reed St Bacup OL13 . . . . . .87 A3
  Burnley BB11 . . . . .127 A4
Reedfield Brierfield BB10 .147 C4
  Clayton Brook PR5 . . . . . .77 C4
Reedfield Pl PR4 . . . . .77 C6
Reedley Dr Brierfield BB10 147 B4
  Brierfield BB10 . . . . .147 C4
Reedley Gr BB10 . . . . .147 B3
Reedley Rd BB10,BB9 . . . .147 C5
Reedmace Wlk LA3 . . . . . .212 E2
Reeds Brow WA11 . . . . .9 C1
Reeds Cl BB4 . . . . .85 A6
Reeds La BB4 . . . . .85 A6
Reeds The
  6 Lancaster LA1 . . . . . . .213 E1
  Ormskirk L39 . . . . .15 D6
Reedsholme Cl BB4 . . . . . .85 A6
Reedy Acre Pl FY8 . . . . . . .89 F4
Reedy Moor Terr BB8 . . . .191 C1
Reedyford Rd BB9 . . . . . . .168 E2
Reedymoor La BB8 . . . . . . .191 C1
Reeford Gr BB7 . . . . .164 D7
Rees Pk L40 . . . . .24 F3
Reeth Way 3 BB5 . . . . . . .102 F4
Reeval Cl BB18 . . . . .201 C2
Reeveswood PR7 . . . . .40 B6
Reform St OL12 . . . . .51 F1
Regal Ave FY4 . . . . .109 E6
Regal Terr 4 LA1 . . . . . . .213 F3
Regency Ave PR5 . . . . .76 D8
Regency Cl PR4 . . . . .112 E5
Regency Gdns PR8 . . . . . . .33 E4
Regent Ave Colne BB8 . . . .169 E6
  Lytham St Anne's FY8 . . . .89 D6
Regent Cl Padiham BB12 . .125 C7
  Southport PR8 . . . . .33 F4
Regent Ct
  4 Blackpool FY1 . . . . . . .129 B6
  Fulwood PR2 . . . . .116 E5
  Lytham St Anne's FY8 . . . .88 D8
  2 Southport PR9 . . . . . . .34 C8
Regent Dr PR2 . . . . .116 D4
Regent Gr PR2 . . . . .116 E5
Regent Park Ave LA3,LA4 212 C3
Regent Park Gr LA4 . . . . .212 D4
Regent Pk PR2 . . . . .116 E5
Regent Pl BB9 . . . . .168 E2
Regent Rd
  Bamber Bridge PR5 . . . . . .96 D4
  Blackpool FY1 . . . . .129 C5
  Chorley PR7 . . . . .42 C4
  Church BB5 . . . . .102 F7
  6 Leyland PR5 . . . . .76 A1
  Morecambe LA4 . . . . .212 C3
  Southport PR8 . . . . .33 F4
Regent Rd E FY1 . . . . .129 C5
Regent St Bacup OL13 . . . .87 A2
  Blackburn BB1 . . . . .100 E5
  Brierfield BB9 . . . . .147 B5
  Coppull PR7 . . . . .41 E1
  Haslingden BB4 . . . . .84 B3
  Lancaster LA1 . . . . .210 E7
  Longridge PR3 . . . . .139 A7
  Nelson BB9 . . . . .168 F2
  Preston PR1 . . . . .95 F6
  Ramsbottom BL0 . . . . .49 A4
  Rochdale OL12 . . . . .51 F1
  Waddington BB7 . . . . . . .186 B4
Regents Cl BB2 . . . . .99 C2
Regents Terr FY6 . . . . .151 E3
Regents View BB1 . . . . . . .121 E1
Regents Way 8 PR7 . . . . . .59 D2
Regentsway 6 PR5 . . . . . .76 E8
Reginald St BB8 . . . . .169 C5
Reigate PR6 . . . . .60 F3
Reiver Rd PR5 . . . . .75 C3
Renacres Hall L39 . . . . . . .22 B5
Renacres La L39 . . . . .22 B5
Rendel St BB12 . . . . .126 C7

Rendsburg Way 15 LA1 . . .210 F8
Renfrey Cl L39 . . . . .15 E8
Rennie Cl PR3 . . . . .178 D6
Rennie Ct LA1 . . . . .210 E5
Rennie St BB10 . . . . .127 C5
Renshaw Dr
  Bamber Bridge PR5 . . . . . .96 E2
  Bury BL9 . . . . .32 C3
Renshaw St 9 BB10 . . . . . .147 B1
Renwick Ave FY4 . . . . .109 D8
Repton Ave Blackpool FY1 .129 C8
  Morecambe LA4 . . . . .213 B4
Reservoir St Burnley BB11 .126 F1
  Darwen BB3 . . . . .80 F1
Reta Dr FY5 . . . . .173 A3
Retford Rd L33 . . . . .1 A2
Revidge Rd BB1,BB2 . . . . .100 C7
Revoe Sch (Jun & Inf)
  FY1 . . . . .129 C3
Rewe Cl BB2 . . . . .80 C8
Rexington Bldgs BB11 . . . .126 C4
Reynolds St Burnley BB11 .126 E3
  2 Lancaster LA1 . . . . . . .213 E1
Rhoda St BB9 . . . . .168 F1
Rhoden Rd Leyland PR5 . . .75 C1
  Oswaldtwistle BB5 . . . . . .102 D2
Rhodes Ave
  Blackburn BB1 . . . . .100 D8
  Haslingden BB4 . . . . .67 A7
Rhodesway PR5 . . . . .97 E2
Rhuddlan St BB4 . . . . .84 B1
Rhyddings Cty High Sch
  BB5 . . . . .102 E4
Rhyddings St BB5 . . . . . . .102 E4
Rhyl Ave BB1 . . . . .100 F2
Rhyl St FY7 . . . . .194 B5
Ribble Ave Brierfield BB10 147 C2
  Darwen BB3 . . . . .80 E4
  Freckleton PR4 . . . . .92 A6
  Great Harwood BB6 . . . . .123 E6
  Grindleton BB7 . . . . .187 B7
  Maghull L31 . . . . .5 E2
  Southport PR9 . . . . .53 C4
  Whalley BB7 . . . . .143 A7
Ribble Bank PR1 . . . . .95 B6
Ribble Bank St PR1 . . . . . .95 E7
Ribble Brook Ho PR1 . . . .116 F1
Ribble Bsns Pk BB1 . . . . . .101 B8
Ribble Cl Freckleton PR4 . .92 A6
  3 Preston PR1 . . . . .95 E6
  Withnell PR6 . . . . .79 A1
Ribble Cres Kirkham PR4 . .113 B5
  5 Preston PR1 . . . . .95 C6
Ribble Ct 2 PR1 . . . . .95 D6
Ribble Discovery Ctr FY8 .89 C3
Ribble Dr Baldingstone BL9 .49 F1
  Hesketh Bank PR4 . . . . . .72 E4
  West Bradford BB7 . . . . . .186 D7
Ribble Hall PR1 . . . . .116 F1
Ribble Ho Blackburn BB1 . .100 F5
  11 Preston PR1 . . . . .96 B8
Ribble La BB7 . . . . .187 D6
Ribble Lodge 10 FY8 . . . . .90 A3
Ribble Rd Blackpool FY1 . .129 C4
  Fleetwood FY7 . . . . .193 F4
  Leyland PR5 . . . . .58 D8
  Shevington Moor WN6 . . . .28 B2
Ribble St Bacup OL13 . . . . .70 A8
  Blackburn BB1 . . . . .100 E4
  Lytham St Anne's FY8 . . . .88 D6
  Padiham BB12 . . . . .125 D8
  Preston PR1 . . . . .95 E7
Ribble View BB7 . . . . .186 F4
Ribble View Cl PR4 . . . . . .91 F6
Ribble Way BB7 . . . . .164 C8
Ribblesdale Ave
  Accrington BB5 . . . . .103 B8
  Clitheroe BB7 . . . . .186 E2
  Wilpshire BB1 . . . . .122 A7
Ribblesdale Cl
  Blackpool FY4 . . . . .110 A8
  Kirkham PR4 . . . . .113 A5
Ribblesdale Ct 5 LA4 . . . .212 E5
Ribblesdale
  Cty High Sch BB7 . . . . . .164 E7
Ribblesdale Dr
  Forton PR3 . . . . .204 B3
  Grimsargh PR2 . . . . .138 C1
Ribblesdale Pl
  Barrowford BB9 . . . . .168 E6
  Blackburn BB2 . . . . .100 C5
  Chorley PR7 . . . . .42 B7
  Preston PR1 . . . . .95 F6
Ribblesdale Rd PR3 . . . . . .140 E3
Ribblesdale St BB10 . . . . .127 B8
Ribblesdale View BB7 . . . .187 E5
Ribbleton Ave PR2 . . . . . .117 E2
Ribbleton Avenue
  Cty Inf Sch PR1 . . . . . . .117 D2
Ribbleton Avenue
  Meth Jun Sch PR1 . . . . .117 D2
Ribbleton Dr BB5 . . . . . . .103 C8
Ribbleton Hall Cres 2
  PR2 . . . . .117 F3
Ribbleton Hall Dr PR2 . . .117 F3
Ribbleton Hall High Sch
  PR2 . . . . .117 F3
Ribbleton Hospl PR2 . . . .117 F2
Ribbleton La PR1 . . . . .117 C1
Ribbleton Pl 6 PR1 . . . . . .96 B8
Ribbleton St 6 PR1 . . . . . .96 B8
Ribby Ave Kirkham PR4 . . .112 F5
  Wrea Green PR4 . . . . .112 C4
Ribby Pl Blackpool FY4 . . .130 B1
  Preston PR1 . . . . .115 F1
Ribby Rd Kirkham PR4 . . . .112 F4
  Wrea Green PR4 . . . . .112 C4

Ribby-with-Wrea
  Endowed CE Prim Sch
  PR4 . . . . .112 B4
Ribchester Ave
  Blackpool FY4 . . . . .130 B1
  Burnley BB10 . . . . .127 D5
Ribchester CE Prim Sch
  PR3 . . . . .140 E3
Ribchester Hospl PR3 . . . .139 F6
Ribchester Rd
  Copster Green BB1 . . . . . .141 A1
  Longridge PR3 . . . . .139 E6
  Lytham St Anne's FY8 . . . .90 D4
  Ribchester BB6,PR3 . . . . .141 C4
  Wilpshire BB1 . . . . .121 E6
Ribchester Way BB9 . . . . .147 C4
Rice Gr FY1 . . . . .129 D8
Richard Burch St 2 BB9 . .32 A3
Richard Durning's
  Endowed Prim Sch L40 . .26 D7
Richard St Blackburn BB2 .100 E4
  Brierfield BB9 . . . . .147 B5
  Burnley BB11 . . . . .127 B5
  Shuttleworth BL0 . . . . . . .49 E7
  Weir OL13 . . . . .87 A7
Richard Thornton's
  CE Prim Sch LA6 . . . . . . .236 B3
Richard's St 7 PR4 . . . . . .112 F6
Richard's Way 7 PR4 . . . .109 E2
Richards Rd WN6 . . . . .28 E3
Richards Way 3 FY1 . . . . .172 F1
Richards Wlk 7 LA1 . . . . .213 D1
Richardson Cl PR4 . . . . . . .92 C6
Richardson St FY1 . . . . . . .129 C4
Richmond Ave
  Accrington BB5 . . . . .103 B5
  Barnoldswick BB18 . . . . .200 A3
  Burnley BB10 . . . . .127 F4
  Burscough L40 . . . . .24 E3
  Cleveleys FY5 . . . . .172 E2
  Haslingden BB4 . . . . .84 C2
  Lancaster LA1 . . . . .213 F4
  Morecambe LA4 . . . . .212 G4
  Wrea Green PR4 . . . . .112 B3
Richmond Cl Brinscall PR6 .61 E8
  Hightown L38 . . . . .2 F2
Richmond Cres BB1 . . . . . .101 E5
Richmond Ct
  7 Blackpool FY1 . . . . . . .129 B3
  Burscough L40 . . . . .24 E3
  Chorley PR7 . . . . .42 C6
  Leyland PR5 . . . . .75 B1
Richmond Gr L31 . . . . .5 E3
Richmond Hill 28 BB1 . . . .100 E5
Richmond Hill La PR3 . . . .204 D2
Richmond Hill St BB5 . . . .103 B5
Richmond Ho
  Lancaster LA1 . . . . .213 F4
  12 Preston PR1 . . . . .96 A7
Richmond Ind Est BB5 . . .103 B5
Richmond Mews L40 . . . . .24 E3
Richmond Pk BB3 . . . . .81 A2
Richmond Rd
  Accrington BB5 . . . . .103 A4
  Barnoldswick BB18 . . . . .200 A3
  Barrowford BB9 . . . . .168 C1
  Blackpool FY1 . . . . .129 B7
  Chorley PR6 . . . . .42 E6
  Eccleston PR7 . . . . .40 C7
  Lytham St Anne's FY8 . . . .88 E6
  Southport PR8 . . . . .33 F2
Richmond St
  Accrington BB5 . . . . .103 A5
  Accrington BB5 . . . . .103 B5
  Burnley BB11 . . . . .126 E5
  Horwich BL6 . . . . .31 B3
Richmond Terr
  17 Blackburn BB1 . . . . . .100 E5
  Clitheroe BB7 . . . . .164 D7
  Darwen BB3 . . . . .81 A2
Rickard Rd BB9 . . . . .147 E6
Ridding La BB7 . . . . .143 B5
Riddings Ave BB10 . . . . . .127 F6
Riddings La BB7 . . . . .143 C6
Ridehalgh La BB10 . . . . . .148 F2
Ridehalgh St BB8 . . . . . . .169 B3
Ridge Ave BB10 . . . . .127 D6
Ridge Cl PR9 . . . . .53 C5
Ridge Ct Burnley BB10 . . .127 C7
  Longridge BB3 . . . . .139 C8
Ridge Gr LA3 . . . . .208 F8
Ridge La
  Lancaster, Bulk LA1 . . . . .214 A1
  Lancaster, Ridge LA1 . . . .214 C2
  Roughlee BB12 . . . . .167 F4
Ridge Prim Sch The LA1 .214 B1
Ridge Rd Burnley BB11 . . .127 B6
  Chorley PR6 . . . . .42 C7
Ridge Row BB10 . . . . .127 D6
Ridge Sq LA1 . . . . .214 B1
Ridge St
  Barnoldswick BB18 . . . . .200 B2
  Lancaster LA1 . . . . .214 A1
Ridge Way PR1 . . . . .95 E4
Ridgeford Gdns PR2 . . . . .116 D5
Ridgemont PR2 . . . . .116 C6
Ridgeway Barrowford BB9 .168 C3
  Barrowford BB9 . . . . .168 D3
  Great Harwood BB6 . . . . .123 B6
Ridgeway Ave BB2 . . . . . . .81 A8
Ridgeway Dr Maghull L31 . . .5 E3
  Thornton FY5 . . . . .151 D8
Ridgeway The
  Fleetwood FY7 . . . . .193 D3
  Nelson BB9 . . . . .147 D7
Ridgeways BB4 . . . . .84 C2
Ridgmont Cl BL6 . . . . .31 F3

Ridgmont Dr BL6 . . . . .31 F3
Ridgway BL6 . . . . .30 C2
Ridgway Ct FY8 . . . . .89 A7
Ridgwood Ave FY3 . . . . . . .129 E5
Riding Barn St BB5 . . . . . .102 F7
Riding Cl BB18 . . . . .200 C2
Riding Head La BL0 . . . . . .49 F8
Riding La L39 . . . . .13 E4
Riding St Burnley BB11 . . .126 E5
  Preston PR1 . . . . .116 F1
  Southport PR9 . . . . .53 B8
Ridings The Burnley BB12 .126 D8
  Lucas Green PR6 . . . . .60 C6
  Southport PR9 . . . . .53 A3
Ridley La Barber's Moor PR5 57 D3
  Maghull L31 . . . . .5 D1
  Mawdesley L40 . . . . .39 F2
Ridley Rd PR2 . . . . .116 C2
Ridley St 2 FY3 . . . . .129 D5
Rifle St BB4 . . . . .84 B2
Rigby Ave BL6 . . . . .30 C2
Rigby Cl PR4 . . . . .92 C6
Rigby Rd Blackpool FY1 . . .129 B3
  Maghull L31 . . . . .5 B3
Rigby St Colne BB8 . . . . . .169 C5
  Nelson BB9 . . . . .147 D8
  Preston PR1 . . . . .96 C8
Rigg La Chipping PR3 . . . .181 B1
  Quernmore LA2 . . . . .226 B7
Rigg St BB9 . . . . .147 E8
Riley Ave FY8 . . . . .88 F5
Riley Cl PR5 . . . . .59 A8
Riley Ct FY8 . . . . .88 F4
Riley Green Switch Rd
  BB2,PR5 . . . . .78 F7
Riley St Accrington BB5 . . .103 B4
  Brierfield BB9 . . . . .147 B5
  Burnley BB11 . . . . .127 B4
  Earby BB18 . . . . .201 B2
Rimington Ave
  Accrington BB5 . . . . .103 A3
  Burnley BB10 . . . . .127 D5
  Colne BB8 . . . . .169 C6
Rimington Cl BB2 . . . . . . .100 F2
Rimington La BB7 . . . . . . .188 D7
Rimington Pl
  Lytham St Anne's FY8 . . . .89 B6
  Nelson BB9 . . . . .169 B1
Rimmer Gn PR8 . . . . .35 D1
Rimmer's Ave Formby L37 . .11 E6
  Southport PR8 . . . . .34 B6
Ring Dyke Way FY8 . . . . . .90 A4
Ring Lows La OL12 . . . . . . .51 F4
Ring O'Bells La L40 . . . . . .25 B2
Ring Way PR1 . . . . .95 F7
Rings St BB4 . . . . .105 A2
Ringstone Cres BB9 . . . . .148 B8
Ringstones La LA2 . . . . . . .233 D4
Ringtail Cl L40 . . . . .24 B4
Ringtail Pl L40 . . . . .24 B4
Ringtail Rd L40 . . . . .24 B4
Rington Ave FY6 . . . . .151 B6
Ringway Chorley PR7 . . . . .42 A7
  Cleveleys FY5 . . . . .172 E4
Ringwood Ave BL0 . . . . . . .49 A4
Ringwood Cl Enfield BB5 . .124 B1
  Lytham St Anne's FY8 . . . .89 F3
Ringwood Rd PR1 . . . . . . .117 C2
Ripley Cl L31 . . . . .5 E1
Ripley Ct LA1 . . . . .210 F6
Ripley Dr FY8 . . . . .89 B6
Ripley St Thomas'
  CE Sec Sch LA1 . . . . .210 F6
Ripon Cl 1 LA1 . . . . .213 F4
Ripon Cl Cleveleys FY5 . . .172 E5
  Great Eccleston PR3 . . . . .154 C5
  Southport PR8 . . . . .34 F3
Ripon Hall Ave BL0 . . . . . .49 B4
Ripon Pl LA3 . . . . .208 E6
Ripon Rd Blackpool FY1 . . .129 C4
  Lytham St Anne's FY8 . . . .89 D5
  Oswaldtwistle BB5 . . . . . .102 C5
Ripon St Blackburn BB1 . . .101 B4
  Nelson BB9 . . . . .147 D7
  Preston PR1 . . . . .116 E2
Ripon Terr PR1 . . . . .117 F1
Rise The LA5 . . . . .216 B6
Risedale Dr PR3 . . . . .139 B7
Risedale Gr BB2 . . . . .80 A7
Rishton Meth Sch BB1 . . .123 B1
Rishton Rd
  Clayton-le-M BB5 . . . . . .123 E3
  Wilpshire BB1 . . . . .122 C5
Rishton St FY1 . . . . .129 C4
Rishton Sta BB1 . . . . .102 A8
Rising Bridge Rd BB4,BB5 .84 A7
Ritherham Ave FY5 . . . . . .172 D3
River Bank Terr BB5 . . . . .124 E6
River Cl L37 . . . . .12 B1
River Dr BB12 . . . . .125 D8
River Hts PR5 . . . . .76 C8
River Lea Gdns BB7 . . . . . .164 F8
River Par PR1 . . . . .95 D6
River Rd FY3 . . . . .173 E3
River St Bacup OL13 . . . . . .86 F1
  Blackburn BB1 . . . . .100 F4
  Colne BB8 . . . . .169 D4
  Darwen BB3 . . . . .80 F2
  Lancaster LA1 . . . . .213 D1
  Preston PR1 . . . . .95 E7
  Ramsbottom BL0 . . . . .49 C6
  Trawden BB8 . . . . .170 C3
River View Glasson LA2 . .205 E5
  Tarleton PR4 . . . . .56 A4
River Way BB9 . . . . .168 D4
Rivermead Ct PR3 . . . . . . .199 C1
Rivermead Dr PR3 . . . . . . .178 C8

Rivermeade PR8 . . . . .34 D4
Rivers St WN5 . . . . .10 E6
Rivers View Fold LA2 . . . .220 A8
Riversedge Rd PR5 . . . . . . .58 C8
Riversgate FY7 . . . . .193 F4
Riverside
  Bamber Bridge PR5 . . . . . .76 E7
  Clitheroe BB7 . . . . .164 B8
  Hightown L38 . . . . .2 F4
  Penwortham PR1 . . . . .95 E5
  Preston PR1 . . . . .95 E5
Riverside Ave PR5 . . . . . . .75 E4
Riverside Cl Halton LA2 . .214 E6
  Leyland PR5 . . . . .75 E4
Riverside Cres PR5 . . . . . . .57 A2
Riverside Ct Garstang PR3 178 C7
  Whitworth OL12 . . . . .70 D4
Riverside Dr
  Hambleton FY6 . . . . .174 B1
  Ramsbottom BL0 . . . . .49 B2
Riverside Fold BB12 . . . . .167 E5
Riverside Ind Pk PR3 . . . .178 C2
Riverside Lofts 11 LA1 . .213 E1
Riverside Mill BB4 . . . . . .169 B4
Riverside Park Ind Est
  LA1 . . . . .214 B4
Riverside Rd PR1 . . . . .95 E5
Riverside Terr 4 BB18 . . .201 B1
Riverside Wlk BB4 . . . . . . .67 C4
Riversleigh Ave
  Blackpool FY1 . . . . .150 C1
  Lytham St Anne's FY8 . . . .89 E3
Riversleigh Ct FY8 . . . . . . .89 E3
Riversway Blackpool FY3 . .129 F6
  4 Lancaster LA1 . . . . . . .213 F2
  Poulton-le-F FY6 . . . . . . .151 F5
  Preston PR2,PR4 . . . . . . .94 D8
Riversway Bsns Village
  PR2 . . . . .95 A8
Riversway Enterprise
  Workshops PR2 . . . . .94 F8
Riversway Managed
  Workshops PR2 . . . . .94 F8
Riversway Motor Pk PR2 .94 D7
Riverview Ct LA4 . . . . .212 E3
Riverway Cl PR5 . . . . .76 D8
Rivington & Blackrod Coll
  Horwich Campus
  BL6 . . . . .31 D2
Rivington & Blackrod
  High Sch BL6 . . . . .31 B6
Rivington & Blackrod
  High Sch (Annexe) BL6 . .31 B4
Rivington Ave
  Adlington PR6 . . . . .30 B7
  Blackpool FY2 . . . . .150 D5
Rivington Cl
  Poulton-le-F FY6 . . . . . . .151 D3
  Southport PR8 . . . . .34 A3
  Tarleton PR4 . . . . .55 F8
Rivington Ctry Pk BL6 . . . .31 A8
Rivington Dr Burscough L40 24 E3
  Orrell WN8 . . . . .10 C7
Rivington Hall Cl BL0 . . . .49 C4
Rivington La Adlington PR6 .30 D6
  Horwich BL6 . . . . .31 A7
  Rivington BL6 . . . . .43 F1
Rivington Pl PR7 . . . . .28 D6
Rivington Rd
  Belmont BL6,BL7 . . . . . . .45 B4
  Chorley PR6 . . . . .60 E1
Rivington St
  Blackburn BB1 . . . . .101 B4
  Blackrod BL6 . . . . .30 D2
  Rochdale OL12 . . . . .51 F1
Riv7ersway Dr BB3 . . . . . . .80 F6
Roach Bridge Cotts PR5 . .97 E6
Roach Rd PR5 . . . . .98 B4
Roach St BL9 . . . . .32 C2
Road La OL12 . . . . .51 D4
Robbin's Bridge L31 . . . . .5 E5
Robert St Accrington BB5 . .103 C7
  Barnoldswick BB18 . . . . .200 B2
  Blackburn BB2 . . . . .100 E3
  Colne BB8 . . . . .169 E5
  13 Darwen BB3 . . . . .80 F2
  Great Harwood BB6 . . . . .123 D5
  40 Lancaster LA1 . . . . . .210 F8
  Newchurch BB4 . . . . .85 F2
  Oswaldtwistle BB5 . . . . . .102 D3
  Ramsbottom BL0 . . . . .67 C1
Roberts Ct LA5 . . . . .217 D6
Roberts St 2 Chorley PR7 .42 C7
  Nelson BB9 . . . . .147 B6
  7 Rawtenstall BB4 . . . . .85 A3
Robertson Ct PR7 . . . . . . .193 F1
Robin Bank Rd BB3 . . . . . .81 A2
Robin Cl PR7 . . . . .41 D3
Robin Croft LA2 . . . . .235 A1
Robin Hey PR5 . . . . .75 B1
Robin Hill Dr WN6 . . . . . . .28 B2
Robin Hill La WN6 . . . . . . .28 C3
Robin Hood La WN6 . . . . . .27 B3
Robin House La BB10 . . . .148 C4
Robin La
  High Bentham LA2 . . . . . .233 D8
  Hill Dale WN8 . . . . .26 C5
  Rimington BB7 . . . . .225 B1
Robin Rd BL0 . . . . .49 B2
Robin St PR1,PR2 . . . . . . .117 D1
Robins Cl FY6 . . . . .151 A4
Robins La Blackpool FY6 . .151 A4
  Carleton FY6 . . . . .151 A6
Robinson La
  BB10,BB12,BB9 . . . . . . .147 A4
Robinson St
  Blackburn BB1 . . . . .101 B7
  Burnley BB10 . . . . .127 A8

Robinson St *continued*
Chatburn BB7 187 E5
Colne BB8 169 C5
Foulridge BB8 191 D1
Fulwood PR2 116 D3
15 Horwich BL6 31 B4
Robraine LA6 238 C1
Robson St BB9 147 B6
Robson Way FY3 151 A2
Roby Mill WN8 19 B3
Roby Mill CE Prim Sch
WN8 19 B3
Rochdale Infmy OL12 51 F1
Rochdale Old Rd BL9 32 D4
Rochdale Rd Bacup OL13 87 A1
Bury BL9 32 B2
Edenfield BL0 67 F2
Ramsbottom BL0,BL9 50 B7
Rochester Ave
Cleveleys FY5 172 F4
Morecambe LA4 212 G3
Rochester Cl OL13 87 A7
Rochester Dr BB10 147 C3
Rochford Ave FY5 172 E1
Rock Bridge Fold BB4 85 E5
Rock Brow PR3 161 B7
Rock Fold BL7 46 F1
Rock Hall Rd BB4 84 B3
Rock La Burnley BB11 127 B3
Darwen BB3 80 A3
Trawden BB8 170 C3
Rock m' Jock LA2 231 B3
Rock St Accrington BB5 103 E2
Clitheroe BB7 164 E8
18 Haslingden BB4 84 B3
Horwich BL6 31 B3
Shuttleworth BL0 49 E7
Thornton FY5 173 B4
Rock Terr Arnside LA5 237 B2
Egerton BL7 46 F1
Pendleton BB7 165 B4
9 Rawtenstall BB4 85 A7
Rock Villa Rd PR6 60 C8
Rock Water
(Bird Conservation Ctr)
BB10 128 C2
Rockburgh Cres PR4 74 A5
Rockcliffe Ave OL13 86 E1
Rockcliffe Dr OL13 86 E1
Rockcliffe Rd OL13 86 F1
Rockcliffe St BB2 100 E2
Rockcliffe Villas OL13 69 E8
Rockfield Gdns 2 L31 5 C2
Rockfield Rd BB5 103 D6
Rockfield St BB2 100 E3
Rockhaven Ave BL6 31 C4
Rockingham Rd FY2 150 D3
Rockliffe La OL13 87 A1
Rockliffe Rd OL13 86 F1
Rockliffe St 5 BB4 85 A3
Rockville BB9 168 E5
Rockville Ave FY5 150 F8
Rockwood Cl BB10 147 E3
Roddlesworth La PR6 62 E8
Roddlesworth
Nature Trail BB3 63 B8
Roddlesworth Vistor Ctr
BB3 63 B8
Rodhill La BB7 224 B3
Rodney Ave FY8 109 E1
Rodney St Blackburn BB2 100 C3
4 Preston PR1 95 F8
Rodwell Wlk FY3 129 F8
Roe Greave Rd BB5 102 D3
Roe Hey Dr PR7 41 F2
Roe La PR9 34 E8
Roe Lee Park Prim Sch
BB1 121 F2
Roe Lee Pk BB1 121 F2
Roe St OL12 51 C1
Roe-Park Mews PR9 34 E8
Roebuck Cl BB2 100 D3
Roebuck Cty Prim Sch
PR2 116 D2
Roebuck St PR2 116 C2
Roeburn Dr LA3 213 B2
Roeburn Pl 5 LA1 213 E2
Roeburn Terr LA2 232 D6
Roeburndale Cres LA3 209 A8
Roedean Ave LA4 213 B4
Roedean Cl Maghull L31 5 D2
12 Thornton FY5 173 A2
Roefield L Ctr BB7 164 B8
Rogerley Cl FY8 90 A4
Rogersfield BB6 122 B8
Rolleston Rd BB2 100 B4
Roman Cres LA2 231 C3
Roman Mus PR3 140 E3
Roman Rd
Blackburn BB1,BB2 81 B8
Preston PR1 96 B7
Whittlestone Head BB3 65 A4
Roman Road Prim Sch
BB2 80 F8
Roman Way Cleveleys FY5 172 F1
Clitheroe BB7 165 A8
Kirkham PR4 113 C4
Red Scar PR2 118 C6
Roman Way Ind Est PR2 118 C6
Rome Ave BB11 126 C4
Romford Rd PR1 117 C2
Romford St 2 BB12 126 C7
Romiley Dr WN8 17 F2
Romney Ave
Barrowford BB9 168 D3
Blackpool FY4 129 D1
Burnley BB11 126 E3
Fleetwood FY7 193 E3
Romney St BB9 147 D7
Romney Wlk BB1 101 C4
Romsey Ave L37 12 B2
Ronald St Blackburn BB1 101 C5
Burnley BB12 126 A5
Ronaldsway Fulwood PR1 117 D3
Nelson BB9 169 B2
Ronaldsway Cl OL13 87 B1
Ronbury Cl 1 BB9 168 C1
Roney St BB2 100 C5
Ronwood Cl PR4 153 F1
Ronwood Ct PR2 95 B8
Roocroft Sq BL6 30 C2
Roods The LA5 217 E6
Rook St Barnoldswick BB18 200 B2
Colne BB8 169 D5
Nelson BB9 168 E1
Preston PR1 117 B1
3 Ramsbottom BL0 49 C6
Rookery Ave WN6 19 E8
Rookery Cl Chorley PR7 42 A6
Penwortham PR1 95 F2
Rookery Dr PR1 95 F2
Rookery Rd
Barnoldswick BB18 200 C3
Southport PR9 52 F1
Rookwood PR7 40 B6
Rookwood Ave Chorley PR7 60 C2
Cleveleys FY5 172 D1
Rooley Moor Rd
Bacup OL12,OL13 69 C4
Rochdale OL12 51 A3
Rochdale, Spotland Fold OL12 51 C1
Rooley St OL11,OL12 51 C1
Rooley View OL13 86 E1
Roosevelt Ave LA1 210 D7
Roots La PR4 134 E2
Rope Wlk PR3 178 C7
Ropefield Way OL12 51 E3
Rosary Ave FY4 129 E1
Roscoe Lowe Brow PR6 30 D7
Rose Acre La LA5 219 F2
Rose Ave Blackpool FY1 129 D2
Burnley BB11 126 E4
Fulwood PR2 116 C3
Rose Bank Lancaster LA1 211 A5
Rawtenstall BB4 85 A3
Rose Bank St OL13 86 F3
Rose Cl PR5 76 E2
Rose Cotts
Low Bentham LA2 233 B8
Preesall FY6 195 C3
Rose Cres
Skelmersdale WN8 17 E1
Southport PR8 20 C2
Rose Ct 1 FY7 193 F4
Rose Fold PR1 95 D4
Rose Fold Cotts PR1 95 D4
Rose Gdns PR4 72 E4
Rose Gr LA2 206 F4
Rose Grove Sta BB11 126 B5
Rose Hill Euxton PR7 59 C4
Ramsbottom BL0 49 B6
Southport PR8, PR9 34 D6
Rose Hill Ave BB1 101 A4
Rose Hill Gr LA7 237 F6
Rose Hill Rd BB2 99 C1
Rose Hill St Bacup OL13 86 F2
Darwen BB3 64 B8
Rawtenstall BB4 105 A1
Rose Hill Terr 7 BB3 64 B8
Rose La PR1 117 C3
Rose Lea PR2 117 D6
Rose Mt BB4 85 F1
Rose Pl L39 15 D2
Rose St Accrington BB5 103 B4
Bacup OL13 86 F2
7 Blackburn BB2 100 E3
Darwen BB3 81 B1
Leyland PR5 76 B3
Morecambe LA4 212 E6
Newchurch BB4 85 E2
15 Preston PR1 96 A7
Rose Terr PR2 116 B2
Rose Vale St BB4 85 B2
Roseacre FY4 109 C5
Roseacre Dr PR4 154 A1
Roseacre Pl
Lytham St Anne's FY8 89 B8
5 Preston PR2 115 E1
Roseacre Rd PR4 133 D6
Rosebank Edenfield BL0 67 D1
Enfield BB5 124 A3
2 Preston PR2 115 C1
Rosebank Ave 3 FY4 109 C5
Rosebay Ave BB2 79 D8
Rosebay Cl L37 12 A3
Roseberry Ave PR4 115 E5
Roseberry Cl BL0 49 C3
Roseberry St OL14 108 B1
Rosebery Ave
Blackpool FY4 109 B6
Lancaster LA1 211 A5
Lytham St Anne's FY8 89 B4
Morecambe LA4 212 F4
Rosebery St Burnley BB10 147 B2
Southport PR9 35 A6
Rosecroft Cl L39 15 E6
Rosedale Ave
Blackpool FY4 130 A2
Heysham LA3 209 A8
Rosedale St BB4 84 F5
Rosedene LA2 213 F7
Rosedene Cl PR4 115 E5
Rosegarth LA2 213 F7
Rosegrove La BB11 126 B5
Rosegrove Prim Sch
BB12 126 A6
Rosehill Ave Burnley BB11 126 E4
12 Nelson BB9 168 F1
Rosehill Bsns Pk 1 PR9 34 D6
Rosehill Dr L39 15 C2
Rosehill Inf Sch BB11 126 F3
Rosehill Jun Sch BB11 126 E3
Rosehill Mans L39 15 C2
Rosehill Rd Burnley BB11 126 F3
Nelson BB8 169 A2
Roseland Ave BB9 147 C6
Roseland Cl L31 5 B4
Roselea Dr PR9 53 C4
Roselyn Ave FY4 109 C5
Rosemary Ave
Blackpool FY4 109 C5
Cleveleys FY5 172 F3
Rosemary Ct 1 PR1 95 C2
Rosemary La Formby L37 11 F3
Haskayne L39 14 B4
8 Lancaster LA1 210 F8
Swillbrook PR4 135 A1
Rosemeade Ave PR5 76 B8
Rosemede Ave FY4 129 F2
Rosemount OL13 87 A4
Rosemount Ave
Barnoldswick BB18 200 A3
Burnley BB11 126 E4
Knott End-on-S FY6 195 A5
Rosendale Cl OL13 87 B3
Rosendale Cres OL13 87 B3
Roseway Blackpool FY4 109 C5
Lytham St Anne's FY8 89 B6
Poulton-le-F FY6 151 C3
Preston PR2 116 A1
Rosewood PR4 115 E5
Rosewood Ave
Blackburn BB1 100 F8
Burnley BB11 126 E3
Haslingden BB4 84 C3
Higher Walton PR5 97 C3
Rosewood Cl
Lytham St Anne's FY8 89 E4
1 Thornton FY5 173 D1
Rosewood Dr PR5 97 B3
Roshaw PR2 138 C1
Rosklyn Rd PR6 42 E7
Rosley St BB8 170 B5
Ross St Brierfield BB9 147 B5
Darwen BB3 64 A6
Rossall Cl Coupe Green PR5 97 E3
Fleetwood FY7 172 D8
Padiham BB12 125 D6
Rossall Ct FY7 193 E3
Rossall Dr PR2 116 C4
Rossall Gate FY7 172 C8
Rossall Gdns FY5 172 D4
Rossall Grange La FY7 193 D3
Rossall Hospl FY7 172 C8
Rossall La FY7 172 E7
Rossall Rd Blackpool FY3 129 D7
Chorley PR6 60 E1
Cleveleys FY5 172 D3
Fulwood PR2 116 C4
Lancaster LA1 213 C2
Lytham St Anne's FY8 89 D4
Rossall Sch FY7 172 C6
Rossall St PR2 116 C1
Rossall Terr BB2 100 E1
Rossendale Ave
Burnley BB11 126 E2
Morecambe LA4 212 F6
Rossendale Ave N FY5 173 B2
Rossendale Ave S FY5 173 B1
Rossendale
General Hospl BB4 84 D2
Rossendale Mus BB4 84 E2
Rossendale Rd
Burnley BB11 126 C3
Lytham St Anne's FY8 89 A7
Rossendale Sch BL0 50 A7
Rossendale Ski Ctr BB4 84 E3
Rosser Ct 14 BB9 147 E8
Rossett Ave FY4 130 C1
Rossetti Ave BB11 126 F3
Rossington Ave FY2 150 E5
Rosslyn Ave FY6 195 A6
Rosslyn Cres FY6 195 B5
Rosslyn Cres E FY6 195 B5
Rossmoyne Rd LA1 211 A4
Rostle Top Rd 6 BB18 201 B1
Rostrevor Cl 4 PR5 75 B1
Rostron Cres L37 11 E1
Rostron Rd BL0 49 B6
Rostron's Bldgs BB4 85 D1
Rothay Ave FY7 193 D2
Rothbury Pl FY8 90 C4
Rotherhead Cl BL6 30 F2
Rotherwick Ave PR7 42 B7
Rothesay Cres LA3 208 D5
Rothesay Rd
Blackburn BB1 101 D3
Brierfield BB9 147 C6
Heysham LA3 208 D5
Rothley Ave PR8 20 A4
Rothsay Rd LA3 208 E5
Rothwell Ave BB5 103 C4
Rothwell Cl L39 15 D5
Rothwell Cres PR2 117 F4
Rothwell Ct PR5 76 A2
Rothwell Dr
Fleetwood FY7 193 D3
Ormskirk L39 15 B2
Southport PR8 20 A4
Rothwell Lodge 5 PR2 117 F4
Rothwell Rd PR6 30 B7
Rothwell St BL0 49 B6
Rotten Row Caton LA2 231 D3
Southport PR8 33 F6
Rough Hey Pl PR2 118 B7
Rough Hey Rd PR2 118 B7
Rough Heys BB5 103 A2
Rough Heys La FY4 109 E7
Rough Hill La BL9 32 E4
Rough Lea Rd FY5 172 D2
Rough Lee Rd BB5 103 C4
Roughlee CE Prim Sch
BB12 167 F4
Roughlee Gr BB10 127 D5
Roughlee St BB9 168 D2
Roughlee Terr BB11 105 B4
Roughwood Dr L33 1 A4
Round Acre
Bamber Bridge PR5 96 A1
Nab's Head PR5 98 E7
Round Barn BL7 65 B3
Round Hill Pl BB10 127 E1
Round Mdws PR5 75 C1
Round Meade The L31 5 C2
Round Wood PR1 95 C7
Roundel St BB10 147 B2
Roundell Rd BB18 200 C3
Roundhay FY4 109 F8
Roundhill La BB4 84 A7
Roundhill Rd BB4,BB5 83 E6
Roundhill View BB5 84 A8
Roundway FY7 172 C8
Roundway Down PR2 116 C7
Roundway The L38 2 F3
Roundwood Ave BB10 147 A4
Row The Knowley PR7 61 D3
Silverdale LA5 218 E3
Rowan Ave Fulwood PR2 118 A4
2 Horwich BL6 31 E1
Oswaldtwistle BB5 102 D2
Rowan Bank LA2 214 E7
Rowan Cl Blackburn BB1 122 B1
Bonds PR3 178 D6
Burscough Bridge L40 24 F6
Penwortham PR1 95 B3
Rochdale OL12 51 B3
Rowan Croft PR6 77 B1
Rowan Gr Burnley BB10 127 C6
Chorley PR6 60 C3
Rowan La WN8 18 B4
Rowan Tree Cl BB5 103 D7
Rowangate PR2 117 C7
Rowans The Ormskirk L39 6 A7
Poulton-le-F FY6 151 A2
Rowberrow Cl PR2 117 D6
Rowen Pk BB2 100 B8
Rowhampton Cl 11 FY5 173 A2
Rowland Ave BB9 148 A8
Rowland Cl FY5 172 F2
Rowland La FY5 172 F2
Rowland St BB5 103 A5
Rowlands Rd BL9 49 D2
Rowley La BB10 127 D6
Rowntree Ave FY7 193 F3
Roworth Cl PR5 96 E3
Rowsley Rd FY8 88 D7
Rowstorne Sports Ctr PR4 92 B6
Rowton Heath PR2 116 C7
Roxburgh Rd FY4 110 A6
Roxton Cl BL6 31 B5
Roy St OL14 108 A1
Royal Ave Blackpool FY3 129 F3
Fulwood PR2 116 E6
Kirkham PR4 113 B4
Leyland PR5 58 E7
Royal Bank Rd FY3 129 E3
Royal Beach Ct FY8 88 D7
Royal Birkdale Golf Links
PR8 33 D3
Royal Brook Ho 6 PR1 117 A1
Royal Cl L37 12 A1
Royal Cres L37 12 A1
Royal Cross Prim Sch
PR2 115 E1
Royal Cross Sch
for the Deaf PR1 118 A1
Royal Ct BB10 147 F3
Royal Fold LA3 208 E8
Royal Lancaster Infmy
LA1 210 F7
Royal Lytham St Anne's
Golf Course FY8 89 B5
Royal Oak Ave BB1 121 E1
Royal Oak Bldgs 16 FY4 129 B1
Royal Oak Cotts BB9 168 B4
Royal Oak Meadow LA2 232 B8
Royal Pl FY8 89 C8
Royal Preston Hospl The
PR2 116 F6
Royal Rd LA4 212 F6
Royal Terr PR8 34 A7
Royal Troon Ct PR4 113 A4
Royalty Ave PR4 95 A1
Royalty Gdns PR4 75 A8
Royalty La PR4 75 A8
Royalty Mall LA4 212 D5
Royds Ave Accrington BB5 103 C3
Morecambe LA3 212 A2
Royds Gr LA3 212 A1
Royds Rd OL13 69 A7
Royds St Accrington BB5 103 C4
Bury BL9 32 D4
Lytham St Anne's FY8 88 E5
Royle Rd 4 Burnley BB12 126 F6
Burnley BB12 126 F7
Chorley PR7 42 C8
Royle St 1 FY1 129 B1
Roylen Ave FY6 151 B5
Royles Brook Cl 8 FY5 173 B3
Royles Brook Prim Sch
FY5 173 A2
Royles Ct FY5 173 B2
Roynton Rd BL6 31 B7
Royshaw Ave BB1 100 E8
Royshaw Cl BB1 100 E8
Royston Cl BL8 48 F1
Royston Rd FY6 151 F5
Royton Dr PR6 60 C5
Ruby St Blackburn BB1 121 F2
Ramsbottom BL0,BL9 49 C3
Rudd St BB4 84 A3
Ruddington Rd PR8 34 E2
Rudman St OL12 51 E2
Rudyard Ave WN6 28 E2
Rudyard Dr BB3 64 D8
Rudyard Pl Blackpool FY3 129 F7
Lytham St Anne's FY8 88 E8
Ruff La L39, L40 16 B4
Rufford Ave L31 5 E3
Rufford CE Prim Sch L40 38 B4
Rufford Dr PR9 53 F5
Rufford New Hall L40 38 B5
Rufford Park La L40 38 A5
Rufford Rd
Bispham Green L40 38 F1
Lytham St Anne's FY8 89 D5
Southport PR9 53 C4
Rufford Sta L40 38 D4
Rufus St PR1 117 C2
Rugby Ave BB5 103 C7
Rugby Dr WN5 10 F8
Rugby St 9 FY4 129 D1
Rumley's Fold BB11 126 E2
Runcorn Ave FY2 150 F2
Rundle Rd PR2 116 D3
Runnel The L39 22 B1
Runnymede Ave FY5 172 D2
Runshaw Ave WN6 19 E8
Runshaw Coll PR5 59 B6
Runshaw La Euxton PR7 59 B3
Runshaw Moor PR7 58 E3
Rupert St Carnforth LA5 217 D3
Nelson BB9 147 C7
Rochdale OL12 51 C1
Rush Hey Bank BB11 106 D8
Rushbed Cotts BB4 85 A6
Rushbed Dr BB4 85 A6
Rushden Rd L32 1 A1
Rushes Farm Cl BB5 102 C4
Rushey Cl BB4 85 A6
Rushley Dr LA2 215 D1
Rushley Way LA2 215 D1
Rushton Ave BB18 201 B1
Rushton Cl BB9 169 B2
Rushton St 5 Bacup OL13 69 E8
Barrowford BB9 168 D3
Great Harwood BB6 123 B4
Rushworth Bldgs OL13 69 C8
Rushworth St E 7 BB10 147 B1
Rushy Field BB5 123 F5
Rushy Hey PR5 76 A7
Rushy Hill View OL12 51 C1
Ruskin Ave
9 Blackpool FY1 129 B2
Colne BB8 169 D6
Leyland PR5 76 A1
Oswaldtwistle BB5 102 C5
Padiham BB12 125 E7
Thornton FY5 173 A3
Ruskin Cl PR4 55 F6
Ruskin Dr
Kirkby Lonsdale LA6 238 C2
Morecambe LA4 213 A6
Ruskin Gr Bolton-le-S LA5 216 A5
Hapton BB11 125 C4
Ruskin Ho LA1 213 E4
Ruskin Rd Freckleton PR4 92 B6
2 Lancaster LA1 213 F3
Ruskin St Burnley BB10 147 A2
Preston PR1 96 B6
Rusland Ave FY4 130 D1
Rusland Dr PR5 97 E4
Ruslands Gdns LA4 212 F4
Russall Ct FY5 172 C5
Russel St OL13 86 F4
Russell Ave Cleveleys FY5 150 D8
Colne BB8 169 E6
Leyland PR5 59 C8
Preston PR1 97 A8
Southport PR9 35 A7
Russell Ct Burnley BB11 127 B4
Lytham St Anne's FY8 88 F6
Southport PR9 53 B4
Russell Dr LA4 213 C4
Russell Pl BB6 123 B5
Russell Rd Carnforth LA5 217 E1
Southport PR9 35 A6
Russell Sq PR6 60 D1
Russell Sq W 8 PR6 60 D1
Russell St Accrington BB5 103 C5
Bacup OL13 86 F4
Blackburn BB2 100 E3
37 Lancaster LA1 210 F8
6 Nelson BB9 147 D8
Russell Terr BB12 125 D7
Russia St BB5 102 F6
Ruth St Edenfield BL0 67 D2
Whitworth OL12 70 D1
Rutherford Pl FY8 109 B4
Ruthin Cl BB1 100 F7
Ruthin Ct PR2 115 F3
Rutland Ave
1 Bamber Bridge PR5 96 D3
Blackburn BB1 101 E4
Burnley BB12 126 A6
Cleveleys FY5 172 E3
Fleetwood FY7 193 F3

Rutland Ave *continued*
Freckleton PR4 . . . .**92** C7
Lancaster LA1 . . . .**211** A5
Poulton-le-F FY6 . . . .**151** C3
Rutland Cl
Clayton-le-M BB5 . . . .**123** F3
Garstang PR3 . . . .**178** B8
Rutland Cres L39 . . . .**15** E7
Rutland Ct FY8 . . . .**89** D5
Rutland Pl 🔲 BB12 . . . .**125** D7
Rutland Rd
Lytham St Anne's FY8 . . . .**89** D5
Southport PR8 . . . .**34** D5
Rutland St Accrington BB5 .**102** F5
Blackburn BB2 . . . .**100** B3
Colne BB8 . . . .**169** F5
🔲 Nelson BB9 . . . .**168** F1
Preston PR1 . . . .**96** C8
Rutland Wlk BB4 . . . .**67** A8
Ryan Cl PR5 . . . .**75** E1
Ryburn Ave Blackburn BB2 **100** B6
Blackpool FY4 . . . .**129** C1
Ryburn Rd L39 . . . .**15** E4
Rycliffe St BB12 . . . .**145** C1
Rydal Ave
Bamber Bridge PR5 . . . .**96** D2
Blackpool FY1 . . . .**129** C3
Darwen BB3 . . . .**64** A8
Fleetwood FY7 . . . .**193** E4
Formby L37 . . . .**11** D3
Freckleton PR4 . . . .**92** A5
Freckleton PR4 . . . .**92** A6
Orrell WN5 . . . .**10** F7
Penwortham PR1 . . . .**95** C3
Poulton-le-F FY6 . . . .**151** D3
Thornton FY5 . . . .**173** B1
Rydal Cl 🔲 Accrington BB5 **124** D1
Blackrod BL6 . . . .**30** C3
Brierfield BB10 . . . .**147** C4
Fulwood PR2 . . . .**117** C4
Padiham BB12 . . . .**145** C1
Rydal Gr
Knott End-on-S FY6 . . . .**194** F6
Morecambe LA3 . . . .**212** A2
Rydal Mount BB1 . . . .**81** F6
Rydal Pl Chatburn BB7 . . . .**187** C3
Chorley PR7 . . . .**42** C6
Colne BB8 . . . .**170** A5
Rydal Rd Blackburn BB1 . .**101** A4
Hambleton FY6 . . . .**174** C2
Haslingden BB4 . . . .**67** C8
Hest Bank LA5 . . . .**215** F4
Lancaster LA1 . . . .**211** A8
Lytham St Anne's FY8 . . . .**88** E8
Morecambe LA3 . . . .**212** A2
Preston PR1 . . . .**117** D2
Rydal St BB10 . . . .**147** A2
Ryddingwood PR1 . . . .**95** B6
Ryde Cl BB4 . . . .**84** C1
Ryden Ave Cleveleys FY5 . .**172** D3
Leyland PR5 . . . .**76** C1
Ryden Rd BB1 . . . .**121** D6
Ryder Cl L39 . . . .**15** C1
Ryder Cres Ormskirk L39 . . .**15** C1
Southport PR8 . . . .**20** E7
Ryding's La PR9 . . . .**54** D8
Rydinge The L37 . . . .**12** A6
Rydings The BB6 . . . .**142** A1
Rye Gdns BB2 . . . .**80** D6
Rye Gr 🔲 BB12 . . . .**125** D7
Rye Moss La L37 . . . .**4** B8
Rye St PR1 . . . .**117** A1
Ryecroft PR6 . . . .**61** A7
Ryecroft Ave FY6 . . . .**174** C1
Ryecroft La BL7 . . . .**45** C5
Ryecroft Pl FY6 . . . .**174** C2
Ryefield PR6 . . . .**61** A7
Ryefield Ave
Haslingden BB4 . . . .**84** B2
Penwortham PR1 . . . .**95** D2
Ryefield Ave W BB4 . . . .**84** B2
Ryefield Pl BB4 . . . .**84** B2
Ryeground La L37 . . . .**12** A5
Ryeheys Rd FY8 . . . .**88** E8
Ryelands Cres PR2 . . . .**94** E8
Ryelands Cty Prim Sch
LA1 . . . .**213** D2
Ryelands Rd LA1 . . . .**213** E2
Ryknild Way LA3 . . . .**213** B3
Ryland Ave FY6 . . . .**151** C3
Rylands Rd PR7 . . . .**42** B7
Rylands St BB10 . . . .**147** B1
Ryldon Pl FY4 . . . .**130** A2
Rylstone Dr
Barnoldswick BB18 . . . .**200** A2
Morecambe LA3 . . . .**212** A1
Rymers Gn L37 . . . .**11** E4
Rysdale Cres LA4 . . . .**212** F4
Ryson Ave FY4 . . . .**129** F1

S

Sabden Brook Ct BB7 . . .**145** A8
Sabden Cty Prim Sch
BB7 . . . .**144** F8
Sabden Pl FY8 . . . .**89** C7
Sabden Rd Higham BB12 .**145** F6
Sabden BB12 . . . .**145** B4
Whalley BB7 . . . .**144** A4
Sabden Wlk BB2 . . . .**100** F2
Saccary La BB1 . . . .**121** A4
Sackville Gdns BB9 . . . . .**147** A5
Sackville St
Barnoldswick BB18 . . . .**200** B1

Sackville St *continued*
Blackpool FY4 . . . .**109** C6
Brierfield BB9 . . . .**147** B5
🔟 Burnley BB11 . . . .**126** F5
🔲 Bury BL9 . . . .**32** A3
Chorley PR6 . . . .**42** E7
Nelson BB9 . . . .**147** F7
Sacred Heart RC
Prim Sch Blackburn BB2 .**100** B6
Chorley PR6 . . . .**42** E7
Church BB5 . . . .**102** F6
Colne BB8 . . . .**169** D7
Preston PR5 . . . .**116** C1
Thornton FY5 . . . .**173** B3
Saddler Nook La LA6 . . . .**235** C8
Saddlers Mews 🔲 BB7 . . .**164** E8
Sadler St 🔲 BB5 . . . .**102** E5
Saer Cl FY7 . . . .**193** D3
Saffron Cl 🔲 BB9 . . . .**168** C1
Sagar Dr PR4 . . . .**92** A6
Sagar Fold L39 . . . .**6** D8
Sagar Holme Terr BB4 . . . . .**85** E5
Sagar La OL14 . . . .**108** D3
Sagar St Eccleston PR7 . . . .**40** C6
Nelson BB9 . . . .**147** E8
Sage Ct PR1 . . . .**95** C2
Sage La PR1 . . . .**117** B3
Sahara Fold 🔲 BB1 . . . .**101** A7
Sailsbury Cl LA3 . . . .**212** E2
St Aidan's Ave
Blackburn BB2 . . . .**100** D2
Darwen BB3 . . . .**64** B8
St Aidan's CE Prim Sch
Bamber Bridge PR5 . . . .**96** F1
Blackburn BB2 . . . .**100** C2
St Aidan's CE Tech Coll
FY6 . . . .**195** B3
St Aidan's Cl BB2 . . . .**100** C1
St Aidan's Rd 🔲 PR5 . . . .**96** E2
St Aidans Pk 🔲 PR5 . . . .**96** E2
St Alban's Cl 🔲 BB1 . . . . . .**100** F6
St Alban's Pl PR7 . . . .**42** D5
St Alban's RC Prim Sch
BB1 . . . .**100** F6
St Alban's Rd
Blackpool FY1 . . . .**129** D4
Darwen BB3 . . . .**80** E4
Lytham St Anne's FY8 . . . .**88** F7
St Albans Rd
Morecambe LA4 . . . .**213** B6
Rishton BB1 . . . .**102** A8
St Ambrose Terr 🔲 PR5 . .**76** B2
St Andrew's Ave
Cleveleys FY5 . . . .**172** D2
Preston PR2 . . . .**116** B2
St Andrew's CE Prim Sch
Blackburn BB2 . . . .**80** B8
Leyland PR5 . . . .**58** F8
Oswaldtwistle BB5 . . . .**102** D4
Preston PR2 . . . .**116** B1
Ramsbottom BL0 . . . .**49** B5
Ramsbottom BL0 . . . .**49** B5
St Andrew's Cl Leyland PR5 **59** A7
Oswaldtwistle BB5 . . . .**102** D4
Ramsbottom BL0 . . . .**49** C4
St Andrew's Ct 🔲 BB5 . .**102** D3
St Andrew's Pl
Blackburn BB1 . . . .**100** D6
Southport PR8 . . . .**34** B6
St Andrew's Rd PR1 . . . . . .**117** A2
St Andrew's Rd N FY8 . . . . . .**88** E7
St Andrew's Rd S FY8 . . . . . .**88** F6
St Andrew's St
Blackburn BB1 . . . .**100** D6
🔲 Burnley BB10 . . . .**147** B1
St Andrews Cl Colne BB8 **169** C3
Euxton PR7 . . . .**59** D4
St Andrews Gr LA4 . . . .**212** G6
St Andrews Maghull
CE Prim Sch L31 . . . .**5** D1
St Andrews Rd BB6 . . . . . .**142** C6
St Andrews Way PR5 . . . . . .**59** A8
St Ann's Sq BB7 . . . .**164** C8
St Ann's St 🔲 BB2 . . . .**100** E3
St Anne Edgeside CE
Church & Day Sch BB4 . .**85** F3
St Anne's Ave LA4 . . . .**213** B5
St Anne's CE Prim Sch
PR4 . . . .**135** D2
St Anne's Cl Caton LA2 . . .**231** C3
Formby L37 . . . .**11** F6
St Anne's Coll Jun Sch
FY8 . . . .**88** E5
St Anne's Cres BB4 . . . .**85** F3
St Anne's Ct WN6 . . . .**19** F5
St Anne's Dr BB12 . . . .**146** D7
St Anne's Old Links
Golf Course FY8 . . . .**109** D2
St Anne's Path L37 . . . .**11** F6
St Anne's Pl 🔲 LA1 . . . . . .**210** F8
St Anne's
Pleasure Island
Family Fun Pk FY8 . . . . . .**88** E5
St Anne's RC Inf Sch
BB5 . . . .**103** D5
St Anne's RC Prim Sch
Blackburn BB2 . . . .**100** D4
Leyland PR5 . . . .**58** D8
St Anne's RC Sch L39 . . . . .**15** C4
St Anne's Rd Formby L37 . . .**11** F6
Leyland PR5 . . . .**76** C3
Ormskirk L39 . . . .**15** D4
St Anne's Rd E FY8 . . . .**88** F7
St Anne's Rd W FY8 . . . .**88** E6
St Anne's St
Padiham BB12 . . . .**125** C7
Preston PR1 . . . .**117** A2
St Anne's Sta FY8 . . . .**88** E7

St Anne's Way BB12 . . . . .**146** D7
St Annes Cl
🔲 Blackburn BB1 . . . .**100** F3
🔲 Church BB5 . . . .**102** E5
St Annes Ct FY4 . . . .**129** C1
St Annes Rd
Blackpool FY4 . . . .**109** D2
🔲 Chorley PR6 . . . .**42** E7
Great Eccleston PR3 . . . .**154** C5
Horwich BL6 . . . .**31** C4
Southport PR9 . . . .**52** F4
St Anselm's RC Prim Sch
OL12 . . . .**70** D2
St Anthony's Cl PR2 . . . . . .**116** C4
St Anthony's Cres PR2 . . . .**116** C4
St Anthony's Dr PR2 . . . . . .**116** C4
St Anthony's Pl 🔲 FY1 . . . .**129** C7
St Anthony's
RC Prim Sch PR2 . . . .**116** C4
St Anthony's Rd PR1 . . . . .**117** A2
St Anthonys Pl PR4 . . . .**113** A4
St Antony's RC Sch BB1 .**101** C3
St Augustine's
RC High Sch BB7 . . . .**143** A4
St Augustine's RC
Prim Sch Burnley BB12 . .**126** B6
Preston PR1 . . . .**96** A7
St Austell Dr BL8 . . . .**48** F2
St Austell Pl LA5 . . . .**216** C8
St Austin's Pl PR1 . . . .**96** A7
St Austin's Rd PR1 . . . .**96** A7
St Barnabas CE Prim Sch
BB3 . . . .**64** C6
St Barnabas St
Blackburn BB2 . . . .**100** C5
🔲 Darwen BB3 . . . .**64** B6
St Barnabas' & St Paul's
CE Prim Sch
BB2 . . . .**100** D5
St Barnabas' Rd PR1 . . . . .**117** A1
St Bartholomew Parish
CE Sch BB6 . . . .**123** C6
St Bartholomew's CE
Prim Sch Blackburn BB2 . .**80** D8
Whitworth OL12 . . . .**51** C8
St Bede's Ave FY1 . . . .**129** B1
St Bede's RC High Sch
Blackburn BB2 . . . .**80** A8
Lytham St Anne's FY8 . . . .**90** C4
Ormskirk L39 . . . .**15** D4
St Bedes Cl L39 . . . .**15** D3
St Bee's Cl BB2 . . . .**100** F1
St Bernadette's
RC Prim Sch FY2 . . . .**150** D5
St Bernadettes
RC Prim Sch LA1 . . . .**211** B4
St Bernard Ave FY3 . . . . . .**129** F7
St Bernard's
RC Prim Sch PR2 . . . .**115** C1
St Bernard's Rd FY4 . . . . .**194** E6
St Brides Cl BL6 . . . .**31** A4
St Catherine Cl FY3 . . . . . .**151** B1
St Catherine's
CE Prim Sch BL6 . . . .**31** B3
St Catherine's Dr PR2 . . . .**116** C4
St Catherine's
RC Prim Sch PR5 . . . .**76** C2
St Catherines Cl 🔲 PR5 . . .**76** C2
St Catherines Ct 🔲 LA1 . .**210** F8
St Catherines Way PR5 . . . .**76** C7
St Cecilia St BB6 . . . .**123** D5
St Cecilia's
RC High Sch PR3 . . . .**139** A6
St Celia's Way LA4 . . . .**213** A6
St Chad's Ave BB7 . . . .**187** D5
St Chad's Dr LA1 . . . .**213** D3
St Chad's CE Prim Sch
PR6 . . . .**60** F6
St Chad's Rd
Blackpool FY1 . . . .**129** B2
Preston PR1 . . . .**117** C1
St Chads Cl FY6 . . . .**151** D2
St Charles'
RC Prim Sch BB1 . . . .**123** B1
St Charles' Rd BB1 . . . .**123** B1
St Christines Ave PR5 . . . . .**76** C4
St Christopher's
CE High Sch BB5 . . . .**103** A7
St Christopher's Rd PR1 .**117** A2
St Christopher's Way
LA4 . . . .**212** G6
St Clair Dr PR9 . . . .**53** A1
St Clair Rd BL8 . . . .**48** F3
St Clare's RC Prim Sch
PR2 . . . .**116** F7
St Clares Ave PR2 . . . .**117** A6
St Clement St
Blackburn BB1 . . . .**101** B4
Blackburn BB1 . . . .**101** B5
St Clement's Ave FY3 . . . .**129** E5
St Clements Ave PR5 . . . . . .**76** C3
St Clements Ct 🔲 BB1 . . .**101** B4
St Clements St BB9 . . . . . .**168** C3
St Crispin Way BB4 . . . .**84** A2
St Cuthbert St BB10 . . . . .**147** C2
St Cuthbert's
CE Prim Sch Darwen BB3 .**80** E3
Halsall L39 . . . .**22** B1
St Cuthbert's Cl
Fulwood PR2 . . . .**116** D3
🔲 Lytham St Anne's FY8 . . . .**90** A3
Southport PR9 . . . .**53** A2
St Cuthbert's
RC Prim Sch FY4 . . . .**109** C8
St Cuthbert's Rd
Bamber Bridge PR5 . . . .**96** A1
Preston PR1 . . . .**117** A2
Southport PR9 . . . .**53** A2

St Cuthberts Cl BB3 . . . . . .**80** E3
St Cutherbert's Ct 🔲 FY8 . .**90** A3
St David's Ave
Blackburn BB2 . . . .**79** E7
Cleveleys FY5 . . . .**172** D2
St David's Gr FY8 . . . .**88** D8
St David's Rd Leyland PR5 . .**76** C2
Preston PR1 . . . .**117** A2
St David's Rd N FY8 . . . .**88** D8
St David's Rd S FY8 . . . .**88** F6
St David's Wood BB5 . . . . .**103** D7
St Deny's Croft BB7 . . . . . .**186** E1
St Edmund Hall Cl BL0 . . .**49** C4
St Edmund's RC
Prim Sch Fleetwood FY7 .**172** E8
Skelmersdale WN8 . . . .**17** F1
St Edmund's Rd FY4 . . . . .**129** E1
St Edmund's St BB6 . . . . . .**123** D5
St Edward's
RC Prim Sch BB3 . . . .**80** E4
St Frances Cl 🔲 BB1 . . . . .**100** F3
St Francis CE Prim Sch
BB2 . . . .**99** F1
St Francis Cl PR2 . . . .**117** A7
St Francis' Rd BB2 . . . .**100** A2
St Francis'
RC Prim Sch PR3 . . . .**159** A2
St Gabriel Cl WN8 . . . .**19** C3
St Gabriel's Ave BB1 . . . . .**121** F3
St Gabriel's CE Prim Sch
BB1 . . . .**121** E2
St George Ct FY1 . . . .**129** D6
St George's Ave
Blackburn BB2 . . . .**100** B1
Cleveleys FY5 . . . .**172** D2
Lytham St Anne's FY8 . . . .**88** E7
St George's CE Prim Sch
PR7 . . . .**42** E7
St George's High Sch
FY4 . . . .**110** A8
St George's La
Cleveleys FY5 . . . .**172** D2
Lytham St Anne's FY8 . . . .**88** E6
St George's Pl PR9 . . . .**34** B7
St George's Quay LA1 . . . .**213** E1
St George's Rd
Blackpool FY4 . . . .**109** C6
Formby L37 . . . .**11** E4
Hightown L38 . . . .**2** F5
Lytham St Anne's FY8 . . . .**88** E6
Preston PR1 . . . .**117** A2
St George's Sh Ctr 🔲 PR1 .**95** F7
St George's Sq FY8 . . . .**88** D7
St George's St PR7 . . . .**42** C7
St George's Terr BB4 . . . . . .**69** A6
St Georges Cl BB8 . . . .**169** C3
St Georges Rd BB9 . . . .**147** F7
St Georges Terr BB3 . . . .**80** F1
St Gerrard's Rd PR5 . . . .**96** A1
St Giles St 🔲 BB12 . . . . . .**145** C1
St Giles Terr 🔲 BB12 . . . . .**145** C1
St Gregory Rd PR1 . . . .**117** B2
St Gregory's Pl PR7 . . . .**42** C5
St Gregory's RC Inf Sch
L31 . . . .**5** C4
St Gregory's RC Jun Sch
L31 . . . .**5** C4
St Gregory's RC Prim Sch
Chorley PR7 . . . .**42** C5
Fulwood PR1 . . . .**117** B3
St Helen's CE Sch LA3 . . .**209** D1
St Helen's Cl PR3 . . . .**178** A2
St Helen's Rd
Clayton Green PR6 . . . .**77** C1
Overton LA3 . . . .**205** E8
St Helens Cl BB5 . . . .**102** F3
St Helens Rd L39 . . . .**16** A2
St Helier Cl BB2 . . . .**80** C8
St Helier's Pl PR3 . . . .**136** A7
St Heliers Rd FY1 . . . .**129** C1
St Hilda's Cl PR7 . . . .**42** C4
St Hilda's RC Girls' Sch
BB11 . . . .**126** C3
St Hilda's Rd FY8 . . . .**88** D8
St Hubert's Rd BB6 . . . . . .**123** C4
St Hubert's St BB6 . . . .**123** D5
St Huberts RC Prim Sch
BB6 . . . .**123** E6
St Ignatius' Pl 🔲 PR1 . . . . .**96** A8
St Ignatius' RC Prim Sch
PR1 . . . .**96** A8
St Ignatius' Sq 🔲 PR1 . . . . .**96** A8
St Ives Ave Blackpool FY1 .**129** E3
Freckleton PR4 . . . .**92** A6
St Ives Cres PR2 . . . .**116** A4
St Ives Rd BB1 . . . .**101** D4
St Jame's CE Prim Sch
BB3 . . . .**81** B2
St Jame's Terr PR5 . . . .**98** E7
St James CE Prim Sch
Blackburn BB3 . . . .**81** A7
Leyland PR5 . . . .**58** B8
St James Cl
Bamber Bridge PR5 . . . .**76** B8
Church BB5 . . . .**102** E7
🔲 Haslingden BB4 . . . .**84** B3
Ormskirk L40 . . . .**16** C5
St James Ct
Blackburn BB1 . . . .**100** E7
Heysham LA3 . . . .**208** E7
🔲 Lancaster LA1 . . . .**210** E8
Standish WN6 . . . .**28** D2
🔲 Tardy Gate PR5 . . . .**76** B8
St James La 🔲 BB1 . . . . . .**127** A6
St James Lodge PR5 . . . . . .**58** B8
St James Mews
Church BB5 . . . .**102** E7
Lancaster LA1 . . . .**213** F1

St James Pl
🔲 Padiham BB12 . . . .**125** D8
Southport PR8 . . . .**34** B5
St James RC Sch WN8 . . . .**18** B4
St James Rd
Blackpool FY4 . . . .**109** C6
Church BB5 . . . .**102** E7
St James Row BB4 . . . .**85** A3
St James Sq 🔟 OL13 . . . . . .**86** F3
St James St Bacup OL13 . .**86** F3
🔲 Rawtenstall BB4 . . . .**85** A3
Southport PR8 . . . .**34** B6
St James The Lesser
RC Prim Sch BB4 . . . .**84** F3
St James' Cres BB3 . . . .**81** B2
St James' Lanehead CE
Prim Sch BB10 . . . .**147** D2
St James' RC Prim Sch
WN5 . . . .**10** D4
St James' Rd
🔲 Barnoldswick BB18 . . . . .**200** B2
Orrell WN5 . . . .**10** D4
St James' Sq 🔟 BB18 . . . . .**200** B2
St James' St
Accrington BB5 . . . .**103** B5
Blackburn BB2 . . . .**100** C1
Rawtenstall, Waterfoot BB4 . .**68** E8
St James' CE Sch BB7 . . . .**164** E7
St James' Dr LA6 . . . .**234** B7
St James' Gdns PR5 . . . . . .**58** B8
St James' Pl
Blackburn BB1 . . . .**100** E7
🔲 Chorley PR6 . . . .**42** E7
St James' Rd
Blackburn BB1 . . . .**100** E7
Preston PR1 . . . .**116** F2
St James' Row 🔟 BB11 . . .**126** F6
St James' St
Brierfield BB9 . . . .**147** B5
🔲 Chorley PR6 . . . .**42** E7
Clitheroe BB7 . . . .**164** E7
St Jerome's
RC Prim Sch L37 . . . .**11** C3
St John Ave FY7 . . . .**193** D2
St John Bosco
RC Prim Sch L31 . . . .**5** B2
St John RC Jun Sch
BB10 . . . .**147** C3
St John Rigby
RC Sixth Form Coll WN5 .**19** F2
St John Southworth
RC Prim Sch BB9 . . . .**147** D7
St John St Bacup OL13 . . . .**86** F3
Colne BB8 . . . .**169** E5
Horwich BL6 . . . .**31** B3
St John Stone
RC Prim Sch PR8 . . . .**20** D2
St John the Baptist
RC Sch BB12 . . . .**125** C7
St John Vianney RC Sch
FY1 . . . .**129** E2
St John with St Michael
CE Prim Sch OL12 . . . .**70** E5
St John's Ave Darwen BB3 .**64** B8
Morecambe LA3 . . . .**212** B2
Poulton-le-F FY6 . . . .**151** E5
Silverdale LA5 . . . .**218** C3
Thornton FY5 . . . .**173** D1
St John's
CE Meth Prim Sch PR6 . . .**61** E7
St John's CE Prim Sch
Accrington BB5 . . . .**103** C7
Burscough Bridge L40 . . . .**24** F5
Coppull PR7 . . . .**28** D6
Galgate LA2 . . . .**207** A3
Garstang PR3 . . . .**220** C1
Nelson BB9 . . . .**148** A8
Pilling PR3 . . . .**196** C6
Southport PR9 . . . .**53** C5
St John's Cl
Accrington BB5 . . . .**103** E2
🔲 Rawtenstall BB4 . . . .**85** A7
Read BB12 . . . .**144** D2
St John's Ct 🔲 Bacup OL13 .**86** F3
🔲 Blackpool FY1 . . . .**129** C5
🔲 Burnley BB12 . . . .**126** C6
🔲 Lytham St Anne's FY8 . . . .**90** C3
St John's Gn PR5 . . . .**75** E1
St John's Gr
Morecambe LA3 . . . .**212** B2
Silverdale LA5 . . . .**218** C3
St John's Mkt FY1 . . . .**129** C5
St John's Pl Nelson BB9 . .**148** A8
🔟 Preston PR1 . . . .**96** A7
St John's Prim Sch
Blackpool FY1 . . . .**129** C5
Great Harwood BB6 . . . .**123** C4
Higham BB12 . . . .**146** A8
St John's RC Inf Sch
BB10 . . . .**147** B1
St John's Rd
🔲 Burnley BB12 . . . .**126** C6
Morecambe LA3 . . . .**212** A2
Padiham BB12 . . . .**125** C7
Southport PR8 . . . .**33** F1
Walton-le-D PR5 . . . .**96** D5
St John's St Darwen BB3 . .**64** B8
Great Harwood BB6 . . . .**123** C4
Lytham St Anne's FY8 . . . .**90** C3
Rawtenstall BB4 . . . .**68** F8
St John's Terr LA3 . . . .**212** F2
St Johns Ave Kirkham PR4 **112** F4
Smallwood Hey PR3 . . . .**196** C5
St Johns Cl PR8 . . . .**20** D4
St Johns RC Prim Sch
WN8 . . . .**18** C1
St Johns Wood FY8 . . . .**89** E3

St Johns'
CE Prim Sch BB1 . . . . .100 E7
St Joseph & St Bede
RC Prim Sch BL9 . . . . .32 B4
St Joseph's Con Ctr WN8 . .19 B2
St Joseph's Inf Sch PR6 . .60 D1
St Joseph's RC Prim Sch
Adlington PR6 . . . . .30 B8
Bacup OL13 . . . . .69 D8
Bacup OL13 . . . . .86 D1
Barnoldswick BB18 . . . . . .200 B3
Chorley PR6 . . . . .60 D2
Darwen BB3 . . . . .64 A8
Gregson Lane PR5 . . . . .97 E1
Hurst Green BB7 . . . . .162 F1
Kirkham PR4 . . . . .112 F7
Lancaster LA1 . . . . .213 B8
Preston PR1 . . . . .117 C1
Ramsbottom BL0 . . . . .49 B6
Withnell BB5 . . . . .79 A1
St Joseph's RC Sch BL6 . .31 E1
St Joseph's Terr **1** PR1 . .117 C1
St Joseph's Wrightington
RC Prim Sch WN6 . . . . . . .28 A3
St Josephs Cl FY3 . . . . . . .129 E5
St Jude's Ave PR5 . . . . .96 D1
St Judes Ave PR5 . . . . .76 C4
St Katherines Dr BL6 . . . .30 C3
St Kentigern's Sch FY3 . .129 D5
St Lames Lodge FY8 . . . . .89 A5
St Laurence's
CE Prim Sch PR7 . . . . .60 D1
St Lawrence Ave BB2 . . . .100 B8
St Lawrence
CE Prim Sch PR3 . . . . . .136 B7
St Lawrence St BB6 . . . . .123 C5
St Lawrence's Ave PR3 . .136 B8
St Leger Ct **11** BB5 . . . . . . .103 C5
St Leonard Ct **5** LA1 . . . . .214 A1
St Leonard's Ave BL6 . . . .31 F1
St Leonard's
CE Cty Prim Sch BB12 . .145 C1
St Leonard's
CE Prim Sch PR5 . . . . .96 C4
St Leonard's CE Sch BB6 142 E2
St Leonard's Cl PR2 . . . . .116 A3
St Leonard's Ct FY3 . . . . . .88 D8
St Leonard's Gate LA1 . . .210 F8
St Leonard's Rd FY3 . . . .130 A3
St Leonard's Rd E FY8 . . .88 F8
St Leonard's Rd W FY8 . . .88 D8
St Leonard's St **8** BB12 . .145 C1
St Louis Ave FY3 . . . . .129 F7
St Luke & St Philip's
CE Prim Sch BB2 . . . . .100 D3
St Luke's Bldg **2** PR8 . . . .34 D6
St Luke's CE Prim Sch
Formby L37 . . . . .11 D1
Lancaster LA1 . . . . .213 E8
St Luke's CE Sch LA2 . . . .213 E8
St Luke's Church Rd
L37, L38 . . . . .2 C8
St Luke's Ct **1** FY4 . . . . . . .109 C6
St Luke's Dr Formby L37 . .11 C2
Orrell WN5 . . . . .10 E4
St Luke's Gr PR9 . . . . .34 E7
St Luke's Pl **9** PR1 . . . . . .117 C1
St Luke's RC Prim Sch
WN8 . . . . .9 E6
St Luke's Rd
Blackpool FY4 . . . . .109 C6
Southport PR9 . . . . .34 D7
St Lukes Ct **2** LA1 . . . . . .210 E8
St Margaret's Ct
1 Blackburn BB1 . . . . .101 B5
Fleetwood FY7 . . . . .194 A4
St Margaret's Gdns BB11 125 C4
St Margaret's Rd
Bolton-le-S LA5 . . . . .216 B6
1 Leyland PR5 . . . . .76 C2
Morecambe LA4 . . . . .212 G6
St Margarets Cl PR2 . . . . .116 A4
St Margarets Way BB1 . .101 B5
St Maria Goretti
RC Prim Sch PR2 . . . . . . .117 F5
St Marie's RC Prim Sch
Kirkby L33 . . . . .1 A3
Southport PR8 . . . . .34 B8
St Maries RC Prim Sch
WN6 .28 C3
St Mark's CE Prim Sch
Bury BL9 . . . . .32 A4
Scarisbrick L40 . . . . .22 D7
St Mark's Pl
Blackburn BB2 . . . . .100 B4
1 Blackpool FY3 . . . . .129 E8
St Mark's Pl E **5** PR1 . . . .95 D8
St Mark's Pl W **4** PR1 . . .95 D8
St Mark's Rd
Blackburn BB2 . . . . .100 B4
Preston PR1 . . . . .95 D8
St Marks RC Sch WN8 . . . .9 E6
St Marlow Ave **3** PR5 . . .76 C3
St Martin's Coll LA1 . . . . .211 B6
St Martin's Ct FY5 . . . . . . .172 F2
St Martin's Dr BB2 . . . . . . .79 D8
St Martin's Rd
Blackpool FY4 . . . . .109 C6
Lancaster LA1 . . . . .211 A7
Preston PR1 . . . . .117 A2
St Martins Cl FY6 . . . . .151 B5
St Mary & St Michael's
RC Prim Sch PR3 . . . . . .178 C6
St Mary Cl FY3 . . . . .151 B1
St Mary Magdalen
RC Prim Sch PR1 . . . . .95 E4
St Mary Magdalen's
CE Prim Sch BB5 . . . . . . .103 B7

St Mary Magdalene's
RC Prim Sch BB12 . . . . . .126 D8
St Mary's & St Andrews
RC Prim Sch PR3 . . . . . .136 A5
St Mary's & St Benedicts
RC Prim Sch PR5 . . . . . . .96 E1
St Mary's & St Joseph's
RC Prim Sch BB1 . . . . . . .100 F3
St Mary's Ave
Bamber Bridge PR5 . . . . . . .96 D1
Barnoldswick BB18 . . . . . .200 D3
St Mary's CE Prim Sch
Eccleston PR7 . . . . .40 C6
Mellor BB2 . . . . .120 D2
Ramsbottom BL8 . . . . .48 C2
Spen Brook BB12 . . . . .167 C3
St Mary's Cl PR5 . . . . .96 D1
St Mary's Ct
Clayton-le-M BB5 . . . . .123 F2
Preston PR1 . . . . .96 B8
St Mary's Dr BB6 . . . . .142 D1
St Mary's Gate
Burnley BB11 . . . . .127 B5
Euxton PR7 . . . . .59 C3
St Mary's Gdns
Mellor BB2 . . . . .120 E2
Southport PR8 . . . . .20 F7
St Mary's Par LA1 . . . . . . .210 E8
St Mary's Pl **4** BB4 . . . . . .84 F2
St Mary's RC High Sch
FY3 .129 F7
St Mary's RC Prim Sch
Accrington BB5 . . . . .102 F4
Bacup OL13 . . . . .87 B2
Bescar L40 . . . . .23 A7
Burnley BB10 . . . . .127 B6
Chipping PR3 . . . . .182 E3
Chorley PR7 . . . . .42 A7
Claughton PR3 . . . . .179 D1
Clayton-le-M BB5 . . . . .123 F3
Euxton PR7 . . . . .59 C3
Fleetwood FY7 . . . . .194 A5
Great Eccleston PR3 . . . . .154 B5
Haslingden BB4 . . . . .84 C2
Horwich BL6 . . . . .31 B4
Horwich BL6 . . . . .31 D2
Leyland PR5 . . . . .75 F1
Morecambe LA4 . . . . .212 F6
Osbaldeston BB2 . . . . .120 D4
St Mary's
RC Primary Sch PR4 . . . .114 F2
St Mary's RC Sch
Langho BB6 . . . . .142 C1
Leyland PR5 . . . . .58 E7
Sabden BB7 . . . . .144 F7
St Mary's Rd
Bamber Bridge PR5 . . . . . . .96 E1
Great Eccleston PR3 . . . . .154 B5
Heysham LA3 . . . . .208 E8
St Mary's
Sixth Form Coll BB1 . . . .100 E7
St Mary's St N **7** PR1 . . .96 B8
Nelson BB9 . . . . .147 C8
Preston PR1 . . . . .96 B8
St Mary's Terr **6** BB4 . . . .85 A2
St Mary's Way BB4 . . . . . . .85 A2
St Mary's Wlk **15** PR7 . . .42 C8
St Marys CE Prim Sch
LA6 .238 B2
St Marys Cl Blackburn BB1 101 B5
Longridge PR3 . . . . .139 A8
8 Preston PR1 . . . . .96 C8
St Marys Wharfe BB1 . . . .100 F3
St Mathew's
RC Prim Sch WN8 . . . . . . .9 D7
St Matthew St BB11 . . . .126 E5
St Matthew's
CE Prim Sch BB1 . . . . . .100 F4
St Matthew's CE Sch PR1 .96 D8
St Matthew's Ct **9** BB11 .126 E5
St Michael & All Angels
CE Prim Sch BB5 . . . . . .169 E8
St Michael & St John's
RC Prim Sch BB7 . . . . . .164 C8
St Michael Rd L39 . . . . .5 F7
St Michael with St John
CE Prim Sch BB1 . . . . . .100 E6
St Michael's
CE High Sch PR7 . . . . . . .60 C1
St Michael's Cl
Blackburn BB2 . . . . .79 E7
Bolton-le-S LA5 . . . . .216 A4
Chorley PR7 . . . . .60 B1
Southport PR9 . . . . .52 F3
St Michael's Cres LA5 . . .216 A4
St Michael's Ct
Barrowford BB9 . . . . .168 C2
1 Blackburn BB1 . . . . . . .100 F6
St Michael's Gr
Bolton-le-S LA5 . . . . .216 A4
Morecambe LA4 . . . . .212 F4
St Michael's La LA5 . . . . .216 A4
St Michael's Pl
Bolton-le-S LA5 . . . . .216 A4
Newsham PR3 . . . . .136 B5
St Michael's Rd
Duncombe PR3 . . . . .156 D4
4 Leyland PR5 . . . . .76 C3
Preston PR1 . . . . .117 A2
St Michael's St **1** BB1 . .100 F7
St Michael's Terr PR5 . . . .57 D7
St Michael's-on-Wyre
CE Prim Sch PR3 . . . . . .155 C6
St Michaels Pk L39 . . . . . . .6 A7

St Michaels Rd
Blackpool FY2 . . . . .150 D3
Kirkham PR4 . . . . .113 C5
St Mildred's Way LA3 . . .208 E6
St Monica's Way FY4 . . .130 D1
St Nicholas Arcs **18** LA1 . .210 F8
St Nicholas Cres LA5 . . . .216 B6
St Nicholas Gr PR4 . . . . . .112 B4
St Nicholas La LA5 . . . . . .216 A6
St Nicholas Rd
Blackpool FY4 . . . . .110 B5
Church BB5 . . . . .102 F7
St Nicholas' Ave BB7 . . . .144 F8
St Nicholas' CE Prim Sch
Blackpool FY4 . . . . .110 A4
Church BB5 . . . . .102 F7
St Ogg's Rd LA4 . . . . .212 F3
St Oswald St LA1 . . . . .211 A6
St Oswald's
CE Prim Sch BB1 . . . . . .101 E4
St Oswald's Cl
Blackburn BB1 . . . . .101 E4
Preston PR1 . . . . .117 C2
St Oswald's RC Prim Sch
Accrington BB5 . . . . .103 A3
Coppull PR7 . . . . .28 D8
Longton PR4 . . . . .74 B8
St Oswald's Rd BB1 . . . . .101 E4
St Patrick's Pl PR5 . . . . . . .96 E4
St Patrick's RC Prim Sch
Heysham LA3 . . . . .209 A8
Southport PR9 . . . . .53 A2
Walton-le-D PR5 . . . . .96 E4
St Patrick's Rd N FY8 . . . .88 E7
St Patrick's Rd S FY8 . . . .88 F6
St Patrick's Wlk LA3 . . . .208 E7
St Paul's Ave
Blackburn BB2 . . . . .100 D5
Lytham St Anne's FY8 . . . .89 B4
Preston PR1 . . . . .117 A1
St Paul's CE Prim Sch
Adlington PR6 . . . . .30 A7
Bury BL9 . . . . .32 B4
Hoddlesden BB3 . . . . .81 F1
Nelson BB9 . . . . .147 D6
Oswaldtwistle BB5 . . . . . .102 E4
Ramsbottom BL0 . . . . .49 C6
St Paul's Cl Adlington PR6 . .30 A8
Clitheroe BB7 . . . . .164 C8
St Paul's Ct
5 Burnley BB11 . . . . .126 F5
12 Oswaldtwistle BB5 . . .102 E4
9 Preston PR1 . . . . .96 A8
St Paul's Dr Caton LA2 . .231 D3
Lancaster LA1 . . . . .210 F5
St Paul's Pas PR1 . . . . .34 A6
St Paul's RC Prim Sch
BB2 . . . . .79 D8
St Paul's Rd Blackpool FY1 129 B8
Lancaster LA1 . . . . .210 F5
Nelson BB9 . . . . .147 E6
Preston PR1 . . . . .117 A1
St Paul's Sq Preston PR1 . .96 A8
Southport PR8 . . . . .34 A6
St Paul's St Blackburn BB2 100 D5
Bury BL9 . . . . .32 A3
Clitheroe BB7 . . . . .164 C8
Oswaldtwistle BB5 . . . . . .102 E4
4 Ramsbottom BL0 . . . . .49 C6
Southport PR8 . . . . .34 A6
St Paul's Terr
Clitheroe BB7 . . . . .164 C8
Hoddlesden BB3 . . . . .81 E2
St Paul's Villas BL9 . . . . . .32 A3
St Paul's Wlk **4** FY8 . . . .89 C4
St Pauls Cl PR5 . . . . .75 F7
St Pauls Mans **4** PR4 . .34 A6
St Peter St Blackburn BB2 .100 E4
2 Rishton BB1 . . . . .123 A1
St Peter's & St Paul's
CE Prim Sch BB1 . . . . . .123 A2
St Peter's Ave Formby L37 .11 A4
Haslingden BB4 . . . . .84 B2
St Peter's CE Prim Sch
Accrington BB5 . . . . .103 A2
Burnley BB11 . . . . .127 A6
Chorley PR6 . . . . .60 C2
Darwen BB3 . . . . .64 B8
Formby L37 . . . . .12 A5
Fulwood PR2 . . . . .116 F7
Heysham LA3 . . . . .208 E7
St Peter's Cl Darwen BB3 . .64 B8
Formby L37 . . . . .11 D4
1 Preston PR1 . . . . .95 F8
Salesbury BB1 . . . . .121 D6
St Peter's Pl
Fleetwood FY7 . . . . .194 B4
7 Haslingden BB4 . . . . . .84 B2
St Peter's RC Cath LA1 . .211 A8
St Peter's RC High Sch
WN5 .10 F7
St Peter's RC Inf Sch
BB2 .100 B2
St Peter's RC Jun Sch
BB2 .100 B2
St Peter's RC Prim Sch
Lytham St Anne's FY8 . . . .90 C5
Newchurch BB4 . . . . .85 E2
St Peter's Rd
Lancaster LA1 . . . . .211 A8
Newchurch BB4 . . . . .85 E2
Southport PR8 . . . . .34 A3
St Peter's Sq **8** PR1 . . . .95 E8
St Peter's Sq Chorley PR6 . .60 C1
2 Preston PR1 . . . . .95 F8
St Peters Mews **16** LA1 .211 A8
St Philip St BB10 . . . . . . .147 A1

St Philip's CE Prim Sch
Nelson BB9 . . . . .147 E8
Southport PR8 . . . . .34 C5
St Philip's Rd PR1 . . . . . .117 A2
St Philip's St
Blackburn BB2 . . . . .100 B3
18 Nelson BB9 . . . . .168 E1
St Pius X Prep Sch PR2 .116 E4
St Richards RC Prim Sch
WN8 .17 D1
St Saviour's CE Prim Sch
PR5 . . . . .76 F7
St Saviour's Cl PR5 . . . . . .76 F7
St Saviour's
Com Prim Sch OL13 . . . .70 A8
St Saviour's Cty Prim Sch
OL13 .69 F8
St Saviours Ct BB3 . . . . . .86 F1
St Silas's CE Jun Sch
BB2 .100 B6
St Silas's Rd BB2 . . . . .100 B6
St Stephen's Ave
8 Blackburn BB1 . . . . . . .101 A7
Blackpool FY2 . . . . .150 B2
St Stephen's CE Inf Sch
BB1 .101 B7
St Stephen's CE Jun Sch
BB1 .101 B7
St Stephen's CE
Prim Sch Burnley BB11 .127 B4
Preston PR1 . . . . .95 E6
St Stephen's Rd
9 Blackburn BB1 . . . . . . .101 A7
Hightown L38 . . . . .2 F4
Preston PR1 . . . . .117 A2
Preston PR1 . . . . .117 B2
Standish WN6 . . . . .28 C1
St Stephen's St **4** BB11 .127 B4
St Stephen's Way BB8 . .169 F6
St Stephens Rd PR4 . . . . .112 F4
St Stephens'
CE Prim Sch PR9 . . . . . . .54 A5
St Teresa's Ave FY5 . . . . .172 D1
St Teresa's RC Prim Sch
Cleveleys FY5 . . . . .172 D1
Orrell WN8 . . . . .19 B1
Penwortham PR1 . . . . .95 A5
Preston PR1 . . . . .117 E1
Southport PR8 . . . . .34 A4
St Theodore's
RC High Sch BB10 . . . . .127 B7
St Theresa's Dr PR2 . . . . .116 E4
St Thereses Ct **1** PR4 . .113 C4
St Thomas CE Prim BB1 .101 B5
St Thomas CE Prim
Sch L31 . . . . .5 D4
St Thomas Cl
Haslingden BB4 . . . . .67 A7
Highfurlong FY3 . . . . .151 B1
St Thomas Ct **3** BL9 . . . .32 A2
St Thomas More
Wlk LA1 . . . . .210 D8
St Thomas Rd PR4 . . . . . .113 A4
1 St Thomas St BB1 . . .101 B4
St Thomas the Martyr CE
Prim Sch WN8 . . . . .10 B7
St Thomas' CE Prim Sch
Bury BL9 . . . . .32 B1
Garstang PR3 . . . . .178 B6
Lytham St Anne's FY8 . . . .88 F6
St Thomas' Pl PR1 . . . . . .116 F1
St Thomas' Rd
Lytham St Anne's FY8 . . . .88 F6
Preston PR1 . . . . .117 A2
St Thomas's St PR1 . . . . .116 F1
St Thomas's Ct WN8 . . . .10 C7
St Thomas's Prim Sch
BB9 .168 D3
St Thomas's Rd
Chorley PR7 . . . . .42 C8
Rawtenstall BB4 . . . . .85 A7
St Thomas's Sq **4** PR7 . .42 C8
St Veronica's
RC Prim Sch BB4 . . . . . . .67 B7
St Vincent Ave FY1 . . . . . .129 C3
St Vincent's
RC Prim Sch OL12 . . . . . .51 A1
St Vincent's Way PR8 . . . .34 A4
St Vincents Rd PR2 . . . . . .116 F5
St Walburga's Rd FY3 . . .129 F7
St Walburge Ave PR2 . . . .95 E8
St Walburges Gdns **8**
PR2 . . . . .95 D8
St Wifrid's CE Inf
& Jun Sch FY4 . . . . .130 C1
St Wilfred's CE Jun
& Inf Schs WN6 . . . . .28 F1
St Wilfred's Dr OL12 . . . . .51 D4
St Wilfred's RC Sch PR1 . .95 F7
St Wilfrid St **2** PR1 . . . . .95 F7
St Wilfrid's CE (Lower)
Sch BB2 . . . . .100 D4
St Wilfrid's CE (Upper)
Sch BB2 . . . . .100 D3
St Wilfrid's CE Prim Sch
LA2 .214 E7
St Wilfrid's Pk LA2 . . . . . .214 E7
St Wilfrid's RC Prim Sch
PR3 .139 A8
St Wilfrid's Rd WN6 . . . . .28 F1
St Wilfrid's Terr PR3 . . . .139 A7
St Wilfrid's Way WN6 . . .28 E1
St Williams Prim Sch
PR3 .196 E6
St Wulstan's
RC Prim Sch FY7 . . . . . .193 E3
St Wulston's Prim Sch
BB6 .123 C5

Salcombe Ave FY2 . . . . . .150 F2
Salcombe Dr PR9 . . . . .53 A5
Salcombe Rd FY8 . . . . . . .109 C1
Salem Mews LA3 . . . . .208 E8
Salem St BB4 . . . . .84 B3
Salerno BB11 . . . . .126 C4
Sales's La BL9 . . . . .50 B3
Salesbury CE Prim Sch
BB1 .121 D7
Salesbury View BB1 . . . . .121 F4
Salford BB1 . . . . .100 E5
Salford Ct PR8 . . . . .20 C5
Salford Rd Galgate LA2 . .207 A3
Southport PR8 . . . . .20 C5
Salford St BL9 . . . . .32 A4
Salisbury Ave FY6 . . . . . .194 E5
Salisbury Ct
Knott End-on-S FY6 . . . . .194 E5
Salisbury Rd
Blackpool FY1 . . . . .129 D4
Brinscall PR6,PR7 . . . . .61 F8
Darwen BB3 . . . . .80 E3
Horwich BL6 . . . . .31 F1
Lancaster LA1 . . . . .210 D8
Preston PR1 . . . . .117 B2
Salisbury St **3** Chorley PR7 42 D7
Colne BB8 . . . . .169 E5
Great Harwood BB6 . . . . .123 E6
15 Haslingden BB4 . . . . . .84 B3
5 Preston PR1 . . . . .117 C1
Southport PR9 . . . . .35 A6
Sallowfields WN5 . . . . .10 C5
Sally's La PR9 . . . . .53 B2
Salmesbury Ave FY2 . . . .150 E2
Salmon St PR1 . . . . .96 C7
Salmsbury Hall Cl BL0 . . .49 C4
Salop Ave FY2 . . . . .150 C4
Salt Aire Sports Ctr LA1 .213 C1
Salt Ayre La
Lancaster LA1 . . . . .213 D1
Morecambe LA1 . . . . .213 B2
Salt Marsh Cl FY6 . . . . . .174 B1
Salt Marsh La FY6 . . . . . .174 B1
Salt Pie La LA6 . . . . .238 C2
Salt Pit La L40 . . . . .39 F3
Saltash Rd FY5 . . . . .173 B5
Saltburn St BB12 . . . . .126 B6
Saltcotes Pl FY8 . . . . .90 D7
Saltcotes Rd FY8 . . . . .90 D7
Salter Fell Rd LA1 . . . . . .213 D2
Salter St PR1 . . . . .116 F1
Salterford La BB10 . . . . . .128 A4
Salterforth La
Barnoldswick BB18 . . . . . .200 E2
Salterforth BB18 . . . . .191 D7
Salterforth Prim Sch
BB18 . . . . .191 D8
Salterforth Rd BB18 . . . . .201 A1
Salthill Ind Est BB7 . . . . .187 A2
Salthill View BB7 . . . . . . .186 F1
Salthouse Ave FY1 . . . . . .129 C3
Saltpit La L31 . . . . .5 E1
Salus St BB10 . . . . .147 C5
Salwick Ave FY2 . . . . .150 D5
Salwick Cl PR9 . . . . .52 F5
Salwick Pl
Lytham St Anne's FY8 . . . .89 A8
Preston PR2 . . . . .115 E1
Salwick Rd PR4 . . . . .134 B3
Salwick Sta PR4 . . . . .114 C5
Sambourn Fold PR8 . . . . .20 A5
Samlesbury Aerodrome
BB2,PR5 . . . . .119 F3
Samlesbury CE Prim Sch
PR5 .118 D3
Samuel St Bury BL9 . . . . . .32 A3
Preston PR1 . . . . .96 D8
Sand Beds La BL0,BB4 . . .68 B5
Sand La LA5 . . . . .217 C4
Sandbank Gdns OL12 . . . .70 C2
Sandbeds La LA2 . . . . .232 A8
Sandbrook Gdns WN5 . . .10 D5
Sandbrook Rd Orrell WN5 . .10 C5
Southport PR8 . . . . .20 D4
Sandbrook Way PR8 . . . . .20 C3
Sandcastle (L Pool) FY4 .109 A8
Sanderling Cl FY5 . . . . . . .150 F8
Sanderling Rd L33 . . . . .1 A3
Sanders Gr LA4 . . . . .212 D4
Sanderson La PR7 . . . . . . .27 A8
Sanderson St **9** BB3 . . . .32 A3
Sandersons Way FY4 . . . .109 F8
Sandfield **4** FY5 . . . . .173 A2
Sandfield Cotts L39 . . . . . .15 D2
Sandfield Ho **6** LA1 . . . .211 A3
Sandfield Pk L39 . . . . .15 D2
Sandfield Rd OL13 . . . . . . .87 A1
Sandfield St **11** PR5 . . . .76 B1
Sandford Dr L31 . . . . .5 D2
Sandford Rd WN5 . . . . .10 D5
Sandgate Blackpool FY4 . .109 D5
Chorley PR7 . . . . .42 D6
Lytham St Anne's FY8 . . . .88 C7
Sandham St **7** PR6 . . . . .42 D8
Sandheys Dr PR9 . . . . .52 F1
Sandhill St BB3 . . . . .64 B5
Sandhills L38 . . . . .2 F3
Sandhills Ave FY4 . . . . . . .109 B5
Sandhills Cl BB18 . . . . . . .191 E8
Sandholme La PR3 . . . . . .179 A4
Sandholme Villas BB18 . .201 A1
Sandhurst Ave
Blackpool FY2 . . . . .150 C5

Sandhurst Ave continued
Lytham St Anne's FY8 . . . .**88** E7
Sandhurst Cl Formby L37 . .**11** C1
 ⑧ Kirkham PR4 . . . .**112** F5
Sandhurst Ct FY8 . . . .**88** D6
Sandhurst St BB11 . . . .**127** B6
Sandhurst Way L31 . . . .**5** B5
Sandicroft Ave FY6 . . . .**174** C1
Sandicroft Pl FY6 . . . .**195** B4
Sandicroft Rd FY1 . . . .**150** C1
Sandilands Gr L38 . . . .**2** E1
Sandiway Ct PR9 . . . .**34** E8
Sandiway Dr BB10 . . . .**147** F3
Sandiways L31 . . . .**5** E1
Sandiways Cl FY5 . . . .**151** C8
Sandon Pl FY4 . . . .**109** C4
Sandon Rd PR8 . . . .**33** F1
Sandon St Blackburn BB2 . .**100** C3
 Darwen BB3 . . . .**81** B2
Sandon Terr BB2 . . . .**100** C3
Sandown Cl PR4 . . . .**112** E5
Sandown Ct
 ⑧ Preston PR1 . . . .**96** A7
 ① Southport PR9 . . . .**34** C8
Sandown Rd
 Haslingden BB4 . . . .**84** C2
 Lancaster LA1 . . . .**211** B3
 Thornton FY5 . . . .**173** B1
Sandpiper Cl
 Blackburn BB1 . . . .**100** F6
 Normoss FY3 . . . .**130** B6
Sandpiper Ct FY5 . . . .**172** C2
Sandpiper Pl ⑩ FY5 . . . . . .**172** F1
Sandpiper Sq ⑦ BB11 . . . .**126** C5
Sandridge Ave PR7 . . . .**42** B7
Sandridge Pl FY4 . . . .**109** B4
Sandringham Ave
 Leyland PR5 . . . .**76** C1
 Thornton FY5 . . . .**173** B1
Sandringham Cl
 Adlington PR7 . . . .**29** E6
 ⑤ Barrowford BB9 . . . .**168** C1
 Blackburn BB1 . . . .**121** E1
 Tarleton PR4 . . . .**56** A6
Sandringham Ct
 Lytham St Anne's FY8 . . . .**89** D4
 Morecambe LA4 . . . .**212** D4
 Southport PR8 . . . .**34** B8
Sandringham Dr
 Brinscall PR6 . . . .**61** F8
 Ramsbottom BL8 . . . .**49** A1
Sandringham Gr ⑨ BB4 . .**84** A1
Sandringham Park Dr
 PR4 . . . .**75** A8
Sandringham Rd
 Bamber Bridge PR5 . . . .**96** D3
 Chorley PR7 . . . .**42** B8
 Darwen BB3 . . . .**80** E4
 Eccleston PR7 . . . .**40** C7
 Formby L37 . . . .**11** E1
 Horwich BL6 . . . .**31** E2
 Lytham St Anne's FY8 . . . .**89** A5
 Morecambe LA4 . . . .**212** D4
 Southport PR8 . . . .**33** C3
 Southport, Ainsdale PR8 . . . .**20** C5
Sandringham Way PR4 . . .**115** E6
Sands Cl BB1 . . . .**123** B2
Sands Rd BB1 . . . .**123** B2
Sands The BB7 . . . .**143** C5
Sands Way FY1 . . . .**129** C3
Sandsdale Ave PR2 . . . .**117** C5
Sandside Dr LA4 . . . .**212** F3
Sandside Rd LA5,LA7 . . . . .**237** D3
Sandwich Cl BB1 . . . .**101** C4
Sandwick Cl PR2 . . . .**116** E7
Sandy Bank Rd BL7 . . . .**47** D5
Sandy Cl FY5 . . . .**172** C3
Sandy Gate La PR4 . . . . . .**136** B2
Sandy La Accrington BB5 . . .**103** E5
 Adlington PR7 . . . .**29** E5
 Barrowford BB9 . . . .**168** C2
 Bispham Green L40 . . . .**38** F2
 Blackpool FY1 . . . .**110** A4
 Brindle PR5,PR6 . . . .**78** C6
 Brinscall PR6 . . . .**61** E8
 Clayton Green PR6 . . . .**77** C3
 Darwen BB3 . . . .**80** E6
 Fleetwood FY7 . . . .**172** D7
 Hambleton FY6 . . . .**174** C1
 Hightown L38 . . . .**3** A3
 Holmeswood L40 . . . .**37** D5
 Holmeswood L40 . . . .**37** E5
 Leyland PR5 . . . .**59** A8
 Lower Bartle PR4 . . . .**115** D7
 Maghull, Holt Green L39 . . . . .**6** B6
 Maghull, Lydiate L31 . . . .**5** C5
 Mawdesley L40 . . . .**39** A1
 Newburgh WN8 . . . .**25** F1
 Ormskirk L40 . . . .**16** D7
 Orrell WN5 . . . .**10** D4
 Out Rawcliffe PR3 . . . .**175** F1
 Pleasington BB2 . . . .**99** C2
 Preesall FY6 . . . .**195** B4
 Skelmersdale WN8 . . . .**17** D1
 Sollom L40 . . . .**38** A8
 Thorpe Green PR6 . . . .**77** E4
Sandy La Ctr WN8 . . . .**17** C1
Sandy Pl ⑧ PR5 . . . .**59** A8
Sandy Way L40 . . . .**37** D4
Sandybeds Cl BB5 . . . .**103** D2
Sandybrook Cl PR2 . . . .**117** E5
Sandycroft PR2 . . . .**117** F2
Sandyfields BB5 . . . .**115** E6
Sandyforth Ave FY5 . . . . . .**173** B3

Sandyforth La PR4 . . . .**116** A8
Sandygate BB11 . . . .**126** F6
Sandyhall La BB9 . . . .**168** A2
Sandylands Arc LA3 . . . . . .**212** A3
Sandylands
 Com Prim Sch LA3 . . . .**212** B3
Sandylands Ct LA3 . . . .**212** B4
Sandylands Prom LA3 . . . .**212** A3
Sanfield Cl L39 . . . .**15** E6
Sangara Dr BB3 . . . .**80** F7
Sangness Dr PR8 . . . .**34** E3
Sanson Ct PR4 . . . .**113** A7
Sanvino Ave PR8 . . . .**20** D5
Sapphire St BB1 . . . .**121** F1
Sarah La PR5 . . . .**56** F5
Sarah St Bacup OL13 . . . .**70** C8
 Darwen BB3 . . . .**81** B1
 Edenfield BL0 . . . .**67** E3
Sarahs Fold FY6 . . . .**174** C7
Sarmatian Fold PR3 . . . . . .**140** D3
Sarscow La PR5 . . . .**57** E2
Saswick Ct PR4 . . . .**133** B7
Saul St PR1 . . . .**95** F8
Saul's Dr LA5 . . . .**218** A8
Saunder Bank BB11 . . . .**127** A5
Saunders Cl BB4 . . . .**85** A7
Saunders Height La BB4 . . .**85** E3
Saunders Mews PR7 . . . .**42** C3
Saunders Rd BB2 . . . .**100** C5
Saunders St PR9 . . . .**52** C1
Saunders' La Hutton PR4 . . . .**94** D2
 Hutton PR4 . . . .**94** E1
Savick Ave PR2 . . . .**115** D1
Savick Cl PR5 . . . .**76** F8
Savick Ct PR2 . . . .**116** D4
Savick Cty Prim Sch PR2 .**115** E2
Savick Rd PR2 . . . .**116** D4
Savick Way PR2 . . . .**115** D3
Saville Ave FY6 . . . .**151** B6
Saville Rd Blackpool FY1 . .**129** C1
 Maghull L31 . . . .**5** C3
Saville St PR7 . . . .**42** C5
Savon Hook L37 . . . .**12** B1
Savoy Ave LA3 . . . .**212** F3
Savoy Cl PR5 . . . .**76** F8
Savoy St Accrington BB5 . . .**102** F5
 ④ Preston PR1 . . . .**95** E7
Sawdon Ave PR8 . . . .**34** E3
Sawley Abbey BB7 . . . .**224** C1
Sawley Ave
 Accrington BB5 . . . .**103** D7
 Blackpool FY4 . . . .**109** D5
 Lytham St Anne's FY8 . . . .**89** C6
 Read BB12 . . . .**144** D1
Sawley Cl BB3 . . . .**64** C8
Sawley Cres PR2 . . . .**117** F2
Sawley Dr BB6 . . . .**123** F5
Sawley Rd Chatburn BB7 . . .**187** E6
 Grindleton BB7 . . . .**187** C8
 Sawley BB7 . . . .**224** C1
Sawmills Ind Est FY1 . . . . .**129** D6
Sawrey Cl BB5 . . . .**123** E2
Sawthorpe Wlk FY6 . . . . . .**151** B3
Sawrey Gr FY4 . . . .**129** F1
Saxby Gr FY4 . . . .**129** F1
Saxenholme PR8 . . . .**33** F5
Saxifield St BB10 . . . .**147** E3
Saxon Cl
 Oswaldtwistle BB5 . . . .**102** C5
 Thornton FY5 . . . .**151** C8
Saxon Hey PR2 . . . .**116** C3
Saxon Hts LA3 . . . .**208** F5
Saxon Rd PR8 . . . .**33** F5
Saxon St BB10 . . . .**127** A7
Scafell Ave LA4 . . . .**212** G5
Scafell Cl BB12 . . . .**126** C8
Scafell Rd Lancaster LA1 . .**214** D2
 Lytham St Anne's FY8 . . . . . .**110** A2
Scaffold La L38 . . . .**3** D4
Scaitcliffe St BB5 . . . .**103** B5
Scale Farm Rd LA1 . . . .**213** C2
Scale Hall La
 Lancaster LA1 . . . .**213** D2
 Newton-with-S PR4 . . . .**114** A2
Scaleber La LA6 . . . .**238** D4
Scar St BB2 . . . .**100** B3
Scarborough Rd
 Blackburn BB2 . . . .**101** A1
 Lytham St Anne's FY8 . . . . . .**110** A1
Scargill Rd LA5,LA6 . . . . . .**216** F1
Scarisbrick Ave
 Parbold WN8 . . . .**26** C2
 Southport PR8 . . . .**34** A7
Scarisbrick Cl L31 . . . .**5** E3
Scarisbrick Ct PR8 . . . .**34** C6
Scarisbrick Cty Prim Sch
 L40 . . . .**23** A3
Scarisbrick New Rd PR8 . .**34** D5
Scarisbrick Pk L40 . . . .**23** A4
Scarisbrick St Ormskirk L39 .**15** E6
 Southport PR9 . . . .**34** B7
Scarlet St PR6 . . . .**42** E7
Scarlett St BB11 . . . .**126** E5
Scarr Dr OL12 . . . .**51** F3
Scarr La BB2 . . . .**100** A6
Scarsdale Ave FY4 . . . .**109** C5
Scarth Hill La L39,L40 . . . . .**16** A2
Scarth La BB12 . . . .**125** B5
Scarth Pk WN8 . . . .**9** C7
Scawfell Rd PR7 . . . .**42** B5
Sceptre Way PR5 . . . .**77** B6
Schleswig St PR1 . . . .**96** A8
Schleswig Way PR5 . . . .**75** C1
Schofield Ave FY3 . . . .**130** B7
Schofield Cl BB4 . . . .**84** F2
Schofield Rd BB4 . . . .**84** F2
Schofield St Darwen BB3 . . . .**80** F2
 Haslingden BB4 . . . .**67** A6

Schofield St continued
 Rawtenstall BB4 . . . .**68** E8
Schola Green La
 Morecambe LA4 . . . .**212** E4
 Morecambe LA4 . . . .**212** E5
Scholars Gn PR2 . . . .**115** C1
Scholefield Ave BB9 . . . . . .**147** E5
Scholefield La BB9 . . . .**147** F5
Scholes Bank BL6 . . . .**31** A5
Scholes St BB3 . . . .**80** F2
Scholey Head La BB10 . . . .**107** A8
School Ave L37 . . . .**11** F3
School Brow PR6 . . . .**60** B7
School Cl Skelmersdale L39 . .**15** C1
 Southport PR8 . . . .**34** B2
School Cotts PR3 . . . .**179** E8
School Ct Egerton BL7 . . . . . .**46** E2
 Ramsbottom BL0 . . . .**67** D2
School Field PR5 . . . .**77** B5
School Fields BB18 . . . .**201** B3
School Hillocks Cotts ④
 PR5 . . . .**76** A8
School House Gn L39 . . . . . .**15** F5
School House Gr L40 . . . .**24** D5
School House La BB5 . . . . . .**103** B1
School House Mews ⑦
 PR6 . . . .**42** E7
School La
 Bamber Bridge PR5 . . . .**96** F2
 Blackburn BB1 . . . .**81** D8
 Brinscall PR6,PR7 . . . .**61** E8
 Burnley BB11 . . . .**127** A7
 Burscough Bridge L40 . . . . . .**24** F5
 Catforth PR4 . . . .**135** A4
 Earby BB18 . . . .**201** B2
 Edgworth BL7 . . . .**47** D8
 Euxton PR7 . . . .**59** D3
 Farington PR5 . . . .**75** F7
 Formby L37 . . . .**11** F3
 Forton LA2,PR3 . . . .**204** B3
 Freckleton PR4 . . . .**92** C7
 Hammerton Mere BB7 . . . . . .**229** E3
 Haskayne L39 . . . .**13** F4
 Inskip PR4 . . . .**155** D1
 Kirkham PR4 . . . .**113** B5
 Laneshaw Bridge BB8 . . . . . .**170** E6
 Leyland PR5 . . . .**76** A1
 Leyland, Moss Side PR5 . . . . .**58** A8
 Longton PR4 . . . .**74** A8
 Lytham St Anne's FY8 . . . .**90** A3
 Maghull L31 . . . .**6** A1
 Mawdesley L40 . . . .**39** C1
 Mereclough BB10 . . . .**128** A1
 Newton-with-S PR4 . . . .**114** A2
 Ollerton Fold PR6 . . . .**78** F4
 Orrell, Roby Mill WN8 . . . . . .**19** B3
 Orrell, Up Holland WN5,WN8 .**10** C7
 Out Rawcliffe PR3 . . . .**175** F2
 Pilling PR3 . . . .**196** C6
 Preesall FY6 . . . .**195** B3
 Simonstone BB12 . . . .**144** F1
 Skelmersdale,
  Pennylands WN8 . . . .**17** E1
 Standish WN6 . . . .**28** D1
 Westhead L40 . . . .**16** E3
 Winmarleigh PR3 . . . .**198** F6
 Wray LA2 . . . .**206** D6
School Rd Blackpool FY4 . . .**110** B5
 Heysham LA3 . . . .**208** E2
 Hightown L38 . . . .**2** F7
 Thornton FY5 . . . .**151** C8
School St Accrington BB5 . .**103** B6
 Bacup OL13 . . . .**69** B8
 Bamber Bridge PR5 . . . .**96** F2
 Bury BL9 . . . .**32** B1
 Colne BB8 . . . .**169** D4
 Darwen BB3 . . . .**81** A1
 Great Harwood BB6 . . . .**123** C4
 Horwich BL6 . . . .**31** C3
 Kelbrook BB18 . . . .**192** A6
 Leyland PR5 . . . .**76** B2
 Nelson BB9 . . . .**147** C8
 Preston PR1 . . . .**95** E7
 Ramsbottom BL0 . . . .**49** B5
 Rawtenstall BB4 . . . .**85** A8
 Rishton BB1 . . . .**123** B1
 Walmer Bridge PR4 . . . .**73** F5
 Whitewell Bottom BB4 . . . . . .**85** F4
School Terr
 Salterforth BB18 . . . .**191** D8
 Whitworth OL12 . . . .**70** D1
School View BL7 . . . .**47** D8
School Villas LA2 . . . .**207** B5
Schoolfold PR4 . . . .**72** E4
Schoolhouse Fold BB11 . . .**125** C3
Schoolhouse La LA2 . . . . . .**214** F7
Schwartzman Dr PR9 . . . . . .**54** A6
Scorton Ave FY3 . . . .**129** F7
Scorton Hall Pk PR3 . . . . . .**199** E6
Scotch Green La PR3 . . . . .**158** A6
Scotforth CE Prim Sch
 LA1 . . . .**211** A4
Scotforth Ct ① LA1 . . . . . .**211** A3
Scotforth Rd
 Lancaster LA1 . . . .**211** A4
 Preston PR1 . . . .**96** C8
Scotland Bank Terr BB2 . .**80** C8
Scotland La BL9 . . . .**32** D8
Scotland Pl ⑪ BL0 . . . .**49** C6
Scotland Rd Carnforth LA5 .**217** E3
 ⑧ Nelson BB9 . . . .**147** D8
 ⑯ Nelson BB9 . . . .**168** D1
Scotshaw Brook Ind Est
 BB2 . . . .**80** E7
Scotswood Ave FY4 . . . . . .**109** D6
Scott Ave Accrington BB5 . .**103** E2
 Morecambe LA4 . . . .**212** C3
 Simonstone BB12 . . . .**144** E2

Scott Cl Blackpool FY4 . . . .**109** F8
 Maghull L31 . . . .**5** D1
 Oswaldtwistle BB5 . . . .**102** D5
Scott Dr L39 . . . .**15** F7
Scott Gr LA4 . . . .**212** D4
Scott Laithe La BB7 . . . . . .**224** E3
Scott Mews FY7 . . . .**109** F8
Scott Park Rd BB11 . . . .**126** E4
Scott Rd LA3 . . . .**212** C3
Scott St Clayton-le-M BB5 . .**123** F3
 Nelson BB9 . . . .**168** D1
 Padiham BB12 . . . .**125** F7
 Southport PR9 . . . .**35** A7
Scott's Terr BB11 . . . .**126** D6
Scott's Wood PR2 . . . .**116** D7
Scout Rd Edenfield BL0 . . . . .**68** A2
 Egerton BL7 . . . .**46** B1
 Newchurch BB4 . . . .**85** F3
Scow Croft La PR6,PR7 . . . .**61** C4
Scowcroft Dr LA4 . . . .**213** A5
Scriffen La LA2 . . . .**207** D3
Scudamore Cres ⑥ FY4 . .**129** D1
Sea View Lancaster LA1 . . .**211** A5
 Longridge PR3 . . . .**159** D2
 Walmer Bridge PR4 . . . .**73** F5
Sea View Cl LA2 . . . .**213** D8
Sea View Dr LA2 . . . .**213** D8
Sea Wall FY7 . . . .**193** C3
Seabank Rd
 Fleetwood FY7 . . . .**194** A5
 Southport PR9 . . . .**34** B8
Seaborn Gr LA4 . . . .**212** G6
Seaborn Rd LA4 . . . .**212** G6
Seabourne Ave FY4 . . . . . .**109** B7
Seabrook Dr FY5 . . . .**150** E8
Seacrest Ave FY1 . . . .**129** C8
Seacroft Cres PR9 . . . .**53** B5
Seafield L37 . . . .**12** A2
Seafield Rd Blackpool FY1 .**129** C8
 Lytham St Anne's FY8 . . . .**89** F3
 Southport PR8 . . . .**20** C6
Seafore Cl L31 . . . .**5** B4
Sealand Ave L37 . . . .**11** E2
Sealand Cl L37 . . . .**11** D2
Seascale Cl BB2 . . . .**101** A1
Seaside Way FY1 . . . .**129** B3
Seathwaite Ave
 Blackpool FY4 . . . .**130** C1
 Morecambe LA3 . . . .**212** B2
Seathwaite Way BB5 . . . . .**103** E8
Seaton Ave FY5 . . . .**172** E4
Seaton Pl WN8 . . . .**17** E3
Seaton Way PR9 . . . .**53** A5
Seattle Ave FY2 . . . .**150** E2
Seaview Way FY7 . . . .**194** B3
Seawell Ave LA3 . . . .**212** A2
Second Ave Blackpool FY4 .**109** C7
 Bury BL9 . . . .**32** D4
 Church BB5 . . . .**103** A8
Second Terr LA3 . . . .**205** B4
Sedberg St PR2 . . . .**116** D3
Sedbergh Ave FY4 . . . .**129** F1
Sedbergh Cl BB5 . . . .**103** D5
Sedburgh St BB10 . . . .**147** C2
Seddon Pl WN8 . . . .**17** E3
Sedge Ct LA3 . . . .**212** E2
Sedgefield PR4 . . . .**73** E8
Sedgeley Mews PR4 . . . .**92** A6
Sedgfield Cl FY4 . . . .**109** F6
Sedgley Ave PR4 . . . .**92** A6
Sedgwick St PR1 . . . .**117** A1
Sedwell Cl FY4 . . . .**89** F4
Seed St Blackpool FY1 . . . . .**129** C6
 Preston PR1 . . . .**95** F8
Seedall Ave BB7 . . . .**164** D7
Seedhill Terr ⑬ BB9 . . . . . .**168** D1
Seedlee Rd PR5 . . . .**77** A6
Sefton Ave
 ④ Burnley BB11 . . . .**126** E5
 Orrell WN5 . . . .**10** D5
 Poulton-le-F FY6 . . . .**151** D1
Sefton Cl Darwen BB3 . . . . . .**64** C6
 Enfield BB5 . . . .**124** A3
 Orrell WN5 . . . .**10** D5
Sefton Ct FY8 . . . .**88** D7
 Lancaster LA1 . . . .**213** D2
Sefton Dr Bury BL9 . . . .**32** A6
 Lancaster LA1 . . . .**213** D2
Sefton Gdns L39 . . . .**6** D7
Sefton La BL6 . . . .**31** D1
Sefton Rd
 Bamber Bridge PR5 . . . .**96** D3
 Formby L37 . . . .**11** C2
 Lytham St Anne's FY8 . . . .**88** F7
 Morecambe LA3 . . . .**212** B3
 Orrell WN5 . . . .**10** D5
Sefton St Brierfield BB9 . . .**147** B5
 Colne BB8 . . . .**169** F5
 Southport PR8 . . . .**34** C5
Sefton Terr ⑱ BB11 . . . . . .**126** E5
Sefton View WN5 . . . .**10** D5
Segar St
 ⑰ Great Harwood BB6 . . . .**123** C5
 Kirkham PR4 . . . .**112** F6
Segar's La PR8, L39 . . . .**20** E4
Selborne Mews BB2 . . . . . .**101** C2
Selborne St Blackburn BB2 .**100** B3
 Preston PR1 . . . .**96** B6
Selbourne BB18 . . . .**201** C2
Selbourne Rd FY1 . . . .**129** D6
Selby Ave Blackpool FY4 . . .**109** D5
 Cleveleys FY5 . . . .**172** F4
 ② Lancaster LA1 . . . .**213** F4
Selby Cl BB5 . . . .**103** E3
Selby Dr L37 . . . .**12** B2
Selby Pl WN8 . . . .**17** D2
Selby Rd PR4 . . . .**112** F5
Selby St Colne BB8 . . . .**169** C5
 Nelson BB9 . . . .**147** E7

Selby St continued
 Preston PR1 . . . .**116** D1
Seldon St ⑪ Colne BB8 . . . .**169** D4
 ⑮ Nelson BB9 . . . .**168** E1
Selkirk Cl ⑥ BB1 . . . .**101** A4
Selkirk Dr PR5 . . . .**96** D2
Selkirk St BB11 . . . .**126** D4
Sellers St PR1 . . . .**117** C1
Selous Rd BB2 . . . .**100** B3
Selside Dr LA4 . . . .**212** E3
Selworthy Rd
 Blackpool FY4 . . . .**33** D3
 Southport PR8 . . . .**33** E3
Senior Ave FY4 . . . .**129** F1
Seniors Dr FY5 . . . .**172** F3
Sephton Dr L39 . . . .**15** F7
Sephton St ⑦ PR5 . . . .**76** A8
Sergeant St PR5 . . . .**76** F8
Serpentine Rd BB11 . . . . . .**126** F4
Serpentine The
 ⑧ Lytham St Anne's FY8 . . . .**90** A3
 Ormskirk L39 . . . .**6** D8
Sett End Rd BB1 . . . .**101** C1
Settle La BB7 . . . .**225** B7
Settle Pl FY8 . . . .**89** C7
Settle Terr BB10 . . . .**147** C2
Seven Acres PR5 . . . .**77** C5
Seven Hos BB1 . . . .**101** D4
Seven Sands PR4 . . . .**94** A1
Seven Stars Prim Sch
 PR5 . . . .**58** D7
Seven Stars Rd PR5 . . . .**58** D7
Seven Trees Ave BB1 . . . . .**101** A8
Sevenoaks PR7 . . . .**42** C4
Sevenoaks Ave PR8 . . . .**20** B5
Sevenoaks Dr FY5 . . . .**150** F8
Seventh Ave FY4 . . . .**109** C6
Severn Ave FY4 . . . .**172** D8
Severn Dr PR5 . . . .**96** D2
Severn Hill PR2 . . . .**116** C8
Severn Ho ⑩ PR1 . . . .**96** D8
Severn Rd FY4 . . . .**109** B7
Severn St PR3 . . . .**139** A7
Seville Ct FY8 . . . .**89** D3
Seymour Ave LA3 . . . .**208** F7
Seymour Ct PR1 . . . .**116** D2
Seymour Dr L31 . . . .**5** E3
Seymour Gr LA3 . . . .**208** F7
Seymour Rd
 Blackpool FY1 . . . .**129** C2
 Fulwood PR2 . . . .**116** C3
 Lytham St Anne's FY8 . . . .**89** D4
Seymour St Chorley PR6 . . . .**42** E8
 ② Fleetwood FY7 . . . .**193** F4
 ⑤ Lancaster LA1 . . . .**211** A8
Shacklady Rd L33 . . . .**1** A4
Shackleton Rd PR4 . . . .**113** B2
Shackleton St
 Burnley BB10 . . . .**127** B8
 Cornholme OL14 . . . .**108** C1
Shade Row FY5 . . . .**195** B3
Shadsworth Cl BB1 . . . .**101** C4
Shadsworth Cty Inf Sch
 BB1 . . . .**101** D4
Shadsworth Cty Jun Sch
 BB1 . . . .**101** C2
Shadsworth Rd BB1 . . . . . .**101** C3
Shady La Clayton-le-W PR5 .**76** E3
 Hest Bank LA2 . . . .**213** E8
Shaftesbury Ave
 Blackpool FY2 . . . .**150** C2
 Burnley BB11 . . . .**126** F3
 Cleveleys FY5 . . . .**172** D5
 Darwen BB3 . . . .**80** E3
 Great Harwood BB6 . . . .**123** E6
 New Longton PR4 . . . .**74** F8
 Normoss FY3 . . . .**130** B6
 Penwortham PR1 . . . .**95** B6
 Southport PR8 . . . .**21** A8
Shaftesbury Cl FY8 . . . .**89** D5
Shaftesbury Ct FY2 . . . . . .**150** C2
Shaftesbury Gr PR8 . . . .**34** A1
Shaftesbury Pl Chorley PR7 **42** B8
 Lancaster LA1 . . . .**210** F1
Shaftesbury Rd PR8 . . . .**34** A1
Shakeshaft St ⑪ BB1 . . . . .**101** A4
Shakespeare Ave BB6 . . . .**123** B4
Shakespeare Prim Sch
 FY7 . . . .**193** E4
Shakespeare Rd
 Fleetwood FY7 . . . .**193** E4
 Lancaster LA1 . . . .**213** C4
 Preston PR1 . . . .**117** D1
Shakespeare St
 Padiham BB12 . . . .**125** D7
 Southport PR8 . . . .**34** B5
Shakespeare Terr PR6 . . . . .**60** D2
Shakespeare Way BB2 . . . .**100** C3
Shalbourn Rd FY8 . . . .**89** A4
Shale St BB12 . . . .**126** D6
Shalgrove Field PR2 . . . . . .**116** C7
Shannon Sq BB10 . . . .**147** C2
Shannon St FY1 . . . .**129** B3
Shap Cl Accrington BB5 . . . .**103** E3
 Barrowford BB9 . . . .**168** C4
Shap Ct FY7 . . . .**193** D1
Shap Gr BB10 . . . .**147** A3
Shard La FY6 . . . .**152** B8
Shard Rd FY6 . . . .**152** B6
Sharley Fold PR3 . . . .**139** B7
Sharman Rd FY8 . . . .**109** F1
Sharneyford
 Cty Prim Sch OL13 . . . . . .**87** C5
Sharoe Bay Ct PR2 . . . .**116** F6
Sharoe Green Hospl PR2 .**116** F4
Sharoe Green La PR2 . . . . .**116** F7
Sharoe Green Pk PR2 . . . . .**117** A5
Sharoe Mount Ave PR2 . .**116** F7

Sharow Gr FY1 ....129 D3
Sharp St
 1 Barrowford BB9 .....168 D3
 Burnley BB10 ....147 B1
Sharpe's Ave LA1 ....211 A5
Sharpes Mill LA1 ....210 F7
Sharples Gn BL7 ....47 D6
Sharples Mdw BL7 ....47 D6
Sharples St
 Accrington BB5 ....102 F5
 Blackburn BB2 ....100 D3
Sharrats Path PR7 ....41 F4
Sharrock St 7 PR8 ......34 B7
Shaw Bridge St 3 BB7 .164 F8
Shaw Brook Cl BB1 .....102 A8
Shaw Brook Rd PR5 .....58 E6
Shaw Brow PR6 ....60 D5
Shaw Cl Blackburn BB2 .100 D5
 Shirdley Hill L39 ....22 A6
Shaw Clough Rd BB4 .....85 F3
Shaw Clough St BB4 .....85 F3
Shaw Cres L37 ....12 B3
Shaw Gn LA7 ....237 F5
Shaw Hill PR6 ....60 B7
Shaw Hill Dr PR6 ....60 B6
Shaw Hill Golf Course
 PR6 ....60 B6
Shaw Hill St PR7 ....42 C7
Shaw La Cornholme OL14 .108 C3
 Haskayne L39 ....13 E6
 Nether Kellet LA6 ......216 F4
 Storth LA7 ....237 F5
Shaw Rd Blackpool FY1 .129 D5
 Horwich BL6 ....31 B5
Shaw Sq 4 BB18 ....201 B2
Shaw St Blackburn BB2 .100 D5
 Bury BL9 ....32 B3
 Colne BB8 ....169 D4
 Haslingden BB4 ....84 B6
 2 Lancaster LA1 ....211 A8
 1 Preston PR1 ....117 A1
Shaw's Ave PR8 ....34 A1
Shaw's La PR3 ....196 A3
Shaw's Rd PR8 ....34 A1
Shawbridge Ct BB7 .....164 F8
Shawbrook Cl PR7 ....59 C5
Shawbury Cl BL6 ....30 D1
Shawcliffe La BB6,BB7 .143 B2
Shawclough Cl OL12 .....51 D3
Shawclough
 Com Prim Sch OL12 ....51 D3
Shawclough Dr OL12 .....51 D3
Shawclough Rd OL12 .....51 C3
Shawclough Way OL12 ....51 D3
Shawes Dr PR6 ....30 C7
Shawfield 4 BB4 ....84 F1
Shawfield La OL12 ....51 A2
Shaws Garth L39 ....22 A6
Shay Head Cotts BB8 ...192 E1
Shay La Longridge PR3 .138 F6
 Slaidburn BB7 ....223 B7
Shay The 8 FY5 ....150 F7
Shays Dr BB7 ....165 A7
Shear Bank Cl BB1 .....100 D6
Shear Bank Gdns BB1 ..100 D6
Shear Bank Rd BB1 ....100 D7
Shear Brow BB1 ....100 D7
Shearwater Dr BB1 .....100 F6
Shed St Colne BB8 ......169 C4
 Oswaldtwistle BB5 ......102 D3
 Whitworth OL12 ....70 D1
Sheddon Gr BB10 ....127 E5
Sheep Gap OL12 ....51 B1
Sheep Gn BB4 ....84 B3
Sheep Hill Brow PR6 ....77 A3
Sheep Hill La
 Clayton Green PR6 ......77 A3
 Clayton Green PR6 ......77 B3
 Clayton-le-W PR5 ....76 F2
Sheep House La BL6 .....44 A3
Sheephill La PR4 ....75 A7
Sheffield Dr PR2 ....115 D1
Sheldon Ave WN6 ....28 E2
Sheldon Ct 1 BB1 .....116 F1
Shelfield La BB10 ......148 F7
Shelfield Rd BB9 ....169 B1
Shelley Cl Bolton-le-S LA5 .216 A5
 Coppull PR7 ....28 F8
Shelley Dr Accrington BB5 .103 E2
 Ormskirk L39 ....15 D6
Shelley Gdns BB6 ......123 B4
Shelley Gr Cleveleys FY5 .150 D8
 Darwen BB3 ....81 C1
 Southport PR8 ....34 F6
Shelley Mews PR2 ......116 C1
Shelley Rd PR2 ....116 C2
Shelley Row PR3 ....178 C2
Shellfield Rd PR9 ....53 A4
Shellingford Cl WN6 .....19 D7
Shelly Dr PR4 ....40 D5
Shelton Dr PR4 ....20 A4
Shenley Way PR9 ....53 D5
Shenstone Rd FY3 ......129 F7
Shepherd Dr FY8 ....89 A7
Shepherd Rd N FY8 .....89 A8
Shepherd St Bacup OL13 .86 F3
 Bury BL9 ....32 A1
 Darwen BB3 ....64 A7
 7 Lytham St Anne's FY8 .90 B3
 Preston PR1 ....96 A7
Shepherd's Ave PR3 ....178 D4
Shepherd's La BB3 ......64 A7
Shepherds Cl Blackrod BL6 .30 C3
 Ramsbottom BL8 ....48 F1
Shepherds Way PR6 .....42 D8
Sheppard St FY1 ....129 B4
Sheraton Pk PR1 ....116 A6
Sherborne Lodge 9 PR2 .117 F4

Sherbourne Cl FY6 .....151 C5
Sherbourne Cres PR1 ...117 B3
Sherbourne Ct FY6 .....151 C5
Sherbourne Rd
 Accrington BB5 ....103 E3
 Blackpool FY1 ....129 C8
 Hambleton FY6 ....174 C2
Sherbourne St 5 PR6 ...42 D7
Sherburn Rd PR1 ....95 E3
Sherburn Sch PR1 ......117 A1
Sherburne Ave 4 PR4 .112 F5
Sherdley Rd PR5 ....76 B7
Sherfin Nook BB5 ....84 B7
Sherfin Side BB5 ....84 B7
Sheridan Rd BB8 ....170 D6
Sheridan St Burnley BB10 .147 E2
 4 Nelson BB9 ....168 F2
Sheriff St OL12 ....51 E1
Sheringham Ave FY5 ...150 D7
Sheringham Way FY6 ...151 E3
Sherrat St WN8 ....17 D1
Sherringham Rd PR8 ....33 E2
Sherwood Ave
 Blackpool FY3 ....129 E8
 Ormskirk L39 ....15 C2
Sherwood Ct BB10 .....127 C5
Sherwood Cty Prim
 Sch PR2 ....117 A7
Sherwood Dr WN8 ....18 D3
Sherwood Ho PR8 ....20 C5
Sherwood Lo PR8 ....33 F5
Sherwood Pl Chorley PR6 .42 D8
 2 Cleveleys FY5 ......172 F1
Sherwood Rd
 Blackburn BB1 ....101 B3
 Lytham St Anne's FY8 ...89 C6
Sherwood Way
 Enfield BB5 ....124 A1
 Fulwood PR2 ....117 A7
Shetland Cl Blackburn BB1 101 C3
 Wilpshire BB1 ....121 F7
Shetland Rd FY1 ....129 C2
Shevington
 Com Prim Sch WN6 .....19 E8
Shevington Cswy PR5 ...57 B2
Shevington La WN6 ......28 B1
Shevington Moor WN6 ...28 A2
Shevington Vale Prim Sch
 WN6 ....19 E8
Shilton St BL0 ....49 B5
Shipley Cl FY3 ....151 B1
Shipley Rd FY8 ....89 B7
Shipper Bottom La BL0 ..49 B5
Shirdley Cres PR8 ....20 C3
Shire La BB7 ....141 D8
Shireburn Ave BB7 .....164 C4
Shireburn Cotts BB7 ...162 E1
Shireburn Rd L37 ....11 D5
Shireshead Cres LA1 ...211 A2
Shirley Cres FY2 ....150 D6
Shirley Gdns BB3 ....79 F2
Shirley Hts FY6 ....151 D4
Shirley La PR4 ....94 A1
Shop La Accrington BB5 .103 D5
 Higher Walton PR5 ......97 B3
 Maghull L31 ....5 C1
Shore Ave BB10 ....147 E2
Shore Cl LA5 ....218 B2
Shore Gn Cleveleys FY5 .172 F3
 Cornholme OL14 ....108 C2
 Silverdale LA5 ....218 B2
Shore New Rd OL14 ....108 B1
Shore Rd Cleveleys FY5 .150 C8
 Hesketh Bank PR4 ......72 C4
 Heysham LA3 ....208 D6
 Silverdale LA5 ....218 B2
 Southport PR8 ....20 B6
Shore The LA5 ....215 F5
Shorefield Mount BL7 ..46 E1
Shoreside Prim Sch PR8 .20 B4
Shorey Bank BB11 .....127 A4
Shorrock La BB2 ....100 B1
Shorrock St BB3 ....64 A8
Shorrocks Ave PR3 ....155 C8
Short Clough Cl BB4 ....85 A6
Short Clough La BB4 ....85 A6
Short Croft La L37 ......12 C1
Short St Bacup OL13 ....69 B8
 Colne BB8 ....169 D4
Shorten Brook Dr BB5 ..124 C1
Shorten Brook Way BB5 .124 C6
Shortlands Dr LA3 .....208 E2
Shortlands The BB12 ...145 C2
Shortridge Rd FY4 .....109 F8
Showfield BB10 ....128 B6
Showley Brook Cl BB1 ..121 E6
Showley Ct BB1 ....121 E6
Showley Rd BB1 ....121 A6
Shrewsbury Cl PR4 .....113 C5
Shrewsbury Dr
 Lancaster LA1 ....211 B5
 Thornton PR5 ....173 A2
Shropshire Dr BB1 .....121 F6
Shuttle Cl BB5 ....103 A6
Shuttleworth Rd PR1 ...116 F2
Shuttleworth St
 Burnley BB10 ....147 B2
 Earby BB18 ....201 B4
 6 Padiham BB12 ......125 C8
 Rishton BB1 ....123 B2
Shuttling Fields La PR5 ..97 B2
Sibbering Brow
 Preston PR7 ....41 C7
Sibsey St LA1 ....210 E7
Siddow's Ave BB7 .....164 D7
Side La BB7 ....189 C2
Sidebeet La BB1 ....101 E7

Sidegarth Gate LA2 ....231 C7
Sidegarth La LA2 ......231 D7
Sidgreaves La PR4 .....115 B4
Siding La Kirkby L33 .....1 C7
 Rainford Junction WA11 ..8 C1
Siding Rd FY7 ....194 A3
Siding St OL13 ....69 C8
Sidings Rd LA3 ....208 F2
Sidings The Bacup OL13 ..70 A8
 Spring Vale BB3 ....64 B7
 Whalley BB7 ....143 C6
Sidmouth Ave BB4 ......84 C2
Sidmouth Rd FY8 ......109 C1
Sidney Ave Becconsall PR4 .72 F3
 Blackpool FY2 ....150 E2
Sidney Rd PR9 ....34 F8
Sidney Terr 4 LA1 .....211 A8
Siemens St BL6 ....31 C2
Silbury Cl BB2 ....81 A8
Silcock's Cotts FY5 ....173 F1
Silk Mill La PR3 ....158 B3
Silloth Cl BB2 ....100 F1
Silly La LA2 ....233 D2
Silsden Ave PR2 ....117 C5
Silsden Cl FY3 ....151 B1
Silver Birch Way L31 .....5 B5
Silver St Clifton PR4 ...114 D1
 Ramsbottom BL0 ....49 C6
Silverburn PR4 ....89 A8
Silverdale Becconsall PR4 .72 F3
 Blackpool FY2 ....150 E6
 Southport PR8 ....33 E4
Silverdale Ave
 Fleetwood FY7 ....193 D1
 Heysham LA3 ....208 F7
Silverdale CE Prim Sch
 LA5 ....218 C3
Silverdale Cl
 Blackburn BB2 ....80 E8
 Brierfield BB10 ....147 B3
 Clayton-le-M BB5 ......123 E2
 Coupe Green PR5 ....97 A4
 Leyland PR5 ....59 B6
Silverdale Ct PR8 ....34 E4
Silverdale Dr PR2 .....117 E5
Silverdale Moss Rd LA5 .218 D7
Silverdale Rd Arnside LA5 .237 B1
 Chorley PR6 ....42 E7
 Lytham St Anne's FY8 ...89 C7
 Yealand Redmayne LA5 .219 E4
Silverdale Sta LA5 ....218 F3
Silverstone Gr L31 ....5 B4
Silverthorne Dr PR9 .....52 F1
Silverwell St BL6 ....31 B4
Silverwood Ave FY4 ...109 D8
Silverwood Cl FY8 ......89 E4
Silverwood Ct 1 FY4 .109 D8
Silvester Rd PR7 ....42 C6
Silvester St BL6 ....30 D2
Silvia Way FY7 ....193 E4
Simfield Cl WN6 ....28 D1
Simmonds Way BB9 ....147 B7
Simmons Ave PR1 ....96 B3
Simmons' St BB2 ......100 D5
Simonstone Bsns Pk
 BB12 ....124 F8
Simonstone CE Prim Sch
 BB12 ....144 F1
Simonstone La BB12 ...124 E8
Simonstone Rd BB12,BB7 .144 F6
Simonswood Ind Pk L33 ..1 B6
Simonswood La Kirkby L33 ..1 A2
 Royal Oak L39 ....6 F3
Simonswood Prim Sch L33 .1 A2
Simonswood Wlk L33 .....1 A2
Simpson Cl BB18 ......200 D3
Simpson St Blackpool FY4 .109 B8
 Hapton BB12 ....125 C4
 Oswaldtwistle BB5 .....102 D3
 10 Preston PR1 ....95 F8
Sinclair Cl PR4 ....89 B7
Sineacre La Bickerstaffe L39 .7 E1
 Kirkby L33, L39 ....7 E1
Singleton Ave Horwich BL6 .31 C5
 Lytham St Anne's FY8 ...89 B8
 Read BB12 ....144 D4
Singleton CE Prim Sch
 FY6 ....152 E1
Singleton Cl PR2 ....116 F7
Singleton Cl 3 FY1 ...129 B4
Singleton Rd Weeton PR4 .131 F4
 Weeton Camp PR4 .....131 E6
Singleton Row 18 PR1 ...95 F8
Singleton St 3 FY1 ...129 B3
Singleton Way PR2 ....116 F7
Sion Cl PR2 ....117 F4
Sion Hill PR2 ....117 F4
Sir Simon's Arc 28 LA1 .210 F8
Sir Tom Finney Way
 PR1,PR2 ....117 B3
Six Acre La PR4 ....74 C6
Sixfields 11 FY5 ....150 F7
Sixpenny La PR8 ....20 C1
Sixth Ave Blackpool FY4 .109 C7
 Bury BL9 ....32 D4
Size House Village 6 BB4 .84 B2
Size St OL12 ....70 D1
Sizehouse St 25 PR1 ....95 F8
Sizer St PR1 ....116 F1
Sizergh Ct LA1 ....210 D7
Sizergh Rd LA4 ....213 A5
Skaithe The BB7 ....223 C7
Skeffington Rd PR1 ....117 C1
Skeleron La BB7 ....189 B6
Skelmersdale Coll WN8 .18 B4
Skelmersdale Coll
 (Westbank Campus)
 WN8 ....18 B1

Skelmersdale Coll
 (Westbank Ctr) WN8 .....9 B8
Skelmersdale Rd L39, WN8 .8 B7
Skelmersdale Sports Ctr
 WN8 ....9 C7
Skelmersdale Tourist
 Information Ctr WN8 .....18 B1
Skelshaw Cl BB1 ....101 A3
Skelton St BB8 ....169 E5
Skelwith Rd FY3 ....130 B2
Skerton 1 LA1 ....213 F2
Skerton Ct LA1 ....213 F2
Skerton High Sch LA1 .213 F2
Skerton Ho 6 LA1 .....213 F2
Skerton Prim Sch LA1 .213 F2
Skiddaw Cl BB1 ....146 C1
Skiddaw Rd Blackpool FY4 109 F8
 Lancaster LA1 ....214 A2
Skiddaw St BB1 ....101 A5
Skip La PR4 ....94 B3
Skippool Ave FY6 .....151 E5
Skippool Rd FY5 ......151 E7
Skipton Ave Carleton FY6 .151 C5
 Southport PR9 ....53 C6
Skipton Cl
 Bamber Bridge PR5 .....96 E3
 Blackpool FY4 ....129 F1
Skipton Cres PR2 ......117 C5
Skipton Gate LA6 .....236 C2
Skipton Old Rd Colne BB8 170 C7
 Foulridge BB8 ....191 E2
Skipton Rd
 Barnoldswick BB18 ....200 B2
 Barnoldswick, Coates BB18 200 D4
 Colne BB8 ....169 C6
 Earby BB18 ....201 B3
 Foulridge BB8 ....191 E2
 Lytham St Anne's FY8 ...89 B6
 Trawden BB8 ....170 B3
Skipton Road Bsns Ctr
 BB18 ....200 C3
Skipton St
 Morecambe LA4 ....212 D5
 Nappa BB7 ....225 E2
Skitham La PR3 ....176 D4
Skull House La WN6 ....19 D8
Skye Cl OL10 ....32 F1
Skye Cres BB1 ....101 C3
Slack BB12 ....145 F6
Slack Booth BB5 ......170 C1
Slack Gate OL12 ....51 F8
Slack House Cotts L39 ..16 A3
Slack La PR2 ....205 C1
Slack's La PR9 ....43 B2
Slackey La PR9 ....53 C4
Slackwood La LA5 .....218 E2
Slade La Padiham BB12 .145 C1
 Padiham BB12 ....145 C2
Slade St PR1 ....95 F7
Sladen St OL12 ....51 F1
Slaidburn Ave
 Burnley BB9 ....127 D5
 Rawtenstall BB4 ....85 A4
Slaidburn Cres PR9 .....53 B5
Slaidburn Dr
 Accrington BB5 ....103 A4
 Lancaster LA1 ....211 A3
Slaidburn Pl PR2 ......118 A2
Slaidburn Rd
 Fulwood PR2 ....118 A2
 Lowgill LA2 ....233 E4
 Waddington BB7 ....186 A5
Slaidburn Wlk 5 FY3 .130 B4
Slape La LA6 ....234 C8
Slate La WN8 ....17 C2
Slater Ave Colne BB8 ..169 D6
 Horwich BL6 ....31 C4
Slater La
 Leyland, Moss Side PR5 .58 D8
 Leyland, Seven Stars PR5 .58 D8
Slater Rd FY5 ....172 C2
Slater St BB2 ....100 C1
Slinger Rd FY5 ....172 C3
Slip Inn La PR4 ....71 B2
Sliven Clod Rd BB4 ....104 E2
Sluice La L40 ....38 B3
Slyne Hall Hts LA2 ....216 A1
Slyne Rd
 Bolton-le-S LA2,LA5 ...216 A2
 Lancaster LA1 ....213 F3
 Morecambe LA4 ....213 C4
Smalden La BB7 ....223 A4
Small La Drummersdale L40 .23 E8
 Ormskirk L39 ....15 F4
 Ormskirk, Clieves Hills L39 .15 A3
Small La N L39 ....22 E2
Small La S L39 ....14 D6
Smalley Croft PR1 ......95 F3
Smalley St Burnley BB11 .127 B4
 Standish WN6 ....28 E1
Smalley Thorn Brow BB6 122 F6
Smalley Way BB2 ......100 E2
Smallshaw Ind Est BB11 .126 C4
Smallshaw La
 Burnley BB11 ....126 B5
 Burnley BB12 ....126 B6
Smallshaw Rd OL12 ....51 A4
Smallwood Hey Rd PR3 .196 C5
Smeaton St BL6 ....31 C2
Smethurst Hall Pk WN5 .10 C2
Smethurst Hall Rd BL9 ..32 F4
Smethurst Rd WN5 .....10 C2
Smirthwaite St BB11 ...126 D5
Smith Ave PR4 ....72 F1
Smith Brow BL6 ....30 C4
Smith Cl PR2 ....138 C1
Smith Croft PR5 ....58 B8
Smith La BL7 ....46 F1

Smith Rd FY5 ....172 D2
Smith St Adlington PR7 ...29 C6
 13 Bamber Bridge PR5 ..76 F8
 Barnoldswick BB18 ....200 A1
 Burnley BB12 ....126 E6
 Bury BL9 ....32 A3
 Chorley PR7 ....42 D6
 Colne BB8 ....169 C4
 3 Kirkham PR4 ....112 F5
 Nelson BB9 ....147 F6
 Ramsbottom BL0 ....49 B5
 Skelmersdale WN8 ......17 D1
 Whittle-le-W PR6 ....60 C8
 Worsthorne BB10 .....128 B5
Smith's La PR4 ....56 A1
Smithills Cl PR6 ....60 C8
Smithills Hall Cl BL0 ....49 C5
Smithy Bridge St 8 BB5 .102 D3
Smithy Brow
 Abbeystead LA2 ....226 F1
 Andertons Mill WN6 ....27 C8
 Haslingden BB4 ....84 B4
 Newburgh WN8 ....26 A1
Smithy Brow Cl BB4 ....84 B4
Smithy Cl Brindle PR6 ...77 F5
 Formby L37 ....12 B4
 Garstang PR3 ....178 C8
 Stalmine FY6 ....174 C7
Smithy Croft FY8 ....89 C6
Smithy Fold Rochdale OL12 .51 C1
 Wrea Green PR4 ....112 B4
Smithy Gn L37 ....12 B4
Smithy How LA6 ......238 E3
Smithy La Brindle PR6 ...77 F6
 Claughton PR3 ....179 B2
 Colne BB8 ....169 B8
 Haskayne L39 ....14 A6
 Heysham LA3 ....208 E6
 Holmeswood L40 ....37 C6
 Hurlston Green L40 ....23 B3
 Lytham St Anne's FY8 ...89 C6
 Mawdesley L40 ....39 C2
 Much Hoole PR4 ....73 E2
 Ormskirk L39 ....6 A6
 Preesall FY6 ....195 B3
 Staining FY3 ....130 E6
 Stalmine FY6 ....174 C7
 Westhouse LA6 ....236 E4
Smithy Lane Ends L40 ...23 D6
Smithy Mews 9 FY1 ...129 C8
Smithy Row BB7 ......162 E1
Smithy St
 2 Bamber Bridge PR5 ..76 F8
 9 Haslingden BB4 ......84 B3
 7 Ramsbottom BL0 .....49 C6
Smithy Wlk 3 L40 .....24 C5
Smithyfield Ave BB10 ..127 F6
Snaefell Rd BB2 ....100 E3
Snape Gn Carr Cross PR8 .22 D8
 Southport PR8 ....35 E1
Snape La LA5 ....219 F1
Snape Rake La PR3 ....180 D4
Snape St BB3 ....80 D4
Snapewood La PR3 .....199 B3
Snell Cres BB8 ....169 E6
Snell Gr BB8 ....169 F6
Sniddle Hill La BB3 .....63 E8
Snipe Cl Blackpool FY3 .130 B6
 Cleveleys FY5 ....172 F5
Snipewood PR7 ....40 B6
Snodworth Rd BB6 ....122 D7
Snow Hill PR1 ....95 F8
Snow St BB1 ....100 F6
Snowden Ave
 Blackburn BB1 ....100 E7
 Morecambe LA3 ....212 A4
Snowden St BB12 .....126 B6
Snowdon Cl FY1 ......129 D3
Snowdon Dr BL6 ....31 C5
Snowdon Rd FY8 ......110 A2
Snowdrop Cl
 Clayton-le-W PR5 ....76 E2
 Haslingden BB4 ....66 F8
Snowhill La PR3 ....199 F6
Snowshill Cres FY5 ....150 F7
Sod Hall La PR4 ....75 A5
Sollam's Cl 4 PR5 .....96 F2
Sollom La PR4 ....56 B2
Solway Ave BB2 ....99 F1
Solway Cl Blackpool FY2 .150 C4
 Penwortham PR1 ....95 E3
Somerby Rd LA4 ......212 C4
Somerford Cl BB12 ....126 D7
Somersby Cl PR5 ....96 E3
Somerset Ave
 Blackpool FY1 ....129 D3
 Chorley PR7 ....60 C1
 Clitheroe BB7 ....186 F2
 Darwen BB3 ....80 F3
 Lancaster LA1 ....211 A6
 Wilpshire BB1 ....121 F5
Somerset Cl BB5 ......102 F3
Somerset Ct FY1 ......129 D3
Somerset Dr PR8 ....20 C3
Somerset Gr BB5 ......102 F7
Somerset Pk BB9 .....169 A1
Somerset Pl PR2 ......116 B7
Somerset Rd Leyland PR5 .76 D2
 Preston PR1 ....117 A1
 Rishton BB1 ....123 A1
Somerset Wlk BB4 .....67 B8
Sorrel Cl FY5 ....172 F5
Sorrel Ct 2 PR1 ....95 C2
Soudan St BB10 ....147 B2

Sough La Belthorn BB1 . . . .**82** A7
Blackburn BB1,BB5 . . . .**101** F2
Sough BB18 . . . .**192** A7
Sough Rd BB3 . . . .**64** B7
South Ave
Barnoldswick BB18 . . . . . .**200** B3
Chorley PR7 . . . .**42** D6
Cleveleys FY5 . . . .**172** C4
Morecambe LA4 . . . .**212** F5
New Longton PR4 . . . .**74** F8
South Cliff St 5 PR1 . . . . .**95** E6
South Clifton St FY8 . . . . . .**90** B3
South Cross St BL9 . . . .**32** A1
South Dr Appley Bridge WN6 **27** C2
Fulwood PR2 . . . .**116** E7
Inskip PR4 . . . .**134** C4
Padiham BB12 . . . .**125** E8
South End PR1 . . . .**95** E5
South Gr Barton PR3 . . . .**136** B8
Fulwood PR2 . . . .**116** E8
Morecambe LA4 . . . .**212** F5
South Hey FY8 . . . .**89** C6
South Holme FY8 . . . .**90** B4
South King St FY1 . . . .**129** C5
South Lawn FY1 . . . .**129** E2
South Meade L31 . . . .**5** B1
South Meadow La PR1 . . . .**95** E6
South Meadow St PR1 . . . . .**96** A8
South Moss Rd FY8 . . . .**89** C7
South Par
8 Barnoldswick BB18 . . . . .**200** B3
Cleveleys FY5 . . . .**172** C4
South Park Dr FY3 . . . .**129** F2
South Pine St BL9 . . . .**32** B2
South Pk FY8 . . . .**90** A4
South Prom FY8 . . . .**88** E5
South Rd Bretherton PR5 . . .**56** F5
Coppull PR7 . . . .**41** E1
Lancaster LA1 . . . .**210** F7
Morecambe LA4 . . . .**212** G5
South Ribble Mus PR5 . . . . .**59** A8
South Ribble St 8 PR1 . . . . .**96** C6
South Shore Hospl FY4 . .**109** C5
South Shore St
Church BB5 . . . .**102** E5
Haslingden BB4 . . . .**84** A3
South Sq Blackpool FY3 . . .**129** D6
Cleveleys FY5 . . . .**172** D5
South St Accrington BB5 . . .**103** C5
Accrington, Hillock Vale BB5 **103** E8
Bacup OL13 . . . .**87** A2
Burnley BB11 . . . .**127** A6
15 Darwen BB3 . . . .**81** A1
Great Eccleston PR3 . . . . .**154** B5
Haslingden BB4 . . . .**84** C1
Lytham St Anne's FY8 . . . . .**90** D4
Newchurch BB4 . . . .**85** E1
Ramsbottom BL0 . . . .**49** D6
16 Rawtenstall BB4 . . . .**85** A3
South Strand FY7 . . . .**172** E7
South Terr Ormskirk L39 . . .**15** E4
Ramsbottom BL0 . . . .**67** C2
South Valley Dr BB8 . . . . . .**169** C3
South View
Bamber Bridge PR5 . . . .**76** B7
Belmont BL7 . . . .**45** C5
Bretherton PR5 . . . .**56** F5
4 Great Harwood BB6 . . . .**123** C5
20 Haslingden BB4 . . . .**84** B3
Kirkham PR4 . . . .**113** A4
2 Lostock Hall PR5 . . . .**76** A7
Nelson BB9 . . . .**147** D7
Saltcotes, Moss Side FY8 . .**111** D1
Simonstone BB12 . . . .**144** E3
South View St 5 OL14 . . . .**108** C1
South View Terr 2 PR5 . . .**59** A8
South Warton St FY8 . . . . . .**90** C3
South Westby St FY8 . . . . . .**90** B3
Southbank Ave FY4 . . . .**110** A7
Southbank Rd PR8 . . . .**34** C5
Southbourne Ave FY6 . . . .**151** C2
Southbourne Rd FY3 . . . . . .**130** A2
Southbrook Rd PR5 . . . .**75** F1
Southcliffe BB6 . . . .**123** B6
Southcliffe Ave BB12 . . . . .**126** C7
Southdene WN8 . . . .**26** B2
Southdown Dr FY5 . . . .**151** D8
Southdowns Rd PR7 . . . .**42** D6
Southern Ave
Burnley BB12 . . . .**126** C7
Preston PR1 . . . .**96** C6
Southern Cl PR3 . . . .**139** A6
Southern Par PR1 . . . .**96** B6
Southern Rd PR8 . . . .**34** A6
Southey Cl PR2 . . . .**116** F7
Southey St 2 BB11 . . . .**126** E6
Southfield PR4 . . . .**73** E3
Southfield Dr
New Longton PR4 . . . .**74** F7
Poulton-le-F FY3 . . . .**130** C8
West Bradford BB7 . . . . . .**186** F5
Southfield Gdns PR4 . . . . . .**73** E3
Southfield La BB10,BB8 . .**148** C7
Southfield Rd BL0 . . . .**49** A2
Southfield Sq BB9 . . . .**147** F8
Southfield St BB9 . . . .**147** F8
Southfield Terr BB8 . . . . . .**170** E6
Southfleet Ave FY7 . . . .**193** E1
Southfleet Pl FY7 . . . .**193** E1
Southfold Pl FY8 . . . .**90** A4
Southgate Fleetwood FY7 .**172** D8
Fulwood PR2 . . . .**116** D5
Morecambe LA3 . . . .**213** A2
Preston PR1 . . . .**116** F1
Whitworth OL12 . . . .**51** C7

Southgates PR7 . . . .**41** D3
Southlands PR4 . . . .**113** A4
Southlands Ave PR5 . . . .**96** C1
Southlands Dr PR5 . . . .**58** C8
Southlands High Sch PR7 .**42** A5
Southport & Formby
District General Hospl
PR8 . . . .**34** E4
Southport Barn Cotts
BB7 . . . .**224** C1
Southport Coll PR9 . . . .**34** C7
Southport General Infmy
PR8 . . . .**34** D5
Southport New Rd
Banks PR4,PR9 . . . .**54** D3
Holmes PR4 . . . .**55** D3
Southport Old Rd L37 . . . . . .**12** B7
Southport Pleasureland
PR8 . . . .**33** F7
Southport Rd Chorley PR7 . .**42** A8
Formby L37 . . . .**12** A5
Haskayne L39 . . . .**14** A6
Hurlston L40 . . . .**23** A2
Maghull L31, L39 . . . .**5** B5
Newtown PR7 . . . .**58** B2
Ormskirk L39, L40 . . . .**15** D8
Scarisbrick L40,PR8 . . . .**22** E7
Southport PR8 . . . .**35** B2
Southport Terr PR6 . . . .**42** E7
Southport Zoo PR8 . . . .**33** F7
Southside PR7 . . . .**59** C3
Southway Fleetwood FY7 . .**193** F1
Skelmersdale WN8 . . . .**18** B1
Southwood Ave FY7 . . . . . .**193** F3
Southwood Cl FY8 . . . .**89** E4
Southwood Dr BB5 . . . .**103** E3
Southworth Ave FY4 . . . . . .**109** E7
Southworth St BB2 . . . .**100** D2
Southworth Way FY5 . . . . .**172** E5
Sovereign Gate FY4 . . . . . .**109** F5
Sow Clough Rd OL13 . . . .**86** D1
Sowerby Ave FY4 . . . .**109** D8
Sowerby Rd PR3 . . . .**155** E3
Sowerby St 4 BB12 . . . .**125** C8
Spa Fold L40 . . . .**17** A4
Spa Garth BB7 . . . .**164** F8
Spa La L40, WN8 . . . .**17** C4
Spa Rd PR1 . . . .**95** D7
Spa St Burnley BB12 . . . .**126** E7
Padiham BB12 . . . .**125** D8
3 Preston PR1 . . . .**95** D8
Spark La L40 . . . .**38** B6
Sparrow Hill WN6,WN8 . . . . .**10** D7
Sparth Ave BB5 . . . .**123** F3
Sparth Rd BB5 . . . .**123** F3
Speakmans Dr WN6 . . . .**19** C6
Speedwell Cl FY5 . . . .**172** F5
Speedwell St BB2 . . . .**100** B2
Speke St BB2 . . . .**100** B2
Spen Brook Cotts BB12 . .**167** C2
Spen Brow LA2 . . . .**233** B6
Spen Cnr FY4 . . . .**129** D1
Spen Farm FY4 . . . .**110** C8
Spen La PR4 . . . .**113** E6
Spen Pl FY4 . . . .**109** F8
Spenbrook Rd BB12 . . . . . .**167** C3
Spencer Ct FY1 . . . .**129** C7
Spencer Gr BB6 . . . .**123** B5
Spencer St Accrington BB5 **103** D6
Burnley BB10 . . . .**147** A1
Ramsbottom BL0 . . . .**49** B5
10 Rawtenstall BB4 . . . .**85** A7
Southport L39 . . . .**21** B3
Spencers Dr PR4 . . . .**56** A8
Spencers Fold BB12 . . . . . .**167** F1
Spencers La WN8 . . . .**9** B7
Spendmore La PR7 . . . .**41** C5
Spenleach La BL8 . . . .**48** D3
Spenser Cl BB10 . . . .**128** C4
Spenser St BB12 . . . .**125** D7
Spey Cl Leyland PR5 . . . .**58** E8
Standish WN6 . . . .**28** D1
Speyside FY4 . . . .**109** D7
Spindle Berry Ct BB5 . . . . .**103** C4
Spinners Cl LA1 . . . .**210** F7
Spinners Gn OL12 . . . .**51** F2
Spinners Sq PR5 . . . .**76** E7
Spinney Brow PR2 . . . .**117** D4
Spinney Cl Lucas Green PR6 **60** B6
New Longton PR4 . . . .**74** F8
Ormskirk L39 . . . .**15** D3
Spinney Croft PR3 . . . .**139** A7
Spinney La LA5 . . . .**218** C8
Spinney The Arnside LA5 . .**218** C8
Blackburn BB2 . . . .**100** A8
Burnley BB12 . . . .**126** D8
Chorley PR6 . . . .**60** C3
Cleveleys FY5 . . . .**150** F7
Edgworth BL7 . . . .**47** C2
Formby L37 . . . .**12** A5
Grindleton BB7 . . . .**187** B7
Heysham LA3 . . . .**209** A7
Lancaster LA1 . . . .**211** B5
Penwortham PR1 . . . .**94** F3
Poulton-le-F FY6 . . . .**151** E4
Rochdale OL12 . . . .**51** D3
Tarleton PR4 . . . .**56** A7
Spinning Ave BB1 . . . .**81** D8
Spinnings The BL0 . . . .**49** C3
Spire Cl BB3 . . . .**64** D8
Spiredale Dr WN6 . . . .**28** F2
Spires Gr PR4 . . . .**115** E5
Spod Rd OL12 . . . .**51** D1
Spodden Cotts OL12 . . . .**70** D2
Spodden Fold OL12 . . . .**51** C8
Spotland Tops OL12 . . . .**51** B1

Spout La LA2 . . . .**235** F1
Spouthouse La BB5 . . . .**124** F1
Spread Eagle St BB5 . . . . .**102** C5
Spring Ave BB6 . . . .**123** C6
Spring Bank
Appley Bridge WN6 . . . .**19** C8
Garstang PR3 . . . .**178** C6
9 Preston PR1 . . . .**95** E7
Rochdale OL12 . . . .**51** D4
Silverdale LA5 . . . .**218** C3
Spring Bank Terr BB2 . . . .**100** C2
Spring Brook Ho BB5 . . . .**123** F2
Spring Cl Kirkby L33 . . . .**1** A5
Ramsbottom BL0 . . . .**49** B6
Southport PR8 . . . .**34** A5
Spring Cres PR6 . . . .**60** E5
Spring Field WA11 . . . .**8** E2
Spring Gardens BB6 . . . . . .**169** D4
Spring Gardens St 4 BB4 . .**68** F8
Spring Gardens Terr 3
BB12 . . . .**145** C1
Spring Gdn St 38 LA1 . . . . .**210** F8
Spring Gdns
8 Accrington BB5 . . . .**103** C5
2 Bacup OL13 . . . .**87** A3
11 Darwen BB3 . . . .**64** C6
Freckleton PR4 . . . .**92** B8
12 Horwich BL6 . . . .**31** B4
Leyland PR5 . . . .**58** F8
Lytham St Anne's FY8 . . . .**109** F1
Penwortham PR1 . . . .**95** F2
Rawtenstall BB4 . . . .**68** F6
Spring Gr BB8 . . . .**170** C6
Spring Hall BB5 . . . .**123** F6
Spring Hill
5 Blackburn BB1 . . . .**100** C5
Freckleton PR4 . . . .**92** D7
Spring Hill Cty Prim Sch
BB5 . . . .**103** B5
Spring Hill Rd
Accrington BB5 . . . .**102** F4
Burnley BB11 . . . .**126** F4
Spring La Blackburn BB2 . .**100** B3
Colne BB8 . . . .**169** D5
Haslingden BB4 . . . .**84** B4
Nab's Head PR5 . . . .**98** C8
Spring Mdws BB3 . . . .**64** D7
Spring Mdw PR5 . . . .**76** E1
Spring Mews PR6 . . . .**60** E6
Spring Pl Colne BB8 . . . .**169** D5
Whitworth OL12 . . . .**70** D3
Spring Rd WN5 . . . .**10** F8
Spring Row BB8 . . . .**170** C6
Spring Side
Rawtenstall BB4 . . . .**68** F6
Whitworth OL12 . . . .**70** D4
Spring Side Cotts BL7 . . . . .**46** A2
Spring St Accrington BB5 . .**102** F4
Bacup OL13 . . . .**86** F1
Bank Lane BL0 . . . .**49** D7
1 Cornholme OL14 . . . . . .**108** C1
Horwich BL6 . . . .**31** B4
6 Leyland PR5 . . . .**76** B1
Nelson BB9 . . . .**147** C7
5 Oswaldtwistle BB5 . . . . .**102** E4
Ramsbottom BL0 . . . .**49** B6
Rawtenstall BB4 . . . .**85** A8
Rishton BB1 . . . .**123** B2
Spring Terr
Accrington BB4 . . . .**104** F2
4 Bacup OL13 . . . .**69** D8
Langho BB6 . . . .**142** D1
Oswaldtwistle BB5 . . . .**102** D4
Rochdale OL11 . . . .**51** A1
Spring Terr S 5 BB4 . . . .**84** E2
Spring Vale PR4 . . . .**204** B3
Spring Vale Garden
Village BB3 . . . .**64** C6
Spring Vale Rd BB3 . . . .**64** B7
Spring View
Blackburn BB2 . . . .**100** C5
Over Town BB10 . . . .**107** A8
Spring Villas 18 OL14 . . . .**108** B1
Spring Wood
Nature Trail BB7 . . . .**143** C5
Spring Wood St BL0 . . . .**49** B7
Spring Yd 3 BB8 . . . .**169** D5
Springbank BB9 . . . .**168** E5
Springbank Ave FY5 . . . . . .**173** C2
Springbank Gdns BB4 . . . .**104** F2
Springbrook Ave FY5 . . . . .**150** F8
Springcroft 1 PR5 . . . .**76** C3
Springdale BB6 . . . .**122** C8
Springfield Arnside LA5 . . .**237** B2
Blacko BB9 . . . .**168** D8
High Bentham LA2 . . . .**233** E8
Springfield Ave
Accrington BB5 . . . .**102** F4
Bacup OL13 . . . .**87** A3
Blackburn BB2 . . . .**99** E1
Earby BB18 . . . .**201** C1
Kirkham PR4 . . . .**112** E5
Springfield Bank BB11 . . .**127** B5
Springfield Cl
Burscough L40 . . . .**24** D2
Formby L37 . . . .**11** C2
Whalley BB7 . . . .**143** D6
Springfield Cres LA2 . . . .**233** E8
Springfield Ct 1 FY3 . . . . .**129** E3
Springfield Dr
Newchurch BB4 . . . .**85** E1
Thornton FY5 . . . .**173** B4
Springfield Flats 7 BB4 . .**64** A8
Springfield Gdns
Bolton-le-S LA6 . . . .**216** F5
Scorton PR3 . . . .**199** E6
Springfield Rd
Adlington PR6 . . . .**30** A8

Springfield Rd continued
Blackpool FY1 . . . .**129** B6
Burnley BB11 . . . .**127** A4
Burnley BB11 . . . .**127** B5
1 Chorley PR7 . . . .**42** C8
Coppull PR7 . . . .**28** E8
Great Harwood BB6 . . . . . .**123** B4
Horwich BL6 . . . .**31** D1
Leyland PR5 . . . .**58** D7
Lytham St Anne's FY8 . . . . .**88** E6
Maghull L39 . . . .**5** F6
Nelson BB9 . . . .**147** E6
Ramsbottom BL0 . . . .**49** A2
Rawtenstall BB4 . . . .**85** B3
Springfield Rd N PR7 . . . . .**28** E8
Springfield St
Blackburn BB2 . . . .**100** B3
Darwen BB3 . . . .**64** A8
Lancaster LA1 . . . .**210** F7
Morecambe LA4 . . . .**212** C4
Oswaldtwistle BB5 . . . .**102** D4
Preston PR1 . . . .**116** E1
Springfield Terr
Blackburn BB2 . . . .**100** A1
Thornton FY7 . . . .**173** A6
Springfield View BB11 . . .**105** C5
Springhill Ave OL13 . . . .**69** D8
Springhill Prim Sch BB5 .**103** A4
Springhill Villas OL13 . . . . .**69** D8
Springmount BB18 . . . .**201** C2
Springmount Dr WN8 . . . . . .**26** C3
Springs Brow PR7 . . . .**28** D5
Springs Rd Chorley PR6 . . . .**60** D2
Longridge PR3 . . . .**139** B8
Springsands Cl PR2 . . . . . .**117** E5
Springthorpe St 7 BB3 . . . .**64** B6
Springvale BB5 . . . .**102** F4
Springvale Bsns Pk 1
BB3 . . . .**64** B6
Springwater Ave BL0 . . . . . .**49** A3
Springwood Cl PR1 . . . .**96** A3
Springwood Dr
Chorley PR7 . . . .**42** E5
Rufford L40 . . . .**38** C5
Springwood Rd BB10 . . . . .**127** E5
Sprodley Dr WN6 . . . .**27** B2
Spruce Ave Bury BL9 . . . . . .**32** B2
Lancaster LA1 . . . .**210** F4
Spruce Cl PR2 . . . .**117** C7
Spruce Ct BB5 . . . .**103** E8
Spruce St BL0 . . . .**49** B5
Spruce Way L37 . . . .**11** C3
Sprucewood Cl BB5 . . . . . .**103** D6
Spurrier St PR5 . . . .**76** A4
Spymers Croft L37 . . . .**12** A6
Square House La PR9 . . . . . .**54** C6
Square La Burscough L40 . . .**24** E3
Catforth PR4 . . . .**134** F4
Square St BL0 . . . .**49** B5
Square The Blackpool FY3 .**130** A2
Brinscall PR6 . . . .**61** F7
Burton-in-K LA6 . . . .**234** B7
Cleveleys FY5 . . . .**172** D5
Cumeragh Village PR3 . . . .**137** F5
Great Eccleston PR3 . . . . .**154** B5
1 Leyland PR5 . . . .**76** B2
Scorton PR3 . . . .**199** E6
Storth LA7 . . . .**237** F5
Waddington BB7 . . . .**186** B4
Squire Rd BB9 . . . .**147** E8
Squire's Gate Rd PR2 . . . .**116** C3
Squires Cl PR5 . . . .**97** E2
Squires Ct
6 Blackpool FY4 . . . .**109** C5
8 Lytham St Anne's FY8 . . .**90** B3
Squires Gate La FY4 . . . . .**109** D5
Squires Gate Link Rd
FY4 . . . .**110** C2
Squires Rd PR1 . . . .**95** C6
Squires Wood PR2 . . . .**117** D6
Squirrel Fold PR2 . . . .**117** F2
Squirrel Gn L37 . . . .**11** C5
Squirrel La BL6 . . . .**31** A4
Squirrel's Chase PR5 . . . . . .**76** A7
Squirrels Cl BB5 . . . .**103** E8
Stable Cl Gisburn BB7 . . . . .**225** B3
Kirkham PR4 . . . .**113** A6
Stable La PR4 . . . .**61** A7
Stables Cl BB4 . . . .**85** A4
Stack Croft PR5 . . . .**77** A2
Stack La OL13 . . . .**70** B8
Stackhouses The 2
BB11 . . . .**127** A6
Stadium Ave FY4 . . . .**109** E5
Staffa Cres BB1 . . . .**101** D4
Stafford Ave FY6 . . . .**151** D1
Stafford Moreton Way L31 .**5** D1
Stafford Rd
10 Preston PR1 . . . .**117** A1
Southport PR8 . . . .**34** A1
Stafford St Burnley BB10 . .**127** A7
Darwen BB3 . . . .**80** F4
Nelson BB9 . . . .**148** A8
Skelmersdale WN8 . . . .**17** D1
Staghills Rd BB4 . . . .**85** D1
Stainburn Cl WN6 . . . .**19** E6
Stainforth Ave FY2 . . . .**150** E5
Staining Ave PR2 . . . .**94** F8
Staining CE Sch FY3 . . . . .**130** D5
Staining Old Rd FY3 . . . . . .**130** D7
Staining Rd FY3 . . . .**130** C6
Staining Rise FY3 . . . .**130** E5
Staining Rd W FY3 . . . .**130** D5
Stainton Dr BB12 . . . .**126** E8
Stainton Gr 1 LA4 . . . .**213** A4
Stakepool Dr PR3 . . . .**196** E4
Stakes Hall Pl BB2 . . . .**100** C2
Stalls Rd LA3 . . . .**208** F2

Stalmine Prim Sch FY6 . .**174** D7
Stamford Ave FY4 . . . .**109** D7
Stamford Ct FY4 . . . .**88** D8
Stamford Dr PR6 . . . .**60** C5
Stamford Pl BB7 . . . .**186** F1
Stamford Rd
Skelmersdale WN8 . . . .**17** D2
Southport PR8 . . . .**34** B2
Stanagate PR4 . . . .**114** C1
Stanah Cty Inf Sch FY5 . .**173** D1
Stanah Cty Jun Sch FY5 .**173** D1
Stanah Gdns FY5 . . . .**173** E2
Stanah Rd FY5 . . . .**173** E2
Stanalee La PR3 . . . .**158** B8
Stanbury Cl OL10 . . . .**32** D1
Stanbury Dr BB10 . . . .**147** E2
Stancliffe St BB2 . . . .**100** C3
Standen Hall Cl BB10 . . . . .**147** E3
Standen Hall Dr BB10 . . . . .**147** D3
Standen Rd BB7 . . . .**164** F7
Standen Road Bglws
BB7 . . . .**164** F7
Standhouse La LA9 . . . .**15** C2
Standing Stone La
BB8,BB9 . . . .**191** A2
Standish Com High Sch
WN6 . . . .**28** C2
Standish St Burnley BB11 .**127** A6
Chorley PR7 . . . .**42** D7
Standridge Clough La
BB18 . . . .**201** D1
Standroyd Dr BB8 . . . .**170** A5
Standroyd Rd BB8 . . . .**170** A5
Stanedge Cl BL0 . . . .**49** C4
Stanford Gdns BB2 . . . .**101** A1
Stanford Hall Cres BL0 . . . .**49** B4
Stang Top Rd BB9 . . . .**167** F6
Stangate L31 . . . .**5** B2
Stanhill La BB5 . . . .**102** C4
Stanhill Rd BB1,BB5 . . . . . .**101** F4
Stanhope Ave LA3 . . . .**213** A3
Stanhope Ct LA3 . . . .**213** B3
Stanhope Rd 1 FY1 . . . .**129** C7
Stanhope St Burnley BB12 .**126** F7
Darwen BB3 . . . .**81** A2
Preston PR1 . . . .**116** E2
Stanier Pl BL6 . . . .**31** C2
Stanifield Cl PR5 . . . .**76** B3
Stanifield La PR5 . . . .**76** C5
Stankelt Rd LA5 . . . .**218** C2
Stanlawe Rd L37 . . . .**11** E6
Stanley Ave Cleveleys FY5 .**172** E2
Hutton PR4 . . . .**94** D2
Leyland PR5 . . . .**76** C4
Penwortham PR1 . . . .**95** E5
Poulton-le-F FY6 . . . .**151** D3
Southport PR8 . . . .**33** F3
Stanley Cl PR3 . . . .**139** B7
Stanley Croft PR4 . . . .**136** B3
Stanley Ct Accrington BB5 .**103** D7
Burscough Bridge L40 . . . . .**24** E5
Chipping PR3 . . . .**182** E3
Kirkham PR4 . . . .**113** B4
Stanley Dr Darwen BB3 . . . .**64** B5
Hornby LA2 . . . .**232** B7
Stanley Fold PR5 . . . .**75** F8
Stanley Gate
Fleetwood FY7 . . . .**193** D3
Mellor BB2 . . . .**120** E2
Stanley Gr Fleetwood FY7 .**193** D2
Horwich BL6 . . . .**31** D1
Penwortham PR1 . . . .**95** A5
Stanley High Sch PR9 . . . . .**52** F4
Stanley Mount 7 OL13 . . . .**86** F3
Stanley Park Cl FY3 . . . . . .**129** F3
Stanley Pl 9 Chorley PR7 . .**42** C8
Lancaster LA1 . . . .**210** D8
Preston PR1 . . . .**95** E7
Stanley Prim & Inf Sch
FY3 . . . .**130** B2
Stanley Range BB2 . . . .**100** B1
Stanley Rd Blackpool FY1 .**129** C4
Fleetwood FY7 . . . .**193** F3
Formby L37 . . . .**11** E6
Kirkham PR4 . . . .**112** F7
Leyland PR5 . . . .**76** C4
Lytham St Anne's FY8 . . . . .**89** D3
Morecambe LA3 . . . .**212** B3
Orrell WN8 . . . .**10** B7
Stanley St Accrington BB5 .**103** D6
Bacup OL13 . . . .**86** F4
Blackburn BB1 . . . .**101** B6
Brierfield BB9 . . . .**147** B6
6 Burnley BB11 . . . .**126** F5
Carnforth LA5 . . . .**217** D1
Colne BB8 . . . .**169** D5
Morecambe LA4 . . . .**113** B4
10 Leyland PR5 . . . .**76** B1
Longridge PR3 . . . .**139** A8
Morecambe LA4 . . . .**212** E6
Nelson BB9 . . . .**147** D8
Ormskirk L39 . . . .**15** F5
Oswaldtwistle BB5 . . . .**102** D3
Preston PR1 . . . .**96** B8
Ramsbottom BL0 . . . .**49** B5
Rochdale OL12 . . . .**51** E1
Southport PR9 . . . .**34** B8
Stanley Terr PR1 . . . .**95** E7
Stanley Villas PR5 . . . .**98** B4
Stanley Way WN8 . . . .**17** E3
Stanleyfield Cl PR1 . . . .**117** A1
Stanleyfield Rd PR1 . . . . . .**117** A1
Stanmore Ave FY4 . . . .**109** F6
Stanmore Dr LA1 . . . .**210** E5
Stannanought Rd WN8 . . . .**18** E2
Stanning Cl PR5 . . . .**58** E8
Stanning St PR5 . . . .**59** A8
Stanrose Cl BL7 . . . .**46** E1

Stansfeld St BB2 . . . . .100 C3
Stansfield Ave L31 . . . . .5 F1
Stansfield Cl 7 BB9 . . . . . .168 D4
Stansfield Rd BB4 . . . . . . .68 E8
Stansfield St
2 Bacup OL13 . . . . .69 C8
Blackpool FY1 . . . . .129 C1
Burnley BB11 . . . . .126 E5
6 Darwen BB3 . . . . .64 A8
Nelson BB9 . . . . .147 B1
Stansfield Terr 14 OL14 . . .108 B1
Stansford Ct PR1 . . . . .95 D4
Stansted Rd PR7 . . . . .42 A7
Stansy Ave LA3 . . . . .212 B1
Stanthorpe Wlk BB10 . . . .147 A1
Stanworth Rd BB9 . . . . . .147 D8
Stanworth St BB10 . . . . . .128 E5
Stanworth Terr 79 B4
Stanzaker Hall Dr PR3 . . .156 D7
Stapleton Rd L37 . . . . .11 D1
Star Bank OL13 . . . . .69 D7
Star La BL6 . . . . .30 F3
Star St Accrington BB5 . . .102 F5
Darwen BB3 . . . . .81 B1
Starbeck Ave FY4 . . . . . . .129 D1
Starfield Cl FY8 . . . . .90 A4
Starkie St Blackburn BB1 . .100 F5
Burnley BB11 . . . . .126 E5
Darwen BB3 . . . . .64 B8
12 Leyland PR5 . . . . .76 B1
Preston PR1 . . . . .95 F6
Starr Gate FY4 . . . . .109 B4
Starrgate Dr PR2 . . . . . . .115 E1
Startifants La PR4 . . . . . . .181 F4
Startifants Lane End PR3 182 A5
Startley Nook PR4 . . . . . . .75 B6
States Rd FY8 . . . . .89 B6
Statham Rd WN8 . . . . .17 E3
Statham Way L39 . . . . .15 E4
Station App
1 Burscough Bridge L40 . . .24 E5
Ormskirk L39 . . . . .15 F5
Station Ave WN5 . . . . .10 D5
Station Brow PR5 . . . . .76 B2
Station Cl Rishton BB1 . . . .102 A8
Wilpshire BB1 . . . . .121 F4
Station Ct LA2 . . . . .232 B7
Station La Burton-in-K LA6 .234 B7
Nateby PR3 . . . . .198 B1
Newsham PR3 . . . . .136 A5
Scorton PR3 . . . . .199 D7
Station Par OL14 . . . . . . .107 F1
Station Rd Adlington PR7 . . .30 A6
Arnside LA5 . . . . .237 C2
Bamber Bridge PR5 . . . . .76 B4
Banks PR9 . . . . .53 F5
Barnoldswick BB18 . . . . .200 B2
Blackpool FY4 . . . . .109 B8
Blackrod BL6 . . . . .30 E1
Burton-in-K LA6 . . . . . . .234 B8
Clitheroe BB7 . . . . .164 E8
Coppull PR7 . . . . .41 F1
3 Cornholme OL14 . . . . .108 C1
Croston PR5 . . . . .57 B3
Edgworth BL7 . . . . .47 C4
Fleetwood FY7 . . . . .194 A4
Foulridge BB8 . . . . .191 D1
Great Harwood BB6 . . . .123 D5
Haskayne L39 . . . . .13 E7
Haslingden BB4 . . . . .84 B4
Haslingden, Bridge End BB4 .67 A7
Hesketh Bank PR4 . . . . . .72 F3
Hest Bank LA2 . . . . .215 D1
High Bentham LA2 . . . . .233 D7
Hoghton PR5 . . . . .98 D2
Hornby LA2 . . . . .232 B7
Huncoat BB5 . . . . .124 E2
2 Kirkham PR4 . . . . . . .112 F5
Lancaster LA1 . . . . .210 E8
Lytham St Anne's FY8 . . . .90 B3
Maghull L31 . . . . .5 A6
Morecambe LA4 . . . . . . .212 E5
New Longton PR4 . . . . . . .74 F8
Ormskirk L39 . . . . .15 F6
Padiham BB12 . . . . .125 C8
Parbold WN8 . . . . .26 C2
Poulton-le-F FY6 . . . . . . .151 E4
Ramsbottom BL8 . . . . . . .48 F1
Rimington BB7 . . . . .188 E3
Rishton BB1 . . . . .123 A1
Rufford L40 . . . . .38 D4
Salwick PR4 . . . . .114 C4
Singleton FY6 . . . . .152 E1
Southport PR8 . . . . .20 C5
Thornton FY5 . . . . .173 D5
Walmer Bridge PR4 . . . . .73 D4
Whalley BB7 . . . . .143 C5
Whitworth OL12 . . . . .70 D3
Whitworth, Broadley OL12 . .51 C5
Wrea Green PR4 . . . . . . .112 B4
Station Sq FY8 . . . . .90 A3
Station Terr
Abbey Village PR6 . . . . . . .79 C2
Blackpool FY4 . . . . .109 B8
Station View BB6 . . . . . . .142 D1
Station Way Garstang PR3 178 C8
Hornby LA2 . . . . .232 B7
Staunton St LA5 . . . . .217 D3
Staveley Ave L40 . . . . .24 E4
Staveley Pl PR2 . . . . .115 E2
Staveley Rd
Skelmersdale WN8 . . . . . .17 E3
Southport PR8 . . . . .20 D4
Staynall La FY6 . . . . .174 B4
Stead St BL9 . . . . .49 C6
Steam Traction Mus BB7 .225 C1
Sted Terr BB1 . . . . .100 E6
Steeley La PR6 . . . . .42 D7

Steeple View PR2 . . . . .95 D8
Steer St BB10 . . . . .147 B1
Steeton Rd FY3 . . . . .151 B1
Stefano Rd 1 PR1 . . . . . . .96 C8
Steiner St BB5 . . . . .103 A6
Steiner's La BB5 . . . . .102 E7
Stella Maris High Sch
FY7 . . . . .194 A5
Step Row OL13 . . . . .86 F5
Stephen St Blackburn BB2 .100 B2
Lytham St Anne's FY8 . . . .88 E7
Stephendale Ave PR5 . . . . .77 B8
Stephenson Dr BB12 . . . . .126 C7
Stephenson St
2 Chorley PR6 . . . . .42 E7
Horwich BL6 . . . . .31 B2
Stephenson Way L37 . . . . .12 C3
Sterling Pl 4 OL10 . . . . . . .32 F1
Sterndale Ave WN6 . . . . . .28 E2
Stevenson Ave 2 BB5 . . . . .76 C3
Stevenson St E BB5 . . . . .103 A5
Stevenson St W BB5 . . . . .102 F5
Steward Ave LA1 . . . . .211 B5
Stewart Cl LA5 . . . . .218 B8
Stewart St Blackburn BB2 . .80 D8
Burnley BB11 . . . . .127 B4
11 Preston PR1 . . . . .95 D8
Stiles Ave PR4 . . . . .94 C1
Stiles The L39 . . . . .15 E5
Stirling Cl Chorley PR6 . . . .42 E7
Clitheroe BB7 . . . . .164 C6
1 Leyland PR5 . . . . .76 C1
Stirling Ct
1 Blackpool FY1 . . . . . .129 D7
Lane Bottom BB10 . . . . .148 B4
Southport PR9 . . . . .53 A2
Stirling Dr BB1 . . . . .100 F4
Stirling Rd Blackpool FY3 . .129 D7
Lancaster LA1 . . . . .211 A7
Stirling St BB1 . . . . .100 B1
Stockbridge Cotts BB7 . . .162 E3
Stockbridge Dr BB12 . . . . .125 E8
Stockbridge Rd BB12 . . . . .125 D7
Stockclough La BB2 . . . . . .79 D6
Stockdale Cres PR5 . . . . . .76 F8
Stockdove Way FY5 . . . . . .172 E3
Stockdove Wood FY5 . . . . .172 E3
Stockholm St BB11 . . . . . .126 B5
Stockley Cres L39 . . . . .7 E6
Stockley Dr WN6 . . . . .19 E8
Stockpit Rd L33 . . . . .1 D2
Stocks Cl PR6 . . . . .78 B1
Stocks Ct 4 FY6 . . . . .151 D3
Stocks La
Barnoldswick BB7 . . . . . .190 A4
Blackpool FY6 . . . . .151 A3
Heskin Green PR7 . . . . . .40 E3
Stocks Lane End PR3 . . . .178 C2
Stocks Park Dr BL6 . . . . . .31 C3
Stocks Rd PR7 . . . . .116 C2
Stocks St 7 PR1 . . . . .95 E8
Stocksgate OL12 . . . . .51 B2
Stockwood Cl BB2 . . . . . . .100 A8
Stockydale Rd FY4 . . . . . . .110 A6
Stoke Ave FY1 . . . . .129 D2
Stokes Hall Ave PR5 . . . . .59 A8
Stone Bridge La BB5 . . . . .102 E3
Stone Cl BL0 . . . . .49 A4
Stone Croft PR1 . . . . .95 D2
Stone Cross Gdns PR3 . . . .178 D2
Stone Edge Rd BB9 . . . . . .168 E6
Stone Edge View BB9 . . . .168 E6
Stone Hall La WN8 . . . . . . .19 A5
Stone Hill Dr BB1 . . . . . . .122 A1
Stone Hill La OL12 . . . . . . .51 A2
Stone Holme Terr BB4 . . . .85 A8
Stone House Fold BB11 . . .106 E6
Stone Moor Bottom
BB12 . . . . .125 C6
Stone Pits BL0 . . . . .67 E3
Stone Row Head LA1 . . . .211 C8
Stone St Haslingden BB4 . . .83 F2
Rawtenstall BB4 . . . . .68 F8
Stonebarn Dr L31 . . . . .5 C3
Stonebridge Cl 6 PR5 . . . .76 C8
Stonebridge Terr PR3 . . . .139 A7
Stonechat FY3 . . . . .130 B6
Stonecroft BB9 . . . . .168 E6
Stonecroft Rd PR5 . . . . . . .58 D7
Stonecrop WN6 . . . . .27 D2
Stonedross La LA6 . . . . . .238 E8
Stonefield Longton PR4 . . . .73 F8
Penwortham PR1 . . . . . . .95 E4
Stonefold Ave PR4 . . . . . . .94 C1
Stonefold CE Prim Sch
BB5 . . . . .84 A7
Stonegate Fold PR6 . . . . . .43 B1
Stonehill Cres OL12 . . . . . .51 A3
Stonehill Dr OL12 . . . . .51 B3
Stonehill Rd OL12 . . . . . . .51 B3
Stoneholme Ind Est BB4 . . .85 A8
Stoneholme Rd BB4 . . . . . .85 A8
Stonehouse Gn PR6 . . . . . .77 B3
Stoneleigh Cl PR8 . . . . . . .20 C4
Stoneleigh Ct LA5 . . . . . . .218 C3
Stoner Rd PR7 . . . . .29 F7
Stones Bank Rd BL7 . . . . . .46 B5
Stones La PR3 . . . . .178 E3
Stoneway Rd FY5 . . . . . . .172 E1
Stonewell 17 LA1 . . . . . . .210 F8
Stoney Brow WN8 . . . . . . .19 B1
Stoney Butts PR2 . . . . .94 D8
Stoney Croft Dr LA5 . . . . .217 E6
Stoney Ct BB8 . . . . .191 E1
Stoney Holt PR5 . . . . .76 E1
Stoney La Adlington PR7 . . .29 E4
Bamber Bridge PR5 . . . . .76 C6

Stoney La continued
Foulridge BB8 . . . . .191 E1
Freckleton PR4 . . . . .92 B5
Galgate LA2 . . . . .207 B3
Hambleton FY6 . . . . .174 C2
Longridge PR3 . . . . .159 C7
Stoney St BB4 . . . . .127 B4
Stoneybutts 8 BB1 . . . . . .100 E5
Stoneycroft BB1 . . . . .128 A5
Stoneycroft Ave BL6 . . . . . .31 D4
Stoneycroft Cl BL6 . . . . . . .31 D5
Stoneycroft Dr LA5 . . . . . .217 E3
Stoneygate Cleveleys FY5 .172 F1
18 Preston PR1 . . . . .96 A7
Stoneygate La WN6 . . . . . .27 B2
Stoneyholme Prim Sch
BB10 . . . . .126 F8
Stoneyhurst Ave
Burnley BB10 . . . . .127 D5
Thornton FY5 . . . . .151 D8
Stoneyhurst Ht BB9 . . . . .147 D4
Stoneyroyd OL12 . . . . .70 D1
Stony Bank Rd BB18 . . . . .201 C2
Stony Croft Pl 2 FY4 . . . . .109 C5
Stony Hill Ave FY4 . . . . . .109 C5
Stony La Cockerham PR3 . .203 F2
Cornholme OL14 . . . . . . .108 E2
Hollins Lane PR3 . . . . . . .204 D3
Parbold WN6,WN8 . . . . . .26 E4
Stonycroft Ave FY4 . . . . . .109 C5
Stonygate La PR3 . . . . . . .140 D6
Stonyhurst PR7 . . . . .42 C4
Stonyhurst Cl
Blackburn BB2 . . . . .100 D4
Padiham BB12 . . . . .125 E6
Stonyhurst Coll BB7 . . . . .163 A3
Stonyhurst Rd BB2 . . . . . .100 D4
Stoop St BB11 . . . . .126 C5
Stoopes Hill BB18 . . . . . .201 C2
Stoops Fold BB2 . . . . .120 E2
Stoops La PR3 . . . . .188 F8
Stopes Brow BB1,BB3 . . . .81 A7
Stopford Ave FY1 . . . . . . .150 E2
Stopford Ct 1 BB5 . . . . . .123 F3
Stopgate La L33 . . . . .1 C7
Stopper La BB7 . . . . .189 B7
Store St Blackburn BB3 . . . .81 A7
17 Haslingden BB4 . . . . . .84 B3
Horwich BL6 . . . . .31 C4
Store Yard PR4 . . . . .114 E7
Storey La Lancaster LA1 . .210 D8
Storey Inst
(Coll of F Ed) LA1 . . . . .210 E8
Stork Cl FY5 . . . . .172 F1
Stork St BB3 . . . . .64 D8
Storrs La LA5 . . . . .219 B4
Storth CE Prim Sch LA7 . .237 F5
Storth Rd LA7 . . . . .237 F3
Stott St 2 Nelson BB9 . . .147 D8
Rochdale OL12 . . . . .51 F1
Stour Lodge PR2 . . . . . . .116 C6
Stourton Rd PR8 . . . . .20 C4
Stourton St BB1 . . . . .123 A2
Stout St BB3 . . . . .100 D4
Straight Up La PR9 . . . . . .35 D8
Strait La LA2 . . . . .226 F1
Straits BB5 . . . . .102 E4
Straits La BB12 . . . . .144 D2
Straits The PR5 . . . . .98 B2
Strand Rd PR1 . . . . .95 D7
Strand St W PR1 . . . . .95 C8
Strand The Blackpool FY1 .129 B6
Fleetwood FY7 . . . . .172 D8
Horwich BL6 . . . . .31 D3
Strang St 9 BL0 . . . . .49 C6
Strange St BB11 . . . . .127 B4
Stransdale Ct PR3 . . . . . .178 B7
Stratford Pl 5 PR5 . . . . . .76 B1
Stratford Cl Lancaster LA1 213 E3
Southport PR8 . . . . .20 A6
Stratford Dr PR2 . . . . . . .116 C4
Stratford Pl Blackpool FY1 129 E2
2 Fleetwood FY7 . . . . . .193 E4
Stratford Rd Chorley PR6 . .42 D8
Lytham St Anne's FY8 . . . .89 B7
Stratford Way
7 Accrington BB5 . . . . .103 A7
Colne BB8 . . . . .169 F5
Strathaven Pl 6 OL10 . . . .32 F1
Strathclyde Rd BB1 . . . . .101 A4
Strathdale PR4 . . . . .109 F7
Strathmore Cl BL0 . . . . . . .49 C4
Strathmore Gr PR7 . . . . . . .42 B7
Strathmore Rd PR2 . . . . . .116 E3
Strathyre Cl FY2 . . . . . . .150 F5
Stratton Cl BB9 . . . . .147 E6
Stratton Gr BL6 . . . . .31 B5
Strawberry Bank BB1 . . . .100 E5
Strawberry Mews 1 LA3 .208 F8
Streatly Wlk BB2 . . . . .81 A8
Street The PR6 . . . . .43 E3
Strellas La LA5 . . . . .216 C1
Stretton Ave FY4 . . . . . . .109 E8
Stretton Dr PR9 . . . . .34 F8
Stretton Rd BL0 . . . . .49 A2
Strickens La PR3 . . . . . . .179 C6
Strickland Dr LA4 . . . . . . .213 A5
Strickland's La FY6 . . . . . .174 D6
Stricklands La PR1 . . . . . . .95 E4
Strike La PR4 . . . . .92 B8
Strike Lane Cty Prim Sch
PR4 . . . . .92 B8
Strine The L40,PR4 . . . . . .56 A1
Stromness Gr 5 OL10 . . . .32 F1
Strongstry Rd BL0 . . . . . . .67 C2
Stronsay Pl FY2 . . . . .150 F6
Stroyan St BB10 . . . . .127 C5

Strutt St 2 PR1 . . . . .117 B1
Stryands PR4 . . . . .94 C1
Sts John Fisher
& Thomas More
RC High Sch BB8 . . . . .169 B2
Stuart Ave Bacup OL13 . . . .69 D8
Morecambe LA4 . . . . . . .212 G6
Stuart Cl 16 Darwen BB3 . .81 A1
Fulwood PR2 . . . . .117 E3
Stuart Rd Fulwood PR2 . . .117 E3
Thornton FY5 . . . . .173 C2
Stuart St Accrington BB5 . .103 B7
5 Barnoldswick BB18 . . .200 C2
Stub La L40 . . . . .24 A2
Stubbins La Catterall PR3 .178 A2
Ramsbottom BL0 . . . . . . .49 C8
Sabden BB7 . . . . .145 A7
Stubbins Prim Sch BL0 . . . .67 C1
Stubbins St BB9 . . . . .67 C1
Stubbins Vale Rd BL0 . . . . .67 C1
Stubbins Vale Terr BL0 . . . .67 B1
Stubbylee La OL13 . . . . . . .69 E8
Stubley Holme 5 OL14 . . .108 A1
Stubley La OL14 . . . . .108 B1
Studfold PR7 . . . . .60 B2
Studholme Ave PR1 . . . . . .95 E2
Studholme Cl 8 PR1 . . . . . .95 E2
Studholme Cres PR1 . . . . . .95 E2
Stump Cross La BB7 . . . . .224 F5
Stump Hall Rd BB12 . . . . .145 F7
Stump La PR6 . . . . .42 D8
Stunstead Rd BB8 . . . . . . .170 C2
Stunstead Rd BB8 . . . . . . .170 C3
Sturgess Cl L39 . . . . .5 F7
Sturminster Cl 5 PR1 . . . . .95 E2
Styan St FY7 . . . . .194 A4
Stydd La PR3 . . . . .140 E4
Sudell Ave L31 . . . . .5 F2
Sudell Cl BB3 . . . . .81 C1
Sudell Cross 20 BB1 . . . . .100 C5
Sudell La L31,L39 . . . . .5 E6
Sudell Rd BB3 . . . . .81 B1
Sudell Prim Sch BB3 . . . . .81 B1
Sudellside St BB3 . . . . .81 B1
Suffolk Ave BB12 . . . . . . .126 A6
Suffolk Cl PR5 . . . . .58 E6
Suffolk Rd Blackpool FY3 . .130 A2
Preston PR1 . . . . .117 A1
Southport PR8 . . . . .21 A8
Suffolk St BB2 . . . . .100 C2
Sugar Stubbs La PR9 . . . . .54 C4
Sugham La LA3 . . . . .208 F8
Sulby Cl PR8 . . . . .33 F3
Sulby Dr Fulwood PR2 . . . .117 F5
Lancaster LA1 . . . . .210 F6
Sulby Gr Morecambe LA4 . .213 A6
Morecambe LA4 . . . . . . .213 A6
Sulby Rd BB2 . . . . .100 E1
Sullivan Dr BB2 . . . . .101 A1
Sullom Side La PR3 . . . . . .179 C5
Sullom View PR3 . . . . . . .178 C6
Sultan St BB5 . . . . .103 B7
Sulyard St LA1 . . . . .210 F8
Summer St Horwich BL6 . . .31 B4
Nelson BB9 . . . . .147 C2
Skelmersdale WN8 . . . . . .18 A4
Summer Trees Ave PR2 . .115 D3
Summerdale Dr BL0 . . . . . .49 B2
Summerer Rd PR4 . . . . . .131 F6
Summerfield PR5 . . . . .75 F3
Summerfield Cl PR5 . . . . . .96 B3
Summerfield Ct 2 BB7 . . .143 C2
Summerfields Coppull PR7 . .28 F7
Lytham St Anne's FY8 . . . .88 C8
Summerhill LA2 . . . . .233 D7
Summerseat La BL0 . . . . . .49 A2
Summerseat
Meth Prim Sch BL9 . . . .49 D2
Summerseat Sta BL9 . . . . .49 C8
Summersgill Rd LA1 . . . . .213 D2
Summerton Wlk BB3 . . . . .81 A2
Summerville 4 FY4 . . . . .109 C6
Summerville Ave FY3 . . . .130 E5
Summerville Wlk BB2 . . . .100 D5
Summerwood Cl FY2 . . . .150 D1
Summerwood La
Halsall L39 . . . . .22 C1
Haskayne L39 . . . . .14 D8
Summit Cl BL9 . . . . .32 F4
Summit Dr PR4 . . . . .92 C6
Summit St OL10 . . . . .32 F3
Summit Works BB11 . . . . .126 E2
Sumner Ave L39 . . . . .13 F4
Sumner Rd L37 . . . . .11 F3
Sumner St Blackburn BB2 .100 C8
Leyland PR5 . . . . .76 A1
Sumner's La PR5 . . . . .39 A7
Sumners Barn PR2 . . . . . .117 E6
Sumpter Croft PR1 . . . . . . .95 E2
Sumpter Ct 3 PR1 . . . . . . .95 F2
Sun St Colne BB8 . . . . . . .169 E5
Lancaster LA1 . . . . .210 F8
Nelson BB9 . . . . .147 C8
Ramsbottom BL0 . . . . . . .49 B7
Sun Terr 7 OL14 . . . . . . .108 B1
Sunacre Ct LA3 . . . . .212 B3
Sunbank Cl OL12 . . . . .51 D2
Sunbury Ave PR1 . . . . .95 D3
Sunbury Dr PR8 . . . . .20 D4
Suncliffe Rd BB9 . . . . . . .147 D4
Suncourt PR8 . . . . .33 F6
Sunderland Ave
Cleveleys FY5 . . . . .172 F4
Hambleton FY6 . . . . .174 D2
Sunderland Dr LA3 . . . . . .212 D2
Sunderland St BB12 . . . . .126 B6
Sunfield Cl FY4 . . . . .110 A2
Sunnindale Ave BB4 . . . . . .86 A1

Sunningdale PR4 . . . . . . .136 B3
Sunningdale Ave
Blackpool FY4 . . . . .130 A2
Fleetwood FY7 . . . . .172 D7
Hest Bank LA2 . . . . .215 D1
Sunningdale Cl PR4 . . . . .113 A4
Sunningdale Cres 2 . . . . .215 D1
Sunningdale Ct FY8 . . . . . .89 A6
Sunningdale Pl PR4 . . . . .134 C8
Sunningdale Gdns
Brierfield BB10 . . . . .147 D3
Formby L37 . . . . .11 E3
Sunny Bank Kirkham PR4 .112 F5
Penwortham PR1 . . . . . . .95 F3
Sunny Bank Ave
Blackpool FY2 . . . . .150 C4
Newton-with-S PR4 . . . . .114 A2
Sunny Bank Cl BB4 . . . . . .67 A6
Sunny Bank Cotts BB4 . . . .66 F5
Sunny Bank Mill 6 PR4 . .112 F5
Sunny Bank Rd
Blackburn BB2 . . . . .100 E1
Haslingden BB4 . . . . .66 F6
Sunny Bank Terr 3 OL14 .108 B1
Sunny Bower Cl BB1 . . . . .122 B1
Sunny Bower Rd BB1 . . . .122 B1
Sunny Brow PR7 . . . . .42 A2
Sunny Dr WN5 . . . . .10 F6
Sunny Lea St BB4 . . . . . . .84 F5
Sunny Rd PR9 . . . . .53 A2
Sunny View PR6 . . . . .79 C2
Sunnybank Dr BB5 . . . . . .102 C2
Sunnybank Rd LA5 . . . . . .216 A5
Sunnybank St Darwen BB3 .81 A1
7 Haslingden BB4 . . . . . .84 A3
Sunnycliff Ret Pk LA3 . . . .212 G1
Sunnyfield Ave
Morecambe LA4 . . . . . . .213 A6
Over Town BB11 . . . . . . .107 A8
Sunnyfields La BB3 . . . . . .65 A8
Sunnyfields L39 . . . . .16 A5
Sunnyhill PR2 . . . . .117 C5
Sunnyhill Cl BB3 . . . . .80 D2
Sunnyhurst Ave FY4 . . . . .109 D6
Sunnyhurst Cl BB3 . . . . . . .80 D2
Sunnyhurst La BB3 . . . . . . .80 D2
Sunnyhurst Rd
Blackburn BB2 . . . . .100 C5
Blackburn BB2 . . . . .100 D4
Sunnyhurst Wood
Visitor Ctr BB3 . . . . . . .80 D2
Sunnymede Dr L31 . . . . . . .5 D3
Sunnymede Sch PR8 . . . . .33 F6
Sunnymede Vale BL0 . . . . .49 A3
Sunnymere Dr BB3 . . . . . .80 E2
Sunnyside
5 High Bentham LA2 . . .233 D8
Ormskirk L39 . . . . .6 C7
Southport PR8 . . . . .33 F3
Sunnyside Ave
Billington BB7 . . . . .143 B4
Blackburn BB2 . . . . .79 E8
Ribchester PR3 . . . . .140 D3
Warton PR4 . . . . .91 E6
Wilpshire BB1 . . . . .122 A7
Sunnyside Cl
Freckleton PR4 . . . . .92 B7
Lancaster LA1 . . . . .210 E7
Rawtenstall BB4 . . . . . . .85 A6
Sunnyside La L1 . . . . .210 E7
Sunnyside Terr FY6 . . . . .195 C3
Sunset Cl L33 . . . . .1 A5
Super St BB5 . . . . .123 E4
Surgeon's Ct PR1 . . . . . . .95 F7
Surrey Ave Burnley BB12 .126 B7
Darwen BB3 . . . . .80 F3
Surrey Cl PR9 . . . . .53 C5
Surrey Rd Barrowford BB9 168 D2
Blackburn BB1 . . . . .101 D5
Surrey St Accrington BB5 . .103 D6
Preston PR1 . . . . .96 C8
Sussex Ave OL10 . . . . .32 E1
Sussex Cl Church BB5 . . . .102 F7
Standish WN1 . . . . .29 B1
Sussex Dr Blackburn BB1 . .101 A4
Garstang PR3 . . . . .178 B7
Haslingden BB4 . . . . .67 B8
Sussex Rd Blackpool FY3 . .129 E6
Rishton BB1 . . . . .101 F8
Southport PR8, PR9 . . . . .34 D6
Sussex St
21 Barnoldswick BB18 . . .200 B2
Burnley BB11 . . . . .127 B4
1 Nelson BB9 . . . . .168 E1
Preston PR1 . . . . .117 A1
Sussex Wlk 10 BB1 . . . . .101 A4
Sutch La L40 . . . . .25 B5
Sutcliffe St Bacup OL13 . . .70 C8
Brierfield BB10 . . . . .147 F3
18 Burnley BB11 . . . . . .126 F6
7 Chorley PR7 . . . . .42 D7
Sutcliffe Terr BB1 . . . . . . .81 F6
Sutherland Cl BB1 . . . . . .122 A7
Sutherland Rd
Blackpool FY1 . . . . .129 C8
Heywood OL10 . . . . .32 F1
Sutherland St BB8 . . . . . .169 C4
Sutherland View 2 FY1 . .129 C7
Sutton Ave Brierfield BB10 147 D2
Tarleton PR4 . . . . .56 A8
Sutton Cres BB5 . . . . .124 F1
Sutton Dr PR2 . . . . .94 D8
Sutton Gr PR4 . . . . .60 F4
Sutton La Adlington PR6 . . .30 B8

Sutton La continued
Tarleton PR4 . . . .**55** F5
Sutton Pl FY1 . . . .**129** C4
Sutton Rd L37 . . . .**11** E1
Sutton St Blackburn BB2 . . .**79** D8
Weeton Camp PR4 . . . . . .**131** E6
Sutton's La L37 . . . .**12** E3
Sutton's Yd FY6 . . . .**151** E4
Swain St OL12 . . . .**51** E1
Swainbank St BB11 . . . . . .**127** B5
Swaine St BB9 . . . .**147** C8
Swainson St FY8 . . . .**89** F3
Swainstead Raike BD24 . . .**230** E8
Swaledale LA2 . . . .**207** B4
Swaledale Ave BB10 . . . . .**147** B4
Swalegate L31 . . . .**5** C2
Swallow Ave 1 PR1 . . . . . .**95** E4
Swallow Cl FY5 . . . .**173** A4
Swallow Ct PR6 . . . .**77** C1
Swallow Dr Blackburn BB1 **100** E6
Bury BL9 . . . .**32** B4
Swallow Field PR4 . . . .**73** E3
Swallow Pk 6 BB11 . . . . . .**126** C5
Swallow Wharf 7 LA1 . . . .**214** A1
Swallowfields
Blackburn BB1 . . . .**100** E8
Cottam PR4 . . . .**115** E5
Swallowfold PR2 . . . .**138** D1
Swan Alley 2 L39 . . . .**15** E5
Swan Delph L39 . . . .**15** C2
Swan Dr FY5 . . . .**172** F1
Swan La L39 . . . .**5** F6
Swan Mdw BB7 . . . .**186** D1
Swan Rd BL8 . . . .**48** F2
Swan St Blackburn BB2 . . .**100** E3
Darwen BB3 . . . .**64** B6
Preston PR1 . . . .**96** C8
Swan Yd 1 LA1 . . . .**211** A7
Swanage Ave **109** B6
Swanage Rd BB10 . . . .**147** C1
Swanfield St BB8 . . . .**170** A5
Swansea St PR2 . . . .**95** C8
Swansey La PR6 . . . .**77** C5
Swanson St 1 FY1 . . . . . .**129** C6
Swarbrick Cl FY1 . . . .**129** D7
Swarbrick Ct PR3 . . . .**139** B7
Swarbrick St PR4 . . . .**113** A4
Sweet Briar Cl OL12 . . . . . .**51** E2
Sweet Briar La OL12 . . . . . .**51** E2
Sweetclough Dr BB12 . . . .**125** F6
Swift Cl BB1 . . . .**100** F5
Swilkin La FY6 . . . .**174** E6
Swill Brook La 1 PR1 . . . .**96** C6
Swinate Rd LA5 . . . .**237** C1
Swinburn Gr WN5 . . . .**10** D1
Swinburne Cl BB5 . . . .**103** E2
Swinden Hall Rd BB9 . . . .**168** E2
Swinden La BB8 . . . .**169** A2
Swindon Ave 6 FY4 . . . . .**109** D8
Swindon St BB11 . . . .**126** D5
Swinless St BB10 . . . .**127** B8
Swinshaw Cl BB4 . . . .**105** A2
Swiss St BB5 . . . .**102** F6
Swithemby St BL6 . . . .**31** A4
Sword Meanygate PR4 . . . .**55** C6
Sycamore Ave
Blackpool FY4 . . . .**109** F5
Burnley BB12 . . . .**126** B4
Euxton PR7 . . . .**59** D3
Garstang PR3 . . . .**178** D8
Sycamore Bglws BB7 . . . .**225** C3
Sycamore Cl
Blackburn BB1 . . . .**100** F8
Burnley BB12 . . . .**126** C6
Fulwood PR2 . . . .**117** C6
Mawdesley L40 . . . .**39** C2
Rishton BB1 . . . .**102** B8
Sycamore Cres Caton LA2 **231** C3
Clayton-le-M BB5 . . . . . .**124** A5
1 Rawtenstall BB4 . . . .**84** F1
Sycamore Ct PR7 . . . .**42** B5
Sycamore Dr Kirkham PR4 **112** D4
Penwortham PR1 . . . .**95** E3
1 Skelmersdale WN8 . . . . .**17** E2
Sycamore Gdns
Foulridge BB8 . . . .**191** D1
Heysham LA3 . . . .**208** E6
Sycamore Gr
Accrington BB5 . . . .**103** E3
Darwen BB3 . . . .**81** B2
Formby L37 . . . .**11** C1
Lancaster LA1 . . . .**210** D8
Sycamore Rd
Bilsborrow PR3 . . . .**157** A5
Blackburn BB1 . . . .**100** F8
Caton LA2 . . . .**231** C3
Chorley PR6 . . . .**60** D2
Fulwood PR2 . . . .**117** C2
Sycamore Rise BB8 . . . . . .**191** D1
Sycamore Trad Est FY4 . . .**109** F5
Sycamore Way SB18 . . . . .**200** A1
Sycamore Wlk 1 BL6 . . . . .**31** E1
Syd Brook La PR5,L40 . . . .**39** E7
Sydenham Terr OL12 . . . . .**51** D3
Sydney Ave BB7 . . . .**143** D5
Sydney St Accrington BB5 .**103** C6
1 Burnley BB11 . . . .**126** F6
Darwen BB3 . . . .**64** B7
Enfield BB5 . . . .**124** A1
Hoddlesden BB3 . . . .**81** F1
Lytham St Anne's FY8 . . .**88** F6
Sydney Terr BB8 . . . .**170** C3
Syke Hill 14 PR1 . . . .**96** A7

Syke House La PR3 . . . . . .**158** E4
Syke La OL12 . . . .**51** F4
Syke Rd OL12 . . . .**51** F4
Syke Side Dr BB5 . . . .**124** E6
Syke St Haslingden BB4 . . .**84** C1
Preston PR1 . . . .**96** A7
Sykefield BB9 . . . .**147** A5
Sykelands Ave LA2 . . . . . .**214** F7
Sykelands Gr LA2 . . . .**214** F7
Sykes St BL9 . . . .**32** A3
Sylvan Dr BB11 . . . .**126** B4
Sylvan Gr PR5 . . . .**97** A2
Sylvan Pl LA3 . . . .**208** E6
Sylvancroft PR2 . . . .**116** A5
Sylvester St LA1 . . . .**210** E7
Symonds Rd PR2 . . . .**116** E3

T

Tabby Nook PR4 . . . .**54** F2
Tabby's Nook
Newburgh WN8 . . . .**26** A1
Skelmersdale WN8 . . . . . .**18** A8
Taberner St WN6 . . . .**28** F1
Tabley La PR2,PR4 . . . .**115** F2
Tabor St BB12 . . . .**126** D6
Tadema Gr BB11 . . . .**126** F2
Tadlow Cl L37 . . . .**11** C1
Tag Croft PR2 . . . .**115** F5
Tag Farm Ct PR2 . . . .**115** F5
Tag La PR2 . . . .**116** A4
Talaton Cl PR9 . . . .**53** A5
Talbot Ave BB5 . . . .**123** F2
Talbot Cl Clitheroe BB7 . . .**164** F7
Rawtenstall BB4 . . . .**67** E8
Talbot Ct 11 Blackpool FY4 **129** B1
3 Lytham St Anne's FY8 . . .**89** A8
Talbot Dr Brierfield BB10 . .**147** F2
Euxton PR7 . . . .**59** D2
Southport PR8 . . . .**34** B6
Talbot Gr BL9 . . . .**32** A6
Talbot House PR7 . . . .**60** C2
Talbot Liby PR1 . . . .**95** D8
Talbot Mkt PR1 . . . .**129** B1
Talbot Rd Accrington BB5 .**103** A8
Blackpool FY1,FY3 . . . . .**129** C6
Leyland PR5 . . . .**75** E2
Lytham St Anne's FY8 . . .**90** C4
Penwortham PR1 . . . .**95** E5
Preston PR1 . . . .**95** D7
Talbot Row PR7 . . . .**59** D1
Talbot Sq PR1 . . . .**129** B5
Talbot St Brierfield BB10 . .**147** F2
Burnley BB11 . . . .**127** B6
Chipping PR3 . . . .**182** E3
Chorley PR6 . . . .**60** E1
Colne BB8 . . . .**169** D6
Fulwood PR2 . . . .**116** D4
Rishton BB1 . . . .**123** C1
Southport PR8 . . . .**34** A6
Talbot Terr 1 FY8 . . . .**90** B3
Tamar Cl PR5 . . . .**59** B7
Tamar St PR1 . . . .**96** E8
Tamneys The WN8 . . . .**17** F1
Tan Hill Dr LA1 . . . .**213** F3
Tan House Ave WN8 . . . . . .**26** C3
Tan House La WN8 . . . .**26** C2
Tan Pit Cotts WN8 . . . .**19** C4
Tancaster WN8 . . . .**17** E1
Tanfield Nook WN8 . . . . . .**26** C2
Tanfields WN8 . . . .**17** F1
Tanglewood PR2 . . . .**117** B5
Tanhouse 6 LA2 . . . .**207** A4
Tanhouse La PR6 . . . .**60** F6
Tanhouse Rd WN8 . . . .**9** E7
Tanner Barn BB5 . . . .**84** B7
Tanner St 11 BB11 . . . . . .**126** F6
Tanners Croft 5 BL0 . . . . .**49** B6
Tanners St BL0 . . . .**49** B6
Tannersmith La L40 . . . . . .**39** F5
Tanpits La LA6 . . . .**234** B7
Tanpits Rd BB5 . . . .**102** F6
Tansley Ave PR7 . . . .**41** D1
Tansley Cl BL6 . . . .**31** C2
Tansy La PR3 . . . .**203** F4
Tanterton Hall Rd PR2 . . .**116** A6
Tanyard Cl PR7 . . . .**41** D1
Tape St 2 BL0 . . . .**49** B6
Taper St BL0 . . . .**49** B6
Tapestry St BB2 . . . .**100** D1
Tarbert Cres BB1 . . . .**101** D4
Tarbet St LA1 . . . .**211** A7
Tardy Gate Trad Ctr PR5 . .**76** A4
Tarleton Ave BB11 . . . .**127** B4
Tarleton CE Prim Sch PR4 **56** A5
Tarleton Cty High Sch
PR4 . . . .**56** A7
Tarleton Cty Prim Sch
PR4 . . . .**55** F7
Tarleton Mere Brow
CE Prim Sch PR4 . . . . . .**54** F2
Tarleton Rd PR9 . . . .**35** A8
Tarleton St BB11 . . . .**127** B4
Tarlscough La L40 . . . .**37** D1
Tarlswood WN8 . . . .**17** F1
Tarn Ave BB5 . . . .**123** F4
Tarn Brook La BB5 . . . .**124** F1
Tarn Brow L39 . . . .**15** C3
Tarn Cl Penwortham PR1 . . .**94** F4
Storth LA7 . . . .**237** F5
Tarn Ct FY7 . . . .**193** D1
Tarn Hows Cl 1 PR7 . . . . .**42** B5
Tarn La LA6 . . . .**234** B6
Tarn Rd Formby L37 . . . . . .**11** D3
Thornton FY5 . . . .**151** D7
Tarnacre La PR3 . . . .**177** E2
Tarnacre View PR3 . . . . . .**178** C6

Tarnbeck Dr L40 . . . .**39** D2
Tarnbrick Ave PR4 . . . .**92** C7
Tarnbrook Cl
Carnforth LA5 . . . .**217** C1
Hest Bank LA5 . . . .**215** F2
Tarnbrook Cotts PR3 . . . . .**196** E5
Tarnbrook Dr FY3 . . . .**130** A7
Tarnbrook Rd
6 Heysham LA3 . . . .**208** F8
2 Lancaster LA1 . . . .**213** D2
Tarnside FY4 . . . .**130** B1
Tarnside Rd WN5 . . . .**10** E6
Tarnsyke Rd LA1 . . . .**213** D2
Tarnwater La LA2 . . . .**206** F2
Tarnway Ave FY5 . . . .**151** D8
Tarradale PR4 . . . .**93** F1
Tarragon Dr FY2 . . . .**150** F4
Tarry Barn La BB7 . . . .**165** A3
Tarvin Cl Brierfield BB10 . .**147** F3
Southport PR9 . . . .**53** D5
Tasker St 14 BB5 . . . .**103** C6
Taskers Croft BB7 . . . .**143** F8
Tatham St PR7 . . . .**193** C1
Tatham Fells
CE (VC) Prim Sch LA2 . .**233** C4
Tattersall Sq BB4 . . . .**85** F3
Tattersall St
6 Blackburn BB2 . . . .**100** E4
Haslingden BB4 . . . .**84** B6
Oswaldtwistle BB5 . . . . .**102** D4
2 Padiham BB12 . . . .**125** D8
Tatton St BB8 . . . .**169** B3
Tauheedul Islam
Girls High Sch BB1 . . . .**100** E6
Taunton Rd BB5 . . . .**100** B5
Taunton St
6 Blackpool FY4 . . . .**129** D1
Preston PR1 . . . .**117** D1
Tavistock Dr PR8 . . . .**20** B6
Tavistock St BB9 . . . .**168** F1
Tawd Rd WN8 . . . .**9** C8
Tay St Burnley BB11 . . . . . .**126** D5
3 Preston PR1 . . . .**95** D6
Taybank Ave FY4 . . . .**109** D7
Taydale Cotts BB10 . . . . . .**147** E3
Taylor Ave Newchurch BB4 .**85** F2
Ormskirk L39 . . . .**16** A5
Taylor Cl BB2 . . . .**100** C3
Taylor Ct BB4 . . . .**84** A3
Taylor Gr LA4 . . . .**213** B6
Taylor Holme Ind Est
OL13 . . . .**69** B8
Taylor St
Barnoldswick BB18 . . . . .**200** A2
Blackburn BB2 . . . .**100** D3
Brierfield BB9 . . . .**147** B6
Burnley BB10 . . . .**127** A8
Bury BL9 . . . .**32** A3
Chorley PR7 . . . .**42** B5
Clitheroe BB7 . . . .**164** F8
Darwen BB3 . . . .**64** A8
Haslingden BB4 . . . .**84** B6
Horwich BL6 . . . .**31** B3
Preston PR1 . . . .**95** D6
6 Rawtenstall BB4 . . . .**85** A3
Rochdale OL12 . . . .**51** F1
Skelmersdale WN8 . . . . . .**17** C1
Whitworth OL12 . . . .**51** D8
Taylor St W BB5 . . . .**103** B6
Taylor's Bldgs BB6 . . . . . .**142** D1
Taylor's La
Fisher's Row PR3 . . . . . .**196** D6
Holmes PR4 . . . .**55** D3
Taylor's Meanygate PR4 . . .**55** A7
Taylors Cl FY6 . . . .**151** C5
Taylors Ct 18 BL6 . . . .**31** C2
Taymouth Rd 5 FY4 . . . . .**110** A6
Taywood Cl FY6 . . . .**151** F4
Taywood Rd FY5 . . . .**173** A4
Teak St BL9 . . . .**32** B5
Teal Cl Blackburn BB1 . . . .**100** D8
Ormskirk L39 . . . .**15** C2
Thornton FY5 . . . .**173** A4
Teal Ct FY3 . . . .**130** D4
Teal Pl PR5 . . . .**58** D7
Teanlowe Ctr FY6 . . . .**151** D3
Tears La WN8 . . . .**17** F8
Teasel Wlk LA3 . . . .**212** E2
Tebay Ave Cleveleys FY5 . .**172** D4
Kirkham PR4 . . . .**113** C5
Tebay Cl L31 . . . .**5** F2
Tebay St LA1 . . . .**213** E4
Tedder Ave Burnley BB12 .**126** B6
Southport PR9 . . . .**35** A7
Teenadore Ave 1 FY4 . . . .**109** E7
Tees Cl FY7 . . . .**193** D2
Tees St PR1 . . . .**117** C2
Teesdale 8 LA2 . . . .**207** A4
Teesdale Ave FY2 . . . .**129** D8
Teil Gn PR2 . . . .**117** E6
Telford St Burnley BB12 . . .**126** C7
Horwich BL6 . . . .**31** D7
Temperance St PR6 . . . .**42** E8
Temperance Terr OL13 . . . .**86** F1
Temple Cl 2 BB1 . . . .**101** B4
Temple Ct 10 PR1 . . . .**95** F7
Temple Dr BB1 . . . .**101** B4
Temple St
10 Blackpool FY1 . . . .**129** B5
Burnley BB11 . . . .**127** B5
Colne BB8 . . . .**169** E6
Nelson BB9 . . . .**147** F8
Temple Way PR6 . . . .**60** D3
Templegate Cl WN6 . . . .**28** F2
Templemartin 2 WN8 . . . . .**17** F2
Templeton Cl BB3 . . . .**81** A2
Ten Row LA2 . . . .**205** E5
Tenby WN8 . . . .**17** E2

Tenby Cl BB1 . . . .**100** E7
Tenby Gr 6 OL12 . . . .**51** C1
Tenby Rd 7 PR1 . . . .**96** A6
Tenby St OL12 . . . .**51** C1
Tennis St BB10 . . . .**127** A8
Tennyson Ave Chorley PR7 .**42** C6
Lytham St Anne's FY8 . . .**90** D4
Oswaldtwistle BB5 . . . . .**102** C4
Padiham BB12 . . . .**125** E7
Read BB12 . . . .**144** D2
Thornton FY5 . . . .**173** A3
Warton PR4 . . . .**91** E6
Tennyson Cl LA5 . . . .**216** A5
Tennyson Dr
Longshaw WN5 . . . .**10** D1
Ormskirk L39 . . . .**15** D6
Tennyson Pl
Bamber Bridge PR5 . . . . .**96** D2
Great Harwood BB6 . . . .**123** B4
Tennyson Rd
Blackpool FY3 . . . .**129** F7
Colne BB8 . . . .**169** D5
Fleetwood FY7 . . . .**194** A4
Preston PR1 . . . .**117** D1
Tennyson St
Brierfield BB10 . . . .**147** F3
Burnley BB10 . . . .**126** D5
6 Hapton BB12 . . . .**125** C4
Tensing Ave FY2 . . . .**150** D5
Tensing Rd L31 . . . .**5** D1
Tenterfield St
28 Preston PR1 . . . .**95** F8
6 Rawtenstall BB4 . . . . . .**68** F8
Tenterheads BB4 . . . .**68** F7
Terance Rd 2 FY4 . . . .**109** E8
Terra Cotta Bldgs BB4 . . .**106** A1
Terrace Row BB7 . . . .**143** C4
Terrace St PR1 . . . .**117** C1
Terrace The 7 LA2 . . . . . .**233** B8
Terry St BB9 . . . .**169** A2
Tetbury Cl BB2 . . . .**79** E8
Teven St 5 PR5 . . . .**96** E1
Teversham WN8 . . . .**17** F2
Teviot 4 WN8 . . . .**17** E2
Teviot Ave FY4 . . . .**193** D3
Tewkesbury 3 WN8 . . . . . .**17** E2
Tewkesbury Ave FY4 . . . . .**109** D5
Tewkesbury Cl BB5 . . . . . .**103** E3
Tewkesbury Dr FY8 . . . .**90** D5
Tewksbury St BB2 . . . .**100** B1
Thames Ave BB10 . . . .**147** C3
Thames Dr WN5 . . . .**10** F7
Thames Ho 8 PR1 . . . .**96** D8
Thames Prim Sch FY4 . . . .**109** B7
Thames Rd FY4 . . . .**109** B7
Thames St PR4 . . . .**113** F2
Thane Row BB11 . . . .**106** D7
Thanet WN8 . . . .**17** F2
Thanet Lee Cl BB10 . . . . . .**127** E1
Thealby Cl WN8 . . . .**17** E2
Theatre St PR1 . . . .**95** F7
Thelma St BL0 . . . .**49** B6
Thermdale Dr PR3 . . . .**178** B7
Thetis Rd LA1 . . . .**210** C8
Thickrash Brow LA2 . . . . .**233** D7
Third Ave Blackpool FY4 . .**109** C7
Bury BL9 . . . .**32** D4
Thirlmere Ave FY7 . . . .**193** C1
Thirlmere Ct LA1 . . . .**214** B1
Thirlmere Ave
Burnley BB10 . . . .**147** A2
Carleton FY6 . . . .**151** C4
Colne BB8 . . . .**169** F6
Formby L37 . . . .**12** A2
Haslingden BB4 . . . .**67** C8
Nelson BB9 . . . .**31** C2
1 Orrell WN5 . . . .**10** F7
Orrell, Hall Green WN8 . .**10** B7
Padiham BB12 . . . .**145** C2
Thirlmere Cl
2 Accrington BB5 . . . . . .**124** D1
Adlington PR6 . . . .**30** B8
6 Blackburn BB1 . . . . . .**100** F6
Knott End-on-S FY6 . . . .**194** F6
Longton PR4 . . . .**74** B8
Maghull L31 . . . .**5** E2
Thirlmere Dr Darwen BB3 . .**81** C2
Longridge PR3 . . . .**138** F5
Morecambe LA4 . . . .**212** D4
Southport PR8 . . . .**20** B3
Withnell Fold PR6 . . . . . .**78** D2
Thirlmere Gdns LA4 . . . . .**212** E4
Thirlmere Rd
Blackpool FY4 . . . .**109** C3
Blackrod BL6 . . . .**30** C3
Burnley BB10 . . . .**127** E5
Chorley PR7 . . . .**42** B6
Hightown L38 . . . .**3** A4
Lancaster LA1 . . . .**214** B2
Preston PR1 . . . .**117** D1
Thirlmere Way BB4 . . . . . .**105** A1
Thirnby Ct LA6 . . . .**238** C1
Thirsk WN8 . . . .**17** E2
Thirsk Ave FY8 . . . .**89** B7
Thirsk Gr FY1 . . . .**129** D2
Thirsk Rd LA1 . . . .**211** B4
Thistle Break LA3 . . . .**209** A2
Thistle Cl Chorley PR6 . . . . .**42** E8
Cleveleys FY5 . . . .**172** F5
Hesketh Bank PR4 . . . . . .**72** E4
Thistle St 15 OL13 . . . .**86** F1
Thistlecroft PR2 . . . .**116** A5
Thistlemount Ave BB4 . . . . .**85** F1
Thistleton Mews 3 PR9 . . .**34** C8
Thistleton Rd Preston PR2 . .**94** E8
Thistleton PR4 . . . .**153** C1
Thomas Gr LA4 . . . .**212** E5
Thomas St Blackburn BB2 .**100** D4

Thomas St continued
Brierfield BB9 . . . .**147** A5
Burnley BB7 . . . .**127** A5
Colne BB8 . . . .**169** C4
2 Cornholme OL14 . . . . .**108** C1
2 Darwen BB4 . . . .**84** A3
Nelson BB9 . . . .**147** E7
8 Oswaldtwistle BB5 . . .**102** D3
4 Preston PR1 . . . .**96** B7
Whitworth OL12 . . . .**70** D2
Thomason Fold BL7 . . . . . .**47** D6
Thompson Ave L39 . . . .**16** B5
Thompson Dr BL9 . . . .**32** C3
Thompson St
Blackburn BB2 . . . .**100** C4
Darwen BB3 . . . .**64** B7
Horwich BL6 . . . .**31** A3
8 Preston PR1 . . . .**112** F6
Padiham BB12 . . . .**125** D7
Preston PR1 . . . .**117** D1
Thonock Rd LA4 . . . .**212** G3
Thorburn Dr OL12 . . . .**51** B7
Thorn Bank OL13 . . . .**87** A2
Thorn Cres OL13 . . . .**87** A2
Thorn Cty Prim Sch OL13 . .**86** F3
Thorn Dr OL13 . . . .**87** A2
Thorn Gdns OL13 . . . .**87** A2
Thorn Gr Blackpool FY1 . . .**129** C8
Colne BB8 . . . .**169** F6
Thorn Hill Cl BB1 . . . .**101** A5
Thorn La PR3 . . . .**139** B2
Thorn St Bacup OL13 . . . . . .**87** A2
Burnley BB11 . . . .**127** A8
Clitheroe BB7 . . . .**164** D8
Great Harwood BB6 . . . .**123** D6
Preston PR1 . . . .**117** C1
Ramsbottom BL0 . . . .**49** C3
Rawtenstall BB4 . . . .**84** F5
Sabden BB7 . . . .**145** A7
Thorn View BL9 . . . .**32** C3
Thornbank FY3 . . . .**130** B7
Thornbank Dr PR3 . . . .**178** D2
Thornbeck Ave L38 . . . .**2** F3
Thornber 1 WN8 . . . .**17** F2
Thornber Ct BB10 . . . .**147** C1
Thornber Gr FY1 . . . .**129** D3
Thornber St BB2 . . . .**100** C3
Thornbridge Ave L40 . . . . .**24** E3
Thornbury WN8 . . . .**17** F2
Thornby 3 WN8 . . . .**17** F2
Thorncliffe Dr BB3 . . . .**64** D8
Thorndale 4 WN8 . . . .**17** F2
Thorne St BB9 . . . .**169** A2
Thorney Bank St 7 BB11 . .**126** F5
Thorneybank Ind Est
BB11 . . . .**125** C2
Thorneycroft Cl FY6 . . . . . .**151** B5
Thorneyholme RC Sch
BB7 . . . .**222** C5
Thorneyholme Rd BB5 . . .**103** C8
Thorneyholme Sq BB12 . .**167** E5
Thorneylea OL12 . . . .**70** D1
Thornfield Lancaster LA1 . .**210** F5
Much Hoole PR4 . . . .**73** E4
Thornfield Ave
Fulwood PR2 . . . .**117** F3
Longridge PR3 . . . .**139** A8
Newchurch BB4 . . . .**85** E1
8 Rawtenstall BB4 . . . . . .**68** F8
Thornton FY5 . . . .**151** D8
Thorngate PR1 . . . .**95** B4
Thorngate Cl PR1 . . . .**95** B4
Thornham Ct FY3 . . . .**129** E5
Thornhill L39 . . . .**6** B8
Thornhill Ave
Knott End-on-S FY6 . . . .**195** A5
Rishton BB1 . . . .**102** A8
Thornhill Cl Blackpool FY4 **109** F5
Ormskirk L39 . . . .**6** B8
Thornhill Rd Chorley PR6 . .**60** E2
Leyland PR5 . . . .**58** D8
Ramsbottom BL0 . . . .**49** A1
Thornhill St BB12 . . . .**126** A6
Thornlea Dr OL12 . . . .**51** B2
Thornleigh Cl 10 FY5 . . . .**173** A2
Thornleigh Dr LA4 . . . .**234** C7
Thornley Ave BB1 . . . .**101** C6
Thornley Pl PR2 . . . .**118** A3
Thornley Rd PR2 . . . .**118** A3
Thornpark Dr 3 PR2 . . . . .**115** D1
Thorns Ave LA2 . . . .**215** D1
Thorns The L31 . . . .**5** B2
Thornton WN8 . . . .**17** F2
Thornton Ave
Fulwood PR2 . . . .**116** B4
Lytham St Anne's FY8 . . .**89** B8
Morecambe LA4 . . . .**212** F6
Thornton Cl
Accrington BB5 . . . .**103** A8
Blackburn BB2 . . . .**80** F8
Rufford L40 . . . .**38** C4
Thornton Cres
Burnley BB10 . . . .**127** E5
Morecambe LA4 . . . .**212** F5
Thornton Ctr 7 FY5 . . . .**173** C1
Thornton Dr
Gregson Lane PR5 . . . . . .**97** D4
Leyland PR5 . . . .**75** E4
Thornton Gate FY5 . . . . . .**172** D4
Thornton Gr LA4 . . . .**212** F5
Thornton La
Morecambe LA4 . . . .**212** F6
Thornton in L LA6 . . . . . .**236** F5
Thornton Manor Ct BD23 **201** A5
Thornton Pl FY5 . . . .**173** A4
Thornton Rd Burnley BB10 **127** E5
Morecambe LA4 . . . .**212** F6
Southport PR9 . . . .**34** F7

Thornton-in-Craven
Cty Prim Sch BD23 . . . .201 B6
Thorntrees Ave
Newsham PR3 . . . . .136 B5
Preston PR2 . . . . .115 D1
Thornway Ave FY5 . . . . .151 D8
Thornwood WN8 . . . . .17 F2
Thornwood Cl
Blackburn BB1 . . . . .121 E1
Lytham St Anne's FY8 . . . .89 E4
Thornylea BB2 . . . . .80 D7
Thorough Way PR3 . . . . .198 E7
Thoroughfare The LA5 . .217 D5
Thoroughgood Cl L40 . . . .24 D2
Thorpe WN8 . . . . .17 F2
Thorpe Ave LA4 . . . . . . .213 B4
Thorpe Cl PR1 . . . . .116 F1
Thorpe St BL0 . . . . .49 B5
Thrang Brow La LA5 . . . .219 C6
Threagill La LA5 . . . . . . .217 F5
Three Lane Ends PR6 . . . .61 C4
Three Nooks PR5 . . . . . . .77 C5
Three Oaks Cl L40 . . . . . .25 B2
Three Pools PR9 . . . . . . .53 C3
Three Tuns La L37 . . . . . .11 F3
Three Turns PR3 . . . . . .141 A8
Threefields PR2 . . . . . . .116 A5
Threlfall PR7 . . . . .59 F2
Threlfall Rd FY1 . . . . . . .129 D1
Threlfall St ■ PR2 . . . . .116 C1
Threlfall's La PR9 . . . . . .52 F2
Threlfalls Cl PR9 . . . . . . .52 F3
Threshers Ct PR3 . . . . . .204 C2
Threshfield Ave LA3 . . . .208 F8
Thrimby LA4 . . . . .212 E4
Thrimby Pl LA4 . . . . . . .212 E4
Thropps La PR4 . . . . .74 D6
Throstle Cl BB12 . . . . . . .127 A7
Throstle Gr LA2 . . . . . . .213 F8
Throstle Nest La PR3 . . .198 C4
Throstle St Blackburn BB1 .100 C4
⊡ Nelson BB9 . . . . .168 E1
Throstle Way ■ FY5 . . . .172 F1
Throstle Wlk LA7 . . . . . .237 F5
Throughs La LA7 . . . . . .237 F5
Throup Pl BB9 . . . . .168 E2
Thrum Fold OL12 . . . . . . .51 D3
Thrum Hall La
Rochdale OL12 . . . . .51 D3
Rochdale OL12 . . . . .51 E3
Thrush Dr BL9 . . . . .32 B4
Thrush St OL12 . . . . .51 C1
Thrushgill Dr LA2 . . . . .214 F7
Thurcroft Dr WN8 . . . . . .17 E2
Thurland Ct LA4 . . . . . . .212 D3
Thurnham Rd PR2 . . . . . .94 E8
Thurnham St LA1 . . . . . .210 F7
Thursby Ave FY4 . . . . . .109 D6
Thursby Cl PR8 . . . . .20 B3
Thursby Pl ■ BB9 . . . . . .168 F2
Thursby Rd Burnley BB10 .147 C1
Nelson BB9 . . . . .168 F2
Thursby Sq BB10 . . . . . .127 A8
Thursden Ave BB10 . . . .147 F3
Thursden Pl BB9 . . . . . . .169 B1
Thursfield Ave FY4 . . . . .109 E8
Thursfield Rd BB10 . . . . .127 B5
Thursford Gr BL6 . . . . . . .30 D1
Thursgill Ave LA4 . . . . .212 F3
Thurston WN8 . . . . .17 E2
Thurston Rd PR5 . . . . . . .76 A1
Thurston St BB11 . . . . . .127 B6
Thwaite Brow La LA5 . . .216 B6
Thwaite La LA2 . . . . . . .233 C5
Thwaites Ave BB2 . . . . .120 C4
Thwaites Rd BB5 . . . . . .102 C4
Thwaites St BB5 . . . . . . .102 C3
Tib St ■ BL0 . . . . .49 B5
Tiber Ave BB11 . . . . . . .126 C4
Tiber St PR1 . . . . .96 B7
Tibicar Dr E LA3 . . . . . .212 A1
Tibicar Dr W LA3 . . . . . .212 A1
Tilbury Gr WN6 . . . . .19 D7
Tilcroft WN8 . . . . .17 E2
Timber Brook PR7 . . . . . .60 A2
Timber St Accrington BB5 .103 C5
Bacup OL13 . . . . .86 F1
Brierfield BB9 . . . . .147 B6
Timberhurst BL9 . . . . . . .32 D2
Timbrills Ave BB7 . . . . .144 F8
Timms Cl L37 . . . . .11 F5
Timms La L37 . . . . .11 F5
Tincklers La PR7 . . . . . . .40 A6
Tinedale View BB12 . . . .145 D1
Tinker's La LA2 . . . . . . .220 B7
Tinkerfield PR2 . . . . . . .116 E2
Tinklers La BB7 . . . . . . .223 E7
Tinline St BL9 . . . . .32 A2
Tinniswood PR2 . . . . . . .116 B1
Tinsley Ave PR8 . . . . . . .34 E3
Tinsley's La
Out Rawcliffe PR3 . . . . . .175 D4
Southport PR8 . . . . .35 A1
Tintagel WN8 . . . . .17 E2
Tintagel Cl BB2 . . . . .79 C7
Tintern Ave Chorley PR7 . .42 D5
Rochdale OL12 . . . . .51 E2
Tintern Cl Accrington BB5 .103 E2
Read BB12 . . . . .144 D1
Tintern Cres BB1 . . . . . .101 B8
Tintern Dr L37 . . . . .12 E6
Tippet Cl BB2 . . . . .101 A1
Titan Way PR5 . . . . .75 B2
Tithe Barn La Knowley PR6 .61 A4
Runshaw Moor PR5,PR7 . . .58 F5
Scorton PR3 . . . . .199 E5
Tithebarn Gate FY6 . . . .151 D4
Tithebarn Hill LA2 . . . . .205 E5

Tithebarn Pl FY6 . . . . . .151 D4
Tithebarn Rd PR8 . . . . . .34 E6
Tithebarn St Orrell WN8 . .10 B7
⊡ Preston PR1 . . . . .96 A7
Preston PR1 . . . . .96 A8
Thornton FY6 . . . . .151 D4
Tittrington Brow BB7 . . .223 C2
Tiverton Ave WN8 . . . . . .17 E2
Tiverton Cl PR2 . . . . . . .116 F8
Tiverton Dr Blackburn BB2 .80 C8
Brierfield BB10 . . . . . . .147 F3
Tockholes CE Prim Sch
BB3 . . . . .80 A3
Tockholes Rd Darwen BB3 .80 F2
Darwen, Tockholes BB3,PR7 .80 A3
Tod Holes La BD23 . . . . .230 E4
Todd Carr Rd BB4 . . . . . .85 F1
Todd Hall Rd BB4 . . . . . .83 F4
Todd La N PR5 . . . . .96 C2
Todd La S PR5 . . . . .76 C8
Todd's La PR9 . . . . .54 A6
Todmorden Old Rd OL13 . .87 B5
Todmorden Rd Bacup OL13 .87 B4
Burnley BB11 . . . . .127 B3
Cockden BB10 . . . . .148 B1
Lytham St Anne's FY8 . . . .88 C8
Todmorden Road
Prim Sch BB10 . . . . . . .127 B5
Toll Bar Bsns Pk OL13 . . .69 C8
Toll Bar Cres LA1 . . . . . .210 F3
Tollgate PR1 . . . . .95 E4
Tollgate Rd L40 . . . . .24 B3
Tolsey Dr PR4 . . . . .94 D2
Tom Benson Way
PR2,PR4 . . . . .115 F4
Tom La BB4 . . . . .85 F2
Tomlinson Rd
Heysham LA3 . . . . .208 F6
Leyland PR5 . . . . .75 F2
Preston PR2 . . . . .116 C2
Tomlinson St BL6 . . . . . . .31 B3
Tonacliffe Cty Prim Sch
OL12 . . . . .51 C6
Tonacliffe Rd OL12 . . . . . .51 C6
Tonacliffe Terr OL12 . . . .51 C7
Tonacliffe Way OL12 . . . .51 C6
Tong Fold OL12 . . . . .70 C2
Tong Ho ⊡ OL13 . . . . . . .87 A3
Tong La Bacup OL13 . . . . .87 B2
Whitworth OL12 . . . . .70 D1
Tongbarn WN8 . . . . .17 E2
Tongues La FY6 . . . . . . .195 C6
Tonine WN5 . . . . .10 C5
Tontine Rd WN5,WN8 . . . .10 C6
Tontine St BB1 . . . . .100 E5
Toogood La WN6 . . . . . . .27 D6
Tootell St PR7 . . . . .42 B6
Tootle La L40 . . . . .38 A3
Tootle Rd PR3 . . . . .139 B8
Top Acre PR4 . . . . .94 C1
Top Acre Rd WN8 . . . . . . .9 C7
Top Barn La BB4 . . . . . . .85 E1
Top Locks L40 . . . . .25 A4
Top o' th' Croft BB2 . . . . .80 D8
Top of Fawna Rd PR3 . . .161 D1
Top Of Heap OL10 . . . . . .32 F2
Top of Wallsuches BL6 . . .31 F4
Top Row BB7 . . . . .144 F8
Topaz St BL9 . . . . .121 F2
Topham St BL9 . . . . .32 A1
Topping Fold Rd BL9 . . . .32 C3
Topping St Blackpool FY1 .129 B5
Bury BL9 . . . . .32 A3
Toppings The PR3 . . . . .178 C6
Tor Ave BL8 . . . . .48 F2
Tor End Rd BB4 . . . . .66 F6
Tor Scar Rd LA6 . . . . . . .236 F6
Tor View Haslingden BB4 . .84 C1
Rawtenstall BB4 . . . . .85 A1
Tor View Rd BB4 . . . . . . .84 C1
Tor View Sch Valley Site
BB4 . . . . .67 D8
Torcross Cl PR9 . . . . .53 A5
Tormore Cl PR6 . . . . .61 A3
Torn Cotts LA5 . . . . .216 C6
Toronto Ave Blackpool FY2 150 E3
Fleetwood FY7 . . . . .193 E2
Toronto Rd BB2 . . . . . . .100 C8
Torquay Ave
Blackpool FY3 . . . . .130 A2
Brierfield BB10 . . . . . . .147 D2
Torra Barn Cl BL7 . . . . . .46 E3
Torrentum Ct FY5 . . . . .173 C1
Torridon Cl BB2 . . . . .99 F1
Torrisholme
Cty Prim Sch LA4 . . . . . .213 B5
Torrisholme Rd LA1 . . . .213 D3
Torrisholme Sq LA4 . . . .213 B4
Torside Gr FY6 . . . . .151 B3
Torsway Ave FY3 . . . . . .129 F6
Torver Cl BB12 . . . . .126 B8
Totnes Cl FY6 . . . . .151 C6
Totnes Dr PR9 . . . . .53 A5
Tottenham Rd BB3 . . . . . .80 F6
Tottington Rd BL7,BL8 . . . .47 F2
Tottleworth BB6 . . . . . . .123 C3
Tottleworth Rd BB1 . . . .123 C2
Toulmin Cl PR3 . . . . . . .178 D2
Tower Ave BL0 . . . . .49 A5
Tower Bldgs ⊡ PR9 . . . . .34 C8
Tower Cl FY5 . . . . .173 A4
Tower Cotts LA3 . . . . . . .208 E7
Tower Ct Chapeltown BL7 . .47 C4
Lancaster LA1 . . . . .210 F7
Tower End L37 . . . . .11 C5
Tower Gn PR2 . . . . .116 F7
Tower Hill Clitheroe BB7 . .186 F1
Ormskirk L39 . . . . .16 A5

Tower Hill Rd WN8 . . . . . .10 B6
Tower La PR2 . . . . .116 F7
Tower Nook WN8 . . . . . . .10 A5
Tower Rd Blackburn BB2 . .99 E2
Darwen BB3 . . . . .64 B8
Tower St ⊡ Bacup OL13 . .86 F2
Blackpool FY1 . . . . .129 B5
Cornholme OL14 . . . . . .108 A1
Edgworth BL7 . . . . .47 C4
Oswaldtwistle BB5 . . . . .102 C5
Tower View Belthorn BB1 . .82 A5
Blackrod BL6 . . . . .30 C3
Darwen BB3 . . . . .81 C1
Penwortham PR1 . . . . . . .95 C7
Towers Ave L31 . . . . .5 C2
Town Brook Ho ⊡ PR1 . .116 E1
Town Brow PR5 . . . . .76 F2
Town End Bolton-le-S LA5 .216 A3
Kirkham PR4 . . . . .113 A5
Slaidburn BB7 . . . . .223 C7
⊡ Thornton FY5 . . . . . .173 A2
Town Gate BB6 . . . . .123 C5
Town Green Ct L39 . . . . . . .6 C4
Town Green Cty Sch L39 . . .6 C4
Town Green La L39 . . . . . . .6 C4
Town Green Sta L39 . . . . . .6 C4
Town Hall Sq ⊡ BB6 . . . .123 C5
Town Hall St
⊡ Blackburn BB2 . . . . .100 E5
⊡ Great Harwood BB6 . .123 C5
Town Head BB18 . . . . . . .200 A1
Town Hill Bank BB12 . . . .145 D1
Town House Rd BB9 . . . .148 B8
Town La Coppull PR7 . . . . .41 C1
Heskin Green PR7 . . . . . .40 C2
Much Hoole PR4 . . . . . . .73 D1
Southport PR8 . . . . .34 E3
Whittle-le-W PR6 . . . . . . .60 D6
Town Rd PR5 . . . . .57 B2
Town View BB1 . . . . .100 F4
Town Wlk BB1 . . . . .100 F4
Towneley High Sch BB11 127 C4
Towneley Rd PR3 . . . . . .139 A7
Towneley Rd W PR3 . . . .139 A7
Towneley St BB10 . . . . . .147 B1
Townely Ave BB5 . . . . . .124 F2
Townfield Ave BB10 . . . .127 F6
Townfield Cl PR4 . . . . . . .73 F7
Townfield La LA2 . . . . . .213 E7
Towngate Eccleston PR7 . . .40 B7
Foulridge BB8 . . . . .191 D1
Leyland PR5 . . . . .58 F7
Preston PR5 . . . . .59 A8
Townhouse Sch BB9 . . . .169 C1
Townley Cl LA1 . . . . .210 D7
Townley La PR1 . . . . .94 D4
Townley Par PR3 . . . . . .139 A7
Townley St Brierfield BB9 .147 B5
Brierfield, Harle Syke BB10 .147 F3
Chorley PR6 . . . . .42 D7
Colne BB8 . . . . .169 E6
Morecambe LA4 . . . . . . .212 E6
Townsend St
Haslingden BB4 . . . . .84 A3
Rawtenstall BB4 . . . . .68 F8
Townsfield LA5 . . . . .218 C6
Townshill Wlk PR4 . . . . .113 A6
Townsley St BB9 . . . . . . .147 E6
Townsway PR5 . . . . .76 C8
Towpath Wlk ⊡ LA5 . . . .217 D1
Toxhead Cl BL6 . . . . .31 A3
Toy & Teddy Bear Mus
of Childhood FY8 . . . . . . .88 D7
Tracks La WN8 . . . . .10 D3
Trafalgar Cl PR2 . . . . . . .116 D3
Trafalgar Rd
Blackpool FY1 . . . . .129 B3
Lancaster LA1 . . . . .211 A6
Southport PR8 . . . . .33 E3
Trafalgar St Burnley BB11 .126 F5
Chorley PR6 . . . . .60 D1
Lytham St Anne's FY8 . . . .88 F7
Trafford St PR1 . . . . .116 E2
Tram La LA6 . . . . .238 C2
Tramway La PR5 . . . . .77 B6
Tranmere Ave LA3 . . . . .212 A1
Tranmere Cres LA3 . . . . .212 A1
Tranmere Rd FY4 . . . . . .129 E1
Tranmoor PR4 . . . . .73 F6
Trans Brittania
Enterprise Est BB11 . . . .126 A3
Trap Hill L37 . . . . .11 C2
Trapp La Sabden BB12 . . .144 F4
Simonstone BB12 . . . . . .144 F2
Trash La Darwen BB3 . . . . .80 B2
Rimington BB7 . . . . .225 B1
Travellers Ct BB7 . . . . . .225 C3
Travera Lo ⊡ PR2 . . . . . .117 F4
Travers Pl PR2 . . . . .95 C8
Travers St BL6 . . . . .31 D1
Travis St BB10 . . . . .127 A8
Trawden Cl BB5 . . . . . . .103 C5
Trawden Cres PR2 . . . . .117 E4
Trawden Forest
Prim Sch BB8 . . . . .170 C2
Trawden Rd BB8 . . . . . . .170 B5
Traylen Way OL12 . . . . . .51 A1
Treales CE Prim Sch PR4 133 C2
Treales Rd PR4 . . . . .114 B6
Trecastle Rd L33 . . . . .1 A4
Tredgold St BL6 . . . . .31 C2
Treen Cl PR9 . . . . .53 B6
Treesdale Cl PR8 . . . . . . .33 F4
Treetop Villas PR9 . . . . . .52 F4
Treetops Ave BL0 . . . . . . .49 A3
Trefoil Cl FY5 . . . . .173 A5

Tremellen St BB5 . . . . . .103 A6
Trengrove St ⊡ OL12 . . . .51 C1
Trent Ave L31 . . . . .5 F2
Trent Cl
Burscough Bridge L40 . . . .24 F5
Lancaster LA3 . . . . .213 B2
Trent Rd Blackpool FY4 . .109 B7
Nelson BB9 . . . . .148 A8
Trent St Longridge PR3 . .138 F7
Lytham St Anne's FY8 . . . .90 D3
Tresco Cl BB2 . . . . .100 B1
Tretower Way FY5 . . . . .173 D2
Trevarrick Ct BL6 . . . . . .31 E2
Trevelyan Dr WN5 . . . . . .10 D1
Trevor Cl BB1 . . . . .100 F7
Trevor Rd Burscough L40 . .24 E4
Southport PR8 . . . . .20 C5
Triangle The
Accrington BB5 . . . . . . .103 E8
Fulwood PR2 . . . . .116 E4
Trigg La PR6,PR7 . . . . . . .61 D5
Trigge House PR7 . . . . . .60 C2
Trinity & St Michael's
CE Prim Sch Croston PR5 .57 B1
Croston PR5 . . . . .57 C2
Trinity Cl Freckleton PR4 . .92 B7
Padiham BB12 . . . . .125 D6
Trinity Ct ⊡ BB1 . . . . . .100 F6
Trinity Fold ⊡ PR1 . . . . . .95 F8
Trinity Gdns Southport PR8 .34 A6
Thornton FY5 . . . . .173 A3
Trinity Gn BL0 . . . . .49 B2
Trinity Mews PR9 . . . . . .34 C7
Trinity Pl ⊡ PR1 . . . . . . .95 F8
Trinity Prim Sch WN8 . . . .17 F1
Trinity Rd PR7 . . . . .42 B7
Trinity St ⊡ Bacup OL13 . .69 C8
Blackburn BB1 . . . . .100 F6
Oswaldtwistle BB5 . . . . .102 D3
Trinity Towers ⊡ BB11 . .126 E6
Trinity Wlks PR4 . . . . . . .56 A5
Trinket La LA2 . . . . .232 E6
Tristan Ave PR4 . . . . .74 A5
Troon Ave Blackburn BB1 .101 C3
Thornton FY5 . . . . .151 D8
Troon Ct PR1 . . . . .95 A6
Trough Rd BB7 . . . . .222 B5
Troughton Cres FY4 . . . .109 E8
Trout Beck BB5 . . . . .123 F4
Trout St ⊡ Burnley BB10 .127 A8
Preston PR1 . . . . .96 C7
Troutbeck Ave
Fleetwood FY7 . . . . .193 D2
Forton PR3 . . . . .204 B3
Maghull L31 . . . . .5 C2
Troutbeck Cl
Burnley BB12 . . . . .126 B8
Hawkshaw BL8 . . . . .48 B2
Troutbeck Cres FY4 . . . .110 D8
Troutbeck Dr BL0 . . . . . .49 C7
Troutbeck Pl PR2 . . . . . .117 C5
Troutbeck Rd Chorley PR7 .42 B5
Lancaster LA1 . . . . .214 A1
Lytham St Anne's FY8 . . .109 C1
Trowbarrow Cotts LA5 . .218 F5
Trower St PR1 . . . . .96 B6
Troy St BB1 . . . . .100 F7
Trumacar Com Prim Sch
LA3 . . . . .208 C5
Trumacar La LA3 . . . . . .208 C5
Truman Ave LA1 . . . . . . .210 C7
Trumley Ct LA3 . . . . . . .212 D2
Trunnah Gdns FY5 . . . . .173 B3
Trunnah Rd FY5 . . . . . . .173 B3
Truro Ave PR9 . . . . .53 B5
Truro Pl ⊡ PR1 . . . . .117 C1
Truro St ⊡ FY4 . . . . . . .129 C1
Truscott Rd L40 . . . . .24 D4
Tucker Hill BB7 . . . . .186 E1
Tucker's Hill Brow WN2 . .30 B1
Tudor Ave Preston PR1 . . .117 C1
Preston, Lea PR2 . . . . . . .115 D1
Tudor Cl Blackpool FY6 . .151 A4
⊡ Cleveleys FY5 . . . . . .172 F1
Darwen BB3 . . . . .81 A2
Langho BB6 . . . . .142 D1
Preston PR2 . . . . .115 D1
Tudor Croft PR5 . . . . .76 C7
Tudor Ct L39 . . . . .15 F6
Tudor Dr PR4 . . . . .113 A2
Tudor Gr ⊡ LA4 . . . . . . .213 A6
Tudor Mans PR8 . . . . . . .33 F6
Tudor Pl FY4 . . . . .109 B6
Tudor Rd
Lytham St Anne's FY8 . . . .88 D1
Southport PR8 . . . . .20 B6
Tuer St PR5 . . . . .75 F2
Tulip Ct OL12 . . . . .51 E3
Tulketh Ave PR2 . . . . . . .116 B1
Tulketh Brow PR2 . . . . . .116 C1
Tulketh Cres PR2 . . . . . .116 C1
Tulketh High Sch PR2 . . .116 B4
Tulketh Rd PR2 . . . . .116 B1
Tulketh St PR8 . . . . .34 B7
Tullyallen St BB3 . . . . . . .80 E3
Tunbridge Pl ⊡ PR1 . . . .117 C1
Tunbridge St ⊡ PR1 . . . .117 C1
Tunbrook Ave PR2 . . . . .138 C1
Tunley Holme PR5 . . . . . .77 C5
Tunley La WN6 . . . . .27 C5
Tunley Moss WN6 . . . . . .27 C4
Tunnel St Burnley BB12 . .126 D6
⊡ Darwen BB3 . . . . .64 C7
Tunstall Dr BB5 . . . . . . .124 B1
Tunstall Ho ⊡ LA1 . . . . .211 A4
Tunstall St LA4 . . . . .212 D5
Tunstead Ave BB12 . . . . .124 F8
Tunstead Cres OL13 . . . . .86 C1

Tunstead La Bacup OL13 . .69 B8
Rawtenstall BB4,OL13 . . . .86 B1
Tunstead Mill Terr ⊡
OL13 . . . . .69 B8
Tunstead Rd OL13 . . . . . .86 C1
Tunstill Fold BB12 . . . . .167 F1
Tunstill St BB10 . . . . . . .147 B1
Turbary Rd LA6 . . . . .236 C2
Turbary The PR2 . . . . . . .116 C3
Turf Moor Football Gd
(Burnley AFC) BB10 . . . .127 B6
Turf St BB11 . . . . .127 B6
Turflands PR5 . . . . .57 B1
Turkey St Accrington BB5 .103 D7
Out Rawcliffe PR3 . . . . . .175 A1
Turks Head Yd ⊡ PR1 . . .96 A7
Turn La BB3 . . . . .63 F8
Turn Rd BL0 . . . . .49 E8
Turnacre L37 . . . . .12 B6
Turnberry WN8 . . . . .17 D2
Turnberry Ave FY5 . . . . .151 D8
Turnberry Cl Kirkham PR4 113 A4
Morecambe LA4 . . . . . . .212 G6
Turnberry Way PR9 . . . . .53 D5
Turnbridge Rd L31 . . . . . . .5 C3
Turnbury Cl PR7 . . . . .59 D4
Turncroft Rd BB3 . . . . . . .64 B8
Turner Ave PR5 . . . . .76 A7
Turner Rd BB9 . . . . .147 B8
Turner St ⊡ Bacup OL13 . .69 C8
⊡ Barnoldswick BB18 . . .200 C2
Clitheroe BB7 . . . . .164 E7
⊡ Preston PR1 . . . . . . .117 A1
Rochdale OL12 . . . . .51 E1
Turner's Pl OL12 . . . . . . .51 E3
Turnerford Cl BL7 . . . . . .46 E1
Turnfield PR2 . . . . .115 F6
Turning La PR5 . . . . .35 A1
Turnpike BB4 . . . . .85 F1
Turnpike Fold LA2 . . . . .213 F5
Turnpike Rd L39 . . . . . . .15 A2
Turnpike The PR2 . . . . . .116 D6
Turnpike Way BB5 . . . . .102 C5
Turnstone FY3 . . . . .130 B6
Turpin Green La PR5 . . . .76 B1
Turton Dr PR6 . . . . .60 E1
Turton Gr BB10 . . . . . . .127 C6
Turton Hollow Rd BB4 . . .85 A8
Turton Rd BL8 . . . . .48 D1
Turton Tower BL7 . . . . . .47 C3
Tuscan Ave BB11 . . . . . .126 C5
Tuson Croft PR4 . . . . . . .73 F8
Tuson Dr PR2 . . . . .95 E8
Tuson House ⊡ PR1 . . . . .95 E2
Tuxbury Dr FY5 . . . . . . .151 D8
Tuxford Ct ⊡ FY8 . . . . . .89 D6
Tuxford Rd FY8 . . . . .89 C6
Tweed St Blackburn BB2 . .80 D8
⊡ High Bentham LA2 . . .233 D1
Nelson BB9 . . . . .148 A8
Tweedy St PR3 . . . . .182 C4
Twemlow Par
Heysham LA3 . . . . .208 F8
Morecambe LA3 . . . . . . .212 A1
Twenty Acre La PR4 . . . . .74 B1
Twickenham Pl ⊡ FY8 . . .89 D6
Twig La L31 . . . . .5 E1
Twin Lakes Ind Est PR5 . .57 A3
Twine Wlk LA6 . . . . .236 C3
Twinegate OL12 . . . . .51 E3
Twist Moor La PR6 . . . . . .62 B8
Twistfield Cl PR8 . . . . . . .33 F5
Twiston La BB7 . . . . .188 D5
Twitter La BB7 . . . . .186 A3
Two Acre La PR1 . . . . . . .95 C1
Two Brooks La BL8 . . . . . .48 B2
Two Gates Dr BB3 . . . . . .81 B2
Two Gates Wlk BB3 . . . . .81 B2
Two Saints Pl ⊡ L39 . . . .15 E5
Twyford Cl L31 . . . . .5 E1
Tyldesley Rd FY1 . . . . . .129 B3
Tyne Ave ⊡ FY3 . . . . . . .129 D4
Tyne Cl PR5 . . . . .172 E5
Tyne St
⊡ Bamber Bridge PR5 . . .96 F1
⊡ Preston PR1 . . . . .95 D6
Tynedale Pl FY3 . . . . . . .151 A1
Tynedale Rd FY3 . . . . . . .151 B1
Tynwald Rd BB2 . . . . . . .100 C1
Tyrer Rd L39 . . . . .15 F7
Tyrer's Ave L31 . . . . .5 A5
Tyrers Cl L37 . . . . .11 F2
Tyrone Ave FY2 . . . . . . .150 D2
Tyseley Gr BB18 . . . . . . .201 A1
Tythebarn St BB3 . . . . . .81 B1

U

Udale Pl ⊡ LA1 . . . . .213 E2
Uggle La LA1 . . . . .210 F3
Uldale Cl Nelson BB9 . . . .147 E6
Southport PR8 . . . . .20 B3
Ulleswater Rd LA1 . . . . .211 A8
Ullswater Ave
Accrington BB5 . . . . . . .124 D1
Fleetwood FY7 . . . . .172 D8
Morecambe LA4 . . . . . . .212 G4
Orrell WN5 . . . . .10 F1
Rochdale OL12 . . . . .51 C1
Thornton FY5 . . . . .173 B1
Ullswater Cl
Blackburn BB1 . . . . .100 F6
Hambleton FY6 . . . . . . .174 C2

Ullswater Cl *continued*
3 Rishton BB1 123 A1
Ullswater Cres
Carnforth LA5 216 E8
Thornton FY5 173 B1
Ullswater Rd
Blackpool FY4 109 C7
Burnley BB10 127 F5
Chorley PR7 42 B6
Fulwood PR2 117 C4
Ullswater Way BB4 105 A1
Ulnes Walton La PR5 58 A6
Ulpha Cl BB12 126 B8
Ulster Rd LA1 211 B5
Ulster St BB11 126 D5
Ulverston Cl
Blackburn BB2 101 A1
Maghull L31 5 E2
Ulverston Cres FY8 89 C7
Ulverston Dr BB1 123 A1
Under Billinge La BB2 99 F4
Underbank Cl 3 OL13 86 F3
Underbank Ho 1 OL13 86 F3
Underbank Rd
Haslingden BB4 83 F3
Rising Bridge BB5 84 A7
Thornton FY5 173 F1
Underbank Way 2 BB4 84 A3
Underley Hall Sch LA6 238 C5
Underley St BB10 147 C3
Underwood PR2 116 C3
Unicon Pk BB4 83 F3
Union Ct 13 OL13 69 C8
Union La PR3 175 C7
Union Pas 6 PR4 113 A5
Union Rd
Oswaldtwistle BB5 102 D3
Rawtenstall BB4 84 D2
Union St Accrington BB5 103 B6
Bacup OL13 86 F2
Bacup, Stacksteads OL13 69 C8
Blackburn BB2 100 E3
Brierfield BB9 147 B5
Chorley PR7 42 C8
Clitheroe BB7 164 C8
Colne BB8 169 E5
Darwen BB3 81 A1
Egerton BL7 46 D2
Haslingden BB4 84 A3
Morecambe LA4 212 D5
11 Preston PR1 95 F8
Ramsbottom BL0 49 C6
Rawtenstall BB4 85 A3
Southport PR9 34 C8
Whittle-le-W PR6 60 C8
Whitworth OL12 51 C8
Union Terr BB4 85 B2
Unit Rd PR8 20 D5
Unity St
3 Barnoldswick BB18 200 C2
Blackburn BB2 100 E2
Kelbrook BB18 192 A6
Unity Trad Est BB2 100 D4
Unity Way BB4 84 F3
Univ of Central Lancashire
PR1 95 E8
Univ of Central Lancashire
Avenham Annexe
PR1 96 A6
Univ of Lancaster LA1 207 B7
Unsworth Ave FY6 195 A4
Unsworth St OL13 69 D7
Up Holland High Sch
WN5 10 C4
Up-Brooks BB7 187 A1
Up-Brooks Ind Est BB7 187 A1
Upholland Rd WN5 10 D2
Upholland Sta WN8 9 F4
Uplands Chase PR2 116 B6
Uplands Dr BB12 146 D7
Upper Ashmount BB4 85 C1
Upper Aughton Rd PR8 34 B4
Upper Cliffe BB6 123 C6
Upper George St 23 OL12 51 F1
Upper Hill Way BB18 191 B7
Upper Lune St FY7 194 B5
Upper Mead BL7 46 F1
Upper Westby St FY8 90 A3
Upphall La LA6 234 C4
Uppingham WN8 17 D1
Uppingham Dr BL0 49 B7
Upton Ave PR8 20 B6
Upton Barn L31 5 C2
Upwood Cl FY2 150 E5
Urban View PR6 61 F8
Ushers Mdw LA1 210 E7

V

Vale Ave BL6 31 A3
Vale Cl WN6 19 E8
Vale Coppice Horwich BL6 31 A3
Ramsbottom BL0 49 C3
Vale Cotts BL6 30 F2
Vale Cres PR8 20 C2
Vale Ct BB5 124 F1
Vale Gr L32 1 A1
Vale House Cl BB7 143 C5
Vale La L40 17 F5
Vale Rd LA1 213 E3
Vale Royal PR4 113 C5
Vale St Bacup OL13 87 A3
Blackburn BB2 100 E2
Darwen BB3 80 F2
Vale St *continued*
Haslingden BB4 84 B4
Vale Terr Calder Vale PR3 179 E8
Rawtenstall BB4 85 F3
Vale The
Appley Bridge WN6 19 D8
Fulwood PR2 116 F5
Valentia Rd FY2 150 D3
Valentines La PR2,PR4 115 E4
Valentines Mdw PR4 115 E4
Valeway Ave FY5 150 D8
Valiants Shireworld
Equestrian Ctr PR3 176 A2
Valley Cl BB9 169 A1
Valley Ctr The 4 BB4 85 A2
Valley Dr
Barnoldswick BB18 200 D4
Padiham BB12 125 D8
Valley Gdns
2 Earby BB18 201 B2
Padiham BB11 125 F4
Valley Rd
Barnoldswick BB18 200 C2
Earby BB18 201 B2
Hoghton PR5 98 F3
Longridge PR3 139 C7
Penwortham PR1 95 D5
Wilpshire BB1 121 F5
Valley St BB11 126 B4
Valley Terr BB12 144 E1
Valley View Chorley PR6 42 E7
Fulwood PR2 117 A4
Whitworth OL12 70 D4
Valley View Rd PR1 96 A3
Valligates BB1 101 B7
Vance Rd FY1 129 B4
Vancouver Cres BB2 100 C8
Vandyck Ave BB11 126 E2
Vardon Rd BB2 100 B2
Varley St Colne BB8 169 F6
2 Darwen BB3 81 A1
Preston PR1 117 A2
Varlian Cl L40 16 C3
Vaughan Cl L37 11 D4
Vaughan Rd PR8 34 B4
Vaughan St BB9 147 F7
Vauxhall St BB2 100 B3
Vauze Ave BL6 30 D1
Vauze House Cl BL6 30 D2
Veevers St Brierfield BB9 147 A6
7 Burnley BB11 126 F6
Padiham BB12 125 D8
Velvet St BB2 80 D8
Venables Ave BB8 169 F6
Venice Ave BB11 126 C4
Venice St BB11 126 D5
Ventnor Pl PR2 116 A4
Ventnor Rd Blackpool FY4 109 B6
1 Chorley PR7 42 B6
Haslingden BB4 84 C1
Venture Ct BB5 124 D5
Venture Rd FY7 173 A6
Venture St 18 OL13 87 A3
Verax St OL13 86 F1
Vermont Gr FY5 150 E8
Vernon Ave Blackpool FY3 129 E3
Warton PR4 91 E6
Vernon Cres LA2 207 A3
Vernon Ct 4 Galgate LA2 207 A4
Southport PR8 34 D5
Vernon Lo FY8 88 F5
Vernon Pk 3 LA2 207 A4
Vernon Rd
Laneshaw Bridge BB8 170 D6
Lytham St Anne's FY8 109 E1
Ramsbottom BL8 49 A1
Southport PR9 35 A8
Vernon St Blackburn BB2 100 E4
Darwen BB3 81 B1
Nelson BB9 147 E7
Preston PR1 116 F1
Verona Ave BB11 126 C5
Verona Ct 6 FY5 173 A2
Veronica St BB3 80 E4
Verulam Rd PR9 53 B3
Vesta St 6 BL0 49 B6
Vevey St PR5 76 A1
Viaduct Rd PR5 98 F2
Vicar St Blackburn BB1 100 F5
Great Harwood BB6 123 C4
Vicarage Ave Caton LA2 231 C3
Cleveleys FY5 172 D3
5 Padiham BB12 125 B8
Vicarage Cl Adlington PR6 30 A8
Burton-in-K LA6 234 C7
Euxton PR7 59 D3
Formby L37 11 D4
Fulwood PR2 116 F4
Lytham St Anne's FY8 88 F7
Morecambe LA3 212 F2
Ormskirk L40 16 B3
Wrea Green PR4 112 B4
Vicarage Dr BB3 64 C8
Vicarage Fold BB7 143 F7
Vicarage Gdns L40 24 D4
Vicarage La
Accrington BB5 103 E1
Banks PR9 53 F7
Blackpool FY4 129 E1
Burton-in-K LA6 234 C7
Churchtown PR3 178 A2
Fulwood PR2 116 F4
Kirkby Lonsdale LA6 238 C2
Newton-with-S PR4 114 A3
Ormskirk L40 16 C3
Samlesbury PR5 118 E1
Wilpshire BB1 121 F6
Rawtenstall BB4 84 F2
Vicarage Rd
Barnoldswick BB18 200 C3
Blackrod BL6 30 D2
Formby L37 11 D4
Kelbrook BB18 192 A6
Nelson BB9 147 D7
Orrell WN5 10 D4
Poulton-le-F FY6 151 E3
Vicarage Rd W BL6 30 C2
Vicarage St 2 PR6 60 D1
Vicarage Wlk L39 15 E5
Vicarsfields Rd PR5 59 A7
Viceroy Ct 3 PR8 34 A6
Victor Ave LA4 213 A6
Victor Mews 6 BB7 164 D7
Victoria Apartments 20
BB12 145 C1
Victoria Ave
Accrington BB5 103 D2
Blackburn BB2 79 E8
Brierfield BB9 147 B6
Chatburn BB7 187 E5
Lancaster LA1 210 F5
Victoria Bldgs Darwen BB3 81 E3
8 Low Bentham LA2 233 B8
Victoria Bridge Rd PR8 34 C6
Victoria Bsns & Ind Ctr
BB5 103 B4
Victoria Cross 4 BB1 100 E6
Victoria Ct
6 Blackburn BB1 100 E5
Broughton PR3 136 C2
Chatburn BB7 187 D5
Fulwood PR2 116 E3
Horwich BL6 31 C3
Padiham BB12 125 E7
Southport PR8 33 F4
Victoria Dr BB4 84 B2
Victoria Gdns BB9 168 C2
Victoria Ho BB1 101 B3
Victoria Lo BB12 144 D2
Victoria Mans PR2 95 A7
Victoria Mews LA4 212 F6
Victoria Par
Morecambe LA4 212 F6
Preston PR2 116 B1
Rawtenstall BB4 68 E8
Victoria Park Ave
Leyland PR5 58 D7
Preston PR2 115 D1
Victoria Park Dr PR2 115 D1
Victoria Pk WN8 17 C1
Victoria Pl Halton LA2 214 E6
6 Lancaster LA1 210 F7
Victoria Quay PR2 95 A7
Victoria Rd
Barnoldswick BB18 200 C2
Blackburn BB2 99 C1
Earby BB18 201 B2
Formby L37 11 D5
Fulwood PR2 117 A4
Horwich BL6 31 C2
Ince Blundell L38 3 E3
Kirkham PR4 112 F5
Lytham St Anne's FY8 88 F5
Ormskirk L39 15 C2
Padiham BB12 125 E7
Poulton-le-F FY6 151 E4
Preston PR1,PR5 96 D5
Victoria Rd E FY5 173 B1
Victoria Rd W FY5 172 E2
Victoria Sq FY5 172 D2
Victoria St Accrington BB5 103 B5
Bacup OL13 69 D8
Bamber Bridge PR5 76 B8
Barrowford BB9 168 D3
25 Blackburn BB1 100 E5
Blackpool FY1 129 B5
Blackrod BL6 30 D2
1 Burnley BB11 126 F5
Burscough Bridge L40 24 E5
Carnforth LA5 217 D1
Chorley PR7 42 D7
Church BB5 102 E6
Clayton-le-M BB5 123 F2
Clayton-le-M BB5 123 F3
Clitheroe BB7 164 D7
9 Cornholme OL14 108 C1
21 Darwen BB3 81 A1
7 Earby BB18 201 B2
Fleetwood FY7 194 B5
Great Harwood BB6 123 D5
Haslingden BB4 84 A3
Longridge PR3 139 A7
Lytham St Anne's FY8 90 C3
Morecambe LA4 212 D5
Nelson BB9 147 D8
Oswaldtwistle BB5 102 D3
Preston PR1 116 E1
Ramsbottom BL0 49 B6
Rawtenstall BB4 85 C1
Rawtenstall, Waterfoot BB4 68 E8
Rishton BB1 123 B1
22 Rochdale OL12 51 F1
Southport PR8 34 B8
Wheelton PR6 61 A7
Whitworth OL12 51 C8
Victoria Terr
Abbey Village PR6 79 B2
12 Bamber Bridge PR5 76 A8
Billington BB7 143 A4
Calder Vale PR3 179 E8
1 Chorley PR6 60 D1
Garstang PR3 178 C7
Glasson LA2 205 F5
6 Leyland PR5 59 A8
Mellor Brook BB2 120 C3
Tockholes BB3 79 F2
Victoria Terr *continued*
Wheelton PR6 61 A7
Victoria Way Formby L37 11 D5
Rawtenstall BB4 85 C2
Southport PR8 33 F7
Victoria Wharf 4 LA1 213 E1
Victory Ave PR9 35 A7
Victory Cl BB9 147 E8
Victory Ctr The 1 BB9 147 E8
Victory Rd FY1 129 C6
Victory Wharf PR2 95 B8
View Rd BB3 80 E5
View St PR7 40 C7
Vihiers Cl BB7 143 C6
Villa Way PR3 178 C6
Village Cl WN8 8 D8
Village Croft PR7 59 D3
Village Dr PR2 117 F2
Village Green La PR2 115 F6
Village Way Blackpool FY2 150 D5
Hightown L38 2 F4
Skelmersdale WN8 8 D8
Villas Rd L31 6 B2
Villas The PR4 115 E5
Villiers Ct PR1 116 E2
Villiers St Burnley BB11 126 C5
Bury BL9 32 A3
Padiham BB12 125 D7
Preston PR1 116 D2
Preston PR1 116 E2
Vincent Ct BB2 80 D8
Vincent Rd BB9 147 F8
Vincent St Blackburn BB2 80 D8
Colne BB8 169 F6
8 Lancaster LA1 211 A7
Vincit St BB10 127 C8
Vine Ct FY2 150 C1
Vine St Accrington BB5 103 A6
Brierfield BB9 147 B5
Chorley PR7 60 C1
Lancaster LA1 210 F6
Oswaldtwistle BB5 102 C3
Preston PR1 95 D8
Ramsbottom BL0 49 A4
Vinery The PR4 74 F8
Viola Cl WN6 28 D2
Violet St BB10 147 A1
Virginia Ave L31 5 D3
Virginia Gr L31 5 C3
Virginia St PR8 34 C6
Vivary Way BB8 169 B5
Vivian Dr PR8 34 A2
Vulcan Rd PR4 113 B1
Vulcan St Burnley BB11 126 F6
4 Nelson BB9 168 F1
Southport PR9 34 C7

W

Wackersall Rd BB8 169 B3
Waddington
& West Bradford
CE Prim Sch BB7 186 C5
Waddington Ave BB10 127 D6
Waddington Ct FY8 89 C6
Waddington Hospl
(Almshouses) BB7 186 B5
Waddington Rd
Accrington BB5 103 D6
Clitheroe BB7 186 E1
Fulwood PR2 118 A2
Lytham St Anne's FY8 89 C7
West Bradford BB7 186 D5
Waddington St
Earby BB18 201 B2
3 Padiham BB12 125 D8
Waddow Gn BB7 164 C8
Waddow Gr BB7 186 C4
Waddow View BB7 186 B4
Wade Brook Rd PR5 57 F6
Wade St BB12 145 D1
Wades Croft PR4 92 C6
Wades Ct FY3 150 F1
Wadham Rd PR1 96 B6
Wagon Rd LA2,PR3 220 B8
Waidshouse Cl BB9 147 E6
Waidshouse Rd BB9 147 E6
Wain Ct BB2 100 B4
Waingap Cres OL12 51 D8
Waingap Rise
Rochdale OL12 51 F4
Whitworth OL12 51 D7
Waingate Grimsargh PR2 138 C1
Rawtenstall BB4 85 B3
Waingate Cl BB4 85 B3
Waingate Ct PR2 138 C1
Waingate La BB4 85 B3
Waingate Rd BB4 85 B3
Waitholme La LA5 234 A7
Wakefield Ave LA4 212 G6
Wakefield Dr LA1 211 A4
Wakefield Rd FY2 150 E4
Walden Rd BB1 121 F4
Waldon St PR1 96 E8
Waldron WN8 8 D8
Wales Rd BB4 85 F1
Walesby Pl FY8 89 D5
Walgarth Dr PR7 42 B7
Walk Mill Pl BB10 127 E1
Walk The Hesketh Bank PR4 72 C4
Southport PR8 34 A5
Walkdale PR4 94 D2
Walker Ave BB5 103 A4
Walker Cl L37 11 F2
Walker Gr LA3 208 F7
Walker La PR2 116 B6
Walker Park Ind Est BB1 81 C7
Walker Pl PR1 96 B7
Walker Rd BB1 81 C7
Walker St Blackburn BB1 100 F4
Blackpool FY1 129 B6
Clitheroe BB7 164 F8
Preston PR1 95 F8
Walker Way FY5 173 B4
Walkers Hill FY4 110 A7
Walkers Ind Est LA3 208 F3
Wall La PR3 153 E5
Wall St Blackpool FY1 129 C7
Newchurch BB4 85 E2
Wallace La PR3 204 C4
Wallbank Dr OL12 51 C7
Wallbrook Ave WN5 10 D1
Wallcroft St WN8 8 E8
Walled Garden The PR6 60 B6
Wallend Rd PR2 94 D7
Waller Ave FY2 150 C5
Waller Hill BB8 191 D1
Walletts Rd PR7 42 B6
Wallhurst Cl BB10 128 B5
Walling's La LA5 218 B4
Wallstreams Ct BB10 128 B5
Wallstreams La BB10 128 B5
Wallsuches BL6 31 F4
Walmer Ct PR8 33 F4
Walmer Gn PR4 73 F5
Walmer Rd
Lytham St Anne's FY8 88 F8
Southport PR8 34 A3
Walmersley Golf Course
BL9 32 B8
Walmersley Old Rd BL9 49 F2
Walmesley Ave BB1 102 B8
Walmsgate BB18 200 B2
Walmsley Bridge La
Bilsborrow PR3 157 E8
Claughton PR3 179 E1
Walmsley Brow BB7 143 B4
Walmsley CE Prim Sch
BL7 46 E1
Walmsley Cl Church BB5 102 E6
Garstang PR3 178 C7
Walmsley Ct BB5 123 F1
Walmsley St Darwen BB3 81 B2
Fleetwood FY7 194 A4
16 Great Harwood BB6 123 C5
Rishton BB1 123 B1
Walney Pl FY3 130 A7
Walnut Ave Bury BL9 32 C3
Haslingden BB4 84 C3
Walnut Cl PR1 95 B3
Walnut St Bacup OL13 86 F3
Blackburn BB1 100 F7
3 Blackburn BB1 101 A7
Southport PR8 34 C4
Walpole Ave FY4 109 B5
Walpole St Blackburn BB1 100 F4
10 Burnley BB10 147 B1
Walro Mews PR9 53 A3
Walsden Gr BB10 127 C6
Walsh Fold BL7 47 D2
Walsh St Blackburn BB2 100 E2
Horwich BL6 31 B4
Walshaw High Sch BB10 147 D1
Walshaw La BB10 147 D2
Walshaw St BB10 127 B8
Walter Ave FY8 110 A2
Walter Pl FY8 110 A2
Walter Robinson Ct FY3 129 D6
Walter St Accrington BB5 103 B6
Blackburn BB1 101 A4
Blackburn BB1 101 B4
Brierfield BB10,BB9 147 B5
Darwen BB3 64 B5
Huncoat BB5 124 E2
Oswaldtwistle BB5 102 D3
Walter Street Prim Sch
BB9 147 B5
Waltham Ave FY4 109 D5
Waltham Cl BB5 103 E3
Waltham Ct LA2 214 E7
Waltho Ave L31 5 E1
Walton Ave
Morecambe LA4 213 B5
Penwortham PR1 95 B3
Walton Cl OL13 87 A1
Walton Cottage Homes
BB9 169 A1
Walton Cres BB2 101 A1
Walton Gn PR5 96 C4
Walton Gr LA4 213 B5
Walton High Sch BB9 169 A2
Walton La BB9 169 A1
Walton St Accrington BB5 124 A1
Adlington PR7 30 A6
Barrowford BB9 168 E4
Colne BB8 169 D4
8 Nelson BB9 168 E1
Southport PR9 34 C8
Walton Summit Rd PR5 77 A7
Walton View PR1 96 D8
Walton's Par PR1 95 E7
Walton-le-Dale
Cty Prim Sch PR5 96 D2
Walton-le-Dale High Sch
PR5 96 F2
Walverden Ave 4 FY4 109 D8
Walverden Cres 3 BB9 147 F8
Walverden Prim Sch BB9 147 F8
Walverden Rd
Brierfield BB9 147 D5
Lane Bottom BB10 148 B4
Walverden Terr BB9 147 F7
Wandales La LA6 238 F2
Wanes Blades Rd L40 25 E5
Wanishar La L39 14 A5

Wansbeck Ave FY7 .....193 D2
Wansbeck House FY7 ...193 D2
Wansfell Rd BB7 ....164 C7
Wanstead Cres FY4 .....129 E1
Wanstead St PR1 ....96 E8
Warbreck Ct FY2 ....150 B1
Warbreck Dr FY2 ....150 B2
Warbreck High Sch FY2 .150 D1
Warbreck Hill Rd FY2 ...150 D1
Warburton Bldgs BB4 ....83 F1
Warburton St BB4 ....83 F1
Warbury St PR1 ....117 E1
Warcock La OL13 ....87 B3
Ward Ave Cleveleys FY5 ...172 D3
Formby L37 ....11 D2
Oswaldtwistle BB5 ....102 C3
Ward Green Cross PR3 ...140 A7
Ward Green La PR3 .....140 A7
Ward St Bamber Bridge PR5 .76 B7
Belmont BL7 ....45 C5
5 Blackpool FY1 ....129 B1
Burnley BB11 ....126 E6
Chorley PR6 ....42 E7
Great Harwood BB6 ....123 C5
Kirkham PR4 ....113 A4
Ward's End PR1 ....96 A7
Warde St 8 BB9 ....147 E8
Wardle Ct PR6 ....60 C6
Wardle Dr FY5 ....172 F3
Wardle St OL13 ....69 D8
Wardley's La FY6 ....174 A3
Wareham Cl BB5 ....124 B1
Wareham Rd FY3 ....150 F1
Wareham St BB1 ....101 A7
Warehouse La BB8 ....191 D1
Waring Dr FY5 ....173 A2
Warings The
Heskin Green PR7 ....40 E4
Nelson BB9 ....147 E6
Warkworth Terr 17 OL13 ...87 A3
Warley Ave LA3 ....213 A4
Warley Dr LA3 ....213 A4
Warley Rd FY1 ....129 C8
Warley Wise La BB8 .....192 F3
Warmden Ave BB5 ....103 E3
Warne Pl LA1 ....213 D1
Warner Rd PR1 ....117 D1
Warner St Accrington BB5 .103 C5
Haslingden BB4 ....84 B3
Warpers Moss Cl L40 ......24 F5
Warpers Moss La L40 ......25 A5
Warren Ave N FY7 ....193 F4
Warren Ave S FY7 ....193 F4
Warren Cl LA2 ....213 E8
Warren Ct PR8 ....33 E5
Warren Dr Bacup OL13 ....70 C8
Barrowford BB9 ....168 C3
Blackpool FY5 ....150 E7
Hest Bank LA2 ....213 E8
Warren Fold BB7 ....141 F8
Warren Gn L37 ....11 D3
Warren Gr Blackpool FY5 ..150 E8
Heysham LA3 ....208 E5
Warren Rd Heysham LA3 ..208 E5
Southport PR9 ....35 A8
Warren St FY7 ....194 B4
Warren The
Blackburn BB2 ....100 A7
Preston PR2 ....117 E6
Warrenhouse Rd L33 ....1 B4
Warrenhurst Ho 1 FY7 ....193 F3
Warrenhurst Rd FY7 ......194 A4
Warrenside Cl BB1 ....122 A4
Warrington St BB1 ....101 A8
Warrington Terr BB6 .....143 D8
Warsicks Cotts FY6 ......152 E1
Warth La Barnoldswick LA6 236 F2
Rawtenstall BB4 ....68 D8
Warton Ave LA3 ....208 E6
Warton Crag
(Nature Reserve) LA5 ..217 C6
Warton Pl PR7 ....42 A8
Warton Rd LA5 ....217 D2
Warton St
Lytham St Anne's FY8 ......90 C3
2 Preston PR1 ....95 E6
Wartonwood View 1
LA5 ....217 D1
Warwick Ave
Accrington BB5 ....103 B7
Clayton-le-M BB5 ....123 F3
Cleveleys FY5 ....172 F4
Darwen BB3 ....80 E3
Lancaster LA1 ....211 A5
Morecambe LA4 ....213 B6
Warwick Cl Church BB5 ...102 F7
Fulwood PR2 ....116 E4
Ramsbottom BL8 ....49 A1
Southport PR8 ....34 B4
Warwick Dr
Barnoldswick BB18 ....200 F1
Brierfield BB9 ....147 D5
Clitheroe BB7 ....186 F2
Padiham BB12 ....125 D7
Warwick Ho 10 PR1 ....96 A6
Warwick Pl Fleetwood FY7 194 A5
Normoss FY3 ....130 B8
Warwick Rd
Bamber Bridge PR5 ....96 D4
Blackpool FY3 ....129 D7
Eccleston PR7 ....40 C7
Leyland PR5 ....58 E7
Lytham St Anne's FY8 ......88 F6
Warwick St Adlington PR7 ...29 F6
Church BB5 ....102 F7
Haslingden BB4 ....84 B3
Longridge PR3 ....139 A8
Nelson BB9 ....147 E7

Warwick St *continued*
Preston PR1 ....95 F8
Southport PR8 ....34 B4
Wasdale Ave
Blackburn BB1 ....101 C3
Maghull L31 ....5 F2
Wasdale Cl Leyland PR5 ....59 B6
Padiham BB12 ....145 C1
Wasdale Gr PR3 ....138 F5
Wasdale Rd FY4 ....110 A8
Wash La BL9 ....32 B2
Washbrook Cl BB7 ....164 D1
Washbrook Way L39 ....15 E4
Washburn Ct LA3 ....213 B2
Washington Ave
Blackpool FY2 ....150 E2
3 Morecambe LA4 ....212 E5
Washington Cl LA1 ....210 D7
Washington Ct FY2 ....150 E2
Washington Dr LA5 ....217 E6
Washington Hall
Fire Brigade
Training Ctr PR7 ....59 F2
Washington La PR7 ....59 F2
Washington St BB5 ....103 C6
Waste La LA2 ....220 C7
Wastwater Dr 4 LA4 ......213 A4
Watchyard La L37 ....12 A4
Water Fold BB4 ....86 A8
Water La Edenfield BL0 .....67 D2
Preston PR2 ....116 D1
Southport PR9 ....53 D5
Water Mdws BB2 ....80 D7
Water Prim Sch BB4 ....86 A8
Water Ski Ctr OL12 ....70 C2
Water St
10 Accrington BB5 ....103 C6
Adlington PR7 ....30 A6
1 Bamber Bridge PR5 ......96 F2
Brindle PR6 ....77 F5
Chorley PR7 ....60 C1
Clayton-le-M BB5 ....123 F5
1 Colne BB8 ....169 E5
Earby BB18 ....201 B2
Egerton BL7 ....46 D2
Great Harwood BB6 ....123 C5
Hapton BB12 ....125 C4
Lancaster LA1 ....213 F1
Nelson BB9 ....147 E8
8 Ramsbottom BL0 ....49 B5
Rawtenstall BB4 ....85 A8
Ribchester PR3 ....140 E3
Whitworth OL12 ....51 C8
Worsthorne BB10 ....128 B5
Water's Edge PR2 ....115 F3
Waterbarn La OL13 ....69 B8
Waterbarn St 3 BB10 .....147 B1
Waterdale FY2 ....150 E5
Waterfall Terr BL7 ....45 C5
Waterfield Ave BB3 ....64 B6
Waterfold La BL9 ....32 C1
Waterfoot Ave
Blackpool FY3 ....129 E6
Southport PR8 ....20 B3
Waterfoot Bsns Ctr BB4 ...85 F2
Waterfoot Cty Prim Sch
BB4 ....68 F8
Waterford Cl Fairview PR6 .43 A1
Preston PR2 ....117 C5
Waterford St BB9 ....168 F1
Waterfront 2 BB1 ....100 F3
Waterfront Marine
& Ind Est FY8 ....90 E3
Waterhead Cres FY5 .....150 C6
Watering Pool La PR1,PR5 .96 B1
Waterloo Cl BB2 ....80 B8
Waterloo Rd
Blackpool FY4 ....129 D1
Burnley BB11 ....127 B4
Burnley BB11 ....127 B5
Clitheroe BB7 ....164 F8
Kelbrook BB18 ....192 A6
Preston PR2 ....116 C1
Southport PR8 ....33 E2
Waterloo Sch
(Prim & Inf) FY1 ....129 D1
Waterloo St Chorley PR7 ...60 D1
Enfield BB5 ....124 A1
Waterloo Terr PR2 ....116 C1
Watermans Cl BL6 ....31 C4
Watermede WN5 ....10 E3
Waters Edge BB1 ....100 F4
Waters Reach
Cleveleys FY5 ....172 C3
Lytham St Anne's FY8 ......89 D3
Waterside Cl PR3 ....178 B7
Waterside Ind Est BB8 ....169 E4
Waterside Mews BB12 ....125 D8
Waterside Pl LA4 ....212 E3
Waterside Rd Colne BB8 ..169 D4
Haslingden BB4 ....84 A2
Ramsbottom BL0,BL8,BL9 ...49 C3
Waterside Terr
11 Bacup OL13 ....86 F3
Waterside BB3 ....81 E3
Waterslack Rd LA5 ....218 E6
Waterworks Rd L39 ....16 A6
Watery Gate La PR3,PR4 .154 D3
Watery La Darwen BB3 ......64 B6
Garstang PR3 ....199 E1
Lancaster LA1 ....213 D3
Preston PR2 ....95 B8
Preston, Fishwick PR1 ......96 E7
Watery Lane Ind Est 2
BB3 ....64 B6
Watford St 5 BB1 ....100 E6
Watkin La PR5 ....76 B7
Watkin Rd PR6 ....60 B8

Watkins Cl BB10 ....147 C4
Watling Cl LA3 ....213 A3
Watling Gate BB6 ....142 C6
Watling St BL8 ....48 A1
Watling Street Rd
Fulwood PR2 ....117 B3
Fulwood, Brookfield PR2 ..117 E5
Watson Ct FY4 ....109 D7
Watson Gdns OL12 ....51 D2
Watson Rd FY4 ....109 C7
Watson St Blackburn BB2 .100 B2
8 Oswaldtwistle BB5 .....102 E4
Watt St Burnley BB12 .....126 C7
Sabden BB7 ....144 F7
Watton Beck Cl L31 ....5 F2
Watts Cl L33 ....1 A4
Watts St BL6 ....31 C2
Wavell Ave PR9 ....35 B7
Wavell Cl Accrington BB5 ..103 F2
Southport PR9 ....35 B7
Wavell St BB12 ....126 C6
Waverledge Rd BB6 ....123 B4
Waverledge St BB6 ....123 C4
Waverley WN8 ....17 D1
Waverley Ave
Blackpool FY1 ....129 C8
Fleetwood FY7 ....193 D3
Waverley Cl Brierfield BB9 147 D4
Read BB12 ....144 D1
Waverley Dr
New Longton PR4 ....74 F7
Tarleton PR4 ....56 A6
Waverley Gdns PR2 ......117 E2
Waverley Pl BB2 ....100 B5
Waverley Rd
Accrington BB5 ....103 E3
Blackburn BB1 ....101 F4
Preston PR1 ....117 D1
Wilpshire BB1 ....121 E4
Waverley St
1 Burnley BB11 ....126 E6
Southport PR8 ....34 A7
Waxy La PR4 ....92 C7
Way Gate FY5 ....172 D5
Way The LA3 ....213 B3
Wayfarers Arc PR8 ....34 B7
Wayman Rd FY3 ....129 D6
Wayoh Croft BL7 ....47 D6
Wayside FY6 ....194 D5
Weald The PR4 ....115 D5
Weasel La BB3 ....80 B2
Weatherhill Cres BB9 ....147 E5
Weaver Ave L40 ....24 F5
Weaver's Brow PR6 ....42 F5
Webb St BL6 ....31 C3
Webber Ct BB11 ....126 A3
Webber Rd L33 ....1 C1
Weber St BB4 ....85 D1
Webster Ave FY4 ....109 E7
Webster Gr LA4 ....213 C6
Webster St PR2 ....116 C1
Wedgewood Rd BB5 ......124 F1
Weeton Ave Blackpool FY4 109 E5
Cleveleys FY5 ....172 D3
Lytham St Anne's FY8 ......89 A8
Weeton CE Prim Sch
PR4 ....131 E1
Weeton Cty Prim Sch
PR4 ....131 E6
Weeton Pl 4 PR2 ....115 E1
Weeton Rd
Great Plumpton PR4 ......111 F7
Kirkham PR4 ....112 F7
Kirkham, Weeton PR4 .....112 C8
Weeton PR4 ....131 F2
Weeton Camp FY6,PR4 ....131 E7
Weets View BB18 ....200 C3
Weind The PR3 ....154 B5
Weir La OL13 ....87 A7
Weir St BB2 ....100 E4
Weirden Cl PR1 ....95 C1
Welbeck Ave
Blackburn BB1 ....101 B8
Blackpool FY4 ....129 E1
Fleetwood FY7 ....193 F3
Welbeck Gdns FY7 ....193 F3
Welbeck Rd PR8 ....34 A4
Welbeck Terr PR8 ....34 A4
Welbourne WN8 ....17 D1
Welbury Cl 5 BB18 ....201 B2
Weld Ave PR7 ....42 C5
Weld Blundell Ave L31 ......5 B5
Weld Dr L37 ....11 D4
Weld Par PR8 ....33 F4
Weld Rd PR8 ....33 F5
Weldale PR8 ....33 F4
Weldbank La PR7 ....42 C5
Weldbank St PR7 ....42 C5
Weldon Dr L39 ....15 F4
Weldon St BB11 ....126 E5
Well Ct WN6 ....28 E1
Well Field BB5 ....124 A2
Well Fold BB7 ....164 F8
Well Head BB8 ....170 B4
Well Head Rd BB12 ....167 A3
Well La Brinscall PR7 ......61 F7
Haskayne L39 ....13 E6
High Casterton LA6 ......238 F2
Little Eccleston PR3 ......153 D6
Warton, Carnforth LA5 ....217 E5
Yealand Redmayne LA5 ...219 E3
Well Orch PR5 ....77 B5
Well St Newchurch BB4 .....85 F3
Padiham BB12 ....125 B8
Rishton BB1 ....123 B2
Well St N BL0 ....67 C2
Well St W 6 BL0 ....49 B5
Well Terr BB7 ....186 F1

Welland Cl FY2 ....150 E4
Wellbrow Dr PR3 ....139 B8
Wellbrow Terr OL12 ....51 D2
Wellcross Rd WN8 ....10 B6
Wellesley St BB12 ....125 F6
Wellfield PR4 ....93 F1
Wellfield Ave PR5 ....75 F1
Wellfield Bsns Pk PR1 ....95 D8
Wellfield CE/Meth Sch
BB12 ....126 D8
Wellfield Dr BB12 ....126 D7
Wellfield High Sch PR5 ....75 F1
Wellfield La L40 ....16 C3
Wellfield Rd
Bamber Bridge PR5 ....76 A7
Blackburn BB2 ....100 C6
Preston PR1 ....95 D8
Wellgate BB7 ....164 F8
Wellhouse Rd BB18 ....200 B2
Wellhouse Sq 17 BB18 ...200 B2
Wellhouse St BB18 ....200 B2
Wellington Ave PR5 ....59 B8
Wellington Ct
7 Accrington BB5 ....103 C5
Burnley BB10 ....127 B5
Wellington Fold 3 BB3 ....81 A1
Wellington Pl PR5 ....96 D2
Wellington Rd
Blackburn BB2 ....100 C3
Blackpool FY1 ....129 B2
Edgworth BL7 ....47 D4
Lancaster LA1 ....211 A5
Preston PR2 ....116 C1
Wellington St
Accrington BB5 ....103 C5
Barnoldswick BB18 ....200 B1
Chorley PR7 ....60 C1
Clayton-le-M BB5 ....123 F2
Great Harwood BB6 ....123 C4
Kirkham PR4 ....112 F5
Lytham St Anne's FY8 ......90 D3
16 Nelson BB9 ....168 D1
Preston PR1 ....95 D8
19 Rochdale OL12 ....51 F1
1 Southport PR8 ....34 A6
Wellington Street
St Johns BB1 ....100 D6
Wellington Terr LA4 ......212 E5
Wellogate Gdns FY4 .....109 D6
Wellow Pl FY8 ....89 C5
Wells Cl Morecambe LA3 ..212 E2
Thornton FY5 ....173 A2
Wells Fold Cl PR6 ....77 C1
Wells St Haslingden BB4 ...84 B3
9 Preston PR1 ....117 D1
Welsby Rd PR5 ....58 D8
Welwyn Ave PR8 ....20 E6
Welwyn Pl FY5 ....172 E1
Wembley Ave
Blackpool FY3 ....129 E8
Penwortham PR1 ....95 B5
Poulton-le-F FY6 ....151 E3
Wembley Rd FY5 ....173 B4
Wemyss Cl 1 LA3 ....208 E7
Wendover Rd FY6 ....151 A6
Wenlock Cl BL6 ....31 C6
Wenning Ave
High Bentham LA2 ....233 D7
Maghull L31 ....5 E2
Wenning Ct LA3 ....213 B2
Wenning Pl LA1 ....213 E2
Wenning St BB9 ....147 F7
Wennington Hall Sch
LA2 ....235 E1
Wennington Rd
Southport PR9 ....34 F7
Wray LA2 ....232 D6
Wennington Sta LA2 ......232 E8
Wensley Ave FY7 ....193 E1
Wensley Cl BB11 ....126 E3
Wensley Dr
Accrington BB5 ....103 D5
Lancaster LA1 ....213 F3
Wensley Fold
CE Prim Sch BB2 ....100 B5
Wensley Pl PR2 ....117 D4
Wensley Rd BB2 ....100 B4
Wensleydale Ave FY3 .....130 A7
Wensleydale Cl Maghull L31 .5 B2
Thornton FY5 ....151 D8
Wentcliffe Dr BB18 ....201 B1
Wentworth Ave
Fleetwood FY7 ....172 D7
Inskip PR4 ....134 C8
Wentworth Cl
Penwortham PR1 ....95 A6
Southport PR8 ....20 C4
Wentworth Cres LA3 .....212 E2
Wentworth Ct PR4 ....113 B4
Wentworth Dr
Broughton PR3 ....136 C3
Euxton PR7 ....59 D4
Thornton FY5 ....151 D8
Wentworth Mews FY8 ......89 A6
Wentworth Pl PR3 ....136 C3
Werneth Cl PR1 ....95 F1
Wescoe Cl WN5 ....10 E5
Wesham C of E Sch PR4 .112 F6
Wesham Cross PR4 ....112 F7
Wesham Hall Cl PR4 ......113 A6
Wesham Hall Rd PR4 .....113 A6
Wesham Park Hospl PR4 112 F7
Wesley Cl LA2 ....233 D8
Wesley Ct 3 FY7 ....194 B5
Wesley Dr LA3 ....208 F7
Wesley Gr BB12 ....126 D7
Wesley Mews FY4 ....110 A7
Wesley Pl Bacup OL13 ......86 E1

Wesley Pl *continued*
Higham BB12 ....145 F6
Wesley St Accrington BB5 .102 F6
Bamber Bridge PR5 ....76 F8
Blackburn BB1 ....100 F7
Brierfield BB9 ....147 B6
Oswaldtwistle BB5 ....102 E5
8 Padiham BB12 ....125 D8
Sabden BB7 ....144 F8
Southport PR8 ....34 B7
Wesley Terr OL13 ....87 A7
Wesleyan Row BB7 ....164 E8
Wessex Cl Huncoat BB5 ...103 F8
Standish WN1 ....29 B1
West Ave
Barnoldswick BB18 ....200 B2
Fulwood PR2 ....116 A6
West Bank PR7 ....42 C8
West Bank Ave FY8 ....89 E3
West Beach FY8 ....90 A2
West Bradford Rd
Grindleton BB7 ....187 A6
Waddington BB7 ....186 C5
West Bradford BB7 ....186 F4
West Bridge L31 ....5 C1
West Cliff PR1 ....95 E6
West Cliff Terr PR1 ....95 E6
West Cliffe FY8 ....90 C3
West Close Ave BB12 .....145 F5
West Close Rd BB18 ......200 B3
West Craven High Sch
BB18 ....200 C1
West Cres Accrington BB5 .103 B8
Broughton PR3 ....136 C3
West Ct FY5 ....172 C5
West Dene WN8 ....26 B2
West Dr Clayton-le-W PR5 ..76 D3
Cleveleys FY5 ....172 E3
Inskip PR4 ....134 C8
Kirkham PR4 ....112 E7
Lancaster LA1 ....213 D2
Whalley BB7 ....143 A7
West Dr W FY5 ....172 D3
West End
Great Eccleston PR3 ......154 A5
Penwortham PR1 ....95 B6
West End Bsns Pk BB5 ...102 B5
West End Cty Prim Sch
Morecambe LA4 ....212 C4
Ormskirk L39 ....15 E7
Oswaldtwistle BB5 ....102 C5
West End La PR4 ....91 B5
West End Rd LA4 ....212 D4
West End Terr PR8 ....34 A7
West Exchange St 7
BB8 ....169 D4
West Field Rd BB18 ....200 A4
West Gate FY7 ....193 D4
West Gdns 1 OL13 ....69 B8
West Gillibrands Ind Est
WN8 ....8 E8
West Hall La LA6 ....235 C6
West Hill BB9 ....168 D4
West Ing La BD23 ....225 D5
West La Downham BB7 ....188 A4
Formby L37 ....11 F6
West Lancashire Light Rly
PR4 ....72 F2
West Leigh Rd BB1 ....100 C8
West Lodge FY6 ....174 C1
West Mdw PR2 ....115 E3
West Meade L31 ....5 B2
West Moss La FY8 ....110 E1
West Mount WN5 ....10 F6
West Paddock PR5 ....58 E8
West Park Ave PR2 ....115 F2
West Park Dr FY3 ....129 E4
West Park La PR2 ....116 A2
West Park Rd BB2 ....100 C6
West Rd Fulwood PR2 .....116 F3
Lancaster LA1 ....210 E8
West Sq PR4 ....74 A8
West St 9 Blackpool FY1 ..129 B5
Burnley BB10 ....127 C8
Chorley PR7 ....42 C7
Colne BB8 ....169 E4
Great Harwood BB6 ....123 C4
Lancaster LA1 ....210 F5
Morecambe LA3 ....212 B4
7 Nelson BB9 ....168 D1
Padiham BB12 ....125 B8
7 Ramsbottom BL0 ....49 B5
Rawtenstall BB4 ....68 E8
Southport PR8 ....34 A7
West Strand PR1 ....95 D8
West Street Cty Prim Sch
BB8 ....169 E4
West View Bacup OL13 .....69 B8
Bamber Bridge PR5 ....76 E7
Blackburn BB2 ....100 B4
Blackpool FY1 ....129 C3
Clitheroe BB7 ....164 D7
Garstang PR3 ....178 C7
Glasson LA2 ....205 E5
Grindleton BB7 ....187 B8
Haslingden BB4 ....84 B4
Haslingden, Bridge End BB4 .67 A7
Hollins Lane PR3 ....204 D2
Kirkham PR4 ....112 F7
Little Eccleston PR4 ......153 F1
Longton PR4 ....74 A8
4 Newchurch BB4 ....85 F1
1 Ormskirk L39 ....15 F5
Oswaldtwistle BB5 ....102 E4
Over Town BB10 ....107 A8

West View continued
Parbold WN8 . . . . .26 C2
Preston PR1 . . . . .117 C2
Ramsbottom BL0 . . . . .67 C2
Waddington BB7 . . . . .186 B4
Wheelton PR6 . . . . .61 A7
West View Ave 8 FY1 . . .129 E5
West View Pl BB2 . . . . . . .100 B6
West View Rd
Morecambe LA4 . . . . .212 D5
Whitewell Bottom BB4 . . . .85 F5
West View Terr
Darwen BB3 . . . . .80 A2
Padiham BB12 . . . . .125 C7
1 Preston PR1 . . . . .95 D8
West Way Chorley PR7 . . .60 C7
Fleetwood FY7 . . . . .172 D8
West Wlk BL7 . . . . .46 D2
Westbank Ave FY4 . . . . .110 A7
Westboro Cl LA3 . . . . . . .212 A1
Westbourne BB4 . . . . .67 A8
Westbourne Ave
Blackpool FY1 . . . . .129 C1
Burnley BB11 . . . . .126 D3
Wrea Green PR4 . . . . .112 B3
Westbourne Ave S BB11 .126 E3
Westbourne Ct FY6 . . . . .194 D5
Westbourne Dr LA1 . . . .210 D7
Westbourne Gdns PR8 . . .33 D4
Westbourne Pl LA1 . . . . .210 D8
Westbourne Rd
Chorley PR7 . . . . .42 B6
Cleveleys FY5 . . . . .172 D5
Heysham LA3 . . . . .209 A2
Knott End-on-S FY6 . . . . .194 D5
Lancaster LA1 . . . . .210 D7
Southport PR8 . . . . .33 D4
Warton, Carnforth LA5 . . .217 C4
Westbrook Cres PR2 . . . .116 A3
Westbury Cl Blackpool FY5 150 C7
Brierfield BB10 . . . . .147 E2
Westbury Gdns BB1 . . . .101 C4
Westby Ave FY4 . . . . . . .109 E5
Westby Ct FY6 . . . . .151 D2
Westby Gr FY7 . . . . .194 B5
Westby Pl PR2 . . . . .115 F1
Westby Rd
Lytham St Anne's FY8 . . . . .88 E8
Westby PR4 . . . . .111 E5
Westby St FY8 . . . . .90 B3
Westby Way FY6 . . . . . .151 D2
Westcliff Inf Sch FY5 . . .150 C5
Westcliffe BB6 . . . . .123 B6
Westcliffe Dr
Blackpool FY3 . . . . .129 E8
Morecambe LA3 . . . . .212 D2
Westcliffe Rd PR8 . . . . . .33 F5
Westcliffe Wlk BB9 . . . .147 E2
Westcote St 8 BB3 . . . . .64 B6
Westcroft PR4 . . . . .73 E3
Westend Ave PR7 . . . . . . .41 D1
Westerdale Dr PR9 . . . . . .54 B5
Westerlong PR2 . . . . . . .115 D1
Western Ave BB11 . . . . . .126 E4
Western Ct OL13 . . . . . . .69 B8
Western Dr PR5 . . . . .75 D2
Western Rd OL13 . . . . . . .69 C8
Westfield
Bamber Bridge PR5 . . . . . . .76 A8
1 Nelson BB9 . . . . .168 D1
Westfield Ave
Blackpool FY3 . . . . .151 A1
Fleetwood FY7 . . . . .193 E4
Normoss FY3 . . . . .130 B7
Read BB12 . . . . .144 D1
Westfield Ct FY5 . . . . . . .173 B4
Westfield Dr
Bolton-le-S LA5 . . . . .216 A6
Fulwood PR2 . . . . .117 E4
Gregson Lane PR5 . . . . .97 D1
Leyland PR5 . . . . .75 E1
Warton PR4 . . . . .91 F5
West Bradford BB7 . . . . . .186 E6
Westfield Gr LA4 . . . . . . .212 D4
Westfield Rd FY1 . . . . . .129 C5
Westfields PR5 . . . . .57 A2
Westgate
Barnoldswick BB18 . . . . . .200 A1
Burnley BB11 . . . . .126 E6
Fulwood PR2 . . . . .116 D5
Leyland PR5 . . . . .58 F8
Morecambe LA3,LA4 . . . . .212 F3
Read BB12 . . . . .144 C1
Skelmersdale WN8 . . . . .8 D8
Whitworth OL12 . . . . .51 B7
Westgate Ave
Morecambe LA3 . . . . .212 E2
Ramsbottom BL0 . . . . .49 A2
Westgate Cl OL12 . . . . . .51 B7
Westgate Cty Prim Sch
LA4 . . . . .212 E3
Westgate Dr WN5 . . . . . . .10 D5
Westgate La LA6 . . . . . .236 E5
Westgate Park Rd LA4 . .212 F3
Westgate Rd FY8 . . . . . .109 C4
Westgate Trad Ctr 2
BB11 . . . . .126 F6
Westham St LA1 . . . . . . .211 A7
Westhaven PR9 . . . . .34 D8
Westhaven Cres L39 . . . . .15 C1
Westhead Ave LA3 . . . . . . .1 A1
Westhead Cl L33 . . . . .1 A1
Westhead Rd PR5 . . . . . . .57 B2
Westhead Wlk
1 Fleetwood FY7 . . . . . . .193 F2

Westhead Wlk continued
Kirkby L33 . . . . .1 A1
Westholme Lower Sch
BB2 . . . . .100 B6
Westholme Sch
Blackburn BB2 . . . . .100 A6
Blackburn BB2 . . . . .99 E6
Westhoughton Rd PR6,PR7 42 F1
Westland Ave BB3 . . . . . . .63 F8
Westlands PR5 . . . . .58 C7
Westlands Ct FY5 . . . . . .151 B8
Westleigh Rd PR2 . . . . . .115 F1
Westminster Ave LA4 . . .212 C4
Westminster Cl
Accrington BB5 . . . . .103 E3
Darwen BB3 . . . . .80 E3
Morecambe LA3 . . . . .212 E2
Read BB12 . . . . .144 D1
Westminster Dr PR8 . . . . .20 A4
Westminster Pl
Eccleston PR7 . . . . .40 A8
Hutton PR4 . . . . .94 D1
Westminster Rd
Blackpool FY1 . . . . .129 C8
Chorley PR7 . . . . .42 C7
Darwen BB3 . . . . .80 E3
Morecambe LA3,LA4 . . . . .212 B3
Westmoor Gr LA3 . . . . . .208 E5
Westmoreland Rd PR8 . . .34 D5
Westmoreland St BB9 . . .147 C8
Westmorland Ave
Blackpool FY1 . . . . .129 D3
Cleveleys FY5 . . . . .172 D4
Westmorland Cl
Leyland PR5 . . . . .58 E7
Penwortham PR1 . . . . .95 B4
Preston PR1 . . . . .95 B4
Westmorland Ho 15
PR1 . . . . .95 F8
Westmorland St BB11 . . .126 D5
Weston La Heads PR4 . . .131 F1
Weston Pl 4 FY1 . . . . . . .129 C5
Weston St 9 PR2 . . . . . . .95 D8
Westover Ave LA5 . . . . . .217 E5
Westover Cl L31 . . . . .5 C1
Westover Gr LA5 . . . . . . .217 E5
Warton, Carnforth LA5 . . .217 E5
Westover St LA4 . . . . . . .212 E5
Westside FY4 . . . . .109 F8
Westway Burnley BB11 . .126 D6
Freckleton PR4 . . . . .92 A6
Fulwood PR2 . . . . .117 A4
Hightown L38 . . . . .2 F4
Maghull L31 . . . . .5 C2
Westway Ct PR2 . . . . . . .117 B4
Westway Sch BB12 . . . . .126 F8
Westwell Gr 2 FY1 . . . . .129 C4
Westwell Rd 3 PR6 . . . . . .60 D1
Westwell St Darwen BB3 . .80 E4
13 Great Harwood BB6 . . .123 C5
Westwood Ave
Blackpool FY3 . . . . .129 E4
2 Fleetwood FY7 . . . . . . .193 E3
Poulton-le-F FY6 . . . . .151 E3
Rishton BB1 . . . . .123 A1
Westwood Cl PR8 . . . . . . .34 E3
Westwood Ct BB1 . . . . . .101 A6
Westwood Mews FY8 . . . .90 A3
Westwood Rd
Blackburn BB1 . . . . .101 B4
Burnley BB12 . . . . .126 C8
Clayton Brook PR5,PR6 . . .77 C4
Leyland PR5 . . . . .76 A2
Lytham St Anne's FY8 . . . . .90 A3
Westwood St BB5 . . . . . .103 B7
Wetherall St PR2 . . . . . .116 D1
Wetherby Ave FY4 . . . . .109 B5
Wetherfield Cl LA1 . . . . .214 A4
Weymouth Rd FY3 . . . . .129 F3
Weythorne Dr BL9 . . . . . .32 F4
Whalley Abbey BB7 . . . .143 B5
Whalley Banks BB2 . . . .100 D4
Whalley CE Prim Sch
BB7 . . . . .143 C5
Whalley Cres Darwen BB3 .81 B1
Staining FY3 . . . . .130 E5
Whalley Dr Formby L37 . . .12 A2
Ormskirk L39 . . . . .6 D8
Rawtenstall BB4 . . . . .85 A4
Whalley Gdns OL12 . . . . .51 B1
Whalley Ind Pk BB7 . . . .143 D8
Whalley La PR4 . . . . .110 A8
Whalley New Rd BB1 . . .121 F1
Whalley Old Rd
Billington BB6,BB7 . . . . . .143 B3
Blackburn BB1 . . . . .101 A7
Sunny Bower BB1 . . . . . . .122 B1
Whalley Pl FY8 . . . . .89 B6
Whalley Range BB1 . . . .100 F6
Whalley Rd
Accrington BB5 . . . . .103 B7
Bank Lane BL0 . . . . .49 E7
Barrow BB7 . . . . .164 D2
Billington BB6,BB7 . . . . . .142 F3
Clayton-le-M BB5,BB6 . . .123 F5
Clitheroe BB7 . . . . .164 D5
Heskin Green PR7 . . . . .40 D4
Hurst Green BB7 . . . . .163 B1
Lancaster LA1 . . . . .213 F4
Langho BB6 . . . . .142 E4
Langho BB6 . . . . .142 D2
Mellor Brook BB2 . . . . . . .120 C3
Padiham BB12 . . . . .125 B8
Read BB12 . . . . .144 D1
Rochdale OL12 . . . . .51 B1
Sabden BB7 . . . . .144 D6
Turner Green BB2,PR5 . . .119 C2

Whalley Rd continued
Wilpshire BB1 . . . . .122 B7
Whalley St
2 Bamber Bridge PR5 . . . .96 F2
Blackburn BB1 . . . . .100 E6
Burnley BB10 . . . . .147 A1
5 Chorley PR7 . . . . .42 C7
7 Clitheroe BB7 . . . . .164 D8
Whalley Sta BB7 . . . . . . .143 B6
Whalley Terr BB3 . . . . . . .80 B6
Whalleys Rd WN8 . . . . . . .18 B5
Wham Bottom La OL12 . . .51 D4
Wham Brook Cl BB5 . . . .102 B5
Wham Hey PR4 . . . . .75 A7
Wham La New Longton PR4 .75 A7
Walmer Bridge PR4 . . . . . . .74 D4
Whams La LA2 . . . . .204 D7
Wharf Ho BB2 . . . . .100 B1
Wharf St Blackburn BB1 . .100 F5
Lytham St Anne's FY8 . . . . .90 C3
Rishton BB1 . . . . .123 C1
Wharfdale LA2 . . . . .207 B4
Wharfdale Ave BB10 . . . .147 B4
Wharfdale Ct FY6 . . . . . .151 C3
Wharfe Ct LA3 . . . . .213 B3
Wharfedale FY4 . . . . . . .109 F7
Wharfedale Ave
Fulwood PR2 . . . . .117 E5
Thornton FY5 . . . . .173 B3
Wharfedale Cl
Blackburn BB2 . . . . .79 D7
Leyland PR5 . . . . .59 A7
Wharfedale Rd LA1 . . . .210 D8
Wharton Ave FY5 . . . . . .173 D1
Whave's La PR6 . . . . .78 D4
Wheat La L40 . . . . .25 A4
Wheat St Accrington BB5 .103 A6
Padiham BB12 . . . . .125 D7
Wheatacre WN8 . . . . .8 E8
Wheatacre La BB6 . . . . . .143 E8
Wheatbeam Cl
Cleveleys FY5 . . . . .172 F5
Penwortham PR1 . . . . .95 B3
Wheatcroft Ave BB12 . . .146 D8
Wheatfield PR5 . . . . .58 A4
Wheatfield Cl 1 FY5 . . . .150 F7
Wheatfield Ct 8 LA1 . . . .210 E8
Wheatfield St
Lancaster LA1 . . . . .210 E8
Rishton BB1 . . . . .123 B2
Wheathead La BB9 . . . . .168 B8
Wheatholme St BB4 . . . . .85 B4
Wheatlands Cres FY3 . . .130 C2
Wheatley Cl Burnley BB12 126 D7
Fence BB12 . . . . .146 D7
Wheatley Dr PR3 . . . . . . .139 B8
Wheatley Gr BB9 . . . . . . .168 C3
Wheatley Lane Prim Sch
BB12 . . . . .146 E8
Wheatley Lane Rd
Barrowford BB9 . . . . .168 B2
Fence BB12 . . . . .146 E8
Wheatsheaf Ave PR3 . . .139 A7
Wheatsheaf Wlk
4 Ormskirk L39 . . . . .15 E5
Standish WN6 . . . . .28 D1
Wheel La PR3 . . . . .196 A6
Wheelton La PR5 . . . . . . .76 A3
Wheelwrights La PR5 . . . .76 A3
Wheelwrights Wharf L40 .22 F4
Whernside FY4 . . . . .109 F7
Whernside Cl BB18 . . . . .200 A1
Whernside Cres PR2 . . . .117 D5
Whernside Gr LA5 . . . . . .217 E5
Whernside Rd LA1 . . . . .213 D3
Whernside Way FY5 . . . . .76 C1
Whimberry Cl 1 PR6 . . . .42 E8
Whimbrel Dr FY5 . . . . . .173 A4
Whin Ave LA5 . . . . .216 B6
Whin Dr LA5 . . . . .216 B6
Whin Gr LA5 . . . . .216 B6
Whin La PR3 . . . . .153 B8
Whinberry Ave BB4 . . . . .85 A4
Whinbrick Cotts PR4 . . .112 B6
Whinbrick Terr PR4 . . . .112 C5
Whincroft BB11 . . . . .126 E2
Whinfell Dr LA1 . . . . .211 A3
Whinfield Ave
6 Chorley PR7 . . . . .60 D1
Fleetwood FY7 . . . . .193 E4
Whinfield La PR2 . . . . . . .95 A8
Whinfield Pl
Blackburn BB2 . . . . .100 A6
Preston PR2 . . . . .95 A8
Whinfield St 8 BB5 . . . . .124 A1
Whinney Brow PR3 . . . . .204 C3
Whinney Heys Rd FY3 . . .130 A6
Whinney Hill Rd BB5 . . . .124 C1
Whinney La Blackburn BB2 100 C8
Langho BB6 . . . . .142 D1
Mellor BB2 . . . . .121 D2
Whinneyfield La PR4 . . . .135 D2
Whinny La Euxton PR7 . . . .59 E3
Knott End-on-S FY6 . . . . .194 E4
Waddington BB7 . . . . .185 E6
Whinnysty La LA3 . . . . . .212 A1
Whinpark Ave FY3 . . . . . .130 A6
Whins Ave BB7 . . . . .144 E6
Whins La Read BB12 . . . .144 E3
Wheelton PR6 . . . . .61 A8
Whins The BB7 . . . . .144 E7
Whinsands Cl PR2 . . . . . .117 D5
Whinsfell View LA4 . . . . .212 E5
Whipp Ave BB7 . . . . .164 D7
Whitaker St BB5 . . . . . . .103 B3
Whitbarrow Sq 8 LA1 . . .211 A8
Whitburn Rd L33 . . . . .1 A4
Whitby Ave Fulwood PR2 .115 F5
Southport PR9 . . . . .53 D6
Whitby Dr BB2 . . . . .101 A1
Whitby Pl PR2 . . . . .115 F7

Whitby Rd
Lytham St Anne's FY8 . . . .110 A1
Morecambe LA4 . . . . .212 F5
White Acre Rd BB5 . . . . .103 E2
White Ash Est BB5 . . . . .102 D4
White Ash La BB5 . . . . . .102 D3
White Birk Cl BB8 . . . . . . .48 F2
White Bull St 4 BB12 . . .126 C6
White Carr La Bury BL9 . . .50 A1
Cleveleys FY5 . . . . .151 A8
Hollins Lane PR3 . . . . .204 E4
Moor Side PR4 . . . . .133 C2
White Cross St LA1 . . . . .210 F7
White Gate Fold PR7 . . . .41 E3
White Gr BB8 . . . . .169 C6
White Hill Cl OL12 . . . . . .51 D4
White Horse Cl BL6 . . . . .31 C5
White Horse La PR3 . . . .156 E1
White Hough Outdoor
Education Ctr BB12 . . . .167 E5
White House La
Drummersdale L40 . . . . . . .36 C1
Lane Heads PR3 . . . . .154 E4
White Lea PR3 . . . . .199 C1
White Lee Ave BB8 . . . . .170 C2
White Lee La PR3 . . . . . .180 C2
White Lund Ave LA3 . . . .212 F2
White Lund Rd LA3 . . . . .212 F2
White Lund Trad Est LA3 212 G2
White Mdw PR2 . . . . .115 E3
White Moss La FY6 . . . . .174 E4
White Moss Rd WN8 . . . . .8 C7
White Moss Rd S WN8 . . .8 D7
White Rd BB2 . . . . .100 B6
White St Burnley BB12 . . .126 B6
Colne BB8 . . . . .169 B4
White Walls Cl BB8 . . . . .169 A3
Whiteacre WN6 . . . . .28 A2
Whiteacre La BB6 . . . . . .143 E8
Whitebeam Cl
Blackburn BB2 . . . . .101 A1
Southport PR8 . . . . .20 B3
Whitebeck La LA6 . . . . . .234 B4
Whitebirk Dr BB1 . . . . . .101 C8
Whitebirk Ind Est BB1 . . .122 C1
Whitebirk Rd BB1 . . . . . .101 D5
Whitechapel
Cty Prim Sch PR3 . . . . . .158 D7
Whitecotes Dr FY8 . . . . . .90 D4
Whitecrest Ave 3 FY5 . . .172 F4
Whitecroft Ave 8 BB4 . . .84 B2
Whitecroft Cl BB4 . . . . . . .84 B2
Whitecroft La BB2 . . . . . .120 E2
Whitecroft Mdws BB4 . . .84 B2
Whitecroft View BB5 . . . .103 E2
Whitefield Cl L38 . . . . .2 C1
Whitefield Cty Prim Sch
BB9 . . . . .147 C8
Whitefield La L40 . . . . . . .38 C3
Whitefield Mdws 5 PR5 . .96 F1
Whitefield Pl LA3 . . . . . .212 F2
Whitefield Prim Sch PR1 .95 A4
Whitefield Rd PR1 . . . . . . .95 A4
Whitefield Rd E PR1 . . . . .95 A4
Whitefield Rd W PR1 . . . .95 A4
Whitefield St BB12 . . . . .125 C4
Whitefriar Cl PR2 . . . . . .116 A5
Whitegate LA3 . . . . .212 G3
Whitegate Cl BB12 . . . . .125 E7
Whitegate Dr FY3 . . . . . .129 E3
Whitegate Gdns BB12 . . .125 E7
Whitegate Lodge 4 FY1 .129 E3
Whitehalgh La BB6 . . . . .142 C1
Whitehall Ave WN6 . . . . .19 E8
Whitehall La Blackrod BL6 .30 D3
Grindleton BB7 . . . . .224 A1
Whitehall Rd
Blackburn BB2 . . . . .100 B7
Darwen BB3 . . . . .64 B7
Whitehall St Darwen BB3 . .64 B5
Nelson BB9 . . . . .168 F1
Rochdale OL12 . . . . .51 F1
Whitehaven Cl
Blackburn BB2 . . . . .101 A1
Southport PR8 . . . . .20 B3
Whitehaven St 7 BB11 . .126 E5
Whitehead Cl FY3 . . . . . .130 D5
Whitehead St
Blackburn BB2 . . . . .100 C5
10 Rawtenstall BB4 . . . . . .85 A3
Whitehey WN8 . . . . .8 E8
Whitehey Rd WN8 . . . . . . .8 E8
Whitehill Rd FY4 . . . . . . .110 E6
Whiteholme Dr FY6 . . . . .151 B6
Whiteholme Pl 3 PR2 . . .115 F7
Whiteholme Rd FY5 . . . . .150 E7
Whitehough Pl BB9 . . . . .169 B1
Whitehouse Ave L37 . . . . .12 A3
Whitehouse La L37 . . . . . .12 A3
Whiteledge Rd WN8 . . . . . .9 B6
Whitelees Way FY6 . . . . .151 D3
Whitelens Ave 4 PR2 . . .115 C1
Whiteley Ave BB2 . . . . . .100 A1
Whiteley St BB4 . . . . .84 C1
Whiteleys La L40 . . . . . . .16 D2
Whitelow Rd BL0 . . . . . . .49 C5
Whitemoor Rd BB8 . . . . .191 C2
Whitemoss Ave FY3 . . . .130 B7
Whitemoss Ave W OL12 . .51 B2
Whitendale 8 LA1 . . . . . .213 D2
Whitendale Cres BB1 . . . .101 A3
Whitendale Dr
Bamber Bridge PR5 . . . . . . .76 E4
Hest Bank LA5 . . . . .215 F2
Whitendale Hall PR1 . . . .116 F1
Whitendale Wlk BB1 . . . .101 A3
Whitepits LA2 . . . . .233 D5

Whiterails Dr L39 . . . . . . .15 D6
Whiterails Mews L39 . . . .15 D6
Whiteray Rd 9 LA1 . . . . .213 D2
Whiteside Fold OL12 . . . . .51 A1
Whiteside St 7 FY1 . . . . .129 C6
Whiteside Way FY5 . . . . .172 E3
Whitestock WN8 . . . . .8 E8
Whitethorn Cl PR6 . . . . . .77 A2
Whitethorn Mews FY8 . . .110 A2
Whitethorn Sq 4 PR2 . . .115 D1
Whitethorne Mews FY5 . .151 C8
Whitewalls Dr BB8 . . . . .169 A4
Whitewalls Ind Est BB8 . .169 A3
Whitewell Cl PR3 . . . . . . .178 D3
Whitewell Dr BB7 . . . . . .164 C7
Whitewell Pl 11 BB1 . . . .100 F6
Whitewell Rd BB5 . . . . . .103 D8
Whitewell Vale BB4 . . . . .85 F2
Whitewood Cl FY8 . . . . . .89 E4
Whitley Ave
4 Blackpool FY3 . . . . . . .129 D5
Cleveleys FY5 . . . . .172 E5
Whitley Rd WN8 . . . . .19 D3
Whitmoor Cl 7 LA4 . . . . .212 E5
Whitmore Dr PR2 . . . . . .118 A2
Whitmore Gr PR2 . . . . . .118 A2
Whitmore Pl PR2 . . . . . .118 A2
Whitstone Dr WN8 . . . . . . .9 D7
Whittaker Ave FY3 . . . . .129 E7
Whittaker Cl BB12 . . . . .126 B8
Whittaker St BB5 . . . . . .100 C5
Whittakers La BB7 . . . . .186 F8
Whittam Ave FY4 . . . . . .129 E1
Whittam Cres BB7 . . . . .143 B6
Whittam Rd Chorley PR7 . .42 B5
Whalley BB7 . . . . .143 B6
Whittam St BB11 . . . . . .126 F5
Whitters La PR3 . . . . . . .198 D2
Whittingham Dr BL0 . . . . .49 C3
Whittingham La
Goosnargh PR3 . . . . .137 C5
Grimsargh PR2 . . . . .138 B2
Whittingham Rd PR3 . . . .138 F7
Whittle Brow PR7 . . . . . . .41 C1
Whittle Cl BB7 . . . . .186 F1
Whittle Dr L39 . . . . .15 E7
Whittle Gn PR4 . . . . .135 E3
Whittle Hill Egerton BL7 . .46 E3
Woodplumpton PR4 . . . . .135 E3
Whittle La WN6,WN8 . . . . .26 F4
Whittle Pk PR6 . . . . .77 B2
Whittle St Haslingden BB4 .84 A2
Rawtenstall BB4 . . . . .85 A3
Whittle-le-Woods CE Sch
PR6 . . . . .60 B8
Whittlefield
Cty Prim Sch BB12 . . . . .126 D7
Whittles St OL13 . . . . .70 B8
Whittlewood Dr BB5 . . . .124 B1
Whitton Mews 5 BL6 . . . .31 B4
Whittycroft Ave BB9 . . . .168 E6
Whittycroft Dr BB9 . . . . .168 E6
Whitwell Ave 4 FY4 . . . .109 C5
Whitwell Cl WN6 . . . . . . .28 D2
Whitwell Gdns BL6 . . . . .31 B5
Whitworth Dr PR7 . . . . . .42 A7
Whitworth High Sch OL12 51 C8
Whitworth Rake OL12 . . . .51 D8
Whitworth Rd OL12 . . . . . .51 F2
Whitworth Sq OL12 . . . . . .51 D8
Whitworth St Horwich BL6 .31 C2
Kirkham PR4 . . . . .112 F6
Whitworth Way BB18 . . . .200 C4
Wholesome La
Drummersdale PR9 . . . . . . .36 E3
New Longton PR4 . . . . .74 C5
Whytha Rd BB7 . . . . .189 D6
Wicken Tree Row BB12 . .144 F3
Wickentree Holt OL12 . . . .51 A1
Wickliffe St 9 BB9 . . . . .168 F1
Wicklow Ave FY8 . . . . . . .90 E5
Wicks Cres L37 . . . . .11 C4
Wicks Gdns L37 . . . . .11 D3
Wicks Gn L37 . . . . .11 C3
Wicks Green Cl L37 . . . . .11 C3
Wicks La L37 . . . . .11 D3
Wickworth St BB9 . . . . . .148 A7
Widford Wlk BL6 . . . . . . .30 E1
Widgeon Cl 5 FY5 . . . . . .172 F4
Widow Hill Rd BB10 . . . . .147 D1
Wigan La
Adlington PR7,WN1 . . . . . .29 D7
Chorley PR7 . . . . .42 E2
Wigan Rd
Bamber Bridge PR5 . . . . . . .76 E7
Euxton PR6,PR7 . . . . .59 C5
Ormskirk L39 . . . . .16 A5
Skelmersdale WN8 . . . . .8 F8
Westhead L40 . . . . .16 A4
Wiggins La L40 . . . . .37 B6
Wight Moss Way PR8 . . . .34 D3
Wignall St 8 PR1 . . . . . .117 C1
Wignalls Mdw L38 . . . . . . .2 F3
Wigston Cl PR8 . . . . .20 B4
Wigton Ave PR5 . . . . .58 D7
Wilbraham St PR1 . . . . . .117 C1
Wilcove WN8 . . . . .17 F1
Wild La FY4 . . . . .110 D4
Wilderswood Ave BL6 . . . .31 C4
Wilderswood Cl PR6 . . . . .77 C2
Wilderswood Ct BL6 . . . . .31 D4
Wilding's La FY8 . . . . .89 B8
Wildman St
3 Blackpool FY3 . . . . . . .129 D2
Preston PR1 . . . . .116 E2
Wildoaks Dr FY5 . . . . . . .151 D8
Wilds Pl BL0 . . . . .49 B5
Wildwood Cl BL0 . . . . .49 A4

Wilfield St **7** BB11 . . . . .126 E6
Wilford St FY3 . . . . .129 E7
Wilfred Dr BL9 . . . . .32 B4
Wilfred St BB5 . . . . .103 C4
Wilfrid's Pl WN6 . . . . .28 F1
Wilkie Ave BB11 . . . . .126 E2
Wilkin Sq BB7 . . . . .164 E8
Wilkinson Ave FY3 . . . . . .129 E4
Wilkinson Mount **6**
    BB18 . . . . .201 B2
Wilkinson St
  Bamber Bridge PR5 . . . . . .76 B8
  Barrowford BB9 . . . . .168 C2
  Haslingden BB4 . . . . .84 B4
  Higham BB12 . . . . .145 F5
  Nelson BB9 . . . . .147 E7
  Rawtenstall BB11 . . . . . . .105 B4
Wilkinson Way FY6 . . . . . .194 F5
Willacy La PR4 . . . . .134 E3
Willacy Par LA3 . . . . .212 B2
Willard Ave WN5 . . . . .10 D3
Willaston Ave BB9 . . . . . . .168 E8
William Henry St **6** PR1 . .96 C8
William Herbert St **13**
    BB1 . . . . .100 F6
William Hopwood St **8**
    BB1 . . . . .101 A4
William St Accrington BB5 . .103 C7
  Bacup OL13 . . . . .70 C8
  Blackburn BB2 . . . . .100 E2
  3 Blackpool FY3 . . . . . .129 E7
  Brierfield BB9 . . . . .147 B6
  Carnforth LA5 . . . . .217 D3
  Colne BB8 . . . . .169 E4
  11 Darwen BB3 . . . . . . .81 A1
  5 Earby BB18 . . . . . . .201 B1
  Enfield BB5 . . . . .124 A1
  Horwich BL6 . . . . .31 A3
  17 Nelson BB9 . . . . . . .168 C1
  Ramsbottom BL0 . . . . .67 C1
  11 Tardy Gate PR5 . . . . .76 A8
  Whitworth OL12 . . . . .70 C1
William Thompson
    Rec Ctr BB11 . . . . .127 A5
William Young Cl PR1 . . . .117 C2
Williams La PR2 . . . . .117 C7
Williams Pl **2** BB9 . . . . .147 F8
Williams Rd BB10 . . . . . . .127 B8
Williamson Rd LA1 . . . . . .211 A8
Willing Dr BB2 . . . . .101 A1
Willis Rd BB2 . . . . .100 A2
Willis St **6** BB11 . . . . . .126 E5
Willoughby Ave FY5 . . . . . .172 D2
Willoughby St **6** BB1 . . .100 E6
Willow Ave BB4 . . . . .85 A4
Willow Bank
  Bilsborrow PR3 . . . . .157 A5
  Darwen BB3 . . . . .64 A6
Willow Bank Ct FY6 . . . . . .151 B5
Willow Bank La BB3 . . . . . .80 F1
Willow Brook
  Accrington BB5 . . . . .103 B6
  Shirdley Hill L39 . . . . .22 A6
Willow Chase PR4 . . . . . . .112 D4
Willow Cl Adlington PR6 . . . .30 B8
  Bamber Bridge PR5 . . . . . .76 A8
  Barrowford BB9 . . . . .168 B1
  Clayton-le-M BB5 . . . . . . .123 E3
  Forton PR3 . . . . .204 B3
  Freckleton PR4 . . . . .92 A5
  Gregson Lane PR5 . . . . . . .97 C3
  Penwortham PR1 . . . . .95 A4
  Thornton FY5 . . . . .173 D1
Willow Coppice PR2 . . . . . .115 E3
Willow Cres
  Burscough Bridge L40 . . . . .24 F6
  Clayton-le-W PR5 . . . . . . .76 D3
  Fulwood PR2 . . . . .117 E2
Willow Ct FY6 . . . . .152 A3
Willow Dr Barrow BB6 . . . . .143 D8
  Charnock Richard PR7 . . . . .41 D3
  Freckleton PR4 . . . . .92 A5
  Garstang PR3 . . . . .199 C1
  Poulton-le-F FY6 . . . . . . .130 D8
  Skelmersdale WN8 . . . . . . .17 C1
  Wrea Green PR4 . . . . .112 C4
Willow End L40 . . . . .24 F4
Willow Field PR6 . . . . .77 C3
Willow Field Chase PR5 . . . .98 B2
Willow Gn **2** Ormskirk L39 . .15 F5
  Preston PR2 . . . . .95 A8
Willow Gr Blackpool FY3 . . .151 A1
  Formby L37 . . . . .11 F4
  Goosnargh PR3 . . . . .137 D6
  Hambleton FY6 . . . . .174 B2
  Morecambe LA4 . . . . .213 B6
  Rufford L40 . . . . .38 A3
  Southport PR9 . . . . .34 E7
  West Bradford BB7 . . . . . .186 D7
Willow Hey
  Skelmersdale WN8 . . . . . . .17 C1
  Tarleton PR4 . . . . .56 A7
Willow La LA1 . . . . .210 D1
Willow Lo FY5 . . . . .89 C7
Willow Mill LA2 . . . . .231 C3
Willow Mount BB1 . . . . . . .121 F3
Willow Pk BB5 . . . . .102 C2
Willow Pl PR4 . . . . .153 F1
Willow Rd Chorley PR6 . . . . .60 C2
  Wymott PR5 . . . . .57 F6
Willow St Accrington BB5 . .103 B6
  Blackburn BB1 . . . . .101 A7
  Burnley BB12 . . . . .126 E6
  Bury BL9 . . . . .32 B3
  Clayton-le-M BB5 . . . . . . .123 E3
  Darwen BB3 . . . . .80 F1
  Fleetwood FY7 . . . . .194 A4

Willow St continued
  Great Harwood BB6 . . . . . .123 C4
  Haslingden BB4 . . . . .84 B3
  Rawtenstall BB4 . . . . .68 E8
Willow Terr FY3 . . . . .130 C6
Willow Tree Ave
  Broughton PR3 . . . . .136 D3
  Rawtenstall BB4 . . . . .84 E2
Willow Tree Cres PR5 . . . . .75 D1
Willow Tree Dr BB1 . . . . . .121 C1
Willow Tree Gdns **3** FY5 .173 D1
Willow Way PR4 . . . . .74 F7
Willow Wlk WN8 . . . . .18 B4
Willow-Dale FY5 . . . . .173 D1
Willowbank Ave FY4 . . . . . .109 E6
Willowbank Cotts PR5 . . . . .57 B2
Willowcroft Dr FY6 . . . . . .174 B1
Willowdene FY5 . . . . .172 E1
Willowhey PR9 . . . . .52 F4
Willowmead Pk FY8 . . . . . .111 F2
Willowmead Way OL12 . . . .51 A2
Willows Ave Cleveleys FY5 .172 E1
  Lytham St Anne's FY8 . . . . .89 E3
Willows La Accrington BB5 .103 A3
  Kirkham PR4 . . . . .112 F5
  Park La PR4 . . . . .139 B8
Willows RC Prim Sch
    The PR4 . . . . .112 F5
Willows The Coppull PR7 . . .28 C4
  Lytham St Anne's FY8 . . . . .89 E3
  Mawdesley L40 . . . . .39 C2
  Mellor Brook BB2 . . . . . . .120 C3
  Southport PR8 . . . . .33 F6
  Whitworth OL12 . . . . .51 C5
Wills Ave L31 . . . . .5 C2
Willshaw Rd FY2 . . . . .150 B1
Willy La L42 . . . . .203 D6
Wilmar Rd PR5 . . . . .76 C2
Wilmcote Gr PR8 . . . . .20 B4
Wilmore Cl BB8 . . . . .169 C5
Wilmot Rd PR2 . . . . .117 E3
Wilpshire Banks BB1 . . . . .121 F4
Wilpshire Golf Course
    BB1 . . . . .122 A6
Wilpshire Rd BB1 . . . . .122 E4
Wilson Cl PR4 . . . . .56 A7
Wilson Dr PR4 . . . . .153 F1
Wilson Fold BB12 . . . . . . .126 B6
Wilson Gr LA3 . . . . .208 E3
Wilson Sq FY5 . . . . .150 D7
Wilson St Blackburn BB2 . . .100 D2
  Bury BL9 . . . . .32 A1
  Clitheroe BB7 . . . . .164 E7
  Foulridge BB8 . . . . .191 D1
  Horwich BL6 . . . . .31 A4
Wilson's Endowed
    CE Prim Sch LA6 . . . . . .231 B1
Wilton Cl LA1 . . . . .214 A4
Wilton Gr PR1 . . . . .95 A4
Wilton Par FY1 . . . . .129 B7
Wilton Pl **3** PR5 . . . . .76 B1
Wilton St Barrowford BB9 . .168 D3
  Brierfield BB9 . . . . .147 B5
  Burnley BB10 . . . . .147 B1
Wiltshire Ave BB12 . . . . . .126 E7
Wiltshire Dr BB4 . . . . .67 B8
Wiltshire Mews PR4 . . . . . .115 D5
Wilvere Ct FY5 . . . . .150 C7
Wilvere Dr FY5 . . . . .150 C6
Wilworth Cres BB1 . . . . . .121 E2
Wimberley Banks BB1 . . . .100 F4
Wimberley Gdns **7** BB1 . .100 E6
Wimberley Pl **8** BB1 . . . .100 E6
Wimberley St BB1 . . . . . . .100 E6
Wimbledon Ave FY5 . . . . . .150 D7
Wimbledon Ct FY5 . . . . . . .150 D6
Wimborne Cl BL6 . . . . .31 F1
Wimbourne Pl FY4 . . . . . . .109 B6
Wimbrick Cl L39 . . . . .15 D4
Wimbrick Cres L39 . . . . . . .15 D3
Winchcombe Rd FY5 . . . . .150 E7
Winchester Ave
  Accrington BB5 . . . . .103 C7
  5 Blackpool FY4 . . . . . .129 D1
  Chorley PR7 . . . . .42 E4
  Lancaster LA1 . . . . .211 B5
  Morecambe LA4 . . . . .212 G6
Winchester Cl
  Morecambe LA3 . . . . .212 E2
  4 Orrell WN5 . . . . .10 F7
Winchester Dr FY6 . . . . . . .151 B6
Winchester Rd
  Longshaw WN5 . . . . .10 D2
  Padiham BB12 . . . . .125 D3
Winchester St BB1 . . . . . . .101 A3
Winchester Way PR3 . . . . .178 B7
Winckley Cl **11** PR1 . . . . . .95 F7
Winckley Rd
  Clayton-le-M BB5 . . . . . . .123 F2
  Preston PR1 . . . . .95 E6
Winckley Sq PR1 . . . . .95 F7
Winckley St **9** PR1 . . . . . .95 F7
Winder Garth LA6 . . . . . . .234 B1
Winder La PR3 . . . . .204 B2
Windermere Ave
  Accrington BB5 . . . . .124 D1
  Burnley BB10 . . . . .147 A4
  Clitheroe BB7 . . . . .164 C7
  Colne BB8 . . . . .169 F6
  Fleetwood FY7 . . . . .172 E6
  Leyland PR5 . . . . .76 A3
  Morecambe LA4 . . . . .212 G4
Windermere Cl **4** BB1 . . .100 F6
Windermere Cres PR8 . . . . .20 C3
Windermere Ct **4** LA4 . . .212 G4
Windermere Dr
  Adlington PR6 . . . . .43 B1

Windermere Dr continued
  Darwen BB3 . . . . .81 C3
  Maghull L31 . . . . .5 E2
  Rainford Junction WA11 . . . .8 E2
  Ramsbottom BL0 . . . . .49 C7
  Rishton BB1 . . . . .123 A1
Windermere Ho PR1 . . . . . .95 B8
Windermere Rd
  Bacup OL13 . . . . .87 A3
  Blackpool FY4 . . . . .109 C8
  Bolton-le-S LA5 . . . . .216 A4
  Carnforth LA5 . . . . .216 E8
  Fulwood PR2 . . . . .117 C4
  Hightown L38 . . . . .3 A4
  Lancaster LA1 . . . . .211 B8
  Orrell WN5 . . . . .10 A4
  Padiham BB12 . . . . .145 C2
  Preston PR1 . . . . .118 A1
Windermere Sq FY8 . . . . . .109 F2
Windfield Cl L33 . . . . .1 A6
Windflower Dr PR5 . . . . . . .76 E2
Windgate Much Hoole PR4 . .73 E2
  Skelmersdale WN8 . . . . . . .17 F1
  Tarleton PR4 . . . . .56 A5
Windham Pl LA1 . . . . .213 C3
Windholme **6** LA1 . . . . . .213 C2
Windle Ash L31 . . . . .5 C2
Windmill Ave
  Kirkham PR4 . . . . .113 C4
  Ormskirk L39 . . . . .15 F5
Windmill Cl FY3 . . . . .130 E5
Windmill Ct **9** LA1 . . . . . .211 A3
Windmill Farm L40 . . . . . . .37 B4
Windmill Hts WN8 . . . . . . .10 A8
Windmill Pl FY4 . . . . .109 F6
Windmill Rd WN8 . . . . .9 F7
Windmill St LA1 . . . . .210 D8
Windmill View PR4 . . . . . . .113 A6
Windrows WN8 . . . . .17 F1
Windrush Ave BL0 . . . . . . .49 A2
Windrush The OL12 . . . . . . .51 C4
Windsor Ave Adlington PR7 . .29 F6
  Church BB5 . . . . .103 A8
  Clitheroe BB7 . . . . .164 C7
  Fulwood PR2 . . . . .116 B2
  Haslingden BB4 . . . . .84 A1
  Lancaster LA1 . . . . .211 B5
  Longridge PR3 . . . . .138 F7
  Morecambe LA4 . . . . .212 D3
  New Longton PR4 . . . . .95 A1
  Newchurch BB4 . . . . .85 E1
  Penwortham PR1 . . . . .95 C3
  Thornton FY5 . . . . .173 B2
Windsor Cl Blackburn BB1 . .101 B3
  Burscough L40 . . . . .24 E3
  Chorley PR7 . . . . .42 B7
  Ramsbottom BL8 . . . . .49 A1
  Read BB12 . . . . .144 D2
Windsor Ct
  Poulton-le-F FY6 . . . . . . .151 E3
  Southport PR8 . . . . .33 E4
Windsor Dr Brinscall PR6 . . .61 E8
  Fulwood PR2 . . . . .116 D6
  Horwich BL6 . . . . .31 E2
Windsor Gdns PR3 . . . . . . .178 B7
Windsor Gr LA4 . . . . .212 D4
Windsor Lodge **3** FY8 . . .89 D4
Windsor Pl
  Barnoldswick BB18 . . . . . .200 D3
  1 Fleetwood FY7 . . . . . .194 B5
Windsor Rd
  Bamber Bridge PR5 . . . . . .96 D3
  Blackburn, Beardwood BB2 .100 B6
  Blackburn, Knuzden Brook
    BB1 . . . . .101 E4
  Chorley PR7 . . . . .42 B7
  Darwen BB3 . . . . .80 F3
  Eccleston PR7 . . . . .40 C7
  Formby L37 . . . . .11 F1
  Garstang PR3 . . . . .178 B7
  Great Harwood BB6 . . . . . .123 D5
  Lytham St Anne's FY8 . . . . .89 A5
  Lytham St Anne's, Ansdell
    FY8 . . . . .89 D4
  Morecambe LA3 . . . . .212 C3
  Normoss FY3 . . . . .130 B7
  Orrell WN8 . . . . .10 A8
  Southport PR9 . . . . .34 D7
Windsor St Accrington BB5 .103 C6
  Burnley BB12 . . . . .126 C6
  Colne BB8 . . . . .169 E5
  Nelson BB9 . . . . .148 B3
Windsor Terr FY7 . . . . . . .194 B5
Windy Bank BB8 . . . . .169 E5
Windy Harbour Rd
  Singleton FY6 . . . . .153 A4
  Southport PR8 . . . . .20 E7
Windy Hill LA2 . . . . .233 E8
Windy St PR3 . . . . .182 E3
Windyhill **35** LA1 . . . . . . .210 F8
Winery La PR1,PR5 . . . . . . .96 C5
Winewall La BB8 . . . . .170 C5
Winewall Rd BB8 . . . . .170 B5
Wingate Ave
  Cleveleys FY5 . . . . .150 D7
  Morecambe LA4 . . . . .212 F4
Wingate Wlk L33 . . . . .1 A3
Wingate-Saul Rd LA1 . . . . .210 E7
Wingates **2** PR1 . . . . .95 C3
Wingrove Rd FY7 . . . . .193 F2
Winifred Ave BL9 . . . . .32 F4
Winifred La L39 . . . . .6 B8
Winifred St Blackpool FY1 . .129 B4
  Ramsbottom BL0 . . . . .49 B5

Winifred St continued
  Rochdale OL12 . . . . .51 B1
Winmarleigh
    CE Prim Sch PR3 . . . . . .198 E5
Winmarleigh Rd
  Lancaster LA1 . . . . .211 A2
  Preston PR1 . . . . .116 B1
Winmarleigh St **3** BB1 . . .101 C5
Winmarleigh Wlk BB1 . . . . .101 C4
Winmoss Dr L33 . . . . .1 A5
Winnipeg Cl BB2 . . . . .100 B8
Winnipeg Pl FY2 . . . . .150 E3
Winscar Wlk FY6 . . . . .151 B3
Winsford Cres FY5 . . . . . . .150 C8
Winsford Wlk BB11 . . . . . .126 B5
Winslow Ave FY6 . . . . .151 B5
Winslow Cl **7** PR1 . . . . . . .95 E2
Winsor Ave PR5 . . . . .59 B8
Winster Cl PR5 . . . . .97 E4
Winster Ct BB5 . . . . .123 E2
Winster Pk LA1 . . . . .213 C2
Winster Pl FY4 . . . . .130 D1
Winster Wlk LA1 . . . . .213 C2
Winsters The WN8 . . . . . . .17 F1
Winston Ave Cleveleys FY5 .172 F2
  Lytham St Anne's FY8 . . . . .89 B6
Winston Cres PR8 . . . . .34 E2
Winston Rd BB1 . . . . .100 D7
Winter Hey La BL6 . . . . . . .31 B3
Winter Hill Cl PR2 . . . . . . .118 C7
Winterburn Rd BB2 . . . . . . .80 C7
Winterley Dr BB5 . . . . .124 E1
Winterton Rd BB3 . . . . .81 A2
Winthorpe Ave LA4 . . . . . .212 G3
Winton Ave Blackpool FY4 . .130 A1
  Fulwood PR2 . . . . .116 F6
Winton Gn BL6 . . . . .31 F1
Winton Rd FY4 . . . . .130 A2
Winward Cl BB3 . . . . .80 F6
Wiseman Cl LA4 . . . . .212 F4
Wiseman St BB11 . . . . . . .126 F6
Wisp Hill Gr LA2 . . . . .214 F6
Wisteria Dr BB3 . . . . .81 B7
Wiswell Cl Brierfield BB10 . .147 E2
  Rawtenstall BB4 . . . . .85 A4
Wiswell La BB7 . . . . .143 D6
Wiswell Shay BB7 . . . . . . .143 E2
Witham Cl WN6 . . . . .28 C1
Witham Rd WN8 . . . . .17 D1
Withens Cl L31 . . . . .5 D3
Withers St BB1 . . . . .100 F4
Witherslack Cl LA4 . . . . . .212 E3
Withgill Piggety Cotts
    BB7 . . . . .163 B6
Within Gr BB5 . . . . .103 D8
Withington La PR7 . . . . . . .40 E2
Withins Field L38 . . . . .2 F3
Withins La L37 . . . . .4 A7
Withnell Fold Old Rd PR6 . .78 E1
Withnell Fold Prim Sch
    PR6 . . . . .78 C3
Withnell Gr PR6 . . . . .60 E1
Withnell Rd FY4 . . . . .109 B8
Withy Ct PR2 . . . . .116 E3
Withy Grove Cl PR5 . . . . . . .96 F1
Withy Grove Cres PR5 . . . . .96 F1
Withy Grove Rd PR5 . . . . . .96 F1
Withy Par PR2 . . . . .116 E4
Withy Trees Ave PR5 . . . . . .96 F1
Withy Trees Cl PR5 . . . . . . .96 F1
Witney Ave BB2 . . . . .79 E8
Witton Ave FY7 . . . . .193 E1
Witton Gr FY7 . . . . .193 E1
Witton Par BB2 . . . . .100 C3
Witton Park Ctry Pk BB2 . . .99 F4
Witton Park High Sch
    BB2 . . . . .100 A4
Witton St PR1 . . . . .96 B8
Woborrow Rd LA3 . . . . . . .208 E8
Woburn Cl BB5 . . . . .103 E3
Woburn Gn PR5 . . . . .76 B2
Woburn Rd FY1 . . . . .129 C7
Woburn Rise PR3 . . . . . . .178 D2
Wold The PR6 . . . . .61 A3
Wolfenden Gn BB4 . . . . . . .68 F8
Wollaton Dr BB7 . . . . .34 F3
Wolseley Cl PR5 . . . . .59 A8
Wolseley Pl **21** PR1 . . . . . .96 A7
Wolseley Rd PR1 . . . . .95 E5
Wolseley St
  Blackburn BB2 . . . . .100 D1
  Lancaster LA1 . . . . .211 A8
Wolsey Cl FY5 . . . . .172 E3
Wolseley Rd Blackpool FY1 .129 B1
  Fleetwood FY7 . . . . .193 F4
Wolverton WN8 . . . . .8 F8
Wolverton Ave FY2 . . . . . . .150 B2
Wood Bank Haslingden BB4 .66 F4
  Penwortham PR1 . . . . .95 C3
Wood Cl BB9 . . . . .168 A5
Wood Close Gdns LA5 . . . .237 B2
Wood Clough Platts BB9 . . .147 A5
Wood End Brierfield BB12 . .146 F3
  Kingsfold PR1 . . . . .95 C1
Wood End Rd PR6 . . . . .77 B2
Wood Gn Kirkham PR4 . . . . .113 B2
  Leyland PR5 . . . . .75 C2
Wood Green Dr FY5 . . . . . .150 F8
Wood Hey Gr OL12 . . . . . . .51 F4
Wood House La BB7 . . . . . .223 A7
Wood La Haskayne L37, L39 . .13 D1
  Heskin Green PR7 . . . . .40 E3
  Hoscar L40 . . . . .25 E5
  Mawdesley L40 . . . . .39 D5

Wood La continued
  Parbold WN8 . . . . .26 D2
  Wrightington Bar WN6 . . . . .27 E8
Wood Lea Bank **9** BB4 . . .68 F8
Wood Lea Rd BB4 . . . . .68 F8
Wood Nook **1** BB4 . . . . . .85 A7
Wood Park Rd FY1 . . . . . . .129 E1
Wood Road La BL8,BL9 . . . .49 C1
Wood St Blackpool FY1 . . . .129 B5
  Brierfield BB9 . . . . .147 B5
  Burnley BB10 . . . . .127 A8
  Church BB5 . . . . .102 E5
  Colne BB8 . . . . .169 E4
  Darwen BB3 . . . . .80 F1
  Fleetwood FY7 . . . . .172 E8
  Great Harwood BB6 . . . . . .123 E5
  Hapton BB12 . . . . .125 C4
  Horwich BL6 . . . . .31 C3
  1 Lancaster LA1 . . . . . .210 F8
  Lytham St Anne's FY8 . . . . .88 E6
  Poulton-le-F FY6 . . . . . . .152 A3
  Ramsbottom BL0 . . . . .49 B5
Wood Street
  Livesey Fold BB3 . . . . .80 F2
Wood Terr BB7 . . . . .187 E5
Wood View Blackburn BB2 . .99 F1
  Burton in L LA6 . . . . .236 C3
Wood View La PR3 . . . . . . .174 C7
Wood's Brow PR3 . . . . . . .140 B6
Wood's La PR3 . . . . .177 A6
Woodacre Rd PR2 . . . . . . .118 A2
Woodale Laithe BB9 . . . . . .168 C3
Woodale Rd PR6 . . . . .77 B3
Woodbank Ave BB3 . . . . . . .80 E2
Woodbine Gdns BB12 . . . . .126 C7
Woodbine Rd
  Blackburn BB2 . . . . .100 B6
  Burnley BB12 . . . . .126 C6
Woodbine Terr OL14 . . . . . .108 B1
Woodbridge Gdns OL12 . . . .51 C2
Woodburn Cl BB2 . . . . . . .100 A8
Woodbury Ave
  Blackburn BB2 . . . . .100 D2
  Fence BB12 . . . . .146 D7
Woodcock Cl FY5 . . . . . . .173 A5
Woodcock Est PR5 . . . . . . .76 B6
Woodcock Fold PR7 . . . . . .40 C7
Woodcock Hill Rd BB2 . . . . .99 B3
Woodcote Cl L33 . . . . .1 A4
Woodcourt Ave BB11 . . . . .126 D3
Woodcrest BB1 . . . . .121 F5
Woodcroft
  Appley Bridge WN6 . . . . . .19 E6
  Skelmersdale WN8 . . . . . . .8 F8
Woodcroft Ave BB4 . . . . . . .84 F5
Woodcroft Cl PR1 . . . . .95 C2
Woodcroft St BB4 . . . . .84 F5
Woodfall PR7 . . . . .60 B2
Woodfall PR5 . . . . .77 C6
Woodfield Ave
  Accrington BB5 . . . . .103 D3
  3 Blackpool FY1 . . . . . .129 B2
  Rochdale OL12 . . . . .51 E2
Woodfield Ct FY5 . . . . . . .173 B1
Woodfield Rd
  Blackpool FY1 . . . . .129 B2
  Chorley PR7 . . . . .60 C1
  Ormskirk L39 . . . . .15 D3
  Thornton FY5 . . . . .173 D1
Woodfield Terr BB9 . . . . . .147 C5
Woodfield View BB7 . . . . . .143 C5
Woodfields BB7 . . . . .163 B3
Woodfold PR1 . . . . .95 B3
Woodfold Cl BB2 . . . . .120 C3
Woodfold La PR3 . . . . .199 C5
Woodfold Pl BB2 . . . . .100 B5
Woodford Copse PR7 . . . . . .42 A7
Woodgate LA3 . . . . .213 B2
Woodgate Ave BL9 . . . . . . .32 D4
Woodgate Hill Rd
  Bury BL9 . . . . .32 C4
  Bury, Woodgate Hill BL9 . . . .32 F4
Woodgates Rd BB2 . . . . . . .99 F5
Woodgrove Rd BB11 . . . . .127 B3
Woodhall Cres PR5 . . . . . . .97 E4
Woodhall Gdns FY6 . . . . . .174 C2
Woodhart La PR7 . . . . .40 C5
Woodhead Cl
  Ramsbottom BL0 . . . . .49 C4
  Rawtenstall BB4 . . . . .86 A2
Woodhead Rd BB12 . . . . . .144 D2
Woodhey High Sch BL0 . . . .49 A3
Woodhey Rd BL0 . . . . .49 A3
Woodhill Ave LA4 . . . . .212 D3
Woodhill Cl LA4 . . . . .212 D3
Woodhill La LA4 . . . . .212 D4
Woodhouse Rd FY5 . . . . . .151 B8
Woodhouse St **1** BB11 . . .127 B4
Woodhurst Dr WN6 . . . . . . .28 D1
Woodland Ave Bacup OL13 . .86 F5
  Bescar L40 . . . . .22 F4
  Thornton FY5 . . . . .173 B2
Woodland Cl
  Hambleton FY6 . . . . .174 D1
  Wrea Green PR4 . . . . .112 B3
Woodland Cres FY6 . . . . . .195 A6
Woodland Dr
  Clayton-le-M BB5 . . . . . . .123 F5
  Poulton-le-F FY6 . . . . . . .151 E2
  Standish WN6 . . . . .28 E2
Woodland Gr
  Blackpool FY3 . . . . .129 E4
  Egerton BL7 . . . . .46 D2
  Penwortham PR1 . . . . .95 B5
Woodland Pk BB7 . . . . . . .143 C5

Woodland Pl BB3 ....80 F7
Woodland Rd OL12 ......51 C2
Woodland Terr OL13 .....86 F4
Woodland View
 Bacup OL13 ....86 F4
 Brinscall PR7 ....61 F7
 Great Harwood BB6 ....123 C6
Woodlands Ave
 Bamber Bridge PR5 .....97 A2
 Blackburn BB2 ....99 E1
 Fulwood PR2 ....117 E2
 7 Kirkham PR4 ....112 F5
 Penwortham PR1 ....95 E2
Woodlands Cl Formby L37 .11 D2
 Newton-w-S PR4 ....113 F3
 Ormskirk L39 ....16 A4
 Southport PR9 ....34 D8
 Storth LA7 ....237 F4
Woodlands Cres PR3 ....136 B5
Woodlands Ct 5 FY8 .....89 D4
Woodlands Dr
 Fulwood PR2 ....116 E8
 Kirkham PR4 ....113 B7
 Leyland PR5 ....75 F1
 Morecambe LA3 ....212 B2
 Shevington WN6 ....19 F4
 Silverdale LA5 ....218 C4
 Warton PR4 ....91 C5
 West Bradford BB7 ....186 D7
 Whalley BB7 ....143 C5
Woodlands Gr
 Darwen BB3 ....80 D2
 Grimsargh PR2 ....138 E1
 Morecambe LA3 ....212 B2
 Padiham BB12 ....145 B1
Woodlands Mdw PR7 .....42 C3
Woodlands Prim Sch L37 .11 D3
Woodlands Rd
 Edenfield BL0 ....67 D2
 Formby L37 ....11 D3
 Lancaster LA1 ....214 A4
 Lytham St Anne's FY8 ...89 D4
 Nelson BB9 ....147 F8
Woodlands Sch PR2 ....117 E2
Woodlands Specl Sch
 FY3 ....129 E4
Woodlands The
 Brockhall Village BB6 ..142 C6
 Garstang PR3 ....178 B8
 6 Preston PR2 ....115 E1
 Southport PR8 ....20 C5
Woodlands View
 Over Kellet LA6 ....231 B8
 12 Ramsbottom BL0 .....49 C6
Woodlands Way
 Longton PR4 ....73 F8
 Newsham PR3 ....136 B5
Woodlea Chase BB3 .....64 C3
Woodlea Cl PR9 ....53 D5
Woodlea Gdns BB9 .....147 D5
Woodlea Jun Sch PR5 ...58 F8
Woodlea Rd
 Blackburn BB1 ....101 B4
 Leyland PR5 ....58 F8
Woodlee Rd PR4 ....72 F2
Woodleigh Cl L31 ....5 B5
Woodley Ave
 Accrington BB5 ....103 C4
 Thornton FY5 ....173 D1
Woodley Park Rd WN8 ..18 B4
Woodman La LA6 ....235 F6
Woodmancote PR7 ......60 B2
Woodmoss La PR8, L40 ..35 E2
Woodnook Cty Prim Sch
 BB5 ....103 C4
Woodnook Rd WN6 ......19 E8
Woodpecker Hill 3
 BB11 ....126 C5
Woodplumpton La PR3 ..136 C2
Woodplumpton Rd
 Burnley BB11 ....126 F1
 Fulwood PR2 ....116 C3
 Woodplumpton PR4 ....135 E2
 Woodplumpton, Moor
 Side PR4 ....135 D4
Woodridge Ave FY5 .....150 C8
Woodrow WN8 ....8 E8
Woodrow Dr WN8 ....26 A1
Woodroyd Dr BL9 ....32 C3
Woodruff Cl FY5 ....172 F5
Woodrush LA4 ....213 B6
Woods Brow BB2 ....119 D5

Woods Cl L39 ....14 A4
Woods Gn PR1 ....95 E6
Woods La PR4,PR7 .....134 E8
Woodsend Cl BB2 ....81 A8
Woodside Chorley PR7 ...42 E4
 Euxton PR7 ....59 C3
 Haslingden BB4 ....84 C1
 Leyland PR5 ....76 C4
Woodside Ave
 Clayton Green PR6 .....77 B1
 Fulwood PR2 ....116 A4
 New Longton PR4 ......74 F7
 Preston PR2 ....117 E3
 Rishton BB1 ....101 F8
 Southport PR8 ....20 B3
Woodside Cl
 Accrington BB5 ....124 F1
 Orrell WN8 ....10 C8
Woodside Cres BB4 .....85 D1
Woodside Dr
 Blackpool FY3 ....130 A5
 Ramsbottom BL0 ....49 A5
Woodside Gr BB2 ....80 A8
Woodside Rd
 Accrington BB5 ....124 F1
 Huncoat BB5 ....103 E8
 Simonstone BB12 .....144 E2
Woodside Terr BB9 .....147 C8
Woodsley St BB12 ......126 B5
Woodstock Ave FY5 ....151 C8
Woodstock Cl 8 PR5 ....76 C8
Woodstock Cres BB2 ....79 E8
Woodstock Dr PR8 ......20 F8
Woodstock Gdns FY4 ..109 B7
Woodstock St 12 OL12 ..51 C1
Woodtop CE Inf Sch
 BB11 ....126 D5
Woodvale Darwen BB3 ..80 F1
 Leyland PR5 ....58 A8
Woodvale Ct PR9 ....54 A5
Woodvale Prim Sch PR8 .20 D3
Woodvale Rd PR8 ....20 E2
Woodville Rd
 Adlington PR6 ....42 F1
 Blackburn BB1 ....101 A4
 Brierfield BB9 ....147 C6
 2 Chorley PR7 ....42 C8
 Penwortham PR1 ....95 D2
Woodville Rd W 5 PR1 ..95 C2
Woodville St
 Lancaster LA1 ....211 A8
 Leyland PR5 ....76 B2
Woodville Terr
 Darwen BB3 ....64 B6
 Lytham St Anne's FY8 ...89 F3
Woodward Rd L33 ....1 D4
Woodway PR2 ....116 C4
Woodwell La LA5 ......218 C1
Wookey Cl PR2 ....117 D6
Woolman Rd FY1 ......129 C4
Woolpack BB8 ....169 E3
Woolwich St BB1 ......101 B5
Woone La BB7 ....164 D7
Worcester Ave
 4 Accrington BB5 .....103 A7
 Garstang PR3 ....178 B8
 Lancaster LA1 ....211 B5
 Leyland PR5 ....59 B8
Worcester Pl PR7 ....42 E3
Worcester Rd
 Blackburn BB1 ....101 C5
 Blackpool FY3 ....130 A3
Worchester Gdns PR4 ..115 D5
Worden La PR5 ....58 F7
Worden La Leyland PR5 .59 A7
 Withnall Fold PR6 ......78 E3
Worden Rd PR2 ....116 D3
Wordsworth Ave
 Blackpool FY3 ....130 B2
 Bolton-le-S LA5 ....216 A5
 Longshaw WN5 ....10 D1
 5 Lytham St Anne's FY8 .90 D4
 Orrell WN5 ....10 F6
 Padiham BB12 ....125 E7
 Thornton FY5 ....173 A2
 Warton PR4 ....91 C6
Wordsworth Cl
 Ormskirk L39 ....15 D6
 Oswaldtwistle BB5 ....102 C4
Wordsworth Ct 1 FY8 ...89 C4
Wordsworth Dr BB6 ....123 B4
Wordsworth Gdns BB3 ..81 B1
Wordsworth Ho LA1 ...213 E4
Wordsworth Pl PR5 .....96 D2

Wordsworth Rd
 Accrington BB5 ....103 A4
 Colne BB8 ....169 D5
Wordsworth St
 Brierfield BB9 ....147 F2
 Burnley BB12 ....126 C6
 5 Hapton BB12 ......125 C4
Wordsworth Terr PR6 ...60 D2
Workshop Rd LA3 .....208 F2
Worrall St 1 OL12 ......51 D2
Worsley Ave FY4 ....109 C7
Worsley Cl FY6 ....194 E5
Worsley Ct 18 BB5 .....102 E4
Worsley Rd FY8 ....89 C5
Worsley St Accrington BB5 103 D4
 Haslingden BB5 ....84 A8
Worsthorne Prim Sch
 BB10 ....128 A6
Worston Cl
 Accrington BB5 ....102 F4
 Rawtenstall BB4 ....85 A4
Worston La BB6 ....123 F6
Worston Pl BB2 ....100 C5
Worswick Cres 3 BB4 ...85 A2
Worthing Cl PR8 ....33 F3
Worthing Rd PR2 ......116 A4
Worthington Rd FY4 ...110 B4
Worthy St PR6 ....42 E7
Wraith St BB3 ....64 A8
Wray Cres
 Wrea Green PR4 ......112 C4
 Wymott PR5 ....57 F6
Wray Ct LA1 ....213 E4
Wray Gr FY5 ....150 D8
Wray-with-Botton
Endowed Prim Sch
 LA2 ....232 D6
Wraywood Ct FY7 .....193 C1
Wren Ave PR1 ....95 E5
Wren Cl Blackpool FY6 .151 A4
 Thornton FY5 ....151 D8
Wren Dr BL9 ....32 B4
Wren Gr FY3 ....129 E2
Wren St Burnley BB12 ..126 C6
 Nelson BB9 ....147 F8
 Preston PR1 ....117 B2
Wrennalls La PR7 ....40 B5
Wright St Chorley PR6 ..42 E8
 Horwich BL6 ....31 B4
 6 Kirkham PR4 ....112 F6
 Southport PR9 ....34 C7
 Weir OL13 ....87 A7
Wright St W 3 BL6 .....31 B4
Wrightington Hospl WN6 .27 D2
Wrightington Mossy Lea
 Prim Sch WN6 ....27 F6
Wrights Fold PR5 ....59 C8
Wrights Terr PR8 ....34 B3
Wrigleys Cl L37 ....11 F5
Wrigleys La L37 ....11 F5
Written Stone La PR3 ..160 E1
Wroxham Cl BB10 .....147 D2
Wroxton Cl FY5 ....150 F7
Wycherley Rd OL12 .....51 B2
Wychnor PR2 ....116 B7
Wycollar Cl BB5 ....103 C4
Wycollar Dr BB2 ......100 A6
Wycollar Rd BB2 ......100 B6
Wycoller Ave BB10 ....127 D5
Wycombe Ave FY4 ....109 B6
Wyfordby Ave BB2 ....100 A7
Wyke Cop Rd PR8, PR9 ..35 D2
Wyke La PR8, PR9 ......35 E6
Wyke Wood La PR9 .....35 F7
Wykeham Gr OL12 ......51 B1
Wykeham Rd FY8 ....90 B4
Wyllin Rd L33 ....1 A2
Wymundsley PR7 ....60 A2
Wyndene Cl PR3 ......139 C8
Wyndene Gr PR4 ....92 B6
Wyndham Gdns FY4 ...109 D6
Wyndham Pl LA4 ......213 B6
Wynfield PR5 ....96 F2
Wynnstay Ave L31 ......5 D3
Wynnwood Ave 1 FY1 .129 D8
Wynotham St BB10 ....147 C1
Wyre Ave PR4 ....113 B5
Wyre Bank PR3 ....155 B6
Wyre Cl
 Great Eccleston PR3 ..154 C5
 Lancaster LA3 ....213 B2
Wyre Cres BB3 ....80 D4
Wyre Ct Fleetwood FY7 .193 E3
 Poulton-le-F FY6 ......152 A3
Wyre Estuary Ctry Pk FY5 173 E3

Wyre Gr FY1 ....129 C3
Wyre Ho LA1 ....210 F7
Wyre La PR3 ....199 D1
Wyre Rd FY5 ....151 F6
Wyre Side Cl PR3 .....178 C8
Wyre St Fleetwood FY7 .193 F3
 Kirkham PR4 ....112 F6
 Lytham St Anne's FY8 ..89 A7
 Padiham BB12 ....125 D8
 Preston PR2 ....116 C1
Wyre View FY6 ....194 E5
Wyredale Ct FY7 ......193 F1
Wyredale Rd FY8 ....88 C8
Wyrefields FY6 ....152 A3
Wyresdale Ave
 Accrington BB5 ....103 A8
 Blackpool FY2 ....150 D4
 Morecambe LA3 ....212 B1
 Poulton-le-F FY6 ......151 C3
 Southport PR8 ....34 D4
Wyresdale Cres
 Fulwood PR2 ....117 D4
 Glasson LA2 ....205 E4
 Scorton PR3 ....199 E7
Wyresdale Ct LA1 .....211 B7
Wyresdale Dr PR5 ......59 B6
Wyresdale Gdns LA1 ..211 B7
Wyresdale Rd
 Knott End-on-S FY6 ...194 D5
 Lancaster LA1 ....211 B6
 Quernmore LA2 ......226 A6
Wyreside Dr FY6 ......174 B2
Wyreside Ecology Ctr
 FY5 ....173 E3
Wyreside Hall LA2 ....220 B7
Wytham St 6 BB12 ....125 D7
Wythburn Ave BB2 .....79 E8
Wythburn Cl BB12 ....126 B8
Wythorpe Croft LA4 ...212 E4
Wyvern Way FY6 ......151 C5

Y

Yale St BL7 ....47 D4
Yans La LA7 ....237 F5
Yardley Ctr L33 ....1 C1
Yardley Rd L33 ....1 C1
Yare St 7 BB4 ....68 F8
Yarlside La BD23 ......225 E4
Yarmouth Ave BB4 .....84 C2
Yarraville St BB4 ....85 A2
Yarrow Ave L31 ....5 F2
Yarrow Cl Croston PR5 ..57 B2
 Withnell PR6 ....79 A1
Yarrow Gate PR7 ....42 E6
Yarrow Gr BL6 ....31 B4
Yarrow Pl PR5 ....58 D8
Yarrow Rd Chorley PR6 ..42 E6
 Leyland PR5 ....58 D8
Yarrow Valley Pk PR7 ...42 A2
Yarrow Wlk LA3 ....212 E2
Yarwood St BL9 ....32 A2
Yates Fold PR2 ....100 F2
Yates Rd PR7 ....42 B5
Yates St FY1 ....129 B6
Yeadon WN8 ....18 B1
Yeadon Gr PR7 ....42 A7
Yeadon Way FY4 .....109 D7
Yeadand Ave LA3 .....208 F6
Yealand Conyers
 CE Prim Sch LA5 .....219 E3
Yealand Dr LA1 ....211 A4
Yealand Gr LA5 ....217 E2
Yealand Rd LA5 ......219 E2
Yeargate Ind Est BL9 ..32 D2
Yellow Hall BB18 .....192 A5
Yellow House La PR8 ...34 B6
Yenham La LA3 ....209 E1
Yeomanry & Cty Mus
 PR5 ....96 B8
Yerburgh Rd BB2 .....120 E2
Yew Ct FY7 ....193 C1
Yew Gn PR4 ....113 B7
Yew St 10 Blackburn BB1 .101 A7
 2 Bury BL9 ....32 A2
Yew Tree Ave Euxton PR7 .59 C4
 Grimsargh PR2 ....138 C2
Yew Tree Cl Garstang PR3 .178 B8
 Newton-with-S PR4 ...113 F3
 Wilpshire BB1 ....121 E6
Yew Tree Dr
 Blackburn BB2 ....121 B1
 Oswaldtwistle BB5 ....102 F3

Yew Tree Gr BB4 ......67 F8
Yew Tree Rd
 Blackpool FY3 ....151 A1
 Ormskirk L39 ....15 E7
Yewbarrow Cl BB12 ..146 C1
Yewdale WN8 ....18 A1
Yewdale Ave LA3 ....208 F6
Yewlands Ave
 4 Bamber Bridge PR5 ..96 F1
 Fulwood PR2 ....116 E6
 Heskin Green PR7 .....40 F3
 3 Leyland PR5 ....76 A1
Yewlands Cres PR2 ...116 E6
Yewlands Dr
 Brierfield BB10 ....147 B3
 Fulwood PR2 ....116 E6
 Garstang PR3 ....199 C1
 2 Leyland PR5 ....76 A1
Yewtree Ave PR2 ......118 A4
Yewtree Cl PR7 ....42 C3
Yewtree Dr LA2 ....233 C8
Yewtree Gr PR5 ....76 A7
York Ave Cleveleys FY5 .172 D2
 Fleetwood FY7 ....193 E3
 Fulwood PR2 ....116 E4
 Haslingden BB4 ....67 B8
 Southport PR8 ....34 A5
York Cl
 4 Bamber Bridge PR5 ..96 D3
 Clayton-le-M BB5 ....123 F3
 Formby L37 ....11 F6
 Leyland PR5 ....58 E2
York Cres BB1 ....121 F3
York Dr
 Great Eccleston PR3 ..154 C5
 Kirkham PR4 ....113 B2
 Ramsbottom BL0 ......49 A4
York Fields BB18 .....200 B1
York Gdns PR3 ....34 A5
York Gr PR3 ....178 B7
York House 28 PR1 .....96 A7
York La BB6 ....122 D8
York Pl Accrington BB5 .103 B7
 Adlington PR6 ....30 A8
 Morecambe LA4 ......212 F5
York Rd Blackpool FY2 .150 B4
 Formby L37 ....12 A3
 Lancaster LA1 ....211 A5
 Langho BB1,BB6 ......122 D6
 Lytham St Anne's FY8 ..88 F5
 Southport PR8 ....33 F4
York St Accrington BB5 .103 B7
 Bacup OL13 ....86 F5
 Barnoldswick BB18 ...200 B2
 Blackburn BB2 ....100 E3
 Blackpool FY1 ....129 B3
 Bury BL9 ....32 A2
 Chorley PR7 ....42 D7
 Church BB5 ....102 E6
 Clitheroe BB7 ....186 F1
 Colne BB8 ....169 F5
 Great Harwood BB6 ..123 D5
 Nelson BB9 ....147 F8
 Oswaldtwistle BB5 ...102 C3
 Rawtenstall BB4 ....85 A7
 Rishton BB1 ....123 A1
York Terr Blackburn BB2 ..79 D8
 4 Southport PR9 ......34 C8
Yorke St 2 BB11 ......126 F5
Yorkshire St
 Accrington BB5 ....103 C4
 17 Bacup OL13 ....86 F3
 Blackpool FY1 ....129 B3
 Burnley BB11 ....127 B6
 Huncoat BB5 ....124 E2
 12 Nelson BB9 ....147 E8
Yorkshire St E LA4 ....212 C4
Yorkshire St W LA3 ...212 B4
Young Ave PR5 ....76 C1
Young St Blackburn BB2 .100 B2
 Ramsbottom BL0 ......49 B6

Z

Zama St 9 BL0 ....49 A4
Zebudah St BB2 ......100 C2
Zetland St Preston PR1 ..96 C7
 Southport PR9 ....34 D7
Zion Rd BB1 ....101 A8
Zion St Bacup OL13 ....87 A3
 Colne BB8 ....169 D4

NG	NH	NJ	NK
NM	NN	NO	NP
NR	NS	NT	NU
NX	NY	NZ	
SC	SD	SE	TA
SH	SJ	SK	TF	TG
SM	SN	SO	SP	TL	TM
SR	SS	ST	SU	TQ	TR
SW	SX	SY	SZ	TV

Any feature in this atlas can be given a unique reference to help you find the same feature on other Ordnance Survey maps of the area, or to help someone else locate you if they do not have a Street Atlas.

The grid squares in this atlas match the Ordnance Survey National Grid and are at 500 metre intervals. The small figures at the bottom and sides of every other grid line are the National Grid kilometre values (**00** to **99** km) and are repeated across the country every 100 km (see left).

To give a unique National Grid reference you need to locate where in the country you are. The country is divided into 100 km squares with each square given a unique two-letter reference. Use the administrative map to determine in which 100 km square a particular page of this atlas falls.

The bold letters and numbers between each grid line (**A** to **F**, **1** to **8**) are for use within a specific Street Atlas only, and when used with the page number, are a convenient way of referencing these grid squares.

Example   The railway bridge over DARLEY GREEN RD in grid square B1

Step 1: Identify the two-letter reference, in this example the page is in **SP**

Step 2: Identify the 1 km square in which the railway bridge falls. Use the figures in the southwest corner of this square: Eastings **17**, Northings **74**. This gives a unique reference: **SP 17 74**, accurate to 1 km.

Step 3: To give a more precise reference accurate to 100 m you need to estimate how many tenths along and how many tenths up this 1 km square the feature is (to help with this the 1 km square is divided into four 500 m squares). This makes the bridge about **8** tenths along and about **1** tenth up from the southwest corner.

This gives a unique reference: **SP 178 741**, accurate to 100 m.

Eastings (read from left to right along the bottom) come before Northings (read from bottom to top). If you have trouble remembering say to yourself "Along the hall, THEN up the stairs"!

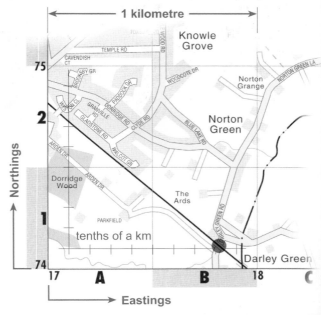

Street Atlases from Philip's

Philip's publish an extensive range of regional and local street atlases which are ideal for motoring, business and leisure use. They are widely used by the emergency services and local authorities throughout Britain.

Key features include:

◆ Superb county-wide mapping at an extra-large scale of 3½ inches to 1 mile, or 2½ inches to 1 mile in pocket editions

◆ Complete urban and rural coverage, detailing every named street in town and country

◆ Each atlas available in three handy formats – hardback, spiral, pocket paperback

'The mapping is very clear... great in scope and value'
★★★★ BEST BUY   AUTO EXPRESS

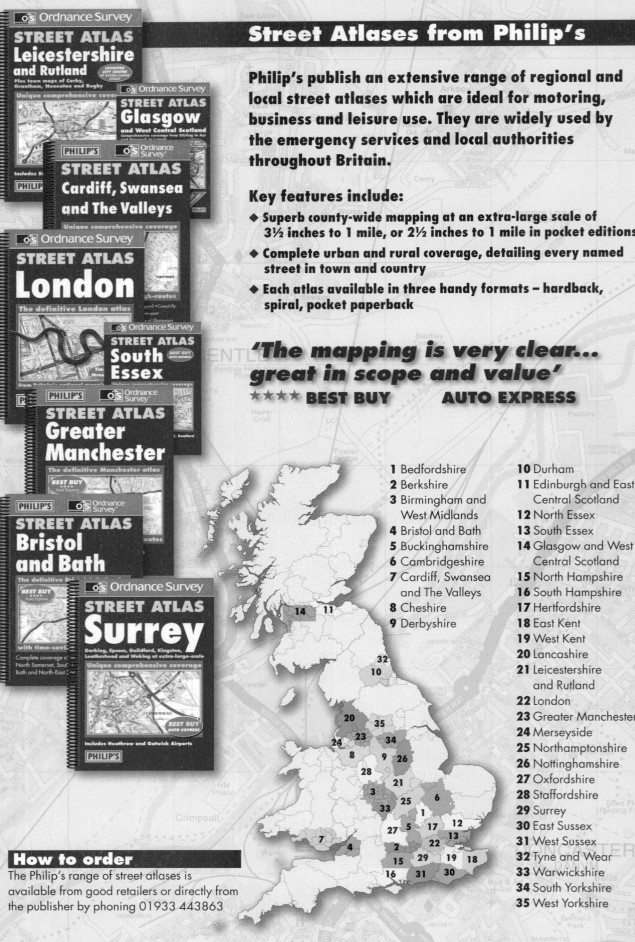

1 Bedfordshire
2 Berkshire
3 Birmingham and West Midlands
4 Bristol and Bath
5 Buckinghamshire
6 Cambridgeshire
7 Cardiff, Swansea and The Valleys
8 Cheshire
9 Derbyshire
10 Durham
11 Edinburgh and East Central Scotland
12 North Essex
13 South Essex
14 Glasgow and West Central Scotland
15 North Hampshire
16 South Hampshire
17 Hertfordshire
18 East Kent
19 West Kent
20 Lancashire
21 Leicestershire and Rutland
22 London
23 Greater Manchester
24 Merseyside
25 Northamptonshire
26 Nottinghamshire
27 Oxfordshire
28 Staffordshire
29 Surrey
30 East Sussex
31 West Sussex
32 Tyne and Wear
33 Warwickshire
34 South Yorkshire
35 West Yorkshire

How to order
The Philip's range of street atlases is available from good retailers or directly from the publisher by phoning 01933 443863